ALAN ROGERS'

GOOD CAMPS GUIDE

EUROPE

1998

Quality Camping and Caravanning Sites

Compiled by: Deneway Guides & Travel Ltd
Cover design: Design Section, Frome
Cover photography: R. Tarn, nr Millau, Aveyron, France
by Michael Busselle

Clive Edwards, Lois Edwards & Sue Smart have asserted
their rights to be identified as the authors of this work.

First published in this format 1997

Published by: Haynes Publishing, Sparkford, Nr Yeovil, Somerset BA22 7JJ
in association with
Deneway Guides & Travel Ltd, West Bexington, Dorchester, Dorset DT2 9DG

British Library Cataloguing-in-Publication Data:
A catalogue record for this book is available from the British Library.

ISBN: 0 901586 80 3

Printed in Great Britain by J H Haynes & Co Ltd

Contents

SELECTED AND INSPECTED CAMPSITES

Foreword

"Each report comprises not only an honest appraisal of the site in question, but also lists all the vital details" - so said Motor Caravan Magazine when they reviewed our Guides in their publication and these few words sum up our philosophy for the last 30 years almost precisely.

Our Europe Guide for 1997 enjoyed a completely new format, thanks to our partnership with Haynes Publishing. Judging by the feedback from readers, campsites and the caravan press, the new format seems to have gone down very well, and has been retained for our 1998 editions.

The Europe Guide now features reports on 23 countries in Europe, including, for the first time, Slovenia. However readers should note that lack of space means that we can only include a fairly limited selection of sites in Britain and France in this guide. A much larger selection of sites in Britain, Ireland and France can be found in our specialist guides for **Britain and Ireland** and **France** respectively.

The introduction of our **Discount Voucher Scheme** in 1996 proved to be very successful and it was extended in 1997. For 1998 we are pleased to have been able to negotiate an even wider range of discounts for readers, and we now include a seven-part discount voucher in every guide which gives readers opportunities to enjoy substantial savings on travel, breakdown, caravan or motorcaravan insurance, on site fees at certain sites, and on their travel arrangements when booked through Sites Abroad or the Caravan & Camping Service, whereby they can recover the full cost of the Guide ! Full details of the 1998 Discount Voucher arrangements are to be found on page 8 and on the vouchers themselves. We would remind readers that the vouchers in this edition are valid only for use during the period 1 January - 31 December 1998.

We hope that all these additions, changes, improvements and 'added value' arrangements will make the 1998 edition of our Europe Guide even more useful, informative and financially attractive than in previous years, and wish all our readers a very happy and enjoyable camping or caravanning season favoured by good weather!

Lois Edwards Cert.Ed, MA, FTS
Clive Edwards BEd, FTS
Sue Smart   Directors

The Guide's Aims and Principles

In producing all our Guides we have a number of aims and objectives designed to:

- Provide readers with the sort of factual information which, from our own extensive experiences, we would wish to know ourselves; for example, most of us want to know if a site is well maintained, if the sanitary facilities are at least adequate, sufficient and regularly cleaned, if electrical connections are available, what sort of shopping, catering and leisure facilities are provided.

- Provide some 'insight' into what a site is like - to try to convey some kind of picture in words that will give the reader an impression of the kind of atmosphere or ambience they can expect. This aspect of our reporting is the most difficult to achieve because what appeals to one person may have exactly the opposite affect on another, but the large number of readers' reports and comments we receive each year is reassuring. We make no claims to infallibility, but this feedback from readers suggests that we get it right most of the time.

- To present the factual information and our assessment of a site in a form that is easily understood, without the use of symbols. Many guides seem to rely on masses of symbols and require their readers to be expert code-breakers. Our Guides have no symbols, and therefore no 'key'.

- To provide basic information concerning tourism, particularly camping and caravanning, in each of the countries featured in the Guide.

- To report on our own experiences in respect of ferry services.

- To provide general information on Camping and Caravanning in Europe, the legal requirements and necessary formalities. This is particularly aimed at those who have never camped abroad before but, as the information is regularly up-dated, it should also provide a useful 'aide-memoire' for the more experienced.

- To provide readers with the opportunity to benefit from a range of discounts through our new **Discount Voucher Scheme**, as detailed above and on the attached vouchers.

Quality Assurance

Having stated our objectives concerning the provision of both factual information and the more subjective aspect of `insight', readers may be interested to know how we set about this. Firstly, we are a small organisation with only three full-time staff and several part-time site assessors. The majority of the sites featured in our Guides have been recommended by readers initially, after which they are visited by one of our site-assessors *before* they are featured in the Guides.

They are then inspected regularly every two/three years to monitor changes and our reports are updated accordingly. In those years when a visit is not made (and we have a total of over 1,500 sites to monitor) the sites are required to return a detailed questionnaire to us which is used to up-date factual information concerning prices, opening dates, etc. To ensure that our reports are consistent, the three of us involved on a full-time basis also undertake a programme of site visits each year designed to monitor the situation as a whole and to make sure that there is a high degree of uniformity in terms of our assessment and reporting procedures. The key personnel directly involved in the Guides now are:

Clive and Lois Edwards (the authors) and Sue Smart (our production/technical director) who are all involved full time, man the office, answer the telephone and readers' letters, typeset the guides, deal with advertisers and make some 200/250 monitoring visits to sites every year.

Currently, our small team of dedicated part-time site assessors, all experienced campers or caravanners, specialising in particular countries and/or areas comprises:

Gerry Ovenden	Switzerland, Austria, Italy, Eastern Europe	Gordon and Joyce Pearce	Denmark, Sweden, Norway, Luxembourg, Belgium
Keith Smart	Scotland, Hungary, Germany, Spain and the Netherlands		Spain, Portugal, Britain
		Rosemary Boyce	Ireland, France, Corsica,
John Seekings	Norway, Slovenia		Finland
Mike Aylott	France, Italy	Thelma and Jack Mitchell	France, Britain
Alan Smith	Southern Italy	Bryan and Eirwen Greves	France

Our thanks are due to them for the many miles they have travelled, their patience with our detailed site reports and their commitment to the philosophy of the guides.

We must also thank our readers for their reports and recommendations, particularly in terms of identifying potential new sites. The other points you raise all receive individual attention, although (with only three of us involved full-time) we cannot always respond as quickly as we would wish, particularly in the summer when two of us are normally away on site visits and in the autumn when we are literally working eighteen hours a day putting the following year's Guides together. We do follow them up and do try to let you know.

On the subject of complaints about any of our featured sites, please bear in mind the following - we are the Authors of the Guide, and we have no contractual arrangements with any of our featured sites, so we cannot actually intervene in any dispute between our readers and any featured site(s) In the event of your having a complaint about a site, ideally this should be addressed to the *campsite owner in person, at the time* - that way you stand the best chance of getting any problem resolved quickly. Of course we are always interested to know about any serious problems encountered by our readers in respect of a particular campsite, as they may well influence our choice of sites for the following year.

How to Use the Guide

The Guide is divided firstly by **country**, subsequently (in the case of larger countries) by region. These are both indicated by the page title lines which should help readers locate their area of interest fairly quickly, although for a particular area the town index provides more direct access. Regions appearing in the title lines are either defined political entities, for example the Départements in France, or more familiar tourist regions such as the Costas in Spain.

The **index** provides an invaluable source of reference, particularly when used in conjunction with the **site number, grid reference** and appropriate **map.** These maps are necessarily diagrammatic, showing the various countries and regions within them, and the approximate location of each site by reference to its site number. Their use is facilitated by dividing each map into 'grid squares', each of which is referenced by two co-ordinates in the form of letters of the alphabet (top line first). These co-ordinate letters are reproduced alongside the site name in the main index. We emphasise however that our maps are intended as a quick reference to the approximate position of sites, and not as basis for navigation.

The **Title Line** for each site seeks to provide the reader with a reasonably accurate idea of the campsite location on a medium-scale map, such as the Michelin Atlas. More precise details can be found in the **'How to find it'** section below the individual site reviews.

Notes on information provided in the site reviews

'Site' and 'Pitch' - the word `site' is used to describe the campsite itself (in Britain more commonly referred to as `parks), and the word `pitch' is used to define individual places on the campsite.

Distances - these are quoted in kilometres and metres

Opening Dates - we give the dates when the site should be open - if we know that facilities on the site, such as restaurants, are open for a shorter period, this is mentioned. However, in some countries (Spain is a frequent culprit), site operators tend to close facilities almost at random. If there are insufficient visitors to justify keeping the pool or the restaurant open on an economic basis they will sometimes simply close it down without warning, so if you are visiting early or late in the season, it is a good idea to check with the site first if you are concerned as to whether a certain facility (or even the site itself!) will be open.

Sanitary Facilities - in years past continental sanitary facilities were by far the biggest cause of complaint from British visitors, but in recent years sanitary facilities in most European countries have improved enormously and, in many cases, are superior to those in the UK. We have tried to give brief details without expanding into a detailed survey. When describing WCs the word `British' denotes the normal (pedestal) type of WC found in the UK - it may or may not have a lifting seat. Some European sites have toilets of the squatting type with a hole at ground level - nowadays these are usually known as `Turkish' style lavatories. So far as personal washing facilities are concerned, on the plus side we normally say if washbasins are in private cabins, whereas on the minus side we say if only cold water is provided. Virtually all sites in this guide have at least good hot showers, sinks for washing dishes and clothes (cold/hot water). Many sites now have washing machines, dryers, etc, and mention is made of these facilities where they exist.

Charges - Some sites have fixed their prices for the following year when our Guides go to print in November, but many have not. We state which year prices refer to, except in those cases when we only have, and can thus only provide, an indication or guide to charges. Some sites accept payment by credit card, which we indicate. In general (not just at campsites) it is wise to check acceptability first, as some of these magnetic type cards are incompatible with European electronic readers.

Self-catering accommodation - e.g. mobile homes, static caravans, chalets, bungalows, apartments, hotel rooms, gites, etc. - in short any accommodation provided by the site which is available for rent. The range of accommodation and prices is far too extensive for us to describe in our individual site reviews, but we do try to mention if such accommodation is available at a site, firstly because some readers may be interested to rent this type of accommodation, and secondly because other readers prefer sites which cater exclusively, or mainly, for campers or caravanners with their own tent or caravan.

Reservations - This is an important subject, but it is difficult to describe comprehensively the various systems operated by all the individual sites. We therefore indicate in our reports whether a site accepts advance bookings or not and, if so, the most important special features of their system. It is important to distinguish between a `booking fee' and a `deposit'. The former is a fee payable by you to the site in addition to the cost of staying on the site and will always be forfeited if you cancel. A deposit, on the other hand, is a payment in advance to be deducted from your final bill. Whether or not a deposit will be refundable if you cancel is dependent on several factors and cancellation insurance is a wise precaution. In general it is best not to send money in the first instance, but rather to write to the site asking for a reservation. If they can offer what you want they will normally write asking for a deposit and/or booking fee to confirm the booking. Most sites will now accept a Eurocheque, obtainable from your bank. Several organisations, including of course the camping tour operators, such as Eurocamp Independent, Select Site Reservations and the Caravan and Camping Service operate systems whereby you can book sites abroad from the UK and details are given in their respective advertisements in this Guide. As to the question of when it is necessary to make a reservation, the peak season in Europe generally runs from about 10 July to 20 August, with some variations between individual countries. Outside of that peak period you stand a good chance of finding space without having booked in advance, except in some particularly popular areas. Occasionally we get complaints from readers who have booked (and sometimes also paid) in advance at a particular site, but after being there for a day or two decide to leave, sometimes because of bad weather, but then have difficulty in recovering their advance payment. The only advice that we can offer in this respect is to consider very carefully the wisdom of parting with a substantial amount of money in advance unless you know the site personally and are prepared to stay for the whole of the period you have booked irrespective of the weather. Frankly the chances of a refund if you book for two weeks but leave after two days are pretty remote and certainly there is no mechanism by which we can assist in such cases.

Telephone numbers are given for most sites, but the numbers quoted assume you are actually IN the country concerned, and are normally nine or ten digit numbers beginning with an `0' (or in Spain a `9'). If you are 'phoning from the UK remember that this `0' should be disregarded and replaced by the appropriate Country Code - for details refer to your telephone directory.

Time: Apart from a period of about three weeks during October, the clocks in most European countries are one hour ahead of those in Britain.

Camping and Caravanning in Europe

When visiting sites featured in this Guide you should not encounter any particular problems and the formalities now required for visiting countries in Western Europe, and even in Hungary, Poland and the Czech and Slovak Republics, are few. The following information may however be useful, particularly for those who do not take their cars abroad all that often.

Sites in Europe - Whether you have a caravan, tent, trailer tent or motorcaravan you will seldom encounter any difficulty with admission to a particular site, with the possible exception of some sites where the terrain is unsuitable for certain vehicles, such as large motorhomes of the American type or occasionally twin axle caravans. It should be noted that motorcaravans are often referred to as 'campers' or 'camping cars', and a sign 'no campers' refers to this type of vehicle, not to people with tents!

Essential Documents and Equipment - The documentation required to take a vehicle abroad is now minimal, and the following list covers both the essential and the advisable items:

☐ **Passport:** a valid full Passport is essential - details from the Passport Office or any main post office.

☐ **Motor Insurance:** although a Green Card is no longer compulsory for countries within the European Community, it is very strongly recommended, and is actually a requirement for some non-EC countries. Your insurance company or broker will advise. Similarly a Bail-Bond is still recommended for Spain

☐ **Driving Licence:** a full (not provisional) British licence of the new type (pink and green) is sufficient in most western European countries, but the old-style British licence is no longer acceptable in several countries, including Spain, Italy, and Austria, without a translation in the local language. The alternative and essential for most East European countries is an International Driving Permit (IDP) - obtainable from the AA or RAC.

☐ **Car Registration Document** (log book).

☐ Letter granting **authority to drive** if the vehicle is not your own.

☐ **GB sign** on rear of vehicle and on rear of caravan or trailer.

☐ **Red Warning Triangle** - from motor accessory shops.

☐ **First-Aid kit.**

☐ **Spare set of vehicle light bulbs.**

☐ **Form E1-11:** this form, now obtainable from main Post Offices, extends your National Health Insurance to the continent, although it may provide for recovery of only about 80% of any medical expenses, so independent medical expenses insurance cover is a wise precaution - see below.

☐ **Travel/Breakdown Insurance:** not absolutely essential, but strongly recommended - we have negotiated special terms for readers of this Guide with Heritage European Rescueline, one of the most reputable (and competitive) insurers for this type of policy; see details between pages 160 and 161. The cover can be arranged to include breakdown insurance, personal accident insurance, cancellation insurance and medical expenses cover. This type of service proved to be very popular when we first introduced it in 1991 and our experience of operating it ever since has been highly satisfactory.

☐ **Camping Carnet:** useful (but by no means essential) if you dislike having to lodge your passport with campsite receptions. They can be obtained from various motoring organisations, including the GB Car Club whose advertisement is in the colour section between pages 16/17.

☐ **Discount Vouchers:** full details of how to use the vouchers attached to this guide are shown on the vouchers themselves, and between pages 160 and 161 .

Naturist Sites - Some years ago we introduced a number of naturist sites into our France Guide. Although naturism is particularly popular in France, where there are very many naturist sites, there is an increasing number of such sites in other European countries too, and we have therefore included a few in our Europe Guide. Those few we include are all of the high quality associated with a majority of naturist sites. Visitors to these sites are, however, normally required to belong to (or join on arrival) one of the recognised naturist associations, membership of which usually involves a fee of around £10 per annum (see advert between pages 32 and 33).

All information given in this guide has been carefully checked for accuracy at the time of going to press and it is believed in good faith to be true. If there should be any errors or omissions, however, due to a change in circumstances or for any other reasons, the publishers and the editors cannot be held in any way responsible for these or for any consequences of them. Any opinions expressed represent honest personal assessments.

ALAN ROGERS' Good Camps Guide

EUROPE 1998 - DISCOUNT VOUCHERS

Between pages 160 and 161
**you will find various Discount Vouchers which will provide you
with potential savings of much more than the cost of the Guide itself!**
(These vouchers are valid 1 January - 31 December 1998 only)

Voucher A   Campsite Discount Voucher

This voucher entitles the holder to the relevant discounts or special offers at those campsites featured in this guide which have a small Alan Rogers' logo beneath their Site Report. This section of the voucher should be retained by the holder, but made available for inspection at the campsite for the purpose of verifying your entitlement to the relevant discount or offer.

Voucher B   Travel and Breakdown Insurance

This voucher entitles the holder to a discount of 10% on Travel & Breakdown Insurance arrangements made via this Guide, as advertised between pages 160 and 161. To arrange cover please complete the proposal and send this, together with the appropriate premium and this voucher to: Deneway Guides & Travel Ltd., Chesil Lodge, West Bexington, Dorchester DT2 9DG. Fax 01308 898017. A proposal form and the discount voucher will need to be completed and sent to Deneway Guides & Travel along with payment for the relevant premium in all circumstances except in very urgent cases (ie. those within seven days of departure) when we can arrange cover via telephone or (preferably) fax .

Voucher C   Caravan or Motorcaravan Insurance

This voucher entitles the holder to a 5% discount on caravan or motorcaravan insurance arranged through Bakers of Cheltenham. Please complete the enquiry form on pages 365/6 and send it, together with this voucher, to Bakers of Cheltenham, Freepost GR1604, The Quadrangle, Imperial Square, Cheltenham GL50 1BR.

Voucher D   Caravan and Camping Service

This voucher entitles the holder to a refund of the full cover price of this guide (£9.99) when booking a travel inclusive holiday arrangement with the Caravan & Camping Service, whose advertisement appears on page 360. To claim your refund, this voucher should be sent to the Camping & Caravan Service, 69 Westbourne Grove, London W2 4UJ when making your booking with them.

Voucher E   Sites Abroad Holidays

This voucher entitles the holder to reclaim the cover price of this Alan Rogers Good Camps Guide 1998 when making a booking with Sites Abroad. Please send the completed voucher to Sites Abroad, Canute Court, Toft Road, Knutsford, Cheshire WA16 0NL, when making your booking.

Voucher F   Camping Cheque

This card entitles the holder to a FREE COPY of the 1998 Camping Cheques Catalogue. Please send the completed card to Camping Cheques, Canute House, Toft Road, Knutsford, Cheshire WA16 0NL

Voucher G   Track Tours

This card entitles the holder to a 15% discount on Track Tours arrangements at the Le Mans 24 Hour Race, as described in Track Tours advertisement in the colour section between pages 64 and 65.

Save Money!

Andorra

Andorra is situated high in the Pyrenees between France and Spain and is an independent principality covering 181 sq. miles. It is a sovereign country and the main occupations are agriculture and tourism. It is probably best known for skiing and tax free goods. The population is 55,000 (1991), density 117 per sq. km. and the capital is Andorra la Vella. The climate is temperate, with cold winters with a lot of snow and warm summers.The language is Catalan, with French and Spanish widely spoken. French francs and Spanish pesetas are both used.

UK Andorran Delegation, 63 Westover Road, London SW18 2RF Tel: 0181 874 4806
(Personal visits by appointment only, telephone morning only)

9143 Camping Xixerella, Erts, nr La Massana

All year site in attractive mountain valley.

Andorra is a country of narrow valleys and pine and birch forested mountains. Xixerella is attractively situated in just such a valley, beside a small river. The site is made up of several sections, accessed by tarmac or gravel roads. There are some terraced pitches, although generally they are not marked out and are on grass, mainly with a small degree of slope. Electricity (3A) is available for most of the 220 places. The site can be very busy from mid-July to mid-August, but otherwise it is usually quite peaceful. The main sanitary building has been refurbished to a satisfactory standard and has British WCs (no paper) with small ones for children and free hot water to the open washbasins (some private cabins), controllable showers and under-cover laundry and dishwashing facilities. There are further modern facilities down inside the round building by the pool, including a laundry, baby bath and dishwashing sinks. There is a pleasant bar with terrace, a cosy restaurant and a small shop. The swimming pool is open mid-June to mid-Sept. and is not depth-marked. Minigolf is also available and there is a well fenced children's play area. Riding is just 3 km. away. Skiing is available at Pal (6 km) or Arinsal (5 km).

How to find it: Site is 8 km. from Andorra la Vella on the road to Pal via La Massana.

General Details: Open all year, as are shop, restaurant and bar. Swimming pool (summer). Minigolf. Chemical disposal. Chalets for hire.

Charges 1997: Per person Ptas 450; child 400; car 450; caravan 450; tent 450; motorcaravan 800; m/cycle 400; electricity (3A) 450; dog 250.

Reservations: Contact site. Address: Carretera de Pals, Erts (La Massana), Andorra. Tel: 836 613. FAX: 839 113.

Liechtenstein

Liechtenstein is an independent principality, bounded on the north by Switzerland and Austria, and on the south and west by Switzerland. One of the smallest independent states in the world, it has a total area of 157 sq. km. (61 sq. miles). The climate is Alpine with mild winters; average temperatures range from -1.1° C (30° F) in January to 21.1° C (70° F) in July. Liechtenstein has a population of 29,868, of whom about one-third are resident aliens (1990 census, 10,218 resident aliens), with an overall density of about 190 people per sq.km. Native-born Liechtensteiners are descended from the Germanic Alamanni people and most still speak an Alamanni dialect of the official language, German. The country's close ties with Switzerland are also important; the Swiss franc is the official currency of Liechtenstein and the two states have operated a customs union since 1924. Liechtenstein is a constitutional monarchy governed by hereditary princes.

758 Camping Mittagsspitze, Triesen, nr Liechtenstein

Attractively and quietly situated site for visiting the Principality.

Mittagsspitze, probably the best site in the region, is on a hillside and has all the scenic views that one could wish. Extensive broad terraces have now been made over the main part of the site so there is a better chance of finding a level pitch on the steep slope. The site has a small swimming pool, not heated but very popular in summer. A good quality sanitary block has all the usual facilities and the older provision near reception has been refurbished recently. British style WCs. This site is mainly used by residential caravans.

How to find it: Site is just off the main Vaduz - Chur road 2 km. south of Triesen.

General Details: Open 1 April - 31 Oct. 36,000 sq.m. Little shade. Electrical connections (6A) in many places. Shop. Swimming pool. Children's playground. Room where one can sit, eat, etc., with cooking facilities. Washing machine, dryer and ironing. Rooms to let.

Charges 1998: Per person Sfr. 8.50; child (under 11) 4.00; car 4.00; caravan or large tent 8.00 - 10.00; small tent 5.00; dog 4.00; electricity 3.00 - 4.00; local tax 6.5%. Discounts: 8 days 5%; 15 days 10%; 21 days 15%.

Reservations: not made. Address: FL-9495 Triesen. Tel: 075/392.36.77 or 392.26.86. FAX: 075/392.36.80.

AUSTRIA

Centrally situated in Europe, Austria is primarily known for two contrasting attractions - its capital Vienna with its fading Imperial glories, and the variety of its Alpine hinterland. Ideally suitable for all year round visiting, either viewing the spectacular scenery and enjoying the various opportunities for winter sports or visiting the historical sites and sampling the cultural attractions. For further information about Austria contact:

Austrian National Tourist Office, 30 Saint George Street, London W1R 0AL.

Tel: 0171 629 0461. Fax: 0171 499 6038.

Population
7,915,000 (1993), density 94.2 per sq. km.

Capital
Vienna (Wien).

Climate
Austria has a moderate Central European climate. The winter season is from December to March (in higher regions the end of May) and warm clothing, including waterproof shoes or boots, is a necessity. Even in summer the evenings in mountain resorts can be quite cool.

Language
German is the usual language but English is widely spoken and understood.

Currency
The unit of currency is the Austrian Schilling which is divided into 100 Groschen. There are bank notes to the value of 5,000, 1,000, 500, 100, 50 and 20 schillings, coins of 20, 10, 5 and 1 schillings and 50 and 10 groschen.

Banks
Banking hours are mainly 08.00 - 12.30 hrs and 13.30 - 15.00 hrs on Mon, Tues, Wed and Fri. Thurs hours are 08.00 - 12.30 and 13.30 - 17.30.
Credit Cards: Most major credit cards are accepted in the larger cities and tourist areas, but few petrol stations (other than Jet stations) accept payment by credit card. Travellers cheques and Eurocheques are widely accepted.

Post Offices
Offices are open Monday to Friday 08.00 -12.00 hrs and 14.00 - 18.00 hrs.

Time
GMT plus 1 (summer BST plus 1).

Telephone
To Austria from the UK the code is 0043, ignoring the '0' at the start of the area code. For calls from Austria to the UK the code is 0044.

Public Holidays
New Year; Epiphany; Easter Mon; Labour Day; Ascension; Whit Mon; Corpus Christi; Assumption, 15 Aug; National Day, 26 Oct; All Saints, 1 Nov; Immaculate Conception, 8 Dec; Christmas, 25, 26 Dec.

Shops
Shops open 08.00-18.30 hrs but many close for 2 hours at lunch and 13.00 on Sats except first Sat in every month, when they open to 17.00.

Motoring
Tolls: It is now (from 1 Jan 97) compulsory to purchase a motorway disc. For visiting cars, motorhomes and towed caravans with a combined weight under 3.5 tons a 'weekly' disc costing 70 schillings (valid up to 10 days Thurs midnight to midnight 2 Sundays later) or 'monthly' (valid for 2 consecutive months) at 150 schillings is available. Motorbikes can only purchase a 'monthly' at 80 schillings. They are available at major border crossings, petrol stations and post offices at present and for cash only. Fines for non-compliance are heavy. Previously levied road and tunnel tolls still apply, but a discount of 15% applies to discholders on the S16 Arlberg Tunnel, A13 Brenner - A9 Pyhon and A10 Tauern motorways.

Speed limits: For caravans and motorhomes (3.5t): 31 mph (50 kph) in built up areas, 62 mph (100 kph) other roads (including motor- ways for caravans) and 81 mph (130 kph) for motorhomes on motorways. There is a lower limit of 68 mph (110 kph) between 2200 - 0500 on the A8, A9, A10, A12, A13 and A14. A min. speed of 37 mph (60 kph) applies on roads with a rectangular blue sign showing a white car.

Towing Restrictions: The maximum overall length for car and caravan is restricted to 12 metres. It is also important that your caravan or motorhome is not overloaded.

Parking: Limited parking (blue zones) with max. parking time of 1.5-3 hrs. Parking clocks can be obtained free of charge from tobacconists (Tabak-Trafik), shops or local police stations. However in Vienna, Graz, Linz, Klagenfurt, Salzburg, Innsbruck and a few other cities there is a charge for parking vouchers which can be obtained in banks, some petrol stations and from tobacconists. They must be clearly displayed on the inside of the windscreen.

Overnighting
It is possible to park outside campsites provided permission has been obtained beforehand from the landowner. Except in Vienna and protected rural areas visitors are permitted to sleep in the camping vehicle but local restrictions can apply and campers are not allowed to set up camping equipment beside their vehicle.

Useful addresses
OCC (Osterreichischer Camping Club) Schubertring 1-3, 1010 Wien.
Tel: 01 771 99/1272. Fax: 01 711 99/1498.
OAMTC (Osterreichischer Automobil-Motorradund Touring Club) Schubertring 1-3, 1010 Wien.
Tel: 01/72990.

Salzburg and the Centre

There is more to Salzburg than 'The Sound of Music' and Mozart, although memorabilia of its most famous composer dominate from confectionery to souvenirs. Pasture-land, curative spas and interesting castles and monasteries abound. The Lake District, set amidst rolling hills, is near, along with salt mines to visit and music, art and drama festivals to enjoy, making a special holiday. Salzburg has its own distinctive cuisine, splendid gardens and ancient castles.

016 Seecamp, Zell-am-See

Excellent lakeside site for summer and winter camping.

Zellersee, delightfully situated in the south of Salzburg province and near the start of the Grossglock-nerstrasse, is ideally placed for enjoying the splendid southern Austria countryside. Seecamp, completely rebuilt in '91, is right by the water about 2 km. from the town of Zell with fine views to the south end of the lake. On entering, one is immediately struck by the order and appearance of the camp, with good level, mainly grass-on-gravel pitches of above average size. All have electricity and about half have water, drainage and TV sockets also. A large, modern building in the centre, houses reception, shop, restaurant (with terrace) and excellent sanitary facilities which include British style WCs, a baby room and special one for the disabled. The lake is accessible for boating and watersports, including both surfing and sailing schools. In summer there is organised entertainment for children and a programme for adults which includes sports, rafting, canoeing, mountain biking, water ski-ing and hiking. Coach excursions are available and glacier ski-ing is possible in summer. All in all, a splendid camp for a relaxing or active holiday amidst the mountains and green pastures of a beautiful country.

How to find it: Follow signs for Thumersbach where site is signed.

General Details: Open all year. 28,000 sq.m. Restaurant (closed Nov). Shop (June-Aug. and Dec). Activity programmes (see text). Beach volleyball. Fishing. Bicycle hire. Children's play area. Winter ski packages with ski passes, etc. Washing machines, dryers and irons. Chemical disposal. Motorcaravan services.

Charges 1997: Per comfort pitch sch. 120, simple pitch 100 or tent pitch 50, all less 25-50% in low seasons; adult 85; child (2-15 yrs) 45; dog 45; electricity, gas. TV connections 30 (once only) plus meters; local tax (over 15 yrs) 7. Special winter package prices.

Reservations: Write to site for application form. Address: Thumersbacherstrasse 34, 5700 Zell-am-See. Tel: 06542/72115. FAX: 06542/7211515.

018 Sport Camp Woferlgut, Bruck a.d. Grossglocknerstrasse, nr Zell

Well equipped site in mountain region for both summer and winter camping.

Opened in 1983, this family run site has been progressively improved to make it one of the best camps in Austria. Surrounded by mountains, the camp is quite flat with an open outlook and is near the start of the Grossglocknerstrasse. The 150 level pitches on grass are of generous size and marked out by shrubs. Each one has electricity connection, water, drainage, cable TV socket and gas point. Two modern sanitary blocks with under-floor heating and music, have excellent facilities with British type WCs and showers on payment. The fitness centre has a fully equipped gymnasium, a small heated pool with 'jet-stream', sauna, Turkish steam bath, solarium, cold spa-baths, exercise and massage rooms, and a bar. In summer there is an activity programme, evenings with live music, club for children, weekly barbecues and guided cycle and mountain tours. There are 3 tennis courts, volleyball, football area, bicycle hire and the site's own lake for swimming and fishing, surrounded by a landscaped sunbathing area. In winter a cross-country skiing trail and toboggan run lead from the site and a free bus service is provided to nearby skiing facilities. The hobby room is equipped with billiards, table tennis and television. A new restaurant has been built and there is a well stocked shop. Apartments, rooms and caravans to let. The management is pleased to advise on local attractions and tours, making this a splendid base for a family holiday.

How to find it: Site is southwest of Bruck. From road B311, Bruck by-pass, take southern exit (Grossglockner) and site is well signed.

General Details: Open all year. 20,000 sq.m.. General room with cooking facilities in room adjoining. Washing machine and dryer. Large children's playground. Watersports and swimming at local lake. Horse riding, hiking, golf, skiing (all year round) nearby.

Charges 1997: Per person sch. 47 - 60, acc. to season + local tax 10; child (under 10) 37 - 50; car 42 - 55; tent 37 - 65 (acc. to season and size); caravan 52 - 65; motorcaravan 62 - 87; m/cycle 32 - 45; cable TV 100; electricity and gas on meter.

Reservations: Contact site. Address: 5671 Bruck a.d. Glocknerstrasse. Tel: 06545/73030. FAX: 06545/73033.

See colour advert
between pages 16/17

AUSTRIA - Salzburg and the Centre

019 Kur-Camping Erlengrund, Badgastein

Mountain site catering for summer and winter.

Visiting this site would mean making a special trip to do so, unless you are taking the Tauern railway tunnel to or from Carinthia (which can take caravans as well as cars) when it is on your route. It is very much a mountain site, over 3,000 feet up, for walking in summer and skiing in winter. There are 250 marked out pitches on flat ground in sizes of 80, 100, and 120 sq. m., all with electricity, water, gas and TV connections and drainaway (only 70 for tourists, the others for permanents). A very good toilet block, heated in cold weather, has British WCs, free hot water in the washbasins with shelf and mirror (some in cabins), the fully controllable showers with screen and seat, and the enclosed washing up sinks. Hair dryers. Dog bath. The site has a small heated swimming pool (12 x 6 m).

How to find it: Turn off the no. 167 road at sign, 1 km. before Badgastein.

General Details: Open all year. Small shop. TV room. Table tennis. Football practice ground. Washing machine, dryer and drying room. Apartments for hire.

Charges 1997: Per person sch. 60 - 67; local tax (over 15 yrs) 15; child (1-12 yrs) 47 - 52; pitch 60 - 87, acc. to size and season; small tent pitch 35 - 40; m/cycle 25; extra car 25; electricity and gas on meter; TV connection 10.

Reservations: made for min. 1 week with deposit. Address: Erlengrund Str. 6, 5640 Badgastein. Tel: 06434/2790. FAX: 06434/2526262.

021 Camping Nord-Sam, Salzburg

Neat little site in suburbs near town and autobahn.

Nord-Sam is very close to the `Salzburg-Nord' autobahn exit, and so makes a convenient stopover for those travelling through. It is also acceptable for a longer stay, being on the edge of the town and with its own small swimming pool (14 x 7 m.). The terrain is divided into about 90 individual marked out pitches, which are not very large but are separated from each other by hedges, etc. which offer some privacy and are also attractive to wild life (including red squirrels)! Pitches are quite well shaded and there are about 60 electrical connections. The site is well tended, with flowers and shrubs. You should find space if you arrive reasonably early. The small, heated sanitary block, situated below the house, is of nice quality with British toilets, individual basins with shelf, mirror and hot water, some in private cabins, free hot water in showers and washing-up sinks. Salzburg is a major railway junction so you should expect some train noise at night. There is a cycle path directly to the centre.

How to find it: Site is signed from the `Salzburg-Nord' autobahn exit and city centre; follow signs carefully.

General Details: Open 1 May - 30 Sept. 13,000 sq.m. Small shop. Room for general use where drinks served. Swimming pool (can be heated). Meals in high season. Unusual small children's play area. Washing machine and dryer. Chemical disposal. Motorcaravan service point. Bicycle hire. Bus service to city (tickets from reception, · change at railway station).

Charges 1997: Per person sch. 43 - 53; child (2-14 yrs) 27 - 34; pitch 79 - 99; dog 15 - 20; electricity 25.

Reservations: Are made - contact site. Address: Samstrasse 22a, 5023 Salzburg. Tel: 0662/660494.

026 Camping Hirschenwirt, St Johann im Pongau

Small, pleasant site with first class sanitary facilities.

This small, but very pleasant camp is ideally placed for those wanting a night stop when travelling on the Salzburg - Badgastein road but could also make an excellent base for seeing this interesting area of mountains, lakes, salt mines, ice caves and famous towns. The flat, open site lies behind the Gasthof Hirschenwirt, with 50 tourist pitches on grass on either side of gravel access roads. All pitches have electrical connections and sockets for satellite TV. The splendid sanitary arrangements are in the basement of the Gasthof. They have under floor heating, British style WCs and some private bathrooms for hire. The sauna and solarium are also here. Small pool for summer use.

How to find it: Site is behind the Gasthof Hirschenwirt at St Johann im Pongau on the main Salzburg - Badgastein road no. 311.

General Details: Open all year except Nov. 8,000 sq.m. Bar/restaurant. Sauna and solarium. Bicycle hire. Electricity and TV points. Swimming pool (June-Sept). Bicycle hire. Children's playground. Music (in restaurant) at weekends. Salzburg, etc. near. Washing machine, dryer and drying room. Baby room. Chemical disposal.

Charges guide: Winter prices in brackets. Per person sch. 44 (64); child (under 14 yrs) 20 (30); pitch 80 (100); electricity 6 per kw.

Reservations: Write to site. Address: 5600 St Johann im Pongau. Tel: 06412/6012. FAX: 06412/6012-8.

 AR Discount
Less 10%

024 Camping Appesbach, St Wolfgang, nr Salzburg

Lakeside site in an attractive region for excursions.

The situation of this site is one of its main assets, being right by the lakeside with a reasonable frontage and with a very pleasant outlook to the high hills on the opposite side. The lake can be used for all types of sailing and sail-boarding; it is possible to leave small boats by the beach and there are also some for hire. There is a possibility of using motor boats, but for restricted hours. Bathing is possible if not too cool. The site is 1 km. from the village of St. Wolfgang and the many excursions possible in the area include Salzburg some 50 km. away. The site has room for about 50 permanent caravans and 150 tourists, but the pitches are not numbered or marked out. Units go on large meadows in rows and could become crowded in the main season. It can be full for July and most of August if the weather is good. There are electrical connections in most parts. The two toilet blocks have British WCs, a good supply of washbasins with shelf, mirror and free hot water, but less numerous free hot showers which in one block require external undressing.

How to find it: Approaching along the no. 158 road from west, turn left at camp sign just past Ströbl and continue round lake to camp which is 1 km. before St. Wolfgang.

General Details: Open Easter - 31 Oct. Shop. Pleasant restaurant/bar with good food, which also serves as general room with TV. Snack bar with terrace. Small children's playground. Tennis nearby. Motorcaravan service point.

Charges guide: Per person sch. 59 - 69, acc. to season, local tax included; child 36 - 39; pitch 50, 80 or 110, acc. to position and size of unit; electricity 30; dog 20; boat 30. Some reductions longer stays off season.

Reservations: made for min. 1 week with deposit. Address: Au 99, 5360 St. Wolfgang (Salzkammergut). Tel: 06138/2206. FAX: 06138/220633.

027 Seecamp-Neumarkt, Neumarkt am Wallersee

Lakeside site north of Salzburg with good facilities.

Surrounded by gentle hills and adorned with trees and flowers, Seecamp is separated from the lake by a narrow public road, although there is access to the water through the municipal bathing station. When seen in mid-week it was very quiet, but one would imagine that it is more lively during weekends in high season. The 170 grass pitches (80 for tourists, the remainder for long stay units) are on either side of gravel roads on a very gentle slope. They are not marked out or numbered but the position of electrical connection boxes allows sufficient space. All pitches have electricity and connections are available for TV/radio, water and drainage. Reception, a restaurant with terrace, very good sanitary facilities, heated in winter (with British type WCs and free hot water) and a first aid room are housed together in a modern, underground block near the lake. Some facilities are used by non-camping members of the public.

How to find it: Approx. 26 km. from Salzburg, on B1/A1 Salzburg - Linz road, take turning for Neumarkt. Follow signs for Strandcamping just before the small town itself. If using motorway use Wallersee Ost exit.

General Details: Open Easter - 31 Oct. 37,000 sq.m. Restaurant with terrace. Shop. Minigolf. Volleyball. Bathing at lake station. Baby room. Ramps on steps to toilets but rather steep. Children's playground. Medical/treatment room. General room with TV.

Charges 1997: High season 15/6-31/8. Per pitch sch. 65 - 95; adult 65; child (2-15 yrs) 35; local tax 5; electricity 25 plus 8 per kw; TV/radio connection 60.

Reservations: Write to site. Address: Uferstr. 3, 5202 Neumarkt (Salzburg). Tel: 06216/4400. FAX: 06216/44004.

Tirol and the West

This is the best known area of Austria as far as British visitors are concerned and the most easily accessible part of the country. It has considerable charm and a wealth of scenic, sporting and historical interest as a centre for both winter and summer tourism. Folk-lore entertainment (Tirolerabend) is on offer outdoors in summer and in Gasthof bars and Hotels in winter. Mountain paths are well marked and maintained and local authorities provide information centres in towns and lay-bys. Innsbruck is the famous capital of the region, good quality camp sites abound and there are many pleasant valleys to explore.

**The sites in AUSTRIA featured in this guide
are shown on the map on page 367**

AUSTRIA - Tirol and the West

001 Seecamping, Bregenz

Busy site with good situation close to the Bodensee.

This site is not directly on the lake but very near - people bathe in the lake and there are small boats for hire. It is a good touring centre with the Vorarlberg region, Germany and Switzerland close at hand. The site is in two parts, with the pitches mainly in flat rows between access roads. Siting is left to campers; it takes large numbers and can be crowded in season. The toilet blocks are good with British WCs and free hot water in showers and basins. The main washrooms are closed at 10 pm. A new block has been added since our visit with washbasins in cubicles, showers and facilities for dishwashing and laundry.

How to find it: Site is on the Swiss side of Bregenz, by the lake; there are camping signs from the main no. 190 road but no site names and there are two other sites on the access road. Seecamping is the last one.

General Details: Open 15 May - 15 Sept. Shade in old part. Shop. Bar; simple hot food served. Children's playground. Washing machine. Electrical connections in most parts.

Charges 1998: Per person 60 sch.+ local tax 17; child (6-15 yrs) 30; car 60; caravan or tent incl. electricity 60, motorcaravan 120.

Reservations: not made and said to be unnecessary. Address: Bodangasse 7, 6900 Bregenz am Bodensee. Tel: 05574/31896.

023 Camping Waldcamping, Feldkirch

Good municipal site on edge of town near borders.

Feldkirch lies near the borders with Germany, Switzerland and Liechtenstein and Waldcamping is part of the Gisingen sports stadium on the edge of the town. The Vorarlberg mountains and Bodensee (Lake Constance) are nearby and there are good sporting facilities at the stadium which is set in a quiet residential suburb, about 4 km from the centre. Tall trees surround the camp and the 170 tourist pitches are on flat grass, either in the centre, or to the side of the hard road which runs round the camping area. In high season an overflow area may be brought into use (without electricity). There are two well constructed sanitary blocks near the entrance, one of which is open and heated in winter plus an older block at the back of the site. British type WCs. A neat, tidy site which caters for winter skiing and summer touring.

How to find it: Follow signs from the centre of town for Gisingen Stadium (4 km.).

General Details: Open all year. 40,000 sq.m. Bar/restaurant 1 km. Shop (May - Sept). Large, heated swimming pool (free for campers). Child's pool and playground. Tennis. Football. Washing machines and dryers. Chemical disposal. Motorcaravan services.

Charges 1997: Per person sch. 50 - 57; child (6-14 yrs) 23 - 30;; local tax 10, young person 5, child free; caravan 46 - 52, over 6 m. 56 - 68; tent 48 - 52, small tent 29 - 34; motorcaravan 66 - 79; car 36 - 42; m/cycle 25 - 30; electricity 25 (plus 4 per kw. in winter).

Reservations: Write to site. Address: Postfach 564, 6803 Feldkirch. Tel: 05522/74308.

020 Sport Camp Tirol, Landeck

Well run site with good facilities and opportunity for white water boating.

There are several medium sized sites in this area bordering the Vorarlberg and Tirol, of which this (previously Camping Huber) is a good example. The area is popular for winter skiing and summer watersports and mountain walking. White water sports are organised on the River Sanna which runs alongside (with access) and the River Inn. On the other side of the narrow site are fir clad mountains which, with many trees on the site, make it a very pleasant place to stop, either for one night whilst passing through, or for longer stays to explore the region. The 100 pitches, all with electricity and 70-100 sq.m, are on either side of gravel roads which run from the hard central road. The pitches are not marked, but campers are shown where to go. There is further space for about 20 tents at the far end. As with most Austrian sites which remain open all year, the sanitary facilities are of a good standard. The ladies' block is central, with the men's block behind reception. There is hot water (pre-set) in showers and sinks and about half the washbasins, British style WCs and a children's washroom. The reception block also has a pizzeria/café and, just outside the entrance, is a shop and restaurant. Children's playground on sand. Good English is spoken by the enthusiastic man and wife team who run the site.

How to find it: Site is on the main Vorarlberg - Tirol road by the river bridge, 1 km. west of Landeck. Signed Camping Huber and/or Sport Camp Tirol.

General Details: Open all year. 11,000 sq.m. Restaurant. Pizzeria/café. Shop. Room for disabled people. Baby room. Table tennis. Children's playground. Volleyball. Programme of watersports, canyoning, rafting, kayak, etc. organised.. Roller skating. Mountain biking. Swimming pool 1 km. Washing machine and dryer. Motorcaravan services. Bungalows and studio to let.

Charges 1997: Per adult sch. 57; child (5-15 yrs) 40; local tax (adults) 6; car 38; m/cycle 27; caravan 90; motorcaravan 108; 1 man tent, 2 man tent 63, family tent 90; electricity 28. Special winter rates.

Reservations: Write to site, no deposit or fee required. Address: Mühlkanal 1, 6500 Landeck. Tel: 05442/64636. FAX: 05442/64037. Internet: http://www.tis.co.at./landeck/sportcamptirol.

14

015 Camping Riffler, Landeck

Small, compact site with good facilities.

This small, pretty site is almost in the centre of the small town of Landeck and being on the main through route from the Vorarlberg to the Tirol, would serve as a good overnight stop. Square in shape, it has just 45 pitches on either side of hard access roads on level grass, with the main road on one side and the fast flowing river on the other edge. Trees and flowers adorn the site giving good shade. The site is open all year except for May, but static caravans are only allowed to stay in the winter period. One small section is kept for groups with tents. The original toilet block was of good quality with British WCs and hot water in washbasins, showers and sinks and a further block has been added. Apart from a washing machine and dryer, there are no other amenities on the site but there is a supermarket just outside the gate and other shops and restaurants about 100 m. away.

How to find it: Site is at the western end of Landeck on the main no. 316 road.

General Details: Open all year except May. 3,000 sq.m. Electricity to all pitches. Washing machine and dryer. Small general room. Children's play area. Table tennis. Restaurants and shops 100 m. in village.

Charges 1997: Per person sch. 50; child (5-14 yrs) 45; car on pitch 25, on car park 20; caravan or motorcaravan 80 - 100; tent 55 - 90; electricity 25; trailer 50; tax 6. Less 5% for stays over 10 days. Winter prices slightly more.

Reservations: Write to site. Address: Bruggenfeldstrasse 2, 6500 Landeck. Tel: 05442/624774. FAX: 05442/624775.

022 Ötztal Arena Camp Krismer, Umhausen

Good site in quiet valley, with excellent toilet facilities.

This is a delightful site in the beautiful Ötz valley, on the edge of the village of Umhausen. Situated on a gentle slope in an open valley, it has an air of peace and tranquillity and makes an excellent base for mountain walking, particularly in spring and autumn, skiing in winter or a relaxing holiday. The 100 pitches are all marked out and numbered and have electrical connections; charges relate to the area available. The single, new reception building houses an attractive bar/restaurant, a TV room (with Sky programmes) and the sanitary facilities. These are of exceptional quality with under floor heating, British style WCs and free hot water in the washbasins (private cabins) and sinks and on payment in the showers. Special baby room with bath and changing area. A small toilet/wash block at the far end of the site has been refurbished for summer use. Good children's playground. Para-gliding, mountain walks and the Stuiben waterfall nearby. The enthusiastic man and wife management team speak good English.

How to find it: Take the Ötztal Valley exit from the Imst - Innsbruck motorway, and Umhausen is 13 km. towards Solden; well signed in village.

General Details: Open all year. 6,800 sq.m. Bar/restaurant (all year). Shops in village (bread can be ordered at reception). Children's play area. TV room with satellite Sky programmes. Ski room. Fishing. Swimming pool, tennis and table tennis 100 m. . Washing machine and dryer, iron from reception, drying room. Chemical disposal.

Charges 1998: Per pitch sch.1 per sq.m. (60 - 80 in winter); person 65; child 50; dog 35; electricity 10 per kw; local tax 10.

Reservations: Write with sch. 500 deposit. Address: 6441 Umhausen 387 (Ötztal-Tirol). Tel: 05255/5390 or 05254/8196. FAX: 05255/5390. Internet: http://www.tiscover.com.oetztal-arena-camp-krismer.

AR Discount
Less 20% on pitch fee in low season

003 Holiday Camping, Leutasch, nr Seefeld

Developing site in mountain setting north of Seefeld.

Rather away from main routes (especially for caravans) this site is not for night stops but could appeal to the active or for touring as it has a fine setting surrounded by mountains. There are about 160 numbered pitches on flat grass, some of 80 sq.m. with electrical and TV connections and 74 of 96 sq.m. with water and drainage also. There should be space in summer. The two toilet blocks, heated in cool weather, are of excellent quality with British type WCs, washbasins all in cabins, showers with long seat and inner door, with push-button and with temperature control, and a dog shower. Hot water is free in all these and in the sinks. A new addition is a superb heated indoor swimming pool complex with sauna, sun-beds, whirlpool and steam bath. This is a friendly site where good English is spoken.

How to find it: Site is 4 km. north of Leutasch. From north Mittenwald - Leutasch direct is banned to trailers, as is Zirlerberg on Innsbruck - Seefeld road coming from the south; these routes are best for cars. With caravans approach either via Seefeld from north or via Telfs - Mosern - Seefeld from the south.

General Details: Open all year except Nov. Small shop for bread and drinks. Restaurant for meals or drinks; music twice weekly. Indoor pool complex (as above). Tennis. Games room with pool, table tennis, etc. Children's playground. Fishing. Bicycle hire. Activity programme. Apartments for hire. Chemical disposal. Motorcaravan service point. Washing machines and dryers. Exchange facilities.

Charges 1998: Winter prices higher. Per unit incl. 2 persons: large pitch (100 sq.m.) with electricity, TV, water and drainage sch. 280 - 320, normal pitch (80 sq.m.) with electricity and TV 270 - 310, tent pitch 200; extra adult 85; child (4-14 yrs) 60; local tax 11 - 13; electricity 8 per kw/h..

Reservations: made for any length with deposit. Address: 6105 Leutasch. Tel: 05214/65700. FAX: 05214/657030. Internet: www.tis.co.at./holiday-camping.

006 Terrassencamping Natterer See, Natters, nr Innsbruck

See colour
advert opposite

Site in quiet lakeside situation above Innsbruck amid fine scenery.

Above Innsbruck, 7 km. southwest of the town, this site is in a quiet and isolated location around two small lakes. One of these is for bathing with a long 67 m. slide - free to campers, on payment to day visitors - while boats such as inflatables can be put on either lake. There are many fine mountain views and a wide variety of scenic excursions. For the more active, signed walks start from the site. The site offers about 200 individual pitches of varying, but adequate size, some on flat ground by the lake, others on higher, level, terraces. Electrical connections are available, with 28 pitches also having water, drain and telephone connections and 42 with drain and telephone. Many are reinforced by gravel (possibly tricky for tents). There are two sanitary blocks of excellent standard with under-floor heating, British type WCs, free hot water in washbasins (some private cabins) and showers, baby baths and facilities for disabled people. For winter camping the site offers ski and drying room and a free ski-bus service. There is a toboggan run and langlauf developed on site and ice skating, ice hockey and curling on the lake. During high season there is an extensive daily entertainment programme for children and adults offering different sports, competitions, amusement and excursions. Occasional services are held in the small chapel. The excellent restaurant with bar and large terrace overlooking the lake has a good menu and takeaway service. Well appointed apartments and rooms to let. Very good English is spoken. This family run camp must rate as one of the best in Austria.

How to find it: From the Inntal autobahn (A12) take the Brenner autobahn (A13) as far as the Innsbruck-sud/Natters exit (no. 3) without payment. From Italy, take exit for Innsbruck-Sud/Natters. Site is signed from the exit (4 km).

General Details: Open all year except 1/10-15/12. Limited shade. Excellent bar/restaurant and good shop (both 15/12-10/1 and 1/3-30/9). 3 children's playgrounds. Sports field. Basketball, beach volleyball and `waterball'. Table tennis. Bicycle hire. Tennis, minigolf and riding nearby. Youth room with games, pool and billiards. TV room with Sky programmes. Electric `bumper' boats and mountain bikes for hire. Animation programmes, child minding (day nursery) in high season. New Indian `tipi' tents. Laundry facilities. Chemical disposal. Motorcaravan service station and car wash. Apartments and rooms to let.

Charges 1997/8: Per person sch. 72 - 93; child (under 14 yrs) 54 - 64; pitch, caravan 98 - 125, motorcaravan or tent 88 - 115; electricity 40 - 45; local tax (adults) 6. Special winter packages.

Reservations: made for min. 7 days with deposit (sch. 350) and fee (150).
Address: 6161 Natters bei Innsbruck (Tirol). Tel: 0512/546732. FAX: 0512/546695.
E-mail: natterer.see@net4you.co.at. Internet: http://www.tiscover.com.

AR Discount
Free bottle of
wine on arrival

010 Camping Seeblick Toni-Brantlhof, Kramsach, nr Rattenburg

Excellent, quiet site by Tirolean lake not far from Inn Valley autobahn.

Austria has some of the finest sites in Europe and Seeblick Toni-Brantlhof is one of the best. In a quiet, rural situation on the edge of the small Reintalersee lake, it is well worth considering for holidays in the Tirol with so many varied excursion possibilities nearby. Kramsach, a pleasant, busy tourist resort is some 3 km. from the site. The mountains which surround the site give scenic views and the camp has a neat and tidy appearance. The 240 level pitches, mostly available for tourists, are in regular rows from hard access roads and are of good size with grass and hardstandings, electricity (10A), TV connections, with 40 having telephone points also. The two sanitary blocks are of quite outstanding quality with free hot water in all basins (some in private cabins), sinks and good showers. The main one, part of the reception/restaurant/shop building has been extended and the second one, on the opposite side of the camping area, as well as providing the usual facilities, has individual bathrooms to let. Both blocks are heated in cool weather and have baby rooms, facilities for the disabled and drying rooms. The large, well appointed restaurant has an adjoining roof-top terrace where one can enjoy a meal, drink or snack and admire the lovely scenery. The rebuilt mini-market is well stocked with food, drink and souvenirs. Path to lake for swimming, boating and sunbathing meadow. With a good solarium, sauna and fitness centre, children's playground and a kindergarten in high season, this makes for an excellent summer holiday and, with ski areas near, an excellent winter holiday also. Family run, good English is spoken and a friendly welcome is given.

How to find it: Take exit for Kramsach from A12 autobahn and follow signs `Zu den Seen' in village. After 3 km. turn right at camp sign. **Note:** there are two sites side by side at the lake - ignore the first and continue through to Seeblick Toni.

General Details: Open all year. 40,000 sq.m. Electricity on all pitches. Restaurant. Snack kiosk. Shop. Fitness centre. Cable TV. Children's playground. Washing machines and dryers. Youth room. Kindergarten in high season.

Charges guide: Per person sch. 70 - 85 + local tax 8; child (under 14 yrs) 55 - 60; pitch 95 - 135; dog 57 - 70; electricity 43.

Reservations: made for min. 1 week with deposit. Address: 6233 Kramsach (Tirol). Tel: 05337/63544. FAX: 05337/63544305.

Your ★★★★★ Holiday Paradise in the Tirol Alps near Innsbruck...

full of life

Natterer See

8 convincing reasons for you to spend your holiday with us:

- the **unique scenic location** in the middle of unspoilt nature
- the **well-placed situation** - also perfect when en route to the South
- the **thrilling water experience** of our own swimming lake (average 22°C)
- the **guarantee of sport, amusement, fun, animation** - ideal for all the family
- the **weekly discounted prices for senior citizens** and bargain hunters
- the comfortable **apartments and guest rooms** for friends and relatives
- the central position in the „**Olympia" ski region** Innsbruck/Seefeld/Stubaital
- the **high praise from ADAC** for the facilities at our site

Facilities•**individual terraced pitches** with water, drainage, electricity and telephone hook-up • motorhome service station • top quality sanitation facilities • mini-market • restaurant with lake terrace • **comfortable guest rooms • holiday apartments** • mini-club • pool room • youth room • sport & games areas • streetball • beach volleyball • swimming lake with 66m giant waterslide • bumper boats • children's swimming bay • archery • mountainbike and cycle hire • indian camp • table-tennis • open-air chess • **top animation programme** • attractive walks

• ski and drying room • ice skating • ice hockey • curling and tobogganing on-site • cross country skiing • "Olympia"ski region • ski bus

ADAC '96 Superplatz

We will be pleased to send you our detailed brochure.

Ⓓ Garmisch

ⒸⒽ Arlberg — INNSBRUCK — Ⓓ München Kufstein

A 13 Innsbruck-Süd Exit 3 Mutters/Natters

1,5 km Natters

2,5 km

Natterer See

Brenner Ⓘ

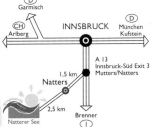

Terrassencamping Natterer See
A-6161 Natters/Tirol/Austria

Tel. ++43(0)512/546732.:.
Fax ++43(0)512/546695...

email: natterer.see@net4you.co.at
http://www.tis.co.at/natterer.see

Servus in Österreich

TOP CAMPING AUSTRIA

Tirol

THE CAMPING AND CARAVANNING CLUB

Carefree TRAVEL SERVICE

The Club's own overseas travel service, Carefree, operates in 14 European countries and can offer everything from simple ferry bookings to all-inclusive holidays.

Offering a complete menu of holiday options, the Club can give substantial savings on every aspect of your holiday, including:

- **Ferry bookings**
- **Campsites abroad**
- **All-inclusive holidays**
- **Guided Tours**
- **French Flavour Holidays**
- **Club Holiday Rallies**
- **Winter Sun Cruises**
- **Travel insurance**

Carefree Travel Service is an exclusive service to Camping and Caravanning Club members. Club membership also offers the opportunity to stay at discounted rates on the Club's 84 UK sites; excellent free sites guides; monthly magazine and access to tailor made insurance, breakdown and financial services.

It's well worth joining!

For further details on Club membership and Carefree Travel Service, telephone **01203 422024** quoting ref no. 9483

or write to:

Carefree Travel Service,
Camping and Caravanning Club,
Greenfields House,
Westwood Way,
Coventry
CV4 8JH

The Camping and Caravanning Club

SCHLOSS-CAMPING VOLDERS

Schlosscamping
Fam. Baron Altenburger
A-6111 Volders/Tirol
Tel/Fax. 05224/52333

AUSTRIA
Tirol

Innsbruck — Hall — Wattens — Kufstein
5km — 2km
Brenner — Volders

Welcome to Eurocamping 'Wilder Kaiser' in Kössen – Tirol, the wonderful region for walking and rambling. Campers tell us that we are one of the top sites in Europe. We offer: Pitches around 100 sq.m. Connections for electricity, gas, water, drainaway and cable TV. Sauna, Solarium, table-tennis room, TV room and general room for relaxation. Heated swimpool with children's paddling pool.

In winter only 300 m. from the well-known Unterberg, 'Langlaufen' direct from site, ice-skating, tobogganning, walking – everything is possible.

EURO CAMPING

«WILDER KAISER»   6345 Kössen-Tirol-Austria Tel. 05375/6444

008 Schloss-Camping, Volders, nr Innsbruck

See colour
advert opposite

Agreeable Tirolean site with solar heated pool near Innsbruck.

Dominated by the castle from which it gets its name, and in a scenic location, this very pleasant, small camp has an enviable position on the edge of the village in the Inn Valley. Being just off a main route, some 15 km. east of Innsbruck, it makes an excellent base for a great variety of excursions to explore Innsbruck, Salzburg, Berchtesgaden, the Royal Castles at Schwangau, the Fern Pass and Bavarian Alps, Brenner Pass and northern Italy on day trips. The 165 pitches are on level or slightly sloping grass and all have electricity (10A) with both 2 and 3 - pin sockets. The good quality sanitary block has hot water in all washbasins, sinks and showers, and British WCs. Near the entrance is a pleasant bar and restaurant with a terrace, a shop for basic supplies and the solar-heated swimming pool. The English speaking Baron, who owns and runs the site, gives a most friendly welcome and has rooms to let in the castle.

How to find it: Site entrance leads off the B171 Innsbruck - Worgl road, 15 km. east of Innsbruck; well signed in village.

General Details: Open 15 April - 15 Oct. 25,000 sq.m. Small shop. Bar/restaurant. Snack bar with terrace. Swimming pool. Minigolf. Children's playground.

Charges guide: Per person sch. 65; child (3-14 yrs) 42; car 40; m/cycle 15; caravan or tent 40; motorcaravan 80; electricity 25; dog 15; local tax 6.

Reservations: made for any length of stay with deposit and small fee. Address: 6111 Volders (Tirol). Tel: 05224/52333.

014 Euro Camping `Wilder Kaiser', Kössen, nr Kufstein

See colour
advert opposite

Good site designed for both summer and winter camping in northeast Tirol.

A modern site, Wilder Kaiser keeps more than half of its 260 pitches for permanent caravans, the remainder being for tourers. Although this is a mountain region which caters very much for winter sports (the winter season is very important here), the site itself is on flat ground. The Unterberg lift is near. The touring pitches are individual ones of some 100 sq.m. all with electricity (10 or 6A) and TV points. Many have water and drainage connections also. The toilet block is of excellent quality and good size with free hot water in all facilities. It has British style toilets, washbasins with shelf and mirror (some in private cabins), a baby bath, showers and footbaths. It is kept immaculately clean and heated in cool weather. Also on site is a small heated swimming pool (16 x 8 m.) which is a deep pool for swimmers, and a small paddling pool. These will be open during summer when weather is suitable. The restaurant with terrace is of above average quality and there is a snack bar in high season. This is a camp which can be recommended without hesitation.

How to find it: Site is well signed around Kössen which is close to the German frontier east of Kufstein; it lies south of the town. Best approaches are: from west via A8/A93 autobahns from Munich and 172 road via Walchsee; from south via the improved no. 312 road from Erpfendorf; from Salzburg via A8 and Ruhpolding.

General Details: Open all year. Self-service shop. Large restaurant. Snack bar (in season). Room for general use with TV. Sauna and solarium. Tennis courts. Table tennis. Large adventure playground. Washing machine. Entertainment programme for adults and children in high season. Motorcaravan service station.

Charges guide: Per person sch. 56 - 72; local tax (over 14 yrs) 9; child (under 14 yrs) 35 - 45; pitch with electricity and TV 61 - 87, with all services (electricity, gas, water, drainage, TV) 71 - 102; dog 37 - 47; electricity 25 - 30, gas connection 49; TV (once only) 55. Reductions for long off-season stays.

Reservations: made with deposit and fee for exact dates in high season; no minimum stay except at Xmas (3 weeks). Address: 6345 Kössen (Tirol). Tel: 05375/6444. FAX: 05375/2113.

007a Camping Kröll, Laubühel, nr Mayrhofen

Good standard site in the Zillertal valley.

The most southerly of the Zillertal camps, this one has some 200 numbered pitches for tourists on flat grass, with nothing between them and with electrical connections for each one. The good quality toilet blocks have British WCs and free hot water in the washbasins (with shelf and mirror), in the fully controllable showers, and in the plentiful sinks for clothes and dishes. There are also facilities for the disabled, a baby room, a dog bathing room and a drying room. It is quite a good supply, with showers least numerous.

How to find it: Site is on northern side of Mayrhofen, signed from the B169 road.

General Details: Open all year (like other sites here of course it caters very actively for winter sports). Basic provisions in shop. Restaurant/bar. Washing machine and dryer. Children's playground. Rooms (with facilities) to let in Gasthof on site.

Charges guide: Per person sch. 55; local tax 9; child (under 14) 35; car 25; tent or caravan 25; motorcaravan 50; m/cycle 20; electricity on meter; dog 20.

Reservations: are made to guarantee admission (no deposit). Address: 6290 Mayrhofen, Laubichl 127, Zillertal. Tel: 05285/2580.

AUSTRIA - Tirol and the West

004 Tiroler Zugspitzcamping, Ehrwald

Mountain site with fine views and excellent modern installations.

Only 100 m. from the base of the Zugspitz cable car lift and standing over 1,200 m. above sea level, this site has about 200 pitches of fair size on flat terraces with fine panoramic views. The two new sanitary blocks, heated in cool weather, are of excellent quality with British WCs, free hot water in washbasins, showers and sinks, with a bath on payment and a baby room. An attractive feature is an indoor and outdoor heated pool complex with sauna, whirlpool and fitness centre. The new restaurant has a terrace and views of the Zugspitz and there is an hotel/restaurant near the cable way station. It provides a comfortable base for walking, climbing and skiing but can become cold at night. Reservation is essential for the winter period.

How to find it: Follow signs in Ehrwald to Tiroler Zugspitzbahn and then signs to site.

General Details: Open all year. 30,000 sq.m. Shop. Bar/restaurant. Hotel. Cable way to mountain summit. Swimming pools. Fitness centre. Table tennis. Sports in Ehrwald. Washing machines and dryers. Apartments to let.

Charges 1997: Per person sch. 137 - 157, acc. to season; child (4-14 yrs) 99 - 112; pitch 75 - 103; electricity 10 per kw/h; local tax 9.50 - 12.50; dog 28; private bathroom 75 - 80. Special seasonal weekly offers.

Reservations: Write with deposit (1,000 sch.) Address: 6632 Ehrwald. Tel: 05673/2745. FAX: 05673/230951.

017 Camping Innsbruck-Kranebitten, Innsbruck

Site with good facilities, just outside Innsbruck.

Formerly known as Aral Camping Innsbruck, this site is on a sloping meadow with good shade cover, in a pleasant situation. The 150 pitches are numbered, but not marked out and there are three separate terraces for caravans and motorcaravans. All pitches have electricity available, though long leads are necessary in parts. By the side of the site, with access to it, is a large open field with a good children's playground and plenty of space for ball games. Being so near to the attractive town of Innsbruck, it makes an excellent base from which to visit the ancient city and also to explore the many attractions nearby. The bar/restaurant also has an attractive terrace and there is a shop for basic supplies. The large, well constructed toilet block has British WCs, free hot water in washbasins (some in private cabins), good, pre-set showers and sinks. The `Innsbruck-Card' gives various discounts for attractions in the city, plus free travel on public transport (park-and-ride from the site, even if you do not stay overnight).

How to find it: From A12 Innsbruck - Arlberg motorway, take Innsbruck - Kranebitten exit from where site signed.

General Details: Open 1 April - 31 Oct. 28,000 sq.m. Electrical connections (2 and 3 pin). Restaurant. Shop. Bicycle hire. Swimming pool 2 km. Large play field adjoining. Washing machines and dryers. Chemical disposal. Motorcaravan services. Tents or caravans to rent. Innsbruck-Card', available from site.

Charges 1998: Per person sch. 69, plus local tax 6; child (4-14 yrs) 45; car 40; tent 40; caravan 45; motorcaravan 60; m/cycle 25; electricity 30. Less 10% for stays over 10 days. Special offers for sporting groups.

AR Discount
Ask at site
for details

Reservations: made for min. 10 days with 10% deposit - contact site. Address: Kranebitter Allee 214, 6020 Innsbruck (Tirol). Tel: 0512/284180. FAX: as phone.

025 Alpencamping, Weer, nr Schwaz

Pleasant Tirol site with outdoor activity programme and a friendly welcome.

This is a good family site run by a family who provide not only a neat, friendly site, but also a variety of outdoor activities. Formerly a farm, they now breed horses, encourage children to take an interest in these and give a free ride each day to youngsters. For children and adults, Herr Mark junior (a certified alpine ski guide and ski instructor) runs courses for individuals or groups in climbing (there is a practise climbing wall on site), rafting, mountain bike riding, tracking, hiking, etc. Guided alpine tours can be arranged and there are pleasant walks up the lower slopes of the mountains directly from the site. Set in the Inn valley, between mountain ranges, the site has 100 flat, grass pitches either side of gravel roads. Trees provide shade in some parts. The old farm buildings house a small, cheerful bar/restaurant, good sanitary facilities (with showers and British style WCs) and a room for washing dishes and clothes. There is an attractive wooden chalet where reception and the activities are administered. Good English is spoken. It could be used for a night stop when passing through, but is even better for a longer stay for adventurous youngsters or for a holiday in the Tirol area. The Mark family would very much welcome visits by rallies in Spring and are happy to arrange programmes of entertainment and excursions.

How to find it: Site is 200 m. east of the village of Weer on the Wattens - Schwaz road no. 171.

General Details: Open 1 April - 31 Oct. 20,000 sq.m. Restaurant. Bread can be ordered. Small heated swimming pool. Activity programme with instruction. Glacier tours. Table tennis. Large children's play area with good equipment. Freezer. Washing machines and dryer. Electricity in all parts. Cabin and 2 caravans to hire.

Charges guide: Per person sch. 60; child (1-13 yrs) 40; pitch for car/caravan or motorcaravan 65; small tent 25; electricity 25; dog 15; local tax 6. Reductions for stays over 14 nights.

Reservations: Necessary for 1/7-15/8 and made without deposit. Address: Maholmhof, 6114 Weer bei Schwaz (Tirol). Tel: 05224/68146. FAX: 05224/681466.

007b Camping Hofer, Zell am Ziller, nr Mayrhofen

Small, family run site near village and sports facilities.

In the heart of the picturesque Zillertal valley, this site has 100 pitches on level meadow-land which are nearly all kept for tourists. Of 70-80 sq.m, they are all marked and have electrical connections, 15 with water and drainage also. The good toilet block has British WCs, washbasins with free hot water, shelf and mirror (some in private cabins for ladies), fully controlled hot showers and facilities for babies. The supply should be adequate. Musical entertainment and a range of activities are provided. All the amenities of the village, such as shops, restaurants, indoor and outdoor swimming pools and tennis courts, are only a short walk. Excellent skiing 1 km. with ski bus from opposite site. A family run site, English is spoken.

How to find it: From the A12 take the Zillertal Valley exit and 20 km. to Zell am Ziller. Site is on the edge of the village and quite well signed.

General Details: Open all year. Shop opposite site entrance. Grill room and bar. Laundry facilities. Simple rooms to let in pension on site. Organised entertainment in high season - guided walks, cycle tours and barbecues. Ski room. Outdoor swimming pool from May '98.

Charges 1997: Per person sch. 50 - 55; local tax (over 15 yrs) 9 - 12; child (under 14 yrs) 40 - 45; pitch 60; dog 20; electricity 7 + meter. Special winter packages.

Reservations: Necessary for July/Aug. and Christmas; made for any length with deposit. Address: Gerlossastr. 33, 6280 Zell am Ziller (Tirol). Tel: 05282/2248. FAX: 05282/2248-8.

007c Komfort Camping Aufenfeld, Aschau, nr Mayrhofen

Pleasantly situated site for summer or winter with good toilet block and indoor pool.

This site is attractively situated in a mountain region with fine views. The main area of the site itself is flat with 120 pitches of 100 sq.m. on grass between made-up access roads, with a further 40 pitches on terraces at the rear. The well kept toilet block in the main building is of excellent quality and size with British WCs, washbasins well spaced out with free hot water, shelf and mirror, several in private cabins for each sex, one with baby bath and one with full bath for ladies and good fully controllable free hot showers; also a dog shower. A second toilet block has private cabins and family rooms. The site can become full mid-July until mid-August and at Christmas, but usually has space at other times. Ski lifts are nearby, one for beginners particularly close. A splendid, indoor swimming pool with whirl pool, sauna and sun-beds have been added and there is a heated outdoor pool, paddling pool, and tennis court for summer use. Most of the site facilities are now housed in the new main building. The site reports that they have created a new lake.

How to find it: From the Inntal motorway, take the Zillertal exit, 32 km. northeast of Innsbruck. Follow road no. 169 to the village of Aschau from which the site is well signed.

General Details: Open all year except 7-30 Nov. Electric points everywhere. TV. Small shop. Restaurant. General room. Fishing. Bicycle hire. Football field. Playground. Riding. Washing machines, dryers. Indoor pool, sauna and sun-beds. Outdoor pool. Tennis court. Chalets and caravans for hire.

Charges 1997/8: Per person sch. 55 - 90, with local tax 8; child (under 13 yrs) 35 - 60; caravan or tent with car 80 - 110; motorcaravan 80 - 110; m/cycle and tent 35 - 48; pitch with water and drainage 100 - 135; dog 40 - 50; electricity 25 - 48; higher prices are for winter.

Reservations: made with deposit and fee for min. 1 week - write to site. Address: Distelberg 1, 6274 Aschau (Zillertal-Tirol). Tel: 05282/29160. FAX: 05282/291611.

011 Tirol Camp, Fieberbrunn, St Johann, nr Kitzbühel

Site in mountain region for summer or winter camping, with good installations.

This is one of many Tirol camps which cater equally for summer and winter (here seemingly more for winter, as reservation is then essential and prices 50% higher). Tirol Camp is in a quiet and attractive mountain situation and has 317 pitches on wide flat terraces, set on a gentle slope. Marked out mainly by the electricity boxes, they are 80-100 sq.m. and all have electricity, gas, water/drainage, TV and telephone connections. The excellent, original toilet block in the main building has British WCs, washbasins (a few in cabins) and good fully controllable, hot showers with seat and screen. Also some private bathrooms on payment. This is supplemented by a splendid heated block at the top end of the camp with washbasins all in private cabins and spacious showers. A small, unheated swimming pool (12 x 8 m.) is on site, with a paddling pool. For winter stays, the site is very close to a ski lift centre and a `langlauf' piste. There is a lake for fishing and a playground and small zoo for children.

How to find it: Site is on the east side of Fieberbrunn, which is on the St Johann-Saalfelden road.

General Details: Open all year. Shop and snacks. Restaurant (closed Oct, Nov and May). Separate general room. Tennis. Fishing in lake. Outdoor chess. Children's playground and zoo. Washing machines, dryers and drying room.

Charges guide: Winter charges higher. Per pitch sch. 50 - 138; adult 55 - 100; child (4-15 yrs) 25 - 60; local taxes 18; dog 60; electricity connection (once only) 25 - 60 + meter; gas 60 + meter; TV/radio 30.

Reservations: made for any length (with deposit in winter only). Address: Lindau 20, 6391 Fieberbrunn (Tirol). Tel: 05354/6666. FAX: 05354/2516.

AUSTRIA - Tirol and the West

009 Camping Zillertal-Hell, Fügen, nr Schwaz

Small site in attractive situation with exceptionally good toilet block.

In the Zillertal, easy to reach and with views of mountains all around, this small site has 120 marked pitches on flat grassy ground. There are special pitches for motorhomes. Although its other facilities are fairly simple, there is a modern sanitary block of top quality, installed to meet winter camping requirements, with British toilets, individual basins with shelf and mirror and free hot water in basins and showers. It can be heated when required and its size should be quite adequate. There is a pleasant and spacious bar where drinks are served. A very neat and well organised site. No dogs are taken.

How to find it: Site is beside the no. 169 road 2 km. north of Fügen.

General Details: Open all year. Many electrical connections. Essential provisions kept in summer. Bar. General room. Washing machine and dryer. Drying room. Car wash. Motorcaravan service station.

Charges guide: Per person sch. 55, plus local tax 7; child (under 14 yrs) 40; pitch 70; electricity 25; rubbish disposal tax 10. Less 10% for stays over 8 days.

Reservations: not made in summer and site can become full in good weather when you need to arrive early. Tel: 05288/62203 for information only.

013 Terrassencamping Schlossberg Itter, Hopfgarten, nr Kitzbühel

Site with good installations west of Kitzbühel.

With some 200 pitches, this well kept site is suitable both as a base for longer stays and also for overnight stops, as it lies right by a main road. It is on a slight slope but most of the numbered pitches are on levelled terraces. All have electricity and cable TV connections, 150 have water and drainage and 25 have telephone sockets also. There is a general meadow for overnight stays. Space is said to be usually available except in the busiest weeks of summer and winter. The site has two remarkable features - the large children's playground has a huge collection of most ingeniously devised fixed apparatus, and secondly, the sanitary facilities which have been added on the floor above the older provision. Both sanitary facilities are of a very high standard. The new section has a large room in which private cubicles have been placed round the walls and as free standing units. Some of these have washbasins set in flat surfaces with others having baths, one a massage type, or showers, with two slightly larger units for families, baby baths and footbaths. British style WCs. Pots of artificial flowers complete the hotel-like atmosphere of 'Washland', all hot water is free and the facilities are heated in cool weather. The site has a pleasant open-air, solar heated swimming pool (16 x 8 m.) and children's paddling pool. Good walks and a wealth of excursions by car are available nearby. Free ski-lift from site in winter, especially suitable for beginners and children; also own toboggan and langlauf runs. Sauna and solarium available on payment.

How to find it: Site is 2 km. northwest of Hopfgarten on B170 road to Worgl (not up by Schloss Itter). The entrance is on a bend opposite a Peugeot/Talbot garage and as much of the site is hidden from the road by trees, care is needed to spot it.

General Details: Open all year. 40,000 sq.m. Small shop, bar/restaurant (both closed Nov). Excellent children's playground. Tennis close. Sauna and solarium. Washing machine and dryer. Cooking facilities. Chemical disposal. Motorcaravan services. Winter facilities see report. Refrigerator boxes for hire. Youth room. Room for disabled people.

Charges 1998: Summer: per person sch. 68; child (under 14 yrs) 44; car 22 - 45; tent or caravan 22 - 45; motorcaravan 44 - 88; m/cycle 30; dog 40; electricity 35; cable TV 48 plus 8 per night; local tax (over 14 yrs) 6. Prices higher for winter. Less 50% on pitch fee in mid-seasons.

Reservations: made with deposit and fee; usually min. 1 week (2 weeks at Christmas). Address: Itter, 6361 Hopfgarten. Tel: 05335/2181. FAX: 05335/2182.

AR Discount
Less 50% for pitch, child and seniors in mid/low season

Vienna and the East

Although Vienna (Wien) is a vibrant centre for culture today, with museums, opera, famous choirs, the Spanish Riding School, well known cafés and the Danube, its glories lie in its illustrious past and the giants of music, architecture and psychology who lived and worked in the Austrian capital during its heyday. This, coupled with its Imperial history, make it a gracious and interesting city to visit. The provinces of Lower Austria, Burgenland and Styria, land of vineyards, mountains and farmland, are off the beaten tourist route, although walkers are attracted to the densely forested hills where hiking paths meander for hundreds of miles over hill and dale. There are less camp sites than in other parts of the country, but enough to provide bases from which to visit Vienna (use public transport) and other places.

028 Camping Stumpfer, Schönbühel

Small, well appointed site between Salzburg and Vienna.

This small site of some 50 pitches is directly on the River Danube, near the small town of Schönbühel, and could make a convenient night stop being near the Salzburg - Vienna autobahn. The sanitary block is part of the main building which also houses a Gasthof, with bar/restaurant of the same name, which can be used by campers. There is shade in most parts and a landing stage for boat trips on the Danube. The facilities are of good quality with British WCs, washbasins and showers, both with hot water on payment. Special facilities for the disabled include ramps by the side of steps up to the washing block. There is a small shop with basic supplies. Pitches are on flat grass, not marked out, with electricity connections available in all parts; the site is lit at night. This is very much a family run site with apartments for hire being added to the main building.

How to find it: Leave Salzburg - Vienna autobahn at Melk exit. Drive towards Melk, but continue towards Melk Nord. Just before bridge turn right (signed Schönbühel and St Polten), at T-junction turn right again and continue down hill. Turn right just before BP filling station (signed Schönbühel) and site is 3 km. on left with narrow entrance.

General Details: Open Easter - 31 Oct. 7,000 sq.m. Restaurant. Children's playground. Washing machine and dryer. Small shop. Swimming pool 5 km. Dogs accepted.

Charges 1997: Per person sch. 40; child (6-14 yrs) 22; tent 30 - 60; caravan or motorcaravan 50 - 70; electricity 30; local tax (over 16 yrs) 10.50. Less 5% for stays over 7 nights. Eurocheques accepted but not credit cards.

Reservations: Write to site. Address: 3392 Schönbühel 7. Tel: 02752/8510. FAX: as phone.

030 Camping Rodaun, Wien-Sud/Vienna

Convenient city site for visiting Vienna.

This good quality site is within the city boundary and is an excellent base for visiting this old, interesting and world famous city. Just 9 km. from the centre of Vienna, there is an excellent public transport system for viewing the sights as car parking is almost impossible in the city. This is also a very pleasant camp in its own right with an excellent sanitary block (British type WCs) and a bar. The site is situated in a southern suburb with a supermarket and a restaurant within 250 m. and a swimming pool, 2 km. It has space for about 100 units on flat grass pitches, neither numbered nor marked, either in the centre or outside the circular tarmac road running round the camping area. There is also a hardstanding area for motorcaravans (but no space for awnings).

How to find it: Take Pressbaum exit from Westautobahn or Vosendorf exit from Sudautobahn and follow signs.

General Details: Open 25 March - 15 Nov. 10,000 sq.m. Bar. Electricity connections in all parts. Little shade. Washing machines, dryers and irons.

Charges guide: Per person sch. 65; child (3-13 yrs) 45; caravan 50 - 60; tent 50; motorcaravan 60; car 12; m/cycle 15; electricity 24 + meter; dog 15.

Reservations: are advised - write to site. Address: 1236 Wien-Rodaun, An der Au 2. Tel: 0222/884154.

031 Schlosscamping Laxenburg, Laxenburg, nr Wien/Vienna

Site with good facilities, next to swimming pool, near Vienna.

Although this site is a little further out (15 km.) than some others, it has better facilities, is in a quieter location, is easier to find - particularly if towing a caravan - and has a bus service from outside the entrance to the city. Close to the historic castle of Laxenburg, it is on the edge of the castle grounds where campers can walk in the extensive park. Adjacent is a pool complex and excellent restaurant with terrace, minigolf, and children's play area. The site has a number of permanent caravans but these are in a separate place on the edge of the tourist area. The seasonal camping part has room for about 300 units, all having electrical points. There are no defined pitches as such, but large flat meadows with a circular tarmac road encircling the main part and units go on each side of this road. Siting can, therefore, be a bit haphazard with a risk of crowding in high season, so arrive as early as possible. The large, single, sanitary block is of a good standard, kept clean with British WCs and hot water in basins (some in cabins), showers and sinks. It is heated in cool weather. Shop. Excursion programme. An excellent base from which to visit the famous city. Parking in Vienna is no easier than any other capital or large town so it makes sense to use a site where the car can be left behind and use made of public transport. There is a bus service to the city from outside the entrance (but last return from Vienna is 9 pm) or from autobahn sign to Praha follow P&R sign to car park at the end of the metro line which runs very late.

How to find it: Laxenburg is south of Vienna, take autobahn exit `Wiener-Neudorf` to Laxenburg village. Turn right at lights in village centre and site is on left beyond village.

General Details: Open 30 March - 31 Oct. 50,000 sq. m. Electric connections for all (long leads in places). Shop. Washing machines. Good restaurant adjacent. Swimming pool (charge for adults). Playgrounds. Minigolf. Excursions to Vienna and Budapest (2 days) with German speaking guides.

Charges guide: Per person sch. 60 - 65, acc. to season; child (4-15 yrs) 35; pitch 56 - 61; electricity 40; local tax 7.

Reservations: Write to camp. Address: Munchendorfer Strasse, 2361 Laxenburg. Tel: 02236/71333 or 71334. Fax: 02236/713348.

AUSTRIA - Vienna and the East

050 Camping Fürstenfeld, Fürstenfeld

Pleasant, small site with basic facilities, near Hungarian border.

Fürstenfeld is the last village on the main route from Graz to Hungary and this site, although small with basic facilities, makes a good staging post when entering (or returning from) Lake Balaton and Budapest. The site is quietly situated on the edge of the village next to a large, well mown, play area with children's playground, space for all types of ball games and a really huge open-air swimming pool complex. This is the size of a football pitch, has a shallow end for paddling, a larger part for general swimming or pool games, an Olympic size racing pool and a diving pool with a 10 m. diving board. There are kiosks for drinks and ice creams, a cafe and changing rooms. The 50 pitches on the site are on terraces on either side of hard access roads, under a covering of trees, with electrical connections available. The single toilet block has British WCs and hot water in washbasins, showers and sinks. The provision is rather cramped and not as good as on most Austrian sites but is clean and acceptable. There is a small bar with TV, but no other facilities on site, but the village shops and restaurants are 2½ km.

How to find it: From Graz - Vienna motorway, take Fürstenfeld exit. Site is at western end of village and is signed.

General Details: Open 15 April - 15 Oct. 3,000 sq.m. Good shade. Electricity in all areas. Bar. Shops and restaurants 2½ km. Large sports park adjacent. Washing machines and dryers. Baby room.

Charges 1997: Per unit incl. 2 persons sch. 125 - 140, acc. to season; extra person 35 - 45; child (6-14 yrs) 10 - 15; dog 5; electricity 15; tax (over 14 yrs) 7.

Reservations: Write to site. Address: Campingweg 1, 8280 Fürstenfeld. Tel: 03382/54940. FAX: 03382/51671.

Carinthia and the South

This gentle, tranquil land of some 200 lakes and mountain scenery deserves to be better known than just as a through route from Salzburg to Italy. The beautiful scenery and rural way of life make it an attractive holiday destination to those who know it. Unfortunately, few British have yet discovered its charms and those who have probably wish to keep the secret to themselves. There are few large towns, but many pleasant villages, good, often uncrowded roads and excellent sites.

048 Komfort-Campingpark Burgstaller, Döbriach, Millstättersee

Excellent large site close to the Millstättersee lake.

This part of Austria deserves to be better known as it is a most attractive region and has some excellent camp sites. Burgstaller is the largest of these and makes a peaceful base from which to explore Carinthia, northeast Italy and Slovenia. The site entrance is directly opposite the lawns leading to the bathing lido, to which campers have free access. There is also a heated swimming pool. The 450 pitches are on flat, well drained grass, backing onto hedges and marked out, on either side of gravel access roads. These vary in size (65-120 sq.m.), all with electricity, water and drainage and there are special pitches for motorcaravans. There are two very good quality sanitary blocks, the larger of which is part of the central complex. It has some basins in private cabins and special facilities for children and the disabled. Both have under floor heating for cool weather. A torch may be useful as site lighting is switched off late evening. There is a large, good quality restaurant with terrace, two children's play areas (one for under 6s, the other for 6-12 yrs). The games room with 3-lane bowling alley and mini bar leads off the restaurant. There is a secluded roof terrace for nude sunbathing. A covered stage and an outdoor arena provide for church services - Protestant and Catholic (in German) - and folk and modern music concerts. Much activity is organised here, including games and competitions for children in summer with a winter programme of skiing, curling and skating. At Christmas, trees are gathered from the forest and there are special Easter and autumn events. This is an excellent family site for winter and summer camping with a very friendly atmosphere, particularly in the restaurant in the evenings.

How to find it: Site is well signed from around Döbriach.

General Details: Open all year. 56,000 sq.m. Restaurant (April - Oct, plus Dec). Shop (May - Oct). Bowling alley. Disco (July/Aug). TV room. Sauna and solarium. Naturist terrace. Children's playgrounds. Bathing and boating in lake. Beach volleyball. Basketball. Special entrance rate for lake attractions. Comprehensive entertainment programmes. Mountain bike area. Horse and pony riding. Chemical disposal. Motorcaravan services.

Charges 1998: Per person sch. 65 - 88; child 40 - 78, under 4 free; local tax (over 18s) 17.50 - 18.50; pitch 80 - 120. Discounts for retired people.

Reservations: Write to site. Address: 9873 Döbriach (Kärnten). Tel: 04246/7774. FAX: 04246/77744. E-mail: dieter-burgstaller@campingpark.telecom.at. Internet: http://www.burgstaller.co.at/burgstaller.

033 Camping Central, Graz

Satisfactory site on outskirts of town with large swimming pool adjoining.

This appears to be the most sensible of the sites around Graz to use. It is of quite satisfactory quality and next door, with free direct access for those staying at the site, is an enormous swimming pool (120 x 90 m.) with sunbathing areas. Half of the 90 tourist pitches are individual, numbered ones on grassy strips between hedges and access roads; the other half are on a general meadow and not marked out. All have electrical connections (10A). Four toilet blocks contain a good supply of washbasins (with hot water) and fewer toilets and rather unexciting, free hot showers. The city centre is about 5 km. and there is a regular bus service from nearby.

How to find it: In spite of its name, site is just outside the town to the southwest, well signed from the 'Graz W' autobahn exit and the B70 road from Klagenfurt. From Salzburg use autobahn exit 'Graz-Sud'.

General Details: Open 1 April - 31 Oct. 30,000 sq.m. In main months restaurant, either self-service or with waiter service, also serving the swimming pool and keeping some basic provisions. Tennis. Table tennis. Children's playground. Jogging track. Minigolf. Excursions organised. Riding near. Washing machines. Caravans for hire.

Charges guide: Prices outside 1/6-31/8 in brackets. Per unit incl. 2 persons and electricity sch. 230 (200); 2 persons and tent 210 (180); extra person 55 (45); child (4-14 yrs) 35 (30); local tax 5.

Reservations: probably unnecessary but will be made if you write. Address: Martinhofstr. 3, 8054 Graz. Tel: 0316/281831. FAX: 0316/28183183.

N036 Rutar Lido FKK-See-Camping, Eberndorf

Secluded naturist site with eight swimming pools.

This is a large (150,000 sq.m.) and very well appointed site for naturist camping and it is a member of the International Naturist Federation (FKK). Situated in the heart of the countryside and surrounded by woodland, the main feature of the site is the provision of no less than 8 swimming pools (6 outdoor and 2 indoor heated ones). As if this is not enough there is also a small lake for swimming. The 365 pitches, all with electrical connections (11A) and some with water and drainage also, are on flat grass marked out by hedges with a special area for campers with dogs. Four sanitary blocks are of good quality with British WCs, some private washcabins and free hot water to the basins and showers and a special block for the disabled. There is a lake for fishing, a small chapel, table tennis, and dances are held in season. Well stocked supermarket, two bar/restaurants and two saunas adjacent to the indoor pools. The village is some distance away. Membership of the FKK or other naturist association is not obligatory but visitors are expected to comply with their rules and ideals.

How to find it: From the Graz - Klagenfurt A2 road, take the B82 at Volkermarkt and follow signs to site.

General Details: Open all year. Some shade. Electrical connections throughout. Supermarket (April - Sept). 2 bar/restaurants (all year). Swimming pools. Laundry facilities. Fishing. Bicycle hire. Children's play area.

Charges 1998: Per large pitch (100 sq.m. with electricity) 80 - 140 sch; small pitch (70 sq.m.) 80 - 100; adult 55 -80; child (3-12 yrs) 40 - 60; tax 12; pitch with water/drainage 10 - 20 extra; dog 30 - 50.

AR Discount
Less 3%;
welcome drink

Reservations: Write to site with sch. 700 deposit. Address: Rutar Lido, 9141 Eberndorf (Carinthia). Tel: 04236/22620. FAX: 04236/2220.

049 Terrassencamping Maltatal, Maltatal

Site with pool and mountain view, 6 km. from autobahn, 15 from Millstättersee.

This site is good for an overnight stop but its pleasant situation and the good sized swimming pool on site encourage many to stay longer. The pool is over 300 sq.m. with a grassy lying out area and is open to all (free for campers). Many walks and excursions are available. There are 200 grassy pitches on shallow terraces (70-100 sq.m.) and mostly in rows on either side of access roads. Numbered and marked, but not separated, all have electricity and 20 also have water and drainage connections. The two toilet blocks, one with under floor heating, have British style WCs and free hot water in the washbasins (with shelf and mirror and about half in private cabins) and in the controllable showers and sinks. 6 family washcabins. They should be a good supply and there are new facilities for babies and children. Water points around.

How to find it: Site is 6 km. up a mountain valley from an exit at the southern end of the A10 Salzburg - Carinthia autobahn. Take autobahn exit for Gmund and Maltatal and proceed up Maltatal 6 km. to camp.

General Details: Open 8 April - 31 Oct. Only basic provisions kept (village 500 m.). Restaurant (all season). Swimming pool (20/5-15/9). Sauna. Entertainment programme for adults and children. Children's playground. Bicycle hire. Riding. Washing machines, dryers and irons. Chemical disposal. Motorcaravan services. Available from site: the Kärnten-card costing sch. 265 per adult (child 6-14 yrs sch. 130) which gives free travel on public transport and free entry to various attractions.

Charges 1998: Per person sch. 69 - 89; child (3-14 yrs) 44 - 54; local tax (over 18 yrs) 15.50; pitch 88 - 138, acc. to season and services; dog 35; electricity incl. Less 5% for stays of over 11 days, 10% for 21 days.

Reservations: Made with deposit - contact site for details. Address: 9854 Malta 6. Tel: 04733/234. FAX: 04733/358. E-mail: pirker-touristik@lieser-maltatal.or.at. Internet: http://www.lieser-maltatal.or.at/pirker.

AUSTRIA - Carinthia and the South

044 Schluga Camping, Hermagor, nr Villach

Attractive site with swimming pool and excellent facilities in rural location.

Schluga Camping, under the same ownership as no. 45 is in a flat valley with views of the surrounding mountains. The 400 tourist pitches, all with electricity and some with water and satellite TV connections, are mainly on grass covered gravel on either side of the hard surfaced access road and divided by shrubs and hedges. Pitch size varies but none is particularly large. The four sanitary blocks (one splendid new one, three good older ones) are well constructed and heated in cold weather. They have British WCs, controllable free hot water to basins (some in cabins) and showers (small dressing space). Some family washcabins are available to rent. There is a heated swimming pool (12 x 8 m), new fitness centre and a sauna. Entertainment in the high season includes a disco and cinema. A weekly programme sheet details events at both Schluga sites and nearby. The site is open all year, to include the winter sports season, and has a well kept tidy appearance, although it may be crowded in high seasons.

How to find it: Site is on the B111 Villach-Hermagor road (which is better quality than it appears on most maps) just east of Hermagor town.

General Details: Open all year. 50,000 sq.m. Shop (May - Sept). Bar/restaurant with terrace (closed Nov). Kiosk for snacks/ice creams. Children's playground. Games room. Bicycle hire. Sauna. Fitness centre. Heated swimming pool (summer only). TV. Room for young people. Badminton. Tennis near. Mobile homes, etc. to rent. Kindergarten programme for small children. Washing machines/dryer. Chemical disposal. Motorcaravan services. English spoken.

Charges 1998: Per person sch. 40.50 - 81; child 6-14 yrs 29.50 - 59, under 6 yrs free; pitch 46.50 - 93, with electricity 74.50 - 121; supplement for water, drainage, TV connection 20 - 35; local tax (over 18) 12 - 14; dog 15 - 54. Special weekly rates for families and senior citizens.

Reservations: Contact site. Address: Obervellach 15, 9620 Hermagor-Presseggersee (Kärnten). Tel: 04282/2051 or 2760. FAX: 04282/288120. E-mail/internet: as for site 045 below.

045 Schluga Seecamping, Hermagor, nr Villach

Pleasant site in attractive out-of-the-way part of Carinthia.

This site is pleasantly situated on natural wooded hillside. Pitches are individual levelled ones, many with light shade. It is about 300 m. from a small lake with clean water, where the site has a beach of coarse sand and a large grassy meadow where inflatable boats can be kept; also a sunbathing area for naturists. Many walks and attractive car drives are available in the area. This part of Carinthia is a little off the beaten track but it still becomes full in season. The sanitary blocks are modern and well constructed, they are of good size, with maybe some waiting for the free hot showers. Facilities include British style toilets, individual washbasins, some in cabins and family washcabins available for rent. Close by is Schluga Camping, under the same ownership, which is open all year.

How to find it: Site is on the B111 road (Villach-Hermagor) 6 km. east of Hermagor town.

General Details: Open 20 May - 20 Sept. 70,000 sq.m. Shade in parts. Many electrical connections. Shop (25/5-15/8). Restaurant/bar by entrance where drinks or meals are served; also takeaway (all 25/5-15/8). Room for young people and children. Kiosk at beach. Surf school. Pony rides. Bicycle hire. Children's playground. Badminton and volleyball court. Tennis (indoor and outdoor) near. Weekly activity programme with mountain walks and climbs. Washing machines and dryer. Chemical disposal. Motorcaravan services. English is spoken.

Charges 1998: Per person sch. 40.50 - 81; child 6-14 yrs 29.50 - 59, under 6 yrs free; pitch 46.50 - 93, with electricity 74.50 - 121; supplement for water, drainage, TV connection 20 - 35; local tax (over 18) 12 - 14; dog 15 - 54. Special weekly rates for families and senior citizens.

Reservations: Contact site. Address: 9620 Hermagor-Presseggersee (Kärnten). Tel: 04282/2051 or 2760. FAX: 04282/288120. E-mail: schlugas-campingwelt@camica.or.at. Internet: http://camica.or.at/schlugas-campingwelt.

047 Camping Mössler, Döbriach, nr Spittal

Friendly family site with heated swimming pool, near a Carinthian lake.

A fairly small, flat, grassy site set in very pleasant surroundings with mountain views, Mössler is close to, but not right on, the Millstättersee, a reputedly warm lake. However, as the camp has a free, well heated swimming pool of 200 sq.m., the 600 m. stroll to the lake, where campers usually have free entry to swimming and boating facilities, is not so important. It is an excellent touring area with mountain lifts and many possible excursions to lakes and mountain. The site has about 200 pitches on flat ground with connections for electricity, water, TV, phone, gas and drainage. In high season cars stand on separate places in front of pitches. The two modern toilet blocks are of exceptional standard and quite luxurious, with under-floor heating. British WCs, washbasins in cabins with automatic light, and good, free showers with full controls. Facilities for disabled people. Bathrooms let weekly.

How to find it: Go to Döbriach, at east end of Millstättersee, and camp is signed.

General Details: Open 1 April - 31 Oct. 30,000 sq.m. Shop and restaurant (both 20/5-30/9). TV facilities. Swimming pools. Children's playground. Sauna. Washing machine. Motorcaravan service station. Caravans for hire.

Charges guide: Per unit incl. 2 persons and all facilities sch. 144 - 444, acc. to type of unit and size of pitch; extra person 64 - 84; child (under 10 yrs) 32 - 42; local tax (over 18s) 18.50. Reductions in low seasons for longer stays.

Reservations: can be made Sat. - Sat., with deposit and fee. Address: 9873 Döbriach am Millstättersee (Kärnten). Tel: 04246/7735. FAX: 04246/773513 (summer) or 721313 (winter).

046 Terrassen Camping Ossiachersee, Ossiach, nr Villach

Popular site of excellent quality on Lake Ossiach.

As its name implies, this modern site has been constructed with terraces on ground which slopes gently down to the lake shore. Because of the thick growth of reeds at the water's edge, there is limited access to the lake via two small clearings. One of these has a beach for bathing and a jetty, and boats may be launched from the other. The site is protected by rising hills and enjoys views across the lake to the mountains beyond. Trees, flowers, hedges and bushes abound adding atmosphere to this neat, tidy site. The 590 pitches are in rows on level grass terraces, which are separated by hard roads. Marked by hedges, each is numbered and has an electrical connection available. It does become full in high season and although there is sufficient room on pitches, it gives the impression, on first sight, that it is overcrowded. Environmental protection is emphasised in this part of Austria and visitors are asked to follow instructions regarding disposal of various forms of waste. A large complex at the entrance includes a good self-service restaurant and well stocked supermarket. In high season a daily 'animation' programme is organised for both children and adults, giving a wide range of sports and activities. Young people are well catered for, with their own playgrounds, games rooms and disco dancing courtyard as well as many sports facilities. Bicycles and mopeds for hire. The lake is available for all forms of water sports including water-skiing and windsurfing schools and there are boats for hire. Although the facilities in the five sanitary blocks are varied, they are all of good quality, heated in cool weather, with British WCs and free hot water in the washbasins (some in private cabins), showers and sinks. The newest block has family washrooms. A friendly, lively site where all ages and sports inclinations are catered for in a scenic location in a very beautiful part of Austria.

How to find it: Directly on the lake shore just south of Ossiach village. Leave the A10 autobahn at exit for Ossiachersee, turn left onto road 94 towards Feldkirchen and then right at Steindorf for Ossiach.

General Details: Open 1 May - 30 Sept. 100,000 sq.m. Shade in parts. Restaurant. Supermarket. Bank. Doctor calls. Entertainment. 5 children's playgrounds. Tennis, volleyball and badminton courts. Football field. Sports area. Bicycles and mopeds for hire. Washing machines, dryers and irons.

Charges guide: Per person sch. 57 - 88; child (2-9 yrs) 40 - 58; pitch 75 - 120, acc. to location and size; small tent pitch 50 - 72; tax 12.50 - 14.50; min. charge (summer) 247 - 284.

Reservations: Write with deposit (3,000 sch) and fee (300). Address: 9570 Ossiach (Kärnten). Tel: 04243/436. FAX: 04243/8171.

040 Camping Arneitz, Faakersee, nr Villach

Site with excellent and comprehensive installations by a Carinthian lake.

Camping Arneitz, directly on Faaker See is one of the best in this area, central for the attractions of the region, watersports and walking. Family run, Arneitz led the way with good quality sanitary facilities. Others have caught up but Arneitz have now gone one further by adding a splendid family washroom. This large, airy room has family cubicles around the walls and in the centre, washbasins at child height in a circle with a working carousel in the middle. British style WCs. There is also a hair washing salon with special basins and hairdryers. This building also houses the children's cinema. There is also a small toilet block nearer the lake. A newly built reception building at the entrance reflects the quality of the site and, apart from booking-in facilities, has a good collection of tourist literature and three desks with telephones for use by guests. Level, individually marked pitches, mainly of gravel, are off hard roads, with electric connections available and some having good shade from mature trees. Grass pitches are available for tents. The well stocked supermarket offers food items, wine, beer, clothes, camping and general articles. This is at the entrance of the site and includes a delightfully appointed restaurant where there is entertainment in high season. On the opposite side of the entrance road is a very well equipped children's playground with fixed climbing frames, go carts and small electric powered boats (on payment) with a large trampoline (small fee). Day trips can be made to Venice and the Postojna Caves and many other parts of northern Italy and the surrounding countryside.

How to find it: Site is southeast of Villach, southwest of Veldon. Follow signs for Faakersee and Egg rather than for Faak village.

General Details: Open 28 April - 30 Sept. 45,000 sq. m. Shade in part. Electric points each pitch included in price. Supermarket. Self-service restaurant, bar and terrace. General room with TV. Small cinema for children's films. Beauty salon. Large sauna/solarium. Minigolf. Children's playground. Football field. Exchange facilities. Doctor visits. Washing machines, spin dryer, irons.

Charges 1998: Per person sch. 88 - 96; child (under 10 yrs) 83 - 91; pitch incl. electricity 120 - 150; plus local tax.

Reservations: only made outside main season. Address: 9583 Faak am See (Kärnten). Tel: 04254/2137. Fax: 04254/3044 or 24535.

BELGIUM

Belgium is a small and densely populated country divided on a federal basis into the Flemish north, Walloon south and Brussels the capital, a culturally varied city. Despite being heavily industrialised Belgium possesses some beautiful scenery, notably the great forest of the Ardennes with its rivers and gorges contrasting with the rolling plains and historic cities of Bruges and Ghent with their Flemish art and architecture and the 40 miles of coastline with safe sandy beaches. For further information contact:

Belgian National Tourist Office, 29 Princes Street, London W1R 7RG Tel: 0891 887799.

Population
10,040,000 (1993), density 329 per sq km.

Capital
Brussels (Bruxelles).

Climate
Belgium's temperate climate is similar to Britain but the variation between summer and winter is lessened by the effects of the Gulf Stream.

Language
There are two official languages in Belgium. French is spoken in the south and Flemish in the north; however, in the eastern provinces, German is the predominant language. Brussels is officially bi-lingual. Road signs and place names maybe written in either language or in some cases both.

Currency
The currency is the franc which is divided into 100 centimes. Notes are 100, 500, 1000 and 5000 francs, coins 0.5, 1, 5, 20 and 50 francs. Note: The Luxembourg currency is interchangeable with the same exchange rate.

Banks
Banking hours are Mon-Fri 09.00-15.30. Some banks open on Saturday mornings.

Credit Cards: Major credit cards are all widely accepted, as are travellers cheques and Eurocheques.

Post Offices
Open Mon-Fri 09.00-12.00 and 14.00-17.00, some opening on Saturday mornings.

Time
GMT plus 1 (in summer BST plus 1).

Public Holidays
New Year; Easter Mon; Labour Day; Ascension; Whit Mon; Flemish National Day, 21 July; Assumption, 15 Aug; All Saints, 1 Nov; Armistice Day, 11 Nov; Christmas, 25 Dec.

Telephone
From the UK the code is 00 32. For calls within Belgium use the local code followed by the number. For calls to the UK the code is 0044 followed by the local STD code omitting initial 0. Telephone cards available from newsagents, post offices and train stations for Fr. 100 or Fr. 500.

Shops
Shops open from 09.00-17.30/18.00 hrs - later on Thursday and Friday evenings but a little earlier on Saturdays. Some close for two hours at midday.

Motoring
For cars with a caravan or trailer: motorways are toll free except for the Liefenshoek Tunnel in Antwerp. The maximum permitted overall length of vehicle/trailer or caravan combination is 18 m.

Speed Limits: Caravans and motorhomes (7.5 tons): 31 mph (50 kph) in built up areas, 56 mph (90 kph) on other roads and 75 mph (120 kph) 4 lane roads and motorways.
The minimum speed on motorways on straight level stretches is 43 mph (70 kph).

Parking: Blue Zone parking areas exist in Brussels, Ostend, Bruges, Liège, Antwerp and Gent. Parking discs can be obtained from police stations, garages, some shops and offices of the RACB - Royal Automobile Club de Belgique.

Overnighting
Not generally permitted except at motorway rest areas.

055 IC-Camping, Nieuwpoort, nr Ostend/Oostende

Large holiday site 4 km. from beach with many on-site amenities.

This large site with over 900 pitches caters particularly for families, with a heated pool complex, many sporting activities, restaurants, takeaway, supermarket, children's farm and playground. The numbered pitches, all with electricity, are in regular rows on flat grass and, with many seasonal units, the site becomes full in July/Aug. A network of footpaths links all areas of the site and a gate to the rear leads to a reservoir reserved for sailing and windsurfing (boards for hire) during certain hours only. The seven functional sanitary units are clean and well maintained, providing British WCs, washbasins in cubicles, showers with dividers, dishwashing and laundry facilities. Hot water is free throughout and the units are accessible to disabled people. The nearest village is 2 km.

How to find it: From E40/A18 junction 4 (Middelkerke-Diksmuide) turn towards Diksmuide, then right onto Ramskapellestraat and follow signs to site.

General Details: Open Easter - 12 Nov. Supermarket. Restaurant. Cafe/bar (all w/ends only from 15/9). 3 swimming pools (1/5-15/9) with waterslide and pool games. Tennis. Football. Adventure playground. Sports/show hall. Entertainment July/Aug. TV. Minigolf. Fishing and bicycle hire near. Laundry. Chemical disposal.

Charges 1997: Per family unit (max. 6 persons) Bfr. 955 in July/Aug. and B.H.s, otherwise 675; electricity 50. Barrier key deposit 750. Largest unit accepted 2½ x 8 m. Less 10% with camping carnet.

Reservations: made with deposit. Address: Brugsesteenweg 49, 8620 Nieuwpoort. Tel: 058/23.60.37. FAX: 058/23.26.82.

056 Camping De Lombarde, Middelkerke-Lombardsijde

Modern, spacious, good value holiday site, 400 m. from sea in popular resort.

Located between Lombardsijde and the coast, this site has a pleasant atmosphere and modern buildings. The 350 pitches are set out in level, grassy bays surrounded by shrubs and all have electricity (16A). Vehicles are parked in separate car parks. There is a good number of seasonal units but still plenty of tourist pitches. The three modern sanitary units are clean and well maintained, with British style WCs, washbasins (some in cubicles), showers with hooks, dividers or curtains, facilities for disabled people, dishwashing and laundry sinks. Hot water is free throughout. Other facilities include a restaurant/bar and takeaway, shop and a large laundry. The children's adventure playground is in the centre of the site. Other activities include tennis, basketball, table tennis, boule, fishing lake and an entertainment programme in season. This is a popular holiday area and the site becomes full at peak times.

How to find it: From traffic lights in Lombarsijde, fork left (towards sea) at next junction, follow tram-lines left into Zeelaan. Continue following tram-lines until crossroads and tram stop, turn right into Elisabethlaan. Site is on right after 200 m.

General Details: Open all year. Shop (July/Aug). Restaurant/bar and takeaway (July/Aug. and weekends). Laundry. Tennis. Table tennis. Basketball. Boules. Fishing lake. TV lounge. Children's playground. Entertainment in season. Chemical disposal. Bungalows for rent.

Charges 1998: Per unit including electricity BFr. 475 - 795.

Reservations: Write or fax for details. Address: Elisabethlaan 4, 8434 Middelkerke-Lombardsijde. Tel: 058/23 68 39. FAX: 058/23 99 08. E-mail: de-lombards@flanderscoast.be.

058 Camping Memling, Sint-Kruis, Brugge

Traditional site, ideal for visiting Brugge, conveniently located in town suburbs.

Located behind a bistro in a quiet suburb, this site is within walking distance of local shops and supermarkets. The 80 unmarked pitches (50 for tourists) are on slightly undulating grass, with gravel roads and a few trees and hedgerows provide some shade. Electricity (5A) is available to 32 places. The sanitary facilities are in older style but are clean and tidy, with British style WCs and washbasins. The refurbished hot showers are on payment. There are dishwashing sinks (H&C), a laundry and a freezer for campers' use. The bistro has a terrace and offers takeaway meals at reasonable prices, but there is no shop on site. There is a tiny playground and bicycles can be hired. The municipal swimming pool and a park are nearby. The Maldegem Steam Centre and narrow gauge railway are 12 km.

How to find it: From the Brugge ring road take the N9 towards Maldegem. At Sint-Kruis turn right at traffic lights, where camp is signed (close to garage and supermarket).

General Details: Open all year. Bistro/grill and takeaway (closed Oct). Children's playground. Bicycle hire. Autobank exchange machine. Chemical disposal.

Charges 1998: Per adult BFr. 105, plus local tax; child (under 12) 65; car 130; caravan 130; motorcaravan 200; small tent 100; electricity 70.

Reservations: Write or fax for details. Address: Veltemweg 109, 8310 Sint Kruis, Brugge. Tel: 050/35 58 45 FAX: 050/35 58 45.

061 Camping Blaarmeersen, Gent (Ghent/Gand)

Comfortable, well managed site on west side of city.

This relaxed municipal site adjoins a sports complex and a fair-sized lake which provide facilities for a variety of watersports, tennis, squash, minigolf, football, athletics track, roller skating and a playground. The 224 individual, flat, grassy pitches are separated by tall hedges and mostly arranged in circular groups; electricity (10A) to all. Separate area for tents with barbecue facility. The four sanitary units are of a decent standard with hot water in the basins (some in cubicles), with provision for the disabled (showers and toilets). Most of the 20 free hot showers are in one block. The café/bar which serves a good range of snacks and meals is open from 10 am. and the shop from 8 am. - both daily. In Gent, tour the markets, free of charge, with the Town Crier (May-Sept, Sunday 10.30). Central Gent is 3 km, the nearest bus stop is 500 m.

How to find it: From the E40/A10 exit 13, turn towards Gent-West, follow dual carriageway for 5 km. Look for Blaarmeersen sign, turning sharp right and following signs to leisure complex. In city avoid overpasses - most signs are on the lower levels.

General Details: Open 1 March - 15 Oct. Shop. Café/bar. Takeaway. Sports facilities. Sauna. Laundry. Playground. Minigolf. Fishing. Bicycle hire. Bottle bank. Chemical disposal. Motorcaravan services.

Charges 1998: Per person Bfr. 110 - 120; child (5-12 yrs) 55 - 60, under 5 free; car 60 - 65; caravan or tent 120 - 130; motorcaravan 165 - 180; electricity 30. Payment accepted in Bfr. or by credit card or Eurocheque only.

Reservations: most advisable in main season; made for any period (no deposit) and kept until 5 pm. Address: Zuiderlaan 12, 9000 Gent. Tel: 09/221.53.99. FAX: 09/222.71.84.

ng Vlaamse Ardennen, Oudenaarde

Goo~ ~~ .~e families in countryside south of Gent.

This site is proud of its range of sporting activities, and the adjacent large lake is available for all manner of watersports. Behind reception is a pleasant paved square with a cafeteria/bar, restaurant, takeaway, and shop. The 369 pitches (170 for tourists), all with electricity (10A), are separated by shrub borders, with good access roads. Some are on a level area, others on sloping grass in small groups. The sections are linked by paved walk-ways, and large areas are given over to meadow-land, lake and recreation. The six modern toilet blocks have British style WCs, washbasins, spacious showers with seats, facilities for dishwashing, laundry and disabled people. Hot water is free throughout and all blocks can be heated. A full programme of activities is organised at B.H.s and high season. There is an attractive swimming pool and an imaginative children's playground complex.

How to find it: From the main N60 (Gent - Ronse), take exit to Avelgem (N453), just north of the Schelde river. Turn west for 2.5 km and follow signs to camp.

General Details: Open Easter - 12 Nov. Shop. Restaurant. Takeaway. Café. Bar. Swimming pool. Games rooms. Entertainment in season. TV. Children's bar/disco in separate building. Playgrounds. Bicycle hire. Boules. Football. Tennis. Volleyball. Minigolf. Fishing.

Charges 1997: Per family unit (max. 6 persons) Bfr. 850 in July/Aug. and B.H.s, otherwise 540; electricity 50. Less 10% with camping carnet.

Reservations: made with deposit. Address: Kortrijkstraat, 9700 Oudenaarde. Tel. 055/315473. FAX: 055/300865.

059 Provincial Domein De Gavers, Geraardsbergen

Modern, organised holiday site, in a peaceful location, with a large sports complex.

Adjacent to a large sports complex, with good security and a card operated barrier, located about 5 km. outside Geraardsbergen, this can be a busy site in season. There are 367 grassy, level pitches (80 for tourists) arranged on either side of surfaced access roads with some hedges and few trees to provide shade in parts. Electricity (5/10A) is available to most. The four main sanitary buildings, plus two portacabin style units, are modern and well equipped, providing British style WCs, hot showers with dividers and seats (on payment), and washbasins (H&C). Facilities include a modern laundry and rooms for disabled people and babies. Within the complex there is also a shop, cafeteria, restaurant, takeaway and bars. The site offers an extensive range of sporting activities, an excellent children's playground and a full entertainment programme over a long season.

How to find it: From E429/A8 exit 26 towards Edingen, take N255 and N495 to Geraardsbergen. Down a steep hill, then left at camp sign towards Onkerzele, through village and turn north to site.

General Details: Open all year. Shop (July/Aug). Restaurant, bar and takeaway (daily April - Sept, otherwise weekends). Tennis. Volleyball. Basketball. Mini-football. Boules. Fishing. Canoes, windsurfers, pedaloes, yachts and row boats for hire. Bicycle hire. Tourist train. Swimming and beach area. Climbing. Entertainment in season. Launderette. Chemical disposal.

Charges 1997: Per unit BFr. 380 - 490. Discounts of 5-30% for longer stays. Credit cards accepted.

Reservations: Write or fax for details. Address: Onkerzelestraat 280, 9500 Geraardsbergen. Tel: 054/416324. FAX: 054/410388. Internet: http://home.virtual-pc.com/althea/gavers.

054 Camping de L'Orient, Tournai

Attractive site in quiet green location, close to historic town, convenient for E42.

An excellent, quality municipal site, L'Orient is immaculately kept by the manager and his wife. The 51 level, grassy, individual pitches (all for tourists) are separated by laurel hedges and have shade in some parts and electricity (10A). There are two modern sanitary units, high quality, spotlessly clean and heated in cool weather. They have British WCs, washbasins (some in cubicles) and roomy hot showers with curtains (on payment). Facilities for laundry, dishwashing and the disabled. Adjoining the site is an attractive restaurant and bar (10 am.- 10 pm. in season) with a superb terrace overlooking the lake where campers can fish and hire pedaloes. Beside the lake are picnic and barbecue areas, a lakeside walk and a children's playground. There is also a new, high quality swimming pool complex and cafeteria with an indoor pool, spectator seating, an outside pool and waterslide and all facilities. Basic provisions are available from reception. Tournai has the oldest belfry in Europe and the Museum of Decorative Arts.

How to find it: Site is well signed from Tournai inner ring road. At exit 32 turn onto N48 Brussels road then turn almost immediately first right, site is signed at junction.

General Details: Open all year. Cafeteria. Bar. Laundry. Swimming pool and waterslide complex. Lake with barbecues, fishing, pedaloes for hire and children's playground.

Charges guide: Per adult BFr 70; child (6-12 yrs) 50; caravan 90; car 70; motorcaravan 160; m/cycle 50; electricity 6 p/kw.

Reservations: Write or phone for details. Address: Vieux Chemin de Mons, 7500 Tournai. Tel: 069/22 26 35.

053 Camping du Waux-Hall, Mons

Convenient, well laid out municipal site, close to town centre and E42 motorway.

This is a useful site for a longer look at historic Mons and the surrounding area. The 75 pitches, all with electricity (10A), are arranged on either side of an oval roadway, on grass and divided by beds of small shrubs; the landscape maintenance is excellent. The single, central sanitary unit is in older style, basic but clean, with British WCs, cold water at washbasins (some in cubicles) and hot showers with dividers and hooks (token from reception). Dishwashing and laundry sinks (H&C) are outside but under cover. There is no shop on site, only a soft drinks machine, ice creams and free tourist information available. Restaurants and shops are within easy walking distance. A large public park with refreshment bar, tennis, children's playground and lake is adjacent, with direct access from the site. Places to visit include the house of Van Gogh, the Fine Art Museum, Decorative Arts, Prehistory and Stamp Museums.

How to find it: From the Mons inner ring road, follow signs for Charleroi, La Louviere, Binche, Beaumont. When turning off ring road, keep to right hand lane, turning for site is immediately first right. (signed Waux-Hall and camping).

General Details: Open all year. Public park adjacent. Shops and restaurants near. Chemical disposal.

Charges 1998: Per pitch for tent/caravan and car plus 1 adult BFr. 171; motorhome plus 1 adult 153; pitch for tent and m/cycle plus 1 adult 159; extra adult 80; child (under 12) 41; electricity more than 2 nights (10A) 6 p/kw.

Reservations: Write or phone for details. Address: Avenue Saint-Pierre 17, 7000 Mons (Bergen). Tel: 65/33 79 23.

MONS (Belgium) CAMPING DU WAUX-HALL

At a short distance from the Town Centre, Camping Waux-Hall ★★ invites you to stay in a quiet and restful place with clean and modern equipment (sanitary facilities, showers, washing machine), with direct access to Waux-Hall park (5 ha. of open spaces, stretches of water, tennis, children's playground, bar . . .)

75 pitches with electricity ~ Open all year

Reservation: 00.32.65/33.55.80 (Tourist Office)
Avenue Saint-Pierre, 17
B-7000 MONS (Belgium)
Tel: 00.32.65/33.79.23 Fax: 00.32.65/35.63.36

069 IC-Camping Bertrix, Bertrix

Secluded Ardennes countryside site with comprehensive sports and leisure facilities.

This attractive, well fenced site has a feeling of well ordered security. The main building houses a restaurant, snack bar, shop, takeaway, with a terrace overlooking an excellent swimming pool complex, plus the main sanitary facilities and a laundry. There are four smaller sanitary units around the site with mostly British style WCs, washbasins (some in cubicles), showers with curtain and shelf, dishwashing and laundry sinks. Free, pre-mixed warm water throughout. The 500 individual, fairly level, grassy pitches are divided by tall beech hedges with mature trees for shade, and all have electricity (10A). There are several excellent playgrounds, including a woodland one with stream and waterfalls. Adjacent to the site is an Arboretum where campers are free to stroll. In high season a full entertainment programme includes daily aerobics lessons. Nearby is the Euro Space Centre at Transinne (15 km).

How to find it: From the church in the centre of Bertrix, turn south on Rue du Culot (towards Mortehan), and site is signed to the right, 2 km. from the town.

General Details: Open Easter - 12 Nov. Shop (July/Aug). Restaurant, snack bar and takeaway (all high season). Playgrounds. Bicycle hire. Tennis. Basketball. Football. Volleyball. Boules. Table tennis. Comprehensive sports and entertainment facilities. Swimming pools (lifeguard in main season, bathing caps required). Laundry. Chemical disposal.

Charges 1998: Per family unit (max. 6 persons) Bfr. 900 in July/Aug. and B.H.s, otherwise 625; electricity 50. Less 10% with camping carnet.

Reservations: Essential mid July - end Aug. and made with deposit.
Address: Route de Mortehan, 6880 Bertrix. Tel: 061/412281. FAX: 061/412588.

AR Discount
Less 10%

BELGIUM

071 Camping International Spineuse, Neufchâteau

Informal small site on outskirts of town, with a friendly, homely atmosphere.

This site is about 2 km. from the town centre, bordered by the river. It is on level grass with trees and shrubs dotted around the 87 large pitches (60 for tourists). Electricity (10 or 15A) is available to most. The sanitary facilities, located in the central building, are modern, comfortable, clean and tidy. They include British WCs, washbasins and good hot showers (on payment). Dishwashing and laundry sinks are located at the end of the building (not under cover) and there is a washing machine and dryer. The owners accommodation is part of this building, which includes a small bistro/bar with a terrace serving good value dishes and drinks, with a nice friendly, family atmosphere. Small shop (main season). Activities include table tennis, boules, a small children's playground, walking, cycling and fishing.

How to find it: Located 2 km. southwest of Neufchâteau on the N85 towards Florenville (there are 3 sites fairly close together, this is the last one on the left hand side).

General Details: Open 16 Feb. - 16 Dec. Shop. Bistro/bar. Laundry. Table tennis. Boules. Children's playground.

Charges guide: Per pitch with electricity BFr. 300, without 250; adult 65; child (under 6) 40; local tax 20. Less 10% out of main season.

Reservations: Not really necessary, write or phone for details. Address: Route de Florenville, 6840 Neufchâteau. Tel: 061/27 73 20.

067 Parc La Clusure, Bure-Tellin, nr Rochefort

Agreeable site in the popular Lhomme Valley touring area, with swimming pool.

Set in a river valley in the lovely wooded uplands of the Ardennes, this site is close to the area's best tourist attractions. The 425 marked, grassy pitches have access to electricity (16A), cable TV and water taps and are mostly in avenues off a central, tarmac road. The three sanitary units (one heated in winter) have free hot water and provide British WCs, washbasins (some in cubicles), showers with dividers/hooks, and facilities for babies. Dishwashing and laundry facilities may be stretched at times. There is a very pleasant, well lit, riverside walk, a heated swimming pool and children's pool with pool-side bar/terrace plus a well stocked shop, snack-bar, tennis courts, restaurant and takeaway. An organised activity programme includes courses in canoeing, mountain biking and climbing. The nearby main Brussels - Luxembourg railway line, though not visually intrusive, can be noisy.

How to find it: Site is signed north off the N803 Rochefort - St. Hubert road at Bure, 8 km. southeast of Rochefort with a steepish, winding descent to site.

General Details: Open all year. Shop. Restaurant. Bars. Snack bar. Takeaway. Laundry. Tennis. Badminton. Volleyball. Swimming pools (open 1/5-15/9). Playgrounds. Motorcaravan service station. Activity programme (July/Aug). Fishing and riding nearby. Bungalows for hire. Bicycle hire. Barrier card deposit 500.

Charges 1997: Per pitch incl. up to 4 persons Bfr. 900 in July/Aug. otherwise incl. 2 persons 490; extra person 140 (90); dog 80; electricity (16A) 80.

Reservations: Advisable for Easter, Whitsun and for July - mid-Aug. Made with deposit and fee (Bfr. 500). Address: Chemin de la Clusure 30, 6927 Bure-Tellin. Tel: 084/36 60 80. FAX: 084/36 67 77.

072 Camping Tonny, Amberloup (Ste Ode)

Family campsite with friendly atmosphere, in pleasant valley by the River Ourthe.

An attractive small site with 75 grassy touring pitches, the wooden chalet buildings here give a Tyrolean feel. The pitches (80-100 sq.m.) are separated by small shrubs and fir trees and electricity (4 or 6A) is available. Cars are parked away from the units and there is a separate meadow for tents. Surrounded by natural woodland, Camping Tonny is an ideal base for walking, cycling, fishing, canoeing and, in winter, cross-country ski-ing. The main chalet has a cafe/bar and open fireplace, small shop, TV lounge/library with a nice shady terrace for relaxing outside and is open all year. There are two sanitary units (one heated in winter) providing British WCs, washbasins and showers with divider/curtain and seat, dishwashing and laundry sinks (all hot water on payment), freezer for campers use, laundry and a baby changing area. Nearby St Hubert has a Basilica, the St Michel Furnace Industrial Museum and a wildlife park, with wild boar, deer and other native species - all worth a visit.

How to find it: From N4 take exit for Libramont (N826), then to Amberloup (4 km.) where site is signed.

General Details: Open all year. Shop. Cafe/bar. TV lounge and library. Sports field. Boules. Games room. Children's playgrounds. Bicycle hire. Fishing. Canoeing. Cross country skiing. Laundry. Chemical disposal. Six mobile homes and two chalets for rent.

Charges 1997: Pitch with electricity BFr. 300; without electricity 250; adult 80; electricity (6A) 6.00 p/kw. Off season discounts for over 55's and longer stays.

Reservations: Essential for high season. Write to or phone site for details. Address: Tonny 35, 6680 Amberloup (St Ode). Tel: 061/688285. FAX: as phone.

074 Domaine de L'Eau Rouge, Stavelot

Attractively located, lively site close to spa and Grand Prix circuit.

In a sheltered valley location, this popular site has a fair number of permanent units but there is usually space for tourists. The main building houses the busy reception, shop, café, bar and the main sanitary facilities. A smaller sanitary unit serves the touring area. These provide good numbers of British WCs, mostly open washbasins, but rather fewer hot showers on payment - which could be stretched at times. Hot water is also on payment for dishwashing and laundry. There are 140 grassy pitches of 110 sq.m. on sloping ground either side of a central road with speed bumps. Baker calls 9.30 am. daily in season. There are plenty of sporting activities available in the area including skiing and luge in winter, and free archery lessons on site 10 am. daily in high season.

How to find it: From A640 Francorchamps - Stavelot road, site is signed (3 km. from Stavelot, 5 km. from Francorchamps).

General Details: Open all year. Shop, Café. Bar. Football. Boules. Table tennis. Archery. Barbecues. Children's playground. Entertainment in season.

Charges 1998: Per unit BFr. 320-400; adult 42; child 32; electricity (10A) 80. Discounts with Carnet.

Reservations: Write to site. Address: Cheneux 25, 4970 Stavelot. Tel: 080/86 30 75. FAX: as phone.

066 Camping Baalse Hei, Turnhout

Friendly forest site peacefully situated close to city.

The 'Campine' is an area covering three-quarters of the Province of Antwerp, noted for its nature reserves, pine forests, meadows and streams and is ideal for walking and cycling, while Turnhout itself is an interesting old town. Baalse Hei is a long-established site and has recently added a separate touring area of 55 large pitches (all with 16A electricity and TV connections and shared water point) on a large grass field which has been thoughtfully developed with young trees and bushes planted. New dishwashing facilities (hot water Bfr. 5), chemical disposal and waste bins are close to the pitches off the hard access road. It is 100 m. from the edge of the field to the modern, heated, sanitary building. This provides hot showers on payment, some washbasins in private cabins and British style WCs (no toilet paper). Facilities for disabled people. Upstairs is a club/TV room. Close to reception is a café/restaurant with bar (July-Sept, then weekends, closed mid Nov-end Jan). No shop but bread can be ordered in high season. Small lake for swimming with beach, boating lake, large fishing lake (on payment), basketball, football pitch, table tennis, 2 hard tennis courts, boules, volleyball and an adventure play area for children on sand. Entertainment and activities organised July/Aug. Walk in the woods and you will undoubtedly come across some of the many red squirrels. Pleasant 1.5 km. riverside walk to next village.

How to find it: Site is northeast of Turnhout off N119. Approaching from Antwerp on E34/A21 go onto Turnhout ring road to the end (not a complete ring) and turn right. Small site sign to right in 1.5 km. then country lane.

General Details: Open all year. Café/restaurant (daily July - Sept, closed Nov - Jan, weekends at other times). Lake swimming. Fishing. Bicycle hire. Tennis. Table tennis. Boules. Volleyball. Basketball. Football. Children's play equipment. Entertainment. Launderette. Chemical disposal. Motorcaravan services. Cars parked away from pitch. Hikers' cabins. Arrival after 4 pm. departure by 10 am.

Charges 1998: Per unit all incl. high season Bfr. 650, otherwise 490; electricity 30.

Reservations: Contact site. Address: Roodhuisstraat 10, 2300 Turnhout. Tel: 014/421931. FAX: 014/420853.

064 Camping de Lilse Bergen, Lille (Gierle)

Spacious lakeside site set in pinewoods, with excellent facilities and convenient to E34.

This attractive, quietly located holiday site has some 500 shady pitches (250 for tourists), all with electricity (10A). Set among pine trees and rhododendrons, on sandy soil and arranged around a large lake, the site has a Mediterranean feel. Cars are parked away from units. The six good sanitary units (two heated in winter) provide British style WCs, mostly open washbasins (H&C), hot showers with seat and divider on payment, dishwashing and laundry sinks, baby baths and facilities for disabled people. The lake has marked swimming and diving areas (adult), a sandy beach, plus a children's pool complex and a most imaginative playground at one end. Lifeguards, a red flag system for safe bathing and the water meet blue flag standard. Other facilities include a restaurant, takeaway and a well stocked shop (open weekends only in low season) and a laundry. There are picnic areas, lakeside and woodland walks, tennis, minigolf, table tennis, boule, cycling and an entertainment programme in high season.

How to find it: From E34/A21 Antwerp-Eindhoven take exit 22 in direction of Eindhoven (exit only northbound), turn towards Beerse and, almost immediately, turn left at camping sign, and follow forest road to site entrance.

General Details: Open all year. Shop (Easter-15/9). Restaurant/bar. Takeaway. Watersports. Tennis. Table tennis. Boules. Minigolf. Bicycle hire. First aid post. Pedalo, windsurfers, lifejackets and bicycles for hire. Playground. Entertainment in season. Chemical disposal. Motorcaravan services.

Charges 1997: Per unit BFr. 180, 370 or 550, acc. to season; dog 100; electricity 40.

Reservations: Write or fax. Address: Strandweg 6, 2275 Gierle-Lille. Tel: 014/557901. FAX: 014/554454.

BELGIUM

065 Camping Floréal Club Het Veen, Sint Job In't Goor, nr Antwerpen

Top quality, good value site with many sports facilities, in woodland area.

A modern site with good security and efficient reception, the 340 marked pitches (60 for tourists) are on level grass, most with some shade and electricity (10A). The four sanitary units are ultra modern and spacious, with coloured fittings, free hot water throughout and providing British style WCs, washbasins (some in cubicles) with quality mixer taps set in marbled surfaces, and roomy hot showers with dividers and hooks. Well equipped facilities for disabled people. Dishwashing and laundry facilities complete the superb installations. The restaurant and bar opens day and evening in July/Aug. (evenings only other times). The well stocked shop and takeaway open daily in high season, at weekends in low seasons. There is an indoor sports hall (charged 150 fr/hr) and courts for tennis (100 fr/hr), football, basketball and softball are outside. Children's entertainment in season, plus a good, safe and exciting playground.

How to find it: From Brecht (exit 4 from E19/A1) follow road to St Job In't Goor, straight on at traffic lights and *immediately* after canal bridge turn left at campsite sign. Continue straight on for about 3 km.

General Details: Open Easter - 30 Sept. Shop. Restaurant, bar, café and takeaway (daily July/Aug. weekends only at other times). Tennis. Badminton. Volleyball. Softball. Basketball. Football. Table tennis. Boules. Fishing. Canoeing. Bicycle hire. Children's playground. Entertainment in season. First aid post. Laundry. Chemical disposal. Motorcaravan services. English spoken.

Charges 1998: Per pitch incl. electricity BFr. 260; person 100; child (3-11) 70; tent + m/cycle 160.

Reservations: Write or fax site. Address: Eekhoornlaan 1, 2960 Sint Job In't Goor.
Tel: 03/636 13 27. FAX: 03/636 20 30.

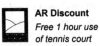

AR Discount
*Free 1 hour use
of tennis court*

BRITISH ISLES

The British Isles (England, Scotland, Wales, Northern Ireland and the Channel Islands) offer the camper or caravanner a choice of just about everything you could imagine in terms of scenery, campsites and weather! Whether you choose to visit the Highlands of Scotland, the English Lake District, Snowdonia in Wales, the Norfolk Broads, England's West Country, the unspoiled beauty of Northern Ireland or the Channel Islands, you are sure to find attractive countryside and/or much of historic interest. Visitors to the British Isles should not encounter any significant problems, other than driving on the left, and the fact that few Britons are proficient in any language other than English.

Population
57,970,200 (93), density 239 per sq.km.

Capitals
London, Edinburgh, Cardiff and Belfast.

Language
Predominantly English, although Welsh also is spoken in many parts of Wales and Gaelic in parts of Scotland and Ireland.

Climate
Changeable and unpredictable - temperatures are generally a little higher in the south and southwest, and rather cooler and wetter in the mountainous regions of Scotland, Wales and the Lake District.

Currency
The Pound Sterling (£) divided into 100 pence.

Banks
Open at least Mon-Fri 09.30-15.30 hrs, except on Public Holidays.

Time
Late October - late March is Greenwich Mean Time (GMT); during the summer (late March - late Oct) clocks are put forward one hour to British Summer Time (BST). For most of the year (11 months) British time is 1 hour behind the time in other EC countries.

Post Offices
Mainly open Mon-Fri at least 09.30-16.30.

Public Telephones
Two main types of public telephone boxes, coin operated and 'phone card operated - cards can be purchased from Post Offices, newsagents, etc.

Public Holidays
New Year; Good Fri, Easter Mon; 1st Mon in May; last Mon in May; last Mon in Aug; Christmas, 25,26 Dec.

Shops
Most shops open at least 09.00-17.30 Monday - Saturday, but some still operate a half day (known as early closing day).

Motoring
In Britain one drives on the left-hand side of the road, and you go round roundabouts clockwise. The overall maximum speed limits are 70 mph (112 kph) on motorways, and 60 mph (96 kph) on other roads, except where a lower limit is indicated by signs. Overall limits are reduced to 60 mph and 50 mph respectively for vehicles towing trailers or caravans. Parking restrictions apply in most towns, and many villages, indicated by yellow lines on the roadside.

Lakeland's Premier Camping & Touring Centre

- **Award Winning range of Family Facilities**

- **Spectacular 'Tranquil Valley' Location**

- Touring Pitches - short stay & full season

- 'State of the art' Holiday Caravans for hire

- Luxurious Holiday Homes for sale

- Only Ten minutes from Lake Windermere

For a full colour brochure or to make a booking please ring (015394)32300 quoting '150' for entry into the 'Tranquil Valley' holiday draw!

Limefitt ♠ Park

Windermere   The Lake District   Cumbria LA23 1PA

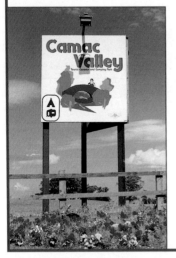

Daily ～ Express

5 DAY RETURN · CAR & 2 ADULTS

FROM
£258
RETURN

A FAST CAR FERRY SERVICE TO
Jersey and Guernsey

Only 2¹/₂ hours to Guernsey and 3³/₄ hours to Jersey with daily departures from Poole, on the high speed Condor Express. Sit back and enjoy the on-board experience of duty free shopping, bar and cafe bar, on one of the world's most advanced fast ferries.

And if you fancy a trip to France, look out for our new high speed Weymouth to St. Malo service from May 1998. Don't forget to pack your passport.

TRAVEL INFORMATION AND BOOKING
01305 761551

Useful Addresses

Tourist information:

English Tourist Board, Thames Tower, Blacks Road, Hammersmith, London W6 9EL. Tel: 0181 846 9000. England is further subdivided into eleven regions, each with its own Regional Tourist Board, details of which can be obtained from the ETB.
Scottish Tourist Board, 22 Ravelston Terrace, Edinburgh EH14 2EU. Tel: 0131 332 2433. Scotland is subdivided into no less than 33 Area Tourist Boards - details from the STB.
Wales Tourist Board, Brunel House, 2, Fitzalan Road, Cardiff CF2 1UY. Tel: 01222 499909, from whom details of the three Welsh Regional Tourist organisations (for North, South and Mid-Wales) can be obtained.
Northern Ireland Tourist Board, 59 North Street, Belfast BT1 1NB. Tel: 01232 231221.
A comprehensive network of over 900 Tourist Information Centres (TIC) covers the British Isles, although their opening hours vary - they are easily identified by the international "i" symbol.

Motoring Organisations:

Automobile Association (AA): at Fanum House, Basingstoke, Hampshire RG21 2EA, and at various other centres such as the major ferry ports.
Royal Automobile Club (RAC): at RAC House, P.O. Box 100, South Croydon CR2 6XW and at various other centres.

B2 Cardinney Camping Park, Crows an Wra, Penzance

Well kept, personally run small park near Lands End beauty spots.

A friendly Geordie welcome awaits from the owners, Liz and Kevin Lindley, when you stay at Cardinney, which is perfectly situated for visiting the famous Lands End beauty spots and tourist attractions and also within easy driving distance of small Cornish beaches and coves. The level field is semi-divided into three camping areas and is neatly kept with some landscaping. The facilities are limited compared to many of the more sophisticated sites in Devon and Cornwall, consisting of one block of 3 metered showers and 6 mirrored washbasins for each sex. Razor points, hair dryers and baby cubicle are also available. The block is situated adjacent to the 105 marked pitches, of which 50 have electrical connections (10A) and 17 hardstanding. The combined café and bar acts as a social point providing breakfasts with fresh croissants, takeaway food at most times and good cheer in the evenings. Children's playground and games room with TV, pool table and video games. Laundry facilities and dishwashing sink with hot water. Fishing and bicycle hire 5 miles. Coastal, cliff top walks nearby, also the Minnack Open Air Theatre.

> **Directions:** Park is signed at Crows an Wra on main Penzance - Lands End A30 road, 5 miles west of Penzance. O.S.GR: SW426285.
>
> **Charges 1997:** Per unit incl. 2 adults £5.50 - £6.50; extra adult £1.50; child (0-14 yrs) 50p - 75p; extra car, tent or awning 50p; electricity £1.50; pets free. Credit cards accepted.
>
> **Open:** 1 February - 30 November.
>
> **Reservations:** Made with £10 deposit. Address: Crows an Wra, St Buryan, Cornwall TR19 6HX. Tel: (01736) 810880.

AR Discount

Apply to park

B4 Trevalgan Holiday Farm, St Ives

Friendly, smàllish, `countrified' park.

Trevalgan is based on a working farm on the cliffs 1½ miles west of St Ives. Providing 120 clearly marked pitches in a level stone walled field, the pitches vary in size as the park is very popular with walkers. A purpose built toilet block has curtained washbasins, controllable hot showers with seat and curtain, plus baby room, laundry and washing up, chemical disposal and even a hot drinks machine. Amenities include reception with a small shop and a 'Farm House Kitchen' with takeaway (mid June - early Sept) and popular for breakfast or evening food with some outside tables only. Games field, children's play area and farm pets corner with baby chickens, two donkeys, etc. A games room in an original barn has table tennis, pool, fruit machines and a comfortable upstairs TV room. Bicycle hire. There is access to the coastal path and it is a 25 minutes walk to St. Ives. Bus service at top of road. With tractor rides, plus farm and hill trails, it is, in all, quite an original type of park.

> **Directions:** Approach park down a narrow Cornish lane from the B3306 St. Ives - Lands End road, following sign. O.S.GR: SW490400.
>
> **Charges 1998:** Per adult £3.00 - £4.80; child 3-14 yrs £2.00 - £3.80, under 3 yrs £1.00 - £1.80; electricity £2.00. Credit cards accepted.
>
> **Open:** 1 May - 30 September.
>
> **Reservations:** Contact park - made for Sat.- Sat. only for electricity in high season. Address: Trevalgan Farm, St Ives, Cornwall TR26 3BJ. Tel: (01736) 796433. FAX: as phone.

BRITISH ISLES - England

B49 Harford Bridge Park, Peter Tavy, nr Tavistock

Attractive, mature park on west Dartmoor with river boundary; holiday caravans and chalets to let.

Harford Bridge has an interesting history - originally a tin mine, Wheal Union, until 1850, then used as a farm campsite from 1930 and taken over by the Royal Engineers in 1939, it is now a quiet, rural park inside the Dartmoor National Park. It is bounded by the River Tavy on one side and the lane from the main road to the village of Peter Tavy, with Harford Bridge, a classical moorland bridge, at the corner. With 16½ acres, the park provides 120 touring pitches well spaced on a level grassy meadow with some shade from mature trees and others recently planted; 40 pitches have electrical hook-ups and 8 have 'multi services'. Out of season or by booking in advance you may get one of the delightful spots bordering the river. Holiday caravans and chalets are also available for hire, neatly landscaped in their own discrete area. The single toilet block, originally built by the Royal Engineers, is older in style but is kept perfectly clean, well decorated and properly maintained. Hot water is free throughout. The facilities include hand and hair dryers (free), baby bathroom, washing up sinks, a good launderette and drying room, freezer pack facility and chemical disposal point. At the entrance to the park a central grassy area is left free for barbecues, the town band, village fete, etc. and is overlooked by the site shop which is well stocked and reasonably priced. While the river will inevitably mesmerise the youngsters and the ducks and chickens attract their interest, a super central adventure play area on a hilly tree knoll will claim them. Formerly the area of the old mine workings, two restored Wickstead stainless steel slides, a 45 year old carnival carousel roundabout, tunnels and model chimney like the original are just part of a well presented, safe and marvellous provision. Games room with table tennis and separate TV room. Tennis court. Fishing (by licence, £2.80 p/day, £10 p/week). Communal barbecues. Well behaved dogs are accepted and a 4 acre exercise field is provided. With its own and the local history, plus its situation, this is a super place to stay.

Directions: Turn off A386 just south of Mary Tavy village, 2 miles north of Tavistock, towards Harford Bridge. O.S.GR: SX504768.

Charges 1997: Per unit, incl. 2 persons £6.00 - £9.00; extra adult £2.00 - £2.50; child £1.00 - £1.50; dog 90p; electricity £2.00; awning £1.00; extra car 50p. Less 10% for stays over 7 days (not electricity or fishing). Credit cards accepted. VAT included.

Open: Late March - early November.

Reservations: Made for any length with first night's fees. Address: Peter Tavy, Tavistock, Devon PL19 9LS. Tel: (01822) 810349. FAX: (01822) 810028.

AR Discount
Ask at park
for details

B61 Ross Park, Ipplepen, nr Newton Abbot

Friendly, relaxed park in attractive surroundings.

The owners of Ross Park, Mark and Helen Lowe are keen to further develop this attractive park with its amazing floral displays and wide range of flowering shrubs and trees. The impressive, heated conservatory sitting area houses yet more named, colourful plants. Connected to the conservatory is the 'New Barn' providing a lounge, gallery bar and restaurant with à la carte menu or bar snacks (all limited hours out of main season). The touring area, with good views (but possibly some wind) across the fruit fields towards Dartmoor, provides 110 pitches, all with electricity (10/16A). They are divided into groups by growing shrubs or hedges and 82 pitches are hardened ones, some larger with an increased gravel area. The modern, unusual sanitary facilities open from under a veranda style roof, with 6 en-suite cubicles, heated in cool weather and recently refurbished. Separate additional shower and toilet (plus 8 new) facilities. Free hot water throughout, shaver points and hairdryers are provided. Fully equipped laundry room and separate dishwashing sinks, freezer and battery charging facilities. A 4 acre park area for recreation has been developed with unusual ornamental shrubs, bowling and croquet greens and an adventure play area on bark for older children. Dogs are welcome with a variety of walks in fields and orchards including a purpose built dog shower with hot water and grooming facilities. Tourist information chalet, shop and games room. A conservation area with information on wild flowers and butterflies, and beautiful views completes the environmentally considered amenities. Facilities may be limited in late autumn and winter. Fishing 3 miles. Bicycle hire available (with delivery to park). Dainton Park 18 hole golf course is adjacent.

Directions: From A381 Newton Abbot - Totnes road, park is signed towards Woodland at Park Hill crossroads and Jet filling station. O.S.GR: SX845671.

Charges 1997: Per unit incl. 2 persons £6.80 - £10.20; extra person over 3 yrs £1.75; electricity (10A) £1.80 - £2.00. VAT included.

Open: All year.

Reservations: Made with £20 deposit. Address: Park Hill Farm, Ipplepen, Newton Abbot, Devon TQ12 5TT. Tel: (01803) 812983. FAX: as phone.

B59 Grange Court Holiday Centre, Paignton

Busy holiday caravan park with good entertainment facilities; touring sections for caravans only.

South of central Paignton, with a short walk to the sea and some views of Torbay, Grange Court's major interest is the complex of 500 holiday homes (with letting service) which totally dominate the site. However there are also 157 touring pitches (no tents) in two sections, each with its own resident wardens. One, probably the quieter of the two, is on flat grass by the entrance, with two fairly standard toilet blocks (washbasins and free pre-set hot showers with push-button). The other is on higher ground with some views and the site shops close by. It is on a gentle slope, with a single, but larger, tiled block of better quality. The individual pitches are of reasonable size, though with some variation, and all have electricity. The park can be full for most of July/Aug. and B.Hs. For those who like entertainment, the central complex is the park's best feature, with a good sized free heated swimming pool (80 x 40 ft. open 6/5-16/9). A super new indoor pool complex with views across the bay and over the outdoor pool has flume, spa bath, sauna, steam room (all free), plus a sun-bed. The clubhouse has a large bar lounge and separate room with dance floor - entertainment is organised almost nightly from Spr. B.H. to end Sept. and at Easter. Supermarket and other shops, takeaway and fast food bar (all Easter - Oct). Games rooms with 2 pool tables and one full size snooker table, and an amusement arcade, playground and large adventure play area (on bark). Launderette. Recycling bins. Up to 30 American motorhomes accepted (30 ft. max). No dogs or pets accepted. Reception is busy, but efficient. Part of the Hoburne group.

Directions: Park is signed (not the normal camp site signs) from outer Paignton ring road. Turn off Goodrington Road into Grange Road. 150 yds from A379 coast road at signs for camp and Marine Park. O.S.GR: SX890585.

Charges 1997: Per unit £8.00 - £20.00, incl. electricity and awning, acc. to season (no tents, trailer tents or pup tents allowed). VAT included. Credit cards accepted.

Open: All year except 15/1-15/2.

Reservations: For 1-6 nights, full payment in advance; 7 nights and over £50 deposit per week (min. 7 days in Jul/Aug and B.H.s). Address: Goodrington, Paignton, Devon TQ4 7JP. Tel: (01803) 558010. FAX: (01803) 663336.

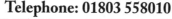

GRANGE COURT
Award Winning Holiday Park
HOLIDAY CARAVANS • TOURING PITCHES
Exciting indoor leisure complex compliments this already striking family Park in the heart of the English Riviera overlooking Torbay.
Close to sandy beaches and Dartmoor.
For FREE colour brochure or credit card bookings please contact:
GRANGE COURT HOLIDAY CENTRE, AR1,
Grange Road, Goodrington Paignton, Devon TQ4 7JP.
Telephone: 01803 558010

B51 Riverside Caravan Park, Plymouth

Good sized touring park with heated pool, close to main routes and city.

Riverside is well placed for those using the car ferries or en-route to Cornwall and is also pleasantly situated for touring Dartmoor and south Devon. Although under 4 miles from the city centre, its location on the banks of the River Plym in a wooded valley is a quiet one. Attractive shrubs and trees, flower beds, well kept grass and tarmac roads give a neat, park-like appearance. Over 230 units of any type are taken on flat, numbered pitches, including 97 with 10A electricity and 40 with hardstandings. There are 65 pitches reserved for tents. A large, hard area is retained for late arrivals. In the centre of the park arranged around a patio are a lounge bar (fully open from July with nightly entertainment), coffee bar and restaurant with takeaway (6-10 pm), games and TV rooms and a play area. A free, sheltered and heated swimming pool (60 x 30 ft), with paddling pool, opens Spr. B.H - mid-Sept. The two sanitary blocks have been modernised and decorated somewhat haphazardly. Both have free hot water in washbasins (some in cabins with toilets for ladies in one block), showers (some pre-set) and indoor dishwashing sinks. Laundry facilities. Good shop at the entrance (Spr. B.H. - mid-Sept). Public phones and post box. Fishing on site, riverside walks up to Dartmoor. One dog per pitch accepted.

Directions: From the A38 dual-carriageway from Exeter, take the Marsh Mill exit (the first signed to Plymouth city centre). Follow good camp site signs to third exit, turning left after a few yards. O.S.GR: SX518576.

Charges 1997: Per adult £2.50 - £3.00; child (3-10 yrs) £1.10 - £1.25; pitch £1.50 - £3.00; electricity £2.00 - £1.75; awning, dog, extra car or boat £1.00.

Open: All year.

Reservations: Made with £15 deposit per week or part week. Address: Longbridge Road, Marshmills, Plymouth, Devon PL6 8LD. Tel: (01752) 344122.

B38 Wooda Farm Park, Bude

Spacious, relaxed, family run farm park with views of sea and countryside.

This well organised and cared for park with some nice touches is part of a working farm situated 1¾ miles from the sandy, surfing beaches of Bude, in peaceful farmland with plenty of open spaces. The 160 pitches, spread over four meadows, are on level or gently sloping grass, 100 with electric connections (10A) and 31 fully serviced with hedging dividers, 15 with hardstanding, plus an additional 5 with hardstanding. There are some holiday letting units situated beside the shop and reception at the entrance. Three well maintained toilet blocks with free hot water provide fully tiled showers with seat and hooks, washbasins in vanity style with shelf and hand dryer, 6 under cover washing up sinks (H&C), a unit suitable for the disabled and a baby room with small bath. Laundry with 2 washing machines, 2 tumbler dryers, sinks with hot water and iron and board. A comprehensive range of facilities are provided from Spr. B.H - Sept. These include a shop with off-licence (8.30 - 8.30 in main season) and a licensed restaurant and bar, Linney's Larder, for meals. A children's play area is provided in a separate field on grass, with plenty of room for ball games, a 9 hole `fun' golf course (golf clubs can be provided), plus a woodland walk (where the pixies can be found) and an orchard walk. There is also a small farm museum and friendly farm animals. Children (and adults) are also welcome to assist at feeding time! Tractor and trailer rides, pony rides, pony trekking, archery and clay pigeon shooting with tuition are provided according to season and demand, likewise barn dances. Games room with TV, table tennis and pool. Bicycle hire. Coarse fishing is also available in a 1½ acre lake (permits from reception, £1.50 per half day, £2.50 per day). Dogs are accepted (not certain breeds) with a large dog exercise field. Finally there is a public telephone and the local village inn is only 5 mins. walk away. There is also much to do in the area - the Leisure Centre and Splash Pool in Bude itself, sandy beaches with coastal walks, and Tintagel with King Arthur's Castle and Clovelly nearby.

Directions: Park is north of Bude at Poughill; turn off A39 on north side of Stratton on minor road for Coombe Valley, following camp signs at junctions. O.S.GR: SS225080.

Charges 1997: Per unit incl. 2 persons £6.25 - £9.50; extra adult £1.00 - £2.00; child (3-16 yrs) 50p - £1.00 - £1.25; awning/pup tent £1.00 - £1.25; dog free - £1.25; electricity (10A) £1.90; fully serviced pitch (incl. electricity) plus £3.00 - £4.25. VAT included. Credit cards accepted.

Open: Easter/1 April - October.

Reservations: Made with £20 deposit. Address: Poughill, Bude, Cornwall EX23 9HJ. Tel: (01288) 352069. FAX: (01288) 355258.

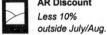

AR Discount
Less 10%
outside July/Aug.

B43 Twitchen Park, Mortehoe, nr Woolacombe

Holiday park with areas for tourers and tents, with extensive family entertainment programme.

Set in the grounds of an attractive Edwardian country house, Twitchen Park's main concern lies in holiday caravans and flats. However, it also provides some 50 marked pitches for tourers and sloping fields for all types of unit. These are at the top of the park, with some views over the rolling hills to the sea. The formal touring pitches, all with hardstanding and electricity, are arranged around an oval access road in a hedged area. These fields are sloping but blocks are thoughtfully provided, with 27 electrical connections (15A) available. There are two sanitary blocks of a fair standard. The larger block is of an unusual design with different levels and rather narrow corridors. Both provide free, pre-set, hot showers (rather small), washbasins in rows and WCs. Dishwashing facilities under cover outside each block and laundry facilities in each, plus a good launderette at the central complex. The touring areas are cared for by wardens who live on site. American motorhomes accepted (up to 30 ft.) depending on the season. A smart, modern entertainment complex incorporates a licensed club and family lounge with snacks, restaurant, adults only bar, teenage disco room, and cartoon lounge, together with games rooms for table tennis, pool, snooker and arcade games, with entertainment during the day and evenings. Shop and takeaway. Outside is a swimming pool (heated mid-May - mid-Sept) and paddling pool with free swimming lessons in high season. A new indoor pool is excellent, with sauna, paddling pool with fountain and viewing area. Super children's adventure play area (on bark), putting green and games field complete the facilities, which make Twitchen very popular for families with children. If they become bored, there are always excellent beaches nearby! No dogs permitted. Part of the Hoburne group.

Directions: From Barnstaple take A361 towards Ilfracombe and through Braunton. Left at Mullacott Cross roundabout towards Woolacombe, then right towards Mortehoe. Park on left before village. O.S.GR: SS466456.

Charges 1997: Per touring pitch, incl. electricity, awning and 1-6 persons £7.00 - £18.00; tent pitch (no electricity available) £7.00 - £15.50; extra person 50p. VAT included. Credit cards accepted.

Open: 1 April/Easter - end October.

Reservations: Made with £50 deposit for tourers, payment in full for tent pitches. Min. period at Easter, May Day B.H. is 4 days, Spr. B.H. 7 days and mid July and Aug, 7 days from Sat. to Sat. Address: Mortehoe, Woolacombe, N. Devon EX34 7ES. Tel: (01271) 870476. FAX: (01271) 870498.

B78 Blue Anchor Park, Blue Anchor, nr Minehead

Beach-side site, for caravans and motorcaravans only, with views across the Bristol Channel.

Although mainly a holiday park, with a large number of holiday homes, Blue Anchor nevertheless offers good facilities for tourers (no tents), providing 103 level touring pitches. All have 16A electricity and are virtually in a separate touring area. Facilities on the park include a good size indoor swimming pool, crazy golf, a small supermarket/shop and an excellent and attractive children's play area. Its situation, directly across the small road from the beach, is unusual and gives some beautiful views across the Bristol Channel to South Wales. Dunster, Exmoor, Minehead and the West Somerset Steam Railway are close. Sanitary facilities include large, free hot showers with push-button, vanity style washbasins and a launderette, in a single, modern block serving just the touring area. Although not actually within the park itself, there are both restaurants and takeaway food facilities within easy walking distance. No dogs allowed. American motorhomes accepted (max. 36 ft). Part of the Hoburne Group.

Directions: From M5 junction 25, take A358 signed Minehead. After 12 miles turn left on A39 at Williton. After 4 miles turn right onto B3191 at Carhampton signed Blue Anchor. Park is 1½ miles on right. O.S.GR: ST025434.

Charges 1997: Per unit, incl. up to 6 persons, electricity and awning £5.50 - £13.50; extra pup tent £2.00. Weekly rate available. VAT included. Credit cards accepted.

Open: 1 March - 31 October.

Reservations: For stays of 1-6 days, payment required in full at time of booking; for 7 nights or more £50 deposit. Address: nr Minehead, Somerset TA24 6JT. Tel: Dunster (01643) 821360. FAX: (01643) 821572.

B93 Freshwater Beach Holiday Park, Burton Bradstock, Bridport

See colour advert opposite page 33

Busy holiday and touring park with direct access to private beach.

Family run parks with direct access to a beach are rare in Britain and this one has the added advantage of being in beautiful coastal countryside in West Dorset. It is an ideal situation to explore the 'Hidden County' and the resort of Weymouth (17 miles) and is next to the sea and a beach of fine pebbles, sheltered from the wind by pebble banks. Approached by a fairly steep access road, the park itself is on level, open ground. The 500 plus touring pitches, over 200 with 10A electricity, are on an open, undulating grass field. Caravan places have wooden pitch locators evenly spaced in lines. Some tent pitches are in the main field, with others spaced around the edge of a slightly sloping extra field. There are many caravan holiday homes for hire. Licensed restaurant and three bars with evening entertainment in season. Daytime entertainment for all ages - don't miss the donkey derby! Supermarket, takeaway and launderette. Heated, supervised outdoor swimming pool and children's pool, adventure play area, pets corner and pony trekking (own stables). Golf course adjacent, fishing from Chesil Bank. Sanitary facilities in three blocks, two fully refurbished with showers, one with washbasins and toilets only, are a good provision for a busy beach park. Both blocks have free hot water, facilities for disabled people and a baby changing room and cleaning and maintenance also seem good. Laundry and washing up sinks. The overall impression is of a large, busy holiday park with a friendly reception and happy atmosphere.

Directions: Park is west of Burton Bradstock village on Weymouth - Bridport road (B3157). O.S.GR: SY980898.

Charges 1997: Per unit incl. up to 6 persons, car and awning £6.50 - £16.00; extra person £1.50; dog £2.50; electricity £1.75; small tent incl. 2 persons walking or cycling £5.50 - £9.50. Single sex groups not admitted. VAT included. Credit cards accepted.

Open: 21 March - 9 November.

Reservations: Min. 1 week with £10 deposit p/week, plus £1 fee. Short break reservations available - ring for details. Address: Burton Bradstock, nr Bridport, Dorset DT6 4PT. Tel: (01308) 897317. FAX: (01308) 897336.

B107 Hoburne Park, Christchurch

Well kept holiday and touring site with many amenities; for caravans and motorcaravans only.

Convenient for Bournemouth or the New Forest, this is a well kept and tidy site with a range of good quality amenities. There are 285 level, grass touring pitches (caravans or motorcaravans only), all with 16A electricity and some with water supply and hardstanding, in three hedged areas. Amenities include an outdoor pool, with paved and grass sunbathing areas, children's pool and an attractive indoor leisure pool with sauna, spa bath, solarium and steam rooms. We continue to be impressed with the attendance to pool safety here and at other Hoburne parks. A large reception area, restaurant, takeaway, well furnished bar with terrace, video games room and snooker room form part of the indoor complex area. A large adventure play area is near this main complex together with tennis, crazy golf and a field area. Organised programme of entertainment for adults and children in season. Well stocked shop and launderette. Sanitary facilities are modern and include free hot showers in blocks central to each field area, with additional facilities attached to the main building. Mother and baby rooms. Many large sites have a frenzied atmosphere in high season. This one can be busy but the atmosphere is pleasantly quiet and relaxed. No tents, trailer tents or pup tents permitted. Dogs not accepted. American motorhomes accepted in limited numbers up to 30 ft. A well managed park, the flag flier of the Hoburne group.

Directions: Park is signed (left) from roundabout 2 miles east of Christchurch on A337. From Lyndhurst, travel south on A35 to junction with A337 - turn left on A337 then left again at first roundabout. O.S.GR: SZ169928.

Charges 1997: Per unit, incl. electricity and awning (up to 3 x 9m.) £9.00 - £22.50. Weekly rates and special weekend breaks. VAT included. Credit cards accepted.

Open: March - October.

Reservations: Made with payment in full (6 days or less) or £50 deposit; min. periods 4 nights B.Hs, 7 nights mid July/Aug. Address: Hoburne Lane, Christchurch, Dorset BH23 4HU. Tel: (01425) 273379. FAX: (01425) 270705.

B105 Sandford Holiday Park, Holton Heath, nr Poole

Pleasant, well run park near popular coastal areas; holiday caravans and large touring section.

Sandford Park has a large permanent section with 248 holiday homes and lodges. However, the touring sections take 460 units of any type, mainly on individual pitches, on level grass with mature hedging in the main area. All have 16A electricity. The main toilet block provides facilities for the disabled and a baby room. It is supplemented by the former main block and subsidiary units (one a bath block). Free hot water in washbasins, set in flat surfaces, and in pre-set showers (under pressure at peak times). Plenty of water points. Dogs permitted in the touring section from 5 Sept. with a walk provided. Sandford is a large, very busy holiday park with a wide range of entertainment. The clubhouse is spacious with dance floor, bar and seating area, and caters for different tastes and age groups. A variety of bars, restaurants (book in busy periods) and simple hot meals and takeaway elsewhere in peak season. The outdoor pool (25 m. long, open May- Oct. and supervised) and a very large play pool (0-2 ft.) with a sandy beach, are attractively situated with a snack bar and terraced area. Large indoor pool with swimming and fun areas (April - Oct and Christmas, also supervised). Large supermarket and other shops (all peak season only). Launderette. Ladies' hairdresser. TV lounges. Children's playground, 2 tennis courts, mountain bike hire, table tennis, 2 short mat bowling greens (outdoor) and large crazy golf course. Public phones. Many activities nearby include riding stables and fishing (9 miles).

Directions: Park is just west off the A351 (Wareham - Poole) road at Holton Heath. O.S.GR: SY940913.

Charges 1997: Per pitch free - £5.50, acc. to season; adult £3.95; child (3-14 yrs) £1.50 - £2.50; extra car free - £1.00; awning free; electricity £2.50; `super hook-up (electricity, TV, water) £4.50; dog after 5/9 (max. 2) £2.50; boat and trailer £1.50 - £2.50; visitor £3.95, child £1.75). Club membership included. Special offers and special interest weeks - details from park. VAT included. Credit cards accepted.

Open: Easter - January incl..

Reservations: Early booking advisable (min. 3 days) - write to park. Address: Holton Heath, nr Poole, Dorset BH16 6JZ Tel: (01202) 631600.

B110 Bashley Park, New Milton

Pleasant park with large section for caravans or motorcaravans, with pools and evening entertainment.

A well run park with a large number of privately owned holiday homes (400 including 80 for hire), Bashley Park also has a very sizeable tourist section and can take 420 touring units (tents, trailer tents and pup tents not accepted). Spread over three flat meadows plus a woodland area with squirrels, pitches are all individual with electricity, marked out but not separated. Ground sheets must be lifted daily, no awnings are allowed in the woodland area. The four toilet blocks, one central to each area, are well constructed buildings, fully tiled with modern fittings. Free hot water, vanity style washbasins and push-button, pre-set showers (no dividers). In pleasant park-like surroundings not far from beaches and the New Forest, the site has a good clubhouse overlooking an 18 m. circular outdoor swimming pool (heated mid-May - mid-Sept) and 18 m. children's paddling pool, fun with its geysers and beach effect. An indoor pool complex has a water flume, sauna, spa bath, steam room and sun-beds. Evening entertainment (and children's entertainment) in the club with live or taped music Spr. B.H. - mid-Sept; it has a ballroom, large lounges and bars, restaurant, simple takeaway all day, TV room. Video arcade and games room. Very well equipped children's play area, crazy golf, nine hole, `par 3' golf course on site and 3 tennis courts. Shop (mid-May to end Sept). Launderette. Up to 6 American motorhomes accepted (40 ft. max). One dog per unit. A popular park with lots going on, part of the Hoburne group.

Directions: Park is on B3055 ¼ mile east of the crossroads with B3058 in Bashley village. O.S.GR: SZ246969.

Charges 1997: Per unit incl. all persons and electricity £9.00 - £25.50; multi service pitch £10.00 - £25.00; pet (1 only) £2.00. Weekly rates available. VAT included. Credit cards accepted.

Open: 2 March - end October.

Reservations: Any length: 1-6 nights payment in full at booking; 7+ nights, £50 p/w. deposit, balance 3 weeks before arrival. Address: Sway Road, New Milton, Hants BH25 5QR. Tel: (01425) 612340. FAX: (01425) 612602.

BASHLEY PARK
Award Winning Holiday Park
HOLIDAY CARAVANS • TOURING PITCHES

ROSE AWARD

Magnificent family Park close to the New Forest and South Coast beaches.
Extensive sporting facilities including indoor leisure pool complex,
Par 3, 9 hole golf course, and football field.
For FREE colour brochure or credit card bookings please contact:
BASHLEY PARK, AR1, Sway Road, New Milton, Hampshire BH25 5QR.
Telephone: 01425 612340

BRITISH ISLES - England

B118 Fishery Creek Caravan and Camping Park, Hayling Island

Friendly, family run park adjoining a tidal waterway of Chichester harbour.

This attractively situated park offers 165 numbered pitches, 120 of which have electrical connections. Some of the central pitches are separated by fences with climbing roses, others around the perimeter lie alongside the creek with mature trees providing shade for some. There is direct access to a slipway (no charge) suitable for small craft and to a footpath which leads to the south beach (5 mins walk). The modern toilet block has vanity style basins with mirrors and hand dryer. Separate shower blocks for men and women are of oldish construction and basic design (open 7.30 am. - 10.30 pm). Dishwashing sinks are under cover, with free hot water throughout. Chemical disposal. Motorcaravan services. Shop with microwave for campers' use, is combined with reception. Also here is a small games room with pool, fruit machines and TV. Behind the toilet block is a fenced children's play area on grass with climbing frame, goal posts and swings. Tractor rides organised around the park in peak season. Fishing possible. Public phones. Pubs, restaurants and shops are within walking distance. A bus service to Havant leaves from the top of the road, also a service to the ferry across to Southsea. The warden lives on site.

Directions: From A27 follow Hayling Island signs on A3023 and cross bridge onto island. Proceed to large roundabout and turn left to Mengham (park signed). Go through town, turn left opposite Hayling Motors, left after 500 yds into Fishery Lane and park is at the end. O.S.GR: SU734985.

Charges 1997: Per unit incl. 2 persons £7.00 - £9.00; extra adult £1.00; child (4-12 yrs) 50p; awning £1.30; dog £1.50; extra car or boat £1.50; electricity £1.80. Credit cards accepted. VAT included.

Open: March - 31 October.

Reservations: Made with deposit (£18.50) and fee (£1.50). Address: Fishery Creek Lane, Fishery Lane, Hayling Island, Hampshire PO11 9NR. Tel: (01705) 462164. FAX: as phone. E-mail: johnadams@hay-isle.demon.co.uk.

B85 Bath Marina and Caravan Park, Bath

Good, purpose-designed touring park for caravans and motorhomes only.

Bath Caravan Park (formerly Newbridge) is under the same ownership as the next door Marina and is a useful, well run park from which to visit historic Bath or Bristol. Indeed, there is a park-and-ride facility for Bath outside the entrance, and the Bath to Bristol cycle path is near. Originally developed by Bath City Council (one can still see signs of this in the design) but now run by John and Gail Churchill, it has 88 pitches for caravans or motorcaravans (no tents). With hardstanding and 16A electricity, they are pleasantly interspersed with grass and flowering trees and bushes. A newer circular area near reception provides landscaped hardstanding for the van only with extra, separate hardstanding for the car. One `super' pitch has full services (electricity, water, drain and TV aerial). The two toilet blocks are heated and have plenty of free hot water. Showers lack shelf space but there are plenty of hooks and stools are outside. Vanity style washbasins are in semi cubicles and hair dryers are provided. Both blocks use a digital security system. En-suite facilities for disabled people, fully equipped laundry room, outside, under cover dishwashing sinks and chemical disposal at each block. The reception/shop has tourist information as well as necessities for the Marina. A gate provides access to the `Boathouse', a bar and restaurant with a terrace fronting the River Avon and useful for bar snacks or more formal meals at the Moorings restaurant. Children's play park. Public phone (card). Fishing 100 yds. A useful park.

Directions: Park is within Bath city limits, north of the Avon just off the A4 Bath - Bristol road, about 1½ miles from the city centre. It is best approached from the direction of Bristol on the A4 to the city limits, where park is signed. O.S.GR: ST720655.

Charges 1997: Per pitch £8.00; `super' pitch £12.00; adult £2.00; child (5-15) 75p; electricity (16A) £2.00; awning £1.50; extra car £1.00; dog 50p. Winter special (1/11-28/2): £12 per unit incl. VAT incl. Credit cards accepted.

Open: All year.

Reservations: Any length with one night's fee as deposit (non-returnable). Address: Brassmill Lane, Bath BA1 3JT. Tel: (01225) 424301 or 428778. FAX: as phone.

BATH'S PREMIER PARK ON THE RIVER AVON

BATH MARINA &
CARAVAN PARK

This beautifully landscaped site overlooks the River Avon only 1.5 miles from the attractions of the historic Roman spa city of Bath. Hard standing for 88 caravans. Electric points, flush toilets, showers, shaver points, laundry, children's playground, on site shop and tourist information. Dogs accepted on leash. Open year round. Sorry no tents.

Contact John and Gail Churchill
Telephone Bath (01225) 428778 or send for our brochure
Bath Caravan Park, Brassmill Lane
Bath, Avon BA1 3TJ

B80 The Isle of Avalon Touring Caravan Park, Glastonbury

Well planned, modern park with excellent facilities, 10 mins walk from town centre.

This pleasant, modern park is under new ownership. Developed on flat, grassy ground, the park has been landscaped to provide 70 individual pitches, well spaced out and connected by hard roads. They have hardstanding with adjacent grass for awning and electrical points. A further 50 tenting spaces are on the adjoining, level field. Water and refuse points are well spaced around and attractively surrounded by trees and shrubs. All units are personally seen to their pitches. A single, excellent, tiled toilet block is purpose built and designed to avoid condensation. It provides large, controllable hot showers, basins in cubicles for women and excellent units for the disabled (plus ramps to the shop and reception). Large laundry room and dishwashing area. Chemical toilet and motorcaravan disposal point. American motorhomes are welcome. A well stocked shop and reception with tourist information has been built at the entrance with a well cared for, attractive and spacious feel with beautiful hanging baskets. There is generally a friendly, welcoming atmosphere. The top area of the tenting field is left clear as a playing field for children and parents. Glastonbury centre, with shops, restaurants and cafés, and the Abbey are a short walk and there are indoor and outdoor swimming pools at Street. Millfield School with its summer activity programme is close. The nearby town of Street is famous for its shoes and the 'Clarke's Village' development with many factory outlets for well known high street names.

Directions: Park is on west side of the town bypass (A39), just off the B3151 (Wedmore Road) with good signs from the bypass. O.S.GR: ST495397.

Charges 1997: Per unit £4.70 - £5.90; hiker or car with small tent £4.50; adult £1.70; child (3-14 yrs) £1.20; awning or small tent £1.30; electricity £1.70; dog 50p; extra car 60p. VAT included.

Open: All year.

Reservations: Any length with £5 deposit.Address: Godney Road, Glastonbury, Somerset BA6 9AF. Tel: (01458) 833618.

The Isle of Avalon Touring Caravan Park

Godney Road, Glastonbury, Somerset BA6 9AF
Please write or telephone for brochure (Tel: 01548 833618)

The Park, which is open all year round, offers a modern architecturally designed service building, with a high standard of cleanliness, All individual level placements have a hard standing, grass area and electric hook-up facility, with provision for tenting on an all grass area. For Guests' convenience, there, there is also a well stocked shop with off licence and Reception Office with useful information for touring the area.

Located in the heart of Somerset, this family run Park within sight of the 520 foot Tor, is a 15 minutes walk from the unique historic town of Glastonbury and famous Abbey ruins. An ideal base for "Discovering Somerset" – We look forward to meeting you.

ANWB (Dutch)
ADAC (German)
England and West Country Tourist Boad Members

The sites in the BRITISH ISLES featured in this guide
are shown on the map on page 369

B125 Cotswold View Caravan and Camping Site, Charlbury

Family run site in rural location with good facilities.

Cotswold View is an interesting example of successful farm diversification providing a spacious, purpose designed site side-by-side with a small working farm of 54 acres (7 are set aside for the site). Visitors are welcome to meet the animals (ask for Simon and observe Rabbit City), book breakfast at the farm kitchen and use the forest or farm trails on the farm land or local bridleways and footpaths. Hedges and trees have grown to give the camping area a more mature, green look and wide, gravel or tarmac roadways give easy access to 90 level, numbered, grassy pitches on a gently sloping site, all with electricity (10A). Good provision of water taps and waste disposal points. The single, tiled toilet block, purpose built from Cotswold stone, provides a separate unit for the disabled, showers with curtain and stool, 4 washbasins in cabins, 2 in the open, shaver points, H&C water, a bath (50p) and baby room. Dishwashing under cover (free hot water). Laundry room with washing machine and dryer, and a freezer for ice packs. The small reception block doubles as a shop and off licence. Good central play area on grass hidden by trees. Dog walks. Hard tennis court. Bicycle hire. Tourist information room. American motorhomes accepted. A well run park, ideal for exploring the Cotswolds area, Oxford and Stratford on Avon, with a warm welcome from the owners. B&B at the farm and self catering farm cottages (with facilities for the disabled). Farmhouse breakfasts need to be booked in advance.

Directions: From A44 Oxford - Stratford-on-Avon road, take the B4022 road to Charlbury, just south of Enstone. Park is 2 miles on left. O.S.GR: SP365210.

Charges 1997: Per unit incl. 2 persons £9.00 - £10.50; extra adult £1.75; child (5-16 yrs) £1.00; electricity £2.00. VAT included.

Open: 1 April - 2 November.

Reservations: Advisable for B.H.s and peak season. Address: Enstone Road, Charlbury, Oxon OX7 3JH. Tel: (01608) 810314. FAX: (01608) 811891.

B176 Cotswold Hoburne, South Cerney, Cirencester

Good touring park with holiday caravans and a variety of watersports amenities close.

Since the park is adjacent to the Cotswold Water Park, those staying will have easy access to the varied watersports there which include sailboarding and water ski-ing. On the park itself there is a lake with pedaloes and canoes for hire. Its range of other amenities include an outdoor heated pool (from Easter, heated from May) and an impressive, indoor leisure complex including pool with flume, spa bath, sauna, steam room (all free) and sun bed. There are 300 well marked touring pitches for any type of unit, all with hardstanding (only fairly level) and grass surround for awning or tent. Of good size but with nothing between them, all have electricity (some need long leads). Also 150 holiday units, mainly to let. Six toilet blocks are quite small and maintenance can be variable. Hot water is free in pre-set showers. Basic facilities for disabled people are in the clubhouse (but locked at night). The site has heavy weekend trade. Large clubhouse with big lounge with giant TV screen, entertainment at times, food service (or food bar in lounge), big games room and a lounge bar which overlooks the outdoor pool and lake with a patio. Supermarket. Football field. Tennis. Good adventure playground on bark. Crazy golf. Launderette. Fishing lake (permits from reception). No dogs accepted. Part of the Hoburne group.

Directions: Three miles from Cirencester on the Swindon road, turn right towards Cotswold Water Park at new roundabout on bypass. Take second right and follow signs. O.S.GR: SU055957.

Charges 1997: Touring pitch incl. electricity £8.00 - £20.00, acc. to season; pup tent £2.00. Weekly rates and weekend breaks available. VAT included. Credit cards accepted.

Open: March - 31 October.

Reservations: Tents: 1-6 nights payable in full at time of booking; caravans with £50 deposit for min 4 days at B.Hs (3 days for May B.H). Address: Broadway Lane, South Cerney, Cirencester, Glos. GL7 5UQ. Tel: (01285) 860216. FAX: (01285) 862106.

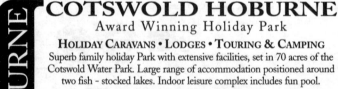

B158 Highfield Farm Camping Park, Comberton, nr Cambridge

Quality, peaceful and very well kept, family run park.

Situated five miles from Cambridge, this eight acre park is a delightfully quiet touring location. Family run, the welcome is warm and the facilities of superior quality. Divided into five enclosures by hedges and conifers, there are also shady glades for those who wish to retreat even further. One enclosure is usually reserved for those without children. Offering 60 numbered pitches for caravans or motorcaravans, and 60 for tents, personal space is further enhanced by the fact that the centre of all enclosures is left free. All pitches have 10A electricity, 40 have gravel hardstanding, and most are level. Three heated toilet blocks provide a more than adequate coverage. The original block offers controllable showers on payment, free hot water to washbasins and an additional set of unisex showers. The other two blocks (fully tiled) provide a combination of showers on payment (10p), free hot water to washbasins, some open plan, others in cubicles, and ample toilets; all of which are outstandingly clean and well maintained. There is no dedicated provision for the disabled, but one block has extra wide doors and easy access. Laundry facilities comprise two washing machines, tumble dryers, spin dryer, iron and board, plus sinks and baby bath. Hot water is free to the 10 covered dishwashing sinks spaced throughout the site. Chemical disposal facilities and motorcaravan service point. Basic provisions are available from reception and there are nearby shops and pubs. Two play areas, swings and tree house, plus further space for football and bicycle hire. Fishing 4 miles. A small kiosk offers tourist information about the area. Public phone and post box. Extensive dog walk. Gates closed midnight - 7.30 am. A member of the Best of British group.

Directions: Park is 5 miles southwest of Cambridge town centre near eastern edge of Comberton village. From M11 take exit 12, the A 603 towards Sandy and right after ½ mile on B1046 to Comberton. From A428 turn south at Hardwick roundabout to Comberton. O.S.GR: TL391571.

Charges 1998: Per caravan/large tent incl. 2 persons £7.00 - £8.50; motorcaravan or small tent £6.75 - £8.00; m/cyclist and tent £5.75 - £6.75; hiker/cyclist and tent £5.50 - £6.50; extra adult £1.50 - £2.00; child (5-16 yrs) £1.00 - £1.50; awning or pup tent £1.00; porch awning 50p; electricity £1.85. VAT included.

Open: 21 March - 31 October.

Reservations: Made for any length with £10 deposit and 50p fee. Address: Long Road, Comberton, Cambridge CB3 7DG. Tel: (01223) 262308. FAX: as phone.

AR Discount
Less 10% in low season for senior citizens (min 3 nights)

B170 Sherwood Forest Caravan Park, Old Clipstone, nr Mansfield

Country park of 22 acres between the M1 and A1 roads.

A quiet country park, taking all types of unit, this is attractively landscaped in pleasant surroundings, and is close to many places of interest. Recently taken over by the Civil Service Club, non-members are also welcome. The touring areas stretch alongside the River Maun, each offering a slightly different aspect, some set aside for dog owners, others overlooking the water. Trees and shrubs enhance the rural atmosphere and wild life abounds (the park is popular with bird watchers). One small lake is especially for inflatables and canoes, the other for fishing (coarse fishing on permit). There are 200 numbered pitches in total on level grass, 137 with electrical connections. The four toilet blocks, refurbished recently, have good, well maintained facilities, with free hot water in washbasins, on payment in showers, under cover washing up, hair care room, laundry, chemical disposal and new facilities for the disabled. Reception and the licensed shop with souvenirs and caravan accessories are central (one-way system in operation) and behind is the barn which provides a mother and toddlers room with toys, TV room and a large room for special events. Attractive children's play areas are located around the park, but perhaps feeding the ducks is more enjoyable. There are barbecue areas, a small wooden kiosk provides visitor information and there are resident wardens on site. Fishing on site, bicycle hire close (½ mile). The Sherwood Forest Visitor Centre is 5 minutes away by car, and a Sherwood Forest Farm Park (rare breeds) is close by. The village is 1½ miles (no public transport) and there are walks from the site.

Directions: Best approach is via the Ollerton - Mansfield road A6075; turn south towards Old Clipstone opposite turning to Warsop and ½ mile to site. Follow signs to Sherwood Forest Farm Park. From M1 take exit 27 from south and 30 from north. O.S.GR: TG423145.

Charges 1997: Per unit incl. 2 persons £9.25 - £10.20; single person £5.30 - £6.80; extra adult £1.65; child (5-15 yrs) £1.20; extra pup tent £1.50; dog 85p; electricity (10A) £2.00 - £2.55. VAT included.

Open: March - 2 November.

Reservations: Made with £5 deposit. Address: Nr Edwinstowe, Mansfield, Nottinghamshire NG21 9HW. Tel: Freephone: 0800 823132. FAX: (01623) 824637.

See colour advert opposite page 33

BRITISH ISLES - England

B196 Golden Square Caravan and Camping Park, Oswaldkirk, Helmsley

High quality, family owned touring park, south of Helmsley.

The area around Helmsley appears very popular, being in the North Yorkshire Moors National Park and around 20 miles from York. Mr and Mrs Armstrong, local farmers, have worked hard to develop the park around old quarry workings, providing a number of split level areas or bays with beautiful views over the surrounding countryside. The 130 pitches, although not separated, have markers set in the ground and back mainly onto grass banks and are on fairly flat grass. The underlying ground is a little hard - steel tent pegs are needed. There are 120 electrical connections (10A) and 24 pitches in the new extension have drainaway also. Six 'de-luxe' pitches provide all services (including waste water, sewage and TV aerial connections) and grass patio with table. The two excellent toilet blocks have washbasins set in flat surfaces with free hot water, shelf and mirror (some private cabins), showers with pre-set, timed hot water on payment, a heated bathroom with baby changing facilities and units for disabled. Mrs Armstrong takes a pride in the provision and pot plants and flower arrangements make them more homely. Covered washing-up sinks, washing machine and dryer, microwave. Chemical disposal. Motorcaravan service facilities. Tourist information. Shop including off licence and craft gifts. Adventure play area, tiny tots area and play field. Games room in the top barn. Bicycle hire on site. Visitors may have membership of nearby Ampleforth College sports centre with indoor swimming pool, tennis, gym etc. Public phone. Pony trekking nearby, fishing 5 miles. The Ebor Way (with access from the park), the Cleveland Way and the Lyle Wake Walk are near for walkers. Pubs with meals at Ampleforth and Helmsley.

Directions: Park is on the Helmsley - Ampleforth road close to the 'caravan route' which avoids the banned Sutton Bank on the A170 Thirsk - Helmsley road. Turn off B1257 to west at camp sign by Golden Square Farm, 1 mile south of junction with A170. O.S.GR: SE605797.

Charges 1997: Per unit incl. 2 persons and all children up to 10 yrs £6.00 - £7.70; extra person (over 10) £1.00; full awning £1.30; extra car £1.00; electricity £2.00; drainage 50p; hikers/bikers £2.60 - £3.30 per person. VAT included.

Open: 1 March - 31 October.

Reservations: Essential for B.Hs and made with £10 deposit. Address: Oswaldkirk, York YO6 5YQ. Tel: (01439) 788269.

B227 Limefitt Park, Troutbeck, Windermere

See colour advert opposite pages 32

Well managed and popular Lake District park.

Limefitt Park is centrally situated for the southern lakes and has fine views and walks, with the beck running alongside. It is a park with various active pursuits nearby and some evening entertainment and is for families or couples. It is very well managed with excellent facilities and 180 pitches. The pitches for touring caravans are good and flat, with hardstanding, electricity (10A) and water, with cars parked at an angle on further hardstanding in front. The remainder of the park is on flat or slightly sloping grass with some terracing and shade provided by trees with numbered pitches for tents or more caravans or motorcaravans. The ground by the beck has been developed for 45 log cabins (for private sale) and there is another field for 20 long stay caravans. The sanitary facilities consist of one large, central block for the tenting area and a smaller block for the caravan area, accessed by combination locks. Both are of excellent quality, amongst the best we have seen and are well maintained and fully tiled with modern fittings including oval washbasins, with mixer taps, flat surfaces, mirrors and side lighting. Hot water is free. Toddlers' rooms with half-size bath and changing facilities. Covered washing-up sinks. Well stocked supermarket and licensed bar lounge with real ales, bar meals and weekly entertainment, both open all season, and takeaway. This should give good coverage all season. Campers' kitchen (metered). Launderette. Sporting activities include walking and fishing, and local facilities, including pony trekking, can be booked from the park. Bicycle hire (4 miles). Games room with many machines. Play field and adventure playground on grass by the river and small beach area with picnic tables. American motorhomes, dogs or boats are **not** accepted. No single persons, no groups and no rallies are accepted - "in order to preserve Limefitt's unique atmosphere and provide restful nights .... we accept families only (with a maximum of two families per caravan and one family per tent)." The park is full and very popular for a long season, reservation is advisable.

Directions: Limefitt Park lies 2½ miles north up the A592 from its junction with the A591 north of Windermere. O.S.GR: NY416030.

Charges 1998: Per unit incl. 2 persons, electricity and TV hook-up £9.50 - £13.00; tent £9.00 - £12.50; extra adult £2.00 - £2.50; child (2-14 yrs) £1.00 - £1.25; awning, pup tent, trailer or 2nd car £2.00 - £2.50. Max. charge 1 family per pitch £11.50 - £15.50 (excl. supplements). Prices are higher for stays not booked in advance. VAT included. Credit cards accepted.

Open: 3 April - 31 October.

Reservations: Made with full payment at time of booking; cancellation insurance available. Address: Windermere, Cumbria LA23 1PA. Tel: (015394) 32300. FAX: (015394) 32848. E-mail: info@limefitt.co.uk.

B256 Disserth Caravan Park, Disserth, nr Llandrindod Wells

Small, family owned riverside park with some caravan holiday homes.

In a secluded situation between the ancient church of Disserth and the Ithon river and sheltered by a wooded cliff formed by river action, yet with handy access to many attractions in mid-Wales, Disserth provides a good base for families with an outdoor disposition. Up to 40 caravans, motorcaravans and tents are taken on one meadow adjacent to the river made attractive with shrubs and trees. The pitches are marked and spacing is generous with electrical hook-ups (10A) for all places. The pride of the park is the homely restaurant/coffee shop with an upstairs bar serving real ales. Small, yet nicely converted from an old barn, this provides a restful evening haven after a day out. Reasonably priced meals are served in the evenings (7.30 - 9.30 pm.) in the main season. The toilet block provides free hot showers (3M 3F) and, for ladies, a hair drying cubicle and 3 washbasins in cubicles. Also provided are a laundry room, separate dishwashing sinks with hot water and chemical disposal facilities. There are colour coded bins for recycling certain rubbish. Other amenities include a small shop, information kiosk, public telephone, private fishing and access to the river with a pebbled beach. Bicycle hire 8 miles. Two holiday homes to let, others privately owned.

Directions: Follow signs for Disserth and Park, either west off A483 at Howey, or east from B4358 around the eastern edge of Newbridge-on-Wye. O.S.GR: SO035585.

Charges 1998: Per unit, incl. 2 adults £6.50 - £7.75; extra adult £1.85; child (3-15 yrs) 95p; full awning 80p, porch 45p; electricity £1.95. Credit cards accepted. VAT included.

Open: 1 March - 31 October.

Reservations: Made with £5 deposit (non-returnable). Address: Disserth, Howey, Llandrindod Wells, Powys LD1 6NL. Tel: (01597) 860277. FAX: as phone.

Graham and Audrey Houghton invite you to

DISSERTH CARAVAN PARK

DISSERTH, HOWEY, LLANDRINDOD WELLS LD1 6NL

Telephone: 01597-860277

<u>D</u>ELIGHTFUL
<u>I</u>DYLLIC
<u>S</u>MALL
<u>S</u>ELECT
<u>E</u>NCHANTING
<u>R</u>ELAXING
<u>T</u>RANQUIL
<u>H</u>IDDEN

IT ALL ADDS UP TO "DISSERTH"
A SECRET PLACE WORTH FINDING

Riverside camping, touring and holiday caravans. Peace and quiet with private fishing

MEMBER

B282 Trossachs Holiday Park, Aberfoyle

Well run, friendly family park, ideal for exploring the Trossachs and Loch Lomond.

Nestling on a hillside 3 miles south of Aberfoyle, this is an excellent base for touring this famously beautiful area. Lochs Lomond, Ard, Venachar and others are within easy reach, as are the Queen Elizabeth Forest Park and, of course, the Trossachs. The park specialises in sales and hire of top class mountain bikes. A very neat and tidy park, there are 45 well laid out and marked pitches arranged on terraces with hardstanding. All have electricity and TV connections and most have water and drainage also. There are trees between the terraces and lovely views across the valley. A modern wooden building houses the sanitary facilities which offer a satisfactory supply of toilets, showers and washbasins, the ladies' area being rather larger, with two private cabins. The building also contains a laundry room and a large games room with TV and lots of seating. There are several items of play equipment on gravel. The park purchased the adjoining oak and bluebell woods in '97. A 'passport' scheme arranged with a local leisure centre (10 miles, 8 passes) provides facilities for swimming, sauna, solarium, badminton, tennis, windsurfing, etc. Nearby are opportunities for golfing, boat launching and fishing (3 miles). A well stocked shop (all season) and the bike shop are either side of reception, where you will receive a warm welcome from Joe and Hazel Norman. Luxury caravans (12) for hire in separate section.

Directions: Park is 3 miles south of Aberfoyle on the A81 road, well signed. O.S.GR: NS544976.

Charges 1998: Per unit incl. 2 persons £8.00 - £10.00; electricity and TV connection £2.00; all services £3.00; porch awning, extra car £1.00; full awning, small extra tent £1.50; extra adult £2.00; child (2-14 yrs) £1.25. Less 10% for weekly stays. VAT included. Credit cards accepted.

Open: 1 March - 31 October.

Reservations: Advisable and made for min. 3 days with £15 deposit. Address: Aberfoyle, Stirling FK8 3SA. Tel: (01877) 382614 (24 hr). FAX: (01877) 382732. E-mail: thp@scotland.force9.net.

BRITISH ISLES - Northern Ireland

Northern Ireland

 The following ferry services are expected to operate between the UK mainland and Northern Ireland in 1998.

Norse Irish Ferries (01232) 779090 - Liverpool - Belfast *(11 hrs overnight, alternate days)*

Sea Cat Scotland (0345) 523523 - Stranraer - Belfast *(1½ hours, 4 daily each way)*

P&O European Ferries (01581) 200276 - Cairnryan - Larne:

Ferry *(2¼ hours, 1 sailing daily each way)*
Jet Liner *(1 hour, 5 sailings daily each way)*

B316 Drumaheglis Marina and Caravan Park, Ballymoney

Well kept site on the banks of the River Bann, convenient for the Causeway coast.

A caravan park which continually maintains a high standard, Drumaheglis is popular throughout the season. Situated on the banks of the lower Bann, approximately 4 miles from the town of Ballymoney, it appeals to watersports enthusiasts or makes an ideal base for exploring this scenic corner of Northern Ireland. The marina offers superb facilities for boat launching, water-skiing, cruising, canoeing or fishing, whilst getting out and about can take you to the Giant's Causeway, seaside resorts such as Portrush or Portstewart, the sands of Whitepark Bay, the Glens of Antrim or the picturesque villages of the Antrim coast road. For tourers only, this site instantly appeals, for it is well laid out with trees, shrubs, flower beds and tarmac roadways. The 47 hardstanding pitches all have electricity (5A) and water points. The toilet blocks are modern and were spotlessly clean when we visited. They house showers which are free, individual wash cubicles, toilets and facilities for the disabled. There are razor points, hand dryers, dishwashing sinks, washing machine and dryer, Chemical disposal. Children's play area. Barbecue and picnic areas. Ballymoney is a popular shopping town and the Riada Centre is a leading leisure establishment with a health suite incorporating a fitness studio, sports hall, etc. There is much to see and do within this Borough and of interest is the Heritage Centre in Charlotte Street.

Directions: From the A26/B62 Portrush - Ballymoney roundabout continue for approx. 1 mile on the A26 in the direction of Coleraine. Site is clearly signed - follow International camping signs.

Charges 1997: Per unit incl. electricity £9.00, per 7 days £54.00; unserviced £8.00, per 7 days £48.00.

Open: Easter - 1 October.

Reservations: Essential for peak periods and weekends. Address: 36 Glenstall Road, Ballymoney, Co. Antrim BT53 7QN. Tel: (012656) 66466. Ballymoney District Council: Tel: (012656) 62280; FAX: (012656) 67659.

B319 LoanEden Caravan Park, Muckross Bay, Kesh

Friendly, family owned park by the shores of Lower Lough Erne.

All caravanners who enter this exceptional park are immediately made welcome and receive the attention of the owners, Noelle and Austyn Loane. Although this site has only been in existence for five years ('93), its reputation is already widespread. An overall neat and tidy appearance is a first impression, with static caravan holiday homes occupying the centre and left hand side of the park, whilst to the right and separated by a tarmac roadway, stand the touring pitches. Flower beds, trees and shrubs are well maintained and an ornamental draw-well and illuminated barbecue give added effect. What makes LoanEden special to tourers is that their needs are thoughtfully catered for and not secondary to the static owners. The 26 touring pitches are level with hardstanding and water, electricity and drainage connections and a rubbish bin; also a dividing grass area on which to erect an awning. Good night lighting. Cleanliness is utmost and the immaculate, ultra modern toilet block is completely tiled inside and houses WCs, facilities for the disabled, showers, washbasins, washing machines, dryers and sinks for dishwashing or handwashing. Nothing has been forgotten - there are soap dispensers, hand dryers, paper towels, clothes hooks and points for hairdryers and razors. A small shop stocks basic foods, confectionery, freshly baked cakes and gas. Children have two play areas and a games room, with plans for a third super play area. Young and old can enjoy pony and horse riding tuition under the supervision of the owners' daughter Victoria, an A.I. instructor, and son Andrew who is an international rider. An additional 30 touring pitches, a second shower and toilet block including a campers' kitchen, a tennis court and various other facilities are also planned.

Directions: Travelling northwest on the A35 Enniskillen - Kesh road, enter village of Kesh. At end of main street, cross over bridge and immediately turn left; park is signed. Continue for ½ mile and site is on right.

Charges 1998: Per caravan or motorcaravan incl. awning and electricity £10.00; tent £6.00; electricity £1.00.

Open: All year.

Reservations: Advisable for high season and B.Hs. Address: Muckross Bay, Kesh, Co. Fermanagh BT93 1TX. Tel: Kesh (013656) 31603. FAX: (013656) 32300.

Welcome to **TULLANS FARM CARAVAN PARK** *and Relax*

Tullans Farm is off the beaten track just 1 mile from Coleraine and about 5 miles from the lovely sandy beaches of Portrush and Portstewart.

Hygienic facilities - launderette, toilet and shower block - chemical disposal Children's play area - TV room - indoor recreation - Awarded *5* ✓

Lamb feeding and sheep shearing in season

Local amenities: pool, bowling, tennis, golf, windsurfing, canoeing, karting.

For information, phone: (01265) 42309

Bed & Breakfast

B322 Tullans Farm Caravan Park, Coleraine

Well run family park in rural setting convenient for the Causeway Coast.

This excellent park, opened in '95, is set to become one of the most popular in the area. Its peaceful and quiet surroundings suggest that it is in the heart of the country, yet the University town of Coleraine is only 1 mile away, the seaside resorts of Portrush and Portstewart are within 5 miles and a shopping centre a 2 minute drive. Tucked in from the busy roads that lead to the coast, Tullans Farm is already earning a reputation for its spotlessly clean toilet block and its well cared for appearance. In a central position in the park, fronted by a large parking space, stands a long white building housing the sanitary facilities, reception, TV lounge and barn which is used for indoor recreation. The toilet and shower rooms, which include a family shower room, are spacious, modern and have facilities for the handicapped. There are washbasins set in marble top units, mirrors, soap dispensers, hand and hair dryers, even flower arrangements. Next to the toilet area is the laundry and washing up room with sinks, washing machine, dryers and a fridge for campers to use. Around the park roadways are gravel and 20 of the 32 pitches have hardstanding, all have electric hook-ups (10A). Trees and shrubs have been planted and will eventually give a more mature look. Chemical disposal, water points, rubbish bins and receptacles for cans and plastic bottles. An outdoor children's play area is another attraction. In season the owners organise barbecues, barn dances and line dancing (funds in aid of charity).

Directions: From the Lodge Road roundabout (south end of Coleraine) turn east onto the A29 Portrush ring road and proceed for 1 mile. Turn right at sign for park and Windy Hall and park is clearly signed on left.

Charges 1998: Per unit incl. all persons and electricity £9.50; awning £1.00; family tent £7.00; 2 man tent £5.00.

Open: March - 31 October.

Reservations: Advisable at peak times - contact park. Address: 46 Newmills Road, Coleraine, Co. Londonderry BT52 2JB. Tel: (01265) 42309.

Caravan Park
Muckross Bay
Co. Fermanagh
N. Ireland

Tel: (013656) 31603/31129
Fax: (013656) 32300

OPEN ALL YEAR - 5✓

★ Award winning caravan park - Calor Green ★
★ Fully serviced pitches ★ Tent area ★
★ Immaculate sanitary facilities ★ Children's play areas ★
★ Quality mobile homes for sale/hire ★
★ Horse riding tuition A.I. instructor ★
★ Special on site feature - barbecue in July ★
★ Extended facilities - new toilet block, 3rd play area, new reception area, campers kitchen ★
★ Boat hire facilities ★ man made beach ★ Marina 5 mins walk
★ Scenic walks ★ Pony trekking ★
★ Village of Kesh - Lough Erne Hotel - Chef of the Year award★

The sites in the BRITISH ISLES (including Northern Ireland) featured in this guide are shown on the map on page 369

BRITISH ISLES - Channel Islands

Jersey

Jersey Tourism, Liberation Square,
St. Helier, Jersey JE1 1BB
Tel: (01534) 500700
Fax: (01534) 500899

Guernsey and Herm

States of Guernsey Tourist Board
PO Box 13, White Rock, Guernsey
Tel: (014581) 26611

Sark

Sark Tourism Office, Sark (via Guernsey),
Channel Islands.
Tel: (01481) 832345.

B366 Rozel Camping Park, St Martin, Jersey

Rurally situated park in quieter northeast of island, close to picturesque harbour.

This family owned park is within walking distance of the famous Jersey Zoo and the pretty harbour and fishing village of Rozel where the north coast cliff path commences. The surrounding countryside is quieter than many areas of the island. A car is probably necessary to reach the main island beaches, although a bus service does run to St Helier from close by. The park itself is quietly situated at the top of a valley (the French coast can be seen on a clear day) and is surrounded by trees providing shelter. There are two main camping areas providing 70 pitches of which some 40 are for campers with their own tents. Some pitches, mainly for smaller tents are arranged on terraced areas. The remainder are on a higher, flat field where pitches are arranged in bays with hedges growing to separate them into groups. Free parking is permitted by the tents and electrical connections available. The clean, bright sanitary facilities are in a block between the two areas (access by steps from the lower part) and provide roomy, controllable hot showers and washbasins in pairs with mirror and shelf, with 2 in private cabins; hand dryers and heater for cooler weather. Dishwashing facilities are under cover. Hot water is free throughout. Laundry and make up room. The park reports a new sanitary block on the lower area with facilities for the disabled and babies. For entertainment there is a good play field with play equipment, an attractive, sheltered swimming pool with child's pool and grass and terrace sunbathing areas, crazy golf, games room, reading room and TV and bicycle hire. A torch would be useful. Public telephone. Breakfast, evening meals and possibly takeaway are offered in high season (closed Mondays) and there is a shop. Fishing 3 miles. In addition to package deals for tent hire and travel, the site offers a good range of camping equipment for hire on a daily basis. Boats are only accepted on site by prior arrangement. No dogs accepted.

> **Directions:** From St. Helier take the A6 through tunnel, northeast to St. Martin's church and on towards Rozel Bay. Park is signed on the right.
>
> **Charges 1998:** Per person £3.70 - £5.70; child (3-11 yrs) half price; electricity £1.40. Tent hire and travel packages. Credit cards accepted
>
> **Open:** 1 May - mid September.
>
> **Reservations:** Made for any length with £20 deposit; balance due 14 days before arrival. Address: Rozel, St. Martin, Jersey, Channel Islands JE3 6AX. Tel: (01534) 856797. FAX: (01534) 856127.

Camping in the Channel Islands

Full details on camping in the Channel Islands and a selection of parks can be found in the Alan Rogers' **BRITAIN and IRELAND** Guide. Camping holidays on the islands are limited to TENTS only. Caravans and motorcaravans are not permitted because of the narrow and sometimes crowded nature of the roads. Trailer tents (with canvas walls and roof) are allowed, but on Jersey advance booking must be made. Tents and camping equipment are often available for hire on site and car hire is easily arranged.

The British and Irish parks featured in this guide are only a small selection of those in our BRITAIN and IRELAND guide

CZECH REPUBLIC

Although the country we have known as Czechoslovakia has a long and distinguished past, it has a chequered history. The combined country of Czechoslovakia only appeared under that name on maps after the Treaty of Versailles in 1918. The latest event in its turbulent history was the split in December 1992 into its two component parts - the Czech Republic in the west and the Slovak Republic in the east (see page 272). The Czech Republic shares frontiers with Germany, Poland, Austria and the Slovak Republic. It is picturesque and hilly, with attractive lakes and valleys, and with many spa towns. The two main regions are Bohemia, including the Giant Mountains (skiing in winter) and Moravia.

Campsites, previously state-owned and run, are being progressively privatised and modernised and are gradually offering facilities more in line with those expected in Western Europe. All the sites we have included have acceptable, if not luxurious, sanitary arrangements. We found them all to be clean with British style WCs and hot water in all washbasins, sinks and showers. However, many shower facilities have no private dressing spaces and, even in the best blocks, often no divider or curtain with just a communal dressing area.

Information about the Czech Republic can be obtained from:

The Czech Centre, 30 Kensington Palace Gardens, London W8 4QY

Tel: 0171 243 7981

Population
10,323,690 (93) , density 131 per sq km.

Capital
Prague (Praha)

Climate
A continental climate with four distinct seasons, average temperatures in summer (July) are 19ºC - 30ºC max. and in winter (January) 1-15ºC.

Language
The official language is Czech. In hotels and restaurants English or German may be spoken.

Currency
Koruna abbreviated to Kc. One Koruna is divided into 100 hellers.

Banks
Open 0830-1630 Mon-Fri. Only notes are exchanged at most border change offices.
Credit cards: The major cards can be used to obtain currency and in some hotels, restaurants, shops and some filling stations. Travellers and Eurocheques are widely accepted.

Post Offices
Offices are open Mon-Sat 08.00-16.00.

Telephone
The code for the Czech Republic is 0042.

Time
GMT plus one hour. Summer BST + 1.

Public Holidays
New Year; Easter Mon; May Day; National Day, 8 May; Saints Day, 5 July; Festival Day, 6 July; Independence Day, 28 Oct; Christmas, 24, 25, 26 Dec.

Shops
Shops are open Mon-Fri 09.00-12.00 and 14.00-18.00. Some shops remain open midday . Sat: 09.00 until midday.

Motoring
There is a good and well signposted road network throughout the Republic and, although stretches of cobbles still exist in parts, surfaces are generally good. There is a motorway from Bratislava (Slovakia) to Prague and others, radiating from the capital, are being expanded with the section to Pilsen nearing completion. New filling stations with well stocked shops (some with snack bars) are replacing the old, rather scarce, ones all over the Republic.

An annual road tax is levied on all vehicles using Czech motorways and express roads. There are three categories: motor vehicle up to 3.5 tons including trailer; with total weight between 3.5 and 12 tons and above 12 tons. The label, which must be fixed to the windscreen, can be purchased at border crossings, post offices and filling stations. The leaflet giving details of this tax shows the designated roads. Anyone driving a vehicle on a toll road without an affixed label is likely to be fined.

Seat belts are compulsory. Full UK licences are acceptable. Drinking and driving is prohibited. Infringing traffic regulations is subject to on-the-spot fines and speed traps abound.
Speed Restrictions: The max. speed limit for cars is 37 mph (60 kph) in built up areas, 56 mph (90 kph) outside them and 69 mph (110 kph) on expressways.
Parking: Cars may be parked only on the right of the road. In Prague, parking is limited and in Wenceslas Square a charge is made.

Overnighting:
Camping is forbidden in places which are not reserved for that purpose.

Useful Addresses
Motoring Organisation:
Ustredi Automotoklub CR (UAMK), FIA & AIT. Information Service for Motorists: Autoturist, Na Rybnicku 16, 120 76 Praha 2. Tel: 249 11830.

All the sites in this guide are regularly inspected by our team of experienced site assessors, but we welcome your opinion too.
See Readers Reports on page 361

CZECH REPUBLIC

465 Autokamping Luxor, Velká Hled'sebe, nr Mariánské Lánzé (Marianbad)

Orderly site near German border for visiting Marianbad.

This site, like some others in the Czech Republic, has now come under the management of a local hotel. Located on the edge of the small village of Velká Hled'sebe, 4 km. from Marianbad, by a small lake, this is a very quiet situation. Pitches are in the open on one side of the entrance road (cars stand on a tarmac park opposite the caravans) or in a clearing under tall trees away from the road. All pitches have access to electricity but connection in the clearings may need long leads. The good sanitary block also serves the bungalows which occupy one side of the site. There is little to do but it is good for a night stop or for visiting the spa town of Marianbad. There is a restaurant with self-service terrace and a good motel restaurant in the village (500 m). A separate block houses a rest room, kitchen and dining room.

How to find it: Site is directly by the Stribo-Cheb road no. 21, 500 m. south of Velká Hled'sebe.

General Details: Open 1 May - 30 Sept. 30,000 sq.m. Restaurant (May - Sept). Motel with restaurant and shops 500 m. Small children's playground. Rest room with TV, kitchen and dining area.

Charges guide: Per person Kcs. 50; child (under 15 yrs) 30; car 30; caravan 50; motorcaravan 60 - 80, acc. to size; tent 50; electricity 60.

Reservations: For information write to Interhotel Cristal Palace, 353 44 Mariánské Lánzé or phone 0165/2056-7. FAX: 0165/2058. Site address: 354 71 Velká Hled'sebe. Tel: 0165/3504.

466 Autocamping Amerika, Frantiskovy Lázné (Franzensbad)

Site near lake outside spa town.

Goethe described this small spa town as 'paradise on earth', although other writers have dismissed it as of little historical interest. However, it has a reputation as a spa centre for the treatment of female ailments and has pleasant parks and leafy streets. Camping Amerika is to the southwest, just outside the town and could make an acceptable night stop when entering West Bohemia from Bayreuth, to explore West Bohemia. The camp is in an open position with slopes in places and, although there are tall trees at one edge, there is little shade in the camping area. There is room for about 50 caravans on a grass area enclosed by hard access roads and 100 tents in another area. There is electricity for about two-thirds of the pitches, which are neither numbered nor marked out. The single sanitary block is showing signs of age but some refurbishment has been done and it is acceptable. Swimming and boating are possible on the lake. There is a restaurant with terrace, a snack bar and a kiosk for basic food supplies.

How to find it: Site is signed from the edge of the town on little Lake Amerika.

General Details: Open Easter - 15 Oct. 12,000 sq.m. Restaurant. Bar. Kiosk. Lake for swimming, boating and fishing. Children's playground. Bicycle hire. Chemical disposal. Large and small bungalows for hire.

Charges 1997: Per person Kcs. 80; pitch 80; electricity 60. Credit cards not accepted.

AR Discount
Less 10%
on pitch fee

Reservations: Write to site. Address: 35101 Frantiskovy Lázné. Tel: 0166/542 518. FAX: 0166/542 843.

467 Autocamping Karlovy Vary-Brezova, Karlovy-Vary (Karlsbad)

Good site by historic and famous spa.

Karlovy Vary, known throughout the West as Karlsbad, has been described as "the undisputed king of the famous triangle of Bohemian spas" and is, after Prague, the most popular tourist town in the Czech Republic with a long history and a list of famous guests. Dvorak's New World symphony had its premier here and each year a Dvorak Music Festival is held. The curative waters and 19/20th century architecture draw visitors from all over the world and it can become crowded during the tourist season. This site makes an excellent base for exploring the town or taking the waters, being in a quiet location outside the town with an electric bus, 'Charlie Express', to take campers into the centre of the town where other vehicles are banned. The town can also be reached on foot (2 km.) through the woods. The camp is in a natural bowl surrounded by hills and tall trees. It is said that there is room for 150 units but, as the pitches of grass on small stones are neither marked nor numbered, placing is rather haphazard and can become crowded. Camping areas are accessed from hard roads and, although there are sufficient electric sockets (10A), long leads are required in some parts. The central sanitary block is of reasonable quality with British WCs, pre-mixed warm water from push-button taps in washbasins and showers. An outside trough with cold water is provided for dishwashing. Electric stoves available for cooking. Excellent heated pool with half price entrance for c ampers. Some motel and other rooms for hire and two good restaurants and a coffee bar. A kiosk supplies drinks and some food items.

How to find it: From Cheb on the Cheb-Karlovy Vary road 6/E48/E49, turn onto road 20/E49 towards Plzen. After about 7 km. fork left leaving the main road where it crosses a dam for camp after 2 km. on the right.

General Details: Open 1 April - end October. 25,000 sq.m. Restaurants. Snack-bar. Kiosk. Heated pool (on payment). Children's play area. Rooms for hire. Cooking stoves. English spoken.

Charges guide: Per person Kcs. 70; child (5-16 yrs) 40; car 90; caravan 90; motorcaravan 170; electricity 30.

Reservations: Write to camp. Address: 36021 Karlovy Vary, Slovenska 9. Tel: 017/25101 or 25224. FAX: 017/25225

468 Autocamping Druhy Mlyn, Chomutov

Small, pleasant site in tranquil setting.

This very pleasant little site on level ground, enclosed by trees and nearby hills, is a world away from the devastation around Chomutov and Most caused by opencast mining. Following the one sign on the edge of town along a narrow, tree lined road, one does begin to wonder where the camp is, but patience is rewarded after about 6 km. The entrance is not too promising but behind the restaurant and car repair shop, over a bridge, it opens out into a level clearing with a circular area for camping. Pitches are neither marked nor numbered but there is room for about 50 units on grass with a clear stream running through. In the centre is a low stone circle for a wood fire with wooden benches around. Sanitary arrangements are in a brick built block which also has four rooms to rent and a kitchen with electric rings. The toilet (British), washbasin and shower areas are tiled. There is a Gasthof (closed Mondays) and a small shop. Druhy Mlyn is an oasis of peace in a noisy world with walks and hill climbing from the camp.

How to find it: From the main Karlovy Vary - Most road no. 13/E442, take the main exit into town, pass a small castle on the left and follow sign at beginning of road to camp.

General Details: Open all year. Restaurant. Small shop. Kitchen. Rooms to hire. 12 electrical connections.

Charges: Not available.

Reservations: Not made. Address: P.O. Box 131, 430 01 Chomutov. Tel: 0396/25918.

469 Camping Slunce, Zandov, nr Ceské Lipy

Pleasant site in rural situation near German border.

Away from larger towns, near the border with the old East Germany this is pleasant rural country with a wealth of Gothic and Renaissance castles. Zandov has nothing of particular interest but Camping Slunce is a popular camp with local Czechs. There is room for about 50 units on the level, circular camping area which has a hard road running round. Outside this circle are wooden bungalows for hire and tall trees. At the camp entrance, but under separate management, is a restaurant (open all year) where live music is played during high season. The general building at the entrance houses the sanitary accommodation, reception, a large, carpeted club room for games and TV and a kitchen with electric rings, full gas cooker and fridges. There is a good outdoor swimming pool.

How to find it: Zandov is 20 km. from Decin and 12 km. from Ceske Lipa on the minor road between these two towns. Signed in the centre of Zandov village.

General Details: Open 2 May - 30 Sept. Restaurant. Kiosk for basics. 36 electrical connections. Tennis. Table tennis. Swimming pool. Volleyball. Mountain bike hire. Children's playground. Well furnished club room with TV. Kitchen with good facilities.

Charges guide: Per person Kcs. 66; child 50; car 66; m/cycle 39; motorcaravan 132; caravan or tent 66; electricity 22 plus meter; local tax 3.

Reservations: Not made. Address: 471 07 Zandov. Tel: 0425/91116.

470 Autocamping Pavlovice, Liberec

Excellent camp in north Bohemia near Polish border.

Although Liberec does not have too much to write home about, it does have a zoo, botanical garden and Renaissance château. It is set in grand countryside near the Jizera mountains and not far from the Polish town of Gorlitz. Autocamp Pavlovice is nicely situated on the edge of the town near the sports ground. Just outside the entrance are the inevitable drab multi-storey workers flats, but trees screen these from view on the site. The Jested mountain at 1,012 m. dominates the distant sky line and is accessible by cable way for winter ski-ing and summer sightseeing. There are 130 pitches, all with electricity (10A), between the excellent bungalows (for hire) and different varieties of trees which give a peaceful air to the camp. Some of the caravan pitches are divided by low hedges on the edge of the site with views across open countryside. Tarmac roads lead to the camping places. The restaurant, with café, snack bar and raised terrace, also houses reception. The single, good quality sanitary block with British style WCs also has a kitchen with electric rings. There is a good-sized, recently rebuilt, swimming pool (open June-Sept) and children's play area, with fixed apparatus, in front of the restaurant. There is a speedway track right next to the camp which could cause noise disturbance when meetings are held on Sundays. This is a neat, tidy and very pleasant camp, good for a night stop or a longer stay.

How to find it: From Decin on road no. 13/E442, turn in direction of Frydlant (road 35), 100 m. before first (and only) traffic lights, to camp on left by sports stadium and large bus stop.

General Details: Open 1 May - 30 Sept. 34,000 sq.m. Restaurant. Snack bar with terrace. Tennis. Table tennis. Swimming pool. Children's playground. Shops outside entrance. Kitchen. Quality bungalows for hire.

Charges guide: Per person Kcs. 50; child (6-15 yrs) 20; tent 50; caravan 40; car 60; motorcaravan 80; m/cycle 20; dog 15; electricity 50; local tax 15.

Reservations: Write to site. Address: Autokempink Automotoklubu Pavlovice, 460 13 Liberec. Tel: 048/512 34 68. FAX: as phone.

CZECH REPUBLIC

474 Transkemp Hracholusky-Lodni Doprava, nr Plzen/Pilsen

Pleasant, waterside site adjacent to hotel.

Set beside the River Mzi where the Hracholusky dam has created a wide basin, Lodni Doprava enjoys a quiet location amidst gentle hills and pleasant trees. The 150 pitches here are spread along three terraces looking over the water with about half having electrical connections. The large, single sanitary block with British style WCs also contains a rest room with TV, kitchen and fridges for campers use. Two kiosks dispense drinks and basic supplies. There is swimming, boating and waterskiing on the lake and, during high season, a steamer makes 40 km. round trips along the river. A pleasant site but the presence of a large car park at the entrance may mean that it becomes crowded with day visitors in the summer.

How to find it: Site is signed on the Pilsen - Nurnberg road no. 5/E50, to the west of Pilsen.

General Details: Open 1 March - 31 Dec. Restaurant. Kiosks. Watersports. Swimming. Table tennis. Boat trips. Kitchen. Rest room with TV. Washing machines, dryers and irons. Rooms, chalets and caravans to let.

Charges guide: Per person Kcs. 20 - 24, acc. to season; child (6-15 yrs) 10 - 12; car 16 - 22; m/cycle 12 - 14; caravan or tent 65 - 90, acc. to size; motorcaravan 70 - 110, acc. to season and size; awning 30 - 40; electricity 35; local tax 5 - 10. Less 10% for stays over 30 days.

Reservations: Write to site. Address: 33034 Hracholusky. Tel: 019/7914 242 or 7914 113.

475 Camping Bílá Hora, Plzen/Pilsen

Site in peaceful location convenient for visiting Pilsen.

Even non-drinkers probably know that Pilsen is famous for its beer (Pils) and as the home of the Skoda car factory. Traffic in the town centre is heavy so, if you wish to visit the city where beer has been brewed since 1295, find a camp site and use the bus. Visits to the brewery may be arranged. Camping Bílá Hora is a suitable site and is situated amidst trees in the suburb of Bílá Hora, about 3 km. from the city centre on the edge of town. Pitches are on a gentle slope in a clearing, but level concrete tracks have been made for caravans and motorcaravans, with electricity available at each pitch. It is a pleasant, quiet site with a new sanitary block (British style WCs, bath and laundry) in the camping area, plus another with the bungalows, and its own restaurant. There are shops at 200 m. and a bus stop at the site entrance. Bungalows for rent are quite separate from the camping area.

How to find it: Site is to the north of the town on the Plzen - Zruc no. 231 road where it is signed.

General Details: Open 15 April - 30 Sept. Restaurant. Kiosk with small terrace. Shops near. Bicycle hire. Children's playground. Table tennis. Volleyball. Fishing 500 m. Swimming and tennis near. Washing machine and iron. Chemical disposal. Motorcaravan services. Kitchen. Chalets for hire.

Charges 1997: Per person Kcs. 50; child (10-15 yrs) 20; car 70; m/cycle 20; caravan or tent 70; motorcaravan 140; electricity 50.

Reservations: Not necessary. Address: Ul. 28.rijna 49, 30162 Plzen. Tel: 019/534905. FAX: 019/7237252.

478 Motel Autocamping Konopiste, Benesov

Camping and motel complex with excellent facilities, south of Prague.

Benesov's chief claim to fame is the Konopiste Palace, the last home of Archduke Franz Ferdinand whose assassination in Sarajevo sparked off the First World War in 1914. Autocamp Konopiste is part of a motel complex situated in a very quiet, tranquil location. On a hillside, rows of terraces separated by hedges provide grassy pitches of average size, all with electricity. One of the best Czech camps, it has many different varieties of trees and much to offer those who stay there. A fitness centre and heated swimming pool are shared with motel guests. The camp has its own bar/buffet in high season with simple meals and basic food items. The two motel restaurants are open all year. The good quality sanitary block is central to the caravan pitches and has British style WCs. The whole complex has a well tended, cared for air. It makes a good centre for visiting Prague (48 km. with public transport available) and to be enjoyed in its own right (see list of activities below). On site, near the motel, is the Stodola restaurant. Open each evening from 6 pm. until 1 am. this attractive replica of an old Czech barn is well worth a visit. With local specialities served by girls in local costume in a candle lit atmosphere and accompanied by a small, live music quartet, it is an evening to remember (booking essential).

How to find it: Site is signed near the village of Benesov at Hotel Konopiste (no connection) and Motel Konopiste on main Prague - Ceske Budejovic road no. 3/E55.

General Details: Open 1 May - 30 Sept. 6,000 sq.m. Bar/restaurant (all year). Snacks (1/6-31/8). Shop (1/6-31/8, another at 200 m). Tennis. Minigolf. Volleyball. Table tennis. Bicycle hire. Badminton. Swimming pool (1/6-31/8). Fitness centre. Children's playground. Kitchen. Club room with TV. Terrace. Chateau and park. Motel restaurants. Washing machine and irons. Chemical disposal. Bungalows to let.

Charges 1998: Per person Kcs. 60 - 110; child (6-15 yrs) 30 - 50; caravan 130 - 310; large tent 120 - 250, small 70 - 120; car 100 - 120; motorcaravan 190 - 380; m/cycle 50 - 100; electricity included. Credit cards accepted.

Reservations: Write to site. Address: 256 01 Benesov u. Prahy. Tel: 0301/22732. FAX: 0301/22053.

AR Discount
Less 10%
all season

477 Camping Dlouhá Louka, Céske Budejovice

Good night stop between Linz and Prague.

The medieval city of Céske Budejovice is the home of Budweiser beer and is also an industrial centre. It lies on the River Vltava with mountains and pleasant scenery nearby. Dlouhá Louka is a motel and camping complex 2 km. south of the town on the Céske Budejovice - Cesky Krumlov road. The camping part is a flat, rectangular meadow surrounded by trees which give some shade around the edges. Pitches, on grass, are not marked out or numbered so pitching can be rather haphazard. There are a few hardstandings. The single sanitary block with British style WCs is at one end making a fair walk for some. There is a very pleasant restaurant (summer only) and a small kiosk for basic food supplies. This is a useful night stop between Prague and Linz or for longer stays if this region is of interest.

How to find it: From town follow signs for Ceske Krumlov. After leaving ring road, turn right at Motel sign. Take this small road and turn right 60 m. before Camp Stromovky. Site name can't be seen from entrance - only 'Motel'.

General Details: Open 1 April - 30 Oct. 30,000 sq.m. Restaurant. Kiosk. Shops 200 m. Tennis. Volleyball. Table tennis. Washing machine and irons. Kitchen with electric rings. Children's playground. Bungalows and rooms to let.

Charges 1997: Per person Kcs. 50; child 30; car 70; tent 60; caravan 70; motorcaravan 110; m/cycle 40; electricity 80; local tax 15.

Reservations: Write to site. Address: Autocamping Motel Dlouhá Louka, Stromovka 8, 370 01 Ceské Budejovica. Tel: 038/7311757. FAX: 038/53141.

479 Sportcamp and Caravancamp, Praha/Prague Motol

Edge of city sites for visiting Prague.

These two camps are side by side, share the same management and have a similar standard of amenities and sanitary arrangements. Both are on sloping ground with some terracing in a quiet location about 8 km. from the centre of Prague. Electricity is available for most caravan places but the grass pitches are neither numbered nor marked out and the camps may become crowded in high season. There are hard access roads. It is a pleasant situation with trees and a hill on one side and some shade in parts. Each camp has its own restaurant and Sportcamp has a kiosk for basic food supplies with shops 200 m. distant. Caravancamp has a swimming pool. There is little to choose between these two camps - Caravancamp is now the larger, with room for about 200 units on flat pitches but is nearer the main road. Sportcamp with about 150 pitches is quieter but more hilly.

How to find them: Sites are well signed on the main highway from Pilsen, road no. 5/E50, near Hotel Golf.

General Details: Both open 1 April - 31 Oct. Restaurants. Kiosk (Sportcamp). Swimming pool (Caravancamp). Tennis. Minigolf. Shops 200 m. Bungalows to let (Sportcamp).

Charges 1998: Per person Kcs. 120 - 140; child (6-12 yrs) 60; tent 90 - 110; car 90 - 120; caravan 120 - 150; motorcaravan 150 - 180; m/cycle 60 - 80; electricity 300. Plus VAT.

Reservations: Write to sites. Address: Sportcamp, Nad hliníkem 1202, 150 00 Praha 5, Motol. Tel: 02/57213080. FAX: 02/57215084. Address: Caravancamp, Plzeñská 279, 150 00 Praha 5, Motol. Tel: 02/524714. FAX: 02/57215084.

481 Intercamp Kotva, Praha/Prague

Riverside city site for visiting Prague.

Kotva is pleasantly situated directly by the River Vltava, 20 mins. by public transport from the city centre. There is some traffic and train noise but the number of trees around and a high bank on the opposite bank of the river give a feeling of being in the country. A train and bus terminal is a few minutes walk. It is best to use the cheap public transport for visiting Prague as parking is very limited and illegally parked cars are swiftly towed away (the site office sells tram tickets which can also be used on the Metro - a tram stops outside the site). Pitches use level grass with hardstanding and electricity, with a separate grass area for tents. A reader reports that drainage is poor in wet weather. None of the pitches is marked out and it could become crowded in high season. The site is owned by a sports club and sanitary arrangements are in the main club building which also houses offices and accommodation. The sanitary facilities, recently enlarged and refurbished, are of good quality but may be under pressure in high season. The site restaurant is now in private hands (and perhaps leaves a little to be desired). There is a shop on the left as you go out of the gate. A well run site, English is spoken at reception and a porter is on duty at night at the entrance.

How to find it: Site is well signed on the southern ring road and on the main road from Pilsen or Ceske Budejovice. Follow signs for Branik.

General Details: Open 1 April - 31 Oct. 12,000 sq.m. Restaurant. Shop near. Fishing and boating on river. Tennis. Table tennis. Volleyball. Minigolf near. Chemical disposal. Bungalows, cabins and rooms to let (all year).

Charges 1997: Per person Kcs. 95; child (6-15 yrs) 45; tent 70 - 100; car 85; m/cycle 50; caravan 170; motorcaravan 200; electricity 60. Plus local tax 17 (child/student 2) and VAT @ 22%.

Reservations: Write to site. Address: Intercamp Kotva, U. ledáren 55, 147 00 Praha 4. Tel: 02/461712 or 461397. FAX: 02/466110.

AR Discount
Less 10%
all year

CZECH REPUBLIC

486 Autocamping Orlice, Kostelec

Pleasant site with good facilities in East Bohemia.

Kostelec does have an ancient castle, although not a lot else to commend it, but is a good centre from which to explore the interesting town of Hradec Kralove, East Bohemia, the Orlicke Hory and other high districts near the Polish border. Autocamping, on the edge of town near the swimming pool, has a river running by and is in a quiet location (except when children play in the weir!) and a pleasant appearance. The central sanitary block, one of the best we have seen in the Czech Republic, has British WCs and hot water in basins, sinks and excellent showers. Unlike most Czech camps, the showers have divider, space for dressing, a door that locks, and even a chair! Surrounded by tall trees, the grass pitches are of generous size although not marked or numbered, on each side of a concrete grid road which runs the length of this rectangular site. There is room for 80 units, half having electric points and with shade in parts. Limited food supplies are available in a bar/lounge during July/Aug. and there is a hotel alongside the camp but advice is to seek a better restaurant in town for meals. The friendly manageress speaks good English and will be pleased to advise on local attractions.

How to find it: Site is signed from the centre of town.

General Details: Open 15 May - 30 Sept. 30,000 sq.m. Bar/lounge. Shop (1/7-31/8). Bungalows for rent. Fishing. Tennis 100 m. Town swimming pool near (from 15/6).

Charges 1997: Per person Kcs. 26 - 34; child (6-15 yrs) 14 - 16; car 44 - 56; m/cycle 22 - 30; motorcaravan 70 - 84; caravan 50 - 60; tent 44 - 56; animal 34 - 38; electricity 44; local tax 2. Credit cards accepted.

AR Discount
Discounts all
season - ask
at site

Reservations: Write to site. Address: 51741 Kostelec nad Orlici. Tel/Fax: 0444/21970 (winter 0444/21691).

487 Autocamping Morava, Mohelnice

Well organised camp in interesting area.

This is an interesting area of contrasts - heavy industry, fertile plains and soaring mountains, with castles, caves and cathedrals. Mohelnice itself is a small industrial town but the camp is in a peaceful setting surrounded by trees on the northern edge. It could make a useful night stop or a base for seeing the locality. The amenities on offer, particularly for children, may tempt one to stay longer. The site is roughly in two halves. The camping area is on a flat, open meadow with hard access road. Pitches are not numbered or marked so siting could be a little haphazard; two thirds have electricity. There is little shade but the perimeter trees should screen out road noise. A swimming pool and a sanitary block are in this section (British style WCs). The other part of the camp is given over to a two storey motel and bungalows with a good quality restaurant between the two sections. An unusual feature of the camp is a driving and cycling learning area, similar to a normal road situation. This is a very pleasant site.

How to find it: Site is signed on the western edge of town on the Olomouc - Hradec Kralove road no. 35/E442.

General Details: Open all year. 20,000 sq.m. Restaurant (all year). Kiosk/snack bar. Small shop (summer only). Live music (high season). Swimming pool. Tennis. Minigolf. Table tennis. Volleyball. Bicycle hire. Road learning track. Children's playground. TV room. Washing machine. Electric cooking rings. English spoken.

Charges 1997: Per person Kcs. 60; child (under 15) 30; car 40; caravan 100; tent 80; electricity 60; local tax 10.

Reservations: Write to site. Address: 789 85 Mohelnice. Tel: 0648/430129. FAX: 0648/51011.

488 Camping Roznov, Roznov pod Radhostem

Good site with pool, on edge of resort town in North Moravia.

Roznov is halfway up the Roznovska Becva valley amidst the Beskydy hills which extend from North Moravia into Poland. It is a busy tourist centre which attracts visitors to the Wallachian open-air museum and those who enjoy walking. The main features of this site are the open air, swimming pool and bungalows for rent. The pitches, some of which are rather small, are on flat grass set amidst a variety of trees. There are electrical connections throughout and shade in some parts. Although right by a main road with some traffic noise, the camp is surrounded by trees and hills and was reasonably quiet during our visit. The good quality central sanitary block has British WCs and hot water in basins and sinks. The rather old showers have a rose water dispenser controlled by a chain. This block also has a large, comfortable TV lounge/meeting room. Local information is well displayed on notice boards and available from the friendly manager and receptionist who will be pleased to advise on local attractions. The shop stocks only very basic food items and the restaurant is not always open. A better bet is to use the restaurant or snack-bar night club at the modern Europlan Hotel some 300 m. towards the town.

How to find it: Site is at eastern end of Roznov on the main 18/E442 Zilina-Olomouc road opposite sports stadium.

General Details: Open May - September. 27,000 sq.m. Swimming pool (25 m. and heated July/Aug). Table tennis. TV lounge and meeting room. Small shop and restaurant.

Charges guide: Per person Kcs. 40 - 60; child (3-15 yrs) 30 - 50; caravan 60 - 70; tent 40 - 50; car 40 - 50; m/cycle 20 - 30; motorcaravan 100 - 110; electricity 50; local tax 17.

Reservations: Write to site. Address: 75661 Roznov pod Radhostem. Tel: 0651/55442. FAX: as phone.

DENMARK

Denmark is the easiest of the Scandinavian countries to visit, both in terms of cost and distance. The countryside is green and varied with flat plains, rolling hills, fertile farmland, many lakes and fjords, wild moors and long beaches, interrupted by pretty villages and towns. There are many small islands but the main land masses which make up this country are the islands of Zealand (Sjælland), Funen (Fyn) and the peninsula of Jutland (Jylland), which extends northwards from the German border at Flensburg. Copenhagen, the capital and Denmark's largest city, is on Zealand and is an exciting city with a beautiful old centre, a good array of museums and a boisterous night life. Camping in Denmark is a delight, with many sites now having facilities that rival, and sometimes even surpass, the best in other parts of Europe. Most sites now offer well designed facilities for disabled people and baby changing, and many now have private family bathrooms which generally include shower, WC and washbasin. You will find kitchens on most sites, many with hobs, ovens, microwaves and the occasional dishwasher. All these facilities are often free of extra charge. You will need either a valid International Camping Carnet, or a Danish Camping Pass (which can be purchased at the first camp you visit in Denmark). Denmark is an ideal destination for those who enjoy watersports of all types, cycling, fishing and sightseeing.

The Danish Tourist Board, 55 Sloane Street, London SW1X 9SY

Tel: 0171 259 5959 Fax: 0171 259 5955

Population
5,162,000 (1992), density 120 per sq.km.

Capital
Copenhagen (København).

Climate
The Danish climate can be changeable throughout the year. In general April-May is mild. June-Aug. is usually warm and sunny. Autumn is often sunny but can be unreliable and the winter months Dec-March tend to be cold, often with a little snow.

Language
The official language is Danish, but English is widely spoken.

Currency
The monetary unit is the Danish Krone (Dkr.) 1 Krone = 100 ore. Bank notes in circulation are: 1,000, 500, 100, and 50; coins are: 20, 10, 5, 2 and 1 krone, 50 and 25 ore.

Banks
In Copenhagen banks are open Mon-Wed & Fri 09.30-16.00. Thurs. to 18.00. Closed Sat. In the provinces opening hours vary from town to town. Note: Danish banks may refuse to exchange large foreign bank notes.
Eurocheques and other well known traveller's cheques are cashed by banks and many hotels, restaurants and shops, which also accept most international credit cards.

Post Offices
Open Mon-Fri 09.00/10.00-17.00/17.30, Sat 09.00/10.00-12.00 (some offices in Copenhagen are closed all day on Saturdays).

Telephone
The dialling code for Denmark is 0045. from Denmark to the UK dial 0044. Phone cards available from Telecom shops (Telebutik).

Time
GMT plus 1 (summer BST plus 1).

Shops
Hours may vary in the main cities. Regular openings are Mon-Thu 09.00-17.30. Fri 09.00-19.00/20.00. Sat 09.00-13.00/14.00. First Sat in every month most shops open 09.00-16.00/ 17.00.

Food and Restaurants
The cost of food is quite high and a stock of basic supplies is useful. However, supermarket prices are now fairly similar to London prices. The price of spirits is prohibitive but for wine and beer almost acceptable! Eating out can be expensive. Try sticking to `Dagens Ret' - the day's speciality which is usually good value. The high point of Danish food culture is the cold table with a large variety of hot and cold fish and meat dishes in which `smorrebrod' (open sandwiches), the great Danish speciality, play an important part.

Motoring
Driving is much easier than at home as roads are much quieter. Driving is on the right. Parking is much easier than ours, apart from main cities, often just off pedestrianised town centres. **Do not drink and drive** - any quantity is liable to immediate drastic action. Dipped headlights are compulsory at all times.
Speed limits: caravans and motorhomes (3.5 tons) 31 mph (50 kph) in built up areas, 44 mph (70 kph) for caravans on all other roads, for motorhomes 50 mph (80 kph) on other roads and 69 mph (110 kph) on motorways.
Parking: In Copenhagen parking discs are required where there are no meters. Meters take 1, 2, 5, 10 and 20 Kr. coins and discs are available from post offices, banks, petrol stations, and tourist offices.

Overnighting
Overnight stays outside camp sites is not permitted without the prior permission of the respective landowner. Camping in car parks and laybys is not permitted either. Strong measures are taken against unauthorised parking in dunes and on beaches - offenders being fined on the spot.

Useful Addresses
National Motoring Organisation:
Forenede Danske Motorejere,
FDM-Huset, PO Box 500, Firskovvej 32,
2800 Lyngby. Tel: 45930800.

DENMARK

2010 Hvidbjerg Strand Camping, Blåvand, nr Esbjerg (Jylland)

High quality, seaside, holiday site, with indoor pools and many activities.

A family owned, 'TopCamp' holiday site, Hvidbjerg Strand is on the west coast near Blåvands Huk, 43 km. from Esbjerg. All 650 pitches have electricity (6A) and 'comfort' pitches also have water, drain and satellite TV. Pitches are in rows on flat sandy grass, with areas divided by small trees and hedges. Four superb sanitary units provide WCs, washbasins (many in cubicles), roomy showers, spa baths, suites for the disabled, family bathrooms, kitchens and two blocks have laundry facilities. The latest unit is thatched in the traditional style with a central glass covered atrium. This includes a children's bathroom decorated with dinosaur characters, racing car baby baths, low height WCs, basins and showers, plus 10 high quality family bathrooms, a suite for the disabled and an excellent kitchen with eight double hobs and sinks, two ovens and adjacent dining area. All hot water and cooking facilities are free. Some family bathrooms may be rented for exclusive use. On-site leisure facilities include an impressive, tropical style indoor pool complex (free outside 1/7-10/8) with water slides, spa baths, Turkish bath and a sauna. A café/restaurant overlooks the pools. Elsewhere are TV rooms, solarium, outdoor barbecue areas with picnic tables, minigolf, horse riding, football, squash, badminton, fishing, many children's play areas, plus the latest indoor suite of supervised play-rooms designed for all ages with Lego, computers, video games, TV etc. (open 09.00-12.30 daily excl. Wed). A Blue Flag beach and windsurfing school are adjacent to the site and the town offers a full activity programme during the main season (mid June - mid Aug). Legoland is 70 km.

How to find it: From Varde take roads 181/431 to Blåvand. Site is signed left on entering the town. (Mind the speed bump on town boundary).

General Details: Open 21 March - 19 Oct. Supermarket. Café. Restaurant. Kitchen and laundry facilities. Pool complex. Comprehensive sporting and leisure facilities. Children's playgrounds. Sauna. Solarium. Dog showers. Car wash. Bicycle hire. Chemicla disposal. Motorcaravan services. Cabins for rent.

Charges 1997: Per adult Dkr. 53; child (0-11 yrs) 38; pitch 28 - 38, payable high seasons and BHs only; electricity (6A) 19; 'comfort' pitch 35. Credit cards accepted.

Reservations: made without deposit. Address: Hvidbjerg Strandvej, 6857 Blåvand. Tel: 75.27.90.40. FAX: 75.27.80.28.

2020 Møgeltønder Camping, Møgeltønder, Tønder (Jylland)

Pleasant family run site with excellent facilities, convenient for ports.

Only 5 minutes walk from one of Denmark's oldest villages and 10 minutes drive from Tønder with its well preserved old buildings and magnificent pedestrian shopping street. The old town of Ribe is just 43 km. A quiet family site, it has 250 large, level, numbered pitches on grass, most with electricity (6A), divided up by new plantings of shrubs and small hedges. Only 25 pitches are occupied by long stay units, the remainder solely for tourists, and there are 15 cabins for rent. Two superb, modern, sanitary units, one built in 1990 the other more recently, provide good roomy showers with divider and seat (on payment), washbasins with either divider/curtain or in private cubicles, British style WCs, plus excellent bathrooms for families and the disabled. In addition there are now two kitchens with hobs and dishwashing sinks (all free), plus a laundry with sink, two washing machines and a dryer. The site also has an excellent outdoor heated swimming pool and children's pool, a good children's playground with bouncing cushion and a range of trolleys, carts and tricycles. Small shop for essentials (fresh bread can be ordered daily), TV and games rooms, minigolf, telephone and tourist information. Golf course and bicycle hire in nearby Tønder.

How to find it: Turn left off the 419 Tønder - Højer road, 4 km. from Tønder. Drive through Møgeltønder village and past the church where site is signed. Note: the main street is cobbled so drive slowly.

General Details: Open all year. Shop. Swimming pool. Children's playground. Minigolf. Kitchen and laundry facilities. Car wash. Chemical disposal. Motorcaravan services. Chalets for rent.

Charges 1998: Per adult Dkr. 45; child (0-12 yrs) 25; electricity 15.

Reservations: Not normally necessary. Address: Sønderstregsvej 2, Møgeltønder, 6270 Tønder. Tel: 74.73.84.60. FAX: 74.73.80.43.

2030 Sandersvig Camping, Haderslev (Jylland)

Attractively laid out family site, in beautiful countryside 300 m. from beach.

This family run site offers the very best of modern facilities in a peaceful location and it is most attractively laid out. The 470 very large grassy pitches are divided up by hedges, shrubs and small trees into small enclosures, many housing only four units, all with electricity (6/10A). The site is well lit, very quiet at night. Water taps close to most pitches. Three sanitary blocks, one by reception, an older one (interior refitted) at the lower end of the site, and the newest at the upper end offer British WCs, washbasins (some in cubicles), and roomy showers (on payment). Also suites for disabled people, six family bathrooms, baby rooms, excellent kitchens with ovens, hobs, dishwashing sinks, plus a very good laundry and separate fish cleaning area. *continued overleaf*

56

2030 Sandersvig Camping (continued)

The site also has a well stocked supermarket and fast food service with a TV lounge/dining room adjacent, an outdoor heated swimming pool which is free to campers, two artificial grass tennis courts, solarium, children's playground with trampolines and Denmark's largest bouncing cushion, games room with TV, pool table, arcade machines, telephones and tourist information. This site makes a very comfortable base for excursions. Visit the restored windmill at Sillerup 4 km. or nearby historic Kolding with its castle, museums and shops. The drive to the island of Fyn takes less than an hour, with miles of country lanes around the site for cycling and walking.

How to find it: Drive from Christianfeld through Fjelstrup and Knud village, turning right 1 km. east of the village from where site is signed.

General Details: Open Easter - 15 Sept. Supermarket (1/4-15/9). Takeaway (15/5-10/8). Swimming pool (15/5-1/9). Games/TV rooms. Solarium. Tennis. Beach. Fishing. Children's playground. Kitchen. Laundry. Chemical disposal. Motorcaravan services.

Charges 1997: Per adult Dkr. 39; child (0-11 yrs) 22; pitch 10 - 20; electricity 6A 17, 10A 25.

Reservations: Essential for high season. Address: Espagervej 15-17, 6100 Haderslev. Tel: 74.56.62.25.

2040 Riis Camping and Fritidscenter, Give (Jylland)

Quality, quiet touring site, 18 km. from Legoland and 3 km. from the Lion Park.

Riis is a friendly, family run `TopCamp' site with 300 large touring pitches, on sheltered gently sloping well tended lawns surrounded by trees and shrubs. Electricity (6A) is available to 220 pitches, and there are 41 cabins and 5 apartments for rent. Two excellent sanitary units provide British WCs, washbasins with divider/curtain, and controllable showers with divider and seat (on payment). There are suites for babies and the disabled, family bathrooms (one with whirlpool bath), solarium, laundry, two excellent kitchens with hobs, ovens, dishwashing sinks, a large dining room/sitting room with TV, plus a covered barbecue grill area. Cooking facilities, family bathrooms and hot water are free, but the showers and whirlpool bath are extra. The outdoor heated pool and water-slide complex (charged) and adjacent small bar serving beer, ice cream, soft drinks and snacks only open in main season. There is also a small, well stocked shop next to reception. Other on site amenities include a comprehensive children's play area, outdoor bowling alley, table tennis, minigolf, TV lounge and bicycle hire. More comprehensive shopping and restaurants are in nearby Give. This is a top class site suitable for long or short stays in this very attractive part of Denmark.

How to find it: Turn onto Osterhovedvej southeast of Give town centre (near Shell Garage) at signpost to Riis and site. After 4 km. turn left into gravel drive which runs through the forest to the site. Alternatively, turn off the 442 Brande-Jelling road at Riis village north of Givskud.

General Details: Open 25 April - 7 Sept. Shop. Pool complex. Cafe/bar. Kitchen and laundry facilities. Dining room. Solarium. Table tennis. Minigolf. Bowling alley. Children's playground. TV lounge. Telephone. Tourist information. Car wash. Chemical disposal. Motorcaravan services. Cabins and apartments to let.

Charges 1997: Per adult Dkr. 49; child (under 12) 32; pitch 35 (23/6-4/8); electricity 18. Credit cards accepted.

Reservations: Site can become full in July/Aug. so reservations are advisable. Address: 7323 Give. Tel: 75.73.14.33. FAX: 75.73.58.66.

2060 Birkhede Camping, Ry (Jylland)

Well managed site, in beautiful quiet countryside on the edge of Lake Knudso.

Birkhede has 250 marked and numbered grassy pitches on two levels, divided by trees and shrubs, all with electricity (10A). Whilst the upper level is terraced, the lower is gently sloping but more suited to larger units. The site also has 7 cabins and motel rooms for rent. Although the entrance driveway is gravel, on-site access is mainly tarmac with a card operated security barrier. The two sanitary units are of excellent quality, the main block behind reception has two complete sets of facilities, only one open outside main season. The other block serves the lower level of the site. These provide British WCs, washbasins in cubicles, controllable card operated showers with divider and seat, family bathrooms, baby room, kitchens, dishwashing and laundry sinks, plus a fridge freezer. Campers buy pre-charged cards (Dkr. 100) to obtain hot water in kitchen, laundry, and showers. The same card operates washing machines, phones and entrance barrier. Takeaway. Mini-market. Free heated outdoor swimming pool (9 x 25 m) with water slide and children's pool (4 x 6 m), an adventure playground, ball games area and TV lounge. The lake provides a bathing area, fishing (licences from reception) and a jetty. Good walks from the site include a climb to a viewpoint which looks out over Denmark's 'Lake District'.

How to find it: Turn off Silkeborg to Ry no. 15 road 4 km. southeast of Laven St. at Alling and campsite sign.

General Details: Open 24 April - 15 Sept. Mini-market and takeaway (May-Sept). Swimming pool (1/6-20/8). Table tennis. Bicycle, boat and canoe hire. Fishing. Windsurfing. Children's playground. TV. Kitchen. Laundry. Chemical disposal. Motorcaravan service point. Chalets and motel rooms for rent.

Charges 1998: Per adult Dkr. 47; child (0-11 yrs) 29; pitch15/6-15/8 only 20 - 35; electricity 14 + 2.00 per Kwh.

Reservations: Essential in high season - contact site. Address: Lyngvej 14, 8680 Ry. Tel: 86.89.13.55. FAX: 86.89.03.13.

DENMARK

2050 Terrassen Camping, Laven St, Silkeborg (Jylland)

Terraced, family run site, overlooking Lake Julso and the countryside.

Terrassen's 260 pitches are arranged on terraces with 6A electricity to most. A small additional tent area (without electricity) is at the top of the site where torches may be required. There are also 20 seasonal units, 9 tour operator units, 10 rental cabins, and 3 site owned caravans on site. The recently extended main sanitary unit is heated and modern and provides British WCs, washbasins (many in cubicles), controllable showers with divider and seat (on payment), 5 family bathrooms, children's bathroom, baby room, and facilities for the disabled. There is also a new kitchen with 10 hobs, 2 ovens and dishwashing sinks. An older re-furbished unit contains another kitchen, plus 4 more shower cubicles with external access - despite their outward appearance they are newly re-tiled and immaculate. Cooking facilities, family bathrooms, hot water and the swimming pool are free, only showers are extra. The solar heated swimming pool (8 x 16 m) has a paved terrace and is well fenced. Other amenities include an adventure playground and pets corner, ball games area with basket and volleyball, a well stocked shop is adjacent to the reception office, games and TV rooms, post box, telephone, tourist information and canoe hire. A restaurant is just outside the site, and fishing and windsurfing are available on Lake Julso. This is a comfortable base from which to explore this area of Denmark where a warm welcome and good English will greet you. Don't forget to take a trip on Lake Julso on Hjejen, the world's oldest paddle steamer.

How to find it: From Silkeborg take the road no. 15 to Linas, turn right to Laven St. village, then right again towards Laven and follow signs to site.

General Details: Open 1 April - 15 Sept. Shop (1/5-15/9). Swimming pool (1/6-1/9). Games/TV rooms. Children's playground. Pets corner. Canoe hire. Fishing and windsurfing on Lake Julso. Kitchen. Laundry. Car wash. Chemical disposal. Motorcaravan services. Cabins and caravans for hire.

Charges 1997: Per adult: Dkr. 45; child (1-11 yrs) 25; pitch 10 - 20; electricity 20.

Reservations: Contact site - essential for high season. Address: Himmelbjergvej 9, Laven St, 8600 Silkeborg. Tel: 86.84.13.01. FAX: 84.84.16.55.

2080 Sølystgård Camping, Fuglsø, nr Ebeltoft (Jylland)

Seaside site with good views in attractive holiday location.

Located in a corner of the delightful Ebeltoft and Møls area, one of the best holiday spots in Denmark, this beach-side site is on Ebeltoft Bay, close to the Helgenæs peninsula, and surrounded by rolling countryside. The spacious site, originally a farm, is divided by hedges and trees into several well tended fields, which have varying slopes. The 280 pitches are unmarked but electricity (4/6A) is available in all areas and many places have sea views. The lovely old, thatched, white walled farm buildings form the central complex incorporating reception, a small shop and other facilities. There are two sanitary units, one a converted thatched barn solely for ladies, the other is more ordinary, with rooms for ladies and men. The former has a kitchen with hobs (on payment), dishwashing sinks (free hot water), baby room and an excellent whirlpool bathroom (on payment) at one end. Other facilities include British WCs, washbasins either in cubicles, with divider and curtain, or open, plus hot showers with divider and seat (on payment). Facilities for disabled people, a sauna and solarium (on payment), laundry, telephone, ice pack service and tourist information. Leisure facilities include a centrally located tennis court and children's play area together with TV and games rooms. The beach offers good bathing with a water chute provided. Fishing is popular and there is a boat to borrow without charge. Golf and riding near.

How to find it: Take road 15 from Århus to Rønde, turn right following signs to Fuglsø where you turn left towards the Helgenæs peninsula. Then left again at camp sign down a narrow lane to the site.

General Details: Open 1 April - 20 Sept. Shop. Sauna. Solarium. Whirlpool bathroom. Tennis. Billiards. Volleyball. Basketball. TV and games rooms. Fishing. Children's playground. Kitchen. Laundry. Car wash. Chemical disposal. Motorcaravan services. Cabins for rent.

Charges 1998: Per adult Dkr. 48 - 55; child (0-13 yrs) 29 - 34; electricity (4A) 20.

Reservations: Essential in high season. Address: Dragsmurvej 15, Fuglsø, 8420 Ebeltoft. Tel: 86.35.12.39.

2090 Krakær Camping, Krakær, nr Ebeltoft (Jylland)

Sheltered, spacious forest site, with swimming pool and bistro.

Situated just north of Ebeltoft Bay in sheltered forest surroundings, but close to beaches and the ferry port of Grenå. Krakær Camping's new family owners have carried out much modernisation work and the 280 marked, but not separated, pitches are mostly on level terraces or in large clearings, together with 13 cabins for rent. Access roads are good and most pitches have electrical hook-ups (10A) but long leads may be necessary. Newer terraces are still maturing and could be muddy in wet weather. There are two modern sanitary units, one below the reception complex, the other nearer the swimming pool. They provide plenty of British style WCs and washbasins in cubicles, but rather fewer hot showers with divider and seat (on payment), which may be pressed in main season. Other facilities include a baby room, family bathrooms, a unit for disabled people, hand dryers, free hairdryers, two kitchens with hobs and dishwashing sinks, plus a laundry with drying room. *continued overleaf*

2090 Krakær Camping (continued)

Hot water, cooking facilities and family bathrooms are free, only showers are extra. A stylish bistro and bar at the entrance (high season) also serves takeaway meals and has a pleasant terrace. Other amenities include a solar heated open-air swimming and toddlers' pools, minigolf, supermarket, TV and games room, telephone, post box and tourist information. Children have an excellent, imaginative adventure playground and pedal car track. Riding, tennis and golf all near. There are glorious walks all around.

How to find it: From road no. 15 at Ronde turn right to Femmøller Strand, then left towards Lyngsbæk. Site is clearly signed 2 km. along country lanes. Take care turning off main road - approach on a blind corner.

General Details: Open all year. Shop (1/4-1/9). Bistro, bar and takeaway (15/6-15/8). TV/games room. Play area. Minigolf. Pool (1/4-15/10). Kitchen. Laundry. Chemical disposal. Motorcaravan services. Cabins for hire.

Charges 1998: Per adult Dkr. 51; child (0-11 yrs) 26; electricity 22. Less 10% outside 15/6-15/8.

Reservations: Write to site for details. Address: GL Kærvej 18, Krakær, 8400 Ebeltoft. Tel: 86.36.21.18. FAX: 86.36.21.87.

2100 Blushøj Camping, Ebeltoft (Jylland)

Comfortable, family run touring site, with views over the Kattegat.

This is a traditional site where the owners are making a conscious effort to keep mainly to touring units - there are only 6 seasonal units and 4 rental cabins. The site has 230 pitches on levelled grassy terraces surrounded by mature hedging and shrubs. Some have glorious views of the Kattegat and others overlook peaceful rural countryside. Most pitches have electricity (10A), but long leads may be required. One sanitary unit provides British style WCs, washbasins with dividers and showers with divider and seat (on payment). The other unit has a kitchen with mini-oven and dishwashing, dining/TV room, laundry and baby facilities. A new heated extension provides six very smart family bathrooms, and additional WCs and washbasins, and is adjacent to the new heated and fenced swimming pool (14 x 7 m) with a water-slide and terrace. Hot water, oven, family bathrooms and the swimming pool are free, only showers are extra. Good children's playground, minigolf, well stocked shop and telephone. The beach below the site provides opportunities for swimming, windsurfing and sea fishing. The owners also arrange traditional entertainment - folk dancing, local choirs, and accordion music some weekends in high season. This is a fine location for a relaxed family holiday, with numerous excursion possibilities including the fine old town of Ebeltoft (4 km), with its shops and restaurants, and the world's largest wooden sailing ship, the Frigate Jylland, now fully restored and open to the public.

How to find it: From road 21 northwest of Ebeltoft turn off at junction where several sites are signed. Follow signs through the outskirts of Ebeltoft turning southeast to Elsegårde village. Turn left for Blushøj and follow camp signs.

General Details: Open from 1 April - 15 Sept. Shop. Kitchen. Laundry. Swimming pool. Minigolf. Children's playground. Beach. Fishing. Chemical disposal. Motorcaravan services. Cabins for rent.

Charges 1997: Per adult Dkr. 45 - 51; child 23 - 25; electricity 15.

Reservations: Advisable for high season - write for details. Address: Elsegårdevej 53, 8400 Ebeltoft. Tel: 86.34.12.38.

2150 Sølyst Camping, Nibe (Jylland)

Family run site beside sheltered Limfjord, with swimming pool.

You will always be near to the water in Denmark, either open sea or, as here, alongside the more sheltered waters of a fjord. Sølyst provides 200 numbered pitches, most with electricity (6A), on gently sloping grass arranged in fairly narrow rows separated by hedges. Also on site are 12 cabins, 3 rooms and 3 mobile homes for rent. There are facilities for watersports and swimming in the fjord, the site also has a small heated swimming pool (8 x 16 m), with a children's pool and paved sunbathing area, and bicycles or paddle boats can be rented. A little train provides rides for children and there is a good playground, minigolf, and TV room. The snack bar (open main season) provides takeaway meals and there are tables outside, under cover. The central sanitary unit provides British WCs, washbasins in cubicles, four family bathrooms, a baby room and facilities for the disabled. There is a kitchen with gas hobs, microwave, oven and dishwashing sinks, and a fully equipped laundry. A second unit provides two more family bathrooms and additional unisex WCs, basins and showers, and is located near the solarium. Hot water (except in washbasins) is charged for. The mini-market at the site entrance is open daily. Good paths have been provided for superb, easy walks in either direction, and indeed right into the nearby town of Nibe (1 km). This is a delightful example of an old Danish town with picturesque cottages and handsome 15th century church. Its harbour, once prosperous from local herring boats, is now more concerned with pleasure craft.

How to find it: Site is clearly signed from the no. 187 road west of Nibe town, with a wide entrance.

General details: Open all year. Mini-market. Snack bar and takeaway. Swimming pool. Children's playground. TV room. Solarium. Bicycle hire. Kitchen. Laundry. Chemical disposal. Cabins for hire.

Charges 1997: Per adult Dkr. 47; child 23; pitch 20 (14/6-16/8 only); electricity 15. Only Visa cards accepted.

Reservations: recommended for peak periods - write for details. Address: Løngstørvej 2, 9240 Nibe. Tel: 98.35.10.62. FAX: 98.35.34.88.

DENMARK

2130 Hobro Camping Gattenborg, Hobro (Jylland)

Imaginatively landscaped site with views over Hobro, Mariager Fjord and Vester Fjord.

This neat and very well tended site has 150 pitches on terraces arranged around a bowl shaped central activity area. Most pitches have electricity (5A) and there are many trees and shrubs. Footpaths connect the various terraces and activity areas. There are also 35 seasonal units and 6 cabins for rent. The main heated sanitary building, towards the rear of the site, provides British style WCs, washbasins in cubicles, and controllable hot showers with divider and seat (on payment), plus two family bathrooms, a kitchen with hobs and dishwashing sinks, and a small laundry with a sink, washing machine and two dryers. A tiny unit in the centre of the site has two unisex WCs and washbasins (cold water only) and a small kitchen, whilst the reception building with a small shop and tourist information, has a covered picnic terrace behind, and also houses a large TV lounge and additional WC and basins. The small, heated, outdoor swimming pool with water-slide is free to campers and open in high season weather permitting. Leisure facilities include a well equipped children's playground, minigolf, basketball and football ground, table tennis, billiards, giant chess, and a woodland moon-buggy track.The site is 500 m. walk from the town, close to the Viking Castle of Fyrkat and the lovely old town of Mariager.

How to find it: From E45 exit 35, take road 579 towards Hobro Centrum. Site well signed to right after rail bridge.

General Details: Open 26 March - 28 Sept. Shop. Swimming pool. Children's play areas. Table tennis. Basketball. Football. Minigolf. TV lounge. Kitchen. Laundry. Chemical disposal. Motorcaravan services. Car wash.

Charges 1997: Per adult Dkr. 44-51; child (2-11 yrs) 24 - 27; electricity 15.

Reservations: Contact site. Address: Skivevej 35, 9500 Hobro. Tel: 98.52.32.88. FAX: 98.52.56.61.

2140 Jesperhus Feriecenter, Nykøbing (Mørs)

Extensive, well run site with pool complex and many leisure activities, adjacent to Blomsterpark.

This large, busy and well organised `TopCamp' site has 723 numbered pitches, mostly in rows, with some terracing, divided by shrubs and trees with shade in parts. Many pitches are taken by seasonal, tour operator or rental units, plus 60 chalets, so advance booking is advised for peak periods. Electricity (5A) is available on all pitches and water points are in all areas. Four first rate sanitary units are cleaned three times daily and the site operates a policy of regular maintenance and upgrading. Facilities include British WCs, washbasins in cubicles or with divider/curtain, controllable showers with divider and seat, family and whirlpool bathrooms, plus suites for babies and the disabled. Superb kitchens have full cookers and hoods, microwaves and dishwashing. All facilities except the whirlpool bathroom and laundry are free. The indoor and outdoor pool complex (daily charge) has three pools, diving boards, water chute, spa pools, saunas, solarium, plus a café. Elsewhere is a separate restaurant/bar, large supermarket, 10 lane bowling centre, minigolf, volleyball, tennis, fishing lake, riding, go-carts and other outdoor sports. An indoor activity hall includes badminton, table tennis, and children's 'play-world'. Although it may appear to be just part of Jutland, Mørs is an island in its own right surrounded by the lovely Limfjord. It is joined to the 'mainland' by a fine 2,000 m. bridge at the end of which are signs to Blomsterpark (Northern Europe's largest flower park which also houses a Bird Zoo, Butterfly World, Terrarium and Aquarium) and the camp site (under the same ownership). The flower park, well to the north of Denmark, is an incredible sight from early spring to late autumn, attracting some 4,000 visitors a day to enjoy over half a million flowering plants and magnificent landscaped gardens. With all the activities an entire holiday could be spent here, but Jesperhus is also an excellent centre for touring a lovely area of Denmark.

How to find it: From south or north, take road 26 to Salling Sund bridge, site signed Jesperhus, just north of bridge.

General Details: Open all year. Supermarket (1/4-1/11) with gas. Restaurant. Bar. Café. Takeaway. Pool complex. Comprehensive leisure, sporting and entertainment facilities. Children's playgrounds. Pets corner. Kitchens. Laundry. Chemical disposal. Motorcaravan services. Chalets for rent.

Charges 1997: Per adult Dkr. 52; child (1-11 yrs) 38; pitch 45 (July, BHs. and w/ends only); electricity 22. Credit cards accepted.

Reservations: Recommended for holiday periods - write for details. Address: Jesperhus Feriecenter, Legindvej 30, 7900 Nykøbing, Mørs. Tel: 97.72.37.01. FAX: 97.71.02.55.

2160 Hirtshals Camping, Hirtshals (Jylland)

Traditional coastal site, close to ferry port for Norway and the North Sea Centre.

This tidy, family run site is well placed for touring the tip of Jutland, and is close to the ferry port (1 km.) from which there are regular crossings to Norway. On the edge of a residential area and facing the Skagerrak (it can be a little windy) it has direct access to the beach. The 130 numbered pitches, all with electricity (10A), are on open, flat, sandy grass and are separated into rows by low wooden rails, with more sheltered pitches for tents behind reception, together with 10 cabins for rent. All amenities, including reception, are in a neat modern block at the entrance. They include good sanitary facilities with modern, bright fittings, including controllable hot showers (on payment), washbasins in cubicles, facilities for babies and the disabled, and a laundry. *continued overleaf*

DENMARK

2160 Hirtshals Camping (continued)

In high season a small `portacabin' style block provides a further shower, washbasin and WC (for each sex) by the pitches furthest from the entrance. Dishwashing sinks with free hot water, gas rings and an oven are in the campers' kitchen. Shop (with takeaway in season), good children's' playground, clubroom with TV. Restaurants, supermarkets and a swimming pool are in the town. For the well protected or warm blooded, the main attraction is the sea, with fishing and watersports. The coast from Hirtshals right up to the tip is almost one long beach with golden sand hard enough even to carry local buses - a quite memorable sight. Just north is Tversted, an ideal forest picnic spot, or 10 km. from Skagen is the fascinating buried church, or you might like to visit the enormous dunes of Råbjerg Mile.

How to find it: Site is clearly signed from road nos. 13, 15 and 55. It is on the outskirts of the town.

General Details: Open 3 May - 14 Sept. Small shop, others and restaurants in the town. Club room and TV. Children's playground. Bicycle hire. Barbecue. Kitchen. Freezer. Laundry. Fish preparation sinks. Chemical disposal. Motorcaravan services. Bus services. Cabins for hire.

Charges 1997: Per adult Dkr. 41 - 48; child (2-12 yrs) 23 - 26; electricity 16.

Reservations: Write to site for details. Address: Kystvejen 6, 9850 Hirtshals. Tel: 98.94.25.35. FAX: 98.94.33.43.

2170 Klim Strand Camping, Klim, Fjerritslev (Jylland)

Large coastal, family holiday site, with quality facilities - a paradise for children.

This privately owned `TopCamp' site has the full complement of quality facilities, including its own fire engine and trained staff. The site has 700 numbered pitches, all with electricity (10A), laid out in rows, many divided by trees and hedges and shade in parts. Some 300 are `luxury' pitches, fully serviced with electricity, water, drain and TV hook-up. Also 24 cabins to rent. The two main, centrally situated, heated sanitary buildings are very large, housing spacious showers (on payment), washbasins (some in cubicles) and British style WCs. A popular feature is the children's room with child size/height WCs, basins and half height showers. Also baby rooms, bathrooms for families and the disabled, sauna, solariums, whirlpool bath, hairdressing rooms, fitness room, and even a dog bathroom. Two smaller sanitary units are by reception and beach and there are well equipped kitchens and barbecue areas with dishwashing sinks, microwaves, gas hobs, and two TV lounges. Activities include an outdoor water- slide complex, indoor pools, tennis, pony riding (all free from '98), numerous children's play areas, adventure playground with aerial cable ride, a crèche, pizzeria and restaurant/bar and supermarket. Live music and dancing twice a week in high season. An 18 hole golf course near. Possible excursions - trips to offshore islands, visits to local potteries, a brewery museum and bird watching on the Bygholm Vejle.

How to find it: Turn off the Thisted-Fjerritslev no. 11 road to Klim from where site is signed.

General Details: Open 15 March - 20 Oct. (incl. all amenities). Supermarket. Pizzeria. Restaurant. Bar. Solarium and sauna. Children's playgrounds. Bicycle and TV hire. Fishing. Comprehensive leisure, sporting and entertainment facilities. Laundry. Kitchens. Chemical disposal. Motorcaravan services. Car wash. Chalets for rent.

Charges 1998: Per adult Dkr. 55; child (0-11 yrs) 40; pitch 35 (21/6-21/8 only); `luxury' pitch 10 - 25 (according to season); electricity 18. Credit cards accepted.

Reservations: Essential for mid June - end August. Address: Havvejen 167, Klim, 9690 Fjerritslev. Tel: 98.22.53.40. FAX: 98.22.57.77.

2180 Nordstrand Camping, Frederikshavn (Jylland)

Excellent site 2 km. from Frederikshavn and ferries to Sweden and Norway.

This is another `TopCamp' site and provides all the comforts one could possibly need with all the attractions of the nearby beach, town and port. The 430 large pitches are attractively arranged in small enclosures of 9-13 units surrounded by hedges and trees. Many of the hedges are of flowering shrubs and this makes for a very pleasant atmosphere. 250 pitches have electricity and drainage, a further 20 have water and there are 16 on hardstandings. There are 64 seasonal units, plus 23 cabins and 3 caravans for rent. Sanitary facilities are in two very large, centrally located, modern blocks and provide spacious showers (on payment), washbasins in cubicles and British style WCs, together with some family bathrooms, rooms for disabled people and babies, and laundry with free ironing. All are spotlessly clean. Good kitchens at each block provide mini-ovens, microwaves, hobs (free) and dishwashing sinks with free hot water. Leisure activities include minigolf, tennis, table tennis, billiards, chess, and fishing. The reception complex also houses a café (high season), with a telephone pizza service at other times. Supermarket. The beach is a level, paved 200 m. walk. Indoor swimming pool complex is 2 km. There is much to see in this area of Denmark and this site would make a very comfortable holiday base.

How to find it: Turn off main no. 40 road 2 km. north of Frederikshavn at roundabout just north of railway bridge.

General Details: Open 1 April - 15 Sept. Supermarket (all season). Café (15/6-15/8). Pizza service. Solarium. Beach. Fishing 200 m. Bicycle hire. Children's playgrounds. Laundry. Kitchens. Tourist information. Telephones. Car wash. Chemical disposal. Motorcaravan services. Chalets and caravans for rent.

Charges 1998: Per adult Dkr. 39 - 49; child (0-11) 25 - 32; pitch 27 - 30; electricity 6A 18. Credit cards accepted.

Reservations: Essential for high season and made with deposit (Dkr. 400). Address: Apholmenvej 40, 9900 Frederikshavn. Tel: 98.42.93.50 FAX: 98.43.47.85.

DENMARK

2200 Bøjden Strandcamping, nr Faaborg (Fyn)

Well equipped family site with beach, in the beautiful 'Garden of Denmark'.

Bøjden is located in one of the most beautiful corners of southwest Fyn (Funen in English) known as the 'Garden of Denmark'. Separated from the beach only by a hedge, many pitches have sea views as the site slopes gently down from the road. Arranged in rows on mainly level grassy terraces and divided into groups by hedges and some trees, the 318 pitches all have electricity (10A). Four special motorcaravan pitches also have water and waste points, and there is also a service point. The new, superb quality, centrally located sanitary building provides British style WCs, washbasins in cubicles, controllable showers with divider and seat (on payment), three family bathrooms, a baby room and excellent facilities for disabled people. Also in this building is a well appointed kitchen with hobs, oven and sinks, plus a laundry with washing machine and dryer. The older unit near reception provides more WCs, basins and showers, and a further kitchen. Cooking facilities and hot water are free, showers are extra. The latest addition is a swimming pool (13 x 9 m), and a paddling pool (8 x 5 m.) with a sun terrace, open during suitable weather conditions. On-site amenities include a well equipped fenced toddlers playground, separate adventure playground, small aviary, games and TV rooms, solarium, fenced dog exercise area, bicycle and boat hire and a barbecue area. Restaurant and bar 100 m. from the site. Everyone will enjoy the beach (Blue Flag) for bathing, boating and water sports. The water is too shallow for shore fishing but boat trips can be arranged. Bøjden is a delightful site for an entire holiday, while remaining a very good centre for excursions.

How to find it: From Faaborg follow road 8 to Bøjden; site is on right 500 m. before ferry terminal (from Fynshav).

General Details: Open 1 April - 15 Sept. Shop. Takeaway. Swimming pool (15/5-1/9). Solarium. Children's adventure playgrounds. TV and games rooms. Bicycle and boat hire. Minigolf. Kitchen. Laundry. Telephones. Tourist information. Chemical disposal. Motorcaravan services. Cabins for rent.

Charges 1998: Per adult Dkr. 48; child (under 12 yrs) 26; pitch (16/6-17/8 only) 20; electricity 19.

Reservations: Recommended for high season - write for details. Address: Bøjden Landevej 12, 5600 Faaborg. Tel: 62.60.12.84. FAX: 62.60.12.94.

2215 DCU Camping Odense, Odense (Fyn)

Ideal base from which to explore this fairy-tale city.

Although within the confines of the city, this site is hidden away amongst mature trees and is therefore fairly quiet. The 225 pitches, of which 145 have electricity (10A), are on level grass with small hedges and shrubs dividing the area into bays. There are a number of seasonal units on site together with 14 cabins for rent. The large new (1997) sanitary unit provides up to the minute facilities including British style WCs, washbasins in cubicles, controllable hot showers with divider and seat, 4 family bathrooms, hand dryers and hairdryers, a baby room, and an excellent suite for the disabled. In addition there is a well equipped kitchen with gas hobs, extractor hoods and dishwashing sinks, plus a laundry with washing machines and dryer. All hot water and cooking facilities are free of charge. Other on-site amenities include a shop, swimming pool complex, games marquee, TV room, large children's playground with bouncing cushion, table tennis, minigolf, ball games field and bicycle hire. A good network of cycle paths lead into the city. The Odense Adventure Pass (available at the site) allows unrestricted free travel on public transport within the city limits, free admission to the swimming baths and a free daily newspaper, with varying discounts on other attractions.

How to find it: From E20 exit 50, turn towards Odense Centrum, site entrance is 3 km. on left immediately beside the Texaco Garage.

General Details: Open 22 March - 20 October. Shop. Laundry. Kitchen. Swimming pool. Table tennis. Minigolf. TV. Children's playground. Bicycle hire. Tourist information. Telephone. Chemical disposal. Motorcaravan services.

Charges 1997: Per adult Dkr. 46 - 50; child 23 - 25; electricity 15 - 20.

Reservations: Contact site. Address: Odensevej 102, Odense S. Tel: 66.11.47.02. FAX: 65.91.73.43.

2205 Løgismosestrand Camping, Hårby (Fyn)

Countryside site with own beach and pool, surrounded by picturesque villages.

The owner of this site is the son of another Alan Rogers' site owner, and was the youngest campsite owner in Denmark when he purchased this site. Since that time he has refurbished the older sanitary unit, also built a new unit and, more recently, a new swimming pool (8 x 14 m) with a paddling pool (6 x 6 m), for which there will be small charge. The 200 pitches, some with a little shade, are arranged in rows and groups divided by hedges and small trees, 190 with electricity (10A). The sanitary units, kept spotlessly clean, have British style WCs, washbasins in private cubicles, roomy showers with seat and divider (on payment), hairdressing and shaving areas, baby room, bathrooms for families and the disabled. The new unit also houses a good laundry with washing machine and dryer, plus an excellent fully fitted kitchen with stainless steel worktops, inset gas hobs, microwave and dishwashing sinks.

continued overleaf

DENMARK

2205 Løgismosestrand Camping (continued)

Cooking facilities and hot water are free, only showers are extra. Other on-site amenities include a large undercover games room, grassy playing field, adventure playground, minigolf, table tennis, bicycle and boat hire, pony riding. Large well stocked shop and snack-bar (in season) with takeaway serving burgers, hot dogs, chicken, fish and chips at reasonable prices.

How to find it: Southeast of Hårby via Sarup and Nellemose to Løgismose Skov. Site is well signed. Lanes are narrow, large outfits should take care.

General Details: Open 27 March - 18 Sept. Shop. Snackbar/takeaway. Kitchen. Laundry. Swimming pool. Beach. Minigolf. Table tennis. Bicycle and boat hire. Pony riding. Children's playground. Telephone. Tourist information. Chemical disposal. Motorcaravan services. Cabins for rent.

Charges 1997: Per adult Dkr. 44; child 22; pitch 20 (23/6-10/8 only); electricity 18.

Reservations: Essential for high season - write for details. Address: Løgismoseskov 7, 5683 Hårby. Tel: 64.77.12.50. FAX: 64.77.12.51.

2220 Billevænge Camping, Spodsbjerg, nr Rudkøbing (Langeland)

Quiet, family run site in a woodland near beach on island of Langeland.

Billevænge is a family owned and managed site - not pretentious, but comfortable, attractive, sheltered, and very acceptable for a quiet relaxing holiday in lovely surroundings. The central point of the site is the duck pond, animal enclosure and children's play area. The 142 pitches are on sloping grass separated into groups by mature hedges and trees, with some pitches flatter than others. Most have electrical connections. A more open area, furthest from reception and the toilet facilities, is mainly reserved for tents. Site facilities are grouped together at the entrance. The original block, which has been refurbished, is kept clean and provides roomy showers (on payment), washbasins, some with partitions and curtain, a baby room, British style WCs, and power points. A nice feature is the family shower rooms including one large and one small toilet. Dishwashing facilities (metered hot water) are in the campers' kitchen (gas rings) and there is a laundry. Lovely walks may be had through the surrounding woods and the beach is reached by footpath (600 m). In addition to bathing, there are facilities for windsurfing and sailing and bicycles can be hired.. Boats can be hired for fishing and the site is proud of its record for really big catches. An excellent example of the Danes' outstanding expertise in bridge building can be seen here when one drives past Svendborg on Funen, across the bridge to Tasinge and then the longer, structure to Langeland - the 'long island'. The island also has many old windmills and castles to visit.

How to find it: From Svendborg, cross bridges to Langeland and Rudkøbing on road no. 9, cross island to Spodsbjerg and ferry (tollbridge planned). Turn right in town following signs 1.8 km. road to site.

General Details: Open 1 April - 31 Oct. Shop. Club room. TV room. Barbecue. Minigolf. Bicycle hire. Tourist information. Telephone. Post box. Children's playground and pets corner. Beach and watersports. Fishing 2 km. Laundry and cooking facilities. Chemical disposal. Motorcaravan service point. Cabins and caravans for rent.

Charges 1997: Per person Dkr. 47; child (0-11 yrs) 25; pitch fee (21/6-3/8 only, not tents) 15; electricity 18.

Reservations: Recommended for high season. Write for details. Address: Spodsbjergvej 182, 5900 Rudkøbing. Tel: 62.50.10.06. FAX: 62.50.10.46. E-mail: billevng@post5.tele.dk.

2240 Lysabildskov Camping and Feriecenter, Lysabildskov, Sydals (Als)

Small, neat, attractive coastal site on island of Als, with excellent facilities and a warm welcome.

In the heart of the country, 600 m. from a small rocky beach, this well laid out, attractive site provides all the comforts one could need for a relaxed holiday or shorter stay. The site has 192 large grassy pitches all with electricity (10A) separated into small secluded areas by mature rose and flowering shrub hedges. The central sanitary block has been totally refurbished inside providing roomy showers, basins with dividers/curtains and British style WCs, plus family bathrooms, facilities for disabled people and baby room with bath. Hot water is free throughout. Laundry and campers' kitchen with sinks and electric hobs. Further facilities serve the pool, apartments and reception complex and house further WCs and washbasins. There is an outdoor heated pool and children's pool (Dkr.6 per day), sauna, solarium, jacuzzi and a billiard room/TV lounge, tennis, ball games area, children's playground and playhouse. Fishing and windsurfing possible from the beach. Well stocked shop with fast food service. The island of Als is connected to mainland Jutland by an excellent toll-free bridge. Many possibilities for day trips to Søndersborg, Flensburg and Aabenra and miles of country lanes for cycling and walking.

How to find it: From Søndersborg drive towards Kegnæs on road no. 427, then towards Vibøge-Lysabild then follow the camp signs to Lysabildskov.

General Details: Open 1 April - 1 Oct. Shop. Takeaway (1/5-1/9). Swimming pool and children's pool (1/5-1/9). Sauna, solarium. and jacuzzi. Table tennis. Trampoline. Billiards. Boules. TV lounge. Barbecue area. Tennis. Ball games field. Children's playground. Fishing 600 m. Windsurfing. Telephones. Tourist information. Laundry. Cooking facilities. Chemical disposal. Motorcaravan services. Apartments (11) and cabins (5) for rent.

Charges 1997: Per person Dkr. 44 - 51; child 24 - 27; dog 5; electricity 17.

Reservations: Essential for high season (late June-mid Aug). Write to site. Address: Skovforten 4, Lysabildskov, 6470 Sydals. Tel: 74.40.43.98. FAX: 74.40.43.86.

DENMARK

2250 Hillerød Camping, Hillerød (Sjælland)

Neat, well run site well placed for touring Sjælland, Copenhagen and ferry to Sweden.

The northern-most corner of Sjælland is packed with interest, based not only on fascinating parts of Denmark's history but also its attractive scenery. Centrally situated, Hillerød is a hub of main roads from all directions, with this neat camp site clearly signed from the town. It has a park-like setting in a residential area with 5 acres of well kept grass divided up by attractive trees. There are 90 or so pitches of which 50 have electricity (10A) and these are marked. The site amenities are all centrally located in modern, well maintained buildings which are kept very clean. The bright and airy toilet block is slightly older in style but provides very good facilities including curtained, free hot showers, washbasins with partitions and curtain and a laundry room (free iron). Facilities for babies can also be used by disabled people. Basic supplies are kept in a small shop located with reception, adjacent to a splendid, large, comfortable club room with sofas, tables and chairs, TV and books. A campers' kitchen adjoins the facilities for dishwashing (free hot water). Tennis, golf and an indoor swimming pool are all within 1 km. The centre of Hillerød, like so many Danish towns, has been pedestrianised making shopping or outdoor refreshment a pleasure. Visit Frederiksborg Slot, a fine Renaissance Castle and home of the Museum of Danish national history. An excellent new electric train service every 10 minutes (20 mins. walk) makes a car unnecessary for a visit to Copenhagen. Hillerød, however is a fine base in itself, only 25 km. from the ferries at Helsingør and the crossing to Sweden.

How to find it: Follow road no. 6 bypassing town to south until sign at junction (signed to Frederiksborg Slot). Turn towards town and site is signed to the right.

General Details: Open 1 May - 13 Sept. Small shop. Good club room with TV. Children's playground. Bicycle hire. Tennis, golf and indoor pool near. Tourist information. Telephone. Laundry and cooking facilities. Cabins and tents to rent.

Charges 1998: Per person Dkr. 53; child (0-11 yrs) 27; electricity 20.

Reservations: Recommended for high season - write for details. Address: Blytækkervej, 3400 Hillerød. Tel: 42.26.48.54 (from 12 May: 48.26.48.54). FAX: as phone. E-mail: hillcamp@post8.tele.dk.

2260 DCU - Camping, Nærum, nr Copenhagen (Sjælland)

Sheltered, friendly site with new enthusiastic management, well situated for visiting Copenhagen.

Obviously everyone arriving in Sjælland will want to visit "wonderful, wonderful Copenhagen", but like all capital cities, it draws crowds during the holiday season and traffic to match. The site is near enough to be convenient but distant enough to afford peace and quiet (apart from the noise of nearby traffic) and a chance of relaxing after sightseeing. Nærum, one of the Danish Camping Union sites, is only 15 km. and very near a suburban railway (400 m. on foot) that takes you to the city centre. The long narrow site covers a large area alongside the ancient royal hunting forests, adjacent to the small railway line and the main road. Power lines cross the site under which camping is not allowed so there is lots of grassy open space. The 275 touring pitches are in two areas - in wooded glades taking about 6 units each (mostly used by tents) or on more open meadows where electrical connections are available. There are two modern toilet blocks. The one in the meadow area has been refurbished and has free, controllable hot showers, partitioned washbasins with hot water and WCs. A new, very good block at reception can be heated and also provides a laundry, dishwashing and a campers' kitchen. Good facilities are provided for babies and the disabled, and four new family bathrooms (free). General amenities include a shop, club room, TV, laundry, barbecue, playing field and playground. A full range of sporting facilities is within easy reach of the site and a café/restaurant within a few hundred metres. Nærum is a useful site to know for Copenhagen, but is also very near to the interesting friendly shopping complex of Rødovre and the amusement park at Bakken.

Note: Should you wish to drive into the city, there is a very useful cheap car park on the quay-side. It is within easy walking distance of the centre and is located where the Kalvebød Brygge meets the Langebrø bridge (suitable for motorcaravans and caravans).

How to find it: Using road no. E55/E47, take Nærum exit 15 km. north of Copenhagen. Turn away from the village and, within a few hundred metres, turn left after railway bridge, where site is signed. Site is 1 km. (by road) from the station, signed.

General Details: Open early April - mid Sept. Shop. Reception and shop closed 12.00 - 14.00 and 22.00 - 07.00. Café/restaurant near. Club room and TV. Laundry and cooking facilities. Barbecue. Minigolf. Children's play field and adventure playground. Bicycle hire. Tourist information. Telephone. Motorcaravan service point and car wash. Train service to Copenhagen.

Charges guide: Per adult high season Dkr. 47.50; child (0-12 yrs) 24; electricity 15; environmental charge 5; cabin 200. Copenhagen Card: 24 hrs 140 adult/70 child, 48 hrs 230 adult/115 child.

Reservations: Write for details. Address: Ravnebakken, 2850 Nærum. Tel: 42.80.19.57. FAX: 42.80.11.78.

Motorsport

A guide for campers, caravanners or motorcaravanners to some of Europe's foremost motor races.

Partly in response to questions from readers, and partly as a result of being motorsport enthusiasts ourselves, we decided to undertake a review, over several seasons, of the most famous of Europe's motor races, particularly from the perspective of campers and caravanners. These include Formula 1 Grand Prix, and the Le Mans 24 hour race.

During the past couple of years we have attended three Grand Prix (in France, Spain and Belgium) and the Le Mans 24 hour race, reports on these appear in this first "Motorsport Feature".

There are a variety of specialist tour operators offering inclusive tour arrangements to many European motor races. However, the sources of "tickets only" are fairly limited and we wanted to be wholly independent, slotting in attendance at some races alongside our Site Inspection Programme. We were therefore fortunate (apart from Le Mans where we were lucky enough to be given press passes courtesy of the Automobile Club de l'Ouest) to obtain basic general admission tickets from Just Tickets who provide an excellent service, and whose advertisement appears in this article.

Over the course of the next couple of years we hope to visit quite a few more GPs and other races to add to this Motorsport Feature. Our ultimate aim is to provide a fairly comprehensive guide to European motor races for the independent camper, caravanner or motorcaravanner.

Belgian Grand Prix
Spa-Francorchamps

The Spa circuit is well-known as one of the most challenging of all the European Formula 1 venues. The circuit (which still uses some closed public roads) is longer than most, and covers quite a large area of countryside, including Francorchamps, Malmedy and Eau Rouge; and Stavelot - where you will find 074 Domaine de l'Eau Rouge: a convenient site featured in this guide, and our choice for the 1997 Grand Prix.

First of all it's worth mentioning that the circuit is not really based at Spa at all,

Spa Francorchamps *(ICN U.K. Bureau)*

Villeneuve, Spain *(ICN U.K. Bureau)*

but at Francorchamps, where there is direct access to the ticket office, main grandstands, pits and paddock. However, it's by no means essential to base yourself here even if you can find a hotel or campsite with any space.

You can indeed camp at several places around the circuit: most of these areas are on a 45 degree slope with only about 10 portaloos in total. When we arrived two days before the race there was no camping/caravanning space left at all, so you'll need to be quite dedicated (and self-sufficient) to consider "rough" camping at Spa. Frankly, we weren't that brave.

Our strategy was to book tickets (basic general admission only) in advance through Just Tickets (see advert in this

article) and similarly to book a pitch in advance at Camping Eau Rouge (No 074 in this Guide): this proved to be a cost-effective and comfortable option. You can arrive on the Friday evening (or even on the Saturday evening) settle onto your pitch and walk to the circuit either along the road or through the woods: it's about 2km to the circuit at Stavelot, where you can get a good close view over two corners and a short straight, plus a more distant view of the following straight. You must get in position really early - the circuit actually opens at 1am on race day, and if you're not in position by 6.30am don't bother trying. There are no stands at Stavelot, so you'll need to take your own chairs unless you're prepared to stand for ten hours. An umbrella and/or parasol is also essential, as it's either very hot sunshine (34 degrees) or torrential rain: Spa is renowned for its unpredictable weather.

Our decision to camp at Eau Rouge, and to book in advance was fortuitous - we arrived on the Friday evening and apart from our reserved pitch there wasn't an inch of free space anywhere: the site was virtually taken over by GP enthusiasts - there was even a Ferrari goodies stand and a Lancia marquee! Given the sheer numbers the site coped quite well, but expect long queues for the few hot showers.

The start of the French Grand Prix *(ICN U.K. Bureau)*

Villeneuve, France *(ICN U.K. Bureau)*

You could of course drive to the circuit, at Stavelot or several other places, but beware of hefty parking charges (about £17), lack of space and a ruthless policy of towing-away illegally parked vehicles. Frankly it's not worth the hassle if you're staying at Eau Rouge. On the other hand a 2km walk back after the race in a temperature of 34 degrees carrying: two chairs, an umbrella, camera, binoculars, VHF radio and thermos flasks isn't a lot of fun either. To say nothing of a similar, if much cooler, walk to the circuit in the dark at 5.30am.

"Was it worth it?" I asked my 19 year old daughter who had never been to a Grand Prix before, and her reply was "Can you get tickets for next year, or could we try Monaco instead - or as well?"

French Grand Prix
Circuit Nevers - Magny-Cours

The Magny-Cours circuit is situated in the heart of the French countryside. Arriving as we did, from the east, the approach to the circuit is via a myriad of tiny country lanes, which are well signposted on the days before the GP.

Given our previous experience at the Spanish GP in May, in addition to our admission tickets we had also obtained a car-parking ticket from Just Tickets. This was for the East car park, which was easy enough to find: on reflection we might have done better to park on the verge of the approach road (a country lane), to avoid at least some of the delay when leaving.

The Magny-Cours circuit is set in a natural bowl in the surrounding hills, and viewing from most parts is quite good. We found "seats" on concrete terracing just before the Adelaide curve, and enjoyed a reasonable view of the straight, the curve itself and the straight beyond it.

You can of course enjoy a better view on TV, but what you don't get on TV is the atmosphere: which is wonderful. In contrast to Barcelona, the commentary, over a quite audible PA system (but also on FM radio if you prefer) was in French and English, so there was no problem keeping track of pit-stops etc. We were also opposite an electronic "scoreboard" which gave updated positions for the leading cars.

The only real problem was getting away afterwards - we sat in a queue of traffic that moved no more than ten metres in an hour! Once you do get out of the circuit the traffic is kept moving by a

(ICN U.K. Bureau)

facilities, although quite clean, were distinctly elderly. The mainly Turkish style WCs were certainly not of a standard one would expect from a more modern four-star campsite.

If you are prepared to travel further, the very comfortable Alan Rogers' inspected/selected site Des Bains (No 5801), at St. Honore les Bains, is only about 80km away: in normal conditions this should be about an hours drive from the circuit - indeed it may well only take that long to get there on race day, but allow about three hours to get back.

The Le Mans 24 Hour Race

variety of police, gendarmes and other military personnel: but progress is still slow.

So far as camping/caravanning is concerned, one option is simply to get a car-parking ticket and take your outfit into the East car park (a very large, reasonably flat, if rather muddy field), where you can choose more or less any spot you like to pitch. There are sanitary facilities in porta-cabins, close to the entrance from the car-park to the circuit itself: these seemed to be kept reasonably clean, apart from mud. To be fair the weather had been terrible for several days prior to the race: so mud was an inevitability wherever you went.

Alternatively, there are several two-star municipal campsites within about 10km of the circuit. However, the one-way system operated, and strictly controlled, by the police precluded our visiting these, although we did visit the four-star municipal "le Halles" at Decize, about 20km from the circuit.

This is an attractive site beside the river, with reasonably sized pitches: all have electricity and are on level grass with ample shade. Unfortunately the sanitary

Traditionally the world famous Le Mans 24 Hour race takes place over the 3rd weekend in June (14/15 June in 1997). The roads around and including the circuit are closed to the public for a week before the race, and practice usually takes place on the Wednesday and Thursday, with the Friday prior to the race being a rest day. The circuit includes the famous Mulsanne Straight, which for most of the year is actually part of the RN138 public highway.

The event is more a "spectacular" than just a motor-race, with many ancillary attractions. It attracts people of every nationality, including quite a few who probably never attend any other race.

Many spectators choose to camp at Le Mans, usually for several days, and there are several "camping fields" around, and even within the circuit. These camping areas are little more than fields of fairly long grass, with basic WCs (often a supervised porta-loo) only: so don't expect true campsite facilities. On the other hand the atmosphere at these informal "sites" is excellent, and they're deservedly popular if for no other reason than conviviality and proximity to the circuit. The organisers normally charge a flat fee for camping, covering anything from one night to a week, depending mainly on which of the several "sites" is chosen - those nearer to the main grandstands/pits etc. being more expensive.

The range of facilities around the circuit is vast, with snack-bars, shops, bars and quite plush restaurants. They also include the Le Mans Motor Museum: a real must for the genuine enthusiast. Track Tours (whose advertisement appears in this article) offer a very interesting tour which includes a visit to this famous museum.

If you choose not to use the circuit's own camping facilities, and to stay at a "proper" campsite, there are a fair number to choose from, including quite a few in the departement of Sarthe (72) some of which are featured in the Alan Rogers' Good Camps Guide to France, but bear in mind that all of these are likely to become very heavily booked-up over the weeks before, during and after the race.

Amongst the several sites within about 30 miles of the circuit are:

Camping Municipal Besse-sur-Braye - (about 45km SE of Le Mans) - An unusual 4-star municipal with around 60 pitches. Tel 02.43.35.31.13

Camping Municipal du Lac, St Calais (about 37km ESE of Le Mans) - Fully described in the Alan Rogers' Good Camps Guide for France (7202M). Tel 02.43.35.04.81

Camping Les Mollieres, Sille Guillaume (about 35km N of Le Mans) - A well-shaded 3-star site with 130 pitches. Tel 02.43.20.16.12

Camping Le Vieux Moulin, Neuville-sur-Sarthe (about 11km N of Le Mans) - Pleasant 3-star site with about 100 pitches. Tel 02.43.25.31.82

Camping Municipal La Route d'Or, La Fleche - (about 50km SW of Le Mans) - Fully described in the Alan Rogers' Good Camps Guide for France (7201M). Tel 02.43.94.55.90

Castel Camping Chateau de Chanteloup, Savigne l'Eveque (15km NE of Le Mans) - Fully described in the Alan Rogers' Good Camps Guide (7203). Tel 02.43.27.51.07.

At the time of going to press (November 1997) we understand that the 1998 race will move from its traditional weekend in mid-June to the previous weekend (6th/7th June) to avoid a clash with the football World Cup.

Frentzen leads in France *(ICN U.K. Bureau)*

The shortest route from the channel ports to Le Mans is from Caen (about 150km): please note that the circuit itself is some distance from the town - all the ferry crossings on the Western Channel routes get heavily booked around the race weekend, so early booking may be necessary.

Race tickets, and tickets for camping at the Circuit are obtainable from Just Tickets (see advertisement in this section) or direct from the Automobile Club de l'Ouest, Siege Social, Circuit des 24 Heures, 72019 Le Mans Cedex. Tel 02.43.40.24.24.

Bear in mind that members of the ACO get a special discount on race tickets, access to their own "club marquee" and other goodies: plus the benefit of all-year-round breakdown cover throughout France. You might like to consider joining the ACO - full details are available from the address above.

Spanish Grand Prix
Circuit de Cataluna - Barcelona

Our visit to the Spanish Formula 1 GP in May 1997 was something of an eye-opener!

Although we had acquired admission tickets in advance, from Just Tickets, we were unable to get to the Saturday qualifying, so getting into the circuit on the Sunday was a new experience. Our first mistake was to take the wrong exit off the autoroute! You'd expect that Exit 13 would be the Exit immediately after Exit 12 wouldn't you? - well, it isn't - there's another unnumbered junction between 12 and 13, which we took by mistake, and ended up driving round a deserted suburb for about half and hour, until we eventually found someone who directed us to the circuit.

Once we found the circuit the problem was to find somewhere to park - there

Former F1 driver Robin Widdows watches the authors negotiate the Grand Prix circuit at Pau in their Lancia Fulvia during the Rallye des Pyrénées *(David Burdon-Bailey)*

are plenty of numbered car-parks, but most are reserved or pre-booked: so unless you are able to attend the Saturday qualifying and buy a car parking ticket in advance, allow yourself plenty of time to find a space (like an hour).

By chance we ended up in the car park next to the camping field, this involved a walk of about 10 minutes to the nearest circuit gate. The camping field was reasonably flat, but the access to it wasn't, and it seemed to be used exclusively by motorhomes. Personally I wouldn't have wanted to manoeuvre a caravan into it: as several thousand cars were also using the entrance to access an adjacent car-parking field.

The camping field had several WCs and showers in porta-cabins, which would have been fine if the car-park adjacent had not been sharing these facilities. As a result the WCs in the camping field were a tad pressed to put it mildly! All in all the camping facilities at the circuit might best be described in one word - primitive.

Our advice would be to do as we did and stay on one of the many excellent sites in the Costa Brava, and drive to the circuit by car. Bear in mind that the circuit is north of Barcelona: about 1km off the autoroute (junction 13) and just over an hours drive from a wide choice of good campsites.

Circuit de Cataluna is in a "bowl" in the surrounding hills, with several good vantage points - we found space on the grassy slope just above turns 1 and 2. We had quite a good view, although not of the pits, so we tended to lose track of the situation after about 15 laps when cars started to pit. Although we could see one of the many giant TV monitors the commentary was all in Spanish and the picture was very faint in the strong sunlight. English commentary was available on FM radio and would have been very useful to keep track of the pit stops etc.

Although you do get a better all round view of a GP from the comfort of your armchair, what you miss is the incredible atmosphere. Next time we'll know better; get there earlier; take a walkman type radio as well as binoculars; and more by way of a picnic. Even allowing for our mistakes, this is an event not to be missed if you enjoy motorsport.

Grand Prix Racing

Just Tickets are the largest UK suppliers of spectator tickets to all Formula One events plus the le Mans 24 hours.

Our **Ticket only** service covers general admission, grandstand seats, also parking at most circuits.

At **Silverstone** and **Monaco** we also book helicopters as well as hospitality, including a new **Speciality Marquee** at Le Mans plus restaurant and private apartment both with viewing terrace at Monaco

Just Motoring offers inclusive self-drive arrangements with hotels, to all European Formula One events.

Brochure available in November
'Phone or fax for price lists

Just Tickets
1 Charter House
Camden Crescent
Dover, Kent
CT16 1LE
Tel: 01304 228866
Fax: 01304 225123

Mr/Mrs/Ms

Address

Postcode

Event   Ref GCG/98

FINLAND

Finland covers an area of 338,000 sq. km. (13,500 sq. miles) and consists of 10% water (forming 187,888 lakes), 69% forest and only 8% cultivated land. The maximum length is 1,160 km. (721 miles), the maximum width is 540 km. (336 miles). Being such a long country, there is a considerable difference in the type of landscape between north and south, with the gently rolling, rural landscape of the south giving way to the hills and vast forests of the north and treeless fells and peat-lands of Lapland. Forests of spruce, pine and birch are inhabited by hares, elks and occasional wolves and bears. It is well worth noting that, every few kilometres, signs are posted depicting an elk warning motorists of the danger involved with these beasts dashing onto the road, with an average of 40 motorists per day being involved in accidents with this animal. If you are unfortunate enough to hit one, it must be reported to the police. International Camping Carnet or Finnish Camping Card required at many sites. We have deliberately chosen the beautiful Saimaa Lake District in the southeast of the country as an introduction, due to its popularity and easy access by excellent roads. Further information can be obtained from:

The Finnish Tourist Board, 30/35 Pall Mall, London SW1Y 5LP.

Tel: 0171 839 4048. Fax: 0171 321 0696

Population
5,054,982 (1993); density 15 per sq. km.

Capital
Helsinki.

Climate
Summer is warm and bright due to the close proximity to the Gulf Stream, with average temperatures in Helsinki ranging from 13.7°C in May to 20.5°C in July; winter months -0.4°C in Dec (31°F) to 6.4°C (44°F) in April.

Language
Finnish - but most young people speak English.

Currency
The Markka or Finnmark, abbreviated to FIM, and divided into 100 pennies (p). Coins are 10p, 50p, 1, 5 and 10 FIM with notes of 20, 50, 100, 500 and 1,000 FIM.

Banks
Open 09.15 - 16.15 hrs Mon - Fri. Outside normal banking hours currency can be exchanged in most hotels or large department stores, or at harbours and railway stations.
Credit cards: are widely accepted in stores, petrol stations and on some campsites.

Post Offices
Open 09.00 - 17.00 hrs, Mon - Fri.

Time
GMT plus 2 hours.

Public Holidays
New Year; Epiphany; Good Fri; Easter Mon; May Day; 1st Sat after Ascension; Whit Sat; All Saints, 1st Sat in Nov; Independence Day, 6 Dec; Christmas, 25, 26 Dec. Other holidays are Vappu Night, 30 Apr, a spring festival and 'Midsummer', nearest Sat to 24 June.

Telephone
The dialling code for Finland is 00358. When calling the UK dial 99044 before the trunk number. Local calls can be made from telephone booths using 1, 5 or 10 FIM coins. Phone-card phones operate on cards purchased in advance (from Teleshops or some post offices).

Shops
Open 09.00 - 17.00 or 18.00 hrs on Mon - Fri and on Sat 09.00 - 14.00 or 15.00 hrs, although supermarkets are usually open to 20.00 hrs during the week. Department stores and shopping malls usually remain open to 18.00 hrs on Sat. The underground shopping arcade adjacent to the main railway station in Helsinki is open until 20.00 hrs every day.
Butane is not available.

Motoring
Main roads in Finland are excellent and relatively uncrowded outside city limits; you can virtually have miles of dual-carriageway or motorway standard roads to yourself. The Finns are very tolerant and cautious drivers and appear to adhere strictly to the speed limits. However, you may encounter a few unsurfaced minor roads off the beaten track but these are usually quite safe for towing, providing you keep your speed down to about 30 mph.
Do not drink and drive as penalties are severe and may even lead to a jail sentence if any alcohol is detected in the blood.
Speed limits: Caravans and motorhomes (3.5 tons) 31 mph (50 kph) in built up areas, caravans 50 mph (80 kph) all other roads, motorhomes 50 - 63 mph (80 - 100 kph) on other roads and 50 - 75 mph (80 - 120 kph) on motorways. Note: there are no emergency phones on the motorway network.
Tolls: There are no toll charges on motorways.

Overnighting
Not allowed outside campsites.

The sites in DENMARK and FINLAND featured in this guide are shown on the maps on page 371

FINLAND

2900 Camping Kokonniemi, Porvoo

Delightful small campsite 50 km. east of Helsinki.

Convenient for the ferry if travelling along the southeast coast, the old town of Porvoo with its waterfront and old wooden houses warrants a stop. This site is 2 km. west of the town and has a garden-like appearance and a white timber reception area with hanging flower baskets. This building, the service buildings and cottages for hire are in an elevated position and backed by tall pines. At a lower level are 36 unmarked caravan pitches (32 with electricity) placed around the perimeter. These pitches are spacious and separated by a variety of shrubs and fruit bushes. Tents are pitched in the more open centre area. Sanitary facilities with white and grey decor are kept very clean and include British style WCs, hot showers (free) with seat, hooks and mat, washbasins with soap, towels, mirror and shaving points. There is a laundry area and a campers' kitchen which doubles for dishwashing. To the side of this building is the barbecue house with pine bench seating. Although beside the Kokonniemi sports centre and lake, on site there is a sauna, volleyball, badminton, bike hire and two children's play areas. Snacks and light meals are available at the café area adjoining reception and a small shop provides milk, bread, ice cream and confectionery.

How to find it: Leave no. 7/E3 Helsinki - Porvoo road at end of motorway and join road 55 for 4 km. Site is clearly signed.

General Details: Open 31 May - 18 August. Small shop. Café. Sauna. Bicycle hire. Badminton. Volleyball. Sports centre and lake adjacent. Barbecue house. Chemical disposal. Cottages for hire.

Charges guide: Per unit FIM 75 with Finnish camping card (85 without) or with Int. camping card 68; every 3rd night 50% off; electricity 18.

Reservations: May be necessary for mid-summer/July: Address: 06100 Porvoo. Tel: (0)19 581 967 or (0)9 6138 3210. FAX: (0)9 713 713.

2903 Camping Kayralampi, Kouvola

Busy southern lakeside site 5 km. from Kouvola in the Province of Kymi.

This campsite appeals to families as it is located near an amusement park which, like the campsite, is run by the Children's Day Foundation. A footbridge leads from the site to the park which is across the road and well away from the site so that no noise carries. The site itself, which is under the control of a manager, is approached by way of a short country roadway leading to reception. Centrally positioned are the timbered service buildings and café. The adequate sanitary blocks with lemon, grey and white decor were very clean when we visited and include British style WCs, facilities for the disabled, washbasins, towels, spacious showers (free) and clothes lockers. There is also a laundry and drying room and a campers' kitchen and dishwashing area. There are 160 unmarked pitches, including the tent area, and 100 have electrical connections (16A). Many pitches are placed between trees and shrubs on level but rough ground, some are in a more open area towards the lake with tents alongside. There are also 35 wooden cottages for hire. Other on site facilities include a double tennis court, minigolf, boats for hire, children's play area, two barbecue houses, 1 smoke and 4 electric saunas. Entrance to the amusement park is free for campers (a pass is given), but amusement rides are charged. Basic food such as bread and milk is sold on site with a supermarket complex within 4 km.

How to find it: Site is at junction of road 6/15, 5 km. east of Kouvola and is clearly signed.

General Details: Open all year. Basic food supplies available. Tennis. Minigolf. Boat hire. Children's play area. Saunas. Barbecue huts. Amusement park. Chemical disposal. Motorcaravan services.

Charges guide: Per caravan or tent incl. 1 person FIM 45, 2-5 persons 70 (without Finnish camping card); with camping card 40 or 65; electricity 16.

Reservations: May be necessary for mid-summer/July: Address: Kanuunakuja 1, 45200 Kouvola. Tel: (0)5 321 1226. FAX: (0)5 321 1203.

2906 Taavetin Lomakeskus Ja Camping, Taavetti

Peaceful campsite on the shores of Lake Kivijärvi.

This campsite is situated in the commune of Luumäki, an area of natural beauty, Kivijärvi being the largest of 50 lakes. At the entrance to the site, just off road no. 6, stand red timbered buildings which house reception, shop, café and restaurant. Beyond this area a road follows the lake to the pitches, sanitary buildings and cottages for hire. There are 28 unmarked caravan pitches all with electrical connections (16A), some amongst the clearing in the trees, others nearer the lakeside. There are also 170 places for tents and 30 cottages for hire. The two sanitary blocks, one of an older design, were clean when we visited with hot showers (free), washbasins, soap dispensers, towels, mirrors, electric points, single WCs, plus some in cabins with washbasins. Other facilities include a campers' kitchen and dishwashing area, washing machine and drying cabinet and waste water point.

continued overleaf

2906 Taavetin Lomakeskus Ja Camping (continued)

The pleasant open style barbecue house, part of the kitchen area, has wooden bench seating. A second is at the beach. There is lake swimming, tennis court, volleyball, crazy golf, TV room, children's play area and 3 saunas. A small shop sells basic groceries such as bread and milk and soft drinks, coffee, snacks, breakfast or dinner can be ordered from the cafe/restaurant. The town of Taavetti is within 4 km, is historically interesting and has an assortment of shops, banks etc.

How to find it: Site is clearly signed, 500 m. from road no. 6 (towards Lappeenranta).

General Details: Open 30 April - 11 August. Small shop. Café/restaurant. Sports facilities as above. Laundry facilities. Chemical disposal.

Charges guide: Per unit FIM 75 - 80 without camping card, with Int. card 58.50 - 60.

Reservations: are advisable for mid-summer/July. Address: 54510 Uro, Taavetti. Tel: (0)5 425 510 or (0)9 6138 3210. FAX: (0)9 713 713.

2909 Camping Ukonniemi, Imatra

Secluded site in South Karelia near one of the highest waterfalls in Finland.

This campsite offers a tranquil location within the Imatra Leisure Centre, 3 km. from the town centre where the incredible Imatra Falls can be seen during the summer season. The Leisure Centre itself covers an area of 600 hectares on the Salpausselka ridge and has a changing terrain to suit many activities, including this 10 hectare campsite. The site is under the control of a manager and is truly 'camping in the trees' with 37 unmarked level pitches, all with electrical connections (10A) and many with water points, plus 84 tent places and 35 cottages. The reception and café area is at the entrance with the sanitary block on the main avenue to the left. Kept clean and well maintained, this is a red timber building with green and white colour scheme. Facilities include free hot showers, washbasins with mirrors, shaver points and cabins with WCs, washbasins, soap dispensers and towels. Facilities for the disabled, dishwashing in a campers' kitchen and a laundry room. There is lake swimming, sauna, fishing, lake cruising, running tracks, a lakeside restaurant, etc. all within the complex. For children, swings are located in the trees plus two play areas with slides, playhouse etc. Bread and milk are on sale at reception with shopping needs, banks, etc. in Imatra. Parts of this town are on the border zone with Russia.

How to find it: From Lappeenranta on road no. 6, site is clearly signed 1 km. after Imatra area sign.

General Details: Open 7 June - 11 August. Cafe. Lakeside restaurant. Bread and milk sold. Children's play areas. Lake swimming. Fishing. Sauna. Chemical disposal. Motorcaravan services.

Charges guide: Per unit FIM 65 with Finnish Camping card, 58 with Int. Camping card; tent incl. 1 person 35; electricity 18.

Reservations: May be advisable for mid-summer/July. Address: Leiritie, 55420 Imatra. Tel: (0)5 472 4055 or (0)9 6138 3210. FAX: (0)9 713 713.

2912 Kultakivi Holiday Village, Punkaharju

Holiday village in forested countryside amid lakes and clearings.

This sprawling, 23 hectare holiday village offers a camping holiday to suit individual needs. You can get away from it all on a quiet secluded lakeside pitch, or participate in the many activities which suit all age groups. At the entrance and parking area stands a large elaborate building housing reception, restaurant and shop. Around this area is the tennis, minigolf, basketball and play area with water slide. The roadways lead into what is best described as a forest park environment with 135 cottages and cabins discreetly situated around the perimeter, mostly at the lakeside. There are 145 caravan pitches with electrical hook-ups (16A) in dry wooded or grassy terrain, with 500 tent places. The main sanitary block, which is well maintained, is situated towards the top of the site beside the TV room, with other WC and shower units at various points. Facilities include British style WCs, washbasins, soap dispensers, towels, mirrors, shaver points and free hot showers. There is a campers' kitchen and a dishwashing and laundry area (incl. in price). Amenities include a barbecue area, 4 family saunas, several beaches and a naturist beach. For the more active there are also jogging tracks and nature trails, fishing, boat and cycle hire. Evening entertainment can include wining, dining or dancing the night away. Although a more lively site, being placed well away from the pitches, the night-time entertainment should not disturb campers.

How to find it: Site is clearly signed off road no. 14, approx. 9 km. south of Punkaharju.

General Details: Open 30 April - 31 Aug. Barbecue area. Jogging and nature trails. Fishing. Boat and bicycle hire. Entertainment. Chemical disposal.

Charges guide: Per unit FIM 70 without camping card, 60 with; electricity 20.

Reservations: Are advisable for mid-summer/July. Address: 58550 Putikko, Punkaharju. Tel: (0)15 645 151. FAX: (0)15 645 110.

FINLAND

2915 Punkaharjun Lomakeskus Ja Camping, Punkaharju

Popular campsite in an area of outstanding beauty.

This campsite is part of a holiday centre and is located near the magnificent Punkaharju ridge. It stands next to the Kesamaa amusement park and enjoys a lakeside environment, making it one of the country's most popular sites. Past the entrance, which is marked by flags, is the reception area and to the right the fun park. There are 500 pitches including tent places, 130 with electrical hook-ups, also many chalets and holiday homes for hire. Some pitches are placed back from the lake, and these are in avenues and separated by shrubs and hedges. Others are by the lakeside and unmarked, with tents to the bottom of the site. The main sanitary block is towards the lake and a smaller one sits further back. Facilities, which are modern and clean, include WCs, washbasins with soap, towels, hand dryer, mirrors, etc. spacious showers (free), and wash cubicles with WCs. Incorporated in the main building are individual campers' kitchens, dishwashing sinks and laundry area. There is also a restaurant and shop with basic groceries, ice cream, etc. The fun park belongs to the campsite but a separate entrance fee is payable. The other on site facilities are netball, tennis, minigolf, lakeside beach, boats and bicycles for hire, barbecue area and 2 saunas. The main attractions outside the holiday centre are the Lusto Forest Museum, Retretti Art Centre and the Valtionhotelli Hotel, the oldest tourist hotel in Finland.

How to find it: Turn off at 'K' sign, 25 km. after Savonlinna on road no. 14 and site is 300 m.

General Details: Camping: 27 May - 26 August; fun park and other accommodation open all year. Restaurant. Small shop. Tennis. Netball. Minigolf. Boat and bicycle hire. Fun park adjacent. Chemical disposal.

Charges guide: Per unit FIM 80 without camping card, with card 75; tent for 1 person 40; electricity 19.

Reservations: Advised mid-summer/July. Address: 58450 Punkaharju 2. Tel: (0)15 739 611. FAX: (0)15 441 784.

2918 Camping Vuohimaki, Savonlinna

Well managed site close to East Finland's most popular resort.

The resort of Savonlinna is built on a chain of islands and is unquestionably the jewel in East Finland's crown. This campsite, on the shores of Lake Pihlajavesi, is only minutes away from the town centre. Although lacking a landscaped appearance it is distinguished by a tall, elegant wooden building, dated late 1800s, which stands to the right of the security barrier and houses reception, restaurant, shop and offices. The camping area is approached by a one way system and there are 100 unmarked pitches for caravans, all with electrical hook-ups, space for 150 tents and 12 cottages for hire. The ground is part sloped, part terraced and the pitches rough but level. This is a more open site than usual, with most of the shade and trees around the perimeter, lakeside and tent area. The two modern sanitary blocks are kept spotlessly clean with grey and white decor and shiny chrome fittings. Facilities include WCs with paper, washbasins, soap and towels, free hot showers and facilities for disabled people. There is a campers' kitchen, dishwashing, barbecue and laundry area with washing machine, clothes line and free hot air dryer. Leisure amenities include volleyball, badminton, minigolf, watersports, boats and bicycle hire and two saunas. For children there are swings and slides. The restaurant serves pizzas, hamburgers, salads, etc. and the shop sells groceries and confectionery.

How to find it: Site is signed off road no. 14, 3 km. west of Savonlinna.

General Details: Open 1 June - mid August. Restaurant. Small shop. Volleyball. Badminton. Watersports. Boat and bicycle hire. Children's play area. Saunas. Chemical disposal. Motorcaravan services.

Charges guide: Per unit FIM 75 with camping card, 85 without; every 3rd night 50% off; 1 person tent 38: electricity.

Reservations: Advisable for mid-summer/July. Address: 57600 Savonlinna. Tel: (0)15 537 353 or (0)9 6138 3210. FAX: (0)9 713 713.

2922 Camping Taipale, Varkaus

Well laid out family run site alongside a lake in North Savo.

The town of Varkaus, known for its paper industry, is surrounded by water and this campsite is located 3 km. from its centre in peaceful surroundings by the water's edge. Its well kept, orderly appearance gives it instant appeal. The reception and café area stand to the left at the entrance and to the right are avenues of individual hardstanding pitches separated by trees and shrubs. There is a total of 90 pitches, some grass and 52 with electrical hook-ups, a large tent area and 16 cottages to hire, placed away from the camping pitches. The grey wooden sanitary block is tastefully decorated with pine interior and grey and white units, all kept spotlessly clean. Facilities include hot showers (free) with curtains, non-slip mats and clothes lockers, WCs with paper, washbasins, long bench mirror and shower for the disabled, etc. There is also a dishwashing area, laundry with drying cabinet and clothes lines. Campers kitchen. Snacks, soft drinks and beer are sold at the café, plus basic foodstuffs and souvenirs. Barbecue house, sauna, lake swimming, beach ball, boat hire, bicycle hire, badminton. For children, wooden toys, slides, etc. are to the fore in a garden like space.

continued overleaf

68

2922 Camping Taipale (continued)

To the rear of the site a gate leads to a park area and a bridge over the old canal, part of the Canal Museum in Varkaus.

How to find It: Site is signed from road no. 5 onto road no. 23, approx. 3 km. from Varkaus at Canal swing bridge.

General Details: Open 25 May - 31 Aug. Café. Sauna. Lake swimming. Boat and bicycle hire. Children's play area. Chemical disposal.

Charges guide: Per unit with camping card FIM 69; without 86; family tent with card 76 or 86; 1 person tent 45.

Reservations: Advised mid-summer/July. Address: Leiritie, 78250 Varkaus. Tel: (0)17 552 6644. FAX: as phone.

2925 Camping Rauhalahti, Kuopio

Large site on the banks of Lake Kallavesi in North Savo.

This site comes highly recommended, with a reputation for being one of the country's finest campsites. It is consistently busy, which creates a constant buzz of activity. Tubs of coloured flowers garland the forecourt and when campers arrive the flag of their country is hoisted, a welcoming touch and a colourful display when all the nations visit. Reception, which offers a 24 hour service, stands close to the entrance and from here the site is laid out in neat avenues with tarmac roads. Pitches are clearly marked and all have hardstanding. The site is level and landscaped, the exception rather than the norm in Finland. This is a more open site than usual, but it still has adequate trees and shrubs with grass areas for awnings separating each of the 237 pitches which include special ones for larger motorcaravans, all with electrical hook-ups. There are also 300 places for tents and 90 cottages for hire. The two timber sanitary blocks were very clean with stainless steel washbasins, mirrors, soap dispensers, electric points, WCs, free hot showers and facilities for the disabled with a shower, WC, and washbasin. There is a baby room, large campers' kitchen/dishwashing, laundry service with free drying cabinets and `Ecopoints' for rubbish disposal. The restaurant offers a choice of menu serving Finnish lunch or snacks, pizzas, etc. and a mini-shop sells basic foodstuffs. This site forms part of the 80 hectare Rauhalahti recreational area and offers a beach and water sports, with equipment for hire and 3 saunas (2 electric 1 smoke). For children there is a play room, puppet theatre, also a TV, swimming pool, tennis courts and much more. It is said Kuopio has three focal points, the Puijo Tower, Kuopio market and its harbour on the shores of the lake, all worth a visit.

How to find It: Site is clearly signed on road no. 5, 7 km. south of Kuopio.

General Details: Open 24 May - 31 Aug. Restaurant (all season). Mini-shop (15/6-15/8). Swimming pool (all season). Fishing. Bicycle hire. Leisure activities detailed above.Chemical disposal.

Charges 1998: Per unit FIM 90 (every 3rd night free); family tent 85; electricity 20. Credit cards accepted.

Reservations: Advisable for mid-summer/July. Address: Kiviniementie, 70700 Kuopio. Tel: (0)17 361 2244. FAX: (0)17 262 4004.

2928 Camping Visulahti, Mikkeli

Excellent campsite and holiday centre within 4 hours drive of Helsinki.

Mikkeli is capital of the Lake District, sitting at the cross-roads of a network of lakes and the labyrinth of Saimaa islands, with more than 3,000 km. of boating routes in its region. On the shores of a Saimaa lake stands this well equipped campsite which appeals to families and varying age groups. The staff are friendly, helpful and dressed in distinctive yellow T-shirts making them easily identified throughout the complex which comprises 30 hectares of landscaped park-land. From reception, immediately beside the security barrier, tarmac roadways lead past the `Dinosauria' and water slides to the right and caravan pitches and tent places to the left. Alongside the camping area stand the restaurant, canteen, coffee pot, shop, vintage car exhibition and wax museum (the only one in Finland we are told). Beyond here the fun park continues with a motor-park and `mini Finland'. Fitting into the layout are cottages and bungalows for hire. There are around 400 pitches for caravans and tents, 200 with electrical hook-ups (16A), unmarked and laid out in avenues. Although it is an open site, shrubs and flower beds divide it into bays in places. Sanitary facilities are housed in two blocks, one facing the caravan pitches and the other by the lakeside. They are kept very clean. There are adequate numbers of WCs, hot showers (free), washbasins with soap, towels, mirrors, etc. and facilities for disabled people. There is also a campers' kitchen, dishwashing and laundry. Barbecue house, sauna and lake swimming. Despite the activity on site the noise level is low, with only slight road traffic during the night. Mikkeli market is worth a visit and a shopping complex with a choice of supermarkets is only minutes away.

How to find It: Site is clearly signed off road no. 5, 5 km. north of Mikkeli.

General Details: Open 18 May - 30 August (Dinosauria, etc. 18 May - 18 August). Fun park with many activities. Restaurant. Barbecue. Sauna. Lake swimming. Chemical disposal. Motorcaravan services.

Charges guide: Per unit FIM 70 without camping card, 60 with card; 1 person tent 35; electricity 17 - 25.

Reservations: Advisable for mid-summer/July. Address: 50180 Mikkeli. Tel: (0)15 18 281. FAX: (0)15 176 209.

FINLAND

2930 Camping Koskenniemi, Hartola

Friendly, family run site in attractive riverside setting.

In the Eastern Hame region, 3 km. from the town of Hartola, this campsite is easily reached from Helsinki within a 2½ hour drive. It is in a delightful, quiet situation tucked in off the road and screened by trees, with a river winding its way through the 5.5 hectare site. Reception is incorporated into the attractive building which is the family home, guest house and restaurant. From here the road follows the river past 150 unmarked pitches for caravans and tents, 80 with electrical hook-ups (16A), sited mostly to the left with 10 wooden chalets spread along the river bank. The terrain is grassy, flat and open with trees interspersed and a pond towards the rear, giving it a garden-like appearance. The excellent sanitary block, adjacent to reception, is clean with modern units. A white wooden building, facilities include British style WCs, washbasins with soap and towels, free hot showers, and good facilities for the disabled with WC, shower and bench. There is a campers' kitchen, dishwashing sinks, laundry area with machines and free drying room. River fishing is available with a licence, and there are boats to hire, minigolf, sauna and conference room, and 2 barbecues, (one outside, one gas under cover). For children there is a play room, a small pool table, TV, books, toys and an outdoor playhouse with sand pit. The restaurant offers a varied menu. Bread and milk can be ordered from reception.

How to find it: Site is clearly signed on left off road no. 59, 3 km. south of Hartola.

General Details: Open all year. Reception. Bread and milk to order. River fishing. Boats to hire. Bicycle hire. Minigolf. Sauna. Barbecues. Play room. Chemical disposal. Motorcaravan services.

Charges 1997: Per unit FIM 75 with camping card; 1 person tent 40; electricity 15.

Reservations: May be necessary for mid-summer/July. Address: 19600 Hartola. Tel: (0)3 716 1135. FAX: (0)3 716 1086.

2932 Camping Sysmä, Sysmä

Family run site with lots of atmosphere, scenically situated on shores of Lake Päijänne.

This site is set on Finland's second largest lake, referred to as 'the pearl of the Finnish lakes' and 'the lake you can drink'. Here the air is pure with miles of countryside all around. Camping Sysmä, within walking distance of the village, has instant appeal. The reception and café area, with flower baskets and a smell of fresh coffee, stands by the entrance. The owner is friendly and smiling and the busy staff were getting the site fully operational for the season when we visited, the week after opening. There are 150 pitches for caravans and tents, 38 with electrical hook-ups (10A), plus 12 bungalows to hire. Pitches are placed amid many varieties of trees and by the water's edge, giving an overall attractive appearance. Although the various buildings of wooden construction that house all the sanitary and other site facilities look their age, even on the dilapidated side, everything inside was neat, tidy and clean. The facilities in the toilet area include British style WCs, washbasins with soap dispensers and towels, hair dryers, free hot showers with mats and bench seating. Plans are in hand to replace the buildings. There is a campers' kitchen, dishwashing sinks and laundry area. For leisure there is a TV room with comfortable chairs and log fire, table tennis, children's swimming pool and play area, water sports and boats and canoes for hire. Snacks are served at the café and there is a shop and garage at the gate, although all necessary shops, banks, etc. are to be found in Sysmä.

How to find it: Site is clearly signed 600 m. from the village of Sysmä on road no. 314.

General Details: Open 1 June - 31 Aug. Café. Shop at gate. TV room. Table tennis. Children's pool. Play area. Watersports. Boat hire. Chemical disposal. Motorcaravan services.

Charges guide: Per unit FIM 55 with camping card; electricity 15.

Reservations: May be necessary for mid-summer/July. Huitilantie 3, 19700 Sysmä. Tel: (0)3/7171386 or (0)3/7177316. FAX: (0)3/7172361. E-mail: raija.hanninen@sci.fi.

N0404 Domaine Naturist Castillon de Provence, Castellane, France

This naturist site with spectacular views in 45 hectares of fairly wild Provencal countryside near the Gorges du Verdon has been in the guide for a number of years but is now up for sale. The owners, Pascal and Malon Pourrier, have asked us to make readers aware of this as perhaps someone may be interested. We have a full site report if any reader requires further information about staying on the site, but any potential buyer should contact the Pourriers direct at:

La Grande Terre, La Baume, 04120 Castellane, France.
Tel: (0)4.92.83.64.24. Fax: (0)4.92.83.68.79 (winter, as telephone).

FRANCE

France has such a variety of scenery from the mountain ranges of the Alps and the Pyrénées, the central massif, the river valleys of the Loire, Rhône and Dordogne, some 1,800 miles of coastline; and is so rich in history with its Gothic cathedrals of the north, the Romanesque churches of the centre and the west, the chateaux of the Loire, the prehistoric cave paintings of the Dordogne that it would take a life time to exhaust all the visit possibilities. Each area of the country looks different, feels different, has its own style of architecture and food, and often its own dialect giving a very strong sense of regional identity. Administratively, France is divided into Régions, which are then subdivided into Départements (95 in total) with an official number which forms the 'root' of the post code. The French Départements are roughly the equivalent of English counties. For further information contact:

The French Government Tourist Office (FGTO), 178 Piccadilly, London W1V 0AL

Tel: 0891 244123 (premium rate). Fax: 0171 493 6594

Population
57,800,000 (94), density 106 per sq.km.

Capital
Paris.

Climate
France has a temperate climate but it varies considerably, for example, Brittany has a climate similar to that of Devon and Cornwall, whilst the Mediterranean coast enjoys a subtropical climate.

Language
Obviously French is spoken throughout the country but there are many local dialects and variations so do not despair if you have greater problems understanding in some areas than in others. We notice an increase in the amount of English understood and spoken.

Currency
French currency is the Franc (subdivided into 100 centimes) in notes of Ffr. 500, 100, 50, and 20, and coins of Ffr. 10, 5, 2, 1 and 50c, 20c, 10c, 5c.

Banks
Open weekdays 09.00-1200 and 14.00-16.00. Some provincial banks are open Tues-Sat 09.00-12.00 and 14.00-16.00.
Credit Cards: Most major credit cards accepted in most outlets and for motorway tolls.

Post Offices
The French term for post office is either PTT or Bureau de Poste. They are generally open Mon-Fri 08.00-19.00 and Saturday 08.00-12.00 and can close for lunch 12.00-14.00. You can buy stamps with less queuing from Tabacs (tobacconists).

Time
GMT plus 1 (summer BST + 1) but there is a period of about three to four weeks in October when the times coincide.

Telephone
From the UK dial 00 33, followed by the 10 figure local number MINUS the initial "0" - in other words from the UK you will dial 0033 followed by the last NINE digits of the telephone number. To the UK from France dial 0044. Many public phone boxes now only take phone cards. (Telecarte) These can be purchased from post offices, tabacs, and some campsites.

Public Holidays
New Year; Easter Mon; Labour Day; VE Day, 8 May; Ascension; Whit Mon; Bastille Day, 14 July; Assumption, 15 Aug; All Saints, 1 Nov; Armistice Day, 11 Nov; Christmas, 25 Dec.

Shops
Often close on Mon, all or half day and for 2 hours daily for lunch. Food shops open on Sun morning.

Motoring
France has a comprehensive road system from motorways (Autoroutes), Routes Nationales (N roads), Routes Départmentales (D roads) down to purely local C class roads.
Tolls: Payable on the autoroute network which is extensive but expensive. Tolls are also payable on certain bridges such as the one from the Ile de Ré to the mainland and the Pont de St Nazaire.
Speed Restrictions: Built-up areas 31 mph (50 kph), on normal roads 56 mph (90 kph); on dual carriageways separated by a central reservation 69 mph (110 kph), on toll motorways 80 mph (130 kph). In wet weather, limits outside built-up areas are reduced to 50mph (80 kph), 62 mph (100 kph) and 69 mph (110 kph) on motorways. A minimum speed limit of 50 mph (80 kph) exists in the outside lane of motorways during daylight, on level ground and with good visibility.
These limits also apply to private cars towing a caravan, if the latter's weight does not exceed that of the car. Where it does by 30%, limit is 40 mph (65 kph) and if more than 30%, 28 mph (45 kph).
Fuel: Diesel sold at pumps marked 'gaz-oil'.
Parking: Usual restrictions as in UK. In Paris and larger cities, there is a Blue Zone where parking discs must be used, obtainable from police stations, tourist offices and some shops.

Overnighting
Allowed provided permission has been obtained, except near the water's edge or at a large seaside resort. Casual camping is prohibited in state forests, national parks in the Départements of the Landes and Gironde, in the Camargue and also restricted in the south because of the danger of fire. However overnight stops on parking areas of a motorway are tolerated but not in a lay-by.

Useful Addresses
Automobile Club de France
FIA, 6-8 Place de la Concorde, 75008 Paris.
Tel: 01 43 12 43 12
Office hours Mon-Fri 0900-1800.
Automobile Club National
 (ACN), FIA & AIT, 5 ruee Auber, 75009 Paris.
Tel: 01 44 51 53 99.

0200 Camping Caravaning du Vivier aux Carpes, Seraucourt-le-Grand

Small, quiet site, close to A26, two hours from Calais, ideal for overnight or longer stay.

This relatively new site is imaginatively set out taking full benefit of large ponds which are well stocked for fishing (cost Ffr. 35). There is also abundant wild life. The 60 well spaced pitches, all at least 100 sq.m. are on flat grass and dividing hedges are growing. All have electricity (6A), some also with water points and there are special pitches for motorcaravans. The site has a comfortable feel, close to the village centre, but quiet. The spacious, clean sanitary block with British style WCs has separate, heated facilities for disabled visitors, also available to other campers in the winter months. Laundry. Upstairs is a large TV/games room with table tennis and snooker. Small children's play area and a petanque court. There is, however, plenty to see in the area, with the cathedral cities of St Quentin, Reims, Amiens and Laon close, Disneyland is just over an hour away, Compiegne and the WW1 battlefields are near and Paris easily reachable by train (1¼ hrs from St. Quentin). Day trips arranged for 10-18 people to Paris (Ffr 160 p.p) or to Disneyland with an English speaking guide. The enthusiastic owners speak excellent English. No restaurant on site, but good, reasonable hotels close. Gates close 10 pm, office open 10-11.30 am. and 5-7 pm. Motorcaravan services. Caravan storage. Rallies welcome.

Directions: Leave A26 (Calais-Reims) road at exit 11 and take D1 left towards Soissons. On entering Essigny-la-Grand (4 km.) turn sharp right on D72 signed Seraucourt-le-Grand (5 km). Site clearly signed (in centre of village).

Charges 1998: Per unit incl. 2 persons and electricity Ffr. 90.00; extra person 15.00; child (under 10 yrs) 10.00; pet 5.00. Discounts for students with tents. Credit cards accepted for min. Ffr. 200.

Open: All year except Xmas - New Year.

Reservations: Recommended for peak season. Address: 10 Rue Charles Voyeux, 02790 Seraucourt-le-Grand. Tel: (0)3.23.60.50.10 (French) or (0)3.23.60.51.02 (English). FAX: (0)3.23.60.51.69.

0401 Hotel de Plein Air L'Hippocampe, Volonne, nr Sisteron

Attractive, friendly site with good pool complex and sports opportunities.

Here is a site set in one of the most beautiful and unspoilt regions of France, the Haute-Provence. The air is clear and the smells of the thyme, lavender and other wild herbs have to be experienced to be believed. The site, started by Mme. Bravay and now in the hands of her sons, has a family feel to it. There are 447 pitches, 350 with 6A electricity, 334 with water also. Pitches are level, numbered and well marked by bushes, olives and cherry trees which not only make an attractive setting but also provide some welcome shade. The toilet blocks vary from quite old to very modern. All WCs are British style, all hot water is free and the washbasins are in cabins. Washing machines, chemical disposal and motorcaravan services. Bar, self service restaurant, takeaway and pizzeria (15/5-15/9). Small shop (July/Aug). The attractively designed swimming pool complex (heated from 1/5) is excellent with a swimming and diving pool, another large pool not quite so deep and a paddling pool. Games, aerobics and club for 7-12 yr olds in high season. Tennis (free outside 3/7-21/8), table tennis and archery. Weekly show. Soundproof disco away from the pitches. Fishing on site. The village is 600 m. The famous Gorge du Verdon is a sight not to miss and rafting and canoeing trips can be arranged from the site information office. Many lesser known gorges and mountains wait to be explored and expeditions are organised. This is a very busy site, with lots going on for teenagers. Mobile homes to hire.

Directions: Approaching from the north turn off N85 across river bridge to Volonne, then right to site. From the south right on D4 1 km. before Château Arnoux.

Charges 1997: Per unit with 2 persons basic pitch: Ffr. 58.00 - 115.00, with electricity 72.00 - 140.00, with water/drainage 100 sq.m. 72.00 - 153.00, 140 sq.m. 72.00 - 173.00; extra person (over 4 yrs) 11.00 - 25.00; extra car or m/cycle 10.00 - 12.00; dog 8.00 - 10.00; local tax 0.50 - 1.50. Low season offers. Credit cards accepted.

Open: 1 April - 30 September.

Reservations: Made with deposit and booking fee (Ffr. 130). Address: Rte Napoléon, 04290 Volonne. Tel: (0)4.92.33.50.00. FAX: (0)4.92.33.50.49.

AR Discount
Less 10%

See colour advert
between pages 96/97

0301 Camping de la Filature, Ebreuil

Small peaceful riverside site with a difference.

This is a lesser known area of France and is consequently quite unspoilt. La Filature was originally developed around a spinning mill and today the hot water is still provided by log fires. The site has an individuality not normally evident in French sites which its English owners hope to maintain. Lying alongside the River Sioule, it has 50 spacious pitches, all grass with a little shade provided by mature fruit trees and electrical connections (3-6A). The sanitary facilities are all in converted original buildings. The majority of the WCs are British style, all the washbasins are in private cabins and the showers are controllable. There is provision for disabled people and a good bathroom with bath and washbasin. Everywhere is tiled and clean with free hot water. Dish and clothes washing sinks also have free hot water and there is a washing machine. The river is shallow in the summer but that means it is safer for paddlers and it is suitable for swimming a 10 minute walk away. Fishing on site. The area is said to be good for mountain biking (bicycle hire near) and facilities for riding, canoeing, bird-watching and tennis are also near. Bread can be ordered daily from the small shop and the restaurant offers traditional French or straightforward English style cooking. Weekly barbecue in high season. The bar has been extended to include tables inside or outside on a terrace. Minigolf, a play area, table tennis and table football are there for the children. Being only an easy 6 km. from the autoroute, it is ideal for a night halt, but you will probably want to stay longer. Mobile homes for hire (details from site).

Directions: Site signed at exit 12 of the A71 autoroute to Clermont Ferrand in the direction of Ebreuil. Site is west of Ebreuil beside the river.

Charges 1997: Per unit incl. 2 persons Ffr. 75.00 - 80.00; extra adult 25.00; child (under 16 yrs) 12.00; electricity 3A 10.00, 6A 18.00. Low season reductions and 'meals included' arrangements. Credit cards accepted.

Open: 31 March - 1 October.

Reservations: Made with deposit (Ffr 200 per week of stay or full amount if stay costs less). Address: 03450 Ebreuil. Tel: (0)4.70.90.72.01. FAX: (0)4.70.90.79.48.

Don't wait to die to go to heaven,

COME TO THE CAMPING DE LA FILATURE!

- Very clean facilities and a bathroom
- Really hot water • Excellent take away with pizza and barbecue evenings in high season
- Bar and terrace with Happy Hour
- Low season bargains for long stays
- Children up to 16 charged child rate
- Near to A71 for stopover or long stay

Camping de la Filature
★ ★ ★ ★
Tel: (00 33) 4 70 90 72 01
FAX: (00 33) 4 70 90 79 48

0402 Castel Camping du Verdon, Castellane

Good site with swimming pool close to 'Route des Alpes' and Gorges du Verdon.

As you drive into Camp du Verdon, the neat and tidy air of the place is very striking. This is a very popular holiday area, the gorge, canoeing and rafting being the main attractions. Two heated swimming pools and numerous on-site activities help to keep non canoeists here. It is a large level site, part meadow, part wooded. The 500 pitches are numbered and separated by newly planted bushes. They vary in size (but mostly over the average) and 420 have 6A electricity, 120 with water and waste water points also. The sanitary blocks are being refurbished. One is already finished with British style WCs and the latest equipment. Showers are pre-set and all facilities have hot water. Three blocks have facilities for disabled people, plus chemical disposal. Washing machines and irons. Motorcaravan services. The restaurant with takeaway is very popular and a pizzeria/crêperie has a terrace and a bar including a room with a log fire for cooler evenings. The two heated swimming pools open all season and a small fishing lake for children is restocked regularly. Children's playgrounds. Minigolf. Archery, volleyball, bicycle hire and table tennis. Entertainers provide games and competitions in July/Aug. Dances and discos suit all age groups (latest finishing time 11 pm). With the facilities open all season, the site is very popular. Used by tour operators. Mobile homes to hire. The river Verdon runs along one edge of the site.

Directions: From Castellane take D952 west towards Gorges du Verdon and Moustiers. Site is 1 km. on left.

Charges 1997: Per unit with up to 3 persons Ffr. 90.00 - 178.00, acc. to season, size and facilities; extra person over 2 yrs 30.00 - 38.00; extra car, tent or caravan 20.00; dog 15.00; local tax 2.00, child (4-12) 1.00.

Open: 15 May - 15 September.

Reservations: Advised for July/Aug. and made for any length with fee (Ffr. 130) and deposit - details from site. Address: Domaine de la Salaou, 04120 Castellane. Tel: (0)4.92.83.61.29. FAX: (0)4.92.83.69.37.

FRANCE - Alpes-Haute-Provence / Alpes-Maritimes

0403 Camping Lac du Moulin de Ventre, Niozelles, Forcalquier

Small, peaceful lakeside site, close to the Luberon.

In the heart of Haute-Provence, near Forcalquier, a busy French town, this is an attractive site situated beside a small lake offering opportunities for swimming (supervised in season), canoeing or for hiring a pedalo and 28 acres of wooded, hilly land available for walking. Trees and shrubs are labelled and the herbs of Provence can be found growing wild. A nature lover's delight - birds and butterflies abound. Some 80 of the 100 level, grassy pitches have electricity (6-10A) and there is some shade from the variety of trees. There is a bar/restaurant with waiter service, takeaway meals and themed evenings (high season). Pizzeria. Children's playground. Sanitary facilities are good, with hot showers, washbasins in cabins and some en-suite cubicles with showers and washbasins. Facilities for disabled people, baby bath, washing machines and fridges for hire. Shop for essentials; supermarket 5 km. Library. Organised activities in high season. Fishing. Apartments, bungalows and caravans to let. Swimming pool with large shallow area (from 1/5). Barbecues permitted in special area only. Site is well situated to visit Mont Ventoux, the Luberon National Park and the Gorges du Verdon. A 'Sites et Paysages' member.

Directions: From A51 autoroute take exit for village of Brillanne and follow N100 east for 3 km. Site is signed near Forcalquier, 3 km. ESE of Niozelles.

Charges 1997: Per unit, incl. 2 persons Ffr. 105.00; extra person 30.00; child (under 4 yrs) 18.00; extra tent 10.00; dog 20.00; electricity (6A) 20.00. Less 20% in low season, 20-60% for longer stays.   `Camping Cheque'

Open: 1 April - 20 October.

Reservations: Advisable for July/Aug. and made with deposit (30% of charge) and fee (Ffr. 100). Address: Niozelles, 04300 Forcalquier. Tel: (0)4.92.78.63.31. FAX: (0)4.92.79.86.92.

0605 Camping La Vieille Ferme, Villeneuve Loubet Plage, nr Antibes

Family owned site with good facilities, open all year, in popular resort area.

La Vieille Ferme is a family owned site with 154 level grass pitches, 106 of them with 2-10A electricity, water and waste water connections and the majority separated by hedges, others simple, small pitches for tents. Also a fully serviced pitch on tarmac for motorhomes. The three toilet blocks (two heated in winter) provide mainly British style WCs, washbasins (some in cabins) and pre-set, well equipped showers. Children's toilets, unit for disabled people, chemical disposal and motorcaravan services. The blocks range from old to brand new, but are all kept very clean. Dish and clothes washing sinks have hot water and there are three washing machines and a dryer. Shop in high season but a drinks, sweets and ices machine is in the TV room for all year use. The swimming pool (20 x 10 m.) is heated and covered for winter use (closed mid Nov-mid Dec) and beside it is a sunbathing area, children's pool and jacuzzi. Table tennis. Boules. Games and competitions organised July/Aug. Bicycle hire. Refrigerator hire and safety deposit boxes. The site aims to cater for all year caravanning and, even though the shop is closed in winter, bread and milk are available to order and there are special winter rates for long stays. English is spoken at reception and the place has a very friendly feel to it. Chalets to let, in winter as well. A 1 km. walk towards Antibes is the railway station, giving access to all the towns along the coast.

Directions: From west take Antibes exit from Esterel autoroute and turn left towards Nice when joining N7 outside Antibes. After 3½ km. on N7 turn left for site. From east take N7 towards Antibes and turn right after Villeneuve Loubet Plage. The turning off the N7, though signed, is not easy to see but, coming from Antibes, it is on the left between Bonne Auberge and Parc de Vaugrenier. Site is 150 m. on right. (Note: avoid N98 Route du Bord de Mer.)

Charges 1997: Per pitch incl. 2 persons: tent Ffr 82.00 - 122.00, caravan 92.00 - 148.00; extra person 21.00 - 26.00; child (under 5) 13.00 - 18.00; extra car 15.00 - 22.00; dog 10.00; electricity 2A 15.00, 6A 20.00, 10A 23.00; local tax 1.00. Less 10-30% for longer stays in low season. Credit cards accepted.

Open: All year

Reservations: Made with 25% deposit and Ffr. 120 fee (high season only); (Sat.-Sat. only in July/Aug. and at Easter). Address: Bvd. des Groules, 06270 Villeneuve Loubet Plage. Tel: (0)4.93.33.41.44. FAX: (0)4.93.33.37.28.

AR Discount
Third person free

0702 Camping-Caravaning L'Ardèchois, St Sauveur-de-Montagut

Well equipped site in spectacular setting.

This site is quite a way off the beaten track and the approach road is winding and narrow in places. It is worth the effort, however, to find such an attractive hillside site offering good amenities and a variety of different types of pitch. All 95 pitches have electricity (6, 10 or 15A) and are said to be 100 sq.m. Some are alongside the small fast-flowing river, while the rest (60%) are on higher, sloping ground nearer the restaurant/bar. The main site access roads are tarmac but are quite steep and larger units may find access difficult to some terraces. The main sanitary block, bar/restaurant, shop and new soundproof 'salle de jeux' have been created by the careful conversion of old buildings and provide modern amenities in an attractive style. (Shop from 15/5, restaurant 1/5). TV room, table tennis, bicycle hire and fishing on site. Heated swimming pool (heated from 1/5) with bar, snack bar and terrace. The sanitary facilities, all recently renovated, are good and provide British toilets, hot showers, washbasins in private cabins etc. A sanitary block of equal quality is beside the riverside pitches. Baths and showers for babies, facilities for disabled people, chemical disposal, dishwashing and laundry rooms are provided. Motorcaravan service point. Chalets and mobile homes for hire. The site owners have developed an extensive and unusual excursion programme for exploring this attractive area on foot or by car. Used by tour operators and popular with the Dutch.

Directions: From Valence take N86 south for 12 km, turn right onto D120 to St. Sauveur de Montagut, then take . the D102 towards Mézilhac for 8 km. to site.

Charges 1998: Per unit incl. 2 persons Ffr 106.00; extra person (incl. children) 20.00; pet 10.00; electricity (6A) 18.00. Less on pitch fees outside July/Aug. Special rate for over 55s outside July/Aug. Credit cards accepted.

Open: 10 April - 20 September. *'Camping Cheque'*

Reservations: Write with deposit (Ffr. 450) and fee (150). Address: 07190 St Sauveur-de-Montagut. Tel: (0)4.75.66.61.87. FAX: (0)4.75.66.63.67.

0705 Camping-Caravaning Le Ranc Davaine, St Alban Auriolles, Ruoms

'Lively but tasteful' - family oriented site in southern Ardèche.

This is a quite large site with an extensive programme of entertainments, especially for families with small children. Although lively, there is nothing 'tacky' about it - even the background music in the attractive partly open air restaurant beside the pool was Baroque, and listening to Bach, Handel and Vivaldi makes a change from Johnny Halliday. The 356 pitches, all of at least reasonable size, are all supplied with electricity (3, 6 or 10A.) and are situated on fairly flat, rather stony, ground under a variety of trees giving plenty of shade. There is an attractive, large, irregularly shaped swimming pool overlooked by terraces and the bar/restaurant which serves a good range of meals in very pleasant surroundings, made more attractive in the evenings by the lighting and floodlighting. The entertainment programme (July/Aug) is extensive and varied with a particular emphasis on the participation by younger children in a quite imaginative way. The five sanitary blocks are all of a good standard, with British style WCs, hot showers with dividers and many washbasins in private cabins. Washing machines, dryer and irons. Amenities include a restaurant, pizzeria and takeaway, large shop, children's play area, tennis, table tennis, archery, minigolf. Extensive programme of watersports and excursions on and to the river Ardèche. Popular with tour operators (45%). A 'Sites et Paysages' member.

Directions: Continue south on D111 after Ruoms. Turn right just before Grospierres on D246, across bridge and then left on D208 towards Chandolas and site.

Charges 1998: Per unit incl. 2 persons Ffr. 85.00 - 138.00, with electricity 107.00 - 160.00; extra person over 2 yrs 24.00 - 32.00; plus local tax; animal free - 12.00.

Open: 1 April - 15 September.

Reservations: Made with deposit (Ffr. 600) and fee (180). Contact site. Address: St Alban Auriolles, 07120 Ruoms. Tel: (0)4.75.39.60.55. FAX: (0)4.75.39.38.50.

FRANCE - Ardèche

0703 Camping Soleil Vivarais, Sampzon, nr Ruoms

Large, quality site bordering the Ardèche river.

Beside the Ardèche river, complete with a sandy beach, Soleil Vivarais offers much to visitors, particularly families with children, be they teenager or toddler. The 200 generously sized, level pitches (23 of which are fully serviced) all have 10A electricity and many are shaded. Four modern, extremely clean sanitary blocks cope well with the demands placed upon them. With a heated babies' and children's room (incorporating several delightful facilities at child height), 6 units for disabled people, ample areas for dishwashing (free hot water), washing machines and dryers, and chemical disposal, there is undoubtedly a full complement of facilities. During the day the proximity of the heated main and toddlers' pools (no bermuda style shorts) to the terraces of the bar and restaurant make it a pleasantly social area. In the evening the stage, with professional lighting and sound, provides an ideal platform for a varied entertainment programme. The disco adjacent to the bar is popular with teenagers (well sound-proofed). The bar/restaurant complex is bright and modern and, in addition to takeaways and pizzas, the restaurant offers a range from set 'table d'hôte' to full 'à la carte' meals. Large shop also with oven for baking bread. An extensive 'animation' programme June, July and Aug. offers water polo, aqua-aerobics, pool games and archery. Minigolf, tennis (both charged), basketball, petanque, table tennis and volleyball. Activities near, many organised with qualified instruction and supervision, include mountain biking (bicycle hire from site), walking, canoeing, rafting, climbing, caving, riding, golf and fishing. Used by tour operators. Chalets, mobile homes and tents available for hire.

Directions: From Le Teil (on N86) take N102 westwards towards and through Villeneuve-de-Berg, disregarding first sign for Vallon-Pont-d'Arc. Continue on N102 before turning left on D103, toward Vogue and Ruoms, then left on D579 to Sampzon. Access to site is via bridge across the river, controlled by lights.

Charges 1998: Per unit incl. 2 persons and electricity Ffr. 109.00 - 174.00; extra person 25.00 - 35.00; child (under 10 yrs) free - 35.00; water/drainage free - 24.00; animal free - 17.00; local tax 2.00 (over 10s). Credit cards accepted.

Open: 1 April - 30 September.

Reservations: Made by fax and credit card or write to site with deposit (Ffr 600) and fee (195). Address: Sampzon, 07120 Ruoms. Tel: (0)4.75.39.67.56. FAX: (0)4.75.93.97.10.

0706 Mondial Camping, Rivière Ardèche, Vallon Pont d'Arc

Attractive family run site beside the river, close to popular, busy resort.

Mondial is a good quality family run site catering for families, and older children should enjoy themselves. It is close to the popular Ardèche resort of Vallon Pont d'Arc but is less frenetic than some of the other sites in this area, with only a few of its 240 pitches taken by tour operators (however, some of these other sites can be noisy). Shrubs separate the pitches and the majority have shade from mature trees. Neatly arranged in short rows, all are of a good size, level and with 6 or 10A electricity. The site itself is quite long and narrow with direct access at the far end to the river for bathing, fishing or canoeing (canoe hire from site) or just watching the river activity. There is a modern bar/restaurant (heated in low season), takeaway and pizzeria, disco 4 nights weekly (until midnight) in high season. Attractive heated pool (no bermuda shorts, etc) with sunbathing areas. All amenities from 1/4. Tennis, volleyball, children's play area, bicycle hire and archery. Shop (28/3-25/9). Three modern sanitary blocks are of a high standard, very clean when seen in high season and with unusually good facilities for disabled people. Comfortable hot showers, a mixture of British and Turkish style WCs (no paper), washbasins in cabins, washing machine and dishwashing. Chemical disposal. Motorcaravan services. The pretty village, with shops, restaurants and bars, is just a short walk, the famous Pont d'Arc is 3 km.

Directions: From Vallon Pont d'Arc take D290 towards Pont St. Esprit - site is on the right side of this road.

Charges 1998: Per unit incl. 2 persons Ffr. 82.00 - 139.00; extra person 30.00 - 34.00; child under 5 yrs 20.00 - 28.00; extra small tent free - 15.00; dog 20.00; electricity 21.00; water/drainage 30.00; local tax 3.00 (over 10 yrs).

Open: 15 March - 30 September.

Reservations: Made with deposit (Ffr. 600) and fee (100). Address: Route Touristiques des Gorges de l'Ardèche, 07150 Vallon-Pont-d'Arc. Tel: (0)4.75.88.00.44. FAX: (0)4.75.37.13.73.

0707 Camping Les Ranchisses, Chassiers, Largentière

Family site on the Route de Valgorge.

The Chevalier family combine farming and wine-making with running a campsite and an Auberge. In a somewhat lesser known area of the Ardèche at Chassiers, on the route de Valgorge, the site started life as `camping à la ferme' but has now developed into a 130 pitch family site with an extensive range of facilities. These include a medium sized, heated pool (from 15/4) with sunbathing areas and, somewhat apart from the pitches, the Auberge developed from an original 1824 building used to house silk-worms. Also open to the public, traditional dishes are served (1/4-15/9) indoors and outside in very attractive surroundings. Shop in high season. The good sized, level, grassy pitches are in two main areas, one older (the original à la ferme) and well shaded, the other newer with recently planted small trees. The great majority have 6A electricity, with 10 fully serviced. *continued overleaf*

0707 Camping Les Ranchisses (continued)

There is frontage onto a small lake which is connected to the river, providing fishing or simple canoeing. Bicycle hire. Two sanitary blocks, one excellent new one with the latest fittings, the other older, smaller one renovated and refurbished to acceptable standards (including British style WCs). Chemical disposal. Washing machine. Both blocks were immaculate when seen in high season. Mobile homes to hire. The medieval village of Largentière (1 km.) has a Tuesday market and a festival in July.

Directions: From Largentière take Route de Valgorge (D24). Les Ranchisses is the first site on the left hand side.

Charges 1998: Per unit incl. 2 persons Ffr. 78.00 - 102.00, comfort pitch 105.00 - 135.00; extra person 16.00 - 25.00; child (under 10 yrs) 12.00 - 20.00; animal free - 6.00; electricity 17.00. Credit cards accepted.

Open: Easter - 27 September.   `Camping Cheque'` `FRENCH FLAVOUR'`

Reservations: Contact site for form; made with Ffr. 500 deposit. Address: Route de Valgorge, Chassiers, 07110 Largentière. Tel: (0)4.75.88.31.97. FAX: (0)4.75.88.32.73.

0709 Castel Camping Domaine des Plantas, Les Ollières-sur-Eyrieux

Good quality campsite in a spectacular setting on the banks of the Eyrieux river.

This site offers an attractive alternative to those in the more popular, and often crowded, southern parts of the Ardèche. The Eyrieux valley is less well known, but arguably just as attractive as those further south and a good deal less crowded, particularly in the main season. Perhaps the only drawback to this site is the narrow twisting 3 km. approach which may present something of a challenge to those with large outfits, although the owners have an ingenious system designed to assist campers on departure. With its own sandy beach beside the quite fast-flowing, but fairly shallow, river (used for bathing) the absence of a swimming pool should present no real deterrent (there are plans to add one). The bar, restaurant and disco are all housed in an original building which is quite impressive with its Protestant history and visible from the main road across the river long before you reach it. Many activities are possible - mountain biking, canoeing, canyoning, riding and `randonnees pedestres'` (sounds better in French!). The pitches are terraced and shaded, so some up and down walking is required. They have 5A electricity (long lead may be needed). One large, central toilet block is in courtyard style with colourful doors, well equipped with washbasins in cubicles, push-button showers, British style toilets and good provision for children. An additional smaller block is for the higher terraces. Washing up, laundry sinks (H&C) and washing machine. Small shop July/Aug, otherwise bread and milk to order. No barbecues July/Aug. Activities and excursions arranged. Adventure play area beside river - near the goats!

Directions: South of Valence exit N86 at La Voulte and follow the D120 west for Les Ollières sur Eyrieux (20 km). After bridge in the village, take left turn and follow sites signs - the road is single track and could be difficult for large units with bends and twists for 3 km. Vans leave the site in timed convoys, otherwise a site car goes in front of you.

Charges 1997: Per unit incl. 2 persons Ffr. 107.00; extra person 20.00; child (under 8 yrs) 10.00; animal 10.00; electricity 20.00; local tax (over 10 yrs) 2.00. Less 30% outside 29/6-25/8.   `Camping Cheque'`

Open: 29 March - 15 September. (all services from 1 June)

Reservations: Made with deposit (Ffr. 400) and fee (120). Address: 07360 Les Ollières-sur-Eyrieux. Tel: (0)4.75.66.21.53. FAX: (0)4.75.66.23.65.

1106 Camping Au Pin d'Arnauteille, Montclar, nr Carcassonne

Peaceful, spacious, developing site with superb views to the Corbières and beyond.

Enjoying some of the best and most varied views, this rather unusual site is ideal for exploring the little known Aude départextement, the area of the Cathars and the walled city of Carcassonne (10 mins drive). However, access could be difficult for large, twin axle vans. The site itself is set in 115 hectares of farmland on hilly ground with the original pitches on gently sloping, lightly wooded land and the new `grand-confort'` ones semi-terraced, on level, hedged places with 3 or 6A electricity, lacking shade at present. A swimming pool with children's pool is in a hollow surrounded by green fields and some of the newer pitches. Sanitary facilities are modern and unisex, the main block part open, part enclosed, with another under the pool, one behind reception and a new small block in the developing area. Facilities include British WCs, hot showers, basins in cabins, dishwashing and laundry, facilities for disabled people. A restaurant in a converted stable block provides plat du jour, grills and takeaway (15/5-15/9). Shop (15/5-15/9 - out of season the site is a little out of the way). Table tennis. Volleyball. Riding. Fishing 2 km. Rafting and canoeing near, many walks with marked paths. Chalets, mobile homes and tents to let. Used by tour operators. A developing site with enthusiastic owners for whom riding is the principle theme with stables on site (note: the French are more relaxed about hard hats, etc).

Directions: On D118 from Carcassonne, bypass village of Rouffiac d'Aude, to small section of dual carriageway. Before end of this, turn right to Montclar up narrow road for 3 km. Site signed sharp left up hill before the village.

Charges 1998: Per pitch incl. 2 persons Ffr. 73.00 - 90.00, pitch with electricity 90.00 - 107.00, with water and drainage 105.00 - 127.00; extra person 18.00 - 23.00; child (under 7 yrs) 12.00 - 15.00; extra car 11.00 - 12.00.

Open: 1 April - 30 September.   `Camping Cheque'`

Reservations: Made with 25% deposit. Address: 11250 Montclar. Tel: (0)4.68.26.84.53. FAX: (0)4.68.26.91.10.

AR Discount
Bottle of quality wine after 5 day stay

FRANCE - Aude / Aveyron

1107 Camping Club Les Mimosas, Narbonne

See colour advert between pages 96/97

Lively site on Mediterranean Littoral, close to beaches at Narbonne and Gruissac.

Being 6 km. inland from the beaches of Narbonne and Gruissac, this site benefits from a somewhat less hectic situation than others in the popular seaside environs of Narbonne. The site itself is, however, quite lively with plenty to amuse and entertain the young while, at the same time, offering facilities for the whole family. Some 75% of the 250 mainly good sized pitches (including a few 'grand confort' ones) have 6A electricity and a reasonable amount of shade. Facilities include a large swimming pool (from mid May) and a smaller one (open earlier) with sunbathing areas, overlooked by a mezzanine level which includes a small lounge, amusements, etc. Three tennis courts, sauna, gym and minigolf, with riding nearby. A lagoon for boating and fishing is accessible via a footpath (about 200 m). The site also includes the rather attractive Auberge Mandirac which offers a comfortable environment and interesting menu for meals. There are four sanitary buildings, two of which have been refurbished to a high standard with baby baths, etc. The other two are of older design but well maintained. The facilities include showers with dividers, some British WCs, washbasins in cabins, hot and cold water, laundry and dishwashing sinks and washing machines. This could be a very useful site offering many possibilities to meet a variety of needs, on-site entertainment (including an evening on 'Cathare' history), and easy access to popular beaches and interesting towns such as Narbonne itself, Beziers or even Carcassonne. Chalets and bungalows to rent.

Directions: From the A9 take exit 38 (Narbonne Sud) and go round roundabout to last exit taking you back over the autoroute (site signed from here). Follow signs to La Nautique then Mandirac and site (total 6 km. from autoroute).

Charges 1997: Per basic pitch incl. 1 or 2 persons Ffr. 63.00 - 84.00, pitch with electricity 84.00 - 99.00, pitch with electricity, water and drainage extra.

Open: 24 March - 31 October.

Reservations: Made with deposit (Ffr. 500) and fee (80). Address: Chaussée de Mandirac, 11100 Narbonne. Tel: (0)4.68.49.03.72. FAX: (0)4.68.49.39.45.

1200 Camping Peyrelade, nr Millau

Attractive site by a pebble beach in the Gorges du Tarn.

Peyrelade is at the foot of the Tarn Gorges, dominated by the ruins of Château de Peyrelade, with the campsite situated on a bend in the river which has thrown up a natural pebble beach. Bathing is safe and the water is clean. Canoes can be hired and the site can arrange for rafting trips and 'canyonning' excursions. There are some 190 level, grassy tourist pitches, all with electrical connections, marked out by trees and shrubs. Shade is very good in most parts. Two conveniently placed toilet blocks with British WCs, one refurbished to a high standard with special miniature facilities for little people! Washing machine, chemical disposal and motorcaravan services. There is a small, attractively designed pool and children's pool (from 1/5) and a children's play area. The site nicely abuts a leisure centre with minigolf and tennis courts, which can be booked at the camp reception. A friendly, comfortable bar and restaurant/pizzeria provides sustenance, including a full takeaway service (all 1/6-1/9). Barbecue area. Games room and mini club. Guided walks and fossil hunting are organised. Fishing. Bicycle hire 200 m. The site is ideal for visiting the Tarn Gorges and other attractions in the area include Roquefort of cheese fame, La Couvertriade (a Knights Templar village) and the eastern Cevennes. The Mediterranean coast is just within range for a day trip. A few tour operator pitches (10%).

Directions: From N9 Sévérac - Millau road, turn east from Aguessac (follow Gorges du Tarn signs). Site is 2 km. past Rivière sur Tarn, on the right - the access road is quite steep.

Charges 1998: Per unit incl. 2 persons Ffr. 85.00 - 110.00; extra adult 16.00 - 20.00; child (under 5) 12.00 - 15.00; dog 7.00; electricity (6A) 18.00; local tax 1.00. Credit cards accepted.

Open: Easter - 15 September.

Reservations: Made with deposit (Ffr. 450) and fee (100). Address: 12640 Rivière -sur-Tarn. Tel: (0)5.65.62.62.54. FAX: (0)5.65.62.65.61.

AR Discount
Free bottle of wine

1202 Les Rivages, Millau

Large site on town outskirts close to Tarn Gorges with good range of sporting facilities.

This site is well organised and is very popular, being close to the high limestone 'Causses' and the various river Gorges, particularly the Tarn, and their associated attractions, such as caves, remote villages, wildlife refuges, etc. Some 314 pitches occupy flat ground adjacent to the Dourbie river, close to its confluence with the Tarn. There is safe river bathing from the river beach. Pitches in the older part of the site are arranged in fours and tend to be a little crowded, with a bare 100 sq.m. space. In a newer, though less shaded part of the site (Camp 2), there is more room. All pitches have electricity (6A), 98 have water and drain points also. Sanitary facilities are good, four modern blocks providing washbasins in cabins, showers and toilets (British and Turkish style), dishwashing and laundry sinks, rooms for disabled people (not all blocks open in low seasons). A special block for children has baby baths, small showers, children's toilets and ironing facilities with a play area beside it. *continued overleaf*

1202 Les Rivages (continued)

A wide range of sporting and cultural options are provided (said to be 26 different activities). On site are indoor and outdoor tennis courts, 2 badminton courts, 2 squash courts, football, volleyball, basketball and two pools. Table tennis. Petanque. Cyclo-cross. Activities on the river, mountain biking, walking, bird watching, fishing and many more, all exclusively for campers in high season. Off-site activities are efficiently publicised. Children's play area and entertainment, with child minding (3-6 yrs). Shop (15/5-15/9), snack bar and restaurant/bar (all season). Gates shut 10 pm.- 8 am. Used by tour operators.

Directions: Site is on the Nant (D991) road out of Millau.

Charges 1998: Per pitch incl. 2 persons Ffr. 74.00 - 107.00, with electricity 85.00 - 125.00, with all services 95.00 - 135.00; extra person (over 3 yrs) 18.00 - 21.00; pet 14.00 - 15.00; local tax (15/6-15/9) 2.00. Credit cards accepted.

Open: 1 May - 30 September.

Reservations: Advisable for Jul/Aug. with deposit (Ffr. 400) and fee (100). Address: Ave. de l'Aigoual, Rte. de Nant, 12100 Millau. Tel: (0)5.65.61.01.07. FAX: (0)5.65.59.03.56.

1201 Castel Camping Val de Cantobre, Nant d'Aveyron, nr Millau

Attractive, terraced site in the valley of the Dourbie.

This site which has been imaginatively and tastefully developed by the Dupond family over a 25 year period, offers a bar, restaurant, pizzeria and takeaway facility. In particular, the magnificent carved features in the bar create a delightful ambience, complemented by a recently built terrace. The ground is hard in summer but reception staff supply robust nails if awning pegs prove a problem. Most pitches (all with electricity and water), are peaceful, generous in size and with views of the valley. Three adjoining swimming pools have a new surround, bedecked by flowers and crowned by a large urn which dispenses water into the paddling pool. The shop, although small, offers a wide variety of provisions; including many regional specialities. Although there are tour operators on many pitches, the terrace design assures peace and privacy. The new sanitary block is impressive and is beautifully appointed, with British WCs and a huge indoor dishwashing area. But it is the activity programme that is unique. Adventurous visitors relish sports like river rafting, white water canoeing, rock climbing or jumps from Millau's hill tops on twin seater steerable parachutes. Around 15 such activities are all supervised by qualified instructors. Passive recreationists appreciate the scenery, especially Cantobre, a medieval village that clings to a cliff in view of the site. Nature lovers will be delighted to see vultures wheeling in the Tarn gorge alongside more humble rural residents. Butterflies in profusion, orchids, huge edible snails, glow worms, families of beavers and the natterjack toad all live here. It is easy to see why - the place is magnificent. Fishing. Mobile homes and chalets for hire.

Directions: Site is 4 km. north of Nant, on D991 road to Millau.

Charges 1998: Per unit incl. 2 persons and 4A electricity 120.00 - 145.00; extra person (4 yrs and over) 20.00 - 32.00; extra car or dog free - 10.00; electricity 10A 10.00. Credit cards accepted.

Open: 15 May - 15 September, with all facilities.   `Camping Cheque' `FRENCH FLAVOUR'

Reservations: Made for any length with deposit (Ffr. 82) and fee (18). Address: 12230 Nant d'Aveyron. Tel: (0)5.65.58.43.00. FAX: (0)5.65.62.10.36.

The following site is included out of order - it should appear on page 93

3206 Camping Lac des Trois Vallées, Lectoure

Large 40 hectare lively site with many facilities.

This site is situated in the Gers countryside in the heart of Gascony, a land of fortified village and `foie gras', near the town of Lectoure which was once the main seat of the Counts of Armagnac and is now a spa town. Lac de Trois Vallées is popular with those who like activities and entertainment. It is, in fact, a large holiday complex and good for families with teenagers. There are three lakes for watersports, fishing, canoeing, surfing and swimming, with four water chutes (open to the public) and an impressive pool complex (with bubble pool), hydro-massage facilities, plus grass and paved sunbathing areas. Lifeguards supervise in season (1/6-10/9). Many activities are organised including tennis, archery and mountain biking, with cabaret and craft activities for all ages. Two restaurants, one beside the pool, the other by the lake (more a snack bar) which also provides takeaway. Three bars include `The Pub' (hours according to season). Mini-market and launderette. We were least impressed with the sanitary provision which is best described as functional. It receives heavy use with maintenance and cleaning suspect at times. There are eight blocks with pre-set hot water, mixed style British and Turkish toilets and open air baby baths. Some up and down walking is required. There are 450 pitches with around 300 for independent units on shaded or open ground, all with electricity (10A). High tour operator presence.

Directions: Site signed 2 km. outside Lectoure to the south, off the N21.

Charges 1997: Per unit incl. 3 persons Ffr. 111.00 - 159.00, with electricity 125.00 - 179.00, with water also 132.00 - 189.00; extra person 26.50 - 38.00; dog 7.00 - 10.00. Special weekly rates available.

Open: Easter - 14 September.   `Camping Cheque'

Reservations: Made with deposit (Ffr. 500) and non-refundable fee (150). Address: 32700 Lectoure. Tel: (0)5.62.68.82.33. FAX: (0)5.62.68.88.82.

1407 Camping de la Vallée, Houlgate

Fresh, well kept site, close to lively little resort of Houlgate.

Camping de la Vallée's owners provide a warm welcome and the attractive site has well maintained, good facilities. Situated on a grassy hillside overlooking Houlgate, the 270 pitches are large and open, with hedging planted and all have electricity. Part of the site is sloping, the rest level, with gravel or tarmac roads. An old farmhouse has been converted to house a rustic bar and comfortable TV lounge and billiards room. Heated swimming pool (from 15/5) and tennis court. Shop. Small snack-bar with takeaway in season (from 15/5). A large grassy area has a children's playground, volleyball and a football field. Tennis. Bicycle hire. Petanque. Organised entertainment in July/Aug. Three toilet blocks of a good standard have free hot water in controllable, well fitted showers; washbasins in cabins; mainly British toilets. Facilities for disabled people and baby bathroom. Dishwashing. Laundry with machines, dryers and ironing boards (no lines allowed), chemical disposal and motor- caravan services. The beach is 1 km, the town 900 m. Championship golf course near. English spoken in season. Popular with tour operators. Very busy in high season, maintenance and cleaning could be variable at that time.

Directions: Site is 1 km. from Houlgate, along D24A (route de Lisieux). Turn right onto D24, rue de la Vallée and look for site sign.

Charges 1998: Per person Ffr. 30.00; child (under 7) 20.00; pitch 45.00, with services 50.00; dog on lead 15.00; electricity 2A 18.00, 4A 20.00, 6A 25.00; local tax 2.00. Less 10% outside main season. Credit cards accepted.

Open: 1 April - 30 September.

Reservations: Made with deposit (Ffr. 400) and fee (100) - write to site. Address: 88 rue de la Vallée, 14510 Houlgate. Tel: (0)2.31.24.40.69. FAX: (0)2.31.28.08.29.

Camping de la Vallée

★★★★

SHOP □ BAR □ GAMES ROOM
HEATED SWIMMING POOL □ TENNIS
CHILDREN'S POOL □ ENTERTAINMENT

88, Rue de la Vallée - 14510 Houlgate
Tel: 02.31.24.40.69

1602 Castel Camping Gorges du Chambon, Eymouthiers, nr Montbron

Attractive family site in pretty, rolling Charente countryside.

This nicely developed site which is under British ownership, is arranged around a restored Charente farmhouse and its outbuildings. It provides high quality facilities in an attractive, spacious setting with 120 large, marked pitches with electrical connections, on gently sloping grass and enjoying extensive views over the countryside. The pitches are arranged in two circular groups with a sanitary block at the centre of each. Built in a traditional style, internally the blocks provide good modern facilities with British style WCs, hot showers and washbasins in private cabins. There are facilities for disabled people, a baby bath, chemical disposal, laundry facilities including tumble dryer, and good dishwashing rooms. To one side is the swimming pool (18 x 7 m) and minigolf. Converted from an old barn with an interesting gallery arrangement, are a bar and restaurant, plus takeaway which includes pizzas (at least 1/6-31/8). Games room, TV and table tennis, etc. Small shop for basics in reception (closes at 7 pm.) where bread can be ordered the night before. Tennis. Bicycle hire. Children's play area. Fishing 200 m. Caravans and gite to let. No animals accepted in July/Aug.

Directions: From N141 Angoulême - Limoges road at Rochefoucauld take D6 to Montbron village. Follow D6 in direction of Piegut-Pluviers and site is signed down country road past holiday complex.

Charges 1997: Per pitch Ffr 38.00; person 28.00; child (under 7 yrs) 14.00; car 12.00; electricity (6A) 20.00; local tax (adults) 1.00. Less 15% (not electricity) outside July/Aug. Credit cards accepted.

Open: 15 May - 15 September.

Reservations: Necessary for July/Aug. Write to site with min. Ffr. 200 deposit and fee (80). Address: Eymouthiers, 16220 Montbron. Tel: (0)5.45.70.71.70. FAX: (0)5.45.70.80.02.

1603M Camping Municipal Le Champion, Mansle

Le Champion is a convenient stop-over on the N10 or a good base to explore the northern Charente area. Beside the Charente river, the site has a cool, relaxing and peaceful atmosphere created by its attractive location, with a natural combination of trees, weirs and running water - ideal for fishermen, and canoes are also allowed. The site itself is mostly open with little shade and has 100 standard sized pitches, all with electricity (10A) and water points. The main sanitary block is kept in immaculate condition and is modern, tiled, with free hot water throughout. An additional smaller, older block is in the tent area at the rear of the site. These provide push-button showers, washbasins in cabins, British WCs and facilities for the disabled. Dishwashing and laundry facilities also. Two privately owned restaurants are situated at the site entrance. One is attractively tented and both have al fresco facilities and snack bar priced food. The town and shops are 200 m. over the bridge (but bread van calls in mornings) with a market on Tuesday and Friday mornings and farm produce on Saturday mornings. Swimming pool in town, recreational area and sports ground next to the site, with plenty of space for children (where most of the town's social activities are held). The local Syndicate d'Initiative calls at the site to advise on trips and activities, eg. cycle tracking (one or two days), coach trips, open air cinema, climbing tuition, canoeing courses, etc. Trout fishing in nearby lake and river fishing (permits needed). Canoe and bicycle hire.

Directions: Site is well signed off the N10 (in town of Mansle), 30 km. north of Angoulême.

Charges 1997: Per pitch Ffr. 15.00; adult 10.00; child (under 7 yrs) 5.00; caravan or tent 10.00; vehicle 10.00; motorcaravan (incl. 2 persons) 60.00; electricity 15.00.

Open: 15 May - 15 September.

Reservations: Bookings accepted without deposit on Alan Rogers' booking form, although not usually necessary. Address: 16230 Mansle. Tel: (0)5.45.20.31.41. FAX: (0)5.45.20.30.40.

1605M Camping Municipal de Cognac, Cognac

If you're a lover of brandy, this area is a must, with abundant vineyards and little roadside chalets offering tastings of Pineau (a Cognac based aperitif) and a vast range of Cognacs. This municipal site by the Charente river is convenient as a night stop or longer stay to visit the area, and for sleeping off the effects of the `tastings' - you probably won't even notice the slight noise from the nearby road! The 165 large pitches, all with 5A electricity, are neatly laid out and separated by shrubs and trees. Two good, modern toilet blocks have mixed British and Turkish style WCs, including children's toilets and chemical disposal. Push-button showers with free hot water, washbasins in private cabins, dishwashing and laundry sinks and a washing machine. There is a small swimming pool on the site (1/6-1/10) or the municipal pool is nearby. Restaurants, bars and shops may be found in the town centre, although the site offers a snack bar and entertainment in July/Aug. Other on-site amenities include bicycle hire, volleyball, table tennis, a children's play area on grass and a sand pit. Motorcycles are restricted. The famous Cognac Houses (Pineau, Hennessy, Martell, Remy Martin, etc.) and the Cognac Museum may be visited but there is no public transport to the town centre (2.3 km). Riverside walks.

Directions: Site is signed from the N141 Saintes - Angoulême road following signs for the town centre. It is to the north of the town beside the river on the road to Ste-Sévère.

Charges 1997: Per pitch incl. 4 persons Ffr. 100.00; extra person 16.00; child (0-7 yrs) 11.00. Less in low season. Less 10% for 4 days, 20% for 7 days.

Open: 1 May - 31 October.

Reservations: Recommended in high season. Write for more information to Office de Tourisme de Cognac, 16 Rue du 14 Juillet, 16100 Cognac. Tel: (0)5.45.82.10.71. FAX: (0)5.45.82.34.47. Address: Bvd. de Chatenay, Rte. de Ste-Sévère, 16100 Cognac. Tel: (0)5.45.32.13.32.

FRANCE - Charente-Maritime / Corsica

1704 Camping International Bonne Anse Plage, La Palmyre

Spacious, well organised, family run site amongst shady pine trees with large pool.

On the edge of the Forêt de la Coubre, just beyond the popular resort of La Palmyre, Bonne Anse has a lovely setting amongst pine trees, just a short stroll from the sweeping sands which almost surround an interesting inlet from the sea (now very tidal). It is a gently undulating site, carefully designed to provide 850 level, marked pitches, of which 600 have electricity (6/8A). Most are shaded by the pines, the ones nearer the sea, less so (these rather sandy). Amenities centred around the well designed entrance include a restaurant/bar with terrace forming the site's social focus. Opposite is a splendid swimming pool complex. Shopping centre (all season) with supermarket, takeaway, other shops and launderette. Good children's playground, video games, TV (satellite) and table tennis. Entertainment and dancing in season, Direct access to cycle tracks (bicycle hire) and many supervised beaches close, also a fitness track. Seven sanitary blocks (two new, with further replacements planned) provide free hot water, washbasins in cabins, British WCs, hot and cold showers and facilities for disabled people and babies. Washing up and laundry sinks under cover. Favoured by tour operators, this is a busy site in an area popular with the British. English is spoken. Motorcaravan services. No dogs. Mobile homes for rent.

Directions: Leave A10 autoroute at Saintes and head for Royan (N150). In Royan take signs for La Palmyre (D25). At La Palmyre roundabout follow signs for Ronce-les-Bains and site is 1 km. on the left.

Charges 1998: Per unit incl. 3 persons Ffr. 157.00; incl. 1 or 2 persons 131.00; local tax 2.00 or child (4-10) 1.00; extra person (over 1 yr) 38.00; electricity (6A) 25.00. Up to 40% discount on reservation. Credit cards accepted.

Open: 24 May - 7 September.

Reservations: Min. 5 days - phone, fax or write for details. Address: 17570 La Palmyre. Tel: (0)5.46.22.40.90. FAX: (0)5.46.22.42.30. E-mail: bonne-anse@wannadoo.fr. Internet: http://oda.fr/aa/bonne-anse-plage.

1705 Camping L'Orée du Bois, La Fouasse, Les Mathes

Large, attractive site amidst beautiful pines and oaks of the Forêt de la Coubre.

L'Orée du Bois has 400 pitches of about 100 sq.m. in a very spacious, pinewood setting. These include 40 extra large pitches with hardstanding and individual sanitary facilities in small blocks of four. Pitches are on flat, fairly sandy ground, separated by trees, shrubs and hedges and all have electricity (6A). There are 45 mobile homes (for hire) and tour operators use the site. The four main sanitary blocks are attractively designed with good modern fittings. British style WCs and free hot water to controllable showers and washbasins in cabins). Three blocks have laundry rooms and washing up is under cover. All have units for the disabled. The excellent bar, restaurant and crêperie have terraces overlooking the large swimming pools, including water toboggan, and paddling pool (proper swimming trunks). Takeaway and shop. Tennis, boules, games room, TV, bicycle hire, children's play areas, volleyball and table tennis. Discos and free children's entertainment in July/Aug. Fairly near are sandy beaches plus walking, riding or cycling in the 10,000 ha. forest. Only gas barbecues allowed. Mobile homes for hire.

Directions: From the north follow D14 La Tremblade road. At Arvert turn onto D141 to Les Mathes and turn east, signed La Palmyre, to second roundabout where site signed. From the south, at Royan take D25 towards La Palmyre, then towards Les Mathes to roundabout where site is signed.

Charges 1998: Per unit incl. 2 persons Ffr 85.00 - 155.00, with private sanitary facilities 125.00 - 205.00; extra person (over 3 yrs) 25.00; local tax 2.00 (child 4-10 yrs 1.00); animal 10.00. Less 10-15% for booked stays.

Open: 15 May - 15 September.

Reservations: Made with 30% deposit plus fee (Ffr 130). Address: 225 Rte. de la Bouverie, La Fouasse, 17570 Les Mathes. Tel: (0)5.46.22.42.43. FAX: (0)5.46.22.54.76. Internet: http://ww.oda.fr/ab/oreedubois.

2001 Camping Arinella Bianca, Ghisonaccia

Very well designed, family run, beach side site on Corsica's east coast.

This site is a tribute to its owner's design skills as it appears to be in entirely natural 'glades' where, in fact, these have been created from former marshland with a fresh water lake. The 300 marked pitches, all with 6A electricity, are on flat grass among a variety of trees and shrubs, providing ample shade. They are irregularly arranged, but all of a good size. The site is right by a sandy beach which extends a long way either side of the attractive central complex of restaurant, shop, bar, amphitheatre, snack bar, etc. (all from 10/5) which, together with the swimming pool, form the hub of this site. Four open plan sanitary blocks have free pre-set showers (some with dressing area), washbasins in cabins and mainly British style WCs. Open air washing up. Laundry with machines and boards. Sports and leisure facilities at or adjacent to the site, include windsurfing, canoeing, bicycle hire, tennis, riding, children's mini-club and play area. Entertainment programme in main season. Used by tour operators. Bungalows for rent.

Directions: From N198 after entering Ghisonaccia look out for 'Route de la Mer' (D144) and site is on left (narrow turn) approaching south end of village (many other sites also signed at turn leading to site).

Charges 1997: Per person Ffr. 43.00; child (up to 7 yrs) 22.00; pitch 19.00; car 11.00; electricity (6A) 18.00; local tax 2.00 (child 1.00). Credit cards accepted.

Open: 1 April - 15 October.   `Camping Cheque'

Reservations: Write to site. Address: 20240 Ghisonaccia. Tel: (0)4.95.56.04.78 or (0)4.95.56.12.54.

2203 Camping Nautic International, Caurel, Mur-de-Bretagne, nr Pontivy

Small, friendly, lakeside site in central Brittany with facilities for watersports.

Nautic is attractively situated on the north shore of the long, sinuous Lac de Guerledan, which is used for all sorts of watersports. There are pleasant walks around the lake, countryside and forests. The site is terraced to the lake shore and provides 120 level pitches, all with electricity (6A), 38 larger and fully serviced, in peaceful, wooded surroundings. An imaginatively designed swimming pool and smaller pool are heated by a wood burning stove in season (15/6-15/9). Two blocks provide mostly British style toilets, hot showers, some wash cabins, a toilet for disabled people and facilities for babies. Shop and limited takeaway (July/Aug), TV and video room. Sauna, solarium and fitness room. Children's play area, games room, tennis, table tennis, volleyball. Fishing. Watersports and riding near. Motorcaravan service point on payment. Super restaurant near, bar/crêperie next door. A `Sites et Paysages' member.

Directions: Turn off N164 between Mur-de-Bretagne and Gouarec to Caurel village and follow camp signs.

Charges 1998: Per person Ffr. 21.00 - 26.00; child (under 7) 12.00 - 17.00; local tax (July/Aug, over 10 yrs) 1.00; pitch 35.00 - 45.00, fully serviced 70.00; car 10.00; electricity (6A) 19.00.

Open: 1 April - 25 September.

Reservations: Write to site. Address: Rte de Beau-Rivage, 22530 Caurel.
Tel: (0)2.96.28.57.94. FAX: (0)2.96.28.02.00.

AR Discount
Free washing machine token

2204 Camping Le Châtelet, St Cast le Guildo, nr St Malo

Pleasant site with views over the bay and steep path down to beach.

Carefully developed over the years, Le Châtelet is pleasantly and quietly situated with views over the estuary from many pitches. It is well laid out, mainly in terraces, with 190 individual pitches of good size marked out by hedge separators; all have electricity and 30 water and drainage also. A `green' walking area is a nice feature around the lower edge. Two toilet blocks, one above the other but with access at different levels, have mainly British style WCs, plentiful washbasins in cabins, pre-set free hot water in these and the showers, and toilets and showers for children. Small night units at the extremities of the site. Chemical disposal. Motorcaravan services. A little lake (unfenced) can be used for fishing. An attractive, landscaped area has a heated swimming pool and children's pool (from 15/5). Small children's play area. Shop and takeaway (from 15/5). Bar lounge and general room with satellite TV, pool table; dancing weekly in season. Games room with table tennis, amusement machines. Organised games and activities in season. A path leads directly down to a beach (about 150 m. but with steps). St Cast, 1 km. to the centre, has a long beach. Popular with tour operators. Mobile homes for hire.

Directions: Best approach is to turn off D786 road at Matignon towards St Cast; just inside St Cast limits turn left at sign for `campings' and follow camp signs on C90.

Charges 1998: Per person Ffr 23.00 - 29.00; child (under 7) 14.00 - 19.00; pitch 67.00 - 88.00, large pitch 75.00 - 99.00; electricity 6A 20.00, 10A 23.00; local tax 2.00 (high season). Credit cards accepted.

Open: 10 April - 12 September.

Reservations: Necessary for July/Aug. and made (min. 1 week) with deposit (Ffr. 200) and booking fee (120). Address: Rue des Nouettes, 22380 St Cast le Guildo. Tel: (0)2.96.41.96.33. FAX: (0)2.96.41.97.99.

2401 Castel Camping Château Le Verdoyer, Champs Romain, nr St Pardoux

Dutch owned site developed in park of restored Château le Verdoyer.

Le Verdoyer is in the lesser known area referred to as the Périgord Vert, with forests and small lakes. The 37 acre estate has two such lakes, one in front of the Château for fishing and one accessed by a footpath, with sandy beach and swimming area where canoeing and windsurfing for beginners are possible. There are 150 marked, level, terraced pitches (ground a little rocky). Of good size (100-150 sq.m), all have electricity, with a choice of wooded area or open field, where hedges have grown well; 120 are 'confort' pitches with more planned. Swimming pool complex with two pools and paddling pool (covered in low season). Activities for children, with a free crêche for 1-5s (July/Aug). Definitely no disco! The toilet block in the old barn buildings is good, containing showers, washbasins in cabins and British WCs. There is another well appointed block and both have facilities for disabled people. Serviced launderette. Motorcaravan services. Shop. The courtyard between reception and the bar is home to evening activities, and provides a pleasant place to enjoy the bar, with snacks and takeaway. Good value bistro July/Aug. Tennis, volleyball, basketball, badminton, table tennis, minigolf and mountain bike hire. Children's play areas. Bungalows and mobile homes to rent. The Château has rooms to let and its excellent restaurant is also open to the public. Used sparingly by a Dutch tour operator.

Directions: Site is 2 km. from Limoges-Chalus-Nontron road, 20 km. south of Chalus; well signed from main road.

Charges 1998: Per person Ffr. 25.00 - 35.00; child (2 -7 yrs) 18.00 - 25.00; pitch 32.00 - 46.00, `confort' 36.00 - 51.00, `grand confort' incl. electricity 73.00 - 97.00; electricity (5A) 17.00. Credit cards accepted.

Open: 1 May - 30 September. `Camping Cheque'`FRENCH FLAVOUR'

Reservations: Write to site. Address: 24470 Champs Romain.
Tel: (0)5.53.56.94.66. FAX: (0)5.53.56.38.70.

AR Discount
Less 5% high season, 15% in low season

FRANCE - Dordogne

2403 Camping Les Périères, Sarlat

Good quality small site with large pitches and swimming pool very close to town.

This little site is in a pleasant setting amid attractive trees on the edge of the town of Sarlat. It has some 100 individual pitches mainly on terraces on a semi-circle of a fairly steep hillside with shade in many parts. They are of very good size and all are equipped with electricity, water connections and drainaway. It becomes full late June - late Aug. so reservation is advisable, but a proportion of the site is not reserved, so space could be found if you are early. The five sanitary blocks, of varying size, are of good quality and should be quite sufficient, providing individual washbasins mostly in private cabins, and free hot water. Washing machines and dryers. On the more level ground there is a small swimming pool, a paddling pool and 2 tennis courts. An indoor spa pool is open all season. The main buildings house a small shop, pleasant bar and just beyond, a terrace restaurant with takeaway (15/6-15/9). The owners have made space for a library, where visitors can read, study or play board games and Dutch billiards. Table tennis, football, fitness track with exercise halts. Good bungalows to let. The site has a spacious air and is quite free from overcrowding - a most thoughtfully improved site. Motorcaravan services.

Directions: Site is east of the town on the D47 road in the direction of `Sous-Préfecture' and towards Croix d'Alon.

Charges 1997: Per unit in high season, incl. up to 3 persons Ffr. 152.00, 2 persons 138.50, in low season incl. 2 persons 108.00; electricity 22.00; extra person 32.50; child (under 7 yrs) 19.00; local tax 2.00.

Open: Easter - 30 September.

Reservations: Made for min. 1 week with deposit (Ffr. 520 per week) and fee (80). Address: Rte. Ste Nathalène, 24203 Sarlat Cedex. Tel: (0)5.53.59.05.84. FAX: (0)5.53.28.57.51.

2404 Castel Camping Le Moulin du Roch, Sarlat

Family run site based around old water mill midway between Sarlat and Les Eyzies.

Set amongst traditional stone buildings, Le Moulin du Roch is ideally situated to visit the medieval Dordogne and prehistoric Vézère valleys. Most of the 195 separated pitches are in rows surrounded by attractive trees and hedges but there are also many levelled places in natural woodland providing shade. All pitches have electrical connections and some have water and drainage. The toilet blocks are of very good quality with free hot water throughout and contain well equipped washing areas and British style WCs. On the site is a swimming pool and children's paddling pool, both open all season. There is a small shop and the site has recently enlarged the bar (with satellite TV, games and billiards) and terrace. There is an excellent takeaway and a cosy restaurant serving local dishes (from 9/5). Children's playground, table tennis, tennis, boules, fishing lake and forest trails for walking. Many mobile homes and tents to let for long stays. In high season daily entertainment, children's club and sporting activities (tennis, aqua gym. arts and craft, etc) are organised. Canoe and riding excursions in mid and high season. English spoken. Used by British tour operators.

Directions: Site is 10 km. from Sarlat on the D47 road to Les Eyzies.

Charges 1998: Per pitch incl. 2 persons Ffr. 70.00 - 121.00, with electricity 88.00 - 139.00, with full services 107.00 - 158.00; extra person (over 4 yrs) 15.00 - 26.00; extra car 5.00 - 12.00; local tax 1.00 per person.

Open: 25 April - 13 September. `Camping Cheque'

Reservations: Accepted from 1/1 with deposit and fee (Ffr. 120) July/Aug. only. Address: Rte. des Eyzies D47 , 24200 Sarlat en Perigord. Tel: (0)5.53.59.20.27. FAX: (0)5.53.29.44.65.

2405 Castel Camping Les Hauts de Ratebout, Belvès, nr Sarlat

Good family site with pool, on a hill away from habitations southwest of Sarlat.

Not a particularly large site, this one has 200 separated pitches, varying in size from 80 - 130 sq.m. and on fairly flat or terraced ground. It is in a fine, hill top situation with different aspects. Almost all pitches have electricity and 155 are fully plumbed. On site is an outdoor, unheated swimming pool (200 sq.m. from 1/5), small children's pool and a new 100 sq.m. heated indoor pool. Amenities, including the pools, are open all season. Four good toilet blocks have British WCs, washbasins in cabins with hot water and free hot showers and facilities for disabled people. Water taps abound. Shop with takeaway, including pizzas. A pleasant restaurant and bar area (from 1/5) opens to the pool-side terrace, which has a small stage for live entertainment. General room with library, pool, football table, TV. Volleyball, table tennis, bicycle hire and two tennis courts. Adventure playground. Washing machines and dryer. Organised activities in season include canoe trips, nightly videos and sports for children. Used by tour operators. No dogs, or discos - it is a site more suitable for families with children under 16 yrs.

Directions: From Belvès, just off the D710 road 60 km. south of Périgueux, proceed 2 km. on D710 then left on D54 at camp sign and follow through to site.

Charges 1998: Per person Ffr 27.80 - 37.00; child (under 8 yrs) 19.50 - 26.00; pitch 39.00 - 52.00; electricity (6A) 18.00; extra car 10.00. Credit cards accepted.

Open: 1 May - 12 September. `Camping Cheque'

Reservations: Made for a few days or more, with deposit Ffr. 420 per week (or 60 per day) and fee (90). Address: Ste Foy de Belvès, 24170 Belvès. Tel: (0)5.53.29.02.10. FAX: (0)5.53.29.08.28. E-mail: ratebout@msn.com.

2408 Camping-Caravaning Le Moulin de David, Gaugeac, Monpazier

Secluded valley site with pool, on southwest of the Dordogne.

This pleasant little site is one for those who enjoy peace, away from the hustle and bustle of larger sites closer to the main Dordogne attractions, yet it is sufficiently close for them to be accessible. Set in 14 ha. of wooded countryside, it has 110 pitches, some large, all with electricity, split into 2 sections; 35 below the central reception complex in a shaded situation, and 75 above on partly terraced ground with varying degrees of shade. Spacing is good. The site has been planted with a pleasing variety of shrubs and trees. Two well appointed sanitary blocks (one in each part) are well kept with British WCs and washbasins in cabins. Baby rooms and washrooms for disabled people in both blocks. Chemical disposal, dishwashing and laundry sinks, plus laundry. The reception block embraces a restaurant, bar with shaded patio and takeaway. Good shop. Two swimming pools, one for small children. Children's play area and small lake with water toboggan. Organised events and games. Boules. Half-court tennis. Table tennis (own bats). Volleyball. Library. Trampoline. Bicycle hire. Canoe trips. Tents, apartments, mobile homes and caravans for hire; used minimally by a tour operator. Delightful wooded walk via long distance footpath (GR 36) to Château Biron, 2-3 km. A `Sites et Paysages' member.

Directions: Site is just south off the Monpazier - Villeréal road (D2), about 2 km. west of Monpazier.

Charges 1998: Per pitch Ffr. 24.50 - 45.00; person 20.00 - 33.50; child (under 2 yrs) free; extra child's tent 7.00 - 10.00; electricity 3A 19.00, 6A 23.00. Credit cards accepted.

Open: 16 May - 12 September.

Reservations: Advisable for Jul/Aug. with Ffr. 300 deposit plus fee (100).
Address: Gaugeac, 24540 Monpazier. Tel: (0)5.53.22.65.25. FAX: (0)5.53.23.99.76.

AR Discount
Welcome drink on arrival

2409 Camping Soleil Plage, Vitrac, nr Sarlat

Spacious site with enviable location beside the Dordogne.

The site is in one of the most attractive sections of the Dordogne, right on the riverside. It is divided into two sections - one of 56 pitches has its own toilet block and lies adjacent to the reception, bar, shop and restaurant complex, which is housed in a renovated Perigourdine farmhouse. It is also close to a small sandy river bank and canoe station, from which canoes and kayaks can be hired for down-river trips or transport up-river for a paddle back to the site. Near the reception area is a swimming pool, paddling pool, tennis court and minigolf. The friendly bar provides an excellent takeaway menu and the attractive restaurant serves excellent Perigourdine menus. The larger section of the site (124 pitches) is about 250 m. from the reception area, and offers river bathing from a sizeable pebble bank. All pitches are bounded by hedges and are of good size. Table tennis, volleyball and children's playground. Fishing. Bicycle hire. Sanitary facilities are provided by two modern blocks, with washing machines, chemical disposal and motorcaravan services. TV room. Used by tour operators. A `Sites et Paysages' member.

Directions: Site is 8 km south of Sarlat. Take D704 and it is signed from Montfort castle. Coming from the west on D703, turn first right 1 or 2 km. after the bridge at Vitrac-Port, and follow the signs.

Charges 1997: Per person Ffr. 32.00; child (under 10 yrs) 20.00; pitch 50.00; local tax 1.00 (over 10s) in high season; dog 10.00; electricity (10A) 20.00. Less outside 20/6-1/9. Credit cards accepted.

Open: 1 May - 30 September.

Reservations: Made for exact dates: min. 1 week with deposit and fee; send for booking form. Address: Vitrac, 24200 Sarlat. Tel: (0)5.53.28.33.33. FAX: (0)5.53.29.36.87.

2415 Camping Les Deux Vallées, Beynac, Vézac

Developing woodland site in the heart of the Dordogne.

This site is enviably situated almost under the shadow of Beynac Castle. There are just over 100 flat, marked touring pitches, divided by trees and shrubs and all with electricity (6A). There is plenty of shade and the general feel is of unspoilt but well managed woodland. The main modern toilet block provides British style WCs and good access for disabled people. A second smaller block is heated for off-season. Chemical disposal and motorcaravan services. Good sized pool and children's pool from mid May. It is a short distance to the Dordogne for bathing or canoeing. A small lake is available for fishing or just sitting beside. Bicycle hire, volleyball, basketball, minigolf, boules, table tennis, table football and an intriguing outdoor pool game. Quiz nights feature in the main season. Shop and bar/restaurant (1/4-30/9) serving good value snacks and more ambitious meals to take away, eat inside or on the terrace. Another surprise is English breakfast! The site is being steadily upgraded by its British/Dutch owners, who assure a friendly welcome. Mobile homes and chalets to rent. Some tour operator pitches.

Directions: Take the D703 from Bergerac, go through Beynac and, just past the village, turn left towards Sarlat on the D57/D49. Shortly after, turn left and the site is signed from here on.

Charges 1998: Per pitch Ffr. 18.00 - 36.00; adult 13.00 - 26.00; child (3-7 yrs) 8.00 - 16.00, free under 3; local tax (over 10) 2.00; electricity 6A 16.00, 10A 20.00. Less 5-10% for stays over 14 days outside 15/7-15/8.

Open: All year.

Reservations: Advised for July/Aug. and made with deposit (Ffr 550) and fee (50). Address: 24220 Vézac. Tel: (0)5.53.29.53.55. FAX: (0)5.53.31.09.81.

FRANCE - Dordogne

2410 Camping-Caravaning Le Moulinal, Biron

Lakeside site with wide range of activities for all ages.

Not only does Le Moulinal provide a good base for exploring the southern Dordogne, but it has extensive wooded grounds to explore with picnic areas. The 265 grassy pitches, all with electricity, are level but of varying size, some a little cramped where access may be difficult for larger units. The sanitary facilities have been built to harmonise with the surroundings and provide mostly British style toilets, washbasins, some in cabins, and hot showers. Good supply of hot water for washing up sinks, laundry with 2 washing machines and dryer, and chemical disposal. Facilities for disabled people and babies. The 5-acre lake with sandy beach is suitable for swimming and boating (canoes available) and fishing. Shop, excellent restaurant serving regional meals (including a 4 course 'menu enfant'!) and bar, also serving snacks and light meals (all from 8/5). Also a snack bar/takeaway on the other side of the lake. A rustic children's play area on grass overlooks the lake. There is a large, heated swimming pool with jacuzzi and children's pool. Ambitious, well organised animation is run as a series of programmes; the 'baby club' (ages 2-6) offering amongst other things ball games, painting and pottery; there is a 'kid's club' for 6-10 year olds, including swimming lessons and football; the 'junior club' for 11-15s, including mountain biking and baseball, and a 'super-club' for active young people or adults - potholing and rock climbing feature. The 'tourist club' and 'art club' add to the variety of programmes. Sport and leisure facilities include canoeing, potholing, tennis, diving, fencing and archery (small charges in high season), volleyball, table tennis, fishing, dance, football and hockey (all free). Bicycle hire. Excursions are organised on foot, on horseback, by car or bicycle. There is a full programme of evening entertainment in high season. Tents, new chalets, bungalows and caravans for hire. The site is popular with tour operators, although the owner has reduced their presence.

Directions: From D104 Villeréal - Monpazier road, 9 km from Villeréal, take D53 south to Biron (3 km). Continue on D53 to Lacapelle Biron (4½ km - the D53 becomes the Dl50 on crossing the regional boundary before reaching Lacapelle Biron). Site is signed to west from Lacapelle Biron on the D255; or, from D911 Fumel - Villeneuve road take D162 and after 6½ km, turn right at sign for Lacapelle Biron.

Charges 1998: Per pitch incl. 2 persons: normal Ffr. 45.00 - 139.00, near lake 55.00 - 150.00. with water and drainage 65.00 - 160.00; extra person (over 7 yrs) 10.00 - 39.00; child (2-7 yrs) free - 33.00; animal free - 10.00; electricity 3A 21.00, 6A 27.00. Credit cards accepted.

Open: 11 April - 12 September, with all services.

Reservations: Made with deposit (Ffr 250) and for high season, fee (150). Address: 24540 Biron. Tel: (0)5.53.40.84.60. FAX: (0)5.53.40.81.49.

86

2602 Castel Camping du Château de Sénaud, Albon, nr Tournon

Pleasant site convenient for the autoroute or a longer stay.

Château du Sénaud, near the N7 south of Vienne, makes a useful stopover on the way south, but one could enjoy a longer stay to explore the surrounding villages and mountains. It is one of the original sites in the Castel chain and is still run with character and hands-on attention by Mme. Comtesse d'Armagnac. There are a fair number of permanent caravans used at weekends, but it also has some 140 pitches in tourist areas, some with shade, some with views across the Rhône valley, and electrical connections are available. There is a swimming pool with water toboggan (from May, depending on the weather) and a tennis court. Four sanitary blocks have constant hot water in basins, showers and sinks, British and Turkish style toilets, washbasins in private cabins, some en-suite with shower in one block, and facilities for babies. Washing machine, chemical disposal and motorcaravan services. Shop (from April). Bar, takeaway and good value small restaurant with simple menu (all from June). On site are fishing, bicycle hire, table tennis, a bowling alley and minigolf. Golf course adjacent. Walks. Possibly some noise from the autoroute. Mobile homes to rent.

Directions: Leave autoroute at Chanas exit, proceed south on N7 for 8 km. then east near Le Creux de la Thine to site. From south exit autoroute for Tain-Tournon and proceed north, approaching site on D122 through St Vallier then D172 towards Anneyron to site.

Charges 1998: Per person Ffr. 26.00; child (under 7) 15.00; pitch 36.00; dog 6.00; visitor 10.00; electricity 6A 18.00, 10A 21.00.

Open: 1 March - 31 October. *`Camping Cheque'*

Reservations: Made with deposit for min. 3 nights. Address: 26140 Albon. Tel: (0)4.75.03.11.31. FAX: (0)4.75.03.08.06.

2603 Camping Le Grand Lierne, Chabeuil, nr Valence

Conveniently and attractively situated family site on the route south.

In addition to its obvious attraction as an overnight stop, fairly convenient to the A7 autoroute, this site provides a pleasant base to explore this little known area between the Ardèche and the Vercors mountains and the Côte du Rhône wine area. The site has 134 marked pitches, mainly separated by hedges or oak trees, with good shade, on flat grass and all with electricity (4-10A). There is a feeling of spaciousness and good views to the mountains on either side of the valley. A varied entertainment programme has a particular emphasis on activities for children, with various excursions, both organised and informal. A disco for teenagers is organised by the owner's sons but is well managed to avoid noise. Two small heated swimming pools, one covered in low season (no bermuda shorts allowed in pool), a children's pool and a new 50 m. water slide. A bar/snack bar with terrace provides both `eating in' and takeaway (all season). Two modern sanitary blocks have hot showers, British style WCs and washbasins in private cabins. Facilities for disabled people and a small WC for children. Partly under cover dishwashing area (H&C). Washing machines and dryer (fairly expensive and no outdoor lines). Shop, tennis, children's playgrounds and trampoline, minigolf, table tennis, volleyball, a football field, small climbing wall and bicycle hire. Library. Bureau de change. Fridge rental. Golf, archery, riding and hang gliding near. American motorhomes not accepted. Bungalows, chalets and tents for hire. No pets allowed. Barbecues allowed on special areas. The site is used by an international tour operator. The owners wish to keep a balance between nationalities and are also keen to encourage rallies and will arrange visit programmes. English spoken. A `Sites et Paysages' member.

Directions: Site signed in Chabeuil about 11 km. east of Valence (18 km. from autoroute). It is best to approach Chabeuil from the south side of Valence via the Valence ring road, thence onto the D68 to Chabeuil itself.

Charges 1998: Per unit, incl. 2 persons and electricity (4A) Ffr 90.00 - 134.00; extra person 30.00; child (under 7 yrs) free - 20.00; electricity 6A 15.00, 10A 20.00; refrigerator rental 25.00; local tax 1.00 per person. Credit cards accepted.

Open: 1 April - 30 September with all services. *`Camping Cheque'*

Reservations: Accepted with deposit (Ffr. 600) and fee (170). Address: BP.8, 26120 Chabeuil. Tel: (0)4.75.59.83.14. FAX: (0)4.75.59.87.95.

How to use the Guide - The Départements of France

France is divided administratively into 95 `départements' (including Corsica) which are approximately the equivalent of our counties but with rather more autonomy. The départements are numbered in alphabetical order and these numbers form the first two digits of all post codes within each département. For example, the Dordogne is département 24, so every large town in the Dordogne has a post code commencing 24. We have adopted a similar system for numbering our French campsites; thus all our sites in the département of Dordogne start with the numbers 24. For the benefit of readers who are not experts on French geography, we include a map on page 125 indicating the location of each département, together with its official number. The map also shows in which Region each département is situated.

FRANCE - Finistère

2901 Castel Camping Ty Naden, Arzano, nr Quimperlé

Country site beside the River Ellé, with swimming pools.

Ty Naden is set deep in the countryside in the grounds of a country house some 18 km. from the sea. It has 220 individual pitches, 160 with electricity, of good size on fairly flat grass, some on the banks of the river with some shade. The two toilet blocks are of an unusual design with access from different levels. They have mixed British and Turkish style WCs and free hot water in the washbasins (in cabins), sinks and showers with push-button. Access for disabled people may be a little difficult although there are facilities in one block. Dishwashing facilities in the ladies' block (!) and laundry room with washing machines and dryers. There are plenty of activities including a heated swimming pool, pool with water slides and paddling pool (all 8/5-5/9), a small beach on the river, tennis, table tennis, pool tables, archery and trampolines. Fishing, canoeing, small roller skating rink and BMX track. Horse and pony rides. Bicycle, skateboard, roller skate and boat hire. Many activities organised in season, particularly sports, excursions, etc. and including mountain bike tours and canoeing trips. Restaurant (w/ends only outside July/Aug), takeaway, bar and shop (all 23/5-5/9). Across the road, by the attractive house and garden, is minigolf and a TV room and delightful crêperie. Tents, mobile homes and chalets for hire.

Directions: Make for Arzano (northeast of Quimperlé on Pontivy road). Turn off D22 west of village at sign.

Charges 1998: Per person Ffr. 28.00; child (under 7) 18.00; pitch 60.00; electricity (10A) 20.00; water/drainage 20.00; dog 10.00. Credit cards accepted.

Open: 8 May - 5 September.

Reservations: Made for exact dates with deposit (Ffr. 200) and fee (100). Address: Rte d'Arzano, 29310 Locunolé. Tel: (0)2.98.71.75.47. FAX: (0)2.98.71.77.31.

AR Discount
Less 5%
on pitch fee

2904 Camping Le Vorlen, Beg-Meil, nr Quimper

Large, informal family site with pool, adjacent to sandy beach - family managed.

This spacious, unpretentious site is on 24 acres of level ground in a rural setting and caters for a wide variety of tastes with good sized pitches providing a choice of sun or shade with mature trees in a number of small `bays' which create an impression of tranquillity unusual in such a large site. Because of its size the site is seldom fully booked. The atmosphere is pleasantly cosmopolitan and relaxed, and the situation provides easy access (about 200 m.) to a long sandy south facing beach. Two thirds of the 600 pitches have electricity. Two modern toilet blocks have ample showers, free hot water, individual cabins, British toilets, and numerous sinks for washing up. The two original blocks, in the older part of the site near the main entrance, have baby baths, a unit for disabled people and British style WCs, all with external entry. Swimming pool (20/6-10/9) and paddling pool at the opposite end of the site from reception. Mini market and takeaway (27/6-1/9). Launderette. Telephones. A torch is useful. Children's play area. Bar in season just outside entrance with some regional music. English spoken in high season. No tour operators; 30 mobile homes for hire.

Directions: Follow signs to Beg-Meil village; site is signed from there.

Charges 1997: Per person Ffr. 22.50; child (under 7) 12.50; pitch 42.00; vehicle 8.00; electricity (6A) 13.00. Less 20% outside 29/6-1/9. Credit cards accepted.

Open: 1 May - 20 September

Reservations: Write with deposit of Ffr. 250 (Eurocheque or credit card). Address: 29170 Fouesnant, Beg-Meil. Tel: (0)2.98.94.97.36. FAX: (0)2.98.94.97.23.

2906 Camping Caravaning Le Pil Koad, Poullan-sur-Mer, nr Douarnenez

Family run, attractive site just back from the sea in Finistère.

Pil Koad provides 200 pitches on fairly flat ground, marked out by separating hedges and of quite good, though varying, size and shape. Nearly all have electrical connections (10A) and original trees provide shade in some areas. Two toilet blocks in modern style have mainly British style WCs and washbasins, some in cabins but mostly not. Free, pre-set hot water in these and the showers. Laundry facilities. The site is 6 km. from Douarnenez and 5 km. from the nearest sandy beach. There is a heated swimming pool and paddling pool, an attractive sunbathing patio and a tennis court. Large room for entertainment with discos and cabaret in July/Aug. Small shop (27/6-30/8) and takeaway (27/6-30/8). Restaurants in the village. Children's playground. Table tennis, minigolf, volleyball, fishing and mountain bike hire. Clubs are arranged for children in season (30/6-30/8) with a charge included in the tariff. Motorcaravan service point. Mobile homes and chalets to rent. Gates closed 11.30 - 7.30 in high season.

Directions: Site is 500 m. from centre of Poullan on road towards Douarnenez. From Douarnenez take circular bypass route towards Audierne; if you see road for Poullan sign at roundabout, take it, otherwise there is camping sign at turning to Poullan from the D765 road.

Charges 1997: Per pitch Ffr. 37.00 - 79.00, services plus 15.00; person 20.00 - 29.00; child (under 7 yrs) 10.00 - 15.00; extra car 10.00 - 15.00; electricity (10A) 22.00; local tax (over 16, 1/6-30/9) 1.00. Credit cards accepted.

Open: 1 May - 15 September

Reservations: Made for min. 1 week with deposit (Ffr. 300) and fee (120). Address: Poullan, 29100 Douarnenez. Tel: (0)2.98.74.26.39. FAX: (0)2.98.74.55.97.

2905 Castel Camping L'Orangerie de Lanniron, Quimper

Beautiful, quiet site in the mature grounds of a riverside and parkland estate, 15 km. from the sea.

This is a peaceful, family site in 10 acres of a XVIIth century, 42 acre country estate on the banks of the Odet river. It is just to the south of Quimper and about 15 km. from the sea and beaches at Bénodet. The family have a five year programme to restore and rehabilitate the park, the original canal, fountains, ornamental Lake of Neptune, the boat-house and the gardens and avenues. The original outbuildings have been attractively converted around a walled courtyard which includes a heated swimming pool (144 sq.m.) with children's pool and a small play area. There are 199 grassy pitches of three types (varying in size and services) on fairly flat ground laid out in rows alongside access roads. Most have electricity and 32 with all three services, with shrubs and bushes providing pleasant pitches. The original sanitary block, along one side of the courtyard, is good, with free hot water in all services. A second modern block serves the newer pitches at the top of the site. They have British toilets, washbasins in private cabins, showers and facilities for the disabled and babies. Shop. Bar, including Cyber café connected to the Web, snacks and takeaway, plus a restaurant in the beautiful XVIIth century Orangerie with very attractive views across the gardens (open daily to the public, reasonably priced and with children's menu). The Gardens are also open to the public and when we visited in May, rhododendrons and azaleas were magnificent, with lovely walks within the grounds. General reading, games and billiards rooms. Tennis court. Minigolf, attractively set among mature trees. Table tennis. Fishing. Archery. Bicycle hire. Children's adventure playground and some farm animals. Karaoke. Animation is provided with a large room for indoor activities, also outdoor activities. TV/video room (cable and satellite). Washing machines and dryers. Motorcaravan service point and chemical disposal. Rooms in the château and 5 cottages in the park to let. The historic town of Quimper, which has some attractive old areas and a cathedral, is under 3 km, two hypermarkets 1 km. Used by tour operators. Mobile homes for hire. All facilities available when site is open. Watch out for the 2-way bike!!

Directions: From Quimper follow `Quimper Sud' signs, then `Toutes Directions' and general camping signs, finally signs for Lanniron.

Charges 1997: Per person Ffr. 27.00; child (2-6 yrs) 17.00; car 17.00; normal pitch (100 sq.m.) 47.00, with electricity (10A) 67.00, special pitch (140 sq.m. with water and electricity) 82.00, (140 sq.m. with electricity, water and drainage) 87.00; animal 17.00. Less 10% outside July/Aug. Credit cards accepted.

Open: 15 May - 15 September.

Reservations: Made with deposit (Ffr. 400) and fee (100). Address: Château de Lanniron, 29336 Quimper Cedex. Tel: (0)2.98.90.62.02. FAX: (0)2.98.52.15.56. E-mail: lanniron@acdev.com. Internet: http://www.acdev.com/lanniron.

`Camping Cheque'

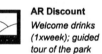

AR Discount
Welcome drinks (1xweek); guided tour of the park

2914 Domaine de Kerlann, Land Rosted, Pont Aven

Newly developed site for holiday homes with a very pleasant touring section.

Developed from an older site known as Le Spinnaker, Haven Europe are investing serious money in updating original touring facilities and developing new facilities for mobile homes. The investment is being imaginatively, environmentally managed by the English project director and much had been achieved when we visited, including an impressive pool complex and much infrastructure work, ie. new drains and new electrical and gas connections, all to a high standard. The sanitary facilities, still in the original two blocks, have been substantially refurbished and now offer an up-to-date provision of a very acceptable standard including British type WCs, plus extensive laundry facilities. Given that the 200 touring pitches account for only 25% of the total provision, we had some misgivings about the suitability of the site for the guide, but our fears on this score were more or less completely assuaged as a result of the care taken with the original landscape (every tree has been mapped and checked by a tree surgeon). The 200 large and level pitches are in tranquil avenues with a small stream and are well shaded and away from the holiday homes and tour operator areas. We felt that independent caravanners and campers could be comfortable (electrical connections available on some pitches) and enjoy the range of facilities on site as well as in the area. Amenities include a bar, restaurant, satellite TV, takeaway, shop, crèche, children's clubs, a range of entertainment, tennis courts, minigolf, BMX track, volleyball, aqua-gym and other activities around the pool which has lifeguards and other attendants.

Directions: From the Tregunc - Pont Aven road, turn south towards Névez and site is on right.

Charges 1998: Per pitch without facilities £10.50 - 16.00, with electricity £12.50 - 17.00, with water and electricity £16.50 - 22.00.

Open: 4 April - 26 September.

Reservations: Contact Haven Europe for information (0990 143285) or reservations (0990 2334777). Address: Land Rosted, 29930 Pont Aven. l: (0)2.98.06.01.77. FAX: (0)2.98.06.18.50.

FRANCE · Finistère

2909 Camping Le Raguenès Plage, Névez, nr Pont-Aven

Well regulated, attractive site in small seaside village, with beach access.

Le Raguenès Plage is personally run by the owner and her family who take great pride in the site, which has many attractive shrubs and trees and is kept very clean and neat. A sandy beach can be reached by footpath (300 m.) and there is a sailing school and small fishing port adjacent to the site. The 287 pitches all have electrical connections and are of good size, on flat ground, arranged in rows on either side of asphalt access roads, separated by hedges and trees. The sanitary facilities are in three well designed blocks of different size and are of very good quality and well maintained. They provide British WCs, pre-set hot showers, washbasins in private cabins, plus free hairdryers and include good baby bathrooms, excellent facilities for disabled people and chemical disposal. Hot water is free throughout. Amenities include a sauna and a new, attractively designed, heated swimming pool with terrace (open from 1/5). Table tennis, volleyball, games room, good play areas and animation are offered for children. A small bar and restaurant (from 15/6) have an outside terrace with lots of flowers; breakfast is served here. Takeaway. Small shop (from 15/5, supermarket 5 km.). Reading, TV rooms and films. Laundry. Exchange facilities. Fishing and watersports near. Bicycle hire can be arranged, with delivery. Motorcaravan service point. Used by British tour operators (20%). Mobile homes for hire.

Directions: From the D783 Concarneau - Pont-Aven road go south to Névez. Site is signed from there, 5 km. on the Raguenès-Plage road.

Charges 1998: Per unit incl. 2 persons Ffr. 130.00; extra person 30.00; child (under 7 yrs) 18.00; electricity 2A 15.00, 6A 20.00; dog 8.00; local tax (over 18 yrs) 1.50. Less 30% in April, May, June, 20% in Sept.

Open: 15 April - 30 September.

Reservations: Recommended in high season, min. 7 days preferred for July/Aug. Write with deposit (Ffr. 300). Address: 19 Rue des Iles, 29920 Névez. Tel: (0)2.98.06.80.69. FAX: (0)2.98.06.89.05.

2912 Camping Manoir de Kerlut, Plobannalec, nr Pont l'Abbé

See colour advert between pages 96/97

Developing site in grounds of manor house on river estuary.

Manoir de Kerlut is on the banks of a river estuary, 2 km. from the beaches of Lesconil and not far from the fishing and watersports opportunities offered by the southwest coast of Brittany. There are pleasant walks in the park and along the river bank. This site, opened in 1990 with strikingly modern buildings, has been constructed on flat grass near the house. It provides 240 pitches, all with electricity (5, 6 or 10A), many with water and drainage also and hardstanding on 10 or so pitches. One area is rather open with hedges planted, the other amongst mature bushes and some trees which provide shade. Amenities are good with a large modern bar with TV (satellite) and entertainment in season, and two heated swimming pools with children's pool. Small shop. Takeaway. Sauna, solarium and small gym. Tennis, volleyball, badminton, petanque. Children's play area. Games room. Bicycle hire. Laundry. Sanitary facilities in two very good blocks provide controllable hot showers, washbasins all in cabins, British style WCs and chemical disposal. Facilities for babies and disabled people. Hot water is free. Gates closed 22.30 - 7.30 hrs. Mobile homes and bungalows to rent. Used by British tour operators.

Directions: From Pont l'Abbé, on the D785, take the D102 road to Lesconil. Site is signed to the left, shortly after the village of Plobannalec.

Charges 1998: Per person 20.00 - 29.00; child (under 7 yrs) 10.00 - 15.00; pitch incl. car 50.00 - 96.00; electricity 2A 10.00, 5A 16.00, 10A 20.00. Credit cards accepted.

Open: 1 May - 15 September.

Reservations: Write to site with deposit (Ffr. 300) and fee (120). Address: 29740 Plobannalec-Lesconil. Tel: (0)2.98.82.23.89 FAX: (0)2.98.82.26.49.

AR Discount
Welcome drink and free tennis

2913 Camping des Abers, Landeda

Attractively situated, family run site in western Brittany.

This delightful 12 acre site is beautifully situated and ideal for younger children, almost at the tip of the Ste Marguerite peninsula on the south shore of L'Aber Wrac'h, with rocky outcrops and islands at high tide and white, soft, sandy beaches. There are 200 pitches at des Abers, spread over some ten quite distinct areas, partly shaded and sheltered by mature trees, all planted and carefully tended over 30 years by the Le Cuff family. These areas have been landscaped and terraced where appropriate, on different levels to avoid any regimentation or crowding. All are easily accessed by good internal roads. Electrical points (5A) are available, with some special pitches for motorcaravans. Modern toilet blocks placed at strategic points, are clean and bright with cubicled washbasins, some British style WCs, good showers (on payment), dishwashing sinks and fully equipped laundry. Facilities for the disabled and for babies have been added. Mini-market (15/6-30/8) and a van with organic vegetables daily. The site offers simple takeaway dishes in high season or there are excellent restaurants nearby at L'Aber Wrac'h, a well known yachting centre, and a crêperie next door. A splendid beach reached direct from the site has good bathing (high tide), fishing, watersports and miles of superb coastal walks. *Continued overleaf*

2913 Camping des Abers (continued)

TV room and indoor games room. Live music, Breton dance and French classes in high season. Tennis and riding close. Mobile homes (4) for rent. Gates locked 22.30-07.00 hrs. Torch useful. The family who own and run the site with 'TLC', make you welcome and speak several languages.

Directions: Cross L'Aber Wrac'h by D13 or D113, then from Lannilis follow signs for Ste Marguerite, 'camping' and des Abers.

Charges 1998: Per person Ffr. 16.00; child (1-7 yrs) 8.00; pitch 25.00; car 6.00; electricity 12.00; dog 5.00. Less 20% outside July/Aug. Credit cards accepted.

Open: 1 May - 30 September.

Reservations: Write to site. Address: 29870 Landeda. Tel: (0)2.98.04.93.35. FAX: (0)2.98.04.84.35.

3003 Camping Abri de Camargue, Le Grau-du-Roi, nr Montpellier

Pleasant site with both indoor and outdoor swimming pools.

This is an agreeable site, which has two swimming pools, one 250 sq.m. and a smaller, indoor heated one (12 x 6 m.) which is overlooked by the restaurant/bar (with heating and air conditioning) and sheltered terrace. The 300 flat pitches are said to average 100 sq.m., but there is some variation in size, and electricity and water are available on most. The site is well shaded, with trees and flowering bushes quite luxuriant in parts. The six toilet blocks have British WCs, washbasins with free hot water in private cabins, and free hot water also in the adjustable showers and sinks. Dishwashing and laundry, chemical disposal and motorcaravan services. Maintenance may be variable - the site lacks a little 'TLC' at present. It is 800 m. from the nearest beach at Port Camargue and 2 km. from the one at L'Espiguette (in July/Aug. a free bus to L'Espiguette beach stops outside). There is a summer fair within walking distance which can be noisy until late. Le Grau-du-Roi is 1½ km. and the old town of Aigues-Mortes 9. TV room. Bar, restaurant, takeaway and shop (all season). Children's playground. Petanque. Very good security. All facilities available when site open. Tennis 800 m. Mobile homes for let. English spoken.

Directions: There is now a road bypassing Le Grau-du-Roi from west as well as the approach from Aigues-Mortes. Turn left at sign to 'Port Camargue' and 'Campings' just northeast of Grau-du-Roi. At next crossroads go left again towards 'Phare de l'Espiguette/Rive Gauche' and after 200 m. you come to site on right. If approaching via the D979 from north, turn onto D62 and D62A towards La Grande Motte at junction north of Aigues-Mortes.

Charges 1998: Per unit incl. 1 or 2 persons and electricity Ffr 115.00 - 250.00, 3-5 persons 130.00 - 250.00; extra person or extra car 30.00 - 60.00; pet, boat or trailer 30.00. Credit cards accepted

Open: April - October.

Reservations: Only required for very high season (10/7-20/8) and made for min. 1 week. (Site will be happy to help with any length of stay - phone and talk to them). Address: 320 Rte. du Phare de l'Espiguette, Port Camargue, 30240 Le Grau-du-Roi. Tel: (0)4.66.51.54.83. FAX: (0)4.66.51.76.42.

Camping-Caravaning-Park ABRI DE CAMARGUE ★★★★
F-30240 Le Grau du Roi ● Tel 0033-4.66.51.54.83 ● Fax 0033-4.66.51.76.42

Two free swimming pools, one covered and heated

Good shady camp-site, pitches totally separated by flowers and trees.

Mobile homes with 2 rooms, shower and WC for hire.

Reservations recommended (booking forms in English). Mediterranean beach only 900m away, gently sloping and suitable for children. Programme of entertainments for adults and children. 2 free Swim-pools. Individual washing cabins. Asphalt paths. International marina with comprehensive water sport facilities. Medieval fortress at Aigues-Mortes (5km). Fishing. Many tennis courts 800m away. Good well-arranged food shop. Doctor available day and night. English spoken. Exchange. Safe deposits, bicycles and mobile homes for hire. Table tennis, volleyball.

From the A9 take exit for Gallargues, then 25km to the site; follow 'Grau du Roi' signs throughout, branching left at the junction before Aigues Mortes. Approaching Grau du Roi follow sign to 'Rive Gauche', then after the canal bridge follow signs for 'L'Espiguette'. The site lies on right side of this road.

For reservations write or phone to: David and Ann Hiscock, 31 Ingram Avenue, Aylesbury, Bucks HP21 9DW. Telephone: (01296) 84084 (after 2 pm.) or contact site direct.

FRANCE - Gard

3005 Camping L'Eden, Le Grau-du-Roi, nr Montpellier

Good modern site close to beaches and Camargue, with swimming pool.

L'Eden is a good example of a modern, well run, purpose built 4-star site. It is on flat ground about 500 m. from a sandy beach, with 377 individual hedged pitches. The flowering shrubs and trees make it cool and very pretty. Shade is available on many of the pitches, electricity on most and some are fully serviced. Reservation is advisable for the main season. The five modern sanitary blocks are of unusual design, tiled blue or pink, and have free hot water everywhere. Toilets (some British style) as so often in France are in shorter supply than washbasins, which are in cubicles or private cabins; free pre-set hot showers, some en-suite with washbasins. Unit with baby bath. Full facilities disabled people. Chemical disposal facilities inside the blocks. There is a very attractive swimming pool with bridge, water toboggan and children's pool on site (from mid April) and a fitness centre next door. Supermarket, boutique, bar and restaurant with takeaway (all open all season). TV room and meeting room. Half court tennis. Minigolf. Archery. Table tennis. Sports area with volleyball and basketball. All activities on site are free. In high season organised events, sports, excursions, entertainment, etc. Mini club for children (1/7-1/9) and special play area for 1-8 year olds. Marina with sailing lessons, riding and tennis nearby. Bicycle hire. Laundry facilities. Free bus service to beach in main season. Some tour operators.

Directions: There is now a road bypassing Le Grau-du-Roi from the west, which is easier if towing, as well as the approach from Aigues-Mortes. Turn left to 'Port Camargue' and 'Campings' just northeast of Grau-du-Roi and follow signs for 'Phare de l'Espiguette' and after 200 m. right at second sign for l'Eden. Note: It is not site with entrance at turn; for l'Eden go hard right onto access road and 200 m. around corner to site on left (it is a busy access).

Charges 1997: Per pitch incl. 2 persons: simple (for small tents) Ffr. 111.00 - 156.00, with electricity and water 111.00 - 184.00, with electricity, water and drainage 111.00 - 199.00, all acc. to season; extra person 10.00 - 21.00; extra car, small boat 20.00; extra small tent 15.00; local tax 1.00. Less 20% for a 2 week stay outside 1/7-26/8 or 5% for a 3 week stay in high season. Credit cards accepted.

Open: 4 April - 4 October.

Reservations: Made from Sat.-Sat. high season only with deposit and fee. Write to site between 1/1 and 15/5. Address: Port Camargue, 30240 Le Grau-du-Roi. Tel: (0)4.66.51.49.81. FAX: (0)4.66.53.13.20.

CAMPING-CARAVANING L'EDEN ★★★★

Port-Camargue, 30240 Le Grau du Roi
Tél: +33 4 66 51 49 81 Fax: +33 4 66 53 13 20

L'Eden is 500 m. from the beach at Port-Camargue (premier pleasure port of Europe). We offer 5 ha. with 377 pitches, a commercial centre, snacks, bazaar, papers, bar/restaurant. For your entertainment: swimming pool with water slide, table tennis, minigolf, halfcourt, archery, multi sports field, children's playground, sauna, sun-bed, gym, bicycle hire and day time and evening animation and miniclub in July/Aug.

SPECIAL OFFER:
50% off our tarif in April, May, 1-14 June and Sept for min.
1 week for reserved stay with this coupon

3002 La Petite Camargue, Aigues-Mortes

Impressive site with large swimming pool on the edge of the Camargue.

This is a large site (400 pitches) with a huge swimming pool complex and other amenities to match, conveniently situated beside one of the main routes across the famous Camargue. Its convenient position alongside this busy road is an advantage for access but could perhaps be a drawback in terms of traffic, although when we stayed overnight in season it was virtually silent. It offers a variety of good sized pitches, regularly laid out, with varying amounts of shade. There are, however, a number of mobile homes interspersed between the touring pitches, but most are set well back from the road. An attractive 'L' shaped pool complex and adjacent bar/restaurant with pizzeria and takeaway, range of shops, etc. are situated between the pitches and the road and are attractively designed, providing a wide range of facilities and activities. The four sanitary blocks provide very good, well maintained, modern facilities including many combined showers and washbasins with controllable hot water and British style WCs. Not only is the site conveniently situated for visiting the Camargue and not far from the sea and beaches (8 km.) and other sport facilities and activities - horse riding for example is available at the adjoining large riding stables - but it also provides a range of on site entertainment. Children's play area. Tennis (charged July/Aug). Table tennis. Laundry facilities. *continued overleaf*

3002 La Petite Camargue (continued)

Hairdresser and beauty centre. Good activity programme and disco. Free bus service to beach (July/Aug). Mobile homes to let. Used by tour operators. A well run, busy site.

Directions: From autoroute A9 take exit 26 (Gallargues) towards Le Grau-du-Roi. Continue past Aigues-Mortes (18 km.) on D62 and site is 2 km. on right, just before roundabout for La Grand-Motte and Le Grau-du-Roi junction.

Charges 1997: Per unit with 1 or 2 persons: standard pitch Ffr. 73.00 - 138.00, with electricity 90.00 - 160.00; extra person (over 4 yrs) 26.00 - 33.00; local tax 1.00; second tent or car 27.00; animal 13.00. Less 30% 26/4-4/5.

Open: 24 April - 21 September.

Reservations: Write to site. Address: 30220 Aigues-Mortes. Tel: (0)4.66.53.84.77. FAX: (0)4.66.53.83.48.

3201 Le Camp de Florence, La Romieu

Attractive site on edge of historic village in pleasantly undulating Gers countryside.

A warm welcome awaits at Camp de Florence from Dutch owners who have sympathetically converted the old farmhouse buildings to provide facilities. There are 135 pitches of 100 sq.m. plus, all with electricity, 3 with hardstanding and terraced where necessary, arranged around a large field with rural views, giving a feeling of spaciousness. The older pitches near the main buildings have good shade but it gets progressively less the newer the pitch. However, 25 are fully serviced and shade will develop. Unisex toilet blocks have British style toilets, free hot water, showers and washbasins, some in cabins. Washing machine and dryer. Chemical disposal and motorcaravan services. A restaurant (also open to the public) serves local specialities and a good value à la carte menu (closed Wed. with a barbecue instead). Swimming pool (15/5-15/9) built with a beach effect so one can walk in on three sides, a paddling pool (supervised July/Aug), children's adventure play area, games area and pets area. Barbecues permitted. Takeaway. Games room. Tennis. Table tennis. Volleyball. Petanque. Bicycle hire. Clay pigeon shooting, video shows, discos, picnics, musical evenings, walks and excursions are organised. Exchange facility. Shop in nearby village (bread on site in season). The 13th century village of La Romieu is on the Santiago de Compostela pilgrim route and the collegiate church is well worth a visit , as is the local arboretum, the biggest collection of trees in the Midi-Pyrénées. The Pyrénées are 2 hour's drive, the Atlantic coast similar. Fishing and riding near. A few tour operator pitches. Mobile homes and chalets for hire (1 night stay possible outside July/Aug. with breakfast).

Directions: Site is signed from the D931 Agen - Condom road. Small units can turn left at Ligardes (signed) and follow D36 for 1 km. and take right turn for La Romieu (signed). Otherwise continue until outskirts of Condom and take D41 left to La Romieu and pass through village to site.

Charges 1998: Per unit incl. 2 persons Ffr. 60.00 - 112.00; extra person 21.00 - 35.00; child (4-9 yrs) 15.00 - 25.00; electricity 3A 15.00, 6A 20.00; water and drainage plus 12.00; dog 10.00; local tax 1.00 (child 4-9 yrs 0.50). Special prices for winter stays, groups, rallies, etc. Credit cards accepted.

Open: 1 April - 31 October.   `Camping Cheque'`

Reservations: Write or phone for information (English spoken). Address: 32480 La Romieu. Tel: (0)5.62.28.15.58. FAX: (0)5.62.28.20.04.

3206 Camping Lac des Trois Vallées, Lectoure

This site is featured out of order - it is on page 79.

3301 Camping de la Dune, Pyla-sur-Mer, nr Arcachon

Busy site with pool and other amenities separated from sea by well known giant dune.

La Dune is a good example of a busy French family site. It is informal, friendly and lively with a comprehensive range of amenities. From its situation at the foot of the enormous dune you can reach the beach either by climbing over the dune (a ladder goes up nearly to the top) or driving round, or you can use the free medium-size swimming pool at the far side of the site. The marked out pitches, some terraced but level, vary in size but all are hedged with shade from pine trees. Nearly half are caravan pitches with electricity, water and drainaway. Some roads are quite narrow and parts quite sandy. Three modern sanitary blocks, plus an existing refurbished one, provide British and Turkish type WCs, washbasins, many in cabins (with H&C) and a good supply of pre-set hot showers. Several small shops. Pleasant little bar and restaurant which can get busy and noisy at times (opens June, other facilities all season), with takeaway. Purpose built barbecue (individual ones not allowed). Fridge hire. Riding. Open-air theatre. Organised sports, etc. mid-June - end Aug. Children's playground with mini-club. Motorcaravan services. Mobile homes and chalets for hire. English spoken in season. No tour operators.

Directions: There is a new road (D259) signed from N250 to Biscarrosse and Dune du Pilat, just before La Teste, avoiding Pyla. At end of new road turn right at roundabout on D218 coast road. La Dune is 2nd site on right.

Charges 1997: Per unit incl. 2 persons: with tent Ffr 70.00 - 110.00; with caravan incl. electricity and water 90.00 - 130.00; extra person 20.00 - 30.00; extra child (under 7) 15.00 - 20.00; extra car 15.00 - 25.00; dog 5.00 - 15.00; local tax (over 18s) 1.10. Credit cards accepted.

Open: 1 May - 30 September.

Reservations: Made for min. 1 week with 25% deposit and fee (Ffr. 150) at least 1 month in advance. Address: Rte. de Biscarrosse, Pyla sur Mer, 33260 La Teste. Tel: (0)5.56.22.72.17. FAX: as phone.

FRANCE - Gironde

3302 Camping de Fontaine-Vieille, Andernos-les-Bains, nr Arcachon

Large site on east side of Bassin d'Arcachon with swimming pool and frontage to Bassin.

Fontaine-Vieille is a large well established site with over 840 pitches on flat grassy ground, some with lovely views, in the residential area of the small town of Andernos. The site stretches along the edge of the Bassin d'Arcachon under light woodland. Pitches are individual, marked by stones or newly planted trees, 540 with electricity. The several sanitary blocks, of rather unusual design, provide an adequate number of hot showers (perhaps on the small side), washbasins, some in cabins, and British style WCs. Facilities for disabled people and children. All the blocks are being refurbished (on a rota basis) to a high standard and maintenance and cleaning appear good. A beach runs along the Bassin which can be used for boating when the tide is in. When out, it is sand and mud but they claim that bathing in the channels is still possible. On site there is also an unheated swimming pool (15/5-20-/9), plus paddling pool, which is charged for - Ffr. 80 leisure card for the entire stay. Shop (from 1/6), bar with terrace and restaurant with takeaway also (all 15/6-31/8) - town shops, etc. near. Communal barbecue. Four tennis courts. TV room. Two children's play areas for little ones, adventure area for older ones. Minigolf. Washing machines. Boat, sailboard and bicycle hire. Organised sports. As good a value site as you will find round the Bassin. No tour operators when seen but mobile homes, chalets and bungalows to rent.

Directions: Turn off D3 at southern end of Andernos towards Bassin at camp sign.

Charges 1998: Per unit with 2 persons Ffr. 60.00 - 85.00, with electricity (5A) 75.00 - 105.00; extra person 15.00 -20.00; child (2-7 yrs) 12.00 - 14.00; local tax 1.10. Credit cards accepted.

Open: 1 May - 21 September.

Reservations: Made for any length with deposit (Ffr. 500) and fee (120). Address: 4 Bvd. du Colonel Wurz, 33510 Andernos-les-Bains. Tel: (0)5.56.82.01.67. FAX: (0)5.56.82.09.81.

☆ ☆ ☆

CAMPING CARAVANNING

FONTAINE VIEILLE

4, Boulevard du Colonel Wurtz
33510 ANDERNOS-LES-BAINS
Téléphone: 05 56 82 01 67

On the edge of the beach, in the Arcachon Basin in the heart of a pine and oak forest. Swimming pool. Mobile homes and chalets for hire/to rent. Reductions in low season and for long stays

3305 Camping Les Ourmes, Hourtin

Pleasantly and conveniently situated site close to lake, providing good value.

Located only 500 m. from the largest fresh water lake in France, only 10 minutes drive from the beach and with its own pool, this is essentially a holiday site. Pitches, marked but in most cases not actually separated, are arranged amongst tall pines and other trees which give good shade. There are 300 pitches some with electricity. Amenities are arranged around a pleasant entrance courtyard and include a bar/restaurant with many outdoor tables and serving snacks and takeaway meals (15/6-31/8), small shop (1/6-10/9), TV and games rooms and boules pitches. Medium sized swimming pool (15/6-10/9) with paved sunbathing area and separate large 'leisure' area with children's play area, volleyball, basketball and table tennis. Evening entertainment in season. Watersports and fishing are possible on the lake, with bicycle hire, tennis and riding near. Sanitary facilities in three blocks are good with free hot showers (with hooks, shelf, but no separate dressing area), some washbasins in cabins and British type WCs. Washing machine in each block. This site has a busy, cosmopolitan feel, with visitors of many different nationalities when we visited. Mobile homes for hire, plus some privately owned. Used by tour operators (10%). Although not the most luxurious site in the area, it seems to offer good value.

Directions: Follow Route du Lac from the town centre and site is signed.

Charges 1998: Per unit incl. 2 persons Ffr. 72.00 - 90.00, with electricity 90.00 - 108.00; extra person (over 2 yrs) 12.00 - 18.00; extra car 8.00 - 10.00; dog 8.00 - 10.00; local tax (over 10 yrs) 1.10.

Open: 1 April - 30 September.

Reservations: Necessary in high season - contact site. Address: Av. du Lac, 3990 Hourtin. Tel: (0)5.56.09.12.76. FAX: (0)5.56.09.23.90.

3306 Camping Le Palace, Soulac-sur-Mer, nr Royan

Large, traditional site close to beach, south of Royan across the estuary.

This large, flat site has good-sized individual pitches regularly laid out amongst a variety of trees including pines which provide good shade. On very sandy ground, pitches for caravans have hardened areas and electricity is available. Most pitches have water taps, some also have sewage connection. There are twelve separate toilet blocks, some smaller and more simple than others. All have British style WCs and free pre-set hot showers, some opening from the outside only. Washbasins in private cabins are provided in some blocks, baby bathrooms (0-24 months) in four others and facilities for disabled people in one. A wide, sandy beach is 400 m. from the site gates and bathing, said not to be dangerous in normal conditions, is controlled by lifeguards. However, the site has its own small swimming pool, also with lifeguards, which is attractively set in a raised, part grass, part tiled area with its own shower facilities, etc. Arranged around a lush green roundabout with a fountain at the centre of the site are a self-service shop, butcher, fish and general shops (mostly 1/6-10/9), restaurant (15/6-10/9) and bar with dancing and concerts. Tennis courts adjacent. Supervised children's playground with paddling pool. Bicycle hire. Programme of sports, entertainments and excursions for adults and children in July/Aug. Washing machines. Treatment room and doctor will call. Mobile homes for hire. English is spoken.

Directions: Site is 1 km. south of Soulac and well signed. The shortest and simplest way is via the ferry which runs from Royan across the Gironde estuary to the Pointe de Grave, but this is quite unreasonably expensive with a caravan. Alternatively make the trip via Bordeaux.

Charges 1998: If reserved: per unit incl. 2 persons, 5A electricity and water Ffr. 88.00 - 118.00, plus drainage 90.00 - 120.00; tent pitch incl. 2 persons 70.00 - 95.00; extra person (over 10 yrs) 18.00 - 24.00; local tax (over 10 yrs, July/Aug) 2.00. Without reservation: per unit incl. 2 persons, 5A electricity and water Ffr. 104.00 - 135.00, plus drainage 107.00 - 137.00; tent pitch incl. 2 persons 90.00 - 116.00; extra person (over 10 yrs) 23.00 - 29.00. Credit cards accepted.

Open: 1 May - 15 September.

Reservations: Made for any length with deposit; contact site for details. Address: B.P. 33, Bd. Marsan de Montbrun, 33780 Soulac-sur-Mer. Tel: (0)5.56.09.80.22. FAX: (0)5.56.09.84.23.

3404 Camping Lou Village, Valras-Plage, nr Béziers

Family owned, good value site with direct access to beach.

Valras is perhaps smarter and is certainly larger than nearby Vias and it has a good number of campsites. Lou Village has direct access to a sandy beach and is a busy site with lots of facilities. Prices are quite competitive and should provide better value than at other sites in the area. However, it will become crowded in the high season as this is a popular area. The swimming pool, children's paddling pool, restaurant, bar (both 8/5-15/9) and shops all form part of the `village centre' where most of the site's activity takes place. There is a raised stage for entertainment, children's club, supermarket, bakery, takeaway, bazaar with daily papers and hairdressing salon. The bar has a large screen for TV and a terrace overlooking the pool. It is a busy site with a pleasant ambience. There are 600 pitches (including a fair number with mobile homes) of which 100 are `grand confort' with electricity, water and waste water facilities. Available everywhere, all electricity is 10A. Pitches further inland are of grass, partly separated by tall trees which provide good shade; nearer the beach the pitches are smaller, sandy and separated by bushes and bamboo hedges. The four toilet blocks, one built in '93 and the older ones recently refurbished, are well situated with reasonable facilities. They provide a mixture of Turkish and British style WCs, free pre-set hot showers with no separator and washbasins, about half in private cabins (H&C). Washing up and laundry sinks are at each block, as are chemical disposal facilities. Considering their heavy use as this is a beach-side site, maintenance (in July) seemed quite satisfactory. Other facilities include a children's playground, football field, bicycle hire, minigolf, volleyball, tennis, etc. There is lots to do off the site - sailing, windsurfing, riding, canoe kayak, river fishing, bike rides and the history of the Languedoc to discover. Mobile homes and tents for hire. English spoken.

Directions: Site is south of Béziers. From autoroute, take Béziers-Ouest exit for Valras Plage and continue for 13-14 km. Follow 'Casino' signs and site is 1 km south of centre of Valras Plage in the direction of Vendres.

Charges 1998: Per unit incl. 2 persons Ffr. 80.00 - 130.00; extra person (over 7 yrs) 12.00 - 20.00; child under 7 free - 15.00; extra car 15.00; electricity (10A)18.00; dog 15.00; local tax 1.90 (over 4 yrs). Credit cards accepted for July/Aug.

Open: 26 April - 12 September.

Reservations: Made with deposit (Ffr. 700) and fee (150). Address: BP 30, 34350 Valras-Plage. Tel: (0)4.67.37.33.79. FAX: (0)4.67.37.53.56.

AR Discount
Welcome drink; discount for `Aqualand'

FRANCE - Hérault

3403 Camping Club International Le Napoleon, Vias Plage

Smaller family site bordering the Mediterranean at Vias Plage.

The town of Vias is in the wine-growing area of the Midi, an area which includes the Camargue, Béziers and popular modern resorts such as Cap d'Agde. The single street that leads to Vias Plage is hectic to say the least in season, but once through the new security barrier and entrance to Le Napoleon, the contrast is marked - tranquillity, yet still only a few yards from the beach and other attractions. Not that the site itself lacks vibrancy, with its own pool, bar and extensive entertainment programme, but thoughtful planning and design ensure that the camping area is quiet, with good shade from the many tall trees. The 200 partially hedged pitches, most with electricity, vary in size from 80-100 sq.m. and two of the three sanitary blocks have been refurbished to a high standard, including British WCs, washbasins in private cabins, baby bath, laundry and facilities for disabled people, all well maintained when seen in peak season. Chemical disposal. Motorcaravan services. The site has its own supermarket and there are plenty of other shops, restaurants, etc. immediately adjacent. Activities include volleyball, bicycle hire, boules and TV. Fishing near. Chalets, mobile homes and apartments to let.

Directions: From Vias town, take the D137 towards Vias Plage. Site is on the right near the beach.

Charges 1998: Per unit incl. 1 or 2 persons and electricity Ffr. 125.00 - 200.00; extra person 18.00 - 30.00; extra tent free - 15.00; extra car free - 18.00; local tax 2.00.

Open: Easter - 30 September (most facilities from May).

Reservations: Taken from 1 Jan. with deposit (Ffr. 500) and fee incl. cancellation insurance (170). Address: Farinette Plage, 34450 Vias sur Mer. Tel: (0)4.67.01.07.80. FAX: (0)4.67.01.07.85.

3407 Camping Village Le Sérignan Plage, Sérignan

Unusual, well equipped, family run site with indoor pool and direct access to sandy beach.

This is a large, but very comfortable site, built in a genuinely unique style. Here you can normally find room even in the high season, with around 500 touring pitches in several areas to choose from and with the benefit of comprehensive amenities. The touring pitches, mostly of a very good size with plenty of shade and virtually all with 5A electricity are mainly on level grass and are fairly separate from a similar number of seasonal pitches and rented accommodation. Perhaps the most remarkable aspect is the cluster of attractive buildings which form a central amenity area amongst which is a small indoor heated pool of unusual design. A large outdoor pool complex is planned for '98. These attractive buildings are virtually a small village, with bar, restaurant, takeaway, disco, small amphitheatre, supermarket, newsagent, outdoor market and even a roof-top bar - all with a lively atmosphere. There are nine unisex sanitary blocks, six older ones of circular design providing for roomy pre-set showers, open plan washbasins and British and Turkish style WCs. These are nearest the central 'village' and thus take the brunt of the wear and tear. The newer blocks, closer to the touring pitches, are of the most modern design, offering excellent facilities including large controllable hot showers with washbasin and WC en-suite, baby rooms and facilities for disabled people. Dishwashing and laundry facilities in all blocks and four washing machines. The site has access to a large sandy beach and adjoining naturist beach, both of which slope very gently (lifeguard in high season). Sailing/windsurfing school on the beach.

Directions: From the A9 take exit 35 (Béziers Est) and follow signs for Sérignan on the D64 (9 km.). Do not go into Sérignan, but take sign for Sérignan Plage for 4 km. At first camping sign turn right (one way) for approx. 500 m. Bear left past two naturist sites (one the sister site to this).

Charges 1997: Per unit incl. 1 or 2 persons Ffr. 65.00 - 142.00, 3 or 4 persons 95.00 - 152.00, 5 or 6 persons 113.00 - 176.00; plus local tax; electricity (5A) 15.00; dog 15.00. Discounts in low season for children.

Open: 15 April - 15 September.   `Camping Cheque'

Reservations: Made from 1 Feb. with deposit (Ffr. 100 - 500, acc. to season) and fee (100). Address: 34410 Sérignan. Tel: (0)4.67.32.35.33. FAX: (0)4.67.32.26.36.

Camping Cheque

An exciting new way of taking your holiday abroad outside July and August.
Pay for your site fees with Camping Cheque vouchers.
Freedom and flexibility at very attractive prices.

51 Quality Sites

All featured in this Alan Rogers Guide (look for *Camping Cheque* in the text)
25 Castels sites. 15 Sites et Paysages sites.
Key facilities open from 15 May to 15 September (minimum).

Easy to Book

One phone call books your Camping Cheques,
your ferry and your insurance.

Competitive Prices

Save between 10%-50% on public tariffs.

£231

2 Adults with
car and caravan
10 nights site fees
Dover-Calais ferry

Special Offers

7 nights for 6
14 nights for 11

Only **£9 per night**
2 adults
pitch + electricity

£199

2 Adults with
motorhome
10 nights site fees
Dover-Calais ferry

Send in discount voucher F in this Guide for your
Free Catalogue (normal cost £1)

or Phone **0541 501030** to find out more

AITO
THE ASSOCIATION
OF INDEPENDENT
TOUR OPERATORS

*W*elcome to a "different France".
If you have chosen France as your
holiday destination and dream of spending
your holiday in the countryside far from the crowds,
on a top-class campsite that stands out from the rest,
and if you consider tranquility, comfort and courtesy
an essential requirement, you won't be disappointed
when you stay with the Castels.

*O*n our
50 4-star
touring
sites, camping has
a completely diffe-
rent meaning. Why ?
Simply because we
have so much more
to offer you !

**LES
CASTELS**

★ ★ ★ ★

CAMPING & CARAVANING

- Address   **LES CASTELS**
                   P I B S - C P 26
                   56038 VANNES CEDEX
- Telephone   **33 2 97 42 55 83**
- Fax   **33 2 97 47 50 72**
- See us on the web   **http/www.les-castels.com**
                   http/www.castels-campings.com

Caravaning
★★★★
l'Etoile d'Argens

TENNIS AND GOLF FREE LOW-SEASON

TEL: 04.94.81.01.41
83370 ST.AYGULF

Manoir de Kerlut

★ ★ ★ ★ Camp Site
in Southern Brittany

You'd have to be potty to take any other ferry to France.

Book now for the lowest prices from Dover to Calais. We guarantee you won't find a better value price. Travel across the channel in a way only the French know how.

le Shuttle

Folkestone ↔ Calais in around 35 minutes • The quicker the journey the longer the lunch. 100 missions a day • For more information call **0990 353535** or your local travel agent.

SAT.PIC.

LAT:5°8"
LON:44°5"

X:158
Y:129

LOC. FR.675

Stena Line leads the way to Europe

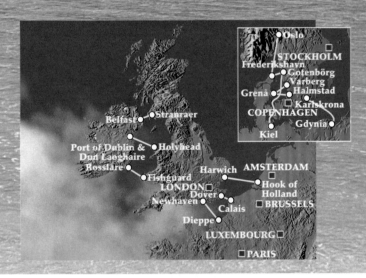

If you are travelling to France, Holland or further afield, Stena Line offers easy access to the continent from England.

Speed across the North Sea to the Hook of Holland in just 3 hours, 40 minutes on our revolutionary new Stena HSS. Or cruise to France on the Stena Empereur, the largest superferry between Dover and Calais.

Whichever route you choose, go with the company that leads the way to Europe. Stena Line.

For reservations and further information call

0990 70 70 70

or see your Travel Agent

The next generation of ferry company

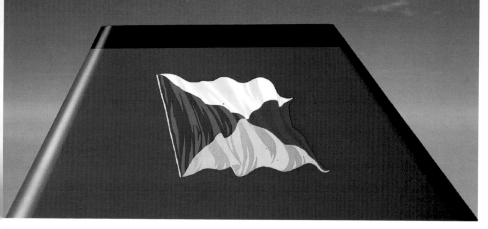

MOTORAIL
The Expressway into Europe

MOTORAIL the safe, comfortable, stress-free, time saving way to travel with your car to the South for your holiday.

For a brochure call our 24 hour Hotline
0181-880 8163

Load the car onto the train in Calais

For bookings call
0171-203 7000

Settle down for a comfortable night's sleep

RAILEUROPE

OUR FRANCE & SPAIN *Direct*

IDEAL FOR ALL OF HOLIDAY FRANCE & SPAIN

LUXURY CRUISE-FERRIES

AWARD-WINNING SERVICE

WIDE RANGE OF DIRECT CROSSINGS

OUTSTANDING VALUE

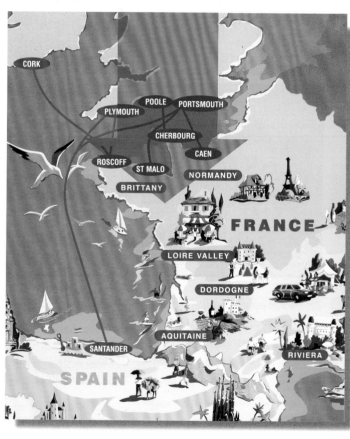

Travelling to Holiday France or Spain?
Why drive the long way round when you can sail direct?
We land you closer to where you'd like to be.

FRANCE

3504 Camping Le P'tit Bois, St Jouan des Guérêts, nr St Malo

Busy, very well kept site near ferry port and yachting centre of St Malo.

This flat, grassy, family oriented site is situated on the outskirts of St Malo, ideal for one night stops or for longer stays in this interesting area. Le P'tit Bois is very neat and clean, with 274 pitches, nearly all with electricity (5A), divided by hedges into groups and separated by shrubs and flowers. Some are under trees giving shade. There are two sanitary blocks, one in the newer area across the lane with facilities for disabled people. A little open in cool weather, they provide British WCs, washbasins in cabins, modern, pre-set showers, baby baths and chemical disposal. Laundry facilities in the ladies' block and free hot water throughout. They could be under pressure at peak times. A bright snack bar (15/5-1/9) with takeaway food is by the swimming pool area which has a terrace, paddling pool and water slide (from 1/5). Good children's playground, TV and games rooms. Small shop (from 15/5). Minigolf, tennis, volleyball. Some entertainment is organised. Motorcaravan service point. Card operated security gate. There are many British tour operators here and site-owned mobile homes, but this does mean that the facilities are open over a long season (15/5-1/9).

Directions: St Jouan is west off the St Malo - Rennes road (N137) just outside St Malo. Site is signed from the N137 (exit St Jouan).

Charges 1998: Per person Ffr. 28.00; child (under 7 yrs) 18.00; pitch and car 60.00 - 84.00; extra car 20.00; dog 25.00; electricity (5A) 19.00; water and drainage 15.00. Credit cards accepted.

Open: 1 May - 12 September.

Reservations: Made on receipt of 25% of total cost, plus fee (120) for July/Aug. Address: 35430 St Jouan-des-Guérêts. Tel: (0)2.99.21.14.30. FAX: (0)2.99.81.74.14.

An ideal setting for your next family holiday
Comfortable
Peaceful
Leisure facilities

SAINT-MALO

"Le P'TIT BOIS"
★★★★ *Camp site*
Near the Rance - Green Site with many flowers
Aquatic Area - water shute/slide, tennis, mini golf, snack, games

WEEKLY HIRING OF MOBILE HOMES AND BUNGALOW TENTS

OPEN 1st MAY - 12th SEPTEMBER, RESERVATIONS ADVISED
35430 SAINT-JOUAN-DES-GUÉRÈTS TEL: 02 99 21 14 30 FAX: 02 99 81 74 14
N137 Rennes road, exit St Jouan

3711M Camping Municipal Les Isles, Veretz, nr Tours

Managed by the Barot family who provide a warm welcome and, in season, live on the site in their caravan, Les Isles is an inexpensive, well laid out site on the banks of the River Cher, with views through tall elm trees to the Château of Veretz. With 64 pitches, most divided by small hedges and all with at least 6A electricity, the site is just outside the town of Veretz where shops, restaurants, bars, etc. can be found. Outdoor swimming pool (July/Aug) 5 km. Bread can be ordered from reception in high season, the nearest supermarket is 500 m. The large, modern, basic sanitary block includes free hot showers, British and Turkish style WCs, under cover dishwashing, chemical disposal, laundry and washing machine. Children's playground and table tennis. Fishing. Bicycle hire available if booked the night before. A new wooden chalet houses reception and plenty of tourist information. Of particular interest is information for railway enthusiasts - restored steam trains and track are in the area and the station at Veretz-Montlouis (3 km.) which uses the last manual signal system in France. This apparently attracts railway 'buffs' from afar. River pleasure trips are now possible between Veretz and Noyers. Bus service from Tours station to Bleré passes site entrance. English spoken.

Directions: Site is at Veretz, via the N76 road, 10 km. southeast of Tours (much better than the municipal at St Avertin en-route).

Charges 1997: Per pitch Ffr. 10.00; adult 11.00; child (under 7 yrs) 5.00; vehicle 10.00; electricity 6A 12.00, 16A 18.00.

Open: end May - 22 September.

Reservations: Contact site. Address: 37270 Veretz. Tel: (0)2.47.50.50.48. FAX: (0)2.47.50.33.22 (Mairie).

AR Discount
Less 10%

3701 Camping de la Mignardière, Ballan-Miré, nr Tours

Pleasant little site quietly situated just southwest of Tours.

The situation of this little site may appeal to many - only 8 km. from the centre of the city of Tours, yet in a peaceful spot within easy reach of several of the Loire châteaux, notably Azay-le-Rideau, and with various sports amenities on or very close to the site. There are 164 numbered pitches, all with electricity and 100 with drainage and water also, on flat grass and of good size. Four modern sanitary blocks have British WCs, free hot water in washbasins (in cabins) and sinks, and premixed hot water in the showers. Unit for disabled people, baby bath in the heated block near to reception, chemical disposal and laundry facilities. Amenities include a shop, two unheated, large swimming pools (15/5-15/9) with sunbathing terrace, a good tennis court, table tennis and bicycle hire. There is a bar and restaurant and crêperie with takeaway (all 15/5- 15/9). Just outside the site is a small `parc de loisirs' with pony rides, minigolf, small cars, playground and some other amusements. An attractive lake catering particularly for windsurfing is 300 m. (boards can be hired) and there is a family fitness run. Fishing 500 m. Barrier gates with card (100 Ffr. deposit), closed 22.30 - 07.30 hrs. Mobile homes (9) and chalets (8) for hire.

Directions: From Chinon along A751, follow signs to site on entering Ballan-Miré. From Tours take D751 towards Chinon. Just after Joué-les-Tours look for and turn right at Campanile Hotel - follow signs to site.

Charges 1998: Per unit incl. 2 persons Ffr. 86.00 - 100.00, comfort pitch with electricity, water and drainage 120.00 - 140.00; extra person 24.00 - 28.00; child (under 7) 16.00 - 18.00; electricity (6A) 18.00; dog 10.00. Credit cards accepted.

Open: 10 April - 30 September.

Reservations: Made for any length with deposit (Ffr. 260) and fee (90). Address: 37510 Ballan-Miré. Tel: (0)2.47.73.31.00. FAX: (0)2.47.73.31.01.

AR Discount
Less 10%

Camping ★ ★ ★ ★

DE LA MIGNARDIERE

37510 Ballan-Miré
Tel: 02 47 73 31 00 Fax: 02 47 73 31 01

All the comforts of a 4 star camp with a wide range of activities for enjoyment and relaxation of adults and children; swimming pool and tennis on site, water sports lake, ponies and minigolf very close, the Loire châteaux and all the attractions of Tours.

6 Mobile Homes and 8 Chalets for hire

From autoroute take exit for Chambray-les-Tours.

3801 Le Coin Tranquille, Les Abrets

Family run site with swimming pool and restaurant, in peaceful surroundings.

Le Coin Tranquille is set in the peaceful Dauphiny countryside in the northeast corner of the Isère département, north of Grenoble and east of Lyon. It is well situated in relation to the Chartreuse Massif, the Savoy regions and the Alps. Developed originally by Martine's parents, who are still very active about the site, the original trees such as walnuts now blend with many varieties of hydrangea and other flowering shrubs to make a lovely environment doubly enhanced by the rural aspect and the marvellous views. It is a pleasant and friendly site with 182 comfortably sized pitches, 60 available for tourers, and is very well maintained. All have electricity (2, 3 or 6A) on grass and separated by hedges. Amenities include a swimming pool (18 x 10 m.) and paddling pool (15/5-30/9) and an excellent restaurant, which is open all year (closed one day a week out of the main season) with a reasonably priced menu and takeaway. An excellent large sanitary block in the centre of the site has washing cabins, British style WCs, controllable water and facilities for children and the disabled. Laundry room. Two other blocks on either edge of the site have been refurbished. All have dishwashing facilities. Shop, two children's play areas, TV/video room with balcony, games room and quiet lounge. High season programmes of games for children, slide shows of the region's attractions, a weekly programme for adults which includes live music and sometimes folk-lore. Bicycle hire. Used by tour operators. A `Sites et Paysages' member.

Directions: Site is northeast of Les Abrets. From the town take the N6 towards Chambery, turning left after about 2 km. where the camp is signed.

Charges 1998: Per pitch incl. 2 persons Ffr. 79.00 - 119.00; extra adult 23.00 - 38.00; child (2-7 yrs) 13.00 - 21.00; extra vehicle 12.00 - 20.00; electricity 2A 8.00, 3A 12.00 or 6A 19.00. Credit cards accepted.

Open: 1 April - 31 October.   `Camping Cheque' `FRENCH FLAVOUR'

Reservations: Write to site with deposit (Ffr. 600) and fee (100). Address: 38490 Les Abrets en Dauphine. Tel: (0)4.76.32.13.48. FAX: (0)4.76.37.40.67.

3803 Camping La Cascade, Bourg d'Oisans, nr Grenoble

Small site amongst the mountains, with heated sanitary facilities.

Although very much among the mountains, with the ski resorts of Alpe d'Huez and Les Deux Alpes close at hand, Bourg d'Oisans, which is in the Romanches valley at 725 m. above sea level, presents no access problems at all for caravanners. You simply drive from Grenoble along the wide N91 Briancon road with no passes or steep gradients. La Cascade is close to, and within sight and sound of, the waterfall from which it takes its name. It has 130 individual pitches of varying but quite adequate size on mainly flat ground and with 6/15A electricity. Two heated sanitary blocks are of top quality with mainly British toilets, washbasins in cabins with light, mirror; good free hot showers, fully controllable. The heated municipal swimming pool is very close but the site has its own pool from 15/5. Bar and snack bar (July/Aug). Children's playground. General room with TV. Animation some evenings. Games/TV room. Table tennis. Volleyball. Boules. Washing machine. Chalets and caravans for hire.

Directions: Site is 400 m. along road to Alpe d'Huez which leads off from N91 just east of Bourg d'Oisans.

Charges 1997: Per unit incl. 2 persons Ffr. 80.00 - 120.00; extra person 20.00 - 28.00; local tax (15/6-31/8) 2.00; electricity (6A) 16.00 (more in winter - 25.00 - 30.00). Credit cards accepted.

Open: All year except 1/10-14/12.

Reservations: Essential for July/Aug; any length with deposit and fee. Address: Rte. de l'Alpe d'Huez, 38520 Bourg d'Oisans. Tel: (0)4.76.80.02.42. FAX: (0)4.76.80.22.63.

AR Discount
Welcome coffee
Discounts in low season

3901 Camping-Caravaning La Plage Blanche, Ounans

Attractive riverside site with good amenities.

Situated in open countryside, along the banks of the River Loue, this site has 220 good sized, marked pitches on level ground, most with electricity (6A). Trees provide fully shaded and semi-shaded pitches. Approximately 1 km. of riverside and beach provide the ideal setting for children to swim and play safely in the gently flowing, shallow water - inflatables are popular. A canoe/kayak base is also on site. Modern, well kept sanitary facilities in three unusual blocks have tiled hot showers with push-button controls, separate washing cabins and British style WCs. Chemical disposal. Dishwashing facilities are provided in blocks of 8 sinks. Bar/restaurant with terrace (1/4-30/9), pizzeria and takeaway (all season). River fishing. Launderette. Table tennis. Riding. Bicycle hire. TV room. Children's play area. Caravans for hire. Used by tour operators.

Directions: Ounans is about 20 km southeast of Dole. Site is best approached from Dole via D405 to Parcey, then N5 towards Poligny/Pontarlier. After 8 km. at Mont Sous Vaudrey take D472 towards Pontarlier to Ounans from where site is signed.

Charges 1998: Per person Ffr. 23.00 plus local tax 1.00 (over 14s); child (under 7 yrs) 12.00; pitch 28.00; extra tent or car 12.00; dog 5.00; electricity (6A) 17.00; local tax (over 14 yrs) 1.00. Credit cards accepted.

Open: 15 March - 31 October.

Reservations: Made with deposit (Ffr. 200) and fee (50) by Eurocheque. Address: 39380 Ounans. Tel: (0)3.84.37.69.63. FAX: (0)3.84.37.60.21.

AR Discount
Welcome drink

3904 Camping La Pergola, Marigny, Lac de Chalain

Hillside, terraced site overlooking lake.

Bordering on Switzerland and overlooking the sparkling waters of Lac de Chalain, Le Pergola is set amidst the undulating, cultivated countryside of the Jura. Not on a main route, it is worth a detour if seeking the restful peace of the country. It is a short distance from the magnificent Cascades du Herrison. This is a very well appointed site with 200 level, mainly stony pitches, separated by small conifers and having some shade on numerous terraces with steep steps between, giving good views over the lake. All have electricity, water and drainage. A tall wire fence protects the site from the footpath which separates it from the lakeside beach but there are frequent gates. The entrance is landscaped with flowers and a small waterfall next to the three pools (two heated) and entertainment area. An excellent sanitary block is on the lowest level and there are four others on different terraces. Washing machines and dryers. Facilities for disabled people, who are advised to select a lower terrace. Good children's play area with children's club. Organised programme in high season includes cycle tours, keep fit sessions and evening entertainment with 2 discos weekly (until midnight). Table tennis and volleyball. Watersports include windsurfing, pedaloes and electric boats for hire. Shop and a large restaurant at the entrance, also used by day visitors who use the lake for watersports. Used by British tour operators.

Directions: Site is 2½ km. north of Doucier on Lake Chalain road D27.

Charges 1997: Per unit incl. 2 persons, electricity and water: lake pitch Ffr. 90.00 - 207.50, plus supplement for lake-side 30.00; standard pitch 90.00 - 177.00; extra person 28.00; child (3-6 yrs) 20.00; baby (0-2 yrs) 10.00; extra car 15.00; dog 5.00; local tax 1.50. Credit cards accepted.

Open: 1 May - 30 September.

Reservations: Write to site with Ffr. 800 deposit and 170 fee. Address: 39130 Marigny. Tel: (0)3.84.25.70.03. FAX: (0)3.84.25.75.96.

`Camping Cheque'

4001 Airotel Le Boudigau, Labenne-Océan, nr Bayonne

Pinewood site close to beach 12 km. north of Bayonne.

Between the Landes and the Basque country, this site is well placed for some interesting excursions as well as being close to a wide sandy beach. This is 500 m. on foot from one side of the camp and rather longer by car (car park available) and includes an area for naturists. The site has a good swimming pool of 25 x 8 m. The 320 pitches are all covered by a pinewood, and of very fair size and numbered, with young shrubs planted to define the pitch area. Although the terrain is basically sandy, most pitches seemed to have a hard core, flat or slightly sloping. About half have electricity. Two identical sanitary blocks in standard modern style, with a further small unit at one end of the site. They have mostly British WCs and washbasins in good cabins with free hot water. There are 40 hot, pre-set showers with push- button, few hooks and no shelf in a separate block. Facilities for the disabled are provided. At the entrance, open to all, are a well stocked supermarket, snack bar, restaurant (15/6-10/9) and separate bar. Cinema weekly. Washing machines and dryers. TV room. Table tennis. Minigolf. Amusement machines. Boules. Children's play area and nursery. Entertainment in season. Folk music. Bicycle hire. Barbecues. Mobile homes, caravans and chalets to let.

Directions: Turn off N10 at Labenne for Labenne-Océan and site is on right in village. From the north, join N10 via St Geours de Maremne.

Charges 1997: Per unit incl. 2 persons Ffr 83.00 - 148.00; extra adult 15.00; local tax: adult 3.30, child (10-18 yrs) 1.65; animal 10.00; extra car 12.00; m/cycle 6.00; electricity (5A) 16.00.

Open: 15 May - 15 September.

Reservations: Made for any length with deposit (25%) and booking fee (Ffr. 140). Address: 40530 Labenne-Océan. Tel: (0)5.59.45.42.07. FAX: (0)5.59.45.77.76.

4002 Camping Les Chênes, Dax

Established, well kept and attractive site on outskirts of busy spa town.

Dax is not a place that springs at once to mind as a holiday town but, as well as being a spa, it has a comprehensive cultural programme of events (concerts, special shows, `courses landaises', corridas, etc.) during the season. Pleasantly situated on the edge of the town amid parkland and close to the river, a number of the 250 pitches are occupied by French seasonal caravans or people taking thermal treatments. Pitches are of two types: good sized `boxes' with hedges including electricity (5A), water and waste water connections, and others on open ground where electricity is also available, some with hardstanding. There are two toilet blocks, one new and very modern with British style WCs, the other of standard French design. Washbasins all in cubicles with hot water and a good supply of pre-set, free hot showers with push-button, facilities for babies and disabled people. Washing machines and dryers. Boules. Bicycle hire. Shop with takeaway, papers, etc. Restaurant opposite (El Callejon) with `tapas' a speciality. The site reports a new swimming pool and a play area for children. Fishing 100m. Riding and golf near, with beaches 28 km. A very reliable site, particularly suitable for adults (many take the waters) or those with older, more independent youngsters. Mobile homes and bungalows for hire.

Directions: Site is west of town on south side of river, signed after main river bridge and at many junctions in town - Bois de Boulogne (1½ km).

Charges 1997: Per pitch incl. 1 or 2 persons and electricity (5A) Ffr. 84.00 - 95.00, pitch with water and drainage also plus 16.00; extra person 18.00; child (under 7) 10.00; local tax 2.00 in high season. Credit cards accepted.

Open: 1 April - 31 October.

Reservations: Only made for the rented accommodation (contact site). Address: 40100 Dax. l: (0)5.58.90.05.53. FAX: (0)5.58.56.18.77.

AR Discount

Less 5%

4004 Camping La Paillotte, Azur, nr Soustons

Very attractive, good lakeside site with an individual atmosphere.

La Paillotte, in the Landes area of southwest France, is a site with a character of its own. The camp buildings (reception, shop, restaurant, even sanitary blocks) are all Tahitian in style, circular and constructed from local woods with the typical straw roof (and layer of waterproof material underneath). Some are now being replaced but still in character. It lies right by the edge of the Soustons lake, 1½ km. from Azur village, with its own sandy beach. This is particularly suitable for young children because the lake is shallow and slopes extremely gradually. For boating the site has a small private harbour where your own non-powered boat of shallow draught can be kept. Sailing, windsurfing (with lessons) and rowing boats and pedaloes for hire. The Atlantic beaches with their breakers are 10 km. Alternatively the site has two swimming pools (from 29/5) with a new water toboggan. All pitches at La Paillotte are marked out individual ones, usually shady, and new shrubs and trees have been planted. Pitches vary in price according to size, position and whether they are equipped with electricity, water, etc. The circular rustic-style sanitary blocks are rather different from the usual campsite installations, but are modern and fully tiled with British WCs and free hot showers in the central enclosed positions, then individual washbasins, partly enclosed with free hot water (some toilets and basins en-suite). Separate `mini' facilities for children. Outside washing-up sinks with hot water, washing machines and dryers, chemical disposal and motorcaravan services. Shop (from 6/5). Good restaurant with very pleasant terrace overlooking the lake and bar (all season). Takeaway (high season). Organised sports, games and activities for children and adults. `Mini-club' room. TV room. Fishing. Table tennis. Amusement room with juke box. Library. Treatment room. Bicycle hire. Mobile homes to let. La Paillotte is an unusual site with its own atmosphere which appeals to many regular clients. New Polynesian style bungalows to rent. Used by tour operators. No dogs accepted. Member `Sites et Paysages' and `Camping Qualité Plus'.

Directions: Coming from the north along N10, turn west on D150 at Magescq. From south go via Soustons.

Charges 1998: Per unit incl. 2 persons: standard pitch Ffr. 98.00 - 155.00; electricity (10A) 20.00 - 28.00; water and electricity 30.00 - 40.00; pitch by lake 20.00 - 40.00; extra person (over 3 yrs) 20.00 - 32.00; local tax (over 10) in July/Aug 1.65.

Open: 21 May - 14 September.

Reservations: Made for Sat. to Sat. only 2/7- 27/8, with deposit (Ffr. 250 per week) and fee (160). Address: Azur, 40140 Soustons. Tel: (0)5.58.48.12.12. FAX: (0)5.58.48.10.73. Internet: http://www.francecom.com/aft/camping/la.paillotte.

4005 Camping Le Col Vert, Vielle-Saint-Girons, nr Castets

Family holiday centre with long frontage to good lake for watersports, 5 km. from Atlantic beaches.

This extensive but natural site, edging a nature reserve, stretches right along the Lac de Léon, a conservation area, for 1 km. on a narrow frontage which makes it particularly suitable for those who want to practise water sports such as sailing and windsurfing. Bathing is also possible; the lake bed shelves gently making it easy for children and the site has a supervised beach, sail-boarding courses are arranged and there are some boats and boards for hire. There are two heated pools (Easter - Sept), both supervised, an open air one with whirl pool and a covered one, with sunbathing areas. An overall charge is made for the leisure activities (see Charges) but this excludes certain facilities, eg. riding, bicycle hire, sauna, tennis, minigolf. The 500 pitches are all flat and covered by light pinewood, most with good shade. They are of around 100 sq.m., only partly separated, some 50 with water and electricity. The four modern toilet blocks, one very large at the far end of the site, are a good supply, with excellent facilities for the handicapped. They have mostly British WCs, washbasins in private cabins or cubicles with free hot water and free hot showers (now in all blocks) with pre-set hot water. There are washing-up sinks mainly with cold water but with hot tap to draw from. A range of facilities on site including shops (20/5-15/9), sports area with tennis and volleyball, a fitness centre and workshops, and sauna and solarium. Sailing school (15/6-15/9). A good terraced bar/restaurant is by the lake (open to all 21/6-7/9). Simple hot takeaway service. Two special areas provided for barbecues. TV room. Table tennis. Amusement machines. Washing machines (4), dryer and dishwasher. Children's playground. Minigolf Walking and cycle ways in the forest and two jogging tracks. Fishing. Stables with riding on site. Much `animation' in season: children's games, tournaments, etc. by day and dancing or shows evenings. Deposit boxes. Chalets and mobile homes for hire. Used by tour operators.

Directions: Roads to lake and site lead off the D652 St Girons - Léon road at Vielle-St-Girons, clearly signed.

Charges 1997: Per unit incl. 2 persons Ffr. 59.50 - 209.00, acc. to season and type; extra person 12.00 - 25.00; child (under 7 yrs) 9.00 - 19.00; local tax (high season only) 2.10, child 1.10; electricity 3A 20.00, 6A 22.50, 10A 32.00. Leisure charge: adults Ffr. 2.00 - 4.00, child (under 7 yrs) 1.50 - 3.00. Discounts for longer stays in low season. Credit cards accepted.

Open: Easter - 1 November.

Reservations: Made for any length with £42 deposit per week booked and £25 fee. Address: Lac de Léon, 40560 Vielle-Saint-Girons. Tel: (0)5.58.42.94.06. FAX: (0)5.58.42.91.88. Internet: http://www.oda.fr/aa/col-vert.

4006 Camping Eurosol, St Girons-Plage, Castets, nr Dax

Well shaded site with swimming pool just back from sea.

Eurosol is 500 m. from a sandy beach with supervised bathing and there are also two swimming pools on site. On undulating ground in a pinewood with numerous tall trees, pitches are marked at the corners but have nothing to separate them and so there is little privacy. On flatter ground are some special caravan pitches with their own water and electrical points. On the site generally, about 300 of the 641 pitches are accessible for caravans (with electricity), so in high season space may be more easily obtainable for tents. Reservation is therefore advisable for caravans especially as only half the site is reserved. There are four main toilet blocks and two smaller units with mainly Turkish type WCs (some British), washbasins in cabins, pre-set free hot showers with pushbutton and hot water to sinks. Three blocks were renovated in '97. Motorcaravan service point. Shop. Large bar, snack bar with takeaway. Two tennis courts, games room with table tennis, minigolf, bicycle hire and a comprehensive recreation programme in July/Aug. with events daily for children and adults, day and evening (a lively atmosphere in the evenings). Play area for young children (3-10 yrs). Plans for '98 include a new entrance, shops and restaurant. Fridges for hire. Deposit boxes. Mobile homes for hire. Used by tour operators.

Directions: Turn off the D42 road at St Girons towards St. Girons-Plage, and site is on left before coming to beach.

Charges 1997: Per unit incl. 2 persons Ffr.50.00 - 107.00, with electricity 55.00 - 132.00, with water and drainage also 55.00 - 137.00; with 3 or 4 pers. respectively 75.00 -158.00, 80.00 - 183.00, 80.00 - 188.00; extra person (over 4 yrs) 25.00; local tax 2.10 (child 1.05). Credit cards accepted.

Open: 1 June - 15 September.

Reservations: Made for min. 1 week with deposit (Ffr. 500) and fee (150). Address: 40560 St Girons-Plage when open or to address in advertisement when closed. Tel: (0)5.58.47.90.14. FAX: (0)5.58.47.76.74.

AR Discount

Less 20% all seasons; tennis, minigolf free in low season. No booking fee.

Camping-Caravaning sites in the Landes
- at Saint Girons Plage:
EUROSOL ★★★★

International leisure centre, tennis, riding, swimming pool, etc.

- at Dax: a Spa and tourist resort.
LES CHENES ★★★★

For reservations write to: CAMPING EUROSOL
Route de la Plage, 40560 Vielle St. Girons
Tel. 05 58 47 90 14

4008 Parc Montana Eurolac, Aureilhan, nr Mimizan

Pleasant, attractively laid out, lakeside site with large pitches and pools, 9 km. from sea.

Now owned by the Parc Montana group, this site, in a peaceful situation by a lake (with a minor road to cross), it is largely used by families but offers a choice of activities - bathing or boating in the lake (with sailing school in season), windsurfing (boards for hire) and a riding school on site. The Atlantic beaches are 9 km. and there are two butterfly shaped swimming pools and a jacuzzi on the site (15/5-15/9). The terrain is flat, grassy and park-like, divided into 475 large numbered pitches, 280 of which have electricity and water connections and with shade from some mature trees. Six sanitary blocks give a very reasonable provision. The newest ones seem good with British and Turkish style WCs, washbasins in cabins and pre-set showers. Hot water is free and can be drawn from a tap for washing-up. Chemical disposal. Activities are organised. Shop (15/5-15/9), bar/restaurant (all season) and takeaway. General room with TV, bar and some special evenings; dancing twice weekly in season. Fishing, tennis, games room, table tennis, volleyball, basketball, minigolf, children's playground, mini-club and bicycle hire. Treatment room. Washing machines. Chalets, caravans and bungalows to let. No pets July/Aug.

Directions: Turn north off D626 at camp sign 3 km. east of Mimizan-Bourg.

Charges 1997: Per tent or caravan incl. 1 or 2 persons Ffr 66.00 - 110.00, motorcaravan 100.00 - 130.00; extra person 15.00 - 20.00; child under 10 free; electricity (6A) 12.00 - 20.00; water connection 10.00.

Open: 1 May - 30 September.

Reservations: Made for any period with 30% deposit and Ffr. 115 fee. Address: Aureilhan, 40200 Mimizan. Tel: (0)5.58.09.02.87. FAX: (0)5.58.09.41.89.

4101 Le Parc du Val de Loire, Mesland, nr Blois

Family owned site with swimming pools, situated between Blois and Tours.

This site is quietly situated away from the main roads and towns, but is nevertheless centrally placed for visits to the châteaux; Chaumont, Amboise and Blois (21 km.) are the nearest in that order. It has 300 pitches of reasonable size, either in light woodland marked out by trees, (30 occupied by British hire tents) or on open meadow with separators. Some 170 pitches have electricity, water and drainaway. The two original toilet blocks are of very fair quality and have British WCs (with external entry), washbasins all in private cabins with free hot water, shelf and mirror, free hot showers at pre-set temperature, and hot water also in sinks. A third toilet block has been built with modern facilities. Units for the disabled and new baby bath facilities. Water points around. There are three swimming pools, the newest (200 sq.m.) with sunbathing area, and heated all season; also a smaller pool with a very popular water slide, and a small children's pool. Tennis court and good children's playgrounds enlarged with skate board facilities. Barbecue area - some organised or DIY (free wood). Large shop. Takeaway all season. Bar adjacent to pools, with restaurant and snack service and TV room. Pizzeria with takeaway. Laundry facilities. Bicycle hire. Table tennis. Minigolf. BMX track. Tennis training wall. Football practise pitch. Basketball. Pony rides and organised sports and competitions in July/Aug. Wine tasting opportunities each Friday and a coach to Paris one day each week. Local walks on marked footpaths (maps Ffr.2). Mobile homes and new chalets for hire. Used by tour operators. Watch for the Rabbit family!

Directions: The village of Mesland is 5 km. northwest of Onzain, accessible from the Château-Renault/Amboise exit of A10 autoroute via D31 to Autrèche, continue 5 km. then left at La Hargardière at camp sign and 8 km. to site.

Charges 1997: Per unit incl. 2 persons: standard pitch (100 sq.m.) Ffr. 100.00 - 140.00, large pitch (150 sq.m.) with water and drainage 110.00 - 150.00; extra person 27.00 - 35.00; child (2-7 yrs) 16.00 - 20.00; electricity (6A) 16.00 - 20.00; animal 8.00 - 10.00. Credit cards accepted.

Open: 6 April - 15 September.

Reservations: Made for min. 4 days with deposit and fee (Ffr. 100). Address: 41150 Mesland. Tel: (0)2.54.70.27.18. FAX: (0)2.54.70.21.71.

4104 Camping Château des Marais, Muides sur Loire, nr Chambord

Impressive site with excellent facilities, near famous royal château.

The château at Chambord, with its park, is certainly impressive and well worth a visit. The nearby Château des Marais campsite is also well situated to visit other châteaux in the `Vallee des Rois'. The recently designed site, providing some 200 large pitches, all with electricity (5A), water and drainage and with ample shade, is situated in the oak and hornbeam woods of its own small château (in which there are rooms to let all year round). It boasts a heated swimming pool and new water slide with its own pool, a pleasant bar/restaurant, bicycle hire, fishing lake, excursions by coach to Paris and an entertainment programme in high season. The village of Muides sur Loire, with a variety of small shops, etc. is within five minutes walk. The four modern, purpose built sanitary blocks have the latest facilities including some large showers and washbasins en-suite, British style WCs, washing machine, etc. with hot water throughout. English is spoken and the reception from the enthusiastic owners and the staff is very welcoming. Used by tour operators. Bungalows and mobile homes to let, as well as the rooms in the château (breakfast included) - useful out of season.

Directions: From the A10 autoroute take exit 7 to Mer, then cross the Loire to join the D951 and follow signs.

Charges 1998: Per pitch incl. vehicle and 2 persons Ffr. 130.00; extra person 30.00; child (under 5 yrs) 20.00; dog 10.00; electricity (5A) 20.00; local tax (over 16 yrs) 2.00. Credit cards accepted (for amounts over Ffr. 1,000).

Open: 15 May - 15 September (rooms in château, etc: all year.)

Reservations: Advised July/Aug. and made with 30% deposit. Address: 41500 Muides sur Loire. Tel: (0)2.54.87.05.42. FAX: (0)2.54.87.05.43.

AR Discount
Low season pitch fee incl. 2 persons Ffr. 110

Château des Marais

CAMPING-CARAVANING-HOTEL
★★★★ GRAND CONFORT

☆ waterslide ☆ canoe & kayak hire
☆ pony rides on site
☆ bungalow & mobile home to let

27, rue de Chambord
41500 MUIDES-SUR-LOIRE
Tél 02 54 87 05 42 Fax 02 54 87 05 43
J. BONVALLET

4103 Sologne Parc des Alicourts, Pierrefitte sur Sauldre

Secluded 21 hectare site in the heart of the forest with many sporting facilities.

This site is in a very secluded, forested area midway between Orléans and Bourges, about 20 km. to the east of the A10. There are 250 pitches of which 200 have electricity (2-6A) and provisions for water are good. Most pitches are 120 sq.m. (min. 100) and vary from wooded to more open areas, thus giving a choice of amount of shade. There are three sanitary blocks, the oldest with British and Turkish style toilets, the two newer ones with all British. Washbasins (open and in cabins) have hot water, showers are controllable and there are baby/toddler bathrooms. Washing machines and drying facilities, chemical disposal and motorcaravan services. There is a restaurant using traditional cuisine (25/5-10/9) plus a takeaway in a pleasant bar with terrace. The shop (from 25/5) has a good range of produce in addition to the basics (the nearest good size town is some distance). Leisure facilities are exceptional: an inviting swimming pool complex (from 1/5) with two pools (one heated), a spa and two water slides, a 7 hectare lake with fishing, bathing, canoes, pedaloes and children's play area, 5 hole golf course (very popular), football pitch, volleyball court, tennis, minigolf, table tennis, boules, cyclo-cross and mountain bikes and a way-marked path for walking and cycling. Organised competitions for adults and children and, in high season, children's club twice a day, disco weekly and a dance for adults. Used by tour operators.

Directions: Site is on a back road, 5 km. from Pierrefitte sur Sauldre and is well signed from this village. From A71 take Lamotte-Beuvron exit.

Charges 1998: Per unit (incl. 2 persons) Ffr. 110.00 - 140.00; extra person over 18 yrs 32.00 - 42.00, 7-17 yrs 22.00 - 32.00, 1-6 yrs 17.00 - 21.00; electricity 4A 25.00, 6A 29.00; dog 25.00; local tax (1/6-15/9) 1.00 p/person. Reductions for low season longer stays.

Open: 1 May - 13 September.

Reservations: Made for min. 7 days for July/Aug. only. Address: Domaine des Alicourts, 41300 Pierrefitte sur Sauldre. Tel: (0)2.54.88.63.34. FAX: (0)2.54.88.58.40.

4405 Camping La Falaise, La Turballe, nr La Baule

Site beside beach and a short walk from resort centre.

This site is unusually situated right by the edge of the sea with direct access to a beach of sand and rocks and a wide range of water sports activities. It is also a walk of only some 400 m. to the centre of the village of La Turballe. It may therefore appeal to many. There is good bathing from a beach just along from the site, especially at high tide. The 150 pitches, on flat sandy/grassy ground with very little shade, are individual ones in rows separated mainly by low hedges but some by stones on frontage. They vary in size but are mostly near 100 sq.m.; about 120 have water and 80 electricity (4/10A). The central toilet block is of good size and fair quality, with British and Turkish style WCs, open washbasins but with free hot water, and good controllable free hot showers. Washing machine and dishwasher. Only bread, milk etc. are kept on site, with a limited takeaway and snack bar, plus a drinks service in season. TV room. There are few other on-site amenities as the village is so near with a supermarket (100 m.) and restaurants. No tour operators but some mobile homes to let (by the night, weekend or week).

Directions: Site is where the main D99 road joins the western exit road from La Turballe.

Charges 1997: Per unit, up to 3 persons with water Ffr. 137.00, with 4A electricity 158.50, 10A 163.50; extra person 24.00; child 0-4 yrs) free; local taxes 4.75. Less outside July/Aug.

Open: 25 March - 31 October.

Reservations: Min. 7 days, Sat. - Sat. only with fee. Address: 1 Bvd. de Belmont, 44420 La Turballe. Tel: (0)2.40.23.32.53. FAX: (0)2.40.62.87.07.

4403 Castel Camping Le Pré du Château, Guérande, nr La Baule

Select, small, quiet site for all units.

In the grounds of the Château de Careil, a building dating from the 14th century which may be visited, this small site, shaded by mature trees, contains less than 50 good sized individual pitches. All are equipped with electricity (6 or 10A), water and drainaway. There is a small swimming pool (10/6-5/9) and a sauna. Otherwise it is a simple site with a quiet atmosphere. Some provisions are kept and bread can be ordered (supermarket near). Children's playground, TV room, volleyball and table tennis. The sanitary facilities, in converted outbuildings, are well kept with British toilets, cubicles for washing, showers and free hot water. Facilities for disabled people. Washing machine. Two restaurants are within walking distance. Tours of the Château in the main season, also by candlelight in July/Aug.

Directions: Take D92 road from Guérande to La Baule and turn east to Careil before the town. From the D99 Guérande - St Nazaire road, turn on to D92, following signs to 'Intermarche' and for Château de Careil.

Charges 1998: Per unit incl. 2 persons and 6A electricity Ffr. 110.00 - 125.00; extra person 25.00; extra child (under 10 yrs) 15.00; 10A electricity 10.00; local tax 2.00.

Open: 1 May - 27 September.

Reservations: Possible with deposit and fee. Address: Careil, 44350 Guérande. Tel: (0)2.40.60.22.99. FAX: as phone. Internet: www.castels-camping.com.

4404 Castel Camping Parc Sainte-Brigitte, La Turballe, nr La Baule

Well established site in the grounds of a manor house, 3 km. from beaches.

A mature and spacious site, Ste Brigitte has about 200 individual pitches, which are of good size. Some are in a circular, park-like setting near the entrance, about 25 with electricity (6A), water and waste water connections. More are in wooded areas under tall pine trees which add to the fresh, open air feel, others are on more open grass, with an unmarked area in addition near the pool. One can walk around much of the areas of the estate not used for camping, there are farm animals to see and a fishing lake is very popular. The main sanitary block has free hot water in all facilities and is of fair quality, supplemented by a second block next to it. They offer British style toilets, washbasins in cabins, with bidets for women; free hot water in basins, fully controllable showers, 2 bathrooms and sinks. Washing machines and dryer (no washing to be hung out on pitches - lines provided). Chemical disposal and motorcaravan services. Children's playground, bicycle hire, boules, volleyball, pool, `baby-foot' and table tennis. A TV room and traditional `salle de reunion' are near the manor house. A swimming pool is heated with a children's pool also (open all season). Small shop for basics and a nice little restaurant/bar with takeaway (both 15/5-15/9). Bread available (baker calls). A quiet place to stay in low season, with few facilities open; in high season, however, it is mainly used by families with its full share of British visitors and can become very busy. Inland from the main road, it is a little under 3 km. from the nearest beach, with a variety of sandy ones near with safe bathing. Used by tour operators.

Directions: Entrance is off the La Turballe-Guérande road D99, 3 km. east of La Turballe.

Charges 1998: Per person Ffr 26.50 plus 1.00 tax; child (under 7) 19.00; pitch 28.50, with water and electricity 57.00; car 15.00; dog 9.50.

Open: 1 April - 1 October.

Reservations: Made for any length with exact dates and recommended for July/Aug, with deposit (Ffr. 400) plus fee (100). Address: 44420 La Turballe. Tel: (0)2.40.24.88.91. FAX: (0)2.40.23.30.42.

PARC SAINTE-BRIGITTE
★ ★ ★ ★ N.N.   HEATED
De Luxe Camping Site   SWIMMING POOL

Close to the fishing village of La Turballe and neighbouring beaches. 10 km. from the well-known resort of La Baule. The charm of the countryside with the pleasures of the seaside. Sanitary facilities as in a first-class hotel.

4410 Camping Caravaning International Le Patisseau, Pornic

Friendly quiet site near fishing port of Pornic with its own pool.

Le Patisseau is a nice friendly site, rurally situated 2½ km. from the sea, with a good welcome from the owners Catherine and Laurent. The older part of the site has an attractive woodland setting, although the pitches are slightly smaller than in the newer 'field' section, but most have water and electricity (4, 6 or 10A). Hedges are growing well in the newer section marking individual pitches. A railway line runs through the bottom of the site with 2 or 3 trains daily, but they finish at 10.30 pm. and the noise is minimal. The site has a small restaurant and bar (both 27/6-29/8) on a terrace near the medium sized pool (all season). Two water slides. Games area with volleyball and table tennis. Children's play areas. With a new reception area and two new sanitary blocks, the site continues to improve its facilities. The blocks are modern, tiled and well cleaned with children's toilets and baby baths, free hot showers, cabins with washbasins and laundry rooms. Shop (all season). Bicycle hire. Pornic is a delightful fishing village and the coastline is interesting with sandy coves and inlets. Chalets, mobile homes for hire.

Directions: Site is signed at the roundabout junction of the D751 (Pornic - Nantes) road, and from the town centre.

Charges 1998: Per unit incl. 2 persons Ffr. 81.00 - 110.00; extra adult 26.00; child (under 7 yrs) 17.00; extra vehicle 20.00; electricity 4A 18.00, 6A 22.00 or 10A 30.00; local tax 1.65.

Open: 1 May - 13 September, with limited facilities outside July/Aug.

Reservations: Made with deposit (Ffr. 300) and fee (100); contact site by letter, phone or fax. Address: Le Patisseau, 44210 Pornic. Tel: (0)2.40.82.10.39. FAX: (0)2.40.82.22.81.

FRANCE - Loire-Atlantique / Loiret / Lot

4409 Castel Camping Château de Deffay, Pontchâteau

Relaxed, family managed site, near the Côte Armor and Brière Regional Natural Park.

Château de Deffay has a rural setting and has been developed to blend into the natural environment of the estate. The 100 good sized, fairly level pitches with views of the lake or farmland are either on level, hedged terraces or informally arranged in a central, semi-sloping wooded area. Most have 6A electricity and some are fully serviced. The natural wild life and old farm buildings combine to produce a relaxed atmosphere. The main sanitary block has been designed to be unobtrusive, in an old barn, but is well equipped with modern free controllable hot showers, British type toilets, washbasins in cabins with hooks and shelves. Provision for disabled people and a baby bathroom. Washing machines, a dryer and chemical disposal. Maintenance variable. Motorcaravan services. Extra facilities are available in the old courtyard area of the smaller château (which dates from before 1400) which is also where the bar and small restaurant with takeaway, well stocked shop and the solar heated swimming pool and paddling pool are located (all 15/5-15/9). The larger château (1880) and another lake stand away from this area providing pleasant walking. It is possible to book dinners in the château with a minimum of 20 persons. The reception has been built separately to contain the camping area. Play area for children on grass, a TV room below the bar and a separate room for table tennis. Animation in season. Tennis and swimming, pedaloes and fishing in the lake, all free. Riding. Bicycle hire. The Guérande Peninsula, La Baule Bay and the natural wilderness of the `Grande Bière' are all near. Golf 5 km. Alpine type chalets (23) for letting have been built overlooking the lake and fit well with the environment. Torches useful. This is a fairly `laid-back' site, not over organised or supervised, but enjoyed by many.

Directions: Site signed from D33 Pontchâteau to Herbignac road near Ste Reine. Also from the D773 and N165.

Charges 1998: Per pitch simple Ffr. 39.00 - 55.00, with electricity (4A) 60.00 - 76.00; with 3 services 69.00 - 95.00; per adult 16.00 - 23.00; child (2-12 yrs) 11.00 - 15.00. Credit cards accepted.

Open: 2 May - 26 September.   `Camping Cheque' `FRENCH FLAVOUR'

Reservations: Accepted for a min. period of 6 nights with deposit (Ffr. 300) and fee (100). Address: BP 18, Ste Reine, 44160 Pontchâteau. Tel: (0)2.40.88.00.57. (winter: (0)2.40.01.63.84) FAX: (0)2.40.01.66.55.

4501 Les Bois du Bardelet, Gien

Attractive, lively family run site with lake and pool complex in eastern Loire.

This site, in a rural setting, is well situated for exploring the less well known eastern part of the Loire Valley. A lake and pools have been attractively landscaped in 20 acres of former farmland blending old and new with natural wooded areas and more open `field' areas with rural views. Bois du Bardelet provides 200 pitches, all more than 100 sq.m. with 80 electrical connections (15A) and some serviced (electricity, water and waste water). The communal areas are based on attractively converted former farm buildings and include two sanitary blocks with controllable hot showers, washbasins in private cabins, British type WCs, facilities for the disabled and for babies. Free hairdryers. Washing machines. The range of leisure facilities includes two swimming pools (1/4/15/9), one with a child's pool, archery, a lake for canoeing and fishing, tennis, minigolf, boules, table tennis and bicycle hire (some activities high season only). A family club card can be purchased to make use of these activities on a daily basis. Shop for basics only (from 1/7, supermarket 5 km). Snack bar and restaurant (1/7-31/8), pizzeria and takeaway service (1/6-15/9), plus a pleasant terraced bar. Various excursions are organised, the most popular being to Paris on Wednesdays, which can be pre-booked. A `Sites et Paysages' member.

Directions: From Gien take D940 towards Bourges. After some 5 km. turn left just before Peugeot garage - follow signs to site for 1.5 km. (narrow road and turning from main road).

Charges 1998: Per unit incl. 2 persons Ffr 110.00, with electricity 132.00; extra person (over 2 yrs) 25.00; animal 8.00. Less 25% in low seasons (40% for over 60s). Credit cards accepted (not Diners or Amex).

Open: 1 April - 30 September.   `Camping Cheque'

Reservations: Made with deposit (Ffr. 350) and fee (100) - contact site for details. Address: Rte. de Bourges, Poilly, 45500 Gien. Tel: (0)2.38.67.47.39. FAX: (0)2.38.38.27.16.

4601 Castel Camping de la Paille Basse, Souillac, nr Sarlat

Site in high rural situation with panoramic views and good swimming pools.

Lying some 8 km. from Souillac, this family owned and managed site is easily accessible from the N20 and well placed to take advantage of excursions into the Dordogne. It is part of a large Domaine of 80 hectares, which is available to campers for walks and recreation. The site itself has a high location and there are excellent wide views over the surrounding countryside. The 250 pitches are in two main areas - one level in cleared woodland with good shade, the other on grass on open ground without shade. They are all a minimum 100 sq.m., numbered and marked, with about 80 having electricity, water and drainaway; electricity is available near all the others. The site has a good swimming pool complex, with a main pool (25 x 10 m.), a second one (10 x 6) and also a paddling pool; they are not heated.

continued overleaf

106

4601 Castel Camping de la Paille Basse (continued)

Solarium and a crêperie adjacent to the pools. Shop. Restaurant, bar with terrace and takeaway. Disco room (twice weekly in season). TV and cinema room. Archery (free) and tennis (charged). Children's playground. Laundry facilities. Doctor calls. The main sanitary installations (there is also a small night unit at one end of site) are in three different sections, all centrally located. All are modern and kept very clean. Activities and entertainment organised in season. Mobile homes for hire (15). The site can get very busy in main season and is popular with tour operators, but there is space from mid Aug.

Directions: From Souillac take D15 road leading northwest towards Salignac-Eyvignes and after 6 km. turn right at camp sign on 2 km. approach road.

Charges 1998: Per person Ffr. 32.00; child (under 7) 20.00; pitch 52.00 or with 3 services 64.00; electricity 3A 19.00, 6A 32.00; local tax 1.00. Less 20% outside 15/6-1/9. Credit cards accepted.

Open: 15 May - 15 September.   `Camping Cheque'

Reservations: Made for min. 1 week with deposit and Ffr. 120 booking fee. Address: 46200 Souillac-sur-Dordogne. Tel: (0)5.65.37.85.48. FAX: (0)5.65.37.09.58.

4605 Camping Le Rêve, Le Vigan

Very peaceful, clean site with pool far from the madding crowd.

Le Rêve is in the heart of rolling countryside where the Perigord runs into Quercy. Pitches are divided by shrubs, and a variety of attractive trees have grown well to provide some shade. There is plenty of space for all units and some pitches are very large. Most have access to electricity. There are 9 pitches in the woods. The toilet block is modern and very clean with free hot showers and washbasins in cabins; facilities for disabled people and a baby room. For '98 the block will be extended to include a heated enclosed area. Washing machine and dryers. The small swimming pool has a large separate children's paddling pool with fountain. The reception area houses a small shop, pleasant bar, restaurant and takeaway, serving snacks and more substantial dishes. A small shaded children's playground, boules area, table tennis and volleyball facilities complete the amenities. A few chalets for hire. Le Rêve continues to impress us with its tranquillity and the young Dutch owners are keen to develop the site in such a way that this will not be lost. A site particularly suitable for families with very young children.

Directions: Follow the N20 from Souillac towards Cahors. About 3 km. south of Payrac, turn right onto the D673 (signed Le Vigan and Gourdon). After about 2 km, Le Rêve is signed on the right down a small lane and the site is some 3 km. further on.

Charges 1998: Per adult Ffr. 21.00; child (under 7 yrs) 10.00; pitch 25.00; electricity 3A 8.00, 6A 12.00. Less 15-25% outside July/Aug.

Open: 25 April - 23 September.

Reservations: Made for any length with deposit (Ffr. 300) and fee (20). Address: 46300 Le Vigan. Tel: (0)5.65.41.25.20. FAX: (0)5.65.41.68.52.

AR Discount
Less 15%
after 15/8

4701 Moulin du Périé, Sauveterre-la-Lémance, Fumel

Immaculate, pretty little site tucked away in rolling wooded countryside.

This site has 125 pitches, well spaced and marked on flat grass. Most have good shade, and pitches on a newer section are already benefiting from extensive planting of attractive trees and shrubs. Grass areas and access roads are kept immaculately clean, as are the three modern, well appointed toilet blocks, which also contain facilities for babies and disabled people. Chemical disposal and motorcaravan services. The attractive main buildings are converted from an old mill and its outhouses. Flanking the courtyard, as well as the restaurant (open air, but covered), are the bar/reception area in which people can meet and keep younger children under supervision (there is even a Lego pit). A small shop sells bread, milk, gas, and various other groceries (good small supermarket in the village, with hypermarkets in Fumel). Bar and restaurant with snacks and takeaway. The site has a clean but rather small swimming pool, with a children's pool much the same size. A small lake next to the pool is used for inflatable boats and swimming. Large games field for football, volleyball, etc. There is a 'boulodrome', two table tennis tables, bicycle hire, a trampoline and a children's playground. Fishing 3 km. A number of activities on and off site in season, including a weekly French meal and barbecues round the lake. It is possible to book inclusive special interest holidays, centred on food and wine, or walking (ring for more details). Some tour operators and a few tents, a caravan and mobile homes for hire. Many clients return again and again, so it is advisable to book early. A `Sites et Paysages' member.

Directions: Sauveterre-la-Lémance lies by the Fumel - Périgueux (D710) road, midway between the Dordogne and Lot rivers. From the D710, cross the railway line, straight through the village and turn left (northeast) at the far end on to a minor road and past the Chateau. Site is 3 km. up this road.

Charges 1998: Per person Ffr. 34.00; child (under 7 yrs) 18.50; pitch and car 47.50; animal 21.00; electricity (6A) 20.50. Credit cards accepted.

Open: 4 April - 30 September.   `Camping Cheque'

Reservations: Advisable for July/Aug. Address: Sauveterre-la-Lémance, 47500 Fumel. Tel: (0)5.53.40.67.26. FAX: (0)5.53.40.62.46.

FRANCE - Lot-et-Garonne / Maine-et-Loire

4703 Castel Camping Château de Fonrives, Rives, Villeréal

Neat, orderly site with swimming pool, in southwest of the Dordogne.

This is one of those very pleasant Dordogne sites set in pretty part-farmed, part-wooded countryside. The park is a mixture of hazelnut orchards, woodland with lake, château (mostly 16th century) and camping areas. Barns adjacent to the château have been tastefully converted - the restaurant particularly - to provide for the reception, the bar, B&B rooms, shop and games areas. The swimming pool is on the south side of this (open 10/5-20/9). There are 160 pitches of 100-150 sq.m. All have electricity, 40 have water also. Those near the woodland receive moderate shade, but elsewhere there is little from young trees. Some `wild' camping is possible. The original sanitary block is clean and adequate with free hot water, push-button showers, washbasins in well appointed cabins and British style WCs. Two additional blocks have private bathrooms (weekly hire), facilities for children and babies and laundry rooms. Chemical disposal. Motorcaravan services. The lake has a small beach and can be used for swimming, fishing or boating. Small field set aside for volleyball and football. Children's play area and paddling pool. Reading room. Minigolf. Bicycle hire. Shop, restaurant, bar and snacks all 10/6-31/8. Organised activities in season, including excursions and walks. Mobile homes, bungalows and chalets for hire.

Directions: Site is about 2 km. northwest of Villeréal, on the Bergerac road (D14/D207).

Charges 1998: Per unit incl. 2 adults Ffr. 81.00 - 110.00; extra person 23.00 - 31.00; child (under 7 yrs) 15.00 - 20.00; electricity 4A 18.00, 6A 20.00, 10A 25.00; dog 15.00; private bathroom 350 per week. Credit cards accepted.

Open: 10 May - 20 September.

Reservations: Advisable for July/Aug. Address: 47210 Rives. Tel: (0)5.53.36.63.38. FAX: (0)5.53.36.09.98.

4901 Castel Camping L'Etang de la Brèche, Varennes-sur-Loire, nr Saumur

Peaceful, spacious family site with swimming pool, adjacent to the Loire.

Towards the western end of the Loire Valley, about 6 km. from Saumur, L'Etang de la Brèche provides an ideal base from which to explore the châteaux for which the region is famous and also its abbeys, wine cellars, mushroom caves and Troglodyte villages. Developed within a 12 ha. estate on the edge of the Loire, the site has a feeling of spaciousness and provides 175 large, level pitches with shade from tall trees, facing central grass areas used for recreation and less shaded. Electricity to most pitches, water and drainage on some. The three toilet blocks have all been modernised to a high standard, providing showers with washbasins, and separate British WCs. Good hot water supply to washing up sinks, laundry, baby facilities and two units for disabled people. Chemical disposal and motorcaravan services. The good restaurant, also open to the public, blends well with the existing architecture and, together with the bar area, provides a social base and is probably one of the reasons why the site is popular with British visitors. The site includes a small lake (for fishing) and wooded area ensuring a quiet, relaxed and rural atmosphere. The swimming pool complex provides three heated pools, plus a water toboggan, for youngsters of all ages. Well organised entertainment programme (July/Aug). Shop, epicerie, takeaway, pizzeria, games and TV rooms. Tennis, basketball, field for football, bicycle hire and BMX track. Child minding arranged in the afternoons. Torches required at night. Used by tour operators.

Directions: Site is 100 m. north off the main N152, about 5 km. southeast of Saumur on the north bank of Loire.

Charges 1997: Per unit incl. 2 persons Ffr. 95.00 - 130.00, 3 persons 110.00 - 145.00; extra adult 26.00; extra child (2-7 yrs) 15.00; electricity 15.00; water and drainage 12.00; extra car 20.00. Credit cards accepted.

Open: 15 May - 17 September.　　　　　　　　　　`Camping Cheque' `FRENCH FLAVOUR'

Reservations: Made for min. 7 days with deposit and fee. Address: 49730 Varennes-sur-Loire. Tel: (0)2.41.51.22.92. FAX: (0)2.41.51.27.24. E-mail: etang.breche@wanadoo.fr.

4902 Camping de Chantepie, St Hilaire-St Florent, Saumur

Pleasant site with swimming pools, close to Saumur with lovely views over the Loire.

Your drive along the winding road bordered by apple orchards and vineyards is well rewarded on arriving at the floral entrance to Camping de Chantepie. The reception and well stocked shop are housed in the tastefully restored ancient farmhouse. The 150 grassed pitches are level and spacious, most with electricity (6A), and separated by low hedges of flowers and trees which offer some shade. They are linked by gravel paths. The panoramic views over the Loire from the pitches on the terraced perimeter of the meadow are stunning, and there is a footpath leading to the river valley. The sanitary block is very clean and facilities are adequate, although they are housed in separate buildings. There is hot water to all the washbasins and showers, which are of the pre-set, push-button variety. WCs are British style. Facilities for disabled people. The two paddling pools and two heated swimming pools are surrounded by an attractive sitting area, well protected by a stone wall.. The new bar and terraced restaurant provide a variety of snacks, takeaway meals and comprehensive menus (from 15/5). For your own cuisine, a well stocked herb garden is at your disposal. Leisure activities are catered for in July/Aug. by the `Chantepie Club'. Pony and donkey cart rides, bicycle and mountain bike hire (maps from reception). Minigolf. Children's play area with wide variety of apparatus. Volleyball, TV, video games and table tennis. Fishing 200 m. Wine tasting evenings, excursions and canoeing expeditions organised.

Directions: Take D751 signed Gennes from Saumur. Turn left in Minerolle as signed and continue 4 km. to site.

Charges 1998: Per adult Ffr. 26.00; child (2-9 yrs) 14.00; pitch incl. car 62.00; electricity 17.00; local tax 2.00 (child 1.00). Less 10-20% in low seasons. Credit cards accepted.

Open: 1 May - 20 September.   `Camping Cheque'

Reservations: Contact site for details. Address: St Hilaire-St Florent, 49400 Saumur. Tel: (0)2.41.67.95.34. FAX: (0)2.41.67.95.85.

5000 Camping L'Etang des Haizes, St Symphorien-le-Valois

Attractive, informal site with small heated pool and pretty lake.

L'Etang des Haizes offers 105 good size pitches on fairly level ground with 100 electrical connections (3 or 6A). They are set in a mixture of conifers, orchard and shrubbery, with some very attractive slightly smaller pitches overlooking the lake. There are 45 mobile homes inconspicuously sited, 25 of which are for hire. The two sanitary blocks are of modern construction, open plan and mixed, with British WCs, free controllable showers and washbasins in private cabins. Units for disabled people, washing up under cover, small laundry with two washing machines and a dryer, chemical disposal and motorcaravan services. The lake offers good coarse fishing for huge carp (we are told!), swimming (with a long slide), pedaloes, a small beach and now, believe it or not, a turtle can sometimes be seen on a fine day! Other facilities include a heated swimming pool, an attractive bar with terrace overlooking the lake and pool (both 20/5-5/9), two children's play areas, bicycle hire, table tennis, TV lounge, pool table, petanque, volleyball and archery, plus ducks and goats. Only milk, bread and snacks (takeaway) on site, but supermarket in La Haye-du-Puits (1 km). Gate locked 22.00 - 07.00. Site is 8 km. from a sandy beach and a 25 km. drive from the Normandy landing beaches. Tour operator mobile homes.

Directions: From Cherbourg follow N13 (Mont St Michel) road as far as Valognes, then the D2 to St Sauveur-le-Vicomte. Continue on the D900 for La Haye-du-Puits, go straight on at new roundabout on the outskirts of town and site is signed almost immediately on the right.

Charges 1998: Per adult Ffr 30.00; child (under 9 yrs) 16.00; pitch plus car 45.00; electricity (6A) 25.00; dog 12.00. Less 20% outside July/Aug.

Open: All year (facilities limited outside May-Sept).

Reservations: Made with 25% deposit. Address: 50250 St Symphorien le-Valois. Tel: (0)2.33.46.01.16. FAX: (0)2.33.47.23.80.

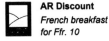

AR Discount
French breakfast for Ffr. 10

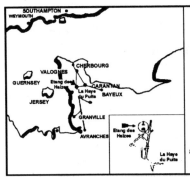

L'ETANG des HAIZES
★ ★ ★ ★
50250 La Haye du Puits

Ideal for an escapade

★ Caravan Park and Storage
★ Chalet and Mobile Home to Hire

For your first night in France, relax and enjoy the comfort and atmosphere. During your stay visit Bayeux, Mont St Michel and enjoy typical Normandy meals with a bottle of real Calvados.

5003 Castel Camping Lez Eaux, Granville

Family site with swimming pools just back from sea on Cotentin coast.

Set in the spacious grounds of a château, Lez Eaux lies in a rural situation just off the main route south, under 2 hours from Cherbourg. The nearest beach is 3 km, St Pair is 4 km. and Granville 7, and it is a very pleasant situation from which to explore this corner of the Cotentin peninsula. However, because of its location, Lez Eaux receives much 'en-route' trade, both from tour operator clients and independent campers on their way further south and at times this can put heavy pressure on the facilities. It has 192 pitches, many taken by British and some Dutch tour operators with special places provided for late arrivals and early departures. Most pitches are of a good size, semi-separated by trees and shrubs on either flat or very slightly sloping, grassy ground overlooking Normandy farm land. All have electricity (5/10A) and some have drainage. Two modern toilet blocks have British WCs, washbasins in cabins and showers with free hot water throughout. They are cleaned three times daily. Full provision for the handicapped. Small heated swimming pool and attractive fun pool with slide and water slide. Shop. Small bar. Snacks and takeaway with set meal each night to order in advance (from 15/5). Adventure play area. Good tennis (Ffr. 40 p/hr high season). Games room with table tennis. Jacuzzi. Fishing. TV room. Washing machine and dryer. Torches required at night. Note: facilities not fully open until 15/5.

Directions: Site access is signed west about 7 km. southeast of Granville on main D973 road to Avranches.

Charges 1997: Per pitch incl. 2 persons Ffr. 105.00 - 110.00, pitch with 5A electricity 127.00 - 142.00, 10A electricity 136.00 - 153.00, with all services 140.00 - 160.00; extra person 32.00 - 36.00; child (under 7 yrs) 17.00 - 20.00. Credit cards accepted.

Open: 1 May - 15 September.   '*Camping Cheque*'

Reservations: Advisable for high season and made for min. 5 days with deposit (Ffr. 200) and fee (100). Address: 50380 St Pair-sur-Mer. Tel: (0)2.33.51.66.09. FAX: (0)2.33.51.92.02.

5604 Camping de Penboch, Arradon, nr Vannes

Quietly situated site on the Golfe du Morbihan with good facilities.

Penboch is 200 m. by footpath from the shores of the Golfe du Morbihan with its many islands, where there is plenty to do including watersports, fishing and boat trips. There are also old towns with weekly markets near and it is 30 minutes walk to Arradon which has a good range of shops and restaurants. The site is in a peaceful, rural area and is divided into two parts - one in woodland with lots of shade, and the other main part, across a minor road on more open ground with hedges and young trees. Well kept, Penboch offers 175 pitches on flat grass, mostly divided into groups; electricity is available on most pitches (6/10A) and there are plenty of water points. Three sanitary blocks, the largest on the main part of the site, have good showers with free hot water, washbasins in cabins and British style WCs. Chemical disposal. Motorcaravan service point. There is a friendly bar with satellite TV, snacks and takeaway, where basic food supplies are also kept (all 15/5-13/9). A heated swimming pool with water slide toboggan and children's pool with 'mushroom' (15/5-13/9) are in the centre of the site and a good children's playground, visible from reception, is provided with interesting play equipment. Games room. Fishing 200 m. Sailing and windsurfing 2 km. Washing machines and dryers. American motorhomes accepted in low season. Barbecues are allowed. Site owned mobile homes and bungalows for rent. Popular with British tour operators. A 'Sites et Paysages' member.

Directions: From the N165 at Auray or Vannes, take the D101 road along the northern shores of the Golfe du Morbihan; or leave the N165 at D127 signed Ploeren and Arradon. Take turn to Arradon, and site is signed.

Charges 1997: Per person Ffr. 23.00; child (under 7 yrs) 16.00; pitch incl. car 30.00 - 78.00; electricity 6A 16.00, 10A 18.00; water/drainage 12.00; extra car 10.00; dog free - 10.00; local tax (over 18) 3.00. Credit cards accepted.

Open: 4 April - 20 September.

Reservations: Recommended for high season and made for min. 7 days for the period 10/7-18/8. Address: Chemin de Penboch, 56610 Arradon. Tel: (0)2.97.44.71.29. FAX: (0)2.97.44.79.10.

5601 Castel Camping La Grande Métairie, Carnac

Good quality site in southern Brittany with many facilities.

La Grande Métairie is quietly situated, a little back from the sea, close to some impressive rows of the famous `menhirs' (giant prehistoric stones). It has much to offer on site and is lively and busy over a long season. There is a feeling of spaciousness with a wide entrance and access road, with 575 individual pitches (with electricity - 30 m. cables needed in parts), surrounded by hedges and trees. Paddocks with ponds are home for ducks, goats and ponies to watch and feed and there is a large playing field with football posts. A heated swimming pool of 200 sq.m. is supplemented by two smaller pools and a children's paddling pool. An entertainment area includes an outside amphitheatre developed for musical evenings and barbecues. The three large, identical toilet blocks are good and well maintained, with free hot water, British toilets, washbasins in cabins, free pre-set showers, hairdryers, and facilities for babies and disabled people, chemical disposal, and each with a laundry room. Other amenities include a shop, boutique, restaurant, good takeaway, bar lounge and terrace, and adjoining TV and games rooms. Occasional dances, etc. (pitches near these facilities may be noisy late at night - the bar closes at midnight). Pony rides from site. Horse riding and golf near. Two tennis courts. Volleyball and basketball. Minigolf. Two children's playgrounds. BMX track. Bicycle hire. Table tennis. Fishing (on permit). Events are organised daytime and evening. Motorcaravan service points. Mobile homes for hire. The nearest beach is about 3 km. by road. Local market at Carnac on Sundays. The site, although large and not cheap, is well known and popular. Limited services before late May. American motorhomes accepted up to 30 ft. It has a large British contingent with many pitches taken by tour operators and British touring caravanners and campers.

Directions: From N165 take Quiberon/Carnac exit onto the D768. After 5 km. turn left on D781 to Carnac and, following camp signs, turn left at traffic lights to the site.

Charges 1998: Per person Ffr. 29.00; child (under 7 yrs) 19.00; pitch incl. car 122.00, with electricity (6A) 140.00 local tax (over 15, 1/6-30/9)2.20. Less 25% 23/5-30/6 and 1-12/9, 40% before 23/5. Credit cards accepted.

Open: 4 April - 12 September, all services from 23/5.

Reservations: Made (min. 1 week) with deposit (Ffr. 300 per week booked). Address: B.P. 85, 56342 Carnac-Cedex. Tel: (0)2.97.52.24.01. FAX: (0)2.97.52.83.58.

5801 Camping Des Bains, St Honoré-les-Bains

Attractive family run site with pool, close to small spa-town.

With 120 large (100 sq.m.) separated pitches, 100 with 6A electricity, and many trees, this is an attractive site, owned and run by the Luneau family who are keen to welcome British visitors and it is well situated for exploring the Morvan area. However, the site is low-lying, pitches can be rather soft in wet weather and it can also be quite cold at night in early or late season. There are opportunities for horse riding, fishing, etc. or for `taking the waters' which, combined with the clean, pollution free environment, are said to be very good for asthma sufferers (cures run for three week periods). The site has its own small swimming pool (12 x 12 m) with a separate aqua slide (15/6-30/9), a children's play area, and two small streams for children to fish in, one of which is warm from the thermal springs. The actual thermal park is next door with added attractions for children. A traditional family bar (1/5-30/9) also provides food and a takeaway service (15/6-30/9). Table tennis. Minigolf. Entertainment weekly for children in July/Aug. The three sanitary units are of varying ages with mostly British WCs, washbasins in separate cabins and ample hot showers. There are dishwashing sinks (with hot water), a baby bath, facilities for disabled people, chemical disposal and laundry facilities. Modern gites for hire all year. A `Sites et Paysages' member.

Directions: From the north approach via the D985 from Auxerre, through Clamecy and Corbigny to St Honoré-les-Bains, from where the site is signed `Village des Bains'.

Charges 1998: Per unit incl. 2 persons Ffr. 90.00; extra person 23.00; child (under 7 yrs) 12.00; local tax extra; electricity (6A) 17.00. Credit cards accepted.

Open: 1 May - 30 September.

Reservations: Write to site with deposit (Ffr. 420) and fee (80). Address: BP 17, 15 Av. Jean Mermoz, 58360 St. Honoré-les-Bains. Tel: (0)3.86.30.73.44. FAX: (0)3.86.30.61.88.

AR Discount
Less 10-30%
outside July/Aug

The French sites featured in this guide are only a selection of those in our ALAN ROGERS' FRANCE guide

5803 Castel Camping Manoir de Bezolle, St Péreuse-en-Morvan

Well situated site for exploring the Morvan Natural Park and the Nivernais area.

This site has been attractively landscaped to provide a number of different areas and terraces, giving some pleasant views over the surrounding countryside. The 140 clearly separated pitches are on level grass with some terracing and a choice of shade or otherwise. The majority have electricity (6A or more). Several features are worthy of special mention including a large swimming pool and children's pool with terrace, a good restaurant with a varied menu, takeaway service (main season only), two small lakes one of which is used for fishing and the Red Indian village with ponies. Sanitary facilities are in 4 units - a small older style unit by the pool and restaurant complex, and a new fibreglass unit containing two tiny family WC/basin/shower suites for rent. Two large more central units of different ages provide the main services. Facilities include baths, pre-set showers, basins in cabins (many with cold water), British WC's, provision for disabled people and a baby bath. Laundry, chemical disposal and motorcaravan services. Shop (15/5-15/9). Riding. Minigolf. Games room. Bicycle hire for children. Table tennis. Fishing. Mobile homes for hire. Used by tour operators.

Directions: Site is mid-way between Châtillon-en-Bazois and Château-Chinon, just north of the D978 by the small village of St Péreuse-en-Morvan.

Charges 1998: Per pitch incl. 2 persons Ffr. 80.00 - 115.00; extra person 20.00 - 30.00; child (under 7 yrs) 15.00 - .20.00; electricity (6A) 24.00, extra 4A 12.00; water and drainage connection 14.00; animal 10.00; visitor 15.00; extra car 10.00; local taxes 3.00. Credit cards accepted.

Open: 15 March - 15 October. `Camping Cheque'

Reservations: Made with deposit (Ffr. 300) and fee (100); contact site for details. Address: 58110 Saint Péreuse en Morvan. Tel: (0)3.86.84.42.55. FAX: (0)3.86.84.43.77.

6001 Camping Campix, St Leu-d'Esserent, nr Chantilly

Unusual, peaceful, modern site in old sandstone quarry, with good access to Paris.

Opened in 1991, this attractive, informal site has been developed in a striking location on the outskirts of the small town. The quarry provides a very sheltered, peaceful environment and trees have grown to soften the slopes. The 170 pitches are arranged in small groups on the different levels with gravel access roads (some fairly steep). Electricity (6A) is available to 150 pitches. There are many secluded corners for additional smaller units and plenty of space for children to explore (parents should supervise - some areas could be dangerous). A footpath leads to the town for shops, restaurants and an outdoor pool (in season). At the entrance to the site, a modern building houses reception, a large social room with open fire, and two modern sanitary units. These have pre-mixed hot showers with dividers and seats, washbasins in rows, some British style WCs, a suite for disabled people, chemical disposal, laundry facilities with washing machine and dryer. Hot water is free. Bread and milk are delivered daily. Snack bar (July/Aug). Bicycle hire. Motorcaravan service station. Bottle bank. The friendly, English speaking owner will advise on places of interest to visit which include Chantilly (5 km), the Asterix Park and the Mer de Sable, a Western theme amusements park. Disneyland is 70 km. It is possible to visit Paris by train (max. 50 mins) from the station in St Leu - ask the site for detailed instructions.

Directions: St Leu d'Esserent is 11 km. west of Senlis, 5 km. west of Chantilly. From the north on the A1 autoroute take the Senlis exit, from Paris the Chantilly exit. Site is north of the town off the D12 towards Cramoisy, and is signed from the peripherique or in the town.

Charges 1998: Per unit Ffr. 20.00 - 30.00; small tent 5.00 - 25.00, acc. to location; person 15.00 - 25.00; child (under 12 yrs) 10.00 - 15.00; dog 5.00 - 10.00; electricity 15.00. Credit cards accepted.

Open: 1 March - 30 November.

Reservations: Advisable for July/Aug. Write for details. Address: BP 37, 60340 St Leu-d'Esserent. Tel: (0)3.44.56.08.48 or (0)3.44.56.28.75. FAX: (0)3.44.56.28.75.

AR Discount
Free ticket for
La Mer de Sable
for a min. 4 day stay.

6203 Camping Château de Gandspette, Eperlecques, nr St Omer

Family run site in grounds of château with swimming pools.

Conveniently situated for the Channel Ports and the Tunnel, this family run site provides useful overnight accommodation as well as a range of facilities for a longer stay. It has the benefit of a large, heated swimming pool - an addition to a smaller older one with paved, sheltered sunbathing area (1/5-30/9). There is also an attractive bar (from 15/4), grill restaurant (from 15/5) and takeaway situated in a 17th century building adjacent to the château. With 120 pitches in all (100 sq.m.), half are taken by semi-permanent French holiday caravans which intermix with some of the touring pitches giving a real French ambience. All have electricity (6A) and are delineated by trees in the corners and some hedging, with circular gravelled access roads and central open spaces so that it is possible to have shade or sun and to see the odd visiting squirrel. The sanitary block is somewhat utilitarian looking but appears satisfactory providing some British style WCs, some washbasins in cabins with H&C, others with cold only and free push-button hot showers in cubicles with separators. *continued overleaf*

6203 Camping Château de Gandspette (continued)

Covered dishwashing sinks with hot water point, washing machine and chemical disposal. Small supermarket in the village (1 km). Children's play area, with a play field; riding nearby (on the campsite at weekends if reserved), walks in the site's 4 ha. of mature woodland. Petanque, tennis, children's room with electronic games and darts! Fishing and bicycle hire 2 km. Entertainment in season. Rooms in the château (B&B). Used by two British tour operators. Market at Watten on Fridays, at St Omer and Dunkerque on Saturdays. A `Sites et Paysages' member.

Directions: From N43 St Omer - Calais (southeast of Nordausques) take D221 east following camp signs (5-6 km).

Charges 1998: Per unit incl. 2 persons Ffr. 100.00; extra person (over 4 yrs) 25.00, under 4 free; extra car 10.00; electricity (6A) 20.00. Credit cards accepted.

Open: 1 April - 30 September. `Camping Cheque'

Reservations: Needed in July/Aug. Address: 62910 Eperlecques. Tel: (0)3.21.93.43.93. FAX: (0)3.21.95.74.98.

6201 Castel Camping Caravaning La Bien-Assise, Guînes, nr Calais

Mature, quality site with pools close to cross channel links.

The chequered history of `La Bien-Assise' goes back to the 1500s, but today the Château, farm and mill are all in the hands of the Boutoille family and they can provide you with a fascinating brief history. However, now the farm buildings house the shop, bar/grill, TV room and takeaway (from early May). The entrance to a more formal restaurant, `La Ferme Gourmande' (open all year, closed Mondays) is in the mellowed farmyard opposite the dovecote with the Auberge du Colombier next door. The pool complex utilises a barn area to provide a partly covered, sheltered and heated pool (16 x 6), and fun pool with toboggan and paddling pool with `mushroom'. There are 200 grass pitches mainly set among mature trees, apart from one new field. Of good size and connected by gravel roads, shrubs and bushes make them `semi-delimité'. Three good, well equipped toilet blocks are ample with free, controllable showers, many washbasins in cabins, mostly British style WCs and provision for babies, clothes and dishwashing. Play areas, minigolf and a tennis court are sheltered by a mature garden wall, which together with the Château itself (hotel rooms and Auberge), combine to give a comfortable, mature feel. Bicycle hire. Used by tour operators; its position 15 mins from Calais, the Channel Tunnel exit 6 km. and Boulogne 20 mins, make it a popular venue en-route north or south, but it is well worth a longer stay. The Boutoille family personally manage the site and reception opens long hours to meet the needs of those crossing the Channel. Local market, walks from the site. `Cloth of Gold' Fete 12-27 July.

Directions: From ferry terminal follow A16 south (Boulogne) for junction 15, turning towards St Pierre de Calais to immediately pick up Guînes signs before going under autoroute following the D127. Continue beside canal to Guînes. Site is just southwest of village on D231 Marquise road. From Tunnel also follow A16 south (Boulogne) to immediately pick up Guînes signs at junction 11 and following D215 past St Tricat to Guînes. From south on autoroute A26, use exit 2 (Ardres, Guînes) onto N43 and D231 (15 km).

Charges 1997: Per pitch Ffr. 56.00; adult 23.00; child (under 8) 16.00; electricity (6A) 18.00. Less 7% in low season. Credit cards accepted (not Diners or Amex). `Camping Cheque'

Open: 25 April - 20 September (full facilities: 6/5-16/9).

Reservations: Advised for July/Aug: deposit required for stays of about a week or more. Rooms in the châteaux, Auberge and restaurant open all year. Address: 62340 Guînes. Tel: (0)3.21.35.20.77. FAX: (0)3.21.36.79.20.

AR Discount
Less 10%
in low season

6405 Camping International Erromardie, St Jean-de-Luz

Good seaside site close to some well known Basque resorts.

Sites right by the sea in this region are not all that numerous but this is a good one with only the access road to cross to reach a beach of fine shingle. It is said to be safe for bathing (some submerged rocks at low tide) although it is supervised by lifeguards. The beach is public and can be busy at weekends. The site is mainly flat, grassy, and consists of several different parts separated by hedges with little shade. All pitches are now individual ones, with electricity, which mainly adjoin access roads and back onto hedges. The two large sanitary blocks are of good quality with free hot water in all facilities, British WCs, washbasins in private cabins and mainly pre-set hot showers. Swimming pool (25/5-30/9) and solarium. Shop (July/Aug), takeaway (July/Aug) and restaurant (15/6-10/9). Boules. Children's play area. Golf courses near. St Jean-de-Luz, an attractive, lively little seaside resort with plenty of history and character, is a short drive. The more select and sedate Biarritz is about 15 km. as is the Spanish frontier at Hendaye and Behobia. Caravans and mobile homes for hire. Used by tour operators.

Directions: Turn off main N10 north of St Jean-de-Luz towards sea by sign to `Campings' and `Plage d'Erromardie', then 1 km. to site. From autoroute A63, take exit for St Jean-de-Luz Nord.

Charges 1998: Per pitch incl. 2 persons and electricity (5A) Ffr. 95.00 - 152.00; extra person 17.50 - 27.50 (under 5 yrs free); local tax (over 10s) 2.00. Credit cards accepted.

Open: 1 May - 27 September.

Reservations: Made for foreigners with substantial deposit and small booking fee for periods of at least a week. Address: 64500 St Jean-de-Luz. Tel: (0)5.59.26.07.74.

FRANCE - Pyrénées-Atlantiques

6409 Camping La Chêneraie, Bayonne

Good class site with swimming pool in pleasant situation 8 km. from sea.

A good quality site in a pleasant setting, La Chêneraie is only 8 km. from the coast at Anglet where there is a long beach and big car park. It also has a medium sized free swimming pool on site, open June-Aug, longer if the weather is fine, which makes it a comfortable base for a holiday in this attractive region. Bayonne and Biarritz are near. There are distant mountain views from the site which consists of meadows, generally well shaded and divided partly into individual pitches and with some special caravan plots with electricity, water and drainage. In the sloping part of the site terraces have been created to give level pitches. A wooded area, not used for camping, is available for strolls. The sanitary installations consist of one very large central block of good quality with British toilets and free hot water in the washbasins (in cabins) and in fully controllable hot showers, and three smaller units in other parts all of which are kept very clean. Baby baths, facilities for disabled people and chemical disposal. Washing machine and dryer. Shop, general kiosk and restaurant with all day snacks and takeaway (shop, restaurant and pool 1/6-15/9). Tennis (free outside July/Aug). Small pool for fishing, boating with inflatables etc. Table tennis. Children's playground. TV room. First aid room. Safe for valuables. Fully equipped tents, bungalows and mobile homes for hire. Used by tour operators. English spoken.

Directions: Site is 4 km. northeast of Bayonne just off the main N117 road to Pau. From new autoroute A63 take exit 6 marked 'Bayonne St. Esprit'.

Charges 1998: Per person Ffr. 24.00; child (under 10 yrs) 14.00; local tax (over 18s) 1.10; pitch 50.00; electricity 18.00. Less 20% outside 1/6-15/9.

Open: Easter - 30 September, full services 1/6-15/9.

Reservations: Made for min. 1 week with deposit (Ffr. 400) and fee (100). Address: 64100 Bayonne. Tel: (0)5.59.55.01.31. FAX: (0)5.59.55.11.17.

6411 Camping du Col d'Ibardin, Urrugne

Family owned site with swimming pool at foot of Basque Pyrénées.

This is a highly recommended site which justly deserves praise. It is well run with emphasis on personal attention, the smiling Madame, her staff and family ensuring that all are made welcome. It is attractively set in the middle of an oak wood. Behind the forecourt, with its brightly coloured shrubs and modern reception area, various roads lead to the pitches. These are individual, spacious and enjoy the benefit of shade, but if preferred a more open aspect can be found. There are electric hook-ups and adequate water points around. The two toilet blocks are kept very clean and house WCs (British style), a WC for disabled people, washbasins, free pre-set hot showers. The second block has been completely rebuilt to a high specification. Dishwashing facilities are in separate open areas close by and a laundry unit with washing machine and dryer is located to the rear of reception. Chemical disposal. A small shop sells basics and bread orders are taken (1/6-15/9), but a large supermarket and shopping centre is 5 km. In July/Aug. there is a catering and takeaway service on site, also a bar and occasional evening entertainment which includes Flamenco dancing. Other amenities include a swimming pool and paddling pool, tennis courts, bicycle hire, boules, table tennis, video games and a children's playground and club with adult supervision. From this site you can enjoy the mountain scenery, be on the beach at Socoa within minutes or cross the border into Spain 14 km. down the road. Used by tour operators.

Directions: Leave the A63 autoroute at St Jean-de-Luz sud, exit no. 2 and join the RN10 in the direction of Urrugne. Turn left at roundabout (signed Col d'Ibardin) onto the D4 and site is on right after 5 km.

Charges 1997: Per unit incl. 2 persons Ffr. 65.00 - 98.00; extra adult 15.00 - 22.00; child (2-7 yrs) 10.00 - 14.00; electricity (4A) 16.00 - 18.00; animal 10.00 (high season only); local tax 1.10 (high season).

Open: 1 May - 30 September.

Reservations: Are accepted - contact site. Address: 64122 Urrugne. Tel: (0)5.59.54.31.21. FAX: (0)5.59.54.62.28.

6601 Camping-Caravaning California, Le Barcarès, Perpignan

Family owned site with swimming pool, not far from beach.

This small site is attractively laid out with much green foliage (formerly an orchard) and has 240 hedged pitches on flat ground. Cool and shaded, the site now has a mature look with an attractive terraced pool bar area and an efficient reception area built in local materials. The pitches, all with electricity and shade, vary a little in size and shape but average about 100 sq.m. The two toilet blocks are of standard modern construction with British style WCs, free pre-mixed hot water in washbasins, showers with push-button, and sinks. Baby bath and small toilets. Chemical disposal. Motorcaravan services. The site is 900 m. from a sandy beach. It has a swimming pool of 200 sq.m. and children's pool (from 1/5), with free water slide (26/6-31/8) in a small separate pool. Restaurant and bar with takeaway, shop (20/6-4/9), wine store and pizzeria. Tennis, TV room, small multi-gym, mountain bike hire and BMX track on site and archery. Fishing 500 m. Washing machine. Car wash. Children's animation in season and some evening entertainment. Only gas or electric barbecues allowed. Bungalows and mobile homes to let.

Directions: Site is on the D90 coast road 2 km. southwest of Le Barcarès centre.

Charges 1998: Per unit with 2 persons Ffr. 105.00, with 10A electricity 121.00; extra person 28.00; child (under 7) 18.00; extra vehicle 17.00; animal 10.00; visitor 17.00; local tax (over 4) 1.00. Less 20-50% outside July/Aug.

Open: 25 April - 26 September.

Reservations: Necessary for high season and made with deposit (Ffr. 500) and fee (80). Address: Route de St. Laurent, 66420 Le Barcarès. Tel: (0)4.68.86.16.08. FAX: (0)4.68.86.18.20.

6607 Camping-Caravaning Le Brasilia, Canet Plage en Roussillon

Excellent, well run site beside beach with wide range of facilities.

La Brasilia is pretty, neat, tidy and well kept with a wide range of facilities and activities. It is large, but does not seem so, with 900 neatly hedged pitches all with 5A electricity. With shade from mature pines and flowering shrubs, less on pitches near the beach, there are neat access roads and many flowers. The nine modern sanitary blocks are well equipped and maintained, with British style WCs (some Turkish) and washbasins in cabins. One block is very modern and impressive with good facilities for children (as does one other block). All have washing up and laundry sinks with hot and cold water. Chemical disposal, laundry room and facilities for disabled people. The sandy beach is busy, with a beach club. However, there is also a large California type pool (1/5-30/9), with sunbathing areas and bar. Sports field beside the tennis courts and sporting activities such as aqua gym, aerobics, football, etc. plus a games and video room (club card required in high season). Bicycle hire. Fishing. The village area with shops, bars and restaurant is busy, providing meals, entertainment (including a night club) and a range of shops. It has a lively atmosphere but is orderly and well run - very good for a site with beach access. Used by tour operators. English is spoken. Bungalows, chalets and mobile homes to rent.

Directions: Site is north of Canet Port. From Canet Plage follow signs for Port, then 'Campings', and then follow site signs (near the American Park).

Charges 1998: Per unit incl. 2 persons Ffr. 150.00; electricity (5A) 16.00; extra person (over 3 yrs) 30.00; second car 10.00; dog 12.00; local tax (over 3 yrs) 2.00. Less 30-40% in low seasons. High season swimming pool entry (1 week) adult Ffr. 50, child (4-10 yrs) 30. Low and mid seasons free. Credit cards accepted.

Open: 4 April - 3 October.

Reservations: Advised for July/Aug - contact site for details. Address: BP 204, 66141 Canet Plage en Roussillon. Tel: (0)4.68.80.23.82. FAX: (0)4.68.73.32.97. E-mail: brasilia@mnet.fr.

7107 Camping-Caravaning Château de l'Epervière, Gigny-sur-Saône

Enthusiastically run rural site in the grounds of a château.

Château de l'Epervière has undergone a transformation under its young owner Christophe Gay. Peacefully situated on the edge of the little village of Gigny-sur-Saône, yet within easy distance of the A6 autoroute, it is in natural woodland, with red squirrels and deer, near the Saône river. With 100 pitches, nearly all with 6A electricity, the site is in two fairly distinct areas - the original with semi-hedged pitches on reasonably level ground with plenty of shade from mature trees, close to the château and fishing lake, and a larger, more open area, still with good shade, with big, hedged pitches on the far side of the lake. A smallish, unheated pool is partly enclosed by old stone walls. Children's play area and paddling pool. Bicycle hire. A good restaurant in the château has a distinctly French menu and takeaway service. Shop for basics. The sanitary blocks, a large one beside the château and a smaller one near the lake, provide modern facilities, including free hot showers, washbasins in cabins and British type WCs. Chemical disposal. Undercover dishwashing and laundry areas, including a washing machine and dryer. Perhaps the most striking feature of this attractive site is the young owner's enthusiasm and the range of activities he lays on for visitors, which include wine tastings and regional tours. He is also the founder and driving force behind French Flavour Holidays, designed to provide an insight into French culture by special theme tours and activities. These weeks appeal more to the British and other nationalities than to the French. *continued overleaf*

FRANCE - Saône-et-Loire / Sarthe

7107 Camping-Caravaning Château de l'Epervière (contunued)

However, a good French ambience has developed and Christophe's wine tastings and château tours are not to be missed. Used by tour operators. Apartments to let in the château.

Directions: From N6 between Châlon-sur-Saône and Tournus, turn east on D18 (just north of Sennecey-le-Grand) and follow site signs for 6.5 km. From the A6, exit Châlon-Sud from the north, or Tournus from the south.

Charges 1998: Per adult Ffr. 25.00 - 30.00; child (under 7 yrs) 15.00 - 20.00; pitch 35.00 - 45.00; electricity 17.00 - 20.00. Credit cards accepted.

Open: 12 April - 30 September.   `Camping Cheque' `FRENCH FLAVOUR'

Reservations: Contact site. Address: 71240 Gigny-sur-Saône. Tel: (0)3.85.44.83.23 or (0)3.85.44.78.79. FAX: |(0)3.85.44.74.20.

7102M Le Village des Meuniers, Dompierre-les-Ormes, nr Mâcon

Opened in 1993, this site is a good example of current trends in French tourism development. The 120 neatly terraced, large pitches are on fairly level grass and all have electricity (15A), with water and drainage shared between 4 or 6 pitches in most parts. They enjoy some lovely views of the surrounding countryside - the Beaujolais, the Maconnais, the Charollais and the Clunysois. The site is 500 m. from Dompierre, a village of 850 people, with all services (banks, shops, etc. closed Sun/Mon). Sanitary facilities are mainly in an unusual, purpose designed hexagonal block, with up-to-date furniture and fittings, all of a very high standard with British WCs. Also a smaller unit in the lower area of the site, plus further WCs in the reception building. Café/bar, shop and takeaway, plus minigolf, bicycle hire and other recreational activities. An attractively designed, upmarket swimming pool complex has three pools with a toboggan (from June). Fishing 2 km. The site has its own high quality wooden gites, operated by Gites de France. This is one of the better municipals we have seen, and as the hedges and trees mature there should be more shade. Motorcaravan service point. An area well worth visiting, with attractive scenery, interesting history, excellent wines and good food. Used by tour operators.

Directions: Town is 35 km. west of Macon. Follow N79/E62 (Charolles/Paray/Digoin) road and turn south onto D41 to Dompierre-les-Ormes (3 km). Site is clearly signed through village.

Charges 1998: Per person Ffr. 20.00 - 25.00; child (under 7 yrs) 10.00 - 15.00; pitch 25.00 - 30.00; electricity 15.00. Family rate (4 or more persons) Ffr. 100.00 - 120.00. Credit cards accepted.

Open: 16 May - 12 September.

Reservations: Contact site. Address: 71520 Dompierre-les-Ormes. Tel: (0)3.85.50.29.43. FAX: as phone in season (winter: (0)3.85.50.28.25).

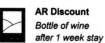

AR Discount
Bottle of wine
after 1 week stay

DOMPIERRE-LES-ORMES

★ 113 pitches ★ 4 star standard
★ 3 Swimming Pools with Toboggan
★ Mini Golf competitions ★ Sports ★ Animation
★ Close to Cluny

A modern purpose-built site with panoramic
views in South Burgundy

For information and reservations
Tel 03 85 50 29 43 Fax 03 85 50 28 25 (low season)
03 85 50 29 43 (in season)

7205 Camping-Caravanning Brulon le Lac, Brulon

Useful, small, picturesque site overlooking an attractive lake, close to autoroute.

Previously a municipal site, but now privately managed, Brulon le Lac offers 65 good size numbered, pitches on flat grass, some divided by new shrubs and bushes; 36 have electricity. The sanitary block, with key system, has British WCs, roomy, pre-set showers and vanity style washbasins, plus a washing machine. Maintenance could be variable. A second block for disabled people has been added. The site is alongside, with direct access to, a large lake and sits in a very attractive valley. Swimming is allowed in the lake, with a lifeguard afternoons in July/Aug. Sailing, windsurfing, canoeing, fishing and archery. Children's play area on sand by the lake. Bicycle hire. Public tennis court. Swimming pool (1/5-30/6), children's paddling pool, minigolf, TV and library room, and a bar/restaurant with lake views (1/5-31/8).

Directions: From A81/E50 (Laval - Le Mans) road, take the D4 (south) to Brulon, where site is signed.

Charges 1998: Per pitch Ffr. 50.00 - 70.00; extra person 10.00 - 15.00; child (under 7 yrs) 8.00 - 12.00; electricity 12.00 - 15.00.

Open: 1 May - 30 September.

Reservations: Contact site. Address: Au Bord du Lac, 72350 Brulon. Tel: (0)2.43.95 68 96. FAX: (0)2.43.92.60.36

7406 Camping La Colombière, Neydens, nr St Julien-en-Genevois

Good small site with pool, near Geneva.

La Colombière, on the edge of the small residential village of Neydens, is a few minutes from the A40 autoroute and only a short way from Geneva. It is a neat, tidy, rectangular site with four rows of pitches of grass on small stones between hard access roads with 100 numbered places separated by fruit and other trees. With mountain ridges to both east and west and a good variety of trees between, this is a quiet peaceful site, well run by the Bussat family. Two good sanitary blocks have British style WCs, the usual amenities, a baby room, facilities for disabled people and chemical disposal. An excellent, good value and quality bar restaurant has a terrace overlooking the heated pool (15/5-15/10). Guided cycle tours (bicycle hire), mountain walks and French country music evenings are arranged in high season. Neydens makes a good base for visiting Geneva and the Lac Leman region and is a very pleasant, friendly site where you may drop in for an en route night stop - and stay for several days!

Directions: Take exit 13 from A40 autoroute south of Geneva, turn towards Annecy on D201 and follow camp signs (Camping Neydens, **not** the name of site).

Charges 1998: Per unit incl. 2 persons Ffr. 90.00; extra person 20.00; child (under 7 yrs) 14.00; electricity 3A 15.00, 5 or 6A 20.00. Less 10% outside July/Aug. Credit cards accepted.

Open: 1 April - 31 October.   `Camping Cheque'`

Reservations: Write to site. Address: 74160 Neydens.

Tel: (0)4.50.35.13.14. FAX: (0)4.50.35.13.40.

AR Discount
Less 15%
in low season

8001 Castel Domaine de Drancourt, St Valéry-sur-Somme, Abbéville

Popular site between Boulogne and Dieppe with swimming pools and other amenities.

A popular, lively, holiday site within easy distance of Channel ports, Drancourt is in four sections. The original section has 100 marked, numbered pitches of good size with shade; an extension taking some 90 units is in light woodland and two newer sections are on flat or gently sloping meadow, with little shade as yet. The total is nearly 300 pitches, many occupied by seasonal or tour operators. Electricity (6A) in all areas. Sanitary facilities in three blocks - the central (oldest) block, a good modern one in the touring section, the third near reception. All have British style WCs, washbasins in cubicles, roomy showers, and free pre-set hot water, some bathrooms and facilities for disabled people, plus laundry and dishwashing, washing machines and dryers. Two free heated pools with waterslide. Shop, takeaway, pizzeria and restaurant (all from 1/5). Bar in the château, pool-side bar with karaoke in season. TV rooms. Disco. Games room. Tennis. Golf practice range and minigolf. Bicycle hire. Riding in season and free fishing. Organised activities and weekly excursions to Paris (June-Aug). Facilities can become busy in peak season. Run very personally by the energetic proprietor, English is spoken.

Directions: Site is 2.5 km. south of St Valéry, near Estreboeuf, and is signed from the St Valéry road N40.

Charges 1997: Per person Ffr. 28.00 + local tax (over 10 yrs) 2.00; child (under 7) 21.00; pitch for caravan or tent 44.00; pitch for motorcaravan 57.00; car 13.00; electricity (4A) 15.00, (6A) 20.00.

Open: Easter - 15 September.   `Camping Cheque'`

Reservations: Made for any length, with deposit for longer stays. Address: B.P. 22, 80230 Saint-Valery-sur-Somme. Tel: (0)3.22.26.93.45. FAX: (0)3.22.26.85.87.

8101 Camping Relais de l'Entre Deux Lacs, Teillet, nr Albi

Small, quiet, family run site between the Rassisse and Bancalié lakes.

This is a lovely little site, run by Belgians Lily and Dion Heijde-Wouters. In part meadow, part semi-cleared woodland, with a small farm alongside, it offers modern amenities including a good sized pool and an excellent bar/restaurant specialising in Belgian cuisine (both 1/5-30/9). It also serves no less than 30 different Belgian beers, as well as French wine. Family attractions include a weekly barbecue and children's activities. The 54 pitches, all with electricity, are on level terraces, mostly with ample shade. The site is well managed and the owners ensure that the generally tranquil atmosphere is not disrupted. Those arriving late or leaving before 8 am. are sited in an adjacent small meadow. Two sanitary blocks, with extra toilets at the lower part of the site. The main one is new with the latest fittings including free, pre-set showers, washbasins in cabins, British WCs and dishwashing under cover (H&C). The older, smaller block in the converted pigeon house, has older style fittings. Heated in winter when the new block is closed, it has facilities for disabled people. Washing machines. Volleyball, table tennis, boules. Children's farm and playground. Bread to order, shop in the village. Bicycle hire. Canoe and kayak hire on Rassisse lake. Caravans and chalets to rent. Guided hikes and tours of Albi or a Gaillac wine cellar.

Directions: From the Albi ring-road, take the D81 going southeast to Teillet (approx. 20 km). Continue through the village on the D81 and site is on the right.

Charges 1998: Per unit incl. 2 persons Ffr. 74.50, with electricity 85.00 - 114.50; extra person 24.00; child (under 7 yrs) 11.50; extra tent 10.50; dog 10.50. Less 20% outside 15/6-31/8 for stays of min. 5 days.

Open: All year.

Reservations: Made with deposit (Ffr. 300) and fee (80). Address: 81120 Teillet. Tel: (0)5.63.55.74.45. FAX: (0)5.63.55.75.65.

8316 Parc Camping-Caravaning Les Cigales, Le Muy

Family run site in a quiet location, convenient for the attractions of this popular area.

In a natural setting of 10 ha. this site is well tucked in, 1 km. from the busy N7. Whilst it offers the opportunity for a peaceful and relaxing stay, it also makes an excellent base for exploring the coast or the hinterland and the Gorges du Verdon. On entering the site (electronic gate operated by card), reception is on the left. Sand based, gravel roads lead to the numbered pitches which vary in size, with some terracing. The terrain is typical of the area with rough, sloped and stony, dry ground, but pitches are mostly level and benefit from the shade given by the abundance of trees which include cork, oak and pine, plus the sweet smelling mimosa and many shrubs that fill the air reminding us that this is Provence. The site has six modern sanitary blocks which more than serve the 180 pitches. Facilities include showers, washbasins in cabins and facilities for disabled people. Dishwashing sinks outside but covered, laundry area with washing machine and chemical disposal. A feature is the swimming pool and sunbathing area, and also the patio at the restaurant/bar which is popular in the evening. Entertainment is organised each evening in season, with a disco twice weekly and daytime activities for children and senior citizens. Salads, fresh food, etc. are available at the restaurant (July/Aug) and there is a shop (June-Sept), but if wanting to get out and about, it is only 2 km. to Le Muy where a Sunday market is held. The N7 is on a bus route or take a train at Les Arcs (8 km). For sports enthusiasts, canoeing, riding and hang-gliding are organised. A `Sites et Paysages' member.

Directions: Site signed off approach to autoroute péage on A8 at Le Muy exit and is 2 km. west of Le Muy on N7.

Charges 1998: Per unit incl. 2 persons Ffr. 65.00 - 97.00; extra person 18.00 - 28.00; child (under 7 yrs) 12.00 - 18.00; electricity 6A 15.00 - 21.00, 10A 20.00 - 29.00; plus local tax. Less 5% for stays over 3 weeks. Credit cards accepted.

Open: 1 April - 30 October.

Reservations: Advisable for July/Aug. Contact site. Address: 83490 Le Muy. Tel: (0)4.94.45.12.08. FAX: (0)4.94.45.92.80.

8307 Camping-Caravaning L'Etoile d'Argens, St Aygulf

See colour advert between pages 96/97

Large, well equipped yet peaceful site near beach, with good pool complex.

L'Etoile d'Argens is a large family site with 493 pitches, and the first impression on entering the gate is that it is spacious, neat, tidy and well cared for. It is family run and for all its size, it has a peaceful air. The swimming pool area has two adult pools and a children's paddling pool. with a large paved sunbathing area around it, and a bar, restaurant, pizzeria and takeaway near. The pitches are in the typical French style, very formal with well clipped hedges and well cut grass. All are of a good size (some very large), 450 of them fully serviced with 10A electricity, water and waste water point. The older part of the site is more shaded with mature trees, but for early and late season the newer part is probably better, giving maximum sunshine. For each row of 25 - 30 pitches there is a small unisex toilet block with British WCs, washbasins (some in cabins) and controllable showers. These blocks are beginning to show their age, but improvements are continuing and they are kept very clean and well maintained. The site provides a small supermarket, four tennis courts, minigolf (both free in low season), table tennis, football pitch and a children's playground. Free tennis coaching, aerobics, swimming games and dances are organised from mid June and there is a children's entertainer in July/Aug. Tour operators take a few of the pitches but are not intrusive. The river runs along one side of the site and a free boat service (15/6-15/9) runs every 40 mins to the beach. It is also possible to moor a boat and to fish from the river. The friendly staff at reception speak English (open 24 hrs).

Directions: Site is 4.5 km. NNW of St Aygulf, where camp signs are not easy to find. You can also approach by turning off the N98 coast road midway between St Aygulf and Fréjus, or from the N7 just outside Fréjus to west. At roundabout on the N7 take D8 signed Roquebrune, St Aygulf. After crossing river bridge with traffic lights site is signed on left (from roundabout 3.5 km).

Charges 1997: Per pitch (100 sq.m.) with electricity and 3 persons Ffr. 206.00; `comfort' pitch (180 sq.m.), incl. 4 persons 270.00; 'luxury' pitch (c. 250 sq.m.) incl. 4 persons 290.00; tent pitch 50.00 - 100.00; extra person 40.00; child (under 7) 28.00. Less 25% in low seasons. Credit cards accepted.

Open: Easter - 30 September, with all services.

Reservations: Made for any period with substantial deposit and fee. Address: 83370 St Aygulf. Tel: (0)4.94.81.01.41. FAX: (0)4.94.81.21.45.

8317 Camping Domaine de la Bergerie, Roquebrune-sur-Argens

Well organised site with a holiday environment to suit all ages and tastes.

This is yet another excellent site near the Côte d'Azur which takes you away from all the bustle of the Mediterranean to total relaxation amongst the natural perfumes of Provence. Here, where cork oak, pine and mimosa flourish, is a 70 ha. campsite which varies from landscaped areas for mobile homes to flat, grassy terrain with avenues of separated pitches for caravans and tents. All pitches average over 100 sq.m. and have electricity, with those in one area also having water and drainage connections. The four sanitary blocks are kept very clean and include hot showers, washbasins in private cubicles, British WCs, facilities for disabled people and for babies, chemical disposal points, plus dishwashing and laundry areas with washing machines. A well stocked supermarket (daily fresh bread) is uphill behind the touring pitches. To the right of this, adjacent to the restaurant, are parking areas as being a spread out site, walking can be tough going. The restaurant/bar, a converted farm building, is surrounded by shady patios, whilst inside it oozes character with high beams and archways leading to intimate corners. Takeaway service. Alongside is an extravagantly designed complex with three swimming pools (15/5-30/9) and a keep fit centre (body building, sauna, gym, etc). There are five tennis courts and two half courts, volleyball, mini football and more. Tournaments and programmes are organised daily and, in the evening, shows, cabarets, discos and dancing at the amphitheatre prove popular (possibly until midnight). Fishing on site, riding, water skiing and rock climbing available nearby - in fact, few activities have been forgotten. When all that the site has to offer has been exhausted, either St Aygulf or Ste Maxime are 7 km, or drive inland and discover the delights of the hinterland.

Directions: Leave A8 at Le Muy exit on N7 towards Fréjus. Proceed for 9 km., then right onto D7 signed St Aygulf. Continue for 8 km. and then right at roundabout onto D8; site is on the right.

Charges 1997: Per unit incl. 2 persons and electricity (5A) Ffr. 95.00 - 127.00; 3 persons and electricity 120.00 - 167.00; 3 persons and electricity, water and drainage 140.00 - 195.00; extra adult 23.00 - 33.00; child (under 7 yrs) 17.00 - 23.00; electricity (10A) 12.00; local tax 2.00.

Open: 1 April - 30 September.

Reservations: Made with deposit (Ffr. 800 by Eurocheque or bank draft). Address: Vallée du Fournel, 83520 Roquebrune-sur-Argens. Tel: (0)4.94.82.90.11. FAX: (0)4.94.82.93.42.

AR Discount
Welcome drink each Sunday in high season

FRANCE - Var / Vaucluse / Vendée

8301 Camping-Caravaning Les Pins Parasols, Fréjus

Family owned site with pool, 5 km. from beach; some pitches with individual sanitary units.

Not everyone likes very big sites, and Les Pins Parasols with its 189 pitches is of a size which is quite easy to walk around. Although on very slightly undulating ground, virtually all the plots are levelled or terraced and separated by hedges or bushes with pine trees for shade. They are of around 100 sq.m. and all with electricity. The most unusual feature is that 48 pitches have their own fully enclosed, tiled sanitary unit, consisting of British WC, washbasin, hot shower and washing up sink, all quite close together. These naturally cost more but may well be of interest. The three normal toilet blocks are of good average quality and give a plentiful supply with washbasins in cabins, free, pre-set showers with push-button, and chemical disposal. Facilities for disabled people. On site is a 200 sq.m. swimming pool with attractive rock backdrop and sunbathing terrace, long slide with landing pool and a small children's pool. Small shop. Restaurant with takeaway (1/5-20/9). General room with TV. Half-court tennis. Bicycle hire 50 m. Bus into Fréjus. The nearest beach is Fréjus-Plage (5½ km). Used by tour operators .

Directions: From autoroute A8 take exit 38 for Fréjus Est. Turn right immediately on leaving pay booths on a small road which leads across to D4, where right again and under 1 km. to site.

Charges 1997: Per normal pitch with electricity incl. 2 persons Ffr 125.00; special pitch with sanitary unit incl. 2 persons 159.00; extra person 33.00; child (under 7 yrs) 22.00; car 9.00; dog 11.00. Less 10% outside 15/6-1/9.

Open: 12 April - 30 September.

Reservations: Necessary for July/Aug. only and made for min. 10 days for exact dates with deposit (Ffr 600) but no fee. Address: Route de Bagnols, 83600 Fréjus. Tel: (0)4.94.40.88.43. FAX: (0)4.94.40.81.99.

8404 Camping Le Jantou, Le Thor, nr Avignon

Family run, attractive site beside River Sorgue.

The nicest feature of this attractive site is the 18th century `mas' (Provencal farmhouse) and outbuildings which, together with a huge plane tree, form a centre piece courtyard. The 143 pitches, around 120 for tourers, are arranged in groups of mainly four pitches, the groups rather than the individual pitches being separated by tall hedges. Mostly of a good size on flat grass, the majority having 3, 6 or 10A electricity and some including water and drainage. The two sanitary blocks provide modern facilities including British style WCs, facilities for disabled people, chemical disposal, dishwashing and laundry sinks with hot water and washing machines and dryers. Snack bar and a little restaurant serving stews, plat du jour, etc. (July/Aug). Shop for essentials, small supermarket within a short walk. Some live entertainment organised in season. Swimming pool, bicycle hire and children's playground. A quite fast flowing river runs past the site (fenced but with unlocked gate) which is suitable for fishing (licences from site), but not swimming due to the current. No tour operators but some mobile homes.

Directions: Leave A7 autoroute at Avignon Nord exit and join D942 towards Carpentras. Turn immediately south on D6 and proceed 8½ km. to join the N100. Turn east for 3½ km. to Le Thor. Site signed before entering village.

Charges 1998: Per adult Ffr. 25.00; child (2-14 yrs) 12.50; pitch 30.50; electricity 3A 15.00, 6A 18.00. 15th night free in high season, 8th in low season. Credit cards accepted.

Open: 28 March - 31 October.

Reservations: Advised July/Aug; made with 20% deposit and Ffr. 50 fee. Address: 84250 Le Thor. Tel: (0)4.90. 33.90.07. FAX: (0)4.90.33.79.84. E-mail: lejantou@avignon.pacwan.net. Internet: http://www.elansud.fr/ lejantou/

AR Discount
Less 5% 4/7-22/8
or 10% other times

8503 Camping La Loubine, Olonne-sur-Mer

Attractive, well run site with friendly atmosphere and good range of facilities.

The original mature parts of this site have been added to, giving a total of 260 pitches, including 143 with all services, plus 40 mobile homes for hire. These individual, marked pitches are particularly large, on flat grass with good shade, except in the new area. Two heated swimming pools with ample sun bathing area, a water slide and an indoor pool with jacuzzi, add to its attraction. Original buildings around a courtyard overlooking the pools have been converted to provide a pleasant bar, takeaway and small shop (15/5-15/9) making a focal point for entertainment nights. A restaurant is near reception. The four toilet blocks are of reasonable quality with mainly British style toilets, washbasins in cabins and free pre-set showers. Facilities for disabled and babies. Washing machines and dryers. Tennis, table tennis, minigolf, badminton net and volleyball. Sauna and fitness room (free). Bicycle hire. Large children's play area and club in high season. TV with Eurosport. Organised activities all season. Site is 1.8 km. from a sandy beach at Sauveterre (or 700 m. walk). No dogs. Popular with tour operators.

Directions: Site is west of Olonne beside the D80 road.

Charges 1998: Per pitch incl. 2 persons, with tent/caravan and car, without electricity Ffr. 119.00, with electricity (6A) 134.00, with all services 144.00; extra adult 25.00; extra child (under 7) 15.00; extra car 10.00. Less 30% outside 23/6-23/8. Credit cards accepted.

Open: 4 April - 26 September (full facilities from 15/5).

Reservations: Made with deposit and Ffr 120 fee (min. 7 days in Jul/Aug.) Address: 1 Route de la Mer, 85340 Olonne-sur-Mer. Tel: (0)2.51.33.12.92. FAX: (0)2.51.33.12.71.

8504 Castel Camping La Garangeoire, St Julien-des-Landes

Rurally situated site in grounds of château, 15 km. from the Atlantic coast.

La Garangeoire, one of a small number of seriously good sites in the Vendée, is 15 km. inland, near the village of St Julien des Landes. One of its more memorable qualities is the imaginative use which has been made of the old 'main road' to Noirmoutiers central to the site which now forms a delightful, quaint thoroughfare. Nicknamed the Champs Elysée, it is quite busy at times with most of the facilities opening directly off it and providing a village like atmosphere. The site is set in the 200 ha. park which surrounds La Garangeoire, a small château. The peaceful fields and woods, where campers may walk, include three lakes, one of which may be used for fishing and boating (life jackets from reception). The site has a spacious, relaxed atmosphere with the main camping areas arranged either side of the old road, edged with mature trees. The 300 hedged pitches, each named not numbered, are especially large (most 150-200 sq.m.) and well spaced. Most have electricity (6A), some water and drainage also. The ample sanitary installations are good and well situated for all areas. The newest block has facilities for babies and the disabled. All have British style toilets, washbasins in cabins and free controllable hot water throughout. Laundry facilities. Two heated pools with water slides, fountain, etc. and a child's pool. Full restaurant, takeaway and crêperie, with attractive courtyard exterior. Large playing field for children's activities, games room, 2 tennis courts, bicycle hire, table tennis, minigolf, archery and volleyball. Riding July/Aug. Good shop. Popular with British tour operators; mobile homes to hire.

Directions: Site is signed from St Julien; the entrance is to the north off D21.

Charges 1998: Per unit incl. 2 persons Ffr. 84.00 - 120.00, with electricity 101.50 - 145.00, with services 109.90 - 157.00; extra person 22.40 - 32.00; child (under 7) 11.20 - 16.00; extra car 10.50 - 15.00. Credit cards accepted.

Open: 15 May - 15 September.   `Camping Cheque'

Reservations: Made for min. 7 days with deposit (Ffr. 280) and fee (120). Address: St Julien-des-Landes, 85150 La Mothe-Achard. Tel: (0)2.51.46.65.39. FAX: (0)2.51.46.60.82.

8502 Camping du Jard, La Tranche-sur-Mer

Neat, developing site, halfway between La Rochelle and Les Sables d'Olonne.

Du Jard is a well planned, neatly laid out site with shade developing from the many attractive trees and hedges which have been planted. The 350 pitches are flat and grassy, and a minimum of 100 sq.m. Most are equipped with electricity, half with water and drainaway also. The site is 700 m. from a sandy beach and also has its own heated pool (from 25/5, no shorts allowed) with a small one for children. An indoor pool is planned for '98. There is a good tennis court, minigolf, table tennis and a sauna, solarium and fitness room with instruction included. Children's play area, games and TV rooms, bicycle hire. The three toilet blocks are well designed and maintained, with excellent facilities for disabled people and for babies. Ample free hot water; a mixture of British and a few Turkish toilets; washbasins, some in private cabins and chemical disposal. Owner managed, one receives a friendly welcome; English is spoken (in season!). Card operated barrier. There is a bar with terrace, restaurant and a small shop for basics (all from 1/6, shops and restaurants nearby). Exchange facilities. Car wash. American motorhomes not accepted. Used by two British tour operators.

Directions: Site is east of La Tranche-sur-Mer, 3 km. from the D747/D46 roundabout, on the D46. From new bypass southeast of La Tranche, take exit for La Grière and then turn east to site.

Charges 1997: Per standard pitch incl. 2 persons Ffr. 115.00, with electricity (4A) 125.00, with electricity, water and drainage 146.00; extra person (over 5 yrs) 22.50; extra child (under 5) 15.00; extra small tent 17.00; visitor 10.00; electricity 10A +11.00; tax (over 9 yrs) 1.10. Less 25% outside 1/7-25/8.

Open: 25 May - 15 September.

Reservations: Advisable for July/Aug. (min. 1 week, Sat.- Sat.) with deposit (Ffr. 500). Address: 123, Route de la Faute, 85360 La Tranche-sur-Mer. Tel: (0)2.51 27 43 79. FAX: (0)2.51.27.42.92.

FRANCE - Vendée

8506 Airotel Domaine Le Pas Opton, Le Fenouiller, nr St Gilles-Croix

Well established site with good installations and swimming pool, 6 km. from sea.

Le Pas Opton is family managed and run and much work has been carried out to make it worth considering for a stay in this popular region. It is 6 km. back from the sea at St Gilles Croix de Vie and quietly situated. With a well established atmosphere, it is a select type of site but at the same time, offers on-site amenities such as a heated swimming pool (from 20/5) with water slide and children's pools and an attractive bar with a pleasant terrace looking across to the pool. There are 200 pitches, most of which have electricity and some hardstanding, water and drainage also. Those in the original part are well shaded by mature trees and tall hedges. The newer areas have less shade but are developing well with a more spacious feel. The four toilet blocks are all of good quality. They have free hot water in all facilities and are kept very clean and in good order, with British toilets, individual washbasins with free hot water, mainly in private cabins for women, partly for men and free hot water in showers and sinks. Unit for the disabled. Laundry facilities available. Other amenities include a shop, bar (both 15/6-31/8), café and takeaway (1/7-31/8), volleyball, table tennis, a children's playground and a car wash area. Entertainment and some dancing is organised in season. The river Vie runs past the rear of the site (fishing possible, licences available in the village) and it is fenced and gated. Non-powered boats can be put on the river, but there can be a current at times. Sailing centre and windsurfing 2 km. markets at St Gilles-Croix 2 or 3 times a week. Chalet and large caravans for hire. Used by a tour operator.

Directions: Site is northeast of St Gilles, on N754 about 300 m. towards Le Fenouiller from junction with D32.

Charges 1998: Per unit incl. 2 persons: without electricity Ffr. 71.50 - 94.50, with electricity (6A) 95.50 - 118.00, with water and drainage also 111.50 - 134.00; extra adult 24.00; child (under 7) 14.00; extra car 8.50; local tax 2.20 per person (over 10 yrs) in July/Aug. Credit cards accepted.

Open: 20 May - 15 September.

Reservations: Advisable for main season and made from Jan. (min. 1 week) with deposit and fee. Address: Route de Nantes, Le Fenouiller, 85800 St Gilles Croix de Vie. Tel: (0)2.51.55.11.98. FAX: (0)2.51.55.44.94.

8508 Camping La Puerta del Sol, St Hilaire de Riez, nr St Gilles-Croix

Well designed, good quality site with swimming pool and other amenities.

We originally described La Puerta del Sol as `a modern site developed on ambitious lines resulting in a very good, environmentally pleasing site with excellent amenities'. Some ten years on this description continues to apply to this excellent campsite, identified as one of the European `Top 30' sites in the main French camping and caravanning magazine. The ambience achieved by the sensitive proprietor is friendly, welcoming and lively, without being intrusive or offensive to those who seek a peaceful and relaxing holiday in an area where so often quite frenzied activity is the order of the day. It has about 193 individual pitches (and 32 chalets), most of about 100 sq.m., on reasonably grassy ground, with plenty of shade. All pitches have electricity, water and drainaway. The three good quality, identical toilet blocks have some British style WCs, washbasins in private cabins with free hot water, shelf, mirror and light, free roomy hot showers plus facilities for the disabled, laundry and babies' rooms. The facilities are very well cleaned and the site well regulated, with friendly staff. The Spanish camp name is reflected in the architectural style of the buildings which contain reception, bar lounge, takeaway and restaurant with well cooked, reasonably priced food. An attractive heated swimming pool of over 200 sq.m., with paddling pool, is by the bar with a terrace. There is a mini-market (20/6-31/8) and a general room also used for `animation' events; sports competitions and games. Mini-club for children (free, 6 mornings a week in the main season), evening entertainment and dancing (until midnight) and organised excursions in July/Aug. Barbecue area with picnic tables, children's adventure play areas (on sand), tennis court and games room with table tennis, amusement machines. The nearest sandy beach is 5 km. and St Jean-de-Monts 7. American motorhomes accepted in limited numbers and with reservation. Chalets for 4-6 persons for hire.

Directions: Site is 1 km. north of Le Pissot (which is 7 km. north of St Gilles Croix-de-Vie on D38) on the D59 road towards Le Perrier. Watch carefully for camp sign, you come on it quite suddenly.

Charges 1998: Per pitch with up to 3 persons, car and caravan or trailer tent, incl. 3 services Ffr 70.00 - 170.00; extra adult 18.00 - 35.00; child (under 7) 8.00 - 24.00; extra tent free - 30.00; animal 7.00 - 24.00; visitor free - 20.00. Credit cards accepted.

Open: 15 May - 20 September.

Reservations: Made for any period with deposit (Ffr. 900) and fee (200). Contact site (as above) when open or reservations address in low season: 47 Rue de Candale Prolongée, 93500 Pantin. Tel or Fax: (0)1.48.44.33.22. Site address: Les Borderies, 85270 St Hilaire de Riez. Tel: (0)2.51.49.10.10. FAX: (0)2.51.49.84.84.

8507 Camping Les Biches, St Hilaire de Riez, nr St Gilles-Croix

Quality site in a pinewood with swimming pools, 4 km. from the sea.

Les Biches is covered by a pinewood, so nearly everywhere has shade. The 380 individual pitches, which are mainly quite large and equipped with electricity, water and drainaway, are on grassy or sandy ground under the trees and there is a spacious and peaceful atmosphere. There are special parts for tents and caravans, the tent part being particularly shady. The four sanitary blocks are of good quality and size, with refurbishment and improvements continuing. They have British style WCs, individual washbasins, many in private cabins (with bidet), with free hot water to all basins and showers, plus laundry facilities. The site is not by the sea but several sandy beaches can be reached in a short drive, the nearest being 4 km. away. There are two heated swimming pools near the site entrance, with children's pool and water slide with splash pool and jacuzzi. Large bar, disco, restaurant and takeaway (from 1/6). Other amenities include a shop (from 16/5) with ice service, crêperie, tennis courts, volleyball, table tennis and games room with amusement machines. There is a private fishing lake, car wash area, new children's playground, a treatment room, TV room with satellite TV, minigolf and bicycle hire. Mobile homes to let. It is a quiet and peaceful type of site, with not so many camp activities as in some places, but it is very popular with British tour operators so can be busy at times.

Directions: Site is about 2 km. north of St Hilaire, close to and well signed from the main D38 road.

Charges 1998: Per pitch incl. 3 persons and car Ffr. 170.00, with electricity (10A) 195.00; extra person 35.00; child (under 7) 17.50; extra car or dog 10.00. Less 20% May, June and Sept. Credit cards *not* accepted.

Open: 15 May - 15 September.

Reservations: Made with dates of both arrival and departure required, with deposit (Ffr. 400) and fee (100). Address: 85270 St Hilaire-de-Riez. Tel: (0)2.51.54.38.82. FAX: (0)2.51.54.30.74.

8519 Le Marais Braud, St Hilaire de Riez, nr St-Gilles-Croix

Small, unsophisticated site with swimming pool, near the sea.

Le Marais Braud occupies a peaceful wooded setting with level, grassy pitches, slightly inland from the busy coastal areas. Sandy beaches are 7 km. by car. Facilities include a small heated swimming pool with slide and children's pool (from 15/6), tennis court and a small lake for fishing, which is also home to white and black swans, plus a cross goose. The friendly bar and crêperie (with takeaway) incorporate a games area with a skittle alley and there is a little shop for basics (all from 1/7). There are 150 pitches of 100 sq.m. with shade and some hedges, half with electricity (6A). One large and one smaller toilet block, both with free hot water, provide showers, wash cabins and mostly British style toilets, chemical disposal and a washing machine. Wooden chalets for rent. No tour operators. The site has a family atmosphere being managed by the owners, M. & Mme Besseau, but is only open for a very short season.

Directions: From St Hilaire de Riez, take the D38 north to Le Pissot, site is signed from the D59 road from Le Pissot to Le Perrier.

Charges 1997: Per unit, incl. 2 persons Ffr. 75.00; extra adult 20.00; child 2-10 yrs 15.50, under 2 yrs 11.50; extra car 7.00; electricity (6A) 15.00; drainage 11.00. Less 15% in low seasons (June or Sept). Credit cards accepted.

Open: 1 June - 15 September.

Reservations: Write to site. Address: 298, Route du Perrier, 85270 St Hilaire de Riez. Tel: (0)2.51.68.33.71. FAX: (0)2.51.35.25.32.

8522 Camping Acapulco, St Jean de Monts

Friendly site, ideal for family holidays.

Situated mid-way between St Jean de Monts and St Hilaire de Riez, and 600 m. from the beach, Acapulco is a young site (opened '95), ideal for family holidays. The medium to large site is level and open with pitches of sandy grass separated by, as yet, small hedges. Some shaded pitches are available at the top end of the site. The three main sanitary blocks boast clean, modern facilities with British style toilets, washbasins in cabins with hot water, free hot showers and facilities for babies and the disabled. There are sinks for laundry and dishwashing, washing machines and a dryer in each block. In the middle of the site a complex comprising a large bar, snack bar and well stocked shop (all season), overlooks the interestingly shaped, heated swimming pool with water slide and paddling pool. A safe attractive play area is adjacent. The young, friendly site owner provides lively entertainment and sporting activities for all ages in high season. Shops, bars and restaurants within 1 km. Used by tour operators. Cottages and mobile homes for hire. Motorcaravan service point.

Directions: Driving south on the D38 St Jean de Monts - St Gilles road, turn right at L'Oasis bar/restaurant in Orouet, signed Les Mouettes. Site is on left after 1 km.

Charges 1997: Per unit incl. 3 persons and electricity Ffr. 162.00; extra person 28.00; child (under 5 yrs) 15.00; animal 10.00. Less 25% in low seasons.

Open: 15 May - 15 September.

Reservations: Contact site for details. Address: Avenue des Epines, 85160 St Jean de Monts. Tel: (0)2.51.59.20.64. FAX: (0)2.51.59.53.12.

AR Discount
Less 5% in all seasons

123

8603 Camping Le Relais du Miel, Châtellerault

New site being developed in the grounds of country house, close to A10 autoroute.

With very easy access from the A10 and N10 roads, in the northern outskirts of Châtellerault, this site is of very promising quality. It is being developed in the 10 acre grounds of a rather grand house dating from Napoleonic times, beside the River Vienne and surrounded by majestic old trees. Twin barns form two sides of a courtyard behind the house, one of which has already been converted very stylishly into reception and a high ceilinged function and games room. Beyond are an orchard and stone gateposts leading onto ground, previously the home farm, which now forms 80 large, flat pitches. The grass is still rather rough but over 1,000 trees and bushes have been planted and all 100-200 sq.m. pitches have electricity and water, 20 drainage also. Tents are pitched in the orchard. Sanitary facilities of first class quality have been created from three sets of outbuildings with free controllable showers, washbasins in cabins, British style WCs, facilities for disabled people, chemical disposal, dishwashing sinks and a washing machine and dryer in one block. A swimming pool with paved surrounds is beside a small restaurant with outdoor tables sheltered by a canopy. A full restaurant is planned on one side of the house with a creeper clad terrace overlooking the old gardens. A bar is now open. You are welcome to stroll in the gardens and there is a gate in the walled grounds to the river bank where you may fish. Children's playground, bicycle hire, boules and games room with electronic games, pool and table tennis. Basic essentials are kept, supermarket 400 m. Takeaway. Futuroscope is 16 km. Good English is spoken by M. and Mme. Mercier who have made a super start in developing their site.

Directions: Take exit no.26 from the A10 autoroute (Châtellerault-Nord) and site is signed just off the roundabout. From the N10 follow signs for Antran north of the town.

Charges 1998: Per pitch incl. 2 persons, electricity and water Ffr. 130.00; extra person over 5 yrs 20.00; extra tent 20.00. Less 15% for 1 week, 20% for 2 weeks. Credit cards accepted.

Open: 1 May - 30 September.

Reservations: Contact site for details. Address: Route d'Antran, 86100 Châtellerault. Tel: (0)5.49.02.06.27. FAX: (0)5.49.93.25.76.

AR Discount
Glass of local wine
(Sauvignon-blanc sec)

8702 Castel Camping du Château de Leychoisier, Bonnac la Côte

Elevated site in the grounds of a château, 10 km north of Limoges.

Just 2 km. from the A20/N20, yet very quiet and secluded, the Château de Leychoisier makes an ideal staging point or a good base for a longer stay. Pitches are very large, individual ones on grassy ground, marked out by trees, some sloping. Of the 80 pitches, 55 have electricity, 10 water and drainage too. The sanitary facilities in part of the old building are a little cramped, but with good hot water, and due for refurbishment. All the toilets are of British type and washbasins are in private cabins with mirrors. Baby bath and changing facilities, provision for disabled people and chemical disposal. Restaurant and a pleasant bar with terrace in an old open-ended barn, part tented. Small shop selling basics and fresh bread each morning. Mini-market 2 km, supermarket 5 km. Swimming pool. Lake with free fishing, boating, canoeing and a marked off area for swimming. Bicycle hire, tennis, table tennis, children's play area, TV room, babyfoot and bar billiards. The large estate is available for walks (watch for roe deer) and there is good terrain in the area for mountain bikes. It is a quiet site where you have plenty of space and where there are no letting units and many people like it for these reasons. Torch useful.

Directions: Take exit (west) signed Bonnac-La-Côte from the A20/N20. The site is well signed from the village.

Charges 1998: Per pitch Ffr. 38.00 - 47.00; person 26.00 - 31.00; child (under 7) 17.00 - 20.00; electricity (4A) 18.00 - 21.00.

Open: 15 April - 20 September.

Reservations: Made with deposit (Ffr. 100) and fee (80), but short low season reservations made without charge. Address: 87270 Bonnac-La-Côte. Tel: (0)5.55.39.93.43. FAX: as phone. Internet: www.castels-campings.com.

AR Discount
Welcome reception
and bicycle ride

8901M Camping de Sous-Rôche, Avallon

This attractive site is in a low lying, sheltered, part wooded situation, 2 km. from the centre of Avallon. There is quite a choice of 100 pitches on the pleasant grassy terrain - on shady terraces, on flat open ground, or by a stream; 60 electrical connections (4A). It may be very busy. The single toilet block is being modernised and now includes British style WCs, including one with basin and ramp for the disabled, individual washbasins (4 in private cabins), showers, traditional sinks for clothes and dishes, all with free hot water. Shop, takeaway (July/Aug) and cooking facilities. Children's playground (on gravel). Fishing on site. Information and reading room with telephone. A very useful night stop on the way to or from Lyon and the south, worth a longer stay. Avallon is a picturesque town and good centre for visiting the wild valleys and lakes of the Morvan mountains.

Directions: From centre of Avallon take N944 to south towards Lormes. After 2 km. turn left at camp sign (a fairly steep, downhill road to site).

Charges 1997: Per person Ffr 18.00; child (under 7) 9.00; car 13.00; pitch 13.00; electricity 18.00.

Open: 15 March - 15 October.

Reservations: Write to La Mairie. Address: Service Camping, Mairie, 89200 Avallon. Tel: (0)3.86.34.10.39. FAX: as phone.

The Départements of France

GERMANY

As a holiday destination it provides a rich variety of scenic and cultural interest. Although the German people are great travellers and can be found on holiday all over Europe, they nevertheless enjoy camping in their own country and good camps can be discovered throughout the 16 'Länder'. Not only does the scenery provide great contrast - from the flat lands of the north to the mountains of the south and the forests of the west and east - but as it was only fully unified as one state in 1871, regional characteristics are a strong feature of German life and give a rich variety of folklore and customs. Medieval towns, ancient buildings and picturesque villages abound all over the country and add to the fascination of visiting Germany. Reunification may have provided many problems for politicians and people but has opened up a whole new area which was previously difficult to explore. Great strides are being made, particularly where investment has been attracted, to improve and modernise campsites. For further information contact:

German National Tourist Office, Nightingale House, 65 Curzon Street, London W1Y 8NE

Tel: 0891 600100   Fax: 0171 495 6129

Population
80,767,591 (1993); density 226 per sq.km.

Capital
Berlin. After unification in 1990, the German parliament chose Berlin as the national capital and voted to move the seat of government from Bonn to Berlin over a 12 year period.

Climate
In general winters are a little colder and summers a little warmer than in the UK.

Language
German. Most Germans speak some English, but it is appreciated if you try to use any knowledge of German that you have retained.

Currency
The unit of currency is the Deutschmark which comes in notes of 10, 20, 50, 100, 200, 500 and 1,000 deutschmark and coins of DM 0.01 (one Pfennig), 0.02, 0.05, 0.10, 0..20, 0.50, 1, 2 and 5. Exchange facilities in the former GDR may be difficult but there are banks in major towns.

Banks
Banking hours are Mon-Fri 08.30-12.30 and 14.00-16.00 with late opening on Thursdays until 18.00 hrs. Closed Sat.
Credit Cards: are becoming widely accepted but only the major cards are accepted in main department stores and restaurants in the large cities. Girocheques are widely accepted.

Post Offices
Open Mon-Fri 08.00-18.00 and Sat 08.00-12.00.

Time
GMT + 1, or BST + 1 in summer.

Telephone
The code to dial Germany from the UK is 0049.

Public Holidays
New Year; Good Fri; Easter Mon; Labour Day; Ascension; Whit Mon; Day of Unity, 17 June; Unification Day, 3 Oct; Christmas, 25, 26 Dec; plus, in some areas, Epiphany, Corpus Christi, Assumption, All Saints and Repentance days.

Shops
Open Mon-Fri 08.30/09.00 to 18.00/18.30, closed Saturday 14.00 (sometimes earlier).

Motoring
An excellent network of (toll-free) motorways (Autobahns) exists in the 'West' and the traffic moves fast. Remember in the 'East' a lot of road building is going on amongst other works so allow plenty of time when travelling and be prepared for poor road surfaces.
Speed limits: Caravans and motorhomes (2.8 tons) 31 mph (50 kph) or 19 mph (30 kph) in built up areas, 50 mph (80 kph) all other roads for caravans, 63 mph (100 kph) other roads and 81 mph (130 kph) motorways for motorhomes. Lower limits for heavier vehicles.
Parking: Don't park on roads with Priority Road signs. Meters and parking disc zones are in use.

Overnighting
If not forbidden by local regulations, then permitted at 'Rast platz' and on streets, but not open spaces.

Miscellaneous
Recycling: By law all sites must have 5 bins: 3 for glass, 1 for paper 1 for household waste.
Signs: 'Müll' - rubbish disposal; 'Einbahnstrasse' - one-way street.
'Mittagsrühe' - Virtually all campsite receptions shut completely for two hours, usually 13.00 - 15.00 hrs, with some slight variations. Barriers are locked, sometimes for pedestrians too.
Fishing: It is compulsory to pass a test (usually available at campsites providing fishing) on recognition of fish breeds, etc. before you fish.

Useful Addresses
National Motoring Organisations:
Automobil-Club von Deutschland (AVD) Lyoner Strasse 16, 60528 Frankfurt am Main Tel: 069 6606-0. Office hours 08.00-17.00 Allgemeiner Deutscher Automobil-Club (ADAC) Am Westpark 8, 81373 München. Tel: 089 76760.

The sites in the GERMANY featured in this guide are shown on the map on page 373

3000 Knaus Camping-Park Wingst, Wingst, nr Bremerhaven

Site in northwest near North Sea coast and River Elbe estuary.

With an impressive landscaped entrance, a shop and restaurant to one side and reception to the other and a barrier which is closed in the evening, this is a good quality site. It is a rural area with attractive villages, plenty of water and woodland, near to the interesting old port of Bremerhaven with its 29 km. of quays and maritime and fishing museums. The heart of this site is a deep set, small fishing lake and beach. Lightly wooded, pitches are accessed by circular roadways on differing levels and terraced where necessary. Because of the design you do not realise that there are 490 pitches, nearly all with electricity and clearly defined by shrubs and trees. There are two toilet blocks, one adjoining reception and one nearer the lake (access to this is by steps from the varying levels). The provision is good and well kept, with one block recently renovated. A swimming pool behind the hotel opposite the site is open to campers at a cost of 50 pf. per day, paid at reception. Zoo for small animals nearby and riding school with Icelandic horses which are small, quiet and very safe for children to learn to ride with good value inclusive daily rate, including lunch.

How to find it: Wingst is on the B73 Cuxhaven - Stade road, approx. 8 km. north of Henmoor.

General Details: Open all year except Nov. Restaurant. Children's playground. Minigolf. Table tennis. Fishing. Bicycle hire. Barbecue facility with roof. Riding and watersports near. Swimming pool opposite (see above). Chemical disposal. Caravans (10) to rent on site; contact site for details.

Charges 1998: Per person DM 8.50; child (3-14 yrs) 4.50; pitch 7.50 - 12.00; small tent with m/cycle 7.50; electricity 3.50.

Reservations: Contact site. Address: Schwimmbadallee 13, 21789 Wingst. Tel: 04778/7604. FAX: 04778/7608.

3005 Camping Schnelsen Nord, Hamburg

Good quality site for visiting Hamburg.

Some 15 km. from the centre of Hamburg on the northern edge of the town, Schnelsen Nord is a suitable base either for visiting this famous German city, or as a night stop before catching the Harwich ferry or travelling to Denmark. This is a relatively new site but shade is now increasing. There is some traffic noise because the autobahn runs alongside (despite efforts to screen it out) and also some aircraft noise. However, the proximity of the A7 (E45) does make it easy to find. The 145 pitches are of good size (100 sq.m.), on grass with access from gravel roads. All have electric points (6A), are numbered and marked out with small trees and hedges. The single sanitary block is a well constructed modern building with good quality facilities and heated in cool weather. It has free hot water in basins (some in private cabins) and on payment for showers and washing up. Only very basic food supplies are stocked in reception as the site is only about 10 mins. walk from the restaurants and shops in town. There is a small children's playground, table tennis, swimming pool, tennis courts, golf and fishing within easy reach. Apart from some road traffic 'hum', as previously mentioned, this is a quiet, well laid out camp. They welcome tourists, but do not allow itinerant workers to stay.

How to find it: From the A7 autobahn take the Schnelsen Nord exit. Stay in outside lane as you will soon need to turn back left; follow signs for the Ikea store and site signs.

General Details: Open 1 April - 31 Oct. Shop (basics only). Children's playground. Facilities for the disabled. Washing machines and dryers. Sports facilities nearby.

Charges guide: Per adult DM 7.00; child (under 13 yrs) 4.00; caravan 12.00; car 4.50; motorcaravan 16.50 - 20.00; tent 10.00 - 12.00; electricity 4.00.

Reservations: Min.1 week without deposit. Address: Wunderbrunnen 2, 22457 Hamburg. Tel: 040/5594225.

3020 Campingplatz `Freie Hansestadt Bremen', Bremen

Small family run site of good quality in pleasant situation just outside the city.

Five kilometres from the city centre and in pleasant `green belt' surroundings, near to the university, a lake used for bathing and sailing, and an indoor swimming pool, this is a nice little site for visits to Bremen and district. Despite being so near the city, this site has a distinctly rural feel with quite an abundance of wildlife! There are good cycle rides and walks in the municpal woodland next door. It has 100 large pitches of at least 100 sq.m. on flat grass marked by stones on frontage, all with electricity and for tourists only. Some special pitches for motorhomes. The toilet block, of good quality, has British WCs, with free hot water in the washbasins with mirror and shelf (4 in private cabins) and in the sinks, and free fully controllable hot showers with seat and screen. Unit for disabled people.

How to find it: From the A27 autobahn northeast of Bremen take the exit for `Universität' and follow signs for University and then for camp.

General Details: Open 22 March - 27 Oct. Shop. Fresh bread (to order). Restaurant for meals and drinks. General room. Washing machines and dryer. Cooking facilities. Children's playground. Bicycle hire. Barbecue area.

Charges guide: Per person DM 7.50; child (under 16) 4.50; caravan 9.50; 2 person tent 5.00; large tent 9.50; car 2.50; motorcaravan 14.00 - 16.00; m/cycle 1.00; dog 2.00. Some discount with camping carnet or for larger families.

Reservations: made for any length, with deposit. Address: Am Stadtwaldsee 1, 28359 Bremen. Tel: 0421/212002. FAX: 0421/219857.

GERMANY - North West

3450 Ferien-Campingplatz Münstertal, Münstertal, nr Freiburg

See colour advert opposite

Very impressive site with indoor pool just on edge of Black Forest, south of Freiburg.

On the western edge of the Black Forest just before the road starts climbing up to Todnau and the Feldberg, this is a site of high quality well worth consideration for your stays in the region. It has some 260 individual pitches on flat gravel, their size varying from 80-100 sq.m. Marked by trees or other means, all have electricity and 180 have waste water drains, 40 with water, TV and radio connection. The site becomes full in season and reservations, especially in July, are necessary. There are two sanitary blocks of truly first class quality in the section with the fully serviced (but slightly smaller) pitches. They have washbasins, half in private cabins, water, showers with glass doors and seat, a baby bath, a unit for the disabled and individual bathrooms for hire. All hot water is free. The third block is to be rebuilt soon to the same standard but is nevertheless very satisfactory. There is a large indoor swimming pool (14 x 7 m.) with sauna and solarium on site.

How to find it: Münstertal lies south of Freiburg. From the A5 autobahn take Bad Krozingen and Colmar exit, turn southeast via Bad Krozingen and Staufen (bypassed) and continue 7 km. to Münstertal, where camp is signed from the main road.

General Details: Open all year. 40,000 sq.m. Shop (all year). Restaurant, particularly good and well patronised (closed Nov). Swimming pool. Tennis. Minigolf. Children's playground. Games room with table tennis. Tennis courses in summer, ski courses in winter - for children or adults. Village amenities are near.

Charges guide: Per person DM 12.00; child (under 10) 6.80; local tax 1.50 for over 16s; pitch 10.90 - 14.90; with TV, water, drainage, radio, phone and electricity connections 18.00; dog 4.00; private bathroom 15.00. Winter prices are similar.

Reservations: are made for min. 7 days, without deposit. Address: 79244 Münstertal. Tel: 07636/7080. FAX: 07636/7448.

This site is featured out of order - it is in South West Germany and should be listed on page 140

3650 Camping Gitzenweiler Hof, Lindau, nr Friedrichshafen

See colour advert opposite

Site with swimming pool in pleasant situation near Lindau.

Gitzenweiler Hof, which is some 3 km. from the Bodensee, is in a pleasant country setting. It is a very spacious site and although it has about 350 permanent caravans, it can still take about 350 tourist units but it is advisable to book for July/Aug. In the tourist section most pitches are without markings with siting left to campers with the remainder in rows between access roads. There are some pitches with water, drainage, telephone and TV connections. The site has a large swimming pool (33 x 25 m.) with an attractive surround with seats, etc. There are three main, well maintained toilet blocks plus one small unit. They have British toilets, individual washbasins with mirrors, some with free hot water, and free hot showers. Hot water also in sinks. A new block opened in '97 which includes children's facilities, shower/WC for disabled people and dog showers. Lindau is an interesting town, especially by the harbour, and possible attractive excursions include the whole of the Bodensee, the German Alpine Road, the Austrian Vorarlberg and Switzerland.

How to find it: Coming from the west on road no. 31, turn left 2 km. before Lindau; from München-Kempten (route 12) turn left 3 km. before Lindau. Camp signs at both places.

General Details: Open all year. Little shade. 300 electrical connections (5A). Shop (limited hours in low season). Restaurant/bar (closed Feb). Swimming pool (summer). Volleyball. Children's playground and playroom with entertainment in summer. Small zoo for children. Ground for football, etc. Free fishing in lake. Table tennis. Minigolf. Club room. Washing machines, dryers and dishwasher. Doctor comes if needed; hospital near. Late arrivals area.

Charges 1997: Per person DM 9.00; child under 10 yrs 3.00, 10-16 yrs 6.00; car 3.00; tent or caravan 6.00; motorcaravan 9.00 - 12.00, acc. to size; m/cycle 2.50; dog 2.00; electricity 3.00. Discounts for stays over 14 days and in winter.

Reservations: made with deposit (DM 180.00) and fee (20.00). Address: 88131 Lindau-Oberreitnau. Tel: 08382/9494-0. FAX: 08382/9494-15.

This site is featured out of order - it is in South West Germany and should be listed on page 150

Sail away to the sites and delights of Denmark, Sweden and Holland.

Camping Holidays in Scandinavia and Holland are perfect for the outdoor life and great value when you sail away, in style, with Scandinavian Seaways.

One, all-inclusive price covers transportation for

you, your family and your car aboard one of our sleek white liners plus camping vouchers to any one of a large selection of superb sites all over Sweden, Denmark or Holland. You get a lot more than you imagine, for a lot less than you think.

See your travel agent or call our 24-hour Brochure Line on 0990 333 666 (quote reference 7B232) for a copy of the Motoring Holidays Brochure.

From £104 per person*

*1997 price

Start your holiday with a Cruise Night out

P&O

Voted No.1 in the Observer Travel Awards for four consecutive years, P&O North Sea Ferries sail each evening from Hull to the Continent saving you a tiring trek south.

You can enjoy a great night out including a five course feast, live entertainment, casino, cinema, fantastic shops and fun for the kids. Plus a comfortable bed in a cosy cabin.

Wake up on the Continent with the whole day ahead of you and excellent road links to all parts of Europe.

Get the full picture in our Cruiseferries Brochure – from your Travel Agent or direct from us on 07000 337743, anytime.

P&O North Sea Ferries has now won The Observer Travel Award's "Best Ferry Company" for 4 years in a row

P&O North Sea Ferries

EVERY NIGHT FROM HULL TO THE CONTINENT

3030 DCC Truma Campingpark, Leeden, Tecklenberg, nr Osnabrück

Large site with swimming pool and other amenities near Osnabrück.

This is a large site taking some 900 units and covers a wide area. Half the pitches (individual ones on mostly flat grassy areas but not separated) are for permanent caravans, leaving 450 for tourists and space is usually available. Many electrical connections. Sanitary installations consist of four good modern blocks (heated in cool weather) with British WCs, washbasins, some in private cabins, with shelf and mirror, controllable hot showers; free hot water in basins, on payment in showers and in sinks for clothes and dishes - it is a good supply. On site is a swimming pool of about 200 sq.m., which can be heated, plus two smaller ones for children; open about mid-May to mid-Sept. No English spoken! Good walks from site - there is woodland not used for camping. Osnabrück is 15 km.

How to find it: Leave A1 autobahn at exit for Tecklenburg and Lengerich. Turn towards Lengerich, left at second traffic lights to `Leeden-Lotte' and follow camp signs. From N take exit for Lotte and follow Lengerich then Leeden.

General Details: Open all year. 300,000 sq.m. Self-service shop (March-Oct). Restaurant/bar (March-Oct and Dec-Jan). Snacks (July/Aug). Swimming pools. Sports field. Minigolf. Children's playground. Dry ski in summer. Youth room with table tennis; occasional disco. Washing machine and dryer in each block. Facilities for the disabled. Cooking facilities. Riding nearby.

Charges guide: Per person DM 7.50; child (4-13 yrs) 5.00; pitch 16.50; hikers' or cyclists' small tent 11.50; electricity 0.50 + 0.75 per kw/h; dog 2.00. 10% off personal charges with camping carnet.

Reservations: Formal ones are complicated and probably unnecessary; send a card to site before arrival. Address: 49545 Tecklenburg-Leeden. Tel: 05405/1007. FAX: as phone.

3025 Campingpark Alfsee, Rieste, nr Osnabrück

Good modern site, 25 km. north of Osnabrück with many watersport facilities.

This is one of those inland sites which, being adjacent to lakes, has made the most of its situation to provide a wide range of watersports opportunities, and with good installations, to offer a base for enjoyable weekends or holidays. The Alfsee itself is a very large stretch of water for sailing, but even closer to the site, a short stroll from the entrance, is a small lake of 100,000 sq.m. where there is both a bathing section with sandy beach (free to campers) and a water-ski automatic tug, ski-lift style, on payment and open to all. The site has 340 pitches on flat grass (160 taken by permanent caravans). They are of irregular shape and size but mostly over 100 sq.m. with separators and there are many electrical connections. The three identical toilet blocks, heated in cool weather, are nice clean ones of good quality, with British style WCs, washbasins with free hot water, shelf, mirror (some in private cabins) and hot showers with screen and seat on payment. A good supply, with a unit for the disabled.

How to find it: From the A1 autobahn north of Osnabrück take exit for Neuenkirchen and Vörden, turn left and follow signs for Alfsee and camp.

General Details: Open all year. Shop and restaurant (both April-Oct). Watersports (see above). Football practice field. Children's playground and entertainment. Grass tennis courts. Trampoline. Minigolf. Go-kart track. General room with amusement machines. Several washing machines and dryers. Cooking facilities.

Charges 1997: Per person DM 6.90; child 4.90; pitch 15.90; dog 3.00; electricity 2.50 (once only) plus meter.

Reservations: made for any length without deposit. Address: 49597 Rieste. Tel: 05464/5166. FAX: 05464/5837.

3010 Kur-Camping Ebsmoor, Soltau

Attractive, small, award winning site, close to many amenities.

Although near to Soltau centre (1½ km), Ebsmoor is an ideal location for visits to the famous Luneburg Heath. Herr and Frau Röders are a happy and dedicated couple who make their visitors most welcome. Herr Röders speaks excellent English. The central feature of the wooded site is a small lake crossed by a wooden bridge. An abundance of trees and shrubs gives a secluded setting to an already well cared for appearance. Ebsmoor only offers a tranquil stay - there are no entertainments. Two modern, very clean sanitary blocks contain all necessary facilities with a laundry room and an excellent, separate unit (including shower) for the disabled. There is an adequate children's play area, a basic shop and a small bar with terrace, but no cafe or restaurant except a breakfast service. Many sports activities are available locally. The site has 100 pitches with electricity and water to hand and with reasonable privacy between positions. Some guest rooms are available in the main building.

How to find it: From Soltau take road no. B3 north and turning to site is on left after 1½ km. (opposite DCC camping sign) at yellow town boundary sign.

General Details: Open all year except 15/1-1/3. Small shop and bar. Breakfast service. Children's play area. Sports activities locally. Rooms available.

Charges 1997: Per pitch DM 16.00; person 7.50; child 6.50; dog 3.00; electricity (6A) 1.00 plus 0.80/kw.

Reservations: Contact site. Address: Röders Park, Ebsmoor 8, 29614 Soltau. Tel: 05191/2141. FAX: 05191/17952.

GERMANY - North West

3015 SüdSee-Camp, Wietzendorf, nr Soltau

Luxury site with extensive activity programme south of Lüneberge Heide, north of Hannover.

This large site has several different types of area, mostly bordering onto the large lake, which has sandy beaches. There are 380 permanent caravans, mostly in pleasant woodland with good privacy, and about 500 tourist pitches. Some flat, individual pitches, with separations, are amid bushes and small trees giving limited shade, others, unseparated, on flat open grass, and others unmarked, under tall trees and close to lake. Electricity and water connections in all parts. Pitches vary in size (mostly 100-140 sq.m.) with a price difference. The lake can be used for bathing or boating with inflatables (but not sailboards) and is open to day visitors. The five sanitary blocks available for tourists are of different types, ages and sizes so the facilities show variations and may come under pressure in busy times. They provide British WCs, washbasins with free hot water, some in cabins, and hot showers mainly controllable and on payment. There are some private cabins (shower, washbasin and WC) at extra cost, two excellent special units for small children with baby baths, low toilets and basins and also ladies' make-up room with hair dryers. The facilities are some distance from areas where short stay visitors may be placed. Over much of season there is a programme of organised events, including excursions to, for example, Legoland in Denmark. The site can be busy in high season and is expensive, although there is lots going on and many facilities. The site reports the addition of a new subtropical indoor pool and a large riding stables.

How to find it: From autobahn A7 take Soltau-Süd exit, take A3 towards Bergen and turn off at signs to site after 3 km. It is 6 km. south of Soltau town.

General Details: Open all year. Large supermarket and general shop. Restaurant/bar. Indoor pool. Riding. Football pitch. Tennis. Volleyball. Table tennis. BMX track. Fitness track. Children's playground. Minigolf. Youth room with disco. TV room. Washing machines and dryers. Programme of organised activities and excursions.

Charges 1997: Per unit incl. 1 or 2 persons DM. 35.00 - 49.50; extra person 5.00 - 7.00; child (3-18 yrs) 3.00 - 5.00; supplement for larger pitches 10-20%; electricity 4A 3.00, 6A 6.00; family washcabin 10.00 - 15.00; dog 3.00 - 6.00. Special price for overnight stay (5 pm. - 10 am.) 25.00 - 30.00.

Reservations: are made, from Sat.-Sat. only in summer, with substantial deposit and fee. Contact site for comprehensive details. Address: 29647 Wietzendorf. Tel: 05196/98016 or 98017. FAX: 05196/98055.

3035 DCC Kur Camping Park, Bad Gandersheim

Good site, easily reached from autobahn and well placed for visiting other Harz resorts.

This well run, formal site has 460 pitches all well marked and easily accessible, divided into long stay and short stay and a section for those with animals. Motorcaravans are not accepted for short stays. Open all year, it provides good amenities for both summer walkers and winter skiers. Although on the edge of the Harz area, the excellent security at the site allows one to leave the van, etc. whilst exploring the twisty and busy roads of the main resort towns. The sanitary facilities are kept very clean. The pretty, old town is a 15 minute stroll.

How to find it: From autobahn A7 (E45), leave at Seesen, then route 64 to Bad Gandersheim. Site is on right, just before town and is well signed.

General Details: Open all year. Bar/restaurant (Easter-31/10, 15/12-10/1, w/ends at other times). Shop (Easter-31/10 and 15/12-10/1). Minigolf. Table tennis. Children's playground. Laundry facilities. Solarium. Dog shower. Tennis, riding, fishing, swimming, sailing, windsurfing all near.

Charges 1997: Per pitch DM 12.50 - 16.50; small tent 11.50; adult 7.50 plus local tax 1.00; child (under 13 yrs) 5.00 plus 0.50 tax; dog 2.00; electricity 0.50 plus meter. Credit cards accepted.

Reservations: Contact site. Address: Braunschweiger Str. 12, 37581 Bad Gandersheim. Tel: 05382/1595. FAX: 05382/1599.

3040 Camping Prahljust, Clausthal-Zellerfeld

Pleasant, large site in a good position to explore the Harz area.

This all year round site is well situated for both winter or summer holidays. It is a gently undulating site sloping down to a small lake. The receptionist/manager speaks good English and provides guests with an excellent information sheet in English. There are 1,000 pitches of which 350 are for permanent units, and three sanitary blocks, one of which has a unit for the disabled. Washing machines and dryers. Amenities include a large, heated swimming pool (with a small charge) and a sauna. Fishing is allowed in the lake (licence essential). A bar, restaurant and a self service shop are close to reception and there is a good children's playground. Entertainment is organised in high season.

How to find it: From autobahn A7 (E45) leave at Seesen and take route 242 for Clausthal Zellerfeld. Go through the town (direction Braunlage) and the site is 2 km. out of the town on the right, well signed. Coming from Braunlage, site is signed 'Rubezahl', on the left.

General Details: Open all year, as are bar, restaurant and shop. Swimming pool (charged). Sauna. Children's playground. Fishing.

Charges 1998: Per pitch DM 6.75 - 8.35; adult 6.55 - 8.15; child (under 14 yrs) 5.60 - 7.35; car 3.50 - 4.20; m/cycle 2.35; electricity 1.00 plus meter; dog 4.70 - 5.00; local tax 1.50.

Reservations: Write to site. Address: 38678 Clausthal-Zellerfeld. Tel: 05323/1300. FAX: 05323/78393.

3045 Knaus Camping Walkenried, Walkenried

Woodland site in the southern Harz with indoor pool.

The southern Harz area offers much for walkers and anglers and this site organises many outings ranging from free walks to coach trips to the highest mountain in the area at Brocken (1,142 m). It also has the benefit of an indoor pool, sauna and solarium. Outdoor activities available in the area include tennis, riding and watersports. There are about 150 touring pitches here of 80-100 sq.m. and arranged in well shaded groups on mainly slightly sloping grass and gravel. Most are separated by bushes or trees and have 4A, 2 pin electrical connections. There are some smaller hardstandings for motorhomes and a separate area for visitors with dogs. The tiled and heated sanitary facilities are satisfactory, with free hot water to the 12 showers and washbasins (private cabins for ladies), British style WCs and a toilet for the disabled, and are all in the main building by the entrance. There is a large children's play area at the side of the site, also a barbecue and some seating here and by the small fishing lake. An indoor swimming pool is free for campers (open 9-12 and 3-6, all year except 1/11-10/12).

How to find it: Walkenried is signed from the B4 Erfurt-Magdeburg road just north of Nordhausen and from the B243 Seesen-Nordhausen road. The site is signed in the town.

General Details: Open all year exc. Nov. Baker calls just after 8 am. Shop and restaurant (both all year). Indoor pool. Sauna and solarium. New children's play area. Small fishing lake. Bicycle hire. Laundry and cooking facilities. Chemical disposal. Caravans (10) and tents to rent on site; contact site for details.

Charges 1998: Per person DM 8.50; child (3-14) 4.50; pitch 7.50 - 12.00; tent with m/cycle 7.50; electricity 3.50.

Reservations: Contact the site. Address: Ellricher Str. 7, 37445 Walkenried. Tel: 05525/778. FAX: 05525/2332.

3280 Camping und Ferienpark Teichmann, Vöhl-Herzhausen, Edersee

Well equipped site for active holidays on the shores of the Edersee.

Attractively situated on the west end of the Eder lake, this site offers many opportunities for watersports and for walking or cycling around the lake or in the Eder hills. The lake provides facilities for windsurfing and swimming (no motor boats are allowed). The site is also suitable for a winter sports holiday (with ski runs near) and the three sanitary blocks for tourers can be heated. Hot showers are free and there are facilities for the disabled. Pitches are on flat ground with electricity available and there is a separate area for tents. The many amenities include a mini-market and café. A good site for families, there are many activities (listed below) and a pitch can usually be found even for a one night stay.

How to find it: From the A44 Oberhausen - Kassel autobahn, take exit for Korbach. Site is between Korbach and Frankenberg on the B252 road, on the south side of Herzhausen, about 45 km. from the A44.

General Details: Open all year. Café and shop (both summer only). Restaurant (Feb-Dec). Watersports. Boat and bicycle hire. Football. Fishing. Minigolf. Beach volleyball (high season). Tennis. Table tennis. Children's playground. Large working model railway. Sauna and solarium. Disco in high season. Holiday homes to rent.

Charges guide: Per person DM 9.00 - 10.00, acc. to season; child (3-13 yrs) 5.30 - 6.30; caravan or motorcaravan 12.50 - 14.00; tent 9.50 - 10.50; small tent 7.40 - 8.40; car or m/cycle 3.40; electricity 3.70.

Reservations: Write to site. Address: 34516 Vöhl-Herzhausen. Tel: 05635/245. FAX: 05635/8145.

3270 Campingplatz Lahnaue, Marburg an der Lahn

Satisfactory site adjacent to swimming pools and within walking distance of town.

This little municipal site should make a satisfactory stop on the main B3 Frankfurt-Kassel road (not the autobahn). Situated on the grassy bank of the river Lahn, there are pleasant walks from the site to the centre of the old university town. An adjoining sports complex includes large swimming pools, tennis, minigolf, playground and general games area. Pitches are all on flat grass, some at the waters edge, numbered but not separated with electric points in most areas. The small sanitary block is modern and should be adequate for the usual numbers. It has hot showers on payment, one washbasin with hot water per sex, the remainder with cold and new facilities for the disabled.

How to find it: Site is at the south end of the town adjoining the ring road (some road noise). Turn off ring road at `Marburg mitte' exit then follow `Freibad' and camping signs.

General Details: Open 1 April - 1 Oct. Some provisions kept. Small restaurant with breakfast served. Washing machine and dryer. Table tennis. Cooking facilities. Minigolf.

Charges guide: Per person DM 6.00; child (2-14 yrs) 3.00; caravan 6.00; tent 4.00 - 5.00; car 3.00; motorhome 8.00; electricity 2.00 plus 1.50 per day.

Reservations: Usually unnecessary, but site address is 35037 Marburg. Tel: 06421/21331.

All the sites in this guide are regularly inspected by our team of experienced site assessors, but we welcome your opinion too.

See Readers Reports on page 361

GERMANY - West Central

3210 Campingplatz Biggesee-Sondern, Olpe-Sondern

High quality leisure complex site, on shores of large lake in Südsauerland National Park.

In an attractive setting on the shores of the Biggesee lake, this site offers many leisure opportunities, as well as high quality camping facilities. It is therefore deservedly popular, and reservation is almost always essential. Well managed, the same company also operates two other sites on the shores of the lake, where space may be available. There are 300 numbered pitches of 100 sq.m, of which about 250 are available for tourists, either in rows or in circles, on terraces. Electricity (6A) and water points throughout. The sanitary facilities are of excellent quality, in two blocks, heated when necessary, with British WCs, washbasins, most in cabins, and good showers (including special ones for children), all with free hot water. With laundry and baby facilities (keys from reception), the provision should be adequate. Watersports on the lake include sailing and windsurfing, with a school. You may launch small boats and swim from the shore. Roller-skating on site and tennis nearby. Playroom and playground for smaller children. Skiing is possible in winter and there are walks around the lake.

How to find it: From the A45 (Siegen-Hagen) autobahn, take the exit to Olpe, and turn towards Attendorn. After 6 km, turn to Bigge-Stausee. Site is signed.

General Details: Open all year. Variable shade. Electricity throughout. Camping shop. Laundry facilities. Watersports and school. Swimming from beach. Football pitch. Table tennis. Roller-skating. Tennis nearby. Children's playground and playroom. Solarium and sauna. Entertainment and excursions. Motorcaravan service points. Car wash area. Cooking facilities. Restaurant and snacks 400 m.

Charges guide: Per unit incl. electricity DM 18.50 - 24.50; person 5.50 - 6.50; child (2-15) 3.00 - 4.00. Less in low season (outside 28/4-31/8).

Reservations: Probably essential for much of the year, but phone site. Address: Erholungsanlage Biggesee-Sondern, 57462 Olpe-Sondern, Am Sonderner Kopf 3. Tel: 02761/944111. FAX: 02761/944122.

3205 Campingplatz der Stadt Köln, Köln-Poll, nr Köln

Convenient overnight site beside the Rhine, very close to motorway.

Adjacent to an autobahn bridge over the Rhine and very conveniently placed for those entering Germany via autobahn from Belgium, this site would also serve for a short visit to the sights of Köln. It receives many British visitors, mostly in transit; these include groups, but the site controls noise. It is a small, neat, grassy site, pleasantly situated on the river bank with electricity available on half the pitches. There is a small, basic toilet block, with free hot water at times in the washing troughs and regularly in the showers, which have external undressing.

How to find it: Leave autobahn A4 at exit no. 13 for Köln-Poll (just west off intersection of A3 and A4). Turn left at first traffic lights, left again at second lights and immediately bear right into one-way street. Continue through built up area and, turning left into park area at camping sign, follow road back along riverside towards motorway bridge.

General Details: Open Easter - 30 Sept. Kiosk (from May). Café adjacent. Cooking facilities on payment. Fishing. Bicycle hire. Washing machine and dryer. Chemical disposal. Motorcaravan services.

Charges 1998: Per adult DM 7.00; child (4-12 yrs) 4.50; caravan 6.00; motorcaravan 8.00 - 10.00; tent 4.00 - 6.00; car 4.00; m/cycle 2.00; electricity 3.00.

Reservations: Write to site. Address: 51105 Köln 91 (Poll). Tel: 0221/831966. FAX: as phone.

3212 Landal GreenParks Wirfttal, Stadtkyll

Site with pools and other facilities near the Belgian border between Cologne and Trier.

Peacefully set in a small valley in the heath and forest of the hills of the northern Eifel, Wirfttal has over 270 numbered pitches of which 60% are for tourists. Not fully separated, they mostly back onto fences, hedges etc. on fairly flat ground of different levels. They are about 80 sq.m. and all have electricity and TV aerial points. Water points around. Also part of the site, but separate from the camping, is a holiday bungalow complex. A short walk up the hill is a swimming pool complex (free for campers) with three pools, one heated, and minigolf. Additionally, at the entrance, is a small, free indoor pool, plus a sauna and solarium on payment, a sports centre with 2 outdoor tennis courts (floodlit), a super adventure playground, volleyball, bowling and an indoor tennis and squash centre. Children and adults will be enchanted by the ducks and swans on the small lake. The site has a main toilet block (heated and the only one open out of main season), and two small units. They should suffice and have free hot water in all washbasins, showers and sinks; all ladies' basins and one for men in the main block are in cabins.

How to find it: Site is 1½ km. south of Stadtkyll on the road towards Schüller.

General Details: Open all year, as are shop and restaurant which front the site and the café by pools (all also open to public). 60,000 sq.m. Riding. Fishing. Bicycle hire. Children's play equipment around site and main adventure playground. Other amenities described above. Windsurfing 3 km. Winter sports. Bicycles and sledges for hire. Animation in season in activity hut. Chemical disposal. Motorcaravan services.

Charges 1998: Per unit incl. up to 5 persons DM 28.00 - 51.00; small pitch, max 2 persons 24.00 - 51.00; extra car, tent or dog 4.50; electricity 4.00.

Reservations: are made and are essential in peak season. Made for Fri.- Fri. only with 50% deposit. Address: 54589 Stadtkyll/Eifel. Tel: 06597/92920. FAX: 06597/929250. Office open 7 days/week.

3215 Campingplatz Goldene Meile, Remagen, nr Bonn

Site on banks of Rhine between Bonn and Koblenz, adjacent to outdoor pool complex.

This site is beside the Rhine (boats of any type can be put onto the river) and adjacent to a large complex of open-air public swimming pools (campers pay the normal entrance). Although there is an emphasis on permanent caravans, there are about 300 pitches for tourists, 17 with water and waste water connections. They are either in the central, more mature area or in a newer area where pitches are arranged around an attractively landscaped small fishing lake. All are now numbered and marked, but with nothing to separate them, and are said to be about 80 sq.m. They claim always to find space for odd nights, except perhaps at B.Hs. The main sanitary installations are in the central block which houses all the washing facilities. This block is of good quality and is heated and kept clean, with British toilets, washbasins partly in cabins, controllable hot showers on payment and new facilities for disabled people. The shower and wash rooms are locked at 10 pm. A smart toilet block serves the newer pitches near the lake. It also has dish and clothes sinks, a washing machine and dryer, and a cooking facility. The central buildings also house a small bar/restaurant and a small shop for basic supplies (including bread to order). This site is in a popular area and, although busy in high season, appears to be well run.

How to find it: Remagen is 23 km. south of Bonn on the no. 9 road towards Koblenz. The site is on the road running close to the Rhine from Remagen to Kripp and is signed from the N9 south of Remagen, which avoids the congested town (signs also for 'Allwetterbad'). From A61 autobahn take Sinzig exit.

General Details: Open all year. Shop and restaurant (weekends only Nov - March). Electrical connections in most areas. Children's playgrounds. Entertainment for children in July/Aug. Volleyball. Football. Bicycle hire. Fishing (permit from reception). Washing machines and dryers. Chemical disposal. Motorcaravan services. Main gate locked at 10 pm. (also 1-3 pm.)

Charges 1998: Per person DM 8.50; child (6-16 yrs) 6.50, under 6 free; caravan pitch 12.50; tent 6.00 - 12.50 acc. to size; dog 2.00; electricity 4.00.

Reservations: can be made for at least a few days. Address: 53424 Remagen/Rhein. Tel: 02642/22222. FAX: 02642/1555.

Campingplatz
»Goldene Meile«
D-53424 Remagen
Tel. (0 26 42) 2 22 22

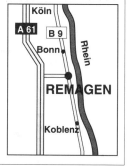

On one of the most beautiful and modern camp sites in the romantic Rhine valley between Bonn (20 km) and Koblenz (40 km) you will find ideal conditions.

For a holiday: water sports on the Rhine and in the heated all-weather pool (86 m chute), sports and keep-fit (indoor and outdoor tennis courts, playing field, volleyball court, football ground), hiking in the Eifel and the Westerwald, boat trips on the Rhine and the Mosel, numerous wine festivals.

For a short stop: convenient location only 7 km from the A 61 motorway (Sinzig-Remagen exit), 2 km to the B 9. Shop, restaurant with terrace, first-class rating from ADAC for many years.

3265 Campingplatz Limburg, Limburg an der Lahn, nr Koblenz

Good municipal site by Cologne-Frankfurt autobahn.

Pleasantly and peacefully situated on the bank of the river Lahn between autobahn and town - both the autobahn viaduct and·the cathedral are visible from the site - this little site makes a good overnight stop for travellers on the Koln-Frankfurt stretch. You may, however, be tempted to stay longer as there are other attractions here, notably a very fine swimming pool complex nearby and the attractive old town of medieval buildings a gentle stroll away. The site is on level grass with numbered pitches on either side of gravel tracks at right angles from the main tarmac road, which runs the length of the site. Being very popular with Dutch and British campers, it can become crowded at peak times, but you should find space. The main sanitary block near reception is rather old but improvements have been made to the facilities. A second small block at the far end of the camp (no hot water) is for night use. Plans are in hand to rebuild this block to a higher standard. A bar/restaurant, open during the evenings, offers drinks, simple meals and takeaway. There is a kiosk for some basic supplies. Some rail noise.

How to find it: Leave A3 autobahn at Limburg-Nord exit and follow road into town and then signs for 'Camping-Swimming'.

General Details: Open 14 April - 30 October. 22,000 sq m. Shade in parts. 170 electrical connections (long leads in parts). Bar/restaurant (evenings). Kiosk. Swimming pool opposite. Boating. Fishing (permit on payment). Children's play area. Washing machines, dryers, cookers. Bicycles and motorcycles for hire. Supermarkets and good range of shops and restaurants in town.

Charges 1997: Per person DM 5.50; child (under 16) 3.00; car 3.00; m/cycle 2.00; caravan 5.00; motorcaravan 8.00; tent 3.50 - 5.00; boat 5.50; dog 2.00; electricity 3.00.

Reservations: Contact site. Address: 65549 Limburg a.d. Lahn. Tel: 06431/22610. FAX: 06431/92013.

133

GERMANY - West Central

3225 Naturpark Camping Suleika, Lorch-bei-Rudesheim

Attractive and comfortable, family run site on steep hillside near popular Rhine town.

Approached by a narrow and steep system of lanes through the vineyards, this situation is not for the faint hearted. Once you reach the site, it is steeply arranged in small terraces, up the side of the wooded hill, with a stream flowing through - the water supply is direct from springs. The surroundings are most attractive, with views over the river below. The Riesling Walk footpath passes above the site. Of the 110 pitches, 60 are available for tourists. These are mostly on the lower terraces, in numbered groups of two or three. There is a special area for younger campers. All have electricity and there are water points around. Cars have to be parked away from the pitches near the entrance. A central block contains a very pleasant restaurant and small shop, with sanitary facilities alongside. These are excellent, heated in cool weather and containing British WCs, washbasins (5, plus 3 in cabins, for each sex), with free hot water. A new block houses free hot showers and there is also a nicely furnished child's washroom, with WC, shower and bath. With steep walks from most pitches to the facilities, this is probably not a site for disabled people; however, it is an attractive situation and reception is friendly.

How to find it: There is a direct entrance road from the B42, between Rudesheim and Lorch, but with a height limitation of 2.35 m. under a railway bridge. Higher vehicles will find the site signed on the south side of Lorch. The site is reached via a one-way system of lanes - follow the signs.

General Details: Open 1 March - 15 Nov. Shade in most areas. Electricity throughout. Water from springs. Restaurant. Small shop. Children's playground. Some entertainment in season. Site open all day. Laundry service. 10 chalets for rent.

Charges 1997: Per adult DM 7.50; child 5.00; caravan 8.00; motorcaravan 10.00 - 12.00; tent 5.00 - 8.00; car 2.50; m/cycle 1.50; dog 3.00; electricity 2.00 plus meter.

Reservations: made with DM 50 deposit, so only worthwhile for a longer stay. Address: Lorch-bei-Rudesheim, 65382 Rudesheim 2 (Ass). Tel: 06726/9464.

3230 Campingplatz Burgen, Burgen, nr Koblenz

Site on banks of Moselle between Koblenz and Cochem.

This site is attractively situated between the road and the river on the flat grassy bank; in fact it suffers sometimes from heavy flooding. Most of the pitches on the river's edge are occupied by permanent caravans and attendant boats, but there are some 120 hardstanding pitches for tourists, with markers and with electricity available, plus a meadow at one end. The site fills up for much of July/Aug. but a few pitches are kept for transit trade. The central buildings have a rather temporary look, but in fact are of a reasonable standard. A single central sanitary block has British toilets; washbasins with free hot water (5 in private cabins), but only 9 showers (on payment). These particularly would be hard pressed in high season. Many water points. With a railway across the water and the road, some noise must be expected.

How to find it: Site is on eastern edge of town, 30 km. from Koblenz (tight turn into site if coming from Koblenz).

General Details: Open 1 April - 15 Oct. 35,000 sq.m. Shop (all season). General room with TV and games, drinks served. Very small swimming pool (9 x 6 m. open Whitsun - 31 Aug). Slipway for boats. Table tennis. Children's playground. Washing machine and dryer.

Charges guide: Per person DM 6.00; child (1-13 yrs) 3.50; pitch 11.00; m/cycle 4.00; dog 2.00; electricity 3.00.

Reservations: are made for any length but with deposit and fee. Address: 56332 Burgen/Mosel. Tel: 02605/2396. FAX: 02605/4919.

3235 Camping am Mühlenteich, Lingerhahn, Laudert, nr Koblenz

Friendly site to west of central Rhine and quite close to autobahn.

Set among trees and fields in the hills at the eastern end of the Hunsrück, this site is only 15 km. from the Rhine at Oberwesel. Bingen, Boppard and Koblenz are also reached easily via the A61 autobahn. Although the majority of the site is occupied by 250 permanent caravans, there are 100 tourist pitches. They are individual ones with nothing between them - some are in the main part of site (for longer stays), others are in a more open situation opposite (caravans and tents are mixed together). Space is usually available. The central sanitary block, in two sections, is large and of good quality. A further block in the permanent area makes a satisfactory supply. Washbasins have free hot water, with some cabins for ladies in two blocks and for men in one; hot showers (controllable) are on payment; British WCs. On site is a pool for swimming (free of charge) fashioned from a natural basin and fed by springs. A splendid building houses reception, a shop and café and there is a disco room for children.

How to find it: From A61 autobahn take exit for Laudert. Site entrance is in Lingerhahn village, between Laudert and Kastellaun and is signed.

General Details: Open all year. Electrical connections everywhere. Small shop. Café (not all year). Baker calls 8.30 am. from April. Cable/satellite TV. Youth disco room. Tennis. Basketball. Bowling. Table tennis. Children's adventure playground. Football field. Wagon rides in season. Barbecue.

Charges guide: Per person DM 6.00; child (under 14) 4.00; car 6.00; caravan or tent 6.00; motorcaravan 12.00; small child's tent 3.00; m/cycle 5.00; dog 3.00; electricity 3.00; cable TV 2.00.

Reservations: Write to site. Address: 56291 Lingerhahn. Tel: 06746/533. FAX: 06746/1566.

CAMPING PLATZ BURG LAHNECK

Lahnstein/Rhein, Ortsteil Oberlahnstein
(Take 'Oberlahnstein' exit from B42 through road)

On the heights near the medieval castle Burg Lahneck and so free from possible Rhine flooding. Beside the public pool. The ideal base for those who want to explore the Rhineland with its wonderful scenery and historic buildings. Beautiful day excursions avaliable in all directions (Rhine, Lahn, Moselle, Nahe, and Ahr valleys). Boarding-point for Rhine steamers.

3220 Campingplatz Burg Lahneck, Lahnstein, nr Koblenz

Orderly, clean site with fine views over Rhine and swimming pool adjoining.
The location of this site is splendid, high up overlooking the Rhine and the town of Lahnstein - many of the pitches have their own super views. Adjacent is a good swimming pool with extensive grassy area, and also the mediaeval castle Burg Lahneck (the home of the camp proprietor, which may be visited). It is in the best part of the Rhine valley, and close to Koblenz and the Moselle. A 'Kurcentrum', under 2 km. from the site, has a thermal bath from warm springs (reduced admission to campers) with sauna and solarium. The site, which consists partly of terraces and partly of open grassy areas, has a cared for look and all is very neat and clean. One can usually find a space here, though from early July to mid-August it can become full. The 125 individual pitches are marked but not separated, all with electricity; campers are sited by the management. The sanitary facilities are in one central block and are of a good standard, but not heated; they are well maintained and cleaned. They have British toilets and washbasins with with some cabins for both sexes. Hot water is free for washbasins and washing-up sinks, showers are on payment (DM 1). Reception staff at the site are friendly and charges reasonable.

How to find it: From B42 town bypass, take Oberlahnstein exit and follow signs 'Kurcentrum' and 'Burg Lahneck'.

General Details: Open Easter or 1 April - 31 Oct. 18,000 sq.m. Shade only in parts. Motorcaravan service point. Small shop. Cafe adjoining site; meals also in Burg Lahneck restaurant. Swimming pool (reduced charges for campers). Children's playground. Washing machine and dryer. Doctors and hospital near. Tennis and riding nearby.

Charges 1997: Per person DM 9.50; child (under 3) free, (under 15) 4.50; car 6.00; tent 7.00 - 9.50, acc. to size; trailer tent or caravan 9.50; motorcaravan 13.00 - 15.50; m/cycle 2.50; dog 1.00; electricity 1.00 plus meter charge.

Reservations: made without deposit. Address: 56112 Lahnstein, Ortsteil Oberlahnstein. Tel: 02621/2765.

**Many continental camp sites, particularly in Germany,
close for 2 or 3 hours at lunch time.**
There are usually parking areas outside where you can park and wait.

GERMANY - West Central

3240 Eifel Ferienpark Im Prümtal, Waxweiler, Bitburg, nr Trier

Pleasant small site next to swimming pools, quietly situated close to town.

This small site in the western Eifel near Belgium and Luxembourg lies rather away from main routes, but is easily accessible from the Prüm-Bitburg-Trier fast road or the A60 autobahn. The 100 numbered tourist pitches, all with electricity, are in two flat sections, one alongside a river and open, the other in groups of 5 or 6 with hedge surrounds. Most average 80 sq.m. but there are 24 of 120 sq.m. also with TV connections. There are 86 well hidden, letting bungalows on sloping ground behind. The sanitary facilities in two blocks have been improved (the toilets are now completely partitioned from the showers) and have free hot water to washbasins and showers. Free admission to nearby municipal pool complex (2 good sized pools) open June to Aug. and a smaller indoor pool open at other times.

How to find it: Site is southwest of Waxweiler off the road to Prüm - access is marked Ferienzentrum. Town is signed from the Prüm-Bitburg (51) fast road and the A60 autobahn.

General Details: Open 31 March - 5 Nov. Shop. Café. Kiosk for snacks. Restaurant quite close and in town. Table tennis. Minigolf, tennis and pools adjacent. Children's playground. Use of football pitch. Free fishing. Washing machines and dryers. No dogs July/Aug. Entertainment programme in high season including `survival' programme with mountain biking, kayaks, etc. for all ages.

Charges guide: Per pitch 35.00 - 51.00; person 4.00; electricity 3.50.

Reservations: are made (Fri.- Fri. only in high season) with deposit (DM 20). Address: 54649 Waxweiler (Eifel). Tel: 06554/427. FAX: 06554/1280.

3242 Country Camping Schinderhannes, Hausbay-Pfalzfeld

Large countryside site with a lake in the Hunsrück.

Set in a `bowl' of land which catches the sun all day long and with trees and parkland all around, this is a very peaceful and picturesque site, very close to, but rather different from, no. 3235. Country Camping also has 250 permanent caravans which are in a separate area from 90 hardstanding overnight pitches which are on two areas near reception. For those staying longer, the site becomes visually more attractive as you drive down into the area around the lake to 160 numbered pitches. These are of 80 sq.m. plus on grass, some with hardstanding and all with electrical connections (10A) and with water points around. You can position yourself for shade or sun. The lake is used for swimming and inflatable boats and for fishing (licence from site). The sanitary buildings, which can be heated, are of a high standard with one section, in the reception/shop building, for the overnight pitches and the remainder close to the longer stay places. They have large, controllable showers, 4 private cabins in total, laundry and facilities for disabled people. Charges are inclusive of electricity and hot water. A pleasant large restaurant features an open fire and includes a rest area with TV and a bowling alley downstairs. English is spoken by the helpful reception staff.

How to find it: From the A61 Koblenz - Ludwigshafen, 30 km. south of Koblenz, take the Pfalzfeld exit and on to Hausbay where site is signed.

General Details: Open all year. No entry or exit 10 pm - 7 am. Restaurant with TV and bowling alley. Shop (both 16/3-31/10 and maybe Xmas). Tennis (on payment). Fishing. Basketball. Laundry facilities. Children's play area and fort. Rallies welcome.

Charges guide: Per adult DM 7.00; child 5.00; pitch 12.00; dog 3.00; electricity included.

Reservations: Contact site. Address: 56291 Hausbay-Pfalzfeld. Tel: 06746/1674 or 8470. FAX: 06746/8214.

3470 AZUR Campingplatz Odenwald, Kirchzell, Eberbach, nr Heidelberg

Odenwald site with indoor pool.

In the nature reserve of the Odenwald and giving the impression of being deep in the forest, this site will appeal most to those who like the peaceful attractions of hills, trees and meadows. It is situated in a low lying valley, away from main through routes although Heidelberg is only an hour away. Over 50% of the pitches are taken by permanent caravans but there are 160 grassy and shaded tourist pitches spread out around the site. There is usually space but it can be full at Easter, Whitsun and in late July. Entertainment is organised at these times. There is a larger than usual, free, indoor swimming pool with sauna. The sanitary facilities, in three main blocks, are of satisfactory quality and are kept clean, with heating in cooler weather. They have British toilets, washbasins with some in cabins for both sexes, and free hot water, plus a toilet and shower for the disabled. Reception is friendly and efficient.

How to find it: Site is 2 km. south of Kirchzell on the Eberbach - Amorbach road.

General Details: Open all year. Many electrical connections. Small shop (April-Sept). Restaurant. Children's playground. Table tennis. Swimming pool, plus sauna and solarium. Barbecue. General room with TV (satellite). Washing machines and dryer. Mobile homes for hire.

Charges 1997: Per adult DM 8.00 - 10.00, acc. to season; child (1-12 yrs) 6.00 - 7.00; pitch 11.00 - 13.00; car or m/cycle 3.00 - 4.00; extra tent 3.00 - 4.00; dog 3.00 - 4.00; electricity 3.80.

Reservations: are made with deposit (DM 15) and fee (15); write to site for details. Address: 63931 Kirchzell-Eberbach. Tel: 09373/566. FAX: 09373/7375.

3245 Landal GreenParks Sonnenberg, Leiwen, nr Trier

Pleasant site of a high standard on hilltop above Moselle valley.

This site is on top of a hill, with views over the Moselle as you climb the approach road, 4 km. uphill from the wine village of Leiwen and the river. An outdoor public swimming pool complex is 1½ km away but the site has recently opened a splendid free indoor activity pool with child's paddling pool, whirlpool, cascade and slides. Combining a bungalow complex (separated) with camping, the site has 145 large, individual and numbered grassy pitches. All have electricity (6A) and TV connections and are spread out in smaller groups on terraces. The toilet block has under-floor heating and is of very good quality. The facilities should be adequate, with British toilets, washbasins in cabins, with shelf and mirror, and free hot showers. Excursions and entertainment are organised in season. There is a restaurant and many amenities, including a leisure centre with indoor tennis courts, bowling, sauna, solarium and fitness room. This site is efficiently managed and reception is friendly and helpful. English spoken.

How to find it: From Trier-Koblenz motorway take exit for Schweich just north of Moselle bridge, turn towards Hetzerath on 49 road, right after 2 km. at Leiwen or Wittlich sign, into Leiwen. Follow signs for Ferienpark, Sonnenberg or Freibad uphill 4 km. to site. From Koblenz on autobahn take Hetzerath exit, go through it on no. 49 road, and 3 km. beyond turn left for Leiwen.

General Details: Open 20 Feb - 6 Nov. 300,000 sq.m. Shop. Restaurant, bar and snacks (all season). Disco, entertainment and excursions at busy times. Indoor leisure centre with tennis. Volleyball. Football pitch. Minigolf. Children's playground. Laundry. Chemical disposal. Motorcaravan services. Bungalows and apartments to let.

Charges 1997: Per unit incl. up to 5 persons DM 41.00 - 52.00; extra person 3.50; electricity, satellite TV 4.00.

Reservations: Write to site with deposit (Fri. - Fri. only in high season). Address: Landal Green Parks Sonnenberg, 54340 Leiwen. Tel: 06507/93690. FAX: 06507/936936.

3250 Landal GreenParks Warsberg, Saarburg, nr Trier

Well organised site with comprehensive amenities including chair lift to town.

On top of a steep hill, approached by a winding road, this site has pleasant views over the town and surrounding area. A chair lift with a terminal near to the site links it to the town and is free for campers - it is well worth a ride. An attractive location, which would only be exposed in the worst weather. Efficiently managed, the site combines holiday bungalows with camping, although the two are divided. There are about 500 numbered tourist pitches, of quite reasonable size, and separated in small groups by trees and shrubs; electrical connections (6A) are available in most places. July is the busiest month and there are some tour operator pitches. The three toilet blocks are of good quality and should suffice, providing British WCs, washbasins, shelf and mirror (most in private cabins for ladies, some for men), fully controllable hot showers, all with free hot water, a unit for disabled and washing machines and dryers. There are many games facilities here, two good quality restaurants and a free heated swimming pool. This is a site which should appeal to all age groups and which has received some positive reports.

How to find it: Site is in the northwest outskirts of Saarburg. From the town take the road signed Trier and follow signs up hill on left for 3 km.

General Details: Open 3 April - 6 Nov. Reception open 9 am. - 5 pm. (Sundays 10-12 only). Shop. Restaurant and snacks, games rooms adjacent. Tennis court and 'platform tennis'. Swimming pool (20/5-15/9). Minigolf. Football field. Large children's playground. Bowling. Outdoor chess and draughts. Entertainment in season for all ages. Washing machines and dryers. Chemical disposal. Motorcaravan services. Many bungalows for hire.

Charges 1998: Per unit incl. 2 persons DM 27.00 - 48.00, 5 persons 32.00 - 48.00; child under 5 yrs free; dog 4.50; electricity 4.00.

Reservations: are made (Fri-Fri only in high season) with deposit of 50%. Address: In der Urlaub, 54439 Saarburg. Tel: 06581/91460. FAX: 06581/2514.

3264 Campingplatz Büttelwoog, Dahn, Pirmasens, nr Saarbrücken

Convenient night stop in attractive countryside between Saarbrücken and Karlsruhe.

There are interesting and unusual rock features at this peaceful, edge of town site, with tall trees all around. In a long, narrowish setting, a tarred access road leading from reception divides flat, unmarked, grassy pitches, all of which have 4A electricity (mainly 2 pin). With a further open section behind reception, there is a total of 100 pitches. By reception are a small shop and a café/bar where breakfast is served. The sanitary facilities here and in a further block in the main part, have free hot water to showers and washbasins, of which a few are in cabins. The showers could be under pressure in peak times. Torch useful. A pleasant site, if not outstanding, in an interesting setting and the welcome is friendly.

How to find it: From Saarbrücken go towards Kaiserslauten on the A6/E50 or road no. 423. Take the Zweibrücken exit, then Pirmasens, finally turning to Dahn at Hinterweidenthal. Site is well signed in Dahn.

General Details: Open all year. Small shop. Café/bar - meals Apr-Oct. Children's playground. Minigolf. Bicycle hire. Swimming pools 300 m. (indoor and outdoor). Washing machine. Chemical disposal. Town 800 m.

Charges 1997: Per adult DM 9.00; child under 12 yrs 5.00, 12-16 yrs 7.00; pitch 10.00; electricity 3.00. Less 10% from 2nd night with camping carnet.

Reservations: Contact site. Address: 66994 Dahn/Pfalz. Tel: 06391/5622. FAX: 06391/5326.

GERMANY - West Central / South West

3260 Knaus Camping-Park Bad Dürkheim, Bad Dürkheim, nr Ludwigshafen

Site with good amenities beside lake, on edge of town.

This large site is comfortable and has some 650 pitches (about half occupied by permanent caravans) but, being the best site at this well known wine town, it is very busy in main season. However, with some emergency areas they can usually find space for everyone. The site is long and narrow with individual pitches of fair size arranged on each side of the central road, which is decorated with arches of growing vines. A lake runs along one side and bathing is possible (much of the lake has a sandy floor and there is a little beach) and non-powered boats can be launched. A new sports programme has been introduced offering guided tours, biking, canoeing and climbing. Three large sanitary blocks are spaced out along the central avenue and they should prove more than adequate. They have British toilets and free hot water in the individual basins, showers and sinks and are heated in cool weather. No dogs are taken. Some noise from light aircraft, especially at weekends.

How to find it: Bad Dürkheim is on the no. 37 road west of Ludwigshafen. Site is on the eastern outskirts, signed from the Ludwigshafen road.

General Details: Open all year except Nov. Some shade - trees are growing. Electrical connections everywhere. Shop (all year). Restaurant just outside gates. Sports programme. Tennis. Sports field. Children's playground. Garden chess. Sauna and solarium. Cooking facilities. Washing machine in each block. Chemical disposal. Motorcaravan services. Caravans (10) and tents to rent on site; contact site for details.

Charges 1998: Per person DM 8.50; child (3-14 yrs) 4.50; pitch with caravan/tent 7.50 - 12.00; tent and m/cycle 7.50; electricity 3.50.

Reservations: made for any length with deposit (DM 50). Address: In den Almen 3, 67098 Bad Dürkheim. Tel: 06322/61356. FAX: 06322/8161.

3405 Camping Bad Liebenzell, Bad Liebenzell, nr Pforzheim

Good municipal site in northeast Black Forest, adjacent to modern swimming pool complex.

This good municipal site is attractively situated on the outskirts of the pleasant little spa town of Bad Liebenzell. It has direct access to an excellent, large, heated thermal swimming pool complex which is free to campers. Recently rebuilt, this includes swimming pools, wave pool and long slide. There is also a children's pool and grassy lying-out area and several tennis courts. The site is often full in high season when reservation is advisable (if not reserved arrive early). The 250 pitches (about 60% for tourists), 200 with electricity, are neatly arranged in rows on flat grass between hedges and trees and the good access roads. Three sanitary blocks are well maintained and have British toilets, individual basins with free hot water, shelf and mirror (in 2 blocks mostly in private cabins) and hot showers. There is provision for the handicapped and babies, and enclosed washing-up sinks. Used by a British tour operator. This is a well run and orderly site.

How to find it: Site is just north of Bad Liebenzell, beside main 463 road; south of Pforzheim (25 km).

General Details: Open all year. Small shop (open all season but for limited hours) - bread to order. Swimming pool complex open from mid-May. 20,000 sq.m. Bar/restaurant with simple, good value meals. Cafe/bar by pool. Large room for general use with TV and library. Tennis (instruction available at weekends). Children's playground. Washing machines and dryers. Cooking facilities. Cycle tracks, nature trails, cross country skiing 8 km. No dogs.

Charges guide: Per person DM 8.00; child (4-16) 5.50; pitch 9.00; electricity on meter; local tax (per person, per night) 16/4-31/10 3.50, otherwise 2.50.

Reservations: Write to site (no deposit). Address: 75378 Bad Liebenzell. Tel: 07052/40460. FAX: 07052/40475.

3410 Campingplatz Aichelberg, Aichelberg, Goppingen

Small, pleasant and friendly municipal site, near Stuttgart-München autobahn.

Being very near the Stuttgart-München autobahn (about midway between Stuttgart and Ulm) and a reasonable drive from the German border at Aachen, this small, shaded site makes an acceptable overnight stop. The pitches, on flat grass and hardstandings, are not marked out but adequate space is allowed. All have electrical connections. The main toilet block is well constructed and should be sufficient for the 90 static units and 36 tourist pitches. British WCs; free hot water in washbasins and sinks; 1 private cabin and 2 showers with free hot water, for each sex and a family washroom. On site are a small shop and bar, a restaurant is 250 m. away. There is a children's playground (on sand).

How to find it: Take autobahn exit Aichelberg in direction of Goppingen. If coming from München turn immediately left to site, if from Stuttgart follow signs.

General Details: Open all year. Well shaded. Shop for basic supplies (all year), village shops 4 km. Bar. Restaurant 250 m. Washing machine and dryer. Children's playground. Swimming pool 5 km.

Charges guide: Per person DM 7.00; child (4-5 yrs) 3.00, (6-15 yrs) 4.00; pitch 8.00; electricity 3.00 + meter.

Reservations: Write to site (not necessary for overnight). Address: 73101 Aichelberg/Goppingen. Tel: 07164/2700.

3420 Freizeitcenter Oberrhein, Rheinmünster, nr Baden-Baden

Large holiday site near the Rhine with excellent facilities.

This large site provides much to do and is also a good base for the Black Forest. There are now three ultra-modern sanitary buildings of excellent quality with automatic doors, free hot water and very smart fittings with a special area of children's showers. One block serves the touring area to the left of the smart reception, where there is also a section of hardstanding for motorhomes. Another block is to the right serving the remainder of the touring pitches. The total of 250 pitches, all with electrical connections (mostly 16A, 3 pin, with 50 6A, 2 pin), include 80 new ones with water and drainage also, which like those to the right of the entrance, are arranged around one of the lakes, which are a feature of the site. Two of the attractive, fair-sized lakes are for swimming and non-powered boating (the water was very clean when we visited), with the third, smaller one for fishing. With facilities including a restaurant, supermarket, snack bar and a variety of activities available, plus local areas of interest to visit, this site is well worth considering for a holiday in Germany.

How to find it: Site is signed from Rheinmünster, 16 km. southwest of Rastatt on 36 road. From north on autobahn A5/E35-52 take Baden-Baden exit and via Hügelsheim; from south take Bühl exit and via Rheinmünster.

General Details: Open all year. Shop (1/4-30/9), local supermarket 3 km. on weekends). Tennis. Table tennis. Bicycle hire. Minigolf. Windsurf school. Swimming and boating lakes. Fishing. Family washcabins to rent. Chemical disposal. Motorcaravan services. Caravans for hire.

Charges 1998: Per pitch with car DM 8.00 - 12.00; adult 8.00 - 13.00; child (7-15 yrs) 5.00 - 9.00, under 6 yrs 4.00 - 6.00; dog 4.00 - 6.00; washcabin 10.00 - 14.00; electricity 3.50.

Reservations: Made for at least a week with deposit (DM 250) and fee (25). Address: 77836 Rheinmünster. Tel: 07227/2500. FAX: 07227/2400.

3430 Schwarzwald-Camping Alisehof, Schapbach, nr Freudenstadt

Agreeable site in quiet central Black Forest situation.

This site, in a beautiful setting in a wooded valley, is for those who want to enjoy the activities of the Black Forest itself. Though very centrally situated in the Forest it is in a quiet position away from the main routes and big towns, with walks available from the camp. Pitches are individual numbered ones of average size in rows on terraces on a slope, steep only at the top part; there are usually 130 on the lower slopes available for tourists. The three sanitary blocks, two on the lower terrace, one beside reception, are first class with free hot water in most washbasins, sinks and showers. There are facilities for the disabled and baby rooms. In high season there is an entertainment programme for children and organised walks for adults. The friendly management speak English.

How to find it: Site is 1 km. northeast of Schapbach, which is southwest from Freudenstadt. From the A5 take the Appelweier/Oberkirch exit towards Freudenstadt turning right to Schapbach.

General Details: Open all year. Electrical connections all parts. Self-service shop (all year). Pleasant bar lounge in old farmhouse on site, open late evening (all year except when very quiet). Restaurant near. Washing machine and dryers. Children's playground. Swimming pool at Schapbach (1 km). Minigolf close. Fishing. Motorcaravan services.

Charges guide: Per person DM 7.50 - 8.50; local tax 1.30; child (under 14) 4.00 - 5.50; pitch 8.00 - 9.00; tent 2.50 - 4.50; dog 3.00; TV connection 1.00; electricity 3.00 plus meter. Less 10% on person charge for stays over 7 days.

Reservations: Write to site before 31 May, with deposit (DM 10) and fee (10) by Eurocheque. Address: 77776 Bad Rippoldsau-Schapbach. Tel: 07839/203. FAX: 07839/1263.

GERMANY - South West

3415 Campingplatz Adam, Oberbruch, Bühl, nr Baden-Baden

Very good lakeside site by Karlsruhe-Basle autobahn near Baden-Baden.

This site is very conveniently situated, only about 1 km. from the Bühl exit on the Karlsruhe-Basle autobahn. For longer stays there is a lake which can be used for bathing or boating, with a long slide installed - the public are admitted to this on payment and it attracts many on fine weekends. You can usually find space here, but the long-term pitches, which are larger and more attractive, might be harder to come by. Pitches for caravans are individual ones, with some special ones near the lake with water and drainage. Tents go along the lake surrounds and there are some places with hard paved centres to eliminate wet weather problems. Overnight caravans may be put on close together hardstandings. The three modern toilet blocks are well maintained and clean. Also serving a permanent caravan section, they include a block with private washing cabins and facilities for babies and disabled people. The provision should be quite adequate with British WCs, individual basins with shelf and mirror and hot showers on payment. The shop and restaurant/bar remain open virtually all year (not Mon. or Tues. in low season), so this is a useful site to use for out of season tours. The site in general has a well tended look and good English is spoken by the pleasant staff.

How to find it: Take Bühl autobahn exit, turn towards Lichtenau, go through Oberbruch and left to site.

General Details: Open all year. 40,000 sq.m. Limited shade. Many electrical connections. Shop. Restaurant. Football. Volleyball. Tennis. Minigolf. Bowling alley and games room with terrace. Children's playground. Fishing. Washing machine and dryer.

Charges 1998: Per person DM 7.50 - 11.00; young person 10 - 16 yrs 5.50 - 6.50, child 3-10 yrs 4.00 - 5.00; pitch 8.00 - 11.00, with services 12.00 - 15.00; electricity 3.00; dog 3.00.

Reservations: Write to site. Address: 77815 Bühl-Oberbruch. Tel: 07223/23194. FAX: 07223/8982.

3435 Terrassen-Camping Sandbank, Titisee

Pleasant, terraced lakeside site, in the Black Forest.

This is a satisfactory site overlooking Lake Titisee in this lovely area of the Black Forest. There are 200 marked pitches for tourists, on gravel with electricity (16A) and on terraces with good views over the lake. Trees provide good shade in some parts. The small town of Titisee is a pleasant 20 minute walk along the lakeside and with the attractions of this part of the Forest near - Freiburg, the Rhine Falls at Schaffausen, the source of the Danube at Donaueschingen, Basle in Switzerland - it is ideal for a long or short stay. The large sanitary block provides free hot water for the washbasins (many in private cabins) and hot showers on payment. There is a shop and a pleasant lakeside restaurant with terrace, which also provides takeaway food. Access to the lake is available for swimming, boating and carp fishing. Walks are organised and there is some music in high season. Reception is friendly and English is spoken.

How to find it: From Freiburg take road no. 31 to Titisee. From the centre follow camping signs then signs for Bankenhof, continuing on less well made up road past this site to Sandbank.

General Details: Open 1 April - 20 Oct. Shop. Bar/restaurant with takeaway. Children's playground. Fishing. Organised walks. Music in season. Infant room (key from management). Facilities for disabled people. Washing machines and dryer. Chemical disposal. Motorcaravan services. Swimming in lake. Boat excursions from Titisee.

Charges 1997: Per person: DM 6.00 - 8.00; child 4.00 - 5.00; pitch 9.50 - 12.00; electricity 2.50; dog 3.00 (2.00); local tax 1.80. Stay 14 days, pay for 10 outside July/Aug. Credit cards accepted.

Reservations: Not made. Address: 79822 Titisee (Hochschwarzwald). Tel: 07651/8243 or 8166. FAX: 07651/8286 or 88444.

3450 Ferien-Campingplatz Münstertal, Münstertal, nr Freiburg

The editorial report for this site appears on page 128 opposite its colour advertisement.

3440 Campingplatz Kirchzarten, Kirchzarten, nr Freiburg

Well equipped Black Forest site with excellent free swimming pools.

This municipal site is on the edge of the Black Forest, within easy reach by car of Titisee, Feldberg and Todnau, and 8 km. from the large town of Freiburg in Breisgau, and may be best suited for families. It is divided into about 460 numbered pitches with electricity (16A), the majority of which are available for tourists in high season. They have made the most of the ground available but most pitches, which are side by side on flat ground, are now of quite reasonable size and marked out at the corners, though there is nothing to separate them. From late June to mid-August it does become full, and it would be advisable to reserve. A fine new swimming pool complex adjoining the site is free to campers and is a main attraction (open 1/6-15/8). The four pools include one of Olympic size which is heated. It is surrounded by spacious grassy lying-out area. The site's sanitary facilities are good, comprising four blocks, one for laundry and dishwashing only. Two blocks are modern with heating. They include British toilets, individual washbasins, free, controllable hot showers, facilities for disabled people and a baby bath. It is only a short stroll from the site to the village centre, which has supermarkets, restaurants, banks, etc.

How to find it: From Freiburg take B31 road signed Donaueschingen to Kirchzarten where site is signed (it is to the south of the village).

General Details: Open all year. 56,000 sq.m. Restaurant/bar. Shop (1/5-30/9). Cooking stoves, washing machines, dryers, irons, sewing machines (all on payment by meter). winming pools adjacent. Large children's playground. Table tennis. Adventure playground, fitness track, tennis and minigolf near (an adjacent covered tennis court can be booked from site); 18-hole course 3 km. Organised recreation in high season. No dogs accepted. Caravans for hire.

Charges 1997: Per person DM 7.50 - 12.50, incl. local tax, acc. to season; child (4-16 yrs) 5.50 - 7.00, third child and above 3.50 - 4.50; pitch 9.00 - 11.00; electricity 2.00 plus meter. Every 15th day free.

Reservations: made for min. 1 week (no deposit). Address: Campingplatz, 79199 Kirchzarten. Tel: 07661/39375.

CAMPING KIRCHZARTEN

A site in the southern Black Forest with every comfort for wonderful holidays. New heated outdoor swimming pool complex.Kurhaus with restaurant and reading room nearby. Riding, tennis, minigolf, children's playground in the wood. Fine walking country. Caravans for hire.

3442 Terrassen Campingplatz, Herbolzheim

Excellent small site on edge of Black Forest.

This first class campsite occupies a quiet location on a heavily wooded slope to the north of Freiburg. It would make a good base from which to explore the Black Forest or as a night stop when travelling between·Frankfurt and Basel, being only a short way from the busy A5 autobahn. There are 70 caravan or motorcaravan pitches available for tourists, all with 10A electricity and with grass surfaces on terraces, plus a separate meadow for tents. The terraces are linked by hard access roads and the many trees, shrubs and plants give the site a pleasant, peaceful atmosphere. The main toilet block is centrally placed near reception with British style toilets and free hot water in washbasins, showers and sinks. There are two cabin toilets near the tent area. Separate provision for clothes and dish washing is under cover and there is a laundry room with drying lines. The pleasant, small bar/restaurant offers a simple menu during the evenings and there is a kiosk for basic food supplies with restaurants and shops in the village about 3 km. Small children's play area and table tennis, volleyball and football with the village swimming pool next door and a Sport Hotel near. The local market is held each Friday morning. Being on the edge of the Black Forest, this is good walking country and Freiburg and Basel are not far away. The Alsace and Vosges areas of France are near on the other side of the Rhine. With only occasional entertainment, the site makes a very pleasant place in which to relax between daily activities.

How to find it: From north on A5 Frankfurt - Basel autobahn take Ettenheim exit, go east to join B3 and south on this to Herbolzheim. From south, use Riegal exit, east to B3 and north to Herbolzheim. Site is signed in village.

General Details: Open 1 week before Easter - 15 October. 6,000 sq. Small bar/restaurant. Table tennis. Volleyball. Football. Washing machines. Swimming pool adjacent. Motorcaravan service point (small). No dogs July/Aug.

Charges guide: Per person DM 9.00; child (2-12 yrs) 5.00; pitch 8.00; electricity 2.00 + 1.00 p/kWh.

Reservations: Write to site. Address: 79336 Herbolzheim. Tel: 07643-1460. FAX: as phone.

3445 Campingplatz Belchenblick, Staufen, nr Freiburg

Quality Black Forest site with good class facilities.

The site stands at the gateway, so to speak, to the Black Forest. Not very high up itself, it is just at the start of the long road climb which leads to the top of Belchen, one of the highest summits of the forest. It is well situated for excursions by car to the best areas of the forest, e.g. the Feldberg-Titisee-Höllental circuit, and many excellent walks are available nearby. Staufen is a pleasant little place with character. The three high quality sanitary blocks have free hot water in all washbasins and the fully controllable hot showers. With British toilets; individual washbasins with shelf and mirror (6 in private cabins), there are 21 family cabins with WC, basin and shower (some on payment per night for exclusive use). Of the 200 pitches, 50 have TV, water and waste water connections. On site is a small heated indoor swimming pool open all year and adjacent is a municipal sports complex building including an open-air pool and tennis courts. Reservation is necessary from early June to late August at this popular site, which is not a cheap one, but the charges include free hot water and the indoor pool.

How to find it: Take autobahn exit for Bad Krozingen, south of Freiburg, and continue to Staufen. Site is south of the town and signed.

General Details: Open all year. 18,000 sq.m. Numerous electrical connections. Shop and general room where drinks and snacks served (both all year). Restaurant near. Indoor and outdoor pools. Tennis. Children's playground with barbecue section. Volleyball. Basketball. Skating. Hockey and football fields. Sauna and solarium. Bicycle hire. Washing machine. Chemical disposal. Motorcaravan services. Apartments for rent.

Charges 1998: Per person DM 8.50 - 13.50; child (2-12 yrs) 5.50; pitch 11.50; dog 3.00; electricity 1.00 p/kwh; TV connection 1.50; drainage 2.00; washcabin 12.00.

Reservations: are made without charge. Address: Münstertäler Str. 43, 79219 Staufen im Breisgau. Tel: 07633/7045. FAX: 07633/7908. E-mail: camping.belchenblick@t-online.de. Internet: http://members.aol.com/campbelche/camp-bel.htm.

3452 Terrassen Camping Alte Sägemühle, Sulzburg

Pretty site beautifully situated in the southern Black Forest.

By a peaceful road leading only to the swimming pool (5 minutes on foot), beyond the picturesque small town of Sulzburg, this attractive location is perfect for those seeking peace and quiet. There are opportunities for walking immediately by the site into the forest. It is divided into terraced areas with another on the other side of the road by the building housing reception, the small shop and the sanitary facilities. These are new and of very good quality, with showers and washbasins (2 private cabins), dishwashing and a washing machine. All 50 pitches have electrical connections (long leads may be needed). The site is operated by the Geuss family - Frau Geuss speaks reasonable English - and they will help with a tractor to site on the higher level. The site has won an award for having been kept natural, for example, no tarmac roads, no minigolf, etc. Prior reservation is recommended.

How to find it: Site is easily reached (25 minutes) from the autobahn A5/E35. Take Bad Krozingen exit just south of Freiburg and take the no. 3 road south to Heitersheim, from where it is clearly signed.

General Details: Open all year. Small shop (all year). Swimming pool adjacent (June-Aug). Washing machine. Chemical disposal. Motorcaravan services.

Charges 1998: Per person DM 8.00; child (1-15 yrs) 6.00; pitch 8.00 - 12.00; electricity 0.80 plus meter; dog 3.00; local tax (from 16 yrs) 1.00.

Reservations: Recommended - contact site. Address: 79295 Sulzburg. Tel: 07634/8550.

At Neuenburg in the Rhine Valley
We offer you a warm welcome and a friendly atmosphere

In the driest and warmest region of Germany. Large, wooded, 1st category site with heated indoor swimming pool, 2 tennis courts, minigolf, bicycle hire. Attractive restaurant, well-stocked kiosk for provisions. Many organised activities for children and adults in main season.

Reservations and brochures from us at:
Gugel's Campingplatz
79395 Neuenburg (Südbaden), West Germany
Telephone: 07631/7719
Fax: 07635/3393

3455 Gugel's Campingplatz, Neuenburg, nr Freiburg and Basle

Large site in natural woodland close to the Freiburg-Basle autobahn.

This site has an attractive setting in natural heath and woodland, with pitches for tents and caravans in numerous clearings. The tourist areas adjacent to woodland have been increased. There are also well spaced individual plots for the permanent caravans (nearly 50%) and longer stay tourists. The terrain is extensive and you should always find room, even if only in the more tightly packed overnight area; it is most full in July. There are three sanitary blocks, one new, the others recently renovated and extended, all of excellent quality. They have British WCs, hot water in all washbasins with some cabins and fully controllable hot showers, with facilities for the disabled and baby rooms in at least one block. Dishwashing and laundry rooms. The facilities and the site itself are well cleaned and have a cared for appearance. In general there seems a good atmosphere on site. Amenities include two small heated and enclosed pools which can be used in all weathers and tennis courts with racquets and balls for hire. A new common room has been added with satellite TV where guests are welcomed with a glass of wine and a slide presentation. Opposite the site is a small lake where one can fish (daily permit) or bathe. The Rhine is within walking distance.

How to find it: From autobahn take Neuenburg exit, turn left at traffic lights, left at next junction (50 m.) and follow signs for 2 km. to site (site is called 'Neuenburg' on most signs).

General Details: Open all year, as is restaurant. 130,000 sq.m. Well shaded. Electrical connections in all parts. Small shop (limited hours April-mid Oct). Popular restaurant/bar. Swimming pools (Easter-end Oct). Tennis courts with courses and racquet/ball hire. Fishing. Minigolf. Table tennis. Bicycle hire. Children's playground. Electric motorcycles for children. Common room with TV. Activity programme: children's sports competitions, organised walks and sightseeing, wine tasting etc, at Easter and July/Aug. 18 hole golf course 5 km. Large pool 2½ km. Washing machine, spin dryer. Chemical disposal. Motorcaravan services.

Charges 1998: Per person DM 8.50; child (2-15) 5.50; caravan/tent 8.50; small tent 5.50; car 6.50; motorcaravan 8.50 - 13.50; electricity on meter. Discount: every 10th night, persons free of charge.

Reservations: made for min. 2 weeks in July/Aug. with deposit; write specifying tent or caravan. Address: 79395 Neuenburg. Tel: 07631/7719. FAX: 07635/3393.

AR Discount
Welcome drink and slide show

Terrassen Camping
Alte Sägemühle
D-79225 Sulzburg / Südl. Schwarzwald
Axel Geuß, Telefon 07634 / 85 50

Ideal for Walking, Cycling and Excursions

25,000 m², 360-380 m. above sea level
12 Terraces, 50 pitches 80-120 m²
Idyllic forest setting by a stream in the very romantic Sulz valley. **Extremely peaceful**

An oasis for genuine campers

Special award form Baden-Württemberg for a fine example of blending with the countryside and outstanding suitability for camping amid nature.

3650 Camping Gitzenweiler Hof, Lindau, nr Friedrichshafen

The editorial report for this site appears on page 128 opposite its colour advertisement.

3465 Camping Wirthshof, Markdorf, nr Friedrichshafen

Site with various sport and recreation facilities near the Bodensee.

Lying 7 km. back from the Bodensee, 12 km. from Friedrichshafen and with Markdorf near at hand to stroll into, this site could well be of interest to Britons with young children. Possible excursions include trips into Switzerland and Austria. The 300 individual touring pitches have electrical connections and are of about 80 sq.m. on well tended flat grass, joining access roads. On site is a pleasant heated swimming pool (25 x 12½ m.) with a grassy lying-out area; it is free to campers but is also open to outsiders on payment so can be busy in season (open perhaps mid-May to mid-Sept). Three well furnished toilet blocks give an ample total provision. Washbasins and showers have free hot water and there is a unit for disabled people. Many activities are organised for children over a long season.

How to find it: Site is on the eastern edge of Markdorf, on the B33 Ravensburg road.

General Details: Open 15 March - 30 Oct. Shade in parts. Shop. Restaurant/bar. Swimming pool (10/5-10/9). Sports field. Adventure playground. Bicycle hire. Minigolf. Tennis near. Washing machines and dryers. Chemical disposal. Motorcaravan services. New caravans for hire. No dogs in July/Aug.

Charges 1998: Per person DM 7.00 - 9.00; child 1-7 yrs 3.00 - 5.00, 7-14 yrs 5.00 - 6.00; pitch 13.00 - 15.00; dog 3.00; electricity 3.00.

Reservations: made with deposit (DM 80) and fee (20). Address: 88677 Markdorf. Tel: 07544/2325. FAX: 07544/3982.

3665 Ferien-Campingplatz Brunnen, Brunnen, Füssen, nr Kempten

Quietly situated lakeside site well placed for excursions.

Right by the Forggen-See, this site has a beach and jetty, although the water level of the lake can be low in early season and not reach up to the site. On slightly undulating ground, the 200 pitches are all individual ones, nearly all with hardstanding, and with some terracing; they vary in size (60-100 sq.m.). There is a separate meadow for tents in summer. Quietly situated, with views of high mountains around, the site is excellently placed for excursions: the Füssen and the famous castles of Neuschwanstein and Hohenschwangau are very close. The satisfactory sanitary facilities are housed in a tiled building with heating; there are several washrooms and toilet rooms (only selected ones opened in low seasons). Hot water is free to the showers and to washbasins, half of which are in cabins. Unit for disabled people.

How to find it: At Schwangau, 3 km. northeast of Füssen on the no. 17 Munich road, turn off at crossroads in village where there are signs to Brunnen and site.

General Details: Open all year except 15 Nov - 15 Dec. 20,000 sq.m. Small shop. Restaurants within 100 m. Children's playground. Washing machines and dryers. Drying room. Cooking facilities. Motorcaravan services.

Charges guide: Per person DM 10.00 - 10.50, incl. local tax; child (2-8) 5.00, (9-15) 8.00; pitch 8.00 - 10.00; electricity (overnight) 2.00; dog or extra car 4.00. Less 10% for stays of over 7 days outside 15/6-31/8 and Xmas.

Reservations: are made for winter only, not summer, so arrive early especially when the weather is good. Address: Seestrasse 81, 87645 Schwangau-Brunnen. Tel: 08362/8273.

3670 Internationaler Campingplatz Hopfensee, Füssen, nr Kempten

Luxury lakeside site, north of Füssen, for caravans and motorcaravans only.

This site has direct access to a lake for sailing of all sorts, canoeing etc., with a place for parking boats. Bathing is possible although the water may be cool. In winter it also caters for winter sports with a ski lift near and `cross-country' tracks. Heated indoor pool (12½ x 7½ m. - free to campers) and complex including sauna, solarium, steam bath and changing rooms, etc. on payment. There is a restaurant and bar. The 382 pitches for tourists are numbered and marked in some way to give 80-100 sq.m. No tents are taken. All have electricity (16A), TV (cable), water and drainage and are on flat or slightly sloping ground with hardstanding for awnings. Although charges are high, the site is full over a long season. The first class toilet block with under-floor heating (quite a step from some pitches) is doubtless one reason. It has British WCs, washbasins with free hot water (some in cabins), good, controllable, free hot showers, facilities for children and disabled people. Large washing-up room and baby room.

How to find it: Site is 4 km. north of Füssen. Turn off no. 16 road to Hopfen to site on the left through a car park. From west on B310, turn towards Füssen at T-junction with B16 and immediately right again for road to Hopfen.

General Details: Open all year except early Nov - 20 Dec. Self-service shop. Restaurant. Bar. Children's playground. Bicycle hire. Tennis. Fishing. Indoor pool and leisure centre. Supervised courses of medicinal baths, massage, etc. Sauna, solarium, steam bath. Ski school in winter. Chemical disposal. Motorcaravan services.

Charges 1998: Per person DM 13.00 - 14.50; child 2-12 yrs 7.50 - 8.80, 12-18 yrs 10.00 - 13.00; local tax (over 18) 2.40 - 3.00; pitch with cable TV and electricity 19.00 - 21.00; plus electricity on meter; dog 5.00 - 5.50; private washcabin 15.00. Eurocheques accepted (no credit cards).

Reservations: made without deposit; min. 14 days between 15/6-1/9 (unless shorter times fits into charts). Address: 87629 Füssen - Hopfen am See. Tel: 08362/917710. FAX: 08362/917720.

3660 Kur-Campingplatz, Bad Wörishofen

Site with treatment centre in southwest Bavaria near the München-Bodensee route 96.

Bad Wörishofen became famous as a hydrotherapy centre when its priest, Father Sebastien Knieppe, perfected his treatment here. The Kur-Campingplatz, situated on the edge of town in a quiet position, has its own treatment centre with fully qualified staff. The 80 pitches, neither marked nor numbered, are on either side of hard access rows with trees separating the rows and providing good shade. Electrical hook-ups are available with long leads needed in some places. Although the camp is primarily for those wishing to take Knieppe treatments, it makes a good night stop or to explore the region. The first class sanitary arrangements are housed on the ground floor of the treatment centre with British WCs and free hot water in basins (some in private cabins), showers and sinks. This is a neat, quiet site.

How to find it: Site is on the north side of Bad Wörishofen, off the Kirchdorf-Bad Wörishofen road from where it is signed.

General Details: Open 15 April - 15 Oct. 11,000 sq.m. Restaurants and shops near. Washing machines and dryers.

Charges guide: Per pitch (caravan or motorcaravan) DM 7.00; tent 3.50; m/cycle 2.00; adult 7.00; child (under 14 yrs) 3.50; dog 1.50; electricity 1.00.

Reservations: Write to site. Address: 86825 Bad Wörishofen, Gottlieb-Daimler Str. 5. Tel: 08247/5446. FAX: 08247/32486.

3630 Donau-Lech Camping, Eggelstetten, Donauwörth, nr Augsburg

Pleasant, friendly site just off the 'Romantische Strasse'.

The Haas family purchased Donau-Lech in '95 and run it very much as a family site, the lake providing swimming and wildlife for children and adults to enjoy. Alongside the lake are 85 marked touring pitches on flat grass arranged in rows either side of a tarred access road. With an average of 120 sq.m. per unit, plus electrical (16A), water, waste water and TV connections, it is a comfortable site with an open feeling and developing shade. There are three separate areas for people with tents (youngsters, cyclists and with cars or motorcycles) with unmarked pitches. All facilities are housed in the main building at the entrance with reception and a large bar area (self-service machines for beer, soft drinks and microwave meals). Downstairs are the sanitary facilities with 8 controllable showers on payment, toilets, washbasins with warm water and a dishwashing and laundry room, all of a satisfactory standard. Basic food supplies are kept. Suitable not only as a night stop on the way south, it is also not far from Munich and the local area is very attractive; you may borrow bicycles from the proprietor.

How to find it: Turn off the main B2 road about 5 km. south of Donauwörth at signs for Asbach-Bäumenheim Nord towards Eggelstetten, then follow camp signs for over 1 km. to site.

General Details: Open all year. Lake for bathing on site; larger sailboarding lake 400 m. Shop on site keeps basics only (April-Oct); shops, restaurants and other amenities a short drive. General room. Youth room. Self service bar. Table tennis. Washing machine and dryer. Perhaps free rides in proprietor's Sinclair cars! Information sheet in English. Motorcaravan service point.

Charges guide: Per person DM 7.30 - 8.00; child (4-12) 4.70; caravan 10.00; tent 8.00; car 2.50; motorcaravan 12.50; electricity 4.00 or on meter; dog 3.50.

Reservations: not needed. Address: 86698 Eggelstetten. Tel: 09002/4044. FAX: 09002/4046.

3640 Campingplatz München-Thalkirchen, München

Reliable municipal site in river conservation area on the city outskirts.

This well run municipal site is quietly situated on the southern side of Munich in parkland formed by the River Isar conservation area, 4 km. from the city centre (there are subway and bus links). Pleasant walks may be taken in the park and the world famous Munich zoo is just 15 minutes walk along the river from the site. The large city of Munich has much to offer and the Thalkirchen site becomes very crowded during the season, when one may have much less space than one would like, particularly if only staying for one night. However, it is well equipped and clean, with a total of 570 pitches (220 for caravans or motorcaravans) of a variety of sizes, marked by posts and rails. Like many city sites, groups are taken in one area. There are five toilet blocks, two of which can be heated, with washbasins with cold water, hot water for showers and sinks on payment. They are hard pressed when the site is full. In low season not all are open and there may be long walks. Facilities for disabled people.

How to find it: From motorways follow 'Mittel' ring road to SSE of the city centre where site is signed; also follow signs for Thalkirchen or the Zoo and site is close.

General Details: Open mid-March - end October. 40,000 sq.m. Electrical connections for caravans. Shop (open 7 am - 8.30 pm). Snack bar with covered terrace (open 7 am - 11 pm). Restaurant 200 m. Treatment room. Washing machines and dryers. Children's playground. Tourist information. Some pitches for American motorhomes.

Charges guide: Per person DM 7.80; child (2-14) 2.50; tent (acc. to size) 5.50 - 7.00; car 8.50; m/cycle 4.00; caravan incl. car 19.00; motorcaravan (acc. to size) 11.00 - 13.00; electricity 3.50. Prices include VAT.

Reservations: not made except for groups - said to be room up to 4 pm. daily. Address: Zentralländstr. 49, 81379 München. Tel: 089/7231707. FAX: 089/7243177.

145

3635 Camping München-Obermenzing, München

Useful site for visits to city or night stops.

This site, on the northwest edge of Munich, makes a good stopover for those wishing to see the city or pass the night. The flat terrain is mostly covered by mature trees. Caravan owners are best off here as they have a special section with individual plots, usually separated from each other and opening off the access roads which are now tarred. For tents and motorcaravans there are quite large, level grass areas. There is an overflow section so space is usually available. The single central sanitary block is large and has been extended. so it should now be adequate in size and cleaning appears satisfactory. It provides British toilets, individual washbasins with shelf and mirror, some in cubicles, and most with free hot water, hot showers on payment (DM 2) and with heating for low season. There is a shop and bar in the main season. Public transport services are available to the city. By car the journey might take 20-30 minutes depending on the density of traffic. Possibly some road noise.

How to find it: Site is very close to the start of the autobahn to Stuttgart and is signed from there. From anywhere around the city follow signs for 'autobahn Stuttgart', but be sure to turn right at the final main junction just before the autobahn begins and keep left to site.

General Details: Open 15 March - 31 Oct. 50,000 sq.m. Mostly shaded. Electrical connections. Shop (all season). 'Tavern' serving drinks and snacks (May - Oct). Cooking facilities on payment. Washing machine and dryers. Chemical disposal. Motorcaravan services.

Charges 1997: Per person DM 7.00; child (2-14 yrs) 4.00; car 5.00; tent 7.50; caravan 8.00; motorcaravan 12.00; m/cycle 4.00; electricity 2.00 plus meter.

Reservations: Not made and said not to be necessary. Address: Lochhausener Str. 59, 81247 München. Tel: 089/811 22 35. FAX: 089/814 48.07.

Camping MÜNCHEN Obermenzing

On your way through Munich follow always the direction sign `Autobahn Stuttgart' until the beginning of the Autobahn **except** when approaching from the Salzburg autobahn. In this case follow `Autobahn Lindau' signs to Gräfelfing; then take Pasing exit and follow `Autobahn Stuttgart'.

A modern camping site located at the beginning of the Autobahn Munich-Stuttgart in a 57,000 sq.m. park.

Open from 15 March to 31 October.

Resident Proprietor: Andreas Blenck
Lochhausener Str. 59, 81247 München
Tel: 0049 89-811 22 35
Fax: 0049 89-814 48 07

* Special plots for caravans.
* Electric supply for light and heating.
* First class sanitary accommodations.
* Hot showers, single cabins with basins.
* Washing machines.
* Dishwashing and cooking house.
* Self-service store for food and beverages.
* Tavern (Hofbräuhaus beer).
* Ca. 20 min. to the city by car.
* Good connections by bus, tram or S-train.

3675 Terrassen-Camping am Richterbichl, Rottenbuch, nr Peiting

Useful overnight site by the main Garmisch-Augsburg road.

This little site, beside the main B23 Garmisch-Augsburg road, has all the features required of a good transit site and might well be interesting for longer stays. About 110 pitches - 40 for permanents and 70 for tourists - are on flat terraces in rows on either side of access roads. They are not marked out but about 80 sq.m. is allowed per unit. Electrical connections in all parts. There could possibly be some road noise at front of site, so choose pitches in higher terraces if possible.

continued on next page

3675 Terrassen-Camping am Richterbichl (continued)

The toilet block, within the main building and kept warm, is satisfactory with free hot water in the washbasins (4 in cabins) and sinks, and on payment in the showers. A little lake on site can be used for bathing or boating with inflatables. The pleasant bar has a TV and a large children's room alongside.

How to find it: Site is beside the B23 road on south side of Rottenbuch (12 km. south of Schongau).

General Details: Open all year. Only basic provisions kept, bread to order (shops 5 mins). Large general room where drinks and breakfast served. Games room with table tennis. Washing machine and dryer. Children's playground. Caravans and apartments for hire.

Charges 1997: Per person DM 8.50; local tax 1.00; child (3-14) 5.00; pitch 7.50; dog 2.00; electricity 2.00 + meter.

Reservations: made for any period without deposit. Address: 82401 Rottenbuch. Tel: 08867/1500. FAX: 08867/8300.

3690 Campingplatz Wagnerhof, Bergen, nr Rosenheim

Small but excellent site close to München - Salzburg autobahn near Chiemsee.

Ringed by hills, with views of distant mountains and a multitude of different trees, Wagnerhof is a well organised, pleasant site in a quiet location on the edge of the village of Bergen. Owned by two brothers, only one of whom speaks good English, there is always a welcome here. With 40 permanent caravans there are also 120 pitches for tourists, part hardstanding, part grass. The new toilet block of excellent quality, has British WCs, free hot water in washbasins (some in cabins) with showers on payment. There is also a small block at reception. The site makes a good night stop for those travelling between Munich and Salzburg by autobahn, but also a peaceful base from which to explore the Chiemsee, Salzburg, mountains and other interesting places nearby. There is no restaurant but these can be found a short distance away in the village.

How to find it: Site is 2½ km. from autobahn; take Bergen exit. Follow road to Bergen where site, in northern part of the town, is signed.

General Details: Open all year. 28,000 sq.m. Electrical connections for all pitches. Self-service shop. General room where drinks served. Tennis. Children's playground. Washing machine and dryer. Cooking facilities. Motorcaravan service point.

Charges 1997: Per person DM 6.50 - 9.00 + 1.20 local tax; child (under 14) 4.00 - 5.00 + 0.60 tax; pitch 9.00 - 12.00; extra car or tent 4.50 - 6.00; electricity 4.00 + meter; dog 3.00.

Reservations: Made with deposit. Address: Campingstrasse 11, 83346 Bergen. Tel: 08662/8557. FAX: 08662/5924.

3685 Camping Allweglehen, Berchtesgaden, nr Salzburg

Hilltop site with spectacular views.

Berchtesgaden is one of the best known districts of Germany and rightly so, as it has magnificent scenery and so much to do, see and explore. It is a land of mountains, lakes, valleys, castles and churches. The spa town of Berchtesgaden began life as a salt mining town and indeed the salt mine is still in operation and well worth visiting where, dressed in miners protective clothing you travel on the `Hunte' 500 m. into the mountain. Hitler built his `Eagles Nest' on top of the Kehlstein (clearly visible from the site) and this is also open to the public (no vehicle access, apart from by bus). Camping Allweglehen occupies a splendid hill top position, some 500 m. above sea level with spectacular views across the pretty Ache valley to the town beyond and the distant sheer rock faces of the Watzmann mountain. The camp access road is steep (14%), particularly at the entrance, but the proprietor will use his tractor to tow caravans for those of a nervous disposition! The 120 pitches, all for touring, are arranged on a series of gravel terraces, separated by hedges or fir trees and all have good views and electrical connections (16A). There is a separate area, on a sloping meadow, for tents. The delightful restaurant, with terrace, offers an excellent menu, including Bavarian specialities, at reasonable prices. There is a swimming pool (16 x 8 m.), heated from May-Oct, a children's play area, minigolf and table tennis. The sanitary facilities are in two adjacent blocks near the restaurant, with British WCs, and free hot water to washbasins, showers and sinks. All in all, a splendid camp where one could just sit and look at the views all day, although this would be a shame as the region has so much to offer.

How to find it: Site is 4 km. from the town on B305 Berchtesgaden - Salzburg road. From autobahn take Salzburg Sud exit and follow the B305 towards Berchtesgaden. It can also be reached on the 305 road from west of Salzburg, signed in Zell and Ruhpolding (the very attractive Alpenstrasse - but this is winding and with 3.1 m. height limit).

General Details: Open all year. Restaurant. Kiosk for essentials. Children's play area. Small heated pool. Solarium. Winter sports. Minigolf. Table tennis. Walks. Excursions. Washing machines, dryers and iron.

Charges guide: Per pitch DM 11.50; adult 7.50; child (4-16 yrs) 6.20; electricity 0.80 per kw. Eurocard accepted.

Reservations: Write to site (in German!). Address: 84171 Berchtesgaden. Tel: 08652/2396. FAX: 08652/63503.

GERMANY - South East

3680 Alpen-Caravanpark Tennsee, Krün, Garmisch-Partenkirchen

Attractive all year site for the active holiday, with excellent facilities.

This is an excellent site in beautiful surroundings, high up (3,000 m.) in the Bavarian Alps with views of the Zugspitze, etc. yet close to many famous places. Oberammergau (26 km) and Innsbruck (44 km) are two of many. Mountain walks are plentiful, with several lifts close by. The site has 139 serviced pitches with individual connections for electricity (up to 16A), gas, TV, radio, telephone, water and waste water disposal. The other 111 pitches all have electricity and some of these are available for overnight guests at a reduced rate. The first class sanitary block has under-floor heating, British style WCs, individual washbasins and hair dryers. There are also many private units with WC, shower, basin and bidet (for rent). Constant hot water (included) is available and a solarium. The unit for disabled people provides the latest in flushing and warm air drying arrangements. There is a baby bath and also a dog bathroom! Well equipped, heated room for ski equipment. Another custom built block houses reception, restaurants (waiter, self service and takeaway), bar, cellar youth room and some well equipped apartments for rent. There is also a well stocked shop. The Zick family run the site in a friendly and efficient manner; they close for a month to mid-December. The site has received high accolades from tourist organisations.

How to find it: Site is just off the main Garmisch-Partenkirchen/Innsbruck road between Kleis and Krün, 15 km. from Garmisch.

General Details: Open all year except 15 Nov - 13 Dec. 30,000 sq.m. Shop. Restaurants with takeaway. Bar. Youth room with table tennis. amusements. Solarium. Bicycle hire. Children's playground. Cash dispenser for Euro cards. Dog bathroom. Cooking facilities. Ski room. Washing machines and dryers. Chemical disposal. Motorcaravan services. Apartments to rent. Many special excursions to local attractions. English spoken

Charges 1998: Prices acc. to season (several price bands, winter charges highest): per person DM 12.00 - 13.00; 1-3 children (3-15 yrs) 6.50 - 7.50; local tax 1.75; pitch 14.50 - 24.00; summer tent pitches in adjacent meadow 10.50; dog 5.50; electricity, etc. on meter. Overnight rate on certain pitches 29.50 plus 10.00 for motorcaravan services. Easter family package 38.50.

Special senior citizens spring, early summer and autumn rate incl. 2 persons 32.50 - 37.50.

Reservations: are made for exact dates: booking fee (DM 30 and deposit (20). Address: 82493 Klais/Krün (Bayern). Tel: 08825/17-0. FAX: 08825/17-236. E-mail: camping.tennsee@t-online.de. Internet: http://www. camping-tennsee.de.

3695 Dreiflusse Campingplatz, Irring bei Passau, Donautal

Good camp overlooking the Danube near Passau.

Although the name of this site suggests an association with the three important rivers here, it is in fact some 9 km. from the confluence of the Danube, Inn and Ilz. Dreiflusse Camping occupies a hillside position to the west of Passau with pitches on several rows of level terraces. The 180 places are not numbered or marked out but electricity boxes determine where units pitch. Trees and low banks separate the terraces which are of gravel with a thin covering of grass. The excellent Gasthof restaurant is part of the reception, shop and sanitary buildings at the entrance. The good sanitary section has British type toilets. There is a small children's pool (high season) and play area. The energetic and very jolly owner is most popular with his regular visitors and he gives the camp a very friendly air. It is a useful en-route stop or for a longer stay to explore the delights of Passau and the southern part of the Bavarian forest. Bus service for Passau from outside site (a little erratic and finishes at 6 pm).

How to find it: From autobahn A3, leave at exit Passau-Nord. Follow signs from Passau on road to west of city and north bank of Danube.

General Details: Open 1 April - 31 Oct. 40,000 sq.m. Restaurant (high season). Shop. Some shade. Electric points. Children's pool and play area. Leisure centre in central Passau with swimming pool, large children's playground. Table tennis. Zoo, breweries, walks and other attractions near.

Charges 1997: Per person DM 7.50; child (4-12 yrs) 5.00; pitch 8.50 - 17.00; electricity 4.80 + kw. charge.

Reservations: Write to site. Address: 94113 Irring 23, Passau/Donautal. Tel: 08546/633. FAX: 08546/2686.

3700 AZUR Ferienzentrum Bayerwald, Gottsdorf, nr Passau

Well run, quiet site with good sports facilities, in southeast Germany.

Attractively situated on high ground above, but not overlooking, the Danube (on which there is a regular boat service), this site has only 160 pitches, of which 40 are for permanent caravans. All are numbered, with electrical connections (11-16A), and stand mostly in rows of 5 or 6 with a high hedge backing each row. Reservations are advisable in season. The heated sanitary block is an excellent modern tiled building, and just about right for the numbers involved; British WCs, free hot water in the individual basins (mainly in cubicles), showers and sinks. Public swimming pools - a heated indoor pool and outdoor one, heated with solar panels - are just below the site (charge for campers DM 6, child DM 3).

How to find it: Leave A3 (E56) Regensburg - Linz autobahn at Passau-Nord exit for the B388 towards Wegescheid. At Obernzell, turn left at Gottsdorf sign and follow to site - entrance is just before village on left.

General Details: Open 15 March - 15 Nov. 120,000 sq.m. Many electrical connections. Self-service shop. Restaurant/bar. TV room. Sports field with football pitch, volleyball, garden chess and extensive children's playground; also adventure playground and running track. Table tennis. Outdoor fitness facilities. Minigolf. Tennis. Swimming pools nearby. Washing machines and dryer. Cooking facilities. 40 bungalows or small houses for hire.

Charges 1997: Per adult DM 7.00 - 9.00, acc. to season; child (1-12 yrs) 5.00 - 6.00; pitch 10.00 - 12.00; car or m/cycle 3.00 - 4.00; extra tent 3.00 - 4.00; dog 3.00 - 4.00; electricity 3.80.

Reservations: made with deposit. Address: Mitterweg 11, 94107 Gottsdorf. Tel: 08593/880. FAX: 08593/88111.

3705 Knaus Camping-Park Lackenhäuser, Neureichenau, nr Passau

Site with good installations and many amenities, including indoor swimming pool.

This extensive site is right at the southeast tip of Germany - at one point on its border is a sign marking the Austrian frontier. There are 7 km. of walks inside the camp perimeter. It is a very popular site and reservations may be advisable mid-June to Sept. Mainly on sloping ground with fine mountain views from some parts, it has 500 pitches, nearly all for tourists, and 40 chalets or caravans for hire. The many amenities (others listed below) include a larger than average indoor pool (free) with child's pool, sauna and fitness room, massage and a new outdoor pool. The site is open all year and has much winter sports trade; own ski lift. The three sanitary blocks, one recently refurbished, are of good quality with free hot water in washbasins (cubicles for ladies), showers and sinks. They have under floor heating for cool weather. Showers could be in short supply. Baby room. Water points fed from pure springs. Rather off the beaten track for British campers, but it is a most pleasant site in a beautiful setting.

How to find it: Turn off road no. 12 to east, about 20 km. north of Passau, and then another 20 km. to Lackenhäuser via Aussernbrünst, Waldkirchen and Jandelsbrunn.

General Details: Open all year except Nov. 146,000 sq.m. Electrical connections all parts. Supermarket. Restaurant/bar. General room for young. Caravan shop. Indoor and outdoor pools. Small lake (ice sports in winter). Fishing. Bowling alley. Massage. Church on site. Organised activities (July/Aug. and Xmas). Cooking facilities. Washing machines and dryers. Chemical disposal. Bungalows and caravans to rent on site; contact site for details.

Charges 1998: Per person DM 8.50; child (3-14 yrs) 4.50; caravan and car 7.50 - 12.00; tent and m/cycle 7.50; electricity 3.50.

Reservations: made for any period without deposit. Address: Lackenhäuser 8, 94089 Neureichenau. Tel: 08583/311. FAX: 08583/91079.

3725 Bavaria Sport Camping Park, Eging am See, nr Passau

New site with excellent facilities, near Passau.

Eging is a Kurbad village of the type found in many parts of Germany where warm and cold water baths are used in a variety of treatments. It is situated in the south west tip of the Bavarian Forest, in good walking country. Bavaria Sport Camp only opened in 1992 so everything is new. It occupies an open hilltop position amidst rolling forest countryside on slightly sloping ground about 200 m. from the small lake, treatment and sports centre. Mainly level pitches of grass or fine gravel are divided by bushes and saplings on either side of tarmac roads. Water and electricity points are widely spaced (long cables may be needed). There is a small bar/restaurant with terrace and another larger one by the lake. A kiosk offers basic food supplies. The single, centrally positioned sanitary block is of excellent quality with free hot water in the basins (some in cabins) and sinks, and on payment in the showers (by slot machine door locks). Facilities for the disabled. Apart from the Kur facilities, a variety of sports are very close - swimming, tennis, table tennis, minigolf, curling, fishing, pedaloes, volleyball, electric go-karts and small motorcycles, billiards, pool, amusement machines, walking and some winter sports.

How to find it: Take Garham exit from A3 Regensburg - Passau autobahn. Pass Eging turn, continuing to main road and turn right, then almost immediately left. Cross level crossing and site is on left. Site also signed in Eging.

General Details: Open all year. Two restaurants. Variety of sports. Washing machines, dryers and irons.

Charges guide: Per adult DM 7.00 - 8.00; child (1-16 yrs) 4.50 - 5.00; pitch 10.00 - 11.00; dog 3.50; electricity 4.30; local tax 0.60.

Reservations: Write to site. Address: Grafenauer Strasse 31, 94535 Eging am See. Tel: 08544/8089. FAX: 08544/7964.

GERMANY - South East

3715 Knaus Camping-Park Viechtach, nr Cham

Excellent site on edge of Bavarian Forest.

Although the Bayerischer Wald is not as well known to the British as it deserves to be, it is an area of great natural beauty with rolling hills rising to over 1,500m at the highest point and ideal for those who wish to enjoy the wide open spaces away from it all. The Bavarian Forest National Park near Grafenau has a 200 km. network of footpaths and a unique collection of primeval flora and fauna. The site at Viechtach is a relaxing place at which to stay, well laid out in a woodland setting on the edge of the village. The variety of trees and shrubs give a 'garden' effect and there is good shade in most parts. A tarmac road winds its way between the grass pitches (some terraced) which are separated by rocks and trees and marked by plaques. Pitch size does vary, from small to sufficient. The site has two sanitary blocks of good quality. One is central to the touring pitches, the second at the far end on the ground floor of a larger building. British WCs and free hot water to washbasins (some cabins), sinks and showers. Attractive bar/restaurant, small shop. Small indoor swimming pool with sauna and solarium. The town swimming pool and tennis courts are near. Whether you are passing through and in need of a night stop or making a longer stay to visit the Bavarian Forest, this site is well worth considering

How to find it: Take the Viechtach exit from the B85 Weiden - Passau road, and follow the campsite signs.

General Details: Open all year except Nov. Restaurant. Shops (basics and camping equipment). Indoor swimming pool. Sauna and solarium. Large, renovated children's playground. Bicycle hire. Small games room. Several rooms for wet weather. Outdoor pool and tennis nearby. Washing machines, dryers and irons. Chemical disposal. Rooms in guest house, caravans (10) and tents to rent on site; contact site for details. English spoken.

Charges 1998: Per person DM 8.50; child (3-14) 4.50; pitch 7.50 - 12.00; tent and m/cycle 7.50; electricity 3.50.

Reservations: Write to site. Address: Waldfrieden 22, 94234 Viechtach. Tel: 09942/1095. FAX: 09942/302222.

3710 AZUR Ferienzentrum Bayerischer Wald, Zwiesel, nr Passau

Good class site with pools adjacent, in southeast Germany.

Pleasantly situated nearly 2,000 feet up (it can be cool at night) on a slight slope, this site has nearly 700 pitches. They are 80-100 sq.m. and numbered but not marked out. The site is mainly for tourists, not for seasonal caravans. There is usually space available and the site is also open for winter camping, with ski-lifts quite near. The two modern tiled sanitary blocks are of good quality with WCs with half seats, individual washbasins, some in cabins; free hot water in basins, showers (with seat and screen) and sinks. Facilities for the disabled. A large swimming pool complex next door comprises a deep Olympic pool, a separate pool for children and non-swimmers and a `natural' pool, open say June-Sept. For other dates or rainy days there is an indoor pool (all are free for campers). The camp is run on quite strict lines, with no vehicles allowed in after 10 pm. or at lunch time. Good camp lighting.

How to find it: Site is on north side of Zwiesel. From autobahn A3 Regensburg-Passau, take Deggendorf exit and then B11 to Zwiesel. Take Zwiesel Nord exit and follow Azur signs.

General Details: Open all year. 160,000 sq.m. Little shade. Numerous electrical connections. Supermarket. Pleasant restaurant/bar. Swimming pools. `Kneippbad' (hot/cold water treatment to do you good). Tennis. Table tennis. Minigolf. Pond for winter skating and curling. Volleyball. Children's playground. Launderette.

Charges 1997: Per adult DM 8.00 - 10.00, acc. to season; child (1-12 yrs) 6.00 - 7.00; pitch 11.00 - 13.00; car or m/cycle 3.00 - 4.00; extra tent 3.00 - 4.00; dog 3.00 - 4.00; electricity 3.80.

Reservations: will be made without deposit. Address: 94227 Zwiesel. Tel: 09922/802595. FAX: 09922/802594.

3610 Campingplatz im Volkspark Dutzendteich, Nürnberg

Satisfactory municipal site just outside the city.

A perfectly acceptable, if not luxurious, municipal site, this is at its best outside the main season. It is some 4 km. from the city centre (a 20 minute walk following signs takes you to the underground station) and 200 m. from the swimming pool and football stadium. Pitches are medium sized on flat grass with electricity and many tall trees. Pitches are not marked and the site does not like to turn people away so at busy times spacing might be close. The two toilet blocks could then be hard pressed but they are normally adequate. They have toilets, washing troughs and some basins for men, some cabins for ladies, all with hot water, and hot showers on payment. The site is quite close to the generally intact remnants of the rise of National Socialism with the Zeppelinfeld, where Hitler addressed 250,000 people, and the Congress Hall, a vast building built on the lines of the Colosseum. Restaurants and bars near here.

How to find it: From autobahns, take Nürnberg-Fischbach exit from A9 München-Bayreuth east of Nürnburg. Proceed 3 km. on dual carriageway towards city then left at camp sign. From city follow `Stadion-Messe' signs and site is well signed (near a large Grundig office block).

General Details: Open 1 May - 30 Sept. Many electrical connections. Café. Kiosk with basic supplies. General room with pool table. Tennis (free). Children's play area. Washing machine and dryer. Motorcaravan services.

Charges guide: Per person DM 8.00; child (3-13 yrs) 4.00; motorcaravan, caravan or tent + car 10.00; hiker or cyclist's tent 5.00; m/cycle 2.00; dog 1.00; electricity 1.00 p/kwh.

Reservations: not made and said to be unnecessary. Address: Hans Kalb Str. 56, 90471 Nürnberg 50. Tel: 0911/811122.

3720 Campingplatz Naabtal, Pielenhofen bei Regensburg

Very pleasant, riverside site with many facilities.

Regensburg is on the edge of the `Bavarian Forest', which though not as well known as the Black Forest, is a lovely area of natural beauty. Regensburg is an ancient city on the Danube, on the autobahn between Nürnberg and Vienna. Naabtal makes an excellent night stop when travelling to or from Austria or Hungary and would also make a good base for exploring this interesting part of Germany. Two-thirds of the site is taken up by static caravans, used for weekends and holidays, and the 100 pitches available for tourists are by the riverside and in an open field. There is good shade in most parts and hills covered with trees rise on the opposite side of the river. This is good walking and mountain cycling country, with marked trails. The two good toilet blocks, part of two large buildings, are heated in cool weather, with British WCs and free hot water in the washbasins, many of which are in cabins, Hot water is on payment in the well designed showers. One of the large buildings contains the shop and bar/restaurant and the other, a large meeting room with tables, catering facilities, a stage and a youth room with table tennis and video games. Sauna and solarium. Alongside, under cover, is a skittle alley and next to this a tarmac curling rink. Children's playground with imaginative apparatus. Small boats can be launched on the placid river (where you may also swim at your own risk) and there are two good size tennis courts.

How to find it: Take Nittendorf exit (before Regensburg) on Nürnberg - Passau autobahn. Follow road to Pielendorf (Camping Naabtal is signed from exit). Cross river and turn right to site. Camp is about 11 km. from autobahn exit.

General Details: Open all year. Bar/restaurant and terrace. Shop for basics, another in nearby village. Washing machines, dryers and irons. Motorcaravan drain station. Sauna and solarium. Tennis. Table tennis. Skittle alley. Curling rink. Youth room with games. Disco in village. Riding near. Walking, cycling. Small boats on river. Reception will advise on local excursions, walks and sports. Bungalows for hire.

Charges guide: Per person DM 7.50; child 5.00; pitch 8.80; dog 3.00; electricity on meter.

Reservations: Needed in high season; contact site. Address: 93188 Pielenhofen. Tel: 09409/373. FAX: 09409/723.

3620 DCC-Campingpark `Romantische Strasse', Dinkelsbühl, nr Ellwangen

Modern site, very close to well-known town on Romantic Road.

Run by the German Camping Club (DCC), this site is by one of Germany's best-known mediaeval towns, from which of course visits can be made to other places on the Romantic Road. There are 475 pitches on broad grassy terraces overlooking a small lake. All are individual and numbered and of about 80 sq.m., though with nothing between them. Most of the pitches are likely to be retained for tourists. A special area is kept for overnight stays. The lake can be used for bathing or one's own non-powered boat. The two large modern toilet blocks are of good quality and should satisfy all demands with British toilets, washbasins with free hot water, some in cabins, plentiful showers with hot water (charge).

How to find it: Site is on the no. 25 road and is signed in Dinkelsbühl towards Dürnwangen.

General Details: Open all year, also shop, (meals at least Easter, then May-end Sept.); 80,000 sq.m. Electrical connections. Shop. General/TV room. Washing machines, dryers and dishwashing. Cooking facilities. Children's playground on sand and grass. Minigolf. Organised daytime activities in season. Bicycle hire.

Charges guide: Per person DM 7.50; child (4-13) 5.00; (10% off these two with international camping carnet); local tax (over 4 yrs.) 1.00; pitch 16.50; dog 2.00; electricity 0.50 + meter.

Reservations: only through DCC and rather complex, costly, and usually unnecessary. Try phoning site shortly before arrival: 09851/7817. FAX: as phone.

3625 Knaus Camping-Park Frickenhausen, Ochsenfurt, nr Würzburg

Pleasant riverside site just south of Würzburg.

This site has been developed recently and now has a small swimming pool and a large children's play area with modern equipment on an `island' surrounded by attractive trees alongside the gently flowing River Main. Young trees are growing well on the site to replace the 300 lost in a violent storm a few years ago. There are 125 fair-sized touring pitches (plus over 90 long stay places, mostly separate nearer the river), most with electricity (6A) on flat grass in sections off a tarred access road with flowers around. All the facilities are in a long block opposite reception where bread may be ordered in low season (Frau Hergeth speaks English). Sanitary facilities have free hot water in the quite large, fully controllable showers, the washbasins and dishwashing sinks. Upstairs is a small supermarket and a restaurant. Just beyond the building is a small swimming pool, with a larger public pool only 300 m. from the site. The ducks are very friendly and will invite you to feed them.

How to find it: Take Ochsenfurt exit from A3 autobahn at Würzburg and continue on B13. Do not cross the Main into town but follow Frickenhausen and site signs; site is shortly on the right.

General Details: Open all year except Nov. Restaurant and cafe/wine bar. Shop. Club room. Small swimming pool. Children's play area and beach volleyball on river island. Table tennis. Fishing. Boat marina. Cooking facilities. Washing machine and dryer. Chemical disposal. Caravans (10) and tents to rent on site; contact site for details.

Charges 1998: Per person DM 8.50; child (3-14) 4.50; pitch 7.50 - 12.00; ten and tm/cycle 7.50; electricity 3.50.

Reservations: Not made. Address: Ochsenfurter Str. 49, 97252 Frickenhausen. Tel: 09331/3171. FAX: 09331/5784.

GERMANY - South East

3605 Camping Rangau, Dechsendorf, nr Erlangen

Overnight halt close to A3 Würzburg - Nürnberg autobahn.

This site makes a convenient stopover, quickly and easily reached from the Würzburg-Nürnberg motorway and may be pleasant enough to stay a bit longer. It has 110 pitches which are mainly for tourists on flat ground, under trees, numbered and partly marked but only about 60-80 sq.m. There are also 60 permanent units. There is usually space and in peak season overnighters can often be put on adjacent football pitch. A reasonable sanitary block, heated when cold, has free hot water in well spaced washbasins with shelf and mirror, and in the controllable showers with seat. An older block provides WCs. A fair sized lake with direct access from the site can be used for sailing or windsurfing or for fishing on permit; boats are for hire. One can also swim here or in a swimming pool 200 m. away. The centre of Erlangen is 5 km.

> **How to find It:** Take exit for Erlangen-West from A3 autobahn, turn towards Erlangen but after less than 1 km. at Dechsendorf turn left by camp signs and follow to site.
>
> **General Details:** Open 1 April - 30 Sept. Restaurant for meals or drinks. Order bread from reception. Children's playground. Laundry facilities.
>
> **Charges 1997:** Per person DM 6.50; child (under 12) 3.00; pitch 8.00; dog 2.50; electricity (6A) 4.00.
>
> **Reservations:** are made without deposit and kept until 6 pm. Address: Campingstrasse 44, 91056 Erlangen-Dechsendorf. Tel: 09135/8866.

3615 Azur Camping Stadtsteinach, Stadtsteinach, nr Bayreuth

Friendly, quality site in the Frankenwald.

Franconia has a wealth of old castles, churches, forests and rivers, to say nothing of its magnificent wine in distinctive bocksbeutels, as well as interesting famous cities such as Bamburg, Coburg, Kronach, Kulmbach and of course Bayreuth with its Wagnerian associations. It may not have the rather sinister beauty of the Black Forest or the splendour of the Bavarian Alps, but it does have much to offer. Stadtsteinach is well placed for exploring this region and the Azur site is a comfortable base from which to do this. Occupying a quiet position in gently undulating countryside, with tree-clad hills rising to the east of the site, there are just 50 static caravans and space for 130 tourers with 80 electrical connections available (16A). Brick main roads give way to hard access roads with pitches on either side. The site is on a gentle slope and pitches have been terraced where necessary and there are some hardstandings for motorcaravans. High hedges and trees separate pitches or groups of pitches in some areas giving the effect of camping in small clearings - the mix giving charm to the site. There is a small restaurant with terrace and a shop. The two sanitary areas, one by the open field, the other part of the administration/restaurant building, are of good quality and include British WCs, free hot water to showers, sinks and basins, some of which are in private cabins. The solar heated public swimming pool near the site entrance is free to campers, there is tennis nearby and this is also good walking country. So, if you are looking for culture interspersed with some physical activity, this would make an ideal base.

> **How to find It:** Stadtsteinach is just north of Bayreuth, off the A9/E51 Nürnberg-Leipzig road, reached by the no. 303 road from this autobahn. The site is well signed.
>
> **General Details:** Open all year. Restaurant and shop (Easter - end Oct). Local shops 800 m. Children's play area. TV. Washing machines and dryers. Facilities for the disabled. Dormitory for young people, cooking rings on payment. Swimming pool, cycle hire and tennis nearby. Walking.
>
> **Charges 1997:** Per adult DM 7.00 - 9.00, acc. to season; child (1-12 yrs) 5.00 - 6.00; pitch 10.00 - 12.00; car or m/cycle 3.00 - 4.00; extra tent 3.00 - 4.00; dog 3.00 - 4.00; electricity 3.80.
>
> **Reservations:** Write to site with deposit (DM 20) and fee (20). Address: Badstrasse 5, 95346 Stadtsteinach. Tel: 09225/95401. FAX: 09225/95402.

Ferien-Campingplatz R. Endres.

Schönrain 97737 Germünden-Hofstetten

Telephone 09351-8645 Fax 09351 8721

Sunny campsite on edge of woodland for restful and relaxing holiday. Range of walks in the adjacent Spessart. Organized coach excursions. Horse riding nearby. Swimming pool. Children's playground with paddling pool. Table Tennis. Good sanitary facilities.
CARAVANS FOR HIRE.

3600 Camping Katzenkopf, Sommerach, nr Würzburg

Pleasantly situated site by the River Main near Würzburg.

If you are looking for a night stop when travelling on the A3 Würzburg-Nürnberg autobahn or wish to spend a few days 'messing about in boats', this bright and lively camp might serve your purpose. It is also in the centre of Franken Wine area for wine buffs who enjoy what is thought by many, to be the finest German wine. Katzenkopf is a popular camp with about 100 permanent caravans and room for slightly more touring units. It is in two parts, nearest reception by a lake and behind the football stadium directly on the river bank (for dog owners). The slow flowing river is ideal for boating and water skiing. There is some shade from the growing trees. The level site has pitches on grass on each side of hard access roads, some unmarked and some separated by hedges. There are restaurants by reception and another at the football stadium. One can fish from the site (on payment) and there are pedaloes for hire with other sporting opportunities near. There a two good quality sanitary blocks, one in each place. The first is on the ground floor of an apartment building and the second a free-standing building. Both have free hot water in the washbasins, sinks and showers, dishwashing, a baby room with bath and facilities for disabled people.

How to find it: Leave the A3 Würzburg-Nürnberg autobahn at the Kitzingen exit northwards towards Volkach and follow site signs.

General Details: Open Easter - 25 Oct. 40.000 sq.m. Small bar/restaurant. Supermarket 2 km. Watersports. Fishing. Bicycle hire. TV room. Swimming pool 5 km. Tennis 800 m. Washing machines and dryers. Chemical disposal. Motorcaravan services.

Charges 1998: Per person DM 7.50 - 8.00, acc. to season; child (1-14 yrs) 4.50 - 5.00; pitch 9.00 - 11.00; electricity 2.50 + 0.90 kw; various extra charges for boats. Less 10% with camping carnet.

Reservations: Not made as site say space is usually available. Address: Am See, 97334 Sommerach am Main. Tel: 09381/9215. FAX: 09381/6028.

3730 Camping Park Bad Kissingen, Bad Kissingen

First class, family owned site adjacent to this pretty spa town and its park.

Although this site was only opened in 1988, it has already been accorded top status by the main German camping organisation. Herr Laudenbach, the friendly English-speaking owner, will greet you and personally conduct you to your pitch. The quiet site is situated by the lakeside and is 1 km. from the town. A grassy, partially shaded site with a tarmac service road, there are only 100 pitches, all well spaced out. Of these 30 are used by permanent units, so reservation is advisable. The simple sanitary block has a room for the disabled and is kept spotless. Showers are on payment (DM 1). The laundry room has 2 washing machines and a dryer. The small, charming restaurant is open every evening and there is folk music to entertain you. Tennis, golf, minigolf, swimming pool are all within easy reach and local excursions leave from the site. Gas barbecues are permitted.

How to find it: Leave autobahn A7/E45 at Hammelburg. Take A287 for Bad Kissingen for 10 km. and site is on the right just before the town approach (and is signed).

General Details: Open 1 April - 15 Oct. Restaurant/bar. Tennis, swimming pool, minigolf and golf nearby. Children's play area. Aviary. Washing machines and dryer. Boats for hire on lake. Car wash.

Charges 1997: Per person DM 9.50; child (under 12 yrs) 5.00; pitch for car/caravan or motorcaravan 11.00; tent 8.00; electricity 3.50; local tax 1.50; dog 2.50.

Reservations: Write to site. Address: Euerdorfer Str. 1, 97688 Bad Kissingen. Tel: 0971/5211. FAX: as phone.

3735 Ferien-Campingplatz Schönrain, Gemünden-Hofstetten, nr Karlstadt

Site in attractive woodland setting with swimming pool.

Situated near the River Main, in an attractive woodland setting, this is a very friendly, family run site. There are now 200 pitches, 100 for tourists. All have electricity and some water and drainage also. A peaceful site, there are opportunities for walking in the adjacent woods and excursions are organised in the main season. The site has an outdoor pool, with a paddling pool for children. Sanitary facilities are satisfactory, with hot showers on payment. There is a restaurant/bar and a shop on site. Frau Endres welcomes British guests and speaks a little English.

How to find it: From the Frankfurt-Würzburg autobahn, take the Weibersbrunn-Lohr exit and then the B26 to Gemünden. Turn over the Main river bridge to Hofstetten. From the Kassel-Wurzburg autobahn, leave at Hammelburg and take the B27 to Gemünden, and as above.

General Details: Open 1 April - 30 Sept. Bar/restaurant (closed Tuesdays). Shop. Swimming pool (15/5-15/9). Children's playground. Table tennis. Bicycle hire. Excursions organised. Horse riding, canoeing, cycling and walking near. Chemical disposal. Motorcaravan services. Caravans for hire.

Charges 1997: Per pitch DM 8.00 - 10.00, acc. to size; person 7.50; child (under 14 yrs) 4.50; electricity 4.00. Less 10% for stays over 14 days.

Reservations: Write to site. Address: 97737 Gemünden-Hofstetten. Tel: 09351/8645. FAX: 09351/8721.

AR Discount

Welcome drink

GERMANY - North East

3845 International Camp Grossbreitenbach, Grossbreitenbach, nr Suhl

Acceptable site in the Thuringian Forest.

If you wish to visit the gently rolling walking country of the Thuringian Forest area or perhaps follow in the footsteps of Goethe and walk the 164 km. Rennsteig long distance footpath which runs over the hills from Horschel near Eisenach to Blankenstein near Hof, this site is in the heart of the region. The height of the forest ensures that there is generally frost for some 150 days a year and this becomes a winter sports area. There is still a number of holiday bungalows, as on most camps in the former East Germany, but there is room for 120 touring units, either on a slightly sloping grassy area surrounded by trees near the entrance, or on an overflow meadow nearby. Pitches are neither marked out nor numbered and space may be limited in high season. There is a fitness centre, with a variety of water treatments, and a large open-air swimming pool right next to the site. Sanitary arrangements are in parts of two modern buildings - a 'Sanitarkomplex' at the fitness centre beyond the bungalows (a 120 m. walk) and as a part of the small restaurant block near the touring area. There are British WCs, free hot water in the basins and on payment in the showers (these have doors and curtained dressing room. The restaurant for simple evening meals, snacks, drinks, etc., is more like a modern hotel coffee lounge with comfortable easy chairs and neat table cloths and is fronted by a terrace with a fountain and colourful flower beds.

How to find it: Leave the Eisfeld-Saalfeld B281 road (southwest of Gera) at Neuhaus for Grossbreitenbach, where the site is situated by the town swimming pool.

General Details: Open all year. Electrical connections throughout (16A). Small restaurant. Fitness centre. Sports area. Children's play area. Swimming pool nearby. Bungalows for rent. Centre for walking and winter sports.

Charges guide: Per caravan DM 6.00; car 3.00; motorcaravan 8.00; tent 5.00 - 8.00; adult 7.00; child (under 14 yrs) 5.00; electricity 3.00.

Reservations: Only made for bungalows. Address: 98701 Grossbreitenbach. Tel: 036781/42398.

3850 Campingplatz Strandbad Aga, nr Gera

Quiet, pleasant site within reach of Dresden, Leipzig and Meissen.

Many sites in the former DDR, starved of investment over many years, are struggling to come to terms with the standards to be found in the West. However, where money has come in from outside, standards have been or are being raised. Now that access has become easier there is much interest in seeing the historic cities of the east and Aga is within reach of Dresden, Leipzig, Meissen, Colditz and other interesting towns. This former municipal site has been privatised and an area next to the permanent caravans has been developed for touring units. Situated in open countryside, on the edge of a small lake, pitches have been levelled and seeded on either side of new rolled gravel access roads. Places of 9 x 9 m. are marked by numbered stones and all have electrical connections. A new sanitary block has been built to one side of but near to all pitches, with free hot water to the basins, most of which are in private cabins and to the sinks; hot showers are on payment. These include a large (4 x 4 m.) room for the disabled. A fine new restaurant has been built and is open 11 am. to 12 pm. There is a well stocked shop and in high season a kiosk for drinks, ice creams, etc. The lake is used for swimming, boating and fishing and there is a small children's playground on one side of the site. Entertainment is organised in July and the friendly, enthusiastic owner is making a great effort to create a first class camp.

How to find it: From the A4 Chemnitz - Erfurt autobahn take the Gera exit; follow the B2 towards Zeitz, turning off onto the unclassified road to Aga which passes the site.

General Details: Open all year except Jan/Feb. Restaurant. Shop. Kiosk (June-Sept). Children's playground. Table tennis. Volleyball. Swimming and watersports in the lake. Entertainment in high season. Riding 1 km. Football 200 m. Go-karts 1 km. Washing machines and dryers. Good facilities for the disabled.

Charges guide: Per adult DM 7.00; child (3-13 yrs) 3.50; motorcaravan 11.00; caravan or tent 8.00; car 3.00; m/cycle 1.00; electricity 3.00 + 0.80 per kw/h; drainage 3.00.

Reservations: Write to site. Address: Strandbad Aga, Reichenbacherstrasse 18, 07554 Aga. Tel: 036695/20209. FAX: as phone.

Camping in Berlin

Like most capital cities, all nearby sites are dreadfully overcrowded in season (we found this to be so at the end of April!) and you really do need to reserve a pitch. Probably the best is:

DCC (German Camping Club), Kladow, nr Gatow: It is not easy to find, although it is well marked for the last two miles. From the autobahn E30 aim for Potsdam, then the A2 for Charlottenburg. From the marked right turn off this road, the signs are excellent. Like all DCC sites, reservations must be made through the Head Office - DCC, Postfach 400428, 8000 München 40 - Tel: 89 33 40 21.

A little further out and on the southeastern outskirts (about 20 miles from city centre) is:

3830 Camping Am Krossinee, Wernsdorf Schmockwitz: Although not tried this seems a well organised attractive lakeside site in pine trees. To find it from autobahn A10 (E30), leave at Niederlehme and take the road to Wernsdorf (about 8 km). The Krossinsee is on the left and is clearly marked from Wernsdorf (on the north side of the lake). Tel: 6758687. Open: 1 May - 30 Oct.

3835 Campingplatz Kim Parke Motel, Altfranken bei Dresden

Quiet site for caravans and motorcaravans only, useful for visiting Dresden.

Dresden is, for a variety of reasons, one of the most popular tourist cities in the former East Germany and Camping Kim Parke Motel, about 10 km. from the city, offers a base for visiting this interesting part of Saxony. New hotels, shops and a large supermarket have been built nearby and roads are being improved, although the site restaurant has been demolished to make way for a block of flats. The site is in two parts. Turning left inside the entrance leads to a sloping, open meadow where some effort has been made to provide level pitches with views of the surrounding countryside and the single toilet block is here. This provision is old but clean, with free hot water in sinks and washbasins and on payment in the showers. The second part, right inside the entrance, consists of gravel hardstandings with pitches in groups of 2 - 5 separated by hedges. There is no toilet block in this section. There is a number of tall trees but not much shade, although the elevated position of the site makes it a pleasant place to stay for a few days. Only caravans and motorcaravans are taken.

How to find it: From autobahn A4 (E4) take Wilsdruff exit, head for Kesselsdorf and B173 to Altfranken where camp is signed. Note: ignore large Kim Parke Hotel on left before Altfranken.

General Details: Open 1 March - 30 Oct. 80,000 sq.m. Washing machines. Small play area. Swimming, 5 minutes.

Charges guide: Per person DM 4.50; child (under 12 yrs) 3.00; pitch: motorcaravan 12.00, caravan 10.00; electricity 2.50.

Reservations: Write to site. Address: 01462 Altfranken bei Dresden. Tel: 0351/ 4102400. FAX: 0351/4102410.

3837 Camping Rehbocktal, Scharfenberg bei Meissen

Small camp near the River Elbe suitable for visiting Meissen.

This small site for about 60 units, 7 km. southeast of Meissen, is situated in a level wooded valley with a small stream running through. Although surrounded by trees there is little shade and with a restaurant 50 m. from the entrance and shops fairly near, amenities on camp are limited to drinks from reception and basic supplies and snacks from a kiosk. Boating is possible on the river which is separated from the site by a main road, but the main purpose in using this site is to visit nearby places of interest like Meissen, Colditz and Dresden for which this would provide a peaceful base. There are two small, old but clean and acceptable toilet blocks with British style WCs, free hot water in basins and sinks and on payment in showers. There is not enough on the site to interest one if wishing to spend all the time there, but it is an acceptable base from which to tour this area by car, on foot, or for boating on the river.

How to find it: Site is 7 km from Keissen on the B6 Meissen - Dresden road.

General Details: Open 1 April - 30 Oct. 13,000 sq.m. Restaurant next door, kiosk for basics and snacks and drinks from reception where there is a small terrace. Electricity most places.

Charges guide: Per person DM 6.00; child (under 12) 3.00; caravan 7.00; tent 4.00 - 5.00; car 3.00; motorcaravan 7.00; electricity 3.00

Reservations: Write to site in German. Address 01665 Scharfenberg bei Meissen. Tel: 03521/452680.

3840 Freizeitpark Grosskoschen, Senftenberg, nr Dresden

Large holiday complex around lake with two camping places.

The leisure lake Senftenbergsee lies between Dresden and Berlin and would make a good night stop if travelling this way. However, Camping Grosskoschen, now privatised and being brought up to date, has more to offer than just a night halt. There are two camp sites here as part of the complex and this is the larger one. Swimming is in the lido in the lake, but high sand banks make the use of boats difficult. The 400 numbered pitches for tourists are grass on sand and their area is determined by the tall trees under which they are situated. Electricity is available to all but some require long leads. Most of the 250 permanent caravans are grouped together. The friendly, helpful, English speaking management (may vary with different receptionists) guide you to your pitch on hard roads (one-way system). There is a good quality, attractive restaurant, an area with snack bars and amusements and elsewhere, a mini shopping centre. There are two large, new toilet blocks of excellent quality and the five older ones are being rebuilt. The second site, Camping Niemtsch, on the opposite side of the lake, is smaller with pitches enclosed by hedges and has easier access to the water for boats. A new toilet block has been built here also but the site lacks the amenities of the larger one and prices are lower. There are steamer trips on the lake and many places of interest to visit by car.

How to find it: On road B96, 5 km. south of Senftenberg.

General Details: Open all year, but no water or facilities except restaurant 1 Nov. - 31 March. 140,000 sq.m. Restaurant. Good variety of shops. Snack bars with terrace. Children's play areas. Swimming (lake, lido). Boating. Volleyball. Bowls. Table tennis. Washing machines and dryers. Many different types of accommodation to rent.

Charges guide: Per person DM 4.00 - 6.00; child (6-14) 2.00 - 3.00; pitch 4.00 - 10.00; tent 4.00 - 7.00.

Reservations: Contact site. Address: Grosskoschen bei Senftenberg. Tel: 03573/8000. FAX: 03573/800801

GERMANY - North East

3827 Camping Sanssouci Gaisberg, Potsdam

Peaceful lakeside site for city visits to Potsdam and Berlin.

There are enough attractions in Potsdam - the famous Sanssouci Park, with its plethora of historical buildings being the main one - to keep you occupied for at least two or three days without even making the one hour train journey to Berlin (day tickets from main station about DM 15). The site is about 2 km. from Sanssouci Park on the banks of the Trempliner See, in a very quiet woodland setting, 1,200 m. along a woodland drive. Tall trees mark out the 120 flat, grassy tourist pitches, all with 6A electricity, and access is good for larger units. Sanitary facilities consist of one smallish toilet block of a good standard and, 50 m. further in, a very modern excellent block containing free hot showers, cabins with hot water, facilities for babies, dishwashing (1 DM). Bread can be ordered from reception where the small shop is also located. Helpful reception with English spoken. Tourist information. It is advisable to leave your vehicle here and make the 1.8 km. walk to the tram terminal or use the free transport offered by the site. Tickets either from machines on the new trams or from Potsdam main station.

How to find it: From A10 take Potsdam exit; follow B1 to within 4 km. of city centre then sign to right for camp. Site is southwest of Sanssouci Park on the banks of the Trempliner See off Zeppelinstrasse.

General Details: Open 1 April - 31 Oct. Shop. Rowing boats, motorboats and pedaloes for hire. Fishing. Children's play area in central woods. Bicycle hire. Washing machine and dryer. Chemical disposal. Motorcaravan services. Camp closed to vehicles 13.00 - 15.00 hrs.

Charges 1998: Per adult DM 10.95 - 12.60; child (under 15 yrs) 1.90; pitch 11.90 - 12.90; local tax 0.90; electricity 3.50. Special low season offers.

Reservations: Not normally necessary. Address: An der Pirschheide/Templiner See 41, 14471 Potsdam. Tel: 03327/55680. FAX: as phone. E-mail: recra@campingweb.com. Internet: http://www.campingweb.com.

3820 Freizeit und Campingpark Helene-See, nr Frankfurt a. d. Oder

Wonderful site for families near Polish frontier.

Helenesee is a large lake with a wide beach sloping gently down to the water and fine sand - a swimmer's paradise. A promenade runs along the lakeside, separated from the shore by a low wall, with various fast food kiosks at intervals, a large supermarket and self service cafeteria plus Murphy's Bar. With pedaloes for hire and bathing, sub-aqua, discos, sporting activities and dancing, there is naturally a lively 'holiday' atmosphere filled with the sounds of happy children, but you can also get peace and quiet by walking a little way round the lake. On arrival at the site there is a car park from where you go to reception which operates a ticket system with a waiting room! The site provides up to 1,000 pitches (320 with 10A electricity), including many for tents in several areas with many tall trees for some shade. There are some holiday homes separate from the touring sections. Several sanitary buildings have free hot water, but all except one are rather let down by poor maintenance. The exception is an excellent block immediately to the right past the entrance, which also happens to be the furthest from the lake.

How to find it: From E30 Hannover autobahn at Frankfurt turn onto B112 (signs for site start here) towards Eisenhuttenstadt and follow signs to Helenesee. Beware large traffic jams on E30 during morning and evening rush hours (Polish border crossing).

General Details: Open all year. Restaurant. Bar. Supermarket. Fast food outlets. Several children's play areas. Lake swimming. Sailing. Sub-aqua school. Discos. Dancing. Volleyball. Washing machine and irons.

Charges guide: Per person DM 6.00; child (under 7 yrs) 3.00; caravan or motorhome 10.00; tent 5.00.

Reservations: Write to site. Address: Freizeitzentrum Helene-See KG, 15236 Helene-See. Tel: 0335/5212202. FAX: 0335/547102.

3815 Azur Camping Ecktannen, Waren am Müitzsee

Large woodland site in German 'Lake District', midway between Berlin and Rostock.

Müritz is the largest of the Mecklenburg lakes with a surface area of 48 square miles. There is said to be room at this site for 1,250 units (all with 10A electricity). The pitches are neither numbered nor marked and are in undulating woodland, either under tall pines or in clearings where tree stumps have been left and small saplings are growing. It is at the northeast tip of the Müritzersee, although trees screen out a view of the lake, and slightly above it. There is direct access to the water with small jetties for boats, a bathing beach of sand and a lakeside restaurant. The toilet arrangements are in two buildings with free hot water in the basins and on payment in the showers and for dishwashing. There is no shop, but tradesmen call each morning with basic foods. If you are looking for a very quiet, simple site 'in the heart of nature', you may well enjoy a stay here. The Azur organisation has recently acquired the site and this should ensure that the anticipated improvements will be carried out.

How to find it: Follow the B192 southeast from Waren following Azur international signs.

General Details: Open 15 March - 15 Nov. Restaurant by lake just outside site. Tradesmen call.

Charges guide: Per adult DM 8.00 - 10.00, acc. to season; child (1-12 yrs) 6.00 - 7.00; pitch 11.00 - 13.00; car or m/cycle 3.00 - 4.00; extra tent 3.00 - 4.00; dog 3.00 - 4.00; electricity 3.80.

Reservations: Not necessary. Address: 17192 Waren am Müritzsee. Tel: 03991/668513. FAX: 03991/664675.

HUNGARY

There are many interesting areas of Hungary for the tourist apart from Budapest (for which you should allow at least a couple of days) and Lake Balaton (around 70% of the visitors here are German) and the British are warmly received. The Danube Bend in the northwest is justifiably popular, as is the northeast hills area (Eger and Miskolc), with the spectacular stalactites in the large cave system at the border with Slovakia in Aggtelek (north of Eger). The interesting towns of the Great Plain to the east of the Danube have a great Magyar tradition and there are many Thermal baths (often at campsites) to enjoy. There are also several notable wine areas and you can purchase quality wines at low prices. West of the Danube appears rather more advanced, while in the east and north it is still common to see agricultural workers with scythes and few tractors. There has been a rapid advance in the general standard of campsites, although the majority still have communal (single sex) changing for showers. All sites, however, have British style WCs. Most sites require payment in cash. It is advisable and convenient to use public transport when visiting Budapest. It is useful to know that the Hungarian tourist organisation (IBUSZ) has offices in most towns where you can also change money. Opening hours Mon-Sat 08.00-18.00/20.00 and 08.00-13.00 on Sundays. Hungarian National Tourist Information is handled in the UK by:

The Danube Travel Agency Ltd, 6 Conduit Street, London W1R 9TG. Tel: 0171 493 0263

Population
10,471,000 (1995); density 113 per sq. km.

Capital
Budapest.

Climate
There are four fairly distinct seasons - hot summer (June-Aug), mild spring and autumn very cold winter with snow.

Language
The official language is Magyar, but German is widely spoken, and English and French are also spoken particularly by those engaged in the tourist industry in the west of the country.

Currency
Hungarian forints (ft) come in notes of 10, 20, 50, 100 and 500 ft. When you change cash keep receipts - necessary to convert money at the end of your visit - it is illegal to export Hungarian currency. You can change money at any IBUSZ or regional tourist office, at most large hotels or campsites. Banks can be slow and exchange rates are the same everywhere.

Banks
Open Mon-Fri 09.00-14.00, Sat 09.00-12.00.

Post Offices
Usually open Mon-Fri 08.00-17.00/18.00, Sat. 12.00-14.00/18.00, but it is quicker to buy stamps at tobacconists.

Telephone
To call from the UK the code is 0036 followed by area code less initial 0, and number. From Hungary dial 06 followed by the area code. International calls from Hungary can be dialled direct from red or grey phone boxes but it may be easier through the international operator (09).

Public Holidays
New Year; 15 March; Easter Mon; Labour Day; Whitsun; Constitution Day, 20 Aug; Republic Day, 23 Oct; Christmas, 25, 26 Dec.

Time
GMT plus 1 (summer BST plus 1).

Shopping
Open Mon-Fri 10.00-18.00, Sat 10.00-14.00. Food shops open Mon-Fri 07.00-19.00, Sat 07.00-14.00. Home produced products, including food and restaurant meals are cheap by western standards. There appears to be no shortage of goods with articles being sold by the roadside and from garages and gardens. Traditionally Hungarians take their main meal at midday so there is a better range of dishes in the restaurants at midday. All eating places display signs indicating their class from I to IV which gives some guide to comparative prices. Set menus are good value.

Motoring
Main roads are very good, as is signposting. Most of the few motorways are single carriage, single lane and care is needed.
Fuel: On motorways and in large towns petrol stations open 24 hours otherwise 06.00-20.00. Eurocard accepted at some petrol stations.
Toll: The M1 from the Austrian border to Györ is the only toll road at present (1300 forints).
Speed Restrictions: Caravans and motorhomes (3.5 tons) 31 mph (50 kph) in built up areas, caravans 44 mph (70 kph) and 50 mph (80 kph) on other roads and motorways respectively, motorhomes 50 mph (80 kph) and 75 mph (120 kph) respectively.
Parking: The centre of Budapest is closed to traffic. Do not park in places where you would not park in the UK.

Overnighting
Not allowed outside campsites.
Note: Camping Gaz can be difficult to obtain.

National Motoring Organisation
Magyar Autoklub (MAK), FIA & AIT, Romer Floris utca 4a, Budapest 11. Tel: 1 212 2938.

**The sites in the HUNGARY featured in this guide
are shown on the map on page 370**

HUNGARY

510 Ózon Camping, Sopron

Peaceful and comfortable edge of town site close to the border.

Sopron was not over-run by the Turks or bombed in WW2, so 350 historic buildings and monuments have remained intact, making it the second major tourist centre after Budapest. It also has a music festival from mid-June to mid-July and is close to the Löverek hills. This surprisingly pleasant campsite is just over 4 km. from the centre, with the modern, chalet style reception at the entrance from where the oval site opens out into a little green valley surrounded by trees. There are also many trees within the site offering shade. The concrete access roads lead to 60 numbered grass pitches, all with electricity (6A). Some with water and waste water also are in the lower level on the left, where siting is more difficult for caravans. They are mostly flat, some with a slight slope, separated by hedges and vary from 40 sq.m. for tents up to 80 sq.m. for larger units. The sanitary facilities are in two buildings which are identical except that the one by reception has a laundry (free) whilst the other, near the swimming pool, has a sauna. They each have 6 fully controllable, curtained, hot showers (communal changing) close to the washbasins, so it could possibly be cramped here. British style WCs. Both blocks have free cookers, fridges and dishwashing. A small open air pool and paddling pool open from the end of May to September. There is a pleasant restaurant with good value meals above the friendly, helpful reception which also offers basic essentials, tourist information and money exchange. No English is spoken but French and German are.

How to find it: From the A3 south of Wien, follow roads 16 (Kingenbach) and 84 to Sopron. Site is on road to Brennerberganya, well signed in Sopron.

General Details: Open 15 April - 15 Oct. Restaurant. Essentials and money exchange at reception. Shops close. Swimming pool (from 15/5). Sauna. Bungalows for hire.

Charges 1998: Per pitch incl. electricity DM 16.00; person 6.50; child (under 10) 4.50; dog 4.50.

Reservations: May be advisable in high season and are made if you write in German. Address: 9400 Sopron, Erdei Malom köz 3. Tel: 99/331 144. FAX: 99/331 145.

512 Camping-Gasthof Pihenő, Győr

Small friendly site on main Budapest - Vienna road.

This privately owned site makes an excellent night stop when travelling to and from Hungary as it lies beside the main no. 10 road, near to the end of the motorway to the east of Győr. It is set amidst pine trees with pitches which are not numbered, but marked out by small shrubs, in a small clearing or between the trees. With space for about 25 units, all with electrical connections (5A), there are also a dozen simple, one roomed bungalows and 4 en-suite rooms for hire. On one side of the camp, fronting the road, are two pleasant restaurants with terrace (menu in English) and the management offer a very reasonably priced package (if desired) which includes pitch and meals. The site has added a new, solar heated swimming pool (10 x 5 m.) open June -Sept, with a children's pool. The single, small toilet block has free hot water in the washbasins. There are just two showers for each sex with pre-mixed hot water (10 forints for one minute) and curtained, communal dressing space. British style WCs. There is a room for washing clothes and dishes with a small cooking facility. A very friendly German speaking owner runs the site and a new restaurant with his wife who speaks a little English.

How to find it: From Austria, continue through Győr following Budapest signs. Continue on road no. 10 past start of motorway for 3 km. and site is on left. From Budapest, turn right on road 10 at end of motorway, then as above.

General Details: Open 1 April - 30 Oct. Restaurant with good menu and reasonable prices. Bungalows and rooms for rent. Bread orders at reception previous evening.

Charges guide: Per pitch DM 4.00; person 2.00; electricity 1.00. Less 10% for stays over 4 days, 20% after 8.

Reservations: Write to site. Address: Oláh Ferenc, 9011 Győrszentivan, Kertvaros 10, es foút 118 km. Tel: 96/316 461. FAX: as phone.

513 Panorama Camping, Pannonhalma, nr Győr

Very peaceful, pretty, hillside site.

In 1982 this became the first private enterprise campsite in Hungary and it offers a very pleasant outlook and peaceful stay at the start or end of your visit to this country. It is situated just 20 km. southeast of Győr, on a hillside with views across the valley to the Sokoro hills. On the edge of the village, it is just below the 1,000 year old Benedictine monastery, which has guided tours. The 75 numbered, hedged pitches (30 with 10A electricity) are on terraces, generally fairly level but reached by steepish concrete access roads, with many trees and plants around. The sanitary facilities are quite satisfactory with a small building near reception and a larger unit half-way up the site. They provide a total of 6 controllable, curtained, hot showers with curtained communal changing, 12 washbasins also with hot water and 8 British style WCs. Hot water is available for dishwashing and laundry.

continued overleaf

HUNGARY

513 Panorama Camping (continued)

There are benches provided and a small, grass terrace below reception from where you can purchase beer, local wine and soft drinks, etc. Occasional big stews are cooked in high season, otherwise there is a good value restaurant 400 m. away in the village and a shop for essentials at 150 m.

How to find it: From no. 82 Györ - Veszprém road turn to Pannonhalma at Ecs. Site is well signed - the final approach road is fairly steep.

General Details: Open 1 May - 30 Sept. Shops and restaurant close by in village. Small children's play area. Table tennis. Rest room with TV. Bar and meals (1/6-15/9). Money exchange. Cooking facilities. Laundry. Chemical disposal. Rooms to let. No English spoken.

Charges 1998: Per adult Forints 400; child (2-14 yrs) 200; pitch 600; electricity 300; local tax 100. Credit cards accepted.

Reservations: Advisable for high season - write in German. Address: 9090 Pannonhalma, Fenyvesalza 4/A. Tel: 96/471 240.

511 Dömös Camping, Dömös, nr Esztergom

Pleasantly situated site on the Danube Bend between river and hills.

The area of the Danube Bend is a major tourist attraction and here at Dömös is a modern, friendly, peaceful site with large pitches and easy access. The Danube is just over 50 m. away and quite fast flowing. With Budapest just 45 km, Esztergom - the ancient capital of Hungary 15 km. and the small town of Visegrad, with its impressive cliff fortress close by, this could make an ideal base from which to explore the whole area. There are about 100 quite large pitches, of which 60 have 6A electricity, in sections on flat grass, numbered and divided by small plants and some with shade from mature trees. Opposite the smart reception which has an under-cover terrace, is a small cafe, also with a terrace, and a little further along is the modern, long, brick built sanitary building. This is tiled and has sliding doors. Beyond the laundry are very satisfactory ample, large showers with individual changing and pre-mixed hot water, open washbasins and then toilets (British style). At the top of the site is an inviting open-air swimming pool (20 x 10 m.) with a grass lying out area and tiny children's pool. Alongside is a large bar with pool tables and table football, beside which is a dishwashing and cooking area (free). A small children's play area on grass is here, just before the 7 self-contained accommodation units for hire.

How to find it: Site is between the village and the Danube off road 11 Esztergom - Visegrad - Szentendre.

General Details: Open 1 May - 15 Sept, as is cafe. Bar (15/5-1/9)/ Shop (1/6-30/9). Swimming pool (all season). Village facilities 300 m. Bicycle hire. Fishing 50 m. Tennis adjacent. Riding school 1 km. Mountain walking tours. Laundry. Chemical disposal. English spoken.

Charges 1998: Per pitch, caravan and car Forints 550; car 160; tent 450; adult 480; child (2-14 yrs) 350; electricity 300; local tax 200. Payment in cash only.

Reservations: Not normally made, but may for British visitors. Address: 2027 Dömös, Dunapart (winter: Dömös Kft, 2500 Esztergom, Bottyán J. u. 11). Tel: 26/397 484 (winter 33/315 740). FAX: 33/414 800.

AR Discount
Less 10% on pitch fees

516 Camping Zugligeti Niche, Budapest

Satisfactory, friendly site with easy access to Budapest.

Car parking is as difficult in Budapest as it is in any large town - Zugligeti Niche is the nearest camp to the tourist centre of the town with good public transport links. The site started life as a tram terminus and when this use was discontinued, it was turned into an acceptable camping site. The narrow entrance has an old tram car on either side, one used as the reception bureau, the other for snacks and basic food supplies. The entrance road, with hardstanding caravan places on either side, passes under a road bridge to similar pitches further up. Small terrace clearings have been made amidst the trees on the steep hill to one side of the caravan area. These are only suitable for small tents and there is parking nearby for cars. The old tram station is now an attractive restaurant. The whole situation is a quiet one near the chair lift to the summit of the Janos mountain. Sightseeing tours are organised. This is a pleasant, friendly site although the sanitary arrangements are not quite up to our normal standards, although hot water is free and toilets are British style.

How to find it: Take the Budakeszi exit from the Austria - Budapest M1 motorway, from where it is well signed at all junctions (look for squirrel logo). From the M0 ring road take M1 exit, then through Budakeszi.

General Details: Open all year. Restaurant. Kiosk (with basic supplies). Chemical disposal. Supermarket 500 m. Swimming pool and other entertainments at Margarit Island, 20 mins. by public transport. English speaking owner who welcomes British guests.

Charges 1997: Per person Ft. 600; child 300; car 500; caravan or motorcaravan 1,300; tent 400; m/cycle 400; electricity 300; dog 300; local tax 50. Payment in cash only.

Reservations: Necessary for August; write to site. Address: Camping Zugligeti Niche, Zugligeti ut. 101, 1121 Budapest. Tel: 01/200 83 46. FAX: as phone.

HUNGARY

515 Fortuna Camping, Törökbálint, nr Budapest

Pretty site close to bus terminal for city centre.

If you are elderly, a courtesy minibus will take you the kilometre to the bus stop for Budapest (journey time 25 minutes) or you may get a ride in the owner's new horse drawn carriage! On your return, there is a large, modern, terraced restaurant with very reasonable prices to save the weary traveller from cooking. An open-air swimming pool, open June - Sept. will also help you to cool off. Fortuna is pleasantly situated in a small valley, with over 100 different trees providing some shade. Concrete and gravel access roads lead to the terraces where there are 120 individual pitches, all with electricity (16A), on mostly sloping ground. They are hedged in the area to the right, otherwise open. Two new sanitary buildings have now been completed which include facilities for disabled people. In the centre of the site is a small, modern building with WCs. Hot water is free. The English speaking owner, Herr Csaba Szücs and his family are keen to make your stay as pleasant as possible and are very helpful with information about the Budapest public transport system.

How to find it: From the M1 Györ - Budapest, exit for Törökbálint following signs for town and then site. Fortuna is beyond and far better than the Flora site. Also accessible from the M7 Budapest - Balaton road.

General Details: Open all year. Restaurant and bar (1/5-30/10). Shop (15/6-31/8 or essentials from reception, order bread previous day). Swimming pool (15/6-31/8). Small children's play area. Excursions organised. Chemical disposal. Motorcaravan services. English spoken.

Charges 1998: Per person DM 6.00; child (4-14 yrs) 4.00; pitch 9.00; electricity 4.00.

Reservations: Recommended for high season. Address: 2045 Törökbálint. Tel: 23/335 364. FAX: 23/339 697.

518 Jumbo Camping, Üröm, Budapest

Modern, thoughtfully developed site in northwest outskirts of Budapest.

On a hillside, with attractive views of the Buda hills and with public transport to the city from 500 m. away, this is a pleasant and comfortable, small site (despite the name). It is possible to park outside the short, steepish entrance which has a chain across. Reception, where you will be given a comprehensive English language information sheet, doubles as a cafe/bar area and bread orders are also taken here. The concrete and gravel access roads lead shortly to 55 terraced pitches of varying size, with hardstanding for car/caravan wheels as well as large hardstandings for motorhomes. All pitches have 6A electricity (may require long leads) and there are some caravan pitches with water and waste water also. They are mostly divided by small hedges and the whole area is fenced. The sanitary facilities are most satisfactory, with large, controllable showers (communal changing) with free hot water also to the washbasins. British style WCs. There is also dishwashing undercover and a terrace with chairs and tables. A small open-air swimming pool is beside the small children's play area.

How to find it: Site is signed on roads to Budapest - nos. 11 from Szentendre and 10 from Komaron. It is also approachable via Györ on M1/E60 and Lake Balaton on M7/E71.

General Details: Open 1 April - 31 Oct. Washing machine, iron and cooking facilities on payment. Cafe where bread, milk and butter available. Shop and restaurant 500 m. Barbecue area. Swimming pool (10/6-10/9). Bus to city 500 m. every 30 minutes. Chemical disposal. English spoken.

Charges 1998: Per pitch DM 2.50 - 8.00, acc. to size and season; adult 5.00; child (3-14 yrs) 2.50 - 3.00; electricity 2.00; dog 2.00. Payable in cash only (Forints).

Reservations: Write to site. Address: 2096 Üröm, Budakalászi ut 23-25. Tel: 26/351 251. FAX: as phone.

522 Pelsöczy Camping, Tokaj, nr Nyiregyhaza

Relaxing, shady, riverside site at small town.

From the middle of June to the middle of September, this site gets quite busy, but either side of these dates it is quiet and very relaxing. Set on the banks of the wide River Tisza, the level grass pitches, about 60 in number, are close together and narrow but quite long, off a hard circular access road so siting should be quite easy. All the pitches have electricity and there is much shade. Basic but clean, the sanitary facilities have external entry WCs (British style) and curtained showers with communal undressing. They are located near the entrance, where there is also the high season reception, shop and restaurant. At other times, site yourself and a gentleman will call during the evening to collect the fee. Shops for basics outside the main season are in the town over the bridge, a 600 m. walk. There may well be some day-time noise from watersports on the river but it is very quiet by night. This is a useful base for visiting northeast Hungary, not far from the Ukraine and Romania.

How to find it: Tokaj is east of Miskolc and north of Debrecen. Site is just south of the river bridge on road no. 38. (Note: beware the noisy campsite signed on the other side of the road).

General Details: Open 15 April - 10 Oct. Shop and restaurant (15 June - 15 Sept). Town 600 m. River sports available. No English spoken (German is).

Charges: Not available - probably modest.

Reservations: Advised for high season, but in German - otherwise arrive early. Address: 3910 Tokaj, Pf.36. Tel: 47/352 626.

Heritage Classic European Rescueline

VEHICLE BREAKDOWN AND RECOVERY
PLUS PERSONAL INSURANCE COVER.

Originally only available for owners of classic cars
- now available to readers of
The Alan Rogers Guide at a specially reduced rate
including a 10% Discount
AND no limit to the age of your car.

Exclusively arranged with
Bishopsgate Insurance in association with
Green Flag National Breakdown and
only available from

Bishopsgate

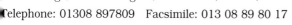

DENEWAY GUIDES & TRAVEL LTD
Chesil Lodge, West Bexington, Dorchester, Dorset, DT2 9DG.
Telephone: 01308 897809   Facsimile: 013 08 89 80 17

"Heritage Classic European Rescueline"

If your car breaks down or you are involved in an accident, a free phone call to Green Flag National Breakdown's European Control Centre will bring rapid assistance. Their English speaking controllers will be able to pinpoint your position and brief the nearest approved garage or agent so you will soon be on your way.

Not only does Heritage Classic European Rescueline provide an excellent breakdown assistance service, but it also provides comprehensive insurance cover for you and your passengers.

Summary of Vehicle Breakdown Cover			Summary of Personal Insurance Cover		
Cover Before Commencement of Travel	To provide a replacement vehicle if your vehicle is lost through breakdown or accident up to 7 days prior to departure	Up to £750	Cancellation and Curtailment	Provides Insurance cover for holiday cancellations from the moment the premium is paid and for unused travel and accommodation not used if you have to curtail your holiday	Up to £3,000*
Roadside Assistance and Towing	Most breakdowns can be repaired quickly at the roadside although occasionally the vehicle may need to be towed to a garage	No financial limit	Medical and Other Expenses	Cover includes medical and hospital fees and additional accommodation charges. In the event of a medical emergency the National Breakdown Controller will contact Assistance International who will contact the relevant hospital and guarantee its charges. They will also arrange repatriation to the UK (including Air Ambulance) when necessary	Up to £2 million*
Emergency Labour Costs	Should your vehicle need repairs to enable you to continue your journey	Up to £100	Additional Hospital Benefits	This is an addition to any amount payable under "Medical and Other Expenses"	Up to £600 (£20 per day)
Location and Despatch of Any Necessary Spare Parts	Where these are not available locally (excluding their actual cost)	No financial limit	Personal Accident	To provide compensation following an accidental bodily injury	Up to £15,000
Alternative Travel Expenses Following Loss of Use of Vehicle	The cost of transporting your party to their original destination, or repatriation to the UK, or the cost of a hire car to allow you to continue your journey	No financial limit, except £750 overall if car hire is provided	Baggage	"New for Old" cover for items less than 2 years old	Up to £1,500*
Extra Accommodation Costs	While awaiting completion of local vehicle repairs	£45 per person per day	Money and Documents	Cover for loss of travel documents and money from 72 hours prior to departure	Up to £500
Vehicle Repatriation	Cost of transporting vehicle and passengers to the UK	No financial limit	Loss of Passport	Additional travel expenses incurred in replacing lost/stolen passport	Up to £250
Vehicle Collection	The additional travelling expenses for one person to collect vehicle (once overseas repairs have been completed)	Up to £600	Additional Expenses	To cover cost of travel and accommodation if your ferry or rail transporter is delayed	Up to £200
Alternative Driver	Cost of chauffeur and additional accommodation costs should only driver become incapacitated	No financial limit	Additional Accommodation	Or tent hire costs if tent becomes uninhabitable during your holiday	Up to £100
Theft	To pay for damage to your vehicle as a result of break in	Up to £175	Delay	Compensation if your ferry crossing is delayed of £20 per 12 hours	Up to £60
Legal Expenses	To cover costs of providing legal defence or in pursuing claims against third parties following a road traffic accident	Up to £25,000	Personal Liability	If you are held to be legally liable for injury or damage to other people or their property, cover is provided to pay for damages and claimants costs and expenses	Up to £1 million
Advance of Funds/Customs Duty	An advance of funds to act as security for bail or to overcome any Customs Duty claim	Up to £4,000	Legal Expenses	To cover cost of pursuing a claim against a third party whilst on holiday	Up to £25,000
				*Excesses: The first £25 of each and every claim per insured is excluded	

Great Value Vehicle Breakdown & Recovery *plus* Personal Insurance Cover

Period of Cover	Vehicle Breakdown	Personal Insurance Adult	Personal Insurance Child*
Cost of Heritage Classic European Rescueline			
1 Day	£19.95	£4.95	£3.45
2 Days	£19.95	£5.95	£3.95
3 Days	£20.95	£6.95	£4.45
4 Days	£21.95	£7.95	£4.95
5 Days	£23.95	£8.95	£5.45
6 Days	£25.95	£9.95	£5.95
7 Days	£27.95	£10.95	£6.45
8 Days	£29.95	£11.95	£6.95
9 Days	£31.95	£12.95	£7.45
10 Days	£32.95	£13.95	£7.95
11 Days	£33.95	£14.95	£8.45
12 Days	£34.95	£15.95	£8.95
13 Days	£35.95	£16.95	£9.45
14 Days	£36.95	£17.95	£9.95
15 Days	£37.95	£18.95	£10.45
16 Days	£38.95	£19.95	£10.95
17 Days	£39.95	£21.95	£11.45
18 Days	£40.95	£21.95	£11.95
Each Additional Week	£8.95	£5.95	£3.95
Caravan/TrailerSupp.	£12.55	-	-
U.K. & EIRE	DEDUCT 40% FROM ABOVE RATES		

*Children from 4 up to 14 years. Children under 4 Free. Premiums include Insurance Premium Tax.

HERITAGE CLASSIC EUROPEAN RESCUELINE DEPARTURE PACK - Available free to all Heritage Classic European Rescueline policyholders - containing a GB sticker, useful tips on preparing your vehicle for the journey, details of documentation required for both vehicle and travellers, and a country guide to motoring abroad.

Please Note:

1. LIMITS OF COVER: Each Section of the insurance has an overall limit per Insured Person, but please note that other limits within the section may apply. For example, the overall limit under the Baggage Section is £1,500 but there is a single item limit of £250, and in respect of valuables as defined under this section a limit of £300 applies.

2. Heritage Classic European Rescueline contains a "7 DAY REFUND GUARANTEE". If the insurance does not meet your needs please return it to the issuing agent within 7 days (and before your date of departure) and the premium will be refunded in full.

3. This insurance is designed to cover most hazards which may affect your holiday, but it does contain certain conditions and exclusions. These are detailed in the full policy wording.

IMPORTANT: This leaflet only gives a summary of the cover provided by Heritage Classic European Rescueline. You are strongly advised to read the full wording of this insurance as it constitutes your "contract of insurance". Full details of the policy wording are available on request but in any event will be provided when you purchase the insurance.

HOW TO APPLY

FOR IMMEDIATE COVER - TELEPHONE 01308 897809 OR FAX 013 08 89 80 17 - ACCESS AND VISA ACCEPTED OR COMPLETE AND RETURN THE APPLICATION FORM OVERLEAF AND SEND IT WITH YOUR CHEQUE TO:

DENEWAY GUIDES & TRAVEL LTD
CHESIL LODGE, WEST BEXINGTON, DORCHESTER, DORSET, DT2 9DG.
TELEPHONE: 01308 897809   FACSIMILE: 013 08 89 80 17

Bishopsgate

HERITAGE CLASSIC EUROPEAN RESCUELINE
APPLICATION FORM

NAME OF APPLICANT (Mr/Mrs/Miss/Ms) ....

ADDRESS..

.... Post Code ....

TEL. NO ....,......... WORK ....

PERIOD OF TRAVEL............................. DAYS COMMENCING ON ....

AGE
(if under 16)

NAMES OF ALL PASSENGERS IN VEHICLE (State Mr/Mrs/Miss/Ms)

1 APPLICANT.. ....

2 ....

3 ....

4 ....

5 ....

6 ....

VEHICLE DETAILS

MAKE & MODEL...

REG. NO...EST. VALUE..YEAR...........................

MOTOR INSURERS...EXPIRY DATE............................

ARE YOU A MEMBER OF A CAR CLUB ....

CARAVAN/TRAILER DETAILS

MAKE & MODEL ....

VALUE .... YEAR ....

COUNTRIES TO BE VISITED

....

....

COVER REQUIRED

PREMIUM

Personal Travel Insurance

.... Adults @ .... each   £ ....

.... Children @ .... each   £ ....

Vehicle Breakdown Insurance   £ ....

Caravan/Trailer (if applicable)   £ ....

Less 10% Alan Rogers Guide Readers Discount   £ ....

Total £ ....

- If personal insurance is taken the driver & all passengers must be covered.
- Please make cheques payable to: **Deneway Guides & Travel Ltd.**
- Please debit my Access ❑   Visa ❑   card (please tick)

Expiry date...........................Card No..Signature.................................

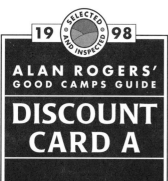

This voucher entitles the holder to the relevant discounts or special offers at those campsites featured in this guide which have a small Alan Rogers logo beneath their Site Report. This section of the voucher should be retained by the holder, but made available for inspection at the campsite for the purpose of verifying your entitlement to the relevant discount or offer

VOUCHER NUMBER

6024

E98/

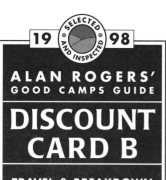

This voucher entitles the holder to a discount of 10% on Travel & Breakdown Insurance arrangements made via this Guide, as advertised between pages 160 and 161. To arrange cover please complete the proposal and send this, together with the appropriate premium and this voucher to: Deneway Guides & Travel Ltd., Chesil Lodge, West Bexington, Dorchester, DT2 9DG - Fax 01308 898017. A proposal form and the discount voucher will need to be completed and sent to Deneway Guides & Travel along with payment for the relevant premium in all circumstances except in very urgent cases (ie those within seven days of departure) when we can arrange cover via telephone or (preferably) via fax

VOUCHER NUMBER

6024

E98/

This voucher entitles the holder to a 5% discount on caravan or motorcaravan insurance arranged through Bakers of Cheltenham. Please complete the enquiry form on pages 365 and 366, and send it, together with this voucher, to Bakers of Cheltenham, Freepost GR1604, The Quadrangle, Imperial Square, Cheltenham, Gloucestershire, GL50 1BR

VOUCHER NUMBER

6024

E98/

CARD A CAMPSITE DISCOUNT VOUCHER

Valid 01 Jan - 31 Dec 1998

NAME:

ADDRESS:

SIGNATURE:

Save Mon A 🚐

CARD B TRAVEL & BREAKDOWN INSURANCE DISCOUNT VOUCHER

Valid 01 Jan - 31 December 1998

NAME:

ADDRESS:

SIGNATURE:

Save Mon A 🚐

CARD C
CARAVAN OR MOTORCARAVAN INSURANCE DISCOUNT VOUCHER

Valid 01 Jan - 31 December 1998

NAME:

ADDRESS:

SIGNATURE:

Save Mo A 🚐

ALAN ROGERS'
GOOD CAMPS GUIDE

DISCOUNT CARD D

**CARAVAN & CAMPING
SERVICE DISCOUNT
VOUCHER**

VALID 01 JAN - 31 DEC 1998

This voucher entitles the holder to a refund of the full cover price of this guide (£9.99) when booking a travel inclusive holiday arrangement with the Caravan & Camping Service, whose advertisement appears on page 360. To claim your refund, this voucher should be sent to the Camping & Caravan Service, 69 Westbourne Grove, London W2 4UJ when making your booking with them

VOUCHER NUMBER

E98/ 6077

Save Money!

ALAN ROGERS'
GOOD CAMPS GUIDE

DISCOUNT CARD E

**SITES ABROAD
DISCOUNT VOUCHER**

VALID 01 JAN - 31 DEC 1998

This voucher entitles the holder to reclaim the cover price of this Alan Rogers Good Camps Guide 1998 when making a booking with Sites Abroad. Please send the completed voucher to Sites Abroad, Canute Court, Toft Road, Knutsford, Cheshire WA16 0NL, when making your booking

VOUCHER NUMBER

E98/ 6077

Save Money!

ALAN ROGERS'
GOOD CAMPS GUIDE

DISCOUNT CARD F

**CAMPING CHEQUES
DISCOUNT VOUCHER**

VALID 01 JAN - 31 DEC 1998

This card entitles the holder to a FREE COPY of the 1998 Camping Cheques Catalogue. Please send the completed card to Camping Cheques, Canute House, Toft Road, Knutsford, Cheshire WA16 0NL

VOUCHER NUMBER

E98/ 6077

Save Money!

ALAN ROGERS'
GOOD CAMPS GUIDE

DISCOUNT CARD G

**TRACK TOURS
DISCOUNT VOUCHER**

VALID 01 JAN - 31 DEC 1998

This card entitles the holder to a 15% discount on Track Tours arrangements at the Le Mans 24 Hour Race, as described in Track Tours advertisement in the Motorsport colour section

VOUCHER NUMBER

E98/ 6077

Save Money!

CARD D CARAVAN & CAMPING SERVICE DISCOUNT VOUCHER
Valid 01 Jan -31 Dec 1998

NAME:

ADDRESS:

SIGNATURE:

Save Mon

CARD E SITES ABROAD DISCOUNT VOUCHER
Valid 01 Jan -31 Dec 1998

NAME:

ADDRESS:

SIGNATURE:

Save Mon

CARD F CAMPING CHEQUES DISCOUNT VOUCHER
Valid 01 Jan -31 Dec 1998

NAME:

ADDRESS:

SIGNATURE:

Save Mon

Haynes
THE BOOK ®

CARD G TRACK TOURS DISCOUNT VOUCHER
Valid 01 Jan -31 Dec 1998

NAME:

ADDRESS:

SIGNATURE:

Save Mon

520 Autós Caraván Camping, Eger

Large, city site in attractive touring area of northern Hungary.

The city of Eger and its surroundings (including the very attractive Bukk mountain area between Eger and Miskolc) provide much for the tourist to see, indeed far too much to list here, but reception will provide lots of information for you. Most of the city attractions are quite close together, with good public transport from close to the site, which is just 2.5 km. from the centre. The site is large, with over 180 pitches, all with electricity (10A). They are on gently sloping hardstanding with much grass, lots of shade and tarred access roads and there is a separate tent area. The quietest part is at the reception end for, at the other side of the camping area, there are many bungalows and dormitory accommodation much used by young people. However, it is quiet at night thanks to 24 hour security patrols. The sanitary facilities are rather basic, with a couple of toilets behind reception, a `portacabin' style facility to the right (nearest for many pitches) with cold water washbasins and a large block at the end of the camping area which was in need of a little maintenance when seen (used by the youngsters) with dishwashing and chemical disposal facilities. A reader recommends the facilities up the steps by the tent area, but this was not open during our stay at the end of May. At the far end of the park is an area with three outlets selling drinks (local wine), snacks and ices, beyond which is a large restaurant and another set in a cave. There are shops just outside the site entrance.

How to find it: Site is in the northern outskirts of the city on the west side of road no. 25. It is well signed (not usual camp signs at entrance) by a Shell station, just before the last high-rise flats.

General Details: Open 15 April - 15 October. Restaurant. Bar. Snacks. Money exchange (including travellers cheques). English spoken.

Charges guide: Per person DM 4.00, child under 6 free; caravan 8.00; motorcaravan 6.00; tent (2 person) 4.00; electricity incl. except for tents (2.00). Discounts: 2nd night 20%, 4th free; 7 nights for 69.00. Student card 20%.

Reservations: Probably not necessary. Address: 3300 Eger, Rákóczi ut 79. Tel: 36/410 558. FAX: 36/411 768. E-mail: egertour@mailagria.hu. Internet: http://www.agria.hu./egertourist.

524 Dorcas Centre and Camping, Debrecen

Friendly, welcoming Christian `Aid Organisation' site.

Debrecen is an interesting old town, close to the Hortobagy National Park and convenient if you are looking for a break travelling to Romania or the Ukraine. Dorcas is a Dutch Christian organisation and the campsite provides holidays for special causes - indeed, while we were there, 40 children arrived from Chernobyl for their first trip abroad. The site is about 10 km. from Debrecen in a forest location, fenced and covered with trees. The 60 flat, grassy pitches, off tarmac access roads, are arranged in four groups. Some pitches are divided by hedges, others marked out by trees and all have electricity available (6A). There is room in the large tenting area for more units, also with electricity, if necessary. The large sanitary building is tiled and of a rather open design. It is situated between the tenting area and the main pitch areas and is of reasonable quality with free hot water to the washbasins and controllable, large, curtained showers (external changing), British WCs; also facilities for dishwashing and laundry (key at reception). There is a very pleasant restaurant and terrace offering very good value meals (menu in English) and a shop for basics. Small swimming pool and several items of children's play equipment next to it on grass. Through the site is an area for walks and a lake for fishing.

How to find it: From Debrecen take road no. 47 south for 4 km. then left towards Hosszupalyi for 6 km. Site is signed on the right.

General Details: Open 1 May - 30 Sept. Shop. Restaurant. Swimming pool (June-Aug). Lake and riding nearby. Good walks. Church services (in English) fortnightly or more often if requested. Bicycle hire. English spoken.

Charges guide: Per unit incl. 2 adults and 2 children DM 17.50. Credit cards accepted.

Reservations: Probably unnecessary. Address: 4002 Debrecen, Pf.146. Tel: 52/441 119. FAX: as phone.

HUNGARY

526 Jonathermal Motel-Camping, Kiskunmajsa, nr Szeged

Large, well run site with marvellous indoor and outdoor pool complex.

Situated 3 km. to the north of the town of Kiskunmajsa, a few kilometres west of road no. 5 (E75) from Budapest (140 km.) to Szeged (35 km.) this is one of the better Hungarian campsites. The camping area is large, reached by tarred access roads and the unmarked pitches are located in several areas around the motel and sanitary buildings. Some shade is available and more trees are growing. All the 120 large pitches have 10A electricity and are set on flat grass where you place the pitch number allocated to you. Reception is part of the smart bar and rest room just to the right of the entrance. Sanitary facilities are in one block over to the left, providing a sufficient number of toilets (British style), washbasins and showers (with the usual communal changing area), plus dishwashing and washing machine (key from reception). All was kept clean during our visit. A kiosk sells bread (to order), fresh fruit and vegetables, groceries, stamps and postcards. The pool complex is accessed via a path through the site fence which leads firstly to the entrance to the fishing lake, then past the restaurant. Entrance to the complex costs 300 forints for adults, 200 for children (weekly tickets available) which gives you free run of a huge 100 x 70 m. open air pool with a beach along one side, the indoor pool, children's pool, thermal, sauna and cold dip. In addition there is an open air thermal pool, a children's playground with carved wooden animals, plus swings on grass, giant chess, volleyball, tennis and minigolf plus various places to eat and drink. Massage is available on payment. This professionally run site is well placed for visiting Szeged, Csongrad or Szolnok, as well as being close to the borders with Romania and the former Yugoslavia.

How to find it: From the no. 5 (E75) Budapest - Szeged road take the Kiskunmajsa exit and site is well signed 3 km. north of the town. Do not use the unmade road via Csengelo to the northeast of the town.

General Details: Open all year. Kiosk on site for bread, etc. (shop opposite entrance, 120 m). Restaurant by pool complex, others near. Large swimming and thermal complex with other facilities (as above). Fishing (day permits available). Bicycle hire. Chemical disposal. Motel rooms for rent. German spoken.

Charges 1997: Per person DM 4.00 - 5.00; child (6-14 yrs) 1.00 - 2.00; pitch 3.00 - 4.00; tent 1.50 - 2.00; electricity 3.50. Less 5-10% for longer stays.

Reservations: Possibly necessary mid-July - mid-Aug. Address: 6120 Kiskunmajsa, Kokut 26. Tel: 77/481 855. FAX: 77/481 013.

AR Discount

Less 10%

530 Kék-Duna Camping Dunaföldvár

Pleasant site on the banks of the Danube.

Dunaföldvár is a most attractive town of 10,000 people and you are in the heart of it in just two or three minutes by foot but, as a 'town site', Kék-Duna is remarkably peaceful and easily reached via the wide towpath on the west bank of the Danube. Apart from the obvious attractions of the river, with a large island opposite and pleasant walks, the ancient town has a most interesting museum, with the 'Burg', with a genuine dungeon and cells, Roman relics and with a panoramic view of the town and river from its top floor. There are too many places of interest within easy reach to list here, but we thoroughly endorse our reader's recommendation of this site. It is small, fenced all round and locked at night, with flat concrete access roads to 40 pitches. All have 3A electricity, the first half being open, the remainder well shaded. The modern, tiled sanitary building has a nicely decorated ladies' section and offers 10 curtained, controllable, free showers with communal changing. British style WCs. The rest of the facilities are also of above average standard. Small shop and café from mid June (otherwise it is a short walk into the town), washing machine and dishwashing (outside with cold water). Thermal swimming pool 200 m.

How to find it: From no. 6 Budapest - Pecs road take exit at Dunaföldvár for Kecskemed road no. 52, and follow until slip road on right which leads on to the riverside towpath. Site is well signed.

General Details: Open 15 April - 30 Sept. Shop and café (from mid June), town shops close. Fishing permits available. Washing machine. Excursion information. English speaking receptionist some days. Bungalows for hire.

Charges guide: Per adult Forints 200 - 340; child 150 - 180; pitch 480 - 580; tent and car 290 - 390; electricity 100; dog 150.

Reservations: Advised for July/Aug. or arrive early. Address: 7020 Dunaföldvár, Häsök Tere 12. Tel: 75/341 529.

504 Autós 1 Camping, Zamárdi, nr Slófok

Large site with own direct access to Lake Balaton.

If you have young children or non-swimmers in your party, then the southern shores of the lake at this site are ideal as you can walk out for nearly 1 km. before the water rises to more than a metre in depth. It is a large site with 545 pitches, most with 6A electricity, and there must be the possibility of noise in high season, although it was peaceful during our visit in early June. There are many tall trees and the more attractive pitches are near the lakeside, some unshaded ones by the water. The rest, in a large central area which comprises the majority of the site, are flat ones on grass. They are hedged and vary from small to quite large. A tent area is at the back of the site, adjacent to three modern, tiled sanitary buildings (plus an old one to the right of the entrance). *continued overleaf*

162

504 Autós 1 Camping (continued)

Free hot water to push-button showers with private changing and warm to washbasins with single taps. British style WCs (no paper). Satisfactory dishwashing and laundry facilities (key from reception). Other amenities include a restaurant and a soft drinks and ice cream bar by the entrance and a bar further in, all with terraces. A shop is only 50 m. Plenty of children's wooden play equipment is on sandy grass by the lake. Next door is a large water slide area and boats for hire.

How to find it: Exit road no. 7/E71 between Balatonföldvár and Siófok towards Tihany, and the site is well signed.

General Details: Open 17 May - 8 Sept. Shop adjacent. Restaurant (from June). Lake swimming, fishing and non-powered boating. Money exchange. Bath (key from reception). Chemical disposal. Table tennis.

Charges guide: Per person DM 5.10 - 7.80; child 2.55 - 3.90; pitch 11.10 - 17.00; tent and car 7.40 - 11.40; electricity 1.50; dog 5.10 - 7.80; local tax (over 18 yrs) 1.00 - 1.50.

Reservations: Write to site. Address: 8261 Zamárdi. Tel: 84/348 863 FAX: 84/348 931. When closed write to Siotour AG Hauptbüro, 8600 Siófok, Szabadság tér 6. Tel: 84/310 900. FAX: 84/310 009.

503 Panorama Camping, Cserszegtomaj, nr Hévíz

Peaceful, hillside site near west end of Lake Balaton.

Sites around Lake Balaton generally have the disadvantage of being close to the main road and/or the railway, as well as being extremely busy in high season. Panorama is popular too, but is essentially a quiet site and also has the benefit of extensive views from the flat, grass terraces. Only the young or very fit are recommended to take the higher levels with the best views of all. There are just 50 pitches varying in size from fairly small to quite large (100 sq.m.), all with 10A electricity, with the lower terraces having fairly easy access. The site is a sun-trap and there is not much shade from the trees. Reception is to the left of the entrance and here also is a small shop and a delightful restaurant, with terrace, offering really good value meals. A little way up is the very satisfactory, tiled and heated sanitary building which has free hot water to large, controllable showers (communal changing), washbasins, dishwashing and British style toilets. Lake Balaton (7 km.), whilst at Hévíz is the famous, large, thermal, warm water lake. The friendly proprietors speak no English but are keen to welcome British visitors and have a dictionary. You will probably find German and or Dutch visitors who would assist if you speak no German at all.

How to find it: Site is 2 km. north of Hévíz on road to Sümeg. Long, hard access road with a large sign.

General Details: Open 1 April - 31 October. Shop (Mon - Sat, 07.30 - 10.00). Restaurant with bar. Washing machine. Ladies' hairdresser. Massage. Many walking and cycling opportunities.

Charges guide: Per person DM 3.50; child (under 14) 2.00; pitch up to 10.00; electricity 3.00.

Reservations: Advisable from mid-July - mid-August, and made in German. Address: 8372 Cserszegtomaj, Panorama Köz 1. Tel: 83/314 412.

508 Diana Camping, Aszófö, nr Balatonfüred

Large, quiet, friendly site in forest near Lake Balaton.

This very large site of about 12 hectares was developed many years ago as a retreat for the 'party faithful'. Now just 4 hectares are used by Mr and Mrs Keller-Toth, who have leased it from the Balatontourist organisation. There is, naturally, much woodland around which you may wander. There are 27 hedged pitches of 120 sq.m. (where two 60 sq.m. ones have been joined) on grass. Many have shade from trees, as have about 65 smaller individual ones. The remainder are amongst the trees which mark them out. There is no exact number of pitches, but about 200 units are taken in all, with 150 electrical connections (2 pin, 6 or 10A) on sloping ground. The toilet facilities are old but kept very clean. The shower block across the path is open 6.30-10.30 am. and 4.30-10 pm. The very smart ladies' section has large, push-button showers with seat, divider and private dressing, whilst the facilities for men are older (with communal changing). Washbasins, for both men and women, are older with just two with hot water for each and many with cold only. At the back of the block is the entrance to a splendid, children's washroom (key from reception), with 3 shower/baths 2 designed for handicapped children. Well stocked shop, with the laundry just beyond (key from reception). A large kitchen has 6 cookers but the cold water dishwashing is probably the least attractive area. The fair-sized restaurant has tables, benches and flowers outside. In front of this area is under cover table tennis and the play area where animation is organised in high season..

How to find it: From road 71 on the north side of the lake, turn towards Azsófö just west of Balatonfüred, through the village and follow the signs for about 1 km. along access road (bumpy in places).

General Details: Open 26 April - 28 Sept. Shop (open 08.00-17.00 low season or 22.00 high season) Restaurant (all season). Children's play area, with animation in high season. Volleyball. Tennis. Table tennis. Post box and telephones. Many walking opportunities. Lake 3 km. Chemical disposal.

Charges 1997: Per caravan, car, electricity and incl. 3 persons DM 16.00 - 20.00, acc. to season; tent 2.70 - 3.00; motorcaravan 6.20 - 7.40; person 2.60 - 3.20; child (6-14 yrs) 1.30 - 1.60; dog 1.30 - 1.60. Local tax (over 18 yrs) 0.80. Special rates for disabled persons. Eurocheques up to 23,000 Forints accepted.

Reservations: are possible - write to site. Address: 8241 Aszófö. Tel: 87/445 013. FAX: as phone.

HUNGARY

531 Sugovica Camping, Baja

Pleasant town site near Croatian and Yugoslavian borders.

If you are exploring Southern Transdanubia or en route south, then Baja is an acceptable stop, on the east banks of the Danube. The site is on a small island, quiet and relaxed, next to the hotel which owns it, where there is a small swimming pool and a terraced restaurant. The 180 fair sized pitches (80 sq.m), all with 10A electricity and 7 with hardstandings for motorhomes, are on flat, grassy, firm ground, easily accessed from tarred roads and with some shade from the many trees. Behind reception are a small shop, TV room, laundry and a kitchen. The reasonable sanitary facilities have British style WCs and free hot water to open washbasins and showers (communal changing), all clean when seen.

How to find it: Site is on Petoti island (sziget), well signed from just southwest of the junction of roads 51 from Budapest and 55 from Szeged, the bridge being close to a cobbled town square.

General Details: Open 1 May - 30 Sept. Shop. Restaurant and swimming pool 50 m. TV room. Table tennis. Riverside walks. Fishing. Chemical disposal. Town facilities close. No English spoken.

Charges guide: Per adult Forints 270; child (6-14) 135; pitch 540; tent 360; electricity 180; dog 140.

Reservations: not made. Address: 6500 Baja. Tel: 79 321 494. FAX: 79 323 155.

509 Balatontourist Camping Füred, Balatonfüred

Large, international camp on lake, with a wide range of facilities.

This is a holiday village rather than just a campsite, pleasantly decorated with flowers and shrubs, with a very wide range of shops, restaurants, fast food bars and sporting activities. Directly on the lake with 800 m. of access for boats and bathing, it has a large, grassy lying out area, a small beach area and various watersports. Mature trees cover about two thirds of the site giving shade, with the remaining area being open. The 1,036 pitches of 60-120 sq.m. and all with electricity (4A), are on either side of hard access roads on which pitch numbers are painted. Along the main road, which runs through the camp, are shops and kiosks, with the main bar/restaurant and terrace overlooking the lake. This building also has a 4-lane bowling alley and video games room. Close by is a street of fast food bars, about 10 in all, with outdoor terraces under trees. Other bars and restaurants are dotted around the camp. A wide range of sporting activities is available, the most spectacular of which is a water ski drag lift Five toilet blocks are at various points around the site. The oldest are showing signs of age, while the two smart, modern blocks have free hot water in the showers (communal changing), with cold water only in washbasins. British style WCs. Good security. Many coach trips and pleasure cruises are organised.

How to find it: Site is just south of Balatonfüred, on the Balatonfüred - Tihany road and is well signed. Gates closed 1-3 pm. except Sat/Sun.

General Details: Open 11 April - 11 Oct. 27,000 sq.m. Numerous bars, restaurants, cafes and food bars (1/5-15/9). Supermarket. Stalls and kiosks with wide range of goods, souvenirs, photo processing. Money exchange. Duty free shop (hard currency). Hairdresser, etc. Sauna and solarium. Post office. Fishing. Water ski lift. Windsurf school. Children's play area and 'bouncy castle'. Bicycle hire. Dodgem cars. Pedaloes. Tennis. Minigolf. Fitness centre. Video games room. Bowling. Washing machines. Chemical disposal. No dogs are allowed. Bungalows to rent.

Charges 1997: (Prices in DM, payable in Forints). Per caravan pitch incl. 3 persons and electricity 70 sq.m. 25.00 - 35.90, 100 sq.m. 28.20 - 42.50; tent pitch (60 sq.m.) incl. 3 persons 18.00 - 27.90; extra person (max. 6) 4.00 - 5.40; local tax 1.60 pp over 18. Credit cards accepted.

Reservations: Write to site. Address: 8230 Balatonfüred. Tel: 87/343-823. FAX: 87/342-341. E-mail: cfured@ balatontourist.hu.

AR Discount
Ask at site
for details

507 Balatontourist Camping Kristóf, Balatonalmádi

Small site with excellent toilet facilities.

This is a delightfully small site with just 33 pitches and many tall trees. Square in shape, the generously sized pitches are on either side of hard roads, on level grass with some shade and 4A electricity. The site lies between the main road and railway line and the lake. There is no direct access to the lake, but a public lakeside area adjoins the camp, and site fees include the entry price. This is a neat little site with a kiosk for breakfast and dinner (steaks, etc) drinks, bread, milk and ice cream, with village shops and supermarket just 50 m. away. The excellent toilet facility is part of the reception building, with British WCs and free hot water in the washbasins and showers (own changing). Good English is spoken. Balatonalmádi is at the northern end of the lake, well placed for excursions around the lake or to Budapest. A small, friendly site without the bustle of the larger camps.

How to find it: Site is on road no. 71 at Balatonalmádi, between the railway line and the lake and is signed.

General Details: Open 11 April - 11 Oct. 1,200 sq.m. Meals from kiosk. Children's playground. Tennis. Laundry room. Kitchen. Sitting room with TV. Chemical disposal. Bungalows for rent.

Charges 1997: (Prices in D.Marks, payable in Forints). Per pitch DM 12.00 - 20.00; adult 4.00 - 6.00; child 2.00 - 4.00; local tax 1.10 pp over 18. Credit cards accepted.

Reservations: Essential July - 20 Aug. Write for form. Address: 8220 Balatonalmádi. Tel: 88/338-902. FAX: as phone. When closed: Balatontourist, 8201 Veszprém, POB 128. Tel: 88/426-277. FAX: 88/426-874. E-mail: ckristof@balatontourist.hu.

AR Discount
Ask at site
for details

IRELAND

The Republic of Ireland, with its green, mist shrouded countryside, its loughs and wild indented coastline, must be explored slowly to enjoy the hospitality and savour the locals love of music - you can expect to find traditional music sessions in the pubs of all the towns of any size along the west coast. Indeed the west coast draws most visitors, be it to visit the mystical lakes and glens of Donegal, Galway and the Aran Islands, or the dramatic peaks of the Ring of Kerry, but Dublin with its mix of youthfulness and tradition and the mountains and monastic ruins of County Wicklow, the cities of Cork and Waterford, are not to be missed. Suffice to say it is not only the landscape but 'the people' which brings visitors to Ireland.

Bord Failte (Irish Tourist Board), 105 New Bond Street, London W1Y OAQ

Tel: 0171 518 0800. Travel Enquiries: 0171 493 3201. Fax: 0171 493 9065

Population
3,500,000, density 50 per sq. km.

Climate
Similar to the UK but even wetter!

Language
English. The traditional tongue Gaelic (Gaeltacht) is spoken mainly in the southwest.

Currency
The Irish pound, known as the punt, divided into 100 pence. Denominations are 1, 2, 5, 10, 20, 50 pence and IR£1, notes of IR£5, 10, 20, 50 and 100.

Banks
Open Mon-Fri 10.00-12.30 and 13.30-15.00 (Thur 13.30-17.00), but note many small country towns are served by sub-offices open only certain days.

Post Offices
Main offices open Mon-Fri 09.00-17.30 and Sat 09.00-13.00. Stamps are sometimes available in shops selling postcards.

Telephone
To call the UK dial 00 44 followed by the local STD code omitting initial 0. From the UK dial 00 353 omitting the first 0 of the code plus number.

Public Holidays
New Year; St Patrick's Day, 17 Mar; Easter; 1st Mon in June; 1st Mon in Aug; last Mon in Oct; Christmas, 25 Dec.

Shops
Open Mon-Sat 09.00-17.30 or 18.00.

Motoring
Allow plenty of time when travelling in Ireland even though the roads are relatively uncongested. Poor road surfaces, unmarked junctions and poor weather conditions can delay. Signposting or the lack of them can be a problem. A good map is a necessity. Drive on the left as in the UK. A Green Card is advised as most policies provide only minimum coverage in the Republic of Ireland
Speed Limits: On certain roads, clearly marked, the speed limits are 40 mph (65 kph) or 50 mph (80 kph) - applying to a car and trailer as well.
Parking: As in the UK. Parking meters are in use - on the spot fines can be levied for offences.

Overnighting
It is possible to camp 'free' in areas where there is no registered site except in state forests (farmers will expect a pound or two).

1325 Gateway Caravan and Camping Park, Ballinode, Sligo

Family run park, convenient for the beauty spots immortalised by the poet W. B. Yeats.

This is the northwest's newest park and straight away it warrants the highest accolade for its excellent design and standards set. Its situation 1.2 km. from Sligo centre means this cultural city is easily accessible, yet Gateway's off-the-road location, screened by mature trees and fencing, offers a quiet relaxing environment. After the park entrance, past the family bungalow and to the left is parking space and the reception and services block which is fronted by columns and an overhanging roof. Flower baskets add decoration and soft background music drifts through the air. Incorporated in this building are three separate rooms - one for TV, snooker and games, the second for satellite TV and the third for selected video viewing. A passageway divides the elongated building which also houses showers, WCs, washbasins with shaver/hairdryer points, hand-dryers and baby changing units in both the male and female areas. Showers, room for the disabled (with WC and shower) are entered from the outside of this block which is centrally heated, has green and white decor and non-slip floor tiling. In an adjacent building is a dishwashing area, laundry room, fully equipped campers' kitchen plus a large indoor games room and a toddlers room. A children's play area faces reception. There are 30 fully serviced touring pitches with hardstanding and satellite TV connection, 10 grass pitches with electrical hook-up for tents and 10 caravan holiday homes for hire. Evening relaxation could mean a 3 km. drive to romantic Half Moon Bay, or a drink in the fascinating surroundings of Farrells Brewery, which faces the caravan park.

Directions: Site is 1.2 km. northeast of Sligo city, off the N16 Enniskillen - Belfast road. Approaching from the north on the N15, turn left at second traffic lights into Ash Lane, continue for 1.1 km. and turn left at traffic lights onto the N16 Sligo - Enniskillen road. Site entrance is on left in 50 m.

Charges 1997: Per unit incl. 2 persons IR£7.50 - 8.50; child free - 50p; family rate IR£7.50 - 10.50; m/cyclist incl. tent IR£7.50; hiker or cyclist incl. tent IR£4.50; electricity (10A) IR£1.00.

Open: All year.

Reservations: Contact site. Address: Ballinode, Sligo, Co. Sligo. Tel: 071 45618. FAX: as phone.

IRELAND

1324 Greenlands Caravan and Camping Park, Rosses Point

Park with excellent facilities in the sand hills adjoining a championship golf course.

This is a well run park at Rosses Point, just off the N15 road and 8 km. from Sligo town. It is thoughtfully laid out with small tents placed to the front of reception and the hardstanding touring pitches separated from the holiday home pitches which occupy the rear. The ground is undulating and adds interest to the overall appearance. Your view depends on where you are pitched - look towards Coney Island and the Blackrock lighthouse which guards the bay, take in the sight of Benbulben Mountain or appreciate the seascape. Sanitary and laundry facilities are modern and kept clean with WCs, washbasins and hot showers (50p token). Dishwashing and laundry sinks, washing machine, dryer and iron. Electric hook-ups available for touring units. Chemical disposal and motorcaravan services. Information point and a TV room beside reception. Sand pit for children and ground chess and draughts sets. A mini market, restaurant and evening entertainment are in the village. An excellent base from which to explore the `Yeats Country' and discover the beauty spots immortalised in his poems, such as Lissadell, Dooney Rock, the Isle of Innisfree and the poet's burial place at Drumcliffe.

Directions: From Sligo city travel approx. 800 m. north on N15 road, turn left onto R291 signed Rosses Point. Continue for 6.5 km. and park is on right after village.

Charges 1997: Per unit high season: IR£7.50 plus 50p per person, low season IR£7.50, no per person charge; all season hiker/cyclist IR£5.00; electricity (5A) IR£1.00.

Open: 22 May - 18 September.

Reservations: Contact park. Address: Rosses Point, Co. Sligo. Tel: (071) 77113 or 45618. FAX: (071) 45618.

1327 Cong Caravan and Camping Park, Cong, nr Connemara

Family run touring park and hostel in a famous and scenic location.

It would be difficult to find a more idyllic and famous spot for a Caravan Park than Cong. Situated on the shores of Lough Corrib, Cong's scenic beauty was immortalised in the film 'The Quiet Man'. This park, which is immaculately kept, is 1.6 km. from the village of Cong, near the grounds of the magnificent and renowned Ashford Castle. The owner's house which incorporates reception, shop and the hostel, stands to the fore of the site. The 40 grass pitches, 36 with electricity, are placed at a higher level to the rear, with the tent area below and to the side. Sanitary facilities and the holiday hostel accommodation are entered from the courtyard area. Tastefully decorated and kept spotlessly clean, the toilet facilities include hot showers with curtains, electric points, mirrors, hairdryers, washbasins, soap and hand towels. Dishwashing area, launderette service, chemical disposal, central bin depot, barbecue, games room and extensive children's play area. Full Irish or continental breakfast, dinner or packed lunch may be ordered, or home baked bread and scones purchased in the shop. Watersports, cycling, walking, climbing, caving and scenic drives can all be pursued. Fishing 500 m. Bicycle hire on site. A mini cinema shows 'The Quiet Man' film nightly all season.

Directions: Leave N84 at Ballinrobe to join the R334/345 signed Cong. Turn left at the end of the R345 (opposite the entrance to Ashford Castle), take next road on the right (approx. 300 m) and the park is on the right (200 m).

Charges 1998: Per adult IR£4.00; child IR£1.00; awning IR£1.50; electricity IR£1.50.

Open: All year.

Reservations: Contact park. Address: Lisloughrey, Lake Road, Cong, Connemara, Co. Mayo. Tel: (092) 46089. FAX: (092) 46448.

 AR Discount
7 nights for the price of 6 (if pre-paid)

1331 Knock Caravan and Camping Park, Knock

Clean, friendly park with many local attractions including religious shrine.

This park is immediately south of the world famous shrine, which receives many visitors. The site is kept very neat and is comfortable and clean. One enters on the tarmac roads to see a square shaped site surrounded by clipped trees. Pitches are of a decent size accommodating 38 caravans or motorcaravans, 20 tents and 14 holiday caravans (for hire). All pitches have hardstandings (5 doubles) and there are 37 electrical connections (13A), with an adequate number of water points. There is also an overflow field. The modern sanitary block, with good facilities for the disabled and a nice sized rest room attached, has 4 controllable hot showers (on payment) and adequate washing and toilet facilities. A laundry and dishwashing room is also part of this building. A children's playground is in the centre of the site. Because of the religious connections of the area, the site is very busy in August and indeed there are unlikely to be any vacancies at all for 14-16 Aug. Besides visiting the shrine and Knock Folk Museum, local activities include golf, riding and fishing. A good centre for exploring scenic Co. Mayo.

Directions: Take the N17 to the Knock site which is just south of the village. Camp site is well signed.

Charges 1997: Per unit IR£5.50 - 6.00, plus 25p per person (weekly IR£30 plus IR£1 per person); hiker or cyclist and tent IR£3.50 - 4.00; electricity IR£1.50.

Open: 1 March - 31 October.

Reservations: Taken for any length, no deposit, but see editorial for August. Address: Claremorris Road, Knock, Co. Mayo. Tel: Knock (094) 88100 or 88223. FAX: (094) 88295.

1334 Kirwans Caravan and Camping Park, Portlaoise

Friendly, peaceful park, ideal for exploring inland, rural Ireland.

One receives a warm welcome at this small `homely' park, located on the edge of Portlaoise and surrounded by trees. The pitches are around the edges of a flat, firm grassy meadow and you site yourself sensibly, choosing morning or afternoon sun. Flowers and shrubs have been planted and secluded seating areas provided. The site offers 16 pitches with electricity (13A) for caravans or motorcaravans and another 14 for tents. There are a couple of static vans and mobile homes for hire. Adequate water facilities with a long hose available. The sanitary block, near the entrance, is very clean and is adequate, without being luxurious. It offers hot showers on payment and additional facilities are being added. Dishwashing facilities and a laundry with washing machine and dryers (not to be used on Sundays). TV and video room and rest room where one can make tea and coffee, plus a kitchen for groups. Children's playground, barbecue and picnic area. Shops, supermarkets, etc. are close by in Portlaoise, where there is a market on Thursdays. Laois is a beautiful inland county of Ireland, with picturesque small towns and many historical connections well worth exploring.

Directions: Approaching Portlaoise from the N7 Kildare - Limerick road, join the M7 bypass and branch off onto R445 signed Portlaoise centre. Continue to roundabout in centre and follow signs for Limerick and Montrath. Site is on right approx. 1 mile from roundabout; watch carefully for campsite sign immediately by entrance.

Charges 1997: Per unit, incl. 2 persons IR£7.00 - 10.00; m/cycle and tent incl. 1 or 2 persons IR£5.00 per person; backpacker or cyclist IR£2.50; child IR£1.00; extra adult, tent, electricity, dog, awning or boat all IR£1.00 - 1.50.

Open: 1 April - 15 October.

Reservations: Made for any length, with deposit. Address: N7 Limerick Road, Portlaoise, Co. Laois. Tel: Portlaoise (0502) 21688.

AR Discount

Third person free

1339 Moat Farm Caravan and Camping Park, Donard

Heart of the country experience within easy driving distance of Dublin or Rosslare.

Camping at its most idyllic is what can be enjoyed at this campsite. Here a true feel of the countryside abounds for it is part of a working farm environment and offers incredible vistas across a scenic landscape. Driving into the village of Donard in West Wicklow you little suspect that alongside the main street lies this tranquil 5 acre site. The entrance is approached by way of a short roadway where the ruins of a Medieval church sit high overlooking the forecourt and reception. Facing down the site is the sanitary block which is kept clean and includes WCs, large showers, sink units with marble effect tops. Facilities for disabled people, well equipped laundry room and TV room with a long window giving a panoramic view over the site and beyond. Chemical disposal is at the end of this building and a campers' kitchen beside the farmyard buildings. Three large barbecues and a patio area. There are 40 pitches for caravans and tents. The pitches with hardstanding to the right, some sheltered by tall trees, occupy both sides of a broad avenue. These are spacious and all have electricity and drainage points. Tents are pitched on the grass area to the centre and left. This site makes a good base for touring or going on foot, for this is a walker's paradise with a 30 minute circular walkway around the perimeter of the site. There is also fishing (3 km), mountain climbing or sites of archaeological interest nearby. Bicycle hire 15 km.

Directions: From south on N81 turn off 14 km. north of Baltinglass at old Tollhouse pub. Site is clearly signed.

Charges 1998: Per caravan, motorcaravan or family tent IR£8.00; adult IR£1.00; child 50p; tent (1 or 2 persons) IR£6.00; m/cyclist incl. tent IR£3.50; hiker or cyclist incl. tent IR£3.00; awning IR£1.50; electricity (10A) IR£1.50.

Open: All year.

Reservations: Contact site. Address: Donard, Co.Wicklow. Tel: 045 404727. FAX: as phone.

IRELAND

I326 Táin Holiday Village, Omeath

Fun packed holiday village, scenically set on Carlingford Lough.

This holiday complex is one of the most extensive in Ireland and is exactly what a family seeking non-stop entertainment might want. The touring park is within the 10-acre village, overlooking Carlingford Lough with views towards the Mourne mountains, whilst nestling at the foot of the Cooley mountains. The area for tourers is to the far right of the main buildings, entrance through a security gate is by key (deposit required). There are 87 pitches with hardstanding and electrical hook-ups, plus 10 pitches for tents. Young trees will eventually add more detail to this well laid out, but open, site. The sanitary block is kept clean and houses WCs, hot showers, washbasins in cubicles with mirrors, etc. and facilities for the disabled. Dishwashing and laundry sinks with hot water, plus washing machines and iron. Included in the site charges is the use of the 40,000 sq.ft. of indoor leisure facilities. These include a heated swimming pool with slides, flumes and rafts, an indoor play area with free fall, ball pool, climbing room and nets, also a new sports hall, gym and games room. Jacuzzi, steam room and sun beds. Not least at The Táin is a hands-on Science Interactive Centre. The licensed restaurant offers varied menus and there is a new lounge and bar. Outdoor activities include two adventure playgrounds, tennis courts, trim track and watersports, not forgetting the pleasant grounds with neat flower beds.

Directions: From Newry take B79/R173 road signed Omeath. Site is 1.6 km. south of Omeath village, on the left.

Charges 1997: Per unit incl. 2 persons on fully serviced gravel pitch IR£16.50 - 18.50; tent on grass area IR£14.50 - 16.50; extra person IR£3.00 - 3.50. Less 10% in July/Aug. for booked stays over 7 days. Credit cards accepted.

Open: All year except Dec/Jan.

Reservations: Made with deposit (caravan IR£15, tent IR£10). Address: Carlingford Lough, Omeath, Co. Louth. Tel: (042) 75385. FAX: (042) 75417.

Táin Holiday Village Omeath, Co Louth

TEL: (UK) 00 353 42 75385 (EIRE) 042 75385

Fun For Families

Enjoy the Tains' Superb Amenities:-
Hostel, Self Catering, Camping & Caravanning and Disabled Accommodation.
Situated on Carlingford Lough & Surrounded by the breathtaking scenery of the Cooley Peninsula area.

Major Attractions Include:-
Indoor:- Swimming Pool & Water Slides, Jacuzzi, Steam Room, Adventure Playground, Childrens Football & Basketball, Games Rooms with Pool Tables & Video Games, Large Screen T.V. etc Hands On Science Learning Centre.
Outdoor:-Tennis Courts, Canoeing, Kayaking, Banana Boat Rides Hill Walking. Tain Animal Farm New for 97

I335 Camac Valley Tourist Caravan and Camping Park, Dublin

See colour advert between pg 32/33

New touring park with top class facilities convenient for ferry ports and Dublin city.

This brand new campsite, opened in July '96, is not only well placed for Dublin, it also offers a welcome stopover if travelling to the more southern counties from the north of the country, or vice versa. Despite its close proximity to the city, being located in the 300 acre Corkagh Park gives it a 'heart of the country' atmosphere. The site entrance and sign are distinctive and can be spotted in adequate time when approaching on the busy N7. Beyond the gate and forecourt stands an attractive timber fronted building. Its design includes various roof levels and spacious interior layout, with large windows offering a view of the site and an exit to what will be a patio area. Housed here is reception, information, reading, TV and locker rooms plus sanitary facilities which include WCs, good sized showers (50p token) and central floor units with washbasins and mirrors.   *continued overleaf*

1335 Camac Valley Tourist Caravan and Camping Park (continued)

Shaver points, hand dryers, facilities for the disabled, baby room, laundry, washing up and chemical disposal. A second well designed and fitted sanitary block is now open. Children's playground. There are 163 pitches, 50 for tents to the fore and hardstandings for caravans laid out in bays and avenues with electricity, drainage and water points. Young trees separate pitches and roads are tarmac. After a day of sightseeing in Dublin, which can be reached by bus from the site, Camac Valley offers a evening of relaxation with woodland and river walks in the parkland or first class restaurants and pubs nearby.

Directions: From north follow signs for West Link and M50 motorway. Exit M50 at junction 9 on N7 Cork road. Site is on right of dual carriageway (beside Green Isle Hotel) after 2 km. Clearly signed on N7 and from ferry ports.

Charges 1997: Per caravan or motorcaravan incl. 4 persons IR£7.00 - 10.00; tent IR£6.00 - 8.00; adult IR£1.50; child 50p; motorcyclist, cyclist or hiker with tent (2 persons) IR£5.00 - 7.00; awning IR£1.00; electricity IR£1.00.

Open: All year

Reservations: Advance bookings not necessary. (max. stay operates at certain times). Address: Corkagh Park, Naas Road, Clondalkin, Dublin 22. Tel: (01) 4640644. FAX: (01) 4640643.

1342 Morriscastle Strand Caravan and Camping Park, Kilmuckridge

Family run park with direct access to sandy beach and convenient for Rosslare Port.

Whether you use this park as a stopover, or choose it as a longer stay destination, you will find it to be in a quiet relaxing location. Situated minutes from the pretty village of Kilmuckridge it offers well maintained and clean facilities. There are a number of privately owned caravan holiday homes on site but these are unobtrusive and kept separate by high hedging. The entrance to the touring park is to the right of reception by way of a tarmac driveway. This leads to the secluded, gently sloping, grass pitches which enjoy an open aspect. They overlook marshland which attracts wild geese and ducks, whilst the sea brings in crabs, eels and fish. To the right of the site lie the sand-hills and paths to the beach. The 105 pitches are numbered and marked by concrete slabs, each has an electrical hook-up (6A) and drainage point. Good night lighting. Two sanitary blocks include spacious WCs, washbasins, mirrors, shaver points, unisex showers (on payment) with divider, seat, hooks and soap dish. There is provision for the handicapped, a baby bath, campers' kitchen, dishwashing area, launderette, chemical disposal and outside cold showers. Shop, snacks and takeaway in high season, also a games room, two tennis courts, football field and children's play area. The beach has a lifeguard in season. Kilmuckridge is approximately 3 km. with an assortment of shops, pubs offering nightly entertainment and top class restaurants, such as The Rafters, a picturesque spot which helps characterise this charming village.

Directions. Site is 25 km. east of Enniscorthy. Travelling south on N11 Dublin/Wexford road branch ontoR741 at Gorey. Continue for 19 km. to Ballyedmund. Turn left at petrol station and follow signs for Kilmuckridge and site.

Charges 1997: Per unit incl. 2 persons IR£6.00 - 9.00; hiker, cyclist or m/cyclist incl. tent IR£2.50 - 4.00; awning IR£1.00; electricity (5A) IR£1.00.

Open: 3 May - 28 September.

Reservations: Contact site by phone or write. Address: Kilmuckridge, Co. Wexford. Tel: (053) 30124/30212; off season (01) 453 5355. FAX: (053) 30365; off season (01) 454 5916.

1341 Tree Grove Caravan and Camping Park, Kilkenny

Orderly, neat touring park within walking distance of Kilkenny.

The entrance to this small family run site is easily spotted off the R700 road. It makes an ideal location for spending time in medieval Kilkenny, known for its elegance and famed for its beer and cats. Tree Grove's young owners have insisted on a logical layout to suit both the terrain and campers needs. It is a terraced site with the lower terrace to the right of the wide sweeping drive laid out with 11 hardstanding pitches for caravans. All 30 pitches have electrical hook-up (10A) and plenty of water points are to be found. On a higher level, to the left is a grass area for hikers and cyclists with further caravan and tent pitches near the elevated sanitary block. If needed more grass pitches face reception, which is temporarily housed in a mobile unit. Whilst there are mature trees at the entrance and around the site perimeter, many young shrubs and flower troughs have been planted. House plants add decoration inside the toilet block giving a well cared for look to this well designed, modern building. Showers are free and a family room with shower, WC and washbasin can be used by the disabled. WCs and washbasins with mirrors, shaver and hairdryer points, are in separate area. An open, covered kitchen for campers adjoins a comfortable games/TV room with pool table. Next to this is a laundry room. On the patio there are bench seats with tables and umbrellas. Tents to rent on site. There is much to see and do around the ancient city of Kilkenny (1.5 km) with its cobbled streets and castle.

Directions: Travelling north on the N10 Waterford/Kilkenny Road turn right at roundabout on ring road. Continue to 2nd roundabout and turn right onto R700. Site is 150 m. on right.

Charges 1997: Per caravan, motorhome or family tent IR£8.00; 1 man tent IR£5.00; 2 man tent IR£6.00; 4 man tent IR£7.00; car IR£1.00; awning IR£1.00; electricity (10A) IR£1.50.

Open: All year.

Reservations: Contact site. Address: Danville House, Kilkenny, Co. Kilkenny. Tel: (056) 70302. FAX: (056) 21512.

IRELAND

1346 Parsons Green Caravan and Camping Park, Clogheen

Small, family run park with excellent on site facilities.

In a tranquil and scenic location, this open style site commands panoramic views toward the Vee Gap and Knockmealdown Mountains. Surrounded by low ranch fencing, it offers 20 pitches for caravans and motorcaravans with hardstanding and electrical connections (6A) and 20 pitches for tents.the sanitary facilities, to the top right of the site close to reception, are kept clean and include WCs, washbasins with mirrors, electric points, etc, free hot showers and good facilities for the disabled (shower and toilet), plus a laundry area with washing machines, dryer and sinks, and three dishwashing sinks. Coffee shop on site and ice cream, confectionery and gifts are sold. The village is within 500 m. with shops, pubs, bank, post office, etc. The wide range of amenities includes a garden area, river walks, picnic area, an extensive farm museum, a pet field with selection of domestic and rare animals and birds, children's playground, pony and trap rides, boating on the small lake and trout fishing river. TV/games room, campers' kitchen and function room. If not enjoying the scenic surroundings or participating in the many activities, there is much to see and do in this area. Caravan holiday homes and chalets for hire.

Directions: Site is in the village of Clogheen, 200 m. off the R665, 24 km. west of Clonmel, 19 km. east of Mitchelstown.

Charges 1998: Per caravan, family tent or motorcaravan IR£8.00; small tent IR£6.00; electricity IR£1.00.

Open: All year.

Reservations: Contact site. Address: Clogheen, Co. Tipperary. Tel: (052) 65290.

AR Discount

7 nights for the price of 6

1347 Carrick-on-Suir Caravan and Camping Park, Carrick-on-Suir

Small, family run, town site in quiet and tranquil setting.

This memorable little site is not only conveniently situated off the main N24 between Waterford and Clonmel, but its owner, Frank O'Dwyer, is an excellent ambassador for his county. On his site campers are guaranteed the finest example of 'Cead Mile Failte' it is possible to encounter - personal attention and advice on where to go and what to see in the area is all part of the service.the entrance to the park is immediately past the O'Dwyers' shop, through a gateway (closed 11 pm). The gravel drive leads past tall hedges and well kept shrubs to the right and several caravan holiday homes (for hire) to the left. The touring park lies to the rear with scenic views to the wooded hills. At the moment there are 30 level pitches, 23 with electrical connections (10A) and several with hardstanding, but this number is to be extended. There are water points, chemical disposal and good night lighting. The excellent, well designed sanitary block includes WCs, showers, basins with mirrors, electric points, hand dryers and plenty of hot water each morning. Laundry room with washing machine and dishwashing. Camper's kitchen with TV. Carrick town centre is a five minute walk where there is a castle open to the public. Within a short drive is the 'magic road', the Mahon Falls, a slate quarry or a romantic river walk.

Directions: Approaching town on N24 road, follow signs for R690 in the direction of Kilkenny. Site is north of town, clearly signed at junction with R697.

Charges 1997: Per unit incl. 2 persons IR£6.50 - 7.50; tent IR£5.00 - 6.00; extra adult IR£1.00; child 50p; electricity (6A) IR£1.00; hiker or cyclist incl. tent IR£2.50 - 3.00; extra car 50p.

Open: All year except 20 Dec - 5 Jan.

Reservations: Contact site. Address: Ballyrichard, Kilkenny Road, Carrick-on-Suir, Co. Tipperary. Tel: (051) 640461.

AR Discount

7 nights for the price of 6

1354 The Meadow Camping Park, Glandore

Small, mature garden park on Ireland's garden route; for tents and motorcaravans only.

The stretch of coast from Cork to Skibbereen reminds British visitors of Devon before the era of mass tourism. This is rich dairy country, the green of the meadows matching the emerald colours of the travel posters. Thanks to the warm and wet Gulf Stream climate, it is also a county of gardens - and keen gardeners. The Meadows lies 1.5 km. east of the fishing village of Glandore. A further 5 km. west is the regional centre, Skibbereen. The owners, who live on the park, have arranged accommodation for 19 pitches among the flower beds and shrubberies of their extended garden. Space is rather tight and towed caravans are therefore not encouraged. There are 6 hardstandings for motorcaravans with 5A electric hook-ups. Facilities are limited but are well designed and immaculately maintained. Among the homely features are a sitting room and a well equipped kitchen (breakfast available). Washing machine and dryer. No dogs. Golf driving range, riding (5 km.), fishing, swimming and sailing at Glandore (15 km.).

Directions: Park is 1.5 km. east of Glandore, off N71 road, on R597 mid-way between Leap and Rosscarbery.

Charges 1998: Per motorcaravan incl. 2 persons IR£7.00 - 8.00; family tent incl. all persons IR£8.00 - 9.00; small tent and car £7.00; extra person IR£2.00; child (under 12) 50p; hiker or cyclist incl. tent IR£3.00 per person; electricity (5A) IR£1.00.

Open: 15 March - 30 September.

Reservations: Phone for details. Address: Glandore, Co. Cork. Tel: (028) 33280.

AR Discount

4 nights for the price of 3

1343 Casey's Caravan Park, Clonea, Dungarvan

Family run site with direct access to the beach.
Set on 20 acres of flat grass, edged by mature trees, this park offers 284 pitches which include 118 touring pitches, all with electrical hook-ups and 30 with hardstanding. The remainder are occupied by caravan holiday homes. The central sanitary block, which is operated on a key system, has good facilities kept spotlessly clean, a top priority for the owner. There are showers on payment (50p), free hot water to open style basins and washing up sinks (10p). Also housed in this block is a small laundry with machine and dryer. A further luxurious and modern block has been added with an excellent campers' kitchen, laundry room and toilet for disabled people. There is direct access from the park to a sandy, blue flag beach with lifeguard in July/Aug. On site facilities include a large children's adventure play area with bark surface, in its own field, (unsupervised). Near the site entrance is a games room with pool table, table tennis and amusements, crazy golf and TV lounge. A highly recommended leisure centre is adjacent should the weather be inclement. There is no shop, but two village stores are near the beach. The park is 5½ km. from Dungarvan, a popular town for deep sea angling, from which charter boats can be hired and three 18 hole golf courses are within easy distance. Recommended drives include the scenic Vee, the Comeragh Drive and the coast road to Tramore. Dogs allowed on a lead.

Directions: From Dungarvan centre follow R675 east for 3.5 km. Look for signs on the right to Clonea Bay and site. Site is approx. 1.5 km.

Charges 1997: Per unit IR£9.50 - 10.00; hiker or cyclist IR£3.75; electricity IR£1.00.

Open: 2 May - 7 September.

Reservations: Are made, but not between 9 July - 15 Aug; contact park. Address: Clonea, Dungarvan, Co. Waterford. Tel: (058) 41919.

 ## Casey's Caravan & Camping Park
Clonea, Dungarvan, Co Waterford Tel: 058 41919

Top class facilities	Two ablution blocks with laundry & kitchen
Playground	Games room and TV room
Electric sites for tents & tourers (5A)	EU Blue Flag beach
Dungarvan town 3½ miles	Two nearby shops with takeaway
Choice of scenic views to visit	Deep sea and river angling
18 hole golf course in easy reach	Adjacent hotel with 19 metre pool
	and leisure centre with bowling alley

1358 Creveen Lodge Caravan and Camping Park, Healy Pass

Immaculately run, small hill farm park, overlooking Kenmare Bay.
The address of this park is rather confusing, but Healy Pass is the well known scenic summit of the road (R574) crossing the Beara Peninsula, which lies between Kenmare Bay to the north and Bantry Bay to the south. Several kilometres inland from the north coast road (R571), the R574 starts to climb steeply southward towards the Healy Pass. Here, on the mountain foothills, is Creveen Lodge, a working hill farm. Although not so famed as the Iveragh Peninsula, around which runs the Ring of Kerry, the northern Beara is a scenically striking area of County Kerry. Creveen Lodge, which commands views across Kenmare Bay, is divided among three gently sloping fields separated by trees. Reception is to be found in the farmhouse which also offers guests a comfortable sitting room. A small separate block, which is well appointed and immaculately maintained, has toilets and showers, plus a communal room with a fridge, freezer, TV, ironing board, fireplace, tables and chairs. Full Irish breakfast is served on request. This park is carefully tended with neat rubbish bins and rustic picnic tables informally placed, plus a children's play area with slides and swings. To allow easy access, the steep farm track is divided into a simple one-way system. There are 20 pitches in total, 16 for tents and 4 for caravans with an area of hardstanding for motorcaravans. Electrical connections are available. This is walking and climbing countryside or, of interest close by, is Derreen Gardens. Fishing 2 km, bicycle hire 9 km, boat launching 9 km. Also available in the area are water sports, horse riding, `Seafari' cruises, shops and a restaurant.

Directions: Park is on the Healy Pass road (R574) 1½ km. southeast of Lauragh.

Charges 1998: Per unit IR£6.00; person IR£1.00; hiker or cyclist incl. tent IR£3.50 per person; electricity £1.00.

Open: Easter - 31 October.

Reservations: Write to site with an S.A.E. Address: Healy Pass, Lauragh, Co. Kerry. Tel: (064) 83131.

IRELAND

1360 Fossa Caravan and Camping Park, Killarney

Mature, well equipped park in scenic location, 5½ km. from Killarney.

A 10 minute drive from the town centre brings you to this well laid out park which is instantly recognisable by its forecourt on which stands a distinctive building housing a Roof Top restaurant, reception area, shop and petrol pumps. The park is divided in two - the touring area lies to the right, tucked behind the main building, and to the left is an open grass area mainly for campers. Touring pitches, with electricity and drainage, have hardstanding and are angled between shrubs and trees in a tranquil, well cared for garden setting. To the rear at a higher level and discreetly placed are a number of caravan holiday homes. These are unobtrusive and sheltered by the thick foliage of the wooded slopes which climb high behind the park. The toilet facilities are modern and kept spotlessly clean. A second amenities block is placed to the far left of the grass area beside the tennis courts. Other facilities, apart from a shop (to end Sept), takeaway and restaurant (July/Aug), include a TV lounge, campers' kitchen, laundry room, washing up area, children's play area, games room, bicycle hire, night lighting and security patrol. Fishing 2 miles. Not only is Fossa convenient for Killarney, it is on route for the famed 'Ring of Kerry', and makes an ideal base for walkers and golfers.

Directions: Park is to the right on the R562/N72, 5½ km. west of Killarney on the road to Killorglin.

Charges 1998: Per unit IR£3.00 - 3.50; adult IR£3.00; child 75p; electricity IR£1.00; m/cycle and tent per person IR£4.25 - 4.50; hiker or cyclist per person IR£3.50 - 4.00; awning IR£1.50; extra car IR£1.50. Credit cards accepted.

Open: 15 March - 31 October.

Reservations: Advisable in high season and made for min. 7 nights with IR£10 deposit. Address: Fossa, Killarney, Co. Kerry. Tel: (064) 31497. FAX: (064) 34459.

FOSSA CARAVAN & CAMPING PARK

★ Ample hardstanding & electric hook-up ★ Separate tent area
★ Modern toilets ★ Shaving points ★ Hairdryers ★ Hot showers ★ Facilities for the disabled
★ Full laundry facilities ★ Campers kitchen ★ Free wash-up facilities
★ On site shop open 7 days Easter to Sept. ★ Restaurant (June-Aug) ★ Take away (July/Aug)
★ Children's playground ★ Tennis court ★ Games room ★ TV room ★ Bicycles for hire
★ Mobile homes for hire ★ Hostel accommodation

FOR FREE COLOUR BROCHURE WRITE TO:
Brosnan Family, Fossa Caravan & Camping Park, Fossa, Killarney, Co. Kerry, Ireland
Telephone: (064) 31497   Fax: (064) 34459

1359 Waterville Caravan and Camping Park, Waterville, Ring of Kerry

Family run park in scenic location overlooking Ballinskelligs Bay.

Drive into Waterville and immediately feel welcome - the Horgan family place emphasis on being hospitable and attentive to their guests. The touring pitches, many with hardstanding, are located in three areas. Some are convenient for reception, whilst others are pitched to the middle and rear. There is also a sheltered corner allocated to campers, with caravan holiday homes for hire, unobtrusively placed around the perimeter and centre, giving the park a spacious, neatly laid out appearance. Sitting high above the bay, the view in all directions is magnificent and the well tended grounds with plants, shrubs and cordyline trees gives a tropical appearance, especially on a fine sunny day. Three sanitary blocks are all well maintained and kept clean, the newest tastefully decorated with white tiles, relieved with rows of decorative black. There are hot showers (50p token), facilities for the disabled, washing up and laundry areas, drying room, quiet room and chemical disposal. Other facilities include a campers' kitchen, shop (June-Aug) and TV room. As well as an outdoor children's play area and above ground swimming pool (June-Aug), there is a play room in an old horse drawn caravan and a timber house with toys and 'upstairs, downstairs'. Waterville is on the 'Ring of Kerry', convenient for all the scenic grandeur and attractions for which the area is famed. Fishing and bicycle hire 2 km, boat launching 3 km. Waterville is also on the 'Kerry Way' walking route.

Directions: Travelling south on the N70, park is 1 km. north of Waterville, 270 m. off the main road.

Charges 1997: Per unit IR£7.00 - 7.50, incl. 2 persons IR£9.00 - 9.50 or family incl. IR£10.00 - 10.50; small tent (1 or 2 persons) IR£6.00 - 6.50; extra adult IR£1.00; child 50p; hiker or cyclist incl. tent IR£3.50; m/cyclist incl. tent IR£3.50 - 4.00; electricity (6A) IR£1.00; awning IR£1.50; hardstanding or extra car IR£1.00.

Open: Easter - 19 September.

Reservations: Made with fee IR£5 plus IR£15 deposit. Address: Waterville, Ring of Kerry, Co. Kerry. Tel: (066) 74191. FAX: (066) 74538.

AR Discount
Less 10%

1365 The Flesk Muckross Caravan and Camping Park, Killarney

Seven acre park at gateway to National Park and Lakes, near Killarney town.

This family run park has undergone extensive development and offers high quality standards.Housed in one of Europe's most modern toilet blocks are well designed shower and toilet areas. Every detail has been added, including soap dispensers, hand dryers, vanity area with mirror and hair dryer, also a baby bath/changing room. Pitches are well spaced out and have electricity (10A), water, and drainage connections; 21 also have hardstanding with a grass area for awnings. Other on site facilities include petrol pumps, supermarket (all year), delicatessen and café (March - Oct) with extra seating on the sun terrace. There is also a laundry room, campers' kitchen with dishwashing sinks, a comfortable games room and chemical disposal point, plus night lighting and night time security checks.The grounds have been well cultivated with further shrubs, plants and an attractive barbecue and patio area. This is situated to the left of the sanitary block and is paved and sunk beneath the level roadway. Surrounded by a garden border, it has tables and chairs, making a pleasant communal meeting place which commands excellent views of Killarny's mountains. Fishing 300 m, boat launching 2 km.

Directions: From Killarney town centre follow the N71 and signs for Killarney National Park. Site is 1½ km on the left beside the Gleneagle Hotel.

Charges 1998: Per unit IR£3.00 - 3.50; adult IR£3.00; child 50p; extra car 50p; tent incl. 1 or 2 persons IR£2.50 - 3.00; m/cylist incl. tent IR£3.75 - 4.00; hiker or cyclist incl. tent IR£3.50 - 3.75; awning IR£1.50; electricity IR£1.00.

Open: 12 March - 31 October.

Reservations: Advisable in peak periods, write to park. Address: Muckross Road, Killarney, Co. Kerry. Tel: (064) 31704. FAX: (064) 35439. E-mail: killarneylakes@tinet.ie.

FLESK MUCKROSS
CARAVAN PARK

Family run, 7 acre park, situated at the gateway to 25,000 acres of National Park and lakes.
AA award winning sanitation facilities 1994/5
Just 1 mile (1.5 km) from Killarney town on the N71 south of Kenmare,
adjacent to Gleneagle Hotel and leisure centre

MUCKROSS, KILLARNEY
CO. KERRY, IRELAND   Prop: Johnny & Sinead Courtney

Phone: 064-31704
Fax: 064-35439

1362 Mannix Point Camping and Caravan Park, Cahirciveen

Quiet and peaceful, beautifully located seashore park.

It is no exaggeration to describe Mannix Point as a nature lovers' paradise. It is situated in one of the most spectacular parts of the Ring of Kerry, overlooking the Portmagee Channel towards Valentia Island. Whilst the park is flat and open, it commands splendid views in all directions, it is right on marshland which teems with wildlife (2 acre nature reserve) and it has immediate access to the beach and seashore. The owner has now planted around 500 plants with plans for around 1,000 more trees and shrubs. There are 42 pitches, 15 for tourers and 27 for tents, with electrical connections (6A) available.A charming old fisherman's cottage has been converted to provide reception and has been extensively renovated in '97. A cosy sitting room with turf fire, and 'emergency' dormitory for campers, is a feature of this site. Toilet facilities, now upgraded and immaculate, have well designed showers and free hot water. There is also a modern campers' kitchen and laundry facilities.The knowledgeable, hospitable owner is a Bord Fáilte registered Local Tour Guide. This park retains a wonderful air of Irish charm aided by occasional impromptu musical evenings. Watersports, bird watching, walking and photography can all be pursued here, but note that dogs are not allowed on site in June, July and Aug. Local cruises to Skelligs Rock with free transport to and from the port for walkers and cyclists. This is also an ideal resting place for people walking the Kerry Way.

Directions: Park is 250 m. off the N70 Ring of Kerry road, 800 m. southwest of Cahirciveen (or Cahersiveen).

Charges 1997: Per caravan or motorcaravan IR£1.00 - 2.00; adult IR£3.00 - 3.25; child IR£1.50; electricity IR£1.00; hiker/cyclist, incl. tent IR£3.00 - 3.25; m/cyclist IR£3.25 - 3.75. Book 7 nights, pay 6. Reductions for groups if pre-paid.

Open: 15 March - 15 October, the rest of the year also, if you write first.

Reservations: Made with deposit. Address: Cahirciveen, Co. Kerry. Tel: (066) 72806. FAX: (066) 72988.

ITALY

Italy only became a unified state in 1861, hence the regional nature of the country today. There are 20 distinct regions and each one retains its own relics of an artistic tradition generally acknowledged to be the world's richest. However, the sharpest division is between the north and south. The north is an advanced industrial area, relatively wealthy, whereas the south is one of the economically less developed areas of Europe. Central Italy probably represents the most commonly perceived image of the country and Tuscany, with its classic rolling countryside and the historical towns of Florence, Siena and Pisa, is one of the most visited areas. Venice is unique and as beautiful as its reputation suggests. Rome, Italy's capital, on its seven hills with its Roman legacy, is independent of both north and south. Naples, the natural heart of the south, is close to some of Italy's ancient sites such as Pompei. An International Camping Carnet is recommended. Further information may be obtained from:

Italian State Tourist Board, 1, Princes Street, London W1R 8AY

Tel: 0171 408 1254 Fax: 0171 493 6695

Population
58,000,000, density 191.7 per sq. km.

Climate
Varying considerably between the north and the south; the south enjoys extremely hot summers and relatively mild and fairly dry winters, whilst the mountainous regions of the north are much cooler with heavy snowfalls in winter.

Language
The language is Italian derived directly from Latin. There are several dialect forms and some German is spoken near the Austrian border.

Currency
The unit of currency is the Lira (plural Lire). Notes are in denominations of 1000, 2000, 5000, 10,000, 50,000 and 100,000; coins: 50, 100, 200 and 500.

Banks
Open Mon-Fri 08.30-13.30 and 15.00-16.00.

Post Offices
Open Mon-Sat 08.00-17.00/18.30. Smaller towns may not have a service on a Saturday. Stamps can also be bought in 'tabacchi'.

Time
GMT plus 1 (summer BST +1).

Public Holidays
New Year; Easter Mon; Liberation Day, 25 Apr; Labour Day; Assumption, 15 Aug; All Saints, 1 Nov; Immaculate Conception, 8 Dec; Christmas, 25, 26 Dec; plus some special local feast days.

Shops
Open Mon-Sat 08.30/09.00-13.00 and 16.00-19.30/20.00, with some variations in the north where the break is shorter and closing is earlier. Food: Pizza must be sampled in Italy - thin and flat and cooked in traditional wood fired ovens. Also sample the ice-cream (gelato). Full meals are generally served in a 'trattoria' or a 'ristorante' (more upmarket). A numbered receipt (Ricevuta Fiscale) for restaurant meals and hotels is compulsory.

Telephone
To call Italy the code is 0039. To phone the UK dial 00 44 followed by the UK code minus the initial 0. As well as coins, tokens (gettone) from Tabacchi, bars and some news stands are used for calls; phone cards are available.

Motoring
Driving Licence: A valid pink EC (all pink or part pink) UK driving licence is acceptable. The older all green UK licence must be accompanied by an official Italian translation (from the Italian Tourist Office or the AA). However, the DVLA will exchange older licences for the pink EC version on payment of the appropriate fee.
Tolls: Payable on the extensive and expensive Autostrada network. If travelling distances, save time by purchasing a `Viacard' from pay booths or service areas.
Speed limits: Caravans and motorhomes (3.5 tons) 31 mph (50 kph) in built up areas, 44 mph (70 kph) and 50 mph (80 kph) for caravans on other roads and motorways respectively, 56 mph (90 kph) and 80 mph (130 kph) for motorhomes.
Fuel: Petrol stations on the Autostrada open 24 hours. Elsewhere times are 07.00-13.00 and 16.00-19.30; only 25% open on Sundays. Most motorway service stations accept credit cards, apart from American Express and Diners.
Parking: There are 'Blue Zones' in all major towns. Discs can be obtained from tourist and motoring organisations or petrol stations. In Venice use the special car parks on the mainland, linked by ferry and bus to Venice. Most major towns now ban traffic in the centre.

Overnighting
Not generally allowed on open land. May be permitted in rest areas and parks where local regulations allow.

Useful Addresses
Automobile Club d'Italia (ACI), Via Marsala 8, 00185 Rome Tel: 06 49981. Touring Club Italiano (TCI), Corso Italia 10, 20122 Milian. Tel: 02 85261. Both clubs have branch offices in most main cities and towns.

Some sites have supplied us with copies of their brochures which we are pleased to forward to readers.
See our Brochure Service on page 359

6400 Camping de Wijnstok, Imperia, nr San Remo

Pleasant, clean site on the Italian Riviera, where good ones are rare.

The Italian Riviera between Genoa and Ventimiglia has few campsites, and most become overcrowded. At de Wijnstok, however, you are at least assured of two important things: sufficient space (pitches are marked out) and a decent toilet block. This has been recently renovated with full tiling in all sections and 3 private washing cabins each for men and women with free hot water in them; mainly British style WCs; hot showers on payment. The site is on grassy soil with a number of trees and shade is also provided in the hot season by overhead matting screens; there is some shade on all pitches. Most pitches have 3A electrical connections. Reservation is advisable for July to mid-Aug., but as part of the site is not subject to reservation there is always a chance of finding space. De Wijnstok is only some 100 yards from the sea, which is reached via a tunnel under the road. The local beach is not one of the most attractive but it has been much improved. Open all year, there are, however, few facilities available outside the main season.

How to find it: Site lies on the western boundary of Imperia very close to the SS1 coast road. From autostrada A10 take exit for Imperia-Ouest and turn right on coast road (SS!).

General Details: Open all year. Approx. 10,000 sq.m. Pizzeria and shop (high season). Supermarket close, on main road. Bar. Toddler's paddling pool. Washing machines. Chemical disposal. Bungalows and caravans for hire.

Charges 1997: Per person L. 7,900 - 8,200; child (0-8 yrs) 6,900 - 7,200; pitch 14,000 - 15,000; extra car or tent 8,000; electricity 3,000.

Reservations: made with L. 90,000 deposit and L 10,000 fee. Address: Via Poggi.2, 18100 Imperia. Tel: 0183/64986.

6405 Camping C'era una Volta, Villanova d'Albenga, Albenga, nr Alassio

Well situated site, back from sea, with swimming pools and other amenities.

A slightly unusual site, this one is about 8 km. back from the sea, situated on a hillside with some panoramic views, and with pitches on terraces in different sections of the site. The pitches - about 100 each for caravans (mainly on hardstandings) and tents - are not very large, perhaps 50 sq.m. and careful siting may be needed, although cars can park in different areas at busy times. In two parts, pitches are equipped with electricity (6A), water and drainaway. The toilet block has been modernised and provides WCs mainly of British style, washbasins with cold water, some with shelves, and free hot showers. The site has a good atmosphere and amenities include a swimming pool of 200 sq.m. and two children's pools in a pleasant setting, open all main season. There is a small section on its own, on the hilltop and fenced off, specially for naturists. Charges are high in season but the site is well organised and maintained. Private beach (4 miles) - reduced cost to campers.

How to find it: Leave autostrada A10 at Albenga, turn left and left again at roundabout for SS453 for Villanova. Follow Villanova signs to T-junction, turn left towards Garlenda, turn right in 200 m. and follow signs to site.

General Details: Open 1 April - 30 Sept. Shade in parts, but trees mostly small. Shop. Bar, pizzeria (April - Sept). Attractive restaurant. Takeaway (high season). Disco (July/Aug). Swimming pool complex (July/Aug). 2 saunas. Tennis. Large adventure playground. Fitness track with exercise points. Small but excellent gymnasium. Riding 500 m. Golf 2 km. Programme of organised sports and other events in season, also dancing or entertainment some nights. Chemical disposal. Bungalows for hire.

Charges 1997: Per pitch incl. up to 3 persons L.30,000 - 64,000, acc. to season and type of pitch; extra person 10,000 - 16,000; VAT and electricity included. Discounts for longer stays in low season.

Reservations: are made for min. of a few days with 30% advance payment. Address: 17038 Villanova d'Albenga (SV). Tel: 0182/580461 or 582871. FAX: 0182/582871.

ITALY - North West

6410 Camping Genova Est, Bogliasco, nr Genoa

Attractive, wooded site above Bogliasco just south of Genoa.

This site of 12,000 sq.m. is close to the Genoa motorways coming from the north or west and although it has limited facilities, it is near the town and the sea. The Buteros who run and own the site both speak good English and are very enthusiastic and anxious to please. The approach from the main road twists and climbs but should present no problem. There are 54 touring pitches. The two modern sanitary blocks are well maintained with hot showers on payment and a washing machine. There is a small shop with a bar and restaurant. Free bus service to the beach.

How to find it: From autostrada A10 take Nervi exit and turn left (south) on the SS1 towards La Spezia. In Bogliasco look for a sharp left turn with a large sign for the site. Follow narrow winding road for 2 km. to site.

General Details: Open 1 Feb - 30 Nov. Electricty available (3/5A). Shop. Bar/restaurant. Towing vehicle available. Chemical disposal. Motorcaravan services. Mobile home and 3 caravans to let. Not suitable for disabled people.

Charges 1997: Per person L. 8,000; child (3-10 yrs) 6,000; small tent 7,500; large tent or caravan 9,000; motorcaravan 12,000; car 4,500; m/cycle 3,500.

Reservations: Contact site. Address: Via Marconi-loc Cassa, 16031 Bogliasco (GE). Tel/Fax: 010/3472053.

6240 Camping Valle Romantica, Cannobio, Lake Maggiore

Attractive site with good facilities in scenic situation.

The pretty little town of Cannobio is situated between Verbania and Locarno on the western shore of Lake Maggiore. It could make a base for exploring the Lake and its islands, although progress along the winding lake-side road, hemmed in by mountains, is slow. Serious mountain walkers are well catered for, and the Swiss resort of Locarno is not far. Steamers cross the Lake, but the only car ferry is between Verbania and Laveno. This lovely (30,000 sq.m.) site was established 40 years ago by the present owner's father, who planted some 20,000 plants, trees and shrubs, and there is much to interest botanists in this tree-clad mountain valley. A swimming pool is in a sunny position, and there is a pool in the river, where, except after heavy rain, children can play. The 130 pitches are on flat grass among the trees, which provide good shade and serve to separate the numbered pitches (but mean some narrow site roads). Three sanitary blocks have British style WCs, free hot water in basins and showers, controlled by taps. Electricity (4A) is available on most pitches, although long cables are necessary in some parts. The small supermarket is well stocked, and there is a pleasant bar/restaurant with waiter service and takeaway. Entertainment (folk music) is provided one night per week in the high season. The owner takes a keen and active personal interest in the site, and English is spoken.

How to find it: From the centre of Cannobio (from where site is signed) take the valley road towards Malesco; site is 1 km. on the right.

General Details: Open 28 March - 30 Sept. Shop. Bar/restaurant. Swimming pool (10/5-20/9). Table tennis. Children's playground. Fishing. Fridge boxes to hire. Washing machine. Chemical disposal. Motorcaravan services.

Charges 1998: Per person L. 10,000 - 11,000; child (1-12 yrs) 6,500 - 7,500; pitch 16,000 - 18,000; extra tent 5,000; extra car 8,000 - 9,000; dog 5,000; electricity 4,500.

Reservations: Made for min. 11 nights with deposit (L. 120,000) and fee (80,000). Address: 28822 Cannobio (Verbania). Tel: 0323/71249. FAX: 0323/71360.

AR Discount
Less 10% in low season

6245 Camping Riviera, Cannobio, Lake Maggiore

Good lakeside site near northern end of Lake Maggiore, with access for watersports.

Under the same active ownership as Valle Romantica, this 22,000 sq.m. site is directly on the lake with scenic views across the water and surrounding mountains. Over 250 numbered pitches, 220 with 4A electricity (long cables may be needed) are on flat grass either side of hard surfaced access roads, and are divided by trees and shrubs. The whole site has a well cared for appearance, and is certainly one of the best lakeside sites in the area. The five sanitary blocks, one new and two with facilities for the disabled, are of good quality with British style WCs and controllable hot water to basins and showers; these are of reasonable size, with hooks, screen and dressing area. The site shop is well stocked and the town is only a short distance away. There is a pleasant bar/restaurant with covered terrace, providing waiter service and a takeaway. Being situated between the main road and the lake, pitches near the entrance may suffer from traffic noise. There is a small jetty and easy access to the lake for boats, swimming and other watersports. Sailing and windsurfing regattas are organised. The site could make a suitable base for exploring the area, although progress on the busy winding road may be slow!

How to find it: Site is by the lake side, just north of the town of Cannobio. There are several sites nearby, and care should be taken not to overshoot Riviera as turning round could be difficult!

General Details: Open 28 March - 18 Oct. Shop. Bar/restaurant with takeaway. Pizzeria. Fridge box hire. Fishing. Boat slipway. Sailing and windsurfing schools. Washing machines. Chemical disposal. Motorcaravan services.

Charges 1998: Per person L. 10,000 - 11,000; child (1-12 yrs) 6,500 - 7,500; pitch 16,000 - 18,000; extra tent 5,000; extra car 8,000 - 9,000; dog 5,000; electricity 4,500.

Reservations: Made for min. 11 nights with deposit (L.120,000) and fee (80,000). Address: 28822 Cannobio (Verbania). Tel: 0323/71360. FAX: as phone.

AR Discount
Less 10% in low season

6215 Camping Villa d'Aoste, Aosta

Small touring site near San Bernado tunnel suitable for overnight stop.

As its name implies, this small, grassy site is just on the outskirts of the small, busy town of Aosta (10-15 minutes walk from the centre), on the SS27 to or from the San Bernado tunnel. Toilets (mostly Turkish style) and washing facilities, including free showers, are in a block near the entrance.

How to find it: Coming from San Bernado the site is on the right just before the town. Coming from Mont Blanc tunnel (SS26) turn left on the town ring road at the sign for the SS27 (San Bernado) and site is on left after ½ km.

General Details: Open 1 June - 30 Sept. Bar and mini-market, but town close.

Charges guide: Per person L. 4,500; child (0-10 yrs) 3,500; pitch 3,500 - 6,000; m/cycle 3,500; electricity 2,000.

Reservations: not made. Tel: 0165/250779.

6220 Camping Mombarone, Torre Daniele

Pleasant, small all year site only suitable for en-route stop.

Mombarone is a pleasant, all year meadow site immediately off the SS26 and close to the small village of Torre Daniele and provides a useful transit stop. A small site, 80 of the 120 pitches are for permanent units. Toilet facilities have British and Turkish style WCs and showers on payment.

How to find it: From A5 Quincinetto exit (north of Ivrea) turn right on SS26. Site is by 45 km. stone, near town.

General Details: Open all year. Electrical connections (2A). Bar. Shops and restaurants close. Chemical disposal.

Charges 1997: Per person L. 4,000; child (under 10 yrs) 3,000; pitch 3,500 - 6,000; car 2,000; electricity 2,000.

Reservations: Write to site. Address: Torre Daniele (TO). Tel: 0125/757907.

6250 Camping Au Lac du Como, Sorico, Lake Como

See colour advert between pages 128/129

Medium size site with good facilities on lakeside.

The owner of Au Lac de Como speaks good English and runs an organised site in that he insists on respect for other residents from all (for example, boisterous football, intrusive barbecues and loud radios are `verboten'). Cars may be parked on the pitch but may only move in and out once daily - there is a large park by the entrance. Pitching can be a little haphazard as places are not defined or numbered. There is one good sanitary block and two smaller basic ones. Most guests are German and Dutch, but British visitors are very welcome. The site is on the lake shore and swimming, boating, etc. are allowed. A bar, restaurant and supermarket are on site, with others nearby. It is well situated for forays into Switzerland, particularly via the imposing Splügen pass.

How to find it: Take SS134 on west side of lake. Site entrance is by the 25 km. sign at northwest corner of the lake. However readers report that, though longer, the eastern approach is easier.

General Details: Open all year. Supermarket. Small hotel and bar/restaurant on site. Tennis courts adjacent. Canoes, kayaks and bicycles for hire. Bungalows for hire.

Charges guide: Per person L. 4,000 - 8,000; child 2,800 - 5,500; pitch 6,500 - 13,000; car 5,000; m/cycle 3,000.

Reservations: Said not to be necessary but site is always full 20/7-15/8. Address: Via Cesare Battisti 18, 22010 Sorico (CO). Tel: 0344/84035 or 84716. FAX: 0344/84802.

6259 Camping Punta d'Oro, Lake Iseo

Pleasant. small site on Lake Iseo.

Lago d'Iseo is the fifth largest of the northern lakes and one of the least known outside Italy. However, it is a popular tourist spot for Italians so has not escaped exploitation. Camping Punta d'Oro, at the town of Iseo in the southeast corner of the lake, is a small, delightful campsite. It slopes gently down to the lake from the railway line (they say, an infrequent local service) and there could be some road noise. The very pretty site, adorned with trees and plants, has 50 grass pitches (with just 15 static caravans) on either side of decorative brick roads with 5A electricity. Trees at the corners define the places. There are good views across the lake to wooded mountains on the opposite shore where small villages shelter down by the water and further mountains rise behind the site. It has a small bar/shop/restaurant with a terrace. The two small sanitary blocks have been refurbished to a high standard with a mix of British and Turkish style WCs and free hot water in washbasins, sinks and showers. There are two narrow slip-ways for launching boats onto the lake which is also used for swimming. It is a good centre for exploring around the lake, Monte Isola (Italy's largest island) by ferry from Iseo or to ascend Monte Gugliemo (1,949 m) which is reported to take about 3½ hours. With no entertainment programme, this could well suit those who are looking for a very pleasant base without the activity of a larger site.

How to find it: Leave A4 (Milan-Venice) autostrada at Ospitaletto exit, go north to Rodengo and then take SS510 to Iseo. Punta d'Oro is at northern end of town - cross the railway line and turn right at corner where site is signed.

General Details: Open 1 April - 25 October. 6,000 sq.m. Electrical connections (5A). Shop. Bar/restaurant. Access to lake. Games room, TV in bar. Washing machine. Chemical disposal.

Charges 1997: Per person L. 6,500 - 8,000; child 5,000 - 6,000; pitch 17,000 - 24,000.

Reservations: Write to site. Address: via Antonioli 51/53, 25049 Iseo (BS). Tel: 030/980084. FAX: as phone.

ITALY - North West

6253 Camping Piani di Clodia, Lazise, nr Verona

See colour advert between pages 192/193

New site on Lake Garda.

As might be expected in a popular area like Lake Garda, there are many camping sites and this new one is a welcome addition. Piani di Clodia, located between Lazise and Peschiera in the southeast corner of the lake, has lovely views across the water to Sirmione's peninsula and the opposite shore. The rectangular site slopes down to the water's edge and has over 1,000 pitches, all with 5A electricity, terraced where necessary and back to back from hard access roads. As yet there is little shade - some mature trees remain but most are young at present. A really good swimming pool complex at the top of the site has three semi-circular pools covering 1,700 sq.m. One can be heated and two have a variety of slides and hydro-massage. The area is fenced with lifeguards in attendance (open 10.00-13.00 and 15.00-18.00 hrs) with a good sunbathing area and a bar. The shopping area is in the centre of the site with an entertainment arena in the open and another on the roof, which is covered. The self-service restaurant with takeaway (open lunch time and evening) and bar (open 07.00-24.00) have a large terrace, part of which is covered. Animation staff provide a variety of entertainment for children and adults and there are facilities for many sports and pastimes (see below). Although there is a fence between the site and the lake, there are access points to a private beach and opportunities for watersports. Seven modern, good quality sanitary blocks are well spaced around the site, with a mix of British and Turkish style WCs and free hot water in washbasins, sinks and showers. All have facilities for the disabled and one has a baby room. Tour suggestions by foot or bicycle and tourist information are available from the reception office where English is spoken. Small British tour operator presence.

How to find it: Site is south of Lazise on road SS249 before Peschiera.

General Details: Open 20 March - 5 October. 220,000 sq.m. Shopping complex with supermarket, general shops for clothes etc. Two bars. Self-service restaurant with takeaway. Swimming pools. Tennis. Table tennis. Gymnastics. Bicycle hire. Riding near. Large grass space for volleyball and other ball games. Good children's playground. Outdoor theatre. Animation programme. Golf 12 km. Caneva acqua park, Gardaland (one of the biggest funfairs in Europe) close. Washing machines, dryers and laundry service. Motorcaravan service point. Chemical disposal.

Charges 1997: Per person L. 7,000 - 12,500; child (under 9 yrs) 4,500 - 8,500; pitch with electricity 16,000 - 27.000, with water also 18,000 - 30,000.

Reservations: Write to site. Address: Localita Bagatta, 37017 Lazise (VR). Tel: 045/7590456. FAX: 045/7590939.

6255 Camping La Quercia, Lazise sul Garda, nr Verona

Large, popular site with very good recreational facilities and excellent beach on Lake Garda.

An extensive, popular site on a slight slope leading down to Lake Garda, La Quercia can accommodate around 1,000 units when full. Pitches are in regular double rows between access roads and are mostly marked by trees. Most pitches are shady, though those furthest from the lake are more open to the sun. Although siting is not always easy, staff do help in high season. The six toilet blocks are perfectly sufficient and are of a very high standard. La Quercia has a fine sandy beach on the lake, with diving jetties and a roped-off section for launching boats or windsurfing. The water is very clear compared to some lake beaches. Much of the activity centres around the Olympic sized swimming pool and terrace bar, restaurant and pizzeria. Also a children's pool and large, landscaped spa pool (small charge). Sports facilities are exceptional, with floodlit table tennis, floodlit football field, multi-gym, archery, volleyball and tennis. A second café/restaurant nearer the beach also houses a large screen TV and ice-cream bar. Prices are so reasonable for both food and drink, it is possible to eat there frequently. Several shops cater for all needs, with supermarkets en route to Verona. The evening entertainment is a little daunting at first, with the young team working hard to involve everyone - smaller children love it! However, the site is a short distance from the exquisite lakeside town of Lazise and is a short drive from Verona, one of Italy's finest cultural centres (the open-air Opera in the Roman Amphitheatre is a unique, and affordable, experience). La Quercia has always been a popular site as, although its prices have been quite high, it does offer a great deal for your money, including a wide choice of activities and amenities, most of which are free. Many courses require enrolment on a Sunday. A reader reports that on Saturday nights in high season there may be late night noise from a disco outside the site. Used by tour operators.

How to find it: Site is on south side of Lazise. From north on Trento - Verona A22 autostrada take Affi exit then follow signs for Lazise and site. From south take Peschiera exit and site is 7 km. towards Garda and Lazise.

General Details: Open 10 days before Easter - 30 Sept. 200,000 sq.m. Shade in parts. Electrical connections (4/6A) to each pitch. Supermarket. General shop. Bar and self-service restaurant. Tennis court. Table tennis. Riding stables. Football. Aerobics and yoga. Facilities for boats on the lake. Supervised children's playground. Minigolf. Organised events (sports competitions, games, etc.) and free courses in swimming, surfboard. canoeing, tennis, archery, climbing, judo. Evening entertainment or dancing. Baby sitting service. Free weekly excursion. Medical service. Laundry. Chemical disposal. Over 100 bungalows with own facilities; details from site. English spoken.

Charges guide: Per person L. 10,100; child (under 5) free - 6,500; pitch 22,250; reserved pitch 25,600. Low season discount for pensioners and rainy days.

Reservations: are made Sat - Sat for certain pitches. Address: 37017 Lazise sul Garda (Verona). Tel: 045/6470577. FAX: 045/6470243.

6285 Camping Zocco, Manerba del Garda, Lake Garda

See colour advert
between pages 192/193

Good lakeside site with access for watersports.

Lake Garda is a very popular holiday area with a good number of sites well placed to explore the many attractions nearby. Camping Zocco is in a quiet, scenic location sloping gently down to the lake where there is a small jetty and good access to the water from a shingle beach. The 270 pitches available for tourists, all with electricity (4A), and from 60-80 sq.m. in size, are either on slightly sloping ground from gravel roads, on terraces or around the perimeters of two open meadows. A variety of trees, including olives which provide oil for the owners, give shade in some parts and the camp has a well cared for appearance. There are some apartments and caravans for hire but no tour operators and only 40 static units. There is a bar with terrace, a new restaurant/pizzeria and a shop. Entertainment is provided for children during July/August, there are two hard tennis courts and a football pitch. Water sports can be enjoyed on the lake. Three tiled sanitary blocks, one of which has been rebuilt, are well spread around the site. They have mainly British style WCs, free hot water in the washbasins, sinks and showers, and facilities for disabled people. The brothers who run this site welcome British visitors.

How to find it: From Desenzano north on road 572 towards Salo. Take minor road to Manerba where Zocco signed.

General Details: Open 4 April - 27 September. 50,000 sq m. Bar. Restuarant/pizzeria. Bar on the beach. Shop (from May). Watersports. Fishing. Bicycle hire. Tennis. Football. Children's play area. Washing machines. Chemical disposal. Motorcaravan services. Apartments and caravans for hire. English spoken.

Charges 1997: Per person L. 7,000 - 8,500; child (3-11 yrs) 5,900 - 7,700; pitch incl. electricity 15,000 - 18,000; small boat 3,800 - 6,500; extra car 3,800 - 6,500.

Reservations: Made for min. 7 days with deposit (L. 100,000) deducted from final bill. Address: via del Zocco 43, 25080 Manerba (BS). Tel: 0365/551605. FAX: 0365/552053 (winter tel/fax: 0365/551036).

AR Discount
Less 10% in low season on pp fee (min 7 days)

6280 Camping Week End, Cisano, San Felice del Benaco

Modern well equipped site with superb views over the lake.

Created among the olive groves and terraced vineyards of the Chateau Villa Louisa, which overlooks it, this site enjoys some superb views over the small bay which forms this part of Lake Garda. Although it is some 400 m. (along a private road from the site) from the lake itself, for many the views resulting from its situation on higher ground will be ample compensation for it not being an actual 'lakeside site'. Being situated above the lake, in quiet countryside, it provides an unusually tranquil environment, although even here it can be very busy in the high season. The site has a good sized swimming pool and a children's pool which compensate for its not actually having frontage onto the lake, and some visitors, particularly families with children, will doubtless prefer this. There are some 220 pitches, all with electricity (from 3A), of which about 30% are taken by tour operators and statics. Touring pitches are in several different areas, mainly on flat grass and many enjoying superb views. The three sanitary blocks, one of which is under the restaurant/shop complex, are modern, well maintained and include free hot water to showers, basins and washing-up. Mainly British style WCs, large showers, a few washbasins in cabins and facilities for disabled people. Large restaurant with terrace and lawn from which again there are lovely views, providing waiter and takeaway meals at reasonable prices, and a well stocked shop.

How to find it: Approach from Salo (easier when towing) and follow site signs.

General Details: Open 26 April - 21 Sept. Bar/restaurant. Shop. Swimming pools. Entertainment programme in season. Children's playground. Windsurfing, water skiing, golf and tennis near. First aid room. Washing machines and dryer. Chemical disposal. Bungalows and caravans for hire. English spoken.

Charges 1997: Per unit incl. electricity L. 15,000 - 22,000; adult 7,500 - 10,000; child (3-10) 6,500 - 8,500; extra car 5,500 - 7,500; extra m/cycle 4,500 - 5,000; dog 4,500 - 5,500.

Reservations: Contact site. Address: Via Vallone della Selva 10, 25010 San Felice del Benaco (Brescia). Tel: 0365/43712. FAX: 0365/42196.

...so unique!! ☆☆☆☆
camping **WEEKEND** villaggio

Quiet family site, well maintained. Modern toilet facilities. Free hot water in the showers and basins. Washing machine, bar, restaurant, pizzeria, small shop. Very scenic. 2 swimming pools, children's playing area, volleyball, table tennis, music and dancing in the evenings. Send for our brochure. Reservations accepted. Caravan, tent and bungalow for hire. New 6 person mobile-homes. Individual washing cubicles.

Via Vallone della Selva, 10 - 25010 SAN FELICE DEL BENACO (BS) -ITALIA- Tel. 0365 43712 Fax 0365 42196

ITALY - North West

6260 Camping Europa Silvella, San Felice del Benaco, Salo, nr Brescia

Site beside Lake Garda with various amenities.

This lakeside site was formed from the merger of two different sites with the result that the 300-plus pitches (about 220 for tourists) are spread among a number of different sections of varying type. The chief difference between them is that the marked pitches close to the lake are in smaller groups and closer together so that one has less space, whereas in the larger, very slightly sloping or terraced grassy meadows further back one can have 80 sq. m. or more instead of 50. There is reasonable shade in many parts and electricity available. 40 new pitches have 4A electricity, water and drainage. Some areas also contain bungalows. The site has frontage to the lake in two places (with some other property in between), with beach, jetty and moorings. Windsurfing can be practised and there is a school in season. There is a new, large modern swimming pool complex with `hydro massage' (jacuzzi) plus a children's pool. New sanitary blocks have been completed in the last two years which include washbasins in private cabins, facilities for the disabled and a children's room with small showers, British WCs and basins. All blocks have free hot water. There is a supermarket and restaurant complex and a new children's playground. A leisure card (costing L. 10,000 for adults, 7,000 for children) is required to participate in the activities.

How to find it: From Desenzano at southerly end of Lake Garda follow S572 north towards Salo. Following signs for San Felice turn off towards lake. Then follow yellow tourist signs bearing camp name.

General Details: Open 1 April - 30 Sept. Self-service shop. Bazaar. Restaurant/bar. Laundry. Swimming pools. Tennis courts. Table tennis. Children's playground. Bowling alley. Surf boards, canoes and bicycles for hire. Animation and entertainment (every night in season). Disco. Tournaments, swimming, surfing and tennis lessons. First aid room. Chemical disposal. Bungalows and caravans to let.

Charges 1997: Per person L. 6,500 - 10,000; child (2-9 yrs) 5,500 - 8,500; pitch with car, electricity, water and drainage 17,000 - 25,000; pitch with electricity only 15,000 - 22,000; small tent pitch, no electricity 14,000; extra car 8,000 - 12,000; trailer 8,000 - 15,000. Rates include VAT.

Reservations: not usually necessary for caravans and tents, but will be made for min. 7 days with 30% deposit and L.25,000 fee. Address: Via Silvella 10; 25010 S. Felice del Benaco (Brescia). Tel: 0365/651095. FAX: 0365/654395.

6275 Fornella Camping, San Felice, Salo, nr Brescia

Good site with pool and access to Lake Garda.

Garda is not only the largest Italian lake, it is also one of the most beautiful and being sheltered in the north by the Dolomites enjoys a very mild climate. It is also central for exploring the many historical, architectural, artistic and cultural gems of northern Italy. Fornella Camping is another of the good sites in this region where one is spoilt for choice. This open site is surrounded by olive and other trees with a backdrop of mountains and good views. Although there is access to the lake, this cannot be seen from all parts of the site as a tree covered hill intervenes. The 260 marked and numbered pitches are separated by access roads on flat grass and terraced where necessary, all with electricity. Mobile homes and bungalows for rent are on the edges of the tourist site and do not intrude. Shade is increasing as young trees grow. The well appointed bar/restaurant and the shop are by the lake side with a terrace giving splendid views over the lake. There is a pizzeria and takeaway at certain times. The pool and children's pool are of good size at the side of the site. Being well away from the main road, this is a quiet, peaceful camp. Three modern sanitary blocks are well dispersed around the site with mainly British type WCs and free hot water (7-10 am. and 5-10 pm. only) in the washbasins (some in cabins), showers and sinks. Facilities for disabled people. The friendly management speak excellent English.

How to find it: From main SS572 Desenzano-Salo road on west side of lake, head for San Felice and follow signs.

General Details: Open 1 May - 30 Sept. 70,000 sq.m. Bar/restaurant. Pizzeria and takeaway. Shop. Swimming pool. Tennis. Table tennis. Volleyball. Two children's playgrounds. Animation for children in season. Washing machines, dryer and irons. Chemical disposal.

Charges guide: Per person L. 7,000 - 9,900; child (3-12 yrs) 5,900 - 7,500; pitch incl. electricity (3A) 14,300 - 19,500; extra car 5,500 - 7,500; boat, trailer 7,000; dog 6,000. Less 20% for 2 week stays in low season.

Reservations: Made with deposit and fee; contact site for details. Address: Via Fornella 1, 25010 San Felice del Benaco (BS). Tel: 0365/62294. FAX: 0365/559418. (Winter: tel/fax: 0365/62200). E-mail: scavazza@gardanet.it.

6270 Villaggio Turistico Camping La Gardiola, San Felice, Salo, nr Brescia

Modern, small site on Lake Garda with access to private beach.

Campsites have mushroomed on this part of Lake Garda as it is a very popular holiday area, and La Gardiola, opened in 1991, is a recent addition. Situated on sloping ground, it is not directly on the lake shore but is only separated by a small private road and has access to a private beach. As yet there is little grass or shade but the 40 tourist pitches are of good size and on flat terraces. All have electrical connections and some waste disposal and water points. The single sanitary block is just below ground level with a lift system and facilities for disabled people. Fully tiled and of excellent quality, it has free hot water in washbasins (cabins), showers and sinks. Small kiosk on site with other shops 100 m.

continued overleaf

6270 Villaggio Turistico Camping La Gardiola (continued)

How to find it: Near San Felice on the SS572 Salo - San Felice road, the site is well signed at San Felice.

General Details: Open 10 April - 30 Sept. 9,000 sq.m. Small kiosk on site with restaurants, shops, pizzerias etc. nearby. Electrical connections in all places. Children's playground. Private beach on lake. Fishing. Laundry room. Chemical disposal. Caravans to rent (12).

Charges 1998: Per person L. 6,000 - 10,000; child (under 6 yrs) 5,000 - 9,000; pitch incl. electricity and water 16,000 - 27,000; dog 3,000 - 8,000. VAT included.

Reservations: Made with L.30,000 deposit. Address: Via Gardiola 36, 25010 S. Felice del Benaco (BS). Tel: 0365 /559240 (winter 0365/520018). FAX: 0365/520690. Internet: http://home.t-online.de/home/777000029631-001/garda.htm.

6265 Villagio Turistico Camping Ideal Molino, San Felice, Salô, nr Brescia

Small Garda lakeside site with an individual garden-like atmosphere.

Molino is a small site with charm and character which may appeal to those who do not like the larger and ordered sites. A friendly family atmosphere is being maintained by the family of the original site owners. English is spoken. The terrain is mainly on fairly level ground along the lake with a hill rising quite sharply behind. It is in two main parts divided by the camp buildings, and pitches vary in character: some by the lake, some for tents on terraces, and many in rows with pergolas, flowering shrubs etc. The size of the individual plots has been increased and, although charges are not low, this attractive site should appeal to the discriminating. Caravan and some tent pitches have electrical (3A), water and drainage connections. It is one of the few Garda sites where one can reserve and in high season this is most advisable. There is a small stony beach at one end; elsewhere one steps straight down into shallow water. The cleanliness of the Garda lake has been much improved by recent measures. Boats can be brought and there is a floating pontoon for sunbathing, diving, boat landing. While all facilities are of good standard they are being continually updated. The three small sanitary blocks, recently renovated, should be entirely adequate. They have British WCs, individual basins with free hot water and free hot showers. The site does not like radios or TVs, or any noise after 11 p.m.

How to find it: From Desenzano at southerly end of lake Garda follow S572 north towards Salô. Turn off towards lake, following signs for San Felice. Then follow yellow signs bearing camp name. Site is about 4 km. outside Salô.

General Details: Open 23 March - 30 Sept. 20,000 sq.m. Well shaded. Electrical and water and drainage connections. Shop. Restaurant/bar. Bicycle hire. Table tennis. Fishing. Waterski-ing. Free organised entertainment. Boat excursions to markets in lakeside towns. Laundry. Chemical disposal. Very well equipped bungalows for hire - details from address below. No dogs accepted.

Charges 1997: Per person L. 7,000 - 11,000; child (2-9 yrs) 5,700 - 8,500; pitch 14,000 - 21,500.

Reservations: made for min. 7 days from February onwards, with booking fee and large deposit. Address: via Gardiola 1, 25010 San Felice del Benaco (Brescia). Tel: 0365/62023. FAX: 0365/559395.

ITALY - North West

6235 Camping Monte Brione, Riva del Garda

New municipal site at northern end of Lake Garda.

The small resort of Riva at the head of Lake Garda shelters under a rocky escarpment and from ancient times has been an important communication and trading centre on the route between Verona and the Alps. Today it is a picturesque tourist resort and a good centre for enjoying the pleasures of the lake and nearby attractions. Camping Monte Brione is quietly situated on the edge of town at the foot of an olive covered hill, about 250 m. from the lake side. There are 101 pitches on flat, well mown grass, marked by trees and posts in groups of 4 around a water and electricity (6A) service point. Unmarked terraces on the hillside take 15 tents. Good tarmac roads dissect the site which has a neat, well tended air. Although near a small residential development, there are good views of the mountains. Two modern sanitary blocks, one at either end of the site, have mixed Turkish and British style WCs and free hot water in washbasins (private cabins), good sized showers and sinks. Facilities for disabled people. Shop for basic supplies, snack bar, bar and covered terrace. Good sized swimming pool with a sunbathing area. Limited entertainment and animation in high season and two children's play areas. The town is within walking distance by a lakeside path and has many shops and restaurants.

How to find it: Leave A22 at Garda-Nord exit for Torbole and Riva. Just before Riva, through short tunnel, then turn right at camp signs.

General Details: Open Easter - early Oct. 33,000 sq.m. Electricity in all parts. Bar with terrace. Small shop. Snack bar. Swimming pool (1/6-30/9). Minigolf. Table tennis. Bowls. TV/video. Bicycle hire. Organised activities. Fishing, riding, sailing, boating and tennis near (reduced rates for campers). Chemical disposal. Motorcaravan services.

Charges 1998: Per person L. 12,000; child (3-12 yrs) 8,000; pitch 18,000; dog 6,000.

Reservations: Write to site with 20% deposit (refundable) of anticipated bill. Address: Via Brione 32, 38066 Riva del Garda (TN). Tel: 0464/520885 or 520890. FAX: 0464/553178.

6230 Camping San Christoforo, Pergine Valsugana, nr Trento

Quiet, mountain site near lake, with views and swimming pool.

This part of Italy is becoming better known by those wishing to spend time by a lake in splendid countryside, but away from the more crowded, better known resorts. Lake Caldonazzo is one of the smaller lakes, but is excellent for watersports, with some twenty lifeguards on duty in the season. San Christoforo is a new site on the edge of the small town of the same name and is separated from the lake by a minor road, but with easy access. The site has 160 pitches on flat grass on either side of hard access roads. The pitches are of a good size with 3A electricity, numbered in front and separated by trees. The modern sanitary block has British style WCs, free hot water in basins (some cabins) and showers; there are footbaths, sinks with free hot water for washing up and laundry and facilities for disabled people. Swimming pool (20 x 20 m.) with sunbathing area and small children's pool. The village shops are close, and the site has a quiet and well cared for air; English is spoken. Used by a tour operator.

How to find it: Site is southeast of Trento, just off the SS47 road; well signed from the village of S. Christoforo.

General Details: Open 22 May - 13 Sept. Electrical connections throughout. Small well stocked shop. Bar/restaurant (all year) with waiter service and takeaway. Swimming pool and child's pool. Bathing, boating and fishing in the lake. Bicycle hire. Minigolf. Washing machine and dryer. Chemical disposal.

Charges 1998: Per person L. 10,000 - 12,000; child 2-5 yrs 6,000 - 7,500, 6-11 yrs 7,000 - 9,500; pitch 16,000 - 16,600; extra car 6,000; dog 6,000. Discounts for longer stays in low season.

Reservations: Not accepted. Address: Loc. San Christoforo, 38057 Pergine Valsugana (TN). Tel: 0461/512707 or 706290. FAX: 0461/707381.

6225 Camping Due Laghi, Levico Terme, nr Trento

Good modern site with swimming pool and mountain views, close to lake and spa town.

This modern site is close to the main road but is quiet and only 5 minutes walk from the Levico lake where it has a small attractive private beach where one can put boats. There are 350 numbered pitches on flat grass, in rows marked by slabs. Most are said to be approx. 80 sq.m. but there are now 60 larger pitches (90 sq.m) with electricity, water, TV and phone connections. On site is a good swimming pool of over 300 sq.m. with a children's pool also. It is therefore suitable for a stay as well as overnight. It is said to become full from 15/7-15/8 but there is always a chance of finding space. The central toilet block is of good quality and very large, with British and Turkish WCs, washbasins with free hot water (some in cubicles), free screened showers with pre-set hot water and a unit for disabled people.

How to find it: Site is 20 km. southeast of Trento just off the S47 road towards Padova (camp sign at turning).

General Details: Open 30 May - 8 Sept. Electrical connections (3A) in all parts. Self-service shop. Sauna. Restaurant, pizzeria and cafe/bar, with takeaway. Music weekly in high season. Tennis courts. Bicycle hire. Children's playground. Laundry. Chemical disposal. Motorcaravan services. Walks from site.

Charges 1998: Per person L. 10,000 - 12.000; child 2-5 yrs 6,000 - 7.500, 6-11 yrs 7,000 - 9,500; pitch 14,000 - 20,000 acc. to size and facilities; extra car 6,000. Discounts for longer stays.

Reservations: are made for at least 1 week in peak season, with substantial deposit and fee. Address: Loc. Costa 3, 38056 Levico Terme (Trento). Tel: 0461/706290. FAX: 0461/707381.

6210 Camping Steiner, Leifers/Laives, nr Bozen/Bolzano

Site with swimming pools and good facilities in central Dolomites, south of Bolzano.

Being on the main S12 which now has a motorway alternative, Camping Steiner is very central for touring with the whole of the Dolomite region within easy reach, as well as Bolzano, Merano and other attractive places. It has its share of overnight trade but is also a camp with much on site activity where one can spend an enjoyable holiday. It is a smallish site with part taken up by bungalows and the tourist pitches, mostly with good shade, are in rows on either side of access roads. They are all individual ones and most are on hardstandings. The two sanitary blocks, one new, can be heated in cool weather and have free hot water in washbasins, sinks and showers and British style WCs. The site becomes full in season. It is run personally by the proprietor's family and one has a friendly reception, with good English spoken. There are two free swimming pools on the site: an open air one, 20 x 10 m. (open May-Sept. and heated in spring), and a 12 x 6 m. enclosed pool (open all season, except July/Aug. and heated to about 25°). The site has an excellent small restaurant and takeaway service, with good choice.

How to find it: Site is on S12 in northern part of Leifers, 8 km. south of Bolzano. From motorway from north, take Bolzano-Süd exit and follow Trento signs for 7 km; from south take Ora exit for 14 km. towards Bolzano.

General Details: Open 28 March - 7 Nov. 20,000 sq.m. Electrical connections (6A) everywhere. Shop. Meals in hotel. Small restaurant and takeaway. Cellar bar with taped music, dancing at times. Swimming pools. General room. Sauna. Children's playground and paddling pool. Table tennis. Golf (18 hole) 30 mins. Chemical disposal. Wooden bungalows for hire for 4 to 5 persons. Rooms available in hotel.

Charges 1997: Per person L. 7,000 - 9,000; child (0-6 yrs) 4,500 - 6,000; pitch incl. car and 6A electricity 18,000 - 22,000; dog 8,000; extra car 6,000. Less 5-10% after 2 weeks stay.

Reservations: are made for minimum one week with reasonable deposit. Address: 39055 Leifers bei Bozen (Südtirol). Tel: 0471/950105. FAX: 0471/951572.

6205 International Camping Dolomiti, Cortina d'Ampezzo

Family run site in mountain setting beside famous resort.

The Cortina region boasts several good sites and this is one of the nearest to the town. It is a grassy site beside a fast flowing river in a broad flat area which is surrounded by mountain scenery - a quiet situation 3 km. from the town centre. The good sized pitches are marked out by white stones on either sides of access roads and most have electricity (4A). Half the site is well shaded. There is a heated swimming pool on site. It makes a good centre for touring the Dolomites or for more active pursuits such as mountain walking. The main toilet block is a large one and the installations, which should be adequate, include mainly Turkish style WCs, with some British, washbasins with hot water sprinkler taps, and free controllable hot showers. A heated block has been added which has facilities for the disabled. With no reservations made, arrive early in the day in the first three weeks of August.

How to find it: Site is south of Cortina, to west of main S51. There are signs from the road.

General Details: Open 15 May - 25 Sept. Small shop (open long hours) and coffee bar. Swimming pool (1/7-10/9). Restaurant 600 m. Basic children's playground (hard base). Chemical disposal. Washing machines and ironing.

Charges 1997: Per person L.7,000 - 13,000; child (under 6 yrs) 5,000 - 8,000; pitch 9,000 - 17,000.

Reservations: Not made. Address: 32043 Cortina d'Ampezzo. Tel: 0436/2485. FAX: 0436/5403.

6200 Camping Olympia, Toblach/Dobbiaco

Dolomite Mountains site on main route with excellent facilities.

Olympia, always good, has been given a face-lift by the redesigning of the camping area and the refurbishment of the already excellent sanitary accommodation. Tall trees at each end of the site have been left, but most of those in the centre have been removed and the pitches re-laid in a regular pattern. They include 12 fully serviced with electricity, water, waste, gas and TV and phone points. The static caravans are grouped together at one end leaving the centre for tourists and with a grass area at the other end for tents. An attractive centre piece has fountain surrounded by flowers. The excellent sanitary provision, on two floor levels, is in the main building which also has reception, restaurant, shop and apartments. Of a very high standard, there are 7 cabins with WC, washbasin and shower to rent. British style WCs and free hot water in washbasins (not in cabins but separated) showers and sinks. Also two small blocks at each end of the camp with WCs and showers. The attractive restaurant is open all day, all year, and opposite is a snack bar. Small swimming pool (10 x 6 m) open when weather permits. In high season, staff arrange an entertainment programme for children and adults.

How to find it: Site is between Villabassa and Toblach/Dobbiaco. From A22 Innsbruck-Bolzano, take Bressanone/Brixen exit and travel east on SS49 for 60 km. From Cortina take SS48 and SS51 northwards then west on SS49.

General Details: Open all year. 45,000 sq.m. Restaurant. Shop. Snack bar with grill meals (not April/May or Oct/Nov). Tennis. Swimming pool. Sauna, solarium, steam bath and whirl pools. Field for games. Table tennis. Minigolf. Fishing (on payment). Bicycle hire. Children's play area. Animation in high season . Horse riding near.

Charges 1997: Per person L. 10,000 - 11,000; child (3-10 yrs) 6,000 - 9,000; pitch 14,000 - 18,000; m/cycle 3,000; car 5,000 - 6,000; small tent 8,000 - 9,000.

Reservations: Write to site. Address: 39034 Toblach (Sudtirol). Tel: 0474/972147. FAX: 0474/972713.

ITALY - North East

6201 Camping Antholz, Antholz-Obertal

All year campsite in the heart of the Dolomites.

Appearances can be deceptive and this is the case with Camping Antholz. At first sight the 130 pitches (with 4A electricity), numbered, but only roughly marked out, make this a very ordinary looking site. Just inside the entrance is a pleasant looking building with reception and a smart restaurant. It is when one investigates the sanitary accommodation that one realises that this is no ordinary site, as the provision is quite superb, with under-floor heating, hair salon, cosmetics room, baby room, British WCs and free hot water in washbasins, sinks and showers. High up in the Anterselva valley, there are splendid views of near and distant peaks. The shop has limited supplies (village 500 m), the bar is open all day and the restaurant, with terrace, opens 18-22.00 hrs. This is good skiing country in winter (ski bus, school, lifts) and, with a new National Park near, provides good walking in summer.

How to find it: From Bressanone exit on A22, go east on SS49 through Brunico and turn north (signed Antholz) for about 12 km. Pass Antholz village and site is on right.

General Details: Open all year. 25,000 sq.m. Restaurant. Shop. Winter sports, summer walking. Children's play area. TV room. Table tennis. Bicycle hire. Tennis near. Washing machine and dryer. Motorcaravan service point.

Charges 1997: Per unit incl. 2 persons and electricity L. 31,500 - 34,500; extra person 8,000 - 9,000; child (2-12 yrs) 5,500 - 6,500; small tent 4,000.

Reservations: Write to site. Address: 39030 Antholz-Obertal (BZ). Tel: 0474/492204. FAX: 0474/492444.

6000 Camping Marepineta, Sistiana, nr Trieste

Site west of Trieste with good swimming pool and sea views over Baia di Sistiana.

This site is 18 km. west of Trieste, on raised ground near the sea, with views over the Sistiana Bay, Miramare Castle and the Gulf of Trieste. A pebbly beach with car park, is just beyond the site, a drive of about 1 km. (free bus service from camp runs every 40 mins from 9 am.-7 pm). Alternatively there is a large swimming pool (unheated), on site with a new terrace. The development of this site continues with modern reception buildings recently completed and refurbished, improved sanitary facilities. Over 350 of the 500 individual pitches are available for tourists. On hardstandings with gravel surface (awnings possible) in light woodland, all have electricity (from 3A) and water near. No animals allowed except in a designated area. Six toilet blocks of varying quality provide hot water in washbasins, including some for children and others in cabins, and free hot showers. British and Turkish style WCs. Facilities for disabled people. Sinks for laundry and dishes, most with hot water. For arrivals outside office hours there is a waiting area with water and toilet facilities. The Rilke footpath runs alongside the site.

How to find it: From west A4 autostrada Duino exit , turn left and camp is 1 km; from east approach on S14.

General Details: Open 1 May - 30 Sept. Shop (15/5-15/9). Bars. Pizzeria. Disco. Swimming pool (1/6-15/9) with lessons. New children's playground. Football, volleyball and mini-basket. Tennis. Table tennis. Games room. Entertainment in season. Fishing and bicycle hire nearby. First aid post. Laundry with dryer and ironing. Chemical disposal. Motorcaravan services. Mobile homes and caravans available for hire.

Charges 1997: Per pitch incl. electricity and water L. 15,000 - 22,000, pitch with view 19,000 - 26,000; person 7,500 - 10,000; child (3-12) 6,000 - 8,000. VAT incl

Reservations: Will be made with 40% deposit and L 30.000 fee. Address: 34019 Sistiana 60/D, Duino-Aurisina (TS). Tel: 040/299264. FAX: 040/299265.

AR Discount
Less 10% in low season on pp fee (min 3 days)

6005 Villaggio Turistico Camping Europa, Grado, nr Trieste

Large seaside site with swimming pools and other amenities.

This large flat site on the edge of the sea can take over 600 units. All pitches are marked, nearly all with good shade and there are electrical connections (4A) in all parts. The terrain is sandy in the areas nearer the sea, where cars have to be left in parking places and not by your pitch. Dogs are taken only in a special section. There is direct access to the beach but the water is shallow up to 200 m. from beach, with growing seaweed. However, there is a narrow wooden jetty stretching out which one can walk along to deeper water. For those who prefer, there is a new swimming pool near the sea and, on the site, a medium sized heated pool and smaller children's pool. The four main toilet blocks are identical with free hot water, half British WCs and hot showers, as well as numerous washing sinks. Facilities for disabled people. A good honest site which, after recent improvements, is probably the best in the area.

How to find it: Site is 4 km. east of Grado on Monfalcone road. On road 35L go through Grado to Grado Pineta.

General Details: Open 10 April - 20 Sept. Supermarket; general shop (May - Sept). Bar, Self-service restaurant, with takeaway (all season). Swimming pools (May-Sept, 10 am.-7 pm). 2 tennis courts. Football. Table tennis. Fishing. Bicycle hire. Children's playground. Dancing and some activities July/Aug. Washing machines. Chemical disposal. Motorcaravan services. Good bungalows and caravans for hire.

Charges 1998: Per person L. 8,000, 9,500 or 13,000; child (3-10) free, 5,500, 8.000; pitch incl. electricity 14,000, 15,000 or 23,000. Less 10% for low season long stays.

Reservations: Advised for high season; made for min. 1 week Sat. to Sat, with deposit in high season (50% of total). Address: PO Box 129, 34073 Grado (Gorizia). Tel: 0431/80877. FAX: 0431/82284.

AR Discount
Less 10% in low season for stays over 10 days

6037 Campeggio Giuliana Bungalow, Ca'Ballarin, Cavallino

Small site, open all year.

This camp is unique in this area in two respects, firstly it is open all year and, secondly it is 500 m. from the sea and not directly by the shore. 40 bungalows and 4 caravans (for hire) are situated along each side of the square shaped camp with space in the centre, under vines, for between 17 and 20 units. Pitches, mainly on sand, are not marked or numbered but some order is given as the resident owner tells campers where to stay. Flowers and the overhead vines make for a pleasant, garden like atmosphere. The small sanitary units have British style WCs and free hot water in basins, showers and sinks. The restaurant `Anna` is open during the summer season but, being in the village, shops and other restaurants are very close. There is musical entertainment in the restaurant twice weekly. Venice is a 40 minute bus/boat ride away, Lido di Jesolo about 25 minutes and other attractions of northern Italy can be reached by car or coach excursions. Small children's play area but the beach is some 500 m. and involves crossing a main road. The friendly owner speaks good English and will help with any information on the locality.

How to find it: From the A4 Venice-Trieste autostrada take airport exit. At airport continue on SS14, follow signs for Jesolo, then Punta Sabbioni and camp will be found at the restaurant Anna in the village of Ca'Ballarin.

General Details: Open all year. Shade most parts. Restaurant (summer only), others and shops near. Small children's play area. Fishing. Bicycle hire. Sports facilities near. Bungalows for hire.

Charges 1997: Per person L. 7,500 - 10,000; child under 2 free; pitch 10,000 - 15,000.

Reservations: Write to site. Address: via Rialto 13, Ca'Ballarin, 30013 Cavallino (VE). Tel: 041/968039. FAX: 041/5370443.

6040 Camping Village Garden Paradiso, Cavallino, Jesolo, nr Venice

Very good medium size, seaside site with swimming pools.

Although there has been much adverse publicity in the media about pollution of the Adriatic sea this has been largely absent in the northern part. However partly to compensate for this and also to add other amenities, sites in this area have added swimming pools. Garden Paradiso has built three of excellent quality in the centre of the site near the restaurant and shopping complex. Compared with other sites here, this one is of medium size with 850 pitches. Most have electricity (from 4A), water and drainage points and all are marked and numbered with hard access roads, under a good cover of trees. Flowers and shrubs abound giving a pleasant and peaceful appearance. The site is directly on the sea with a beach of fine sand. There are four brick, tiled sanitary blocks around the site with a mix of British and Turkish style WCs, free hot water in the basins, showers and sinks, and facilities for babies. The restaurant, with self-service at lunch time and waiter service at night, is near the beach with a bar/snack bar in the centre of the site. Entertainment, animation and excursions are offered in high season.

How to find it: Leave the Venice-Trieste autostrada either by taking the airport or Quarto d'Altino exits; follow signs to Jesolo Punta Sabbioni. Take the first road on the left after Cavallino and site is a little way on the right.

General Details: Open 1 May - 30 Sept. 13,000 sq.m. Restaurant. Snack bar. Shops. Tennis. Table tennis. Minigolf. Swimming pools. Entertainment in season. Bicycle hire. Children's play area. Washing machines and dryers. Chemical disposal. Motorcaravan services. Caravans and maxi-caravans for hire.

Charges 1997: Per person L. 5,250 - 12,500; junior (1-6 yrs) or senior (over 60 yrs) 3,700 - 9,800; pitch 11,600 - 29,300. Less 10% for stays over 30 days (early) 20 days (late) season. Credit cards accepted.

Reservations: Made with deposit (L. 250,000 - 300,000) - write to site for details. Address: 30013 Cavallino (VE). Tel: 041/968075. FAX: 041/5370382.

6035 Camping Mediterraneo, Treporti, Jesolo, nr Venice/Venezia

Large site with a wide range of amenities including large swimming pools.

This big site has been considerably improved in recent years and is near Punta Sabbioni from where boats go to Venice. Mediterraneo is directly on the Adriatic Sea with a 480 m. long beach of fine sand which shelves gently and also two large pools and a whirlpool. Sporting, fitness and entertainment programmes are arranged and sea swimming is supervised by lifeguards. The 800 pitches, of which 500 have electricity (from 4A), water and drainaway, are partly in boxes with artificial shade, some larger without shade, with others in unmarked zones under natural woodland equipped with electric hook ups where tents must go. The eight modern sanitary blocks are good with British type WCs and free hot water in the washbasins, showers and sinks. The commercial centre near reception has a supermarket and other shops with a restaurant, bars and a pizzeria near the pools. An organised and efficient site.

How to find it: Site is well signed from Jesolo-Punta Sabbioni road near its end after Ca' Ballerin and before Ca' Savio. Follow camp signs, not those for Treporti as this village is some way from the site.

General Details: Open 1 May - 30 Sept. 170,000 sq.m. Shop. Large bar and snack bar by pool. Restaurant. Tennis. Minigolf. Table tennis. Surf and swimming school. Programme of sports, games, excursions etc; dancing or shows in main season. Refrigerator hire. Washing machines. Chemical disposal. Motorcaravan services.

Charges 1998: Four rates. Per person L. 5,400 - 12,600; child (3-5 yrs) 3,800 - 9,500; pitch with electricity 11,000 - 25,500, with 3 services 11,700 - 29,500; tent with electricity 8,200 - 22,500. VAT included. Credit cards accepted.

Reservations: made with deposit. Address: 30010 Ca'Vio-Treporti (VE). Tel: 041/966721 /22. FAX: 041/966944.

6020 Camping Union Lido Vacanze, Cavallino, Jesolo, nr Venice/Venezia
6010 Camping Capalonga, Bibione Pineda, Bibione, nr Venice/Venezia
6015 Camping Residence Il Tridente, Bibione Pineda, Bibione

The editorial reports for these sites appear on pages 192/3 opposite their colour advertisements

6025 Camping Residence, Cavallino, Jesolo, nr Venice/Venezia

Pleasant, well run site by beach with first class, clean installations.

The Litorale del Cavallino has a large number of excellent sites, giving a good choice for those wishing to visit and stay in this area near Venice. Residence is a very good site with a sandy beach directly on the Adriatic and is well kept, with many floral displays. Pitches are marked out with small fences or pines, which give good shade, and are laid out in regular rows on level sand. These boxes vary in size with those for caravans larger than those for tents and all have electricity (6A). A medium size site (for this region) of 300 tourist pitches, it is smaller than 6020 but has the same strict rules regarding noise (no radios or dogs, quiet periods) but is less formal and more personal. The beach fronting has been enlarged and improved and the sea bed shelves gradually making it safe for children. Excellent swimming pools and sunbathing areas. Good animation in high season for children and adults. Venice can be easily reached by bus to Punta Sabbioni and ferry across the lagoon and there are organised excursions. The three large sanitary blocks are very clean with full facilities including free hot water in basins, sinks and showers with British style WCs. Although of good quality, they are being refurbished.

How to find it: From the A4 Venice-Trieste autostrada leave at exit for Airport or Quarto D'Altino, follow signs for Jesolo and then Punta Sabbioni. Take first left after Cavallino and camp is 800 m. on right (well signed).

General Details: Open 24 March - 15 Sept. 70,000 sq m. Supermarket, separate shops for fruit and other goods. Restaurant with separate bar. Takeaway. Children's playground. swimming pools. Dancing or disco by beach until 11 pm three times weekly June-August and entertainment programme. Fitness programme. Boat moorings at nearby marina. Ladies hairdresser. Car wash. Table tennis. Small tennis court. Video games room. Post office. Bureau de change. Minigolf. Doctor will call. Chemical disposal. Modern apartments, bungalows and maxi-caravans for hire.

Charges guide: Per person L. 5,500 - 10,500; child (under 5 yrs) 3,800 - 8,200; pitch 12,000 - 24,000.

Reservations: Made for min. 1 week with L. 150,000 deposit. Address: via F.Baracca 47, 30013 Cavallino (Venezia). Tel: 041/968027 or 968127. FAX: 041/5370164.

6050 Camping Caravanning della Serenissima, Oriago, nr Venice/Venezia

Convenient site for overnight stay or for visiting Venice and other places in this region.

This is a delightful little site of some 125 pitches (120 with 16A electricity) where one could stay for a number of days whilst visiting Venice (12 km), Padova (24), Verona (24), Lake Garda (135) or the Dolomites. There is a good service by bus and boat to Venice and the site is situated on the `Riviera', a section of a river with some very large old villas. The site is used mainly by Dutch and British with some Germans, and is calm and quiet. It is long, narrow and flat with numbered pitches on each side of a central road. There is good shade in most parts with many trees, plants and grass. The single sanitary block is just adequate, has been and still is being improved, with free hot water in washbasins, showers and sinks. Mainly Turkish style WCs. The management is very friendly and good English is spoken.

How to find it: From the east take road S11 at the roundabout SSW of Mestre towards Padova and site is 2 km. on your right. From the west, leave autostrada A4 at Dolo exit, follow signs to Dolo, continue on main road through this small village and left at T-junction (traffic lights). Continue towards Venice on S11 for site about 6 km on your left.

General Details: Open Easter - 10 Nov. Shop (all season). Restaurant and bar (from May). Children's play area. Fishing. Bicycle hire. Reduced price bus/boat ticket to Venice if staying for 3 days. No organised entertainment but local markets etc. well publicised. Chemical disposal. Motorcaravan services. Bungalows and mobile homes to rent.

Charges 1997: Per unit L. 16,000 - 18,000; adult 9,000; child (3-12 yrs) 8,000. Credit cards accepted.

Reservations: are made. Address: 30030 Oriago (Venezia). Tel: 041/921850. FAX: 041/920286.

6030 Camping dei Fiori, Treporti, Lido del Cavallino, nr Venice

Excellent small site with swimming pools and special hydro-massage pools.

The peninsula Lido del Cavallino, stretching from the outskirts of Lido del Jessolo to Punta Sabbioni, has almost 40 good camps directly on the Adriactic sea and convenient for visiting Venice and other interesting places in northeast Italy. Dei Fiori stands out amongst the other small camps in the area. As its name implies, it is aflame with colourful flowers and shrubs in summer and presents a neat and tidy appearance whilst providing a quiet atmosphere. About a quarter of the pitches are taken by static units, many for hire. The 400 tourist pitches, with 5A electricity, are either in woodland where space varies according to the trees which have been left in their natural state, or under artificial shade where regular shaped pitches are of reasonable size. Well built bungalows for hire enhance the site and are in no way intrusive, giving a village-like effect. Shops and a restaurant are in the centre next to the swimming pools. Nearby is the hydro-massage bath which is splendidly appointed and reputed to be the largest in Italy. This is under the supervision of qualified staff, as is the fitness centre. A charge is made during middle and high seasons but not in low season. The long beach is of fine sand and shelves gently into the sea. The resident animation team offer a daily programme for children and activities for adults which includes games, tournaments and entertainment. Regulations ensure the site is quiet between 11 pm. - 7.30 am. and during the afternoon siesta period. Three sanitary blocks are conveniently situated around the site and are of exceptional quality with British style WCs, well equipped baby rooms, good facilities for the disabled, washing machines and dryers and free hot water in all facilities. Venice is about 40 minutes away by bus and boat and excursions are arranged from the site. The site is well maintained by friendly, English speaking management.

How to find it: Leave the A4 Venice-Trieste autostrada either by taking the airport or Quarto d'Altino exits and follow signs for Jesolo and then Punta Sabbioni and camp signs just after Ca'Ballarin.

General Details: Open 27 April - 4 Oct. 10,000 sq.m. Restaurant. Shops . Tennis. Table tennis. Minigolf. Basketball. Entertainment and excursions. Adult and children's swimming pools. Children's play area. Children's club. Windsurfing. Hydro-massage bath, fitness centre and programmes. Bicycle hire near. Washing machines and dryers. Chemical disposal. Motorcaravan services. Bungalows and caravans for rent. English spoken.

Charges 1998: Four seasons. Per person L. 6,900 - 13,200; child (1-5 yrs) 5,200 - 10,200; pitch with 3 services 14,000 - 31,300, pinewood pitch with electricity 13,000 - 27,500; tent pitch in pinewood with electricity 10,000 - 25,000. Credit cards accepted. *Min. stay 7 days in high season (4/7-29/8).*

Reservations: Advised for high season (incl. Whitsun) and made for min. 7 days. Write for application form as early as possible. Address: 30010 Treporti (VE). Tel: 041/966448. FAX: 041/966724.

6055 Villagio Turistico Isamar, Sa. Anna di Chioggia, nr Venice/Venezia

Seaside site south of Venice with six good swimming pools.

Many improvements have been made here over the years and these continue, making it difficult to itemise all the amenities. Although directly by the sea, with its own beach of fine sand, it is a fair way from the entrance to the sea. The largest camping area, under pines, is grouped around a swimming pool, the large modern sanitary block, shops, etc. near reception. There is a smaller area under artificial shade near the beach with an Olympic size, salt-water swimming pool, children's pool and four new pools. Here also are a covered entertainment section, pizzeria, bar/restaurant and small toilet block. Between these sections are well constructed bungalows available for rent. A third camping area has been developed but as yet with little shade. The pitches, on either side of hard access roads, vary in size and all have electrical connections. The site may become crowded in high season. The main toilet block is of good quality with British WCs (small block has only Turkish style), and free hot water in washbasins, showers and sinks. An extensive entertainment and fitness programme is offered for adults and there is supervised play for children over 4 years of age, a disco and a games room with pin tables. The site has a much higher proportion of Italian holidaymakers than many other sites and it is also popular with the Germans and Dutch. No dogs permitted.

How to find it: Turn off main 309 road towards sea just south of Adige river about 10 km. south of Chioggia, and proceed 5 km. to site.

General Details: Open 13 May - 24 Sept. Supermarket and general shopping centre. Large bar/pizzeria and self-service restaurant. Tennis. Hairdresser. Swimming pools. Children's playground. Fridges for hire. Disco. Entertainment programme.

Charges guide: Four rates acc. to season (highest 22/7-19/8): Per person L. 5,000 - 12,500; child (2-5 yrs) 4,000 - 10,500, under 2 yrs 3,000 - 6,500; pitch with full facilities 13,000 - 30,000; tent pitch 6,500 - 19,000. Less 10% for stays over 3 weeks.

Reservations: made for min. 7 days with deposit (L. 30,000) from Sat. or Thurs. Address: Isolaverde, 30010 Sa. Anna di Chioggia (VE). Tel: 041/498100. FAX: 041/490440.

ITALY - North East

6065 Camping Tahiti, Lido delle Nazioni, nr Ravenna

Site with swimming pools and other amenities north of Ravenna.

Tahiti is a well run but informal site, ¼ mile from the sea. It has a medium sized swimming pool, small children's pool and new water play area with shallow pools, small waterfall and lying out area. About 25% is taken up by Italian seasonal units but it has over 500 individual pitches of reasonable size, under shade. Some 36 pitches have a private WC with cold water washbasin. It can be full from mid-July to mid-August when reservation is advisable. There is one large and three smaller toilet blocks, plus a new one. They are of satisfactory quality with British and Turkish style WCs and free hot water in individual basins and in the pre-mixed hot showers. No dogs are allowed.

How to find it: Turn off S309 35 km. north of Ravenna to Lido delle Nazioni (north of Lido di Pomposa) and follow camp signs.

General Details: Open 16 May - 20 Sept. 80,000 sq.m. Electrical connections (3A) throughout. Supermarket. Self service restaurant. Pizza bar. Swimming pools. 2 children's playgrounds. Bicycle hire. Tennis. Table tennis. Minigolf. Volleyball. Football pitch. Sailing school on beach. Dancing and cinema once weekly. Organised events in season. Daily medical service. Washing machines. Chemical disposal. Bungalows for hire (20).

Charges 1997: Per person L. 10,900; child (under 8) 9,900; pitch incl. electricity 20,900; private toilet 6,000 - 12,000. Less 40% in low season.

Reservations: made for min. 1 week (2 weeks 6/7-23/8) with deposit. Address: 44020 Lido delle Nazioni (Ferrara). Tel: 0533/379500. FAX: 0533/379700. E-mail: info@tahiti.com. Internet: http://www.campingtahiti.com.

6075 Camping Cesenatico, Cesenatico, nr Ravenna

Large, edge of town site with access to private beach.

The northern Adriatic coast of Italy is popular with British visitors and this is a well appointed site about midway between Rimini and Ravenna. It is a large site under trees on flat grass at the northern end of Cesenatico. Apart from the nearby attractions of San Marino, Ravenna and Rimini, Florence and Venice are within easy reach for day visits. However the site also provides attractions of its own, with access to a private beach (free umbrellas), many sports, disco and entertainment for children. There are 800 pitches, of which half are for tourers, numbered and marked out by trees, so size varies but is adequate; 4A electricity to all places. An unusual feature is the 37 small toilet blocks around the site. These are of mixed construction and quality, but acceptable with mainly Turkish style, some British WCs, free hot water to some basins, showers and dishwashing points, plus washrooms for disabled people.

How to find it: Site is on the SS16 on north edge of Cesenatico, and is well signed.

General Details: Open 1 April - 25 Sept. Good shade. Bar/restaurant and takeaway. Supermarket. Hairdresser. Bazaar. Tennis. Minigolf. Table tennis. Watersports. Disco. Washing machines and dryers. Motorcaravan services.

Charges 1997: Per adult L. 6,000 - 10,500, acc. to season; child (3-8 yrs) 5,000 - 8,500; car, tent, caravan or motorcaravan 13,500 - 18,000, with electricity 16,500 - 24,500; small tent incl. 2 persons 21,000 - 30,000; extra car 6,500 - 10,000. Minimum price per pitch 28,000 - 42,000.

Reservations: Write to site. Address: Via Mazzini 182, 47042 Cesenatico (FO). Tel: 0547/81344. FAX: 0547/672452. E-mail: gesturist@linknet.it.

6070 Camping Park Adriano, Punta Marina Terme, nr Ravenna

Large, well shaded site with swimming pool, near beach on Adriatic Riviera.

This quietly situated site is about 8 km. to the north of Ravenna and has many attractive amenities for a family holiday. Tall, mature trees determine pitches and give excellent shade in all parts. Some 700 pitches have 4A electricity and satellite TV connections. The beach is about 200 m. from the site entrance, but the camp has an excellent swimming pool and many sports and recreational facilities, including a small theatre with nightly entertainment of films and dancing. There is a 'nature track' amongst the trees on one side of the site. The camp's reserved section of the beach has a bar with snacks and beach equipment for hire. A nearby sailing centre has windsurf boards and boats for hire. Trips are organised to famous towns and beauty spots. Five toilet blocks around the site are fairly old but fully tiled and clean, with British and Turkish WCs, hot water in some basins, showers and sinks and have facilities for disabled people. Snack bar by the pool. The bar, restaurant, pizzeria and a shopping centre with supermarket, bazaar, greengrocer, ice cream parlour, tobacconist and newsagent are near reception.

How to find it: From the SS309 Ravenna - Venice road, follow signs to Lido Adriano and camp signs from there. Site has many road side advertising boards some distance from the camp but these give no directions.

General Details: Open 23 April - 30 Sept. 140,000 sq.m. Good shade. Restaurants, bars and shops as above. Children's play park. Swimming pool (May-Sept). Minigolf. Handball court. Bowls area. Football field. Table tennis. Games room with video games and billiards. TV room. Jogging track. Entertainment and excursions in high season. Washing machines, dryers and irons. Chemical disposal. Motorcaravan services. Bungalows to rent.

Charges 1997: Per unit L. 12,000 - 21,000; person 5,800 - 11,400; child (under 8 yrs) 4,500 - 10,300; electricity connection included; TV connection 500. Credit cards accepted.

Reservations: Write to site. Address: Via dei Campeggi 7, 48020 Punta Marina Terme (Ravenna). Tel: 0544/437230. FAX: 0544/438510.

6060 Camping Comunale Estense, Ferrara

Very useful municipal site, on outskirts of city.

Ferrara is, somewhat surprisingly, an interesting and historic city, well worth a short visit. The old city, surrounded by ancient walls, is attractive and mainly pedestrianised, with several museums, a cathedral and a wealth of architectural interest, but as a result of an apparent lack of publicity, has relatively few foreign visitors. The recently established municipal campsite, on the northern outskirts offers comfortable facilities for all types of unit and includes fairly large pitches, with numerous electrical connections, and two adjacent well fitted sanitary blocks (one heated) with large free hot showers, British and Turkish style WCs, etc. The showers have no separated dressing area, the hooks are on outside walls and the tiled floors become very slippery. In summer the two blocks seem to open on alternate days, presumably to save on cleaning and one suspects this may be a bit variable. However, despite the somewhat uncared for overall appearance, it proved to be perfectly adequate and comfortable, with a friendly reception and (for Italy) reasonable prices. No on-site facilities other than those described above, but there is an excellent trattoria within walking distance (1 km.) and a wide choice of other eating places in the city itself.

How to find it: Site is well signed from the city and is situated on the northern side of the ring road.

General Details: Open all year.

Charges 1997: Per person (over 8 yrs) L. 5,000; pitch 10,000; dog 2,000.

Reservations: Policy not known - contact site. Address: Via Gramicia, 80, 44100 Ferrara. Tel: 0532/752.396. FAX: 0532/239.389. Tourist information office: Tel: 0532/209370. FAX: 0532/212266. E-mail: infotur.comfe@ fe.nettuno.it.

6602 Camping-Hotel Citta' di Bologna, Bologna

Good quality site in historic city.

This site was established as recently as 1993 on the edge of the Trade Fair Centre of this ancient and historic city. Although near enough to the motorway to be aware of traffic 'hum', the site is surrounded by fields and trees giving a peaceful atmosphere. The intention was not only to make a camp site, but to provide high quality motel-type rooms for use by those visiting trade fairs. Although the bungalows are self-contained, a fine sanitary block for campers' use has been constructed in the centre of the camping area. Hot water is free in washbasins and sinks and on meter in the showers. There is excellent provision for the disabled (with British WCs and free showers) with alarms which ring in reception. WCs, except for two in each section are Turkish style. The pitches are numbered and marked out by young trees (60-75 sq.m.) on level grass with hardstandings (open fretwork of concrete through which grass can grow) in two areas. A restaurant is planned but there is no date for completion. The site is excellent for an overnight stop or for longer stays to explore Emilia-Romagna.

How to find it: Site is well signed from 'Fiera' exit on the autostrada on the northeast of the city.

General Details: Open all year (except 10 days at Christmas). 63,000 sq.m. Electrical connections (6A) in all areas. Excellent facilities for the disabled. Bar. Soft drinks and snacks available from machine. Small children's play area. Table tennis. Football. Minigolf. Volleyball. Shops and restaurant 500 m. Medical room - doctor will call. Washing machines. Chemical disposal. Motorcaravan services. Bus service to city centre from site.

Charges 1998: Per person L. 6,000 - 8,500; child (3-8 yrs) 5,000 - 6,500; pitch 13,000 - 17,000; electricity incl.

AR Discount

Less 10%

Reservations: Write to site. Address: Campeggio Citta' di Bologna, Via Romita 12/4a, 40127 Bologna. Tel: 051/325016. FAX: 051/325318.

6608 Camping Torre Pendente, Pisa

Pisa's most central site.

Camping Torre Pendente is within walking distance of the famous leaning tower. It is a friendly site, well run by the Signorini family who speak good English and make everyone feel welcome. Obviously the excellent position means it is busy throughout the main season. A medium sized site, it is on level, grassy ground with tarmac or gravel access roads and some shade. There are 220 touring pitches, 160 with 5A electrical connections. Sanitary facilities are very adequate with hot showers and mainly British style toilets. A swimming pool is planned, but meanwhile there is a municipal pool nearby. The shop, bar and restaurant cater for all pockets; the meals sampled were very good. Consider a visit in mid-June to coincide with the town fiesta - the candle-lit river banks and leaning tower are something to behold.

How to find it: From autostrada A12, exit at Pisa Nord and follow signs for 5 km. to Pisa. The site is well signed at a left turn into the town centre (Viale delle Cascine) and is then a short distance on the left hand side.

General Details: Open week before Easter - 15 October. 24,000 sq.m. Shop. Bar. Restaurant. Bicycle hire. Children's playground. Chemical disposal. Motorcaravan services. Caravans and bungalows for hire.

Charges 1997: Per adult L. 9,500; child (3-10 yrs) 4,500; car 5,000; tent 8,000; 1 person tent 4,500; caravan 9,000; motorcaravan 13,000; m/cycle 3,000; trailer 3,000.

AR Discount

Welcome drink

Reservations: Contact site. Address: Viale delle Cascine 86, 56122 Pisa. Tel: 050/561704. FAX: 050/561734.

ITALY - Central

6600 Camping Barco Reale, San Baronto, nr Pistoia

Beautiful site in Tuscany hills, with fine views.

Just 40 minutes from Florence and an hour from Pisa, this site is beautifully situated high in the hills with fine views. Part of an old, walled estate, there are pleasant walks available in the grounds. A quiet site of 7.5 ha, and with good shade from mature pines and oaks, there are 175 numbered pitches, all for tourists but not all easily accessible for towed units. All have electricity (3, 5 or 10A) and 25 pitches with water and drainage are being added for '98. Two modern sanitary blocks are centrally positioned and are kept very clean with British and Turkish type WCs, free hot water throughout and with two toilets for disabled people. Bathrooms and baby rooms are planned. The site has an attractive bar, a very smart restaurant with terrace and a good sized swimming pool. Live music and other entertainments, including games for children, are arranged in high season. There is a small shop on site and others in the village 1 km. away. Outside the site itself but part of the estate are other leisure facilities listed below. A lake for fishing, a disco and an indoor pool are 5 km. away. This is an attractive site which will appeal to those who prefer a quiet site but with plenty to do for all age groups. No fires are permitted.

How to find it: From Pistoia take the Vinci - Empoli - Lamporecchio signs to San Baronto. From Empoli follow signs to Vinci and San Baronto. Final approach is around a sharp bend and up a steep slope.

General Details: Open 1 April - 30 Sept. Restaurant. Bar. Disco. Small shop, other 1 km. Swimming pool. Children's playground. Table tennis. Volleyball. Football. Chess. Bowls. Golf, indoor pool and fishing near. Entertainment and excursions organised (July/Aug). Laundry facilities. Chemical disposal. Motorcaravan services. Caravans (3) for hire.

Charges 1998: Three charging periods. Per person L. 8,500 - 11,800; child 0-3 yrs 4,500 - 6,500, 3-12 yrs 6,000 - 8,000; tent 7,400 - 9,100; trailer tent or caravan 9,500 - 12,500; motorcaravan 13,000 - 17,500; car 4,500 - 6,500; m/cycle 3,000 - 4,500; electricity 2,500. Tax included.

Reservations: Write to site. Address: Via Nardini 11/13, 51030 San Baronto-Lamporecchio (PT). Tel: 0573/88332. FAX: as phone.

CAMPING BARCO REALE

IN THE HEART OF TUSCANY
Swimming pool - Volleyball - Outdoor draughts
Skittle alley - Trekking - Football field - `Boccia'
Children's playground - Supermarket - Restaurant
- Tennis (3 km).
The campsite lies in the midst of a forest of pines
and magnificent old oaks, on a hill with panoramic
views. The birth place of **Leonardo Da Vinci** is
very close and nearby are the towns of **Florence,**
Pistoia, Pisa and **Lucca,** all reached easily by good roads. An ideal place to
stay for holidays in the Tuscany hills or an ideal starting point on the **Culture Trail.**

via Nardini 11/13
I-51030 S. Baronto (PT)
Tel & Fax 0573/88332

6610 Camping Panoramico, Fiesole, Florence/Firenze

Hilltop site with fine views on the outskirts of Florence.

This is a good site in a fine hilltop situation, appreciably fresher and quieter than near the town, and with good installations. However, it can become overcrowded in main season with too many pushed in and a steep final access on which it is difficult for caravans to restart when halted by parked cars. The site will assist with a jeep if required and we still rate it one of the best sites around Florence if you want to stay a while, though further from the centre (7 km.) than some of the others. There is a bus service from Fiesole to the centre of Florence (tickets from site office) but it is a long uphill walk back to the camp. The pitches are on terraces and steep walks to and from various facilities could cause problems for people with mobility problems. The sanitary installations are not too large but of quite good quality, with mainly British style WCs, and free hot water in washbasins and showers. If you only want a quick overnight stop for a rapid tour round Florence, you could try Camping Internazionale, on southwest side of, and quite close to the city, and quickly reached from the Certosa exit of autostrada A1.

How to find it: From A1 take Firenze-Sud exit and follow signs to Fiesole (which lies NNE of central Firenze). From Fiesole centre follow `Camping Fiesole' - not `Panoramico' which is only on site entrance - 1 km.

General Details: Open all year. 25,000 sq.m. Shade in many parts. All pitches have 3A electrical connections. Shop (30/3-30/10). Bar (30/3-30/10). Snack bar (15/7-15/9). Motorbike rental. Fridges, irons and little cookers for campers' use. Washing machines. Chemical disposal. Motorcaravan services. Bungalows and caravans for hire.

Charges 1997: Per person L. 11,500, incl. local tax; child (3-12 yrs) 8,000; pitch 20,000; extra car 5,000. Credit cards accepted.

Reservations: Not taken and said to be unnecessary if you arrive by early afternoon. Address: Via Peramonda 1, 50014 Fiesole (Firenze). Tel: 055/599069. FAX: 055/59186.

6605 Camping Mugello Verde, San Piero a Sieve, nr Firenze

Friendly, all year, inland site, north of Florence.

Mugello Verde is in the hills 20 km. north of Florence, but near to route 65. It is quietly situated in pretty countryside 2 km. from San Piero. With plenty of hardstanding and shade, there are 100 unmarked places for tourists and 34 bungalows of very good standard. The shop is well stocked and the bar/restaurant both good and reasonably priced - try Michele's tortellini! The two toilet blocks are very adequate, with mostly British style WCs and facilities provided for disabled people.

How to find it: From A1 autostrada exit for Barbarino. From SS65, aim for San Piero a Sieve. Site signed locally.

General Details: Open all year. Electrical connections (6A). Swimming pool (from June). Tennis. Restaurant (March - Oct). Play area. Table tennis. Boules. Riding and fishing near. Cinema. Daily bus service to Florence except Sun. (1 hr). Washing machines. Chemical disposal. English spoken.

Charges 1997: Per person L. 8,500 - 11,000; child (3-12 yrs) 5,000 - 7,000; pitch 10,000 - 20,000; second car 11,500; water, electricity and VAT incl.

AR Discount
Less 10%

Reservations: accepted with 30% deposit: Address: 50037 San Piero a Sieve (Firenze). Tel: 055/848511. FAX: 055/8486910.

6612 Camping Norcenni Girasole Club, Figline Valdarno, nr Florence/Firenze

Secluded haven for campers in the heart of Tuscany.

A busy, well run site in a picturesque, hilly situation 32 km. south of Florence, the Norcenni Girasole Club has been most efficiently operated by the Cardini family since 1982. An excellent swimming pool with water slide, a heated covered pool, fitness centre and a most attractive bar and restaurant, grouped together, are of particular note.There are over 200 places for touring units, all with 4A electricity, with many others taken by tour operators. Although on a fairly steep hillside, pitches are on level terraces accessed from good, hard roads. Sanitary facilities are good with mixed British and Turkish style WCs. Free warm water with push-button taps. Five family bathrooms for hire (popular, so book in advance). Weekly animation with music and activities for children. A number of excursions is on offer with one evening tour of Florence which includes a five course dinner in a historic palace. Courses in the Italian language and Tuscan cooking are available.

How to find it: From Florence take Rome A1/E35 autostrada and take Incisa exit. Turn south on route 69 towards Arezzo. In Figline turn right for Greve and watch for Norcenni signs - site is 4 km up a twisting, climbing road.

General Details: Open 1 March - 31 Oct. 110,000 sq.m. Supermarket and gift shop. Bar and restaurant with terrace. Pizzeria. Washing machines and dryers. Two flood-lit tennis courts. Swimming pools. Fitness centre with jacuzzi and Turkish bath. Chemical disposal. Riding. Excursions. Bungalows to rent. English is spoken.

Charges 1997: Per person L. 11,200 - 12,500; child (under 12 yrs) 6,500 - 7,200; car 6,200 - 6,900; m/cycle 5,200 - 5,800; caravan 9,700 - 10,700; tent 8,900 - 9,800; motorcaravan 15,600 - 17,200; electricity 2,100 - 2,300.

Reservations: Made with deposit. Address: Via Norcenni 7, 50063 Figline Valdarno (FI). Tel: 055/959666. FAX: 055/959337.

6623 Centro Turistico San Marino, San Marino

Good modern site with swimming pool.

According to one guide book, the Republic of San Marino is "an unashamed tourist trap which trades on its falsely preserved autonomy". It has its own mint, produces its own postage stamps, issues its own car registration plates and has a small army, but in all other respects, is part of Italy. However, tourists do seem to find it interesting, particularly those with patience to climb to the castles on the three highest ridges. Centro Turistico San Marino is a good 4 km. below this, standing at 400 m. above sea level and spreading gently down a hillside, with lovely views across to the Adriatic. It has a good variety of trees but, as most of these are young, not much shade as yet. The main caravan pitches are on level terraces with hardstanding, accessed from tarmac or gravel roads, separated by hedges and with water, waste and electricity connections (5A). There are smaller pitches on lower terraces for tents. Four good quality sanitary blocks are well spread around the site with British and Turkish style WCs and free hot water in washbasins, sinks and showers. The attractive, almost circular, swimming pool has hydro-massage and solarium. Shop with limited supplies. Restaurant with terrace which overlooks the swimming pool and has good views. In high season, staff organise activities for children and adults. The presence of a tour operator is obvious, but not intrusive. Good English is spoken and British campers are welcomed.

How to find it: From A14 autostrada Rimini-Sud exit (or SS16 where signed) follow SS72 west to San Marino.

General Details: Open all year. 100,000 sq.m. Shop (all year, closed Tues. in winter). Restaurant (all year). Swimming pool Hydro-massage. Solarium. Children's play area. Table tennis. Volleyball. Football. Archery. Boules. Tennis. Games room. Lounge with satellite TV. Small amphitheatre for entertainment. Animation programme (high season). Electricity (5A). Washing machines. Motorcaravan services. Chemical disposal. Bungalows for hire.

Charges 1997: Per person L. 7,000 - 12,000; child (4-10 yrs) 3,500 - 10,000; tent 6,000 - 11,000; caravan 6,000 - 16,000; car 2,500 - 7,000; motorcaravan 7,000 - 21,000; satellite TV connection 1,000 - 5,000.

Reservations: Write to camp. Address: Strada San Michele 50, 47031 Cailungo, R.S.M. Tel: 0549/903964. FAX: 0549/907120. E Mail: cturistico@omniway.sm.

6020 Camping Union Lido Vacanze, Cavallino, Jesolo, nr Venice/Venezia

Superb, well organised seaside site with aqua-park and excellent facilities.

This well known site is extremely large but has first class organisation and it has been said that it sets the standard that others follow. It lies right by the sea with direct access to a long and broad beach of fine sand which fronts the camp. Shelving very gradually, the beach, which is well cleaned by the site, provides very safe bathing. The site is laid out regularly with parallel access roads under a covering of poplars and pine trees which serve also to mark out numbered pitches of adequate size. There are separate parts for caravans, tents and motorcaravans, plus one mixed part. All have 5A electricity and 956 have water and drainaway also. The redesigned entrance now provides a large off-road overnight parking area with electrical connections, toilets and showers for those arriving after 9.00 pm. An aqua-park, opened on the site's 35th anniversary in 1990, includes a swimming pool, lagoon pool for children, heated whirlpool and a slow flowing 160 m. long 'river' for paddling or swimming. Covering 5,000 sq.m. this is under lifeguard supervision and is open mornings and afternoons. There is also a heated pool for hotel and apartment guests, available to others on payment.

Amenities are varied and numerous. The 16 sanitary blocks, which open and close progressively during the season, have free hot water in all facilities and are kept very clean. They have British WCs, washbasins with shelf and mirror, (many in cabins for ladies) hot showers, footbaths and deep sinks for washing dishes and clothes. 6 blocks have facilities for the disabled. A comprehensive main shopping area, set around a pleasant piazza, has a wide range of shops including a large supermarket. There are 7 restaurants and several pleasant and lively bars. A selection of sports is offered in the annexe across the road and fitness programmes under qualified staff are available in season. The golf 'academy' with professional in attendance, has a driving range, pitching green, putting green and practice bunker. There are regular entertainment and activity programmes for both adults and children. Union Lido is above all an orderly and clean site and this is achieved partly by strict adherence to regulations suiting those who like comfortable camping undisturbed by others and good management.

How to find it: From Venice-Trieste Autostrada leave at exit for airport or Quarto d'Altino and follow signs first for Jesolo and then Punta Sabbiono, and camp will be seen just after Cavallino, on the left.

General Details: Open 1 May - 30 Sept. 600,000 sq.m. Good shade in all parts. Many shops (see text above), open till late. Restaurants, bars, pizzerias. Ladies' and gent's hairdressers. Tennis. Riding. Windsurfing school in season. Table tennis. Minigolf. New skating rink. Two fitness tracks in 4 ha. natural park with children's play area and supervised play for children. Boat excursions. Bicycle hire. Recreational programme of events for adults and children, daytime and evening. Italian language lessons. Golf academy. Church service in English in Jul/Aug. Launderette. First aid centre with treatment room and camp ambulance. Luxury apartments, bungalows, caravans and mobile homes for hire and site owned hotel by entrance.

Charges 1997: Three different rates: (i) high season - 28/6-30/8; (ii) mid-season - 17/5-28/6 and 30/8-13/9, and (iii) off-season - outside these. Per person L. 12,600/10,800/9,000; child under 3 yrs 8,500/7,200/5,500, under 12 yrs 11,000/9,400/7,500; pitch without electricity (high season only) 24,000; with electricity 28,000/18,500/15,500; with water and drainaway also 31,000/22,000/20,000; extra car 8,500/6,500/4,500. VAT included. Min. stay in high season 1 week.

Reservations: made for the letting units only, but site provides 'priority cards' for previous visitors. Address: 30013 Cavallino (Venezia). Tel: 041/968080 or 2575111. FAX: 041/5370355. Internet: http://www.omninet.com/union/. UK contact: G. Ovenden, 29 Meadow Way, Heathfield, Sussex TN21 8AJ.

This site is featured out of order - it should be listed on page 186

See colour advert opposite

6625 Camping La Montagnola, Sovicille, nr Siena

Quiet, clean site close to Siena, Volterra and San Gimignano.

An agreeable alternative to sites closer to the centre of Siena, Montagnola is set in secluded woodland to the north of the village of Sovicille. The owners have worked hard to provide a good basic standard of amenities. The 66 pitches are of good size (80 sq.m), clearly marked and have reasonably good shade. All are suitable for caravans and motorcaravans with electrical connections (5A). Water points are plentiful and the pitches furthest up the hill are arranged in a circle around a central barbecue area. There is an overflow field for tents with no shade and another for sports. A single toilet block provides free hot showers and sufficient washbasins (cold water) and mainly British style toilets - not luxurious, but adequate and clean. A friendly bar/shop area offers snacks and basics; large supermarket 6 km. (San Rocco a Philli or Rosia), a small one 6 km (Sovicille). Two restaurants are in the village. This site could make an excellent touring base for central Tuscany and is not too far from the motorway for short stays, perhaps including a visit to Siena (10 km. with an hourly bus service from the site)

How to find it: From north on the Firenze - Siena motorway take Siena Ovest exit onto SS73 Ponente road from where site is signed. From south (Grosseto) take SS223 turning at crossroads to Rosia from where site is signed.

General Details: Open Easter - 30 Sept. Small shop. Bar. Restaurants and supermarkets near. Chemical disposal.

Charges 1997: Per person L. 9,000; child (4-12 yrs) 5,000; pitch 8,000; electricity 2,000.

Reservations: not really necessary. Address: 53018 Sovicille (Siena). Tel: 0577/314473. FAX: as phone. (Winter address: SS73 Ponente 190, Siena. Tel and fax: 0577/349286).

The pleasant holiday park with quality, style and atmosphere in a friendly environment right on to the Venetian Cavallino coast.
Open from 1st May to 30th September.

★ ★ ★ ★

I - 30013 CAVALLINO - VENEZIA
Tel. Camping (041) 968080, 2575111
Tel. Hotel (041) 968043, 968884
Telefax (041) 5370355

Camping - Caravan - Bungalow

Spacious, fitted pitches on grass under pines and poplars, for tents, caravans and motorcaravans. Many caravan pitches have water and drainage points. Caravans and mobile homes for hire, with shower and WC.
Bungalow "Lido" with kitchen-living room, 2 double bedrooms (twin beds), shower and separate WC and terrace including some for disabled guests.

e-mail: unionlid@tin.it
http://www.omninets.com/union/

UNITER®
UNI EN ISO 9002

NEW: the first campsite in Europe to be granted UNI EN ISO 9002 certification.

Fitness - Sport - Play Park

Spacious area with games and keep-fit equipment, with trained staff, Multi-use sportsground for roller blading and other activities, volley ball, swimming instruction, wind surfing school, diving centre with school and diving excursions at sea, table tennis, minigolf, tennis and riding school. Archery and football competition. Golf Academy.
The Happy Place! Children's play area with much equipment. Climbing games, supervised play.

Park Hotel Union Lido

3 Star hotel with modern airy rooms, some of which have been completely refurbished. Self-catering complex with 24 two-storey flatlets. Heated swimming pool, with splash and whirlpool also available in the early and late season for our Hotel and self-catering guests.

Animation - Entertainment - Activities

Amphitheatre for concerts and music shows. Organised activities: Painting courses, artistic activities, games & recreation by trained staff.

Aqua Park

An experience! 5000 sq metres of water landscape with a gentle river, a lagoon for the children, swimming pool, whirlpools and a waterfall (15.5 - 30.9).

Scout camp for 8-12 yr olds on holiday with their parents in July-August.

Swimming pools, nature and organised activities in a park which is all for you.

Imagine an oasis with all the comforts of a 4 star holiday park: 24 hectares of countryside close to the lake, panoramic view, bungalows with from 2 to 5 beds, ample, well-equipped camping spaces, every type of service, 3 splendid swimming pools with waterslides and hydromassage... And then tennis, basketball, volleyball, bicycles, exercise walk, windsurfing, canoeing, courses, championships and organised activities directed especially at children. At Piani di Clodia the daytime is spent enjoying yourself, whereas the evenings are even better, with shows, entertainment, music and dancing. Piani di Clodia: this is a real holiday!

With us summer begins on 28 March!

PIANI DI CLODIA
★ ★ ★ ★

Loc. Bagatta, 37017 Lazise - (Verona - Italy)
Tel.++39.45.7590456 - Fax ++39.45.7590939
www.pianidiclodia.it

Camping CAPALONGA
NATURE AT THE SEASIDE

6010 Camping Capalonga, Bibione Pineda, Bibione, nr Venice/Venezia

Quality site with a very good beach and excellent sanitary blocks.

Capalonga is a large, well developed and cared for site, right beside the sea. The pitches are of variable size (70-90 sq.m.) and nearly all marked out; some can be reserved. All have electrical connections (4A) and there is good shade almost everywhere. The site is pleasantly laid out - roads run in arcs which avoids the `square box' effect. Some pitches where trees define the pitch area may be tricky for large units. The beach is a very wide sandy one which is cleaned by the site and never becomes too crowded; a concrete path leads out towards sea to avoid too much sand-walking. The sea bed shelves extremely gently and is very safe for children and the water is much cleaner here than at most places along this coast. Along the other side of the site runs a large lagoon, where boating (motor or sail) can be practised. The site provides a landing stage and moorings. There is also a swimming pool (25 x 12½ m.). The site has seven toilet blocks with hot water throughout; they are well and frequently cleaned. Two newer blocks built side by side have special facilities for disabled people and very fine children's rooms with washbasins and showers at the right height. British and some Turkish style toilets, individual basins, some in private cabins, and a whole wall of mirrors. Large new playing field with exercise stations, football pitch and area for ball games. Capalonga is an excellent site, with comprehensive facilities.

How to find it: Bibione is about 80 km. east of Venice, well signed from afar on approach roads. 1 km. before Bibione turn right towards Bibione Pineda and follow camp signs.

General Details: Open 1 May - 30 Sept, with main shop and restaurant. 250,000 sq.m. Electrical connections (4A). Large supermarket. General shop for campers and beach goods, cards, papers, etc. Self-service restaurant and separate bar. Swimming pool. Boating. Fishing. Launderette. Children's playground. Sports field. First-aid room. Car wash. Chemical disposal. Motorcaravan services. Caravans and bungalows for hire.

Charges 1997: Four charging seasons. Per person L. 8,000 - 15,000; child 1-4 yrs 4,000 - 8,000, 5-8 yrs 6,000 - 10,000; pitch with electricity 16,000 - 32,000; pitch with water and drainage also 18,000 - 34,000; extra car 4,000 - 8,000; boat 9,000 - 20,000 acc. to season and size.

Reservations: Recommended for July/August and made from Sat. to Sat. only, with large deposit and fee. Address: Viale della Laguna 16, 30020 Bibione Pineda (VE). Tel: 0431/438351.

This site is featured out of order - it is in North East Italy and should be listed on page 186

See colour
advert opposite

6015 Camping Residence Il Tridente, Bibione Pineda, Bibione

Natural woodland site on Adriatic, with Residence and excellent facilities.

This is an unusual site as only half the area is used for camping. Formerly a holiday centre for deprived children, it occupies a strip of woodland 200 m. wide and 400 m. long stretching from the main road to the sea. It is divided into two parts by an apartment block of first class rooms with air conditioning and full cooking and bathroom facilities which are for hire. The 230 tourist pitches are located amongst tall pines in the area between the entrance and the Residence. Pitch sizes vary according to the positions of the trees, but they are of sufficient size and have 4A electrical connections. The ground slopes gently from the main building to the beach of fine sand and this is used as the recreational area with two swimming pools - one 25 x 12½ m. and a smaller children's pool - tennis courts, table tennis and sitting and play places. The three sanitary blocks, two in the main camping area and one near the sea, are of excellent quality. All have similar facilities: mixed British and Turkish style WCs in cabins with washbasins, good showers, with free hot water throughout and facilities for disabled people. The Residence includes an excellent restaurant, bar and well stocked supermarket. An animation programme includes activities for children in high season. Boats may be kept at the quay on the sister site, Capalonga (no. 6010), about 1 km. away. With thick woodland on both sides, Il Tridente is a quiet, restful site with excellent facilities.

How to find it: From A4 Venice - Trieste autostrada, take Latisana exit and follow signs to Bibione and then Bibione Pineda and camp signs.

General Details: Open Easter - 30 Sept. 54,500 sq.m. Restaurant. Bar. Supermarket. Swimming pools. Children's playground. Tennis. Table tennis. Mini-football. Volleyball. Animation. Washing machines and dryers. Chemical disposal. Motorcaravan services. Caravans for hire.

Charges 1997: Per person L.8,000 - 15,000; child 1-4 yrs 4,000 - 8,000, 5-8 yrs 6,000 - 10,000; caravan or tent 16,000 - 29,000; extra car 4,000 - 8,000. VAT included.

Reservations: are made; contact site for details. Address: via Baseleghe 12, 30020 Bibione Pineda. Tel: 0431/439600 (winter: 0431/438351).

This site is featured out of order - it is in North East Italy and should be listed on page 186

6630 Camping Montescudaio, Montescudaio, nr Cecina

Well developed site, with swimming pool, south of Livorno.

This site has been fashioned out of a very extensive area of natural undulating woodland (with low trees) and has its own character. There are about 300 individual pitches for tourists plus 150 permanent bungalows or large caravans, in separate clearings. They vary in size, some quite small, and there is varying shade. Electrical connections (3A) are available in all parts. With installations of good quality and a comprehensive range of amenities, this is an attractive site which has almost arrived at the end of its development. It is 4 km. from the sea at the nearest point but there is a large free swimming pool on the site with separate children's pool. The modern sanitary blocks are well appointed with hot water in the two main blocks. The facilities are comprehensive and should provide a good supply, with British style toilets, individual washbasins with shelves, free warm water (premixed) in some basins and showers and baby baths. Used by tour operators. The site should usually have space.

How to find it: From new autostrada (Livorno-Grosseto) take Cecina, Guardistallo, Montescudaio exit. Follow signs to Guardistallo, **not signs to Montescudaio**. The site is on the Cecina-Guardistallo road, 2 km. from Cecina.

General Details: Open 1 May - 20 Sept. 250,000 sq.m. Shops. Bar. Restaurant in main season. Open-air pizzeria at one end of site with bar, many tables and small dance floor for nightly family disco from mid-June. Swimming pool. Tennis. Minigolf. Bicycle hire. Good children's playground. Table tennis. Organised events programme in main season. Medical service. Chemical disposal. Motorcaravan services. Bungalows (13) and caravans (71) for hire.

Charges 1998: Per person (any age) 7,800 - 10,000; pitch (any unit) incl. electricity 17,000 - 23,000.

Reservations: Write to site with deposit (L. 100,000). Address: Casella Postale no. 4, 56040 Montescudaio (Pisa). Tel: 0586/683477. FAX: 0568/630932. E-mail: mocamp@luda.livorno.it. Internet: www.campingmontescudaio.com.

AR Discount

Less 5%

CAMPING & VILLAGE
MONTESCUDAIO

250.000 SQ MT OF FOREST - CECINA - TUSCANY
4 KM FROM THE SEA. EXCELLENT GEOGRAPHICAL POSITION
TO REACH THE SPLENDID CITIES OF TUSCANY:
FLORENCE, PISA, SIENA,
VOLTERRA, SAN GIMIGNANO AND LUCCA.

Pitches, Bungalows and Caravancasa's
Isolated and immersed in the forest. First class shops and services.
Bungalows with washrooms for 4 people.
Caravancasa's with washroom for 4/6 people.

I - 56040 Montescudaio - Italy - Via del Poggetto km 2 •Tel. 0039 (0)586/683477 - Fax 0039 (0)586/630932
Visit our WWW site: www.camping-montescudaio.com - E-mail: mocamp@luda.livorno.it

6637 Camping Il Gineprino, Marina di Bibbona

New, small site near Mediterranean coast in Tuscany.

This is a pleasant part of Tuscany with many interesting places within visiting distance. Il Gineprino is on the edge of Bibbona but not directly on the coast. As the camp was only opened in 1995, the ground is a bit bare in parts and the young trees not grown enough yet to provide shade. It is small (15,000 sq.m) when compared with most sites in this area with about 60 spaces for tourists, but it does have a swimming pool and an excellent restaurant. Cars have to be parked in a separate place opposite the site entrance. The 60 touring pitches are numbered and marked by saplings at the corners and all have a water tap and electricity (4A). There is entertainment provided on two or three evenings each week in high season and excursions can be arranged. The beach is about 400 m. and can be reached on foot through a pine wood.

continued overleaf

6637 Camping Il Gineprino (continued)

The two sanitary blocks, one at each end, have British and Turkish style WCs and free hot water in washbasins and showers, with cold for dish and clothes washing. There is a family room (on payment) with WC, washbasin and shower and facilities for disabled people. The friendly owner, who speaks some English, is keen to welcome British guests.

How to find it: Site is signed on the approach from the main road SS1 coast road between La California and Marina di Bibbona.

General Details: Open April - end Sept. 15,000 sq.m. Shop. Restaurant with terrace (open all season). Swimming pool. Games room. TV room. Table tennis. Bicycle hire. Some entertainment in high season. Excursions.

Charges 1997: Per person L. 12,000; child (under 8 yrs) 9,000; car 5,200, tent or caravan 11,800; motorcaravan 16,900.

Reservations: Write to site. Address: Via del Platani, 57020 Marina di Bibbona. Tel/fax: 0586/600550. (Winter address: Arch. Roberto Valori, via F.lli Rosselli 7, 57023 Cecina (LI). Tel: 0586/683500. FAX: as phone).

6635 Camping Le Pianacce, Castagneto Carducci, nr Donoratico

Terraced site in Tuscan hills 6 km. back from sea with pleasant pool; south of Livorno.

In a quiet situation 6 km. back from sea at Donoratico, this site has an attractive medium-sized swimming pool and a new children's pool with water games which are overlooked by a terrace leading from the bar. Said to be suitable for tents and caravans the site is, however, on steeply rising ground. The 150 individual pitches for tourists, all with 3A electricity, are in tiered rows on fairly narrow terraces. Access to most is not easy because the limited space between the small dividing hedges and the high bank of the next terrace restricts manoeuvring so installation is now made by the site's tractor. All pitches are shady. There are now three toilet blocks, including a newer small one at the top of the site. They have all been refurbished to a high standard; British style WCs, individual washbasins with hot water; free hot showers. The site is almost entirely for tourists, with very few seasonal units, but it is likely to be full from about mid-July to 20 Aug. It is a quiet site and peaceful at night. There is a nature reserve adjacent and the sandy beach is 20 km. long so there are no restrictions.

How to find it: Turn off the main S1 just north of Donoratico in hamlet of Il Bambolo at signpost to Castagneto Carducci. After 3 km. turn left signs to Bolgheri and site, then follow camp signs. Single track final approach.

General Details: Open 1 April - 15 Oct. 80,000 sq.m. Shop. Restaurant/bar. Swimming pool and new children's pool with water games. Tennis court. Minigolf. Bicycle hire. Children's playground. Riding near. Motorcaravan service point. Chemical disposal. New mobile homes for hire.

Charges 1998: Four charging seasons. Per person L. 6,500 - 12,000; child (0-10 yrs) free - 9,000; motorcaravan or caravan/tent, incl. car 11,000 - 20,000; 2 man tent incl. m/cycle 8,000 - 14000; extra car 2,500 - 5,000; dog 5,000 - 8,500. Some special offers in low season.

Reservations: made with deposit; contact site. Address: Via Bolgherese, 57022 Castagneto Carducci (LI). Tel: 0565/763667. FAX: 0565/766085.

6640 Camping Pappasole, Vignale Riotorto, nr Follonica

Large, well run site on coast with many sporting activities.

This lively site offers plenty of sporting activities and is located 250 m. from its own sandy beach, facing the island of Elba. It is a large site on flat, fairly open ground offering 450 pitches of 90 sq.m. many with electricity (3A) and water, others with electricity, water and waste water connections. Some 344 of the pitches have their own individual sanitary facility with WC, shower and washbasin, and next to these a compartment with 4-burner gas stove, fridge, sink with H&C and drainer, and 5 cupboards (extra cost for this about £5 per night). Pitches are separated by bushes with some shade from medium sized trees and artificial shade in other areas. There may be some road or rail noise in certain areas. There are three modern sanitary blocks with free hot water for the washbasins and showers and mainly Turkish but with some British style WCs. These facilities may be a fair walk from some of the pitches. Laundry facilities are provided. The central focus of the site is a covered area (a very tall, open marquee type structure, floodlit at night) for dancing, music and entertainment which is surrounded by the main camp buildings. There are many sporting opportunities including archery, windsurfing and sailing, tennis, excellent swimming pools and activities and excursions are organised.

How to find it: Site is north of Follonica just off the `new' SS1 and well signed.

General Details: Open 2 April - 17 Oct. Restaurant. Snacks. Bar. Shop. Swimming pools (15/5-26/9). Children's play area. Tennis. Table tennis. Bowls. Archery. Handball. Watersports. Minigolf. Bicycle hire. Entertainment, activities and excursion programmes (17/5-6/9). Fridges for hire. Medical services. Safety deposit boxes. Laundry facilities. Chemical disposal. Motorcaravan services. Bungalows for rent.

Charges 1998: Per person L. 6,000 - 14,000; child (3-10 yrs) 4,500 - 8,500; caravan/tent and car or motorcaravan 15,500 - 37,000, electricity included; individual sanitary facility 7,000 - 18,000. Credit cards accepted.

Reservations: are made for whole weeks, Sat. - Sat. Write to site. Address: Loc. Carbonifera, 57020 Vignale Riotorto (LI). Tel: 0565/20420. FAX: 0565/20346.

AR Discount
Less 10% in low season

ITALY - Central

6620 Campo Norina, Pesaro

Small, seaside site with own private beach on Adriatic Riviera.

This small, rectangular site is sandwiched between mountain, road and railway and the coast. The private beach of fine sand runs the 320 m. length of the site and as the shore is said to slope gently, could make a base for a family holiday as well as for visiting the attractions nearby, both inland and along the northern Adriatic coast. The main access road runs near the railway line, with pitches arranged either side of smaller roads at right angles to the shore. The places are marked by numbered stones and backed by hedges, all having electrical connections (3A). There is a children's play area and a small platform for dancing during the high season. Stone groynes, running parallel to the shore, some 70 m. from it, should make for calm water. The site has a family atmosphere. The pleasant bar/restaurant has a pizzeria as well as specialising in local sea food. The three toilet blocks, although showing signs of age, are tiled and clean with British and Turkish style WCs. Cold water only in washbasins and dishwashing sinks, with hot water on payment in the showers. English is spoken by the friendly management.

How to find it: Site is mid-way between Pesaro and Fano. From autostrada, take Fano exit and follow signs on the SS16 for Pesaro and Rimini. The access road goes under the railway (high enough for motorcaravans), which it shares with Camping Marinella, and care is needed to enter Norina rather than its rival.

General Details: Open 7 April - 15 Oct, as is bar/restaurant. 25,000 sq.m. Shade in some parts. Shop and bazaar (open during season). Washing machine. Chemical disposal. Electricity in all parts. Small children's playground. Dancing (July/Aug). Tennis 400 m. Riding 1 km. San Marino 40 km. and other attractions near.

Charges 1997: Per adult L.7,500 - 12,000; child (0-6 yrs) 4,500 - 7,500; pitch incl. electricity 15,000 - 22,000, small pitch for tent 8,000 - 10,000; dog 3,000 - 5,000; boat 5,000 - 7,500. VAT included.

Reservations: Necessary for August, with deposit and fee - write to site. Address: Marina Ardizia 181, 61100 Pesaro. Tel: 0721/55792. FAX: 0721/55165.

6645 Parco-Campeggio Delle Piscine, Sarteano

See colour advert between pages 192/193

Site with thermal swimming pools, 6 km. from A1 autostrada southeast of Siena.

Sarteano is a spa and the main feature of this site is the three swimming pools fed by the natural thermo-mineral springs and held at a temperature of 24°. Two of these (one large with whirlpool), set in a park-like ground with picnic tables, are free to all those staying on the site; a third, also good sized, on the site itself, is opened in main season for exclusive use of campers. Even apart from the pools, the site itself is a good one which is worth considering, either as a sightseeing base or as an overnight stop from the Florence - Rome motorway (site is 6 km. from exit). The 450 flat pitches, all for tourists, though many are occupied by long-stay clients, are all individual ones, fully marked out with hedges. They claim they will always find space and reservations are not usually made. Two toilet blocks, one new and of excellent quality, provide very reasonable provision. Mainly British style WCs; washbasins with free hot water, shelf, mirror; free hot showers of different types; particularly numerous sinks for clothes and dishes, with hot water. A friendly welcome. Dogs are not taken. Used by a tour operator.

How to find it: From autostrada A1 take Chiusi/Chianciano exit, from where Sarteano (6 km.) and site are signed.

General Details: Open 1 April - 30 Sept. Electrical connections (6A) all parts. Shop (town only a 200 m. stroll). Restaurant/bar. Takeaway. Newspaper kiosk. Telephones. Swimming pools (one all season). TV room and videos. Tennis. Table tennis. Volleyball. Exchange facilities. Free guided cultural tours. Local market on Fridays. Chemical disposal. Motorcaravan services.

Charges 1998: Per adult L. 12,500 - 16,000; child (3-10 yrs) 9,500 - 11,000; car 5,000 - 6,000; tent or caravan 12,500 - 16,000; motorcaravan 17,500 - 22,000; electricity 4,000. Less 10% for stays over 25 days.

Reservations: May be possible if you write to site, but probably not necessary (see above). Address: 53047 Sarteano (Siena). Tel: 0578/26971. FAX: 0578/265889. E-mail: bagnosanto@kranet.it. Internet: http://www.evols.it/bagnosanto.

6650 Camping Kursaal Hotel, Passignano sul Trasimeno

Well located, orderly site on north east edge of Lake Trasimeno, 1 km. from town.

Anna Posta, the charming manager of this pretty, well run site speaks some English and would give a real welcome to British guests. The lake is checked for water quality every week and the site has its own small beach. All water sports are available. The attractive bar and restaurant are complemented by a small well stocked shop, all open 8 am.-11 pm. daily. Part of the site is very shady with coniferous trees and part is open with flowering trees giving a total of 160 pitches, each of 80 sq.m. but not all marked. Plentiful electrical connections (15A) and no static pitches. Two sanitary blocks, well arranged and spotless, provide mainly British type toilets, free hot showers and facilities for disabled people and babies. A family atmosphere is encouraged but this is not a place for the uninhibited. There is a 16 room hotel which could be of interest, for example to families who have older parents with them.

How to find it: Take 'Passignano est' exit from Perugia spur of Florence-Rome autostrada; site signed from there.

General Details: Open 25 March - 30 Oct. Bar/restaurant (live music in bar in high season). Shop - supermarket 500 m. Good swimming pool (free). Small play area for children. Fishing. Chemical disposal. Motorcaravan services. Hotel and bungalow accommodation (apply to site for details).

Charges 1998: Per adult L. 9,000 - 10,000; child 0-3 yrs 3,000, 4-10 yrs 7,000 - 8,000; pitch with electricity 14,000 - 18,000; car 3,000; dog 2,000. Credit cards and Eurocheques accepted.

Reservations: Accepted with 30% deposit (by Eurocheque payable to Camping Kursaal). Address: 06065 Passignano sul Trasimeno. Tel: 075/828085. FAX: 075/827182.

AR Discount
Less 10%
excl. July/Aug.

6654 Camping Badiaccia, Castiglione del Lago

Lakeside camp with on-site activity and excursion possibilities.

Lake Trasimeno is not Italy's most beautiful lake, as the immediate environs are rather flat, although within sight of distant mountains. However, it does provide a base from which to visit interesting places in this part of central Italy or as a night stop when travelling to Rome, being near the Al autostrada. Badiaccia, being directly on the lake, gives an almost seaside atmosphere and it has a good selection of sporting opportunities with four staff in high season to organise activities. Being well tended and maintained, it has a pleasant appearance enhanced by a variety of plants and flowers and, although some pitches are smaller than average, there is good shade in most parts. The 195 pitches for touring are numbered and separated by trees and bushes in rows from hard access roads. As well as swimming in the lake, there is a good sized pool (20 x 10 m) and small one (6 x 3 m) for children. A large area right by the lake has access from the site. Guided excursions to Rome and Florence are organised in high season. Open all season are a pleasant restaurant, snack bar and a shop. The two centrally positioned sanitary blocks have Turkish and British style WCs and free hot water in washbasins, sinks and showers. At the time of our visit, good English was spoken by the Dutch receptionist. Accommodation to rent.

How to find it: From A11 Milan-Rome autostrada take Val di Chiana exit and turn east towards Perugia on the SS75bis. Leave this at Castiglione exit and go south on SS71 to Castiglione where site is well signed.

General Details: Open 1 April - 30 Sept. 55,000 sq.m. Restaurant. Shop. Snack bar. Electricity (4A). Swimming pool and children's pool. Play area. Tennis. Table tennis. Boules. Minigolf. Riding near. Volleyball. Football. Beach volleyball. Windsurfing. Fishing. Boat hire. Entertainment and excursions in high season. Washing machines.

Charges 1997: Per person L. 7,500 - 8,500; child under 3 free; tent 7,000 - 8,000; caravan 8,000 - 9,000; motorcaravan 9,000 - 9,500; car 3,000.

Reservations: Write to site. Address: Via Trasimeno 1 - Voc. Badiaccia 91, 06061 Castiglione del Lago (PG). Tel: 075/9659097. FAX: 075/8230103.

6653 Camping Listro, Castiglione del Lago

Small, unpretentious site on the western edge of Lake Trasimeno.

A simple, pleasant, flat site right on the shore of the lake, Camping Listro is a few hundred yards north of the historic town of Castiglione. It provides 100 pitches all with electricity. The sanitary facilities are clean and adequate, although most of the WC's are of the Turkish type. Facilities on the site are fairly limited with only a small shop and snack bar, but there are bars and restaurants close by, as are sporting facilities, including a good swimming pool and tennis courts. There is a small children's play area and a private beach on the lake shore. Dogs are accepted in the low season only. Barbecues are permitted. No organised entertainment. English is spoken and British guests are particularly welcome.

How to find it: From A1/E35 Florence-Rome autostrada take Val di Chiana exit and join Perugia (75 bis) superstrada. After 24 km. take Castiglione exit and follow town signs. Signs to site are clear just before the town.

General Details: Open 1 April - 30 Sept. Bar. Shop. Snack bar. Children's play area. Table tennis. Volleyball. Private beach. Tourist information. Motorcaravan services.

Charges 1997: Per person (over 3 yrs) L. 6,000 - 7,000; caravan or motorcaravan 6,000 - 7,000; tent 5,000 - 7,000; acc. to season and size; car 2,000 - 2,500; m/cycle 1,500; electricity incl. Less 10% for stays over 8 days.

Reservations: Contact site. Address: Via Lungolago, 06061 Castiglione del Lago (PG). Tel: 075/951193 (winter: 075/9658235). FAX: 075/9658200.

ITALY - Central

6665 Camping Le Soline, Casciano di Murlo, nr Siena

Small, terraced site with most facilities, some 20 km. south of Siena.

A country hillside site, 800 m. from the village of Casciano, Le Soline has room for 100 caravans and 40 tents set on seven terraces beneath the main buildings. They range in size from 36-80 sq.m. and all caravan pitches have electricity (6A). In high season cars must be parked away from the pitches. The site has its own power supply, and occupying an area of 70,000 sq.m, there are many olive and other small trees which do not, however, provide much shade for the pitches. There are also a few bungalows for hire. The restaurant, pizzeria (all season), shop (closes Oct) and heated swimming pools are by the entrance, which has a large visitors car park. Horse riding available from site. A good quality sanitary block is on the third terrace, providing mixed British and Turkish style WCs, washbasins (most with hot water) and hot showers on payment, dishwashing (cold water only) and a toilet for the disabled. The site reports a new block with facilities for babies. There are excellent panoramic views of the surrounding countryside and the site is well positioned to visit the many historic and cultural places in the area.

How to find it: From Siena, turn off the SS223 Siena - Grosseto road to the left to Fontazzi (about 20 km.) and keep right for Casciano, following signs.

General Details: Open all year. Restaurant (closed 8/11-8/12). Pizzeria. Shop (Easter - 5/11). Swimming pools (Easter - 20/10). Children's playground. Riding. Volleyball. Mini-football field. Bicycle hire. Barbecue area (not allowed on pitches). Laundry. Car wash area. Chemical disposal. Motorcaravan services. Bungalows for rent.

Charges 1998: Per person L.10,000; child (2-12 yrs) 7,000; car 3,000; m/cycle 2,000; caravan 10,000; tent 9,000 (family) or 7,500 (2 person); motorcaravan 11,000; electricity 2,000. Credit cards accepted.

Reservations: Write to site. Address: 53010 Casciano di Murlo (Siena). Tel: 0577/817410. FAX: 0577/817415.

AR Discount

Less 10% on pp fees after 3 days, 10% on total bill after 14 days.

6660 Camping Maremma-Sans-Souci, Castiglióne della Pescaia, nr Grosseto

Seaside site on Mediterranean coast between Livorno and Rome.

Family owned and run, this seaside site is in natural woodland, in which the minimum amount of undergrowth has been cleared to provide 430 individually marked and hedged, flat pitches for tourists. They are mostly small and cars may not remain with tents or caravans but must go to a numbered, shaded and secure car park near the entrance - an inconvenience to those who rely on the car for lighting, though it does mean less vehicle movement on the site. Roads are mostly narrow and bordered by trees (this is a protected area, and they cannot fell the trees) so access to some parts is difficult for caravans, and each pitch is earmarked either for caravans or for tents. A good sandy beach is less than 100 m. from one end of the camp (say 400 m. from the other) and is normally used only by campers. There are five small, acceptable toilet blocks strategically situated around the site. Three have large private cabins each with WC, basin and shower; this has considerably increased the supply of hot showers, which are on payment. Mainly British, some Turkish style toilets. Maremma is a friendly site right by the sea which should appeal to many people who like its style of relaxed camping. This particular region enjoys a very sunny climate with minimum rainfall, and there are occasional water problems. The sea was clean when we visited in May. No dogs taken between 16/6-31/8.

How to find it: Site is 2½ km. northwest of Castiglione on road to Follonica.

General Details: Open 1 April - 31 Oct. 100,000 sq.m. overall. Access not easy inside site. Electrical connections (3A) for all caravan pitches. Shop. Excellent restaurant (self service in season) serving a range of local fish and fresh pasta. Bar with pizzas and other snacks. Volleyball. Washing machines. Car wash. Chemical disposal. Excursions organised to Elba and Rome. Sailing school. Caravans for hire. Good English spoken.

Charges 1997: Per person L. 7,000 - 12,000; child (under 6 yrs) 5,500 - 7,500; pitch and car 10,000 - 18,000.

Reservations: necessary for July/Aug. and will be made for min. 1 week with deposit (L. 5,000). Address: 58043 Castiglione della Pescaia (Grosseto). Tel: 0564/933765. FAX: 0564/935759.

6663 Camping Amiata, Castel del Piano

Mountain campsite in Tuscany, open all year.

Mount Amiata, the highest point in Tuscany, is accessible by car and becomes very crowded in the height of summer. However, there are splendid views and, away from the summit, the woods and paths of the lower slopes are beautiful with forests of chestnut and beech inhabited by deer and wild boar. The lush vegetation and fresh mountain air make for superb walking. Situated on a hill-top some 8 km. from Mt Amiata, Camping Residence Amiata, open all year, is in a nice situation. The site is heavily wooded which provides good shade and pitches, on slightly sloping ground, are separated by hedges which, in parts, offer more privacy than most sites. A narrow road leads from the main road to a small square which has reception, shop and pleasant bar/restaurant. From here a hard road leads to side roads with pitches on either side on slightly sloping ground. A platform with good views can be used for picnics and is where limited musical entertainment is offered in high season. The sanitary accommodation has been, or is, being refurbished and in the main block (heated) behind the restaurant, is mainly in cabins with British style WCs, washbasins and showers, all with free hot water. ***continued overleaf***

6663 Camping Amiata (continued)

In some parts the blocks are unisex. More a base from which to explore than one to remain on all day as the dense tree cover restricts the views.

How to find it: From SS223 (Grosseto-Siena), turn east at Paganico and signs to Castel del Piano or, from SS2 (Siena-Rome) turn west to Abbadia San Salvatore and signs for Castel del Piano.

General Details: Open all year. 42,000 sq.m. Electrical connections (3,6 or 10A). Shop. Restaurant. Snacks. Some entertainment in high season. Games and TV rooms. Play field. Washing machine. Chemical disposal. Flats for hire.

Charges 1997: Per person L. 6,800 - 10,200; child (1-6 yrs) 5.600 - 7,000; pitch 6,800 - 15,000.

Reservations: Write to site. Address: via Roma 15, 58033 Castel del Piano (GR). Tel: 0564/956260. FAX: 0564/955107.

6656 Camping Il Collaccio, Preci

Unusual campsite with good amenities in rural Umbria.

Tuscany has grabbed the imagination and publicity, but parts of nearby Umbria are just as beautiful and deserve to be better known. Preci or, to give it its full name, Castelvecchio di Preci, is tucked away in the tranquil depths of the Umbrian countryside. The natural beauty of the Monti Sibillini National Park is near and there are walking and cycling opportunities with many marked paths and guided excursions. Historic Assisi and Perugia and the walled market town of Norcia are worth exploring and distinctive Umbrian cuisine to be enjoyed. Il Collaccio is owned and run by the Baldoni family who bought the farm over 30 years ago, rebuilt the derelict farmhouse in its original style and then decided to share it by developing a campsite and accommodation for hire. The farming aspect was kept and its products can be bought in the shop and sampled in the excellent restaurant. The camping area has been carved out of the hill-side which forms a natural amphitheatre with splendid views. At first sight the narrow steep entrance seems daunting (the owner will assist) and the road which leads down to the camping terraces takes one to the exit. The 100 pitches are on level terraces but the thousands of trees, planted to replace those cut down by the previous owner, are not yet mature enough to provide much shade. An interesting feature is a tree plantation on a lower slope where they are experimenting with cultivating truffles - patience is needed here as the results will not be known for ten years! Three modern sanitary blocks are spaced through the site with British and Turkish style WCs, cold water in washbasins and hot, pre-mixed water in showers and sinks. There is an excellent, heated swimming pool (25 x 12.5 m) and children's pool, a good tennis court, volleyball, basketball, small football pitch, boules and mountain biking. With sparsely populated villages across the valley on the mountain slopes and surrounded by stunning scenery, this site is unusual with peace and quiet, activities for those who wish it, good excursions and some entertainment in high season. Small, but not intrusive, tour operator presence.

How to find it: From SS77 Foligno-Civitonova Marche road turn south at Muccia for Visso where Preci signed.

General Details: Open 7 April - 15 Oct. 100,000 sq.m. Electrical connections (6A) - long lead useful. Restaurant Shop (basics, high season). Swimming pool and children's pool. Play area. Tennis court. Volley and basket ball. Football. Table tennis. Boules. Cycling and walking. Canoeing (2 km). Fishing (2 km). Riding near.Washing machine. Motorcaravan services. Chemical disposal. Dormitories for groups and chalets and rooms for hire.

Charges 1997: Per person 9,000 - 10,000; child (3-12 yrs) 4,500 - 5,000; tent 9,000 - 10,000; caravan or motorcaravan 11,000 - 12,000; car 3,000 - 4,000.

Reservations: Write to site. Address: Centro Agrituristico Il Collaccio, 06047 Preci (PG). Tel: 0743/939005. FAX: 0743/939094.

6655 Camping Internazionale, Assisi

Modern, well equipped site with good restaurant and a fine view of the city.

Camping Internazionale is on the west side of Assisi and has new facilities which provide tourers with a good base to visit both St. Francis' city and nearby Perugia and Lake Trasimeno. The toilet block is well appointed and clean, with free hot showers, plenty of washbasins, mainly Turkish style WCs (4 British) and facilities for disabled people. The restaurant has a large garden, and the city is lit up in the evenings to provide a beautiful backdrop to a reasonably priced meal (closed Tues). The 250 pitches are large and clearly marked, on flat grass, and all have electricity (16A). As yet, there is little shade - the trees will take a while to reach full maturity, and it can be very hot in this part of Italy (a pool is planned). However, Assisi boasts one of the finest cathedrals in Christendom, among many other attractions. At the time of publication (Nov '97), the campsite had not been damaged by recent tremors.

How to find it: Site lies on the south side of the SS147, which branches left, off the SS75 Perugia - Foligno road. Follow Assisi signs, and it is clearly signed just over 1 km. from the city.

General Details: Open Easter - October. Restaurant/pizzeria with self-service section. Bar with snacks. Shop. Kitchen for campers. Table tennis. Video games. Bicycle hire. Tennis. Volleyball. Roller skating area. Excursions to Assisi centre, local swimming pool, Rome and Siena. Bus service to city. Chemical disposal. Motorcaravan services.

Charges 1997: Per adult L. 8,000; child (3-10 yrs) 6,000; tent 7,000; caravan or motorcaravan 9,000; car 3,000; m/cycle 2,000; electricity included.

Reservations: made for 1 week stays in high season, but not really necessary. Address: San Giovanni in Campiglione 110, 06081 Assisi (Perugia). Tel: 075/813710 or 816816. FAX: 075/812335.

ITALY - South

6810 Camping Seven Hills, Rome

Excellent, busy, hillside site with easy access to Rome.

A number of sites are available for visiting the `Eternal City' and campers needs and preferences will vary. If you are looking for a site away from the centre, Seven Hills makes an excellent base. In a delightful valley, surrounded by two of the seven hills of Rome, just off the Autostrada ring road to the north of the city, 4 km. from the centre. The site runs a bus shuttle service to the city with the frequency dictated by demand. Arranged in two sections, the top half, near the entrance, restaurant and shop, consists of small, flat, grass terraces with 2-4 pitches on each, with smaller terraces for tents, all from hard access roads. Access to some pitches may be tricky. The flat section at the lower part of the site is reserved for tents used by British (and one Dutch) tour operators who bring guests by coach. These tend to be younger people, but they have their own disco near the pool and are not too obtrusive. The site is a profusion of colour with flowering trees, plants and shrubs and a good covering of trees provides shade. A feature is a `mini-zoo' - a few small animals are enclosed and peacocks strut around. The 80 pitches for tourers are not marked, but the management supervise in busy periods and all should have sufficient space. The excellent central buildings house the well stocked shop and attractive restaurant and bar terrace. English is spoken. Three soundly constructed sanitary blocks are well situated around the site, with open plan washbasins with cold water, free hot water in the average sized showers and British style WCs. Dishwashing under cover with cold water. All cash transactions on the site are made with a plastic card (similar to a BT phone card) from reception. As with all city sites, it can be busy and perhaps a little noisy. Bungalows to hire but they are of average standard.

How to find it: Take exit 3 from the autostrada ring-road on to Via Cassia (signed SS2 Viterbo - NOT Via Cassia Bis) and look for camp signs. Turn right after 1 km (13 km. stone) and follow small road for about 1 km. to site.

General Details: Open mid-March - mid-Oct. 50,000 sq.m. Shade in most parts. Electrical connections (3A) to some pitches. Shop. Bar/restaurant and terrace. Money exchange. Bus service to Rome. Table tennis. Volleyball. Swimming pool (salt water). Disco. Horse riding. Golf (good course 4 km). Washing machines and irons. Chemical disposal. Excursions and cruises arranged.

Charges 1997: Per person (over 4 yrs) L.12,000; tent 6,000 - 9,000; caravan 11,000; car 6,000; motorcaravan 15,000; m/cycle 3,000.

Reservations: Write to site. Address: Via Cassia 1216, 00191 Rome. Tel: 06/30310826. FAX: 06/30362751.

6812 Happy Camping, Rome

A 'proper' camping site with no bungalows or static caravans.

This site, just 10 km. north of Rome, is well situated to visit the glories of the Eternal City. The 36,000 sq.m. are set in a sloping country area in two sections and it is surprising how remote it seems. There are 166 pitches arranged on terraces and trees provide shade in most parts. The two sanitary blocks are well positioned and hot water is free in the shower, washbasins and dishwashing sinks. Good shop, pleasant bar and a very acceptable restaurant. The large swimming pool and children's pool have safety attendants. Bus service every 30 minutes to the metro station. Sig. Bordini and his staff speak English.

How to find it: From the Rome ring road (GRA) take exit 5 on Cassia Bis. Black on white 'Happy' signs are well sited all the way (about 1 km).

General Details: Open April - 31 Oct. 36,000 sq.m. Shop. Bar. Restaurant. Swimming pool. Washing machine and dryer. Motorcaravan service point.

Charges 1997: Per person L. 9,000 - 10,500; child (3-14 yrs) 3,000 - 3,500; tent 4,800 - 5,500; caravan 7,000 - 8,500; motorcaravan 9,000 - 10,500; car 4,800 - 5,500.

Reservations: Contact site. Address: Via Prato delle Corte 1915, 00123 Roma. Tel: 06/33626401. FAX: 06/33613800. Internet: www.webeco.it/happycamping.

AR Discount

Less 10%

6808 Camping La Genziana, Barrea

Unsophisticated campsite high in the Abruzzi mountains.

This is the place to get away from it all. At night you can almost hear the flowers grow. Situated in the middle of Italy, it is well away from towns, yet only an hour or so from Rome or Pescara. This is a simple site with adequate facilities but Sig. d'Amico makes everyone so welcome. There are 110 pitches, of which 100 have 3A electricity, with 50 more for tents. Mountain walking tracks start from the site and facilities for swimming, riding and fishing are all nearby. Not suitable for disabled people.

How to find it: From autostrada A25, either take route 83 from Celano and site is signed 4 km. before Barrea, or take route 17 from Pratola/Sulmona to Castel di Sangro, then route 83 through Barrea to site.

General Details: Open all year. Bar and small shop but Barrea has most things just 500m down the road. Motorcaravan service point.

Charges 1997: Per person L. 8,000; child (under 9 yrs) 5,000; caravan 12,000; tent 11,000 - 12,000; motorcaravan 12,000; car 5,000; pet 5,000; electricity 2,000.

Reservations: Contact site. Address: Loc. Tre Croci, Parco Nazionale d'Abruzzo, 67030 Barrea (AQ). Tel: 0864/88450. FAX: 0864/88101.

6815 Fondi Holiday Camp, Salto di Fondi, nr Sperlonga

Picturesque seaside site with unusual cultural activity, midway between Rome and Naples.

Fondi is a big but peaceful site, midway between Rome and Naples, 300 m. off the main road. Largely covered by a pinewood, carefully tended flowers and trees and the white painted buildings make it a very pleasant site. Sand dunes protect from offshore breezes and during high season there are cultural and sporting activities. A troop of ballet dancers entertain and teach, plays and shows are staged in the open-air theatre and a mini judo festival is held with the British and Italian champions taking part. Films are shown and there is a wardrobe of over 400 costumes for the children's use. The management also sponsor theatre activity in the town. As well as the Mediterranean beach of fine sand, there are two swimming pools in the entertainment area near the restaurant, just back from the sea. With tennis courts, table tennis and a disco, there appears to be always something going on during the main season. The 100 pitches available for tourists are at the back of the site. They have some shade and are on flat grass, all with 3/5A electricity. The one large and 5 smaller toilet blocks are of modern construction and have mainly Turkish, but some British type WCs. The showers have hot water on payment, with cold water in the washbasins and dishwashing. There are 2 family washrooms with hot water. The large restaurant offers self service at lunch times with waiter service during the evenings serving mainly Italian and regional cuisine. The private beach is 250 m. wide, so there is always space. Signora Banotti, the lady owner speaks excellent English. All in all, an excellent site.

How to find it: Sperlonga is on the coast road SS213 between Gaeta and Terracina, 7 km. from Terracina. It is reached from the Rome - Naples autostrada, depending on approach, from several exits between Frosinone and Ceprana. Site is signed from Sperlonga and Terracina.

General Details: Open 1 April - 28 Sept. 40,000 sq.m. Good shade. Bar/restaurant, pizzeria, snack bar (all June-Sept). Supermarket. Greengrocer. Bazaar. Hairdresser. Chemical disposal. Main and children's swimming pools (instructor). Tennis. Table tennis. Handball. Disco. TV. Live theatre and ballet. Organised excursions possible to Rome, Capri, Naples, Pompei, Monte Cassino, etc. (with local agency). Facilities for the disabled. Washing machines and dryers. Dogs and pets not permitted.

Charges 1997: Per pitch incl. 2 persons L.30,000 - 65,000 acc. to season; extra person 9,000 - 20,000.

Reservations: Write to site. Address: Via Flacca km 6,800, 04020 Salto di Fondi (LT). Tel: 0771/555029 or 556282. FAX: 0771/555009.

6820 Camping Baia Domizia, Baia Domizia, Mondragone, nr Napoli

Large, formal seaside site north of Naples with many amenities.

This very large site, about 70 km. north west of Naples, is largely covered by a pinewood, much of which has been left in its natural state. There are 1,000 touring pitches, often in clearings on ground which may be grassy, a bit sandy, or on a hardstanding. Finding a good pitch may take time, but staff help in season and there are many individual pitches numbered for reservation purposes. Many varieties of bushes, roses and other flowers have been added to the natural surroundings. The site is run on strict lines, with various regulations (eg. no dogs or radios) but it is not a regimented site, and the general atmosphere is quiet but easy-going. Although the site is so big, there is never very far to walk to the beach, though from the ends it may be some 300 m. to the central shops and restaurant. Near these is a good sized swimming pool, recently refurbished and a pleasant alternative to the sea on windier days, with a smaller children's pool. There are seven good toilet blocks, all with British style WCs and constant hot water in all washbasins (many in cabins) and showers. Facilities for the disabled. A wide range of sports and other amenities is available. No dogs accepted. Charges are undeniably high, but this is a site with some class about it.

How to find it: The turning to Baia Domizia leads off the Formia-Naples road 23 km. from Formia. From the Rome-Naples autostrada, take the Cassino exit to Formia. The site is to the north of Baia Domizia itself.

General Details: Open 1 May - 30 Sept. 450,000 sq.m. Many parts well shaded, but in full sun near beach. Electrical connections (3A) in all parts. Large supermarket and general shop. Large bar and self-service restaurant with pizzeria. Ice cream parlour. Sports ground. Children's playground. Bicycle hire. Windsurfing hire and school. Tennis nearby. Excursions to Rome, Naples, Ischia, Capri. Bureau de change. Doctor on site daily. Washing machines, spin dryers. Chemical disposal. Motorcaravan services.

Charges 1997: Per person L. 5,800 - 13,500; child charged as adult; car or m/cycle 3,500 - 5,800; tent or caravan 8,800 - 18,800; motorcaravan 10,200 - 21,800; electricity included. Reductions for stays of over 14 days in low season.

Reservations: none, but min. 1 week stay in high season (July/Aug). Address: 81030 Baia Domizia (Caserta). Tel: 0823/930164 or 930126. FAX: 0823/930375.

The sites in the ITALY featured in this guide
are shown on the map on page 374

ITALY - South

6800 Camping Europe Garden, Silvi Marina, nr Pescara

Site with swimming pool and views to the sea, 13 km. northwest of Pescara.

Although not many Britons seem to visit these parts, this is somewhere decent to stay on the south east Italian coast. It lies just back from the coast (2 km) on raised ground with views over the sea. The 250 pitches, all with 10A electricity, are nearly all on terraces - if installation of caravans is difficult a tractor is always available to help. Cars stand by units on about half the pitches, in nearby parking spaces for the remainder. A fair amount of shade is available. There is a good swimming pool of 300 sq.m. on site, plus small children's pool, and a private sandy beach at Silvi about 2 km. away to which there is a bus service provided in July and August. There are two good toilet blocks which are well cleaned and provide mixed British and Turkish style WCs, washbasins with free hot water, not fully enclosed, and free hot showers. Free weekly coach excursions to different parts of the Province (10/7-30/8).

How to find it: Turn off inland S16 coast road at km. 433 stone for Silvi Alta and follow camp signs. From autostrada A14 take Pineto exit from north and Montesilvano exit from south. Signing is very good.

General Details: Open 1 May - 20 Sept. Electrical connections in all parts. Self-service shop. Restaurant. Bar. Tennis. Children's playground. 30 good bungalows for hire.

Charges 1997: Three charging seasons. Per person L.6,500 - 10,500; child (3-8 yrs) 5,000 - 7,500; pitch 15,000 - 22,500; m/cycle and 2-man tent 10,500 - 19,500; hiker and 2-man tent 9,000 - 19,500; electricity 2,500. Discounts for longer stays outside high season.

Reservations: made with L.150.000 deposit for first 2 weeks of Aug. (min 2 weeks), other times without deposit. Address: 64028 Silvi (Teramo). Tel: 085/930137 or 932844-5 (winter 085/75035). FAX: 085/932846. E-mail: nsantare@tin.it

6805 Camping Heliopolis, Pineto

Attractive site with individual sanitary arrangements and with direct access to beach.

Heliopolis is an attractive, well run site with a friendly English speaking lady owner. We just had to include this site - it is so spacious, although orderly, with an individual shower, WC and kitchen for 140 of the 250 touring pitches. Electrical connections (4A) are available on 16 places and cars are parked near the entrance. The site opens directly onto a wide sand and shingle beach which is very safe for children. Like most Adriatic sites, it is close to the railway, and there is some noise from passing trains. There are two excellent toilet blocks for campers, one for men and one for women. A pleasant bar, a games room, a sizeable, attractive pool and children's pool, plus a good restaurant, plus various beach facilities are all available. Like most Italian sites, this one is very full in July/August.

How to find it: Site is to the north of the town, clearly signed from A14 road (exit Pineto) and SS16 (in town centre). If coming from the north, it is worth the extra money to take the A14; the SS16 is busy and boring.

General Details: Open 1 April - 30 Sept. Bar/restaurant. Shops. Laundry facilities. Swimming pool (from June). Tennis and play pitches. Children's playground. Entertainment organised in high season. Doctor attends 2 hrs daily. A good site for the disabled. Chemical disposal. Caravans and tents for hire.

Charges 1997: Three charging seasons. Per standard pitch L.18,000, 22,000 or 32,000; pitch with private facilities 32,000, 35,000 or 45,000; small tent pitch 8,000, 10,000 or 13,000; person 6,000, 8,000, 10,000; child (3-12 yrs) 5,000, 7,000, 9,000; electricity included.

Reservations: Write to site for details. Address: Contrada Villa Fumosa 1, 64025 Pineto (TE). Tel: 085/9492720 -30 or -50. FAX: 085/9492171.

6830 Villagio Turistico Costa Alta, Piano di Sorrento, nr Napoli

Pleasant, shady site on headland above the sea.

Although sites like Camping Pini and Giardino delle Esperidi (San Agnello) are of a similar standard and price, Costa Alta is better located. We do not recommend any sites beyond Sorrento town centre because of the daily, chaotic congestion on the only main road. Costa Alta has 118 pitches, 50 of which are permanently reserved, and there are also 60 bungalows. The site is on a gentle slope. The toilet blocks provide altogether, 22 showers and WCs of the seatless type. Hot water is free but only one small sanitary block is suitable for the disabled. The swimming pool (25 x 12 m.) charges on a daily rate (L 5,000) and is open from 15 June. Facilities include a snack bar and a well run restaurant. A supermarket and other shops are just 100 m. away. There is tennis and table tennis and evening entertainment in July and August. Lift access to the small area of so called beach.

How to find it: Piano di Sorrento is 2 km. before Sorrento centre approaching on the SS145 from Castellamare. Site is well signed, but Camping Riposo nearby has clearer signs to follow.

General Details: Open 15 March - 31 Oct, as are restaurant and bar. Shade in most parts. Electrical connections spread around. Tennis. Table tennis. Dancing and video shows July/Aug. Bungalows and chalets for hire.

Charges 1997: Per person L. 10,000 - 14,000; child (2-6 yrs) 5,500 - 8,000; caravan 9,000 - 13,500; large tent 8,500 - 13,000; car 4,000 - 6,500; small tent 7,500 - 10,000; motorcaravan 13,000 - 16,000; m/cycle 3,000 - 4,500; electricity 4,000. In March, April and Oct. there are reduced prices by negotiation.

Reservations: are made for any period, with 10% deposit. Address: Via Madonna di Roselle 20/A, 80063 Piano di Sorrento (NA). Tel: 081/5321832. FAX: 081/8788368.

Villaggio-Camping **EUROPE GARDEN** 64028 Silvi (TE)
tel. 0039/85/930137 - fax 0039/85/932846§
E-mail: nsantare@tin.it

Send immediately for our 20 page colour brochure
RESERVATIONS POSSIBLE

6842 Camping Sant' Antonio, Seiano, Vico Equense

Peaceful base from which to explore Pompei, Herculaneum and Sorrento.

This pretty little site, just across the road from Seiano beach, would suit caravanners who like a peaceful (for Italy) location. There are only 150 pitches which are in shade offered by orange, lemon and walnut trees. The single sanitary block provides hot and cold showers, washbasins and British style WCs. Hot water is on payment. There is a regular 15 minute bus service to the Circumvesuviana railway which runs frequently to Sorrento, Pompei, Herculaneum and Naples - the only sensible way to travel for non-party sightseeing.

How to find it: Take route SS163 from Castellamare to Sorrento. Just after the tunnel by-pass around Vico Equense, watch for the hard right turn for Seiano beach and follow the signs down the narrow road.

General Details: Open 15 March - 15 Oct. 10, 000 sq.m. of flat, shady ground with easy access. Electricity to all pitches (3A). Small shop, bar and restaurant. Barbecues allowed. No static caravans. Caravans for rent.

Charges 1997: Per person L. 9,000 - 10,500; caravan 9,000 - 10,500; motorcaravan 11,000 - 13,500.

Reservations: Contact site. Address: Via Marina d'Equa, Seiano, 80069 Vico Equense (NA). Tel: 081/8028576.

AR Discount

Less 10%

6845 Centro Turistico San Nicola, Peschici, Gargano Peninsula

Busy, top class site on most attractive, sandy cove (but 80 km. from the autostrada).

This is a really splendid site occupying a hill side, sloping down to a cove with a 500 m. beach of fine sand, protected by cliffs at each end. Surrounded by tree clad mountains, it is a quiet, well regulated site which is part of, but separate from, a tourist holiday complex. Hard access roads lead to well constructed, grassy terraces, under shade from mature trees. By the beach is another camping area on grass, but with little shade and minimal space. There are 750 pitches of varying size, all with 5A electrical connections. Cars may have to be parked away from the pitches in high season. There are no static caravans but bungalows are available for rent. Six excellent, modern toilet blocks, 2 in the beach part, the others situated around the site, are of superb quality with British and Turkish style toilets and free hot water in the washbasins (some with toilets in private cabins), showers and dishwashing facilities. The shopping complex (open during busiest seasons) has a supermarket, greengrocer, fish stall, hairdresser and bazaar for holiday items. The large bar/restaurant with another small shop and two small bars are by the beach. Entertainment for young and old by the restaurant in high season. The site is fairly remote with some tortuous roads towards the end of the 80 km. trip from the autostrada. With a neat, tidy appearance, the many flower beds provide a garden atmosphere of calm serenity. The helpful staff all wear San Nicola shirts for identification. The site is popular with German campers (tannoy announcements and most notices in German only!) Dogs not accepted in July/Aug.

How to find it: Leave the Autostrada A14 at exit for Poggio Imperiale, and proceed towards Peschici and Vieste. When signs for Peschici and Vieste diverge, follow Vieste signs keeping a sharp lookout for San Nicola. Then follow black signs for Centro Turistico San Nicola and pass Camping Baia San Nicola (on your left) just before site. It will take at least 1½ hrs from the motorway. Note: There is also a San Nicola Varano en-route which must be ignored.

General Details: Open 1 April - 15 Oct. 120,000 sq.m. Shade in main part. Supermarket, fruit and fish shops, bazaar. 2 beach bars (open 1 May). Bar/restaurant (open all season). Electrical connections all parts (5A). Chemical disposal. Tennis. Watersports. Children's playground. Organised recreational activity July/Aug. Cash point. Coach and boat excursions. Washing machines and dryers. Bungalows for rent.

Charges 1997: Four charging seasons. Per adult L. 6,500 - 14,000; child (1-8 yrs) 4,500 - 10,000; tent 6,500 - 14,000; caravan or trailer tent 8,500 - 17,000; car 5,000 - 8,500; motorcaravan 12,000 - 21,000; m/cycle 4,500 - 7,500. Min. stay 7 days 18/6-3/9.

Reservations: Only made for site's own accommodation (min. 1 week). Address: 71010 Peschici (Foggia), Gargano. Tel: 0884/964024. FAX: 0884/964025.

ITALY - South

6835 Camping Riposo, Piano di Sorrento, nr Napoli

Small site with few facilities but reasonable charges.

Just 300 m. from the picturesque port of Piano di Sorrento is the tiny site of Camping Riposo. Simple, pretty and clean, this is only for those who just want a secluded place to park their 'van whilst they explore this famous area. There are no entertainments and no pool - just a tiny bar and shop. The Scalici family offer a courteous and helpful service. The site is shaded by citrus trees and there are three excellent food shops nearby. Electrical connections are available and there is free hot water.

How to find it: From Meta follow plentiful directions for either Riposo or Costa Alta (no. 6830) off main road SS145 (to Sorrento from autostrada at Castellamare). Access could be tricky for large units but gates open wide.

General Details: Open 1 June - 30 Sept. Small bar and shop. Caravans for hire.

Charges 1997: Per person L. 7,000; child (1-6 yrs) 5,000; tent 6,000 - 8,500; caravan 8,500; motorcaravan 11,000; car 5,500; m/cycle 3,000; electricity and tax included.

AR Discount

Less 10%

Reservations: Write to site. Address: Via Cassano 12/14, 80063 Piano di Sorrento (NA). Tel: 081/8787374.

6850 Sea World Village, San Giorgio, Bari

Seaside site in the far south of Italy, with new name and management.

There are few good sites in this part of Italy but Sea World Village (formerly Camping Internazionale San Giorgio) is acceptable as a transit stop or short stay. The new owners are livening up the old, rather neglected site. Bari is a busy city, but Sea World Village is on the southern edge. There are 20 tourist pitches, all with electricity, well separated from the static pitches. Access to the sea is via rocks and concrete platforms, with a small swimming pool at the water's edge, plus a separate, man-made, sandy beach which is cleaned daily. The large car park and many changing cabins means the site is crowded at weekends with day visitors. The modern sanitary block has British style WCs and free hot showers. There are 42 bungalows, several built in the local 'Trulli' style, for hire on a weekly basis.

How to find it: Take the Bari exit from autostrada A14 and follow signs for Brindisi on the dual carriageway ring road (Tangenziole). After exit 14 watch carefully for the San Giorgio exit. Turn left and site is signed 200 m. ahead, across traffic lights.

General Details: Open all year. 50,000 sq.m. Bar/restaurant, pizzeria and market open during season. Writing room. Doctor calls. Roller skating, hockey, football and tennis areas. Bowling. Disco. Watersports.

Charges 1997: Per person L.10,000; car 7,000; m/cycle 3,000; tent 6,000 - 8,000; caravan, motorcaravan or large tent 10,000; electricity 2,000.

Reservations: Only made for bungalows. Address: San Giorgio, ss Adriatica 78, 70126 Bari. Tel: 080/5491202.

6852 Village Camping Marina di Rossano, Rossano

Excellent site in the far south.

This is the most welcoming site we have visited in this area. Most of the staff in reception, the shops, bar and restaurant speak English with a smile. The location is not so far as it seems - it can be reached by either the west or east autostrada, without the final tortuous or very busy roads to some nearer coastal sites. It took us over 4 hours from Naples and it is approximately 2 hours from Bari. There are about 200 pitches, all under tall, shady poplar trees. It is entirely secluded and leads directly to a large stretch of private beach. There are several toilet blocks mostly with free hot water. Dogs are only accepted with medical clearance and payment. Very suitable for disabled people, their own facilities are provided. There are many apartments and bungalows to rent. The site has an excellent swimming pool and sporting facilities, with attentive entertainment staff, at reasonable prices.

How to find it: From the north take the east coast highway (route 106 - Ionica). Leave at Rossano exit and a football stadium is immediately opposite with a site sign to its left. Follow signs for 1 km. to site. From the south, at Rossano exit turn left under road bridge. Turn left immediately before football stadium.

General Details: Open 1 April - 30 Sept. Shops. Bars. Restaurants. Swimming pools. Private beach. Basketball. Volleyball. Bicycle hire. Apartments and bungalows for hire.

Charges 1997: Per pitch L. 32,000 - 38,000; adult 6,000 - 10,000; child (3-5 yrs) 6,000 - 7,000; second car 2,000 - 3,200; dog 2,500 - 4,000; electricity incl. Credit Cards accepted.

Reservations: Contact site. Address: C. da Leuca, CP98, 87069 Rossano (Cosenza). Tel: 0983/516054. FAX: 0983/512069. Internet: www.masternet.it/itwg/itw01997.htm.

6803 Camping Villagio Athena, Paestum

Compact, well run site by the sea and 1 mile from the Greek temples.

This level site, which has direct access to the beach, has most facilities to hand. Some of the site is in woodland, but sun worshippers will have no problem here. The access is easy and the staff are friendly. There are 150 pitches, of which only 20 are used for static units and these are unobtrusive. Sanitary facilities are in two blocks with mixed British and Turkish style WCs, washbasins (cold water only) and hot showers on payment.

continued overleaf

6803 Camping Villagio Athena (continued)

Dishwashing and laundry sinks, and toilets for disabled people. No disco, but there are cabaret shows in July/Aug. Dogs and barbecues not permitted.

How to find it: Take the SS18 through Paestum and, at southern end of town, turn right and follow road straight down to sea. Site is well signed.

General Details: Open 1 April - 30 Sept. 20,000 sq.m. Shop and bar. Restaurant (open all day June - mid Sept). Riding available. Tennis 1 km. Watersports. Chemical disposal. Hourly bus service. Bungalows for hire.

Charges 1997: Per person L. 7,000 - 9,000; pitch 15,000 - 23,000.

Reservations: Contact site. Address: Via Ponte di Ferro, 84063 Paestum (SA). Tel: 0828/851105 (winter 0828/724725).

Sardinia

There are regular ferries to the islands of the north coast and to Corsica. For ferry information contact:

Southern Ferries Ltd, 179 Piccadilly, London W1V 9DB. Tel: 0171 491 4968

6860 Camping Capo d'Orso, Palau

Pretty seaside site on northern edge of Costa Smerelda.

This is a well established and decidedly pretty site on a hillside sloping down to the sea and facing Caprera Island and several beaches, some 4½ km. from the village of Palau. The terrain is fairly rocky but the 450 pitches are on level, sparsely grassed terraces, with quite good access roads. Most have 3A electricity and are of a fair size (40-80 sq.m). Cars are parked away from the pitches in July/Aug. This side of the island seems generally to be hotter and more sheltered from the wind, but there is not a lot of shade. The restaurant, bar, pizzeria, takeaway and shop are only open from 1 June, and other facilities, including scuba-diving, sailing school and boat excursions to the nearby small islands only operate in the main season. Other facilities include caravans and bungalows for hire, tennis, an underground disco, children's and adults entertainment (in high season). There are moorings for boats and boat hire in high season. Sanitary facilities, in three blocks, are adequate, with hot showers (on payment in season, free at other times), open plan washbasins, washing-up and laundry sinks (cold water) and mainly Turkish, but with some British, type WCs. They seemed to be well maintained when we visited in late May, although not all the blocks were open at that time. A useful alternative to our other site on Sardinia, being somewhat cheaper, smaller and less formally organised, but with significantly less shade.

How to find it: Site is 5 km. from Palau, in the northeast, on the coast opposite (southwest of) Caprera Island.

General Details: Open 1 April - 30 Sept. Bar/restaurant. Pizzeria. Takeaway. Shop (all from 1/6). Disco. Chemical disposal. Entertainment programmes and excursions. Scuba diving, windsurfing, sailing (all main season). Boat hire and moorings. Tennis. Bungalows and caravans for hire.

Charges guide: Per pitch L. 9,000 - 16,000; tent pitch for 2 persons 6,000 - 11,000; adult 6,000 - 11,000; child 4,000 - 8,000; car or m/cycle 2,000 - 6,000; extra tent 3,000 - 7,000; electricity 3,000.

Reservations: Contact site for details. Address: 07020 Palau (SS). Tel: 0789/702007. FAX: 0789/702006.

6855 Camping Baia Blu La Tortuga, Aglientu, nr S. Teresa di Gallura

Aptly named, large site situated on a bay of startling blue sea and golden sand.

La Tortuga is in one of the nicest corners of this island, enjoying welcome breezes and convenient for the ferry at St Teresa di Gallura (for Corsica). The site is under the same ownership as Marepineta (no. 6000) and La Gardiola (6270) and has excellent facilities including some very modern sanitary installations. The four blocks of a similarly unusual design provide an exceptionally good ratio of facilities to pitches. The most unusual feature is combined shower/washbasin cabins, with controllable hot showers (on payment) and free hot water to basins. Apart from the large number of showers, British and Turkish style WCs and washbasins, there are footbaths, basins for children, sinks for dishes and laundry (hot water am. clothes, pm. dishes) and facilities for disabled people. Washing machines, dryers and irons. The 700 pitches, all with 3A electricity, are arranged in rows between tall pines, eucalyptus and shrubs with good access and plenty of shade. Catering facilities include an attractive restaurant, pizzeria and takeaway and a small, pleasant bar. A large and still developing site with direct access to the beach and an extensive range of amenities, both on site and nearby. Used by tour operators.

How to find it: Site is on the north coast between the towns of Costa Paradiso and S. Teresa di Gallura (18 km.) at Pineta di Vignola Mare.

General Details: Open 6 April - 3 Oct. Bar. Restaurant, pizzeria, snack bar and takeaway (May-Sept). Supermarket. Children's playground. Tennis. Volleyball. Football. Table tennis. Games and TV rooms. Disco 50 m. Barbecue area. Chemical disposal. Wind surfing school. Facilities and school for divers. Entertainment and sports activities organised in season. Riding near. Excursions. 50 mobile homes and 37 caravans for hire.

Charges 1998: Four charging seasons. Per person L. 7,500 - 16,500; junior (under 10 yrs) or senior (over 60 yrs) 5,500 - 13,000; pitch 10,500 - 26,500; electricity 3,500.

Reservations: made with L. 30,000 deposit. Address: Pineta di Vignola Mare, 07020 Aglientu (SS), Sardegna. Tel: 079/602060 (winter: 0365/520018). FAX: 079/602040. (winter: 0365/520690).

LUXEMBOURG

The Grand Duchy of Luxembourg is an independent sovereign state, 999 square miles in area lying between Belgium, France and Germany. Geographically, the Grand Duchy is divided into two sections: in the north the uplands of the Ardennes, a hilly and scenic region, in the south mainly rolling farmlands and woods, bordered on the east by the wine growing area of the Moselle Valley. Luxembourg City is one of the most spectacularly sited capitals in Europe and home to about one fifth of the population. Luxembourg is essentially a Roman Catholic country.

For further information contact:

Luxembourg Tourist Office, 122, Regent Street, London W1R 5FE

Tel: 0171 434 2800 Fax: 0171 734 1205

Population
389,800; density 151 per sq. km.

Capital
Luxembourg City.

Climate
A temperate climate prevails, the summer often extending from May to late October.

Language
Letzeburgesch is the national language, with French and German also being official languages.

Currency
Luxembourg Franc interchangeable with the Belgium Franc. Divides into 100 centimes and comes in coins worth 5, 10, 20 and 50 francs and notes worth 100, 500, 1000 and 5000 francs.

Banks
Open 08.30/09.00-12.00 and 13.30-16.30.
Credit Cards: are widely accepted.

Post Offices
Open 08.00-12.00 and 14.00-17.00 (but those in villages often operate more restricted hours).

Time
GMT plus 1 (summer BST +1).

Telephone
For calls from Luxembourg to the UK the code is 0044 followed by the STD code omitting initial 0. To call Luxembourg from the UK the code is 00 352 followed by the number (no area codes).

Public Holidays
New Year; Carnival Day, mid-Feb; Easter Mon; May Day; Ascension; Whit Mon; National Day, 23 June; Assumption, 15 Aug; All Saints; All Souls; Christmas, 25, 26 Dec.

Shops
Open Mon 14.00-18.30. Tues to Sat 08.30-12.00 and 14.00-18.30, (grocers and butchers close at 15.00 on Sat).

Motoring
Speed Limits: Caravans and motorhomes (3.5 tons) 31 mph (50 kph) in built up areas, caravans 46 mph (75 kph) and 56 mph (90 kph) on other roads and motorways respectively, motorhomes 56 mph (90 kph) and 75 mph (120 kph). Fuel: Visa and Eurocard are accepted.
Parking: A Blue Zone area exists in Luxembourg City (discs from ACL, police stations, tourist offices) but parking meters are also available.

Overnighting
Generally only allowed on camp sites.

Useful Addresses
Motoring Organisation:
Automobile Club du Grand-Duche de Luxembourg (ACL)
54 route de Longwy, 8007 Bertrange. Tel: 450045. Offices hours ; Mon-Fri 08.30-12.00 and 13.30-18.00

Tourist Information:
Tourist Information Societies (Syndicat d'Initiative) with offices in most towns. Closed lunch time - times vary. The National Tourist Office in London is very helpful.

During 1997 The Microsoft Corporation released their new version of 'AUTOROUTE Express' which features a campsite database. This database includes and highlights virtually all our Alan Rogers' Inspected and Selected sites throughout the UK, France and the rest of Europe. It also includes a large number of other sites too, which have not been subject to our rigorous inspection process.

770 Camping Gaalgebierg, Esch-sur-Alzette

Good quality site near French border

Occupying an elevated position on the edge of town, this pleasant site is run by the local camping and caravan club. Although surrounded by hills and with a good variety of trees, not all pitches have shade. There are 150 pitches (50 for tourists) 100 sq.m., on grass, marked out by trees, some on a slight slope. All have 16A electricity and TV points. The site has an entertainment and activities programme in peak season. There is a small bar/restaurant with terrace, a shop for basics, plus table tennis and a children's playground. The sanitary units, which can be heated, provide British WCs, washbasins with free hot water (some in cubicles), hot showers on payment, excellent facilities for disabled people and babies, and dishwashing and laundry sinks. All have been re-furbished and have a key-card entry system.

How to find it: Site is well signed from the centre of Esch, but a sharp look out is needed as there are two acute right-handers on the approach to the site.

General Details: Open all year. Shop. Bar/restaurant. Laundry. Children's playground. Volleyball. Table tennis. Boules. Badminton. Swimming pool and tennis nearby. Entertainment in season.

Charges guide: Per pitch LFr. 120; adult 120; child (3-12 yrs) 60; electricity (16A) 50; local tax per person 20.

Reservations: Write to site with deposit. Address: 4001 Esch-sur-Alzette. Tel: 541069. FAX: 549630.

772 Camping Steinfort, Steinfort

Traditional small site in southwest of country, en-route from Arlon to Luxembourg.

An ideal transit site, being close to the E25, this site has a friendly, family atmosphere, backs onto open fields and is quiet at night. The 100 marked, grassy pitches, 75 with electrical connections, are slightly sloping with some trees for shade. There are a number of residential and long stay units, but there is usually space for tourists - arrive early in season. This site's main attraction is that it is open all year and reception, the good value restaurant and the well stocked shop are always open late. The single sanitary unit is functional and clean providing British WCs, washbasins (cold water), hot showers with dividers, seats and hooks (on payment), facilities for babies, with dishwashing sinks (H&C) outside under cover. Re-cycling is important here, with separate containers for glass, paper and metal.

How to find it: From E25 take Steinfort exit, then left at crossroads, site entrance is on the left between two filling stations and immediately alongside the motel.

General Details: Open all year. Shop, restaurant and bar (all year). Snack bar and takeaway. Laundry. Freezer. Children's pool (25/6-10/9). Bicycle hire. Table tennis. Badminton. Games machines. Fishing licences. Entertainment in season. Children's playground and ball games area. Nearby are tennis, bowling, archery, fishing and go-karting. Chemical disposal.

Charges 1998: Per pitch LFr. 240; pitch with electricity 290; adult 95; child (2-10 yrs) 65; small pitch 125. Less 10% in low season.

Reservations: Advised for main season. Address: 72 Rte de Luxembourg, 8440 Steinfort. Tel: 398827. FAX: 397410.

AR Discount
Free drink when you buy a meal

776 Camping Europe, Remich

Useful touring site by River Moselle, close to town activities.

This municipal site is the best we could find on the road which runs alongside the Moselle. Its facilities are acceptable and clean, but not luxurious, and it is convenient for the town centre. We recommend that you arrive early in season as the site fills up quickly. The 110 marked pitches, all with 10A electricity, are on level grass with no static or long stay units. The municipal swimming pool and ice skating complex is at one end of the site (no direct access). The sanitary building contains British WCs, washbasins with cold water only and free hot showers. The town is a picturesque and popular resort with a tree shaded promenade along the river bank, wine cellars and facilities for wine tasting, many sporting facilities, entertainment and restaurants.

How to find it: From Rue de Moselle (running alongside river) just south of the river bridge, turn (by large car park) into Rue de Camping, and site is on left.

General Details: Open 5 April - 16 September. Chemical disposal. Within easy walking distance of all facilities.

Charges guide: Per pitch LFr. 130; adult 120; child 60; electricity 35.

Reservations: Write to site for details. Address: Rue de Camping, 5550 Remich. Tel: 698018.

764 Camping 'Auf Kengert', Larochette

Agreeable site with good shop and restaurant, northeast of Luxembourg city.

A friendly welcome awaits you at this peacefully situated, family run site, 2 km. from Larochette, with 181 individual pitches, all with electricity (4/16A). Some are in a very shaded woodland setting, on a slight slope with fairly narrow access roads. There are six hardened pitches for motorcaravans on a flat area of grass, complete with motorcaravan service facilities. Further pitches are in an adjacent and more open meadow area. The well maintained sanitary installations are in two parts with free hot water throughout; the modern unit has British WCs, washbasins (some in cubicles), and excellent, fully equipped, dedicated cubicles for the disabled. The showers (older in style) and a laundry room are located below the central building which houses the restaurant, large well stocked shop, etc. There is a good swimming pool for the summer months. This site is popular in season, so early arrival is advisable, or you can reserve.

How to find it: From Larochette take the N8 (towards Mersch) and just outside town turn right on CR119 towards Schrondweiler, site is 2 km. on right.

General Details: Open 20 Feb - 8 Nov. Self-service shop. Bar. Restaurant. Laundry. Children's playground. Sauna and solarium. Swimming pool (Easter - Sept). Paddling pool. Chemical disposal. Motorcaravan services. Bottle bank. Good English spoken.

Charges 1998: Per person LFr. 320 - 400; child (2-18 yrs) 160 - 240; electricity 80; walkers and cyclists less 10%.

Reservations: Write to site. Address: 7633 Larochette/Medernach. Tel: 837186. FAX: 878323. E-mail: linda@ camping.lu.

AR Discount
Welcome drink;
bottle of wine.
Luxembourg card.

Camping »Auf Kengert«

L-7633 Larochette / G.D. of Luxembourg • Tel. 00 352-837186 • Fax 878323

Situated in the heart of Luxembourg

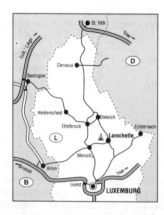

1st class camp – large supermarket – Restaurant with open fire and French cuisine – self-service washers and dryers – children's playground – new modern sanitary installations too for the disabled – service station – Calor gas & others – sauna – solarium – money-exchange – swimming pool for children and adults. **English spoken.**

---

775 Camping Bettembourg, Bettembourg

Small municipal site, exclusively for tourists with immaculate modern facilities.

This small site on the southern outskirts of Bettembourg is beautifully maintained. The 25 pitches, accessed from a central paved roadway, have some neatly trimmed dividing hedges and all have 16A electricity. The sanitary facilities are exceptional with British WCs, washbasins in cubicles, spacious showers with dividers, seat and hooks, a superb suite for the disabled, fully equipped baby room, dishwashing and laundry facilities, all with free hot water. The warden is justifiably proud of them. A cosy club room with TV and coffee bar is available should the weather be inclement.

continued overleaf

LUXEMBOURG

775 Camping Bettembourg (continued)

A brochure showing the local cycle path network and other tourist information may be obtained from reception.

How to find it: From the town centre follow camping signs, site lies to the south of the town, near the railway station and marshalling yard (not noticeably noisy at time of visit).

General Details: Open 15 April - 30 September. Clubroom with coffee bar and TV. Laundry. Chemical disposal. Reception closed 12.00-14.00; barrier closed 23.00-07.00. Only French spoken.

Charges guide: Per pitch LFr. 150; adult 150; child (3-14 yrs) 70.

Reservations: Write to site for details. Address: Parc Jacquinot, 3241 Bettembourg. Tel: 513646. FAX: 520357.

762 Europacamping Nommerlayen, Nommern, Larochette

Modern, terraced holiday site in central Luxembourg with excellent pool complex.

This is a top quality site with fees to match, but it has everything! A large, central building housing most of the services and amenities opens onto a terrace around an excellent swimming pool complex with two main pools, plus an imaginative watery playground. The 423 individual pitches (70-120 sq.m.), all with access to electricity (2, 10 or 16A) and water taps, are on grassy terraces. There is little shade on the newer open, grassy section - this is a deliberate policy so as not to obscure views over the surrounding countryside. A large, high quality, modern sanitary unit provides British WCs, washbasins (some in cubicles), showers with dividers, facilities for disabled people, family and baby rooms. Hot water is free throughout. There is an additional small `portacabin' unit for peak season in the newer section.

How to find it: Site is 5 km. from Larochette, on the west side of Nommern village.

General Details: Open 13 Feb. - 7 Nov. Restaurant. Snack bar. Bar. Laundry. Swimming pools. Bowling. Table tennis. Snooker. Billiards. Volleyball. Football. Children's playground. Large screen TV. Entertainment in season. Motorcaravan service station. Car wash. Bicycle hire. Bottle bank. Returnable deposits required for: barrier keycard Lfr 1,000, water tap key Lfr 100 and pool bracelet Lfr 150.

Charges guide: Per unit July/Aug Lfr. 700-1,490 acc. to pitch and facilities; extra person 120; electricity 16A 100.

Reservations: Essential for high season. Address: 7465 Nommern. Tel: 878078 or 878093. FAX: 879678.

781 Caravaning-Parc Martbusch, Berdorf

Relaxing, well tended site on edge of town, with excellent facilities.

A municipal site adjacent to the sports facilities of an elegant small town, this site is kept neat and tidy by the parks department. The touring section is well screened from the long stay area and shaded by mature trees. The 100 grassy, numbered pitches are divided by hedges, all with electricity (10A) and accessed from tarmac roadways. The sanitary facilities are housed in two good quality modern buildings which provide British WCs, washbasins (some in cubicles), spacious showers with dividers, seats and hooks, dishwashing and laundry facilities, units for babies and disabled people. Free hot water throughout. Shop and snack bar, TV and games rooms and a `salle de séjour'. Adjoining the site is a recreation complex which includes minigolf, tennis, indoor swimming pool (adults LFr 70; child 40; open July/Aug), fitness centre, playgrounds, marked walks and rock climbing in the surrounding area.

How to find it: Site and recreation centre are well signed from the Consdorf - Echternach road in Berdorf centre.

General Details: Open 1 March - 15 November. Shop. Snack bar. Laundry. Chemical disposal. Children's playground. TV and games room. Bottle bank. Recreation centre adjacent.

Charges guide: Per pitch LFr. 160; person 160; child (3-14) 100; (less 10% low seasons); electricity 60.

Reservations: Write for details to: Tourist Info-Service CR, 5 Rue de Consdorf, 6551 Berdorf. Tel: 79643. Site address: 3 Bäim Maartbësch, 6552 Berdorf. Tel: 79545.

765 Camping de la Sûre, Reisdorf

Riverside site, with pleasant atmosphere, popular with fishermen.

On the edge of this small town, this site has 160 numbered pitches, most with electricity (16A) and arranged around a tarmac access road. Some are on the river bank (heaven for keen anglers - advance booking advised). They are not separated but are marked with small trees. There are some static units, but these are nearest the road in their own fenced area, leaving the prime pitches for tourists. The town centre is within easy walking distance, and cycle ways abound. When we visited the sanitary facilities were in an older building, but were modern and clean with British WCs, some washbasins in cubicles, showers with dividers, and free hot water throughout. A new extension was close to completion and this should now be open. New paths and roads were also under construction. Other services include a small shop, a café/bar with takeaway meals, a playground, minigolf and fishing.

How to find it: From river bridge in Reisdorf, take road to Echternach, de la Sûre is the **second** campsite on left.

General Details: Open 1 April - 30 October. Small shop. Café/bar. Takeaway. Laundry. Chemical disposal. Children's playground. Minigolf. Sports field. Canoeing. Fishing.

Charges guide: Per pitch LFr. 200; adult 180; child 80; electricity 80. Discounts for long stays and off season.

Reservations: Write to site for details. Address: 23 Rue de la Sûre, 9390 Reisdorf. Tel: 86509 or 86246.

209

LUXEMBOURG

791 Camping Kalkesdelt, Ettelbruck

Agreeable, good value site on a hilltop overlooking the town.

Quietly located about 1 km. from the centre of Ettelbruck, this municipal site has a nice atmosphere with well tended gardens and grass. The modern main building includes reception, a 'salle de séjour' (with library and TV), some excellent new WCs and washbasins, a room for the handicapped and a laundry. Two older sanitary units (one used high season only) provide British WCs, washbasins (cold water) and free hot showers with divider, shelf and hooks. All can be heated in cool weather. The 150 marked pitches are generally slightly sloping, some on terraces backed by banks and trees, others on an open area at the top of the site. All are accessed from tarmac roadways and have electricity available (16A). The restaurant, snack bar and takeaway are open each evening in season. A baker calls daily at 7.30 am. (order day before). Breakfasts can also be served. Reception has good tourist information and There is a small playground, table tennis and children's entertainment in high season.

How to find it: Site is signed off N15 on western outskirts of Ettelbruck; approached via short one-way system.

General Details: Open 1 April - 30 September. Restaurant. Snack bar and takeaway. Bicycle hire. Playground. Table tennis. Entertainment in season. Laundry. Chemical disposal. Bottle bank. English spoken.

Charges guide: Per pitch LFr. 130; adult 120; child (3-14 yrs) 50; electricity 80; local 'Eco' tax 20.

Reservations: Write to site for details Address: Rue de Camping, 9022 Ettelbruck. Tel: 812185. FAX: 819839.

769 Camping Romantique, Walsdorf, nr Diekirch

Peacefully situated country site in a valley, in eastern Luxembourg

This friendly, family run site is located beside a stream and surrounded by fields and woods - a most tranquil haven especially during low season. There are several marked walks around the area and one can visit the nearby hydroelectric power station - the site provides a free and comprehensive tourist information pack with full details of this and other local attractions. The 190 spacious, numbered pitches are arranged on long flat open terraces on either side of well surfaced access roads, with shade in parts and electricity (6A) available to most. There is a special area for young campers. The main sanitary installations are of a good standard, with British WCs, washbasins (some in cubicles), roomy showers, facilities for babies, laundry, dishwashing and a freezer for campers. Hot water is free throughout. There is an additional small sanitary unit on the upper terrace. The site has a good restaurant and bar with a pleasant terrace.

How to find it: Off the N17 road from Diekirch - Vianden, site is signed.

General Details: Open 1 April - 31 Oct. Bar with snacks, restaurant (both limited hours, closed Wed). Laundry. Freezer. TV. Children's playground. Chemical disposal.

Charges 1998: Per pitch incl. 2 persons LFr. 700; extra person 100 (less 33% in low season); electricity 75. Credit cards accepted.

Reservations: Essential in July/August. Address: 9465 Walsdorf. Tel: 834464. FAX: 834440.

767 Camping des Ardennes, Hosingen

Good value site in a very attractive small town, noted for its floral displays.

This small municipal site is located on the edge of this most attractive town with an easy level walk to all amenities and parks and floral arrangements to admire during the summer season. The 50 level, open, grassy pitches all have electricity (10A) and are arranged on either side of surfaced roadways, with a few trees providing a little shade in places. The single sanitary unit, which can be heated in winter, is well appointed, modern and very clean, with British WCs, large shower cubicles (with full screens), and open washbasins in separate men's and women's facilities. Hot water is free throughout. Dishwashing and laundry facilities with washing machine and dryer (instructions in English), also clothes lines. The site has a tiny inflatable type swimming pool principally for children, a small playground, barbecue, café/bar and boule pitch. Skis and winter sports equipment for hire.

How to find it: Site is off the main N7 road north of Diekirch and is signed from the centre of the town, with the sports complex.

General Details: Open all year. Café/bar (opening variable). Laundry. Children's pool and playground. Boule. Barbecue. Winter sports equipment for hire. Rooms for rent. Adjacent sports complex with tennis and football, etc.

Charges guide: Per pitch LFr. 120; adult 120; child 60; electricity 60.

Reservations: Write to site for details. Address: 9809 Hosingen. Tel: 91911.

LUXEMBOURG

771 Camping Trois Frontières, Leiler

Attractive, friendly site with pool, in beautiful location in northeast Luxembourg

Conveniently located close to the German and Belgian borders, this well established, good quality site has some stunning views from the terrace over the surrounding countryside. An attractive `Spanish' style building houses the sanitary installations which are modern and clean with British WCs, washbasins in cubicles, and facilities for the disabled. The spacious showers are housed in a separate room under the main building (heated in cool weather), together with a well equipped baby room. Free hot water throughout. The 120 pitches (100 sq.m.) are arranged in bays for around 10 units each, either side of a central roadway. All have access to electricity (4A). Other services include a small bar/restaurant, takeaway, heated swimming pool and a good quality children's playground. A baker calls daily in season. The site also offers an entertainment programme in high season. Clervaux Abbey is just a short drive away.

How to find it: Approaching Leiler from the west, site is on right hand side as you enter the village.

General Details: Open all year. Small shop. Takeaway. Restaurant. Bar. Laundry. Swimming pool and terrace. Children's playground. Table tennis. TV lounge. Boule. Motorhome service point. Bottle bank.

Charges guide: Per pitch LFr. 200; person 160; child (under 12 yrs) 80; extra tent or car 50; electricity 60; local tax per pitch/day 20.

Reservations: Write to site for details. Address: Maison 1, 9972 Leiler. Tel: 998608. FAX: 979184.

773 Camping Kaul, Wiltz

Excellent quality municipal site on outskirts of attractive small town.

This is a large site in area, with 240 pitches for tourists in two sections, either side of the swimming pool complex. One area open and grassy, the other with individual pitches divided by hedges, and all with access to electricity (6A). There are three sanitary buildings - two in the open area, one of which is of outstanding quality. It has ultra-modern fittings and tiling and includes dishwashing and laundry facilities and a dedicated baby room. The other, a tiny unit at the top corner of the site, has only basic facilities. The third block, serving the individual pitches, is older but is well maintained and serviceable. Both main units have some British style WCs, washbasins (some in cubicles), and good sized showers with seats, dividers and hooks. Free hot water throughout. The municipal swimming pool complex with children's pool is excellent (charged for). There is a café/bar with takeaway opposite reception, a small playground and boule pitch.

How to find it: Site is well signed in Wiltz town centre and from the N15.

General Details: Open Easter - 31 October. Café/bar. Takeaway. Laundry. Swimming pool complex (discount for campers) with lifeguards and café. Children's playground. Boules. Tennis nearby. First aid post.

Charges guide: Per pitch LFr. 160; person 160; child (3-14 yrs) 80; electricity 70.

Reservations: Essential for July/August. Address 9550 Wiltz. Tel: 95 03 59. FAX: 95 97 47.

774 Camping an der Schleif, Schleif

New, good value, municipal site, close to Belgian border.

In an attractive, tranquil location overlooking a valley, this site nestles in the heart of a conservation area and lies on the route of a traffic free 20 km. cycle route (part of an old railway track). The sanitary building, formerly the elegant old station, is well maintained and fitted with modern facilities in three rooms, the ladies toilets and showers new in 1996. There are British WCs and hot showers (separate women's and men's), and open washbasins (unisex) in a central room. Dishwashing and laundry sinks are outside under cover. Hot water is free throughout. The 80 level, grassy pitches are marked, divided by small hedges and arranged around a tarmac access road. Electricity (6A) is available to most. A café/bar with terrace is adjacent, also a small children's play area and table tennis. There are also 5 well appointed apartments for rent, plus conference and restaurant facilities which open according to demand. Fishing licences issued.

How to find it: From Bastogne (Belgium), cross the border on the N15 towards Wiltz, and turn towards Schleif, where the site is signed.

General Details: Open 1 April - 31 Oct. Cafe/bar. Restaurant. Bread and milk usually available (shop 3 km). Fishing. Bicycle hire. Children's playground. Table tennis. Washing machine. Self catering apartments for rent.

Charges 1997: Per pitch LFr. 100; adult 100; child 50; electricity (6A) 60 dog 40.

Reservations: Recommended for July/Aug; write for details. Address: Maison 1, 9654 Schleif. Tel: 95 07 12. FAX: as phone.

NETHERLANDS

The Netherlands offers a warm welcome to British visitors, and the general standard of campsites has improved considerably during the last few years. It is a country partly reclaimed from the sea (one-fifth of the country lies below sea level). A flat fertile landscape is punctured by dykes, windmills, church spires and marvellously ornate gabled terraces flanking peaceful canals, broken by the forests of Arnhem, the bulb fields in the west, the Ijsselmer and unique and independent Friesland (with its own language) in the north. Amsterdam is the liberal, sometimes irreverent, capital with its horseshoe of 17th century canals, tall elegant houses and 62 museums. The Hague is the seat of government as well as a royal city home to Queen Beatrix and Rotterdam is the world's greatest port. Cycling is extremely popular - an estimated 14 million bicycles, that is one per man, woman and child of the population, so take care when driving or take your own with you and join them!

For further information contact:

Netherlands Board of Tourism, PO Box 523, London SW1E 6NT

Tel: 0891 200277. Fax: 0171 828 7941.

Population

15,200,000, density 447 p/sq. km.

Climate

The sea has a great affect on the climate of the Netherlands. The average winter is mild - although a sudden cold snap in January or February will have the skaters out with a vengeance on the water- ways. Summers are warm with temperatures averaging 16-17°C centigrade in July and August. In the east and southeast winters are colder and summers warmer. Spring is the driest season.

Language

Dutch is the native tongue. English is very widely spoken, so is German and to some extent French. In Friesland a Germanic language, Frisian is spoken. The Dutch are very language- conscious partly because they are great travellers, to be found in all parts of the world - often running camp sites!

Time

GMT + 1 (summer BST + 1).

Currency

Dutch currency is the Guilder or Florin written as Dfl. or Nfl. and made up of 100 cents. Notes are 10, 25, 50, 100 and 250, coins are 5, 10, and 25 cents pieces and 1, 2.50, and 5 Nfl.

Banks

Open Mon-Fri 09.00-16.00/1700. Exchange offices (GWK) are often open longer hours.

Post Offices

Open Mon-Fri 08.30-17:00. Some offices open Sat 08.30-12.00.

Telephone

To call the Netherlands from the UK the code is 00 31, the UK from the Netherlands, 00 44.

Public Holidays

New Year; Good Fri; Easter Mon; Queen's Birthday, 30 Apr; Liberation Day, 5 May; Ascension; Whit Mon; Christmas, 25, 26 Dec.

Shops

Shops open Mon-Fri 09.00/ 09.30 -17.30/18.00. Sat. closing 16.00/ 17.00. In big cities, stores have late opening Thurs. or Fri. and close Mon. morning. The Dutch are early diners - restaurants open 17.30-22.00/23.00.

Motoring

There is a comprehensive motorway system but, due to the high density of population, all main roads can become very busy, particularly in the morning and evening rush hours. There are many bridges which can cause congestion.

Tolls: There are no toll roads but there are a few toll bridges and tunnels notably the Zeeland Bridge, Europe's longest across the Oosterschelde. **Speed Limits:** Built up areas 31 mph (50 kph), other roads 50 mph (80 kph) and motorways 62 mph (100 kph) or 75 mph (120 kph). Cars towing a caravan or trailer are limited to 50 mph (80 kph) outside built-up areas.

Parking: Blue Zones exist in most towns and free parking discs are available from police stations.

Overnighting:

Prohibited outside campsites.

Useful Addresses

Motoring Organisations:

Koninklijke Nederlandsche Automobiel Club (KNAC), Westvlietweg 118, Leidschendam. Tel: (070) 399 7451. Offices hours Mon-Fri 09.00-17.00.

Koninklijke Nederlandsche Toeristenbond (ANWB), Wassenaarsweg 220, The Hague. Tel: (070) 3141420 Offices hours Mon-Fri 08.00-17.30

Tourist Information:

The Netherlands has 440 Tourist Information Offices (VVV) throughout the country which claim to be able to deal with any enquiry.

The sites in the NETHERLANDS featured in this guide are shown on the BENELUX map on page 368

DISCOVER THE NETHERLANDS

By Caravan, tent or camper

25 top campsites in the Netherlands, situated along beautiful scenic routes, play host under the name of **Holland Tulip Parcs** and offer high-quality facilities. **Holland Tulip Parcs** guarantee their visitors a splendid site, even during the high season.

Ask for our brochure.

Netherlands Board of Tourism (NBT)	**Holland Information line** Tel: **0891 200 277**
P.O. Box 523	(calls cost 39 pence per minute cheap rate,
LONDON SW1E 6NT	and 49 pence per minute at all other times

HOLLAND
TULIP PARCS
CAMPING & CARAVANNING

HTTP://www.hollandtulipparcs.nl
E-mail: info@hollandtulipparcs.nl

Members of the HTP group in this guide are numbers:
551, 558, 560, 563, 565, 570, 576, 579, 581, 583, 587, 595

597 Camping De Paal, Bergeyk, nr Eindhoven

First class campsite, especially suitable for families with young children.

A lot of money has been invested in this touring site (no static mobile homes) and the excellent facilities mean that reservation in July/Aug. is essential. In 34 hectares of woodland, there are 544 touring pitches (plus 70 seasonal pitches) offering a choice of sunshine or shade (the site map shows the choice for each pitch). All have 6A electricity, water, waste water and a bin, ranging in size up to 150 sq.m. Numbered and generally separated by trees in shaded areas, there is also a choice of area for parking, either on the pitch or in special car parks, affording extra safety for the children whose importance here is paramount. Each group of pitches is provided with a play area (31 in all) with additional facilities comprising a very large open sand-based area with adventure play equipment (with safety inspection certificate) and a large 'barn' for wet weather. In high season an animation team provides further entertainment. The high quality indoor heated swimming pool is open all season and consists of play pools for children and a smaller, deeper one for parents, supervised in high season. Heated outdoor and toddlers pools also. Two ultra modern sanitary buildings, specifically designed with families in mind, have magnificent facilities. Toilets are separate at either side of the buildings. There are dishwashing and laundry sinks plus a spin dryer just inside the main entrance, then wash-cabins and showers with family rooms (bath, shower, washbasin), baby bathrooms, and standard showers, all with lots of space, plus 2 children's toilets. Rooms for wheelchair users are at the back. Two other older buildings are also very well fitted out. A new bar, reception and restaurant complex is planned for '98. Currently these are quite satisfactory, but in older buildings (the old schoolhouse). Maps can be purchased in reception showing some of the many walking and cycling opportunities in this attractive area, whilst a short walk from the entrance is a tennis complex with 6 indoor courts (Sept-May) with 10 outdoor all weather courts (equipment for hire) and a pleasant lounge bar. Whilst catering splendidly for children, outside the high season there are many regular adult visitors to this comfortable, friendly site, very capably run by the Martens family and staff.

How to find it: From E34 Antwerpen - Eindhoven road, take exit 32 (Eersel) and follow signs for Bergeyk and site (2 km from town).

General Details: Open Easter/1 April - 31 Oct. Shop, bar and snacks (all season). Restaurant (high season). Indoor pool (all season). Outdoor pool (May - Sept). Bicycle hire. Tennis. Children's play areas. Theatre. Bicycle storage room. Laundrette. Chemical disposal. Motorcaravan services. Trekkers' huts for rent.

Charges 1997: Per pitch incl. 2 persons and services Nfl 51.00; extra person (over 1 yr) 6.00; cyclist 13.50; dog 6.00. Discounts outside 5/7-16/8 daily 30%, over 7 days 35%, (over 55's 40% for more than 7 days).

Reservations: Essential for July/Aug. and made for min. 1 week Sat to Sat. Address: De Paaldreef 14, 5571 TN Bergeyk. Tel: 0497/571977. FAX: 0497/577164.

NETHERLANDS

593 Camping De Dousberg, Maastricht

Spacious site in leisure park on outskirts of historic city.

Founded by the Romans, Maastricht is the Netherlands' oldest and most southern city. Situated in South Limburg, the Belgian and German borders are very close. Dousberg Parc, 4 km. from the city centre, incorporates a wide range of sporting facilities including very large outdoor and indoor swimming pools, partly `subtropical' (free for campers), a tennis centre with indoor and outdoor courts, cycling training track, climbing wall and artificial ski slope. Camping de Dousberg, situated 300 m. up a gentle hill from the park entrance, forms part of this centre. It has 300 large pitches, most with electricity and TV connections and easy access to water, arranged in hedged bays which radiate outward from the centre. Three similar toilet blocks around the site offer functional facilities of a good standard. Hot water is on payment for showers but free for dishwashing. British style WCs. There is a small shop at the centre and a cafe/bar at the entrance. It is quite a busy site, with visitors of many nationalities, some of them groups of youngsters, but it is well run and well situated for visiting a lively, interesting city.

How to find it: From north on Eindhoven - Liège motorway (A2/E25) take Maastricht/Hasselt exit and follow signs for Hasselt and then municipal signs for `Dousberg'. From Liège follow signs for `Centrum' then `Dousberg'.

General Details: Open 26 March - 1 Nov. Small shop (5/4-15/9). Bar/restaurant (5/4-15/9). Tennis centre. Large outdoor and indoor pools (1/3-1/11). Climbing wall. Artificial ski slope, Cycling track. Children's play areas. Laundry facilities.

Charges 1997: Per person Nfl. 7.00; child (under 12 yrs) 5.50; tent or caravan 7.50; motorcaravan 10.00; car 4.00; m/cycle 2.75; electricity 4.00; local tax 1.50.

Reservations: Write to site. Address: PO Box 2860, 6201 MB Maastricht. Tel: 043/3432171. FAX: 043/3430556.

592 Vakantiecentrum De Zwarte Bergen, Luyksgestel, nr Eindhoven

Large woodland site with swimming pools, south of Eindhoven.

In a pleasant woodland setting, De Zwarte Bergen is a holiday type of site with many permanent caravans and bungalows (some to let) but there are also plenty of touring spaces. These are mainly situated in a newly cleared area near the swimming pools which has 250 numbered pitches of up to 120 sq.m. arranged in circles of 8-10, with car parking adjacent. Water, electricity and TV connections are available. It is an attractive setting with quite a few tall pines left standing and young bushes and trees planted to separate the groups. Towards the centre of the site is a central complex with a large entertainment, bar and restaurant facility, a snack bar and supermarket. There are three sanitary blocks, two close to the main touring area which are supplemented by a small portacabin style unit. They provide small, close together washbasins with some in private cabins with cold water and free hot showers and, whilst very clean and tidy, are becoming slightly dated. This is an area with easy access to a number of tourist attractions and, taking account also of the range of amenities listed below, it is a site which does offer something for longer stays.

How to find it: Site is near the Belgian border south of Eindhoven, northwest of Luyksgestel. From A21/E34 motorway (Antwerpen - Eindhoven) near Eersal take Luyksgestel exit. Turn left at traffic lights to Luyksgestel; site is signed before Weebosch.

General Details: Open all year. Complex of heated open air swimming pools (1/5-10/9), free to campers but open to others on payment. Supermarket (1/4-31/10). Restaurant and bar, disco, snack bar (weekends and holidays). . Recreation programme July/Aug. 3 playgrounds, animals and birds. Minigolf. 2 petanque courts. Basketball. 2 all-weather tennis courts. Football field. Launderette. Motorcaravan services. Tourist information. Bungalows for hire.

Charges guide: Per unit incl. 2 persons with all services Nfl 31.95; person (over 3 yrs) 4.80; local tax 0.60; extra person (over 3 yrs) 4.80; hiker or cyclist pitch incl. 2 persons 25.00. Credit cards accepted.

Reservations: are made with 50% payment in advance, Sat.- Sat. only in July/Aug, any period at other times. Address: P.B. 50, 5575 ZH Luyksgestel. Tel: 0497/541373. FAX: 0497/542673.

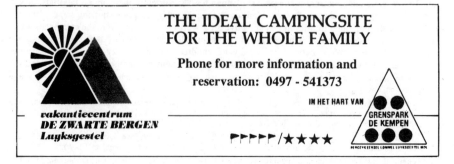
214

594 Vryetydspark Elfenmeer, Herkenbosch, nr Roermond

Large professionally managed site with swimming pools and other amenities.

In the southern part of the country between the borders with Germany and Belgium (both quite close), this is a big site with amenities on holiday camp scale. Situated in the Meinweg National Park, it is very popular for weekend breaks, even out of season, and the facilities are also offered on a daily basis. These include two very good outdoor heated swimming pools, both 25 x 15 m. one deep, one shallow, and a small children's pool (open about 7 May-7 Sept). Sunbathing areas extend down to the grassy surrounds of a lake used for boating and swimming. These are free to campers except for initial fee for identity pass. There are many permanent large caravans or seasonal tourers, but around half of the 800 pitches are available for touring units, with electrical connections (4A) in most areas. Also many bungalows for rent in a separate area. Pitches average about 90 sq. m. and are mostly in separate enclosures of 10 or so pitches, backing on to hedges, etc. Part is light woodland, part open grass. The new or refurbished toilet blocks were clean and probably an adequate provision (at the time of our visit the block in the 'Zomerveld' area was the best). They provide WCs with either lifting or fixed seat, individual basins with shelf and cold water, pre-set free hot showers, babies' room and toilets for disabled people. Launderette. Fishing lake. Minigolf. Bowling alley. Organised sports programme in season. Supermarket. Restaurant/bar (April-Oct) and seasonal takeaway facilities. Large, efficient reception, with English spoken.

How to find it: From Roermond take Wassenberg road to southeast (to find this exit you can also follow white signs to 'Roerstreek' industrial estate); pass turning to right to Herkenbosch after 6 km. and turn left to site about 1 km. further on.

General Details: Open 28 March - 25 Oct. Supermarket. Restaurant/bar (April-Oct). Takeaway. Organised sports programme. Fishing lake. Large children's playground on grass and sand. Riding and sailing and windsurfing courses arranged nearby. Minigolf. Bowling alley.

Charges guide: Per person (from 2 yrs) Nfl 4.75 - 5.75; pitch (any unit) 8.00 - 14.00; electricity (4A) 5.25. Package arrangements available.

Reservations: made only Sat. to Sat. and recommended in peak weeks, perhaps from 7/7-10/8, with full payment in advance. Address: Meinweg 1, 6075 NA Herkenbosch (L). Tel: 0475/53 16 89. FAX: 0475/53 47 75.

590 Camping Hilvarenberg and Safari Camping, Beekse Bergen, nr Tilburg

Large, impressive lakeside leisure complex, with many amenities.

Beekse Bergen is an impressive leisure park set around a very large, attractive lake. The park offers a range of amusements which should keep the most demanding of families happy! These include not only water based activities such as windsurfing, canoeing, jetski, rowing and fishing, but also a small amusement park, a cinema, tennis, minigolf and many more. The lake is bordered by sandy beaches, playgrounds, swimming areas and water slides. Transport around and across the lake is provided by a little 'train' or a sightseeing boat. These and most of the amenities are free to campers. Part of the resort is the Beekse Bergen Safari Park with reduced entry for campers, where you can see the many wild animals from either your own car, a safari bus or two safari boats, the Stanley and the Livingstone. On the far side of the lake, as well as bungalows and tents for hire, there are two distinct campsites - one on flat meadows surrounded by hedges and trees near the lake, the other in a more secluded wooded area reached by a tunnel under the nearby main road. The 600 numbered pitches are about 100 sq.m, and all have electricity. The lakeside area has a very good waterside restaurant, a cafe and takeaway, supermarket and indoor children's pool. The Safari Campsite has a 'typical safari environment' and a viewpoint over the Safari Park (with free entry for campers). A central complex has catering, a playground and launderette, plus an entertainment team. Sanitary facilities are adequate in numbers and cleanliness and include British WCs, free hot showers and some washbasins in cabins. This is an area with many other recreational activities, including the award winning Effteling amusement park.

How to find it: From A58/E312 Tilburg - Eindhoven motorway, take exit to Hilvarenbeek on the N269 road. Park and campsite are signed Beekse Bergen.

General Details: Open 28 March - 25 Oct. Restaurants, cafes and takeaway (weekends only in low seasons). Supermarket. Children's playgrounds and indoor pool. Beaches and lake swimming. Watersports including rowing boats (free) and canoe hire. Amusements. Tennis. Minigolf. Fishing. Recreation programme. Bicycle hire. Launderettes. Motorcaravan services. Bungalows, cabins and tents to rent. Twin axle caravans not accepted.

Charges 1998: Per person (from 2 yrs) Nfl 6.80; pitch 19.00 - 31.00; electricity included; local tax 1.10 per person. Discounts for weekly stays, camping packages available. Credit cards accepted.

Reservations: Necessary for high season and B.Hs. Address: Leisurepark Hilvarenberg, Beekse Bergen 1, 5081 NJ Hilvarenbeek. Tel: 013/536 00 32. FAX: 013/536 67 16.

NETHERLANDS

591 Vakantiecentrum De Hertenwei, Lage Mierde, nr Tilburg

Large, spacious site in southern Netherlands with swimming pools.

Set in the southwest corner of the country quite close to the Belgian border, this relaxed site covers a large area. In addition to 100 quite substantial bungalows with their own gardens (some residential, 30 to let) and about 125 privately owned static caravans, the site has some 400 touring pitches. These are in four different areas on oblong meadows surrounded by hedges and trees, with the numbered pitches around the perimeters. There is a choice of pitch size (150, 100 or 64 sq.m.) and all have 4A electricity, many water and drainage as well. The most pleasant area is probably the small one near the entrance and main buildings - these are a long walk from some of the furthest pitches. The range of amenities includes a small indoor heated swimming pool (12 x 6 m.) open all year (with admission charge), sauna, jacuzzi and solarium. Three outdoor pools open late May to early Sept. A modern building houses a restaurant, canteen and snack bar with a disco in the basement. Four toilet blocks of slightly differing types but all of quite good quality are well spaced around the site. They have British style WCs, virtually all washbasins in cabins, good, controllable showers and can be heated in cool weather. Hot water for all facilities is free. Some blocks have units for the disabled, hair washing and baby baths.

How to find it: Site is by the N269 Tilburg - Reusel road, 2 km. north of Lage Mierde and 16 km. south of Tilburg.

General Details: Open all year. Supermarket (1/4-27/10, nearest 2 km). Bar by indoor pool. Restaurant, cafeteria with snack bar (all year). Disco. 2 tennis courts. Children's playgrounds and play meadows. Sauna, solarium and jacuzzi. Bicycle hire. In season recreation programme with films, dances or disco, sports, bingo, etc. Bus service to Tilburg or Eindhoven with stop at entrance. Launderette. Chemical disposal. Motorcaravan services.

Charges 1998: Per unit incl. 2 persons and electricity Nfl. 38.50 - 48.50, acc. to type; extra person 5.75; local tax 0.60; extra car 5.75. Special 25-40% in low seasons.

Reservations: are made for min. 1 week, in summer Sat to Sat. only, with deposit. Address: Wellenseind 7-9, 5094 EG Lage Mierde. Tel: 013/509 12 95.

588 Vrijetijdspark Vinkeloord, Vinkel, nr s'Hertogenbosch

Large, pleasant holiday site with many amenities.

Run by the same group as Beekse Bergen (590), Vinkeloord is a large site with motel accommodation and a bungalow park in addition to its 500 camping pitches. These are divided into several grassy areas, many in an attractive wooded setting, and 350 with electrical connections. There are also some new fully serviced pitches. Open all year, the site is a popular holiday choice with activities organised in the main seasons. The varied amenities are located in and around a modern, central complex. They include heated outdoor swimming pools, an indoor leisure pool with slide, fitness room, 10 pin bowling alley, minigolf and tennis courts. There is also a small, landscaped lake with sandy beaches suitable for swimming and inflatable boats, overlooked by a large, modern children's play area. Some of the touring pitches also overlook the water. Campers have free entry to the adjacent `Autotron' attraction. The eight toilet blocks are well situated for all parts of the site. The clean and simple facilities are a bit of a mixture (some unisex) with some warm water, some individual washbasins and pre-set showers.

How to find it: Site is signed from the N50/A50 road between s'Hertogenbosch and Nijmegen, approx. 10 km. east of s'Hertogenbosch at Vinkel.

General Details: Open all year. Supermarket. Bar. Modern, up-market restaurant. Snack bar/takeaway (high season only). Free outdoor heated swimming pools (May - early Sept). Indoor leisure pool (on payment). Sauna, solarium and fitness room. 10 pin bowling alley. Tennis. Minigolf. Table tennis. Sports field. Bicycle hire. Fishing. Barbecue area. Children's play areas. Many organised activities in season. Motel bedrooms and bungalows for hire.

Charges 1997: Per person (from 2 yrs) Nfl 4.65 - 8.20; pitch simple: 7.70 - 14.10, serviced (water and TV connections) 13.35 - 17.95, with waste water 16.00 - 20.00, fully serviced with own sanitary facility 40.00; electricity 5.90 - 7.50. Special camping packages available. Credit cards accepted.

Reservations: Recommended for high season - write for details. Address: Vinkeloord 1, 5382 JX Vinkel (North Brabant). Tel: 073/532 29 66. FAX: 073/532 16 98.

595 Camping-Caravanning Heumens Bos, Heumen, nr Nijmegen

Friendly site, family run for families.

The area around Nijmegen, the oldest city in the Netherlands, has large forests for walking or cycling, nature reserves and old towns to explore, as well as being quite close to Arnhem. A warm welcome from the Grol family awaits you at this well run site. It covers 30 acres and is open over a long season for touring families (no groups of youngsters) and all year for bungalows. It offers 186 level, grass pitches (all with 6A hook-ups), numbered but not separated, in glades of 10 and one large field. Cars are parked away from caravans. One small section for motorcaravans has some hardstandings. The main, high quality sanitary building, plus another new block, are modern and heated, with showers on payment, British style WCs, rooms for families and disabled people and free hot water to private cabins and other washbasins. External, covered dishwashing. Another smaller building has acceptable facilities. The restaurant, which offers a quality menu (the owners are former restaurateurs) is close to the comfortable bar and there is a snack bar. An open air swimming pool with a small children's pool is maintained at 25°C by a system of heat transfer from the air. A glade has play equipment on sand and grass. Entertainment in July/Aug. and large wet weather room. Founder member of Holland Tulip Parc group.

How to find it: From the A73 Nijmegen - Venlo take exit 3 (4 km. south of Nijmegen) and follow site signs.

General Details: Open 1 April - 1 Nov. (bungalows all year). Shop (1/4-14/9). Bar, restaurant and snack bar (all season). Heated swimming pool (1/5-1/10). Bicycle hire. New all weather tennis courts. Boules. Table tennis. Activity and excursion programme (high season). Golf and riding near. Launderette. Chemical disposal. Motorcaravan services. Modern bungalows, caravans and tents for hire.

Charges 1998: Per pitch incl. 2 persons, caravan or tent Nfl. 30.00 - 38.00, motorcaravan 36.00 - 45.00; extra person (over 4 yrs) 6.00; electricity 4.50. Special low season weekends (incl. meal) . Credit cards accepted.

Reservations: Made without charge and advisable for July/Aug. Address: Vosseneindseweg 46, 6582 BR Heumen. Tel: 024 358 1481. FAX: 024 358 3862.

CAMPING-CARAVANNING HEUMENS BOS

is just beneath Nijmegen and is an ideal base for visits in the area, like Nijmegen, Arnhem and Germany (Aken, Kleef, Xanten). A perfect place to start your Holland discovery.

Heumens Bos has a lot of facilities: heated swimming pools, tennis court, modern toilet buildings with a baby room, facilities for the disabled and a family shower. Special motorhome service point, playground, supermarket, luxurious launderette, snack bar and à la carte restaurant with a cosy bar and terraces. All these things make Heumens Bos a complete family campsite. During high season we have a recreation programme.

Heumens Bos offers you: bicycle hire, cycle and walking routes and lots of information about things to see in the area like: Liberation Museum Groesbeek, Afrika Museum, Biblical Open Air Museum, Bicycle Museum, Burgers Zoo/Bush/Desert, Dutch Open Air Museum, Themeparc The Efteling, Autotron, Het Loo, National Parc De Hooge Veluwe.

Heumens Bos is easy to reach by motorway A73, Nijmegen/Venlo/Keulen, exit 3, Heumen.

heumens bos ★★★★ A.N.W.B.

Heumens Bos, Vosseneindseweg 46, 6582 BR Heumen NL
Tel: +31 24 358 1481   Fax: +31 24 358 3862.

---

589 Kampeercentrum Klein Canada, Afferden, nr Nijmegen

Pretty site with good facilities in the Maas valley, close to German border.

Pleasant, farm style buildings house this site's amenities and there is a sheltered atmosphere with many ornamental trees. There are two touring areas, one on an island surrounded by an attractive, landscaped moat used for fishing, the other on flat ground on the other side of the entrance. They provide 120 large, numbered pitches, all with 4A electricity, water, drainage and TV connections. Some 190 permanent and seasonal pitches form other areas to the back of the site. The island pitches have excellent, unisex sanitary facilities with free hot water, private cabins, controllable showers and family facilities in fully tiled and heated rooms alongside the bar. The other pitches are served by a good block with push-button showers. There is a small indoor pool, sauna and solarium and an outdoor pool (with large slide) and children's pool with a grassy sunbathing area. A traditional looking bar has takeaway facilities tucked away behind. Small shop (bread to order). A good quality site in charming surroundings.

How to find it: Afferden is on the N271 road between Nijmegen and Venlo, just south of the A52/E31 motorway into Germany. Site is on the N271 and is signed.

General Details: Open all year. Bar, restaurant, snack bar, takeaway and shop (all April - Oct). Outdoor pool (May - Sept). Indoor pool. Sauna and solarium. Table top minigolf. Tennis. Fishing. Children's playground. Bicycle hire.

Charges 1997: Per unit: high season incl. up to 4 persons Nfl. 49.50, low season incl. 2 persons 37.00; extra person 6.25; dog 4.00; local tax 1.25 per person.

Reservations: made with Nfl. 10 deposit Address: Dorpsstraat 1, 5851 AG Afferden (Limburg). Tel: 0485/53 12 23. FAX: 0485/53 22 18.

NETHERLANDS

587 Camping De Vergarde, Erichem, nr Tiel

Family oriented site in a quiet setting.

Situated north of s'Hertogenbosch and west of Nijmegen and Arnhem, De Vergarde has two sections on either side of a lake. Static holiday caravans are on the left, with 175 touring pitches in named sections on the right (about one third seasonal). With good access, pitches are numbered on flat grass and include 30 new ones with electricity (6A) and TV connections. There are trees all round the perimeter (but no shade on the pitches) and the site has a spacious, open feeling with the lake adding to its attractiveness. Sanitary facilities are in three blocks of an excellent standard, with British style WCs, family showers, washing machines and baby bathrooms. Most, but not all, hot water is on payment. The shop opens daily and the restaurant/bar in high season plus weekends in low season. There is a heated pool each for adults and children, the latter also being catered for with minigolf, pony riding, pets corner, horse drawn wagons, large play area, volleyball and a large indoor games room for wet days. Two tennis courts. Lots of ducks and geese gather around the lake, which can be used for fishing (but not swimming).

How to find it: From A15 Dordrecht/Nijmegen road exit at Tiel West and follow signs to Erichem village.

General Details: Open 1 April - 1 Nov. Swimming pools (1/5-1/9). Shop (1/5-1/10). Restaurant (1/5-1/10). Minigolf. Pony riding. Pets corner. Bicycle hire. Children's play area. Volleyball. Basketball. Games room. Tennis courts. Fishing. Chemical disposal. Motorcaravan services.

Charges 1998: Per unit incl. 2 adults and services (electricity, water and drainage) Nfl. 33.00 - 38.00; extra person 6.00; dog 5.00. Weekly rates. Low season less 25%.

Reservations: Contact site. Address: Erichemseweg 84, 4117 GL Erichem. Tel: 0344/572017. FAX: 0344/572229.

AR Discount
Less 10% for
2 week stay

CAMPING DE VERGARDE

- Modern family campsite with excellent facilities
- Pony riding, children's farm, heated swimming pool, etc.
- In the centre of Holland
- Near the historical town of Buren, with old mill
- Everything is present for a successful holiday

Looking forward to seeing you,
Fam. Staal

Highway A15 exit Tiel-West; follow signs

HOLLAND
TULIP PARCS

☆☆☆☆   Erichemseweg 84, NL-4117 GL   Erichem/Tiel. Tel: +31 344 57 20 17, Fax: +31 344 57 22 29

569 SVR Camping De Victorie, Meerkerk

Nature at its best on a family run site convenient to North Sea ports.

Within an hour's drive from the port of Rotterdam you can be pitched on this delightful site in the 'green heart of Holland'. De Victorie, a working farm and a member of a club of small, 'green' sites, offers an alternative to the bustling seaside sites. Everything about it is surprising and contrary to any preconceived ideas. To the left of the entrance stands a modern building which houses reception, open plan office and space with tables and chairs, where the friendly owners may well invite you to have a cup of coffee. Adjoining is the main sanitary block which is kept spotlessly clean and is tastefully decorated with grey tiled walls and floors. Facilities include British style WCs, washbasins, mirrors, etc. and showers with stool, hooks and divider (on payment). There is a dishwashing area and laundry room, plus additional sanitary facilities situated around the spacious site. The 70 grass pitches are level and generous in size with 4A electricity supply. You can choose to be pitched in the shade of one of the orchards, or in the more open meadow area. The freedom of the farmland is especially enjoyed by children. Apart from the farm animals, wildlife and tractor rides, there is a trampoline, table tennis, fishing, bicycle hire and a play field for football. The farm shop sells milk, eggs, cheese and ice cream.

How to find it: From Rotterdam follow A15 to junction with A27. Proceed 6 km. north on A27 to Noordeloos exit (no. 25) and join N214. Site is signed approx. 200 m. after roundabout at Noordeloos (do not enter vilage).

General Details: Open 15 March - 31 Oct. Shop. Children's play area. Bicycle hire. Fishing. Chemical disposal.

Charges 1998: Special price for SVR Club and AR readers: Per person Nfl. 2.50; caravan, tent or motorcaravan 2.50; car 1.00; large motorcaravan 3.50; electricity (4A) 2.50; local tax 0.35.

Reservations: Contact site. Address: Broekseweg 75-77 4231 VD Meerkerk. Tel: 0183-352741 or 351516. FAX: 0183-351234.

AR Discount
See text

586 Camping Betuwestrand, Beesd, nr Utrecht

Pleasant, conveniently situated site for night stop or longer stay.

Just off the A2/E25 motorway (Utrecht - s'Hertogenbosch, exit 14), this is a large site with 200 places for tourers (all with 10A electricity, most with drainage) in addition to 500 well established permanent units. The touring pitches are in four distinct areas with many around the edges of an attractive lake with a large sandy beach. The toilet blocks are of a good standard and include British WCs, family rooms and facilities for disabled people. Hot water is on payment in both showers and washbasins in cabins. The site has a restaurant (open to the public), shop, bar, TV room and children's play area. An area of the lake is cordoned off for swimming and it is also suitable for windsurfing.

How to find it: Site is 25 km. SSE of Utrecht, clearly signed from both directions on the A2/E25 road between Utrecht and s'Hertogenbosch. Take the exit 14 (Beesd) and site is 200 m.

General Details: Open 1 April - 30 Sept. Shop. Restaurant. Bar/TV room. Playground. Good lake fishing. Bicycle hire. Launderette. Tennis. Mobile homes for hire. No dogs accepted.

Charges 1997: Per unit incl. up to 2 persons, electricity and tourist tax Nfl 31.00; extra person 6.00.

Reservations: Contact site. Address: A. Kraalweg 40, 4153 XC Beesd. Tel: 0345/68 15 03. FAX: 0345/68 16 86.

582 Camping de Hertshoorn, Garderen

Attractive, good quality site with woodland pitches.

Although this is quite a large site, this is not immediately apparent with its woodland location. Careful design has allowed both single pitches in little glades and groups on cleared grassy areas with plenty of gentle shade. Around 300 of the pitches are for tourists with some seasonal units placed around the edges of the site. All have 4A electrical connections, over 200 with water and drainage also. Cars must be parked on the entrance car park. Three excellent toilet blocks provide comprehensive facilities with a variety of cabins and showers with free hot water (showers electronically timed), British style WCs, dishwashing facilities and freezers. An older block houses a well equipped laundry. The very smart reception (more like a hotel than a camp site!) provides information packs in English, with a pleasant restaurant at the rear which the owners, the Selderijk family, call `a living room for guests'. Well kept, small animal paddocks and stables entertain the children and there is a variety of play equipment around the site. There are indoor heated swimming and paddling pools and outdoor paddling pools. Garderen is a pretty village, 1 km. away, and the area is very suitable for cycling.

How to find it: From A1/E30 between Amersfoort and Apeldoorn, take Garderen exit. Cross the N344, through village and site is signed on Putten road.

General Details: Open 31 March - 30 Oct. Supermarket. Restaurant (closed Mondays). Snacks. Swimming and paddling pools. Minigolf. Children's farm. Play areas. Bicycle hire. Entertainment for children in high season. Baby equipment hire. Laundry facilities.

Charges 1998: Per unit incl. electricity and 2 persons Nfl. 25.00 - 50.00; extra person 5.00; local tax 0.92 per person. Weekly family packages - details from site.

Reservations: Recommended for high season. Address: Putterweg 68-70, 3886 PG Garderen. Tel: 0577/461529. FAX: 0577/461556.

N580 Flevo-Natuur, Zeewolde

Large, well equipped naturist site in quiet forest location.

This large naturist site, set amongst the densely wooded area of the southern Flevoland polder, is well equipped and well organised. The central feature of the site is an island recreation area with a sandy beach, sunbathing lawns, children's animal enclosure, volleyball and boules areas. There are two large swimming pools, outdoor and indoor, and a small children's pool directly linked to the main pool. Adjacent are a sauna and solarium. A daily events programme has activities for children and adults. Other amenities include tennis courts, a restaurant/bar, small snack bar with takeaway and supermarket. The 750 pitches, about half for tourists, are in groups separated by hedges. Cars must be parked at the entrance. Visitors with motorcaravans are at a disadvantage as they are placed in a more remote area (with inferior portacabin style sanitary facilities). The main sanitary facilities consist of three blocks, one of which can be heated. They have British style WCs, free hot showers (communal) and facilities for the disabled. This is a friendly site where naturist cards are unnecessary - entrance is open to all and day visits are possible. Nudity is obligatory in all areas when the temperature reaches 20°C.

How to find it: From the A28/E232 motorway (Amersfoort-Zwolle) take the Nijkerk exit, and turn towards Zeewolde. After 500 m. cross lifting bridge onto Flevoland then follow signs for Flevo-Natuur. From the opposite direction (ie. Almere) follow signs to Nijkerk, and then site.

General Details: Open all year. Supermarket (1/4-31/10). Bar. Restaurant (closed Oct - Dec). Swimming pools. Sauna and solarium. Table tennis. Minigolf. Boules. Volleyball. Entertainment programme. Launderette. Library.

Charges 1997: Per tent or caravan Nfl 12.50, with electricity 16.00; person 13.50; child (4-14 yrs) 7.00. Less outside high season. Credit cards accepted. Arrival after 15.00 hrs.

Reservations: Recommended for July - mid-Aug. and school holidays especially for electricity. Address: Wielseweg 3, 3896 LA Zeewolde. Tel: 036/552 82 41.

NETHERLANDS

584 Camping De Pampel, Hoenderloo, nr Arnhem/Apeldoorn

Tranquil forest site in De Hoge Veluwe National Park.

A site with no static holiday caravans is rare in the Netherlands and this adds to the congenial atmosphere at De Pampel, which is enhanced by its situation deep in the forest, with 9 ha. of its own woods to explore. This peaceful park offers many opportunities for interesting outings with the two National Parks in the vicinity, the Kroller-Muller museum and the city of Arnhem. The area has excellent cycle paths which can be joined from a gate at the back of the site. Therre are 180 pitches (20 seasonal). You can choose to site yourself around the edge of a large open field with volleyball, etc. in the middle, or pick one of the individual places which are numbered, divided by trees and generally quite spacious. All have 4A electricity (no heaters allowed) but the furthest pitches are some distance from the sanitary facilities. The swimming pool and child's pool are open Easter to October but are probably not warm enough until at least June. Modern play equipment has special safety surfaces. There is just one building which houses reception, a restaurant, bar, snack bar, laundry and dishwashing, and the sanitary facilities, which are modern and a very good new addition at the end (showers on payment, British style WCs). Full catering facilities are provided in high season (6 weeks of July/Aug), otherwise at weekends only. Shop. Pets corner. Barbecues by permission only, no open fires.

How to find it: From the A50 Arnhem-Apeldoorn road exit for Hoenderloo and follow signs.

General Details: Open all year. Swimming pool (Easter - Oct). Restaurant. Bar. Snack bar. Shop (1/4-31/10). Children's play area. Sports area. Chemical disposal.

Charges 1997: Per adult Nfl. 7.50; child (under 11 yrs) 5.00; pitch 10.00; electricity (4A) 5.00. Less 10% 1/9-25/3.

Reservations: Made with deposit (Nfl. 100). Address: Woeste Hoefweg 33-35, 7351 TN Hoenderloo. Tel: 055/378 17 60. FAX: 055/378 19 92.

To tourist campers "De Pampel" is the most attractive camp-site of the Netherlands

The site is the most centrally located in the "green heart" of the Netherlands, less than two kilometres from the entrance of the "Hoge Veluwe" National Park in Hoenderloo, and offers a wide diversity of tourist possibilities.
"De Pampel" is an excellent camp-site.
Come and see for yourself!

Camping "De Pampel"   tel. +31 55 378 1760
Woeste Hoefweg 33-35, 7351 TN HOENDERLOO   fax. +31 55 378 1992

---

581 Rekreatiepark De Luttenberg, Luttenberg, nr Zwolle

Large, peacefully set park with many facilities.

This woodland site is near the Sallandse Heuvelrug nature reserve in a hilly location and is well placed for relaxing walking and cycling tours. It is a large park with 125 seasonal pitches around the perimeter and 225 touring pitches (all with 4A electricity) in a central area off tarred access roads. The individual, numbered and separated, large pitches are in rows divided by hedges and trees, with easy access, on mainly gently sloping or undulating grass. A separate cluster is for dog owners. A new heated sanitary block gives a satisfactory overall provision with two other facilities each offering 4 pre-set hot showers on payment, 12 open washbasins (4 with free hot water) and 8 British style WCs. Outside are under cover dishwashing points. Small shop for essentials with fresh bread. Large bar and eating area with terrace and small, separate restaurant (low season: Tues. and Fri-Sun). Barbecue with seating. The fair-sized swimming pool and a small one for children, plus boules, football, tennis, table tennis, minigolf, volleyball and an animal enclosure provide plenty to keep younger visitors happy. Member of the Holland Tulip Parc group.

How to find it: From N35 Zwolle - Almelo turn onto N348 Ommen road east of Raalte, then turn to Luttenberg and follow signs. From A1 (Amsterdam - Hengelo) take exit 23 at Deventer onto N348 then as above.

General Details: Open 28 March - 4 Oct. Shop. Bar. Restaurant. Swimming pool (15/5-15/9). Tennis. Table tennis. Volleyball. Boules. Bicycle hire. Minigolf. Riding 4 km. Chemical disposal. Bungalows for hire.

Charges 1998: Per pitch incl. 2 persons and electricity Nfl. 30.00, 3 persons 35.00, 4 persons 40.00; car or m/cycle 5.00; cyclists, 2 persons 25.00; extra person (over 3 yrs) 6.00; dog 7.00.

Reservations: Made with fee Nfl 10.00. Address: Heuvelweg 9, 8105 SZ Luttenberg. Tel: 572 30 14 05. FAX 572 30 17 57.

CAMPING KERKENDEL

Fam. Van Asselt
Kerkendelseweg 49
NL-3775 KM Kootwijk

Tel.: 0031-577-45 62 24
Fax: 0031-577 45 65 45
http://www.kerkendel NL

TULIP PARCS

ANWB *****

- Large heated pool for all the family 28° ● Large heated outdoor pool 23°
- Tennis, badminton and volleyball courts, table tennis
- Restaurant, snackbar and mini-market ● Activity programme for school holidays
- Situated in the heart of the Veluwe, near to the biggest sand-drift in Western Europe
- Easy to find: Motorway Amsterdam-Apeldoorn, exit Kootwijk, then follow signs

583 Camping Kerkendel, Kootwijk, nr Arnhem

Friendly, family site with high quality amenities.

Kerkendel is a good quality touring site, small enough to allow friendly, personal attention from the owners, the Van Asselt family. Very suitable for families with young children, the 170 pitches are arranged in small groups with play equipment in many of the central open spaces. Cars are parked on car parks at the entrance. Hedges and attractive trees provide shade and electrical connections (3A) are available on all pitches. A super new sanitary block has under-floor heating and a room with a wide range of washing and shower facilities with the emphasis on families (baby rooms, family shower rooms, low washbasins, etc). Another excellent new building with no children's facilities, is for those who prefer a quieter environment. Hot water is free throughout and entry is controlled by a card system. The adjacent fully equipped dishwashing (dishwasher!) and laundry room is of the same high standard. Two small blocks with WCs (British style) only will be replaced within the next few years which will ensure that there are adequate facilities when the site is busy. A range of activities includes a small indoor and a heated outdoor swimming pool, tennis courts (small charge), volleyball and table tennis. Also a children's playground, TV room, a good restaurant and snack bar, and a small supermarket. Plenty of tourist information and advice are available from reception and bicycles are available for hire to try out the network of cycle paths in the area. The site is surrounded by woodland and sandy open spaces (this is the largest sand `dune' in Western Europe) and is very close to two National Parks and the city of Arnhem with its Burger Zoo and Open Air Museum.

How to find it: Kootwijk is 10 km. west of Apeldoorn. From A1/E30 motorway, take Kootwijk exit and site is signed.

General Details: Open 1 April - 1 Nov. Shop. Restaurant. Snack bar with takeaway. TV room. Indoor and outdoor swimming pools. Tennis. Bicycle hire. Volleyball. Children's playground. Laundry facilities. New animation chalet. Simple wooden chalets to rent.

Charges 1998: Per unit incl. 2 persons NLG 27.00 - 49.50; extra person 5.00; dog 8.50; local tax 0.92 per person; electricity included. Credit cards accepted.

Reservations: Made free of charge - write for details. Address: Kerkendelweg 49, 3775 KM Kootwijk. Tel: 0577/45 62 24. FAX: 0577/45 65 45. E-mail: kerkendel@tref.nl. Internet: http://www.kerkendel.nl.

Rekreatiepark "De Luttenberg"

Camping de Luttenberg is situated in the part of Holland called `Salland'. This part of the country shows a variety of nature such as woods, meadows and hay-fields. It is nice to walk and bike or to visit one of the Attraction parks or nice cities in the neighbourhood. Pitches on the park are grassy and marked with bushes, all with electricity. We also rent chalets and caravans. The sanitary facilities are modern, heated and clean. In high season a team of animators will fulfil your entertainment wishes.

Ask for our brochure and prices: Tel.+31.572.301405 Fax.+31.572.301757.
Recreatiepark `De Luttenberg' Heuvelweg 9, NL-8105 SZ Luttenberg

HOLLAND
TULIP PARCS
CAMPING & CARAVANING

NETHERLANDS

578 Recreatiecentrum D'Olde Lantschap, Wateren, Meppel, nr Zwolle

Family site with swimming pool, in pretty countryside.

This site is situated in the historic and beautiful area of Drente, on the borders of Friesland amid small lakes and pretty villages, and is set well away from main roads. The 280 pitches, all with electricity (4A) are of ample size, sited around the perimeter of about ten small or partitioned level fields. The hedges are mature and there are many tall trees surrounding and sheltering the site. One large sanitary block and another smaller block which services the furthest fields provide British WCs and free hot showers, but they are both a fair walk from some of the pitches. The site amenities are all near the entrance and include a thatched bar and a shop for provisions. Popular with Dutch families, entertainment is organised for young children and adults in the season. There is a sports field, a heated indoor pool, a lake for fishing and another larger lake for swimming with a beach.

How to find it: Site is about 24 km. north of Meppel. When approaching from the south (Zwolle) on the A28 turn onto the N32 to Meppel and then Diever. From Diever follow road to Wateren, from where the site is signed.

General Details: Open 1 April - 1 Nov. Indoor swimming pool. Bar. Snack bar (all season). Restaurant 500 m. Fishing lake. Bicycle hire. Entertainment at times. Children's play areas. Laundry facilities.

Charges 1997: Per person (over 2 yrs) Nfl 3.95; pitch 14.95 plus 1.65 tax; cyclist or hiker's tent pitch 11.75; electricity 3.65; dog 3.75; local tax 0.80 per person.

Reservations: Made without deposit. Address: Schurerslaan 4, 8438 SC Wateren. Tel: 0521/38 72 44. FAX: 0521/38 75 93.

579 Camping 't Kuierpadtien, Wezuperbrug, nr Emmen

Large, friendly site in northeast with its own dry-ski slope.

This all year round site is suitable as a night stop, or for longer if you wish to participate in all the activities offered in July and August (on payment). These encompass canoeing, windsurfing, water shutes and the dry-ski slope, which is also open during the winter so that the locals can practise before going en masse to Austria. There are three opportunities for swimming with an indoor pool supplemented by a heated outdoor pool (June-Aug) and the lake itself. Sauna, solarium, whirlpool and tennis also. Children's play areas, volleyball and basketball. There are plenty of local attractions and brochures for these are available at reception. Restaurant (all year but weekends only in winter), supermarket (May-Aug, bread all year). The site itself is in a woodland setting on the edge of the village. The pitches, all with electricity (4A) are of reasonable size and are flat and grassy. There are four quite acceptable sanitary blocks with British style WCs and free hot showers (available 17.30 - 10.00 in July/Aug).

How to find it: From N34 Groningen-Emmen road exit near Emmen onto N31 towards Beilen. Turn right into Schoonord where left to Wezuperbrug. Site is at beginning of village on the right.

General Details: Open all year. Supermarket. Restaurant. Indoor and outdoor pools. Sauna. Solarium. Tennis. Volleyball. Basketball. Children's play areas.

Charges guide: Per person (over 1 yr) Nfl. 5.00; pitch 15.75, 21.75 or 29.50, acc. to season; car 5.00.

Reservations: Recommended for July/Aug. and made with deposit. Address: Oranjekanaal NZ 10, 7853 TA Wezuperbrug. Tel: 0591/38 14 15. FAX: 0591/38 22 35. E-mail: kuierpad@icns.nl. Internet: www.kuierpad.nl.

576 Recreatioord-Watersportcentrum De Kuilart, Koudum

Well run, modern site by Friesland's largest lake, ideal for watersports.

With its own marina and private boating facilities, De Kuilart attracts many watersports enthusiasts. The marina provides windsurfing and sailing lessons and boat hire, and there are special rates at the site for groups and sailing clubs. However, the site has an excellent indoor swimming pool as well as an area for lake swimming and on land there are sports facilities including tennis, a sauna and solarium, and woods for cycling and walking. It may also therefore appeal for a relaxing break in a pleasant area not much visited by British campers. Pitches at De Kuilart (some with electricity, water, waste water and TV connections) are set in groups of 10 to 16 on areas of grass surrounded by well established hedges. Four modern sanitary blocks are well spaced around the site and are of above average quality, although showers are on payment and most washbasins (half in private cabins) have only cold water. British style WCs. The restaurant provides good views of the lake and woodland. Dogs are not accepted. A member of the Holland Tulip Parks group.

How to find it: Site is southeast of Koudum, on the Fluessen lake. Follow the camping sign off the N359 Bolsward - Lemmer road.

General Details: Open 21 March - 31 Oct. Restaurant/bar. Supermarket (May - 1 Sept). Launderette. Sauna and solarium. Sports field. Indoor pool (3 sessions daily, 1 swim free). Lake swimming area. Children's playground. Recreation team (high season). 400 berth marina with windsurfing, boat hire and boat shop. Garage at harbour.

Charges guide: Prices outside 2/7-20/8 in brackets. Per unit incl. 2 persons Nfl 31.00 (25.00), with electricity 34.50 (28.50); all service plus 3.00; extra person 6.00; extra car 3.25; boat on trailer 3.50; tourist tax and babies under 1 year included. Special weekend rates at B.Hs.

Reservations: Recommended as site is very popular; made from Sat. - Sat. only in peak season. Address: Kuilart 1, 8723 CG Koudum. Tel: 0514 52 22 21. FAX: 0514 52 30 10.

De KUILART ®

- A camping site with all the facilities you can imagine, situated close to the forests of Gaasterland and the lake "IJsselmeer".
- Comfortable bungalows and luxury chalets to rent.
- Individual surfing and sailing lessons can be arranged.
- A large marina and great fishing waters.
- Surfing piers and sailboat hire.
- Playground, tennis court, sports grounds and bicycles to rent.
- Indoor swimming pool with jet stream, slide, jacuzzi-bench and a natural swimming pool.
- Sauna and solarium.
- An active recreation team.
- After sports: a spacious bar restaurant.
- Supermarket and launderette.

DE KUILART

You can count on us for a memorable holiday! Call us, write or send a fax so we can answer all your questions and send all details to your home address.
Telephone: +31 514 52 22 21 • Fax: +31 514 52 30 10
Kuilart 1 8723 CG KOUDUM

HOLLAND
TULIP PARCS

577 Camping Stadspark, Groningen

Woodland site for city visits or passing through night halt.

The Stadspark is a large park to the southwest of the city, well signed and with easy access. The campsite is within the park with many trees and surrounded by water. It has 200 pitches (50 seasonal), of which 130 have 4A electricity. The separate tent area is supervised directly by the manager. There are two sanitary blocks, of which the newer and better is near reception with hot water for showers and dishwashing on payment, although the other block does have a free hot tap for this. Shop daily, cafe April - mid-Sept. Leisure facilities include bicycle hire, fishing and canoeing. The Paterswoldse Lake is near for windsurfing, swimming or sailing. Buses to the city leave from right outside and timetables and maps are provided by Mr. Wessels, the helpful, English speaking manager.

How to find it: From Assen on the A28 turn left onto the A7. Turn onto N370 and follow site signs (Stadspark, quite close).

General Details: Open 15 March - 15 Oct. Shop. Café (April - mid-Sept). Bicycle hire. Fishing. Canoeing.

Charges guide: Per adult Nfl. 4.45; child (1-8 yrs) 3.05; caravan or tent 4.45; car 4.45; motorcaravan 9.50; electricity 3.30.

Reservations: Contact site. Address: Campinglaan 6, 9727 KH Groningen. Tel: 050-251624.

NETHERLANDS

575 Camping De Kleine Wielen, Leeuwarden

Lakeside site in wooded park near historic town of Leeuwarden.

Situated 5 km. from the historic town of Leeuwarden, this site is set in the attractive Groene Ster recreation park in an area of woods, small canals, lakes and fields. Most of the 200 touring pitches are on an island in the lake which has a cove for swimming and sunbathing. Other pitches are either in wooded clearings or on open fields in separate areas from the 130 seasonal and permanent units. There are two sanitary buildings on the island which provide hot showers on payment, washbasins with free hot water and cabins, and British style WCs. Dishwashing at both. Very pleasant grassy areas surround the lake which is used for swimming, fishing and small boats. Amenities within walking distance include a heated swimming pool, minigolf and a jogging track of 1,800 m. for the more energetic camper! An Otter Park is next to the site where fresh water animals (otters, beavers, polecats, etc.) can be seen in a natural environment. Evening entertainment is a bus ride away in Leeuwarden.

How to find it: Site is 5 km. east of Leeuwarden on the N355 road to Hurdegaryp and Groningen and is signed.

General Details: Open 1 April - 30 Sept. Shop (limited hours). Launderette. Chemical disposal. Licensed canteen for snack meals. Youth room. Watersports and swimming in lake. Good children's play equipment on sand. Swimming pool/minigolf near. Bus stop 200 m. Caravans/chalets to rent.

Charges guide: Per caravan/tent Nfl 5.00; motorcaravan 11.00; person 5.25; child (2-12 yrs) 3.00; car 5.00; m/cycle 3.75; dog 3.00; electricity 3.50; shower 1.00.

Reservations: Necessary for high season. Address: Groene Ster 14, 8926 XE Leeuwarden. Tel: 0511/43 16 60. FAX: 0511/43 25 84.

574 Camping Sint Maartenszee, Sint Maartenszee, nr Den Helder

Excellent family site with good facilities in North Holland.

Situated within easy travelling distance of the attractive and interesting towns of North Holland, especially Alkmaar, this family site is separated from the sea by 900 m. of grassy dunes. With the dune environment, the ground is basically sandy but grass has grown well and hedges are now established. Specialising in family holidays, unusually for the Netherlands only touring units are taken (with a bungalow park adjacent). The 300 pitches are arranged in lines backed by high hedging; 200 have electricity and 150 are fully serviced with water, drainage and cable TV connections. In low, neat buildings, all facilities are of a high standard, particularly both first class, modern sanitary blocks. Hot water for showers is free (with a fascinating panel demonstrating how solar power helps to heat the water!), and it includes wash-cabins, family shower rooms and baby bathrooms. Raised level showers for children are a nice special feature. A dishwashing and laundry room has hot water on payment with a microwave provided. Each block has a resident couple to clean and maintain standards throughout the day. A good restaurant/bar, with attractive terrace overlooking the minigolf, has a sitting area with open fire and board games. This is a pretty and interesting area of the Netherlands and Sint Maartenszee is quite near the fascinating man-made barrier built to form the Ijsselmeer.

How to find it: From Alkmaar, take the N9 northwards towards Den Helder. Site is signed after approx. 18 km. towards the sea at St-Maartensvlotbrug.

General Details: Open 21 March - 21 Sept. Restaurant/bar (all season). Supermarket (all season). Minigolf. Volleyball. Basketball. Children's play areas. Bicycle hire. Bus service from village to Alkmaar (cheese market on Fridays April - Sept). No dogs or transistors accepted.

Charges 1997: Per unit: 60 sq.m. pitch Nfl. 16.00 - 21.00, with electricity 22.50 - 27.50; 90 sq.m. pitch 25.50 - 34.00, fully serviced 28.50 - 40.50; person 5.50, plus local tax 1.10.

Reservations: Made for approx. 100 pitches (all with electricity) with deposit (details from site) but 40% are kept free from reservation for any length of stay. Address: Westerduinweg 30, 1753 BA Sint Maartenszee. Tel: 0224 56 14 01. FAX: 0224 56 19 01.

ALAN ROGERS' Good Camps Guide

EUROPE 1998 - DISCOUNT VOUCHERS

Between pages 160 and 161 you will find various Discount Vouchers which will provide you with potential savings of much more than the cost of the Guide itself!

(These vouchers are valid 1 January - 31 December 1998 only)

Voucher A Campsite Discount Voucher	Voucher B Travel and Breakdown Insurance
Voucher C Caravan or Motorcaravan Insurance	Voucher D Caravan and Camping Service
Voucher E Sites Abroad Holidays	Voucher F Camping Cheque
Voucher G Track Tours	

Save Money!

Taking your own **CAMPING** equipment abroad?

Eurocamp Independent
FREEPOST ALM1584
KNUTSFORD
Cheshire
WA16 0BR

Eurocamp Independent

The easy way to take your own tent, trailer tent, caravan or motorhome to Europe.

One phone call will book your whole holiday

•

Choose from over 120 of Europe's best sites

•

Use of Eurocamp Couriers and Children's Couriers

•

Free comprehensive Travel Pack

•

Competitive prices

•

Friendly and efficient service

To receive your copy of the 1998 brochure, complete the attached card or call

01565 625544

AITO — THE ASSOCIATION OF INDEPENDENT TOUR OPERATORS

ABTA

Never travelled abroad? Phone Now for FIRST TIME ABROAD VIDEO - cost £5.00

Mr/Mrs/Miss   Initials

Surname

Address

Postcode

How many adults are in your party? _____

If applicable what are the ages of your children? _____

Do you have a:

tent ☐   trailer tent ☐   caravan ☐   motorhome ☐

Have you ever taken your own equipment abroad before?   Yes ☐   No ☐

If 'Yes' how many times? _____

Would you be interested in pursuing any of the following interests whilst on holiday with your own equipment?

Golf ☐   Birdwatching ☐   Fishing ☐

Wine ☐   Cooking ☐

Tick if you do not wish to receive direct mail from other carefully screened companies whose products or services we feel may be of interest ☐

Eurocamp Independent

EIAR

570 Molengroet Recreatieverblijven, Noord-Sharwoude, nr Alkmaar

Pleasant site close to lake for watersports.

Whether you wish to stop over on the way to the Afsluitdijk across the top of the Ijsselmeer or partake in watersports, this is a modern site, just 40 km from Amsterdam. The enthusiastic manager, Tom van den Ham, believes you must cater for all ages ('young people are our future') and he provides a range of facilities to meet the varying needs. Therefore, the 300 touring pitches are grouped according to services provided, ranging from simple pitches with no services, to those with 10A electricity, TV, water and waste water 'comfort pitches'. These pitches also have the best sanitary facilities in a modern heated building with free, pre-set hot showers. Two other buildings are to be renewed for '98. A large shop is open April to October, but bread and milk may be obtained at other times from reception. The restaurant is open all year (low season 12.00 to 20.00, closed Mon/Tues) and there is a snack bar in high season - order snacks from the restaurant otherwise. Hotel accommodation is also available. Bicycles, surfboards and small boats may be hired and there are opportunities for tennis, squash, sauna, horse riding and swimming nearby. The nearby lake with surf school is an attractive proposition, particularly for those with teenagers. A site bus can take you to the local pool or the beach. Friendly multi-lingual reception staff provide local information and a range of on-site entertainment is carefully controlled by Tom.

How to find it: From Haarlem on A9 to Alkmaar take the N245 towards Schagen. Site is southwest of Noord Sharwoude, signed to west on road to Geestermerambacht.

General Details: Open all year. Shop (Apr-Oct). Restaurant (all year, not Mon/Tues. in low season). Snack bar (high season). Fishing. Bicycle hire. Watersports close by. Entertainment in high season and weekends. Chemical disposal. Motorcaravan services. Hotel (catering more for group accommodation). Camping cottages for rent.

Charges 1997: Per small tent incl. 3 persons Nfl. 9.00, large tent 13.25; incl. 2 persons plus car: non-service pitch 29.00, with 4A electricity and TV 37.00, 10A electricity, TV, water, waste water 44.50; extra person 5.85; child (under 5) 2.90; car 4.10; m/cycle 2.50; dog 3.50. Reductions in low season and for longer stays.

Reservations: Made with 50% deposit on booking, balance 3 weeks before arrival. Write to site. Address: Molengroet 1, Postbus 200, 1722 ZL Noord-Scharwoude. Tel: 0226 39 34 44. FAX: 0226 39 14 26.

565 Camping Club Soleil, Noordwijk, nr Den Haag

Quality site not far from Amsterdam.

The facilities here are first class, including an indoor heated swimming pool with 'massage water' and watershute, a plunge bath for children, tennis court and sun-trap terrace all free of charge. The children's play equipment is very satisfactory and they also have an activity room and an animal enclosure. The shop, launderette and restaurant (Indian speciality and Dutch meal of the day) plus takeaway are all of a high standard. A 1,500 m. dune beach is 1.5 km. The site provides just over 100 pitches of 80 sq.m. plus on flat grass, mainly individual ones separated by small trees or hedges and all having electricity, TV and water. Some hardstandings for motorhomes. The main sanitary building is modern and has free hot water to showers (some with external entry), washbasins, some in cabins, baby room and dishwashing facilities. A secondary 'portacabin' style facility is of an excellent standard (open in high season). Much thought has gone into the design of this park and the cars for the seasonal pitches and bungalows are parked outside the camping area. There was little noise apparent from aircraft (Schipol airport).

How to find it: From Amsterdam to Den Haag A4/A44 take exit 3 towards Noordwijk and follow ANWB camping signs (not frequent, just keep going). Take turning to right (small sign) shortly after Camping De Wijde Blick.

General Details: Open 1 April - 31 Oct. Shop (summer). Restaurant. Takeaway. Indoor pool and tennis (both free). Launderette. Animal enclosure. Chemical disposal. Bungalows and mobile homes for hire.

Charges guide: Per family pitch incl. TV connection, electricity and water Nfl 65.00 plus local tax 1.32 per person. Low season discounts 10-30%.

Reservations: Made for Sun.-Sun. only in high season. Write to site. Address: Kraaierslaan 7, 2204 AN Noordwijk. Tel: 0252 37 42 25. FAX: 0252 37 64 50.

NETHERLANDS

572 Camping-Jachthaven Uitdam, Uitdam, nr Monickendam

Large waterside site for sailing and windsurfing enthusiasts, northeast of Amsterdam.

Situated beside the Markermeer which is used extensively for watersports, this large site has its own private yachting marina (320 yachts and boats). It has 350 seasonal and permanent pitches, many used by watersports enthusiasts, but also offers marked pitches on open, grassy ground overlooking the water for tourers. Electrical connections are available and amenities include a shop, TV room, tennis, children's playground and a bar/cafe. Sanitary facilities are rather basic in fairly open buildings with hot showers on payment and British style WCs. There is a special area for campers with bicycles. Very much dominated by the marina, this site will appeal to watersports enthusiasts, with sailing, windsurfing and swimming opportunities, but it is also on a pretty stretch of coast, only 15 km. from Amsterdam.

How to find it: From the A10, take the N247 towards Volendam then the Monnickendam exit south in the direction of Marken, then Uitdam.

General Details: Open 1 April - 1 Nov. Shop. TV room. Tennis. Children's playground. Bar/restaurant (weekends and high season). Yacht marina (with fuel) and slipway. Watersports facilities. Entertainment in high season.

Charges 1997: Per unit incl. 2 persons Nfl 35.00 (tent 27.50, without car 21.50); extra person 7.50; dog 5.00; boat on land 7.50, in marina 2.00 - 2.50 per metre. Less 20% outside July/Aug. excl. B.Hs.

Reservations: Contact site. Address: Zeedijk 2, 1154 PP Uitdam. Tel: 020/4031433. FAX: 020/4033692.

CAMPING AND WATERSPORT IN A DUTCH WAY

Camping and Yacht harbour "Uitdam" direct to the Markerwaard and near to Amsterdam (12 km) and Volendam, Marken, Monnikendam and Edam.

• Mobile homes and cottages for hire • swimming and fishing • Supermarket, laundry, cafeteria, restaurant and bar • Tennis courts, children's playground & swimming pool.

• Sailing, catamaran sailing, surfing,

Camping/jachthaven "Uitdam", Zeedijk 2, 1154 PP Uitdam. Tel: +31 20 403 14 33. Fax: +31 20 403 36 92

---

560 Recreatiecentrum Delftse Hout, Delft

Well run, modern site within easy reach of Delft.

Pleasantly situated in Delft's park and forest area on the eastern edge of the city, this site is part of the Koningshof group. It has 200 tourist pitches quite formally arranged in groups of 4 to 6 and surrounded by attractive young trees and hedges. All have sufficient space and electrical connections. Buildings near the entrance house the site amenities. These include modern toilet facilities with free hot showers and a spacious family room. A good sized first floor restaurant serves snacks or full meals and has an outdoor terrace overlooking the swimming pool and pitches. There is also a bar and recreation room. Reception provides friendly service and tourist information and also houses a shop for basic food and camping items. A small outdoor pool, volleyball, basketball and an adventure playground are in one corner. Walking and cycling tours are organised and there is a recreation programme in high season. A special package deal can be arranged including tickets to local 'royal' attractions and a visit to the Royal Delftware factory.

How to find it: Site is 1 km. east of Delft; take the Delft/Pijnacker exit no. 9 from the A13 motorway, turn towards Pijnacker and then right at first traffic lights, following camping signs through suburbs and park to site.

General Details: Open all year. Restaurant. Bar. Shop (all 1/4-1/11). Outdoor swimming pool (15/5-15/9). Children's play area. Table tennis. Recreation room. Bicycle hire. Regular bus service to Delft. Laundry. Motorcaravan services. Chemical disposal. Chalets and caravans to let.

Charges 1998: Per caravan or tent plus car incl. 2 persons Nfl 38.00; motorcaravan 36.00; extra person (over 3 yrs) 3.00; local tax 1.00; electricity 4A 4.00, 10A 7.00; cable TV connection 2.00; dog (1 per pitch) 4.00. Low season discounts and for senior citizens (over 55). Special packages. Credit cards accepted.

Reservations: Essential for high season (not made by telephone). Address: Korftlaan 5, 2616 LJ Delft. Tel: 015/213 00 40. FAX: 015/213 12 93.

566 Camping Het Amsterdamse Bos, Aalsmeer, nr Amsterdam

Neat municipal site in large park area quite close to city.

Het Amsterdamse Bos is a very large park to the southwest of Amsterdam, one corner of which has been specially laid out as the city's municipal site. Close to Schiphol Airport (we noticed little noise), it is about 12 km. from central Amsterdam. A high season bus service runs from the site every 35 mins. during the day to the city (local service at other times 300 m.). The site is well laid out alongside a canal, with unmarked pitches on separate flat lawns mostly backing onto pleasant hedges and trees, with several areas of hardstanding. It takes about 450 tourist units, with 150 electrical connections. An additional area is available for tents and groups. The four older style sanitary blocks were clean when we visited but rather let the site down, appearing somewhat small and well used. Hot water is on payment to the washbasins but there are free pre-set hot showers; British style WCs. Near the entrance are laundry and snack bar facilities.

How to find it: Amsterdamse Bos and site are west of Amstelveen. From the A9 motorway exit for either Amstelveen or Aalsmeer (easier), turn towards Aalsmeer and look out carefully for camp signs.

General Details: Open 1 April - 31 Oct. 50,000 sq.m. for camping. Small shop. Cafe/bar and snack bar. Children's sand pit. Fishing. Riding, fishing, boating, pancake restaurant in park. Some 2 or 4 berth camping huts to rent. Laundry facilities. Chemical disposal. Motorcaravan services.

Charges 1997: Per person Nfl 8.25; child (4-12 yrs) 4.25; car 4.25; motorcaravan 10.25; tent 5.25; caravan 6.25; m/cycle 2.25; dog 2.25; electricity 4A 3.25. Camping huts 33.00 (2 person) - 60.00 (4 person) per night. Group reductions. Credit cards *not* accepted.

Reservations: A limited number only will be made for `serious enquirers'. Address: Kleine Noorddijk 1, 1432 CC Aalsmeer. Tel: 020/641 68 68. FAX: 020/640 23 78.

567 Gaasper Camping, Gaasper, Amsterdam

Well laid out site near Metro station, southeast of Amsterdam.

As Amsterdam is probably the most popular destination for visits in the Netherlands, a second site here may be useful. Gaasper is on the southeast side, a short walk from a Metro station with a direct 20 minute service to the centre. Situated on the edge of a large park with nature areas and a lake (with sailing facilities and new swimming beaches), there are also opportunities for relaxation. The site is well kept and neatly laid out on flat grass with attractive trees and shrubs. There are over 400 pitches in two main areas - one more open and grassy, mainly kept for tents, the other more formal with numbered pitches mainly divided by shallow ditches or good hedges. Areas of hardstanding are available and all caravan pitches have 4/10A electrical connections (20 tent pitches have 4A connections). Some 60 seasonal and permanent units have their own area. In high season the site becomes very crowded and it is necessary to arrive early to find space, especially since reservations are not taken. The three modern toilet blocks for the tourist sections should be adequate. Unisex in some sections, they have washbasins (cold water), some in cabins and pre-set hot showers. Hot water for showers and some washing-up sinks is on payment. British style WCs. Facilities for disabled people. Although this is a typical, busy city site, it is better than many and there is a friendly welcome, with good English spoken.

How to find it: Take the exit for Gaasperplas from the section of A9 motorway which is on the east side of the A2. Note: do not take the Gaasperdam exit which comes first if approaching from the west.

General Details: Open all year except 1/1-14/3. Small shop (15/3-15/10). Cafe/bar plus takeaway (1/4-15/10). Shopping centre and restaurant nearby. Children's play area on grass. Washing machine and dryer. Chemical disposal. Motorcaravan services.

Charges 1997: Per person Nfl. 6.25; child (4-12 yrs) 3.50; car 5.75; m/cycle 3.00; caravan 8.25; motorcaravan 10.50; tent 6.50 - 8.50, acc. to size; electricity 4.50; dog 3.75.

Reservations: are not made for Easter, Whitsun, July or August. Address: Loosdrechtdreef 7, 1108 AZ Amsterdam. Tel: 020/696 73 26. FAX: 020/696 93 69.

NETHERLANDS

562 Camping Duinrell, Wassenaar, nr Den Haag (The Hague)

Very large site adjoining pleasure park and impressive tropical pool complex.

Duinrell means 'well in the dunes' and the water theme is continued in the adjoining amusement park and in the extensive indoor pool complex which are Duinrell's main attractions. Entry to the popular pleasure park is free for campers - indeed the camping areas surround and open out from the park. The 'Tiki' tropical pool complex, redesigned in 1994, has attractions which include slides ranging from quite exciting to terrifying (according to your age!), whirlpools, saunas and many other features. There are also free outdoor pools and the centre has its own bar and cafe. Entry to the 'Tiki' complex is at a reduced rate for campers. Duinrell is open all year and a ski school (langlauf and Alpine) with 12 artificial runs, is a winter attraction.

The campsite itself is very large with 1,300 tourist places on several flat grassy areas and it can become very busy in high season. As part of a continuing improvement programme, 700 pitches are now marked and have electricity, cable TV, water and drainage connections. Six toilet blocks, including two very good new ones, serve the tourist areas. They have British WCs, washbasins with warm water, free hot showers and can be heated in cool weather. The amenities shared with the park include restaurants, a pizzeria and pancake house, supermarket and a theatre (shows in high season). The original 900 permanent units have been reduced to around 400, gradually being replaced with smartly furnished 'Duingalows', self catering bungalows available to rent all year. Accommodation in family rooms is also provided in the estate's old coach house.

How to find it: Site is signed from the N44/A44 Den Haag-Amsterdam road, but from the south the turning is about 5 km. after you pass the sign for the start of Wassenaar town - then follow camp signs.

General Details: Open all year. Amusement park and Tiki tropical pool complex as detailed above. Restaurant, cafes, pizzeria and takeaways (weekends only in winter). Supermarket. Laundry facilities. Entertainment and shows in season. Bicycle hire. Bowling. Winter ski school. Fishing.

Charges 1997: Per 'comfort' pitch incl. electricity Nfl. 20.00, with cable TV 22.50; 'nature' pitch 17.50; person (over 3 yrs) 17.50, over 65 12.50; car 7.50; m/cycle 2.50; dog 10.00. Overnight stays between 17.00-10.00 hrs. (when amusement park closed) less 25%.

Reservations: Recommended in high season, Easter and Whitsun (min. 1 week), 50% payment required 6 weeks in advance plus fee (15.00). Address: Duinrell 1, 2242 JP Wassenaar. Tel. 070/515 52 57. FAX: 070/515 53 71.

Some sites have supplied us with copies of their brochures which we are pleased to forward to readers.

See our Brochure Service on page 359

563 Camping Koningshof, Rijnsburg, nr Leiden

Relaxed, well run site between Den Haag and Amsterdam.

Koningshof is not far from site no. 562 but is of an entirely different type. Much smaller, it is run in a personal and friendly way with about 175 numbered pitches divided into separate small groups of 4-12 by hedges and trees. Electrical connections (4 or 10A) are available in all areas. Cars are parked in areas around the perimeter. There are also about 125 static caravans, some for hire. Sanitary facilities are provided in three good blocks, one of which is a new one with under floor heating. They have British WCs, washbasins partly in private cabins (with hot water) or in general washrooms (cold water only), free controllable hot showers and facilities for the disabled. The reception, a pleasant restaurant, bar and snack bar are grouped around a courtyard style entrance decorated with seasonal flowers. On site is a small heated swimming pool (13½ x 7 m.), with separate paddling pool (open May - Sept) and imaginative children's play equipment. It is 5 km. to a sandy beach, 15 to Den Haag and 30 to Amsterdam. The site has a number of regular British visitors from club connections and the welcome is friendly, with English spoken. A very useful local information booklet (in English) is provided.

How to find it: From the N44/A44 Den Haag - Amsterdam motor road, take exit 7 for Oegstgeest and Rijnsburg. Turn towards Rijnsburg and follow camp signs.

General Details: Open all year. Shop (1/4-15/9). Restaurant (15/5-15/9). Bar with snacks and takeaway (1/4-30/10). Entertainment in high season. Adventure playground and sports area. Tennis courts. Fishing pond (free). Bicycle hire. Small swimming pool (unsupervised, 1/5-1/10). Solarium. Room for shows. Washing machines and dryers. Chemical disposal. Motorcaravan services. Chalets for hire.

Charges 1998: Per pitch incl. 2 persons Nfl 38.00, motorcaravan pitch 36.00; extra person (over 3 yrs) 3.00; second car (in car park) 4.00; extra small tent free; electricity (10A) 5.50; cable TV connection 2.00; local tax per person 1.00. Low season and senior citizen discounts; special group rates. Security barrier key deposit 25.00 (refundable). Credit cards accepted.

Reservations: Necessary for July/Aug. and made for any length with deposit and fee (payable by credit card). Address: Elsgeesterweg 8, 2231 NW Rijnsburg. Tel: 071/402 60 51. FAX: 071/402 13 36. E-mail: koningshof@tours.nl.

Drive on the wrong side ....
but choose the right site!

HOLLAND TULIP PARCS

KONINGSHOF
Camping
Caravanning
Chalets

DE ZUIDDUINEN
Camping
Caravanning
Chalets

DE NOORDDUINEN
Camping
Caravanning
Chalets

HOLLAND TULIP PARCS

DELFTSE HOUT
Camping
Caravanning
Chalets

Elgeesterweg 8	Campingweg 1	Zuidduneseweg 1	Korftlaan 5
2231 NW Rijnsburg	2221 EW Katwijk	2225 JS Katwijk	2616 LJ Delft
Holland	Holland	Holland	Holland
Tel.+31 71 402 6051	Tel.+31 71 402 5295	Tel.+31 71 401 4750	Tel.+31 15 213 0040
Fax.+31 71 402 1336	Fax.+31 71 403 3977	Fax.+31 71 407 7097	Fax.+31 15 213 1293

For a list of sites which are open all year - see page 359.
Also: Alan Rogers' Good Camps Guide ALL YEAR ROUND
features campsites throughout Europe for All Year touring.

NETHERLANDS

556 Zeeland Camping de Wijde Blick, Renesse, nr Zierikzee

Neat, well kept site in popular North Sea coast holiday area.

This site is run in a friendly and personal way by the owners, the van Oost family. Within walking distance of the village of Renesse, it is in a quiet, rural location. Laid out in a fairly formal way, with attractive trees and hedges, the site has 170 numbered tourist pitches arranged in groups of 4 to 8, all with electrical (4A) and TV connections. Cars are parked away from the pitches by the access roadways. Sanitary facilities in two blocks are very modern with first class, clean facilities. Washbasins in cabins, controllable showers, facilities for the disabled and babies, and dishwashing sinks all have free hot water and are arranged around glass roofed courtyards with seating, plants and music. There is a bath on payment. The main amenities at the entrance to the site include an outdoor swimming pool with sunbathing terrace, an informal, timber clad bar/restaurant, a supermarket and a laundry (with cartoons for the children to watch). Many activities are organised for children - the campsite mascot, Billy Blick, is amusing as he welcomes the children. Very much a busy holiday area, there are restaurants and shops in the village (market on Wednesdays) and the sandy beach is 2 km. from the site.

How to find it: Renesse is on the near 'island' of Schouwen on the Haamstede - Zierikzee road. This road bypasses the centre of Renesse and the site is signed to the east of the village.

General Details: Open all year. Swimming pool (1/5-15/9). Shop. Restaurant/bar (both Easter - Oct). Good children's play area on sand. Table tennis. No dogs accepted. Cabins to rent. Tennis, minigolf and riding close. Motorcaravan services. No dogs are accepted.

Charges 1997: Per unit incl. 2 persons Nfl. 29.00 - 33.00, with electricity 36.00 - 40.00; extra person 6.50; local tax 1.50 per person.

Reservations: Recommended for high season - contact site. Address: Hogezoom 112, 4325 CK Renesse, (Zeeland). Tel: 0111/46 14 44. FAX: 0111/46 22 22.

561 Camping De Oude Maas, Barendrecht, by Rotterdam

Peaceful riverside site convenient for Rotterdam.

The entrance is the least inspiring part here and you have to drive right up to the barrier in order to activate the intercom. Once through this, you pass a long strip of mixed seasonal and touring pitches. There are two more attractive touring areas, one for 12 units with electricity, water and waste water connections in a hedged group near to the reception, shop, restaurant and river. They have their own small, mediocre sanitary building, but there is a more modern one a short walk away. This has free hot water to the showers, private cabins and washbasins, British style WCs, facilities for the disabled, baby room and dishwashing. The third section is in a woodland setting, well back from the river on flat grass. It has a small 'portacabin' type facility but again it is not far from the main sanitary building. The site is easily accessed from the A15 southern Rotterdam ring road and is situated right by the river, so it is well worth considering if you are visiting the city or want a peaceful stop.

How to find it: From the Rotterdam ring road south take exit 20 (Barendrecht) and follow signs to Achterzeedijk and Oude Maas.

General Details: Open all year. Restaurant, bar and snacks (all year). Shop (1/6-31/8, town 3 km). Fishing. Bicycle hire. Swimming pool and golf near. Launderette. Chemical disposal.

Charges 1997: Per adult Nfl 5.90; child (under 15 yrs) 2.90; car 5.90; motorcaravan 7.70; caravan or tent 5.90; electricity (10A) 3.20; dog 3.20. Credit cards accepted.

Reservations: May be advisable high season. Write to site. Address: Achterzeedijk 1a, 2991 SB Barendrecht. Tel: 0786 77 24 45. FAX: 0786 77 30 13.

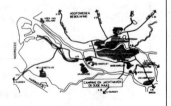

564 Recreatiecentrum Kijkduinpark, Den Haag

Rapidly developing park close to long beach.

This used to be a site with 1,700 touring pitches plus further statics, but its transformation into an ultra-modern, all year round centre is well under way, with many huts, villas and bungalows built along with a brand new reception. The new, wooded, touring area is immediately to the left of the entrance, with pitches in shady glades of bark covered sand. There are simple ones for tents, some pitches with electricity only and many with electricity (6A), water, waste water and cable TV connections. When we visited the sanitary facilities were in temporary `portacabin' style units (with free hot water). These are to replaced with brand new facilities, as are the supermarket, snack bar, shop and restaurant. The main attraction here is the Meeresstrand, 500 m. from the site entrance, which is a long, wide, sandy beach with flags to denote suitability for swimming and popular with windsurfers.

How to find it: Site is southwest of Den Haag on the coast and Kijkduin is well signed as an area from all round Den Haag.

General Details: Open all year. Snack bar and shop. Restaurant. Supermarket (all April-Sept at present). Launderette. Accommodation to rent. Entertainment and activities organised in summer.

Charges guide: Per basic family pitch incl. car Nfl 15.50, with electricity 21.50, all services 29.50; adult 5.50; child (under 15) 2.95; youth pitch 17.00 + car 5.50, m/cycle 3.00; dog (max 1) 5.00 plus tourist tax. Discounts in low seasons.

Reservations: Advisable for high season, write to site. Address: Machiel Vrijenhoeklaan 450, 2555 NW Den Haag. Tel: 070 3 25 25 10. FAX: 070 3 23 24 57.

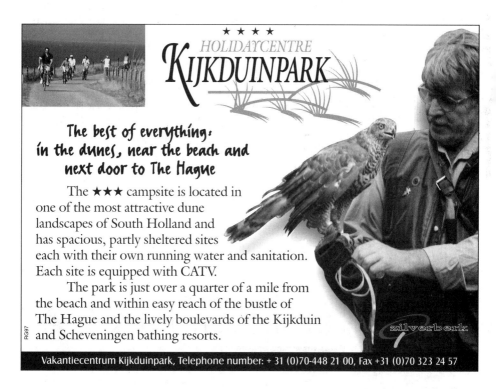

The sites in the NETHERLANDS featured in this guide are shown on the BENELUX map on page 368

559 Camping Rondeweibos, Rockanje

Holiday site near North Sea coastal resort.

This site is situated near the pleasant seaside resort of Rockanje, quite convenient for the North Sea ferry ports. Very much a holiday caravan site (privately owned or to let), it is large, with lines of static units separated by semi-wild hedges and trees. Of nearly 1,000 pitches, just 85 are available for tourers. However, these have their own pleasant area, separated from the rest of the site by the main access road. The pitches here are on grassy/sandy ground and divided into groups by more formal hedges. All have electricity and cable TV connections available with water points near. Sanitary facilities are in two blocks, one near the touring area, which can be heated. They provide neat, clean, acceptable facilities with hot showers on payment and British style WCs. A good range of amenities (listed below) includes a popular medium sized outdoor swimming pool with a slide and whirlpool. Rockanje is situated on Voorne (which used to be an island), an area of beaches, dunes, woods and lakes. A popular area with Dutch holidaymakers, beach activities and watersports opportunities are plentiful. Rockanje's beach is a 10 minute walk.

How to find it: From the N15/A15 motorway towards `Europoort' take exit marked Brielle-Hellevoetsluis onto the N57 and over the bridge. After 7 km. take the Rockanje exit and site is signed at next junction and in Rockanje itself.

General Details: Open: mid-March - late-Oct. Supermarket (limited hours in low seasons). Cafe, restaurant and bar (weekends only in low seasons). Tennis. Boules. Good children's playground. Swimming pool (15/5-15/9). Children's games room and organised activities in high season. Launderette. Bus service 100 m.

Charges guide: Per person Nfl 6.00; caravan or tent 9.00; motorcaravan 15.00; car 4.00; m/cycle 1.00; electricity 4.00; dog/cat 3.50.

Reservations: Essential in high season - contact site. Address: Schapengorsedijk 19, 3235 LA Rockanje. Tel: 0181/40 19 44. FAX: 0181/40 23 80.

558 Camping de Veerhoeve, Wolphaartsdijk, nr Goes

Family run site, near the shores of the Veerse Meer, ideal for families.
Situated in a popular area for watersports, this is a site well suited for sailing, windsurfing or fishing enthusiasts. As with most sites in this area there are many mature static and seasonal pitches. However, part of the friendly, relaxed site is reserved for tourists with 150 marked pitches on grassy ground, 100 with electrical connections. Sanitary facilities, in three blocks, have been well modernised with full tiling and include British style WCs and hot showers on payment. Other amenities include a good shop, TV, sports field and a children's playground. Slipway for launching boats and horse riding nearby.

How to find it: From N256 Goes-Zierikzee road take Wolphaartsdijk exit. Follow through village and signs to site.

General Details: Open: 3 April - 30 October. Restaurant. Shop. Snack bar. Tennis court. Children's playground. Watersports, boat launching and horse riding near. Laundry facilities. Accommodation for groups. Mobile homes, chalets and tents for hire.

Charges 1998: Per pitch incl. 2 persons Nfl. 30.00 - 34.00; small tent (2 persons) 19.00 - 24.00; electricity 5.00; dog 5.00. Tax included.

Reservations: Write to site. Address: Veerweg 48, 4471 NC Wolphaartsdijk. Tel: 0113/581155. FAX: 0113/581944.

CAMPING AT THE VEERSE MEER

➤ Family Campsite

➤ Luxurious fully complete tents for hire; Log cabins, mobile homes and bungalows

➤ Ideal for Anglers, Surfers and Divers

➤ Tennis court

➤ For nature lovers and those looking for rest and relaxation

DE VEERHOEVE

Veerweg 48, 4471 NC Wolphaartsdijk Tel. +31 113 581155 Fax. +31 113 581944

557 Camping de Molenhoek, Kamperland, nr Middelburg

Quietly situated Zeeland site near watersports centre.
This family run site makes a pleasant contrast to the livelier coastal sites in this popular holiday area. It is rurally situated 3 km. from the Veerse Meer which is very popular for all sorts of watersports. Catering both for 300 permanent or seasonal holiday caravans and for 100 touring units, it is neat, tidy and relatively spacious. The marked touring pitches are divided into small groups with surrounding hedges and trees giving privacy and some shade, and electrical connections are available. Sanitary facilities, in one old (partly refurbished) and one newer block, include some washbasins in private cabins with free hot water and showers, dishwashing and clothes sinks with hot water on payment, British style WCs, plus toilet and shower facilities for the disabled and provision for babies. Other amenities, grouped in front of a pleasant, open, grassy area with a children's paddling pool, playground and small animals enclosure, include a shop and a simple bar/restaurant with terrace and TV room. Entertainment is organised in season (dance evenings, bingo, etc.) as well as a disco for youngsters. An indoor pool and tennis courts are nearby. Although the site is quietly situated, there are many excursion possibilities in the area including the towns of Middelburg, Veere and Goes and the Delta Expo exhibition.

How to find it: Site is west of the village of Kamperland on the `island' of Noord Beveland. From the N256 Goes - Zierikzee road, exit west onto the N255 Kamperland road. Site is signed south of this road.

General Details: Open 29 March - 25 Oct. Restaurant/bar (high season only). Well stocked shop (all season). Entertainment in high season. Children's playground, pool and animals. TV room. Bicycle hire. Indoor pool, tennis, fishing and watersports close. Chemical disposal. Motorcaravan services. Caravans for hire.

Charges 1997: Per unit, incl. 2 persons and electricity Nfl. 40.75, 6 persons 45.75; dog 5.00. Less 25% outside high season.

Reservations: Are made - details from site. Address: Molenweg 69a, 4493 NC Kamperland. Tel: 0113/37 12 02.

NETHERLANDS

552 Vakantiepark Zeebad, Breskens

Large, friendly site near beach and ferry port.

Under the same ownership as no. 550 Pannenschuur, Camping Zeebad is just along the coast road. It is partially surrounded by small lakes and is adjacent to the beach. The established areas are well shaded but these are mainly reserved for seasonal units. However, there are 120 numbered touring pitches of 80 - 100 sq.m. with growing hedges. Cars are not allowed beside the pitches but alternative parking is provided. One tiled sanitary block near the entrance (some distance from the touring pitches) is supplemented by two rather cramped mobile units. Hot water is on payment and facilities at the main block include separate wash cabins, a family room and laundry facilities. British style WCs. There is an organised activity programme for children in high season. Swimming pools and minigolf are nearby and the town of Breskens is within walking distance (15 mins). An indoor pool and sports complex is planned, hopefully for '98.

How to find it: From Breskens take the coast road west and site is less than 1½ km. on the left.

General Details: Open all year. Electricity available in all parts. Restaurant with outdoor terrace. Bar. Snack bar. Supermarket. Games room. Children's playground. Activity programme for children. Weekly disco. Bicycle hire. Mobile homes for hire.

Charges 1997: Per person (over 2 yrs) Nfl 5.00; pitch 25.00; dog 5.00; local tax 1.00. Less in low seasons.

Reservations: Contact site for details. The site is very busy 20/7-15/8, but some pitches are normally kept for short stays. Address: Nieuwesluisweg 5, 4510 RG Breskens. Tel: 0117/38 13 38. FAX: 0117/38 31 51.

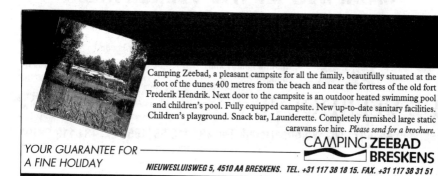

Camping Zeebad, a pleasant campsite for all the family, beautifully situated at the foot of the dunes 400 metres from the beach and near the fortress of the old fort Frederik Hendrik. Next door to the campsite is an outdoor heated swimming pool and children's pool. Fully equipped campsite. New up-to-date sanitary facilities. Children's playground. Snack bar, Launderette. Completely furnished large static caravans for hire. *Please send for a brochure.*

YOUR GUARANTEE FOR
A FINE HOLIDAY

CAMPING ZEEBAD
BRESKENS

NIEUWESLUISWEG 5, 4510 AA BRESKENS. TEL. +31 117 38 18 15. FAX. +31 117 38 31 51

551 Camping Groede, Groede, nr Breskens

Friendly, family run site two minutes from dunes and sandy beach.

Camping Groede is a friendly, fair sized site on the same stretch of sandy beach as no. 550. Family run, it aims to cater for the individual needs of visitors and to provide a good all-round holiday. Campers are sited as far as possible according to taste - in family areas, in larger groups or on more private pitches for those who prefer peace and quiet. In total, there are some 540 pitches for tourists (with seasonal units also), 275 with electrical connections (4A) and 260 with water and drainage connections also. Sanitary facilities are good with a high standard of cleanliness, British style WCs, free hot showers and some washing cabins also with hot water. A restaurant/bar provides a friendly service and there is also a snack bar (both weekends only in low season). Visitors are invited to join locals in archery and card games. Other activities include football, volleyball and plenty of activities for children in peak season. Groede is ideally sited for ferry stopovers and short stay visitors including hikers are very welcome, as well as long stay holiday makers. Run by the family van Damme who ask visitors to complete a confidential questionnaire to ensure that their site offers the best possible service and provide you with a comprehensive information booklet (in English).

How to find it: From Breskens take the coast road for 5 km. to site. Alternatively, the site is signed from Groede village on the more inland Breskens - Sluis road.

General Details: Open 27 March - 31 Oct. Shop, restaurant and snack bar (all until 13/9). Sports area. Several children's play areas (bark base). Bicycle hire. Fishing. Recreation room. Chemical disposal. Motorcaravan services.

Charges 1997: Per pitch incl. 2 persons Nfl 22.50 - 30.00, with 4A electricity 25.00 - 33.50, with water and drainage also 27.50 - 36.50; extra person 3.00 - 4.00 (incl. taxes); dog 2.65 - 3.50.

Reservations: Will be made (with Nfl 25 fee) but half the pitches are kept unreserved. Address: Zeeweg 1, 4503 PA Groede. Tel: 0117/37 13 84. FAX: 0117/37 22 77.

550 Recreatiecentrum Pannenschuur, Nieuwvliet, nr Breskens

Seaside site near Belgian border with new indoor pool complex.

This is one of several coastal sites on the narrow strip of the Netherlands between the Belgian frontier near Knokke and the Breskens ferry. Quickly reached from the ports of Ostend, Zeebrugge and Vlissingen, it is useful for overnight stops or for a few days to enjoy the seaside. A short walk across the quiet coast road and steps over the dike bring you to the open, sandy beach. Quite a large site, most of the pitches are taken by permanent or seasonal holiday caravans but there are also 150 pitches for tourists mostly in their own areas. In short rows backing onto hedges, all have electricity (4A) and (from '98) water and drainage connections. A new sanitary building provides first class facilities including a children's washroom, baby room and some private cabins (shower tokens from the supermarket). The other star attraction is the recently completed complex which provides a super indoor heated swimming pool with baby and children's sections, jacuzzi, sauna, Turkish bath and solarium. Also leading off the central café style area are a restaurant, snack bar and launderette. Overall, a very good site.

How to find it: At Nieuwvliet, on the Breskens - Sluis minor road, 8 km. southwest of Breskens, turn towards the sea at sign for Nieuwvliet-Bad and follow signs to site.

General Details: Open all year. Supermarket (all year except 4/1-20/2, restricted hours in low seasons). Restaurant, snack bar and takeaway (all year except 12/1-22/1). Swimming pool (all year except 12/1-22/1). Sauna and solarium. Large games room for young with snooker, pool tables, amusement machines, soft drinks bar. Children's playground and play field. Bicycle hire. Bungalows and caravans for hire. Organised activities during season. Launderette. Chemical disposal. Motorcaravan services.

Charges 1998: Per person (over 2 yrs) Nfl. 6.00, plus tax 1.20; pitch incl. electricity 28.00; dog 6.00. Rates available for weekly stays. Credit cards accepted.

Reservations: Recommended (high season Sat.- Sat. only) and made with deposit and fee. Address: Zeedijk 19, 4504 PP Nieuwvliet-Bad (Zeeland). Tel: 0117/37 23 00. FAX: 0117/37 14 15. E-mail: info@pannenschuur.nl.

NORWAY

Norway has the lowest population density in Europe, which is not surprising when one realises that about one quarter of its land is above the Arctic Circle. It is a land of contrasts, from magnificent snow capped mountains, dramatic fjords, vast plateaux with wild untamed tracts, huge lakes and rich green countryside. Oslo is the oldest of the Scandinavian capitals and one of the most prettily sited, whilst Bergen is the fjord capital, Trondheim is an atmospheric city with its medieval heart intact, and Tromsø, with its stunning 'Arctic Cathedral', likes to think of itself as the capital of the North. You can see the Northern Lights (Aurora Borealis) between November and February, north of the Arctic Circle, which lies between Mo i Rana and Bodø. During certain freak weather conditions it may be seen further south. The Midnight Sun is visible north of the Arctic Circle in summer - at Bodø between early June and early July, at Tromsø from late May to mid July, and at Nordkapp from mid May until late July. However you can never guarantee these experiences - it depends on meteorological conditions. Midsummer night's eve is celebrated all over the country, with thousands of bonfires along the fjords.

Conservation of the environment was a practical reality in Norway long before it became a fashionable International issue. This, and the more recent improvements in the infrastructure, with many new tunnels and upgraded roads replacing some of the older more tortuous sections, explains why tourism is increasing rapidly. With main roads throughout the country now perfectly adequate for average sized caravan and motorcaravan outfits, the most popular regions and routes do become busy during the short summer season from June to August. Although there are still gravel surfaced roads in places, you will be unlikely to encounter many when visiting the main tourist areas. 1997 saw more changes to the Norwegian road numbers with an upgrade to the new E-road status on a number of routes.

Further information may be obtained from:

Norwegian Tourist Board, Charles House, 5-11 Lower Regent Street SW1Y 4LR

Tel: 0171 839 6255 Fax: 0171 839 6014

Population
4,300,000 (1997); density 13 per sq. km.

Capital
Oslo.

Climate
The Gulf Stream follows the coast from south to north and the weather is less extreme on the west coast. Generally weather in both summer and winter is unpredictable (it can be very wet). Average temperatures 18.2° in Oslo, 14.5° in Bergen, 12.7° in Tromso during July whilst in Jan. -3.7° in Oslo, 1.5° in Bergen, and -4.7° in Tromso. Daylight hours in Oslo are 6 hrs 3 mins in Jan. and 18 hrs 41 mins in July whilst Tromso in Jan. has no daylight and in July, 24 hours

Language
Norwegian, but English is widely spoken, particularly by the young.

Currency
The Norwegian krone, divided into 100 ore. Denominations are 10, 50, 100, 500, and 1000 kr.

Banks
Open Mon-Fri 09.00-15.00. Every largish village and town in Norway has a bank, although rural branches may have restricted opening hours. Some, e.g. NOR Bank and Dennorske Bank, allow you to withdraw cash against a credit card.

Post Offices
Opening hours vary but are generally 08.00/08.30- 16.00/ 17.00 Mon-Fri, 08.00-13.00 on Saturdays.

Time
GMT plus 1 (BST plus 1 in summer).

Telephone
To phone from the UK, the code is 0047 plus the number. From Norway to the UK, the code is 095 44, plus the number (omitting the initial 0).

Shops
Normal hours: Mon-Fri 09.00-16.00/17.00, Thu 09.00-18.00/20.00 and Sat 09.00-13.00 /15.00. There are 2,600 tax-free shops in Norway. If you buy goods for more than 308 kr make sure you get a tax refund. After deduction of a handling charge you'll get 11-18% of the buying price back in cash, at ports or major border crossings.

Food: more expensive than in the UK, except for very good vegetables, fruit and some fish. Smoked and fresh salmon are excellent and reindeer steak very tender. A small beer in a cafe can cost £3.

Camping Gaz: Not readily available, though some larger sites stock 904 and 907 refills. You can buy camping gaz from Statoil and AGA Progas, which have outlets throughout Norway.

Motoring
Roads are generally uncrowded except in and around Oslo and Bergen but be prepared for tunnels and hairpin bends. Certain roads are forbidden to caravans or best avoided (an advisory leaflet is published by the Norwegian Tourist Office). Vehicles must have sufficient road grip and in the winter it may be necessary to use winter tyres with or without studs or chains. Towed caravans up to 2.3 m. wide are permitted; if between 2.3 and 2.5 m. (max permitted width) the car towing it must be at least as wide as the caravan. Drink driving laws are extremely strict.

Tolls: Vehicles entering Bergen on weekdays must pay a toll. Vehicles up to 3.5 tonnes entering Oslo pay a toll. Tolls are also levied on certain roads.

Speed Limits: Caravans and motorhomes (3.5 tons) 31 mph (50 kph) in built up areas, caravans 50 mph (80 kph) on all other roads, motorhomes 50 mph (80 kph) on other roads and 56 mph (90 kph) on motorways.

Motoring (continued)

Fuel: Mon-Fri petrol stations are closed between 19.00 and 05.00. At weekends stations are closed other than in closely populated areas. Major credit cards accepted in larger petrol stations.

Parking: Parking regulations in towns are very strict and subject to fines. Yellow parking meters give 1 hour, Grey -2 and Brown - 3 hours.

Overnighting

You can camp in open areas provided you are at least 150 m away from houses or cabins. Caravans may not park on laybys or picnic sites. Open fires forbidden 15 April - 15 September.

Note: Mosquitos can be a problem in summer (from June) - go prepared.

Useful Addresses:

Motoring Organisations:
Kongelig Norsk Automobilklub (KNA), Drammenasveien 20-C, Oslo. Tel: 02 561000.
Norges Automobil-Forbund (NAF), Storgt. 2, Oslo 1. Tel: 02 429400.

Camping Clubs:
Norsk Campingbilforening, Postboks 18, Lysejordet, 0312 Oslo 3.
Norsk Caravan Club Landsforbund, Solheimveien 18, 1473 Skarer. Tel: 02 974920.

Camping in Norway

There are more than 1,000 campsites in Norway and you have the option to take your own tent, caravan or motorcaravan, or to use cabin (Hytte) accommodation. Camping costs for a unit incl. two persons with electricity is around Nkr. 80-150 per night, whilst a cabin will cost Nkr. 200-600 per night depending on size, number of beds, and level of facilities. The Norwegian Public Roads Administration (Statens Vegvesen), in conjunction with local authorities, has in recent years started creating roadside campsites with basic facilities (known as Bobil parks). These are primarily designed for motorcaravans to overnight, some are free, others operate an honesty box system. With an ever increasing number of 'wild-campers', and these new facilities, it is not surprising that in certain areas commercial campsites are reluctant to spend money on expensive refurbishment or renewal work, opting instead to increase the static or cabin accommodation to supplement reducing income.

So few British were going to Norway in the early 'nineties that it was an act of faith on our part to extend our guide north of Denmark. We must admit to have been heavily influenced by the arrival on the scene of Color Line who adopted a positive approach to the British camping market. More recently, the Scandinavian Seaways service to Göteborg in Sweden, has become equally popular as an entry route to Norway, for those who live closer to Harwich. In our first year entries were heavily concentrated around Bergen, this being the area traditionally favoured by British visitors, but since then we have steadily expanded our coverage. This year, to enable the more adventurous to reach the Arctic Circle and Nordkapp, we have expanded north with a small selection of sites including the most northerly campsite in the world. The main E6 'Arctic Highway' is a good tarmac surfaced road, running some 2,000 km. from Oslo until it joins the E69 north of Alta, which then takes you the final 100 km. on to Nordkapp itself. During '98 the ferry linking Kåfjord to Honningsvåg is due to be replaced by a new tunnel and road section, the charges being similar to the existing ferry service.

We continue to give low priority to the coast to the south of Stavanger/Oslo or to the valleys to the east of Oslo/Trondheim, although these are deservedly popular among Norwegian campers, they are of least interest to British campers. Norway is primarily touring country, very few campers spend more than two nights in any one camp, preferring to move on in search of wonderful scenery just around the corner. To fit in with this we have arranged our sites in a loose circuit starting at Stavanger and Haugesund, moving north via Bergen through fjordland to Trondheim. From here one can either travel north to the Arctic Circle or Nordkapp (returning through Norway or via our new sites in Sweden), or turn south and continue the circuit via the eastern valleys and Oslo. Such is the attraction of the dramatic rural scenery that few campers will wish to linger long in Norway's urban gateways; we have accordingly resorted to the unusual practice of describing briefly the camping situation in each of the main gateways rather than restricting our information to one or more key sites.

There are several negatives which deserve mention. Norway can be very expensive. With few exceptions most things cost double what they cost in Britain (dependant on the exchange rate). Although it is not good normal practice, campers should buy as much food and drink as possible before leaving Britain. Norway's west coast and central mountains and fells can also be very wet; only the well equipped should consider relying entirely on tented accommodation.

The sites in NORWAY featured in this guide are shown on the SCANDINAVIA map on page 377

NORWAY

Camping at the Gateways

Traditionally, British campers view Bergen as the usual gateway to Norway. If the visitor expects to tour only in the fjord country to the north and immediately inland then it makes sense to return to Bergen. However, for the visitor looking further afield, beyond the three main fjords, there is much to be said for considering the two other west coast gateways of Stavanger and Haugesund, both now well served by Color Line from Newcastle. Along the south coast there are several gateways served by cross-Baltic ferries from Denmark and Germany. For the long distance driver prepared to drive via Sweden, Oslo will be the obvious entry point. The following notes provide a quick guide to the camping situation at the four main gateways.

Bergen

Unless there is little choice, we do not recommend camping in built-up Bergen. There are four sites within 10 km. of the focal old harbour:

Camping Sandviken - a congested overnight camping site for motorcaravans in the industrial harbour within walking distance of the Color Line quay.

Bergenshallen Camping - a small tract set aside for camping in a suburban shopping complex at Landas, 5 km. south of the town centre.

Paradis Caravan Camping - a van parking site at a suburban sports complex 7 km. south of the centre.
Midttun Motel - adjacent to a small motel in Nesttun, 9 km. south of the town centre, near the airport.

Further out of town, going inland on the main 580 highway which leads to Hardangerfjord from Nesttun, are three more attractive sites which until now we have been hesitant to recommend but which have been steadily upgraded to the point where they deserve consideration. The first to be reached is **Grimen Camping**, a very small site just off the 580 on the shore of an attractive lake. At weekends and during the school holidays it is usually fully occupied by knowing Norwegians visiting Bergen. The owner runs a nice general store next door. He also offers a good choice of small lake-side huts at prices which are unusually low by Norwegian standards. Only a few hundred metres further on the opposite side of the 580 is another lakeside site, **Bratland Camping**, which is larger but which also tends to be fully occupied at popular times. A few miles further down the 580 is an even larger lakeside site, **Lone Camping**, which has been very sensibly developed in recent years to the point where it deserves recommendation, despite its distance (nearly 20 km) from central Bergen.

Fredrikstad

For those arriving in Norway via Gothenburg, Fredikstad is not only the obvious gateway but it is one of Norway's most interesting cities and certainly deserves at least a day or two. It has a delightful waterfront, bubbling with cheerful nautical activity. Its historic old town, across the river from the newer town, is one of the best preserved in Europe and is also bustling with life. There are many other attractions, including a choice of two good camps sites. Within walking distance of the old town, from where the new town can be reached by frequent foot ferry, is a small greenfield municipal site, **Fredrikstad Motel and Camping**. Further south, along route 107, at Torsnes is a very different proposition, **Bevo Camping**, which occupies woodland on the fjord shore, commanding a wonderful view of this very attractive stretch of coast. Although Bevo attracts many statics, there is usually space for tourers - the friendly manager like to guide visitors to a suitable site on his bike!

Haugesund

Now served by Color Line, Haugesund is well worth considering as a departure port. It is a well preserved small town, with traditional wood buildings predominant, and a lively marine atmosphere and it has a better choice of campsites than any other major Norwegian town. About ten miles east of the town centre, just off the main route 11 leading to Oslo, there is the very large, very well equipped and imaginatively designed **Grindafjord Naturcamping** (named after its entertaining animal life!). Along the coast of the unspoilt southern half of neighbouring Karmoy island (reached by bridge) there are several rather basic but spectacularly sited waterfront sites (Karmoy deserves a visit to wander around the picturesque old fishing port of Skenshaveñ) but our favourite is the municipal site on the northern outskirts of the town, but only a mile from the town centre! Named **Haraldshaugen** after the neighbouring monumental obelisk - a national shrine honouring the Viking hero Harald the Fairhaired - this site is formed by a boulder strewn meadow on the shore of Haugesundfjord. It has an excellent sanitary block and a small shop.Unlike Grindafjord where statics predominate, no statics are permitted at Haraldshaugen. Another plus is the friendly atmosphere; the site is managed by the local Red Cross, run by volunteers, and all profits go into charitable medical services in the community.

Grindafjord Naturcamping: 5570 Aksdal. Tel: 47 52 77 57 40.

Haraldshaugen Camping: Post boks 1309, Gard, 5501 Haugesund. Tel: 52 72 80 77.

Oslo

In general, the sites in Oslo (like most major city sites) are large and very crowded. If you do need to stay in Oslo, two sites are available, both operated by NAF, the Norwegian motoring organisation:

Bogstad Camp and Turistsenter is 9 km. to the north of the city in a residential, lakeside area. It can take 1,200 units. There are 170 numbered pitches with electricity. Open all year, there is a petrol station, supermarket and a restaurant adjoining. Sanitary facilities are in three modern blocks, the best of which can be heated in winter. The site is a 5 min. walk from Bogstad Lake. To reach the site follow signs from the E18 through suburbs. Also signed from 120 ring-road. Address: Ankervn 117, 0757 Oslo 7.

Ekeberg Camping is on a hilltop with panoramic views across the city. Very busy in high season, the undulating grassy areas are unmarked. Only open 1 June - 31 Aug, it accepts about 700 units (including groups). When full the sanitary facilities are fully stretched. Site is well signed (Ekeberg) from E18 running southeast to Sweden in a suburb. Address: Ekebergvein 65, 1181 Oslo 11.

On Oslo's southern boundary **Stubljan Camping** deserves consideration. It is extremely convenient, lying between the E18 and the fjord and there is a regular park and ride bus service to central Oslo. It is a well laid out and attractive, occupying a series of grass ledges sloping down to the fjord which is one of Oslo's most popular bathing beaches. There are few statics and it is open all year.

Stavanger

Although most British tourists head for Bergen, Stavanger is also well worth considering as a gateway. Despite its reputation as an `oil town', Stavanger is very attractive and compact and in no sense inferior to Bergen. It is well served by Color Line - indeed Color's late night departure schedules in effect offer the motorist an extra half day in Norway compared with Bergen. It is a most convenient gateway for exploring south Norway and, unlike Bergen, has a campsite which we can highly recommend. **Mosvangen Camping** (Henrik Ibsens grt 21, 4021 Stavanger) is only 2 km. from the centre and only just off the E18 road as it enters the town from the south. It is on the shore of the lake from which it takes its name. Gently undulating. well shaded and divided by trees, it has 200 pitches and is very well equipped.

2315 Ringoy Camping, Ringoy (Hordaland)

Simple site by Upper Hardangerfjord.

Although the village of Ringoy is quiet and peaceful, it occupies a pivotal position, lying not only midway between two ferry ports of Upper Hardangerfjord (Kinsarvik and Brimnes), but also by the junction of two key roads (7 and 13). There are several sites at the popular nearby resort town of Kinsarvik but none compares for situation and atmosphere with the small, simple Ringoy site. Basically a steeply sloping field running down from the road to the tree-lined fjord, there are flat areas for camping along the top and the bottom. The toilet block is small and simple (with metered showers and British style WCs), but well designed and maintained. On arrival find a place - someone calls between 8 and 9 pm.

> **How to find it:** Site is on route 13, midway between Kinsarvik and Brimnes.
>
> **General Details:** Open all year. Simple facilities, possibly inadequate during peak holiday weeks in July. No shop but village mini-market and garage within a minute's walk. Rowing boat available (free).
>
> **Charges guide:** Per unit Nkr. 80; electricity (10A) 15.
>
> **Reservations:** Write to site. Address: 5782 Ringoy. Tel: 53.66.39.17.

2325 Sundal Camping, Mauranger (Hordaland)

Excellent gateway site for fjordland, from either Stavanger or Bergen.

Maurangerfjord is a steep-sided arm leading off the eastern shore of the middle reaches of the Hardangerfjord. The village of Mauranger commands magnificent views across the waters. Cutting through the village is a turbulent stream, popular with those in search of trout. Its waters are ice-cold, for they descend from the nearby Folgafonn ice-cap and its renowned glacier, an hour's brisk walk from the village. Sundal Camping is divided into two sections: a wooded, waterfront site between the local road and the fjord, which combines camping with a small marina; and an open meadow site uphill of the local road. Both are served by well equipped toilet blocks. Sundal is not only ideally situated for Folgafonn; it is also the nearest good site to the charming small town of Rosendal.

> **How to find it:** Route 48 crosses Hardangerfjord by ferry from Gjermundshavn to Lofallstrand from where a clearly marked local road runs northeast for 16 km. along the fjord waterfront to Mauranger.
>
> **General Details:** Well equipped with most facilities. Stream and lake fishing. Canoe and rowing boat hire. Small shop. Pleasant small hotel adjacent with attractive restaurant and bar.
>
> **Reservations:** Contact site. Address: P.O. Box 5476, Mauranger, (Hordaland). Tel: 53.48.41.86.

NORWAY

2320 Odda Camping, Odda (Hordaland)

Neat, lakeside municipal site, just within walking distance of Buar glacier and the Vidfoss Falls.

Bordered by the Folgefonna glacier to the west and the Hardangervidda plateau to the east and south, Odda is an industrial town with electro-chemical enterprises based on zinc mining and hydro-electric power. At the turn of the century Odda was one of the most popular destinations for the European upper classes - the magnificent and dramatic scenery is still there, together with the added interest of the industrial impact which is well recorded at the industrial museum at Tyssedal. This municipal site has been attractively developed on the town's southern outskirts, just over a kilometre from the centre on the shores of the Sandvin lake (good salmon and trout fishing) and on the minor road leading up the Buar Valley to the Buar glacier and Folgefonna ice-cap. It is possible to walk to the ice face but in the later stages this is quite hard-going! The site is spread over 2½ acres of flat, mature woodland, which is divided into small clearings by massive boulders deposited long ago by the departing glacier. Access is by well tended tarmac roads which wind their way among the trees and boulders. There are 50 tourist pitches including many with electrical connections. A single timber building at the entrance houses the reception office (often unattended) and the simple, but clean sanitary facilities which provide, for each sex, 2 WCs, one hot shower (on payment) and 3 open washbasins. There is also a small kitchen with dishwashing facilities and a washing machine and dryer in the ladies washroom. The site fills up in the evenings and can be crowded with facilities stretched from the end of June to early August.

How to find it: Site is on the southern outskirts of Odda, signed off road to Buar, with a well marked access.

General Details: Open 1 June - 31 Aug. Town facilities close. Washing machine and dryer. Kitchen.

Charges guide: Per tent and car Nkr. 75; caravan and car 90; m/cycle 65; electricity 20.

Reservations: write to site. Address: Borsta, 5750 Odda (Hordaland). Tel: 53.64.34.10.

2330 Eikhamrane Camping, Nå, Sorfjord (Hordaland)

Small, neat site among orchards on western shore of Sorfjord.

Sorfjord, well known for its fruit growing, has long been on a popular route for travellers across Norway via Utne (where Norway's oldest hotel is a tourist attraction in its own right) and a short ferry crossing across Hardangerfjord. Travellers are also attracted by the Folgefonn ice cap, the most accessible of the great glaciers, which lies at the head of Sorfjord. About halfway along the western shore of Sorfjord is Eikhamrane Camping. Arranged on a well landscaped and partly terraced field which slopes alongside the road to a pebbly lakeside beach, it was formerly part of an orchard which still extends on both sides of the site and uphill across the road. There is room for 50 units (about 20 caravans or motorcaravans and 30 tents) on unmarked, well kept grass with 20 electrical hook ups. There are attractive trees and good gravel roads, with areas of gravel hardstanding for poor weather. Many pitches overlook the fjord where there are also thoughtfully positioned picnic benches. There are two small timber sanitary blocks, one for toilets with external access, the other for washbasins (open) and showers (on payment). Both are simple but very well kept. Small kitchen with dishwashing (hot water on payment) and 2 laundry sinks outside, under cover. The office (where you can order bread and where home-grown fruits are available) is in the old farmhouse, home of the owners, the Mage family. The site is well situated for watersports (sailing, canoeing and rowing), fishing and the nearby Digranes nature reserve (birdwatching).

How to find it: Site is on road no. 550 just outside the village of Nå, on the western shore of Sorfjord, 32 km. south of Utne and 16 km. north of Odda.

General Details: Open 1 June - 31 August only. Some supplies kept at reception office - bread and milk to order. Watersports and fishing in lake. 5 cabins to let (Nkr. 180 - 250).

Charges guide: Per person Nkr. 10; child (4-12 yrs) 5; pitch 50; extra tent 30; awning 20; electricity 10.

Reservations: write to site. Address: 5776 Nå (Hordaland). Tel: 53.66.22.48.

2370 Botnen Camping, Brekke (Sogn og Fjordane)

Good first stop for those going north from Bergen.

For those setting forth north on route 1 from Bergen there are suprisingly few attractive sites until one reaches the southern shore of mighty Sognefjord. At Brekke is a well known tourist landmark, the remarkable Breekstranda Fjord Hotel, a traditional turf-roofed complex which tourist coaches are unable to resist. A mile or two beyond the hotel, also on the shore of the fjord, is the family run Botnen Camping. An isolated, simple (2-star) site which slopes steeply, it is well maintained. It has its own jetty and harbour, complete with rowing boats and canoes for hire and commands a splendid view across the fjord to distant mountains.

How to find it: Site is 2 km off the coast road running west from Brekke.

General Details: Open 1 May - 1 Sept. Children's play area. Swimming, fishing and boating in fjord. Boats and canoes for hire.

Charges guide: Per person Nkr. 10; child 5; caravan 40; tent 30; electricity 15.

Reservations: Contact site. Address: 5950 Brekke. Tel: 57.78.54.71.

NORWAY

2340 Mo Camping, Norheimsund (Hordaland)

Simple, well kept family site in scenic location with friendly welcome.

The main road leading inland from Bergen (route 7) is pleasant but perhaps unexciting until it reaches Norheimsund where is joins Hardangerfjord, one of the `Big Three' of Norway's spectacular fjords. Mo Camping is a very attractive site on what appears to be a small lake but is actually an arm of the main fjord. At the head of this arm (within walking distance of the site, but along the side of the road) are the spectacular Steinsdals Falls which draw half a million visitors annually to view the falls from behind! This little site is part of a small working farm run by the Mo family. It has some 40 unmarked touring places, with 25 electrical connections, on a curve of flat, well kept grass. There are also two small areas of hardstanding for poor weather. The camping area is divided from the working part of the farm by a line of charming, traditional, wooden farm buildings which include the family home, the office and the sanitary facilities (in a converted barn). Rather cramped, these include for each sex a shower (on payment) and 2 WCs with washbasins opposite. They are hard-pressed when the site is full. Laundry, dishwashing and drying facilities. Shop at a nearby filling station (200 m.). Although offering only basic facilities, this site is fastidiously looked after with good walks, free fishing and a 2-seater canoe for hire.

How to find it: Site is by the no. 7 road just over 1 km. west of Norheimsund.

General Details: Open 1 June - 31 August only - minimal facilities, but town 1 km. and shop 200 m. Fishing. Chemical disposal. Motorcaravan services.

Charges 1997: Per person Nkr. 5; child (under 12 yrs) 3; caravan, motorcaravan or tent with car 60; tent without car 35; m/cycle 35; local tax 40; electricity (16A) 20.

Reservations: Write to site. Address: 5600 Norheimsund, Hardaland.

2350 Espelandsdalen Camping, nr Ulvik (Hordaland)

Basic, farm campsite, but `a glimpse of untamed Norway'.

If one follows Hardangerfjord on the map and considers the mighty glacier which once scooped away the land along its path, it is easy to imagine that it started life in Espelandsdalen. Here is the textbook upper glacial valley. Espelandsdalen runs from Granvin to Ulvik, both of which lie at the heads of their respective arms of Hardangerfjord. A minor road (route 572) links the two small towns with sharp climbs at either end (tricky for caravans). The valley bed here is occupied by a series of connected lakes, popular with canoeists. For generations farmers have struggled to make a living out of the narrow strip of land between water and rock. One of these farmers has converted a narrow, sloping field bisected by the road (572) into a modest lake-side camp site taking about 40 units. The section above the road has a sanitary block (washing trough with hot water, a shower on payment and WCs) and a neat row of chalets for hire. The grassy pitches below the road run down to the shore. Campers come for fishing (boat hire), walking or skiing, or just to marvel at the views of the valley and towering mountain sides.

How to find it: The northern loop of the 572 road follows Espelandsdalen and the campsite is on this road, about 6 km. from its junction with route 13 at Granvin (steep gradients - see above).

General Details: Open all year.A few electrical hook-ups (8-10A). Some basic foodstuffs kept in office. Swimming, fishing and boating in lake. Ski track 2 km. Ten cabins to let (Nkr. 200 per night).

Charges guide: Per unit Nkr. 50; person 10; child (4-12 yrs) 5; hikers tent 20; electricity 20.

Reservations: Contact site. Address: 5736 Granvin (Hordaland). Tel: 56.52.51.67. FAX: 56.52.51.67.

2360 Ulvik Fjord Camping, Ulvik (Hordaland)

Small, quiet, orchard site on outskirts of Ulvik, on the fjord.

Ulvik was discovered by tourists 150 years ago when the first liners started operating to the head of Hardangerfjord, and to this day, a regular stream of cruise liners work their way into the very heartland of Norway. A century and a half of visitors has meant that Ulvik is now a well-established tourist destination, describing itself as `the pearl of Hardanger' but, with only just over 1000 inhabitants, it still manages to retain an unspoilt village atmosphere. Access is by narrow, winding roads, either along the side of the fjord or up a steep road behind the town - probably not to be recommended for caravans. This pretty little site is 500 m. from the centre of the town occupying what was once a small orchard. There is room for about 30 units on undulating ground which slopes towards the fjord, with some flat areas and a few electrical connections. A small wooden building houses reception, a small kitchen (with a cooker and a sink) and the sanitary facilities. Well kept, these comprise for each sex, 2 open washbasins, WCs and 2 modern showers on payment. Slipway for small boats and swimming or fishing is possible in the fjord. Meals may be taken at the hotel opposite and the town shops, etc. are close.

How to find it: Ulvik is reached by road no. 572; site is on southern side of town, opposite Ulvikfjord Pension. There is a ferry from road 7 at Brimnes. Note: Cars and caravans can now connect with road 7 via a new tunnel.

General Details: Open 20 May - 31 Aug. Kitchen. Boat slipway, fishing and swimming in fjord. Hotel opposite, shops and restaurants in town. 10 cabins for hire.

Charges guide: Per motorcaravan or tent Nkr. 60, caravan 65; person 15; child (4-12 yrs) 10; electricity 20.

Reservations: write to site. Address: 5730 Ulvik. Tel: 56.52.65.77.

241

NORWAY

2380 Tveit Camping, Vik/Vangsnes (Sogn og Fjordane)

Charming, neat, family run site, ideally placed for exploring the Balestrand area.

Located in the district of Vik on the south shore of Sognefjord, 4 km. from the small port of Vangsnes, Tveit Camping is part of a small working farm. Reception and a kiosk open most of the day in high season, with a phone to summon assistance at any time. Four terraces provide 45 pitches with electricity (10A) to 30. There are also 10 cabins on site. Modern heated sanitary facilities provide British style WCs, washbasins (one per sex in cubicle), controllable hot showers with divider and seat (on payment), a unit for the disabled, kitchens with facilities for dishwashing and cooking, and a laundry with washing machine, dryer and iron (hot water on payment). Other on-site facilities include TV rooms, a fenced playground and a slipway. A shop, café, pub and post office are by the ferry terminal in Vangsnes 4 km. away. On the campsite you will find a restored Iron Age burial mound dating from 350-550AD, whilst the statue of Fritjov 'The Intrepid' towers over the landscape at Vangsnes. Visit the Kristianhus Boat and Engine Museum or see traditional Gamalost cheese making in Vik, and in Fjærland across the fjord you can find the Norwegian Glacier Museum.

How to find it: Site is by the Rv 13 between Vik and Vangsnes, 4 km. south of Vangsnes.

General Details: Open 15 April - 15 Oct. Kiosk (15/6-25/8). Laundry. Kitchen. Motorcaravan service point. Car wash. TV rooms. Children's playground. Slipway and boat hire. Cabins for rent.

Charges 1997: Per unit Nkr. 50 - 60; person (over 5 yrs) 10; electricity 20.

Reservations: Write to site. Address: 5865 Vangsnes, Sogn og Fjordane. Tel: 57.69.66.70.

2385 Sandvik Camping, Gaupne (Sogn og Fjordane)

Compact, popular, small site on edge of town and close to the Nigardsbreen Glacier.

This small site has 60 touring pitches, 32 with electrical connections (8/16A), arranged on fairly level grassy terrain either side of a gravel access road, on the edge of this small town. A large supermarket, post office, banks, etc. are all within a level 500 m. stroll. The single central sanitary unit provides British style WCs, washbasins with dividers, and two hot showers per sex (on payment). In addition there is a multi-purpose unit serving the needs of families or the disabled with facilities for baby changing and a further WC, basin and shower with ramp for access. A small campers' kitchen provides dishwashing facilities, hot-plates, oven and fridge (all free of charge) together with tables, chairs and TV. The separate laundry has sinks with free hot water and a washing machine and dryer. The owner tells us that these facilities are scheduled for refurbishment at the end of the 97 season so campers can look forward to even better standards for 98. A café in the reception building is open mid June-August for drinks and meals. The small shop sells ices, soft drinks, sweets, crisps, etc. This is a useful site for those using the spectacular Rv 55 high mountain road from Lom to Sogndal or for visiting the Nigardsbreen Glacier and Jostedalsbreen area of Norway.

How to find it: Signed just off the Rv 55 Lom-Sogndal road on the eastern outskirts of Gaupne.

General Details: Open May - Sept. Shop. Cafeteria (mid June-Aug). Kitchen. Laundry. TV. Children's playground. Cabins for rent.

Charges 1997: Per pitch Nkr. 50; tent, caravan or motorcaravan 30; adult 20; child (4-14 yrs) 10; electricity 20. Credit cards accepted.

Reservations: Write to site. Address: 5820, Gaupne. Tel: 57.68.11.53. FAX: 57.68.16.71.

2390 Kjornes Camping, Sogndal (Sogn og Fjordane)

Simple farm site in a prime fjordside location, ideal for those on a budget.

Occupying a long open meadow which slopes down to the tree lined waterside this site is ideal for those who prefer the simple life, just enjoying the peace and quiet, the lovely scenery or a spot of fishing. Access is via a narrow lane with passing places, which drops down towards the fjord 3 km. from Sogndal. The site takes 100 touring units, but there are only 36 electrical connections (16A). There are also 8 cabins for rent but no static caravans. The sanitary unit is basic but clean, providing British style WCs, mostly open washbasins, and 2 hot showers per sex (on payment). A small kitchen has a dishwashing sink with free hot water, plus a double hot-plate and fridge (also free). The laundry is 'al fresco' with a small roof covering the sink, washing machine and dryer. A scenic route (Rv 55) runs along the entire north shore of Sognefjord and the Sogndalfjord to Sogndal and then continues across the Jotunheimen mountain plateau towards Lom.

How to find it: Site is off the Rv 5, 3 km. east of Sogndal, 8 km. west of Kaupanger.

General Details: Open 1 June - end Aug. Kitchen. Laundry. Chemical disposal. Cabins for rent.

Charges 1997: Per unit Nkr. 45; adult 15; child 5; small tent 30; electricity 20.

Reservations: Write to site. Address: 5800 Sogndal, Sogn og Fjordane. Tel: 57.67.45.80.

2400 Camping Jolstraholmen, Vassenden (Sogn og Fjordane)

Well presented, family run site on the E39 between Sognefjord and Nordfjord.

This attractive site is located between the road and the fast-flowing Jolstra River (renowned for its trout fishing), 1.5 km. from the lakeside village of Vassenden, and behind the Statoil filling station, restaurant and supermarket complex which is also owned and run by the site owner and his family. The 60 pitches (some marked) are on grass or gravel hardstanding all with electricity (10A) and some have water and waste points. A river tributary runs through the site and forms an island on which some additional tent pitches are located, and there are also 19 cabins. The main heated sanitary facilities, in rooms below the complex, provide British style WCs, open washbasins, controllable hot showers (on payment), plus one family bathroom per sex. A further small unit is on the island. Two small kitchens provide dishwashing and cooking (free of charge) and the laundry has a washing machine and dryer. Children's playground, 50 m. waterchute (open summer, weather permitting), minigolf, covered barbecue area, and boat hire. Ski slopes are within 1 km., guided walking tours are organised, and a riverside and woodland walk follows a 1.5 km. circular route from the site and has fishing platforms and picnic tables along the way.

How to find it: Site is beside the E39 road, 1.5 km. west of Vassenden, 18 km. east of Førde.

General Details: Open all year. Supermarket. Restaurant. Garage. Laundry. Kitchens. Barbecue area. Children's playground. Minigolf. Waterchute. Rafting. Fishing. Guided walks. Boat hire. Cabins for rent.

Charges 1997: Per unit Nkr. 30 - 40; small tent 20 - 30; adult 15 - 20; child (5-15 yrs) 5 - 10; electricity 30. Credit cards accepted.

Reservations: Write to site. Address: 6840 Vassenden, Sogn og Fjordane. Tel: 57.72.71.35. FAX: 57.72.75.05.

2436 Byrkjelo Camping, Byrkjelo, nr Sandane (Sogn og Fjordane)

Pretty, good value site, in village location, ideal base for Nordfjord and Jostedalsbreen.

This neatly laid out and well equipped small site offers 50 large marked and numbered touring pitches, 40 with electrical connections (10A) and 15 with gravel hardstandings. At the time of inspection the owners were just completing their excellent new drive-over motorhome service point. The neatly mown grass, attractive trees and shrubs and the warm welcome from the young and enthusiastic owners make this a very pleasant place to stay. The good heated sanitary unit provides British style WCs, washbasins, and 5 shower rooms each with washbasin, changing space and seats (showers on payment). In addition, a multi-purpose unit serves the needs of families and the disabled, with facilities for baby changing and incorporating a further WC, basin and shower with handrails, etc. The campers' kitchen has dishwashing sinks, hot-plates and dining area, all free. A separate laundry provides a sink, washing machine, dryer and airing rack. Fishing is available in the river adjacent to the site and a riding stables are 5 km. Reception and a small kiosk selling ices, sweets and soft drinks, is housed in an attractive cabin and there is a bell to summon the owners should they not be on site when you arrive. A garage, mini-market and cafe are just 100 m. from the site and the lively town of Sandane is 19 km.

How to find it: Site is beside the Rv 1 in the village of Byrkjelo, 19 km. east of Sandane.

General Details: Open 1 May - 1 Sept. Kiosk. Laundry. Kitchen. Motorcaravan service point. TV room. Minigolf. Small children's playground. Fishing. Cabins for rent.

Charges 1997: Per unit Nkr. 55; adult 10; child 5, electricity 20.

Reservations: Advisable in peak season. Address: 6867 Byrkjelo. Tel: 57.86.74.30.

2480 Bjorkedal Camping, Volda (Møre og Romsdal)

Interesting, excellent value, boat builder's campsite in outstanding location.

On the Rv 1 north of the Nordfjord, in Møre og Romsdal, is a lovely bowl shaped valley famous throughout Norway for traditional boat building. Bjorkedal Camping is on a grassy open plateau about 300 m. off the main road and overlooking the farmland and mountains around the lake. There is space for 25 tents or vans with 10 electricity connections (16A) and also 5 nicely designed cabins for rent. The small, modern and spotlessly clean sanitary unit provides British style WCs, washbasins with dividers and curtains, one controllable hot shower per sex with changing space, curtain and seat (on payment), plus a WC and washbasin unit with ramped access for disabled people. Kitchen with dishwashing sink and a full cooker (free), laundry with sinks and washing machine, and cosy TV lounge. For a thousand years boats have been hand built in this valley by the Bjorkedal family. Site owner, Jakob Bjorkedal, will be pleased to show you the old water powered saw mill which he has reconstructed, and there are usually some examples of his boat building craft in the magnificent workshop with a most spectacular cathedral style timber roof. An extensive network of footpaths both in the valley and leading up into the surrounding circle of mountains where you can see the old cabins of the herdsmen, one dating back to the 17th century. Amongst the other activities available are small game hunting and freshwater fishing.

How to find it: Signed off Rv 1, midway along western side of Bjorkedal lake, 21 km. north of Nordfjordeid.

General Details: Open all year. Laundry. Kitchen. TV lounge. Small game hunting. Freshwater fishing.

Charges 1997: Per unit Nkr. 40; adult 10; child 5; electricity 15.

Reservations: Write to site. Address: 6120 Folkestadbgd. Tel: 70.05.20.43.

NORWAY

2460 Prinsen Strandcamping, Alesund (Møre og Romsdal)

Lively, fjordside site, just outside the attractive small town of Alesund.

Although 5 km. from the town centre, this is a more attractive option to the more crowded sites closer to town, even so, this is mainly a transit and short-stay site. Divided by trees and shrubs, and sloping gently to a small sandy beach with views down Borgundfjord, the site has 125 grassy pitches, 25 cabins and 7 rooms, 110 electricity connections (16A) and 75 cable TV hook-ups. The main heated sanitary unit, in the reception building, has British style WCs, mostly open washbasins, controllable hot showers with divider and seat (on payment), plus a sauna for each sex. A small kitchen has cooking facilities but only 2 dishwashing sinks, and the laundry has a sink, 2 washing machines and a dryer. Further older facilities mainly serving rooms and cabins, include a multi-purpose bathroom for the disabled, families and baby changing. A hatch by the central road serves as a chemical disposal point and a motorcaravan service point (not drive over - difficult for some units). Reception shares space with the small shop (bread to order). Small children's playground, barbecue areas, slipway and boat hire. Alesund has lovely Art Nouveau architecture, Sunnmøre Folk Museum has 50 old houses, a boat collection and medieval and Viking artefacts, and on the island of Giske we recommend a visit to the 'Marble Church'.

How to find it: Turn off the E136 at roundabout signed to Hatlane and site. Follow signs to site.

General Details: Open all year. Shop (1/6-1/9). Sauna. TV room. Children's playground. Slipway. Boat hire. Fishing. Bicycle hire. Kitchen. Laundry. Chemical disposal. Cabins and rooms for rent. Restaurant 800 m.

Charges 1998: Per unit incl. up to 6 persons Nkr. 130.00; electricity 20.00. Credit cards accepted.

Reservations: Write to site. Address: Ratvika, 6015 Alesund. Tel: 70.15.52.04. FAX: 70.15.49.96.

2470 Åndalsnes Camping and Motel, Åndalsnes (Møre og Romsdal)

Leafy, sheltered site, close to town and the spectacular Trollstigen Mountain Road.

This attractive, popular site is situated in mature woodland beside the Rauma river 1 km. from the town centre, and close to Romsdalfjord and the breath-taking Trollstigen mountain road with its 11 giant hairpins that scale the sheer rock face. The reception, well stocked shop and cafeteria complex are on the opposite side of the road to the main touring area. The 213 grassy pitches are arranged informally between the many trees and shrubs, with 180 electric hook-ups (16A, long leads may be required). Two heated sanitary units provide British style WCs, washbasins (some in cubicles), controllable hot showers with divider and seat (tokens on payment), hairdryers, plus facilities for the disabled. Kitchens and laundries have facilities for cooking, dining, dishwashing, ironing plus token operated washing machines and dryers. The cafeteria, which doubles as a function room/TV lounge, serves breakfast and dinner and is open daily though times vary according to demand.

How to find it: Turn off Rv 1 by bridge south west of town, towards Trollstigen and Romsdalfjord. Site is signed.

General Details: Open 1 May - 15 September. Shop and cafeteria (15/5-30/8). Kitchen. Laundry. Minigolf. Bicycle hire. Canoe and boat hire. Fishing. Children's playground. Chemical disposal. Motorcaravan services. Chalets and cabins to rent.

Charges 1998: Per caravan or motorcaravan Nkr. 70; cyclist or m/cyclist and tent 50; extra tent 45; adult 15; child (4-12 yrs) 7.00; electricity 22. Credit cards accepted.

AR Discount
Less 10%

Reservations: Contact site. Address: 6300 Åndalsnes. Tel: 71.22.16.29. FAX: 71.22.62.16.

2450 Bjølstad Camping, Malmefjorden (Møre og Romsdal)

Delightful rural retreat on Malmefjorden, close to the Atlantic Highway.

This small site, which slopes down to Malmefjorden, a sheltered arm of Fraenfjorden, has space for just 40 touring units on grassy, fairly level, terraces either side of the tarmac central access road. A basic, clean sanitary unit provides British style WCs, one controllable hot shower divider and shelf per sex (token on payment), plus washbasins with dividers and one cubicle (for ladies). A small kitchen has two dishwashing sinks and a hot-plate, whilst the laundry has a washing machine and dryer. A delight for children is a large, old masted boat which provides hours of fun, plus the more conventional swings, etc. At the foot of the camp is a waterside barbecue site, shallow paddling area for children and a jetty. Both rowing and motorboats (with lifejackets) can be hired and one can swim or fish in the fjord. This is an ideal base for visiting Molde International Jazz Festival (mid-July), or the famous Varden viewpoint with its magnificent views over this 'Town of Roses', the fjord and 222 mountain peaks, both only 15 minutes drive. Further afield, the small town of Bud is famous for its WW2 German coastal fortress, or one can drive the fantastic and scenic Atlantic Highway (toll road).

How to find it: Turn off Rv 64 on northern edge of Malmefjorden village towards the village of Lindset (lane is oil bound gravel). Site is 1 km.

General Details: Open 20 May - 1 Oct (maybe earlier if pre-booked). Laundry. Kitchen. Children's playground. Boat hire. Fjord fishing and swimming. Cabins for rent. No dogs. Credit cards accepted.

Charges 1998: Per unit Nkr. 60 - 70; small tent 30; adult 10; child 5; electricity 15.

AR Discount
Less 5-10%

Reservations: Write to site. Address: 6445 Malmefjorden, More og Romsdal. Tel: 71.26.56.56 or 94.66.02.23.

2490 Skjerneset Camping, Averoy (Møre og Romsdal)

Extraordinary island site with fishery museum near Kristiansund.

The tiny island of Ekkilsøya lies off the larger island of Averoy and is reached via a side road and bridge (no toll) from the main Rv 64 just south of Bremsnes from where the ferry crosses to Kristiansund. Although the fishing industry here is not what it used to be it is still the dominant activity and Skjerneset Camping has been developed by the Otterlei family to give visitors an insight into this industry and its history. Most of the old `Klippfisk' warehouse is now a fascinating 'fisherimuseum' and aquarium, with the remainder housing the sanitary installations, 3 small 4-bed apartments, a kitchen, laundry and lounges. There is space for 20 caravans or motorcaravans on gravel hardstandings around a rocky bluff and along the harbour's rocky frontage and all have electricity connections (16A). A small grassy area for 10 tents is under pine trees in a hollow on the top of the bluff together with the children's swings and 5 fully equipped cabins. Sanitary facilities are heated but basic, unisex, and perhaps a little quirky in their layout, but they provide British WCs, washbasins in cubicles and controllable hot showers with divider and shelf. Free hot water throughout. The kitchen provides 2 full cookers plus a hot-plate and dishwashing sinks, and the small laundry has a sink and washing machine. All were free of charge. A new small sanitary unit with a motorcaravan service point is planned for the '98 season. The small reception kiosk also has small stocks of packet foods, crisps, ices, sweets, postcards etc. Other on-site amenities include motor or rowing boat hire, sea-fishing or sightseeing trips in the owner's new sea-going boat, and for non-anglers who want a fish supper, fresh fish are always available on site. *Please note: this is a working harbour with deep unfenced water very close to pitches.*

How to find it: Site is on the little island of Ekkilsøya which is reached via a side road running west from the main Rv 64 road, 1.5 km. south of Bremsnes.

General Details: Open all year. Kiosk. Kitchen. Laundry. TV. Boat hire. Fishing.

Charges 1997: Per unit Nkr. 90 (Less 20% outside 20/6-20/8); electricity 20.

Reservations: Write to site. Address: Ekkilsoya, 6553 Bremsnes, More og Romsdal. Tel: 71.51.18.94. FAX: 71.51.18.15.

2495 Vegset Camping, Snåsa (Nord-Trøndelag)

Pleasant site north of Snåsa, beside the E6 road.

Only 7 km. from Snåsa on the banks of Lake Snåsavatn, this site consists of 10 chalets and an extensive area for touring units, mainly on quite a slope. A new, well equipped sanitary block provides showers (Nkr. 5), plus a shower with toilet suitable for disabled people. There is a kitchen, TV room and a kiosk selling groceries. Snåsa is a centre for the South Lapp people who have their own boarding school, museum and information centre there. The Bergasen Nature Reservation is close to the village and is famous for its rare flora, especially orchids. The Gressamoen National Park is also near.

How to find it: Site is just off the E6 road, 7 km. from Snåsa.

General Details: Open Easter - 10 Oct. Kiosk. Kitchen. TV room. Swimming, fishing and boat hire.

Charges 1997: Per unit Nkr. 80.

Reservations: Contact site. Address: 7760 Snåsa. Tel: 74.15.29.50.

2485 Krokstrand Camping, nr Storforshei (Nordland)

Cosmopolitan and popular riverside site only 18 km. from the Arctic Circle.

Attractively arranged amongst the birch trees, with a fast flowing river and waterfall alongside, and views of snow covered mountains, this site is a popular resting place for all nationalities on the long trek to Nordkapp. There are 60 unmarked pitches and electrical connections (16A) for 20 units. The well maintained, spotlessly clean, small sanitary unit provides British style WCs, open washbasins and 2 controllable hot showers per sex, with curtain and seat (on payment). The laundry has a washing machine and dryer, and the small kitchen a double hot-plate and dishwashing sink. There is also a chemical toilet emptying facility and a conveniently located water tap and hose for motorcaravan tank filling. The small reception kiosk is only open for a short time mornings and evenings, but campers are invited to find a pitch and pay later. Directions in English are given to the owner's house (within walking distance) for emergencies. An excellently maintained and brightly painted children's playground includes a trampoline, and families can enjoy a game of minigolf on the equally well tended course. Being only 18 km. drive from the Arctic Circle with its Visitor Centre, this site is in an ideal location. The small village just outside the camp entrance has a hotel with restaurant, a souvenir shop, and those interested in WW2 history will find the neatly tended grave of a Russian soldier by the site gate. The nearest town for shopping is Mo-i-Rana (60 km).

How to find it: Entrance is off the E6 at Krokstrand village opposite the hotel, 18 km. south of Arctic Circle.

General Details: Open 1 June - 20 Sept. Kitchen. Laundry. Children's playground. Minigolf. Restaurant near.

Charges 1997: Per unit Nkr. 60; adult 10; child 5; extra tent/hiker's tent 40; electricity 20.

Reservations: Write to site. Address: Krokstrand, 8630 Storforshei. Tel: 75.16.60.74.

NORWAY

2475 Saltstraumen Camping, Saltstraumen (Nordland)

All weather site on `coastal route', close to the largest Maelstrom in the world.

The site is rather ordinary but it is conveniently located within walking distance of an outstanding phenomenon, the strongest tidal current in the world, where in the course of 6 hours between 33,800 and 82,700 billion gallons of water are pressed through a narrow strait, at a rate of about 20 knots. The effect is greatest at new or full moons, check tide tables to determine the best time to visit. The 60 touring pitches are mostly level gravel hardstandings in rows, with electricity (10A) available to all, but a few `softer' pitches are for tents. The heated sanitary facilities are basic but clean, and provide British style WCs, open washbasins and free hot showers. The latter are just shower heads with dividers between and communal changing, although in the ladies' there are some shower curtains. Kitchen with cookers, laundry with washing machine and dryer. Site is 33 km. from Bodø and 50 km. from Fauske.

How to find it: From the Rv 80 (Fauske -Bodø) turn south on to the Rv 17, site is 12 km. at Saltstraumen adjacent to the Statoil station.

General Details: Open all year. Kitchen. Laundry. TV room. Children's playground. Minigolf. Fishing. Chemical disposal. Motorcaravan services. Filling station adjacent with shop, hairdresser. Hotel and cafeteria nearby.

Charges 1997: Per caravan Nkr. 100; motorcaravan 85; tent 75; electricity 25. Visa cards accepted.

Reservations: Write to site. Address: Boks 85, 8056 Saltstraumen. Tel: 75.58.75.60. FAX: 75.58.75.40.

2465 Lyngvær Lofoten Bobilcamping, Lyngvær (Lofoten Islands)

Superbly positioned site by the sea on the Lofoten Islands.

This well laid out site, built in 91/92, has room for 200 units, half with access to electrical connections. The facilities are new, clean and good, although there are rather few of them. Showers, a little cramped, are on payment (Nkr. 10). There are extra unisex showers and toilets beside reception. A communal kitchen has cooking and washing up facilities and a large sitting area with satellite TV. There are several play areas and boat hire is available (rowing and motor boats, canoes and pedaloes). The site has its own salmon and sea trout fishing. It is a good area for walking, both by the sea and in the mountains.

How to find it: Site is signed from the ferry terminal.

General Details: Open 15 March - 31 Aug. Kitchen. TV lounge. Children's play areas. Boat hire. Fishing.

Charges 1997: Per unit Nkr. 80; electricity 20. Fifth night free.

Reservations: Write to site. Address: Postboks 30, 8310 Kabelvåg. Tel: 76.07.87.81.

2455 Ballangen Camping, Ballangen (Nordland)

Pleasant, lively site with small pool and waterslide, on the E6 outside of town.

This site is on the edge of a fjord with a small rocky beach, with direct access off the main E6 road. Reception shares space with the well stocked shop and takeaway (main season). The 150 marked pitches are mostly on sandy grass, with electricity (10/16A) to 120. There are a few hardstandings, also 50 rental cabins. The sanitary facilities are housed in an older style building, but the fittings are more modern and provide British style WCs, washbasins (some in cubicles), and controllable hot showers (on payment). The kitchen with dishwashing sinks, a full cooker, hot-plates and a covered seating area, plus a laundry are also in the same building. Facilities for the disabled, sauna and solarium are in a much older building which the owner intends to replace. TV room with tourist information, coffee and games machines, small outdoor pool and waterslide (charged), tennis, minigolf, children's playground, free fjord fishing and boat and bicycle hire. Supermarket in Ballangen (4 km.). An interesting excursion is to the nearby Martinstollen Mine where visitors are guided through the dimly lit Olav Shaft 500 m. into the mountain. Narvik with it's wartime connections and museums is 40 km.

How to find it: Access is off the E6, 4 km. north of Ballangen, 40 km. south of Narvik

General Details: Open all year. Shop. Takeaway. Kitchen. Laundry. Sauna and solarium. TV/games room. Swimming pool and waterslide. Tennis. Minigolf. Fishing. Boat and bicycle hire. Car wash. Cabins for rent.

Charges 1997: Per unit, incl. 4 persons Nkr. 100; electricity 20; small tent 80; m/cycle or cycle and tent 60. Credit cards accepted.

Reservations: Contact site. Address: 8540 Ballangen. Tel: 76.92.82.97. FAX: 76.92.81.50.

2445 Slettnes Fjordcamp, Oteren (Finnmark)

Useful stopover southeast of Tromso beside the E6 road.

Beside a narrow fjord and surrounded by snowy capped mountains, this is a large site mainly for permanent caravans but with room for 20 touring units. A very well kept site, there are neat flower beds. Sanitary facilities consist of two toilets for each sex, washbasins, etc. and three showers each, communal but with no charge and good hot water. A kitchen houses a sink unit, full size cooker and microwave.

How to find it: Site is beside the E6 road near Oteren.

Charges 1997: Per unit Nkr. 100.

Reservations: Contact site. Address: 9047 Oteren. Tel: 77.71.45.08.

2435 Solvang Camping, Alta (Finnmark)

Old-style site, with relaxed, welcoming atmosphere, on the Altafjord.

This restful little site is set well back from the main road, so there is no road noise. The site overlooks the tidal marshes of the Altafjord, which are home to a wide variety of bird-life, providing ornithologists with a grandstand view during the long summer evenings bathed by the Midnight Sun. The 30 pitches are on undulating grass amongst pine trees and shrubs, and are not marked, but there are 12 electric hook-ups (16A). The heated sanitary facilities are basic and in a fairly old building, but provide British style WCs, mostly open washbasins and free controllable hot showers, together with a kitchen containing two full cookers and dishwashing sinks, plus a small laundry with a washing machine and spin dryer. In its own little kiosk outside is the modern stainless steel chemical disposal point and outside a waste water drain which, with a little ingenuity, is possible to use for draining a motorcaravan tank. The site is run by a church mission organisation, consequently only limited funds are available for repairs and refurbishment. However, all facilities are clean and in good order (out of season, the site provides holidays for needy children). Of interest are the Alta Museum with ancient rock carvings, and Savco Canyon, with the controversial Alta Power Station and 100 m. dam at its upper end.

How to find it: Site is signed off the E6, 10 km. north of Alta.

General Details: Open 1 June - 10 Aug. Kitchen. Laundry. TV lounge. Football field. Children's playground. Cabins and rooms for rent. Chemical disposal.

Charges 1997: Per unit Nkr. 90; cyclist tent 70; electricity 30. Credit cards not accepted.

Reservations: Write to site. Address: Transfarelv, 9500 Alta. Tel: 78.43.04.77.

2425 Kirkeporten Camping, Skarsvåg, Nordkapp (Finnmark)

The most northerly campsite in the world (71° 06' 50").

This is a superb site with the most modern sanitary installations. In two under-floor heated buildings, linked by a covered timber walkway they provide British style WCs, open washbasins and free controllable hot showers, sauna, plus two family bathrooms, baby room, and an excellent unit for the disabled. A laundry and a kitchen with dining area complete the facilities. All have quality fittings and beautiful woodwork - the owner is a carpenter by profession. Considering the climate and the wild unspoilt location this has to be one of the best sites in Scandinavia. An added bonus is that reindeer come right into the site to graze. The 30 pitches, 22 with electricity (16A), are on grass or gravel hardstanding in natural `tundra' terrain beside a small lake, together with 10 rental cabins and 5 rooms. The reception/cafeteria at the entrance is open daily. Sea fishing and photographic trips by boat can be arranged and buses run 4 times a day to Honningsvåg or the Nordkapp Centre. Follow the marked footpath over the hillside behind the campsite, to photograph `Nordkapp' at midnight if the weather is favourable. We also advise you pack warm clothing, bedding and maybe propane for this location.

Note: Although overnighting at Nordkapp Centre is permitted, it is on the very exposed gravel car-park with no electric hook-ups or showers. 1997 prices: Car parking and Visitor Centre Nordkapp - Nkr. 175 per person. Single ferry fare (6 m. vehicle + 2 persons) Kåfjord-Honningsvåg 222 Nkr. Ferry to be replaced by a tunnel and bridge, due to open Nov 1997, but charge will be similar.

How to find it: On the island of Magerøya, from Honningsvåg take the E69 for 20 km. then fork right signed Skarsvåg. Site is on left after 3 km. just as you approach Skarsvåg.

General Details: Open 10 May - 10 Sept. Cafeteria. Kitchen. Laundry. Sauna. Motorcaravan services. Cabins and rooms for rent.

Charges 1997: Per unit Nkr. 110; person 20; small tent 80; electricity 20. Credit cards not accepted.

Reservations: Not usually necessary. Address: 9763 Skarsvåg, Nordkapp. Tel: 78.47.52.33. FAX: 78.47.52.47.

2415 Kautokeino Camping, Suohpatjávri, Kautokeino (Finnmark)

Newly developed, friendly, lakeside site, 8 km. south of Kautokeino.

The 30 pitches here are not marked and are generally on a firm sandy base, amongst low growing birch trees, with 20 electric hook-ups (10A). There are also 8 cabins and 7 motel rooms for rent and these are very attractively designed and furnished. Although the grass is trying to grow, the ground is frozen from Sept - May so it takes many years to establish. The sanitary building is modern, heated and well maintained, with 2 British style WCs, 2 open washbasins and 2 controllable hot showers (on payment) per sex. A small kitchen has a full cooker, dishwashing sinks and refrigerator, the laundry has washing machine, dryer and ironing facilities. Separate bathroom for disabled people and baby changing. The site rents canoes, boats and pedaloes. Free fishing in the lake. During the season the owner arranges an evening campfire around two Sami tents, with `lectures' about the Sami people. Good walks to special Sami sites, shops and other services in Kautokeino (8 km). Site is 35 km. north of the Finnish Border.

How to find it: Site is 8 km. south of Kautokeino on Rv 93 (do not confuse with another site of similar name).

General Details: Open 1 June - 30 Sept. Kitchen. Laundry. Chemical disposal. Football. Boat hire. Fishing.

Charges 1997: Per unit Nkr. 65-75; adult 10; child 5; hikers tent 45; electricity 25. Visa card accepted.

Reservations: Write to site. Address; Suohpatjávri, 9520 Kautokeino. Tel: 78.48.57.33. FAX: as phone.

NORWAY

2500 Trasavika Camping, Viggja, nr Orkanger (Sør Trøndelag)

Terraced site with glorious views and sandy beach, 40 km. from Trondheim.

On a headland jutting into the Trondheimfjord and some 40 km. from Trondheim, Trasavika occupies such an attractive site that the extra distance into town is bearable. The 65 pitches are on an open grassy field at the top of the site, or on a series of terraces below which run right down to the small sandy beach, and are easily accessed via a well designed gravel service road. There are 40 electricity connections (10A). To one side, on a wooded bluff at the top of the site, are 14 rental cabins and the neat, sanitary unit. Facilities include British style WCs, open washbasins and 2 controllable hot showers per sex (on payment). Hot water also on payment in the kitchen and laundry which have a hot-plate, dish and clothes washing sinks, washing machine and dryer. A new entrance has been constructed leading down to the reception complex which also houses the small shop, licensed café (20 June-end Aug), and a TV/sitting room. Other amenities on site include a jetty and boat hire, free fjord fishing, and a children's playground. Nobody travelling as far as mid-Norway would dream of not visiting the unusually interesting and attractive historic city of Trondheim, for long the capital of Norway.

How to find it: Site is on the edge of Viggja on the Rv 65 between Orkanger and Buvik, 17 km. from the E6 and 40 km. west of Trondheim.

General Details: Open 1 May - 30 Sept. Shop. Café. Kitchen. Laundry. TV/sitting room. Children's playground. Jetty and boat hire. Cabins and apartments for rent.

Charges 1997: Per caravan or motorcaravan Nkr. 100; tent 90; small tent 70; electricity 25. Credit cards accepted.

Reservations: Write to site. Address: 7354 Viggja, Sør Trondelag. Tel: 72.86.78.22.

2505 Magalaupe Camping, Oppdal (Sør Trøndelag)

Rural, good value, riverside site, close to Dovrefjell National Park.

Lying in a sheltered position with easy access from the E6, this site offers fairly simple facilities but a host of unusual activities in the surrounding area, including caving, canyoning, rafting, gold panning, mineral hunting, and musk oxen, reindeer and elk safaris. In winter the more adventurous can also go snow-mobiling or skiing in the high Dovrefjell National Park. The 70 unmarked and grassy touring pitches, 36 with electrical connections (10/16A), are in natural surroundings amongst birch trees and rocks on several different levels and served by gravel access roads. There are also 8 attractive and fully equipped cabins for rent. The small, but very clean, heated sanitary unit provides a British style WC, 3 washbasins (1 cubicle) and 2 hot showers (on payment) per sex. This is supplemented by 2 further WC/washbasin units in the building which also houses the reception and kiosk for ices, soft drinks, etc., the TV lounge, plus a bar open mid June - Aug. As the site rarely fills up, these simple facilities should be adequate at most times. Small kitchen with dishwashing facilities, hot-plate and freezer, plus a combined washing/drying machine. Supermarkets and other services can be found in Oppdal (11 km).

How to find it: Site is signed to the western side of the E6, 11 km. south of Oppdal.

General Details: Open all year. Kiosk. Bar (mid June - Aug). Kitchen. Laundry. Motorcaravan service point. Car wash. TV lounge. Fishing. Cabins for rent.

Charges 1997: Per unit incl. 4 persons and electricity Nkr. 90; small tent without electricity 50; extra person 10.

Reservations: Write to site. Address: Rute 5, 7340 Oppdal. Tel: 47.72.42.46.84.

2510 Håneset Camping, Roros (Sør Trøndelag)

Acceptable, high plateau site, close to the UNESCO World Heritage town of Roros.

At first sight Håneset Camping it is not promising, lying between the main road and the railway, and nor is the gritty sloping ground of the site very imaginatively landscaped - for grass, when it grows up here, is rather coarse and lumpy. However, as we soon discovered, it is the best equipped campsite in the town, and ideal to cope with the often cold, wet weather of this bleak 1,000m. high plateau. The 50 unmarked touring pitches all have access to electricity (10/16A), and most facilities are housed in the main complex building. These include reception, shop and cafeteria, a huge sitting/TV room and two well equipped kitchens which the owners, the Moen family, share fully with their guests, plus 9 rooms for rent. Heated sanitary installations provide three separate rooms for each sex with British WCs, open washbasins and controllable hot showers (on payment). A washing machine and two sinks are in one of the ladies' rooms. People flock from all over Europe to visit this remarkably well preserved mining town. For over 300 years it was one of Europe's leading copper mines, and during all that time it never suffered serious fire. As a result it occupies a special place on UNESCO's world heritage list for its unique concentration of historic wooden houses. The walk to the town takes around 20 minutes.

How to find it: Site is on the Rv 30 leading south from Roros to Os, 3 km. from Roros.

General Details: Open all year. Shop and cafeteria (mid June-August). Kitchen. Laundry. Children's playground. Chemical disposal. Cabins and rooms to let.

Charges 1997: Per caravan or motorcaravan Nkr. 110; tent 90; electricity 20.

Reservations: Write to site. Address: 7460 Roros, Sør Trondelag. Tel: 72.41.13.72. FAX: 72 41 06 01.

2515 Gjelten Bru Camping, Alvdal (Hedmark)

Cosy, village site in wooded riverside location, close to the small town of Alvdal.

Located just a few kilometres west of Alvdal, this peaceful little site with its traditional turf roof buildings, makes an excellent base from which to explore the area. The 48 touring pitches are on level neatly trimmed grass, served by gravel access roads, and with electricity (10A) to 37. Some pitches are in the open and others under tall pine trees along the river bank. The heated sanitary facilities are housed in two buildings. One unit was being refurbished, the other was newly constructed. These provide a good supply of British style WCs, a mix of conventional washbasins and stainless steel washing troughs, and controllable hot showers on payment. A separate unit has WC, basin, shower and handrails for disabled campers. Two small kitchens, one at each block, provide dishwashing facilities, hot-plates and an oven all free. Across the bridge on the other side of the river and main road, the site owners also operate the local, extremely well stocked mini-market and post office where you will also find the public telephone. The UNESCO World Heritage town of Roros is 75 km. to the northeast of this charming little site, and the Dovrefjell National Park is also within comfortable driving distance.

How to find it: On the Rv 29 at Gjelten 3.5 km. west of Alvdal. Turn over the river bridge opposite the village store and post office, and site is immediately on the right.

General Details: Open all year. Kitchen. Fishing. Supermarket near. Children's swings. Chemical disposal.

Charges 1997: Per unit Nkr. 95 - 100; electricity 15.

Reservations: Write to site. Address: 2560 Alvdal. Tel: 62.48.74.44.

2555 Lom Motell & Camping, Lom (Oppland)

Mountain resort site, 500 m. from town and Stave Church.

This small site provides pitches for 60 touring units on slightly sloping grass on either side of a modern motel only 500 m. from the centre of this famous town and its beautiful medieval wooden Stave Church. There are 52 electrical connections (10A). The single large heated sanitary unit provides a good supply of British style WCs, washbasins in cubicles, but only 2 hot showers per sex (on payment). A further free hot shower is available for those using the sauna/solarium (Nkr 30), or the very comprehensive, free gymnasium facilities, plus a unit for families, babies or the disabled. Small campers' kitchen with two dishwashing sinks with free hot water, and hot-plates for cooking (also free). A separate laundry room houses washing machines, dryers and sinks again with free hot water. Also on site is a ski preparation room, a children's playground, plus 16 cabins, 4 apartments and 8 motel rooms for rent. Reception shares space with the small shop, and the licensed motel cafeteria serves both dinners and breakfasts (times vary according to season and demand). Besides the lovely mountain views from the site and the attractions of Lom, the site is a good base from which to explore the mountains, take a trip to see the Briksdal Glacier or visit the Norwegian Mountain Museum and Fossheim Mineral Centre.

How to find it: Site is 500 m. from roundabout in centre of Lom, beside the Rv 55 towards Sogndal.

General Details: Open all year. Kiosk. Cafeteria. Kitchen. Laundry. Sauna and solarium. Gymnasium. Motorcaravan services. Children's playground. Ski preparation room. Cabins and motel rooms for rent.

Charges 1997: Per unit incl. 5 persons Nkr. 125; small motorcaravan + 2 persons 110; m/cycle and tent 90; bicycle and tent 70; electricity 25. Visa cards accepted.

Reservations: Write to site. Address: Postboks 88, 2686 Lom. Tel: 61.21.12.20. FAX: 61.12.12.23.

2545 Rustberg Hytteulerie & Camping, Øyer, nr Lillehammer (Oppland)

Traditional family site, convenient for visiting the 'Olympic area' of Norway.

Conveniently located beside the E6 and just 20 km. from Lillehammer, this attractive terraced site provides a comfortable base for exploring the area. Like all sites along this route it does suffer from road noise at times, but the site facilities and nearby attractions more than compensate for this. There are 90 pitches with 60 for touring units, most reasonably level and with some gravel hardstandings and 50 electrical connections (10A). Heated sanitary facilities provide British style WCs, washbasins (mostly in cubicles) and hot showers (on payment), plus two luxurious family bathrooms and a unit for the disabled each with WC, basin and shower. The newly rebuilt campers' kitchen and dining room provides facilities for dishwashing together with a microwave and double hob (all free). Separate laundry with sinks, washing machine, dryer and drying cupboard. Good children's playground, an unusual billiard golf game, and a small open air swimming pool with water-slide open June-Aug. (weather permitting). The small reception building also houses a kiosk stocking basic foods, beer, ices, sweets, postcards and stamps. The Maihaugen Folkmuseum and Lillehammer town are 20 km, Hunderfossen (5 km.) has the Norwegian Road Museum and the more adventurous can ride the Olympic bobsleigh track.

How to find it: Site is well signed from the E6, 20 km. north of Lillehammer.

General Details: Open all year. Kiosk. Kitchen. Laundry. Swimming pool and water-slide. Billiard golf. Children's playground. Motorcaravan services.

Charges 1997: Per unit Nkr. 125; small tent 110; electricity 20. Visa cards accepted.

Reservations: Write to site. Address: 2636 Øyer. Tel: 61.27.81.84. FAX: 61.27.87.05.

NORWAY

2550 Strandefjord Camping, Leira, nr Fagernes, Valdres (Oppland)

Mature, wooded, lakeside site in the Valdres district just outside Fagernes.

Fagernes lies on the north shore of an impressive glacial lake - Strandefjorden, and just 4 km. to the southeast at Leira, on a corner of this lake, is Strandefjord Camping. This undulating, woodland site behind a light industrial estate, has 70 touring pitches, but can take up to 250 units in scattered clearings amongst the trees and beside the lake. Many pitches are only suitable for tents and only 75 have electricity (10A). Also 30 seasonal units, 31 cabins and rooms on site. The main heated, but rather basic, sanitary unit could be hard pressed in high season. It has British WCs, washbasins (some in cubicles), but only 2 hot showers per sex (on payment). Separate rooms house a small kitchen with dishwashing and cooking facilities (free of charge), and a laundry. More showers and WC's can be found together with saunas (which are equipped with TV!) under the main site complex which also houses reception, a licensed restaurant, and conference room. Other on-site facilities include a fitness track, tennis and beach volleyball courts, children's play areas, minigolf, boat hire. Fishing and swimming in the lake are possible. It is a 2 minute walk to the village mini-market.

How to find it: Turn off the E16 Oslo road onto the Rv 51, at Leira village 4 km. east of Fagernes. The site entrance is within 50m.

General Details: Open all year. Restaurant (June-Aug). Laundry. Kitchen. Sauna. Children's play areas. Conference room. Lake swimming. Fitness track. Tennis. Beach volleyball. Minigolf. Boat hire. Chemical disposal.

Charges 1997: Caravan or motorcaravan Nkr. 120; tent and car 100; cycle or m/cycle and tent 85; electricity 25. Credit cards accepted.

Reservations: Write to site. Address: 2920 Leira. Tel: 61.36.23.65. FAX: 61.36.24.80.

2570 Fossheim Hytte and Camping, nr Gol, Hallingdal (Buskerud)

Idyllic touring site beside the Hallingdal river on the 'Adventure Road'.

Centred on the country town of Gol is one of Norway's favourite camping areas, Hallingdal. This small touring site lies just 4 km. west of the town, on the river bank, and is shaded by elegant tall birch trees. Despite being just below the main road and with a railway in the trees on the opposite side of the river, surprisingly little noise penetrates this idyllic setting. There are 50 grassy touring pitches, with electricity (10/16A) available to 40, and most overlook the river. In addition there are 13 cabins and 4 rooms for rent, but no static caravans are permitted. The site is well equipped, with a modern heated sanitary unit providing British style WCs, washbasins (some in cubicles), free controllable hot showers with dividers and seats, a separate unit for disabled people and a sauna. Small kitchen and laundry rooms provide cramped facilities for dishwashing and cooking (free of charge), plus sinks for clothes washing and a washing machine and dryer. Other facilities include a large, very comfortable TV lounge, a children's play area, canoe hire, and trout fishing with a specially constructed wooden walkway and platform for disabled anglers. A small shop is open in season with bread to order. (Note: there is another site of similar name in the adjoining Hemsedal).

How to find it: Site is 4 km. west of Gol on route Rv 7 leading to Geilo.

General Details: Open all year. Shop (1/6-31/8). TV lounge. Sauna. Children's play area. Bicycle hire. Trout fishing and canoeing. Laundry. Kitchen. Chemical disposal. Motorcaravan services. Cabins and rooms for rent.

Charges 1998: Per unit incl. 2 persons Nkr. 95 - 125; incl. 3 persons 105 - 130; (peak season is 21/6-15/8); electricity 25. Credit cards accepted.

Reservations: Write to site. Address: 3550 Gol. Tel: 32.07.33.16. FAX: 32.07.33.52.

2590 Camping Sandviken, Tinnsjo (Telemark)

Remote, lakeside site, in scenic location, suitable for exploring Hardangervidda.

With its own shingle beach, at the head of Tinnsjo Lake, Camping Sandviken provides 130 grassy, mostly level, pitches. In addition to the 30 seasonal units and 13 cabins, there are 80 numbered tourist pitches with electricity (5A), plus an area for tents, under trees along the waterfront. The tidy heated sanitary unit has British WCs, washbasins (some in cubicles), hot showers with dividers and seats (on payment), a sauna, solarium and a dual purpose disabled/family bathroom with ramped access and baby changing mat. Kitchen and laundry rooms provide facilities for cooking, dish and clothes washing (hot water on payment). The office/reception kiosk also sells sweets, soft drinks, ices etc. and a baker calls daily in July. A 1 km. stroll takes you to the tiny village of Tinn Austbygde which has a mini-market, bakery, café, bank, garage and post office. On-site leisure facilities include minigolf, TV and games rooms, a children's play area, watersports and fishing.

How to find it: Easiest access is via the Rv 37 from Gransherad along the western side of the lake.

General Details: Open all year. Kiosk (May-15 Sept). Kitchen. Laundry. Sauna. Solarium. Minigolf. Children's playground. Fishing. Boat hire. TV and games room. Motorcaravan service point. Chemical disposal. Cabins for rent.

Charges 1997: Per person Nkr. 15; child (4-18 yrs) 10; caravan or motorcaravan 70 - 85, acc. to season; tent 60 - 75; m/cycle 40 - 50; electricity 20. 'Quickstop' (8 pm-9 am) 65 - 80.

Reservations: Write to site. Address: 3650 Tinn Austbygd. Tel: 35.09.81.73.

2600 Rysstad Feriesenter, Setesdal (Aust-Agder)

High quality site in spectacular setting within easy reach of Stavanger and Kristiansand.

Setesdal is on the upper reaches of the Otra river which runs north from the southern port of Kristiansand right up to the southern slopes of Hardangervidda. It offers a wide range of scenery, often spectacular where the valley cuts through high, steep sided mountains. It is an area famous for its colourful mining history (silver) and for its vibrant art (especially music) and folklore. Thanks to a major new hydro-electric project, a spectacular mountain road has now opened linking Setesdal with Sirdal to the west, bringing Setesdal within easy and pleasant driving range of Stavanger. At the junction of this new road and Setesdal is the small village of Rysstad, named after the family who have developed camping in this area. Trygve Rysstad now runs the Rysstad Feriesenter, founded by his father in the '50s. The site occupies a wide tract of woodland between the road and the river towards which it shelves gently, affording a splendid view of the valley and the towering mountains opposite. The site is in effect divided into two sections; one is divided by trees and hedges into numbered pitches, some occupied by chalets to hire, the other is an adjacent open field. Good modern sanitary facilities are found under the reception block with showers on payment, washbasins in cubicles, washing up sinks and cooker. There is an attractive area on the river's edge for barbecues and entertainment with an arena type setting. The little village is within walking distance.

How to find it: Site is about 1 km. south of the junction between route 39 (from Kristiansand) and the newly extended route 45 (from Stravanger).

General Details: Open 1 May - 1 Oct. Electrical connections (20). Children's play area and amusement hut. Sports field. Fishing, swimming and boating (boats for hire). Fitness track. Bicycle hire. TV room. Laundry facilities with washing machine. Campers' kitchen. Centre includes café, shop, bank, garage and restaurant.

Charges 1997: Per person Nkr. 10; caravan or tent 100; hiker's tent 35; electricity 25. Credit cards accepted.

Reservations: Write to site. Address: Midt i Setesdal, 4692 Rysstad. Tel: 37.93.61.30. FAX: 37.93.63.45.

2610 Neset Camping, Byglandsfjord (Aust-Agder)

Modern site by lake in Otra valley, good for activity holidays in south Norway.

On a semi-promontory on the shores of the 40 km. long Byglandsfjord, Neset is a good centre for activities or as a stop en route north from the ferry port of Kristiansand (from Denmark). Byglandsfjord offers good fishing (mainly trout) and the area has marked trails for cycling, riding or walking in an area famous for its minerals. The site has a stone workshop where your finds can be identified and courses in stone polishing are organised. Climbing, rafting and canoe courses (including trips to see beavers) are organised and there are bicycles, canoes and pedaloes for hire. Ski-ing is possible in the area in winter, the site being open all year. Neset is on well kept grassy meadows by the lake shore with the water on three sides and the road on the fourth. It provides 180 unmarked pitches, most with electricity. The main building houses reception, a small shop and a restaurant with fine views over the water. Three modern sanitary blocks can be heated, two with comfortable hot showers on payment, washing up facilities (metered hot water) and a kitchen. Chalets and three caravans to hire. Barbecue area and children's play equipment around the site. This is a well run, friendly site where one could spend an active few days.

How to find it: Site is on route 39, 2½ km. north of the town of Byglandsfjord on the eastern shores of the lake.

General Details: Open all year. Restaurant. Shop. Kitchen. Children's playground. Lake swimming, boating and fishing. Bicycle, canoe and pedalo hire. Courses in stone polishing. Climbing, rafting and canoeing courses.

Charges guide: Per unit Nkr. 105; tent and m/cycle 70; adult 10; child (5-12 yrs) 5; electricity 20.

Reservations: Write to site (also for details of courses). Address: 4680 Byglandsfjord. Tel: 37.93.42.55.

2612 Holt Camping, Tvedestrand (Aust-Agder)

Useful little site on outskirts of popular small Norwegian resort.

Tvedestrand is an attractive small resort with a pretty harbour, which is very popular with the Norwegians for their own holidays. Holt Camping is quite pleasantly situated beside the main E18 road, some 3 km. from the town - there is a little noise from the road during the day but we were not disturbed when staying overnight. The campsite is part level, part sloping grassland and about half of the pitches have 16A electrical connections. There are the usual cabins for hire. The single small sanitary block has excellent, well maintained facilities including hot showers on payment (1 per sex), washbasins (H&C) and provision for dishwashing and laundry (washing machine and dryer). Serving both the touring pitches and the cabins, the facilities may well be under pressure during busy times. A shop and café are immediately outside the site. This site could be very useful for those seeking a break in a part of Norway frequented more by the Norwegians themselves than by visitors from abroad.

How to find it: Site is beside the main E18 coast road (which actually bypasses the town), about 1 km. south of the turn off to the town itself.

General Details: Open 1 June - 31 Aug (huts all year). Shop/café outside. Laundry facilities. Children's play area.

Charges guide: Per unit incl. 2 persons and electricity Nkr. 100.00, without electricity 80.00.

Reservations: Contact site. Address: 4900 Tvedestrand. Tel: 37.16.02.65.

NORWAY

2615 Olberg Camping, Trøgstad (Østfold)

Peaceful, village farm site, close to Lake Øyeren within easy reach of Oslo.

A newly developed, delightful small site, Olberg Camping is located on neatly tended grassy meadow with newly planted trees and shrubs. There are 35 large, level pitches and electricity connections (10A) are available for 12 units. The excellent heated sanitary facilities are housed in a purpose built unit, created in the end of a magnificent large, modern barn and have a ramp for wheelchair access. They provide controllable hot showers, British style WCs and washbasins, with one bathroom for families or the disabled. Laundry and dishwashing share the same facilities at present, with a sink, washing machine and ironing board provided. A small kitchenette has a full size cooker and food preparation area. Free hot water throughout. The reception building also houses a small gallery with paintings, glasswork and other crafts. A short drive down the adjacent lane takes you to the beach on Lake Øyeren, and there are many woodland walks in the surrounding area. Oslo is only 30 km, the old church and museum at Trøgstad, and Båstad church are all worth visiting. Bicycles can be hired and the local tennis court is also available. Children will love the ducks, rabbits, cats, sheep and hens, as well as the small playground with its sand-pit, trampoline, swings and climbers, but please bear in mind that this is a working farm, with the attendant potential dangers for small children.

How to find it: Site is signed on Rv 22, 20 km. north of Mysen on the southern edge of Båstad village.

General Details: Open all year. Kiosk. Craft gallery. Laundry and cooking facilities. Children's playground. Bicycle hire. Tennis and riding nearby. Cabins for rent.

Charges 1997: Per unit incl. 2 adults Nkr. 110; extra adult 10; extra child 5; electricity 20.

Reservations: Write to site. Address: 1860 Trøgstad. Tel: 47.69.82.86.10. FAX: 47.69.82.85.55.

The Good ArctiCamps Guide

Very few British campers are to be seen in North Norway, beyond the Arctic Circle. Except for a few enthusiasts with several weeks to spare, it is too far to drive. Yet it has much to offer.

The best way to get to North Norway is to take advantage of the special promotional fares offered by Braathens via Bergen or Oslo and then travel on by road or by ferry from Trondheim or Bodo. Car hire in North Norway is hideously expensive. However, there is an alternative: public transport. To the annoyance of taxpayers in South Norway the Norwegian government pours subsidy into North Norway and much of this goes into a remarkable network of transport services by ferry, coach and bus. These services are operated with modern vehicles to regular published timetables and all carefully interconnect. Full details are provided in a comprehensive timetable available from the Norway Tourist Board in London. This includes the amazing Hurtigruten - the 100 year old coastal 'steamer' - which links all the main coastal towns on a daily basis in each direction and which can be used for hopping from town to town starting from Bergen. Backpackers use their youth rail passes to travel by train from Oslo or Stockholm to the Arctic rail gateways of Bodo and Narvik and then explore North Norway by bicycle or public transport. However, for those who are not into lightweight camping there are two forms of camping which are unique to the Arctic and which require virtually no equipment whatsoever: rorbu camping and sjohus camping.

Arctic Norway happens to be the world's most important cod fishing coast. Every spring thousands of fishing folk pour into the coastal towns and villages to catch and process cod. Over several centuries two forms of accommodation have developed to serve this massive migration; small huts on the waterfront, like boathouses, for the fishing crew, known as rorbu, and large sheds on the quayside for the workers in the fishery, known as sjohus (sea house). The rorbu traditionally has only one or two bunk-bedrooms, plus sitting room, kitchen and washroom. The sjohus usually has three floors with cod processing on the ground floor, ample public rooms on the second floor and bunk-bedrooms on the second and third floors. In effect the rorbu is a fisherman's flat while the sjohus is a fishery hostel. Over the past twenty years, the rorbu and sjohus have been adapted for use by campers during the summer when the cod have fled elsewhere. Most are spartan, offering what might be described as bunk-house accommodation. However, some conversions (and modern versions) are in the de luxe category and charge over £100 per room per night. The normal charges range between £10 and £20 per person per night.

Although this might seem expensive by most camping standards it is very cheap by Norwegian standards and it does provide a form of camping which is highly appropriate to Arctic Norway. As a result the rorbu and sjohus tend to be heavily booked by Scandinavian visitors during the peak holiday month of July but in the months on either side of July there is usually plenty of available space (look for the sign 'ledig' for vacancy) and off-season bargains are often on offer.

The Good ArctiCamps Guide (continued)

For the first time camper to this area we recommend three basic options: the immediate area around Tromsø; the neighbouring island of Senja; and the offshore islands of Lofoten. These offer convenient local transport; a wide range of rorbu and sjohus accommodation; and - last but not least - a fascinating landscape which combines one of the world's most spectacular coastal mountain ranges with a thriving and picturesque fishing and sea faring community.

Tromsø Environs There is one rather unexciting conventional campsite on the outskirts of Tromsø. If an overnight stay in the town is needed, we would recommend the central Skipperhuset, the last remaining guest house for sea captains. There is a large conventional site with a spectacular view across the fjord about 15 miles north of Tromsø; this site, **Skittnelv**, has a range of small plank huts for hire by the night. About 20 miles south of Tromsø there is a most unconventional site, **Straumhella**, where rooms are available in an outdoor museum of part-restored historic rural buildings, again in a spectacular location overlooking the turbulent sound, but to get the feel of authentic rorbu and sjohus camping one should venture forth by local Tromsbuss and ferry to either of two small islands, 35 miles north of Tromsø, **Sandoy** and **Vannoy**, each of which has one traditional fishery converted into simple camping facilities.

Senja Easily reached either by Hurtigruten or by the faster and more frequent express ferry, Senja can be explored by bus. Scattered around the island, mostly on the wilder western shore, are almost a dozen rorbu/sjohus campsites. The tiny islet of Husoy, on the northern tip of Senja, has a particularly enchanting sjohus, famed for its fresh fish cafe. Expensive, but worth a visit just to witness the location, is Hamn, an isolated fishery now being transformed into a sjohus resort. Other good centres for Arcticamping are Mefjordvaer, Gryllerfjord and Torsken, with Hamn all on the north-west coast.

Lofoten Separated from the mainland by the wide (and often wild) Vestfjord, the Lofoten group of islands can be reached easily by air or ferry from Tromsø, Senja or Bodo, or by road via the neighbouring Vesteralen island group. Even more dramatic than Senja, the jagged mountain backbone - long known to sailors as the Lofoten Wall - provides what must be one of the world's most spectacular camping scenes. Hugging the protected eastern shore is a series of fishing villages, where the fishing industry is still alive and well, and which offer several score sites providing rorbu and sjohus accommodation. See our selected site, no. 2465, on page246. We were particularly impressed by the following (going down the coast from northeast to southwest):

Lofoten Rorbuferies at Kabelvag (only a few miles from the island capital of Svolvaer);
Henningsvaer Rorbuer and Giavers Sjohus at Henningsvaer;
Nusfjord Rorbu at the UNESCO - recognised village of Nusfjord;
The abundant choice of rorbu/sjohus accommodation at the picturesque adjacent villages of Reine and Hamnoy (among the best is Captain Nyboen's little establishment);
The youth hostels (Vandrerhjem) in Stamsund and Å, both in sjohus and both welcoming adults (although now both so popular among backpackers that many visitors have to be turned away).

There are also several good conventional campsites on Lofoten, one of which is outstanding both for its location and its management (its toilets are serviced three times a day). So impressive is the view from this site, **Fredvang**, that people travel from elsewhere in Lofoten just to stand and stare. The owners have installed several cabins for hire.

Information There are three levels for provision of tourist information. At the national level the Norway Tourist Board (NORTRA) has offices in Britain at Charles House, Lower Regent Street, London SW1Y 4LR. At the regional level - corresponding to counties - Nordland Reiseliv, Storgaten 4A, PO Box 434, N-8001 Bodo, includes Lofoten in its territory; Troms Reiser, Storgaten 63, PO Box 1077, N 9001 Tromsø covers Tromsø, the surrounding area and Senja; and Finnmark Opplevelser, PO Box 1223, N-9501 Alta, covers the area to the north of Troms, including North Cape. Each of the three areas highlighted in this report has its own local tourist board and these can usually provide material of a much more detailed nature, including local bus timetables, large-scale local maps and accommodation guides; these are: Tromsø Arrangements, 61/63/3 Storgaten, PO Box 312, N-9001 Tromsø; Senja Tour, Radhusveien 1, PO Box 326, N-9301 Finnsnes; and Destination Lofoten, PO Box 210, N-8301 Svolvaer.

The sites in NORWAY featured in this guide are shown on the SCANDINAVIA map on page 377

POLAND

The first Polish state was established about the year 1,000 and since that time has been subjected to invasions from its German, Russian and Austrian neighbours. The course of time has seen its borders reduce and expand and produced a race of rugged fighters, fierce patriots and a deeply religious nation. It was in the forefront in leading the revolt against Soviet influence with strikes and riots in the Gdansk shipyards which brought about the disintegration of communism in Eastern Europe in 1989. Now it struggles to come to terms with a free-market economy which encourages tourism to share its natural delights and historic associations. Although much of the country is flat and parts having some of the worst environment polluting industrial centres in Europe, the gentle beaches of the Baltic, the lake district in the northeast and the mountain region in the southeast have much to offer to tourists who are looking for something a little different. For further information contact:

Poland National Tourist Office, Reno House, 310-312 Regent St, London WlR 5AJ

Tel: 0171 580 8811

Population
38,736,000 (1995); density 121 p/sq km.

Capital
Warsaw (Warszawa)

Climate
Cold winters, moderate summers.

Language
Polish. Some Russian, German and English.

Telephone
The code for Poland is 0048.

Time
GMT + 1 hour. BST + 1 hour in summer.

Currency
Zloty (Zl) divided into 100 groszy (gr). The New Zloty was introduced in 1995 (10,000 old Zl = 1 new Zl). The Old Zl was not valid after 1996. The import/export of Zl is prohibited.

Banks
Hours are Mon-Fri 0800 to 1800. Sat 0800 to 1400. Private banks 'Kantor' 0900 to 1800 and frontier change offices will only exchange notes. Credit cards are gradually being introduced.

Public Holidays
New Year; Easter Mon; Labour Day; Constitution Day, 3 May; Corpus Christi; Assumption, 15 Aug; All Saints, 1 Nov; Independence Day, 11 Nov; Christmas, 25, 26 Dec.

Shops
Open 1000 to 1800 with some food shops from 0600 to mid afternoon.

Motoring
Wide main roads throughout. Mainly local numbers with increasing use of E numbers. Road surfaces very poor in parts, particularly in large towns often with stretches of uneven cobbles. More than 0.2% alcohol in blood illegal.
Fuel: There are frequent filling stations - diesel 'NO' or 'O'. There are few motorways.
Speed limits: In built-up areas 37 mph (60 kph), other roads 56 mph (90 kph), motorways 68 mph (110 kph). Caravans are limited to 44 mph (70 kph) outside built up areas.
Parking: In towns, only park in secure guarded parks.

Overnighting
Not advised outside organised camps and forbidden on sand dunes at the coast and in national parks (except on an organised campsite).

Useful Addresses
Polski Zwiazek Motorowy (PZM), FIA & AIT, 66 Kazimierzowska Street, Pl-02518 Warszawa. Tel: 22 499 361 or 212. Office hours Mon-Fri 0745-1545. Touring Office: Autotour ssrl, 85 Solec Street, 00950 Warszawa. Tel: 22 498 449. Office hours Mon-Fri 0800-1600.

301 Camping Lesny Nr. 52, Zielona Góra

Pleasant, quiet campsite on edge of town.

The Silesian town of Zielona Gora largely escaped damage during the war and, although without any notable sights, it has a variety of architectural styles, a population of 100,000 and has become the centre of the textile industry. The very pleasant campsite is 5 km. from the centre of town at the rear of the rather drab looking Hotel Lesny and one books in at the hotel reception which is open 24 hours. With tall trees on two sides of the square site and a small area for tents under the pines, it is a quiet site, ideal for a night stop in transit or for a longer stay if wishing to explore the southwest part of Poland. The hotel occupies one side of the camp with direct access to the 24 hour restaurant. The 200 flat tourist pitches are grass on sand between concrete access roads. They are not marked out although some are numbered and where you park is determined by electric connection boxes which have points for 4 units. The single, very good quality sanitary block is in the centre of the site. It has British WCs and hot water in washbasins, sinks and showers. There is no shop but these can be found about 10 mins walk away or in the town, together with sports facilities in the nearby stadium. With good security and surrounded by a wire fence, the gate is kept locked with keys being provided when one books in at reception.

How to find it: Site is 5 km. north from town centre off no. 3/E65 road towards Sulechow, near the stadium.

General Details: Open May - October. 14,000 sq.m. Restaurant in hotel (24 hrs). Washing machine. Play area.

Charges guide: Per person Zlts 5.00; car 2.00; caravan 5.00; motorcaravan 7.00; tent 5.00; electricity 5.00.

Reservations: Write to site. Address: 65 454 Zielona Góra, ul. Sulechowska 39. Tel: 068 254446 or 253636. FAX: 068 2704 29.

303 Motel-Camping International Nr. 111, Poznan

Popular quiet site in forest near lake.

Poznan is about half-way between Berlin and Warsaw and makes a convenient stop when travelling between these cities or on the way to the Baltic. Founded in the 9th century, this elegant city, centre of culture and learning, has grown over the centuries and is now home to some 600,000 souls and important today for its Annual International Trade Fair. The Old Market Square with its beautiful Renaissance Town Hall is a great tourist attraction. Camp Nr 111 is nicely situated on the northwest outskirts of the town in a birch and pine forest near Lake Strzeszynskie, which is a popular watersports centre. The oblong site, under tall trees, has a neat, tidy air and pitches of varying sizes are grass on sand amidst the holiday bungalows. Some pitches would be difficult for very large caravans to manoeuvre but twin concrete tracks are provided to give hardstanding. There is a separate area for tents. The brick and tile sanitary block near entrance is old but clean with British WCs and hot water in washbasins, sinks and (small) showers. A restaurant with separate bar operates June to September and there is another by the lake with a small shop for basic food supplies in high season. Apart from watersports, where a lifeguard is on duty during high season, clay pigeon shooting is also available at this time. Other local attractions include walking. Dutch groups rally here and English is spoken at reception.

How to find it: From Poznan centre, follow road 2/E30 towards Szczecin and then after 7 km. camp signs.

General Details: Open 1 May - 15 October. 30,000 sq.m. Restaurant. Bar. Family kitchen. Chemical disposal. Satellite TV. Swimming and watersports in nearby lake. Bungalows for hire. Motel near.

Charges guide: Per person Zlts. 2.35; tent 3.21 - 5.35; caravan 5.89 - 8.03; car 4.28; motorcaravan 14.98; electricity 6.72. Less 20% discount April/May and Sept/Oct.

Reservations: Write to site. Address: 60 480 Poznan, ul. Koszalinska. Tel: 061 483129. FAX: as phone.

305 Camping Tramp Nr. 33, Torun

Pleasant transit camp near river bridge.

Like so many Polish towns, Torun, once a Hanseatic trading centre, has a long, interesting and troubled history. Famous as the birth place of Copernicus, it is today a prosperous university city on the wide River Wisga with cultural and architectural interests. Camping Tramp has a pleasant appearance and lies in a basin below the level of the roads which run on both sides of the site. A variety of trees cover about half the camp where pitches with electricity mingle with holiday bungalows, with the other half being on an open meadow. Places, reached from hard access roads, are neither marked nor numbered but the position of electric boxes define where to go. The well built central sanitary block is tiled with British WCs and hot water in sinks, washbasins and showers. Like most Polish camps, showers are open (no curtains or doors) and lack dressing space. In high season a small bar/shop provides basic supplies with shops and restaurants 2 km. away in the town. The site is very well lit at night. The main E75 runs along one side of the camp just before a busy junction and river bridge resulting in continuous traffic noise although we did not find this too intrusive. Whilst we would not recommend this as a `holiday' base, it makes a good night stop when travelling from between Germany and the Baltic coast.

How to find it: Site is on the south side of the main river bridge.

General Details: Open 1 June - 30 October. 26,000 sq.m. Small shop/snack bar.

Charges guide: Per person Zlts. 4.00; caravan 8.00; tent 4.50 - 5.00; electricity 6.00.

Reservations: Write to site. Address: Kazimierz Lubnav, 87 111 Torun, ul. Kujawska 14.

307 Camping Lesny Nr. 21, Leba

Barely acceptable site in popular Baltic resort.

Situated at the mouth of a small river with a marina, and just north of the village of Leba, Camping Lesny is one of three which are about 500 m. from the sea and 200 m. from the village. Pleasantly situated in a quiet location with a number of mature trees, there is room for 200 units on the open meadow with pitches which are neither marked nor numbered, of grass on sand which could result in haphazard pitching when the camp is full. The ground is uneven in places. Two identical sanitary blocks are rather old and, as they are not fully enclosed, rather draughty. The facilities - British WCs and hot water in sinks, washbasins and showers - are very basic and not as good as we would expect for an Alan Rogers' site, but are just about acceptable. As with so many camps in former Warsaw Pact countries, showers have no dressing space. However, many caravanners prefer to use their own provision and might like to do so here. A small bar/shop with basics in high season, with shops and restaurant in village.

How to find it: From road no. 6/E28 Koszalin-Wejherowo, turn north on the 214 at Lebork to Leba. Follow signs to camps on left on main street and continue to site.

General Details: Open 1 May - 30 Sept. 25,000 sq.m. Small bar/shop (15/6-1/9). Play area. Volleyball. Football. Table tennis. Washing machine. Community room with TV and cooking facilities.

Charges guide: Per person Zlts. 6.50; car 4.00; tent 3.00 - 4.00; caravan 10.00; motorcaravan 8.00; electricity 5.00; local tax: adult 0.60, child 0.30.

Reservations: Write to site in Polish ....! Address: 34 360 Leba, ul. Turystyczna 3. Tel: 059 663180.

POLAND

309 Mister Camping Nr. 19, Sopot, nr Gdynia

Good site for visiting the Baltic coast mid-way between Gdansk and Gdynia.

Sopot is a popular seaside resort on the Golf of Gdansk with a sandy beach, promenade and pier against a background of wooded hills. There are many attractions nearby including 'Opera-in-the-Woods' with 5,000 seats, an annual pop concert and other centres of historic interest. Camp 19 is set back from the beach and, by Polish standards, is a large site with 400 tourist pitches, some of which are back to back on either side of concrete access roads, with others in open meadows. Places are numbered but not marked out, of grass on sand and 300 pitches have an electrical supply. During our early season visit the grass was well mown and the camp very neat and tidy. There are many tall trees around the camp although not much shade in camping areas. There are four sanitary provisions, two in the ground floors of adjacent hotels and two free standing blocks. Although these are old, they are clean and acceptable with British WCs and hot water in sinks, washbasins and small showers which have curtains but no dressing space. There is a small snack bar/restaurant in high season and the Shell garage near the camp entrance has a good shop for basic food supplies. Dutch clubs rally here and the whole camp has a pleasant quiet atmosphere, although there is some road noise in the part near the entrance.

How to find it: Site is 2 km. north of Sopot on main road behind Shell garage.

General Details: Open 1 May - 30 Sept. 40,000 sq.m. Bar/restaurant, another at 50 m; Beach 300 m. Volleyball. Play area 300 m. Washing machine.

Charges guide: Per unit incl. 2 adults + 1 child, with electricity Zlts. 31.50 - 33.00.

Reservations: Write to camp in German. Address: 81 718 Sopot, ul. Zamkowa Gora. Tel: 058/518011.

311 Camping Stegna Nr. 180, Stegna, nr Gdansk

Wooded, hilly site on Baltic Sea.

With so much of Poland being very flat, it is surprising to find wooded hills so near the sea. Stegna is about 25 km. east of Gdansk in pleasant countryside and camp 180 is right by a sandy beach. The presence of a restaurant and kiosks at the entrance and the beach access suggest that it attracts many day visitors in summer. However, the beach stretches a long way so it should not become overcrowded. The very pleasant site has 100 terraced pitches, all with 10A electricity, on slopes under tall pines within sight and sound of the sea shore. Some of these are rather small depending on the disposition of the trees. The camp is rather let down by the state of the sanitary block. The WC sections are excellent but the parts with washbasins and showers are very basic. However, there are three good showers at the end of the block which are kept locked with key available at reception. The site would suit those looking for a beach holiday or a respite from touring, particularly if you have your own washing facilities.

How to find it: From the no. 7/E77 Gdansk - Elbag road take the 502 at Nowy Dwor signed 'Stegna' to Stegna, turn right to enter village and then left at church signed 'Stegna Port' with camp sign.

General Details: Open 1 May - 15 Sept. 46,000 sq.m. Washing machine.

Charges guide: Per person Zlts. 6.00; child 4.50; tent 3.50 - 6.50; caravan 5.50 - 7.50; motorcaravan 10.00; awning 4.50 - 5.50; car 4.00 - 6.00; m/cycle 3.50; electricity 4.50; local tax: adult 0.50, child 0.25.

Reservations: Write to camp. Address 82 103 Stegna, ul. Morska 15. Tel: 055/478284.

313 Camping Kretowiny Nr. 247, Kretowiny, nr Morag

Excellent site on western edge of Mazurian Lake District.

Mazuria, 'land of a thousand lakes', is a very popular holiday region in the northeast corner of Poland. A sparsely populated area of thick forests, it attracts walkers, naturalists, watersports enthusiasts and campers. This, combined with much historical interest, makes it a good location for those who seek rest and relaxation away from noise and the trappings of modern tourism. Camping Kretowiny is a well organised site and unusual in Poland in having individual pitches divided by hedges, rather than the overcrowding that can occur where no places are clearly defined. Scenically situated on Lake Jezioro Narie on a gentle slope, the 100 level, enclosed pitches are grass on sand, back to back between hard access roads and all have electricity. Also an open lawn for about 60 tents. The two very good quality sanitary blocks are well tiled with British WCs and hot water in sinks, washbasins and on payment in the showers. Restaurant, bars, shops and limited entertainment in high season. The lake is used for swimming (lifeguard in summer), windsurfing, boating and fishing. Rooms and bungalows for hire and the company who own the camp also have hotels nearby. With a most pleasant appearance with many trees, shrubs and flowers this is considered to be one of the most beautiful sites in the country.

How to find it: Site is signed about 7 km. south of Morag on the no. 527 Olsztyn-Morag road.

General Details: Open 1 May - 31 October. 20,000 sq.m. Restaurant, bars and shops. Watersports. Cycle hire. Horse riding. Rooms and bungalows to let.

Charges guide: Per person with tent Zlts. 2.20, with caravan 3.80; tent 3.95; pitch 3.95; caravan 4.85; car 3.80; motorcaravan 6.50; m/cycle 2.20; electricity 3.80.

Reservations: Write to camp. Address: 14 331 Zabi Rog, Kretowiny, Morag. Tel: 08985 2668. FAX: as phone.

No Stamp
Required

Sites Abroad
FREEPOST ALM1584
KNUTSFORD
Cheshire
WA16 0BR

Sites ABROAD

For the more experienced camper and caravanner

Booking made easy
One phone call will book your whole holiday - sites, channel ferry or shuttle crossings and insurance.

Variety of sites
From 4 star sites with a full range of facilities to well-run municipal sites.

Quality and Service
All sites meet rigorous standards for safety and cleanliness.

Value for money
A competitive package at a price you will find hard to beat.

Book with Sites Abroad and we will reimburse the cost of this guide.
To claim your refund return the discount card in this guide with your booking.

For a brochure call now on:
01565 625525

Title _____ Initials _____

Surname _____

Address _____

_____

Postcode _____

How many adults are in your party? _____

If applicable what are the ages of
your children? _____

Do you have a:

tent ☐ trailer tent ☐ caravan ☐ motorhome ☐

Have you ever taken your own   Yes   No
equipment abroad before?   ☐   ☐

If 'Yes' how many times? _____

Would you be interested in pursuing any of the
following interests whilst on holiday with your own
equipment?

Golf ☐   Birdwatching ☐   Fishing ☐
Wine ☐   Cooking ☐

Tick if you do not wish to receive direct mail from
other carefully screened companies whose
products or services we feel may be of interest ☐

Sites ABROAD

SAAR

315 Camp Park Wilamowek, Grabowo

Quiet, isolated camp by lake.

When you leave the hard road following signs for Camp Wilamowek along a narrow, undulating sand road, you do wonder just where you are going, but if you are looking for a restful camp on the shores of a lake amidst the forests of the Mazurian Lake District where you can fish, walk or enjoy boating, this might well suit you. The main building which houses reception, a fine restaurant with separate bar and rooms to let, is elevated above the lake with the excellent quality sanitary block nearby. The camping area is right down by the lake with a climb up to these facilities. The 55 grass on sand pitches all have electricity, are neither numbered nor marked out and have little shade. There is a WC here. In winter, caravans are placed near the main building and use the toilet and cooking facilities of the apartments. The friendly owner speaks some English. Wilamowek is not for those who want bright lights and discos, but would suit those wishing to get away from it all.

How to find it: Site is signed at Sorkwty on road no. 16, 12 km. west of Mragowo.

General Details: Open all year. 80,000 sq.m. Bar. Restaurant. Basic supplies. Washing machine. Rooms to let. Watersports. Fishing. Walking.

Charges guide: Per person DM 3.00; child (6-16 yrs) 1.50; caravan 6.50; motorcaravan 9.00; tent 3.50 - 5.50; car 3.00; m/cycle 1.50; electricity 3.00; local tax 0.50.

Reservations: Write to camp. Address: 11 705 Grabowo. Tel: 089 84 8151.

317 Hotel Camping Park Mazurski Eden, Jznota Bartlowo, nr Ukta

Very remote, quiet camp with hotel on large lake.

Mazurski Eden is in the centre of the beautiful Mazurian Lake District surrounded by the interesting flora and fauna of the Piska forest. It is a quite amazing place approached by a 6 km. sand road, easily negotiable by caravans, with the entrance flanked by tall pine posts of carved figures. Wood carvings abound with statues by the waters edge, on buildings and inside the hotel. The camping area with room for 50 units, is grass on sand under tall trees which determine pitches, with electrical connection boxes topped with lamps for night illumination. The well built, wood clad, brick sanitary block stands to one side of the camping area and is an excellent provision with British WCs and hot water in sinks, washbasins and good showers. Dish and clothes washing facilities are outside but under cover. A wealth of activities is available with organised photographic safaris, canoeing and hiking trips, bicycle excursions, visits to nature reserves with wolves, bison, beavers and other wild life. Sailing and other watersports are arranged and even fishing under the ice in winter. Parties, picnics and barbecues are offered with dancing and folk bands. Various national days are noted, with open air workshops for painters and sculptors and church festivals are celebrated in a family atmosphere. The Manager has a great interest in the social history of the ancient people of this area and this is reflected in the entertainment offered to group conferences being held in the hotel, to which campers are also invited.

How to find it: Turn south at Mikogajki on road no. 16 (Mragowo-Elk) and follow sign `Nw Most'. Continue on unmade road to camp.

General Details: Open all year. 80,000 sq.m. Restaurant. Grotto bar. Hotel. Watersports and entertainment.

Charges guide: Per unit incl. 2 adults, 1 child, pitch, caravan and electricity DM 16.00 - 31.00.

Reservations: Write to camp. Address: Camping Park Pension Galindia Mazurski Eden, Iznota nr Mikogaji, 12 210 Ukta. Tel: 0117 31669. FAX: 0117 31390.

319 Camping Pension Kruska, Wygryny, nr Ukta

Simple camp with excellent sanitary facilities by lake.

If looking for a cheaper option with just room for camping and no frills, this small camp for about 70 units might suit. Pitches which are neither marked out nor numbered, are on slightly sloping ground between the Pension and the lake. There is no shade, units group around the electrical boxes and it could become crowded in high season. However, the brick built sanitary block is of excellent quality with British WCs and hot water in sinks, washbasins and very good showers. There is a small jetty by the lake which can be used for a variety of watersports. A separate bar and small restaurant are available in the Pension.

How to find it: Wygryny is signed from road no. 610 Ukta - Rciane-Nida.

General Details: Open all year. 12,000 sq.m. Bar. Restaurant. Shop 100 m. Swimming, fishing and watersports in lake. Rooms to rent.

Charges guide: Per person DM 3.00; tent 3.00; caravan 5.00; car 2.00; motorcaravan 6.00; electricity 4.00.

Reservations: Write to camp in German. Address: Wygryny 52, 12 210 Ukta. Tel: 0117 31597. FAX: as phone.

POLAND

321 Astur Camping Nr. 123, Warsaw (Warszawa)

Good city camp in quiet location in south of town.

Camp 123 is inside the city boundary about 4 km. (20 minutes by bus) from the centre of the Polish capital. What is more, if approached from the south on roads 8/E67 or 7/E77 which merge on city outskirts, it is easy to find. Although a main road runs past the entrance, tennis courts on one side and a small park with a swimming pool on the other, along with the trees on the site, make this a very pleasant quiet base from which to explore this historic and interesting city. The site, with room for about 50 caravans and tents, is in two parts with an oblong section leading from reception and entrance and another square section beyond the sanitary provision and rented bungalows. Grass pitches on sand are on either side of concrete paved roads and all have electric connections. 'Portacabin' type buildings house the toilet facilities which have British WCs and hot water in washbasins and small showers. Campers are given a key to use these as the other more open block is used by those renting bungalows where groups of children are sometimes brought to stay. There is a small hotel with a shop for basic supplies which also offers a limited menu of simple snack meals. The Vera Hotel opposite the site has a good restaurant.

> **How to find it:** From the south on roads 7 and 8, continue into city to concrete monument in the centre of the tramway which divides carriageways. Turn left at traffic lights and camp is on left after Hotel Vera.
>
> **General Details:** Open all year. 8,000 sq.m. Snack bar. Kiosk. Restaurant opposite. Shops 300 m. Tram 200 m. for city. Hotel rooms and bungalows to rent.
>
> **Charges guide:** Per person Zlts. 7.00; caravan 7.00 - 8.00; tent 4.00 - 6.00; car 7.00 - 8.00; motorcaravan 12.00 - 15.00; electricity 8.50; m/cycle 5.00; cycle 1.00.
>
> **Reservations:** Write to site. Address: 02 366 Warszawa (Warsaw), ul. Bitwy Warszawskiej 1920 N 15/17. Tel: 022 276778. FAX: 022 271472.

323 Camping Olemka Nr. 76, Czestochowa

Pleasant, leafy site near famous monastery.

Czestochowa's main claim to fame is the famous Jasna Gora monastery, one of Europe's main pilgrimage centres. The Black Madonna icon, displayed in the monastery, has attracted thousands of pilgrims for 600 years and still does today. Camp 76 is located right behind the huge monastery car and coach park, on a slight slope with level pitches of grass on sand and some hardstandings. Electricity boxes determine pitches which are otherwise not marked or numbered. There is room for about 100 units with the many mature trees which enhance the site, giving shade in some parts. The two identical toilet blocks which are quite acceptable but not luxurious, have British WCs and hot water in sinks, washbasins and rather small showers which, as with most in Poland, have no dressing space. There is a restaurant and shop in high season, with others a short distance away in the town. This site could make a useful night stop when passing through or for a day or two if visiting the monastery.

> **How to find it:** Follow signs for 'Jasna Gora' (the monastery which being on a hill, is very obvious from most parts of town) and then camp signs.
>
> **General Details:** Open all year. Bar/restaurant (main season). Shop. Washing machine. Drying room. Iron. Bungalows for rent.
>
> **Charges guide:** Per caravan Zlts. 9.00; tent 5.00; car 6.00; motorcaravan 8.00; electricity 8.00 - 10.00.
>
> **Reservations:** Write to camp. Address: 42 200 Czestochowa, ul. Olenki 10/50. Tel: 034 247495.

325 Auto Camping Nr. 215, Katowice

Good edge of town site for night stop.

Although the industrial complex of Katowice and the surrounding area is not a tourist centre, camp 215, being near a lake and 5 km. from the town centre in a leafy suburb, makes a good one night stop when travelling from the west to Kracow or for a few days if visiting Auschwitz. A main road runs along one corner of the camp but we did not notice undue noise during our one-night stop. Five rectangular grass lawns, separated by hard access roads provide unmarked pitches with some being under trees and some in the open and all having electricity. The well constructed, single toilet block stands to one side of the camp with British WCs and pre-mixed warm water in sinks, showers and half the washbasins. The block is heated in cool weather. There is a bar/restaurant/shop in high season, a club room with TV and a separate community room with kitchen, barbecue style grill, and tables and benches under cover. For recreation the site has a tennis court and sauna with a lake opposite for water sports.

> **How to find it:** Site is signed at the junction of roads nos. 1 and 93 in Katowice between Czestochowa and Bielsko-Biala.
>
> **General Details:** Open 1 May - 30 Sept. Restaurant. Shop. Club room (high season). Sauna. Tennis. Lake near.
>
> **Charges guide:** Per person Zlts. 4.20; child (3-10 yrs) 2.10; caravan 5.00 - 8.00; car 4.00; tent 3.00; motorcaravan 7.00; m/cycle 2.00.
>
> **Reservations:** Write to camp. Address: 48 266 Katowice. ul. Murchowska. Tel: 155/5388 or 156/5939.

PORTUGAL

Portugal occupies the southwest corner of the Iberian peninsula and is a relatively small country, bordered by Spain in the north and east and the Atlantic coast in the south and west. However, for a small country it has tremendous variety both in its way of life and traditions. The Portuguese consider the Minho area in northern Portugal to be the most beautiful part of their country with its wooded mountain slopes and wild coast line, a rural and conservative region with picturesque towns. Central Portugal (the Estremadura region) with its monuments, evidence of its role in the country's history, has fertile rolling hills and adjoins the bull-breeding lands of Ribatejo (banks of the Tagus). The huge, sparsely populated plains south east of Lisbon, the cosmopolitan yet traditional capital, are dominated by vast cork plantations supplying nearly half the world's cork, but it is an impoverished area, and visitors usually head for Evora. The Algarve compensates for the dull plains south of Evora and has attracted more tourist development than the rest of the country. Portugal is therefore a land of contrasts - the sophisticated development of the Algarve as against the underdeveloped rural areas where time has stood still. There is a more liberal constitution now but the country is still poor and the cost of living generally low, although there has been a marked increase in prices in the Algarve. For British visitors, with large distances to travel, longer stays out of season are particularly attractive and most camp sites are actively encouraging this type of visitor. For further information contact:

ICEP Portuguese Trade & Tourism Office, 22/22a Sackville Street, London W1X 1DE

Tel: 0171 494 1441. Fax: 0171 494 1868.

Population
9,900,000, density 106.6 per sq.km.

Capital
Lisbon (Lisboa)

Climate
The country enjoys a maritime climate with hot summers (sub-tropical in the South) and mild winters with comparatively low rainfall in the South, heavy rain in the North.

Language
Portuguese, but English is widely spoken in cities, towns and larger resorts. French can be useful.

Currency
The currency unit is the escudo, divided into 100 centavos and its symbol - the dollar sign - is written between the escudo and centavo units. Notes are issued for 5,000$00, 1,000$00, 500$00, and 50$00. Coins are issued for 50$00, 25$)), 20$00, 10$00, 5$00, 2$50, 1$00, and $50. One thousand escudos is a 'conto'.

Banks
Open Mon-Fri 08.30-11.45 and 13.00-14.45. Some large city banks operate a currency exchange service for tourists 18.30-23.00

Post Offices
Offices (Correios) normally open Mon-Fri 09.00-18.00, some larger ones on Saturday mornings.

Time
From the last Sunday in Sept to the last Sunday in March, the time in Portugal is GMT. During summer it is GMT + 1 hr (as the UK).

Telephone
To telephone Portugal from the UK dial 00 351. To the UK from Portugal dial 00 44. You need to be patient to get a line. Phone cards available (500 /1200 esc) from post offices, and tobacconists.

Public Holidays
New Year; Carnival (Shrove Tues); Good Fri; Liberty Day, 25 Apr; Labour Day; Corpus Christi; Portugal, 10 June; Saints Days: Lisbon 13 June, Porto 24 June; Aassumption, 15 Aug; Republic Day 5 Oct; All Saints, 1 Nov; Independence Day, 1 Dec; Immaculate Conception, 8 Dec; Christmas, 24, 25 or 25, 26 Dec.

Shops
Open Mon-Fri 0900-1300 and 1500-1900. Sat 0900-1300. Shopping centres are open much longer hours.
Food: Along the Atlantic coast fresh fish and shellfish are to be found on every menu - Caldeirada is a piquant mixed stew. However, Portugal is perhaps best known for Port and Maderia but don't forget the Vinho verde - marvellous with freshly caught sardines!

Motoring
The standard of roads is very variable - even some of the main roads can be very uneven. The authorities are making great efforts to improve matters, but other than on motorways or major highway routes (IP's) you should be prepared to make slow progress. Watch Portuguese drivers, as they tend to overtake when they feel like it.
Tolls: Tolls are levied on certain motorways (auto-estradas) out of Lisbon, and upon southbound traffic at the Lisbon end of the giant 25th Abril bridge over the River Tagus.
Speed Limits: Car - Built-up areas 31 mph (50 kph), other roads 56 mph (90 kph), Motorways min. 25mph (40 kph) Max. 75mph (120 kph). For towing vehicles in built-up areas 31 mph (50 kph), other roads 43/50 mph (70/80 kph) and Motorways min. 25 mph (40 kph) max. 62mph (100 kph).
Fuel: Petrol stations are open from 0700-2200/2400 and some 24 hours. Credit cards are accepted but Visa is preferred. Use of a credit card incurs a surcharge of 100 esc.
Parking: Parked vehicles must face the same direction as moving traffic. Some towns have 'Blue Zones', discs available from ACP or the police.

Overnighting
Generally not allowed and fines may be imposed.

Useful Addresses
National Motoring Organisation
Automovel Club de Portugal (ACP)
Rua Rosa Araujo 24-26, 1200 Lisbon.
Tel: 563931.
Office hours Mon-Fri 09.00-13.00, 14.00-17.00.

PORTUGAL - West Coast

801 Orbitur Camping Mata do Camarido, Caminha, nr Viana do Castelo

Pleasant site in northern Portugal close to the Spanish border.

Only a short 200 m. walk from the beach, this small site has an attractive and peaceful setting in woods alongside the river estuary that marks the border with Spain. Fishing is possible in the estuary and bathing, either there or from the rather open, sandy beach. The site is partly shaded by tall pines with other small trees planted to mark the sandy pitches. The clean, well maintained and extended toilet block is centrally located. It has British style toilets, washbasins (cold water) with shelf, hook and mirror, and free hot showers, plus beach showers, extra dishwashing and laundry sinks (cold water).

How to find it: Turn off main coast road (N13-E50) along estuary 3 km. south of Caminha at sign to site.

General Details: Open 16 Jan - 30 Nov. Restaurant, snacks and supermarket (all May - Sept). Tennis. Children's playground. Telephone and post box. Medical post. Laundry with ironing boards. Motorcaravan services. Bus service 800 m. Gates are locked at 11 pm. English spoken.

Charges 1997: (to 31 May 98) Per person esc. 580; child (5-10 yrs) 290; car 490; m/cycle 340; tent 480 - 810; caravan 570 - 890; motorcaravan 710 - 960, all acc. to size; boat 360; electricity 360. Off season discounts (up to 70%). Credit cards accepted.

Reservations: Contact Orbitur - Central de Reservas, Rua Diogo do Couto, 1-8°, 1100 Lisboa. Tel: (0)1/811 70 00 or 811 70 70. FAX: (0)1/814 80 45. E-mail: info@orbitur.pt. Internet: http://www.orbitur.pt.

802 Orbitur Camping Viana do Castelo, Viana do Castelo

Site in northern Portugal with direct access to sandy beach.

This site is worth considering as it has the advantage of direct access, through a gate in the fence (locked at night), to an excellent sandy beach, very popular for windsurfing. There are around 187 pitches on slightly undulating, sandy ground - most with good shade. As usual with Orbitur sites, pitches are not marked and it could be crowded in July/August. There are some hardstandings for caravans and electricity (15A) in all parts. Some pitches are very sandy. The clean, well kept sanitary facilities are in two blocks and have mostly British style WCs, washbasins with cold water, and only 4 free hot showers with many more cold ones - facilities may be pushed to cope in high season. A pleasant restaurant terrace overlooks the site and a ferry crosses the river to the town centre. The site is also convenient for visiting the medieval town of Ponte de Lima (24 km), with its whitewashed houses, towers and Roman bridge, and Viana do Castelo is famous for its beautiful embroideries and festival processions.

How to find it: Turn off N13 coast road 2 km. southeast of Viana do Castelo towards Cabedelo and the sea. Site is the second camp signed.

General Details: Open 16 Jan - 30 Nov. Supermarket, restaurant with terrace and bar (all April - Oct). Reading room with TV, video and fireplace. Children's playground. Adjacent swimming pool (from 15/6). Tennis. Telephone and post box. Laundry. Motorcaravan services. Bus service 200 m. English spoken. Bungalows for hire.

Charges 1997: (to 31 May 98) Per person esc. 580; child (5-10 yrs) 290; car 490; m/cycle 340; tent 480 - 810;' caravan 570 - 890; motorcaravan 710 - 960, all acc. to size; boat 360; electricity 360. Off season discounts (up to 70%). Credit cards not accepted.

Reservations: Contact Orbitur - Central de Reservas, Rua Diogo do Couto, 1-8°, 1100 Lisboa. Tel: (0)1/811 70 00 or 811 70 70. FAX: (0)1/814 80 45. E-mail: info@orbitur.pt. Internet: http://www.orbitur.pt.

803 Camping Rio Alto, Estela, nr Povoa de Varzim

Well managed site with good facilities adjacent to beach and golf course.

This site makes an excellent base for visiting Porto which is some 35 km. south of Estela. It takes around 600 units on sandy terrain, and is adjacent to what is virtually a private beach (access via a tunnel under dunes), and also to an 18 hole golf course. It has some hardstandings for motorcaravans and electricity (5A) to most pitches. The area for tents is furthest from the beach and windswept, stunted pines give some shade. There are arrangements (cheaper) for car parking away from camping areas. Four well equipped sanitary blocks have large shower cubicles including free hot water, British type WCs, washbasins and dishwashing and laundry sinks under cover. Units for disabled people. Unusually for a seaside site, a swimming pool is across the road from reception where tennis courts are also located. The beach tunnel is open 9 am.-7 pm. and the beach has a lifeguard from 15 June.

How to find it: Site is reached via a cobbled road leading directly off the EN13 coast road towards the sea (just north of Estela), 12 km. north of Póvoa de Varzim. Then turn right onto a private road to site (beware speed bumps).

General Details: Open all year. Restaurant (1/5-30/9) Bar and snack bar (all year). Mini-market (every day 1/5-30/9, weekends other times). Swimming pool (1/6-30/9). Tennis. Children's playground. Games room. TV. Golf (reduced rate for campers). Fishing. Bicycle hire. Telephone and post box. Medical post. Laundry. Car wash. Chemical disposal. Motorcaravan services. Evening entertainment twice weekly in season.

Charges 1998: Per adult Esc. 305 - 635; child (4-11 yrs) 140 - 270; car on site 250 - 690, in car park 250 -360; m/cycle 250 - 400; tent 310 - 900, caravan 530 - 1,280, both acc. to season and size; motorcaravan 690 - 1,200; electricity 310 - 360. Credit cards accepted.

Reservations: Not normally made (except for groups). Site becomes full in July/Aug - anyone arriving before noon should find space, those arriving in the afternoon may not be so lucky. Address: Estela, 4490 Póvoa de Varzim. Tel: 052/615699 or 615599. FAX: 052/611540.

804 Parque de Campismo da Prelada, Porto

Interesting wooded camp within the limits of a great trading City.

Porto is a fine city and the port industry opens its doors to tourists for both tastings and to demonstrate its technology and traditions. Once past the somewhat overplayed security at the entrance, this site proved to be one of the most attractive inner-city sites we have encountered. Pitches are grouped in small clearings, bounded by shrubs and trees. There is plenty of shade and the vegetation creates a peaceful park-like atmosphere, a world away from the bustling traffic of the wine trading city beyond its walls. The two toilet blocks are just adequate, with reasonably modern installations which could have been a little cleaner. As in most Portuguese sites, only cold water is provided generally, but hot showers are available on payment. The site is open all year but the inexpensive restaurant and bar only in the main season. Children's playground and tennis courts. A bus service is available from the site gates to the city centre. We visited in early August and there was plenty of space.

How to find It: It is situated in the Rua do Monte dos Burgos... best policy is to take the N12 northern ring road and look for 'Prelada' signs - you will need to turn southwards. **Note:** a massive road building programme has been underway in the city for some years which makes the site very difficult to find. Allow plenty of time.

General Details: Open all year, although 1 Oct - 1 April Park is closed 1pm - 8pm. 100,000 sq.m. Well shaded. Many electrical connections. Shop (May-Sept), restaurant and bar (June-Sept.). General room. Tennis. Boats for hire on lake. Children's playground. Bureau de change. Doctors call. Public transport from camp to city centre.

Charges: Not available.

Reservations: Not made but priority for admission is given to those with international camping carnet. Address: R. Monte dos Burgos, 4200 Porto. Tel: 02/812616. FAX: 02/723718.

805 Orbitur Camping São Jacinto

Small site in attractive location on a peninsula between sea and lagoon.

This is a typical Orbitur pinewood site, near the tip of the peninsula on the northern shore of the Aveiro Ria (lagoon), with views to the mountains beyond. The area is a weekend resort for locals and can be crowded in high season; therefore it may be difficult to find space at times, particularly for larger units. Swimming and fishing are both possible in the adjacent Ria, or the sea, 20 minutes walk from a guarded back gate. It is not a large site, taking 200 units on unmarked pitches, but in most places trees help provide natural limits. Two toilet blocks were clean when inspected, and contain the usual facilities including free hot showers. Dishwashing and laundry sinks on a tiled loggia. Small shop, restaurant and bar. The children's playground has also been recently refurbished.

How to find It: Turn off N109 at Estarreja to Torreira and São Jacinto; bypassing Murtosa. Road is well surfaced, with just a short cobbled section at Estarreja.

General Details: Open all year except Dec. Shop (May-Sept). Restaurant/bar (June-Oct). Children's playground. Table tennis. Telephone and post box. Laundry. Motorcaravan services. Bus service 20 m. English spoken. Orbitur bungalows for hire.

Charges 1997: (to 31 May 98) Per person esc. 570; child (5-10 yrs) 280; car 480; m/cycle 330; tent 460 - 800; caravan 560 - 890; motorcaravan 690 - 970, all acc. to size; boat 370; electricity (6A) 360. Off season discounts (up to 70%). Credit cards not accepted.

Reservations: Contact Orbitur - Central de Reservas, Rua Diogo do Couto, 1-8°, 1100 Lisboa. Tel: (0)1/811 70 00 or 811 70 70. FAX: (0)1/814 80 45. E-mail: info@orbitur.pt. Internet: http://www.orbitur.pt.

807 Orbitur Camping Praia de Mira

Small well kept site on quiet inlet close to beach.

A seaside site set in pinewoods, Praia de Mira is situated to the south of Aveiro and Vagos, in a quieter and less crowded area. It fronts onto a lake at the head of the Ria de Mira, which eventually runs into the Aveiro Ria. A back gate leads directly to the sea and a wide quiet beach. The site has around 350 pitches which are not marked but with trees creating natural divisions. Electricity and water points are plentiful. Two toilet blocks include British style WCs, 14 free hot showers and washing machines. The site provides an inexpensive restaurant, snack bar, lounge bar and TV lounge. A medium sized supermarket is well stocked, with plenty of fresh produce. The Mira Ria is fascinating - brightly painted boats collect seaweed which is used to enrich the soil for growing vegetables. It will be probably be some time before watersports and intensive tourism dislodge these centuries old traditions.

How to find It: Turn off the N109 at Mira, about 27 km. south of Aveiro towards Praia de Mira. A small sign after about 5 km. shows a left turn which leads direct to the site. If you miss it, the site is signed from the beach resort. Make sure you ask for the **Orbitur** site if stuck - there are others here which are not as pleasant!

General Details: Open 1 Feb - 30 Nov. Shop and restaurant/bar (May-Sept). Snack bar. TV room. Laundry. Children's playground. Telephone and post box. Motorcaravan services. Bus service 150 m. English spoken.

Charges 1997: (to 31 May 98) Per person esc. 580; child (5-10 yrs) 290; car 490; m/cycle 340; tent 480 - 810; caravan 570 - 890; motorcaravan 710 - 960, all acc. to size; boat 360; electricity (5A) 360. Off season discounts (up to 70%). Credit cards accepted.

Reservations: Contact Orbitur - Central de Reservas, Rua Diogo do Couto, 1-8°, 1100 Lisboa. Tel: (0)1/811 70 00 or 811 70 70. FAX: (0)1/814 80 45. E-mail: info@orbitur.pt. Internet: http://www.orbitur.pt.

PORTUGAL - West Coast

809 Orbitur Camping Gala, Figueira da Foz, nr Coimbra

Large site close to resort and with path to nearby private beach.

This site, for around 1,500 units, is on sandy terrain in a pinewood. Some pitches near the road may be rather noisy. One can drive or walk the 300 m. from the back of the site to a private beach; bathing needs caution when windy - the warden will advise. The site fills quickly in July/Aug. and units may be very close together, but there should be plenty of room at other times. There are a few individual pitches with electricity and water (only 50 sq.m), the majority (70 sq.m) unmarked with electricity throughout (15A). The three toilet blocks, one recently refurbished, have British and Turkish style toilets, individual basins (some with hot water) and 16 free hot showers. All were clean at time of inspection despite heavy usage. Besides the beach, Coimbra and the nearby Roman remains are worth visiting.

How to find it: Site is 4 km. south of Figueira beyond the two rivers; turn off main road over 1 km. from bridge on southern edge of Gala, then 600 m. to site.

General Details: Open all year. Supermarket, restaurant/bar (all May-Sept). Lounge. Children's playground. Tennis. TV room planned. Telephone and post box. Laundry. Car wash area. Motorcaravan services. Orbitur bungalows for hire. No dogs permitted. English spoken.

Charges 1997: (to 31 May 98) Per person esc. 580; child (5-10 yrs) 290; car 490; m/cycle 340; tent 480 - 810; caravan 570 - 890; motorcaravan 710 - 960, all acc. to size; boat 360; electricity 360. Off season discounts (up to 70%). Credit cards accepted.

Reservations: Contact Orbitur - Central de Reservas, Rua Diogo do Couto, 1-8°, 1100 Lisboa. Tel: (0)1/811 70 00 or 811 70 70. FAX: (0)1/814 80 45. E-mail: info@orbitur.pt. Internet: http://www.orbitur.pt.

840 Campismo `De Klomp', nr Louriçal

Peaceful countryside site, with homely atmosphere, flowers and fruit trees.

The Dutch owners are sure to give you a warm welcome at this delightful little touring site where they, aided by family and friends, have built all of the quality installations and laid out the site of which they are so justifiably proud. The site is within walking distance of local shops and services and is very popular with mature couples and winter campers. It is not really suitable for families with young children who need to be entertained. The 100 good sized pitches are separated by cordons of fruit trees, ornamental trees and flowering shrubs, on level grassy ground. There is electricity (16A) to 72 pitches and 5 pitches are suitable for large motorhomes. The site is lit and there is nearly always space available. The single sanitary block, just behind the owners house at the front of the site, provides spotlessly clean and generously sized facilities. British style WCs, pre-set showers and washbasins in cabins (with easy access for disabled people). Dishwashing and laundry sinks outside under cover. Hot water is free. The owners keep a wide range of provisions and local produce and there are bread and milk deliveries daily. Market in nearby Louriçal every Sunday. One can fish or swim in a nearby lake, and the resort beaches are a short drive. Possibly some road noise on pitches at the front of the site.

How to find it: From N109 (Leira-Figuera de Foz) road, 25 km. south of Figuera in Matos de Carriço, turn on to N342 road (signed Louriçal 6 km). Site is 1.5 km. on left-hand side; look for distinctive yellow `clog' signs.

General Details: Open all year. Library and TV room/lounge. Supermarket 800 m. Washing machine. Milk and bread deliveries daily. Bicycle hire. Chemical disposal. Bungalows for rent.

Charges 1998: Per adult Esc 350 - 400; child (up to 5 yrs) 150; tent, caravan or trailer 300; car 200; m/cycle 100; motorcaravan 500; dog 80; electricity 340. Discounts of 10-30% for off season long stays. Credit cards not accepted.

Reservations: Contact site. Address: O Tamanco Lda, Casas Brancas, 3100 Louriçal. Tel/Fax: 036-952551.

810 Orbitur Camping Sao Pedro de Moel, nr Leira

Pleasant, well maintained seaside site close to small resort in central Portugal.

Arguably one of the more attractive sites in the Orbitur chain, this one is tranquilly situated under tall pines, on the edge of this rather select small resort. The attractive, sandy beach, about 500 m. walk downhill from the site, (you can take the car, although parking may be difficult) is sheltered from the wind by low cliffs. Four toilet blocks have mainly British style toilets (some with bidets), individual basins (some with hot water) and free hot showers mostly in one block. The shady site can be crowded in July/Aug, when units might be rather too close for comfort, but there are some individual pitches of 50 sq.m. with electricity (15A) and water. Very few permanent units. Over 400 electrical connections overall. There are areas of soft sand, but there should be no problem in finding a firm pitch.

How to find it: Site is 9 km. west of Marinha Grande, on the right as you enter São Pedro de Moel. The busy road from Marinha Grande is a combination of cobbles and very rough and badly patched surfaces - take it slowly!

General Details: Open all year. 75,000 sq.m. Supermarket, restaurant and bar with terrace (May-Sept). TV and games room. Children's playground. Tennis. Swimming pool planned for '98. Telephone and post box. Medical post. Laundry. Car wash. Motorcaravan services. Bus service 100 m. Orbitur bungalows for hire.

Charges 1997: (to 31 May 98) Per person esc. 580; child (5-10 yrs) 290; car 490; m/cycle 340; tent 480 - 810; caravan 570 - 890; motorcaravan 710 - 960, all acc. to size; boat 360; electricity 360. Off season discounts (up to 70%). Credit cards accepted.

Reservations: Contact Orbitur - Central de Reservas, Rua Diogo do Couto, 1-8°, 1100 Lisboa. Tel: (0)1/811 70 00 or 811 70 70. FAX: (0)1/814 80 45. E-mail: info@orbitur.pt. Internet: http://www.orbitur.pt.

846 Camping-Caravanning Vale Paraiso, Nazaré

Well managed, shady site near the coast, open all year.

This pleasant campsite is by the main N242 road in 8 ha. of undulating pine woods and provides over 600 pitches, many of which are on sandy ground only suitable for tents. For other units there are around 250 individual pitches of varying size on harder ground with electrical connections (4/6A) available. Sanitary facilities are good, with free hot water for washbasins, showers, laundry and dishwashing sinks. Nearly all WCs are British style and there are facilities for disabled people. A range of sporting and leisure activities includes a good outdoor swimming pool with sunbathing areas and a new children's adventure playground. There is a shop also selling newspapers, a bar and restaurant with regional cuisine. Access roads, walkways and car parking have been recently improved. Several long beaches of white sand are within 2-15 km. allowing windsurfing, sailing, surfing or body-boarding. Nazaré is an old fishing village with narrow streets, a harbour and marina and many outdoor bars and cafés, with a lift to Sitio. There is much of historical interest in the area although the mild Atlantic climate is also conducive to just relaxing. The owners are keen to welcome British visitors.

How to find it: Site is 2 km. north of Nazaré, on the EN242 Marinha Grande road.

General Details: Open all year. Shop. Restaurant (March - Sept). Bar and café (all year). Swimming pool (March - Sept). Volleyball. Basketball. Football. Badminton. Leisure games. Amusement hall. Bicycle hire. Washing machine. Chemical disposal. Motorcaravan services.

Charges 1997: Per person esc. 345 - 575; child (3-10 yrs) 150 - 250; tent 295 - 600; caravan 355 - 720; motorcaravan 415 - 860; car 285 - 470; m/cycle or trailer 185 - 310; electricity 4A 265, 6A 365; pet 120 - 200. Credit cards accepted.

Reservations: Contact site. Address: EN 242, 2450 Nazaré. Tel: 062/561800. FAX: 062/561900. E-mail: camping.vp.nz@mail.telepac.pt.

CAMPING CARAVANING ***

VALE PARAÍSO

NATURE·SEASIDE·BEACH·TRADITION·CULTURE·ENTERTAINMENT·QUIET·CLEANLINESS·SECURITY

NAZARÉ - Portugal

845 Parque de Campismo Colina do Sol, S. Martinho do Porto

Well appointed touring site, near to beach, with own swimming pool.

Only 1 km. from the small town of S. Martinho do Porto, Colina do Sol has around 350 pitches marked by fruit and ornamental trees on grassy terraces. Electricity (6 or 10A) is available to all, although some may need long leads. The attractive entrance with its beds of bright flowers, is wide enough for even the largest of outfits, with a warm welcome from the receptionist and good English spoken. Two large, clean and modern sanitary blocks provide British style WCs (some with bidets), washbasins - some with hot water, shelves etc, and showers with dividers. Hot water is free throughout. Dishwashing and laundry sinks are outside but covered and ironing facilities are available. A well stocked supermarket and a restaurant, cafeteria, and bar are open in peak season, with a delightful paved terrace beside the large clean swimming pool. The beach is at the rear of the camp, with access via a gate which is locked at night (22.00-08.00). The site is a convenient base for exploring the Costa de Prata and for excursions to old town of Leiria, with its crenellated walls towering high above the rock faces, and to the famous shrine of Fátima. Market in S. Martinho do Porto on Sunday.

How to find it: Turn from EN 242 (Caldas-Nazaré) road northeast of San Martinho do Porto. Site is signed - do not go into town centre.

General Details: Open all year except 15/12-15/1. Supermarket. Restaurant/cafe with bar (high season). Swimming pool. Lounge. Children's playground. Telephone and post box. Medical post. Car wash.

Charges guide: Per adult Esc. 520; child (4-10 yrs) 250; small tent 450, large 530; caravan or motorcaravan 550; car 430; m/cycle 290; electricity 290.

Reservations: Contact site. Address: 2465 S. Martinho do Porto. Tel: 062/989764. FAX: 062/989763.

PORTUGAL - West Coast

811 Orbitur Camping Valado, Nazaré

Popular site close to busy resort on central west coast.

This site is on the edge of the old, traditional fishing port of Nazaré which has now become something of a holiday resort and popular with coach parties. The large beach in the town, about 2 km. downhill (steeply) from the site, is sheltered by headlands and provides good bathing. The campsite is on undulating ground under tall pine trees, takes around 500 units and, although some smallish individual pitches with electricity and water are available for reservation, the bulk of the site is not marked out and units could be close together especially during July/August. About 420 electrical connections are available. There are three toilet blocks with British and Turkish style WCs, washbasins and showers (cold water), and 17 free hot showers with seat, divider and curtain, plus dishwashing and laundry sinks under cover. All were reasonably clean when inspected - some repairs were needed and we were assured by the management that these were in hand.

How to find it: Site is on the Nazaré - Alcobaca road - 2 km. east of Nazaré.

General Details: Open 1 Feb - 30 Nov. Supermarket. Bar, snack bar and restaurant with terrace. TV/general room. Children's playground. Tennis. Telephone and post box. Medical post. Laundry. Car wash. Motorcaravan services. English spoken. Bus service 20 m. Bungalows for hire.

Charges 1997: (to 31 May 98) Per person esc. 570; child (5-10 yrs) 280; car 480; m/cycle 330; tent 460 - 800; caravan 560 - 890; motorcaravan 690 - 970, all acc. to size; boat 370; electricity 360. Off season discounts (up to 70%). Credit cards accepted.

Reservations: Contact Orbitur - Central de Reservas, Rua Diogo do Couto, 1-8°, 1100 Lisboa. Tel: (0)1/811 70 00 or 811 70 70. FAX: (0)1/814 80 45. E-mail: info@orbitur.pt. Internet: http://www.orbitur.pt.

813 Orbitur Camping Guincho, Areia, nr Cascais

Convenient site for visiting Lisbon, with nearby beach.

Although this is a popular site for permanent or long stay caravans, it is nevertheless quite attractively laid out among low pine trees and with the new A5 autostrada connection to Lisbon (30 km), it provides a useful alternative to sites nearer the city. Located behind sand dunes and a wide, sandy but somewhat windswept beach, the site offers a wide range of facilities. These include a bar/restaurant, supermarket, general lounge and TV room and laundry. There is a choice of pitches (small - mainly about 50 sq.m.) mostly with electricity (15A), although siting amongst the trees may be tricky, particularly when the site is full. The three sanitary blocks in the older style, were in need of some refurbishment when visited, but were clean. These provide British type WCs, washbasins with cold water and one block has free hot showers. Facilities for dishwashing, and disabled people.

How to find it: Approach from either direction on N247. Turn inland 6½ km. west of Cascais at camp sign. Travelling direct from Lisbon site is signed at the end of the A5 autopista.

General Details: Open all year. 70,000 sq.m. Supermarket, Restaurant, bar and terrace (open March-Oct). General room with TV. Tennis. Children's playground. Entertainment in summer. Excursions. Telephone and post box. Medical post. Laundry. Car wash. Motorcaravan services. Bungalows for hire.

Charges 1997: (to 31 May 98) Per person esc. 680; child (5-10 yrs) 330; car 590; m/cycle 410; tent 600 - 930; caravan 710 - 980; motorcaravan 840 - 1,100, all acc. to size; boat 540; electricity 400. Off season discounts (up to 70%). Credit cards accepted.

Reservations: Contact Orbitur - Central de Reservas, Rua Diogo do Couto, 1-8°, 1100 Lisboa. Tel: (0)1/811 70 00 or 811 70 70. FAX: (0)1/814 80 45. E-mail: info@orbitur.pt. Internet: http://www.orbitur.pt.

THE ORBITUR CHAIN OF CAMPS

The Orbitur organisation runs a large chain of sites in Portugal ensuring consistency in standards and operating a central booking service. The sites are spread throughout Portugal and can provide comfortable holidays, especially if you avoid the peak weeks when they may be very full. The booking system would however ensure a place at these times. A few have a large number of permanent caravans but most are wholly for tourists - the reports in this guide make this clear.

The following Orbitur sites have not been inspected for this guide:

    Orbitur Camping Visieu   Orbitur Camping Angeiras   Orbitur Camping Montargil

    Orbitur Camping Portalegre   Orbitur Camping Madalena-Gaia

Reservations for any of the sites should be made through the central office (not to individual sites):

    Orbitur - Central de Reservas,

Rua Diogo do Couto, 1-8°, 1100 Lisboa.

Tel: (0)1/811 70 00 or 811 70 70. FAX: (0)1/814 80 45.

E-mail: info@orbitur.pt. Internet: http://www.orbitur.pt.

See colour advert
between pages 288/9

Membership of the Orbitur Camping Club, taken either with your booking or at any site (free for pensioners) grants a 10% discount on site charges. Camp charges are reasonable and there is a general reduction of 40% to 70% (depending on length of stay) from October to March inclusive.

814 Parque Municipal de Campismo de Monsanto, Lisbon

Acceptable site outside the city with swimming pool and other amenities.

The park-like entrance, with a wide avenue of trees, lawns and flowering shrubs leading up to the swimming pool, is probably this site's most attractive feature. The camp is on sloping ground with many levelled pitches and is well shaded by trees and shrubs. This extremely large site, with many permanent caravans and transit units of varying quality, can hold 7,000 people when full and is very impersonal. There is also a confusing booking-in procedure (no English spoken) with a separate fee. However, it is the closest site for visiting Lisbon. The twelve, rather basic toilet blocks, could be hard pressed to cope if site was full, could have been cleaner, and were in need of some refurbishment when inspected. They contain washbasins in tiled surrounds and British style toilets. There are free hot showers in each block. Separate units with hot water for clothes and dish washing. The site is 8 km. from central Lisbon with a public bus service (with organised excursions), and 10 km. from a decent beach, but it has a swimming pool (open only in high season and charged for).

How to find it: From Lisbon take motorway towards Estoril, camp signed at one of first exits to Sintra and Alges.

General Details: Open all year. 340,000 sq.m. Electrical connections. Shops and restaurants. Hairdressers. Tennis. Minigolf. Sports field. Playground. General and TV rooms. Launderette. Post office. Bank. Medical post. Car wash. Organised excursions. No dogs permitted.

Charges guide: Prices vary according to size and season. Per adult Esc 125 - 390; child under 10 yrs free; tent 100 - 740 (acc. to size); caravan 125 - 1050; car 100 - 255; motorcaravan 190 - 520; m/cycle 80 - 190.

Reservations: not made. Address: Estrada da Circunvalacao, 1400 Lisboa. Tel: 01/702061 or 2 or 3. FAX: 01/702062.

815 Orbitur Camping Costa da Caparica, Costa da Caparica, nr Lisbon

Site with small touring section at coastal resort 20 km. from Lisbon with quick access.

This is very much a site for 600 permanent caravans but it has very easy access to Lisbon (10 km.) via the motorway, by bus or even by bus and ferry if you wish. It is situated in a small resort, favoured by the Portuguese themselves, which has all the usual amenities plus a good sandy beach (200 m. from camp) and promenade walks. There is a small area for touring units which includes some special pitches for motorcaravans. The toilet blocks have mostly British style toilets, washbasins with cold water and free hot showers. Facilities are provided for the disabled.

How to find it: After crossing the Tagus bridge (toll) on the E4 motorway going south, immediately take the turning for Caparica. Turn right for Trafaria before entering Caparica.

General Details: Open all year. Supermarket. Large bar/restaurant (Feb-Nov). Children's playground. Some organised activities and shows in season - outdoor disco/entertainment area. Excursions. Washing machine. Treatment room; doctor calls daily in season. Motorcaravan services. Bungalows for hire.

Charges 1997: (to 31 May 98) Per person esc. 660; child (5-10 yrs) 330; car 590; m/cycle 410; tent 590 - 930; caravan 700 - 980; motorcaravan 830 - 1,100, all acc. to size; boat 540; electricity 400. Off season discounts (up to 70%). Credit cards accepted.

Reservations: Contact Orbitur - Central de Reservas, Rua Diogo do Couto, 1-8°, 1100 Lisboa. Tel: (0)1/811 70 00 or 811 70 70. FAX: (0)1/814 80 45. E-mail: info@orbitur.pt. Internet: http://www.orbitur.pt.

839 Parque de Campismo de Milfontes, Vila Nova de Milfontes

Pleasant site with good facilities, within walking distance of town and beach.

This popular site has the advantage of being open all year and being within walking distance of the town and beach. As such, it makes a perfect base for those visiting out of main season or for long winter stays when fees are heavily discounted. It is well lit, fenced, with a gate-man on duty at all times. The site has around 500 shady pitches on sandy terrain, which are marked out and divided by hedges and nicely paved paths. Electricity (6A) is available in all parts. The four toilet blocks (one new) are clean and well maintained and two blocks have suites for disabled people with ramps. There is a good supply of mainly British style WCs, bidets, washbasins (some with hot water), hot and cold showers, footbaths and some children's facilities, in a mix of combinations and styles. Hot water is free. Dishwashing and laundry sinks with cold water outside under cover. The site also has a restaurant and bar complex and a well stocked supermarket. Opportunities for fishing, canoeing and swimming from the resort beaches.

How to find it: From N120 coast road at Cercal, turn on E390 and continue into Vila Nova de Milfontes. Turn right in town following camp signs. Site on right at end of no through road. Do not confuse with site on left before it.

General Details: Open all year. Supermarket (1/4-30/9). Bar and snacks (1/4-30/9). Restaurant (June-Sept). TV room. Children's playground. Telephone. Laundry. Car wash. Chemical disposal. Motorcaravan services. Mobile homes and cabins for hire. English spoken. Dogs not permitted.

Charges 1998: Per person Esc 300 - 540; child (5-10 yrs) 150 - 270; small tent 220 - 410, large tent 240 - 450; caravan or motorcaravan: small 285 - 490, large 340 - 550; car 180 - 370; m/cycle 160 - 285; electricity 300. Credit cards accepted.

Reservations: Contact site. Address: 7645 Vila Nova de Milfontes. Tel: 083/96140 or 96693. FAX: 083/96104.

AR Discount
Less 10%
(excl. rental uints)

PORTUGAL - Algarve

841 Parque de Campismo de Armação de Pêra

Modern, attractive site with excellent facilities and own pool.

A wide attractive entrance with a parking area, and a gate-man to greet you - this well managed site has no shortage of staff, including a lifeguard on duty at the swimming pool. The 1,200 pitches on level grassy sand, marked by trees which provide some shade, are easily accessed from the tarmac and gravel roadways. Electricity (10A) is available for most pitches. Three modern, clean, well maintained sanitary blocks, provide British and Turkish style WCs, some with bidets, washbasins, and showers with hot water on payment. Excellent suite for disabled people. The restaurant/self service café and bar, and well stocked supermarket should cater for most needs, and you can relax around the swimming pool with a children's pool. The disco near to the entrance and café complex is soundproofed which should ensure peaceful nights. The site is within easy reach of Albufeira, Portimão and is 40 km. from Faro and makes an excellent base for stays in this region and for winter sun-seekers. Fishing, hunting and surfing near.

How to find it: Turn off EN125 road in Alcantarilha, taking the EN269-1 towards the coast. Site is on left side before Armação de Pêra. There are other sites in the area, so be sure to find the right one.

General Details: Open all year. Supermarket. Restaurant/self service café. 3 bars. Kiosk. Laundry. Games and TV rooms. Tennis. Children's playground. Swimming pool. Disco. Medical centre. Telephone and post box. Car wash.

Charges 1997: Per adult Esc 550; child (4-10 yrs) 275; tent or awning 500 - 650, acc. to size; caravan or motorcaravan 550 - 700; m/cycle 400; electricity 400. Less 50% in off season.

Reservations: Write to site. Address: 8365 Armação de Pêra (Algarve). Tel: 082/312296 or 312260. FAX 082/315379.

843 Parque de Campismo de Sagres, Sagres

Pleasant and extremely well maintained site at western tip of the Algarve.

Not very far from the lighthouse in the unspoilt southwest corner of Portugal, this site has 920 sandy pitches located amongst pine trees, which give good shade. There are some hardstandings for motorhomes and electrical connections (5A) throughout. The three modern, spacious sanitary blocks are excellently maintained and cleaned, providing hot and cold showers (hot showers are free with a token from reception), British style WCs, bidets, washbasins with cold water and footbaths. Dishwashing and laundry sinks are under cover outside the blocks. The restaurant, bar and cafe/grill provide reasonably priced meals including breakfast, and there is a supermarket. A swimming pool has been added, tennis courts are planned. A very good site for those seeking winter sun, or as a base for exploring this `Land's End' region of Portugal, away from the hustle and bustle of the more crowded resorts. The beaches and the town of Sagres (the departure point of the Portuguese navigators) with its fort, are a short drive.

How to find it: Turn off road EN268, approx 2 km before Sagres, site is signed.

General Details: Open all year. Supermarket, restaurant/bar and cafe/grill (all 1/4-15/10). TV room. Swimming pool (on payment). Bicycle hire. Barbecue area. Children's playground. Medical post. Laundry. Car wash. Chemical disposal. Motorcaravan services. English spoken.

Charges 1998: Per adult Esc. 500 - 700; child (4-10 yrs) 250 - 350; small tent or awning 400 - 600, medium 500 - 750, large 600 - 850; caravan small 500 - 750, large 600 - 850; car 250 - 450; m/cycle 150 - 250; motorcaravan small 600 - 800, large 600 - 950; electricity 250 - 350.

Reservations: Write to site. Address: 8650 Vila do Bispo (Algarve). Tel: 082/624351. FAX: 082/624445.

820 Orbitur Camping Valverde, Praia da Luz, nr Lagos

Large, well run site with many individual pitches and good range of amenities.

A little over 1 km. from the village of Praia da Luz and its beach and about 7 km. from Lagos, this site is certainly worth considering for your stay in the Algarve. Taking around 1,000 units, it has 600 individual, numbered pitches, mostly 40-60 sq.m., some larger - up to 100 sq.m. which are enclosed by hedges. All are on flat ground or broad terraces with good shade in most parts from established trees and shrubs. Six large, clean, toilet blocks, have British style WCs, washbasins and sinks, some with cold water only, and free hot showers. Units for disabled people. On site is a swimming pool with slide (200 sq.m), children's pool (under 10's free - adults charged). An excellent, well maintained site with good security, it attracts a good number of long-term winter visitors who are actively encouraged by Orbitur, and the site is extremely well managed by Senhor Pinto and his wife, who are helpful and friendly.

How to find it: Fork left on N125 road 3 km. west of Lagos to Praia da Luz and site is under 1 km.

General Details: Open all year. 100,000 sq.m. Supermarket, shops, restaurant and bar complex with both self-service and waiter service in season (April - Oct). Takeaway. Swimming pool with water slide (June-Sept). Children's pool. Playground. Tennis court with markings for other sports. General room with TV. Excursions. Telephone and post box. Laundry. Motorcaravan services. Bungalows, apartments and caravans to let.

Charges 1997: (to 31 May 98) Per person esc. 700; child (5-10 yrs) 350; car 590; m/cycle 410; tent 600 - 930; caravan 720 - 980; motorcaravan 890 - 1,100, all acc. to size; boat 540; electricity (6A) 400. Off season discounts (up to 70%). Credit cards accepted.

Reservations: Contact Orbitur - Central de Reservas, Rua Diogo do Couto, 1-8°, 1100 Lisboa. Tel: (0)1/811 70 00 or 811 70 70. FAX: (0)1/814 80 45. E-mail: info@orbitur.pt. Internet: http://www.orbitur.pt.

821 Camping Albufeira, Albufeira, nr Faro

Attractive, high quality site, with many amenities, close to town and beaches.

One of the better sites on the Algarve, with installations and amenities well above the usual standard, and of which the English speaking staff are justifiably proud. The 1,500 pitches are on fairly flat ground with some terracing, small trees and shrubs give reasonable shade in most parts. There are some marked and numbered pitches of 50-80 sq.m. Winter stays are encouraged, with many facilities remaining open including a heated pool. An attractively designed complex of traditional Portuguese style buildings on the hill which forms the central area of the site, is surrounded by a variety of flowers, shrubs, well watered lawns and a fountain. The waiter and self-service restaurants, a pizzeria, bars and a sound proofed disco, have views across the three swimming pools and a waterslide pool. There are five good, clean toilet blocks. One is heated for winter use and all have British style toilets, washbasins, controllable showers, laundry and dishwashing sinks with free hot water throughout. They may be hard pressed when the site is full (July/Aug) and are some distance from some pitches.

How to find it: From N125 coast road or N264 (from Lisbon) at new junctions follow signs to `Albufeira'. Site is approx. 1 km. from junctions, on left.

General Details: Open all year. Supermarket and shops. Restaurants. Bars. Disco. Swimming pool complex. TV room. Hairdresser. Safe deposit. Children's playground. Bicycles/motorbikes for hire. Tennis. Minigolf. Sports park. Excursions and organised entertainment. Telephone and post box. Medical post. Laundry. Car wash. Camp bus service to Albufeira (2 km). Caravans and apartments for rent.

Charges guide: Per adult Esc 795; child (4-10) 395; car 795; caravan or tent 795 - 895, acc. to size; motorcaravan 1170 - 1,790; m/cycle 530; electricity 450. (50% discount winter season).

Reservations: are made to give individual pitch, no deposit or fee. Address: 8200 Albufeira (Algarve). Tel: 089/587629. FAX: 089/587633.

842 Parque de Campismo Caliço, Vila Nova de Cacela

Neat, tidy site, with own pool, set back from the coast in eastern Algarve.

This refurbished site is on higher ground with good views, with around 300 unmarked pitches on sparse, undulating grass with some terracing. There is good access for most units on gravel site roads. Electricity (5A) is available to most pitches, although some may need long leads. The sanitary blocks are well cared for and provides free hot, or cold showers in cubicles, cold water in washbasins (some in curtained cubicles), British style WCs, bidets and footbaths. There are dishwashing and laundry sinks (cold water), and a washing machine. Extra toilet and shower facilities are with the changing rooms for the excellent, clean, swimming pool. The restaurant/bar has an attractive terrace (with oleanders and bougainvillias) overlooking the pool. There are relatively few good sites at this end of the Algarve but Caliço should make a comfortable stop-over in this region.

How to find it: Turn from EN125 at Km stone 147.3, and drive through Vila Nova de Cacela (site is signed). Continue over railway bridge turning left at camp sign, follow lane to site past water tower.

General Details: Open all year. Shop. Cafe/bar and terrace. Restaurant. Swimming pool. Games room. Children's playground. Laundry. Chemical disposal. Telephone and post box. Medical post. Some English spoken.

Charges guide: Per adult Esc. 240 - 385; child (over 4 yrs) 120 - 180; small tent 185 - 290, large tent 295 - 480; caravan 185 - 290; car 150 - 240; m/cycle 60 - 90; small motorcaravan 240 - 385, large 280 - 475; electricity 285 - 380; awning 125 - 195.

Reservations: Write to site. Address: Vila Nova de Cacela (Algarve). Tel: 081/951195 or 951360.

822 Orbitur Camping, Quarteira, nr Faro

Algarve site near the sea on the outskirts of Quarteira.

This is a large site on undulating ground, taking around 795 units. On the outskirts of the popular Algarve resort of Quarteira, it is 600 m. from a sandy beach which stretches for 1 km. to the town centre. Many of the unmarked pitches have shade from tall trees and there are a few small individual pitches of 50 sq.m. with electricity and water for reservation. There are 680 electrical connections (15A). The five sanitary blocks provide British and Turkish style toilets, individual basins with cold water, shelves and mirrors, and free hot showers plus new facilities for the disabled. Like others along this coast, the site encourages long winter stays. Swimming pool planned for '98.

How to find it: Turn off N125 south towards Quarteira in Almancil (8 km. west of Faro). Site 5 km. from junction.

General Details: Open all year. 10.6 ha. Supermarket, self-service restaurant (Feb - Nov). Separate takeaway (from late May). General room with bar and TV. Tennis. Kiosk. Open air disco. Medical treatment room. Doctor on call. Washing machines. Car wash area. Motorcaravan services. Orbitur bungalows for hire.

Charges 1997: (to 31 May 98) Per person esc. 720; child (5-10 yrs) 360; car 590; m/cycle 410; tent 600 - 930; caravan 730 - 990; motorcaravan 900 - 1,100, all acc. to size; boat 540; electricity 400. Off season discounts (up to 70%). Credit cards accepted.

Reservations: Contact Orbitur - Central de Reservas, Rua Diogo do Couto, 1-8°, 1100 Lisboa. Tel: (0)1/811 70 00 or 811 70 70. FAX: (0)1/814 80 45. E-mail: info@orbitur.pt. Internet: http://www.orbitur.pt.

PORTUGAL - Algarve

823 Camping Olhão, Pinheiros de Marim, nr Olhão

Large, well laid out and acceptable site in eastern Algarve.

This site, taking around 2,000 units and open all year, has been developed in the grounds of an old house and mature trees provide reasonable shade. The pitches are marked, numbered and in rows divided by shrubs with electricity and water to all parts. There are many permanent and long stay units and the tourist pitches fill up quickly between June and August - so arrive early. Amenities include swimming pools and tennis courts (both charged for), a restaurant/ bar and a café/bar with TV and games room. The eleven sanitary blocks which were reasonably clean when seen but in need of some refurbishment, are specifically sited to be a maximum of 50 m. from any pitch. Each has British toilets, bidets and a free hot shower. There is some noise nuisance from an adjacent railway. The large, sandy beaches in this area are on offshore islands reached by ferry and are, as a result, relatively quiet; some are reserved for naturists. There is a bus service to the nearest ferry at Olhao.

How to find it: Just over 1 km. east of Olhão, on EN125, take turn to Pinheiros de Marim. Site is 300 m. on left.

General Details: Open all year, as are all facilities. Supermarket. Kiosk. Restaurant. Bar. Laundry. Children's playgrounds. Swimming pool (all year). Tennis. Volleyball. Bicycle hire. Café with TV. Telephone and post box. Medical post. Car wash area. Chemical disposal. Bus service 50 m. Mobile homes and caravans to hire.

Charges 1997: Per adult esc. 300 - 600; child (5-12 yrs) 150 - 300; car 250 - 500; tent 200 - 400, 300 - 600 or 500 - 1,000, acc. to size; caravan or motorcaravan 400 - 800 or 600 - 1,200; m/cycle 125 - 250; electricity 210. Less for longer winter stays.

Reservations: Contact site. Address: 8700 Olhão (Algarve). Tel: 089/700 1300. FAX 089/700 1390. E-mail: sbsicamping@mail.telepac.pt. Internet: http://www.sbsi.pt/camping.

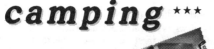

844 Parque de Campismo Quintos dos Carriços, Praia de Salema

Attractive, peaceful, valley site with naturist area, in unspoilt western Algarve.

A traditional tiled Portuguese style entrance gateway leads you into this excellent and well maintained site which has a village atmosphere. The site has been developed over the years by the Dutch owner and his family and there are plans to build a further new sanitary block. The camp is spread over two valleys (which are real sun-traps), with the partially terraced pitches marked and divided by small trees and shrubs (oleanders and roses). A small stream (dry when seen) meanders through the site. The more remote part of this site has been `adopted' by naturists, but it is also open to ordinary campers - dress or non-dress optional! Although the site is lit, torches may be required in the more remote corners. The four current sanitary blocks are modern, spacious, well tiled with quality fittings, and are spotlessly clean. These provide British style WCs, washbasins with cold water, and hot showers on payment. There are dishwashing and laundry sinks and a washing machine plus an excellent facility for disabled people. Open daily (including Sundays) throughout the year is a well stocked mini-market. The restaurant and bar open daily in season. A very popular site for summer and winter sun-worshippers, within easy driving distance of resorts. The many fine beaches in the region provide ample opportunities for diving, swimming and fishing. Also available nearby are tennis, squash, riding, golf and there are excellent walks from the site.

How to find it: Turn off RN125 (Lagos-Sagres) road at junction to Salema (17 km. from Lagos); site is signed.

General Details: Open all year. Mini-market (all year). Restaurant (daily 1/3-15/10). Bar (once a week only 15/10-1/3). TV room. Telephone and post box. Bicycles, scooters, mopeds and m/cycles for hire. Safety deposit. Money exchange. Laundry. Car wash. Chemical disposal. Apartments for rent.

Charges 1998: Per adult Esc. 640; child 310; tent 640 - 825; caravan 885; car 640; m/cycle 460; motorcaravan 980 - 1,130; electricity 210. Discounts for long winter stays. Credit cards accepted.

Reservations: Contact site. Address: Praia de Salema, 8650 Vila de Bispo (Algarve). Tel: 082/695201, 695400 or 695401. FAX: 082/695122.

835 Camping Markadia, Barragem de Odivelas, nr Alvito

Superb, lakeside touring site, miles from anywhere!

This site will appeal most to those nature lovers who want to 'get away from it all' and to those who enjoy country pursuits such as walking, fishing or riding. The lake is in fact a 2,500 ha. reservoir, and more than 120 species of birds can be found in the area. The open countryside and lake provide good views and a very pleasant environment, albeit somewhat remote. This is an outstanding site by any standards with some of the best installations to be found on a campsite anywhere in Europe. There are 130 unmarked pitches on undulating grassy ground with ample 16A electrical connections. The Dutch owner tries to ensure that each pitch has its own (numbered!) small oak tree to provide shade. Four very modern, spotlessly clean, and superbly equipped sanitary blocks, are built in traditional Portuguese style. They have controllable showers, British style WCs and bidets, washbasins, dishwashing and laundry sinks (open air); free hot water throughout. Washing machines and ironing boards. The bar/restaurant with terrace is open daily in season but weekends only during the winter. One can swim in the reservoir (free) and rowing boats, pedaloes and windsurfers are available for hire. You may bring your own boat, although power boats are discouraged on environmental grounds. Dogs not permitted July/Aug. Facilities and amenities may be reduced outside the main season.

How to find it: Site signed from N2 between Torrao and Ferreira do Alentejo, 7 km. from village of Odivelas.

General Details: Open all year. Swimming pools (1/6-15/9). Bar. Restaurant (Oct - March weekends only or on request). Shop (all year). Lounge. Laundry. Children's playground. Telephone. Medical post. Fishing. Boat hire. Bicycle hire. Tennis. Horse riding. Car wash. Chemical disposal. Motorcaravan services. Apartments for rent.

Charges 1997: Per adult Esc. 680; child (5-10 yrs) 340; tent or caravan 680; car or m/cycle 680; motorcaravan 1,360; electricity 340. Discounts of up to 60% acc. to season. Credit cards not accepted.

Reservations: are made - write to site for details. Address: Aptdo 17, Barragem de Odivelas, 7920 Alvito. Tel: 084/76141. FAX: 084/76294.

AR Discount
Less10% on camp site fees

834 Orbitur Camping Evora, Evora

Well equipped site with swimming pool, close to historic walled town.

Situated some 1½ km. from the historic former provincial capital, this is one of the most modern and well equipped sites in the Orbitur chain with the benefit of a good sized, new swimming pool (for which there is a separate charge). There is also a pleasantly constructed small restaurant on site, popular also with locals, in addition to another snack bar/small bar. A new sanitary block with free hot showers and modern British style WCs, in addition to another, older block should be sufficient provision. Most of the 500 pitches have 15A electricity and those in the older part of the site (some 250) have well developed shade. A small market sells essentials and a range of local specialities. It is a useful site from which to explore the town and surrounding area with its megalithic monuments.

How to find it: Site is 1½ km. southwest of the town on the N380 road to Alcacovas.

General Details: Open all year. Restaurant, bar, snack bar and shop (April-Oct). Swimming pool (May - Sept). Tennis court. Children's play area. Shop. Laundry. Motorcaravan services.

Charges 1997: (to 31 May 98) Per person esc. 580; child (5-10 yrs) 290; car 490; m/cycle 340; tent 480 - 810; caravan 570 - 890; motorcaravan 710 - 960, all acc. to size; boat 360; electricity 360. Off season discounts (up to 70%). Credit cards accepted.

Reservations: Contact Orbitur - Central de Reservas, Rua Diogo do Couto, 1-8°, 1100 Lisboa. Tel: (0)1/811 70 00 or 811 70 70. FAX: (0)1/814 80 45. E-mail: info@orbitur.pt. Internet: http://www.orbitur.pt.

836 Parque de Campismo, Barragem de Idanha-a-Nova, nr Castelo Branco

Smart, new, good value site, with pool and quality installations, in attractive location.

This very attractive, well laid out municipal site is located in quiet, unspoilt countryside beside a reservoir, near the small town of Idanha-a-Nova. The site has around 500 unmarked pitches on wide grassy terraces and there is a little shade from young trees. Electricity (16A) is included in the price. The four large sanitary blocks, built in the traditional Portuguese style, provide a plentiful supply of British style WCs (some with bidets), washbasins, some in private cabins, free hot showers with dividers, shelves and hooks, foot baths and facilities for the disabled. Dishwashing and laundry sinks (cold water). Amenities include tennis courts with stadium-style spectator seating and a good sized swimming pool with child's pool, together with several children's playgrounds. A good supermarket, restaurant, bar and terrace complex is located centrally on site.

How to find it: Approach from the south using the N240. Turn off at Ladoeiro on to N354 and follow signs to Barragem and site. Do not approach via the town of Idanha-a-Nova.

General Details: Open all year. Supermarket. Cafe, bar and restaurant (open main season). Swimming pool. Tennis courts. TV room. Laundry. Telephone and post box. Medical post. Car wash. Canoe hire. Bungalows for hire.

Charges guide: Per adult Esc 200; child (4-10) 100; tent (small) 100, (large) 300; caravan 400; car 200; m/cycle 100; motorcaravan 400; electricity incl. Discounts for long stay off season.

Reservations: Write to site. Address: Barragem de Idanha-a-Nova, Castelo Branco. Tel: 077/22793.

PORTUGAL - Inland

832 Orbitur Camping Guarda, Guarda

Inland site perched on a hill-top, with a good panoramic view.

This site takes around 135 units and is just 50 km. from the Spanish frontier, on perhaps the most popular route for entering Portugal, so it makes a very good night stop. It is therefore mainly a transit site, although some people stay on if the weather is good. The well fenced and gated site is partly covered by mature pine trees, and is on terraced or undulating ground partially surrounding a public park. There are some level pitches for caravans and the site is well lit at night. The two sanitary blocks are an adequate supply with British and Turkish style toilets, washbasins with cold water and 3 free hot showers per sex. Electrical connections (long leads may be required) and water points to all parts. Tenters may have difficulty getting tent pegs into the hard, somewhat gritty, ground. Guarda has some old buildings and the region is also noted for its colourful markets, Serra cheese, handicrafts of all descriptions, religious festivals and winter sports.

How to find it: Site is 5 km. from the new bypass road on a hill-top on western side of town. Follow signs for the centre of Guarda then camp signs.

General Details: Open 1 March - 30 Oct. Mini-market, restaurant, bar (May - Sept). General room with TV. Telephone and post box. First aid. Laundry. Motorcaravan services. Bus service 50 m.

Charges 1997: (to 31 May 98) Per person esc. 580; child (5-10 yrs) 290; car 490; m/cycle 340; tent 480 - 810; caravan 570 - 890; motorcaravan 710 - 960, all acc. to size; boat 360; electricity 360. Off season discounts (up to 70%). Credit cards accepted.

Reservations: Contact Orbitur - Central de Reservas, Rua Diogo do Couto, 1-8°, 1100 Lisboa. Tel: (0)1/811 70 00 or 811 70 70. FAX: (0)1/814 80 45. E-mail: info@orbitur.pt. Internet: http://www.orbitur.pt.

831 Orbitur Camping Castro Daire, Castro Daire

Traditional small touring site beside the Carvalhal spa.

Situated in the mountains in the Dao Lafóes tourist region, between Castro Daire and Visieu, only the main road (somewhat noisy but quite well screened) separates the site from the sulphur spa and hotel complex. This has a swimming pool and tennis court (open from June). The site is small, very attractive with a garden-like atmosphere, and has two of the best toilet blocks we have seen in Portugal. These have free hot showers, British toilets and washbasins with cold water. There are sinks for clothes and washing up at various points through the site. The pitches are on level grass, terraced in places, with some shade from pine and oak trees. There are 60 electrical connections (15A). A small 'cottage' has an open fire to barbecue food and there is a snack bar. This is a comfortable base from which one can explore the historic old spa towns and villages of this most beautiful and unspoilt mountain region.

How to find it: Site is 5 km. south of Castro Daire beside the A2 road to Visieu.

General Details: Open 1 June - 30 Sept. Bar (July/Aug). Barbecue house. Children's playground. Telephone and post box. Laundry. Tourist information. French spoken.

Charges 1997: (to 31 May 98) Per person esc. 480; child (5-10 yrs) 240; car 430; m/cycle 300; tent 400 - 700; caravan 500 - 770; motorcaravan 610 - 950, all acc. to size; boat 360; electricity 360. Off season discounts (up to 70%). Credit cards not accepted.

Reservations: Contact Orbitur - Central de Reservas, Rua Diogo do Couto, 1-8°, 1100 Lisboa. Tel: (0)1/811 70 00 or 811 70 70. FAX: (0)1/814 80 45. E-mail: info@orbitur.pt. Internet: http://www.orbitur.pt.

833 Orbitur Camping Arganil, Sarzedo, nr Arganil

Quiet, inland site attractively situated on the hillside above the river Alva.

The site is located in the hamlet of Sarzedo, some 2 km. from the town of Arganil. A spacious and well planned site, delightfully situated among pine trees above the River Alva where one can swim, fish, canoe and windsurf. The 150 pitches, most with electricity (15A), are of a reasonable size and are mainly on flat sandy grass terraces shaded by tall trees. Access roads are tarmac. There is a bar/restaurant and shop (closed on Tuesdays!) and a children's play area. Sanitary facilities are clean and well maintained, with mainly British WCs, controllable free hot showers, washbasins in semi-private partitioned cabins and hairdressing area with electric sockets. Ramped entrances make it suitable for the disabled. Laundry facilities include washing machines. The site also has 5 attractive A-framed timber chalets, with views over the river and countryside, for rent. There is a swimming pool in Arganil.

How to find it: From EN17 Guarda-Coimbra road, take EN342 towards Arganil. Site is signed in the village of Sarzedo, about 2 km. northwest of Arganil.

General Details: Open all year. Restaurant. Bar (July/Aug). Children's play area. TV room. Tennis. Telephone and post box. Laundry. Car wash. Bus service 50 m. Bungalows for hire.

Charges 1997: (to 31 May 98) Per person esc. 480; child (5-10 yrs) 240; car 430; m/cycle 300; tent 400 - 700; caravan 500 - 770; motorcaravan 610 - 950, all acc. to size; boat 360; electricity 360. Off season discounts (up to 70%). Credit cards not accepted.

Reservations: Contact Orbitur - Central de Reservas, Rua Diogo do Couto, 1-8°, 1100 Lisboa. Tel: (0)1/811 70 00 or 811 70 70. FAX: (0)1/814 80 45. E-mail: info@orbitur.pt. Internet: http://www.orbitur.pt.

837 Parque Campismo de Cerdeira, Campo do Gerês

Quiet, inland, `away from it all' site with excellent facilities, in National Park.

Situated in the National Park of Peneda Gerês, amidst spectacular mountain scenery, this fairly new site offers modern facilities in a truly natural area. The National Park is home to all manner of flora, fauna and wildlife, including the roebuck, weasel, badger, wolf and wild boar. The well fenced, quiet, site has some 350 unmarked, mostly level, grassy pitches in a shady woodland setting. Electricity (5 or 10A) is available for most pitches, though some long leads may be required. Although the site is lit, a torch would be useful. There are three very clean sanitary blocks with mixed style WCs, washbasins and controllable showers. Free hot water throughout. Dishwashing and laundry sinks under cover. A timber, lodge style complex near the site entrance provides a restaurant serving a full range of good value meals (including breakfasts), a bar and terrace, takeaway and mini-market. Small playground for children. Opportunities in the area for fishing, riding, swimming, canoeing, mountain biking and climbing.

How to find it: From the N103 (Braga-Chaves road), take N308 towards Campo Do Gerês and Gerês. Proceed down a steep hill and across bridge over lake, to a roundabout. Take `straight on' exit and camp is signed (14 km). Follow signs, and enjoy the scenery.

General Details: Open all year. Mini-market. Restaurant/bar and takeaway (1/4-15/10, except school holidays). Children's playground. Bicycle hire. TV room. Telephone and post box. Medical post. Laundry. Motorcaravan services. Tourist information. Bungalows for hire. Good English spoken.

Charges 1997: Per adult Esc 500 - 600; child (5-11 yrs) 300 - 350; tent: small 400 - 500, medium 600 - 700, large 700 - 800; caravan: small 700 - 800, medium 800 - 900, large 900 - 1,000; car 450 - 550; m/cycle 300 - 350; motorcaravan: small 800 - 900, medium 900 - 1,000, large 1,000 - 1,100; electricity 5A 350, 10A 750. Credit cards accepted.

Reservations: Contact site. Address: Campo do Gerês, 4840 Terras de Bouro. Tel: 053/351005 or 357065. FAX: 053/357065.

838 Parque Natural de Vilar de Mouros, nr Seixas

Traditional, small and friendly site, in quiet country location, with own pool.

Located some 15 minutes walk (downhill) from the village of Vilar de Mouros and very close to the Spanish border, this small site is ideal for those looking for a more traditional campsite. The 45 marked pitches for caravans and motorcaravans, all with electricity (2 or 5A), are on slightly sloping, grassy terraces, with a separate unmarked area for tents, all set amongst trees and vines on a hillside. There are two toilet blocks, very much in the quainter, older Portuguese style, providing British style WCs (some with bidets), washbasins (cold water), and free hot showers, they also had soap and paper towel dispensers. Dishwashing and laundry sinks (cold water) under cover. The site has a good range of other amenities which include a tennis court, unusual small stone swimming pool and children's pool (free to campers), a good cafe/bar (open 8 am.-11 pm), takeaway service, a self-service restaurant with shady terrace, and a mini-market. By far the most popular attraction is the regular Saturday evening organised gastronomic and folklore trips (with free mini-bus transport) to the site owners own hotel 2 km. away. French and a little English spoken.

How to find it: Site is signed from the N13, just north of Seixas, turn towards Vilar de Mouros. Site is on right just before village.

General Details: Open all year. Mini-market. Cafe/bar. Self-service restaurant. Swimming pool. Tennis court. TV room. Washing machine. Children's pool and playground. Telephone and post box. Medical post. Bicycle hire. Local folklore entertainment trips. Hotel rooms for rent.

Charges guide: Per adult Esc. 500; child 240; tent (small) 400, (large) 450 - 500; caravan 450 - 550; car 400; m/cycle 350; motorcaravan 480 - 550; electricity 350.

Reservations: Contact site. Address: Vilar de Mouros, 4910 Caminha. Tel: 058/727472. FAX: as phone.

ALAN ROGERS' Good Camps Guide

EUROPE 1998 - DISCOUNT VOUCHERS

Between pages 160 and 161 you will find various Discount Vouchers which will provide you with potential savings of much more than the cost of the Guide itself!

(These vouchers are valid 1 January - 31 December 1998 only)

Voucher A Campsite Discount Voucher	**Voucher B** Travel and Breakdown Insurance
Voucher C Caravan or Motorcaravan Insurance	**Voucher D** Caravan and Camping Service
Voucher E Sites Abroad Holidays	**Voucher F** Camping Cheque
Voucher G Track Tours	

Save Money!

SLOVAKIA

Slovakia became an independent republic on 1st January 1993, following the split of the former Czechoslovakia into its two component parts - the Czech Republic in the west and Slovakia in the east. It is situated in central Europe, sharing boundaries with the Czech Republic, Austria, Poland, Hungary and the Ukraine. It is hilly and picturesque, with historic castles, thick forests, mountain streams, valleys and lakes, and the culture reflects a strong Hungarian influence in terms of music, food and architecture. The Danube flows briefly into Slovakia and then along the border with Hungary. Spa towns and good skiing are winter attractions. For further information contact:

Slovak Tourist Centre, 25 Kensington Palace Gardens, London W8 4QY. Tel: 0171 243 0803

Population
5,403,500 (94); density 110 per sq. km.

Capital
Bratislava

Climate
Cold winters and mild summers. Hot summers and some rain in the eastern lowlands.

Language
The official language is Slovak. Some English or German in hotels and restaurants.

Currency
Koruna or Crown (Skr) = 100 halierov. Notes are Sk. 50, 100, 200, 500 and 1000; coins are Sk. 1, 2, 5,10,20 and 50.

Banks
Hours are Mon-Fri 08.00-13.00 and 14.00-17.00; banks are closed on Sat. Only notes exchanged at most border change offices
Credit cards: The major ones can be used to obtain currency and in some hotels, restaurants shops and some petrol stations in towns and tourist areas. Travellers cheques and Eurocheques are widely accepted.

Post Offices
Offices are open Mon-Sat 08.00-16.00.

Telephones
The dialling code for Slovakia is 0042.

Time
GMT plus one hour, BST + 1 in summer.

Public Holidays
New Year; Easter Mon; May Day; Liberation Day, 8 May; Saints Day, 5 July; Festival Day, 6 July; 28 Oct; Christmas, 24, 25, 26 Dec.

Shops
Open Mon-Fri 09.00-12.00 and 14.00-18.00. Some remain open at midday. Sat: 09.00-midday.

Motoring
The major route runs from Bratislava via Trengin, Banska, Bystrica, Zilina and Poprad to Presov. A full UK driving licence is acceptable. Petrol stations on international roads and in main towns are open 24 hours.
Tolls: A windscreen sticker which is valid for a year must be purchased at the border crossing for use on certain motorways.
Speed limits: Caravans 31 mph (50 kph) in built up areas and 50 mph (80 kph) on all other roads. Motorhomes (3.5 tons) 31 mph (50 kph) in built up areas 56 mph (90 kph) other roads and 69 mph (110 kph) on motorways.
Parking: Vehicles must be parked on the right.

Overnighting
Not allowed on open land. Elsewhere permissible where a toilet is in situ.

Useful Addresses
HEPEX Ltd (the agency for tourism), P.O. 32, 94501 Komarno, Slovakia.
National Motoring Organisation.
Ustredni Automotoklub SR Wolkrova ut 4, 85101 Bratislava. Tel: 07 850 911.

490 Autocamping Trusalová, Turany

Small, quiet site on edge of National Park.

Autocamping Trusalová is situated right on the southern edge of the Malá Fatra National Park, north east of the historic town of Martin which has much to offer to tourists, despite being best known for the engineering works which produced most of the tanks for the Warsaw Pact countries before the recent revolution and change to a more democratic regime. Paths from the site lead into the Park making it an ideal base for walkers and serious hikers who wish to enjoy this lovely region. The site is in two halves, one on the left of entrance and the other behind reception each having its own old, but clean and acceptable, sanitary provision of British WCs and hot water in basins, sinks and showers. Surrounded by trees with a stream rushing along one side, pitches are grass from a hard road with room for about 80 units and there are bungalows to rent. The area behind reception is on a slight slope. There is a bar just outside the camp and shops in the village about 3 km. away. There is a large, outdoor chess board, volleyball, table tennis and a TV lounge. Each section has a covered barbecue area with raised fire box, chimney, tables and chairs. Information on the area is available from reception. We received a most friendly welcome from the German speaking staff. A quiet, orderly and pleasant camp.

How to find it: Turn north at Motorest Fatra on the road 18/E50 near village of Turany to camp.

General Details: Open 1 June - 15 Sept. 40,000 sq.m. Volleyball. Table tennis. TV lounge. Chemical disposal. Bungalows to rent.

Charges 1998: Per person Sks. 53; child (6-15 yrs) 25; tent 55; caravan 75; motorcaravan 100; car 50; m/cycle 30; electricity 50; dog 20; local tax 9.

Reservations: Write to site in German. Address: 03853 Turany. Tel: 0842/292636 or 292667.

495 Autocamping Zlaté piesky, Bratislava

Edge of town site by large lake.

Bratislava undoubtedly has charm, being on the Danube and having a number of interesting buildings and churches in its centre. However, industry around the city, particularly en-route to the camp from the south, presents an ugly picture and gives no hints of the hidden charms.Zlate piesky (golden sands) is part of a large, lakeside sports complex which is also used during the day in summer by local residents. The camp is on the edge of town with about 200 pitches - 120 with electrical connections - on level grass under tall trees. There are 20 well equipped and many more simple bungalows for hire spread around the site. There are two restaurants, one with waiter service, the other self service and many small snack bars around the camp and adjoining lakeside recreation area. The lake is available for swimming and watersports with pedaloes for hire and there is a fitness area in the park. There are four sanitary blocks, two for campers and two for day visitors and these may be hard pressed during high season. At the time of our visit, privatisation was imminent and the very friendly (English speaking) management were uncertain of the future direction of the camp. It could suit for a night stop or a short stay. If you are looking for a quieter site with fewer facilities, Intercamp may suit.

How to find it: Follow signs on road no. 61 for Zillina and airport and pick up signs for camp. Zlaté piesky is on the left on entering the sports area, Intercamp is on the right.

General Details: Open 1 May - 15 Oct. 90,000 sq.m. Restaurants. Snack bars. Shops. Lake for swimming and watersports with large beach area. Table tennis. Minigolf. Room with billiards and electronic games. Disco. Doctor calls. Children's play areas. Bungalows and chalets to rent.

Charges guide: Per person Sks. 30 - 60, acc. to season; child (6-15 yrs) 15 - 40; caravan 30 - 60; motorcaravan 40 - 140, acc. to season and size; tent 15- 50; electricity 35 - 70; local tax (summer) 10, child 5.

Reservations: Write to site. Address: 82104 Bratislava. Tel: 07/257373 (reception).

494 Autocamping Neresnica, Zvolen

Small site on main route from Budapest to Warsaw.

If you are travelling through Slovakia from Hungary to Poland and looking for a night stop or exploring the central Slovak area, Neresnica is well situated, being on the main 66/E77 highway just to the south of the town. There could be some traffic noise but we did not notice this during our one night stay. The glories of Zvolen lie in the past rather than the present, but the camp, under private ownership, is surrounded by trees with a rushing steam along one side. The level site has room for 65 units with unmarked pitches of grass from tarmac roads and electrical connections (10A) for about 60%. The two sanitary blocks, one at either end of camp, are basic rather than luxurious but clean with British WCs, hot water in troughs and cold in cabins for washing and hot water for washing dishes under cover. Special covered areas have barbecue pits with tables and benches. The restaurant (at entrance) has an extensive menu with good value meals and sometimes provides music from a violin, cello, zither trio. Well designed bungalows for hire. Apart from Slovak, only German is spoken.

How to find it: From Zvolen centre take road 66/E77 towards Sahy. Site is signed as Neresnica at junction with 50/E571 road to Lucenec.

General Details: Open all year. 25,000 sq.m. Restaurant. Shops and swimming pool 200 m. Bungalows for hire.

Charges guide: Per person Sks. 40; child (under 10) 5; tent 50; caravan 70; car 30; motorcaravan 70; electricity 60.

Reservations: Write to site in German. Address: 96001 Zvolen. Tel: 0855/22651.

493 Autocamp Tourist Club Kosice Hamre, nr Kosice

Neat, rural site for winter and summer sports.

There is much of natural and historical interest in this part of Eastern Slovakia and T.C. Kosice is situated in beautiful mountain scenery north west of the ancient town of Kosice. Surrounded by tree clad mountains and rolling hills and by a lake, this neat, orderly site provides a quiet base for winter ski-ing (with a drag lift from the camp) and for water sports and walking in the summer. There are more simple bungalows to rent than there are pitches which are not numbered or marked out on flat grass near the lake. There are two sanitary blocks with one for campers near the lake and one for the bungalows near the restaurant. The well appointed, large restaurant also has a separate bar and terrace and a kiosk in the camping area carries basic food supplies and snacks. There is an excellent children's playground and minigolf as well as a games room with mini-bar.

How to find it: Site is signed on the Kosice - Margecarney road.

General Details: Open all year. Restaurant. Bar. Snack bar/kiosk for basics. Ski drag lift. Minigolf. Children's playground. Swimming, boating and other watersports. Games room. Bungalows for hire.

Charges guide: Per person Sks. 30; caravan or tent 40; car 40; motorcaravan 50; electricity (15A) 33.

Reservations: Contact site. Address: 04465 Kosice Hamre, Kosice. Tel: 095/961144.

SLOVAKIA

492 Autocamping Trencin, Trencin

Small, neat site on river near sports centre.

Trencin is an interesting town with a long history and dominated by the partly restored castle which towers high above. The small camp with room for 30 units - all with electricity - and rooms to let, stands on an island about 1 km. from town centre opposite a large sports complex. Pitches occupy a grass area surrounded by bungalows, with the castle high on one side and woods and hills on the other. The sanitary block, also used by occupants of the bungalows, is old but tiled and clean with British WCs and hot water in the washbasins (in cabins with curtains) and showers (doors and curtains) under cover but not enclosed. A good sized room has electric cookers, fridge/freezer, tables and chairs. Hot water for washing clothes and dishes. There is a bar in summer with restaurant at 200 m and shops at 300 m. Tennis near, boating and fishing in river. Some road and rail noise. A very neat, tidy friendly camp with English spoken during our visit.

How to find it: Site is signed in places in town, otherwise head for town sports centre.

General Details: Open 15 May - 31 Sept. 20,000 sq.m. Little shade. Bar in high season. Restaurants and shops near. Tennis, boating, fishing.

Charges guide: Per person Sks. 75; child (6-15 yrs) 35; caravan 60; car 60; tent 30 - 60, acc. to size; dog 25; electricity 60; local tax 5.

Reservations: Write to site. Address: 91101 Trencin. Tel: 0831/34013.

491 Autocamping Turiec, Martin

Small country camp in northeast Slovakia.

Turiec is situated 1½ km. from the small village of Vrutky, 4 km. north of Martin, at the foot of the Lucanska Mala Fatra mountains and with castles nearby. Holiday activities include hiking in summer, skiing in winter. There is room for about 30 units on slightly sloping grass inside a circular tarmac road with shade from tall trees. Electrical connections are available for all places. A wooden chalet by the side of the camping area has a TV rest room and a small games room. Some snacks are available in season with a shop outside the entrance. There is one acceptable sanitary block to the side of the camping area, but in winter the facilities in the bungalow at the entrance are used.

How to find it: Site is signed from E18 road (Zilina - Martin) in the village of Vrutky, 3 km. north of Martin. Follow signs to Martinské Hole.

General Details: Open all year. Snack bar in summer. Badminton. Volleyball. Bicycle hire. Swimming pool 1½ km. Rest room with TV. Small games room. Laundry room with electric cooking facilities. Covered barbecue. Bungalows and rooms for hire.

Charges guide: Per caravan Sk. 20 - 55; tent 15 - 45; car 15 - 45; m/cycle 10 - 20; motorcaravan 25 - 65; electricity 50.

Reservations: Contact site. Address: 03608 Martin 8. Tel: 0842/284215.

SLOVENIA

With the collapse of former Yugoslavia in the early 'nineties we withdrew that country's sites from our guides. With the recovery of tourism in Slovenia we are now including a small section of 12 inspected sites in our '98 edition. Next year we plan to also include Croatia. Despite the tourism recovery very few British registered vehicles are yet to be seen in Slovenia. This is partly because the country has been concentrating its promotional efforts since becoming independent on its neighbours, in particular Germany, Austria and Italy. However, it is also because of the daunting driving distance from the UK. Whether via France or Germany, the Slovenian border is about 1,000 miles from Calais; this means that the return journey, including a tour of the country, can amount to 3,000 miles.

Nevertheless, having re-visited Slovenia, we are convinced that it fully deserves a place in our guide. The scenery almost everywhere is attractive, often spectacular; there is much of interest to enjoy; the road network is quite adequate; price levels are generally lower than Britain or mainland Europe; the people are relaxed and friendly; and last but not least, there is an ample choice of good campsites with sanitary facilities mainly on a par with those found in the more popular European destinations.

Because of difficulty in identifying and remembering Slovene place names we have arbitrarily divided the country into four quarters, with the Ljubliana area in the centre. The northwest is the quarter of prime interest to British visitors as it is not only the usual entry from Austria but it includes the awesome Julian Alps with the lakes of Bohinj and Bled to the east and the Upper Soca Valley to the west. For those with less than a week available to spend in Slovenia, there is much to be said for keeping to this alpine region. We have included six sites in this region.

The southwest quarter includes Slovenia's short stretch of Adriatic coast in which the historic port of Piran and the adjacent resort of Portoroz will be of particular interest to British visitors. Unfortunately the campsites on the coast are grossly overcrowded during the summer holiday season, mainly by Slovenes and Italians, and dominated by their static caravans.

Next the centrally situated capital Ljubljana. As the national road network radiates from Ljubljana many foreign tourists find it a convenient stop-over. Yet the old town is both interesting and attractive and fully deserves at least a full day's visit. Also deserving a visit is its historical rival, the nearby small unspoilt town of Kamnik. We include one site in each of these places.

The northeast quarter has two very different areas of attraction. The Savinja valley, in particular its upper section in the Savinja Alps, is almost as spectacular as the Julian Alps. However, it is less accessible and there is little suitable choice of campsites so we have selected only one small site in this area. The far northeast, beyond the Savinja, is a gentle rural area, largely given over to vines (home of Lutomer Riesling). We have not included any sites beyond the Savinja as this distant area is unlikely yet to attract British campers in any number.

In the pleasant rolling countryside of the southeast, the main attractions are to be found on the banks of the slow flowing Krka river. We have had no difficulty selecting a good site here as this is a popular area for those Slovenes who prefer the countryside to mountains or beaches.

Population
Just over 2 million.

Capital
Ljubljana (pop. approx 1/4 million).

Language
Slovene, with German often spoken in the north and Italian in the west. English is generally understood except by the elderly.

Currency
The basic unit is the Slovene Tolar (abbreviated as SIT) of which there are several hundred to the pound sterling (the official rate in autumn '97 was 270). Any unused Tolars should be exchanged on or soon after departure.

Banks
Now run on efficient conventional western lines. Cash machines in most towns. Banks open week-days 8.30-16.30 with a lunch break 12.30-14.00, plus Saturday mornings 8.30-11.30.

Credit cards: Main credit cards accepted, including most filling stations.

Post Offices
Opening hours as for banks.

Time
Central European Time (one hour ahead of UK).

Telephone
To call Slovenia, prefix code is 386. To call the UK prefix code is 0044. Most call boxes require a phone card. Phone system being converted from analogue to digital, therefore many numbers need to be checked.

Shops
Shops usually open by 8 in the morning, sometimes 7. Closing times vary widely.

Food: Readily available in shops and street markets. General quality a little below West European standards but rather cheaper.

Drink: Usual range readily available. Prolific choice of Slovenian wines but confusingly labelled (in Slovene) and not generally cheaper than in Britain or western Europe. Limited choice of pleasant but unexciting local beers.

Motoring
Small but expanding network of motorways radiating from Ljubljana (tolls being introduced-check with motoring organisations for latest situation). Other main roads not usually dualled and some in need of maintenance. Secondary roads often poorly maintained. Tertiary roads are often all weather graded limestone gravel (known locally as 'white roads' and shown thus on road maps).

Fuel: Filling stations readily available except in remote rural areas. Fuel is very cheap (kept at low price as an anti-inflation measure), say one-third below UK level.

Speed Limits: Driving standards mixed as privatisation of economy has resulted in presence of many high-performance cars with low-performance drivers. Overtaking on blind corners by adolescents is one result. The normal speed limit is 80 mph (130 kph), faster on motorways - slower in built up areas. Road markings and signs are generally good.

Parking: Not a problem, even in Ljubljana (except in old town). In a few towns some central streets are pedestrianised.

Overnighting
Not permitted except on private land with owners permission.

Further Information
Most towns have well marked and helpful tourist information centres. Best guidebook (very good) is Lonely Planet `Slovenia'.

The sites in SLOVENIA featured in this guide are shown on the map on page 367

SLOVENIA - North West

410 Spik Autocamp, nr Kransjska Gora

Large, well equipped site in spectacular setting near the Austrian border.

Most British motorists enter Slovenia on the E55 from Villach over the demanding Wurzen pass, or through the easy Karawanken tunnel. On the Slovenian side they will rejoin national route 1 and normally proceed to Kransjska Gora, this pleasant resort town being the main northern gateway for the Julian Alps. Close by the turn to Kransjska Gora is the small village of Gozd Martuljek and here, directly on route 1, is Spik Camping, named after the peak which dominates the spectacular view from the site of the jagged Julian Alps skyline. This is the highest site in Slovenia (altitude 750 m., nearly 2,500 ft). It is large and flat, covering 8 ha of spruce woodland. The site is shared with the modern Spik Hotel and facilities are extensive, including excellent recreational amenities. As a result of its spectacular location and its extensive facilities many of the pitches are occupied by caravans which may not be statics but which are clearly not tourers. The complex is owned by the giant Petrol fuel enterprise and this could account for the somewhat impersonal manner in which the site appears to be run.

How to find it: Site is well signed on the A1 just outside Gozd Martuljek.

General Details: Open all year. All facilities expected of modern tourist complex.

Charges 1997: Per person SIT 850 - 1,100; child (5-12 yrs) less 30%; electricity 360; dog 300; local tax 80.

Reservations: Contact site. Address: Jezerci 21, 6482 Gozd Martuljek. Tel: 064/880 120. FAX: 064/880 115.

415 Kamp Kamne, Mojstrana

Small, friendly family-run site between Kransjska Gora and Jesenice.

For visitors proceeding down the A1 towards the prime attractions of the twin lakes of Bled and Bohinj, a delightfully informal little site is to be found just outside the village of Mojstrana. Owner Frank Voga opened the site as recently as 1989, on a small terraced orchard, immediately before the collapse of Yugoslavia. Although business was affected, he has steadily developed the facilities, a small swimming pool being added and then a tennis court (' hacked out of the rock with my own hands'). The latest addition is a set of three delightful Alpine `bungalows' which are let at DM20 (about £7) per night per person. These have proved so popular that he is working on another six. The little reception doubles as a local bar where locals wander up for a beer and a chat while enjoying the view across the valley of the Julian Alps. The site is particularly popular with walkers as three valleys lead west into the mountains from Mojstrana, including the trail to the ascent of Triglav, at nearly 3,000 m. the highest point of the Julian Alps. Franc's English is rather basic but his daughter Anna is fluent.

How to find it: Site is well marked on the north side of the A1, just to the west of the exit for Mojstrana.

General Details: Open all year. Basic facilities only (classified as third class) but of high quality and well maintained.

Charges 1997: Per person SIT 540 - 720; child (7-14 yrs) less 25%; electricity 270; local tax 90.

Reservations: Contact site: Address: Dovje 9, 64281 Mojstrana. Tel: 064/891 105.

420 Kamp Zaka, Bled

Excellent site on the Bled waterfront, within walking distance of the town.

Visitors to Bled are well provided with camping facilities, there being two very large sites nearby. About 3 km. to the east of the lake, in a flat pine forest just off the main road leading from the A1 to Bled, is the heavily publicised Sobec site. Although this is very professionally managed and equipped to a very high standard, thus explaining its ranking in several guides as one of the best in Europe, the location cannot compare with that of Zaka which is actually on the western tip of Lake Bled. The Zaka waterfront is a small public beach immediately behind which gently runs a sloping narrow wooded valley. Unlike Sobec there is no pitch allocation, visitors being free to pitch anywhere on the grass covered 6 ha site. Unlike many other Slovenian sites the number of statics (and semi-static) appears to be carefully controlled with touring caravans, motorcaravans and tents predominating. Like many other large sites designed to accommodate over 1,000 guests, and built in the sports-orientated period of Socialist rule, the reception and toilet facilities are of a very high standard, as are the extensive sports facilities. Some visitors might well be disturbed by the noise coming from above of trains as they hurtle out of a high tunnel overlooking the campsite on the line from Bled to Bohinj. But this is a small price to pay for the pleasure of being in a pleasant site from which the lake, its famous little island, its castle and its town can be explored on foot or by boat.

How to find it: From the town of Bled drive along the south shore of the lake to its western extremity (some 2 km); Zaka campsite lies behind the large public restaurant of the same name which faces the beach.

General Details: Open 1 April - mid-Oct. Full range of facilities.

Charges 1997: Per person SIT 765 - 1,080; child (7-14 yrs) less 30%; electricity 360; local tax 90.

Reservations: Contact site. Address: Kidriceva 10A, 64260 Bled. Tel: 064/77 325. FAX: 064/78 776.

425 Camping Danica Bohinj, Bohinj

Although not on the lake, the best site for Bohinj.

Until recently the best site for those visiting the famous Bohinj valley, which stretches like a fjord right into the heart of the Julian Alps, was the Zlatorog camp on the western tip of the lake. Appropriately named after the chamois, Zlatorog also happens to lie at the foot of a spectacular amphitheatre of Alpine peaks which rise seemingly sheer several thousand feet above the lake. However, in the wake of post-Socialist reconstruction the campsite lost much of its waterfront to its pre-Socialist owners and the available waterfront is now so packed with Slovene campers that visitors from abroad are well advised to chose the more spacious Danica site in the valley about 3 km. downstream of the lake. Danica was set up in '89 by the Bohinj Tourist Association to supplement the camping accommodation then only available at Zlatorog. The fact that the manager on the site, Marjan Malej, is the director of the local tourist association is an indication of the local community's well deserved pride in their own campsite. Danica occupies a rural site originally of 2.5 ha. but recently expanded to 4 ha. which stretches from the main road leading into Bohinj from Bled to the bank of the newly formed Sava river. It is basically flat meadow, broken up by lines of woodland. That this is essentially a site for real campers rather than budget holiday makers is evident from the predominance of touring units and the absence of statics.

How to find it: Driving from Bled to Bohinj the well signed site lies just behind the village of Bohinjska Bistrica on the right-hand (north) side of the road.

General Details: Open June - Sept. All essential services incl. small shop and café. Limited recreational facilities.

Charges 1997: Per person SIT 800 - 1,000; child (7-14 yrs) less 25-30%; electricity 300; local tax 100.

Reservations: Contact site. Address: 64264 Bohinjska Bistrica. Tel: 064/721 055.

423 Camp Soca, Soca

Family run site on the Soca river at entrance to Lepena Valley.

From Kranjska Gora an amazing road runs southwest to the upper Soca valley. This road was built by Russian prisoners of war during WW1 in order to allow Austria to move troops and supplies towards the Italian frontier. Those with large motorcaravans or towed caravans should note that it is tough going with over 50 hairpin bends! Those who have successfully negotiated the 1,600 m. summit usually drop down to the busy small town of Bovec where there are several campsites. These have little to commend them except to canoeists for the turbulent waters of the Soca in this area are world famous among kayak and raft enthusiasts. Fortunately for non-canoeists there is Camp Soca in the spectacular Lepena valley which is one end of a wonderful mountain trail, the other end of which is Bohinj (this trail was also opened by the Austrian army in WW1). Camp Soca is just off the main road on a shelving bluff formed by a wide curve of the Soca River. The site is literally theatrical as its two upper terraces and its large lower platform form a natural amphitheatre from which the mountains at the head of the Lepena valley can be readily admired. Facilities are limited to a small but well equipped toilet block and a small reception office/shop. Those in need of a good restaurant or bar, a game of tennis or a ride on a Lipizaner can cross the Soca on a wobbly wire and plank bridge which leads from the camp, through the woods on the opposite bank, to a small, tasteful holiday resort which boasts an even better view of the Lepena. Campsite owner Bostjan Komac and his father are usually on site to give help and advice.

How to find it: Site is on the main road between Kranjska Gora and Bovec, between the villages of Soca and Podklanec, just to west of the side road to Lepena.

General Details: Open May - Sept. Basic services only.

Charges 1997: Per person SIT 675 - 805; child (7-14 yrs) less 25%; electricity 240.

Reservations: Contact site. Address: Soca 8, 5232 Soca. Tel: 065/89 318.

427 Kamp Koren, Kobarid

Pleasant riverside site within walking distance of the rather special town of Kobarid.

British history teaches little of the terrible mountain warfare between Austria and Italy which went on in the Julian Alps throughout WW1. This macabre struggle, involving half a million casualties, is commemorated in the military museum at Kobarid and in the well-preserved fortifications and cemeteries in the neighbourhood. Kobarid itself is a pleasant country town, with easy access to nearby rivers, valleys and mountains which alone justify a visit to Camp Koren. But most British visitors will remember it for the opportunity it provides to fill that curious gap in their knowledge of European history. The camp occupies a flat, tree-lined meadow on a wide ledge which drops down sharply to the Soca river. It is deservedly very popular with those interested in outdoor sports, including canoeing, and this generates a pleasantly athletic atmosphere. The attractive log-built toilet block is of a standard worthy of a high class private sports club and the on-site café dispenses light meals, snacks and drinks apparently without much regard to closing hours.

How to find it: Site is on side road leading east out of Kobarid, just beyond `Napoleon's Bridge', signed on left.

General Details: Open mid-March - Oct. A small but well-equipped site.

Charges 1997: Per person SIT 720 - 900; child (7-14 yrs) less 50%; electricity 260; local tax 90.

Reservations: Contact site. Address: 65222 Kobarid. Tel: 065/85 312. FAX: as phone.

SLOVENIA - South West/ Central

430 Hotel-Camping Belvedere, Izola

Not an ideal site but the best for the Slovenian Riviera.

On paper, with the choice of no fewer than six sites, there should be no difficulty in selecting a recommended site for the Slovenian Riviera. In fact, it is very difficult, not because the sites are unsuitable, but because the sheer pressure of customers on restricted space is too heavy. Two factors exacerbate this situation. For the many Italians living in the Trieste area, and for Slovenes, the Slovenian Riviera is the nearest place for a cheap beach holiday. This is coupled with willingness by site operators to allow permanent or long seasonal letting of pitches, usually in the better positions. This not only means that touring visitors have difficulty in obtaining a satisfactory pitch, it also means that it is very difficult for site operators to maintain standards. Of the six sites the only site we can recommend happens to be the only one which is not on the waterfront. Belvedere is so named because it occupies the ridge of a high hill, half a mile's walk or drive from the sea, commanding a stunning view of the coast. During the Socialist period the site was developed into a massive leisure complex of which the camping facilities are a small part. Thanks to its inland location, it is the only coast site where the pressure on facilities is such that the management can maintain the standards we judge to be necessary.

How to find it: Follow the main A2 coast road west just beyond the Izola by-pass; the site is clearly signed but the exit is on a rather confusing summit road junction.

General Details: Open May - Oct. Limited space dedicated for tourers; very comprehensive leisure facilities including a huge swimming pool, restaurant, night club (can be very noisy late into the night) and hotel.

Charges 1997: Per person SIT 600 - 1,100; child (under 10 yrs) less 30%; car 300; electricity 500; dog 200; local tax 130.

Reservations: Contact site. Address: Hotel Belvedere, Dobrava 1A, 6310 Izola. Tel: 066/605-100. FAX: 066/65 583.

433 Camping Pivka Jama, Postojna

Highly recommended forest site within a day-trip distance of the Riviera or Ljubljana.

Postojna is renowned for its extraordinary limestone caves which form one of Slovenia's prime tourist attractions. Among campers it is also renowned for the campsite situated in the forest only 4 km. from the caves. Deservedly recognised by the Slovenian chamber of commerce as the best campsite in the country, Pivka Jama also happens to be a most convenient site for the foreign visitor, being mid-way between Ljubljana and Piran and only about an hour's pleasant drive from either. The site is deep in what appears to be primeval forest, very cleverly cleared to take advantage of the broken limestone forest bedrock. Pitches are not clustered together but nicely segregated under trees and in small clearings, all connected by a neat network of paths and slip-roads. The facilities are both excellent and extensive and run with obvious pride by enthusiastic staff. It even has its own local caves which can spare its visitors the commercialisation of Postojna.

How to find it: Take the side road leading west from Postojna (just off the trunk A10) to neighbouring Pojnska Jama and on to Pivka Jama (all well signed).

General Details: Open May - Sept. Extensive service and recreational facilities, including 24 4-bed, A-frame bungalows.

Charges 1997: Per person SIT 1,400; child (7-14 yrs) less 30%; electricity 400; local tax 90.

Reservations: Contact site. Address: HOT Postojna, Jamska Cesta 28, 6230 Postojna. Tel: 067/24 168. FAX: 067/24 431.

435 Autocamp Jezica, Ljubljana

Convenient base for Ljubljana, only minutes by bus from the historic old town.

The Sava river slices across Slovenia from northwest to southeast, passing through the northern outskirts of Ljubljana. Jezica is actually on the south bank of the river but a thick hedge and a heavy wire fence means that many campers are unaware of the Sava's presence. The site is basically a large 3 ha. flat grass expanse, punctuated with birch trees. It has a large, modern, well designed but under managed toilet block. Ample sporting facilities are available locally, but it is essentially a convenient base for visiting or transiting Ljubljana rather than a holiday centre. The under management evident in the toilet block appears to pervade the running of the site in general, indicating a lack of direction from above. For instance, one side of the site is occupied entirely by caravans which appear to be derelict, suggesting that the dead shadow of bureaucratic socialism is still lurking here. Bearing in mind its value as a Ljubljana base we shall be surprised if action is not taken soon to raise standards.

How to find it: Follow the main road leading due north from the city, across the ring road, continuing straight ahead (not bearing right) towards Jezica suburb. Turn left immediately before the Sava bridge crossing; site is well signed.

General Details: Open all year. All basic facilities.

Charges 1997: Per person SIT 860; child (7-12 yrs) less 40%; pitch 180 - 260; electricity 350; local tax 170.

Reservations: Contact site. Address: Dunajska 270, 61000 Ljubljana. Tel: 061/371 382. FAX: 061/313 649.

437 Autocamp Resnik, Kamnik

Convenient place for Kamnik, despite borderline facilities.

Nobody should visit central Slovenia without stopping off to wander around the unspoilt small country town of Kamnik which was once Ljubljana's main trade rival. The town is delightful and is only five minutes walk from the campsite. At first sight the site is rather unprepossessing, comprising a small open field with two very basic prefabricated toilet units, which are not as well serviced as they should be. However, there are compensations. Although the actual camping area is but 1 ha. it is only the edge of a much larger meadow. The site is also only part of the Kamnik sports complex which boasts a large swimming pool, and many tennis, badminton and squash courts. On the campsite is a friendly bar/café, patronised by both campers and players. On the opposite side of the road is a pleasant family inn, Pod Skalo; proprietor Michael Resnik, also runs the campsite. Ljubljana is only an easy hour's drive to the south.

How to find it: Site is 200 m. on the left along the main road leading north from Kamnik.

General Details: Open May - Sept. Basic facilities only.

Charges 1997: Per person SIT 300; child (under 10 yrs) less 50%; pitch 200 - 400; electricity 300; dog 100; local tax 100.

Reservations: Contact site. Address; Maistrova 15, 1240 Kamnik. Tel: 061/831 233.

440 Camp Dolina, Prebold

Tiny but perfectly run site, a good base for the Upper Savinja valley.

Prebold is a quiet village about 15 km. west of the large historic town of Celje. It is only a few kilometres from the remarkable Roman necropolis at Sempeter. To serve these two places there are two small campsites in Prebold. Our choice, Dolina, is little more than the garden of the house belonging to Marta Vozlic and her son who look after the site and its guests with loving care. The small toilet block would certainly qualify for Slovenia's 'best loo' award. However, the proximity of Celje and Sempeter are not the main reason for our choice. To the south of Prebold lies some of Slovenia's best walking country and to the north lies the upper Savinja valley. It is an easy drive up the Savinja to its spectacular source in the Logar Valley; beyond its semi-circle of 2,000 m. peaks lies Austria. Although there are other campsites on the upper Savinja our preference is for Dolina.

How to find it: Site is well signed in a small side street on the northern edge of Prebold. Best reached via a signed exit on the Ljubljana - Celje highway (now the A10 but due to become a motorway in '98).

General Details: Small family run site with minimal facilities.

Charges 1997: Per person SIT 1,000; electricity 300; dog 200.

Reservations: Contact site. Address: Dolenjska vas 68, 63312 Prebold. Tel: 063/723 501.

442 Hotel Grad Otocec Camp, nr Novo Mesto

Rather exclusive site in the grounds of an ancient castle on the Krka River.

Unlike the turbulent Soca and Savinja upper rivers, the Krka flows slowly through the fertile farmland of southeast Slovenia. There are several well known campsites along its banks and, with one exception, these are part of large spa complexes which generally have little appeal to British travellers, however well equipped and well run. The exception is a quiet wooded stretch of the Krka river, immediately opposite the small island on which the 16th century fortress of Otocec is to be found. The fortress has recently been turned into a 5 star hotel and is now owned by a major leisure company. Campers have to drive or walk across the wooden bridge to register at the hotel's opulent reception desk. Once registered they are given a key which allows entry to the superior toilet block on the actual campsite. During mid-week the area is fairly quiet but at weekends the campsite and neighbouring area liven up with Slovenes attracted for canoeing, fishing, cycling and horse riding (equipment for all these can be readily hired).

How to find it: About 7 km. northeast of Novo Mesto on route 1 (E70), take the clearly signed Otocec exit on right. Cross the old road running along the north bank of the Krka river and on over the bridge to the island hotel (the campsite lies beyond on the south bank via a second bridge).

General Details: Open May - Sept. Small 2 ha. river-front site with limited but excellent essential facilities on site but with a wide range of other facilities within walking distance.

Charges 1997: Per person SIT 500 - 700; child (under 7 yrs) free; tent 300; car 250; caravan 350; motorcaravan 600; electricity 450.

Reservations: Contact hotel. Address: 68222 Otocec. Tel: 068/21 830. FAX: 068/23 413.

SPAIN

Spain, which occupies the larger part of the Iberian peninsula, is the third largest country in Europe, with extremes of climate, widely contrasting geographical features and diversity of language, culture and artistic traditions. The peninsula's dominant feature is the Meseta, the immense plateau at its centre, where the summer heat is intense and the winters long and rigorous. The area to the north, with the mountains of the Pyrenees and the Asturian Picos de Europa, is the exact opposite with no extremes of temperature - green and lush. The east and south coast, protected by the Sierra ranges, enjoy a typically Mediterranean climate and in the extreme south there is virtually no winter season. In Almeria and Murcia, lack of rain as on the Meseta, gives rise to an almost desert landscape, however, the coastline has become a Mecca for those seeking sun all the year. Great monuments survive from a history affected by the Romans, Moors and the Renaissance, but modern Spain is breaking out as the '90s develop. Already Spain has hosted the Olympics, the World Fair and Madrid has been the Cultural Capital of Europe; a long cry from the 33 year dictatorship of Franco. There is a vitality about Spain now and in the cities there is always something happening - in politics, in fashion, in the clubs, on the streets, not forgetting the more traditional fiestas. Tourism is important to Spain, as the 'Costas' have proved, but there is a new awareness of the needs of the more discerning independent traveller, a new, albeit long overdue, concern for the environment and generally a more welcoming attitude.

Spain's capital is, of course, Madrid, but the country is divided, like the USA or Germany, Austria or Switzerland, into 17 different federal states called `autonomias', each with its own capital. For example the capital of Catalunya is Barcelona, that of Galicia is Santiago de Compostela; each federal state has its own government and parliament, and its own prime minister. The central government in Madrid retains power over the national economy and foreign affairs, for example, but other matters such as tourism are the exclusive preserve of the autonomias, which explains why there are different regulations for camping, caravanning and campsites in the various different autonomias. These differences extend to matters such as `wild camping', `overnighting' and even the classification (grading) of campsites.

So far as campsites are concerned, Spain has much to offer in terms of some of the best large sites in Europe, such as Playa Montroig, but it also has many attractive smaller sites which will appeal to many of our readers. There are quite a lot of sites which claim to be open all year, but services on most may well be limited to a minimum (eg. only one sanitary block operating and the shop open at weekends only). Even though all the sites featured in this guide have indicated positively that they will be open during the periods stated, we would still advise anyone contemplating a visit out of season to check first rather than rely entirely on information provided so far in advance! Readers should also bear in mind that a pitch of 80 sq.m. is considered to be large in Spain (worth remembering if you have a large outfit), although many sites, particularly in Catalunya, are now increasing pitch size to 100 sq.m. Finally we should mention that there has been a growing tendency in recent years for what we call `Spanish weekenders' - domestic tourism, whereby the Spanish themselves take pitches for an extended period to use as a weekend `holiday home' - this tends to give some sites a rather strange appearance during the week when many pitches are occupied by caravans, tents, etc. but not a soul is to be seen.

Spanish National Tourist Office, 57/58 St James's Street, London, SW1A 1LD
Tel: 0171 499 0901. Fax: 0171 629 4257

Population
39,000,000, density 77 per sq. km.

Capital
Madrid

Climate
Spain has a very varied climate depending where you are and the time of year. Temperate in the north, which also has most of the rainfall, dry and very hot in the centre, subtropical along the Mediterranean coast . The average winter temperature in Malaga is 57°F.

Language
Castilian Spanish is spoken by most people with Catalan (northeast), Basque (north) and Galician (northwest) also used in their respective areas.

Currency
Spanish peseta which circulates in coins of 1, 5, 10, 25, 50, 100, 200 and 500 ptas, and notes of 500, 1000, 2000, 5000 and 10,000 ptas.

Banks
Open Mon-Fri 09.00-14.00 Sat 09.00-13.00 (only certain towns). In tourist areas you will also find 'cases de cambio' with more convenient hours.

Post Offices
Offices (Correos) open Mon-Sat 08.00-12..00. Some open late afternoon, while some in the large cities open 08.00-15.00. Queues can be long and stamps can be bought at tobacconists (tabac).

Time
GMT plus 1 (summer BST + 1).

Telephone
From the UK, the code is 00 34 followed by the internal area code, omitting the initial 9, and exchange number. To call the UK dial 0744. Make international calls from 'telefone internacional' boxes or from 'Telefonica' offices.

Public Holidays
New Year; Epiphany; Saint's Day, 19 Mar; Maundy Thurs; Good Fri; Easter Mon; Labour Day; Saint's Day, 25 July; Assumption, 15 Aug; National Day, 12 Oct; All Saints Day, 1 Nov; Constitution Day, 6 Dec; Immaculate Conception, 8 Dec; Christmas, 25 Dec.

Shops
Open Mon-Sat 09.00-13.00/14.00, afternoons 15.00/16.00-19.30/20.00. Many open longer.

Food: The Spanish in general eat much later than we do. Lunches start at 13.00 or 14.00 and evening meals 21.00-22.00, so the streets remain lively until late. You can go to a 'restaurante' for a full meal or to a 'bar' where you have a succession of 'tapas' (small snacks) or 'raciones' (larger ones). Fish stews (zarzuelas) and rice based 'paellas' are often memorable.

Motoring

The surface of the main roads is on the whole good, although secondary roads in some rural areas can be rough and winding and have slow, horse drawn traffic. In Catalan and Basque areas you will find alternative names on the signposts, for example, Gerona - Girona and San Sebastian - Donostia.

Tolls: Payable on certain roads - A1, 2, 4, 6, 7, 8, 9, 15, 18, 19, 66, 68 and for the Cadi Tunnel , the Vallvidrera Tunnel (nr. Barcelona) and the Tunnel de Garraf on the A16.

Fuel: Petrol stations on motorways often open 24 hrs. Credit cards are accepted at most stations.

Speed Limits: Built-up areas 31 mph (50 kph) or less for both car and car towing. Other roads 56/62 mph (90/100 kph). On motorways, 75 mph (120 kph). For cars towing: other roads 43/50 mph (70/80 kph), on motorways 50 mph (80 kph).

Parking: 'Blue' parking zones (zone azul) are indicated by signs and discs are available from hotels, the town hall and travel agencies. In the centre of some large towns there is a zone 'ora' where parking is allowed only against tickets bought in tobacconists.

Overnighting

There are different regulations in the various different autonomias (see introduction).

Useful Addresses

Real Automovil Club de Espana (RACE), José Abascal 10, 28003 Madrid 3 . Tel: 4773200.

Costa Brava

The Costa Brava was the archetype Spanish destination in the early years of mass tourism and the tower blocks in some of the resorts are a dubious testimony to the days of the £50 package holiday. Fortunately package holiday trends changed before the developers could wreak total havoc and many villages and resorts remain very attractive and retain their charm, helped enormously by the towering cliffs and sheltered coves which give this coast its name - the `Wild Coast'. There are of course some distinctly lively resorts, such as Lloret, Tossa and Calella in the province of Barcelona, but also several quieter ones. The coastal scenery is often spectacular and the climate pleasant - somewhat less hot than further south - making this one of the most attractive areas for the British, particularly for those who drive through France, since it is possible to reach the Costa Brava with only one night stop en-route.

8050 Camping Aquarius, Sant Pere Pescador, nr Figueres

Well run family site in quiet seaside situation suited to families and sun-lovers.

Aquarius has direct access to a quiet sandy beach with a gentle slope and good bathing, and is a site for those who really like sun and sea, with a quiet situation. One third of the site has good shade with a park-like atmosphere. An extension with less shade provided an opportunity to enlarge the pitches and they are now all at least 70-100 sq.m. which is good for Spain. A total of 430 are all numbered with 400 6A electrical connections. The main sanitary facilities are in attractive, large tiled blocks with British toilets, washbasins set in flat surfaces, all with hot water (some in cabins for each sex) and free hot showers, fully controllable. Facilities for disabled people provided plus baths for children and there is hot water in the sinks. An excellent new block has under-floor heating, so is open all season, features family cabins with showers and basins. A large terrace area outside the bar/restaurant is unusually designed with split level terraces and attractive flower and water arrangements by the German owner who not only has an architectural background, but also has a wealth of knowledge on the whole Catalan area and culture. He has written a booklet of suggested tours (from reception). The whole family are justifiably proud of the site, which is strictly and efficiently run. They continue to make improvements (eg. a good new tarmac access road completed recently). There is a 50 sq.m. `play centre', open all season with a qualified attendant and a playground near the beach. The sea is shallow for quite a long way out. The beach bar complex with shaded terraces and minigolf has marvellous views over the Bay of Roses. The `Surf Center' with rentals, school and shop is ideal for enthusiasts and beginners alike.

How to find it: Turn off main road by bridge south of Sant Pere Pescador and follow camp signs; the site reports that the access road has now been resurfaced.

General Details: Open Easter - 18 Oct. New supermarket with butcher. Pleasant restaurant and bar with terrace. Restaurant and bar by beach. `Surf Center'. Takeaway. Children's playground and games hall. Play centre (all season). Table tennis. Volleyball. Minigolf. Bicycle hire. Football field. Boules. Barbecue and dance once weekly when numbers justify. Special animation for children. Dogs allowed in one section. Laundry facilities. Car wash. Chemical disposal. Motorcaravan services. Site is run by a German family who speak good English.

Charges 1998: Per adult 400 - 700 ptas; child (1-10) 250 - 500; car 400 - 700; m/cycle 300 - 550; tent or caravan 750 - 1,400; motorcaravan (up to 3.6 tons) 1,150 - 2,100; animal 225 - 400; electricity 400. All plus 7% VAT. Discounts for pensioners on longer stays.

Reservations: are made for any length with £50 deposit and £15 fee.
Address: 17470 Sant Pere Pescador (Girona). Tel: 72/52.00.03. FAX: 72/55.02.16.
E-mail: camping@aquarius.es. Internet: www.aquarius.es.

AR Discount
Free bike hire and minigolf

SPAIN - Costa Brava

8020 Camping-Caravaning Internacional Amberes, Empuria Brava

Large, friendly site 50 m. from wide, sandy beach.

Situated in the 'Venice of Spain', Empuria Brava is interlaced with inland waterways and canals, where many residents and holiday-makers park their boats directly outside their homes on the canal banks. Internacional Amberes is 50 m. from the wide, sandy beach, which is bordered on the east and west by the waterway canals (no access into them from the beach, only by car on the main road). The site can arrange temporary moorings for boats at Empuria Brava on request. The sea breeze here appears regularly during the afternoon so watersports are very good and hire facilities are available. Amberes is a surprisingly pretty, friendly and hospitable site where people seem to make friends easily and get to know other campers and the staff, who organise the sports and children's programmes. The site has 650 hedged pitches with light shade from many smallish trees, 550 with electricity and water connections, and there are pleasant views from some parts. Sanitary facilities are provided in four blocks, all recently renovated and with hot showers, British style WCs and vanity style washbasins. The restaurant and bar are located on entry to the site rather than around the pool area. The small, pleasant restaurant adjoining the bar area serves excellent food in copious quantities and tables outside add to the intimate atmosphere. The swimming pool is on an elevated terrace, raised out of view of most onlookers, with a small children's pool adjoining. Football and volleyball are organised by the management and a 'secret garden' style minigolf course is special to this site. Rented accommodation includes mobile homes, bungalows and apartments (with private facilities and bath) in a complex opposite the pool.

How to find it: Site is signed from the main roundabout leading into Empuria Brava from the Roses - Castello d'Empuries road (4 km. from Roses).

General Details: Open 15 May - 30 Sept. Supermarket. Restaurant/bar. Disco bar and restaurant. Takeaway. Watersports - windsurfing school. Boat moorings. Fishing. Organised activities and entertainment. Swimming pool. Football. Table tennis. Tennis. Bicycle hire. Horse riding. Volleyball. Minigolf. Children's playgrounds (one new). Washing machines. Chemical disposal. Motorcaravan services. Accommodation for rent.

Charges 1997: Per adult ptas. 410 - 560; child (2-12 yrs) 305 - 460; tent or caravan 720 - 1,350; car 410 - 560; m/cycle 375 - 520; motorcaravan 950 - 1,750; electricity 405. Less 20% pensioners 15 days or over in low seasons.

Reservations: Contact site for booking form. Address: 17487 Empuriabrava (Girona). Tel: 972/45.05.07 (1/5-30/9). FAX: 972/67.12.86 (all year).

8015 Camping-Caravanning La Laguna, Empuria Brava

Unusually relaxed spacious site on isthmus, with direct access to beach and estuary.

La Laguna is aptly named, the site actually being spilt into two halves joined by a bridge over the lagoon. The approach to the site is by a long (4 km.), more or less, private road. This is quite an unusual site for this area, being laid out very informally among mature pine trees, in contrast to other large more formally designed sites nearby. More trees have been planted in newer areas on the other side of the lagoon. There are over 750 pitches clearly marked on grass and sand, all with 6A electricity (a long lead may be useful). The facilities, particularly the sanitary installations, are quite elderly and the site's attraction is much more in terms of its informality, friendliness and value for money (particularly for long stays) than its amenities. Four toilets blocks, placed to avoid long walks, are simple in design but adequate, with free hot water, plenty of dishwashing sinks, well equipped laundry room and chemical disposal. An attractive bar restaurant overlooks the lagoon and a swimming pool and riding school are on site (May-Sept), likewise a bar and shop. There is beach frontage with a sailing school. It is said to be possible to cross over to Empuria Brava when the tide is out. The river is hidden by a high bank with a path along the top.

How to find it: Site is signed from the Castello d'Empuries bypass at the junction with the road for Sant Pere Pescador. Follow approach road for approx. 4 km.

Charges 1997: Per person ptas. 470 - 730; child (5-10 yrs) 400 - 600; tent or caravan 470 - 730; car 470 - 730; motorcaravan 830 - 1,280; m/cycle 400 - 600; electricity 400. Discounts for longer stays and pensioners.

General Details: Open 15 March - 20 Oct. Bar. Restaurant. Shop. Swimming pool (May - Sept). Tennis (free in low seasons). Minigolf. Sailing school. Horse riding. Chemical disposal. Mobile homes for hire.

Reservations: Contact site. Address: 17486 Castello d'Empuries (Girona). Tel: 972/45.05.53 (when closed 972/20. 86.67). FAX: 972/45.07.99 (or 972/20.86.67). E-mail: laguna@grn.es. Internet: http://www.6tems.grn.es/laguna.

8035 Camping Caravaning L'Amfora, Sant Pere Pescador

8040 Camping Las Dunas, Sant Pere Pescador, nr Figueres

8060 Camping La Ballena Alegre 2, Sant Pere Pescador, nr Figueres

The editorial reports for these sites appear on pages 288/9 opposite their colour advertisements

8072 Camping Les Medes, L'Estartit, nr Gerona/Girona

See colour advert
between pages 288/9

Small, attractive, family site with pool, 2 km. from centre of L'Estartit.

Les Medes is a refreshing change from some of the `all singing, all dancing' sites so popular along this coast. The friendly owners are justifiably proud of their neat, well equipped and well run site. Set back from busy L'Estartit itself, it is a peaceful and pretty oasis and a little train runs from near the site (June-Sept) to the town, The nearest beach is 800 m. With just under 200 pitches, the site is small enough for the owners to know their visitors and being campers themselves, they have been careful in planning their facilities and keep the site immaculate. The level, grassy pitches range in size from 60-80 sq.m. depending on your unit. All have electricity and the larger ones (approx. half the provision) also have water and drainage. All are clearly marked in rows, but with no dividers and the trees are growing and providing shade. Both toilet blocks are clean and well maintained, providing British toilets, hot and cold water in washbasins (in private cabins), good sized showers with dividers and shelves, very good facilities for disabled people and baby baths. Washing machines are provided in each block and there is hot and cold water for dishes and clothes washing. The pool area is attractively landscaped in front of the old Catalan farmhouse buildings which house reception and the small, air conditioned bar and restaurant, providing a grassy sunbathing area and an open air dance floor for twice weekly music evenings (in season). The site has well equipped apartments with central heating and TV to rent. A small indoor pool (heated) with sauna and solarium and good access for disabled people is a new addition.

How to find It: Site is signed from the main Torroella de Montgri - L'Estartit road GE641. Turn right after Camping Castel Montgri, `Joc's' hamburger/pizzeria and follow signs.

General Details: Open all year. Bar and snacks (all year). Restaurant (1/4-15/9). Shop (all year). Outdoor swimming pool (15/6-15/9) Indoor pool with sauna, solarium and masseur (1/1-15/6 and 15/9-31/12). Children's play area with small hut for games. Converted stables for indoor children's area and TV room, from where animation and excursions are organised in July/Aug. Large chess. Table tennis. Volleyball. Boules. Bicycle hire. Car wash. Chemical disposal. Motorcaravan services. Extra parking area. No dogs allowed. Apartments to let.

Charges 1998: Per person 600 ptas; child (0-10 yrs) 435; pitch 1,350; electricity 430. All plus 7% VAT. Less in low seasons and special offers for longer stays in low seasons.

Reservations: Recommended for July/Aug. with 5,000 ptas. deposit. Address: 17258 L'Estartit (Catalunya). Tel: 972/75.18.05. FAX: 972/75.04.13. E-mail: campinglesmedes@cambrescat.es. Internet: http://www.info3.es/campinglesmedes.

8080 Camping El Delfin Verde, Torroella de Montgri, nr Gerona/Girona

Large, good quality, friendly site with own beach and extremely large swimming pool.

A popular, busy site in a quiet location, El Delfin Verde has its own long beach, which campers have to themselves, stretching along its frontage. An attractive large pool in the shape of a dolphin is a feature of the site with a total area of 1,800 sq.m. with lifeguard (no bermuda shorts). A large bar, full restaurant and separate pizzeria are open in the main season and overlook the pool area. There is a further restaurant with slightly cheaper, good value food in the main complex with an open air arena. This is a large site with nearly 6,000 persons at peak times. Level grass pitches nearer the beach are marked by indicators and there are now many separated by small fences and newly planted hedging. All have electrical connections and access to water points. There is shade in some of the older parts and a particularly pleasant area of pine trees in the centre with pitches marked but not separated, sandy and not so level. There are five excellent large sanitary blocks and a further new sixth smaller block, all with resident cleaners. In this new block and the second newest, half the washbasins are in private cabins. All blocks have free hot water in the washbasins, fully controllable showers (2 taps) of good, comfortable size with seat, plus British style toilets. El Delfin Verde is a large and cheerful holiday site with many good facilities, sports and free entertainments and is well worth considering for your Costa Brava holidays. Used by a number of British tour operators. Dogs not allowed 18/6-25/9.

How to find It: A very long approach road leads off the road from Torroella de Montgri to Palafrugell (watch carefully for the sign, particularly if coming from Palafrugell); there is a sign to site at the end of it.

General Details: Open 1 April - 27 Sept, including shops, one restaurant and one bar. 290,000 sq.m. Supermarket and other shops. 2 restaurants, grills and pizzerias. 3 bars; small bar by beach open in season. `La Vela' barbecue and party area. Sports area. 8 tennis courts. 2 km. exercise track. Dancing and shows in season. Disco. Excursions. General room with TV. Video room. Bicycle hire. Fishing. Minigolf. Children's playground. Trampolines. Badminton. Hairdresser. Laundry. Car repairs, servicing, and washing. Chemical disposal. Motorcaravan services.

Charges 1998: Per pitch, incl. electricity 3,900 ptas (1,600 or 3,300 outside 19/6-26/8); per person 350; child (2-9 yrs) 300; dog (low season only) 350; extra car 1,000 - 1,500; boat 350. All plus 7% VAT.

Reservations: Only a guarantee to admit - no specific pitch allocated. Write (all year) with deposit of ptas. 10,000. Address: Apdo Correos 43, 17257 Torroella de Montgri (Gerona). Tel: 972/75.84.50. FAX: 972/76.00.70. For bungalows and apartments, from 1/10-30/6, write to 08021 Barcelona, c/Muntaner 415 or from 1/7 - 30/9 to site.

See colour advert
between pages 288/9

SPAIN - Costa Brava

8070 Camping La Escala, La Escala
Neat and tidy, small site within walking distance of beach and town.

Under the same ownership as Las Dunas (no. 8040), but a complete contrast, this is one of those sites where you can walk both to the beach and to the centre of a modest sized but lively, yet historical, popular holiday resort. It is therefore not very large, but the pitches are level, marked and well shaded. They have managed to carve over 200 out of the area so they are small - just room for the car and caravan or tent - but all pitches have electricity, water and drainage. The central toilet block is basic but clean, with British toilets (no paper), washbasins, 2 in cabins for ladies, with shelf, mirror and free hot water and 25 free showers. In season there is a supermarket and small bar with terrace. The site has 12 modern 2-tier bungalows to let at reasonable charges.

How to find it: On entry to La Escala at first roundabout turn right, at second roundabout turn left and then continue 1 km. to site on right. Watch for gate in high wall.

General Details: Open Easter - 25 Sept. Most well shaded. Shop. Bar (high season). Restaurant. Dishwashing and laundry sinks with hot water. Bungalows for hire. Good value English restaurant (Angela's) at the port area.

Charges 1997: Per person 350 ptas; child (2-9 yrs) 275; pitch incl. electricity 1,375 - 2,125. All plus 7% VAT.

Reservations: Not necessary. Address: Apdo. Correus 23, 17130 La Escala, Costa Brava (Gerona). Tel: 972/77.00.08 or 77.00.84. FAX: 972/55.00.46.

8103 Camping El Maset, Sa Riera, Begur, nr Gerona/Girona
Little gem of a site in lovely surroundings, close to beaches.

This is a delightful, tiny site with 109 pitches, of which just 14 are for caravans or motorcaravans, the remainder suitable only for tents. The site entrance is steep and access to the caravan pitches can be quite tricky. All these pitches have electricity, water and drainage with some shade. Access to the tent pitches, which are more shaded on terraces on the mountainside (more of a hill really!) seems quite straightforward, with parking for cars not too far away - of necessity the pitches are fairly small. There are also seven traditional Catalan style 'bungalows' to rent (4-6 persons, fully equipped and with sun terraces). For such a small site the amenities are quite extensive and there is a swimming pool. The facilities include a bar/restaurant, with terrace and takeaway, children's games room and play area on sand and a supermarket. Sanitary facilities, in three small blocks, were clean and include free hot showers, British style WCs, soap and hot-air dryers, hot water to washbasins in two blocks and a baby bath. Under cover washing up area (H&C) and washing machine. This small site provides the standard of service normally associated with the best of the larger sites. It is situated in the tiny resort of Sa Riera with access to beaches (300 m), including a naturist beach (via a longer uphill path). Begur, with its beautiful, small, quite unspoilt bay and beach, is 10 minutes by car.

How to find it: Site is 2 km. north of Begur (or Bagur). Follow signs for Playa de Sa Riera and camp. Site has a steep entrance.

General Details: Open 3 April - 26 Sept. Bar/restaurant, takeaway (all season). Shop (from May). Children's play area. Area for football and basketball. Games room. Swimming pool (all season). Solarium. Fishing, watersports and riding near. Chemical disposal. No dogs allowed. Bungalows to rent.

Charges 1998: Per person 550 - 690 ptas; child (1-10 yrs) 420 - 550; car 550 - 690; m/cycle 360 - 460; tent 550 - 730; caravan 670 - 860; motorcaravan 700 - 900; electricity 400 (tent) or 525 (caravan). Credit cards accepted.

AR Discount
Less 10% in low season for min. 1 week stay

Reservations: Write to site. Address: Playa de Sa Riera, 17255 Begur (Gerona). Tel: 972/623023. FAX: 972/623901.

8101 Camping Playa Brava, Platja de Pals, nr Gerona/Girona

Surprisingly `green' and quiet, beach-side site with good facilities.

As well as having direct access to a large beach and to watersports facilities on both beach and river, this is a very grassy, level site. Shade is provided by a mixture of fir and broad-leaf trees for most of the 500 pitches. These all have electricity (10A), a third with water and drainage also, and are of a good size ranging from 75-100 sq.m, with many large ones. There is an air of spaciousness and general tidiness. The 4 modern sanitary blocks have British WCs, controllable hot showers, with dressing area and hooks, washbasins with hot water, undercover dishwashing facilities and 6 washing machines. Facilities are provided for the disabled. Amenities include a medium sized pool and children's pool, with a large grass sunbathing area, two tennis courts, volleyball, children's play area on grass and an entertainment programme during July and August. There is a good golf course close by. The bar/restaurant, with terrace, provides both waiter service and takeaway meals, and there is a supermarket.

How to find it: Site is 3 km. north of the village of Pals, in the direction of Platja de Pals. Follow road for 3 km. past golf course to beach; well signed.

General Details: Open 16 May - 20 Sept. Bar/restaurant. Takeaway. Supermarket. Swimming pool (from 1/6), with large, grassy sunbathing area. Tennis. Volleyball. Minigolf. New children's play area. Fishing. Watersports on river and beach, including sheltered lagoon for windsurfing learners. Chemical disposal.

Charges 1998: Per person ptas. 300; child (2-9 yrs) 250; pitch incl. electricity 3,400. Less in low seasons. All plus 7% VAT. Discount for longer stays in low season.

Reservations: Write to site. Address: 17256 Platja de Pals (Gerona). Tel: 972/636894. FAX: 972/636952.

8150 Camping Internacional de Palamós, Palamós, nr Gerona/Girona

Site with good swimming pool quite close to town.

This site has a large swimming pool, surrounded by a grass sunbathing area and with its own bar/terrace. It is 1 km. from the town and only 400 m. to the nearest beach. It might have space when others are full and has over 500 level, terraced pitches on a gentle slope, of moderate size, with variable shade. Electrical connections (6A) are available in most parts. Three toilet blocks, one of which is large and modern providing good facilities with free hot water in washbasins, pre-set showers with push-button and facilities for disabled people. The two more elderly, smaller blocks are somewhat basic, with mostly Turkish, but some British WCs and cold showers. There are some tour operator pitches and mobile homes and bungalows to rent.

How to find it: Cars can approach site from central Palamós, but town streets are too narrow for caravans which should turn off C255 road just outside Palamós to north by Renault garage, signed to Kings Camping and La Fosca, turn right just before Kings and from there follow Internacional signs.

General Details: Open 26 March - 9 Oct. Swimming pool (36 x 16 m.), with paddling pool. Self-service shop. Restaurant and bar. Laundry room with washing machines etc. Hourly bus services to town.

Charges guide: Per person 325 ptas; child (under 10) 250; pitch for car and tent/caravan 1,635, 1,850 or 2,150, acc. to season; tent (m/cycle but no car) 1,100, 700 or 540; electricity 400; water/drainage 200. All plus 7% VAT.

Reservations: Write to site with 5,000 ptas deposit. Address: Apdo Correos 100, 17230 Palamos (Girona). Tel: 972/31.47.36. Office tel: 972/31.49.48 or 31.49.48. FAX: 972/31.85.11.

SPAIN - Costa Brava

8090 Camping Caravaning Cypsela, Platja de Pals, nr Gerona/Girona

Impressive, de-luxe site, 2 km. from the sea, with many amenities.

The most striking feature of this site is its rather sumptuous complex of sport facilities and amenities near the entrance. This consists of a fine swimming pool, a good children's pool and playground, 2 excellent squash courts, a tennis court, volleyball and table tennis, a restaurant and bar with terrace and other entertainment rooms. These include a children's playroom with organised entertainment (video screen), an amusements room with pool, football tables and video games, and a lounge for adults entertainment, with piano for twice weekly concerts. The bar/restaurant is very pleasant, with set meals at low cost, as well as a full menu and takeaway. The main part of the camping area is pinewood, with 1,170, clearly marked pitches of sandy gravel of a good size for Spain. The newer extensions at the rear have more grass with pitches hedged with a mixture of trees. The four sanitary 'houses' are of excellent quality with comprehensive cleaning schedules, providing all British toilets, three with washbasins in cabins, free hot water and adjustable showers. Three have children's rooms with baby baths and larger ones for older children. Good provision for the disabled and many hot water sinks. Cypsela is a busy, well organised site which one can thoroughly recommend, especially for families, very efficiently run, with everything clean and maintained to a high standard. Gates closed at night. Several tour operators.

How to find it: Cypsela is on the road running from the Torroella de Montgri to Bagur down to Platja de Pals.

General Details: Open 15 May - 30 Sept. 200,000 sq.m. Access easy but care needed with trees in places. Electrical connections in all parts. Supermarket and other shops. Well appointed restaurant. Cafeteria. Bar. Lounge. Hairdressers. Swimming pools. Tennis. Squash. Table tennis. Football field. Minigolf. Social room/TV. Lounge with drinks/snacks. Dancing weekly in season. Organised sports and games. Barbecue and party area. Children's playroom with organised activities. Games room with pool tables, etc. Free hourly bus service to beach. Serviced launderette. Ironing. Car wash. Doctor on site; well equipped treatment room. Air conditioned telephone parlour! No dogs taken.

Charges 1997: Per person ptas. 560 - 700; child (2-10 yrs) 395 - 495; pitch incl. vehicle 1,840 - 2,300; extra vehicle 670 - 840; electricity 420; water/drainage 250. All plus 7% VAT. Less 5-15% for long stays in low season.

Reservations: Write to site for details. Address: Ctra. Pals-Playa de Pals, km. 3, 17256 Pals (Girona). Tel: 972/66.76.96. FAX: 972/66.73.00.

8120 Kim's Camping, Llafranc, nr Palafrugell

Pleasant, attractive, terraced site near the sea. with swimming pool.

Situated on the wooded slopes of a narrow valley leading to the sea, this steep site provides 322 grassy and partly shaded, terraced pitches, with many larger pitches on a plateau with the pool and shop. They are connected by winding driveways, narrow in places, and most have electrical connections (6A). There is adequate sanitary provision including free warm showers, British style WCs and laundry facilities. Amenities include a children's playground, an excellent pool area with adult and small children's pools, a bar, restaurant and 'al fresco' eating. All amenities are offered at a high standard of cleanliness and efficiency. The site is under 1 km. from the beach at Llafranc. This is a good place for holidays to enjoy the bustling atmosphere of Llafranc town and beach, but staying in a quieter environment. There is an outstanding view along the coastline and of the Pyrenees from Cap Sebastian close by. English is spoken by the very friendly management and staff.

How to find it: Turn off for Llafranc from the Palafrugell - Tamariu road at turning signed 'Llafranc, Caella, Club Tenis'. Site is 1 km. on, next to the El Paraiso hotel.

General Details: Open Easter - 30 Sept. Shop (1/5-30/9). Bar (1/5-30/9). Cafe/restaurant (15/6-15/9). Swimming pools (1/6-30/9). TV room. Children's play area. Car wash. Chemical disposal. Bungalows, mobile homes for hire.

Charges 1998: Per person 450 - 725 ptas; child (3-11 yrs) 365 - 450; car 450 - 725; m/cycle 400 - 500; tent 550 - 775; caravan 550 - 875; motorcaravan 650 - 1,200; electricity 450. Plus 7% VAT. Credit cards accepted.

Reservations: Made with deposit (ptas. 10,000). Address: 17211 Llafranc-Palafrugell (Girona). Tel: 972/30 11 56 or 61 16 75. FAX: 972/61 08 94. E-mail: kims@grn.es. Internet: http://www.6tems.com/ckims.

286

Your family
deserves luxurious holidays...

...in beautiful nature, under splendid pine-trees, surrounded by phantastic beaches, with magnificent installations, excellent service and animation activities for the whole family, and with special attention to the children.

Please consult our offers

✉ CAMPING CYPSELA - 17256 PALS (Girona)
☎ (34-72) 66 76 96 - Fax (34-72) 66 73 00
PLATJA DE PALS - COSTA BRAVA

SPAIN - Costa Brava

8035 Camping Caravaning L'Amfora, Sant Pere Pescador

See colour advert opposite

Spacious, medium sized site with direct access to the beach.

This is a friendly, colourful site with a Greek theme to its appearance. There are 440 pitches, all with electrical connections and most with water tap, on level grass with small trees and shrubs. Of these, 64 pitches are large (180 sq.m.) and have their own, individual sanitary facilities. This rare feature consists of small blocks of four units (toilet, shower and washbasin), each unit `owned' by one pitch for their stay - virtually `en-suite' camping. The other main sanitary blocks offer free hot water, washbasins in cabins, hairdryers and baby rooms. Further new, separated pitches of 95 sq.m. have been developed with limited shade as yet. Access is good for disabled people. Laundry facilities are also available with washing machines. There is extra provision near the pool area. An inviting terraced bar and self-service restaurant overlook two large swimming pools (one for children), which are divided by an attractive arch and fountain. A restaurant, takeaway, pizza service and supermarket are available. Sports facilities include two tennis courts, basketball and horse riding (in season). Evening entertainment (pub, disco, shows) and children's animation organised in season and watersports activities available on the beach.

How to find it: From A7 motorway take exit 3 (N-11) towards Girona/Barcelona. Exit for Figueres/Roses towards Roses on the C260 and, 9 km. before Roses turn right to San Pere Pescador.

General Details: Open Easter, then 15 May - 30 Sept. Bar. Self service and waiter service restaurants. Takeaway. Pizza service Swimming pools. Horse riding. Table tennis. Tennis. Fishing. Windsurfing. Sailing. Bicycle hire. Minigolf. Football. Volleyball. Children's playground. Entertainment and organised activities for children. Supermarket. Exchange facilities. Car wash. Laundry facilities. Bungalows and mobile homes to rent.

Charges 1998: Per person ptas. 450; child (2-9 yrs) 350; pitch (100 sq.m.) 1,590 - 3,200, pitch (90 sq.m.) with individual sanitary arrangements 2,150 - 4,500, large pitch (160 sq.m.) with sanitary 2,500 - 5,200; electricity (5A) included. Plus 7% VAT. Discounts for pensioners for longer stays.

Reservations: Made with deposit (ptas. 10,000) and fee (2,500) - write to site. Address: Av. Josep Tarradellas 2, 17470 Sant Pere Pescador (Girona). Tel: 972/52.05.40 or 52.05.42. FAX: 972/52.05.39.

This site is featured out of order - it should be listed on page 282

8060 Camping La Ballena Alegre 2, Sant Pere Pescador

See colour advert opposite

Very large site in quiet position by long beach, with own swimming pool.

La Ballena Alegre 2, sister site to the Ballena Alegre south of Barcelona, is a big, relaxed site taking 1,700 units, partly in a lightly wooded setting, and with some 1,600 m. of frontage directly onto a sandy beach. The grass pitches are individually numbered and of adequate size (over 200 are 100 sq.m.) with pitching informally arranged. Electrical connections (5A) are available in all parts and there are 48 fully serviced pitches. The site is under new management and all five of the toilet blocks have been refurbished to a very high standard. These feature large pivoting doors for showers, wash cabins, etc, special low facilities for children, baby baths and unusual floors of slatted wood aid drainage. All looks and feels good and seems very functional. A unit for the disabled is in the block nearest reception. There are restaurant and bar areas beside the terraced, 300 sq.m. swimming pool and smaller children's pool and there is a good shop and bakery on site (with bread delivered by bike). A little train ferries people along the length of the site. Plenty of entertainment and activities are offered, including a large shop for watersports, with a centre for hire and lessons, and a new open air fitness centre beside the beach bar!

How to find it: Best approach is from the Figueres-La Escala road, turning to the north 2 km. west of La Escala at sign to San Martin d'Empúries and following camp signs. Access has now been entirely asphalted.

General Details: Open 15 May - 27 Sept. 250,000 sq.m. Swimming pools (all season). Supermarket. Bar. Self-service restaurant (23/6-28/8). Takeaway (22/5-27/8). `Croissanterie' (15/6-28/8). Full restaurant (evenings all season) and beach bar in high season. 3 tennis. Table tennis. Watersports centre. Fishing. Bicycle hire. Fitness centre. Children's playgrounds. Sound proofed disco. Dancing twice weekly and organised activities, sports, entertainments, etc. in season (23/6-24/8) but generally a quiet site. Golf and go-karting nearby with bus service. Safe deposit. Cash point. Resident doctor and site ambulance. Car wash. Dog showers. Launderette. Chemical disposal. Motorcaravan services. New bungalows to rent (11).

Charges 1998: Per pitch incl. electricity (5A) ptas. 1,700, 3,300 or 3,650, acc. to season; pitch with drainage plus 200; person 350; child (3-9 yrs) 275. All plus 7% VAT. Discount of 10% on pitch charge for pensioners all season.

Reservations: made with deposit (ptas. 12,000), min. 10 days 10/7-10/8; contact site for details. Address: 17470 Sant Pere Pescador (Girona). Tel: 972/53.03.02 or 52.03.26. FAX: 972/52.03.32. E-mail: infb2@ballena-alegre.es. Internet: http://www.ballena-alegre.es. Winter address: Ave. Roma 12, 08015 Barcelona. Tel: 93/226.13.02. FAX: 93/226.65.28.

This site is featured out of order - it should be listed on page 282

les medes

Camping Caravaning
COSTA BRAVA

E-17258 L'ESTARTIT (Girona)

Paratge Camp de L'Arbre
Tel. (34-72) 75 18 05 • Fax (3472) 75 04 13

Quiet, flat holiday site only 2 km from L'Estartit, surrounded by fields en inmidst of nature. At only 800m from beach, ideal f. children and watersport. All pitches are properly laid out and w. electr. conn. Modern ablution blocks (baby room, complete bath room f. disabled) w. free hot water. Swimming pool, superm., bar, restaurant, meals to take away, washing machines, car-wash w. hoover, table tennis, boules game, volley, children's playground, organised activities, bikes f. hire. **Bungalows for hire.** *New at the Costa Brava: Familiar campsite open throughout the year with heated indoor swimming-pool, solarium, sauna and heated ablution blocks.*

HOLIDAY ON THE BEACH...

...AND IN THE POO.

Waiting for you at EL PINAR BEACH CAMP:
300 metres of fine soft sand beach,
pine woods, easy motorway access
and organised events for everybody,
every day. And that is not all!
There is also a superb freshwater
swimming pool in a carefully landscaped
garden, a snack bar, a supermarket,
organised activities, etc...

elPinar BEACH CAMP
COSTA BRAVA

C/ Villa de Madrid
E-17300 - Blanes (Girona)
Tel. (34 72) 33 10 83

Now at EL PINAR BEACH CAMP-more of everything! Discover us.

Camping Caravaning

el delfin verde

E-17257 TORROELLA DE MONTGRÍ -GIRONA- Tel. (34-72) 75 84 50
COSTA BRAVA ESPAÑA Fax (34-72) 76 00 70

One of the most beautiful and spacious camping and caravanning sites of the COSTA BRAVA.

In quiet tranquil surroundings by a magnificent wide and mile-long sand beach with the largest fresh-water swimming pool of the Costa Brava and generously-sized pitches and sites. Many green areas and groups of pine trees. Commercial centre. Fresh water plant.

Gastronomy: 3 bars, 2 restaurants, 2 grills, 2 pizzerias, 2 snack bars and 1 beach-bar
Sports: Multi-use sports area (hand-ball, volley, basketball, badminton, football, 8 tennis courts, minigolf (3000 sq.m. 18 holes), windsurfing school.
Activities: Organised fiestas. Disco "Light" excursions, dancing, sports competitions, movie/video shows. 7 modern ablution blocks with hot water everywhere. Money exchange, safe, medical service, telephones.
Bungalows and apartments for hire. We speak English.

SPECIAL
off-season fees
Open:
1.4 - 27.9

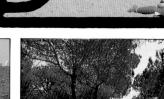

LA SIESTA
CARAVANING CAMPING

E-43840 SALOU
(Tarragona)
C/ Norte, 37
Tel. (34-77) 38 08 52
Fax (34-77) 38 31 91

A real holiday site, situated in the centre of the elegant, intern. holiday resort of SALOU, in the always sunny prov. of Tarragona. Excellent installations as swimming pool and paddling pool, free hot water, electr. conn. f. tent and caravan, supermarket, restaurant, bar, cafeteria, etc. At only 100m from a large, magnificent beach and at 900m from the theme-leisure park "PORT AVENTURA".

BUNGALOWS AND MOBILE HOMES FOR HIRE OPEN 14.3 - 3.11.

Very reasonable of-season fees and 10% P/N reduction from 14.3 till 15.6 and in Sept. and Oct.

CAMPING & BUNGALOWS
Sangulí Salou
SALOU (TARRAGONA) - COSTA DAURADA - ESPAÑA

SPECIAL OFF-SEASON OFFERS

CAMPING & BUNGALOWS SANGULI, situated in Salou in the heart of the Costa Dorada and only 50m from the beach, offers all amenities only a high-class camping site can offer.

– An animation programme for young and old; daily entertainment in an exceptional amphitheatre with a capacity of 2000 seats.
– 6 swimming-pools, 2 supermarkets, 4 bars, 2 children's playgrounds, gift-shop, restaurant, take-away meal, pub discotheque, launderette, etc . . .
– sports facilities, such as tennis, mini-golf, squash, indoor football, basketball, petanque, volleyball, etc . . .
– 7 modern sanitary blocks, offering the highest level of hygiene and comfort. (Facilities for the disabled and babies, etc . . .)

All this, surrounded by a unique nature and precious gardens, makes CAMPING AND BUNGALOWS SANGULI your ideal holiday destination.

camping sangulí
Prolongació carrer E, s/n
E-43840 SALOU (Tarragona) - España
Tel. (34-77) 38 16 41 & 38 16 98
Fax (34-77) 38 46 16

http://www.salou.org/camping/sanguli   E-mail: sanguli@salou.org

PLAYA MONTROIG
CAMPING & BUNGALOW PARK
vacaciones **VIVAS**

A family holiday park equipped to the highest standards, surrounded by large tropical gardens and with a spectacular swimming pool. Situated in front of a wonderful sandy beach; PLAYA MONTROIG is a very safe and clean holiday park, that offers, among other things, the following services and installations: wide variety of leisure activities (including tournaments, shows, excursions, etc...), Hobby Centre (workshop), Sport Club (tournaments and sport activities), Junior Club & Teenager Club. Sport area with basketball and football fields, skateboard track, archery, jogging track. Fitness, tennis, minigolf, a large shopping centre, restaurants, bars and discotheques.

Dream Holidays

COSTA DAURADA - MONT-ROIG - TARRAGONA
CATALUNYA · ESPAÑA

*Splendid Holidays
in contact with Nature*

Take notice of our special offers!

For further information & reservation:
Apartado de Correos 3
E-43300 Mont-roig [Tarragona] · ESPAÑA
Tel.: 34/77/81.06.37 · Fax: 34/77/81.14.11

http://www.playamontroig.com
E-mail: info@playamontroig.com

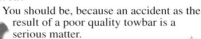

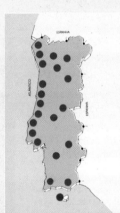

Cala Llevadó camping

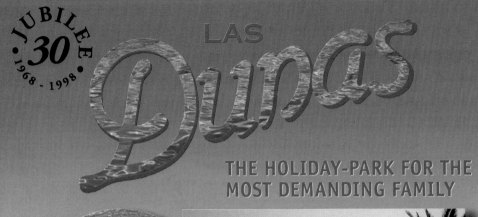

8040 Camping Las Dunas, Sant Pere Pescador, nr Figueres

See colour advert opposite

Large, well organised site beside sandy beach, with pool and many on-site activities.

Las Dunas is right by a sandy beach (with direct access) which stretches along the site for nearly 1 km. with a windsurfing school and beach bar. There is also a much used swimming pool (30 x 14 m.) with small children's pool. Las Dunas is a very large site with 1,500 individual pitches, now increased in size to 100 sq.m. which is good for Spain. They are laid out on flat ground in long regular parallel rows, hedged and with shade available in the older parts of the site. Space is usually available even in the main season. A special area is set aside for campers with dogs. Five excellent large sanitary blocks with resident cleaners (7-9) have British style toilets (no paper - a policy of the management), mostly controllable hot showers and washbasins in cabins. There are facilities for babies and disabled people. There is a large bar with terrace and also a pleasant, more secluded pub-type bar with slightly higher prices. A magnificent disco club, in a soundproof building is reputedly the biggest on the Costa Brava! Beach bar in main season. With free entertainment in season and good security arrangements, this site is good for families with teenagers. Used by British tour operators.

How to find it: Use autostrada exit no. 5 towards Escala and turn north 2 km. before reaching La Escala at sign to St Martin de Ampurias.

General Details: Open 10 May - 26 Sept. Electrical connections in most parts. Large supermarket and other shops. Exchange facilities. Big self-service restaurant. Takeaways. Large bar with terrace. Refurbished laundry facilities. 2 tennis. Minigolf. Disco club. Beach bar in main season. Children's playgrounds. Football and rugby pitches. Basketball. Volleyball. Sailing/windsurfing school and other watersports. Organised programme of events for children and adults 15/6-31/8 - sports, children's games, evening shows, music and entertainment, partly in English. Motorcaravan services. Large caravans for hire. Dogs taken in only one section mid June-mid Sept.

Charges 1997: Per pitch (any unit) incl. electricity 1,400, 1,825, 3,000 or 3,200 ptas; adult 350; child (2-9 yrs) 275. All plus 7% VAT.

Reservations: can be made for numbered pitches with deposit and fee. Address: Apdo. de Correus 23, 17130 La Escala, Costa Brava (Girona). Tel: 972/520400 or 520401. FAX: 972/550046.

This site is featured out of order - it should be listed on page 282

8200 Camping Cala Llevadó, Tossa de Mar, nr Gerona/Girona

See colour advert between pages 288/9

Beautifully situated cliff-side site with excellent facilities.

For splendour of position Cala Llevadó can compare with almost any in this book. Situated on high ground, it has fine views of the sea and coast below and is shaped something like half a bowl. There are flat terraced areas for caravans and tents on top of the two hills at the sides and a great many individual levelled pitches for tents along the slopes leading down to the sea. There is usually a car access (may be narrow) not far from these. Many electrical connections cover all caravan sectors and one tent area. High up in the centre with a good aspect is the attractive restaurant/bar with a large terrace overlooking the high quality children's play area and the free swimming pool (20 x 10 m.), which is much frequented, plus paddling pool. There is a rather steep road leading right down to one of the four sandy or pebbly coves (one naturist) with a car park at the foot. Some other pleasant little coves can also be reached by climbing down on foot. Some up-and-down walking must clearly be expected on this site and should be considered if older or disabled people are included in your party. There are four very well equipped sanitary blocks well spaced around the site and built in an attractive style, with fully controllable, free hot water in washbasins (some in cabins) and in well equipped showers, baby baths and British style toilets. Water points around. The reception area has post office/telephone facilities. Cala Llevadó is luxurious and has character, with many regular clients and the atmosphere is informal and friendly. Only 150 of the 630 pitches are accessible for caravans, so reservation in season is vital. It is peacefully situated but only five minutes away from the busy resort of Tossa. Torches needed at night. There are lots of watersports activities locally.

How to find it: Cala Llevadó leads off the new Tossa-Lloret road about 3 km. from Tossa; the approach from either direction now presents no problems.

General Details: Open 1 May - 30 Sept, including all amenities. Large supermarket. New restaurant/bar with terrace. Swimming pools. Tennis. Three children's play areas. Sailing, water ski and windsurfing school. Fishing. Scuba diving. Post office/telephone. Washing machines and dryer. Laundry service. Chemical disposal. Motorcaravan services. Tents (7) and caravans (7) for hire.

Charges 1998: Per person 580 - 850; child (3-14 yrs) 360 - 475; car or m/cycle 580 - 850; tent 580 - 850; caravan 660 - 920; motorcaravan 950 - 1,320; electricity 450. Plus 7% VAT.

Reservations: accepted with deposit and fee. Address: Apdo 34, 17320 Tossa de Mar (Girona). Tel: 972/340314. FAX: 972/341187. E-mail: calalleva@grn.es. Internet: http://www.6tems.grn.es/calalleva.

AR Discount
Less 10% on person charge

8102 Camping Mas Patoxas, Pals, nr Gerona/Girona

Unpretentious site with satisfactory facilities in main season, set back from the coastal resorts.

This is a useful site for those who prefer to be apart from but within easy travelling distance of the beaches (5 km) and town (1 km) in high season. It has very easy access, being set on a slight slope with level terraces providing some 600 grassy pitches of a minimum 72 sq.m. All have electricity (5A) and water, 150 have drainage as well. There are some pleasant views but not a lot of shade. Although there are some 80 static units, there is the impression of more as they are sited together near the entrance and pool. There are no tour operators. The three sanitary blocks are of modern construction, with one rebuilt in 97. They offer controllable hot showers, with dressing area, some washbasins with hot water, British style WCs, baby bath and three children's cabins with washbasin and shower. There are dishwashing facilities under cover (H&C) and five washing machines. A restaurant/bar provides both waiter service meals and takeaway food to order, and there is a shop (all open all season). Activities include a medium sized swimming pool with sunbathing area and entertainment during the main season. Although there are no specific facilities for the disabled, access throughout the site looks to be relatively easy.

How to find it: Site is approx. 1½ km. south of Pals on the left hand side going towards Palafrugell on the GE650.

General Details: Open 1 April - 30 Sept. Restaurant/bar. Pizzeria. Takeaway. Shop. Swimming pool (1/6-15/9). Tennis courts. Table tennis. Volleyball. Football field. Entertainment in high season. Laundry facilities. Chemical disposal. Bungalows and mobile homes to rent (details from site).

Charges 1998: Per person 400 - 700 ptas; child (1-10 yrs) 300 - 425; caravan pitch 1,300 - 1,950, tent pitch with car 1,100 - 1,500. Plus VAT @7%. Discounts of 5-18% for stays over 7 days in low season. Credit cards accepted.

Reservations: Write to site. Address: Ctra. Palafrugell-Torroella km.5, 17256 Pals (Girona). Tel: 972/636928 or 636361. FAX: 972/667349.

CAMPING CARAVANING

MAS PATOXAS

tel. 972-63 69 28
PALS (Girona)

AN ALL ROUND HOLIDAY SITE!

E-17256 PALS (prov. Girona)
On the road Palafrugell to Torroella de Montgri, km 5, situated between the beach at Pals (5 km) and the beaches at Begur.
Tel. (34-72) 63 69 28 & 63 63 61
Fax. (34-72) 66 73 49

COSTA BRAVA

OPEN: 1.4-30.9.
Mobile homes, wooden bungalows and Trigano tent-bungalows for hire. Interesting fees.
Write to us for more information.

For a list of sites which are open all year - see page 359.

Also: Alan Rogers' Good Camps Guide ALL YEAR ROUND features campsites throughout Europe for All Year touring.

SPAIN - Costa Brava

8075 Camping Estartit, Estartit

Friendly, Belgian run site with small swimming pool, 300 m. from Estartit town.

Although facilities at this site are fairly limited, a short walk down the hill brings you into the heart of the extremely popular Estartit with its authentic tapas bars and street entertainment. Set in tall pine trees in a valley situation, this is a peaceful site with 160 pitches, all with electrical connections (2/6A), terraced and mostly suitable for tents (with some steep drops between terraces). However there are two long sand/gravel areas for motorhomes and caravans, separated by a canal. The site itself is surprisingly quiet, considering its proximity to the town - there is no need to use a vehicle once on site. One modern, fully tiled sanitary block provides hot and cold showers (small fee for hot water), small laundry with washing machines and a separate baby area. On site facilities include a bar/restaurant and shop (high season). There is a small swimming pool with a children's section, with a play area next to it, plus an attractive shaded area beside the bar. Access around the site could be difficult for disabled people.

How to find It: Site is signed from Estartit town centre.

General Details: Open Easter/1 April - 1 Oct. Bar/restaurant and shop (1/6-15/9). Swimming pool (all season). Children's play area. Children's activities and adult social events arranged (barbecue, bingo, etc). Laundry facilities. Chemical disposal. Apartments for rent. Site is guarded day and night.No dogs 20/6-20/8.

Charges 1997: Per person 550 ptas; child (2-10 yrs) 400; caravan or family tent 575; small tent 475; motorcaravan 950; car 525; m/cycle 425; electricity 2A 300, 6A 375. Plus 7% VAT. Less 10-30% outside high season (10/6-31/8).

Reservations: Contact site for details. Address: 17258 Estartit (Girona). Tel: 972/75.89.09 or 75.19.09. FAX: 972/75.09.91. Winter address (15/10 -15/3) Vrancken Joss, Plantenstraat 74, 3500 Hasselt, Belgium.

AR Discount
Less further 10% in low season; welcome drink in high season

8140 Camping Caravaning Treumal, Calonge, Platja d'Aro, nr Girona

Very attractive terraced site on hillside with direct access to small beaches.

This pretty site has been developed in the attractive gardens of a large private house (used for some of the main facilities), creating the effect of a private, personal place that has adapted itself beautifully to camping with a tranquil atmosphere. It is in a quiet situation (although some noise may be expected from the busy coast road on pitches nearer the entrance) on a pine-wooded hillside leading down to the sea, with around 500 pitches on well shaded terraces. Because of trees and difficult access, only perhaps 300 are accessible to caravans; also, cars may not park by tents or caravans in high season, but must be left on car parks or roads. This is not a site for large units. Electrical connections are available in all parts. The three well maintained sanitary blocks have British toilets and free hot water in both the washbasins (with some in private cabins) and the controllable showers, and a tap to draw from for the sinks. Drinking water may be salty. There is access from different parts of the site to the main beach of coarse sand, with good bathing, and direct access to two smaller pretty coves.

How to find It: Access to site is signed from the C253 coast road 3 km. south of Palamos.

General Details: Open Easter/1 April - 31 Oct. Supermarket. Bar. Takeaway. Good restaurant with attractive shaded terrace (15/5-15/9). Table tennis. Fishing. Children's play area and sports area. Washing machines. Chemical disposal. Motorcaravan services. Traditional Spanish-style rooms and small mobile homes to let.

Charges 1998: Per person ptas 450 - 750; child (4-10 yrs) 249 - 415; caravan 690 - 1,150; motorcaravan 930 - 1,550; tent 615 - 1,025, car, m/cycle or boat 492 - 820; extra tent 312 - 520; electricity 480. Plus 7% VAT.

Reservations: are made to guarantee admission (needed more for caravans than for tents) with deposit. Address: Aptdo Correos 348, 17250 Playa de Aro (Girona). Tel: 972/65 10 95. FAX: 972/651671.

SPAIN - Costa Brava

8160 Camping Cala Gogo, Platja d'Aro, nr Gerona/Girona

Large, successful and vibrant site by sea with swimming pool and many amenities.

One of the best known campsites in Spain, its situation on a wooded hillside leading down to a small cove with a sandy beach is one of considerable natural beauty. In a high central position there are two good sized pools (25 x 12 m.) and children's pool - an excellent provision. Close by are shops, restaurant and a bar with adjoining terrace with views over the pools down to the beach, all open for the whole season. A second floodlit restaurant and bar are down by the beach (reached via a tunnel under the main road - possibly some road noise) and is open from June. The resort of Platja d'Aro is 2 km. Cala Gogo is divided into over 1,000 individual pitches, some shaded, others with artificial shade. These range in size from 50-100 sq.m. without the car, which stands in front of or near your unit (there are now many more of the larger pitches and some have water connection). The site is an active, bustling place, with over 3,000 campers when full. The distance from the busy beach with good bathing, depends on the position of your pitch. Some are now right by the beach, others up to 800 m. uphill, but two `Gua gua' (South American Spanish for bus) tractor trains, operating all season, take people up and down and add to the sense of fun and energy that the camp generates. A programme of animation which includes sports, tournaments, entertainment, etc. for children and adults is arranged free of charge (7 nights a week), as are the sports centre facilities of tennis, volleyball, basketball, etc. and the minigolf, plus a `mini-club' and crèche for small ones. Also fairly close is a new aqua-park offering waterslides, wave simulation etc. with a bus from the camp. There is another quieter beach adjacent. The seven sanitary blocks are quite satisfactory and are continuously cleaned. The newest one, in a section at the top of the site, is fully tiled with British WCs, free hot water in the washbasins set in flat surfaces (some private cabins), and free hot showers. The gates are closed to cars at midnight and the site is well supervised.

How to find it: Site is on the main road between Palamos and Platja d'Aro, 4.5 km. south of Palamos.

General Details: Open 9 April - 27 Sept, including amenities. 160,000 sq.m. Artificial or natural shade on most pitches. Electrical connections. Large supermarket. General shop. Tobacconist. Restaurants and bars in two places. Swimming pools and paddling pool. Children's playground and crèche. Sports centre. Table tennis. Sailboards and pedaloes for hire. Fishing. TV/video room. Grass minigolf. Bureau de change. Telephones. Medical service; nurse daily, doctor alternate days. Good 24 hr security service. Laundry. Chemical disposal. No dogs July/Aug. Small number of tour operators. Bungalows, Trigano tents and mobile homes to rent.

Charges 1998: Per person 455 - 760 ptas; child (under 10) 235 - 380; car 465 - 810; tent 500 - 985; caravan or trailer tent 610 - 1,155; motorcaravan 760 - 1,285; electricity (5A) 475. All plus 7% VAT. Credit cards not accepted.

Reservations: are made for min. 1 week with deposit (10,000 ptas.), no fee. Address: Apdo 80, 17250 Platja d'Aro (Girona). Tel: 972/651564. FAX: 972/650553.

 AR Discount
Less 10% in low season, 6% in high season. Show guide on arrival

First categorie holiday site bordering the sea and beautiful sand beach in the very centre of the COSTA BRAVA

COSTA BRAVA ☆ CALONGE ☆ PLAYA DE ARO

We offer you: well shaded pitches, 2 swimming pools, children's playground, supermarket, 2 restaurants, snack bar, grill, pizzeria, souvenirs, laundry, modern anblution block, etc. Multilingual reception service, safe deposit, automatic telephone service, medical assistance. Guarded day and night. Comfortable, well equipped mobile homes can also be rented direct in the reception. Organised games and activities for children and adults, dicotheque, excursions, etc. Important discounts for camping and mobile homes, except from 22.6 - 31.8.

Open: 9.4 - 27.9

For inf. and reservation write to:
CALA GOGO
Apartado 80,
E-17250 Platja d'Aro
(Girona)
Tel. (34-72) 65 15 64
Fax (34-72) 65 05 53.

OFF - SEASON -35%

AutoRoute Express

During 1997 The Microsoft Corporation released their new version of `AUTOROUTE Express' which features a campsite database.

This database includes and highlights virtually all our Alan Rogers' Inspected and Selected sites throughout the UK, France and the rest of Europe. It also includes a large number of other sites too, which have not been subject to our rigorous inspection process.

8130 Camping Internacional de Calonge, Platja d'Aro, nr Gerona/Girona

Smart, efficient, spacious site with wide range of amenities, open all year.

Although perhaps not as luxurious as some of its neighbours, this is a family site with a good pool, plus large sunbathing area and a range of amenities which include a comfortable restaurant serving good food at reasonable prices. It is situated beside the coast road with good bathing beaches just across the busy road (possibly some road noise), with access by footbridge. The site is set on sloping ground and is quite large with 700 pitches, all with electricity, of which some 400 are suitable for caravans, the remainder being set on attractively landscaped terraces. Access to some pitches may be a little difficult. There is good shade from the tall pine trees. Some sites which are nominally 'open all year' offer nothing but a pitch during winter, but Calonge has a heated sanitary block and the bar/restaurant is fully open April - Oct. and in the evenings even during the winter with a log fire. The satisfactory sanitary installations in the new and renovated blocks include British style WCs, free hot showers and some washbasins in cabins. Some British tour operators and some mobile homes, mainly in their own areas.

How to find it: Site is on inland side of coast road between Palamos and Platja d'Aro, just south of Sa. Calonge and 4 km. south of Palamos.

General Details: Open all year. Electrical connections throughout. Shop (Easter-30/10, supermarket 500 m). Bar/restaurant (Easter- 30/10). Swimming pool (1/4-30/10). Children's playground on sand. Fishing. Bicycle hire. Table tennis. Tennis. Volleyball. Cash machine. Exchange. Hairdresser. Laundry facilities. Chemical disposal. Motorcaravan services. Good security. Tents and mobile homes to let.

Charges 1998: Per adult 425 - 715; child (2-10 yrs) 220 - 385; tent 550 - 855; caravan 580 - 855; car 570 - 800; motorcaravan 850 - 1,195; m/cycle 405 - 570; electricity 475. All plus 7% VAT. Discounts for retired people for longer stays Oct - end May.

Reservations: Write to site with deposit (6,000 ptas). Address: Aptdo. Correos 272, 17251 Calonge (Girona). Tel: 972/65 12 33. or 65 14 64. FAX: 972/65 25 07. Internet: http://www.abaforum.es/cic. E-mail: zubarosi@abaforum.es. UK contact: Mr J Worthington, 0161-799-1274.

8230 Beach Camp El Pinar, Blanes, nr Gerona/Girona

See colour advert between pages 288/9

Pleasant, family orientated, smallish site adjoining good beach.

Previously named Camping El Pinar, this is essentially a family site without tour operators or mobile homes. The new name sums up the direction in which the owners are developing the site, with an emphasis on a more participatory approach to camping with an increase in the amount of activities and facilities offered - mostly directed towards sports. It is situated at the southern edge of Blanes beach, with direct access, and is about 2 km. from the town. The 495 pitches, all with electricity and a min. 60 sq.m. are mostly shaded by pine or broad leaf trees. The site is in two sections, the second across the road, with its own sanitary block only used in July/Aug. Modern, tiled sanitary facilities have British style WCs and controllable hot showers with dressing area. Baby baths and open plan washbasins (cold water). Dishwashing facilities are under cover. A café and takeaway are amongst the facilities, plus an aerobic centre with professional instructor (but no real gym equipment when we visited). Beach activities and games are organised. A swimming pool is planned. Small supermarket. Well enclosed, children's play area on grass. This site will appeal particularly to families seeking easy access to a long beach (shelves quite steeply) and the attractions of a major resort. Regular bus service into Blanes.

How to find it: Site is the last travelling south from Blanes town centre. Follow camping signs in Blanes until you see the El Pinar sign.

General Details: Open 1 May - 30 Sept. Bar/restaurant with takeaway. Small supermarket. Volleyball. Table tennis. Children's playground. Activities for adults and children organised in season (2/5-16/9), including Spanish classes, dancing, bicycle excursions, aerobics. Excursions. Watersports near. Bungalows and mobile homes to let.

Charges 1997: Per person 440 - 575 ptas; child 385 - 465; pitch incl. electricity 1,390 - 1,675; plus 7% VAT.

Reservations: Write or phone site (no deposit). Address: Villa de Madrid s/n, 17300 Blanes (Girona). Tel: 972/33.10.83. FAX: 972/33.11.00.

SPAIN - Costa Brava / Costa Daurada

8240 Camping Botànic Bona Vista (Kim), Calella de la Costa, nr Barcelona

Delightfully attractive, small site on hillside south of Calella de la Costa.

While Calella itself may conjure up visions of mass tourism, this site is set on a steep hillside some 3 km. out of the town. Apart from perhaps some noise from the nearby coast road and railway, it is a quite delightful setting, with an abundance of flowers, shrubs and roses (1,700), the design successfully marrying the beautiful botanic surrounds with the attractive views of the bay. The 160 pitches, all with electricity, are 60-80 sq.m. or more and are situated on terraces with some shade. The access roads are steep and many of the pitches enjoy lovely views. There are quite good beaches, including a naturist beach, just across the road and railway, accessible via a tunnel and crossing. The standard of the sanitary installations in 3 blocks is quite outstanding for a small site (indeed any site). They include controllable, free hot showers, with dressing area, British WCs and (in the newest block) some washbasins (H&C) in cabins, a bidet in the ladies' and a baby room. Dishwashing facilities with hot water, under cover and washing machines. The bar/restaurant is unusual in having a circular, central open-hearth fire/cooker, and serves both eat-in and takeaway meals, with roof top terrace. No shop but essentials are kept in the bar. Children's playground, satellite TV, with 2 pool tables in a separate room and a recreation park (2,000 sq.m.) with table tennis, football, petanque, etc. A barbecue and picnic area has been added. On arrival, park at the restaurant and choose a pitch - the owner is most helpful with siting your van.

How to find it: From the N11 coast road site is signed travelling south of Calella (at km. 665), and is on right hand side of road - care is needed as road is busy and sign is almost on top of turning (next to Camping Roca Grossa). Entrance is very steep. From Barcelona, after passing through Sant Pol de Mar, go into outside lane shortly after 'Camping 800 m.' sign and keep signalling left. Site entrance is just before the two lanes merge.

General Details: Open all year. Bar/restaurant (weekends only in winter). Takeaway. Electricity throughout. No shop, but essentials from bar. Large children's playground. Recreation park. Satellite TV. Games room. Barbecue and picnic area. Fishing. Bicycle hire. Watersports near. Chemical disposal.

Charges 1998: Per person ptas. 500; child (3-10 yrs) 425; car 500; tent or caravan 500; motorcaravan 1,000; m/cycle 425; electricity (6A) 435. All plus 7% VAT.

Reservations: Write to site. Address: Ctra. N-ll, Km.665, PO Box 38, 08370 Calella (Catalunya). Tel: 93/7692488. FAX: 93/7695804. E-mail: bonavista@redestb.es. Internet: http://www.datum.es/bonavis.htm.

Costa Daurada

The 'Golden Coast' is aptly named with a fine band of pale yellow sand stretching almost continuously along its length. It covers the shores of Barcelona and Tarragona provinces, from the Rio Tordera to the Ebro. The section south of Barcelona includes the well known resorts of Sitges, Tarragona and Salou and is backed by pine-covered hills. The northern section includes Arenys and Calella, and is flatter country, with a fair penetration of industry. The area is famed for its fresh vegetables and fish and in Barcelona boasts one of the most exciting cities in the world.

8310 Camping La Ballena Alegre, Castelldefels, nr Barcelona

Spacious, well laid out site on beach, with comprehensive shops and restaurant/bars.

La Ballena Alegre is one of the best known sites in Spain. About 16 km. from the centre of Barcelona, it has a super sandy beach more than a kilometre long and 100 m. wide, although some may prefer the 25 x 13 m. swimming pool (and small children's pool). It is a very large site, most of which is covered by a pinewood and divided into 1,570 pitches of about 70 sq.m. with tourers going on the left hand side. Space is not usually a problem, certainly outside July/Aug. The sanitary blocks have been much improved and are all good, although they still vary in size and type, two being new. All have free warm water in washbasins and the new blocks have some cabins, Free controllable hot showers with screen, mostly British style WCs, units for the disabled. Cleaning is good. Attractive bar/restaurant and pool terrace with entertainment in season. Although not a quiet site, with a lively atmosphere in high season and some aircraft noise, this is nevertheless a well run one, with personal supervision.

How to find it: From Barcelona on the N11 you can turn off on to the C245 road to Gava and Castelldefels or take the motorway A2 spur towards Castelldefels - El Prat de Llobregat and continue to Castelldefels. Entrance leads directly off C246 dual carriageway 'Autovia Castelldefels' on coast side of the road, by a service station.

General Details: Open 1 April - 30 Sept. Probably some 260,000 sq.m. Mostly well shaded. Electrical connections of 220v. everywhere. Large supermarket and other shops. Restaurants (self and waitress service), and adjoining bar and snack bar. Hairdressers. Soundproofed disco. Organised sports activities: aerobics, squash, roller skating, bicycle track, swimming, football etc., and entertainment twice weekly in season. Sports area. Tennis. Children's playground. Garage (petrol and servicing) by entrance. Washing machines. Bureau de change. Treatment room with nurse. Doctor calls daily. Roman amphitheatre where folk dances, shows etc. are staged. Chalets and bungalows to rent.

Charges 1998: Per person ptas. 575; child (under 10) 260; pitch incl. car and electricity 1,425 - 2,650, with tent 1,100 - 1,600. All plus 7% VAT.

Reservations: only made in the sense of guaranteeing admission. Site address: Autovia Castelldefels km.12.5, 08840 Viladecans (Barcelona). Tel: 93/658.05.04. FAX: 93/658.05.75. Winter: Aptdo de Correos 438, 08080 Barcelona. Tel: 93/226.13.02. FAX: 93/226.65.28.

8390 Camping Vilanova Park, Vilanova i la Geltru, Sitges

See colour advert
between pages 288/9

Hillside site with views to sea, good quality installations and large pool complex.

This large modern site has been equipped with costly installations of good quality. The most remarkable feature is the swimming pool complex with one very large pool with water jets and a coloured floodlit fountain. Together with a smaller children's pool, this covers an area of some 1,000 sq.m. In the same area is the shopping centre and the large bar and restaurant, set around old Catalan farm buildings where dancing or entertainment takes place when numbers permit. The site is 4 km. from Vilanova town and beach, and 11 km. from Sitges. At present there are 1,100 pitches on the site with a very significant proportion occupied by a variety of static units. They are divided by markers at the front and mostly of good average size, say 70 sq.m. for caravans and a bit less for tents. The site has developed some larger pitches (100 sq.m.) with electricity, water and drainage. The terrain, hard surfaced and mostly on very gently sloping ground, has many trees and considerable shade. The two large, well maintained sanitary blocks are of excellent quality and can be heated, but they may be a fair walk from the touring pitches and have some steps to negotiate. British WCs, washbasins (over half in cabins) with free hot water, and others of standard type with cold water. Free controllable hot showers and hot water for washing dishes, cold for clothes; also serviced laundry. A new attraction is a Wildlife Park, inhabited by deer and bird-life. Very pleasant, it has picnic areas and footpaths. Barcelona is easily accessible - buses every hour in the main season or electric train from Vilanova i la Geltru every 20 minutes.

How to find it: Site is 4 km. northwest of Vilanova i la Geltru towards L'Arboc. From Barcelona-Tarragona autopista take exit 29 and turn towards Vilanova. There is no exit at 29 from Tarragona direction; from here take exit 30, into Vilafranca and turn right for Vilanova. Vilanova bypass now open so one need not go into town. Alternatively from N340 from L'Arboc directly on attractive but very winding road for 11 km. signed Vilanova i la Geltru.

General Details: Open all year (full services May - Oct). Electrical connections throughout (6A). Supermarket, souvenir shop. Full restaurant and larger bar with many tables where simpler meals served. Swimming pools. Tennis. Launderette. Chalets, bungalows, caravans and 6 newly built self contained cabins available to rent.

Charges guide: Per person 760 ptas; child (3-9 yrs) 475; car 760; tent/caravan 760; motorcaravan 1,375; m/cycle 575; electricity (6A) 450. Less in low season. All plus 7% VAT.

Reservations: are made in sense of guaranteeing to admit, with deposit. Address: Aptdo 64, 08800 Vilanova i la Geltru (Barcelona). Tel: 93/8933402. FAX: 93/8935528.

8410 Park Playa Bara, Roda de Bara, nr Tarragona

See colour advert
between pages 288/9

Excellent, well maintained site near beach, with comprehensive amenities.

This is an impressive site which is family owned and has been carefully developed over the years. On entry you find yourself in a beautifully sculptured, tree lined drive with an accompanying aroma of pine and woodlands. Considering its size, with over 850 pitches, it is still a very green and relaxing site with an immense range of activities. It is well situated with a direct access to a long sandy beach (via a tunnel under the railway and 50 m. walk). An important feature is the attractive, medium sized heated pool of irregular shape in the centre of the site, with separate small pool for children, landscaped with grass and trees surrounding and additional terraced sunbathing areas. A new heated pool has been added with toboggan slides, jacuzzi and spa bath. There is an adjacent bar when the pool is open. Pitches vary in size but are larger than the Spanish average, the older ones terraced and well shaded with pine trees, the newer ones more open, with a variety of trees and bushes forming separators between them and with electricity (5A) and water. Arrive early to find space in peak weeks. The toilet blocks are of different sizes and types, but all very good, with British style WCs, free hot water in washbasins and showers and in many of the sinks. There are some cabins for both sexes in some blocks, children's baths, basins and toilets and facilities for disabled. The water is rather salty here but spring water is available from special taps. The site is well laid out with an attractive central roadway. Much care with planning and in the use of natural stone and flowering plants gives a pleasing appearance, which particularly shows in the Roman-style amphitheatre, part of the comprehensive amenity complex at the front of the site. Modern fitness suite complete with up-to-date equipment and instructor. Used by some British tour operators.

How to find it: Site entrance is off the main N340 just opposite the Arco de Bara. From autopista A7, take exit 31.

General Details: Open 10 March - 30 Sept. with all amenities. Electrical connections (5A) in all parts. Supermarket and other shops. Full restaurant and larger bar where simpler meals and takeaway served, bars also in 3 other places, and self-service restaurant on beach. Swimming pools. 'Frontennis' ground and tennis courts (both floodlit). Roller skating. Football and basketball. Sports area for children. Windsurfing school. Volleyball. Basketball. Bicycle track. Gymnasium. Petanque. Minigolf, arranged on a map of Europe. Washing machines. Fishing. Entertainment centre: amphitheatre with stage and dance floor, large busy room for young with pool, football, table tennis, machines; bar, video room with seating, satellite TV, disco room open 11 to 4 am. (weekends only outside high season). Exchange facilities, cash point. Hairdresser. Chemical disposal. Motorcaravan services.

Charges 1997: Per person 430 - 860 ptas; child (1-9 yrs) 310 - 620; car 860; large tent or caravan 860; motorcaravan 1,500; small tent 620; m/cycle 620; electricity 495. All plus 7% VAT. Low season reductions for pensioners and all sports charges reduced by 90%. CCI members 10% discount (min. 10 days) in high season.

Reservations: Contact site for details. Address: 43883 Roda de Bara (Tarragona). Tel: 977/80 27 01. FAX: 977/80 04 56. E-mail: barapark@lix.intercom.es. Internet: http:/www.barapark.es.

SPAIN - Costa Daurada

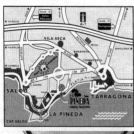

CAMPING LA PINEDA DE SALOU
Ctra. de la Costa Tarragona a Salou, Km 5
E-43480 LA PINEDA - Tarragona COSTA DAURADA
Tel. (34-77) 37 21 76
Fax (34-77) 37 06 20

The ideal camping site due to its microclimate and exceptional beach

Situated at the beach of La Pineda, only 2,5 km from the holiday theme park Port Aventura, 3 km from the centre of Salou and 6 km from Tarragona (with its Roman amphitheatre, walls, museums, casteIIers –human towers–, gastronomy, fishing).

OFFER-96 / Campsite and Bungalows	
Special season from 01-03 to 08-07 and from 24-08 to 30-10	
Period of stay	Pay only
8 days	6 days
11 days	8 days
15 days	11 days

Pitch reservation.
Completely equipped
wooden bungalows for rent

- A quiet and **pleasant** camping site with more than a thousand trees to give you shade; gardens and well defined 70 m² plots.
- Two swimming-pools, 2.000 m² solarium, kindergarten, games area, TV room, all this just 400 m from the magnificent **beach of La Pineda.**
- Children's baths, free hot water, independent toilets, chemical WC, laundry, medical attention.
- Cafeteria, restaurant with a terrace, barbecue, supermarket, autovending section, **bed and breakfast.**

- Day and night-time **animation**, special activities for children, games, sports. Information on visits and excursions (**Port Aventura**, Santes Creus, Montserrat, Barcelona). Bus stop just in front of the camping site with services to Tarragona, Salou, and Port Aventura.
- **Acquapark** (the best waterworld in Catalonia), discos (Pachá, Pineda Drink), pubs, tennis, mini-golf just 300 m away).
- Just 2,5 km away from the entrance to the **Port Aventura** theme park. An exotic and fascinating journey.

The campsite is open from 01-03 to 30-10. The bungalows stay open throughout the year.

8480 Camping Sanguli, Salou, nr Tarragona

See colour advert between pages 288/9

Large, spacious site close to beach and within town, with pools and entertainment.

Owned, developed and managed by a local Spanish family, this large site lies little more than 100 m. from the good sandy beach, across the coast road and a small, manned railway level crossing (some train noise at times). Although large, Sanguli manages to convey the intimacy of smaller, family run sites. There are three attractive, good sized pools (with children's pools), one with grassy lying-out area partly shaded near the entrance, and a second deep one as part of the sports complex with tennis court, 2 squash courts, a `fronton', minigolf and football practice area. The third is part of the new amphitheatre area at the top of the site. This will allow over 4,000 campers to sample the free nightly entertainment and enjoy the attractively designed new pool. All the pools have adjacent amenity areas, bars, etc. and from mid-June to mid-Sept. there is a comprehensive programme of entertainment. Excellent sports facilities. The site is also fortunate to be placed near the centre of Salou and so can offer the attractions of a busy resort while still being private. It is only 3 km. from Port Aventura. The sanitary facilities have been comprehensively updated and improved including a further new block for '98. They provide mostly hot water in showers and basins, including many individual cabins with `en suite' facilities. The new blocks provide excellent facilities, the showers mostly with dividers and shelves. British style WCs. All are kept very clean. The general appearance of the site has greatly improved over the years, with trees growing well to indicate the boundaries of the pitches. There is provision for 1,1,80 places, with pitch size being increased to 90 sq.m. The new pitches at the top of the site are provided with 10A electricity (whereas the rest of the site is up to 8A). Trees provide natural sha de on these pitches. This is a large, busy site providing something for all the family, but still big enough to give peace and quiet for those looking for it. The management are friendly and very efficient. Used by British tour operators.

How to find it: On west side of Salou about 1 km. from centre, site is well signed from the coast road to Cambrils and from the other town approaches.

General Details: Open 13 March - 26 Oct, with shop, meals and facilities available all season. 150,000 sq.m. Many electrical connections. Two supermarkets. Bars and restaurant with cooked meals to take away. Swimming pools. Sport complex with tennis, squash, football practice ground, etc. Children's playground. First-aid room. Launderette with service provided. Security service. Chemical disposal. Motorcaravan services.

Charges 1998: Per adult 600; child (3-10 yrs) 400; standard pitch (70-75 sq.m.) 2,000 - 3,200, `special' pitch (90 sq.m.) 2,000 - 3,600, `master' pitch (90 sq.m.) incl. water 2,200 - 3,900; car 590 - 810; electricity included. All plus 7% VAT. Less 25-35% in low seasons for longer stays. Long stay offers for senior citizens. Credit cards accepted.

Reservations: made up to 1 March with sizeable booking fee. Address: Aptdo de Corrreos 123, 43840 Salou (Tarragona). Tel: 977/381641 or 381698. FAX: 977/384616. E-mail: sanguli@salou.org. Internet: http://www. salou.org/camping/sanguli.

8482 Camping La Pineda de Salou, La Pineda

Useful site for Port Aventura and Acquapark.

La Pineda is just outside Salou towards Tarragona and this site is just 300 m. from the Acquapark and 2.5 km. from Port Aventura, to which there is an hourly bus service from outside the camp entrance. On site there is a medium sized swimming pool and children's pool, open from mid June, with a large lying out terrace with sun loungers, as well as various entertainments aimed at young people. The shop, restaurant and bar are open all season and there are acceptable sanitary facilities. These include British style WCs, free hot water to the washbasins, showers, baby bath, dishwashing and laundry sinks. There are two washing machines in each block. The second building is opened in high season only. The 336 flat pitches (280 for touring) are mostly shaded and of about 70 sq.m. All have 5A electricity. The beach is only about 400 m. away. This is a friendly and convenient site, without being outstanding.

How to find it: From A7 just southwest of Tarragona take exit 35 and follow signs to Port Aventura then site signs.

General Details: Open 15 March - 15 Oct. Restaurant, bar, snacks and shop (all season). Swimming pools (from mid-June). TV room. Bicycle hire. Games room with videos and drink and snack machines. Chemical disposal.

Charges 1998: Per person ptas. 430 - 590; child (1-10 yrs) 310 - 460; car 415 - 650; caravan 530 - 800; motorhome 810 - 1,100, electricity 395 - 425. Credit cards accepted.

Reservations: Made for high season (min. 7 nights) contact site. Address Ctra de la Costa Tarragona a Salou, km 5, 43480 La Pineda (Tarragona). Tel: 977/37 21 76. FAX: 977/37 06 20.

8470 Camping La Siesta, Salou, nr Tarragona

See colour advert between pages 288/9

Lively site in centre of Salou with swimming pool.

La Siesta is only 250 m. from the sandy beach and not very much more from all the life of Salou, which is very popular with the British and has just about all that a highly developed Spanish resort can offer. For those who do not want to walk this distance, there is a swimming pool of 300 sq.m., free of charge and open all season, on the camp itself, with filtered water. The site is divided into 400 individual pitches which are large enough and have electricity connections (10A), with smaller ones for tents. There is one box for the tent or caravan and a shared one for the car, with some shade from the trees and shrubs that are part of the site's atmosphere. In July/Aug. siting of campers is carried out by the management, who are friendly and helpful. There are three satisfactory sanitary blocks, the best of which is on the left in the quieter area of the site. There are 48 free hot showers. Young campers are sited to the rear of the restaurant. Reservation is advisable from 1/7-20/8.

How to find it: Both new roads from Tarragona and Reus end at a large roundabout from where the camp is only about 200 m. and signed through a one way system in the town.

General Details: Open Easter - 31 Oct. (shop and restaurant all season to 15 Oct.). 50,000 sq.m. Large supermarket. Swimming pool (all season). Self-service restaurant and bar with terrace overlooking pool; also cooked dishes to take away. Dancing some evenings till 11 pm. Many other shops, restaurant and dancing near. Children's playground. Medical service daily in season.

Charges 1997: Per person 490 - 660 ptas; child (4-9 yrs) 400 - 490; car 490 - 660; tent or caravan 490 - 660; motorcaravan 700 - 950; electricity 385 - 400. All plus 7% VAT.

Reservations: made in sense of guaranteeing a shady place, with electricity if required. Deposit asked for. Address: 43840 Salou (Tarragona). Tel: 977/38.08.52. FAX: 977/38.31.91. E-mail: siesta@tinet.fut.es. Internet: http.www.fut-es/nsiesta.

8535 Camping-Pension Cala d'Oques, Hospitalet del Infante

Peaceful, simple site right beside the sea.

As a change from the sophisticated, well equipped sites of the Costa Daurada, you may wish to spend some time at this simple, tranquil site. Its attraction is its position, right by the sea with a wide beach of sand and pebbles, and with a mountain backdrop. As you enter the site, past the guard-geese house, you can go right onto a wide, level section or left up to the terraces. The 234 large pitches are among trees which provide little shade. Electricity is available (10A) but long cables may be needed. Sanitary facilities, by reception, are clean, with hot water for the showers which are small with no divider (shower heads from reception). Hot water in 6 washbasins (of 36) and for dishwashing; British style WCs. It is a long site so you could have a long walk to use them, although there are now toilets at the far end. Rooms available in the pension at the entrance which also houses a shop and restaurant/bar with terrace (open Easter-Sept).

How to find it: Hospitalet del Infante is south of Tarragona, accessed from the A7 (exit 38) or from the N340. From the south take first exit to Hospitalet del Infante. Follow signs in the village, site is 2 km. south, by the sea.

General Details: Open all year. Restaurant/bar and shop (both Easter-Sept). Rooms. Village facilities 1½ km.

Charges 1997: Per person ptas. 595 - 715; child (under 10 yrs) 500 - 595; tent or caravan 595 - 715; car or m/cycle 595 - 715; motorcaravan 845 - 995; dog 350 - 395; electricity 435 - 495.

Reservations: Contact site. Address: 43890 Hospitalet del Infante (Tarragona). Tel: 977/82.32.54. FAX: 977/82.06.91.

SPAIN - Costa Daurada

8481 Camping Cambrils Park, Salou, nr Tarragona

Modern site with first-class facilities.

An impressive entrance drive, lined with palm trees and flowers, leads from the large reception building at the entrance of this site to the pitches and facilities. It is set some way back from the beach in a generally quiet setting. The 611 slightly sloping, grassy pitches of around 90 sq.m. are numbered and separated by trees. All have 10A electricity, 50 also with water and waste water connections. They are served by three excellent sanitary buildings which have free hot water to the washbasins (half in cabins), showers, units for the disabled, dishwashing, laundry and baby bath sections. Hand and hairdryers are provided and there is also a serviced laundry. The large supermarket, souvenir shop and 'panaderia' (fresh-baked bread and croissants) are open daily with a break from 2-4 pm. The takeaway and restaurant offer a wide selection and from 10 June the very large bar between the pool and games area is open. There is also a bar on the central island in the 1,000 sq.m. swimming pool, which has a slide and a thickly carpeted grass lying out area. There are many sporting opportunities here, with a football pitch (on sand), multi-games court, tennis, basketball, volleyball and petanque. Children have a large adventure fortress on sand, daily animation from 10 June, pool, table football and other games. In high season there is a daily show on the 'island' in the pool. At present there is a very small number of tour operator pitches. It is a walk of about 500 m. to the beach and 4 km. to Port Aventura.

How to find it: Site entrance is signed 700 m. west of Camping Sanguli, off coast road from Salou, in Cambrils.

General Details: Open 1 May to 30 Sept, including all amenities. Restaurant. Takeaway. Supermarket. Swimming pools. Football. Basketball. Volleyball. Animation. Entertainments. Souvenir shop. Doctor on site July/Aug. Chemical disposal. No dogs accepted.

Charges 1998: Per person ptas. 600; child (under 10 yrs) 400; pitch incl. electricity 3,000, with water and waste water 3,400; all plus 7% VAT. Less 40% outside 21/6-31/8. Credit cards accepted.

Reservations: Contact site. Address: Apdo de Correos 123, 43840 Salou (Tarragona). Tel: 977/35 10 31. FAX: 977/35 22 10.

8483 Camping Caravaning Tamarit-Park, Tamarit, nr Tarragona

Well cared for, modern site with direct access to beach.

This is a modern, well designed site, situated at the foot of Tamarit castle (church service Sunday, 10 am), with direct access to a good beach. It is only 8 km. from Tarragona and 15 km. from Port Aventura. The 550 pitches are mainly on grass (some a little sandy) and are marked with some separated by hedges. All have electricity (6A) and are 70, 90 or 100 sq.m. in area. Sanitary blocks are modern and tiled, the one nearest the beach provide excellent facilities with British WCs and some washbasins in private cabins with showers. Dishwashing facilities are under cover with hot water and laundry facilities, including washing machines, are provided. Catering includes a beach-side waiter service restaurant, terrace and takeaway. There is a tennis court and an animation programme in season. An excellent new swimming pool with bar and solarium has been added. The site is approached by a long, but improved access road, reached across a new bridge (6 m.) over the railway line (little or no train noise on the site). This is a well designed and maintained site, with good facilities and security.

How to find it: Site is 8 km. north of Tarragona, signed from the N340 (km. 1172). Continue on narrow road for 1 km. to site entrance, on the left side at the end of the road. Note: Take care to ensure you get the correct reception as there is another site next door.

General Details: Open all year with shop, reception and one heated sanitary block, otherwise from 25 March. Bar/restaurant. Takeaway. Supermarket. Swimming pool (15/5-30/9). Tennis. Volleyball. Petanque. Minigolf. Table tennis. Children's playground. Washing machines. Exchange facilities. Car wash. Bungalows (20) and Trigano tents (15) to let.

Charges 1998: Per person 600 - 800 ptas; child (1-9 yrs) 400 - 600; pitch incl. car 2,200 - 2,500; electricity 500. All plus 7% VAT. Discounts for students, pensioners, large families and longer stays in low season.

Reservations: Write to site. Address: Platja Tamarit, 43893 Tarragona (Catalunya). Tel: 977/650128. FAX: 977/650451. E-mail: tamaritpark@tamarit.com.

See colour advert between pages 288/9

Some sites have supplied us with copies of their brochures which we are pleased to forward to readers. See our Brochure Service on page 359

8484 Camping-Caravaning Gavina, Creixell de Mar

Modern, friendly site with direct access to 400 m. beach.

Gavina is sister site to Camping Tamarit (no. 8483) and is a modern, friendly beach site. It has 40 pitches (60 sq.m.), of which 220 have electrical connections (6A), set on flat grass and sand, separated by tall hedges which provide adequate shade. The wide, sandy beach is adjacent to the site with opportunities for a wide range of watersports - including sailing, windsurfing and water skiing. There are two sanitary buildings, the second being of good quality, tiled with free hot water to the showers and some washbasins. In the first block, the showers have no dividers and hooks outside. There are no facilities for use by the disabled. Laundry facilities with washing machines. The attractive restaurant/bar has a terrace overlooking the sea and entertainment is arranged in high season. Well stocked supermarket. There is a children's play area, a tennis court and a sports area.

How to find it: Take exit 32 from A7 Barcelona - Tarragona autopista and follow N340 towards Tarragona until km. 1181 sign. Take road for Creixell Platja and follow well signed road to site (by the sea).

General Details: Open Easter/1 April - 30 Sept. Bar/restaurant. Supermarket. Children's play area. Tennis. Table tennis. Telephones. Exchange facilities. Safe deposit boxes. Laundry facilities. Sports area. Bungalows for rent.

Charges 1998: Per person ptas 500 - 600; child (under 10 yrs) 350 - 450; pitch (any unit) 1,700 - 2,000; electricity 500. Plus 7% VAT.

Reservations: Write to site for details. Address: 43839 Creixell de Mar (Tarragona). Tel: 977/801503. FAX: 977/800527.

8530 Camping Caravaning Playa Montroig, Montroig, nr Tarragona

One of Europe's top sites with excellent facilities and pool complex, beside sandy beach.

Playa Montroig is about 30 km. beyond Tarragona set in its own tropical gardens with direct access to what amounts to a private section of a very long sandy beach. This offers good bathing, windsurfing, surfboarding and a diving raft in the sea. The main part of the site lies between the sea and the railway (there is an underpass). The whole site is divided into individual pitches of acceptable size, mainly marked out at front and back and with good shade provided by a variety of lush vegetation including very impressive palms set in wide avenues. There are now over 2,000 pitches, all with electricity and 330 with water and drainage connections also. The site has two outstanding features. There is an excellent swimming pool complex near the entrance with two heated pools (one for children) and a larger unheated one adjoining. The other feature is the 15 sanitary buildings, many of them small but of very good quality with toilets and washbasins, plus really excellent, air conditioned larger buildings housing large showers, washbasins (many in private cabins) and separate WCs. There are several launderettes and special facilities for the disabled and for babies. A 24 hour cleaning service operates. Water points around site (water said to be very pure from the site's own wells).

There are two restaurants (500 places in each) and four bars. One in the camp itself has video and activity room upstairs and an adjoining bar and small dance floor, air conditioned, for more traditional dancing in a club atmosphere. The one by the main road at the entrance has a smart restaurant and a separate open-air dance floor for livelier dancing till late. Two takeaways also. Multi-purpose hall, the 'Eurocentre', with 250 person capacity and specially equipped for entertainment and activities, large screen videos, films, shows and meetings (air conditioned). Fitness suite. Children's day care centre (multi-lingual staff). Camp theatre 'La Carpa', a spectacular open air theatre, an ideal setting for shows and beach parties. New 'Tam-Tam Eco Park, a 20,000 sq.m. forest zone where an expert will introduce you to the natural life of the area. No dogs taken and TVs, sometimes very obtrusive on Spanish sites, are not allowed. Mid-day rest period 13.00-16.00 hrs. A range of bungalow accommodation to hire. This is an excellent site for those who like sunshine and sea and can be recommended without hesitation.

How to find it: The entrance is off the main N340 nearly 30 km. southwest from Tarragona. From the motorway take Cambrils exit and turn west on N340.

General Details: Open 1 March - 31 Oct. About 150,000 sq.m. Good shopping centre with supermarket, greengrocer, butcher, fishmonger, tobacconist and souvenir shops. Restaurants and bars. Dancing, shows, films and videos (see Eurocentre and La Carpa above). Eco-park (see above). TV lounges (3) incl. satellite. Also beach bar. Children's playground. Free kindergarten with multi-lingual staff. Junior and teenage clubs. Fitness centre. Skate-boarding. Jogging track. Activities centre with tourist information. Sports area for volleyball, football and basketball. Tennis. Minigolf. Table tennis. Organised activities for children and adults including pottery and gardening classes. Windsurfing and water skiing courses. Surfboards and pedaloes for hire. Boat mooring. Launderettes. Ladies' and men's hairdressers. Car wash. Bicycle hire. Bureau de change. Safety deposit boxes. Special telephone service. Doctor always available. Mobile homes, bungalows to rent - details from site.

Charges 1997: Per person 450 - 800 ptas; child (under 10) 350 - 700; standard pitch B with electricity 1,900 - 3,200, standard pitch A with electricity 2,100 - 3,900, premium pitch with water also 2,300 - 4,200; extra car or boat 350 - 700. All plus 7% VAT. Discounts for longer stays and for pensioners.

Reservations: possible and made with refundable booking fee (4,000 ptas). Address: Dept de Reservas, Apdo 3, 43300 Montroig (Tarragona). Tel: 77/81.06.37. FAX: 77/81.14.11.

See colour advert between pages 288/9

8520 Camping Caravaning Marius, Montroig, nr Tarragona

Agreeable site with family atmosphere and personal touch, by a sandy beach.

A quiet, well tended site which is not too huge, Marius has a pleasant atmosphere. It is right beside a good sandy beach, with direct access and no roads to cross - you can almost fall out of bed and on to the beach! The site is divided into individual pitches of adequate size so does not become too overcrowded. They are quite shady with 300 electrical connections and 8 pitches with water and drainage also. Dog owners go on one half of the site. Two sanitary blocks have been completely renovated and there is free hot water in both showers and half the washbasins, plus the 21 private cabins, British style WCs, plus an excellent new shower block also. The use of TV sets and bicycles on site is not permitted. The site is near nos. 8540 and 8530, and the lively fishing port of Cambrils where you can buy freshly caught fish, is about 7 km. An excellent watersports venue in high season. Some train noise.

How to find it: Entrance is 28 km. ?? from Tarragona on the Valencia road (N340).

General Details: Open 1 April - 15 Oct. 4 ha. Bar and restaurant (June-Sept). Supermarket (all season). Children's playground. Fishing. Windsurfing. Table tennis. Water ski near. Washing machine. Chemical disposal.

Charges 1998: Three charging seasons. Per person 400, 500 or 700 ptas; child (under 10) 200, 300 or 400; pitch 1,900, 1,700 or 2,200. Plus 7% VAT.

Reservations: Contact site. Address: 43892 Miami-Playa (Tarragona). Tel: 977/810684. FAX: as phone.

8540 Camping Caravaning Club La Torre del Sol, Montroig, nr Tarragona

Large, pleasant site beside beach with good amenities and pools complex.

A member of the French Airotel chain, Torre del Sol occupies a good position with direct access to the beach and has many on site activities. It can offer good shade on a high proportion of the individual numbered pitches, which are mostly of about 70-80 sq.m. There is usually space for odd nights but for good places between 10/7-16/8 it is advisable to reserve. Dog owners go to a special section.The site has the sort of very comprehensive amenities (listed below) found at some of the good large Spanish sites and there is always plenty to do. There is a new complex of three swimming pools, of which two are heated (fully open May - Sep/Oct.) A pizzeria, bar and ice cream service adjoins. The site offers much 'animation' with an organised programme of events, for children and adults, in high season. The tiled, sanitary facilities consist of four well maintained blocks giving a good provision with hot water and with some nice tiled units added on to three blocks comprising private cabins with washbasins and hot showers. British style toilets, units for disabled and babies. Radios and televisions are banned. Mobile homes and caravans for hire and also Etapes Andre Trigano (special tents popular in France) for hire. Part of the site is between the railway and the sea so there may be occasional train noise.

How to find it: The entrance is off the main N340 road about 30 km. from Tarragona towards Valencia. From motorway take Cambrils exit and turn west on N340.

General Details: Open 15 March - 15 Oct, amenities form 1 April. 24 ha. Electrical connections in all parts. Large supermarket and other shops at entrance, open to public. Full restaurant Takeaway. Bar with large terrace where shows and dancing held daily in high season. Beach bar. Pizzeria. Cinema with seating for 500; 3 TV lounges (satellite); separate room for films or videos shown on TV screen. Soundproofed disco. Ladies' and gents' hairdresser. Swimming pools. Solarium. Sauna. Tennis. Table tennis. Squash. Minigolf. Bicycle hire. Fishing. Windsurfing school; sailboards and pedaloes for hire. Children's playground and crèche. Medical service with treatment room. Safe deposit. Bureau de change. Telephone service. Car repair and car wash service. Washing machines. Chemical disposal. Motorcaravan services. Bungalows, mobile homes and tents for hire.

Charges 1998: Per person ptas. 400 - 950; child (under 10 yrs) 300 - 800; tent, caravan with car 1,800 - 2,800; motorcaravan and electricity 1,850 - 2,900. All plus 7% VAT. Less in low season for longer stays.

Reservations: Made only for Jul/Aug. before 15 June, in sense of guaranteeing admission, with booking fee (3,000 ptas). Address: 43892,Miami Playa (Tarragona). Tel: 977/810486. FAX: 977/811306.

Costa del Azahar

The `Orange Blossom' Coast runs down the east coast from the Ebro to Oliva, with the great port of Valencia in the middle. Orange groves grow right down to the coast, particularly in the northern section and the area is rich in fresh food from land and sea. Wine, fruit and flowers play large parts in the local economy and Paella and Zarzuela are said to have originated here. Most of the best beaches are found in the area of Peñiscola or to the south of Valencia and the area is very, very sunny.

8580 Camping Bonterra, Benicasim, nr Castellón/Castelló

Appealing, Mediterranean style site by the main road but with surprisingly little noise.

If you are looking for a site which is not too crowded and has good facilities, you will be welcomed here. It is not right by the sea but it is near enough to a good, shady beach to walk (say 300 m.) and parking is not too difficult if you want to take the car. Good beach for scuba or underwater swimmers - hire facilities at Benicasim. There is also a small, free swimming pool on the camp itself with a children's pool, attractively laid out with bar, restaurant and terrace overlooking. The camp has been extended, with extra toilet blocks, giving nearly 400 pitches at peak times which are marked out at their corners giving a min. 70 sq.m. Around half are opened up from July. Bonterra has a clean and neat appearance with reddish soil mixed with some grass and quite a number of trees which are gradually giving good shade. Some rail noise (20 trains per day). Four quite attractive, well maintained sanitary blocks are sensibly laid out with British style toilets, some cabins and washbasins with hot water, others with cold, 56 free hot showers with solar heating. Showers and WCs for the disabled. A well run site.

How to find it: Site is east of Benicasim village, with entrance off old main N340 road running a little back from the coast. From north, turn left at sign `Benicasim por la costa'. On A7 from north use exit 45, from south exit 46.

General Details: Open Easter - 30 Sept. 5.5 ha. Reasonable shade. All pitches have electrical connections. Restaurant. Bar. Snacks all season. Children's playground (some concrete bases). Disco. Adjacent supermarket. Bicycle hire. Laundry service. Chemical disposal. Motorcaravan services. Mobile homes and new chalet style bungalows to let (details from site). No dogs Juy/Aug.

Charges 1998: Per adult ptas. 240 - 440; child (3-9 yrs) 220 - 400; car 280 - 500; m/cycle 190 - 345; caravan or tent 660 - 1,200; motorcaravan 940 - 1,710; pitch Easter, July/Aug, 1,850 - 2,300; electricity 6A 400, 10A 735. All plus 7% VAT. Special long stay rates excl. July/Aug. Credit cards accepted.

Reservations: made if you write at least a month in advance. Address: Avda. de Barcelona, Aptdo 77, 12560 Benicasim (Castelló). Tel: 964/30.00.07. FAX: 964/30.00.60. When closed: 964/30.02.00.

Camping-Caravaning

BONTERRA

Holiday site with luxurious installations, very near to the beach of Benicasim with its golden yellow, clean sand and to the centre of the village. Free swimming pool. Sites with electricity, bar, restaurant, large supermarket, safe, money exchange, hot water showers, children's playground, well shaded. No dogs in July/August.
Special fees in off-season and for long term stays

E-12560 Benicasim (Castellón)
Tel. 964/30.00.07. Fax. 964/30.00.60

8755 Camping-Caravanning Moraira, Moraira

Well shaded site in pine woods close to the sea.

Sympathetically developed over the past few years, this is now an attractive modern site with the latest facilities, yet still in harmony with its rural surroundings. Approached down a winding road and in a pine forest, the site offers 105 pitches on several terraces with ample shade and all with electricity. Some pitches also have water and drainage connections. The owners are rightly proud of their modern sanitary facilities which are well above average in terms of provision and quality, with polished granite floors and marble fittings. British style WCs. They have recently been improved for winter use. Bar/restaurant and a shop on site, both open all year. Various sports and leisure facilities include a new swimming pool, also used for sub-aqua instruction. A pretty, sheltered bay and beach are 350 m.

How to find it: Turn west 1 km. south of Moraira on AP1347, then ½ km. up hill to site. From A7 take exit 63.

General Details: Open all year. Bar/restaurant. Shop. Swimming pool. Tennis courts. Sub-aqua with site boat and instruction available. Laundry facilities.

Charges 1997: Per person ptas. 550; caravan 550; tent 500; motorcaravan 850; pitch incl. car and unit 1,550. Less 15-60% in low season.

Reservations: Write to site for details. Address: Apdo. Correos 38, 03724 Moraira-Teulada (Alicante). Tel: 96/574.52.49 or 96/574.53.15.

SPAIN - Costa del Azahar

8615 Camping-Caravaning Kiko, Playa de Oliva

Small, efficient, family run site beside Blue Flag beach.

This site is located with direct access onto a spectacular, white, fine sandy beach that runs for miles - Kiko is towards the northwest end, which leads into a beautifully situated small marina and yacht club. Unfortunately the beach is not visible from the campsite itself, which is set at a lower level, behind a grassy bank. There are 215 pitches with hardstanding, all with 16A electrical connections and adequate shade. Cars are parked away from the pitches. Four modern sanitary blocks, fully tiled with free hot water, have large showers, washbasins (a few in cabins), British style WCs, hair dryers and facilities for disabled people. A small bird sanctuary is at the entrance, opposite the bar and supermarket. A larger beach bar and a new restaurant, with entertainment in season, is on the beach itself, which is good for swimming. The yacht club also offers its facilities of swimming pool, bar, restaurant and TV room to campers at Kiko. The footpath to the marina leads into the town, about 10 minutes walk. This is an excellent site for water sports enthusiasts and medium sized boats can be trolleyed onto the beach by means of a ramp. Windsurfing is reputed to be very good and there is a diving school from mid-June.

How to find it: From A7 north of Benidorm take exit 61 to the town and then the beach; site is at the northwest end.

General Details: Open all year. Bar. Beach-side bar and restaurant (all year). Supermarket (open all year, excl. Sundays). Children's playground. Watersports facilities. Entertainment for children from mid-June. Telephones. Exchange facilities. Laundry. Petanque. Bicycle hire. Beach volleyball. Motorcaravan services Bungalows for rent.

Charges 1997: Per person 620 ptas; child 475; pitch 2,100; electricity (16A) 225 plus meter. Plus 7% VAT. Low season discounts (10-40%) for longer stays and for pensioners. Credit cards accepted.

Reservations: Write to site for details. Address: Apdo. 70, 46780 Playa de Oliva (Valencia). Tel: 96/2850905: FAX: 96/2854320.

8560 Camping Playa Tropicana, Alcossebre, nr Castellón/Castelló

Upmarket, pleasant site with pool in quiet seaside situation beside a good beach.

Playa Tropicana has a beautiful position away from the main hub of tourism, right by a good sandy beach which shelves only gently for bathing. A shingle beach for fishing is nearby and a promenade in front of the site. It is a quiet position and it is a drive rather than a walk to the centre of the village resort. The site has been extended to take 300 units and the individual pitches are all marked out and separated by lines of flowering bushes. The larger pitches (up to 100 sq.m.) are in the newer area where shade has developed. The original ones have been enlarged to 80 sq.m. with good shade. Movement of cars may need care when the site is full. An excellent, fully tiled toilet block has been added to the improved original one to give a good supply. British WCs, and free hot water in well spaced washbasins, including 16 in cabins, in the fully controllable showers (with screen) and the sinks. Baby baths. Some units with WC, basin and shower, and facilities for disabled people. Water points around. A swimming pool (18 x 11 m.) and terrace with an individual style and flair and a children's pool (8 x 4 m.) have been added to the restaurant complex. A site which appeals to discerning campers.

How to find it: Alcoceber (or Alcossebre) is between Peniscola and Oropesa. Turn off N340 at campsite sign towards the town and follow signs along coast road to south of town, to site.

General Details: Open 15 March - 31 Oct. 31,000 sq.m. Electrical connections everywhere. Large supermarket (all season). Large restaurant (from Easter). Drinks served on terrace. Swimming pool (from Easter). Children's playground. Volleyball. Table tennis. Treatment room. Washing machine. Chemical disposal. Apartments and villa to let. No dogs are taken. No TVs allowed in July/Aug.

Charges 1998: Per person 905 ptas; child (1-10 yrs) 715; per unit incl. electricity (4A) 2,750 - 3,950, acc. to size; extra car 700; extra tent 900. All plus 7% VAT. Less 20-45% outside July/Aug. Special promotion in July - less 20% for min. 14 days. Credit cards accepted.

Reservations: made for min. 15 days with substantial deposit (5,000 ptas) and fee (5,000). Address: 12579 Alcossebre (Castellón). Tel: 964/41.24.63. FAX: 964/41.28.05. Internet: http://www.ctv.es/azahar/ccarav.htm.

camping ★ caravaning ★ bungalows

KIKO

E-46780 PLAYA DE OLIVA - VALENCIA
Tel.(34-6) 285 09 05 . Fax (34-6) 285 43 20

● Right on the Golden beach of Oliva and shaded by a very Mediterranean vegetation.
● Excellent, new sanitary installations.
● Bungalows, mountain bikes, canoes and windsurf-boards to rent, Windsurfing school.
● Our restaurant serves you the typical dish of the region: "Paella" among many other delicious meals.
● OPEN THROUGHOUT THE YEAR

1ˢᵗ Category
Special fees in
winter. Up to
70% discount

Costa Blanca

The Costa Blanca (the White Coast) derives its name from its 170 miles or so of silvery-white beaches along the central section of the Spanish Mediterranean coastline. There are many sheltered bays and most beaches shelve quite gently. The countryside behind the coast remains largely untouched by mass tourism and is well worth exploring, as are places such as Alicante, Cartegena and Valencia. The most popular resort is Benidorm, which has very much shed its 'lager lout' image. Large sums of money have been spent building a beautifully paved promenade stretching the whole length of the beach, with palm trees at regular intervals. The beach itself is cleaned every night and the whole town presents a very well cared for image with plenty of police patrols in evidence. However, don't be too complacent as petty pilfering does occur. In the winter the town is filled with older people who never pose a problem, whilst in summer it is noisier and more boisterous with families and younger people on holiday.

8680 Camping Armanello, Benidorm

Friendly site with swimming pool just behind the town.

About 1 km. back from the northern Benidorm beach (the one on the other side of the town is less crowded), Armanello is quietly situated just far enough away from the main coast road to avoid excessive noise and is a natural, 'green' site, with pitches in orange and olive groves. There is a small and much-used swimming pool. About 130 units are taken on flat ground with 10A electricity. Two toilet blocks (back to back) have washing and shower facilities with hot and cold water, British toilets, some washbasins in cabins, hot showers and baths. Hot water also for laundry and dishwashing. New facilities near reception include a washroom, shower and WC for the disabled. The site is popular with long stay Spanish units in winter.

How to find it: From the new bypass (N332) take the Levante Beach road into Benidorm; watch for site signs after 1 km. directly off this road.

General Details: Open all year. 25,000 sq.m. Some shade. Electrical connections in all parts. Well stocked shop (all year). Bar. Public telephones (card). No meals but restaurants near. Washing machine. Aviary.

Charges guide: Per person 500 ptas.; child (under 10) 400; car 500; m/cycle 450; tent 500; caravan 600; motorcaravan 1,500. Plus 7% VAT.

Reservations: Advised all year - contact site. Address: 03500 Benidorm. Tel: 95/85.31.90.

8681 Camping Villasol, Benidorm

Excellent, modern site with large swimming pool and views, close to town and beach.

Benidorm is increasingly popular for winter stays and Villasol is a genuinely excellent site, purpose built in '89 with a very attractive, large swimming pool complex with a smaller indoor pool. There is a paved terrace and a grass sunbathing area. The pool is overlooked by the bar/restaurant and restaurant terrace. The restaurant offers good value. The modern, well fitted sanitary blocks provide free, controllable hot water to the showers and washbasins and British WCs. The site is terraced, with tarmac roads and gravel pitches (80-85 sq.m.), all of which have electricity and satellite TV connections. Shade is mainly artificial as yet. The town and Levante beach are 1 km. within easy walking distance. There is an evening entertainment programme. For first class amenities in pleasant and fairly quiet surroundings, this site would make an excellent choice. Reservation is advised even in winter.

How to find it: From autopista take Benidorm exit (65) and turn left at 2nd set of traffic lights. After 1 km. at more lights turn right, then right again at next lights. Site on right in 400 m. From northern end of N332 bypass follow Benidorm Playa Levante. In 500 m. at traffic lights turn left, then right at next lights. Site is on right after 400 m.

General Details: Open all year. Electricity throughout. Restaurant. Bar. Shop. Swimming pools, outdoor and indoor. Children's playground. Satellite TV. Laundry facilities. No dogs are accepted. Mobile homes to rent.

Charges 1997: Per person ptas. 525 - 700; child (1-9) 400 - 500; car 525 - 700; tent 550 - 750; large tent/caravan 550 - 1,275; motorcaravan 1,075 - 1,975; electricity (1,000w) 425. All plus 7% VAT. Good winter discounts.

Reservations: Write to site. Address: Avda. Bernat de Sarriá, s/n, 03500 Benidorm (Alicante). Tel: 96/585.04.22 or 680.08.98. FAX: 96/680.64.20.

SPAIN - Costa Blanca

8683 Camping Benisol, Benidorm

Mature site with golf driving range.

Camping Benisol is older than the other three sites we feature in Benidorm. It is run by Jean and Brigitte Picard who provide a friendly atmosphere with a range of languages being spoken. The site is mature with well developed hedging and trees giving a good degree of privacy to each pitch. The trees are severely pruned in winter but make tremendous growth by the summer enhanced by extra artificial shade. In total there are 250 touring pitches (60-80 sq.m.), all with electrical hook-ups (4-6A) and 75 with drainage also. The connecting roads are not all tarmac. The modern sanitary facilities, heated in winter and kept very clean, have free hot water to the washbasins, by token (50 ptas) to the showers and for clothes and dish washing. Amenities include a swimming pool with cascade and water slides and the sports facilities listed below. According to our site assessor, the golf driving range is the only one on a campsite in Spain. It is free to campers, although a charge is made for a bucket of balls.

How to find it: From the autopista take Benidorm exit (no. 65) and turn left at the second set of traffic lights then, after 1 km. right at another set of lights. At next lights go straight on and site is on right in 300 m. From northern end of N332 bypass follow signs for Benidorm Playa Levante. In 500 m. turn left at traffic lights, then straight on at next lights for 300 m. to site on the right.

General Details: Open all year. Electrical connections throughout. Restaurant with terrace. Bar. Swimming pool. Sports ground. Small children's play area. Minigolf. Table tennis. Jogging track. Tennis courts. Golf driving range. Laundry facilities. Bungalows, caravans and rooms to let. Caravan storage adjacent.

Charges 1997: Per unit ptas. 1,400 - 1,600 for 60 sq.m. pitch, 1,600 - 1,800 for 70 sq.m; person 475 - 500; child (1-10 yrs) 375 - 400; extra tent or car 475 - 500; m/cycle 375 - 400; electricity (220v) 375 per kw/hr. All plus 7% VAT. Less 15-60% in low seasons.

Reservations: Contact site for details. Address: Avda. de la Comunidad Valenciana, s/n, 03500 Benidorm. Tel: 96/5851673. FAX: 96/5860895.

8685 Camping Caravaning El Raco, Benidorm

New site with good facilities, close to Levante beach.

This is a brand new site, opened in '96, with excellent facilities and with wide access from the Runcon de Loix road (no problem with access for larger units). It is the nearest of all the sites to the Levante beach and town, being less than 1 km. The road has footpaths and a cycle track into Benidorm, so the car can be left on site. Tarmac roads lead to all 80 sq.m. pitches, of which there are 250 at present although the site is still expanding. The pitches are of hard, rolled grit, divided by newly planted leylandii so there is little privacy and no shade as yet. The whole site is on a slight downward slope away from the entrance and affords excellent views of the rugged mountains in the hinterland, although this open aspect could be a disadvantage in windy weather. The facilities are excellent. The two toilet blocks are large and well provided with showers, washbasins, laundry and dishwashing sinks - all with free hot water. The shop is well stocked and the prices reasonable. The swimming pool is a lovely feature surrounded by a grass sunbathing area. No slides or diving boards - and no shade, except perhaps parasols. New indoor pool planned for '98. A clean, tidy and good quality site.

How to find it: From the autopista take Benidorm exit (no. 65) and turn left at the second set of traffic lights. After 1 km. at another set of lights turn right, then straight on at next lights for 300 m. to site on right. From northern end of N332 bypass follow signs for Benidorm Playa Levante. In 500 m. at traffic lights turn left, then straight on at next lights for 300 m. to site on right.

General details: Open all year. Restaurant. Swimming pool. Shop. Laundry facilities. Satellite TV connections. Exchange facilities. Children's playground. Caravan storage (2,500 ptas. per month).

Charges 1997: Per person ptas. 575 - 610; child (1-9 yrs) 375 - 425; car 525 - 610; tent 525 - 610; caravan 630 - 690; motorcaravan 850 - 990; electricity (220v) 393 - 435. Discounts for longer stays. VAT @ 7% incl.

Reservations: Contact site for details. Address: Avda. Doctor Severo Ochoa, s/n, 03500 Benidorm (Alicante). Tel: 96/5868552. FAX: 96/5868544.

8741 Camping Florantilles, Torrevieja, nr Alicante

Modern site with good views, some 4 km. behind the coast.

Florantilles is a very well laid out, attractive, terraced site with good views over the top of the orange groves to the distant salt lake. Although it is not very old, the trees have grown quickly to provide plenty of shade to the pitches, the majority of which are of a good size (90 sq.m.) although some are only suitable for smaller units. On four large terraces, all pitches have good access, plus electrical connections, water and drainage. Sanitary facilities are good and well maintained with British style WCs and controllable hot showers. There are several small blocks dotted around the site, but in the winter months the main block (part of the reception area) is the only one with hot water. The laundry room is in the same area, with sinks, one hot tap and two washing machines. The attractive site entrance has a large parking area with car wash facilities, with the entrance to the pitch area protected by a barrier (key). Good size swimming pool, plus a children's pool, restaurant bar, and a well stocked shop (limited opening in low seasons). *continued overleaf*

8741 Camping Florantilles (continued)

Keep fit classes, discos, barbecues and line dancing are arranged in season. Watersports in nearby Torrevieja. The site is very popular with British visitors in winter months.

How to find it: 1 km. south of Torrevieja turn inland (northwest) onto the C3323 signed San Miguel. In 4 km. turn right at sign 'Les Montesinos' and campsite sign. Site is on left after 200 m.

General Details: Open all year. Electricity, water and drainage throughout. Bar/restaurant. Shop (limited hours in low seasons). Swimming pool. Tennis. Squash. Minigolf. Boules. Table tennis. Children's playground.

Charges 1997: Per person ptas 500; child 400; caravan/car or motorcaravan 1,200; electricity 350. All plus 7% VAT. Discounts outside July/Aug.

Reservations: Contact site. Address: 03193 San Miguel de Salinas (Alicante). Tel: 96/5720458. FAX: 96/6723250.

8742 Camping Internacional La Marina, La Marina, nr Santa Pola

Holiday site close to beach, with good facilities.

Although run by a Belgian family, this site is very popular with the Spanish themselves, with around half of the pitches taken by seasonal units and tour operators. For touring units, there are four different type and size of pitch ranging from about 50 sq.m. for tents to 100 sq.m. with electricity, TV, water and drainage. Shade is available and the pitches are well maintained on fairly level, gravel ground. A special area for tents only is in a small orchard. The site has a good sized swimming pool, paddling pool and `plunge' pool and beside the pools is a bar/restaurant with terrace (Spanish menu including tapas). These are very busy in season and tickets are required for the pool. A fitness centre and covered, heated pool (14 x 7 m.) have been added. The sanitary facilities, recently modernised and improved, can now be heated. In tiled blocks they have controllable hot showers, British style WCs and some washbasins in private cabins with hot water. An access gate to the beach has been created.

How to find it: Site is a little to the west of La Marina, which is on the seaward side of the N332 road, between Guardamara de Segura and Santa Pola.

General Details: Open all year. Bar/restaurant and supermarket (all year also). Swimming pools (Easter - Oct). Fitness centre. Tennis. Table tennis. Children's playground (recently improved). Laundry facilities incl. irons. Exchange facilities. Car wash. Chemical disposal. Motorcaravan services. Bungalows (5 persons) to rent.

Charges 1998: Per person ptas. 550; child (under 10 yrs) 400; pitch 1,200 (50-70 sq.m.), 1,900 (70-90 sq.m.) or 2,400 (100 sq.m.); pitch with water, sewerage 2,400; electricity 350. Plus 7% VAT. Less in low season, plus good discounts for longer stays 16/9-14/6, excluding Easter. Credit cards accepted.

Reservations: Write to site. Address: Ctra N332 km.76, 03194 La Marina (Alicante). Tel: 96/541.90.51. FAX: 96/541.91.10.

AR Discount

A Gift

Why don't you do like the sun and spend your holidays on ...

CAMPING INTERNACIONAL
LA MARINA

Only 29 km from Alicante and 16 km from Elche, Viviana and her team are pleased to welcome you on their 1st cat. camping site equipped with modern installations, also thought for longer stays during winter. Clean sanitary installations, now with heating, and hot water in every tap, washing and drying machines, possible to iron. Medical service daily. Marked sites with connection for electricity, water and sewage. Parabolic antenna RTL 4 and 5, car wash, children's playground, half olympic-size swimming pool, paddling pools, tennis, indoor heated (28°C) swimming pool (7 x 14 m) and fitness room, table tennis, hairdresser, bar-restaurant and supermarket. Bungalows (5 persons) for rent. Only 500 m from a fine sandy beach (ideal for windsurfing) next to a beautiful pine-tree forest (protected nature reserve) made for long walks. Excellent climatic conditions throughout the year.

2 km from the village of LA MARINA and 8 km from SANTA POLA. Bus stop right at camp. The site with all its installations is open all year. Various types of trees spread a lot of shade. Sunny places for winter. Special fees during winter season.

At the end of your stay a present upon presentation of this guide.

We are waiting to hear from you. Further information please write to:

Camping Internacional La Marina
(N-332, km 76) E-03194 LA MARINA (ALICANTE)
Tel: (34-6) 5419051 Fax: (34-6) 5419110

SPAIN - Costa Blanca

N8752 Camping Naturista El Portus, Cartagena

Naturist campsite on the shores of the Mediterranean - open all year.

Set in a secluded south-facing bay, El Portus is a large site beside the beach and enjoying magnificent views. It has 400 pitches (250 of 100 sq.m, 150 of 60 sq.m.) over half with 5/10A electrical connections, with more planned. The majority are on level ground, although some are terraced, and there is a fair number of trees with more being planted. The ground here is distinctly hard, so good quality pegs are needed! Sanitary facilities include four modern blocks, with other older ones being upgraded. They include free hot showers, washbasins with only cold water, British style WCs, dishwashing and laundry facilities. All were clean when seen and are conveniently situated for the pitches, but whilst the overall provision seems adequate, we suspect that they could be hard-pressed at peak periods. Two swimming pools (unsupervised outside main season), one solar-heated, are set in nicely landscaped surroundings of lawns and trees and there is a paddling pool for children. The site offers a quite wide range of activities (listed below) and there are discos three evenings per week (until midnight) in the main season. Recently constructed children's play area. Barbecues are dependent on the prevailing conditions and risk of fire. The campsite restaurant is open daily in the main season, but only at weekends during the rest of the year, and the hours of the site shop are also dependent on the time of year. The site's publicity claims that 'the sea here is nearly always warm enough for swimming, and the sun shines almost every day'.

How to find it: Site is on the coast, 10 km. west of Cartegena, via Canteras. Follow signs to Pryca commercial centre, then to Canteras/El Portus.

General Details: Open all year. Restaurant. Shop. Swimming pools. Tennis. Volleyball. Table tennis. Petanque. Yoga. Scuba-diving. Windsurfing. Chemical disposal. Motorcaravan services. Bungalows and mobile homes to rent.

Charges 1998: Per person ptas. 775; child (3-7 yrs) 570; pitch 1,630, with electricity 2,300; extra tent 400; extra car or m/cycle 475; dog 525. Discounts for longer stays in low season. Credit cards accepted.

Reservations: made with large deposit - contact site. Address: 30393 Cartagena. Tel: 968/55.50.52. FAX: 68/55.30.30.53. E-mail: portus@hipocom.es. Internet: www.hipocom.es/portus/

8750 Camping Los Gallardos, Los Gallardos

Good quality, English owned and managed site with all year round facilities.

Since 1991, Anthony and Shirley Jackson have built this site up from barren land into the comfortable, homely site one finds today. They seem to have the knack of making trees grow quickly so shade is available now, as well as the flowers, which add to the pleasing atmosphere created by the site's open position with its views of the surrounding mountains. There are over 100 good sized pitches marked by trees and with easy access and firm surfaces. The majority have 5 or 10A electricity. The central sanitary block is kept in pristine condition with free hot water for washbasins and showers, with one hot tap for dishwashing. British style WCs. There are covered areas for food preparation and laundry. The Jacksons are keen to help visitors get the best out of their stay in Spain and organise plenty of activities all year round. The swimming pool, with sunbathing area, sunbeds and keep fit sessions, is open all year, as is the adjacent bar/restaurant (daily 9-4, 7-late) where special dish evenings, Sunday roasts, bridge mornings and games evenings are organised regularly. Excursions to Granada, local restaurants and places of interest are arranged. A good area for walking and beaches are within about 10 km. New reception and small shop with English foodstuffs and fresh bread each day. There is some road noise.

How to find it: Leave the CN340 at km. 525, 8 km. from Mojacar, and follow signs.

General Details: Open all year, as are shop, bar, restaurant and pool. Spit roast chicken to order. Washing machine and dryer. Hairdresser weekly. Animal farm. Boules. Bridge mornings. English breakfasts. Spanish lessons. Exchange library, video and jigsaw hire. Golf and riding near. Excursions. Full information sheets on request.

Charges 1997: Per person ptas. 400; car 400; caravan or tent 400; motorcaravan 700; m/cycle 300; electricity 300. Discounts for longer stays and up to 65% in winter.

Reservations: Write to site. Address: 04280 Los Gallardos (Almeria). Tel: 950/52.83.24.

Costa del Sol

The Costa del Sol stretches from Gibraltar north-eastward along the Mediterranean coast for some 250 miles and, even in April and October, averages 7-8 hours of sunshine daily, with average temperatures of around 20`C. The most popular (and most commercialised) resorts are Torremolinos and Marbella, both of which have much to offer, but there are several quieter and more tranquil resorts such as Fuengirola and Nerja. For sightseeing, there are many historic towns and cities within range, including Seville, Granada, and Cordoba, as well as a host of Andalucian villages.

8780 Camping Torre del Mar, Torre del Mar, nr Malaga

Good site for those who like to be in the heart of things.

This site is at the end of the sea-front of the main town of Torre del Mar. It is well equipped, with marked, separated pitches, regularly laid out. They are quite large, most with a fair degree of shade. A swimming pool complex at the far end consists of one large, Olympic size pool complete with water slide and two adjoining smaller pools. There is also a restaurant, bar and shop unit, although the main life goes on in the town itself. Although not in the same league as some of the very large sites further up the Golden Coast, this site holds its own in terms of facilities. Two sanitary blocks are modern and clean and seem about adequate for the camp size. Washing up and laundry sinks. Rather lacking in character.

How to find it: On the sea-front at Torre del Mar, on N340, Malaga to Nerja road.

General Details: Open all year. Shop (June - Sept, but town close). Restaurant/bar. Swimming pools (June/Sept).

Charges 1997: Per person 550 ptas; child (2-10 yrs) 430; tent 550; caravan 585; car 550; m/cycle 430; motor-caravan 1,100; electricity 325. Discounts of 10-30% for long stays in low season (1/10-25/3, OAPs until 31/5).

Reservations: Write to site. Address: Paseo Maritimo S/N, 29740 Torre del Mar (Malaga). Tel: 952/54.02.24.

8760 Camping Mar Azul, El Ejido, nr Almeria

Sea-front site, on its own by beach, with good sized pitches and many sporting activities.

Right beside the sea, on flat ground and with direct access to a sandy beach, Mar Azul is in a dry and sunny area of Spain where there are not many other camping sites. The landscape is dominated by the Sierra Nevada (but is rendered somewhat unsightly behind the site by local farmers' use of acres of plastic cloches, as along most of this coast). The site normally has space as it has not yet become widely known. About 450 individual, numbered pitches are quite attractively laid out with palm trees between them and at 90 sq.m. are larger than most in Spain. Artificial shade is provided on most pitches. The four toilet blocks are of good quality with British style toilets, washbasins and free hot showers. A circular, unheated swimming pool with child's pool, terrace and sun-beds, is near the beach, a further pool is in the centre of the site, where there is a large area set aside for many different sports, a third pool has been added. The site lies out on its own, but the large development of Almerimar with golf course, large hotel, restaurant, some shops, etc. is little over 1 km. along the beach. El Ejido is 8 km.

How to find it: Turn off main N340/E15 road at km. 409 (El Ejido-Almerimar) exit. Site is on east side of El Ejido, from where it is signed.

General Details: Open all year. Supermarket (1/4-15/10). Bar (1/4-15/10 and winter weekends). Restaurant (1/4-15/10). Swimming pools and child's pool (1/4-15/10). Tennis. Fronton. Squash. Table tennis. Fitness centre. Boules. Volleyball. Badminton. Basketball. Horse riding. Archery. Bicycle hire and circuit. Roller skating. Minigolf. Football. Fishing. Windsurfing school and equipment for hire. Activities organised for children. Washing machines. Treatment room; doctor visits in season. Chemical disposal. Motorcaravan services. Bungalows to rent.

Charges 1998: Per person 300 - 625 ptas.; child (2-10 yrs) 200 - 550; tent or caravan 300 - 625; car 300 - 625; motorcaravan 600 - 990; electricity 300 - 450. All plus 7% VAT. Credit cards accepted.

Reservations: are made for any length. Address: Apdo. Correos 39, 04700 El Ejido (Almeria). Tel: 950/497585 or 497505. FAX: 950/497294. E-mail: cmazul@a2000.es.

AR Discount
Less 10% on person price

8711 Nerja Camping, Maro-Nerja

Spectacularly situated small site with swimming pool and glorious views.

So many Spanish camp sites seem to look like local authority car parks that it is nice to be able to report on one that is about as unlike a car park as you could possibly get! Set on the lower slopes of the Sierra Almijara, some 5 km. from Nerja and 2 km. from the nearest beach, Nerja Camping is a delightful small site of 60 pitches (30 with 15A electricity) with impressive views of the surrounding mountains and nearby Mediterranean. Being situated slightly above but alongside the main coast road, it is easy to find - the price you pay is some traffic noise but this seems hardly to detract from the relaxing and almost idyllic ambience. The pitches are of reasonable size on flat terraces with mainly artificial shade, whilst the roads, although quite steep, are newly surfaced and should present little problem except perhaps to drivers of really huge motorhomes. The site also boasts a small swimming pool, a bar/restaurant serving simple fresh dishes and even large breakfasts, all cooked and served by the Irish owner Peter Kemp and his Spanish wife Make on the terrace beside their magnificent carob tree. The single sanitary block is of modern design and construction with British type WCs, some free hot showers, washbasins (1 only with hot water), dishwashing sinks (cold water) under cover and laundry facilities.

How to find it: Site is signed from the main N340 coast road about 5 km. north of Nerja. If coming from Nerja, go 50 m. past site entrance to cross main road.

General Details: Open all year except Oct. Swimming pool (Easter-Sept). Bar/restaurant (Jan-Sept). Essentials from the bar. Pool table. Mountain bike hire. Chemical disposal. Bus service nearby.

Charges 1998: Per person ptas. 500; child (2-10 yrs) 400; tent 500 - 650; caravan 600; car 500; motorcaravan 750; m/cycle 350; electricity 400. All plus 7% VAT. Less 20-40% outside 1/6-30/9. Special rates for long stays.

Reservations: Write to site. Address: Ctra. N340 - km. 297, 28787 Maro - Nerja (Malaga). Tel: 95/25.29.714.

SPAIN - Costa del Sol / Costa de la Luz

8800 Camping-Caravaning Marbella Playa, Marbella

See colour advert between pages 288/9

Modern site on northern outskirts of Marbella, with good pool.

This site is on the outskirts of the internationally famous resort of Marbella with public transport available to the town centre. A sandy beach is about 150 m. with direct access. There are 400 individual pitches of up to 70 sq.m. with limited shade (some artificial shade provided), and electricity. A large swimming pool complex with a restaurant/bar provides an attractive feature with palm trees. The three sanitary blocks are modern and kept clean with free hot showers, 2 small baths, 2 cabins and 6 washbasins in each. The site can get busy at weekends, but staff are friendly and the site is well run.

How to find it: Site is 12 km. north of Marbella with access close to the 193 km. point on the main N340 road.

General Details: Open all year, as are supermarket, bar, restaurant and café. Swimming pool (April-Sept). First aid centre. Children's playground (on gritty sand). Bureau de change. Laundry facilities.

Charges guide: Per person 490 ptas; child (1-10 yrs) 420; car 490; caravan/tent 830; m/cycle 450; motorcaravan 1,160; electricity 335. Min. pitch fee 2,300. All plus 7% VAT. Less for long stays and outside 16/6-31/8.

Reservations: Write to site. Address: Ctra N-340, Km. 192,800, 29600 Marbella (Malaga). Tel: 95/283.39.98. FAX: 95/283.39.99.

8801 Camping La Rosaleda, Los Boliches, nr Fuengirola

Satisfactory smaller site with pool, on outskirts of Fuengirola.

This is quite a cosmopolitan site attracting campers from many different countries, situated on the outskirts of the fashionable resort of Fuengirola and very convenient for visiting Torremolinos and the famous Tivoli Park. The site enjoys some good views towards the mountains and over the town down to the sea. There is an attractive, medium sized swimming pool with paved surround and grass sunbathing area. Pitches are of about 80 sq.m. and on flattish, grassy/sandy ground with a good proportion having electrical connections. Many are separated by chain link fencing, some with young hedges and there is some shade in most places. The two sanitary blocks are of fairly modern construction and design and appear to be quite adequate, if not luxurious, providing some free hot showers, British type WCs, dishwashing sinks under cover and 2 washing machines. The site is very busy in July/August.

How to find it: Although signed from new bypass going round the back of Fuengirola, you are still directed into the town centre and then back out again over the autopista! However, it is well signed from the town centre.

General Details: Open all year. Bar/restaurant (1/6-30/9) with takeaway. Small supermarket (1/7-30/9). Swimming pool (15/3-30/10) with bar in main season. Telephone. Washing machines and dryer. Chemical disposal.

Charges 1997: Per adult ptas. 600; child 300; tent, caravan or motorcaravan 750; electricity 300.

Reservations: Write to site. Address: Aptdo. 288, Los Boliches, 29649 Fuengirola (Malaga). Tel: 952/460191. FAX: 952/581966.

AR Discount
Less 10% (if no other discounts taken)

Costa de la Luz

This is the stretch of coast running from Gibraltar in the east to the Portuguese border in the west. Despite being even further south, it does not enjoy quite the same climate as the Costa del Sol as it borders the Atlantic rather than the Mediterranean - but this may be an advantage during high summer. The eastern end of this coast is quite attractive with many wonderful views across to Africa and we feature several sites in this area. However, the western end, apart from the Donana National Park and some large beaches, is rather different. We searched this coast, running from La Rocia up to Huelva, looking for a site and, so far, have found just one at this end up to guide standards (at Punta Umbria).

8830 Camping Torre de la Pena I, Tarifa, nr Algeciras

Pleasant seaside site for the young at heart on terraces overlooking the Straits of Gibraltar.

Claimed to be Europe's most southerly camp site, this one is west of Tarifa on the main coast road. It is a pretty site with good views across the straits and a sandy beach adjacent. With a sloping entrance, the main part is on a steep hillside, with pitches on terraces properly and attractively formed with stone walls but with considerable up and down walking. Flat ground on the far side of the road, next to the beach, has also been developed. The beach-side pitches are well shaded by mature trees and are favoured by younger campers, mostly windsurfing enthusiasts. This area is likely to be crowded and noisier. A total of 250 pitches with electricity for about half. Five toilet blocks have free hot showers, some basins in cabins, British toilets. Should this site be full Torre de la Pena II is 4 km. along the road.

How to find it: Site is beside main N340 road about 10 km. northwest of Tarifa.

General Details: Open all year. 15,000 sq.m. Shop. Attractive regional-type restaurant/bar right beside the beach. Windsurfing school with hire facilities. Washing machine. Satellite TV. Garage. Bungalows to rent.

Charges 1997: Per person 575; child (2-12 yrs) 550; tent or caravan 450; car 425; motorcaravan 775; m/cycle 350; electricity (6A) 400. All plus 7% VAT. Reductions for long winter stays.

Reservations: made for any length July/Aug. Address: C.N.340 km.78, 11380 Tarifa (Cadiz). Tel: 956/68.49.03.

8850 Camping Paloma, Tarifa, nr Algeciras

Attractively situated site close to beaches, 30 km. west of Algeciras.

A spacious, neat and tidy, family orientated site, Paloma is 300 m. from the nearest beach which has good facilities for bathing and also windsurfing. There are some 380 pitches on flat ground of quite reasonable size and shaded and separated by mature trees; 200 have electricity. The main central toilet block is of good size though a fair step from one end of site. It has mostly Turkish style WCs, some British, washbasins with cold water (some cubicles and with bidets for women) and 12 free controllable hot showers. It was very clean when seen. A small (free) swimming pool with paved sunbathing area and an attractive, thatched, stone bar have been added, together with a number of new pitches (not yet any shade) and a modern, open plan sanitary block including facilities for the disabled (steepish ramp).

How to find it: Site is adjacent to the N340 Cadiz road at Punta Paloma, about 10 km. northwest of Tarifa at km. 74 point. Watch carefully for the site sign - no advance notice.

General Details: Open all year (no electricity from Nov.- March). Shop. Busy bar and good Italian restaurant. Swimming pool with adjacent bar (high season only). Children's playground. TV lounge. Excursions. Washing machine. New fully equipped bungalows to rent.

Charges 1997: Per person 575 ptas; child 525; car 425; m/cycle 350; tent or caravan 425; motorcaravan 775; electricity 400. Plus 7% VAT. Discount of 40% from 1/11-31/3 (no electricity).

Reservations: made for one part of site, for any length and without deposit. Address: Ctra. Cadiz-Malaga Km. 70, 11380 Tarifa (Cadiz). Tel: 956/68.42.03.

8860 Camping Fuente del Gallo, Conil de la Frontera, nr Cadiz

Small site on a sloping, grassy position close to two good beaches.

Fuente del Gallo is situated reasonably close to one beach (100 m.) and slightly further from a second (300 m), both beaches being ideal for bathing and watersports (although no hire facilities were available when we visited). Although beautiful beaches, access to them is down stony paths and may not be suitable for older or disabled persons, particularly when returning up to the camp site. The approach road from the village passes through a very pretty avenue of palm trees. One of the owners is Irish and the general atmosphere and home-made entertainment reflects the Irish humour. The attractive bar and restaurant facilities are of a good standard with very reasonable prices (breakfasts served). The pitches are marked and numbered, nearly all with electricity, and there are trees and bushes separating them in many parts. The sanitary blocks, recently renewed, are modern, clean and well looked after, with hot water available on payment. There is also a new block with facilities for disabled people and babies. A recreation area with two swimming pools was added in '97. Tennis court and games area. The main features of this site are the beautiful beaches, very natural surroundings and the enjoyable atmosphere.

How to find it: From the Cadiz-Algeciras road (N340) at km. 21.9, follow signs to Conil de la Frontera town centre, then shortly right to Fuente del Gallo and 'playas' following signs.

General Details: Open week before Easter - 1 Oct, with all amenities. Restaurant/bar. Shop. Children's playground. Watersports on beach. Excursions. Car wash area. Laundry room with 2 washing machines. Chemical disposal. Motorcaravan services.

Charges 1998: Per person 495 ptas; child 395; tent 425; caravan 475; car 415; m/cycle 325; motorcaravan 825; electricity 390. Plus 7% VAT. Credit cards accepted.

Reservations: Write to site. Address: Apto. 48, 11140 Conil de la Frontera. (Cadiz). Tel: 956/44.01.37 or 44.20.36. FAX: 956/44.20.36.

AR Discount
Less 5% in high season, 10-30% in low season

8870 Camping Derena Mar, Punta Umbria, nr Huelva

Useful site for overnight stops en route to or from Portugal or for a longer stay by the beach.

The long, golden sandy beach, 200 m. from the site across a small road, may tempt you to spend some time here. The site has a pleasant, open feel and is reasonably sheltered from any road noise by its situation in a bowl in the ground. The 200 level pitches for caravans are of varying, but quite large size for Spain. Marked by trees which give moderate shade (watch out when reversing), these pitches are very sandy. Places for cars and motorcaravans are firmer and all have electricity (6A) and water. About 30% of the pitches are taken by the site's own tents. Open areas around the site are available for small tents. Three modern sanitary blocks have British WCs and free, controllable hot showers. The site can be very busy in July/August.

How to find it: From Portugal on the N431/E1 road follow sign for Huelva and then for 'Playas' and Punta Umbria. From Seville on A49 or N431, take Punta Umbria/Huelva Nord exit and follow signs again for playas and Punta Umbria. Site is on right at km. 11 point.

General Details: Open all year, as is bar/café. Pub. Restaurant (April-Oct, Fri-Sun only). Barbecue area. Supermarket (summer only with bread, milk and butter available at café in winter). Public telephones.

Charges guide: Per person 520 ptas; child (3-13 yrs) 425; tent 500; caravan 500; car 475; m/cycle 350; motorcaravan 800; 400; electricity 360 - 450. Low season discounts for longer stays.

Reservations: Recommended for July/Aug. and made for min. 7 days. Address: 21100 Punta Umbria (Huelva). Tel: 959/312004. FAX: 959/315096.

SPAIN - North

Northern Spain

This area includes the Costa Verde, the Basque Coast, the Pyrenees and inland Spain north of a line between Valladolid and just north of Burgos (lat. 42°). The Costa Verde is largely unspoiled, with clean water, sandy beaches and rocky coves against a backdrop of mountains including the magnificent Picos de Europa. The beaches and countryside on the Basque Coast are rather more developed in terms of tourism and industry and tend to be very popular, particularly during July and August. Both these areas are easily accessible from the ports of Santander or Bilbao. The Pyrenees stretch from the Bay of Biscay in the west (with the highest peaks) to the Mediterranean in the east, and include two spectacular natural parks, the Ordesa in Aragon and Aigues Tortes in Catalonia. The mountain gorges and valleys remain largely unspoiled. Visitors will find much of `Old Spain' in gastronomy and the way of life generally.

9024 Camping As Cancelas, Santiago de Compostela

Hillside site, with quality facilities, overlooking the pilgrims' city.

As Cancelas has 156 marked pitches (30-70 sq.m), arranged in terraces and divided by trees and shrubs, on a hillside overlooking the city. Access to some pitches can be difficult for large units. Electricity (5A) is available. Regular bus service into the city from the bottom of the hill, and a small mini market (open late) is 5 minutes level walk. The site has a well kept, unsupervised, swimming pool and children's pool. The two ultra modern, luxurious toilet blocks provide British WCs, washbasins in marble tops, hand dryers, spacious controllable showers with dividers and marble seats and a suite for the disabled with ramped access. The quality and cleanliness are outstanding. Free hot water throughout. Lounge bar with TV (open all year), restaurant and mini market (open July/Aug) and small children's playground. No English spoken. Santiago, with its legendary festivals and processions, is the destination for Christians, who find their way to the city across the centuries old pilgrims' routes.

How to find it: From N550 La Coruna - Santiago road, at large roundabout, exit to Lugo (C547)/La Coruna (A9), and immediately turn left into Rua das Cancelas (site is signed), turn right at stadium, site is 800 m. on left.

General Details: Open all year. Mini market. Restaurant. Bar. Laundry. Swimming pools. Children's playground. Telephone and post box. Safe deposit. Medical post.

Charges guide: Per adult ptas. 400-520; child (up to 12 yrs) 325 - 415; car 400 - 550; tent 400 - 550; caravan 425 - 575; m/cycle 325 - 415; motorcaravan 800 - 1,100; electricity 425. All plus VAT.

Reservations: Write to site. Address: Rue do 25 de Xulio 35, 15704 Santiago de Compostela. Tel: 981/58.04.76 or 58.02.66. FAX: 981/57.55.53.

9028 Camping Leiro, Leiro, Orense

Pleasant, peaceful riverside site, deep in heart of mountainous region.

This site would make an attractive base from which to explore the coasts of southern Galicia, the Ribeiro wine region and mountains around Orense. The entry to the site is alongside a high quality riverside restaurant and lounge bar, which is under the same ownership. The pitches are on level ground with easy access and are marked by newly planted shrubs and hedges. Electricity (16A) is available to all 108 pitches. Sanitary facilities are well tiled and clean, with a newly refurbished block for the ladies to a very high standard, large shower cubicles, British WCs and plenty of washbasins. The men's, at present in older style, is not quite so luxurious. Free hot water throughout. Dishwashing and laundry sinks are under cover at one end of the block. One can swim or fish in the river beside the site. No English or French spoken. The site also has some very good quality bungalows for hire.

How to find it: Turn off N120 at Ribadavia towards Carballiño for 10 km., turn left into village - site is signed.

General Details: Open Easter - 30 Sept. Shop. Restaurant. Bar/lounge with terrace. Riverside picnic area. Money exchange. Telephone and post box. Safe deposit. Medical post. Bungalows for hire.

Charges 1997: Per adult ptas. 475; child 400; tent 450; caravan 500; car 500; m/cycle 450; motorcaravan 1,000; electricity 425. All plus VAT. Credit cards accepted.

Reservations: Write to site for details. Address: 32420 Leiro (Orense). Tel: 988/48.80.36.

310

8942 Camping Los Manzanos, Santa Cruz, nr La Coruña

Clean site with good pool well placed for visiting Galicia.

This site is to the east of the historic port of La Coruña, not far from some ria (lagoon) beaches and with good communications to both central and north Galicia - it is only an hour and a half drive from Santiago de la Compostela, for example. The site is divided by a stream into two main sections, linked by a wooden bridge, and has some interesting sculptures to create focal points. Pitches for larger units are marked and numbered, all with electricity (10A) and, in one section, there is a fairly large field for tents. There are two good toilet blocks with modern installations and free hot showers. The site impressed us as being very clean, even when full, which it tends to be in high season. The swimming pool (1-1.75m deep) was clean, with a lifeguard, free to campers, and stays open most of the day and evening. Small shop with fresh produce daily, and restaurant/bar serving good food and a range of wines at reasonable prices. Señor Sanjurjo speaks good English and visitors are assured of a friendly welcome.

How to find it: From the E50 motorway, do not go right into Coruña, but take the N-VI link road across the bridge, following signs towards Meiras and Lugo. Just over the bridge turn left towards Santa Cruz. Turn right at the centre of Santa Cruz and the site is signed from there.

General Details: Open Easter - 15 Sept. Swimming pool. Shop. Restaurant/bar. Children's playground. Barbecue area. Telephone and post box. Medical post.

Charges 1997: Per adult ptas 590; child 490; tent 590; car 590; caravan 600; motorcaravan 1,190; electricity 475. All plus 7% VAT.

Reservations: Write to site. Address: Ctra. Sta Cruz - Meiras, km. 0.7, La Coruña. Tel: 981/61.48.25.

8941 Camping Valdovino, Valdovino, nr Ferrol

Site with top class facilities close to supervised beach.

This site is on the edge of the village, about 300 m. from the beach. The sea here can be lively but at the back of the beach is a calm ria (lagoon) suitable for younger children. The camping area is divided into small enclosures with space for four to six large units each and takes about 70 units in all. They are well shaded by trees and surrounded by hedges of the most beautiful blue hydrangeas which flower all summer. All have access to electricity (16 or 25A), with some night lighting. The one large toilet block is central, as clean and luxurious as any we have seen in Spain, with baby baths, facilities for disabled people, spacious pre-set warm showers, British WCs, a good supply of washbasins, and was pleasantly decorated with plants. In front of the site is a large and low priced supermarket, which also serves the villagers. An excellent restaurant and bar complex offers attractively priced food via waiter service, cafetería or takeaway. Also an ice-cream parlour. The owner, Señora Soto Lopez, speaks good English, and can provide information about visits in the area.

How to find it: From Pontedueme on the N-VI, drive north, but at Fene branch towards Cedeira rather than Ferrol. The road meets the C646 at the coast in Valdovino itself, and the site is almost opposite, down the road to the beach.

General Details: Open 1 June - 30 Sept. Supermarket. Restaurant/bar. Cafe. Takeaway and ice-cream parlour. New children's playground. Bicycle hire. Fishing. Basketball. Fronton courts. Telephone and post box. Safe deposit. Laundry. Medical post. Chemical disposal. Motorcaravan services. Apartments for rent.

Charges 1998: Per adult ptas 575; child 475; tent 615; car 615; caravan 635; m/cycle 475; motorcaravan 1,230; electricity 450. Plus 7% VAT. Credit cards accepted.

Reservations: Write to site. Address: Apdo 104 (Ferrol), Valdovino (La Coruña). Tel: 981/48.70.76. FAX: 981/486131

8940 Camping Los Cantiles, Luarca, nr Oviedo

Well maintained cliff-top site to west of Gijón and Oviedo.

Luarca is a picturesque little place with an inner harbour and two sandy beaches adjoining. Los Cantiles is 2 km. to the east of the town on a cliff-top jutting out into the sea, with good views. The site has no permanent units and is a pleasant place to stop along this undeveloped coastline. The 238 pitches, 83 with electricity (3A), are mostly level grass divided by shrubs. There is a separate area for late arrivals. You can take the car to the Luarca beaches and the small town is within walking distance downhill (remember you have to walk back up!) There is a friendly welcome from the Dutch owner. There are two modern, clean sanitary blocks, one renovated and one newer and very smart. Mainly British toilets; individual basins with hot water and free hot showers. Unit for disabled people and baby bathroom. The site is 300 m. from a new indoor swimming pool, sauna and fitness centre, also close to riding stables There is a disco and pub and restaurants in the town 1.4 km. away.

How to find it: Turn off main N634 road at km. 502.7 point east of Luarca; site is signed.

General Details: Open all year, as is small shop. Bar with hot snacks (main season only). Lounge/reading room. Laundry. Freezer service. Telephone and post box. Safe deposit. No dogs in main season. English spoken.

Charges 1997: Per person 425 ptas; child (4-10 yrs) 375; family tent 500; individual tent 400; caravan 525; motorcaravan 775; car 425; m/cycle 250; electricity 300. Plus 7% VAT.

Reservations: advisesd for mid-July - end-Aug. Made by post with deposit (1,500 ptas). Address: 33700 Luarca (Asturias). Tel: 98/5640938.

SPAIN - North

8950 Camping Costa Verde, Colunga

Busy but acceptable site by a good beach.

This site is some 1½ km. from the town of Colunga and has adequate rather than luxurious facilities which are beginning to show signs of heavy usage. Further afield are the towns of Ribadesella, Gijón and Oviedo. The most attractive feature is a spacious, supervised beach with a low tide lagoon which is ideal for younger children. The 160, regularly laid out pitches which cater for some 630 campers will all be full in high season and, indeed, were fairly full when we visited in June. Electricity (6A) is available throughout. The single toilet block has a mixture of British and Turkish style toilets (all British for ladies). Showers are large (without separators) but you do need a token from the camp shop for hot water. The shop is well stocked and the bar is friendly. The owner makes his own cider!

How to find it: From Santander take the N634 to Ribadesella, and continue for 21 km. along the N632 coast road towards Gijón. Take the right turn towards Lastres from the centre of Colunga.

General Details: Open Easter - early Oct. Shop. Bar/cafe. Laundry. Sports field. Children's playground. Telephone and post box. Safe deposit. Little English spoken.

Charges guide: Per adult ptas 440; child (over 5) 390; tent 390 - 440; caravan 490; car 390; m/cycle 300; motorcaravan 750; electricity 290. VAT included. Credit cards accepted.

Reservations: essential for peak weeks and made for exact dates with deposit. Send for booking form. Address: 33320 Colunga (Asturias). Tel: 98/585.63.73.

8962 Camping La Isla - Picos de Europa, Potes

Relaxed and friendly family site, with good shade and mountain views.

La Isla is beside the road from Potes to Fuente Dé, with mountain views and good shade, which makes it a popular camp for families with young children. A warm welcome awaits you from the lady owner, who speaks good English. The 160 unmarked pitches are arranged around an oval gravel track (one-way system), under a variety of fruit and ornamental trees. Electricity (3A) is available to all pitches, though some may require long leads. The single sanitary block is clean and in the older style, but is steadily being up-graded. It provides British WCs, washbasins with cold water, and free hot showers. There is also a washing machine plus laundry and dishwashing sinks (cold water only). A small bar/cafe is situated by the (very clean) stream adjacent to the site, serving good value meals and takeaway; the small shop provides a good variety of essentials. There is also a barbecue and picnic area under the trees beside the stream, alongside the children's playground. The small heated swimming pool (bathing cap compulsory) is not supervised. Potes with its Monday morning market is only 4 km. away, whilst the monastery at Toribio is also within easy reach. There are opportunities for horse riding and 4x4 safaris in the region, together with all the other mountain sports and active outdoor pursuits.

How to find it: Site is on the right hand side, 4 km. outside Potes, on N621 Potes to Fuente Dé road.

General Details: Open 1 April - 30 Sept. Small shop. Cafe/bar and terrace. Takeaway. Small swimming pool. Children's playground. Laundry. Freezer service. Barbecue and picnic area. Telephone and post box. Safe deposit.

Charges guide: Per person ptas. 400; child (0-10 yrs) 300; tent large 400, small 375; caravan or trailer tent 425; car 400; m/cycle 250; motorcaravan 550; electricity 300. All plus VAT. Credit Cards accepted.

Reservations. Write to site. Address: Potes - Turieno (Cantabria). Tel: 942/73.08.96.

8955 Camping Arenal de Moris, Caravia Alta

Rural site, very close to sea and mountains.

This site is close to three fine sandy beaches and is surrounded by mountains in the natural reservation area known as the Sueve. A hunting reserve, this is important for a breed of short Asturian horses, the `Asturcone'. The Picos de Europa are only 35 km, Covadonga and its lakes is near and Ribadesella is 12 km. It is an ideal area for sea and mountain sports, horse riding, walking and cycling. Camping Arenal's 350 grass pitches (40 - 70 sq.m.) are terraced with little shade. There are three sanitary blocks with hot and cold water and laundry facilities. The restaurant is said to be in typically Asturian style and good. There is a supermarket. This site has been recommended by our Spanish agent and a fuller report will follow next year.

How to find it: Site is signed from the N632 Ribadesella - Gijón road at km. 14 point.

General Details: Open 1 April - 30 Sept. Shop. Restaurant. Swimming pool. Tennis. Laundry. Chemical disposal.

Charges 1998: Per person ptas. 510; child 485; car 495; m/cycle 395; caravan 625; tent 510; motorcaravan 857; electricity 340

Reservations: Contact site. Address: Ctra. 632, 33344 Caravia Alta (Asturias). Tel: 985/85 30 97 or 85 30 50. FAX: 985/85 30 97.

8963 Camping La Viorna, Potes

Well appointed terraced site, with magnificent mountain views in heart of Picos de Europa.

The wonderful views from the open terraces of this site make it an ideal base for a stay in this region and it is especially popular with mature couples and motorcaravanners. The 110 pitches of around 70 sq.m. are marked by newly planted trees which will, in time, provide some shade - but not for a few years yet. There is good access for all sizes of unit and electricity to all pitches (3 or 6A). The single sanitary block is neat and attractive and surrounded by beds of flowers. Its interior is clean and modern with British WCs, washbasins (cold water) with soap dispensers, and good hot showers with divider and seat. The laundry room has plenty of sinks, a washing machine and ironing board, and there is a dishwashing room with 15 sinks (all cold water). Well stocked shop and restaurant/bar (open in season) with a terrace overlooking the excellent swimming pool (23 x 13 m.), and children's pool (bathing caps are compulsory). The pools are not supervised but are heated and free. The site is only 2 km. from Potes, capital of the Picos (market every Monday), close to the Toribio Monastery and a short, but spectacular, drive from Fuente Dé.

How to find it: Take road N621 from Unquera to Potes. After town take left fork signed Toribio de Liebana and site is on right after 800 m.

General Details: Open Easter - 30 Oct. Shop. Restaurant/bar with terrace. Swimming pools. Laundry. Children's playground. Games room. Telephone and post box. Medical post. Tourist information. A little English spoken.

Charges guide: Per adult ptas. 375-400; child 300 - 325; large tent 375 - 400; caravan 375 - 425; car 375 - 400; m/cycle 300 - 325; motorcaravan 550 - 575; electricity 250. All plus VAT.

Reservations: Write to site. Address: Ctra Potes-Santo Toribio, Potes - Mieses (Cantabria). Tel: 942/732021 or 732101.

8964 Camping El Molino de Cabuérniga, Sopeña

Rural `alpine meadow' location, close to old Spanish village.

Located in a peaceful valley beside the river Saja and only a short walk from the old and attractive village, this site is on an open, level, grassy meadow. There are 102 marked pitches, all with electricity (3A), although long leads may be needed. The site is lit at night. A single, modern sanitary block provides free hot showers in curtained cubicles, British WCs and washbasins (cold water only). Dishwashing and laundry sinks are outside the block (also cold water only). There is a small laundry with washing machine (tokens from reception) and ironing facilities. The site also has a small shop for basic needs, cafeteria, bar and barbecue area (open in main season). There is a small, but very simple, children's playground. This comfortable site is very good value and ideal for a few nights whilst you explore the Cabuérniga Valley which forms part of the Reserva Nacional del Saja. The area is great for indulging in active pursuits with opportunities for mountain biking, climbing, walking, swimming or fishing in the river, riding, hunting, paragliding and 4x4 safaris. Sopeña Fiesta is in mid-July each year.

How to find it: From the N634 at Cabezon de la Sal turn on to the C625, continue to km. 42 where site is signed, turn into village (watch out for low eaves/gutters on buildings), keeping to the right turns.

General Details: Open all year. Shop. Cafetería. Bar. Barbecue. Terrace. Children's playground. Telephone and post box. Safe deposit. Money exchange. Tourist information. Laundry. New apartments to rent. No English spoken.

Charges guide: Per adult ptas. 425; child 350; tent 425; caravan 450; car 425; m/cycle 350; motorcaravan 650; electricity 275. All plus VAT. Credit cards accepted.

Reservations: Write to or fax site. Address: 39515 Sopeña de Cabuérniga (Cantabria). Tel: 942/706259. FAX: as phone.

313

8960 Camping La Paz, Vidiago, nr Llanes

Superb and unusual terraced site, by the sea, with spectacular views.

La Paz is arranged on several terraces with sea views, with a lower area in a valley. The way down to the beach is steep but the views, both to the Picos de Europa and to seaward, from the upper terraces are impressive. There are 434 pitches of between 30-70 sq.m, quite a few only suitable for tents, and electricity (3 or 5A) is available. Because of the steep access, units are positioned on upper terraces by site staff with Landrovers. The area at beach level is more suitable for very large units. The four, first class sanitary blocks, with some interesting and unusual design features, are modern, well equipped and spotlessly clean. These have British WCs, washbasins, hot showers (tokens from reception), and baby bath. There are also full laundry and dishwashing facilities. Spring water is available from a number of taps throughout the site. A cliff-top café/restaurant and bar overlook the beach. Mini-market. It is best to book in high season since the site is deservedly popular and one of the best managed along this coast with a policy of respecting the maximum capacity. La Paz is above Vidiago beach where there are opportunities for swimming, windsurfing and fishing. It is also well placed for excursions to the eastern end of the Picos de Europa. Llanes 10 km. to the west, will appeal to inveterate shoppers.

How to find it: From Santander take the N634 towards Llanes. Site is signed from the main road at km.292, before you arrive in Vidiago.

General Details: Open 1 June - 20 Sept. Cafe/restaurant and bar. Mini market. Laundry. Lounge. Watersports. Table tennis. Games room. Telephone and post box. Safe deposit. Medical post. Tourist information. English spoken.

Charges 1997: Per adult ptas 535; child 485, car 525; m/cycle 450; tent 535; caravan 690; motorcaravan 925; electricity for tent 300, caravan 375. All plus VAT @ 7%.

Reservations: Recommended for peak weeks. Address: Km.292 C.N.634 Irun-Coruna, Playa de Vidiago, 33597 Llanes (Asturias). Tel: 985/41.10.12. FAX: 985.41.12.35.

8970 Camping Las Arenas, Pechon

Pleasant, green and spacious touring site, with mountain views and beach access.

This campsite is in a very quiet location bordering the sea and a river, with views to the mountains. It is a very green, 10 ha. site with lots of shade from acacias, oak and poplar trees, and is good value for your holiday budget. Taking 337 units, half of the site is divided into marked, grassy pitches (60 sq.m) in various bays or on terraces. Electrical connections (5A) are available and the roads are asphalted. The clean, and well tiled sanitary facilities are in the older style. The three blocks provide a good supply of British WCs and washbasins, with hot showers (token on payment), plus dishwashing, laundry sinks and washing machines. Well stocked supermarket, restaurant and snack bar. There are opportunities for fishing, swimming, diving, windsurfing or cycling from the site. For older teenagers a disco/bar is only a kilometre away.

How to find it: Turn off the N634, Santander-Coruna road, just east of Unquera on road to Pechon. Site is 2 km.

General Details: Open 1 June - 30 Sept. Restaurant. Snack bar. Supermarket. Children's playground. Fishing. Windsurfer and bicycle hire. Telephone and post box. Safe deposit. Medical post. Money exchange. Laundry. English spoken. Apartments to let.

Charges 1998: Per adult ptas 550; child 450; tent 550; car 550; caravan 675; motorcaravan 900; m/cycle 390; electricity 325; All plus 7% VAT. Credit cards accepted.

Reservations: Contact site. Address: 39594 Pechon. Tel: 942/717188. FAX: as phone.

Camping - Caravaning

E-33597 Vidiago - LLANES (ASTURIAS)
Road N-634 (E-70), km 292.
Tel. (34-85) 41 10 12 • Tel. & fax (34-85) 41 12 35.
In extraordinary quiet, very beautiful surroundings and
directly at the fantastic, very clean beach. 170.000 sqm.
surface with very good installations. At only 45 km from the
famous mountain chain **"PICOS DE EUROPA"**. The country
side is really very beautiful; a "must" for all nature lovers.

8971 Camping Caravaning Playa de Oyambre, San Vicente de la Barquera

Excellent quality modern site with own swimming pool, near good beaches.

This exceptionally well managed site is ideally positioned to use as a base to visit the spectacular Picos
de Europa or one of the many sandy beaches along this northern coast. The site is set back from the
coast in lovely countryside, 5 km. from San Vicente de la Barquera. The 200 marked pitches are mostly
of a good size (the largest ones often taken by seasonal units). They are arranged on wide terraces with
little shade and with electricity (5A) available to all. The excellent sanitary facilities, in one main block,
are spotless with cleaners on duty all day and evening. The showers are spacious with a divider and
hooks; British WCs, a good supply of washbasins and facilities for babies and the disabled. Free hot
water throughout. Dishwashing (H&C) and laundry sinks (cold only) and washing machines (tokens
from reception) are also provided. The site is lit and a guard patrols at night. The local doctor visits 3-4
pm. daily in high season. A well stocked supermarket is open until 10 pm. and there are fresh fish
deliveries 3 days a week. Good, clean and homely restaurant, and a large bar with TV and games
machines. The fair sized swimming pool and a children's pool have a lifeguard on duty, and there is also
a basketball and football court. English spoken.

How to find it: Site signed at junction to Comillas, at km. 265 on E70, 5 km. east of San Vicente de la Barquera.

General Details: Open Easter - 30 Sept. Supermarket (1/6-15/9). Restaurant. Bar/TV lounge. Games room with
machines. Swimming pools (1/6-15/9). Children's playground. Basketball. Football. Telephone and post box. Safe
deposit. Medical post. Laundry. Chemical disposal. Motorcaravan services. Hotel rooms for rent.

Charges 1998: Per adult ptas. 475; child 425; pitch 1,000; electricity 325.
All plus VAT. Credit cards accepted.

Reservations: Advised, particularly if you have a large unit. Write to site.
Address: San Vicente de la Barquera, 39547 Los Llaos (Cantabria).
Tel: 942/711461. FAX: 942/711530. E-mail: oyambre@ctv.es.

AR Discount
Less 5-15%
acc. to season

8961 Camping El Helguero, Ruiloba, nr Santillana del Mar

Well designed site with pool, good facilities for the disabled, close to good beaches.

Although this site is surrounded by tall trees, there is little shade for the pitches. It caters for around 250
units on slightly sloping ground, with many marked out pitches on different levels, all with access to
electricity (6A). There are also attractive tent and small camper sections amongst interesting rock
formations. Two toilet blocks, although showing signs of age, are clean and cared for, with free hot
water in all installations. These include British WCs, washbasins and soap dispensers, showers with
curtains, plus facilities for the disabled, dishwashing, laundry sinks and washing machine. There is a
good, clean swimming pool and children's pool (bathing caps compulsory - sold on site). We were
pleased to see the pool also had an access lift for the disabled. A well stocked shop provides fresh food
and other goods, and the bar and restaurant complex is busy and friendly. This is a good site for disabled
people, in a peaceful location, and is excellent value out of main season. One can generally find space
here even in high season, but arrive early.

How to find it: From C6316 road Santillana del Mar - Comillas, turn left at Sierra. Site signed 'Camping Ruiloba'.

General Details: Open Easter - 30 Sept, including all facilities. Shop. Restaurant/bar. Swimming pool with
lifeguard. Children's playground. Bicycle hire. Games machines. Telephone and post box. Tourist information.
Medical post. Laundry. Chemical disposal. Motorcaravan services.

Charges 1997: Per adult ptas 450; child (4-10 yrs) 375; caravan or
tent 450; car 450; m/cycle 250; motorcaravan 900; electricity 325.
Less in low seasons. Credit cards accepted.

Reservations: Write to site. Address: 39527 Ruiloba (Cantabria).
Tel: 942/72 21 24. FAX: 942/72 10 20.

AR Discount
Special for July:
less 25% after
5th days' stay

SPAIN - North

8980 Camping Municipal Bella Vista, Santander

Municipal site on approach to Cabo Mayor lighthouse.

An agreeable site, with a well cared for look, Bella Vista is on raised ground in a quiet location. There are good views and walks and the site is about 300 m. from a sandy cove which is approached by flight of steps down the cliff. The long, narrow site is grassy with a tarred access road but without too much shade, providing 207 marked pitches. An area under pine trees at one side, gives a degree of shelter for small tents. Electricity (6 or 10A) is available, some pitches with water and drainage also. A restaurant, shop and laundry are on site, together with a basketball and football court, children's playground plus minigolf and petanque. The six toilet blocks (3 men's and 3 women's in separate buildings) are well maintained. They have British style WCs, vanity type washbasins, controllable, free hot showers with excellent dressing area, but no dividers or seat, plus dishwashing and laundry sinks. The site is lit at night. This is primarily a transit site, very popular with British and Dutch visitors, and space is usually available. An excellent stop-over for those arriving at, or departing from, the port of Santander.

How to find it: Site is northeast of town. On leaving ferry terminal turn right on coast road for approx. 5 km.

General Details: Open all year, including amenities. Shop. Café. Children's playground. Basketball and football court. Minigolf. Petanque. Telephone and post box. Safe deposit. Medical post. Money exchange. Laundrette and ironing facilities. Chemical disposal. Bus service. Tourist information. English spoken. Bungalows for hire.

Charges 1998: Per adult ptas. 615; child 460; pitch 1,540, with electricity, water and drainage 2,050; small tent 460 - 665; car 615; m/cycle 410; electricity 385.

Reservations: No stated policy, but site address is Carretera del Faro S/N°, 39012 Santander. Tel: 942/39.15.30 or 39.15.36. FAX: 942/39.15.36.

 AR Discount
Less up to 50% for longer stays in low season

9000 Camping Playa Joyel, Noja, nr Santander

High quality, comprehensively equipped busy site with pool, by superb beach.

This very attractive holiday and touring site is 40 km. from Santander and 70 km. from Bilbao, with 1,000 well shaded, marked and numbered pitches (70-80 sq.m.). Electricity available (3A). Six spacious toilet blocks have British WCs, vanity style washbasins, large showers, baby baths (free hot water) and dishwashing plus a large laundry. The swimming pool complex with lifeguard is free to campers (caps compulsory). Other facilities include a superb restaurant and bar, well stocked supermarket, good value takeaway, hairdresser, kiosk, and a general shop with souvenirs, camping gaz, etc. There is no shortage of entertainment on site with a soundproof pub/disco (July/Aug), large indoor games hall with minigolf, video and table games, plus tennis, riding, animal park, children's playgrounds, recreation area and sports field, and the superb beach (cleaned daily 15/6-20/9). `No cycling' rule July/Aug. Security patrols at night. Although prices are higher, this well managed camp has a lot to offer for family holidays.

How to find it: From A8 (E70) toll-free motorway at Beranga (km.185) take the N634 then, almost immediately, take the S403 for Noja. Follow signs to site.

General Details: Open Easter - 30 Sept. Restaurant (July/Aug). Bar, café and snacks (all season). Takeaway (July/Aug). Supermarket (all season). General shop. Kiosk. Swimming pools (15/5-15/9). Tennis courts. Pub/disco (July/Aug). Games hall. Children's playground. Pharmacy - doctors visit daily in season. Riding. Animal park. Barbecue area. Laundry. Hairdresser (July/Aug). Car wash. Telephone and post box. Safe deposit. Money exchange. Freezer service. Motorcaravan services. English spoken.

Charges 1997: Per adult ptas 425 - 700; child 325 - 580; pitch 1,450 - 1,550; electricity 360 - 380. Plus 7% VAT.

Reservations: made for 1 week or more. Early arrival or reservation is essential in high season. Address: 39108 Noja (Cantabria). Tel: 942/63.00.81. FAX: 942/63.12.94.

See colour advert between pages 288/9

9035 Camping Portuondo, Mundaka

Attractive terraced site suitable only for tents or small units.

This site is a good base from which to explore the local area and the old Spanish town. However, the entry to this well cared for site is steep (18%) and at an oblique angle to the road and the pitches are not suitable for large outfits. In fact, caravans are not accepted at all 15 July - 20 Aug. The site is partly terraced, with pitches marked and numbered and there is some shade in parts. Most pitches are very slightly sloped and all have electricity (5A - some may need long leads). The good quality sanitary facilities include controllable hot showers, washbasins, hand and hairdryers, and mostly British WCs. Dishwashing and laundry sinks are outside under cover and there is a washing machine. Free hot water throughout. The owner also runs a restaurant (at site entrance) with a full range of meals and takeaway. There is a large covered patio with tables and benches above the shower block and a barbecue area.

How to find it: From N634 or autopista (S. Sebastian-Bilbao), turn at Amorebieta onto the C6315 road to Gernika/Bermeo. Approach site from Bermeo direction due to oblique access.

General Details: Open all year. Shop. Restaurant. Bar. Cafeteria. Takeaway. Laundry. Barbecue area. Telephone and post box. Safe deposit. Table tennis. Bungalows for rent. English spoken.

Charges 1997: Per adult ptas 525; child 470; pitch 1,125, with electric 1,525. Plus 7% VAT. Credit cards accepted.

Reservations: Contact site. Address: 48630 Mundaka (Bizkaia). Tel/Fax: 946/87.77.01.

 **AR Discount**
Less 15% on all incl bungalows excl. 15/6-15/9

316

9038 Camping Orio, Orio

Typical seaside site, suitable for first/last night of tour.

This site has 400 pitches, with many long stay units and privately owned statics, but there should always be adequate space for tourers. As it is only 50 m. from the beach, there is no shade. The pitches are in rows divided by tarmac roads and hedges, all with electricity (5A). The main sanitary block has recently been refurbished and provides showers (pre-set hot water) with large changing rooms, washbasins, British WCs and baby baths. Hot water is free throughout. A large kitchen is provided with additional dishwashing and laundry sinks (cold water) outside under cover. Good facilities for wheelchairs. Two additional smaller, older sanitary blocks on site are opened in the main season. Small swimming pool, children's pool (unsupervised), squash and tennis courts, with fishing in the nearby river and the sea. A cafe/bar and mini market are open in July/Aug. This site is fairly expensive in high season, with the cheaper pitches furthest from the beach, but closer to the sanitary installations. Dogs not accepted. No English spoken.

How to find it: Turn off N634 road at km. 12.5 in centre of Orio (sign is easy to miss), and follow signs to site. Take care, the streets in Orio town centre are not wide.

General Details: Open 1 Jan - 31 Oct. Cafe. Bar. Mini market. Money exchange. Swimming pools. Barbecue area. Children's playground. Squash and tennis courts. Fishing. Telephone and post box. Safe deposit. Medical post. Mobile homes for rent.

Charges 1997: Per unit incl. 2 persons ptas. 1,655 - 3,300 (area A - nearest beach), 1,585 - 3,175 (area B - central) or 1,530 - 3,055 (area C - furthest from beach); extra adult 270 - 540; child (2-10 yrs) 225 - 445. VAT included. Credit cards accepted.

Reservations: Write to site. Address: 20810 Orio (Gipuzkoa). Tel: 943/83.48.01. FAX: 943/13.34.33.

9030 Camping Igueldo, San Sebastian

Site on high ground just outside the town.

Igueldo has an imposing situation on top of a hill, by the side of San Sebastian, with a fine panoramic view on the land side. It is also quite a pleasant site in a part of Spain where Britons may want to find a camp and where there are not many available. Although not a luxurious one, it is a friendly place. The sanitary blocks have been extended and improved to give a much more satisfactory provision. The terrain has been divided into 289 individual pitches, though they are not very large - 70 sq.m. They are of two types, 191 with electricity (5A) and water. There are also some tiny tent pitches of 20 sq.m. San Sebastian is a large, pleasant and quite fashionable town which has all the shops, restaurants, entertainment and night life that one could want, as well as some sandy beaches, which are usually busy in the season. The nearest beach is about 5 km. from the site.

How to find it: The turning to Igueldo is on the west side of the town and is well signed from the main road.

General Details: Open all year. 33,000 sq.m. Little shade. Shop. Bar. Restaurant with takeaway food.

Charges 1997: Per unit, incl. car, 4 adults, and with services ptas. 3,100, without services 2,700; extra adult 395; child (3-10) 275; small tent pitch, incl. car, 2 adults 1,300; electricity 350. All plus 7% VAT. Special winter prices.

Reservations: none made. Address: 20190 Igueldo. Tel: 943/214502. FAX: 943/280411.

9070 Camping Pirineos, Santa Cilia de Jaca, nr Jaca

Pretty site with attractive swimming pool, convenient for touring in the Pyrenees.

This all year site has a quite mild climate, being near the River Aragon and not too high. Unusually for Spain the trees are mainly oak and provide reasonable shade. Although there is space for caravans, it is possibly more suited for motorcaravans, owing to the kerbs and trees to be negotiated. The large number of permanent units detracts a little from the overall impression and there is some daytime road noise along one side. However, there is an attractive swimming pool and children's pool with bar and terrace which is open from mid-June to end of August, as is the supermarket. The restaurant and bar are open all year lunch-times and evenings. One heated sanitary block is open all year, providing a quite satisfactory supply, with hot water for the showers, washbasins, dishwashing and laundry sinks. A second, very modern block is open June to August only. Both have British WCs. It is a friendly site which is also useful for off-season camping on the all-electric(6A), mostly level and quite large pitches.

How to find it: Site is 15 km. west of Jaca on the N240 (65 km. northwest of Huesca).

General Details: Open all year. Shade in parts. Restaurant and bar (open all year). Supermarket (high season, otherwise essentials kept in bar). Swimming pools (July/Aug). 2 tennis courts. Table tennis. Children's playground. Fishing. Petanque. Launderette. Chemical disposal. No dogs accepted in high season. Small hotel recently added and accommodation to let.

Charges 1998: Per adult 650; child (2-9 yrs) 625; car 650; caravan or tent 650; motorhome 1,150; electricity 575; all plus 7% VAT: Credit cards accepted.

Reservations: Contact site. Address: Centro de Vacaciones, Ctra N240 km 300, 22791 Santa Cilia de Jaca (Huesca). Tel: 974/377351. FAX: as phone. Internet: http://www.pirinet.com/pirineos/

AR Discount
Less 20% in
low seasons

317

SPAIN - North

9100 Camping Casablanca, Zaragoza

Small city site suitable for overnight stop.

Although not a perfect site, Casablanca is reasonable for overnight or for a short stay. On flat meadow (with little grass) there are 180 pitches with 10A electricity. It does lack shade, and it can be hot here. It has a medium sized swimming pool on site, although this is only open July/Aug. The sanitary block is basic with little hot water and could be hard-pressed at busiest times. British style WCs.

How to find it: Site is just outside town to southwest in the Val de Fierro district; access roads lead off N11 Madrid road (km. 316) or N330 Valencia road and are well signed, if a little difficult to follow.

General Details: Open 1 April - 15 Oct. Shop and restaurant/bar (from 1/6). Town shop 200 m.

Charges 1997: Per adult ptas. 565; child 460; car 565; tent/caravan 565; motorcaravan 900; electricity 420.

Reservations: can be made to Campings Betsa, C/Nov. 139, 17600 Figueras (Gerona). Tel: 976/753870. FAX: 976/753875.

9105 Camping Lago Park, Nuevalos, nr Zaragoza

Attractively situated site with many visitors for the Monasterio de Piedra.

The drawbacks here are the rather steep access, possible up and down treks to the sanitary block (which might not cope with a full site) and possible noise from the disco (although soundproofed), which doubtless gets very busy with the many tent pitches. If you can accept all this or visit out of the main season, you will be rewarded with a site which is positioned just outside the ancient village, between lake and mountains, and which is very suitable as a base for exploring this really attractive area. On a steep hillside, the 250 pitches are on terraces. With only a few pitches suitable for large caravans, just over 50% have electrical connections (10A). They are numbered and marked by trees. The single sanitary block has British style WCs (some Turkish for men), washbasins with cold water and some controllable hot showers (no dividers). If you are placed on the left side of the site, the pool toilets are more easily accessible. Facilities include the swimming pool and a restaurant/bar and shop. A bull-ring is now apparently used as children's play area, although the brochures show young bulls in action.

How to find it: From Zaragoza (120 km.) take fast A2/N11/E90 road and turn on C202 road beyond Calatayud to Nuevalos (25 km). From Madrid exit A2 at Alhama de Aragon (13 km). Follow signs for Monasterio de Piedra from all directions.

General Details: Open 1 April - 30 Sept. Restaurant/bar (open June-Sept). Shop (all season). Swimming pool (late June-Sept). Chalets (4 persons) to rent.

Charges 1997: Per person ptas. 600; child (3-10 yrs) 575; car 530; m/cycle 525; caravan or tent 650; motorcaravan 1,250; electricity 550. Credit cards accepted.

Reservations: Contact site. Address: 50210 Nuevalos. Tel: 976/8490.38, 84.90.48 or 84.90.57.

9142 Camping Solana del Segre, Bellver de Cerdanya, nr Puigcerda

Pleasantly situated all year round site.

The Sierra del Cadi offers some spectacular scenery and the Reserva Cerdanya is very popular for skiing. This site is beside a river where trout fishing is apparently very good and there are views of the mountains. It is in two sections, the lower one nearer the river being the main tourist one, mainly flat and grassy with pitches of 70 sq.m. or more, mostly marked out by trees and all with 6A electricity and quite easy access. There are 300 pitches in total. The sanitary facilities are in three sections and are of satisfactory quality, with free hot water. Showers are of fair size with seats outside. The shop and bar/ restaurant open Easter - mid Sept. and Christmas, otherwise at weekends only, but the town is very close. Fair-sized swimming pool and children's play area, games room/disco, volleyball and petanque. Skiing, riding, golf, hang-gliding and climbing are all available in the vicinity.

How to find it: On the N260 from Puigcerda, the site is just beyond Bellver de Cerdanya towards La Seu (Seo).

General Details: Open all year except 14 Sept - 10 Oct. Shop, Bar/restaurant (see text). Children's play area. Games room. Swimming pool. Many sports in area. Motorcaravan service point. Chemical disposal.

Charges 1997: Per person ptas 630; child (under 10) 550; tent, caravan, car all 630; motorcaravan 1,300; electricity 600. Credit cards accepted.

Reservations: Generally not necessary. Address: Ctra N-260, Km 198. 25720 Bellver de Cerdanya (Lleida). Tel: 973/510310. FAX: 973/510698

9123 Camping El Solsones, Solsona

Useful nightstop in a peaceful situation.

Situated on a hillside, 2 km. from Solsona with pleasant views of the hills on three sides and an open feeling, this all year site would make for a pleasant short stop, with all facilities open. There are many weekend units here, but still room for 100 vans and 100 tents out of the total of 312 pitches. These are slightly sloping, with some shade available and 4, 6 or 10A electricity. The modern sanitary facilities are in two buildings, with free hot water to the showers, washbasins, laundry and dishwashing sinks.

continued overleaf

318

9123 Camping El Solsones (continued)

There is a swimming pool for the high season, a small aviary and children's play equipment. For winter visitors, the 'Ski Port del Conte' is 18 km. and there are facilities for riding, golf and walking in the vicinity. A friendly welcome is provided by the owner who has no English, but good French.

How to find it: Solsona is at the junction of the L301, C1410 and C149 in Lleida, 45 km. northwest of Manresa. The site is 2 km out of town on the LV4241 signed to Sant Llorenc de Morunys and Ski Port del Comte.

General Details: Open all year as are shop, restaurant and bar. Bicycle hire. Children's play area. Petanque. Fronton. Aviary. Swimming pools. Golf, riding and skiing nearby. Motorcaravan service point. Chemical disposal.

Charges 1997: Per person ptas. 560; child (2-10 yrs) 490; car and caravan or tent 1,120; motorcaravan 900; electricity (4A) 300: Plus 7% VAT. Credit cards accepted.

Reservations: Contact site for high season (in French). Address: Ctra Sant Llorenc, Km 2. 25280 Solsona. (Lleida). Tel: 973/482861. FAX: 973/481300.

9060 Camping Peña Montañesa, Labuerda, nr Ainsa

Large, riverside site by the Ordesa National Park in the Pyrenees.

Although situated quite high up in the Pyrenees, Pena Montanesa is easily accessible from Ainsa or from France via the Bielsa Tunnel, and is ideally situated for exploring the beautiful Pyrenees. The site is essentially divided into three sections opening progressively throughout the season and providing progressively less shade as the trees in the newer section grow. The 525 pitches on fairly level grass are of approximately 75 sq.m. and 10A electricity is available on virtually all of them. The newer pitches (open in the main season) have the benefit of a brand new sanitary block, heated when necessary. It has free hot water for the showers, cold for the open plan washbasins, facilities for the disabled, a small baby bathroom and British style WCs. The older pitches are served by an older sanitary block of nevertheless satisfactory standard, with similar provision. This is quite a large site which has grown very quickly and as such may at times be a little hard pressed. Near the entrance are grouped the facilities that make the site so attractive. Apart from a fair sized outdoor pool and children's pool, there is a heated indoor pool with jacuzzi and sauna (all year) and an attractive bar, restaurant (with open fire) and terrace. The supermarket and takeaway are opposite. Used by tour operators and 58 bungalows for rent.

How to find It: Site is 2 km. from Ainsa, on the road from Ainsa to France.

General Details: Open all year. 80,000 sq.m. Bar. Restaurant. Takeaway. Supermarket. Outdoor swimming pool and children's pool (March - Oct). Indoor pool with jacuzzi and sauna. Children's playground. Boules. Minigolf. Table tennis. Canoeing near. Washing machine. Caravans and bungalows to rent.

Charges 1997: Per person ptas. 650; child (1-9 yrs) 560; pitch 1,850; dog 260; electricity 550. All plus 7% VAT.

Reservations: are made for camping with ptas. 10,000 deposit by visa, giro or eurocheque (25,000 ptas. for a bungalow). Address: Ctra. Ainsa-Bielsa, km.2, 22360 Labuerda-Ainsa (Huesca). Tel: 974/50.00.32. FAX: as phone. E-mail: penemontanesa@pirineo.com. Internet: http://pirineo.com/pena montanesa.

SPAIN - North

9121 Camping de la Vall d'Ager, Ager, nr Lleida

Very peaceful all year round site in lovely setting.

Ager is not on a through-route to anywhere, so if you are coming here it is for a specific reason, hence the peaceful situation. One of the main reasons for being here is that it is a hang glider's paradise, the Montsec mountain (1,677 m.) overlooking the site in the Catalan pre-Pyrenees, being the launch point. When you also consider that climbing, walking, mountain biking, canoeing and other water sports are all available in the vicinity, you may well wish to visit this pleasant site. There are 180 touring pitches on slightly sloping ground, marked out by trees and with some shade. Electricity (10A) is available to all. The central sanitary building provides good facilities, with soap and paper towels in the toilet sections and free hot water in the washbasins and large showers (with divider and lots of room to change). The building also houses separate rooms for disabled people, dishwashing (hot water) and laundry (cold) facilities, plus a washing machine and dryer downstairs. There is a large bar with snack area and a restaurant which opens all year. The small shop is open April - Sept. only, but the village is only 3/400 m. The swimming pool is open in high season and there is a well provisioned area of children's play equipment.

How to find it: The site is on the edge of the village, which is on the L904, either direct from Balaguer (which is 28 km. NNE of Lleida) or from the C147 Balaguer/Tremp road. Either way, the L904 (which is being modernised) has old, narrow sections requiring caution.

General Details: Open all year, as are the bar, snack bar and restaurant. Shop (main season only). Bicycle hire. Delta-wing store. Swimming pools. Children's play equipment. Chemical disposal. Accommodation to let.

Charges 1997: Per person ptas. 550; child (under 10 yrs) 500; tent, caravan, motorcaravan all 550; electricity (10A) 600. Credit cards accepted.

Reservations: Unlikely to be needed. Address: 25691 Ager, La Noguera (Lleida). Tel: 973/455200/1/9. FAX: 973/455202.

9125 Camping Lago de Barasona, La Puebla de Castro, nr Huesca

Hillside site by lake in the pre-Pyrenees.

This site is beautifully positioned in terraces by the shores of the Lago de Barasona (a large reservoir), with views of hills and the distant Pyrenees. The local administration has put together some excellent tourist information (in English) and a brochure detailing the local way-marked walks and the owner has matched this with his own quality brochure. The recently discovered Roman town of Labitolosa, just 1.5 km. away on foot, direct from the site, is best seen in high summer when further excavations take place. The site has its own canoes for hire and waterskiing is available also in July and August. You may also swim and fish in the lake which has a very shallow area extending for 20 m. or so. If you prefer, the site offers its own outdoor pool, open from as early as April when the weather is often quite warm. The very friendly, English speaking owner would welcome more British visitors, especially in the spring, when the area is very attractive. The grassy, fairly level pitches are up to 100 sq.m. in size for larger units and all have 6A electricity connections. Many are well shaded and views of the lake and/or hills are available. Some up and down walking is necessary to the shop (July/Aug), bar/restaurant, swimming pool and the two sanitary units. The lower, recently modernised building is nicely presented, although hot water is only available in the cabins (3 for ladies, 1 for men) and the smallish showers (no divider), and some dishwashing and laundry sinks. Volleyball, football and a new children's play area were all under construction. A pleasant and peaceful site in a lovely area.

How to find it: Site is on the west bank of the lake, close to km. 25 on the N123, 4.5 km. south of Graus (approx. 80 km. north of Lleida/Lerida).

General Details: Open 1 April - 30 Sept. Bar/snack bar and restaurant (all season). Swimming pool. Money exchange. Shop (July/Aug but bread always available). Lake swimming, fishing, canoeing etc. Walking. Mountain bikes for hire. Accommodation to let.

Charges 1997: Per person ptas. 560; child (2-10 yrs) 460; car 640; caravan 640; tent 640; motorcaravan 990; electricity 460. Credit cards accepted.

Reservations: Not needed outside mid-July - mid-August. Address: Ctra N-123, km. 25, 22435 La Puebla de Castro (Huesca). Tel: 974/54 51 48. FAX: as phone. E-mail: camping-lago-barasona@spicom.es.

All the sites in this guide are regularly inspected by our team of experienced site assessors, but we welcome your opinion too.
See Readers Reports on page 361

8506 Camping-Caravaning Serra de Prades, Vilanova de Prades, nr Reus

Tranquil site on edge of village, nestling in granite foothills.

On the edge of the village of Vilanova, on the lower mountain slopes with good views, this is a welcoming and peaceful site. The 215 pitches are on terraces formed with natural stone and with good access, 189 have electrical connections (176 with 6A, 13 with 10A). Hedges and trees have been planted to separate pitches which provide a green environment and shade. All facilities are at the entrance to the site and include a modern, very well maintained sanitary block with British style WCs and which can be heated in winter. Solar power is used to ecologically supplement the hot water supply. The bar/restaurant offers a wide range of meals including regional dishes. There is plenty to do on the site and in the area and the site has facilities for horse riding (with guided treks) and for the hire of 4x4 vehicles. The helpful staff will give you many leaflets and brochures to guide you to interesting visits, including the attractive, old village itself. Organised activities for children and adults. The village swimming pool is 100 m. and is free for campers.

How to find it: From autopista A2 take exit 8 (L'Albi) or 9 (Montblanc) and follow CN240 to Vimbodi. Take the TV7004 road for 10 km. to Vilanova de Prades and site.

General Details: Open all year. Shop. Bar/restaurant. Archery. Basketball. Volleyball. Tennis. Riding with guided treks. 4x4 vehicle hire. Entertainment organised in season. Swimming pool 100 m. Laundry facilities. Safety deposit. Exchange facilities. New bungalows (5) to rent.

Charges 1998: Per person ptas. 575; child (under 10 yrs) 475; tent 550; caravan 575; car 575; m/cycle 450; motorcaravan 1,150; m/cycle 575; boat 575; electricity 495. Plus 7% VAT.

Reservations: Write to site. Address: c/Sant Antoni s/n, 43439 Vilanova de Prades (Tarragona). Tel: 977/86.90.50. FAX: as phone.

Central

This area comprises the whole of inland Spain, south of a line just south of Burgos (Lat. 42°) excluding the coastal strip - see map on page 375.

9021 Camping Municipal Fuentes Blancas, Burgos

Comfortable, municipal site, within easy reach of Santander ferries.

Burgos is an attractive city, ideally placed for overnight stop en route to the south of Spain. The old part of the city around the cathedral is quite beautiful and there are pleasant walks along the river banks. Fuentes Blancas is a municipal site with clean, modern, sanitary facilities in five blocks, although some may not be open outside July/Aug. These include British WCs, vanity style washbasins, free hot showers and facilities for babies. There are around 400 marked pitches of 70 sq.m. on flat ground, 112 with electrical connections (6A) and there is good shade in parts. A small shop caters for most needs and the terraced snack bar is friendly without being noisy. A swimming pool is open in main season only. The site has a fair amount of transit trade and reservations are not possible for August, so arrive early.

How to find it: From the cathedral, cross the river and turn left. Follow the Cartuja de Miraflores road alongside the river for about 3 km. Site is signed to the right, about 1 km. further on. Signs are small and not easy to spot.

General Details: Open 1 April- 30 Sept. Small shop (May-Sept). Bar/snack bar (all season). Swimming pool (from May). Children's playground. Table tennis. Basketball. Football. Telephone and post box. Safe deposit. Medical post. Money exchange. Chemical disposal. English spoken.

Charges 1998: Per pitch incl. caravan and electricity ptas 1,625 (package); adult 525; child (2-10 yrs) 375. Plus 7% VAT. Credit cards accepted.

Reservations: Not made. Address: Ctra. Cartuja Miraflores, 09000 Burgos. Tel: 947/48 60 16. FAX: as phone.

9250 Camping Costajan, Aranda de Duero

Good night stop en route to or from ferries, 75 km. south of Burgos.

This site has approximately 100 pitches (with electricity) available for all types of tourer. Large units may find access to the variably sized pitches a bit tricky among the pine trees and on the slightly undulating ground. Ignore the few unsightly static caravans, as this is a shady, clean and friendly spot for an overnight stop. Sanitary facilities are satisfactory, with hot and cold water and just one water point. New bungalows to rent - details from site.

How to find it: Turn off the N1 at km. 162, just north of Aranda de Duero and follow signs to site (under 1 km).

General Details: Open 1 April - 30 Sept. Shop (all season). Cafe, swimming pool and bar (all June-Sept). Tennis. Football. Minigolf. Exchange facilities. Bungalows for rent.

Charges 1997: Per person ptas. 450 - 500; child 425 - 475; tent or caravan 450 - 500; car 450 - 500; motorcaravan 685 - 735; m/cycle 350 - 400; electricity 375.

Reservations: Said to be unnecessary. Address: Ctra. no.1, km. 162, 09400 Aranda de Duero (Burgos). Tel: 947/502070. FAX: 947/511354.

SPAIN - Central

9023 Camping Camino de Santiago, Castrojeriz, nr Burgos

Small countryside site with outstanding views, slightly remote with a superb location.

This site lies to the west of Burgos on the outskirts of Castrojeriz, an unspoilt original Spanish small town. In a superb location, almost in the shadow of the ruined castle high on the adjacent hillside, it will appeal to those who like perfect solitude and a true touring campsite without all the modern trimmings, at a reasonable cost. The 50 marked pitches are level, grassy and divided by hedges, with electricity available to all. Sanitary facilities are adequate, with showers (2 hot per sex), British and Turkish style WCs, and washbasins with cold water only. All of these are in the older style, but are well maintained and were clean when visited. A further small block is next to the barbecue area. Small shop with basic necessities, shares space with the bar/coffee shop and reception and there is a shady terrace outside. Games room with table football, pool table and table tennis. Two tennis courts complete the facilities.

How to find it: From N120 (Osorno-Burgos) road, turn onto BV404 for Villasandino and Castrojeriz. Turn left at crossroads on southwest side of town and then left at campsite sign.

General Details: Open 1 June - 30 August. Shop. Bar. Cafeteria/coffee shop with terrace. Washing machine. Telephone and post box. Safe deposit. Medical post. Games room. Tennis courts. Barbecue area.

Charges guide: Per person ptas. 350; child 300; tent small 300, large 350; caravan 350; car 300; m/cycle 150 - 250; motorcaravan 575; electricity 300. All plus VAT.

Reservations: Write or fax site for details. Address: Casco Urbano, 09110 Castrojeriz (Burgos). Tel: 947/377255. FAX: 983/359549.

9025 Camping Regio, Salamanca

Convenient, touring site, next to hotel complex with good pool.

Salamanca is one of Europe's oldest university cities, and the old town has much to commend it. It is also a useful staging post en route to the south of Spain or central Portugal. The site is some 4 km. outside the town on the road to Madrid. It is behind the Hôtel Regio and shares with it a quality restaurant, somewhat cheaper cafeteria and a very good swimming pool and children's pool (small charge). Other facilities include tennis and basketball courts, and a children's playground. The 200 pitches are on slightly sloping ground, with some shade in parts and very sparse grass, the site was dusty when we visited. The pitches are marked out but not too formally, with electricity points (15A) in little red-roofed towers and enough for all; water points are plentiful. The two large toilet blocks in the older style, one for women and one for men, provide British WCs, washbasins and free hot showers - all reasonably clean when seen but in need of some refurbishment.

How to find it: Take the N501 route from Salamanca towards Avila and Madrid. Hôtel Regio is on the right after about 4 km.

General Details: Open all year. Restaurant, cafe and swimming pool at adjoining hotel. Shop. Laundry. Telephone and post box. Safe deposit. Money exchange. Medical post. Car wash. Tennis and basketball courts. English spoken.

Charges guide: Per adult ptas. 425; child 375; tent (small) 375, (large) 425; car 425; caravan 425; m/cycle 375; motorcaravan 675; electricity 425. Credit cards accepted.

Reservations: Write to site. Address: Ctra. de Madrid, km 4, 37900 Santa Maria de Tormes. Tel: 923/130888. FAX: 923/130044.

9090 Camping El Greco, Toledo

Quiet, spacious site with attractive pool.

Toledo was the home of the painter and the site that bears his name boasts a beautiful view of the city from the restaurant, bar and pool. Ivy clad pergolas run down each side of the swimming pool (charged: adult ptas. 350, child 250) with tables in the shade - it can be very hot here. There is an hourly air conditioned bus service to the city centre from the gates, which tours the outside of the walls first. There is always plenty of space and reservation is said not to be necessary. A recent addition for caravans are 21 pitches of 80 sq.m. with electrical connections but, as yet, little shade although trees have been planted. Access to some pitches may be tricky for caravans (narrow and at an angle). All the facilities are reasonably modern and kept clean. The site stretches along the Tagus but fishing in it is a better bet than swimming. This is worth a few days for Toledo and the pool alone, but it is only an hour's drive from Madrid and thus makes a good base for a longer stay.

How to find it: Site is on the C502 road on the edge of the town, signed towards Puebla de Montelban; site signs also in city centre. From Madrid on the N401, turn off right towards Toledo city centre but turn right again at the gates to the old city. Site is signed from the next right turn. Don't be misled by the 'Camping' signs on the road into Toledo from Madrid - these lead to an inferior site.

General Details: Open all year. Swimming pool (1/6-5/9). Restaurant/bar (all year) with good menu and fair prices. Shop in reception (all year). Laundry facilities. Volleyball. Children's playgrounds.

Charges 1997: Per person ptas. 550; child (3-10 yrs) 450; car 550; m/cycle 480; caravan or trailer tent 625; tent 570; motorcaravan 1,120; electricity (6A) 450. Plus 7% VAT.

Reservations: not necessary and not made. Address: Ctra. Comarcal 502, 45004 Toledo. Tel: 925/22.00.90. FAX: as phone.

9200 Camping Caravaning El Escorial, El Escorial, nr Madrid

Site with swimming pools and other amenities 50 km. northwest of Madrid.

There is a shortage of good sites in the central regions of Spain, but this is one, well situated for sightseeing visits with the El Escorial monastery and the enormous civil war monument of the Valle de los Caidos very close and Madrid and Segovia both 50 km. away. There are over 1,300 marked, individual pitches, of which over 450 are occupied by permanent caravans, which is an improvement on past years. There are another 200 `wild' spaces for tourists on open fields, with improving shade (long cables may be necessary for electricity) and there should usually be space. There are three large new or refurbished toilet blocks, plus two smart, new small toilet blocks for the `wild' camping area. British WCs, some without seats; washbasins with free hot water, shelf and mirror (some in private cabins), and hot showers with push-button but controllable temperature. Baby baths. The blocks can be heated in cool weather. The general amenities on site are good and include three swimming pools (unheated) and a children's pool in a central area with a bar and plenty of grassy sitting out areas.

How to find it: From El Escorial-Guadarrama autopista A-6, take exit 47 and M600 towards El Escorial town. Site is 3.5 km.

General Details: Open all year. Large supermarket (open for 1 hour daily in winter) and boutique. Restaurant/bar. Disco-bar. Swimming pools. 3 tennis courts. 2 football pitches. Basketball. `Fronton'. Well equipped children's playground on sand.

Charges 1997: Per person 650 ptas; child (3-9) 625; caravan or tent 650; car 650; motorcaravan 1,150 - 1,800, acc. to size; electricity 400. VAT included.

Reservations: to guarantee admission made if you write but considered unnecessary. Address: Apdo. Correos 8, 28280 El Escoril, Madrid. Tel: 91/890.24.12.

E-28280 EL ESCORIAL (Prov. MADRID) • Tel. (34-1) 890 24 12 • Fax (34-1) 896 10 62

Situated in the most beautiful part of Castille, 3 km from the impressive National Monument VALLE DE LOS CAIDOS (Valley of the Fallen, a memorial to the dead in the Spanish Civil War, where Francisco Franco is also buried) and 8 km from the famous Monastery of SAN LORENZO DE EL ESCORIAL, pantheon of the Spanish kings since Charles I.

Restaurant • Cafeteria • Supermarket
• hot water in showers and wash-basins
• disco-pub • 90 m2 pitches
with electr. conn.

3 swimming pools • 3 tennis courts
• 2 fronton (basque ball game, similar to squash) courts, basket ball.

9091 Camping Soto del Castillo, Aranjuez, nr Madrid

Useful stop-over municipal site with good facilities, near Madrid.

Situated near the centre of the royal town of Aranjuez, with its beautiful palaces and gardens and 44 km. south of Madrid, this is a very useful site, convenient either as a night stop en-route from the Santander ferry, or for visiting the Spanish capital. Aranjuez, itself, is an interesting, royal town, with leafy avenues, worthy of a visit. The site is near the town centre and close to the River Tajo and historic palaces. The 225 touring pitches, all with electricity, are set on flat grass amid tall trees. Pitches are not marked and siting is informal and left to the individual, but they should be of moderate size. The site has good facilities including a swimming pool (June-Sept), small supermarket and restaurant (quite expensive, also open to the public) with takeaway, TV room, children's play area and volleyball court.

continued overleaf

9091 Camping Soto del Castillo (continued)

There are three sanitary blocks - the largest is very well equipped, with roomy tiled hot showers, some basins in cabins and British WCs. The two smaller blocks, of more open design, appear somewhat older but have been updated and provide less good facilities. Maintenance may be variable. Washing up facilities are adequate, although with only cold water. Chemical disposal point and laundry facilities.

How to find it: Site is just north of the town centre (from where it is signed) Aranjuez is bypassed by the old NIV, so ensure you follow the signs for the town, some 44 km. south of Madrid. Watch for sign to site - a sharp left turn off the main road with little notice, at the end of a small archway of trees.

General Details: Open 1 April - 30 Sept. Electricity throughout. Bar. Restaurant. Takeaway. Small shop. Swimming pool (June-Sept). Children's play area. Volleyball. TV room. Bicycle hire. Walking distance of palace, gardens and museums, etc. Bungalows for hire.

Charges 1997: Per person ptas. 600; child (3-10 yrs) 475; car 500; caravan 675; motorcaravan 750; tent 525 - 650; electricity 500. Discounts for groups or long stays.

Reservations: Write to site. Address: Aranjuez, 28300 Madrid. Tel: 91/891.13.95.

9095 Camping Ciudad de Albarracin, nr Teruel

Satisfactory site for visiting interesting, historic town in southern Aragon.

Albarracin is a much frequented, fascinating town with a Moorish castle and other antiquities to see, set in the 'Reserva Nacional de los Montes Universales', with some wonderful scenery around. The site is set on a hillside at the back of the town, with views of it and a walk of perhaps 500 m. to the centre. It is modern and long, set on fairly flat ground, sloping for the last third. There are 70 pitches (increasing to 130 for 1998), all with electrical connections, separated by trees and ranging in size up to 70 sq.m. The modern sanitary building has British style WCs for ladies and mixed British and Turkish for men. The vanity style washbasins have free hot water, as do the showers, which are quite large but have no divider. There is a baby bath in the ladies' and provision in between for dishwashing and laundry with one machine. No shop but essentials available from the bar. The bar/restaurant, with terrace and TV, is said to be open all season, but there are shops, bars and restaurants in the town as well. A municipal swimming pool, just 100 m. away, is open in high season and there is a small children's play area. No English spoken yet, until the owner's children gain in confidence!.

How to find it: From Teruel north on N330 for about 8 km. then west on A1512 for 37 km. Well signed in town.

General Details: Open 1 April - 31 Oct, as is bar/restaurant. Essentials from bar. Town shops 500 m. Special room for barbecues with fire and wood provided.

Charges 1997: Per person ptas. 350; child (under 14) 250; car, caravan and tent 700; motorhome 600; electricity 300. Credit cards accepted.

Reservations: No English spoken; policy not known but probably not necessary. Address: Ciudad de Albarracin, Amparo Hernandez Lozano, 44100 Albarracin (Teruel). Tel: 978/71 01 97 or 07.

9270 Camping Suspiro Del Moro, nr Granada

Impressive site in Sierra Nevada mountain range, useful for sightseeing.

Suspiro Del Moro is 11 km. south of Granada on the N323 Motril road or, alternatively, can be approached on the scenic mountain road from Almunecar (lots of bends this way). Many places of interest are within reasonable distance of the site, including La Alhambra, Granada and the Parador of La San Francisco. Based high in the Sierra Nevada mountain range, the area offers spectacular views from just outside the site, with trees and fences inhibiting the views inside. Cool and peaceful, the site is beautifully kept, with gravel paths leading to laid out flat, grass pitches. The one main sanitary block is modern with British WCs, free hot showers, washbasins with shelves and mirrors. Laundry and washing up facilities also. Three small toilet blocks are situated around the camping area. A very attractive Olympic sized swimming pool, together with a restaurant with bar tables, umbrellas and waiter service, covers a large area behind the main camping site. The restaurant offers a large, varied menu and, like the site itself, shows a professional image. A smaller bar and TV lounge is available, and also a supermarket. This is an impressive site all round.

How to find it: On the N323 road, 11 km. from Granada on the road to Motril.

General Details: Open all year. Supermarket, restaurant/bar (both all year). Bar. TV lounge. Swimming pool, with children's end (high season only). Small children's play area on gravel. Table tennis. Table football. Bus service from outside site to Granada. Bungalows to rent.

Charges guide: Per person 450 ptas; child 350; pitch 850; electricity 250. Less 20% in low season. Visa cards accepted.

Reservations: May be made for high season. Write to site. Address: N323, km. 145 (Cruce Ctra. Almunecar), 18630 Granada. Tel: 958/55.51.05 or 55.54.11. FAX: 958/55.51.05.

9280 Camping-Motel Sierra Nevada, Granada

Good site with swimming pool, useful for visiting Granada.

This is a good site either for a night stop or for a stay of a few days while visiting Granada. Quite a large site with an open feeling and, to encourage you to stay a little longer, a medium sized swimming pool of irregular shape (open at least June - Sept) with a smaller child's pool (admission charge 175 ptas). Granada has much to offer for sightseeing, including the Alhambra; it also has some interesting shops and there are usually one or two excellent shows. The camp fills up considerably each evening in the season, so the earlier you arrive, the better your chances of securing a good pitch. There is quite good shade and electrical connections are available. There are two main toilet blocks (one very modern), with a separate new unit with free hot showers and facilities for the disabled and babies. Extensive facilities by the pool which can be made available at peak times. Mostly British style toilets some with bidets, individual basins with mirrors and free hot showers.

How to find it: Site is just outside the town to the north, on the road to Jaén and Madrid. From the autopista, take Granada North - Almanjayar exit 126 (close to the central bus station). Follow road back towards Granada and site is shortly on the right, well signed.

General Details: Open March - Oct, as are shop and restaurant. About 10,000 sq.m. Self-service shop. Bar/café by pool. Rather expensive restaurant. 2 tennis courts. Children's playground (with hard surface). Doctor lives on site. Washing machine. Frequent bus service to city centre from outside site. Motel apartments (2 persons, incl. bath/WC).

Charges 1997: Per person 535 ptas; child (3-10 yrs) 435; car 535; tent 435 - 535; motorcaravan 660; caravan 575; electricity 350. All plus 7% VAT.

Reservations: are made for camping or motel. Address: 18014 Granada. Tel: 958/15.00.62.

9080 Campamento Municipal El Brillante, Cordoba

Very busy site with some shade.

Cordoba is one of the hottest places in Europe - the `frying pan' of Spain - and the pool here is more than welcome, being large and bordered by pleasant terraced gardens. If you really want to stay in the city, then this site is acceptable. Most pitches are now covered with artificial shade but, to get the best ones, it is essential to arrive early in any season as the site becomes very crowded. The entrance is narrow and may be congested. The toilet facilities were barely adequate - do not expect the same standards as at long-stay sites - and when the site was full they only just coped. We are told that a new block is to be added with facilities for babies and the disabled. The bar/restaurant is cheap and cheerful, with plenty of shade. Cordoba is a fascinating town and the Mosque/Cathedral is one of the great buildings of Europe and not to be missed.

How to find it: Entering by the NIV/E25 road from Madrid, drive into the city centre. After passing the Mosque/Cathedral, turn right onto the main avenue, keep going bearing right, and follow signs for the campsite and/or the district of El Brillante.

General Details: Open all year. Bar, restaurant, new shop, swimming pool, all high season only. Large supermarket 300 m. Bus service to city centre from outside site.

Charges 1997: Per adult ptas. 550; child 390; car 500; tent 354 - 550, acc. to size; caravan 550; motorcaravan 850; electricity 350.

Reservations: are not made. It is essential to arrive early in high season. Address: Avda. del Brillante 50, 14012 Cordoba. Tel: 957/282165.

9085 Camping Carlos III, La Carlota, nr Cordoba

Good alternative site for Cordoba, 25 km. from the city.

If you don't care for the very busy municipal site in Cordoba with its hard-pressed facilities, then the trip to La Carlota may suit you better. With its bar and catering services open all year, the site has an open feel. The touring areas offer some shade for the 300 pitches which are level and separated by trees, on grassy, sandy ground. Around two thirds have 5A electrical connections. Sanitary facilities, in two modern blocks, have mixed British (40%) and Turkish WCs and hot showers in the block near reception. Permanent units, mobile homes and bungalows (to rent) are in a separate area, where there are sporting facilities. There may be some slight road noise.

How to find it: From the N-IV Cordoba-Seville motorway take La Carlota exit at km. 429 point; site is well signed.

General Details: Open all year. Bar/restaurant, shop (all year). Swimming pool (high season). Aviary. Table tennis. Boules. Children's play area. Volleyball. Football. Chemical disposal. Motorcaravan services. Bus service outside site. Village 2 km.

Charges 1998: Per person ptas. 475; child (under 12 yrs) 375; car 475; m/cycle 300; tent 475; caravan 500; motorcaravan 725; electricity (5A) 350. Plus 7% VAT. Discounts (10-30%) for longer stays and outside high season. Credit cards accepted.

Reservations: Probably necessary in July/Aug. Address: Ctra. Madrid-Cadiz km. 430.5, 14100 La Carlota. Tel: 957/300697. FAX: as phone.

AR Discount
Less 10% in
low seasons

SPAIN - Central

9081 Camping Villsom, Dos Hermanas, nr Seville

Clean, fairly shady site with attractive pool and bar area.

This is a fine city site with an excellent new sanitary block supplementing the well renovated existing facilities to give a very good quota now. Together with a new minigolf and table tennis area, this has resulted in the number of pitches being reduced slightly to around 180. The oranges from the trees, which almost enclose a very pretty outdoor bar area, are sold to Britain for marmalade. The site has a small shop and a most inviting small pool. Temperatures can be hotter here than almost anywhere in Spain and the pool seems essential, as are the orange trees. There is satellite TV in the bar/café (breakfast served 9-12 daily). Restaurant 80 m, supermarket 400 m. Bus service from outside site to city. It is essential to book if intending to visit this site in peak weeks.

How to find It: You need to be about 10 km. from Seville on NIV to Cadiz. Look for 'Continente' sign on left and soon afterwards turn right on road to Salida dos Hermanas - Isla Menor; site is on right.

General Details: Open all year. Bar/café with satellite TV. Swimming pool (June-Sept). Minigolf. Table tennis. Small shop (at reception). Laundry facilities. Children's playground. Restaurant and supermarket close.

Charges guide: Per adult 435 ptas; child 385; tent 450; caravan 475; car 450; motorcaravan 560; m/cycle 380; electricity 275. All plus 7% VAT.

Reservations: Write to site. Address: Ctra. Sevilla-Cadiz, km. 554.8, 41700 Sevilla. Tel/Fax: 95/472.08.28.

9083 Camping Monesterio, Monesterio

Attractive, conveniently located new site.

This brand new, modern site, located on the Ruta de la Plata in the Sierra de Tudia, is ideal for those travelling to or from Seville or the eastern Algarve. The traditionally styled, modern sanitary installations include WCs, washbasins and showers with facilities for the disabled and children, plus dishwashing and laundry sinks. Hot water is free throughout. All pitches have electrical connections (16A). Also on site is a good swimming pool (2.5 m. deep), launderette, supermarket and horse riding facilities. Although newly planted, this well laid out site has shade in parts and is well fenced and lit.

How to find It: Site is on western side of CN 630 (Merida-Seville) just south of Monesterio, turn off at km. 726 (new access road).

General Details: Open from Easter. Supermarket. Launderette. Swimming pool. Horse riding.

Charges guide: Per adult ptas 425; child 375; tent 425; car 500; caravan 425; motorcaravan 750; m/cycle 375; electricity 350; all plus 7% VAT.

Reservations: Contact site. Address: CN 630 Km 726, Monesterio, Badajoz. Tel: 924/516352. FAX: as phone.

9087 Camping Mérida, Mérida

Attractive well maintained site, close to architecturally interesting town.

Camping Mérida is ideally located to serve both as a base to tour the local area and as an overnight stop en route when travelling either north/south or east/west. The site lies behind camp buildings, beside the main road to Madrid but is quite well shielded from road noise, with easy access. There are 130 good sized pitches, most with some shade and on level ground, with ample electricity connections (long leads may be needed). The excellent sanitary facilities provide showers (some hot, some cold) with hooks and seat outside in a changing area, British WCs, and washbasins. Free hot water. Dishwashing (H&C) and laundry sinks (cold only) are at the end of the block under cover. Also on site is a cafe/bar and restaurant, adjacent to a medium sized swimming pool (with lifeguard), and a small shop. No English is spoken, but try your French. Reception open until midnight. Mérida is an interesting town with a Roman amphitheatre and other ruins, a classical Theatre Festival, and a National Museum of Roman Art.

How to find It: Site is alongside road NV (Madrid-Lisbon), 5 km. east of Mérida, at km. 336.6 point.

General Details: Open all year. Shop. Restaurant/cafeteria. Bar. Swimming pool. Children's playground. Telephone and post box. Safe deposit. Money exchange. Medical post.

Charges 1997: Per adult ptas 450; child 400; caravan and car 900; motorcaravan 650; electricity 375. + 7%. VAT

Reservations: Contact site. Address Ctra. N-V Madrid-Portugal km 336, Mérida (Extremadura). Tel: 924/30.34.53.

9089 Camping Despeñaperros, Santa Elena   *late entry*

New site in strategic position.

A new, very useful site for those travelling from Madrid towards the Costa del Sol, Despeñaperros is located in a 30 year old pine grove which is part of the Despeñaperros nature reserve. Readers tell us that it has a charming restaurant and bar, new sanitary facilities and friendly staff. Also that everything is very clean. There are wonderful views, especially from the swimming pool.

How to find It: On the E5 'autovia de Andalucia' at km. 257, at the village of Santa Elena.

General Details: May be open all year, but not yeat confirmed; phone site out of the main season..

Charges 1997: Per unit incl. 2 adults and 1 child 2,355 ptas.

Reservations: Contact site. Address: 23213 Santa Elena (Jaén). Tel: 953/66 41 92.

SWEDEN

Sweden covers an area almost twice that of the UK but has a population only one seventh of ours, with over half the land surface covered by forests and lakes. Stretching from north of the Arctic circle for 1,000 miles to a southern limit about level with Glasgow, inevitably the roads are quiet and almost traffic free with a range of scenery varying from the vast, wild open spaces of Lapland to the rich forests of the south and a choice of climate to match. The very beautiful southwest region, the 'Swedish Lake and Glass country', makes a perfect introduction to this fascinating land. It is easily reached, either by a wide choice of ferries or overland from Norway. The area is dominated by the two great lakes, Vänern (2,000 sq. miles) and Vättern (750 sq. miles), Europe's second and third largest lakes. Stockholm, the capital, is a delightful place built on a series of fourteen small islands, housing monumental architecture and fine museums giving it an ageing, lived-in atmosphere and providing the country's most active culture and night life. Today Sweden enjoys one of the highest standards of living in the world and a quality of life to go with it. For further information contact:

Swedish Travel and Tourism Council, 73 Welbeck Street, London W1M 8AN
Tel: 0171 487 3135. Fax: 0171 935 5853.

Population
8,700,000, density 19.3 per sq. km.

Capital
Stockholm

Climate
Sweden enjoys a temperate climate thanks to the Gulf Stream. The weather is similar to Britain's, apart from the fact that there is generally less rain and more sunshine in the summer.

Language
English is fairly widely spoken but a phrase book is advised.

Currency
Swedish currency is the Krona (plural Kronor) made up of 100 öre. It comes in coins of 50 öre, 1 kr, 5 kr and 10 kr, and notes of 20, 50, 100, 500, 1,000 and 10,000 kr.

Banks
Open Mon-Fri 09.30-15.00. Some city banks stay open til 17.30/18.00. All are closed on Sats.

Post Offices
Open 09.00-18.00 on weekdays and 09.00/10.00 - 13.00 on Saturdays. You can also buy stamps at stationers and tobacconists.

Telephone
To dial Sweden from the UK, dial 00 46 followed by the area code (omitting the initial zero) followed by number. For Britain dial 009 44.

Time
GMT plus 1 (summer BST +1).

Public Holidays
New Year; Epiphany; Good Fri; Easter Mon; Labour Day; Ascension; Whit Sun/Mon; Mid-summer, Sat between 20-26 June; All Saints, Sat between 31 Oct-6 Nov; Christmas, 24-26 Dec.

Shops
Open Mon-Fri 09.00-18.00. Sat 09.00-13.00/16.00. In some large towns department stores remain open until 20.00/22.00.

Food: The Swedes generally eat fairly early. Lunch can start at 11.00, the evening meal at 18.00. A typical Swedish 'Smorgasbord' can be enjoyed all over the country.

Motoring
Roads are much quieter than in the UK. Secondary roads may be gravel surfaced but are still good. Dipped headlights are obligatory.

Speed Limits: Caravans and motorhomes (3.5 tons) 31 mph (50 kph) in built up areas; 50 mph (80 kph) on other roads for caravans. Motorhomes 44 - 56 mph (70 - 90 kph) on other roads and 56 - 69 mph (90 - 110 kph) on motorways.

Fuel: Away from large towns, petrol stations rarely open 24 hrs. Buy diesel during working hours, it is rarely available at self service pumps. Credit cards generally accepted except in some 24 hr stations where payment must be made in 20/100 kr notes.

Parking: Meters are in use in several larger towns.

Overnighting
Allowed in most areas, with the permission of the landowner.

Note: Mosquitos can be a problem in summer (from June) - go prepared.

Useful Addresses

National Motoring Organisations:
Motormannens Riksforbund (M),AIT, Sturegatan 32, Stockholm. Tel: 08 7823800.
Kungl Automobil Klubben (KAK)FIA, Gyllenstiernsgatan 4, 11526, Stockholm. Tel: 0860 0055.

The Gothenberg Gateway

Gothenberg is unusually well served for visiting campers with no fewer than five sites, four of which are run by leisure giant Liseberg (operator of the city's renowned theme park). Most central is Liseberg's **Karralund** site in a pleasant suburb only 2 miles east of the town centre; this is magnificently equipped but rather regimented and likely to be congested. Close by, in a lovely small nature park, is **Delsjo Camping**. Also run by Liseberg as a Karralund overflow, this site is basic and only open during peak summer holiday weeks. On the southern outskirts of the town are two sites: the small but friendly independent **Krono Camping**, located in a convenient but uninteresting suburb and Liseberg's leisure beach complex, **Askim Strand**, where tourers tend to be dominated by holiday villas, chalets, huts and statics. Although further out of town, Liseberg's latest acquisition, **Lilleby Havsbad**, is closest to Scandinavian Seaways Terminal. *continued overleaf*

SWEDEN - South

The **Lilleby Havsbad** campsite is easily accessible for the town centre by car or bus and is delightfully located in a rustic coast setting. With only 123 pitches it is also the smallest and there are no huts or statics. All the usual facilities are provided and serviced to a high standard. Details are as follows:

How to find it: Turn off E6 going north from Gothenberg on to Torslanda side road and then follow campsite signs.

General Details: Open May - September. Modern block with all facilities, including cooking. Small shop.

Charges 1997: Per unit Skr. 125 - 140.

Reservations: Contact site. Address: Lillebyvagen, 42353 Torslanda. Tel: 031/560 867. FAX: 031/561 605.

2645 Råå Vallar Camping, Råå, Helsingborg (Skåne)

Large, privately managed, seaside site with good facilities and swimming pool complex.

Convenient for the ferry terminal at Helsingborg, this is a very busy site and there is no doubt that it can become very crowded in high season and periods of good weather. Nevertheless, it provides a good stop over for those using the ferry port of Helsingborg on journeys to and from Denmark. The site has 450 marked and numbered pitches separated by tarmac roads and small hedges and shrubs, 218 of these have electricity (10A). The site also has 17 statics, 7 cottages and 5 caravans for hire. There are 5 sets of sanitary facilities (including those in the pool complex) which should be sufficient even when site is full. These have a good mix of showers (some without dividers and all without curtains) all have communal undressing and hot water on payment, washbasins (free hot water) and British style WCs. Although they are clean, the proximity to the beach means that sand and water is walked in all the time. Large laundry and three well equipped campers' kitchens, together with facilities for the disabled and babies. Other facilities include a new restaurant and bar complex, which serves reasonably priced meals until 11 pm. Takeaway. Small well stocked supermarket, video games arcade, TV room, children's playgrounds and bicycle hire. The excellent outdoor swimming pool complex is heated, with swimming instructors on hand daily and a lifeguard at all times. There are separate pools for children, beginners, and experienced swimmers. The pool complex is charged for but campers have 50% discount. Although some facilities are open very late, the site was fairly quiet at night when inspected.

How to find it: Turn off E6 motorway 5 km. south of Helsingborg Centrum onto road no 111 for Råå, drive towards the coast and follow campsite signs to site.

General Details: Open all year. Supermarket (24/5-31/8). Restaurant. Bar. Takeaway (all 30/4-31/8). Laundry. Cooking facilities. Swimming pool complex (1/6-18/8). Beach and promenade. Video games arcade. TV room. Children's playgrounds. Bicycle hire. Telephone. Caravans and cottages for hire.

Charges guide: Per unit Skr.90 - 105, acc. to unit size and season; electricity 6A 20 - 25, 10A 30 - 35.

Reservations: Essential in high season. Write to site for details. Address: Kustgatan, 252 70 Råå. Tel: 042/10.76.80. FAX: 042/26.10.10.

2640 Krono Camping Båstad-Torekov, Torekov, nr Båstad (Skåne)

Good quality site in natural woodland edging the sea on western Swedish coast north of Helsingborg.

This Krono camp is 500 m. from the fishing village of Torekov, 14 km. west of the home of the Swedish tennis WCT Open at Båstad on the stretch of coastline between Malmö and Göteborg. Useful en route from the most southerly ports, it is a very good site and worthy of a longer stay for relaxation. It has 450 large pitches, all numbered and marked, mainly in attractive natural woodland (mostly pine and birch), with some on more open ground close to the shore. Of these, 350 have electricity and cable TV, 77 also having water and drainage. Three very good sanitary blocks include a modern high quality one and two older blocks. Free hot water throughout and facilities in each block for cooking, dishwashing, babies and the disabled. A laundry is at the reception complex. This modern complex is professionally run and is also home for a good shop, two small boutiques, a snack bar with takeaway, restaurant, minigolf, and a new fisherman style bar (Zorba's), open until 1 am. The spacious site covers quite a large area and there is a cycle track along the shore to the beach with bathing. Tennis and golf close and fishing possible from the site. Several good children's play areas (games organised in high season) and an outdoor stage for musical entertainment and dancing (also in high season). This well run site is a pleasant place to stay.

How to find it: From E6 Malmö - Göteborg road take Torekov/Båstad exit and follow signs for 20 km. towards Torekov. Site is signed 1 km. before village on right.

General Details: Open 19 April - 15 Sept. Restaurant. Snack bar with takeaway. Bar. Shop and kiosk. Laundry. Cooking facilities. Minigolf. Sports fields. Children's play areas. Games, music and entertainment in high season. Bicycle hire. TV room. Beach. Tennis and golf close. Fishing. Motorcaravan service point. Telephone. Tourist information. Bungalows, tents and cabins for hire.

Charges guide: Per unit Skr. 130 -170; electricity/TV connection 40. Credit cards accepted.

Reservations: Write to site for details. Address: 260 93 Torekov. Tel: 0431/64525. FAX: 0431/64625.

2650 Skånes Djurparks Camping, Jularp, Höör (Skåne)

Unique, small, friendly, family run site in conservation area with unusual features and attractions.

This site is probably one of the most unusual we featur. It is adjacent to the Skånes Djurpark, a zoo park with Scandinavian species, and has on site a reconstructed Stone Age Village. The site is in a sheltered valley and has 90 large, level grassy pitches all with 10A electricity, a few with waste water drain, and a separate area for tents. A small, heated, family swimming pool is behind reception, a mini shop and a children's playground. A restaurant is just outside the entrance. The most unusual feature is the sanitary block - it is underground! The air-conditioned building houses superb and ample facilities including roomy showers in private cubicles, washbasins and British style WCs, 2 fully equipped kitchens, laundry and separate drying room and an enormous dining/TV room. Facilities for disabled people and baby changing. Free hot water. The site has a number of underground, caveman style, 8 bed (dormitory type) holiday units for families or groups. They open onto a circular courtyard with barbecue/camp fire area and have access to the kitchens and dining room in the sanitary block. There are good walks through the nature park and around the lakes, where one can see deer, birds and other wildlife. A site for discerning campers who want something distinctly different.

How to find it: Turn off no.23 road 2 km. north of Höör (at roundabout) and follow signs for Skånes Djurpark. Camp entrance is off the Djurpark car park.

General Details: Open all year. Mini-shop. Swimming pool. Restaurant nearby. Cooking facilities. Laundry. Children's playground. Stone Age Village. Apartments for hire. Telephone. Tourist information. Chemical disposal.

Charges 1998: Per unit Skr. 110; electricity 20 (summer) - 30 (winter). Credit cards accepted.

Reservations: Recommended for high season (July/Aug). Write to site for details. Address: Skånes Djurparks Camping, Jularp, 243 93 Höör. Tel: 0413/53270. FAX: 0413/200 61. E-mail: lotta.nordstrom@hoor.mail.telia.com.

2655 Tingsryds Camping, Tingsryd (Småland)

Pleasant, well managed municipal site by Lake Tiken, well placed for Sweden's Glass District.

Tingsryds' 129 large pitches are arranged in rows divided by trees and shrubs, with some along the edge of a lakeside path (public have access). All have electricity (10A) and there is shade in parts. Access is from a tarmac perimeter road and the facilities are housed in buildings near the entrance, with the reception building having the restaurant, cafe, bar and a small shop. The sanitary installations are in two buildings, one housing showers with curtains (on payment, communal undressing), washbasins and British style WCs, the other a campers' kitchen with hobs and dishwashing sinks and further sinks outside under cover (hot water from separate tap), laundry, facilities for the disabled, and changing rooms for the sports activities. Although these facilities are in the older style, all are well maintained and very clean. Adjacent is a small beach, children's playground, 3 tennis courts and a riding stables. Hire of canoes, fishing and minigolf are on site (public access also). Two large supermarkets, a heated indoor 'Waterworld', bowling alley, and further shops and restaurants in the town (1½ km), which can be reached via a level footpath/cycle track. The town hosts a Folk Festival and Market in July. This site is an ideal place from which to explore the factories and shops of the 'Kingdom of Crystal'.

How to find it: Site is 1½ km. from Tingsryd off road no. 120. Well signed around the town.

General Details: Open 1 April - 20 Oct. Shop (1/5-15/9). Restaurant, cafe, bar (1/5-15/9). Tennis. Riding. Minigolf. Children's playground. Lake swimming. Canoe hire. Fishing. Telephones. Tourist information. Laundry. Site lit at night. Cooking facilities. Chemical disposal. Motorcaravan services. Cabins for rent.

Charges 1998: Per unit incl. electricity Skr. 110 - 130. Credit cards accepted.

Reservations: Recommended for high season. Write to site. Address: 362 32 Tingsryd. Tel: 0477/10554 (season) or 0477/11825 (off-season). FAX: 0477/11825. Internet: www.camping.se.

2660 Ägårds Lantgårdscamping, Hillerstorp (Småland)

Small, tranquil site with simple facilities, home cooking and a warm welcome.

On an old Swedish farm, this site is adjacent to the Store Mosse National Park. The most delightful thing about this family run site, apart from its quiet location, is the wonderful home cooking straight from the farmhouse kitchen. Fresh bread is available every morning and you can sample traditional meals and barbecues (order in advance). The site has 80 large pitches set on open meadows near the farmhouse and facilities, 50 of these with electricity (10A). The simple new sanitary block houses roomy hot showers, washbasins and British style WCs, facilities for babies and the disabled, with dishwashing sinks at one end (free hot water). The site is not lit. Children will love it here with a variety of farm animals and birds to watch. Swimming and fishing are possible in local lakes and the nearby Store Mosse National Park provides ample opportunities for walking, cycling and naturalist pursuits.

How to find it: Site is 4 km. south of Hillerstorp on road no.152. Turn at sign to Ägårds and site.

General Details: Open all year. Shop, home cooking and meals (both 30/4-30/9). Telephone. Tourist information. Farm animals. Children's playground. Walking, swimming, cycling and fishing near. 3 or 4 mobile homes to rent.

Charges guide: Per unit Skr. 100; electricity 25. Credit cards accepted.

Reservations: Nearly always space. Address: 330 33 Hillerstorp. Tel: 0370/22007. FAX: 0370/22270.

SWEDEN - South

2665 SweCamp Rosenlunds, Jönköping (Småland)

Town site overlooking Lake Vättern, ideal for visiting the important city of Jönköping.

Rosenlunds is a good site, useful as a break in the journey across Sweden or visiting the city during a tour of the Lakes. It is on raised ground overlooking the lake, with some shelter in parts. There are 350 pitches on well kept grass which, on one side, slopes away from reception. Some pitches on the other side of reception are flat and have hardstandings and there are 200 electrical (10A), 100 cable TV and 40 water connections. The owners have refurbished and extended the sanitary facilities which include hot showers (some in cubicles), washbasins and British style WCs, plus provision for the disabled and babies. There is a laundry, dishwashing facilities, a well stocked shop and a TV room. Swimming pools are close and a `Sommarland' (leisure centre with pools and activities) in the city. Jönköping is one of Sweden's oldest trading centres with a Charter dating back to 1284 and several outstanding attractions. These must include the Calle Ornemark wood carving centre at Riddersberg Manor, the museums of the `Safety match', ceramics and weaponry and, particularly, the superb troll artistry of John Bauer.

How to find it: Site well signed from E4 on eastern side of Jönköping. Watch carefully for exit on this fast road.

General Details: Open all year. Shop. Restaurant 500 m. Swimming pools close. Playground. TV room. Bicycle hire. Minigolf. Laundry facilities. Telephone. Tourist information. Caravans, rooms and cottages for hire.

Charges guide: Per unit incl. all persons Skr. 110; electricity 25.

Reservations: Recommended for July - write to site for details. Address: Korallvägen 26, 554 54 Jönköping. Tel: 036/122863. FAX: 036/126687.

2670 Grännastrandens Familjecamp, Gränna (Småland)

Large, lakeside site with modern facilities and busy continental feel, below the old city of Gränna.

Flat fields separate Gränna from the shore, one of which is occupied by the 25 acres of Grännastrandens where there are 500 numbered pitches, including a tent area and some pitches which are seasonally reserved. The site is flat, spacious and very regularly laid out on open ground with only a row of poplars by the lake to provide shelter, so a windbreak may prove useful against any onshore breeze. About 260 pitches have electrical connections and there is a good internal road system. There is one large, sanitary block in the centre of the site with modern, well kept facilities which include British style WCs, some with external access, washbasins and hot showers in private cubicles (on payment). There are dish and clothes washing sinks, laundry facilities and provision for disabled people, with a further small, older block by reception. Part of the lake is walled off to form an attractive swimming area with sandy beaches, slides and islands. Obviously the great attraction here is the lake. It offers beaches, bathing, fishing, sailing and superb coastal walks. Outstanding, however, is the 30 minute ferry crossing from the tiny harbour next to the site to Visingsö, the beautiful island reputedly inhabited for over 6,000 years, complete with its gentle tour by horse drawn `remmalag'. Gränna is also the home of the famous peppermint rock which you can watch being made. In the Hallska Gården in the old city centre you will also find potteries, paper makers, basket weavers and goldsmiths. Gränna is also the centre of hot air ballooning and on 11 July each year there are ascents from Sweden's only `balloon airport'.

How to find it: Take Gränna exit from E4 road (no camping sign) 40 km. north of Jönköping. Site is signed in the centre of the town, towards the harbour and ferry.

General Details: Open 1 May - 30 Sept. Shop. Café outside site (1/5-31/8) or town restaurants close. TV room. Children's playground. Lake swimming area. Boating and fishing. Telephone. Laundry and drying. Cooking facilities. Chemical disposal. Cabins and rooms to let.

Charges 1998: Per unit Skr. 120, with electricity 150. Credit cards accepted.

Reservations: Write to site for details. Address: Grännastrandens Familjecamp, Box 14, 563 21 Gränna, Småland. Tel: 0390/10706. FAX: 0390/30059.

2675 Lysingsbadet Camping, Västervik (Småland)

Large site with unrivalled views of the `Pearl of the East Coast' - Västervik and its fjords and islands.

One of the largest sites in Scandinavia, Lysingsbadet has around 1,000 large, mostly marked and numbered pitches, spread over a vast area of rocky promontory and set on different plateau, terraces, in valleys and woodland, or beside the water. It is a very attractive site, and one which never really looks or feels crowded even when busy. There are 83 full service pitches with TV, water and electricity, 163 with TV and electricity and 540 with electricity only, the remainder for tents. Reception is smart, efficient and friendly with good English spoken. The 10 modern sanitary blocks of various ages and designs house a comprehensive mix of showers, basins and WCs. All contain good quality fittings and are kept very clean. There are several campers' kitchens with dishwashing sinks, cookers and hoods, also 4 laundry rooms. Free hot water throughout and all facilities free of charge. Campers are issued with `key cards' which not only operate the entrance barriers, but are used to gain access to sanitary blocks, swimming pool complex and other facilities. A further sanitary block with showers, changing rooms, basins, lockers and British style WCs serves the pool complex. An hourly bus service to Västervik runs from the site entrance May-Sept. *continued overleaf*

330

2675 Lysingsbadet Camping (continued)

On site are a full golf course, minigolf, heated outdoor swimming pool complex, children's playgrounds, boat hire, tennis, basketball, volleyball and fishing. A licensed restaurant is supplemented by a café/takeaway and a range of shops. For children, Astrid Lindgren's World theme park at Vimmerby is an easy day trip and for adults the delights of the old town of Västervik and its shopping.

How to find it: Turn off the E22 for Västervik and keep straight on at all junctions until you see the first campsite sign. Follow signs to site.

General Details: Open all year. Supermarket and shops, restaurant and café/takeaway (all 1/6-31/8). Cooking facilities. Laundries. Hairdresser. Swimming pool complex (1/6-31/8). Golf. Minigolf. Tennis. Basketball. Volleyball. Boat hire. Fishing. Entertainment and dances in high season. Children's playgrounds. Quick Stop service. Telephones. Motorcaravan services. Hotel rooms, cabins and caravans for rent. Tourist information. Bus service.

Charges guide: Per unit Skr. 70-150, acc.to unit, pitch type and season; electricity 30. Credit cards accepted.

Reservations: Advisable for peak season (July/Aug). Write to site for details. Address: 593 53 Västervik. Tel: 0490/36795. FAX: 0490/36175.

2680 Krono Camping Saxnäs, Färjestaden (Öland)

Large site well placed for touring Sweden's Riviera - fascinating and beautiful island of Öland.

This family owned site, part of the Krono group, has 490 marked and numbered pitches arranged in rows on open, well kept grassland dotted with a few trees, all with electricity (10A). A further unmarked area without electricity can accommodate around 60 tents. 320 of these pitches also have TV connections and a further 116 also have water connections. The site has about 125 long stay units and 16 cabins for rent. Reception is efficient and friendly with good English spoken and comprehensive tourist information. Three sanitary blocks provide a good supply of roomy private showers, washbasins, some washbasin/WC suites and WCs. There are also facilities for babies and the disabled. Good, well equipped laundry room and good campers' kitchen facilities with cookers, microwaves and dishwasher (free) together with dishwashing sinks. Free hot water throughout. The site has a licensed restaurant, pizzeria, café, shop, minigolf, volleyball and football field and a good children's playground. In high season a crèche and children's games are organised. Dances are held on Wed/Sat in season with other activities on other evenings. The beach is sandy, slopes very gently and is very safe for children. Nearby attractions include the 7 km. long Öland road bridge, Kalmar and its castle, museums and old town on the mainland, Eketorp prehistoric fortified village, Öland Djurpark and many old windmills.

How to find it: Cross the Öland road bridge from Kalmar on road no. 137. Take exit for Öland Djurpark/Saxnäs, then follow campsite signs. Site is just north of the end of the bridge.

General Details: Open 2 May - 20 Sept. Shop (May-Aug). Pizzeria, licensed restaurant and café (all May-Aug). Children's playground and crèche. Beach with volleyball. Fishing. Bicycle hire. Minigolf. Football. Family entertainment and activities organised. Telephones. Tourist information. Laundry. Cooking facilities. Chemical disposal. Motorcaravan services. Cabins for rent.

Charges 1998: Per unit Skr. 125 - 175, with electricity 155 - 205 with TV also 165 - 220. Weekend and weekly rates available. Credit cards accepted.

AR'Discount

Less 10%

Reservations: Essential for high season (July/Aug). Write to site. Address: 386 95 Färjestaden, Öland. Tel: 0485/35700. FAX: 0485/35664. E-mail: kronocamping.saxnas@saxnasturism.se.

2700 Borås Camping, Borås (Västergotland)

Pleasant municipal site in a park setting 2 km. north of the city centre.

Borås Camping is within easy walking distance of a swimming pool complex, Djurpark and shopping centre, and is convenient for ferries to and from Göthenberg. On the outskirts of Borås, this tidy, well managed site provides 490 large, numbered, level pitches, carefully arranged in rows on well kept grass with good tarmac perimeter roads. There is some shade. Seven good, clean sanitary blocks provide hot showers, washbasins, WCs and facilities for babies and the disabled, in various combinations, most opening directly from outside. Good campers' kitchens with hobs and dishwashing sinks (free of charge) and laundry facilities are provided. Many activities are available both on the site and nearby, many free to campers; the excellent outdoor heated pool complex, Alidebergsbadet, is only 400 m. Canoes and pedaloes are available on the small canal running through the site. Small shop for necessities and fast food service. Also on site is a Youth Hostel and many cabins for rent. The shopping precinct at Knalleland is only 500 m, the Zoo (Djurpark) is 400 m. The site can issue the 'Boråscard' which gives free and discounted access to city car parks, transport, museums and attractions during your stay.

How to find it: Exit road no. 40 from Göthenberg for Borås Centrum and follow signs to Djurpark and road no. 42 to Trollhåtten through the town. Turn left to site.

General Details: Open all year. Shop. Takeaway. Laundry. Cooking facilities. Several children's playgrounds. Minigolf. Swimming, tennis, frisbee, badminton, football, croquet, table tennis, jogging tracks, basketball all nearby. Telephones. Motorcaravan service point. Tourist information. Cabins for rent.

Charges guide: Per unit Skr. 135; motorcycle and tent 95; electricity 25.

Reservations: One should always find room here. Address: 500 04 Borås. Tel: 033/121434. FAX: 033/140582.

2710 Krono Camping Lidköping, Lidköping - Lake Vänern (Västergotland)

High quality, attractive site with lake and leisure facilities.

This attractive site provides about 430 pitches on flat, well kept grass. It is surrounded by some mature trees, with the lake shore as one boundary and a number of tall pines have been left to provide shade and shelter. There are 274 pitches with electricity (10A) and TV connections and 91 with water and drainage also, together with 60 cabins for rent. A tour operator takes a few pitches. Excellent, modern sanitary facilities are provided in two identical blocks with under-floor heating, attractive decor and lighting (and music), and there is free hot water throughout. They have controllable hot showers (in roomy private cubicles with divider, hooks and seat), partitioned washbasins, British style WCs, make up and hairdressing areas with mirrors, electric points and shelves, baby room and facilities for the disabled. Dishwashing sinks are outside each block. Good kitchens with cookers and microwaves. There is a laundry, a small shop (shopping centre very close) and a coffee bar with conservatory seating area in the reception complex. Very good playgrounds are provided for the children, together with a play field, TV room (cartoon videos shown) and an amusement and games room. Solarium, bicycle hire, minigolf and volleyball. The lake is available for watersports, boating and fishing with bathing from the sandy beach or there is a swimming pool complex (free for campers) adjacent to the site.

How to find it: From Lidköping town junctions follow signs towards Läckö then pick up camping signs turning right at second roundabout. Continue to site on left (½-1 km).

General Details: Open 13 April - 15 Sept (full services 13/6-14/8). Small shop. Coffee bar with snacks. Minigolf. Volleyball. Solarium. Children's playgrounds. TV room. Games and amusements room. Bicycle hire. Play field. Laundry facilities. Cooking room. Swimming pool adjacent. Lake swimming, fishing and watersports. Motorcaravan services. Telephone. Tourist information.

Charges guide: Per unit on pitch with electricity Skr. 121 -151; pitch with electricity and TV connection 161 - 191; with water and drainage also 181 - 211; cyclist or m/cycle with tent 91.

Reservations: Write to site. Address: Läckögatan, 531 54 Lidköping. Tel: 0510/26804. FAX: 0510/21135.

2720 Hökensås Holiday Village and Camp Site, Tidaholm (Västergotland)

Well run site and holiday complex in wild, unspoiled national park.

This good site is part of a holiday complex including wooden cabins for rent. It is relaxed and informal, with over 200 pitches either under trees or on a more open area at the far end, divided into rows by wooden rails. These are numbered and electricity is available on 130. Tents can go on the large grassy open areas by reception. The original, recently refurbished, sanitary block near reception has been supplemented by a newer one in the wooded area. These provide free hot showers with communal undressing and curtained cubicles, open washbasins and WCs. Separate saunas for each sex and facilities for the disabled and babies. A campers' kitchen is at each block with cooking, dish-washing and laundry facilities (irons on loan from reception). A children's playground, tennis court and minigolf are provided near the entrance and there is a small, but well stocked shop with a comprehensive angling section. A café with tables on a terrace outside also serves takeaway snacks. Hökensås is located just west of Lake Vättern and south of Tidaholm, in a beautiful national park of wild, unspoiled scenery. The park is based on a 100 km. ridge, a glacier area with many impressive boulders and ice age debris but now thickly forested with majestic pines and silver birches, with a small, brilliant lake at every corner. The forests and lakes provide wonderful opportunities for walking, cycling (gravel tracks and marked walks) angling, swimming and when the snow falls, winter sports.

How to find it: Approach site from no. 195 western lake coast road. at Brandstorp, about 40 km. north of Jönköping, turn west at petrol station and camp sign signed Hökensås. Site is about 9 km. up this road.

General Details: Open all year. Café with takeaway. Sauna. Laundry. Cooking facilities. Children's playground. Tennis. Minigolf. Shop. Lake swimming. Fishing. Telephone. Tourist information. Cabins for hire.

Charges guide: Per unit Skr. 93-110 (more for Midsummer celebrations); electricity 28.

Reservations: Write to site for details. Address: Blåhult, 522 91 Tidaholm. Tel: 0502/23053.

2730 Ekudden Camping, Mariestad - Lake Vänern (Västergotland)

Well established site on the eastern shore of Lake Vänern with swimming pools adjacent.

Ekudden occupies a long stretch of the lake shore to the south of the town, in a mixed woodland setting, and next door to the municipal complex of heated outdoor pools and sauna. The lake, of course, is also available for swimming or boating and there are bicycles, tandems and canoes for hire. The spacious site can take 425 units and there are about 160 electrical hook-ups (10A). Most pitches are under the trees but some at the far end of the site are on more open ground (without electricity) with good views over the lake but some distance from the facilities. Sanitary facilities are provided in three low wooden cabins all of which have been recently refurbished or renewed. These have hot showers (on payment with token from reception) some with curtains and communal undressing, some in private cubicles, and both open and cubicled washbasins .   *continued overleaf*

2730 Ekudden Camping (continued)

There are facilities for the disabled with good access ramps and baby changing rooms. All are clean and well maintained. There are two kitchens with dishwashing (free hot water) and other covered sinks, outside in groups of four (cold water only) around the site. The site becomes very busy in high season.

How to find it: Site is south of the town and well signed at junctions on the ring road and from E20 motorway.

General Details: Open 1 May - 15 Sept. (full services 15/6-16/8). Shop. Takeaway (in high season). Cooking facilities. Swimming pools adjacent. Canoes, bicycles and tandems for hire. Children's playground. Minigolf. TV room. Laundry. Lake swimming, boating and fishing. Telephone. Tourist information. Mobile homes for hire.

Charges guide: Per unit Skr. 95 - 120, acc. to season; electricity 30.

Reservations: Essential in high season. Write to site. Address: 542 01 Mariestad. Tel 0501/10637.

2740 Laxsjöns Camping Och Friluftsgård, Dals Långed (Dalsland)

Lakeside site with swimming pool in beautiful Dalsland region.

Laxsjöns is an all year round site, catering for winter sports enthusiasts as well as summer tourists. On the shores of the lake, the site is in two main areas - one flat, near the entrance, with hardstandings and the other on an attractive, sloping, grassy area adjoining. In total there are 300 places available for caravans or motorcaravans, all with electricity, plus more for tents. Rooms and cabins are also available for rent. A good, modern toilet block has hot showers on payment (communal undressing), open washbasins, WCs and a hairdressing cubicle with free dryer. With a further small block at the top of the site, the provision should be adequate. Other services include a shop, laundry, clothes drying rooms for bad weather, cooking rooms for tenters and provision for the disabled. Outside there is a good swimming pool (1.9 m, open 10 am - 9 pm.) with paddling pool, minigolf, unusual table top minigolf, tennis, trampoline and a playground. There is a restaurant at the top of the site with a good range of dishes in high season. In addition, there is a lake for swimming, fishing and canoeing (boats available). The site is located in the centre of Dalsland, west of Lake Vänern, in an area of deep forests, endless lakes and river valleys, and is one of the loveliest and most interesting regions in this always peaceful and scenic country.

How to find it: From Åmål take road no. 164 to Bengtfors, then the 172 towards Dals Långed. Site is signed about 5 km. south of the town 1 km. down a good road.

General Details: Open all year. Restaurant (high season). Shop. Laundry and drying facilities. Cooking facilities. Tennis. Minigolf. Sauna. Children's playground. Swimming pool. Lake for swimming, Fishing and boating. Telephone.

Charges guide: Per unit up to 4 persons Skr. 95 - 120, with electricity 140; tent 100 - 105; 1 person tent 75; additional person 40; shower 5 (3 mins).

Reservations: Advisable in peak season. Write to site for details. Address: 660 10 Dals Långed, Dalsland. Tel: 0531/30010. FAX: 0531/30555.

2750 Sommarvik Fritidscenter, Årjäng (West Värmland)

Good quality site in beautiful surroundings beside lake Västra Silen, for family holidays.

Sommarvik has some 250 large, separated and numbered pitches arranged in terraces on a pine wooded hillside, some overlooking the lake; 100 of these have electrical connections and 30 are all service pitches. It offers much in the way of outdoor pursuits and peaceful countryside. The site is served by 5 sanitary blocks which house a good mix of private shower cubicles (hot water on payment), washbasins (free hot water), WCs, family bathrooms, and facilities for the disabled and baby changing. All are kept clean. In addition there are good campers' kitchens with cookers and sinks, and laundry facilities. The site has 43 cabins for rent, 40 long stay units, with a youth hostel and conference centre. A very large and smart restaurant offers a full range of meals, soft drinks, beers and wines, plus takeaway. Activities include swimming in the lake from a sandy beach (safe for children), canoe hire, windsurfing, rowing boats, fishing, sauna, tennis, football field, organised Elk safaris, minigolf, quizzes, guided walks, horse riding, and there are good children's playgrounds. The site also organises local folk music during the main season. You can ride trolleys around the area on disused railway tracks or take a day trip to go gold panning. The site is within easy reach of the Norwegian border and Oslo. Skiing is available (when there is snow) and an indoor swimming pool complex is 3 km. in Årjäng. This is a very scenic region and one which makes an ideal base for a family holiday with lots of activities and sightseeing trips.

How to find it: Site signed from road no. 172 - 1 km. south of Årjäng Centrum. Site is 3 km.. from town centre.

General Details: Open all year. Restaurant and takeaway (2/6-25/8). Shop (1/5-25/9). Cooking facilities. Laundry. Minigolf. Lake swimming. Canoe, row boat and windsurfer hire. Fishing. Tennis. Sauna. Football field. Children's playgrounds. Horse riding. Range of organised activities. Telephone. Motorcaravan services. 'Quick stop' pitches for overnight stays. Cabins for hire. Tourist information.

Charges guide: Per tent Skr. 90 - 140; caravan or motorcaravan 110 - 200; electricity included. Credit cards accepted.

Reservations: Recommended for peak seasons (summer and winter). Write to site for details. Address: 672 00 Årjäng. Tel: 0573/12060. FAX: 0573/12048.

SWEDEN - West / Central

2760 Frykenbaden Camping, Kil (Värmland)

Quiet, friendly site on the shores of Lake Fryken.

Frykenbaden Camping is in a wooded area and takes 250 units on grassy meadows surrounded by trees. One area nearer the lake is gently sloping, the other is flat with numbered pitches arranged in rows. There are 125 pitches with electricity, satellite TV and phone connections and a further 25 with electricity only. Reception, a small shop and takeaway are located in a traditional Swedish house surrounded by lawns sloping down to the shore, with minigolf, a children's play barn and playground, with pet area, also close by. The main sanitary block is also here. It is of good quality and heated in cool weather with showers on payment, open washbasins, a laundry room and room for families or the disabled. With a further small block with equally good facilities, the overall supply is better than average for Swedish sites. Well equipped camper's kitchen with ovens, hobs and sinks together with tables and benches and separate fish cleaning sinks near the lake. Swimming and canoeing are possible in the lake as well as fishing in the sites' own area (payment per kg. caught). There is a good value restaurant at the adjacent golf club which can be reached by a pleasant walk. Fryken is a long, narrow lake, said to be one of the deepest in Sweden, and it is a centre for angling. Frykenbadens Camping is on the southern shore, and is a quiet, relaxing place to stay away from the busier, more famous lakes. There are plenty of other activities in the area (golf, riding, ski-ing in winter) and Kil is not too far from the Norwegian border.

How to find it: Site is signed from the no. 61 Karlstad - Arvika road, then 4 km. towards lake following signs.

General Details: Open 15 May - 15 Sept. (full service 15/6-16/8). Small shop. Snack bar and Takeaway. Minigolf. Children's play barn and playground. Campers' kitchen. Fishing from site with rods for hire. Lake swimming. Canoes and bicycles for hire. Telephone. Tourist Information. Cabins for rent.

Charges guide: Per unit 13/6-16/8 Skr. 110, other times 90, electricity 25; TV connection 15; showers 3-5.

Reservations: Write to site. Address: Frykenbaden PL. 1405, 665 00 Kil. Tel: 0554/40940.

2800 Glyttinge Camping, Linköping (Östergötland)

Top quality site with enthusiastic and friendly management.

Only 5 minutes by car from the new Ikea Shopping Mall and adjacent to a good swimming pool complex, Glyttinge is a most attractive site with a mix of terrain - some flat, some sloping and some woodland. It is maintained to a very high standard and there are flowers, trees and shrubs everywhere giving it a cosy garden like atmosphere. There are 239 good size, mostly level pitches of which 125 have electricity (10A). The main centrally located sanitary block (supplemented by additional facilities at reception) is modern, well constructed and exceptionally well equipped and maintained. It provides showers in cubicles with divider, washbasins, and WC suites with basins, hand dryers and soothing music! Excellent separate facilities for disabled people, a solarium, laundry and baby rooms. The superb kitchen and dining/TV room is equipped with everything you could possibly need to prepare and enjoy a meal. Hot water is free throughout. Children are well catered for with a wonderful fenced and safe children's play area and parents can rent (minimal charge) tricycles, pedal cars, scooters and carts. Wet weather playroom for children, shop with gifts, fresh bread, milk, soft drinks and ices are sold. Takeaway snacks. Minigolf, football field and bicycle hire. Adjacent is a heated outdoor swimming pool complex with 3 pools (charged). Bus stop at camp gate. Attractions nearby include the town of Linköping, Aviation Museum, Land Museum and the new Ikea Shopping Mall.

How to find it: Exit the E4 Helsingborg - Stockholm road north of Linköping at signs for Ikea and site. Turn right at traffic lights and camp sign and follow signs to site.

General Details: Open 1 April - 31 Oct. Shop and takeaway (24/6-26/8). Cooking facilities and dining/TV room. Laundry. Swimming pool complex (adjacent. 1/5-26/8). Minigolf. Football. Bicycle hire. Children's playground. Cabins for hire. Motorcaravan services. Telephones. Bus stop. Tourist information.

Charges 1997: Per unit Skr. 115 - 140; electricity 30. Credit cards accepted.

Reservations: Recommended for July/Aug. Write to site for details. Address: Berggardsvagen, 582 49 Linköping. Tel: 013/174928. FAX: 013/175923.

2810 Vätterviksbadet Camping, Vadstena, Östergötland (Lake Vättern)

Large and busy, municipal site on the shore of Lake Vättern.

This is an acceptable site for overnighters or short stays on one of the main north south routes. The site has some 550 mostly marked and numbered pitches separated by low wooden rails on flat grass between the road and lake. Of these, 292 have electricity (10A). Some shade in parts and although the main areas of the site are lit, torches may be required at the furthest extremities. The site is very long and narrow and it is quite a walk to facilities from the distant ends of the site. There is some road noise and many long stay units on site. The site is fenced and the barrier is locked promptly at 10 pm. The three sanitary blocks are of varying ages and designs, the oldest at the northern end of the site. All contain a mix of cold water and free hot water facilities. *continued overleaf*

334

2810 Vätterviksbadet Camping (continued)

There are some private shower cubicles, some with divider seat and curtain and some with communal undressing. There is a good supply of washbasins, but rather fewer WCs and hand dryers. In addition there are limited facilities for the disabled and a baby changing room. Two small kitchens have basic facilities, and there is a small laundry at each of the two newer blocks - mostly cold water. The site has a good shop and take-away service, a waterslide pool and one can swim from the safe sandy beach at the lake. The water is very shallow here and safe for children.

How to find it: Site is alongside the no. 50 Jönköping - Örebro road, 3 km. north of Vadstena.

General Details: Open 30 April -13 Sept. Shop. Takeaway. Laundry. Cooking facilities. Lake swimming. Waterslide pool. Minigolf. Volleyball. Children's playground. Telephone. Car wash. Tourist information.

Charges guide: Per unit Skr. 110; electricity 25.

Reservations: Essential for peak season (July/Aug). Write to site for details. Address: 592 80 Vadstena. Tel: 0143/12730. FAX: 0143/15190.

2820 Skantzö Bad Camping, Hallstahammar (Västmanland)

Attractive, well maintained municipal site beside Strömsholms Kanal between Örebro and Stockholm.
A very comfortable and pleasant site just off the main E18 motorway from Oslo to Stockholm, this has 186 large marked and numbered pitches, 150 of these with electricity (10A). The terrain is flat and grassy and there is good shade in parts. The site is well fenced and locked at night. There are 17 new alpine style cabins for rent with window boxes of colourful flowers. Reception is very friendly. The sanitary block serving the camping area is located in the reception area and is maintained and equipped to a high standard, providing free hot showers (now in private cubicles with washbasin), basins (free hot water) and WCs, facilities for disabled people and baby changing. In addition there are good campers' kitchen facilities, a good laundry with drying room/lines, washing machine and dryer. Barbecue grill area. Cafeteria, fresh bread and milk, etc sold. Very large, fenced, outdoor, heated swimming pool and waterslide, children's playground, tennis courts, minigolf and games area complex (free to campers). Direct access to the towpath of the Stromsholms Kanal and nearby is the Kanal Museum. The site provides hire and transportation of canoes for longer canal tours.

How to find it: Turn off E18 at Hallstahammar and follow road no. 252 to north of town centre and signs to site.

General Details: Open 1 May - 31 August. Cafeteria and shop (10/5-20/8). Swimming pool and waterslide (20/5-23/8). Minigolf. Tennis. Children's playground. Bicycle hire. Canoe hire. Telephone. Conference room. Tourist information. Cooking facilities. Laundry. Chemical disposal. Motorcaravan services. Cabins for hire.

Charges 1997: Per unit Skr. 100; electricity 30. Credit cards accepted.

Reservations: Write to site. Address: Box 506, 734 27 Hallstahammar. Tel: 0220/24305. FAX: 0220/24187.

2830 Ängby Camping, Bromma (Stockholm North)

Good short stay or transit site on the edge of Lake Mälaren, close to central Stockholm.
Of all the sites close to central Stockholm, this appears to be the best option, being only some 500 m. walk from the Metro that takes you to the heart of the city in 15 minutes. The site also sells the famous `Stockholm Card' which gives unlimited access to transport and most attractions throughout the city. The site can accommodate around 150 units with easy access. Some level pitches are behind reception, others on the wooded hillside area nearer the lake - all with electricity (10A), satellite TV to around half the pitches. There is a separate area for tents. Reception is friendly with good English spoken. The sanitary installations are in two recently refurbished and heated blocks, one serving the camping area, the other the cabins. They provide hot showers on payment with divider and curtain (communal undressing), basins (free hot water), and WC/hand basin units (cold water). Campers' kitchens have sinks, ovens and hobs and a laundry (hot water on payment). Facilities for the disabled. A cafeteria serves coffee, pastries, beer, soft drinks and takeaway. Breakfasts served in main season. There is some road noise and campers do leave early and return very late, as one would expect in this situation. There is a guard in reception all night, a guard dog is kennelled at the gate, the owner lives opposite and the police visit regularly - it all adds to the feeling of security for campers. The site is adjacent to a small park with a water slide and pool (open when weather warm enough), minigolf, children's playground, café and bathing beach. Fine lakeside walks on good footpaths and a jogging track from the site. Fishing and canoe hire. It is also possible to hike or cycle to Drottningholm Palace and gardens from the site.

How to find it: Leave E18 at exit for road no.275 and drive towards Vallingby/Brommaplan; then turn right off the 275 for S. Angby and site.

General Details: Open all year. Cafeteria and takeaway (15/5-31/8). Small shop (15/5-31/8). Sauna. Fishing. Minigolf. Water slide. Children's playground. Games room. Jogging track. Canoe hire. Good security. Telephone. Tourist information. Cooking facilities. Laundry. Chemical disposal. Motorcaravan services. Cabins for rent. Tennis courts, supermarket and restaurant 400 m. Indoor swimming pool 1 km.

Charges 1998: Per unit Skr. 120 - 190, acc. to unit type and season; electricity 25;

Reservations: Essential in peak season. Write to site for details. Address: Blackebergstr. 27, 168 50 Bromma. Tel: 08/370420. FAX: 08/378226.

SWEDEN - East

2840 Stockholm SweCamp Flottsbro, Huddinge

Neat, quiet lakeside site with ski slope and good security 18 km. south of Stockholm.

Flottsbro is a small site with good quality facilities and very good security, located some 18 km. south of Stockholm. There are 74 large numbered pitches for caravans and motorhomes and a separate unmarked area for tents. Pitches are arranged on level terraces, but the site itself is sloping and the reception and restaurant are at the bottom with all the ski facilities and further good sanitary facilities with sauna. The main site road is tarmac. At the time of inspection, there was only one sanitary block on the camping area but an additional one has been opened to serve the tenting area. The modern facilities include free private hot showers, WCs and washbasins, a suite for disabled people, baby changing facilities and a family bathroom. An excellent campers' kitchen has electric cookers and sinks with hot water, all free of charge. Small laundry with washing machine, dryer and sink. The reception area is remote from the entrance but a very good security system is in place, campers have keys to the barrier and sanitary installations, there is a night guard and an entry phone/camera surveillance system on the entrance for good measure. Once you have negotiated the entry phone you will find a friendly and more personal service at reception. Do not be tempted to walk to reception from the gate, it is a long way down and a steep climb back. Other facilities on site include the ski slope and lift, restaurant which serves simple meals and snacks, beer, tea, coffee and soft drinks. The site has a small lakeside beach and grassy lying out area with children's playground and plenty of room for ball games. Also minigolf, volleyball, frisbee, jogging track, canoe hire. A large supermarket and the local rail station are 10 minutes by car. The area is also good for walking, cycling and cross-country skiing.

How to find it: Turn off the E4 at Vårby/Huddinge and turn left on road no.259. After 2 km. turn right and follow signs to Flottsbro.

General Details: Open all year. Restaurant. Sauna. Minigolf. Volleyball. Frisbee. Jogging track. Canoe hire. Children's playground. Telephone. Tourist information. Cooking facilities. Laundry. Chemical disposal. Motorcaravan services. Cabins for rent.

Charges 1997: Per unit Skr. 160 with electricity, 130 without; small tent 95. Credit cards accepted.

Reservations: Advisable for both summer and winter peak times. Write to site for details. Address: Box 1216, 141 25 Huddinge. Tel: 08/7785860. FAX: 08/7785755.

2835 Orsa Grönklitt Camping, Orsa (Dalarna)

Quiet, budget priced site, adjacent to the Grönklitt Bear Park

Primarily designed for winter, with a ski slope adjacent, the site is a rather large and featureless, gravel hardstanding, providing room for more than 50 units with electricity (10A) available to all, but particularly good for larger motorcaravans. In summer, this quietly located site rarely has more than a dozen occupants, yet it is half the price of the crowded, often noisy sites in Orsa town 14 km. away. The excellent, very modern, small sanitary unit is heated. It has one unisex WC with external access and, inside for each sex, there is one WC and washbasin cubicle, and two hot showers with curtains and communal changing area plus a seat and hooks. There are also hairdryers and soap dispensers, a suite for the disabled and drying room. A well equipped kitchen has two hobs and two dishwashing sinks. All showers, hairdryers, hot water, drying and kitchen facilities are free of charge. Reception is located in the holiday centre with its rental cabins, inn, tourist information and other services, about 1 km. below the camping area, and one should book in here and obtain a key for the sanitary unit before proceeding to the site. The Grönklitt Bear Park, with bears, wolves, and lynx is within a short scramble up the hillside from the site and there are magnificent views over this scenic lakeland area.

How to find it: From Orsa town centre follow the signs to Grönklitt and `Björn Park'. Site is 14 km.

General Details: Open all year. Kitchen. Drying room. Chemical disposal.

Charges 1997: Per unit, incl. all persons Skr. 75.00; electricity 30. Credit cards accepted.

Reservations: Not necessary. Address: Box 23, 794 21 Orsa. Tel: 0250/462 00. FAX: 0250/461 11. E-mail: fritid@orsa-gronklitt.se. Internet: www.orsa-gronklitt.se.

2845 Svegs Camping, Sveg (Jamtland)

Neat, riverside municipal site, on the `Inlandsvagen' route through Sweden.

The town centre is only a short walk from this friendly municipal site, with two supermarkets, café and tourist information office adjacent. The 160 pitches are in rows, on level grass, divided into bays by tall hedges, and with electricity (10/16A) available to 70. The sanitary facilities provide British style WCs, stainless steel washing troughs, controllable hot showers with communal changing areas, and a unit for the disabled. These are in the older style, functional rather than luxurious, and although a little short on numbers will probably suffice at most times as the site is rarely full. The kitchen and dining room with TV, has four full cookers and sinks, plus more dishwashing sinks outside under cover. Free hot water throughout. Laundry facilities include a washing machine and dryers, and an ironing board (iron on loan from reception).

continued overleaf

2845 Svegs Camping (continued)

The site has boats, canoes, cycles and rickshaws for hire, and the river frontage has a barbecue area with covered seating and fishing platforms. Alongside the river with its fountain, and running through the site is a pleasant well lit riverside walk. The town has a lovely church and adjacent gardens, there are some interesting old churches in surrounding villages, and 16th Century Remsgården is 14 km. to the west.

How to find it: Site is off road 45 behind the tourist information office in Sveg.

General Details: Open all year. Kitchen. Laundry. TV. Children's play area. Minigolf. Canoe, boat, rickshaw and bicycle hire. Fishing. Chemical disposal.

Charges 1997: Per unit Skr. 110; tent and car 90; cyclist and tent 90; electricity 25 - 30. Credit cards accepted.

Reservations: Contact site. Address: Kyrkogränd 1, 842 32 Sveg. Tel: 0680/107 75 FAX: 0680/103 37.

2850 Östersunds Camping, Östersund (Jamtland)

Extensive, modern, woodland site, a good base for exploring central Sweden.

Östersund lies on Lake Storsjön, which is Sweden's Loch Ness, with 200 sightings of the monster dating back to 1635, and more recently captured on video in 1996. Also worthy of a visit is the island of Frösön where settlements can be traced back to pre-historic times. This large site has 300 pitches, electricity (10A) and TV socket available on 120, all served by tarmac roadways. There are also 41 tarmac hardstandings available, and over 200 cottages, cabins and rooms for rent. The sanitary facilities are in three units, two providing British style WCs, washbasins and controllable hot showers (on payment) with communal changing areas, plus suites for the disabled and baby changing; the third has four family bathrooms each containing WC, basin and shower. There are two kitchens, each with full cookers, hobs, fridge/freezers and double sinks (all free of charge), and excellent dining rooms. Laundry facilities include three washing machines (charged) and dryers and drying cabinet (free). Also on site is a very good motorhome service point suitable for all types of unit including American RVs, and a children's playground. Adjacent to the site are the municipal swimming pool complex with cafeteria (indoor and outdoor pools), a Scandic hotel with restaurant, minigolf, and a Statoil filling station. A large supermarket and bank are just 500 m. from the site, and Ostersund town centre is 3 km.

How to find it: Site is to the south of the town off road 605 towards Torvalla, turn by Statoil station and site entrance is immediately on right (well signed from around the town).

General Details: Open all year. Kitchen. Laundry. Motorcaravan service point. Children's playground. Cottages, cabins and rooms for rent.

Charges 1997: Per unit Skr. 125 - 150 (incl. electricity/TV), 90 - 150 (without). Credit cards accepted (not Amex).

Reservations: Contact site. Address: Krondikesvagen 95, 831 46 Östersund. Tel: 063/14.46.15. FAX: 063/14.43.23.

2855 Flogsta Camping, Kramfors (Västernorrland)

Delightful small municipal site, a good base to explore the `High Coast'.

Kramfors lies just to the west of the E4, and travellers may well pass by over the new Höga Kusten bridge (one of the largest in Europe), and miss this friendly little site. The area of Ådalen and the High Coast, which reaches as far as Örnsköldsvik, is well worth a couple of days of your time, also Skuleskogen National Park, and Norfallsvikens, an old fishing village with many original buildings. The attractive garden-like campsite has around 50 pitches, 21 with electrical connections (10A), which are arranged on level grassy terraces, separated by shrubs and trees into bays of 2-4 units. All overlook the municipal swimming pool complex (one day free admission to campers), and attractive minigolf course. The non-electric pitches are on an open terrace nearer reception, and there are 16 rental cabins on site. Excellent sanitary facilities consist of nine well equipped family bathrooms, each with British style WC, basin with soap dispenser and hand dryer, shower (on payment), plus a laundry with washing machine and dryer. These are supplemented by more WCs and showers in the reception building with a free sauna facility. A separate building houses the kitchen, with hot-plates, fridge/freezer and TV/dining room (all free of charge). Also on-site is a small children's play area on a sandy base. The reception building has a small shop and snack-bar and is staffed 07.00-23.00 hours from 9/6-11/8. Outside these dates a warden calls daily. The town centre with supermarkets and restaurants is a 20 minute easy walk through a housing estate, and do use the excellent covered and elevated walkway to cross the main road and railway to the pedestrian shopping precinct with its floral arrangements and fountain.

How to find it: Well signed from road 90 in the centre of Kramfors, the site lies to the west in a rural location beyond a housing estate and by the Flogsta Bad, municipal swimming pool complex.

General Details: Open May - end Sept. Shop. Snack-bar. Laundry. Kitchen. TV. Children's playground. Cabins for rent.

Charges 1997: Per unit Skr. 85 - 95; cyclist/hiker and tent 55; electricity 25.

Reservations: Contact site. Address: 872 80 Kramfors. Tel: 0612/100 05. FAX: 0612/71.13.13.

SWEDEN - North

2860 Umeå Camping, Umeå (Västerbotten)

Good quality municipal site, on outskirts of university city.

An ideal stop-over for those travelling the E4 coastal route, or a good base from which to explore the area, this campsite lies 6 km. from the town centre, almost adjacent to the Nydalsjön lake, ideal for fishing, windsurfing and bathing. There are 320 grassy pitches arranged in bays of 10-20 units, divided by shrubs and small trees, all with electricity (10A), and some are fully serviced (electricity, water, waste water). The large, heated, central sanitary unit is modern and well equipped with British style WCs, open washbasins, controllable hot showers with communal changing areas, and a sauna. There is a well equipped kitchen with a large dining room adjacent, and a laundry with five washing machines (on payment), two dryers and ironing boards. The showers, kitchen facilities, hot water and dryers are all free of charge. These facilities are supplemented in high season by a basic smaller unit, plus a `portacabin' style unit both with WCs and handbasins only. Outside the site adjacent to the lake, but with direct access, are football pitches, a small open-air swimming pool with waterslide, minigolf, mini-car driving school, skateboard ramp, beach volleyball, a mini-farm and there are cycle and footpaths around the area. Umeå is also a port for ferries to Vasa in Finland (4 hrs).

How to find it: From the E4 on the northern outskirts of the town, turn at traffic lights, where site is signed.

General Details: Open all year. Shop. Snack-bar. Kitchen. Laundry. Volleyball. Children's playgrounds. Car wash. Boat hire. Chemical disposal. Cabins for rent (34).

Charges 1997: Per unit Skr. 115; electricity 30; serviced pitch 150. Credit cards accepted.

Reservations: Contact site. Address: Nydala Fritidsområde, 901 84 Umeå. Tel: 090/16.16.60. FAX: 090/12.57.20.

2865 Camp Gielas, Arvidsjaur (Norrbotten)

Modern site with excellent sporting facilities on outskirts of town.

This site is well shielded on all sides by trees, providing a very peaceful atmosphere. The 150 pitches, 80 with electricity (16A) and satellite TV connections, are level on sparse grass and accessed by tarmac roadways. There are two modern heated sanitary units with British style WCs, open washbasins and controllable hot showers with divider and seat (on payment), a unit for the disabled, well equipped kitchens (free of charge), also a laundry with washing machine and dryer. The unit by the tent area also has facilities for the disabled and baby changing. The sauna at the sports hall is free to campers, who may also use all the indoor sporting, gymnasium and solarium facilities at the usual rates. Also on site is a snack-bar. The lake on the site is suitable for boating, bathing and fishing and other amenities include tennis courts, minigolf, canoe and boat hire and children's playgrounds. Hunting trips can be arranged.

How to find it: Site is well signed from road 95 in the town.

General Details: Open all year. Snack bar. Kitchen. Laundry. Sauna. Solarium. Sporting facilities. Minigolf. Car wash. Children's playgrounds. Boat and canoe hire. Lake swimming. Swimming pool and 9-hole golf course near. Motorcaravan services. Chemical disposal. Cottages, cabins and apartments (65) for rent.

Charges 1997: Per unit Skr. 100; hiker's tent 70; electricity 20. Credit cards accepted.

Reservations: Contact site. Address: Jarnvägsgatan 111, 933 22 Arvidsjaur. Tel: 0960/556 00 FAX: 0960/106 15.

2870 Jokkmokks Turistcenter, Jokkmokk (Norrbotten)

Attractive municipal site in a popular tourist area, 8 km. from Arctic Circle.

Large and well organised, this site is bordered on one side by the river and with woodland on the other, just 3 km. from the town centre. It has 220 level, grassy pitches, with an area for tents, plus 59 cabins and 26 rooms for rent. Electricity (10A) is available to all 159 touring pitches. The heated sanitary buildings provide British style WCs, mostly open washbasins and controllable showers - some are curtained with a communal changing area, a few are in cubicles with divider. A newly refurbished unit (by reception) has a baby bathroom, a fully equipped suite for the disabled, games room, plus a very well appointed kitchen and launderette. A further unit with WCs, basins, showers plus a sauna and solarium is adjacent to the heated open-air swimming pool complex (25 x 10 m. main pool with water slide, two smaller pools and a paddling pool with lifeguard). All facilities, hot water and the pools are free of charge. There is a very smart restaurant and bar, plus a takeaway. Free river fishing (licences sold). There are opportunities for snow-mobiling, cross-country skiing in spring, or ice fishing in winter. Nearby attractions include the first hydro-electric power station at Porjus, built 1910-15, with free tours between 15/6-15/8, Vuollerim (40 km.) reconstructed 6,000 year old settlement, with excavations of the best preserved ice-age village, or try visiting for the famous Jokkmokk Winter Market (First Thurs-Sat February) or the less chilly Autumn Market (end of August).

How to find it: Site is 3 km. from the centre of Jokkmokk on road 97.

General Details: Open all year. Restaurant/bar (Feb-Sept). Takeaway (main season). Sauna and solarium. Children's playground. Swimming pools. Fishing. Minigolf. Football field. Kitchen. Laundry. Motorcaravan services.

Charges 1997: Per unit Skr. 110; hiker/small tent 70; car/small tent 90; electricity 30. Credit cards accepted.

Reservations: Contact site. Address: Box 75, 962 22 Jokkmokk. Tel: 0971/123 70. FAX: 0971 124 76.

338

SWITZERLAND

This land locked country, with 22 independent Cantons sharing languages with its four neighbours, has some of the most outstanding scenery in Europe which, coupled with its cleanliness and commitment to the tourism industry, makes it a very attractive proposition. The Swiss are well known for their punctuality and hard work and have the highest standard of living of any country in Europe, which makes Switzerland one of the most expensive yet problem free countries to visit. The Berner Oberland is probably the most visited area with a concentration of picturesque peaks and mountain villages, though the highest Alps are those of Valais in the southwest with the small busy resort of Zermatt giving access to the Matterhorn. Zurich in the north is a German speaking city with a wealth of sightseeing. Geneva, Montreux and Lausanne on the northern shores of Lake Geneva make up the bulk of French Switzerland, whilst the southernmost canton, Ticino, is home to the Italian speaking Swiss, with the resorts of Lugano and Locarno. For further information contact:

Swiss National Tourist Office, Swiss Centre, Swiss Court, London W1V 8EE

Tel: 0171 734 1921 Fax: 0171 734 4577

Population
6,800,000, density 165.5 per sq.km.

Capital
Bern.

Climate
No country in Europe combines within so small an area such marked climatic contrasts. In the northern plateau surrounded by mountains the climate is mild and refreshing. South of the Alps it is warmer, coming under the influence of the Mediterranean. The Valais area is noted for its dryness.

Language
The national languages of Switzerland are German 65% (central and east), French 18% (west), Italian 10% (south), Romansh - a derivative of Latin 1% (south east), and others 6%. Many Swiss, especially those involved in the tourism industry speak English.

Currency
The unit of currency is the Swiss franc, divided into 100 centimes, coming in coins of 5, 10, and 20 centimes and Sfr 0.5, 1, 2, 5. Notes are Sfr 10, 20, 50, 100, 500, 1000.

Banks
Open Mon-Fri 08.30-16.30. Closed for lunch in Lausanne and Lucerne 12.30-13.30/14.00

Post Offices
Open Mon-Fri 07.30-12.00 and 13.45-18.30. Sat 07.30-11.00 or later in some major city offices.

Time
GMT plus 1 (summer BST +1).

Telephone
From the UK, the code is 00 41 followed by the area code (omitting the initial zero) followed by number. Phone cards are available.

Public Holidays
New Year; Good Fri; Easter Mon; Ascension; Whit Mon; Christmas, 25 Dec; Other holidays are observed in individual Cantons.

Shops
Generally open Mon-Fri 08.00- 12.00 and 14.00-18.00. Sat 08.00-16.00. Shops often close Monday mornings.

Food: The cost of food in shops and restaurants can be expensive; it may be worthwhile to consider 'stocking-up' on basic food necessities purchased in the UK, or elsewhere in Europe. Note that, officially,only 2.5 kgs per head of foodstuffs may be imported into the country The local specialities to try if there is money in the budget are 'Fondue' or 'Raclette' in French Switzerland and 'Rösti' in German Switzerland.

Motoring
The road network is comprehensive and well planned. If the roads are narrow and circuitous in parts, it is worth it for the views. An annual road tax is levied on all cars using Swiss motorways and the 'Vignette' windscreen sticker must be purchased at the border (credit cards not accepted), or in advance from the Swiss National Tourist Office, plus a separate one for a towed caravan or trailer .

Fuel: On motorways, service stations are usually open from 0600- 2200/2400. On other roads it varies 0600/0800-1800/2000. Outside these hours petrol is widely available from 24 hr automatic pumps - Sfr 10/20. Credit cards are generally accepted.

Speed Limits: Cars in built-up areas 31 mph (50 kph), other roads 50 mph (80 kph), and motorways 75 mph (120 kph). For towing vehicles on motorways 50 mph (80 kph).

Parking: Blue Zones are in operation in certain cities, discs obtainable from most petrol stations, restaurants and police stations.

Overnighting
Only permitted at a few motorway rest areas.

Useful Addresses

National Motoring Organisation
Automobile Club de Suisse (ACS) FIA 39 Wasserwerkgrasse, 3000 Berne 13. Tel: 031 328 3111.
Touring Club Suisse(TCS), AIT, 9 rue Pierre Fatio, 1211 Geneve 3. Tel: 022 737 1212.

The sites in SWITZERLAND featured in this guide are shown on the map on page 376

SWITZERLAND

900 Camping Waldhort, Reinach, Basel/Basle

Satisfactory site for night halts or visits to Basel.

Although there are almost twice as many static caravans than spaces for tourists, this is a quiet site on the edge of a residential district, within easy reach of Basel. The site is flat, with level pitches on grass with access from the tarmac road which circles round inside the site. Trees are now maturing to give some shade. All pitches have electricity (6A) available and are near the good quality, central sanitary block. This has British WCs and free hot water, except in the sinks. Owned and run by the Camping and Caravanning Club of Basel, it is a neat, tidy and orderly site and there is usually space available. An extra, separate camping area has been added behind the tennis club which has pleasant pitches and good sanitary facilities. Reinach is within walking distance from where there is a tram service into Basel.

How to find it: Take Basel - Delémont motorway spur, exit at 'Reinach-Nord' and follow camp signs.

General Details: Open 13 March - 18 Oct. 23,000 sq.m. Small shop with terrace for drinks. Children's playground with 2 small pools. Swimming pool and tennis next to site. Facilities for the disabled. Washing machine and dryer. Chemical disposal. Motorcaravan services.

Charges 1997: Per person Sfr. 6.50; child (6-14 yrs) 4.30 (reduction with camping carnet); car 3.50; tent 4.00 - 6.00; caravan 6.00 - 8.00; motorcaravan 8.50 - 14.50; electricity included. Credit cards accepted.

Reservations: made for main season; advance payment asked for single nights, otherwise no deposit. Address: Heideweg 16, 4153 Reinach bei Basel. Tel: 061/7116429. FAX: 061/3022481.

905 Camping Bois du Couvent, La Chaux-de-Fonds

Hill-top site at 1,060 m. in the Swiss Jura.

The road from Lake Neuchatel to Chaux-de-Fonds, which stands just inside the Swiss border with France in the northwest of Switzerland, has been greatly improved with parts to motorway standard. La Chaux-de-Fonds is the biggest watch and clock making centre in Switzerland and one of the largest agricultural centres. Completely destroyed by fire in 1794, it was rebuilt to a geometric plan. Postage stamps for Switzerland and many foreign countries are printed here. Camping Bois du Couvent is situated at the southern end of the town on a hill-top with splendid views. More than half the pitches are taken by static caravans but the 70 places for tourists, with 10A electrical connections, although not marked, are obvious, with an open lawn for tents. The camp has a pleasant appearance and tarmac and gravel roads link the terraces, some of which have shade from tall trees. There is a nice restaurant, but no shop as there is a supermarket 1 km. away in town. Very little English is spoken but the warden has good tourist information available. Two sanitary blocks have British style WCs, free hot water in washbasins and on payment in sinks and showers.

How to find it: Site is signed and is at the south end of La Chaux-de-Fonds. Coming from Neuchatel, turn left at 2nd roundabout after tunnel.

General Details: Open all year. 60,000 sq.m. Restaurant (open all year except Tues, 08.00 - midnight). Shop 1 km. Children's playground. Some entertainment for children in summer. Minigolf 300 m. Bicycle hire and tennis 100 m. Clock museum 1 km. Heated pool 500 m. Washing machine and dryer. Chemical disposal.

Charges 1998: Per person Sfr. 3.50; child (4-16 yrs) 1.20; caravan 9.50; motorcaravan 14.00; family tent 8.00; car 3.00; m/cycle 2.00; electricity 3.00. Chalets, bungalows and caravans for hire.

Reservations: Write to site. Address: 2301 La Chaux-de-Fonds. Tel: 079/240 50 39.

903 Camping Paradis Plage, Colombier, nr Neuchatel

Pleasant lakeside site with good facilities, near French border.

This area of Switzerland deserves to be better known as there is much of interest here near the French border. Paradis Plage is nicely situated on the shores of Lake Neuchatel, with access to the lake. The 160 pitches available to tourists are numbered and marked out on flat grass under a covering of tall, mature trees. All have electricity (10A) and some have gravel hardstanding for caravans and motorcaravans. There are separate areas of grass where pitches are not marked, including a small overflow section for individuals or groups. The 200 static pitches are occupied mainly at weekends and high season and are neatly set out together in rows. Although a motorway runs over the site near the entrance, we did not notice any undue noise as this seemed to be screened out by the trees. Access to the site is rather narrow but adequate. A very pleasant restaurant with a large terrace, well stocked shop and takeaway (all to end Sept) form the focal point in the centre with views through the trees to the lake. Three sanitary blocks, well sited around the site, have been refurbished and make a good provision with British style WCs. Laundry rooms have electric rings for free use. Friendly, English speaking management. Well placed for walking in the Jura or touring the Bernese Oberland.

How to find it: Leave the short stretch of motorway at Colombier from where the site is signed.

General Details: Open 1 March - 31 Oct. 40,000 sq.m. Restaurant and shop (1/3-1/10). Small children's pool (20/6-20/8). Children's play area. Table tennis. Bicycle hire. Fishing. Boating. Sports complex near camp with indoor and outdoor tennis courts, horse riding, squash, bowls and football. Washing machines and dryers. Chemical disposal. Motorcaravan services.

Charges 1998: Per person Sfr. 5.50; child (6-15 yrs) 2.00; tent or caravan 7.00 - 12.00; motorcaravan 8.00 - 13.00; car 1.00 - 2.00; electricity 3.25; local tax 2.00 per pitch. Discounts for stays over 17 days (10%) up to 30 days (23%). Credit cards accepted.

Reservations: Write to site. Address: 2013 Colombier. Tel: 032/841 24 46. FAX: as phone.

906 TCS Camping Caravaning Kappelenbrücke, Bern

Fairly new site for overnight or longer stay, near city.

This relatively new site, being just outside the Federal Capital, is conveniently placed either for an overnight stop, or for exploring the city and surrounds. A frequent bus service to the city passes the entrance. The 305 pitches (230 for touring) are numbered but not marked and you choose your own place; cars are parked away from the pitches. All have electricity (4A or more). There are some static units but there should always be room. The two new toilet blocks of exceptional quality, have British WCs, enclosed washbasins with free hot water; also in the showers. One block is heated in cool weather. Sinks for washing clothes and dishes have free hot water and are under cover. Shop also serving drinks which can be taken to a pleasant rest room nearby or to the terrace. This pleasant, well cared for site is near a small lake which is unsuitable for bathing, although there is now, however, a swimming pool and children's pool on site. It is probably the best site for visiting Bern.

How to find it: Take the 'Bethlehem' exit from N1 motorway on western side of Bern, towards Aarberg, and site will be seen on right before river.

General Details: Open all year except 6-18 Feb. 35,000 sq.m. Electrical connections throughout. Special pitches for motorcaravans. Shop/bar. TV room. Day room. Children's playground. Table tennis. Fishing. Baby room. Washing machines and dryers. Chemical disposal.

Charges 1997: Per person Sfr. 4.40 - 6.00; child (6-16 yrs) 2.20 - 3.00; tent or caravan 5.20 - 17.00, acc. to type; motorcaravan 18.00; electricity 2.50 or 4.00; local tax 1.40.

Reservations: Write to site. Address: Wohlenstrasse 62c, 3032 Hinterkappelen (BE). Tel: 031/901 10 07. FAX: 031/901 25 91.

909 Camping Avenches Port-Plage, Avenches

Large site with good boating possibilities on Lake Murten.

This is a large site by Swiss standards, located in a quiet, open situation directly on Lake Murten with its own marina and excellent access to the water. The camp is well cared for, with 200 out of the 700 pitches available for tourists. These are of reasonable size (80 sq.m.) with shade in parts from tall trees and electrical connections are available (6A). It is, above all, a site for those interested in watersports. At the centre of the site is a large building which houses a general shop, butcher, baker and the main sanitary facilities. A separate restaurant is nearer the lake shore. There are three toilet blocks, all of excellent quality with British style WCs.

How to find it: Site is signed near Avenches on the Bern - Lausanne road no.1 (not the motorway).

General Details: Open 1 April - 30 Sept. 80,000 sq.m. Electrical connections most pitches. Restaurant. Shop, butcher and baker. First aid room. Children's playground. Pedaloes. Chemical disposal. Motorcaravan services.

Charges 1998: Per person Sfr. 7.00; child (4-16 yrs) 4.00; car 4.00; caravan 10.00; tent 6.50 - 10.00, acc. to size; motorcaravan 14.00; electricity 3.50; local tax 1.00.

Reservations: Write to site with Sfr. 20 fee. Address: Camping-Port-Plage, 1580 Avenches. Tel: 026/675 17 50. FAX: 026/675 44 69.

SWITZERLAND

912 Camping Lido Luzern, Lucerne/Luzern

Site in good touring area popular with the British.

Luzern is a traditional holiday resort of the British and this site has many British visitors. It lies near the shore of Lake Luzern, just outside the town itself. Next to the site (but not associated with it so you have to pay for entrance) is the Lido proper, which has a large sandy beach, bathing in the lake and sports fields. The town of Luzern has excellent shopping and sightseeing; one could walk there along the lake in about 20 minutes, or nearby buses run into town up to midnight. The site is divided into separate sections for caravans, motorcaravans and tents; the first two have hardstandings which, in effect, provide rather formal and small individual pitches. There are about 80 electrical connections (10A). Quiet in early season, from late June to late August it usually becomes full and, especially in the tent section, can at times seem rather crowded. The sanitary installations are in three sections, two being close to the reception area. A large and very modern block incorporates toilets, basins, showers, washing facilities, a rest room and cooking area with electric rings (pre-payment). British WCs: mostly individual basins, some in cabins for women, with hot water; hot water for showers and sinks is on payment. The blocks can be heated. Good English is spoken and the charges are reasonable.

How to find it: Follow Lido signs out of Luzern and a large sign to Lido will be seen on right just outside of town.

General Details: Open 15 March - 31 Oct. 23,000 sq.m. Shade in parts. Smallish shop. Takeaway. Community room. Organised excursions. Doctor on call. Chemical disposal.

Charges 1997: Per person Sfr. 6.50 (with camping carnet 6.00); child (6-16) 50%; local tax (over 11s) 1.20; car 5.00; tent 3.00; caravan 6.00 - 10.00; motorcaravan 12.00 - 17.00; m/cycle 3.00; dog 3.00; electricity by meter.

Reservations: Write to site. Address: Lidostr. 6, 6006 Luzern. Tel: 041/370 21 46. FAX: 041/370 21 45.

913 Terrassencamping Vitznau, Vitznau, nr Lucerne/Luzern

Quiet site scenically positioned on shores of Lake Luzern.

Camping Vitznau is situated in the small village of the same name, above and overlooking the lake, with splendid views across the water to the mountains on the other side. It is a small, neat and tidy site very close to the delightful village on the narrow, winding, lakeside road. The 120 pitches for caravans or motorhomes (max length 7 m.) have 15A electricity available to most. They are on level, grassy terraces with hard wheel tracks for motorcaravans and separated by tarmac roads, and although of sufficient rather than large size, with single rows on each terrace, all places have unobstructed views. However, larger units might have difficulty manoeuvring onto the pitches. There are separate places for tents. The single, well constructed sanitary block has British WCs, washbasins in flat vanity tops and free hot showers. Dish and clothes washing is under cover with metered hot water. There is a general room for wet weather, a games room and a well stocked shop but no restaurant as the village ones are about 5 minutes walk away. Trees provide shade in parts and this delightful camp makes an excellent base for exploring around the lake, the town of Luzern and the nearby mountains.

How to find it: Site is signed from the centre of Vitznau.

General Details: Open 1 April - 5 Oct. 20,000 sq.m. 1,446 feet above sea level. Shop. Swimming pool and children's splash pool. Watersports near. Washing machines and dryers. Chemical disposal.

Charges 1998: Per person Sfr. 7.50 - 9.00; child under 6 yrs 2.50, 6-16 yrs 5.00; pitch 13.00 - 17.00; local tax 1.60; electricity 4.00. Credit cards accepted.

Reservations: Write with deposit (Sfr 20). Address: 6354 Vitznau. Tel: 041/397 12 80. FAX: 041/397 24 57.

915 Camping Seebucht, Zürich

Busy lakeside site quite close to the city.

Being a smallish site only 4½ km. from the centre of the important town of Zürich and in a pleasant situation with well kept lawns, Seebucht has more demands on space than it can meet. With 300 touring pitches (136 with 6/10A electricity), it may well pack units rather closely in season but there is much transit trade so there are usually plenty of vacancies each day if you are early (reservations not made). Caravans go on flat hardstandings (cars cannot always stand by them); tents, for which space may be easier to find, go on lawns. The grassy strip alongside the lake is kept free for recreational use. The single toilet block might be stretched at the busiest times. It provides British style toilets, with some Turkish style for men, individual washbasins (cubicles for women) with cold water and hot water on payment for the showers.

How to find it: Site is on the southern side of the town and the western side of the lake, at Wollishofen; well signed from most parts of town and at motorway exit.

General Details: Open 1 May - 30 Sept. 20,000 sq.m. Shop. Café for meals or drinks. Bathing possible into fairly deep water. Fishing. Jetty where small boats can be launched. Chemical disposal. Motorcaravan services.

Charges 1997: Per person Ffr. 6.00; child (4-16 yrs) 3.00; small tent 10.00; large tent, caravan or motorcaravan 12.00 (plus 5.00 if over 6 m); car 3.00; electricity 3.00; plus local tax 1.20.

Reservations: not made; for information only: Address: Seestrasse 559, 8038 Zürich-Wollishofen. Tel: 01/482 16 12. FAX: 01/482 16 60.

918 Campingplatz Buchhorn, Arbon

Small, well ordered site on Lake Bodensee in northeast Switzerland.

This small but clean and pleasant site is directly on Lake Bodensee in the town's park. There is access for boats but powered craft must be under a certain h.p. and advice on this should be sought from the management. There are splendid views across this large inland sea and interesting boats ply up and down between Constance and Lindau and Bregenz. The town swimming lido in the lake, with a restaurant, is quite close. The site is well shaded with pitches by the water's edge and an overflow field for tents next door. There are a number of static caravans but said to be room for 100 tourists, pitches being on a mixture of gravel and grass, flat areas on either side of access roads, most with 6A electricity. A railway line runs directly along one side but one gets used to the noise from passing trains, and pitches near the lake should be requested. A single, well constructed set of buildings comprise reception, shop (small terrace for drinks), sanitary and washing arrangements. Sanitary facilities, which should just about suffice in high season, are clean and modern with free hot water in basins, showers and sinks. British WCs. The site is well placed for touring Lake Bodensee, the Vorarlberg province of Austria, Liechtenstein and northeast Switzerland. Watersports and steamer trips on the lake, walks and marked cycle tracks around it and a nature reserve is near. The weather can be unsettled in this region.

How to find it: On Arbon-Konstanz road 13, signed 'Strandbad' and 'Strandbad Camping' on leaving Arbon.

General Details: Open 5 April - 18 Oct. Well shaded. Shop (basic supplies, drinks and snacks - all season). General room. Children's playground. Town swimming lido 400 m. Tennis 150 m. Watersports and excursions on lake. Washing machine, dryer and drying area. Fridge. Chemical disposal. Gates closed 12-14.00 hrs daily.

Charges 1998: Per person Sfr. 6.70; child (6-16 yrs) 3.10; small tent 5.65; large tent, caravan or motorcaravan 11.35; car 3.10; m/cycle 1.05; electricity 2.05.

Reservations: Write to site. Address: 9320 Arbon. Tel: 071/446 65 45. FAX: 071/446 48 34.

Arbon *Camping Buchhorn*

One of the finest camping sites on the shores of Lake Constance
♦ 100 yards of own sandy beach
♦ idyllic site under old, high trees
♦ perfect, new sanitation equipment
♦ shop with Camping-Gaz
♦ free entrance to the Lido, 200 yds
♦ closed daily from 12 am to 2 pm
Edi+Lotty Hurter, CH-9320 Arbon
071 446 6545 Fax 071 446 4839

921 TCS Camping Pointe à la Bise, Vésenaz, nr Geneve/Geneva

Lakeside site within easy reach of Geneva.

Although the majority of campers only stop for a few nights at this site whilst visiting Geneva, and it is well placed for this, TCS have rebuilt the main building and refurbished the sanitary block to a high standard giving the site a new appearance which may tempt for a longer stay. Pointe a la Bise is directly on the lake and has superb views of the lake and surrounding mountains. The 200 pitches, 70 with electricity (4/10A) are not marked so you do not have a defined place which might make for crowding in high season. Tall trees provide some shade. It is possible to swim in the lake and there is a small children's pool. Windsurfing and small boats under 10 hp may be used from the camp. Away from the main road, this is a quiet, relaxed site - no disco, but occasional live music in high season and organised activities July/Aug. The pleasant bar/restaurant is open all day with takeaway meals which may be eaten on the terrace or in the community room which has tables, chairs and TV, with a baby room next door. The terrace overlooks the pool and small children's playground. The improvements have lifted this from a reasonable site to a good one and the friendly, English speaking manager will advise on nearby attractions. He also organises a bicycle ride weekly in high season which includes lunch in a French restaurant. The sanitary block has British style WCs and free hot water in washbasins, sinks and showers. A number of static caravans are grouped one side of the tourist area.

How to find it: Follow lakeside road from city centre towards Thonon (lake on left) for 6.5 km. and site is signed.

General Details: Open Easter - 25 October. 32.000 sq.m. Shop. Bar/restaurant with takeaway (until late Sept). Baby room. Community room with TV. Children's pool and playground, lake swimming and watersports. Fishing. Bicycle hire. Washing machines and dryers. Chemical disposal. Motorcaravan services.

Charges 1997: Per person Sfr. 4.80 - 5.80; child (6-15 yrs) less 50%; pitch 6.50 - 19.00 acc. to size and season; motorcaravan 22.00; electricity (4/10A) 3.00; local tax 0.50. Credit cards accepted.

Reservations: Write to site, Address: 1222 Vésenaz. Tel: 022/752 12 96. FAX: 022/752 37 67.

SWITZERLAND

924 TCS Camping Le Petit Bois, Morges

Pleasant site by Lake Geneva near Lausanne, with swimming pool adjacent.

This site is most attractively situated amid a complex of municipal sports fields, by the shore of Lake Geneva, with a view of the mountain across the lake. Almost next door is an excellent, heated swimming pool which is free to campers (better here than bathing in the lake). The small harbour adjoining the site has some moorings for campers' boats. It is an easy walk into Morges. The terrain is divided up regularly into pitches, 170 for tourists, which are said to be all 80 sq.m. Cars stand on the wide road at the front. There are 140 electricity connections (4A) and 8 large pitches for motorhomes with water, electricity and drainage. Sanitary installations are good with free hot water in washbasins, controllable showers and washing-up sinks. British WCs. Hair dryers. Unit for disabled people.

How to find it: Coming from Lausanne leave the Lausanne - Geneva autoroute at the exit for 'Morges-ouest', from Geneva exit at 'Morges'. Proceed towards the town and turn left at T-junction and then sharp right to reach site.

General Details: Open Easter - 19 Oct. 36,000 sq.m. Well stocked shop. Bar/restaurant (with service) and takeaway. Washing machines, dryers and irons. Baby room. Small general room. Children's playground. Treatment room; doctors will call. A little 'animation' in season. Sports area. Chemical disposal. Motorcaravan services.

Charges 1997: Per person Sfr 4.80 - 6.00; child (6-16) less 50%; pitch 6.30 - 19.00 acc. to facilities and season; dog 1.00; car 2.00; m/cycle 1.00; local tax 0.80.

Reservations: Made for min. 1 week with deposit (Sfr 80) and fee (20). Address: 1110 Morges (Vaud); Tel: 021/801 12 70. FAX: 021/803 38 69.

927 Camping de Vidy, Lausanne

Friendly site in popular city on Lake Geneva.

The interesting and ancient city of Lausanne - its first cathedral was built in the 6th century - spills down the hillside towards Lake Geneva until it meets the peaceful park in which this site is situated. The present owners took the site over from the City council in '87 and have enhanced its appearance by planting many flowers and shrubs. Although minutes from the city centre, only a gentle hum of traffic can be heard and the site exudes peace and tranquillity. A public footpath separates the site from the lakeside, but there is good access. The World HQ of the Olympic movement is adjacent in the pleasant park. Hard access roads separate the site into sections for tents, caravans and motorcaravans, with 10A electrical connections in all parts, except the tent areas. Pitches are on flat grass, numbered but not marked out, with 245 (of 315) available for tourists. A few apartments for hire. Two excellent sanitary blocks, one near reception (heated) and one on the opposite side of the site, have mostly British, some Turkish style WCs, free hot water in washbasins, sinks and showers with warm, pre-mixed water. Facilities for disabled people. A third small block of the same standard has been added. The lakeside bar/restaurant (also open to the public) provides entertainment in season in the various rooms so that the young and not so young can enjoy themselves without impinging on each other. The keen young couple who manage the site speak good English, whom they welcome. The site has a neat and tidy appearance. There is a frequent bus service into Lausanne and boat excursions on the lake.

How to find it: Left of the road to Geneva, 500 m. west of La Maladière. Take autobahn Lausanne-Süd, exit La Maladière, and follow signs to camp (very near). Care needed at motorway exit roundabout.

General Details: Open all year. Shop (1/5-30/9). Self-service bar/restaurant with takeaway in season. Children's playground. Evening entertainment mid-June - Aug. Chemical disposal. Motorcaravan services.

Charges 1998: Per person Sfr. 6.50; student 6.00; child (6-16 yrs) 5.00; car 2.50; m/cycle 1.50; tent, caravan or motorcaravan 10.00 - 12.00; 2 person tent 7.00; local tax 1.40 (caravan) 1.20 (tent). Credit cards not accepted.

Reservations: Write to site. Address: 1007 Lausanne-Vidy (Vaud). Tel: 021/624 20 31. FAX: 021/624 41 60. Internet: http://www.campinglausannevidy.ch.

930 Camping Le Bivouac, Les Paccots, Châtel St Denis, nr Lausanne

Pleasant, small site with swimming pool, in mountains north of Montreux.

A nice little mountain site, Le Bivouac has its own small swimming pool and children's pool. Most of the best places are taken by seasonal caravans and there are now only about 20 pitches for tourists. Electricity (10A) is available and there are five water points. Also open for winter sports caravanning, all the sanitary facilities are heated. The good provision has British style toilets, pre-set free hot water in washbasins, showers and sinks, and a baby room. New facilities have been added in the main building with more showers, free hot water and laundry facilities. Entertainment is organised for adults and children in high season. Used by tour operators. A good centre for walking and excursions.

How to find it: From N12/A12 Bern-Vevey motorway exit Châtel St Denis turn towards Les Paccots (about 1 km).

General Details: Open all year. Shop (15/5-15/9). Room for general use adjoining. Café with takeaway (15/5-15/9). Swimming pool (1/6-15/9). Table tennis. Fishing. Laundry facilities. Chemical disposal.

Charges 1998: Per person Sfr. 6.00 plus local tax (adults) 1.20; child (6-16 yrs) 4.00; pitch incl. car 15.00; electricity (10A) 3.00. 10% off with camping carnet.

Reservations: Advised for July/Aug. and made for 1 week with deposit (Sfr. 20) and booking fee (10). Address: 1618 Châtel St Denis. Tel: 021/948 78 49. FAX: as phone.

AR Discount
Less 10%
(excl. tax)

344

933 Camping Bettlereiche, Gwatt-Thun

Small, lakeside site with good facilities, in popular area.

Bettlereiche is an ideal site for those who wish to explore this part of the Bernese Oberland and who would enjoy staying on a small site in a quiet area, away from the larger sites and town atmosphere of Interlaken. There are 90 numbered, but unmarked pitches for tourists, most with 4A electricity available, and about the same number of static units, with hard access roads. Cars must be parked away from the pitches. Although there are some trees, there is little shade in the main camping area. Direct access to the lake is available for swimming and boating. The single sanitary block is well constructed and modern with British WCs. Free hot water is provided for the washbasins in cabins (cold otherwise) and in the showers controlled by a single tap and facilities should be just adequate in high season. The site has a cared for air and the friendly management speak good English. Well stocked shop. Part of the restaurant is reserved for young people. Some animation in high season.

How to find it: From Berne-Thun-Interlaken autoroute, take exit Thun-Süd. Follow signs for Gwatt and site.

General Details: Open Easter - 5 Oct. 15,000 sq.m. Shop. Restaurant (no alcohol). Room for disabled. Washing machine and dryer. Lake swimming. and boating. Chemical disposal. Motorcaravan services.

Charges 1997: Per person Sfr. 4.60 - 6.20; child 50%; pitch 6.30 - 19.00; local tax 2.40.

Reservations: Write to site. Address: 3645 Gwatt. Tel: 033/336 40 67. FAX: 033/336 40 17.

939 Camping Vermeille, Zweisimmen, nr Gstaad

Attractive, small mountain site with good facilities, for families.

This small, well run camp is about 1,000 m. above sea level, on a road followed by many tourists and can serve either as a night stop or as a holiday base for those who like a mountain site with many attractive excursion possibilities. In summer there are 40 pitches for tourists, in winter 25 (the remainder of the 125 total being seasonal lets), with 130 electrical connections (from 6A) available. There is a small free swimming pool which can be heated, open mid-May to late September if weather permits. The site is equipped for winter sports camping and a fair proportion of the available space, therefore, consists of hardstandings for caravans on stony ground. However, there are also lawns for tents. The sanitary installations have been upgraded and now include a baby room and facilities for disabled people. In the main building, they are fully enclosed and heated in winter. The facilities are kept extremely clean and include British WCs, troughs and washbasins for washing with a few private cabins, and hot water for washing up (new facilities) and showers on payment.

How to find it: Site is north of the town on no. 11 road. Turn off where signed and go past different camp on left of access road. From N6 motorway take exit for Wimmis/Spiez (From Spiez before town, from Saanen after town).

General Details: Open all year. 9,000 sq.m. Limited shade. Shop for food and sports goods. Restaurant 100 m. on main road and in Zweisimmen. Two rooms for general use, one with sink and cooking facilities. Children's play area and trampoline. Mountain bike hire. Washing machine. Chemical disposal. Motorcaravan services.

Charges 1998: Per person Sfr. 6.60; child 6-12 yrs 3.80, under 6 2.20; local tax 0.80 (0.40); pitch 8.00 - 13.50; m/cycle with tent 7.00; bicycle with tent 5.00; electricity 2.00 (winter 2.00 - 9.00). Less 10% pp outside July/Aug.

Reservations: Made for min. 5 nights with deposit (Sfr. 40) and small fee (10). Address: 3770 Zweisimmen. Tel: 033/722 19 40. FAX: 033/722 36 25.

944 Camping Jungfraublick, Interlaken

Pleasant site on edge of town with splendid mountain views.

Interlaken is a very popular holiday town and we offer a second site here which contrasts with the larger one on the opposite side of the town. Situated in the district of Matten, within walking distance of the centre and handy for excursions to Grindelwald, Lauterbrunnen and the Jungfrau, Jungfraublick faces up the Lauterbrunnen valley towards the majestic Jungfrau mountain. The Interlaken by-pass motorway runs along one side of the camp but, being in a deep cutting, the noise of traffic is screened out. There is some noise from the access road but an earth bank has been constructed to cut this down. The 135 marked pitches are on flat grass with hard access roads and 80 have electrical connections (2-6A). Although there are a number of trees, there is not too much shade. It is a very pleasant site with friendly, English speaking management and a neat, tidy appearance. The sanitary facilities are divided between two buildings near the entrance and there is a small swimming pool. Small shop for basic requirements, with shops and restaurants near (1 km).

How to find it: Take the Lauterbrunnen/Grindelwald motorway exit (where the site is signed as no. 7), turn towards Interlaken and site is on the left hand side.

General Details: Open 1 May - 25 Sept. 13,000 sq.m. Children's play area. Small swimming pool (mid June - end Aug). Bicycle hire. Heated room with TV. Washing machines and dryers. Chemical disposal. Motorcaravan services.

Charges 1998: Per person Sfr. 5.40 - 6.20; child 3.20 - 3.80; pitch 14.00 - 28.00; dog 3.00; local tax 1.60.

Reservations: Write to site with deposit (Sfr 30) and fee (10). Address: Camping Jungfraublick (7), Gsteigsttr. 80, 3800 Matten, Interlaken. Tel: 033/822 44 14. FAX: 033/822 16 19.

AR Discount
Low season discounts
- ask at site

942 Camping Manor Farm, Interlaken

946 Camping Jungfrau, Lauterbrunnen, nr Interlaken

These sites are featured out of order - they are on pages 352/353 opposite their colour advertisements

936 Camping Grassi, Frutigen, nr Spiez

Small, quiet site on the road to Kandersteg.

This is a small site with about half the pitches occupied by static caravans, used by their owners for weekends and holidays. The 70 or so places available for tourists are not marked out but it is said that the site is not allowed to become overcrowded. Most places are on level grass with two small terraces at the end of the site. There is little shade but the site is set in a river valley with trees on the hills which enclose the area. It would make a useful overnight stop en-route for Kandersteg and the railway station where cars can join the train for transportation through the Lotschberg Tunnel to the Rhône Valley and Simplon Pass, or for a longer stay to explore the Bernese Oberland. Electricity (6 or 8A) is available for all pitches but long leads may be required in parts. The well constructed sanitary block has good quality installations including British style WCs and also a rest room with TV. There is a kiosk for basic supplies, but shops and restaurants are only a 10 minute walk away in the village.

How to find it: Take the Kandersteg road from Spiez and leave at `Frutigen Dorf' from where the camp is signed.

General Details: Open all year. 15,000 sq.m. Kiosk. Children's play area. Mountain bike hire. Outdoor and indoor pools, tennis and minigolf in Frutigen. Ski-ing and walking. Washing machine and dryer. Chemical disposal.

Charges 1998: Per person Sfr. 6.20 + local tax 0.80; child (1-6 yrs) 1.00, (6-16 yrs) 3.00 + 0.40; pitch 6.00 - 12.00; electricity (8-10A) 1.50.

Reservations: Write to site. Address: 3714 Frutigen. Tel: 033/671 11 49 or 671 37 98. FAX: 033/671 11 49.

FRUTIGEN
CAMPING GRASSI

Located off the road, alongside the Engstligen stream, this is the location for the quiet and well equipped site in the summer holiday resort of Frutigen - inexhaustible choice of excursions - free loan of bicycles.
Winter Camping - Ski-ing resort of Adelboden, Kandersteg, Elsigenalp Swiss ski-school only 10-12 km distance.
Inf': W. Glausen, CH-3714 Frutigen
Tel: 033/671 11 49 / 671 37 98

954 Camping Lido Sarnen, Sarnen, nr Luzern

Good lakeside site in a popular area.

Sarnen is about 20 km. south of Luzern on the main road to Interlaken and is, therefore, ideally placed for ski-ing in winter and sightseeing in summer. The summit of the well known Mt. Pilatus can be reached by mountain railway (the steepest of its type in the world) from Stansstad, about halfway between Luzern and Sarnen, and steamer trips on Lake Luzern can also be made from here. The camp site is on flat ground directly on the lake with views of near and distant mountains. Suitable for long or short stays, it makes an ideal base for this part of Switzerland or for a night stop if passing through. The 220 pitches, 80 for tourists with 10A electricity, are of 80-90 sq.m. on grass with hard access roads (some narrow). There is shade in parts and the location is a quiet one on the edge of the small town. The exceptionally good sanitary arrangements, which are heated in cool weather and include a special baby room, are in the main reception building at the entrance to the site. Hot water is free to washbasins, on payment in the showers and sinks. British style WCs. The site is part of the town Lido complex with a large, heated swimming pool and child's pool and facilities for non-powered boats. The restaurant, which has a large terrace, is self-service at lunch time and waiter service at night.

How to find it: Follow signs from southern junction where town road meets the main road from Interlaken.

General Details: Open all year. 20,000 sq.m. Shop. Restaurant. Tennis. Table tennis. Watersports. Swimming pools. Good children's playground. Room for the disabled. Washing machines and dryers. Chemical disposal. Motorcaravan services.

Charges 1997: Per person Sfr. 6.00 - 7.50; child (6-11 yrs) 3.00 - 4.00, under 6 free; local tax 1.00, child 0.50; lakeside pitch 9.00 - 12.00; inner pitch 7.00 - 9.00; car by pitch 3.00; m/cycle 2.00; electricity 3.00.

Reservations: advised for high season and made with Sfr. 30 deposit. Address: 6060 Sarnen. Tel: 041/660 18 66. FAX: 041/662 08 66.

948 Camping Gletscherdorf, Grindelwald, nr Interlaken

Small site with good toilet block quite close to town.

On flat ground in a valley with mountains around, this site has a scenic situation with views to the Eiger. It has 80 pitches for tourers (40 permanents in addition), most of which are individual, marked ones in the main section, with an unmarked overflow field. Electrical connections are available (10A). The sanitary block is tiled and of excellent quality with free hot water. However, it is only small and might be barely adequate in peak weeks. However, it is kept very clean and has British WCs, washbasins with shelf and mirror and controllable, free hot showers. There are good walking opportunities in the area and a mountain climbing school in the village.

How to find it: To reach site, go into town and turn right at camp sign after town centre; approach is quite narrow and steep down hill but there is an easier departure road.

General Details: Open 1 May - 20 Oct. for tourists (in winter, seasonal lets only). Small shop. Washing machines and tumble dryer. Chemical disposal. Motorcaravan services. No dogs accepted.

Charges 1997: Per person Sfr. 6.50 plus local tax 2.50; child (6-16 yrs) 3.00; pitch 4.00 - 14.00, acc. to size; electricity 3.00 - 3.50.

Reservations: essential for July/Aug. Write to site. Address: 3818 Grindelwald. Tel: 033/853 14 29. FAX: 033/853 31 29.

GRINDELWALD GLETSCHERDORF 31

The especially quiet camping ground with lots of wonderful ramble possibilities.
New sanitary block. In winter only: seasonal caravan pitches.

After the village, turn right. Follow signs Gletscherdorf 31.

Fam. D. Harder-Bohren,
Gletscherdorf,
CH3818 Grindelwald

Tel. 033/853 14 29
Fax. 033/853 31 29

951 Camping Aaregg, Brienz, nr Interlaken

Lakeside site east of Interlaken.

A very good site in a delightful lakeside setting, Aaregg is suitable for overnight or longer stays. Situated at the eastern end of Brienzersee with splendid views of lake and mountains, there is room for 213 outfits. The pitches are on flat grass and now include 15 of 100 sq.m. with hardstanding, water and drainage. There are some permanent units and the site could become full in high season. Pitches fronting the lake have a surcharge. There are electrical connections (10A) in most parts and good shade in some. Good quality sanitary blocks have British style WCs, washbasins with free hot water, shelves and mirrors (some in private cabins), hot showers (on payment) and facilities for disabled people. The site is owned and run by Frau Zysset and her sons, and English is spoken.

How to find it: Site is on road no. 6 on east side of Brienz with entrance between B.P. and Esso petrol stations, well signed. From new Interlaken-Luzern motorway take Brienz exit and turn towards Brienz, site then on left.

General Details: Open 1 April - 31 Oct. Shop. Café with terrace. Takeaway in season. Children's play area. Laundry facilities. Chemical disposal. Motorcaravan services.

Charges 1997: Per person Sfr. 7.00; child (6-16 yrs) 3.50, (1-6 yrs) 1.00; local tax 2.00; tent 13.00; car 3.00; caravan 13.00; motorcaravan 12.00 - 15.00; m/cycle 2.00; dog 2.00; electricity 3.00; extra small tent 4.00; pitch with services plus 8.00; lakeside pitch (in season) plus 10.00. Discount in low season.

Reservations: Made for any period (except Jul/Aug when min. is 14 days) with deposit (Sfr 20). Address: 3855 Brienz. Tel: 033/951 18 43. FAX: 033/951 43 24.

For a list of sites which are open all year - see page 359.
Also: Alan Rogers' Good Camps Guide ALL YEAR ROUND features campsites throughout Europe for All Year touring.

SWITZERLAND

949 Camping Eigernordwand, Grindelwald

Mountain site at the foot of the Eiger.

Grindelwald is a very popular summer and winter resort and Eigernordwand, at 950 m. above sea level, is dramatically situated very close to the north face of the famous mountain in a delightful situation. The slightly sloping pitches have gravel access roads but are not marked out. There are some trees around but little shade, although there are splendid views of surrounding mountain peaks. Being so high it can become cool when the sun goes down. Excursions to the Jungfrau and climbing or walking tours are organised. Some static caravans remain during the winter with about 140 places for tourists in summer. Electrical connections (10A) are available. There is a good quality restaurant and hotel at the entrance. The new sanitary block, heated in cool weather, is of excellent quality and has British style WCs, a drying room and facilities for disabled people.

How to find it: 800 m. before entering Grindelwald bear right past Grund railway station. Turn right over bridge, follow railway line for 500 m. and cross stream to camp on right.

General Details: Open all year. 12,000 sq.m. Restaurant. Hotel. Kiosk for basic supplies. Children's playground. Barbecue hut. Ski lifts, cable cars near. Washing machines. Drying room. Chemical disposal. Motorcaravan services.

Charges 1998: Per person Sfr. 8.00; child (3-12 yrs) 4.00; tent 7.00 - 9.00; caravan 9.00 - 11.00; motorcaravan 9.00 - 11.00; car 3.00; m/cycle 2.00; electricity 3.00 (summer); dog 4.00; local tax 2.50. After 10 days, 1 day free.

Reservations: Write to site. Address: 3818 Grindelwald. Tel: 033/853 42 27.

Grindelwald - Eigernordwand

• The ideal place for your summer or winter holiday • Peaceful and sunny • Picturesque views of the Eigernordwand mountains
• Heated swimming pool nearby
• New sanitary building with first class facilities
• Impeccable motorcaravan service station
• Free hot water • Hotel*** restaurant for campers' friends and family.

TURN OFF BEFORE VILLAGE TOWARDS GRUND
Tel: 033-853 42 27

957 Camping Eienwäldli, Engelberg, nr Lucerne/Luzern

This site is featured out of order - it is on page 353 opposite its colour advertisement

963 Camping Sémiramis, Leysin

High level mountain site in well known winter and summer resort.

Leysin came to fame at the end of the last century when it was found that the pure mountain air was conducive to the cure of turberculosis. The discovery of antibiotic drugs in 1955 made the lengthy natural treatment redundant and Leysin turned to tourism as a summer and winter resort. At 4,500 feet above sea level in the Vaudois Alps, there are spectacular views over the Rhône valley. Reputably enjoying more hours of sunshine than anywhere in Switzerland, Leysin has become a well equipped resort with ski-ing facilities including a new cable way to a revolving restaurant. The village straggles up the mountain side and Sémiramis is at the start of this. With 125 pitches and on a slight slope with static caravans on the upper level, the meadow at the entrance provides 70 places for touring visitors. No places are marked out and long leads may be required for the 6/15A hook ups. There is little shade but the views are breathtaking and mountains protect the camp to the north. There are two sanitary blocks, heated in cool weather, one on the ground floor of the hotel and one next to the snack bar, shop and reception. British style WCs. Free hot water is dispensed through a single tap in washbasins, showers and sinks. Tennis courts and the town's large ice rink (open all year) are next to the camp with restaurants and shops nearby. This neat, compact site has very friendly, English speaking management and provides an excellent base to enjoy the amenities of the region.

How to find it: Take the Leysin road at Le Sepey on the Aigle-les Diablerets road and turn left immediately after the town sign (just past the Subaru garage).

General Details: Open all year. 12,000 sq.m. Shop. Snack bar. Children's play area. TV room in bar. Boules. Table tennis. Badminton. Washing machine and dryer. Chemical disposal. Motorcaravan services. Caravans for hire.

Charges 1998: Per person Sfr. 5.80 - 6.20; child (6-16 yrs) 3.00 - 4.70; tent 3.00 - 4.00; caravan 7.00 - 7.20; car 4.00 - 5.50; m/cycle 2.00; motorcaravan 12.00 - 15.00 or 12.50 - 15.50, acc. to size and season; electricity 2.70 plus meter; local tax 3.25 (child 1.70). Higher prices in winter.

Reservations: Write with deposit (Sfr. 50). Address: 1854 Leysin. Tel: 024/494 18 29. FAX: 024/494 20 29.

960 Camping Rive-Bleue, Le Bouveret, nr Lausanne

Site by Lake Geneva with good swimming pool and lakeside installations.

At the eastern end of Lac Léman, the main feature of this site is the very pleasant lakeside lido only a short walk of 300 m. from the site and with free entry for campers. It has a swimming pool (25 x 15 m.), with a water toboggan and plenty of grassy lying-out areas, a bathing area in lake, boating facilities with storage for sailboards, canoes, inflatables etc, sailing school, pedaloes for hire. Also here and, like the lido, under same ownership as the camp, is a quality hotel which at the rear has a cafe for food and drinks with access from the lido. The camp itself has 200 marked pitches on well kept flat grass, half in the centre with 6A electricity, the other half round the perimeter. Two decent toilet blocks with British WCs, washbasins with shelf, mirror and cold water in the old block, hot in the new, pre-set free hot showers with seat and screen, push-button operated but water runs on well.

How to find it: Approach site on Martigny-Evian road no. 21 and turn to Bouveret-Plage south of Le Bouveret.

General Details: Open 1 April - 30 Sept. Shop, restaurant by beach (both all season). Bicycle hire. Fishing. Covered area for cooking with electric rings and barbecue. Drying room. Chemical disposal. Euro-relais station for motorcaravans.

Charges 1998: Per person Sfr. 7.10 - 8.50, plus local tax 0.60; child (6-16 yrs) 5.00 - 6.00, plus local tax 0.30; car 1.70; tent 6.00 - 9.60, acc. to season and size; caravan 7.70 - 10.50; motorcaravan 9.30 - 12.00; electricity 3.10.

Reservations: are recommended and made for any length with Sfr. 20 non-refundable reservation fee. Address: Bouveret-Plage, 1897 Le Bouveret. Tel: 024/48 42 42 (reservation 481 21 61). FAX: 024/481 21 08.

RIVE-BLEU, BOUVERET PLAGE
Lake Geneva

Tel: (information) 024/482 42 42
(reservation) 024/481 21 61
Fax: 024/481 21 08

New, 1st category international tourist site Natural beach, heated swimming pool, tennis, sailboarding, shop and restaurant. Modern toilet blocks with free hot water.

971 TCS Camping Les Iles, Sion

Pleasant, well organised campsite in the Rhône Valley.

Sion is an ancient and interesting town on the main route from Martigny to Brig and the Simplon Pass into Italy. Les Iles is an excellent, well organised and pretty site, useful for a night stop when passing through or for a longer stay to explore the region or relax in a pleasant area. Although it is near a small airport, it is understood that no planes fly at night. The rectangular site has 440 level pitches for tourists, 340 with 4A electricity and 22 serviced with water and waste water also. Well laid out, a profusion of flowers, shrubs and trees lead to a lake which supplements the pool for swimming and may be used by inflatable boats. There is a good area of grass for sunbathing and two playgrounds for children. Six good sanitary blocks are spaced around the site with British style WCs, free hot water in washbasins, showers and sinks, as well as baby rooms and provision for disabled people. The site has a popular restaurant with terrace and a well stocked shop (both all year) with others in the town (4 km). A entertainment programme for children and adults is offered in July/Aug. with organised excursions (extra cost) and a wealth of interesting activities near including watersports, mountain biking, para-gliding, etc from Swissraft. Good English is spoken and the warden is pleased to give advice on places to visit.

How to find it: Site is about 4 km. west of Sion and is signed from road 9 and the motorway exit.

General Details: Open all year exc. 1 Nov - 19 Dec. 80,000 sq.m. Electrical connections (4A). Shop. Restaurant. Swimming pool (12 x 10 m. mid May - mid Sept). Children's play areas. Football field. Table tennis. Tennis 100 m. Golf and horse riding 6 km. Good animation programme in July/Aug. and many sporting opportunities nearby. Bicycle hire. Washing machines and dryers. Baby rooms. Chemical disposal. Motorcaravan services.

Charges 1997: Per person Sfr. 5.20 - 6.60; child (6-16 yrs) 50%; pitch 6.20 - 22.00; electricity 4.00; local tax 0.80.

Reservations: Write to site. Address: 1951 Sion. Tel:027/346 43 47. FAX: 027/346 68 47.

The sites in SWITZERLAND featured in this guide are shown on the map on page 376

SWITZERLAND

966 Camping des Glaciers, La Fouly, nr Martigny

Mountain site with first-class facilities and spectacular views.

Situated at 1,600 m. above sea level, Des Glaciers is set amidst magnificent mountain scenery in a very quiet, peaceful location in the beautiful Ferret Valley. Being just off the main Martigny - Grand St Bernard route, it could make a night stop when travelling along this road but as this would entail a 13 km. detour along a minor road, it is more convenient for a longer stay. Those seeking peace, quiet and fresh mountain air or an opportunity for mountain walking would be well suited here. Marked tracks bring Grand St Bernard and the path around Mont Blanc within range, among many other possibilities with an abundance of flora and fauna for added interest. Guides are available if required. The camp offers two types of pitches - about half in an open, undulating meadow with campers choosing where to go and the proprietor advising if numbers require this and the rest being level, individual plots of varying size in small clearings either between bushes and shrubs or under tall pines. Equally suitable for all units from small tents to large caravans. A small stream runs through the site. Of the 170 places, 150 have 15A electricity so a small heater can be used if evenings become chilly. There are three sanitary units, all of exceptional quality and heated when necessary. The oldest and smallest is under reception, there is another in the centre of the open area and a new block in the centre of the site. Hot water is free in all basins (some in private cabins), showers and sinks. British style WCs. Each block has washing machines and dryers and the older block a drying room. A special baby room has been incorporated in the new block. An interesting feature of the site is a large, half-oval tent structure with beds and kitchen facilities for the use of those who wish to pack the evening before departure and a new wet weather room has been added for campers. There are sports facilities and swimming pools at 18 and 25 km. but this is, above all, a camp for those who wish to enjoy the mountain atmosphere, get close to nature or walk in the mountains where there are also refreshment stops at mountain huts. The charming lady owner, fluent in 6 languages, is always ready not only to welcome you to this peaceful haven but also to give information on the locality. The site has a small shop for basic supplies with restaurants and village shop about 5 minutes walk away.

How to find it: Leave the Martigny-Gd St Bernard road (no. 21) at Orsieres and follow signs to La Fouly. Site is signed on right at end of La Fouly village.

General Details: Open 20 May - 30 Sept. 70,000 sq.m. Shade in parts. Shop for basics. Children's playground. Bicycle hire. Washing machines and dryers. Baby room. Chemical disposal. Motorcaravan services.

Charges 1998: Per person Sfr. 6.00; child (2-12 yrs) 3.50; pitch 10.00 - 16.00; electricity 3.00; dog 1.00. Credit cards accepted.

Reservations: Made without deposit; write to site. Address: 1944 La Fouly (VS). Tel: 027/783 17 35. FAX: 027/783 36 05.

973 Camping Gemmi, Susten, nr Sion

Small, friendly, family site in Rhône Valley.

The Rhône Valley is a popular through route to Italy via the Simplon Pass and a holiday region in its own right. Enjoying some of the best climatic conditions in Switzerland, this valley, between two mountain regions, has less rainfall and more hours of sunshine than most of the country. It is an area of vines and fruit trees with mountain walks and the majestic Matterhorn nearby. Gemmi is a delightful small camp in a scenic location with 70 level pitches, all with 16A electricity, on well tended grass amidst a variety of trees, many of which offer shade. There are some pitches for motorcaravans with water and drainage. The modern, central sanitary block, part of which is heated, is of excellent quality and kept very clean. It has British WCs and free hot water in washbasins (some in private cabins), showers and sinks. Private bathrooms are available for hire on a weekly basis. The pleasant, friendly owner speaks fluent English, maintains high standards and has bucked current trends by establishing a camp for tourists with no resident static units. An attractive wooden building at the entrance includes a well stocked shop and small bar/restaurant where snacks and a limited range of local specialities are served.

How to find it: From east (Visp), turn left 1 km. after sign for Agarn Feithieren. From west (Sierre), turn right 2 km. after Susten by Hotel Millius, then after 300 m. right at sign for Camping Torrent.

General Details: Open 24 April - 10 Oct. 10,000 sq.m. Shop. Terrace bar and snack restaurant. Modern electricity connections. Tennis, swimming and walking near. Children's playground. Washing machines and dryers. Chemical disposal. Motorcaravan services.

Charges 1998: Per adult Sfr 6.00 - 7.00; child 1-6 yrs 3.50 - 4.50, 6-16 yrs 4.50 - 5.50; pitch 10.00 - 14.00; pitch with drainage 14.00 - 18.00; electricity 3.00; private sanitary facility 150.00 per week; local tax 0.60 (0.30, under 16); dog 2.00.

Reservations: Necessary for high season - no charge. Address: Briannenstrasse, 3952 Susten-Leuk. Tel: 027/473 11 54. FAX: 027/473 42 95.

969 Camping Swiss-Plage, Salgesch, Sierre

Large, well run site with natural lake, in the Rhône Valley.

This is a good site and is well run by its English speaking owner and, although about half is occupied by static caravans, there are still 250 pitches for visiting tourists. The site is also slightly unusual in that much of the terrain has been deliberately left in its natural state. The wooded section gives good shade and tree formations and access roads determine where units go. There is a central open meadow and some quiet spots are a little further from the amenities. Most pitches, although unmarked, have 10A electric points available. Some new, marked pitches have electricity, water and drainage. One part of the site may be reserved but some space is usually available. The centre of the site has a natural lake which is kept dredged and clean and is suitable for small boats (not windsurfers) and for bathing - the site say the water is tested weekly. It is possible to stroll along the banks of the Rhône and good walks are nearby. The main sanitary block in the centre has been refurbished to a high standard and can be heated in cool weather. Although the two other blocks are showing signs of age, the total provision should be sufficient. British style WCs, free hot water in basins in the new block, cold in some of the others, and hot showers on payment. Outside the excellent restaurant is a snack bar which offers good grill meals and 30 different pizzas which can be eaten on the terrace or taken away.

How to find it: From either direction on road no. 9 or more recent bypasses, follow Salgesch signs which should bring you past site entrance 3 km. northeast of Sierre. Care required to spot first sign in Sierre at multi-road junction.

General Details: Open Easter - 3 Nov. 11,000 sq.m. Self-service shop. Bar/restaurant with terrace. Takeaway food. Lake. Paddling pool. Children's playground. Table tennis. Fishing (on payment). Volleyball. Badminton. Some entertainment in high season. Washing machine and dryer. Chemical disposal. Motorcaravan services.

Charges 1997: Per person Sfr. 6.30, plus local tax 0.60; child (4-14 yrs) 3.00 plus tax 0.20; pitch 14.00; electricity 2.50; dog 2.00. Less 10% in low season. Credit cards not accepted.

Reservations: necessary and made for any length with deposit. Address: 3960 Sierre-Salgesch (Valais). Tel: 027/455 66 08 or 481 60 23. FAX: 027/481 32 15.

Camping Swiss-Plage, Sierre-Salgesch (Valais) Switzerland

The only camp in the Valais region with its own natural bathing lake (entry free for campers), with temperature around 18°C. Part sunny, part shaded pitches. Well maintained sanitary facilities. Restaurant. Self-service shop. Starting point for innumerable excursions (Val d'Anniviers, etc). Sports centre (tennis, badminton, beach volleyball, sauna, climbing wall, fitness centre, etc) 800 m.

972 Camping Bella Tola, Susten, nr Sion

Site with good facilities, swimming pool and individual pitches.

An attractive site with good standards, Bella Tola is on the hillside above Susten (east of Sierre) with good views over the Rhône valley. It boasts a good sized heated swimming pool and children's pool (both free to campers) which, like the restaurant and bar overlooking them, are also open to non-campers and so more crowded at weekends and holidays. In the low rain climate of the Valais the pool is naturally much used. Pitches are nearly all on sloping ground which varies in steepness, but extensive terracing is being carried out and about 50 plots had been completed when seen. Some 200 of the 260 individually numbered pitches have 16A electrical connections. The fullest season is 10/7-10/8, but they say that there is usually room somewhere. Three good quality modern sanitary blocks should provide sufficient coverage with British style toilets, individual basins (some cabins), with free hot water in some ladies' basins, showers and sinks. Torches advised. Further improvements are underway including facilities for disabled people. Very pleasant management. Used by tour operators. Guests are requested to comply with environmental rules by sorting rubbish as directed.

How to find it: Turn south from main road at Susten where camp is signed.

General Details: Open 16 May - 27 Sept. (as are shop and restaurant/bar). 200 electrical connections - long leads may be needed. Swimming pool (29/5-20/9). Tennis courts. General room with TV. Baby room. Films, organised sports, activities, guided walks etc. in July/Aug. Riding near. Washing machines, dryers and irons. Car wash. Chemical disposal. Motorcaravan services.

Charges 1998: Per person Sfr 7.00 - 9.50, plus local tax 0.80; child 2-6 yrs 2.50 - 4.50, 6-16 yrs 4.50 - 6.00, plus 0.40; pitch 10.50 or 10.00 - 25.00; electricity 3.50; dog 2.20. Credit cards accepted.

Reservations: made with deposit and fee (Sfr. 25). Address: 3952 Susten. Tel: 027/4731491. FAX: 027/4733641.

SWITZERLAND

942 Camping Manor Farm, Interlaken

See colour
advert opposite

Lakeside site in the Bernese Oberland popular with the British.

Manor Farm has, for some years, had a large proportion of Britons among its guests, for whom this is one of the traditional touring areas. The site lies outside the town on the northern side of the Thuner See, with most of the site between road and lake but with one part on the far side of the road. Interlaken is rather a tourist town but the area is rich in scenery, with innumerable mountain excursions and walks available and the lakes and Jungfrau railway near at hand. The flat terrain is divided entirely into individual, numbered pitches which vary considerably both in size (from 40-100 sq.m.) and price; 450 are now equipped with electricity (10A), water, drainage and cable TV connections. Reservations are made, although you should find space except perhaps in late July/early August, but the best places may then be taken. The ground becomes a little muddy when wet. Around 30% permanent or letting units. There are seven separate toilet blocks which are practical and soundly constructed but mostly fairly small, although they have been much improved recently. They have British toilets, washbasins or troughs for washing with mirrors and showers, with free hot water in all blocks for washbasins, showers and baths. Twenty private units are available for rent. Site is used by tour operators (15%). Bathing is possible in the lake at two points and boats can be brought if a permit obtained. The site is efficiently and quite formally run, with good English spoken.

How to find it: Site is about 3 km. west of Interlaken along the road running north of the Thuner See towards Thun. Follow signs for 'Camp 1'. From the motor road bypassing Interlaken (N8) take exit marked 'Gunten, Beatenberg', which is a spur road bringing you out close to site.

General Details: Open all year. 70,000 sq.m. Shade in some places. Shop (15/4-15/10). Site-owned restaurant adjoining (1/3-31/12). New snack bar with takeaway on site (1/6-30/9). TV room. Football field. Children's playground and paddling pool. Minigolf. Bicycle hire. Table tennis. Sailing and windsurfing school. Boat hire. Fishing. Daily activity and entertainment programme in high season. Excursions. Bureau de change. Tourist information. Dishwasher. Washing machine, dryer, ironing. Car wash. Chemical disposal. Motorcaravan services. Bungalows, caravans and tents to let.

Charges 1998: Per person Sfr. 5.70 - 9.10; local tax 1.60; child (6-15 yrs) 2.60 - 4.30 (under 6 free); pitch 6.50 - 29.00, acc. to season and type (see description above); boat 2.00 - 6.00; electricity 0.80 - 4.00. acc. to amperage. (0.5, 4 or 6A). Various discounts for longer stays. Credit cards accepted.

Reservations: Taken for high season (min. 3 days) with booking fee (Sfr. 20). Address: 3800 Interlaken-Thunersee. Tel: 033/822 22 64. FAX: 033/823 29 91.

This site is featured out of order - it should be listed on page 346

967 Camping de Molignon, Les Haudéres-Evoline

Mountain site with stunning views in the Herens Valley.

The uphill drive from Sion in the Rhône Valley is enhanced by the Pyramids of Eusegeine, through which the road passes via a short tunnel. These unusual structures, cut out by erosion from masses of morainic debris, have been saved from destruction by their unstable rocky crowns. De Molignon, surrounded by mountains, is a quiet, peaceful place where, although there may be some road noise, the rushing stream and the sound of cow bells are likely to be the only disturbing factor in summer. The 100 pitches for tourists are on well tended, level terraces leading down to the river. Some 72 have electricity and are marked by numbered posts. They have a small shop for basic supplies (mid-July to mid-Sept) and a pleasant restaurant (open all year) with a good menu at reasonable prices. Although this is essentially a place for mountain walking (guided tours available), climbing and relaxing, there is a geological museum in Les Haudéres, which has links with a British University, cheese making and interesting flora and fauna. Skiing and langlauf in winter. The two sanitary blocks, heated in cool weather, have British style WCs, free hot water in sinks and washbasins and on payment in the showers. Good English is spoken by the owner's son who is now running the site, who will be pleased to give information on all that is available from the camp.

How to find it: Follow signs southwards from Sion for the Val d'Herens through Evoline to Les Haudéres where the site is signed on the right of the road.

General Details: Open all year. 15,000 sq.m. 1,450 m above sea level. Electrical connections (10A). Basic food supplies (high season). Restaurant. Small playground. Guided walks, climbing, geological museum, winter skiing. Fishing, tennis and hang-gliding near. Washing machines and dryer. Motorcaravan service point. Chemical disposal.

Charges 1997: Per person Sfr. 4.50; child (4-16 yrs) 2.00; pitch 8.00 - 12.00; electricity 2.00; local tax 1.10.

Reservations: Write to site. Address: 1984 Les Haudéres-Evoline. Tel: 027/283 12 40. FAX: as phone.

Touring *Britain, France and Europe*

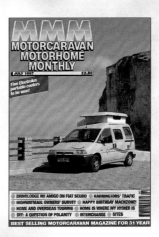

For tests and touring features 12 months of the year choose Britain's premier caravan and motorhome magazines.

946 Camping Jungfrau, Lauterbrunnen, nr Interlaken

See colour
advert opposite

Friendly site with good quality installations, in attractive mountain surroundings.

This site has a very imposing situation in a steep valley with a fine view of the Jungfrau at the end. You can laze here amid real mountain scenery, though it does lose the sun a little early. There are naturally many more active things to do - mountain walks or climbing, trips up the Jungfrau railway or one of the mountain lifts or excursions by car. The site itself is quite extensive and is grassy with hard surfaced access roads. It is a popular site and, although you should usually find space, in season do not arrive too late. All 391 pitches (250 for touring) have electrical connections (10-15A) and 50 have water and drainage also. There are three sanitary blocks, the new one at the far end of the site being a good modern one with hot water in all basins and showers, and the others having been thoroughly renewed and modernised. All have British toilets, individual washbasins and free hot showers. Hot water in all basins and for washing-up. There are new facilities for the disabled, baby baths and footbaths. Water taps on site. Also open for winter camping, the installations are heated in cool weather. The site is owned and run by the von Allmen family who provide a warm welcome (English is spoken). Improvements over the last few years have made this an excellent and most recommendable site. About 30% of the pitches are taken by seasonal caravans. The site is used by a tour operator and by groups of youngsters from many different countries - pitches at the top of the site may be quieter. Bungalows and caravans to let. Hostel accommodation in winter only. Free bus to ski station (winter only).

How to find it: Go through Lauterbrunnen and fork right at far end before road bends left, 100 m. before church. The final approach is not very wide.

General Details: Open all year, including shop. 50,000 sq.m. Good shade in parts. Supermarket. New self-service restaurant with takeaway. Good general room with wooden tables and chairs, TV, jukebox, drink vending machines, amusements, with second one elsewhere. Well equipped and cared for children's playgrounds and covered area for children also. Washing machine, spin dryer and ironing. Hair dryer. Excursions and some entertainment in high season. Mountain bikes for hire. Bungalows and mobile homes for hire. Doctor very close, will call. Chemical disposal. Motorcaravan services.

Charges 1997: Per person Sfr. 6.20 - 7.60, plus local tax 2.00; child (6-15 yrs) 3.10 - 3.80, plus 0.80; car 3.50; caravan 9.00 - 15.00; motorcaravan 9.00 - 15.00, acc. to size; tent 6.00 - 15.00; hiker's tent 4.00; electricity 2.50 + meter. Discounts for camping carnet and for stays over 3 nights outside high season.

Reservations: made for any period with deposit; write for details. Address: 3822 Lauterbrunnen. Tel: 033/856 20 10. FAX: 033/856 20 20.

This site is featured out of order - it should be listed on page 346

957 Camping Eienwäldli, Engelberg, nr Lucerne/Luzern

See colour
advert opposite

Quiet mountain site south of Luzern.

This is a delightful site surrounded on all sides by mountains, in a beautiful setting at over 1,000 m. above sea level, on the edge of the lovely village of Engelberg. This area is famous for winter sports and summer walking, and the site is open all year except for November. Half the site is taken up by static caravans but there is space for some 160 tourist units on a flat grass meadow with numbered and marked pitches on either side of hard access roads and a good provision of hardstandings. The reception building has been extended to include a small, well stocked self service shop, snack bar/cafe (which looks into the heated indoor swimming pool) and hotel. A Gasthof/restaurant is opposite. The toilet block has been refurbished to an excellent standard with British style WCs, washbasins set in flat surfaces with free hot water with private cabins for ladies, and hot showers on payment. A laundry room has been added in the basement below. Free hot water in sinks. Car entrance is closed 8 pm.-7.30 am.

How to find it: From the Gotthard motorway, leave at Stans-Sud exit and follow signs to Engelberg. Turn right at T-junction on edge of town and follow signs for 'Wasserfall' or camp.

General Details: Open all year (except Nov.). 40,000 sq.m. Electrical connections everywhere (10A). Shop. Restaurant. Indoor swimming pool. Snack bar/café. Small lounge. Ski facilities. Children's playground. Golf driving range and 9 hole course (480 m). Sauna. Washing machines and dryers. Chemical disposal.

Charges 1998: Per person Sfr. 6.50; child (6-15 yrs) 3.50, under 6 yrs free; local tax 1.90; caravan 11.00; motorcaravan 13.00; tent 7.00 - 11.00; electricity 2.00 + meter; cable TV 2.50.

Reservations: necessary for summer and winter and made with Sfr. 50 deposit. Address: 6390 Engelberg. Tel: 041/6371949. FAX: 041/6374423.

This site is featured out of order - it should be listed on page 348

SWITZERLAND

977 Camping Santa Monica, Raron

Neat and compact all year campsite in the Rhône Valley.

We offer several different styles of campsite in the Rhône Valley and now add this pleasant, well tended site which stays open all year. The Simplon Pass is the only main route from Switzerland to Italy which avoids motorways and the need to buy the Swiss motorway vignette. It is also an easy pass for caravans which is only closed occasionally in winter and, even then, this way is possible by using the Brig-Iselle train ferry through the mountain. About half the site is occupied by static caravans and the site's own accommodation, but these are to one side leaving two flat, open meadows, bisected by the hard access road, so do not intrude on the tourist area. The 140 level pitches, all with 16A electricity, are roughly defined by saplings and electrical connection boxes. There is a small (12 x 4 m) swimming pool with another smaller one for children and a shop/bar/restaurant (open in high season) in the reception building, with other shops and restaurants near. Being right beside the main road 9, one does not have to deviate to find a night stop but it would also make a good base for exploring the area. It has an air of peace although, being so near the road, there is some traffic noise. Mountain views, close on south side, distant across interesting valley. The single, heated sanitary block is towards the entrance, has British style WCs and free hot water in washbasins and sinks and on payment in the showers. There are facilities for the disabled. Table tennis on site and tennis courts next door. Two cable ways start near the site entrance for winter skiers and summer mountain walkers.

How to find it: On the south side of road 9 between Visp and Susten, signed.

General Details: Open all year. 40,000 sq.m. Electricity (16A). Bar/restaurant/shop (July/Aug). Small pool and child's pool. Children's playground. Table tennis. Walking country, cable cars near. Chemical disposal. Motorcaravan services (Euro-Relais).

Charges 1997: Per person Sfr. 5.00 - 6.00; child (6-16 yrs) 3.00 - 4.00; tent (max 3 persons) 7.00 - 8.50; caravan 9.50 - 12.00; electricity 3.00 (winter 5.00); local tax 0.50.

Reservations: Write to site. Address: 3942 Raron (VS). Tel: 027/934 24 24. FAX: 027/934 24 50.

987 Camping Piccolo Paradiso, Avegno, nr Locarno

Pleasant, popular site in mountain valley setting.

Locarno, in the most southern of Swiss cantons, Ticino, is a very popular holiday area with activities associated with lakes and mountains. Being on the south of Locarno, Avegno is also a good base from which to visit Lake Maggiori and this part of northern Italy. There are a number of very good camps around to which we add this one to give as much choice as possible. During our stay we were impressed with the friendly, happy atmosphere, much of which is engendered by the owner who appears to know visitors who return year after year and greets them enthusiastically. The lively social life revolves around the central bar/restaurant and terrace. However, all noise has to cease at 11 pm. The 300 tourist pitches are on two level terraces in a river valley, marked by numbered stones set into the ground. Spaces are not over-large but seem to suffice. There are 200 electrical connections, in all areas except the areas set aside for small tents. Three sanitary blocks are spread the site and, although not too large, should be enough. Hot showers are on payment. British style WCs. The owner has a hut in the mountains in which campers can spend the night if climbing. Children are welcome and catered for with two playgrounds, a small pool and organised games in high season making this an ideal family site.

How to find it: From Locarno follow signs for 'Valle Maggia' and then camp signs to site (6 km.).

General Details: Open 1 March - 31 Oct. 4.5 ha. Self-service bar/restaurant (mainly Italian type fast food) with terrace. Shade in parts. Children's pool. 2 children's play areas. River bathing (summer). Boating. Table tennis. Volleyball. Mountain bike hire. Entertainment in high season. Washing machines and dryers. Chemical disposal. Motorcaravan services.

Charges 1998: Per person Sfr. 7.00 - 8.00; child (4-14 yrs) 5.00 - 6.00; caravan, motorcaravan or large tent 10.00 - 18.00, acc. to unit and season; dog 3.00; electricity (10A) 4.00.

Reservations: Write to site with Sfr. 50 deposit. Address: 6670 Avegno, v. Maggia. Tel: 091/796 15 81. FAX: 091/796 31 70.

988 Camping Lido Mappo, Tenero, nr Locarno

Orderly but friendly site with good installations on Lake Maggiore.

Lido Mappo lies on the lakeside at the northeast tip of Lake Maggiore, about 5 km. from Locarno, and has views of the surrounding mountains and hills across the lake. A wide variety of trips can be made from here by car, lake steamer or mountain lift. The site has its own narrow beach with a frontage of some 400 m., mainly sandy, but the lake, shelving very gradually, has a stony floor. Boats can be brought and left on the shore or at moorings; a jetty has been constructed for these. The site is attractively laid out in rows of individual, numbered pitches, half for tents and half for caravans and mostly split up by access roads or hedges. *continued overleaf*

988 Camping Lido Mappo (continued)

The pitches (430 for touring) vary in size, those by the lake costing more and most are well shaded. Electricity (10A) is available on all pitches. Although reservations are only made for longer stays, there is always a fair chance of finding a vacant place. The five toilet blocks, which can be heated in cool weather, are always well kept but some are newer than others. They have been improved with more individual washbasins, all in cabins for women and some for men, free hot water and British WCs. Facilities for disabled people. With helpful staff who speak good English, it is a quiet site which celebrated its 40th anniversary in 1997.

How to find it: On the Locarno side of Tenero, a road with sign to camp will be seen leading off the Bellinzona - Locarno road to the south.

General Details: Open 27 March - 25 Oct. as are all amenities. 65,000 sq.m. Supermarket. Restaurant/bar. Takeaway (high season). Large children's playground. Bathing raft in lake. Fishing. Bicycle hire. First-aid post. Washing machines and dryers. Cooking facilities. Refrigerated compartments for hire. Chemical disposal. Motorcaravan services. No dogs accepted.

Charges 1998: Per unit incl. 2 persons Sfr. 32.00 - 45.00, on lakeside 47.00 - 65.00, acc. to season; extra person (over 3 yrs) 6.00 - 7.00; extra car 5.00 - 6.00; m/cycle 3.00 - 4.00; trailer 4.00 - 5.00; electricity included. Less 5% for stays over 15 days.

Reservations: Min. 1 week (2 weeks lakeside) July/August, or 2 weeks at other times. Large deposit and smaller fee. Address: 6598 Tenero (Ticino). Tel: 091/745 14 37. FAX: 091/745 48 08. E-mail: gpedrazzini@tinet.ch.

990 Camping Delta, Locarno

Good lakeside site within walking distance of central Locarno.

Camping Delta is actually within the Locarno town limits, only some 800 m. from the centre, and it has a prime position right by the lake, with bathing direct from the site, and adjacent to the municipal lido and sports field. Boats can be put on the lake and the site also has some moorings on an estuary at one side, with a jetty. It has 300 pitches on flat ground of 80-100 sq.m.; they are marked out at the rear but have nothing between them. There are also 30 smaller 'student pitches' for those without a car. The single central toilet block is kept very clean and should be about large enough though it could be hard pressed at the busiest times. Hot water is free in the washbasins (some in cabins for women), fully controllable showers and sinks; WCs are British type. Delta is a well run and well situated site. No dogs are accepted.

How to find it: From central Locarno follow signs to Camping Delta, Lido or Stadio along the lake. Beware that approaching from south there are also Delta signs which lead you to Albergo Delta in quite the wrong place.

General Details: Open 1 March - 31 Oct. 65,000 sq.m. Partly shaded. Electrical connections (10A) all parts. Small supermarket. Restaurant/bar with limited menu. Fitness room. Sauna. Children's playground. Table tennis, amusements. Washing machine and dryer. Chemical disposal. Caravans for hire.

Charges 1997: Per person Sfr. 9.00 - 13.00; child (3-18 yrs) 5.00; normal pitch 20.00 - 30.00; lakeside pitch 30.00 - 45.00; electricity 4.00; boat 7.00 - 44.00; trailer 7.00; local tax 1.00.

Reservations: made for any length with booking fee (Sfr. 100). Address: 6600 Locarno. Tel: 091/751 60 81. FAX: 091/751 22 43.

991 Park-Camping Riarena, Cugnasco, nr Bellinzona

Site with swimming pool between Bellinzona and Locarno.

An agreeable site close to the route from the St. Gotthard to the south, Riarena may appeal both to those who are looking for a convenient night stop and to those seeking a holiday site, as it has a medium sized swimming pool and children's pool. Most of the site is covered by tall trees and it is in a peaceful setting, far enough from the main road to be away from noise. The sanitary block is of good quality and has British toilets, individual basins with shelf and mirror (a few in private cabins) and free hot water in all facilities. It is however small for the size of the site, though showers have been increased to 16 and facilities for the disabled added. The 200 pitches are now all individually marked with 10A electrical connections available. July is busiest; there is usually space at other times. Used by tour operators.

How to find it: From motorway exit Bellinzona south in the direction of Locarno. After 10 km. at large roundabout turn to Gudo-Bellinzona for 2.5 km. and follow signs for Cugnasco from where site is well signed.

General Details: Open 1 April - 20 Oct. 38,000 sq.m. Well shaded. Electrical connections available. Shop (1/4-15/9). Restaurant. Takeaway. Play area. Swimming pools (25/5-15/9). Mountain bike hire. Siesta time 12.00-14.00 hrs. Washing machines and dryers. Chemical disposal. Motorcaravan services.

Charges 1998: Per unit incl. 2 persons and tax 27.00 - 35.00; extra adult 7.00 - 8.00; child under 6 yrs 3.00 - 4.00, 6-14 yrs 4.00 - 5.00; dog 3.00; electricity 3.50.

Reservations: Made without charge. Tel: 091/859 16 88. FAX: 091/859 28 85.

SWITZERLAND

993 Camping Al Censo, Claro, nr Bellinzona

Tranquil site on old Gotthard - Bellinzona road.

A most agreeable, pretty site on the old Gotthard - Bellinzona road, Al Censo is suitable for those wanting a peaceful night away from the motorway. There is a number of permanent caravans, but room for 90 touring pitches, 52 with electricity (6A) on both sides of reception but not marked out. The site is on a very gentle slope amidst mainly mature trees. The two small sanitary blocks are well appointed and should be sufficient even in high season. British type toilets. Warm water is supplied through a single tap into washbasins. Free hot showers. The site is well maintained and regularly cleaned.

How to find it: Site is well signed at the northern end of Claro on the old St Gotthard-Bellinzona road. From motorway take Bellinzona-Nord exit and head north on old pass road. From the north, take Biascon exit and go south on old pass road.

General Details: Open 1 April - 31 Oct. 20 ha. Good shade in most parts. Shop (limited supplies), drinks served. Play area. Unheated swimming pool. Whirlpool (in season). Games room (3 pin ball tables). Table tennis. Washing machines and dryers. Chemical disposal. No entry to site 12-14.00 hrs.

Charges 1998: Per person Sfr. 7.00; child (1-12 yrs) 5.20; pitch 9.00 - 18.00; tax 1.30; electricity (6A) 3.00.

Reservations: made without charge. Address: 6702 Claro. Tel: 091/863 17 53.

995 TCS Camping Piodella, Muzzano, nr Lugano

Excellent lakeside site with sandy beach.

This modernised site, on the edge of Lake Lugano facing south down the lake must rank as one of the best in Switzerland. There are 210 numbered tourist pitches of good size, with shade in the older part nearest the lake and young trees in the new area. Cars must be parked in the car park, not by your pitch. Roads have been relaid and a marina has been added. The former sanitary block has been refurbished and a splendid new one has been built. This includes a baby room, bathroom for the disabled, British style WCs and free hot water in the washbasins, sinks and good sized showers. As the site is now open all year, these facilities are heated in cool weather. A large swimming pool and a child's pool have been constructed and one can also bathe from the sandy beach. There is a children's playground on a safe base with good, fixed apparatus and two new tennis courts. The site is a short way from the end of Lugano's airport but there appears to be no night flying or movements by large aircraft. There is a new bar/restaurant with a pleasant terrace. Although the site is well placed for exploring Lugano, southern Switzerland and northern Italy, many will be content to stay put and enjoy the facilities of the site.

How to find it: Piodella is on the Bellinzona-Ponte Tresa road; take motorway exit for Ponte Tresa and turn left at T-junction in Agno. Follow signs for Piodella or TCS. Site is at south end of the airport.

General Details: Open all year except 3-14 March and 3-28 Nov. Electricity connections in all areas (4, 6 or 10A). Shop. Bar/restaurant. Motorcaravan service point. Swimming pools. Tennis. Day and TV rooms. Children's playground. Washing machines and dryers. Chemical disposal. Motorcaravan services.

Charges 1997: Per person Sfr. 5.50 - 7.00; child (6-16 yrs) 50%; pitch 9.00 - 28.00, acc. to season and type; motorcaravan 23.50 - 28.00; local tax 1.25; electricity 2.40 - 4.00, acc. to amps.

Reservations: Write to site. Address: 6933 Muzzano. Tel: 091/994 77 88. FAX: 091/994 67 08.

981 Camp Au, Chur

Satisfactory site on through route in attractive part of country.

This modern site has some 120 individual pitches, not very big (say 60 sq.m.) but all with electricity (10A), and about an equal number of unmarked ones on an open meadow, all on flat grass. The toilet block is also modern and of good quality but would frankly be too small if the site were full. It has British style toilets, washbasins with free hot water, shelf and mirror, hot showers on payment and is heated in cool weather. There are no water points outside the block. Despite this drawback Camp Au is a good site for a night stop or a few days exploring this attractive mountain region. It is rarely full and with much short-stay trade, usually has vacancies. About 400 m. walk away is a sports centre including both an indoor and outdoor swimming pool, and the centre of Chur, said to be the oldest town in Switzerland. is about 3 km. The main entrance to the camp is reached by passing under a bridge with only 3.05 m. clearance - there is an alternative but with only 3.30 m.

How to find it: Site is on south side of town; from motor road take 'Chur N' exit from north and continue on obvious main road - signs eventually appear. From south 'Chur S' exit and follow signs. See above for height limit.

General Details: Open all year. Small shop. Swimming and tennis centre (next to camp) have restaurants. General room with drinks served. Children's playground. Table tennis. Washing machine and dryer. Chemical disposal. Motorcaravan services.

Charges 1998: Per person Sfr. 6.00; child (6-12 yrs) 3.00; local tax (over 12s) 0.80; 1 or 2 person tent 6.0, 3 or 4 person 8.00, family tent 12.00; caravan 12.00; motorcaravan 14.00; car 4.00; m/cycle 2.00; electricity 3.30 (p/kw. in winter); dog 1.50; local tax (over 12) 0.30.

Reservations: made if you write to site. Address: Felsenaustrasse 61, 7000 Chur. Tel: 081/284 22 83. FAX: 081/284 56 83.

982 Campingplatz Pradafenz, Churwalden

Mountain site with excellent facilities and services.

In the heart of the village of Churwalden on the Chur - St Moritz road, Pradafenz makes a convenient night stop and being amidst the mountains, is also an excellent base for walking and exploring this scenic area. There are 38 ski lifts serving the district with one starting from the camp entrance both for winter ski-ing and summer walking. Being at 1,200 m. above sea level and surrounded by pine clad mountains, the views are breathtaking and the air fresh and clean. The absence of entertainment on site makes this a quiet, peaceful place although a variety of entertainment is offered in the region. At first sight, this appears to be a site for static holiday caravans but the owner has made a large rectangular terrace at the rear for 30 touring units. This area has a hardstanding of concrete frets with grass growing through and 'super-pitch' facilities of electricity (10A), water, drainage, gas and TV sockets. Cars must be parked in a separate park. A flat meadow is also available for tents or as an over-flow for caravans. Although the gravel road which leads to the tourers' terrace is not very steep, the friendly German speaking owner will tow caravans there with his tractor if this is required. The single sanitary block is half underground and is very well appointed with free hot water in all washbasins (some in private cabins) and sinks, with showers on payment. British style WCs. There is a baby room and another with hair dryers. A warm temperature is maintained all year. Because of its nearness to a ski lift, campers are provided with a key for the block during their stay. There is also a sm all community room. During high seasons a kiosk at the entrance provides basic food items with the village supermarket about 300 m. along with other shops and restaurants.

How to find it: Site is 300 m. from the main road, signed in the centre of the village.

General Details: Open all year except April - mid-June. 13,000 sq.m. General room. Washing machines. Kiosk for basic foods. Restaurants and shops 300 m. Walking. Skiing. Washing machines, dryers and separate drying room. Chemical disposal.

Charges 1997: Per person Sfr. 6.00 - 6.50; child (up to 12 yrs) 4.00 - 4.50; local tax 1.80 (child 0.80); caravan 7.00 - 10.00; car 3.00; tent small 4.00, large 8.00; motorcaravan 8.00 - 12.00; electricity 2.00 (metered in winter). Prices higher in winter.

Reservations: Advisable for winter; write to site. Address: 7075 Churwalden. Tel: 081/382 19 39. FAX: 081/382 19 21.

983 Camping Sur-En, Sent, nr Scoul

All year campsite with excellent facilities.

Sur-En is at the eastern end of the Engadine valley, about 10 km. from the Italian and Austrian borders. The area is, perhaps, better known as a skiing region, but has summer attractions as well. At nearby Scoul there is an ice-rink and thermal baths, plus a wide range of activities including mountain biking, white water rafting and excursion possibilities. As you approach on the road 27 and spot the site way below under the shadow of a steeply rising, wooded mountain, the drop down may appear daunting. However, as you drive it becomes reasonable, although the site owner will provide assistance for nervous towers. A level site, it is in an open valley with little shade. They say there is room for 150 touring units on the meadows where pitches are neither marked nor numbered; there are 80 electrical connections. The modern, heated sanitary block near the restaurant, shop and reception building is of a high standard and there is a further small provision in the main building when required. British WCs and free hot water in washbasins and showers. The good restaurant with a covered terrace overlooks the children's play area so that adults can enjoy a drink and keep watch on their children whilst enjoying the mountain views. Entertainment for both adults and children is arranged in July/Aug. and a symposium for sculptors is held during the second week in July. Excursions are also arranged in high season. The friendly, English speaking owner seems to have created a very pleasant atmosphere and although the camp might be used for a night stay during transit, it could well attract for a longer period.

How to find it: Site is clearly visible and also signed from main road 27 to the east of Scoul.

General Details: Open all year. 20,000 sq.m. Electrical connections (6A). Shop (all year). Restaurant (closed Nov. and April and on Tues. and Wed. in low season). Takeaway (high season). Good children's playground. Animation in high season. Activities near - see text above. Washing machine and dryer. Bus service to Scoul for train to St Moritz. Motorcaravan service point. Chemical disposal.

Charges 1997: Per person Sfr. 5.80; child (6-16 yrs) 2.90; caravan 13.40 - 15.00: tent 9.90 - 13.40; motorcaravan 13.40 - 15.00.

Reservations: not made. Address: 7554 Sur-En/Sent. Tel: 081/866 35 44. FAX: 081/866 32 37.

SWITZERLAND

985 TCS Camping Farich, Davos

Small, pleasant site on road to the Fluela Pass.

Davos extends for about 4 km. between Davos-Dorf and Davos-Platz between the Fluela Pass and Klosters. A ski centre in winter, Davos has the largest ice rink in Europe and cable cars to nearby peaks. Farich is situated on the edge of Davos-Dorf, at the start of the Pass road and, as the road rises as it passes the campsite, there is some road noise particularly at weekends and public holidays when hoards of motorcyclists race round two passes - Fluela and Julier - with scant regard for other road users. The 90 pitches, mainly under tall pines, are on either side of a fenced river with bridges between. These are not marked or numbered but the centre road and the 50 electricity points roughly determine where units go. A small shop provides basic food items and a pleasant bar serves good grill meals during the evenings. There is a small children's play area, table tennis and bicycle hire, with a swimming pool 1 km. away. The single sanitary block is at the rear of reception with British style WCs and free hot water in washbasins, sinks and showers.

How to find it: On the main road at eastern end of Davos-Dorf at the start of the Fluela Pass.

General Details: Open 16 May - 28 Sept. 13,000 sq.m. Electrical connections (4A). Shop, Grill meals. Children's playground. Bicycle hire. Table tennis. Swimming pool 1 km. Chemical disposal. Motorcaravan services.

Charges 1997: Per person Sfr. 5.80; child 6-15 yrs) 2.90; pitch 5.20 - 13.50; electricity 4.00.

Reservations: Write to site. Address: 7260 Davos-Dorf. Tel: 081/416 10 43.

984 Camping St Cassian, Lenz, nr Lenzerheide

Mountain site with good facilities in scenic area.

Although St Cassian caters mainly for static holiday caravans, it has room for 30 touring units and is suitable for a night stop travelling to or from St Moritz, or for a longer stay. The camp is on a gentle slope but the 40 touring pitches (out of 150) are terraced between the statics under a cover of tall pines. Being 1,415 m. above sea level in a north-south valley, this is a peaceful location surrounded by scenic views and abundant sunshine; 140 signed walking paths of various degrees of difficulty start from the site. Although there is no organised entertainment on the site, there are many opportunities at the holiday resort of Lenzerheide Valbella 3 km. Tennis, 18 hole golf course, bars and discos, heated swimming pool and a lake for fishing and watersports are near. Good bus services (with a stop outside the entrance) serve the region and many places of interest are accessible by car. The small, heated, good quality sanitary facility is in the main block which also houses reception and an excellent restaurant. Free hot water in washing troughs and sinks and on payment in the showers. British style WCs.

How to find it: Site is 20 km. from Chur on the no. 3 Chur-St Moritz road, between Lenzerheide and Lantsch/Lenz.

General Details: Open all year. Restaurant. Shop for basics. Washing machine and dryer. Chemical disposal.

Charges 1997: Per person Sfr. 6.50 - 7.00; child (6-16 yrs) 4.00 - 4.50; car 2.50; m/cycle 1.50; caravan 8.50; motorcaravan 11.00; tent large 8.50, small 5.50; electricity (10A) 2.50.

Reservations: Made with Sfr. 20 deposit. Address: 7083 Lantsch bei Lenzerheide. Tel: 081/384 24 72. FAX: 081/384 24 89.

980 Camping Silvaplana, Silvaplana, nr St Moritz

Family run site on edge of lake in the Engadine region.

Silvaplana is situated at the junction of the road from Italy over the Malojapass, the road from northern Switzerland via the Julierpass, and the road which continues through St Moritz to Austria. Camping Silvaplana, therefore, might be useful for a night stop if travelling this way. Although the surrounding scenery across the lake is very pleasant, there is nothing remarkable about the site except that it was reported that a wind blows along the lake most afternoons which is used by wind surfing enthusiasts. However, it is probably the best campsite in the area, with facilities next to the site for volleyball and football and good walking possibilities. There is a shop for basic supplies and a restaurant just away from the entrance which is open all day June-Oct. The site is mainly level and the 200 pitches for tourists are numbered and marked by posts or tapes, with 120 electical connections (10A). To be fair, our visit was the day after they had opened and the brother and sister who had taken over the running from their parents, seemed keen and enthusiastic to make changes. The sanitary accommodation is old, but acceptable, with British style WCs and free hot water in washing troughs, sinks and showers. There are no washing machines for campers but staff provide a laundry service. A fenced river runs through but the lake shore is unprotected (with access for boats to the lake).

How to find it: Look for camp signs on main road to the west of town, entrance to site is by underpass.

General Details: Open 15 May - 20 Oct. 50,000 sq m. Restaurant outside site (June-Oct). Shop. Watersports, climbing, walking, sports centre near, swimming in lake - pool 4 km. in St Moritz. Small children's play area. Fishing, tennis near. Laundry service. Chemical disposal. Motorcaravan services.

Charges 1998: Per person Sfr. 7.60; child 5-12 yrs 4.00, 12-16 yrs 6.00; tent 5.00 - 7.00; caravan 7.00; motorcaravan 8.00 - 10.00; car 7.00; m/cycle 3.00; electricity 2.80.

Reservations: Write to site. Address: 7513 Silvaplana. Tel: 081/828 84 92.

OPEN ALL YEAR

The following sites are understood to accept caravanners and campers all year round, although the list ***also includes some sites open for at least 10 months***. For sites marked ★ please check our report for dates and other restrictions. In any case, it is always wise to phone as, for example, facilities available may be reduced.

Andorra
9143

Austria
3*, 6*, 007B, 007C*, 9, 10, 11, 13, 14, 15*, 16, 18, 19, 20, 22, 23, 26*, 036N, 44, 48

Belgium
53, 54, 56, 58, 59, 64, 66, 67, 71*, 72, 74

British Isles
B61, B51, B59*, B60, B65, B319

Czech Republic
468, 474, 487

Denmark
2090, 2150

France
0200, 0605, 2415, 3803*, 5000, 8101

Germany
3000*, 3010*, 3015, 3025, 3030, 3035, 3040, 3045*, 3210, 3215, 3235, 3242, 3260*, 3264, 3280, 3405*, 3410, 3415, 3420, 3430, 3440, 3445, 3450, 3455, 3470, 3615, 3620, 3625*, 3630, 3650, 3665*, 3670, 3675, 3680*, 3685, 3690, 3705*, 3710, 3715*, 3720, 3725, 3820, 3840, 3845, 3850

Hungary
515, 526

Ireland
I325, I326*, I327, I335, I339, I341, I346, I347*

Italy
6037, 6200, 6250, 6400, 6610, 6665

Luxembourg
770

Netherlands
550, 556, 560, 561, 562, 563, 564, 579, 580, 584, 588, 591, 592

Norway
2315, 2350, 2400, 2460, 2480, 2510, 2570, 2590, 2610

Poland
315, 317, 319, 321, 323

Portugal
804, 814, 815, 820, 821, 822, 823, 833, 834, 835, 836, 837, 838, 839, 840, 841, 842, 843, 844

Slovak Republic
491, 493, 494

Spain
8072, 8130, 8240, 8390, 8506, 8535, 8615, 8680, 8681, 8711*, 8742, 8750, 8752, 8755, 8760, 8761N, 8780, 8800, 8801, 8830, 8850, 8870, 8940, 8964, 8980, 9024, 9025, 9030, 9035, 9070, 9080, 9081, 9085, 9087, 9090, 9200, 9270

Sweden
2650, 2665, 2675, 2745, 2750, 2840

Switzerland
936, 939, 942, 946, 949, 954, 995*

SITE BROCHURE SERVICE

The following sites have undertaken to supply us with a quantity of their brochures. These leaflets are interesting and useful supplements to our editorial reports and most contain colour photographs or other illustrations of the site which cannot be reproduced in this guide. If you would like any of these simply cut out or photocopy this page, tick the relevant boxes and post it to us. Please enclose a large, stamped, self addressed envelope (at least 9" x 6") addressed to yourself and stamped (on average, 5 brochures will weigh 100 gms, =31p 2nd class post). Please note that we cannot accept requests over the phone and that our supplies are normally exhausted by the end of August. Send your requests to:

Deneway Guides Ltd, Chesil Lodge, West Bexington, Dorchester, Dorset DT2 9DG

British Isles
- B110 Wooda Farm ☐

France
- 0401 L'Hippocampe ☐
- 0403 Moulin de Ventre ☐
- 0701 Mondial ☐
- 01107 Les Mimosas ☐
- 1202 Rivages ☐
- 1603M Champion ☐
- 1702 Puits l'Auture ☐
- 2403 Les Périères ☐
- 2404 Moulin-Roch ☐
- 2409 Soleil Plage ☐
- 2603 Grand Lierne ☐
- 2901 Ty Naden ☐
- 2906 Pil Koad ☐
- 2909 Raguenes ☐
- 3305 Les Ourmes ☐
- 3404 Lou Village ☐
- 3504 P'tit Bois ☐
- 3901 Plage Blanche ☐
- 4004 La Paillotte ☐
- 4005 Col Vert ☐
- 4410 Patisseau ☐
- 4501 Bois Bardelet ☐
- 5801 Des Bains ☐
- 6001 Campix ☐
- 6203 Gandspette ☐
- 6411 Col d'Ibardin ☐
- 6601 California ☐
- 8101 Deux Lacs ☐
- 8316 Les Cigales ☐
- 8403 Le Jantou ☐
- 8508 Puerta del Sol ☐
- 8603 Relais de Miel ☐

Ireland
- Irish Caravan Council ☐

Germany
- 3735 Schònrain ☐

Italy
- 6020 Union Lido ☐
- 6275 Fornella ☐

Luxembourg
- 764 Auf Kengert ☐

Portugal
- Orbitur Camping ☐

Spain
- 8035 L'Amfora ☐
- 8040 Las Dunas ☐
- 8060 Ballena Alegre II ☐
- 8072 Les Medes ☐
- 8080 Delfin Verde ☐
- 8090 Cypsela ☐
- 8102 Mas Patoxas ☐
- 8103 El Maset ☐
- 8120 Kim's ☐
- 8130 Calonge ☐
- 8150 Palamos ☐
- 8160 Cala Gogo ☐
- 8200 Cala Llevado ☐
- 8230 El Pinar ☐
- 8390 Vilanova ☐
- 8410 Playa Bara ☐
- 8470 La Siesta ☐
- 8480 Sanguli ☐
- 8482 Pineda-Salou ☐
- 8483 Tamarit ☐
- 8530 Playa Montroig ☐
- 8560 Tropicana ☐
- 8580 Bonterra ☐
- 8615 Kiko ☐
- 8742 La Marina ☐
- 8755 Moraira ☐
- 8800 Marbella Playa ☐
- 8955 Arenal-Moris ☐
- 8960 La Paz ☐
- 8970 Las Arenas ☐
- 9000 Playa Joyel ☐
- 9024 As Cancelas ☐
- 9060 Pena Montanesa ☐
- 9200 El Escorial ☐
- Garoa Campings ☐

PLEASE NOTE: These are the sites' own brochures, the contents of which we have no control over. We cannot therefore accept any responsibilities for errors, omissions, inaccuracies or misleading information contained therein. We make every effort to fufill requests as promptly as possible, but this offer is subject to stocks being supplied to us and still being available at the time of receiving your request.

REPORTS BY READERS

We always welcome reports from readers concerning sites which they have visited. Generally reports provide us with invaluable feedback on sites already featured in the Guide or, in the case of those not featured in our Guide, they provide information which we can follow up with a view to adding them in future editions. However, *if you have a complaint about a site, this should be addressed to the campsite owner, preferably in person before you leave.* When contacting us, please make your comments either on this form or on plain paper. It would be appreciated if you would indicate the approximate dates when you visited the park and, in the case of potential new sites, provide the correct name and address and, if possible, include a site brochure. Send your reports to:

Deneway Guides & Travel Ltd, Chesil Lodge, West Bexington, Dorchester DT2 9DG

Name of Park and Ref. No. (or address for new recommendations):

....

....

Dates of Visit: ....

Comments:

Reader's Name and Address: ....

....

....

....

REQUESTS FOR INFORMATION

For your convenience, we have printed below some slips which you may cut out and fill in your name and address to obtain further information from any of the sites in the guide in which you are interested. Send the slip *to the site concerned* at the address given in the site report, not to us.

✂

ALAN ROGERS' GOOD CAMPS GUIDE - 1998
ENQUIRY FORM

To (name of site): ....

Please send me a copy of your brochure and details of your conditions for making reservations.

We have our own trailer caravan / motor caravan / tent / trailer tent (delete as appropriate).

Name: ....

Address: ....

....

CAR FERRY INFORMATION

Many ferry companies operate services between the UK mainland and continental Europe, providing an extensive choice of routes. The actual choice of route is a matter of personal preference, influenced by such factors as where you live, your continental destination, the cost, and whether or not you enjoy sea travel and consider a longer crossing itself as part of your holiday.

In general terms travel by ferry, especially on the longer routes, is now far more comfortable than in the past as a result of the introduction of larger, faster and more luxurious vessels which, whilst able to accommodate large numbers of vehicles, are in many respects more similar to passenger liners than to ferries as they used to be. For anyone wanting to combine a 'mini-cruise' with their camping holiday, and save considerable driving time and fuel costs, these services are well worth serious consideration.

However, the British fondness for the sea does not extend to everyone, and there are many travellers for whom the sea-crossing represents a necessary evil rather than a pleasure, and for whom the shortest possible crossing is the best crossing, and this is borne out by the increasing popularity of the Channel Tunnel (Le Shuttle). Details of our experience of this service to date are to be found on page 363.

Taking these many personal preferences into account makes it virtually impossible to recommend any particular service as being 'better' than any other, but one consideration which may influence your choice in favour of a short crossing is the fact that if you arrive at the departure point late or without a booking, the frequency of services on these routes means that, apart from the peak weekends, if you cannot get onto the first departure, the chances are that you will get on the next one, or at worst the one after that.

As a result primarily of the fierce competition on cross-channel services following the opening of the Tunnel, many operators had not finalised their schedules or fares when we went to press in November '97. The following, therefore, is a preliminary list of services for 1998 based on the latest information available. Readers are advised to contact the operators direct (or their local travel agent) in the New Year for definitive details of services to be operated in 1998.

Destination	Ferry Company	Routes	Time
FRANCE	Brittany Ferries	Plymouth-Roscoff	6-8 hrs
		Portsmouth-St Malo	9-11 hrs
		Portsmouth-Caen	7-8 hrs
		Poole-St Malo	8-9 hrs
		Poole-Cherbourg	4-7 hrs
		Cork-Roscoff/St Malo	13 hrs
	Hoverspeed	Dover-Calais	35 mins
		Folkestone-Boulogne	55 mins
	P&O European Ferries	Dover-Calais	75 mins
		Portsmouth-Le Havre	5¾ hrs
		Portsmouth-Cherbourg	5-9 hrs
	Stena Line	Dover-Calais	45-90 mins
		Newhaven-Dieppe	2-4 hrs
		Southampton-Cherbourg	6-8 hrs
	Condor Ferries	Weymouth-St Malo	2½ hrs
	Irish Ferries	Rosslare-Cherbourg	18 hrs
		Rosslare-Le Havre	5¾ hrs
		Cork-Cherbourg/Le Havre	18-22 hrs
BELGIUM	North Sea Ferries	Hull-Zeebrugge	14 hrs
	Holyman Sally	Ramsgate-Ostend	110 mins
NETHERLANDS	North Sea Ferries	Hull-Rotterdam	14 hrs
	Stena Line	Harwich-Hook (ferry)	6-8 hrs
		Harwich-Hook ('fastcraft')	3¾ hrs
GERMANY	Scandinavian Seaways	Harwich/Newcastle-Hamburg	20-23 hrs
SPAIN	Brittany Ferries	Plymouth-Santander	24 hrs
	P&O European Ferries	Portsmouth-Bilbao	28½ hrs
DENMARK	Scandinavian Seaways	Harwich-Esbjerg	20 hrs
NORWAY	Color Line	Newcastel-Stavanger/Bergen	c. 24 hrs
SWEDEN	Scandinavian Seaways	Harwich/Newcastle-Gothenburg	c. 24 hrs

Ferry Company Addresses and Phone Numbers:

Brittany Ferries (& Truckline)
Millbay Docks,
Plymouth PL1 3EW
Tel: 01752 221321
Fax: 01752 255065
See advert between pages 96/7

Sally Ferries
Argyle Centre, York Street,
Ramsgate CT11 9DS
01843 595522

Hoverspeed
Maybrook House, Queens
Gardens, Dover CT17 9UQ
Tel: 01304 240241
Fax:(01304 211801

Stena Line
Charter House, Park Street,
Ashford TN24 8EX
Tel: 01233 647047
Fax: 01233 202241

P & O European Ferries
Channel House, Channel View
Road, Dover CT17 9TJ
Tel: 01304 203388
Fax: 01304 223223
See advert between pages 96/7

P&O North Sea Ferries
King George Dock,
Hedon Road, Hull HU9 5QA
01482 77177
See advert between pages 128/9

Scandinavian Seaways
Scandinavia House, Parkeston
Quay, Harwich CO12 4QG
01255 240234
See advert between pages 128/9

SeaFrance
Room 106, Eastern Camber
Office, Eastern Docks, Dover,
Kent CT16 1JA
Tel: 01304 212696
Fax: 01304 240033
See advert between pages 96/7

Color Line
Tyne Commission Quay,
North Shields, NE29 6EA
0191 296 1313

Irish Ferries
2/4 Merrion Road, Dublin 2
Tel: 016 610511
Fax: 0171 491 7961

Condor Ferries
Newharbour Road South,
Hamworthy, Poole BH15 4AJ
Tel: 01202 207207
Fax: 01202 685184
See advert between pages 32/3

Ferry Reports

Lack of space prevents us from reporting in this Guide on all the many services we have used over the last year. As our France Guide features reports on many of the services to France, we have included in this Guide only those services we have used in the last year to destinations other than France.

Brittany Ferries - Plymouth/Santander

This service is operated by Brittany Ferries flagship, the 'Val de Loire'. Although this is a long crossing, which on the face of it appears relatively expensive, if you are travelling to Spain, Portugal or even the Basque area of France, the higher ferry cost may well be offset by the saving in fuel, autoroute tolls or overnight accommodation en route, so it's well worth making a comparative calculation of the **total** cost of your journey! Facilities on the Val de Loire are almost up to cruise liner standards, and the 24 hour voyage itself can be very enjoyable indeed, with plenty to keep you occupied or pleasantly relaxed - a good choice of restaurants, cinema, sun-decks, etc. all add to the `cruising' atmosphere.

North Sea Ferries Hull - Rotterdam, and Hull - Zeebrugge

We have used these services on several occasions during the last two or three years, and our opinion is generally favourable. The two ferries on which we have travelled recently (the 'Norstar' and 'Norsea') are designed as a 'floating hotels', with first class facilities, plenty of space and ample entertainment; unfortunately the ticket price no longer includes a five-course evening meal and full English breakfast! The cabins are situated towards the forward end of the ship, away from the public rooms, providing the opportunity of an undisturbed night's sleep. The decor is above average, and there are private facilities available; a nice touch was early morning tea served in your cabin, which helps soften the blow associated with an early start! Overall, North Sea Ferries provide an excellent service, neatly illustrated by their getting us and our car on-board at Europort (Rotterdam) even though we arrived at the terminal (after an horrendous drive) actually at the precise time that the vessel was due to sail! This route must be a particularly attractive proposition for those living in the north or in Scotland.

Color Line - Newcastle/Bergen

Last year, having never previously travelled to Scandinavia by sea, we were quite excited at the prospect of this crossing, and we weren't disappointed, despite the irritation of a two hour check-in time! In fact the two hours are necessary, as vehicles have to be loaded according to their port of disembarkation, because, unlike most ferries, this service calls at several ports. Finally arriving on board, I must confess that we wished we'd booked a better cabin - the standard inside cabins are pretty small and somewhat claustrophobic, so next time we get the opportunity to travel on this service we'll opt for one of the much nicer (but somewhat more expensive) outside cabins. *continued overleaf*

The views, despite some very indifferent weather, as the vessel nosed her way into Bergen were rather spectacular, and we regretted having to disembark at the first port of call instead of being able to enjoy the views as the voyage continued down the coast. All in all a thoroughly enjoyable way to get to Norway. We used the 'Venus' which operates the thrice weekly service on this route - although built in 1975, this vessel has been extensively and continuously upgraded and now provides a modern smart and comfortable service in keeping with the length of the crossing. Catering is now of a very high standard; particularly impressive are the good-value Norwegian breakfasts. The whole operation gives the impression of a well-run company. Color Line is also doing a good job in marketing Norway, and the encouragement given to us in the last three years since we extended the Good Camps Guides to include Scandinavia is only one example of Color's efforts to gain media support for Norway.

The decor and overall design on board is distinctly different from what we're used to on the cross-channel ferries, so we spent quite a lot of time exploring the ship, sampling the restaurants, etc, hence the time passed all too quickly. We were generally very impressed with everything about this service (even the more or less mandatory briefing about disembarkation arrangements was presented in a quite amusing fashion!)

At first sight the fares might seem rather high, but it must be remembered that this is a crossing that takes the best part of 24 hours, and saves a drive of some 2,000 km! Color's policy is, therefore, to offer a service which is equivalent to a holiday cruise rather than a ferry; reference to the cabin accommodation has already been made, but to be fair there is actually a wide range of overnight accommodation on offer, including four different grades of cabin, bunk-type couchettes, and airline-type reclining seats (which are, by the way, equivalent to an airline's first class).

Scandinavian Seaways - Newcastle/Gothenburg - Harwich/Gothenburg

Travelling with Scandinavian Seaways from Newcastle to Gothenburg on board the 'Princess of Scandinavia' line added 22 hours cruising time to our journey. This leisurely crossing provided the perfect opportunity to relax and unwind after a hectic, pre-travel rush. Once on board, we found all services to be efficiently run without fuss by a friendly crew. Our twin berth outside cabin with en-suite facilities was comfortable, airy and spacious. Catering facilities included an à la carte restaurant offering Scandinavian and German cuisine, the popular Smörgasbord/carvery, a traditional Scandinavian feast, or the cafeteria and bistro is another option. Discounts for children are a plus, with under fours eating free and under twelves getting 50% discount on buffet meals.

The list of on board activities is equally extensive with live entertainment, disco, casino, cinema, sauna, solarium, swimming pool, etc. There are shops and a bureau de change; vouchers, received with our travel documents, meant discount on certain duty free items. A most important factor on any journey is the cost, but with fare structuring and book in advance deals, we believe Scandinavian Seaways offers excellent value for money. Arriving in Gothenburg thoroughly refreshed, we also had to agree that the top AA rating awarded to the Princess of Scandinavia is well deserved.

The Channel Tunnel - *"Le Shuttle"*

The lorry fire at the French end of the tunnel undoubtedly dented confidence as well as disrupting schedules. The advantage of a 'turn up and go' system had to be abandoned and it became necessary to book in advance. These troubles are behind them and the previous arrangement is now in force. We used the service in July and September and were well satisfied. The duty free shops at both terminals had been enlarged with an increase in the number of check-out points. It is worth pointing out that if one person is doing the shopping for more than one allowance, those whose duty-free cards are being used must also be present when paying. Traffic was less than experienced before the fire but this was due, partly, on the outward journey, to an accident which closed the M20 delaying vehicles including coaches. When we checked-in at Folkestone with an open ticket, we were asked if we were using the service area before leaving and given a suitable departure time. After shopping, we had a clear run right through to the train after the gas bottle on our motorcaravan had been checked and left on time. The whole operation was smooth and efficient and, being able to drive straight off at the French end without immigration controls, we soon joined the autoroute system and proceeded on our way. The return, six weeks later, mirrored the outward journey and, although we missed the on-board services of a conventional ferry, it was a slick operation. Having a slight disability at the time, the fact that no stairs had to be climbed was a great advantage. There will always be a place for the conventional ferries but it is nice to have this alternative, particularly for those who do not like sea travel and on the rare occasions when bad weather prevents boats from sailing.

Gerry Ovenden
who travelled as a guest of Eurotunnel.

Put a smile on the face of your touring caravan...

...by insuring it with 'The Caravan Insurance Centre'

And bring a smile to your face too when you receive details of our excellent policies and competitive premiums.

As our name suggests we specialise in caravan insurance and are able to offer the <u>very best</u> cover at very competitive premiums - with discounts for the over 50's, for all types of touring caravans, trailer tents and, incidentally, static holiday caravans and motorcaravans.

CLAIM YOUR
ALAN ROGERS
READERS DISCOUNT
-See below

We offer a choice of either new for old or market value cover with or without a policy excess. **We include 6 months continental use free (additional cover costs a little more)** and also provide generous loss of use benefits and third party liability cover. For full details complete and return the coupon below. By utilising this coupon you will benefit from a special discount only available to readers of an 'Alan Roger's publication.

Please send me by return full details of Touring Caravan Insurance   **AR**

Name   ....

Address ....

....

....

Postcode ....

THE
CARAVAN
INSURANCE
CENTRE

**FREEPOST GR1604, THE QUADRANGLE,
IMPERIAL SQUARE, CHELTENHAM GL50 1BR**

BAKERS
OF CHELTENHAM

MAP - Austria

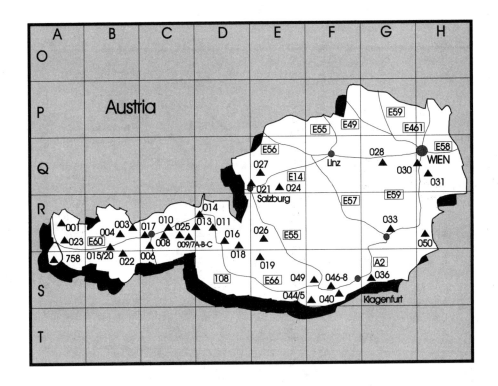

MAP - Slovenia

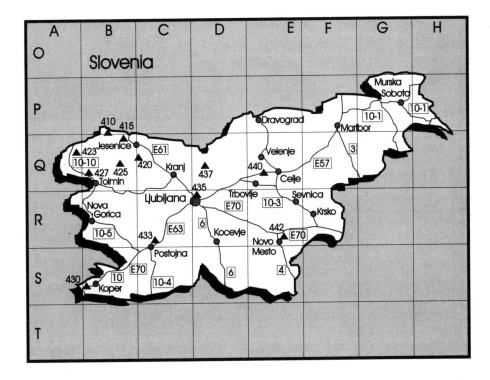

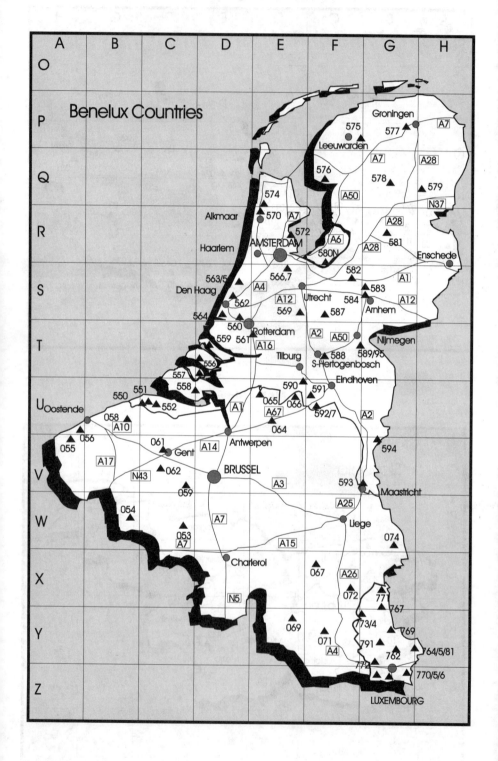

Benelux Countries

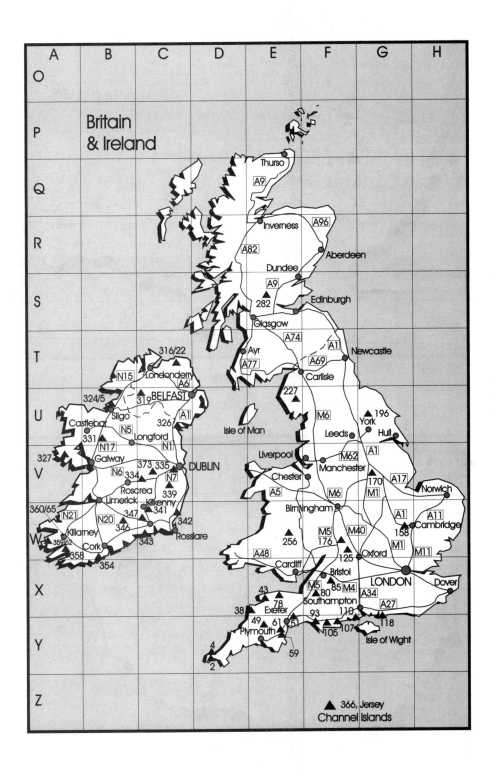

MAP - Czech and Slovak Republics

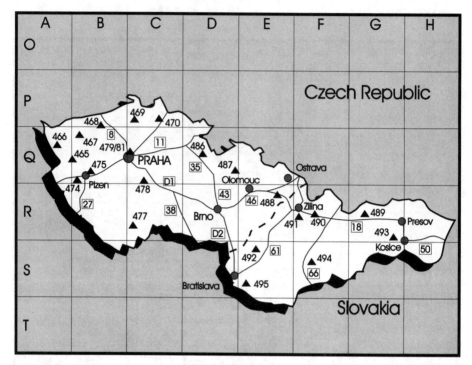

MAP - Hungary

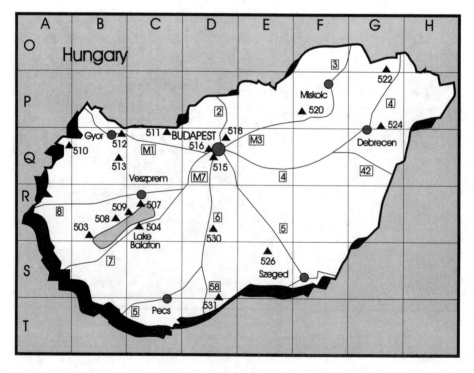

MAP - Denmark

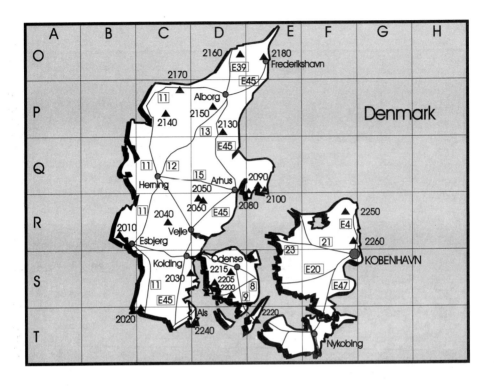

MAP - Finland

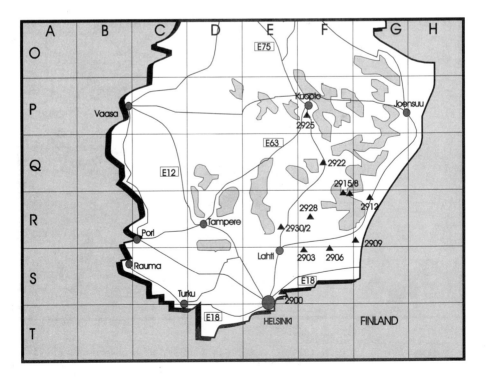

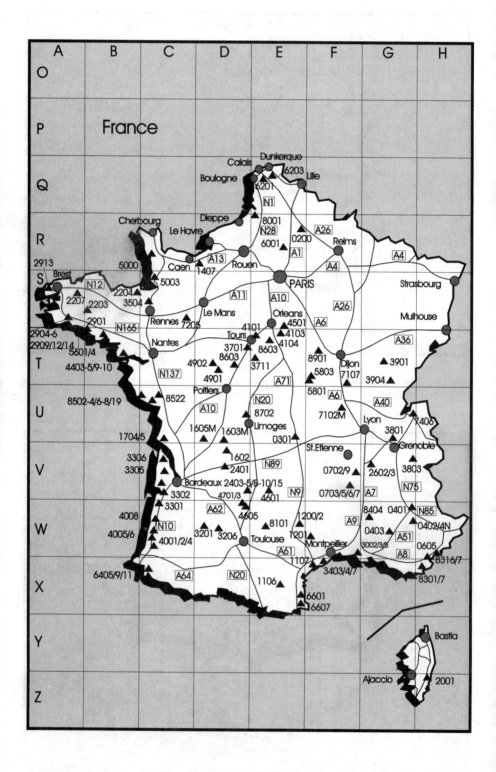

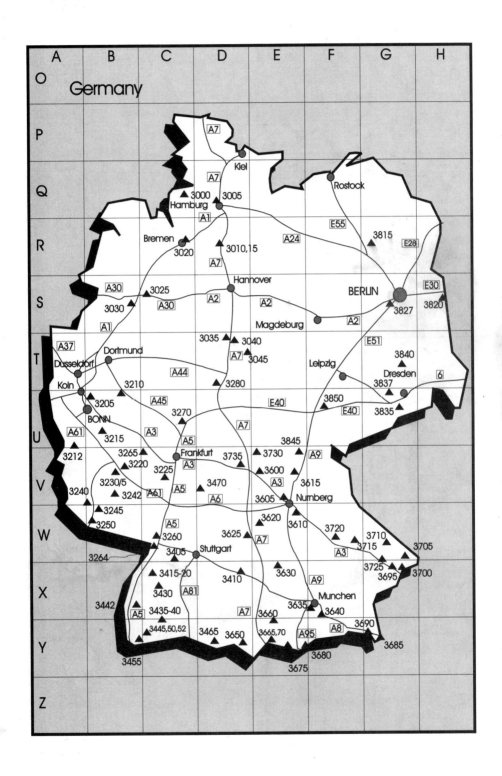

MAP - Italy

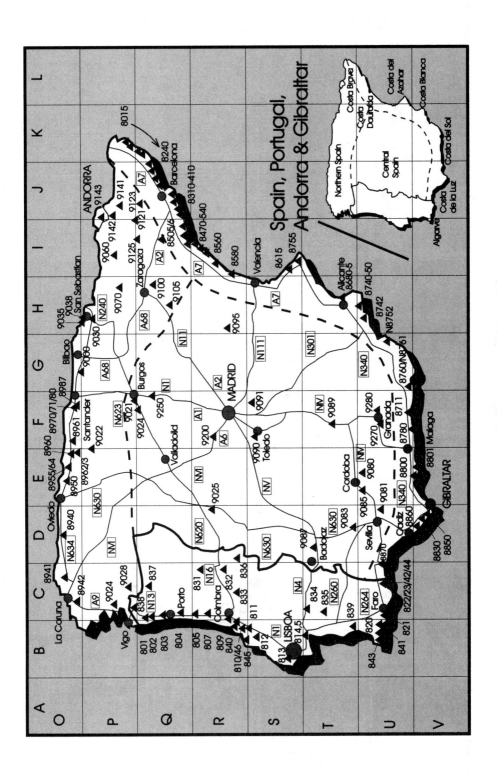

Spain, Portugal,
Andorra & Gibraltar

MAP - Poland

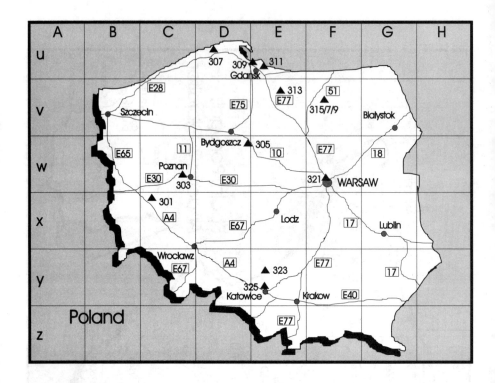

MAP - Switzerland

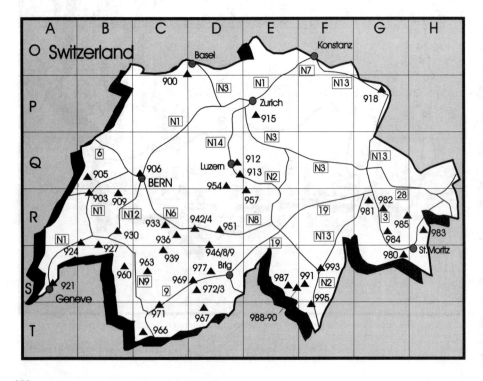

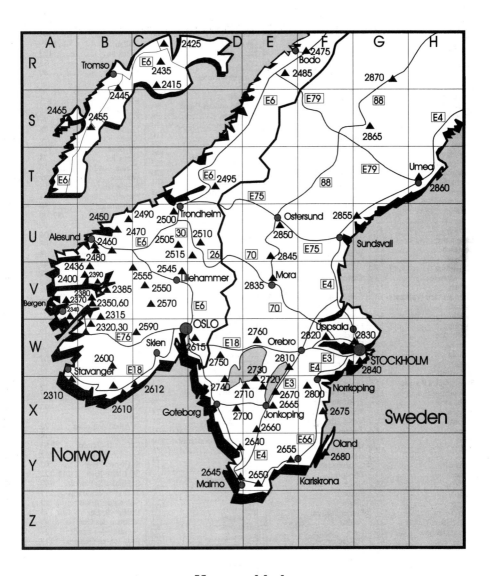

Maps and Index

The Site Index: The Site Index at the back of the guide (starting on page 381) comprises a listing of all the sites featured in this guide in the order in which they appear giving a page number together with a grid reference related to the appropriate country map – e.g. taking Germany, site number 3635 is to be found in grid square FX on page 146.

New sites: Sites that are new to the guide this year are highlighted in bold text in the index.

The Town Index: Comprises an alphabetical town name index to each country giving the names of all the towns where sites are featured.

The Maps: The maps are included on the preceding pages. These may be used to identify the approximate location of sites; each site is identified on the appropriate map be reference to an individual site number and we include a grid system for each map. One can therefore identify the grid square (e.g. square BY) in which a particular site is situated.

TOWN and VILLAGE INDEX

Index of Campsites

381

map	ref	page		map	ref	page		map	ref	page
833	Arganil	CR 270		8741	*Florantilles*	HU 304		2710	Lidköping	EX 332
837	Cerdeira	CQ 271		8742	Int. La Marina	HU 305		2720	Hökensås	EX 332
838	Vilar de Mouros	CP 271		8750	Los Gallardos	HU 306		2730	Ekudden	EX 332
				8752	Nat. El Portus	GU 306		2740	Laxsjöns	DX 333
Slovakia				8711	Nerja	FU 307		2750	Sommarvik	DW 333
490	Trusalová	FR 272		8760	Mar Azul	GU 307		2760	Frykenbaden	EW 334
493	Kosice Hamre	GR 273		8780	Torre del Mar	FU 307		2800	Glyttinge	FX 334
494	Neresnica	FS 273		8800	Marbella Playa	EU 308		2810	Vätterviksbadet	EW 334
495	Zlaté piesky	ES 273		8801	La Rosaleda	EV 308		2820	Skantzö Bad	FW 335
491	Turiec	FR 274		8830	Torre-Pena I	DV 308		2830	Ängby	GW 335
492	Trencin	ES 274		8850	Paloma	DV 309		2840	Flottsbro	GW 336
				8860	Fuente del Gallo	DV 309		*2835*	*Orsa Grönklitt*	EV 336
Slovenia				8870	Derena Mar	CU 309		*2845*	*Svegs*	EU 336
410	*Spik Autocamp*	BP 276		9024	As Cancelas	CP 310		*2850*	*Östersunds*	EU 337
415	*Kamp Kamne*	BQ 276		9028	Leiro	CP 310		*2855*	*Flogsta*	GU 337
420	*Kamp Zaka*	CQ 276		8941	Valdovino	CO 311		*2860*	*Umeå*	HT 338
423	*Camp Soca*	AQ 277		8940	Los Cantiles	DO 311		*2865*	*Geilas*	GS 338
425	*Danica Bohinj*	BQ 277		8942	Los Manzanos	CO 311		*2870*	*Jokkmokks*	GR 338
427	*Kamp Koren*	BQ 277		8962	La Isla	EO 312				
430	*Belvedere*	BS 278		8950	Costa Verde	EO 312				
433	*Pivka Jama*	CR 278		*8955*	*Arenal de Moris*	EO 312		**Switzerland**		
435	*Jezica*	DR 278		8963	La Viorna	EO 313		900	Waldhort	CO 340
437	*Resnik*	DQ 279		8964	El Molino	EO 313		*905*	*Bois-Couvent*	BQ 340
440	*Dolina*	EQ 279		8970	Las Arenas	FO 314		903	Paradis Plage	BR 341
442	*Otocec*	ER 279		8960	La Paz	EO 314		906	Kappelenbrücke	CQ 341
				8961	El Helguero	FO 315		909	Avenches	BR 341
Spain				8971	Playa Oyambre	FO 315		912	Lido Luzern	DQ 342
8050	Aquarius	KP 281		8980	Bella Vista	FO 316		913	Vitznau	DQ 342
8015	*La Laguna*	KP 282		9035	Portuondo	HP 316		915	Seebucht	EP 342
8020	Int. Amberes	KP 282		9000	Playa Joyel	GO 316		918	Buchhorn	GP 343
8072	Les Medes	KP 283		9038	Orio	HP 317		921	Pointe à la Bise	AS 343
8080	El Delfin Verde	KP 283		*9070*	*Pirineos*	HP 317		924	Le Petit Bois	BR 344
8070	La Escala	KP 284		9030	Igueldo	HP 317		927	De Vidy	BR 344
8103	El Maset	KP 284		9105	Lago Park	HQ 318		930	Le Bivouac	BR 344
8150	Int. de Palamós	KQ 285		*9123*	*El Solsones*	JQ 318		933	Bettlereiche	CR 345
8101	Playa Brava	KP 285		9100	Casablanca	HQ 318		939	Vermeille	CS 345
8090	Cypsela	KP 286		*9142*	*Solana-Segre*	JP 318		944	Jungfraublick	DR 345
8120	Kim's	KQ 286		9060	Peña Montañesa	IP 319		936	Grassi	CR 346
8060	Ballena Alegre 2	KP 288		*9121*	*Vall d'Ager*	JQ 320		942	Manor Farm	DR 346
8035	L'Amfora	KP 288		*9125*	*Barasona*	IQ 320		946	Jungfrau	DS 346
8040	Las Dunas	KP 289		9021	Fuentes Blancas	FP 321		954	Lido Sarnen	DQ 346
8200	Cala Llevadó	JQ 289		8506	Serra de Prades	IQ 321		948	Gletscherdorf	DS 347
8102	Mas Patoxas	KP 290		9250	Costajan	FQ 321		951	Aaregg	DR 347
8140	Treumal	KQ 291		9023	Camino-Santiago	FQ 322		949	Eigernordwand	DS 348
8075	Estartit	KP 291		9025	Regio	DR 322		957	Eienwäldli	ER 348
8160	Cala Gogo	KQ 292		9090	El Greco	FS 322		963	Sémiramis	CS 348
8130	Int. de Calonge	KQ 293		9200	El Escorial	FR 323		960	Rive-Bleue	CS 349
8230	Beach Camp	JQ 293		9091	Soto-Castillo	FS 323		*971*	*Les Iles*	CT 349
8240	Bona Vista	JQ 294		9270	Suspiro-Moro	FU 324		966	Des Glaciers	CT 350
8310	Ballena Alegre	JQ 294		*9095*	*Albarracin*	HR 324		973	Gemmi	DS 350
8390	Vilanova Park	JQ 295		9080	El Brillante	EU 325		969	Swiss-Plage	DS 351
8410	Playa Bara	JQ 295		9280	Sierra Nevada	FU 325		972	Bella Tola	DS 351
8480	Sanguli	IQ 296		9085	Carlos III	EU 325		942	Manor Farm	DR 352
8535	Cala d'Oques	IQ 297		9081	Villsom	DU 326		*967*	*De Molignon*	DT 352
8470	La Siesta	IQ 297		9087	Mérida	DT 326		946	Jungfrau	DS 353
8482	*Pineda de Salou*	IQ 297		9083	Monesterio	DT 326		957	Eienwäldli	ER 353
8481	Cambrils Park	IQ 298		*9089*	*Despeñaperros*	FT 326		*977*	*Santa Monica*	DS 354
8483	Tamarit-Park	IQ 298						987	Piccolo Paradiso	ES 354
8530	Playa Montroig	IR 299		**Sweden**				988	Lido Mappo	ES 354
8484	Gavina	IR 299		2640	Krono-Torekov	DY 328		990	Delta	ES 355
8520	Marius	IR 300		2645	Råå Vallar	DY 328		991	Riarena	FS 355
8540	Torre del Sol	IR 300		2650	Skånes Djurparks	EY 329		981	Camp Au	CR 356
8580	Bonterra	IR 301		2655	Tingsryds	EY 329		993	Al Censo	FS 356
8755	Moraira	IS 301		2660	Ågårds	EX 329		995	Piodella	FT 356
8560	Playa Tropicana	IR 302		2665	Rosenlunds	EX 330		982	Pradafenz	GR 357
8615	Kiko	IS 302		2670	Grännastrandens	EX 330		*983*	*Sur-En*	HR 357
8680	Armanello	HT 303		2675	Lysingsbadet	EX 330		*980*	*Silvaplana*	GS 358
8681	Villasol	HT 303		2680	Krono-Saxnäs	FY 331		984	St Cassian	GR 358
8683	*Benisol*	HT 304		2700	Borås Camping	DX 331		*985*	*Farich*	GR 358
8685	*El Raco*	HT 304								